Handbook of
Personal Relationships
Second Edition

Handbook of
Personal Relationships

Theory, Research and Interventions

Second Edition

Edited by
Steve Duck
University of Iowa, USA

Sections Edited by

Rosemary S.L. Mills, University of Manitoba, Canada
William Ickes, University of Texas, USA
Kathryn Dindia, University of Wisconsin, USA
Robert M. Milardo, University of Maine, USA
Barbara R. Sarason, University of Washington, USA

JOHN WILEY & SONS
Chichester · New York · Brisbane · Toronto · Singapore

Copyright © 1997 by John Wiley & Sons Ltd,
Baffins Lane, Chichester,
West Sussex PO19 IUD, England

National   01243 779777
International (+44) 1243 779777
e-mail (for orders and customer service enquiries): cs-boosks@wiley.co.uk
Visit our Home Page on http://www.wiley.co.uk
or http://www.wiley.com

Other Wiley Editorial Offices

John Wiley & Sons, Inc., 605 Third Avenue,
New York, NY 10158-0012, USA

Jacaranda Wiley Ltd, 33 Park Road, Milton,
Queensland 4064, Australia

John Wiley & Sons (Canada) Ltd, 22 Worcester Road,
Rexdale, Ontario M9W 1L1, Canada

John Wiley & Sons (Asia) Pte Ltd, 2 Clementi Loop #02-01,
Jin Xing Distripark, Singapore 129809

Library of Congress Cataloging-in-Publication Data

Handbook of personal relationships: theory, research, and
    interventions/edited by Steve Duck; sections edited by Rosemary.
    Mills . . . [et al.].—2nd ed.
        p.   cm.
    Includes bibliographical references and index.
    ISBN 0-471-95913-8 (cloth)
    1. Interpersonal relations.   I. Duck, Steve.
HM132.H3325   1996
302.3′4—dc20   96-10234
                                                           CIP

British Library Cataloguing in Publication Data

A catalogue record for this book is available from the British Library

ISBN 0-471-95913-8

Typeset in 10/12pt Times by Best-set Typesetter Ltd., Hong Kong
Printed and bound in Great Britain by Bookcraft (Bath Ltd), Midsomer Norton.
This book is printed on acid-free paper responsibly manufactured from sustainable
forestation, for which at least two trees are planted for each one used for paper production.

Contents

About the Editor

Steve Duck, *Department of Communication Studies, 105 Communications Studies Building, University of Iowa, Iowa City, IA 52242, USA*

Steve Duck is the Daniel and Amy Starch Distinguished Research Professor at the University of Iowa and has been a keen promoter of the field of personal relationships research since it was formed. He co-founded the first International Conference on Personal Relationships in 1982, and was founder and first editor of the *Journal of Social and Personal Relationships*, first President of the International Network on Personal Relationships, the professional organization for the research field, and editor of the first edition of the *Handbook of Personal Relationships*. The Steve Duck New Scholar Award was endowed and named in his honor by a group of independent scholars to recognize his promotion of the work of younger professionals and his dedication to developing the field.

Contributors

Linda K. Acitelli, *Department of Psychology, University of Houston, Houston TX 77204-5341, USA*

Graham Allan, *Department of Sociology and Social Policy, University of Southampton, Southampton, Hampshire SO9 5NH, UK*

Arthur Aron, *Psychology Board, SUNY Stony Brook, Stony Brook, NY 11794-2500, USA*

Elaine N. Aron, *2095 California Street, Apartment 204, San Francisco CA 94109, USA*

Ximena Arriaga, *Department of Psychology, University of North Carolina, Chapel Hill, NC 27599-3270, USA*

Karen Caplovitz Barrett, *Department of Human Development and Family Studies, Colorado State University, Fort Collins, CO 80523, USA*

Leslie A. Baxter, *Department of Communication Studies, University of Iowa, Iowa City, IA 52242-1498, USA*

Victoria Hilkevitch Bedford, *Department of Psychology, University of Indianapolis, Indianapolis, IN 47401, USA*

Rosemary Blieszner, *Department of Family and Child Development, Virginia Polytechnic Institute, Blacksburg, VA 24061-0416, USA*

Arthur P. Bochner, *Department of Communication, University of South Florida, Tampa, FL 33620-5550, USA*

Rebecca M. Buchanan, *Department of Psychology, University of Maryland, College Park, MD 20742-4411, USA*

Heather M. Coon, *Survey Research Center, University of Michigan, Ann Arbor, MI 48109, USA*

Teresa M. Cooney, *Department of Individual and Family Studies, Allison Hall, University of Delaware, Newark, DE 19716, USA*

Patricia M. Crittenden, *Family Relations Institute, 9481 SW 147 St., Miami, FL 33176, USA*

Ann C. Crouter, *S-110 Henderson Human Development Building, Pennsylvania State University, University Park, PA 16802, USA*

Kathryn Dindia, *Department of Communication, University of Wisconsin, PO Box 413, Milwaukee, WI 53201, USA*

Steve Duck, *Department of Communication Studies, 105 Communication Studies Building, University of Iowa, Iowa City, IA 52242, USA*

Carolyn Ellis, *Department of Sociology, University of South Florida, Tampa, FL 33620-5550, USA*

Stanley O. Gaines, *Department of Psychology, Pomona College, Claremont, CA 91711, USA*

Richard Gonzalez, *Department of Psychology, NI-25, University of Washington, Seattle, WA 98195, USA*

Dale Griffin, *School of Cognitive and Computing Sciences, University of Sussex, Falmer, Brighton, Sussex BN1 9QH, UK*

Regan A.R. Gurung, *Department of Psychology, University of Washington, NI-25, Seattle, WA 98195, USA*

Cindy Hazan, *Department of Human Development & Family Studies, MVR Hall, Cornell University, ITHACA, NY 14853, USA*

Kenneth Heller, *Department of Psychology, Indiana University, Bloomington, IN 47401, USA*

Heather Helms-Erickson, *S-110 Henderson Human Development Building, Pennsylvania State University, University Park, PA 16802, USA*

Jordan B. Hiller, *Department of Psychology, Harvard University, 33 Kirkland Street, Cambridge, MA 02138, USA*

Jill M. Hooley, *Department of Psychology, Harvard University, 33 Kirkland Street, Cambridge, MA 02138, USA*

William Ickes, *Department of Psychology, University of Texas, Room 313, Life Science Building, Arlington, TX 76019, USA*

Michael P. Johnson, *Department of Sociology, Pennsylvania State University, 211 Oswald Tower, University Park, PA 16802, USA*

Krzystof Kaniasty, *Department of Psychology, Indiana University of Pennsylvania, Indiana, PA 15705-1087, USA*

Douglas T. Kenrick, *Department of Psychology, Arizona State University, Tempe, AZ 85287, USA*

Renate Klein, *Department of Human Development, 16 Merrill Hall, University of Maine, Orono, ME 04469, USA*

Archie B. Kwan, *Department of Applied Psychology, Ontario Institute for Studies in Education, 252 Bloor St. W., Toronto, Ontario M5S 1V6, CANADA*

Brent Mallinckrodt, *Department of Counseling Psychology, College of Education, University of Oregon, Eugene, OR 97403, USA*

Sandra Metts, *Department of Communication, Illinois State University, Fell Hall, Normal, IL 61790-4480, USA*

Robert M. Milardo, *Department Human Development and Family Studies, University of Maine, 17 Merrill Hall, Orono, ME 04469-5749, USA*

Rosemary S.L. Mills, *Department of Family Studies, Faculty of Human Ecology, University of Manitoba, Winnipeg, Manitoba R3T 2N2, CANADA*

Barbara M. Montgomery, *School of Humanities and Social Sciences, Millersville University, Millersville, PA 17551, USA*

Fran Norris, *Department of Psychology, Georgia State University, University Plaza, Atlanta, GA 30303-3083, USA*

Robin O'Neil, *Department of Psychology and Center for Family Studies, University of California, Riverside, CA 92521, USA*

Ross D. Parke, *Department of Psychology and Center for Family Studies, University of California, Riverside, CA 92521, USA*

Malcolm R. Parks, *Department of Speech Communication, University of Washington, DL-15, Seattle, WA 98195, USA*

Samantha E. Poisson, *Department of Applied Psychology, Ontario Institute for Studies in Education, 252 Bloor St. W., Toronto, ONTARIO M5S 1V6, CANADA*

Karen S. Rook, *Program in Social Ecology, University of California, Irvine, CA 92717, USA*

Caryl E. Rusbult, *Department of Psychology, University of North Carolina, Chapel Hill, NC 27599-3270, USA*

Maria von Salisch, *Freie Universität Berlin, Institut für Soziologie der Erziehung, Berlin 14195, GERMANY*

Barbara R. Sarason, *Department of Psychology, University of Washington, NI-25, Seattle WA 98195, USA*

Irwin G. Sarason, *Department of Psychology, University of Washington, NI-25, Seattle, WA 98195, USA*

Barry H. Schneider, *Department of Applied Psychology, Ontario Institute for Studies in Education, 252 Bloor St. W., Toronto, Ontario M5S IV6, CANADA*

Andrea Smith, *Department of Applied Psychology, Ontario Institute for Studies in Education, 252 Bloor St. W., Toronto, Ontario M5S IV6, CANADA*

Lisa M. Tillman-Healy, *Department of Communication, University of South Florida, Tampa, FL 33620-5550, USA*

Edison J. Trickett, *Department of Psychology, University of Maryland, College Park, MD 20742-4411, USA*

Melanie R. Trost, *Department of Communication, Stouffer Hall, Box 871205, Arizona State University, Tempe, AZ 85287-1205, USA*

Joseph Veroff, *Survey Research Center, University of Michigan, Ann Arbor, MI 48109, USA*

Kathy Werking, *Department of Communication, University of Louisville, Strikeler Hall, Louisville, KY 40292, USA*

Lee West, *Department of Communication Studies, 105 Communication Studies Building, The University of Iowa, Iowa City, IA 52242, USA*

Amy M. Young, *Survey Research Center, University of Michigan, Ann Arbor, MI 48109, USA*

Debra Zeifman, *Department of Human Development and Family Studies, MVR Hall, Cornell University, Ithaca, NY 14853, USA*

About the Authors

Linda K. Acitelli is an Associate Professor in the Department of Psychology at the University of Houston. She is the principal investigator of a 5-year research project on relationships funded by the National Institute of Mental Health. In 1995, the International Network on Personal Relationships awarded her the Gerald R. Miller Award for her early career achievements. She is interested in examining the effects of thinking and talking about relationships on married and unmarried partners.

Graham Allan, PhD, is Senior Lecturer in Sociology at the University of Southampton. He is the author of *Friendship: Developing a Sociological Perspective* (1989), *Family Life: Domestic Roles and Social Organisation* (1985) and *A Sociology of Friendship and Kinship* (1979).

Arthur Aron received his PhD from the University of Toronto in 1970 in social psychology. His main research interests are in motivation and cognition in personal relationships and the role of personal relationships in intergroup relations. He is currently Associate Editor for the Interpersonal Relations and Group Processes of the *Journal of Personality and Social Psychology*. He teaches in the Psychology Department at the State University of New York at Stony Brook.

Elaine N. Aron received her PhD from Pacifica Graduate Institute in 1995 in clinical psychology with a specialization in depth psychology. Her research interests are personal relationships, adult temperament and the depth psychology of culture. Her most recent book is *The Highly Sensitive Person* (Carol/Birch Lane Press, 1996). Elaine consults and maintains a private practice in San Francisco.

Ximena Arriaga is a graduate student in the Department of Psychology, University of North Carolina at Chapel Hill; she completed her PhD work in the spring of 1996. Her research concerns developmental processes in close relationships; she is particularly interested in how variability over time in adherence factors influences the stability of ongoing relationships.

Karen Caplovitz Barrett, who received her Bachelor's degree in human development and family studies from Cornell University and her Master's and PhD in developmental psychology from the University of Denver, is currently Associate Professor of Human Development and Family Studies at Colorado State University. She is the author of a number of articles on her functionalist approach to emotional development, including a chapter in the recent volume *Self-conscious Emotions: The Psychology of Shame, Guilt, Embarrassment and Pride* (Guilford) and a recent article on the development of non-verbal communication of emotion in Volume 17 of the *Journal of Nonverbal Behavior*. Her empirical work concerns emotional development in the context of the parent–child relationship with particular focus on the development of the "social" emotions such as shame, pride and guilt.

Leslie A. Baxter, Professor of Communication Studies at the University of Iowa, has published widely in the area of communication in personal relationships. Her theoretical interests focus on the role of contradictions in relating; she has just completed a book on this subject with Barbara M. Montgomery and the two are currently co-editing a volume on similarities and differences among various dialectical perspectives on relating.

Victoria Hilkevitch Bedford is Assistant Professor of Psychology in the Department of Psychology at the University of Indianapolis. She received her PhD from Rutgers University in developmental psychology with a concentration on lifespan development. Recent publications include *Handbook of Aging and the Family* (with Rosemary Blieszner), "Memories of parental favoritism and the quality of parent–child ties in adulthood" (*Journal of Gerontology*), and several chapters on adult sibling relationships. Her primary research interests are in family relationships of middle and old adults and lifespan development.

Rosemary Blieszner is Professor of Gerontology and Family Studies in the Department of Family and Child Development and Associate Director of the Center for Gerontology at Virginia Polytechnic Institute and State University. She received her PhD from the Pennsylvania State University in human development–family studies with a concentration in adult development and aging. Her research focuses on family and friend relationships and well-being in old age. She is co-editor with V.H. Bedford of *Handbook of Aging and the Family*, co-author with R.G. Adams of *Adult Friendship*, and co-editor with R.G. Adams of *Older Adult Friendship: Structure and Process*. Her research has been published in gerontology, family studies, and the *Journal of Social and Personal Relationships*.

Arthur P. Bochner is Professor of Communication and Chair of the Department of Communication, University of South Florida. He has published more than 40 monographs and research articles on interpersonal relationships, communication theory and narrative. His current projects focus on local naratives that show how couples jointly construct relationship meanings.

Rebecca M. Buchanan is a doctoral candidate in clinical and community psychology at the University of Maryland. She received her MA degree in the same field from the University of Maryland in 1994 after earning a BA in psychology from Williams College in 1990. Her research interests focus on the acculturation and adaptation of adolescent refugees and immigrants as they negotiate family and school transitions. Specifically, she has conducted research on the adolescent–family adjustment of immigrants from El Salvador and is currently studying the adjustment of Evangelical Christian refugees from the former Soviet Union. As a contractor for the Refugee Mental Health Branch, Center for Mental Health Services, Substance Abuse Mental Health Services Administration, she has also prepared documents conceptualizing the social adjustment issues and available resources for Bosnian refugees and Evangelical Christian refugees from the former Soviet Union. She also serves as the editorial assistant for the *American Journal of Community Psychology*.

Heather Coon graduated from Mount Holyoke College in 1988 and subsequently worked as a research assistant for Teresa Amabile, conducting studies on creativity and intrinsic motivation at Brandeis University. She is currently a graduate student in the social psychology area at the University of Michigan and is interested in understanding cultural norms. Her recent work has investigated the consequences of endorsing cultural norms for Black and White couples in the USA.

Teresa M. Cooney received her doctorate in human development and family studies with a minor in demography from the Pennsylvania State University. Upon completion of her degree she was awarded an NICHD-funded postdoctoral research position studying family demography and the demography of aging at the Carolina Population Center, University of North Carolina, Chapel Hill. Currently, she is an Associate Professor in the Department of Individual and Family Studies at the University of Delaware, where she has taught since 1989. Her research focuses primarily on the impact of sociodemographic changes on adult child–parent relationships. She recently completed a 5-year project, funded by an NIMH First Award, in which she examined the consequences of recent parental divorce for young adults' family and personal relationships, life-course transitions and mental health and well-being.

Patricia M. Crittenden has a multidisciplinary background in developmental and clinical psychology and special education. She received her PhD from the University of Virginia, under the guidance of Mary D.S. Ainsworth and has been a member of the faculties of the University of Miami and San Diego State University. She has published approximately fifty articles and chapters on maltreatment and attachment as well as two books on cross-cultural aspects of parent child adaptation. Her most recent work consists of a series of theoretical papers on the development of psychopathology across the life-span. These papers address issues of multidimensional risk, the non-linear process of development and the implications for prevention and treatment. Currently she consults on developmental psychopathology and attachment assessment techniques and is engaged in cross-cultural research in a number of countries.

Ann C. Crouter is Professor of Human Development at Pennsylvania State University, where she has served on the faculty since 1981. Her research focuses on the connections between parental work and family life, and the implications of these dynamics for the daily activities and family experiences of school-aged children and adolescents. Together with her colleague, Susan McHale, Professor Crouter is conducting two longitudinal studies of families, both funded by the National Institute for Child Health and Human Development. The first study focuses on gender role socialization in middle childhood. The second explores the linkages between parental work, family processes and adolescent development. A theme in both studies is "within-family variability" in the experiences and perceptions of family members—mother, fathers, brothers and sisters—as they interact and develop over time, as well as the implications of these differences for family members' developing competencies, interests and psychological well-being.

Kathryn Dindia is a Professor in the Department of Communication at the University of Wisconsin Milwaukee, where she has taught for 15 years. She received her PhD in Speech Communication from the University of Washington in 1981. She has published articles on self-disclosure, communication and relationship maintenance and sex-differences in communication in both communication and psychology journals. She was the Associate Editor for Communication for the *Journal of Social and Personal Relationships* from 1990 to 1993. She co-edited with Dan Canary a Special Issue on Relational Maintenance and in 1993 also hosted the Conference of the International Network on Personal Relationships of which she became President in July 1996.

Carolyn Ellis is Professor of Communication and Sociology at the University of South Florida. She is the author of *Final Negotiations: A Story of Love, Loss, and Chronic Illness* (Temple University Press), *Fisher Folk: Two Communities on Chesapeake Bay* (University Press of Kentucky), and co-editor of *Investigating Subjectivity: Research on Lived Experience* (Sage), as well as other edited collections and articles on qualitative methods and emotions. Her current work focuses on narrative, auto-ethnography and emotional experience.

Stanley O. Gaines Jr is Assistant Professor in the Department of Psychology at Pomona College and in the Intercollegiate Department of Black Studies at The Claremont Colleges. His primary research interests include cultural value orientations, ethnicity, personality characteristics and gender as influences on interpersonal resource exchange, responses to partners' dissatisfaction, and other personal relationship processes. He has published conceptual and empirical articles in a number of journals, including *Journal of Black Psychology*, *Journal of Social and Personal Relationships*, *Basic and Applied Social Psychology*, and *American Psychologist*.

Richard Gonzalez was raised in Southern California, received a BA in psychology from UCLA and a PhD in social psychology from Stanford University. His current research interests include mathematical modeling, interpersonal relations and group decision-making.

Dale Griffin was raised in Vancouver, Canada, received a BA in psychology from the University of British Columbia and a PhD in social psychology from Stanford University. His current research interests include social prediction, interpersonal relations and medical decision-making.

Regan A.R. Gurung is a graduate student in the Social Personality Program at the University of Washington. He has carried out research on the role of self and other perceptions in close relationship satisfaction and the influence of personality factors, relationship history and cultural expectations on behavior in close relationships.

Cindy Hazan received her PhD in Personality and Social Psychology from the University of Denver in 1988, and is currently Associate Professor in the Department of Human Development and Family Studies at Cornell. For more than a decade, she has been investigating romantic relationship phenomena within the framework of ethological attachment theory. Currently, she is PI on a four-year grant from the National Science Foundation to study attachment formation processes.

Kenneth Heller is Professor of Psychology and Director of the Training Program in Clinical Science at Indiana University. He has been a Visiting Scholar at the Andrus Gerontological Research Center, University of Southern California, Visiting Professor at the School of Social Ecology, University of California, Irvine, Visiting Scholar at the Aging and Mental Health Program at the University of California Medical School, San Francisco and at the School of Public Health, University of California, Berkeley, Visiting Scholar at the Institute for Social Research, University of Michigan, and Special Research Fellow at the Laboratory of Community Psychiatry, Harvard University. His formal training is in clinical and community psychology. His specific research interests are in understanding the factors involved in the effects of social ties on health and well-being, and in the design and evaluation of community-based intervention programs.

Heather Helms-Erikson received a MS degree in Family Studies with a specialization in marriage and family therapy from the University of Maryland in 1992. She is currently a doctoral candidate in the Department of Human Development and Family Studies at the Pennsylvania State University. Her research interests encompass issues pertaining to the work–family interface as it relates to marital and family relationships, including gender-role issues in marriage, parenting and work concerns of dual-earner couples, and the gender-role socialization of children in dual-earner families.

William Ickes is Professor of Psychology at the University of Texas at Arlington. His early research focused on personality influences on behavior in unstructured dyadic interactions. His current research is focused on empathic accuracy and other aspects of intersubjective cogition. He is co-editor (with John Harvey and Robert Kidd) of the three-volume series, *New Directions In Attribution Research*, and is editor of *Compatible and Incompatible Relationships* and *Empathic Accuracy* (forthcoming).

Michael P. Johnson is Associate Professor of Sociology and Women's Studies at the Pennsylvania State University. He has published broadly in the area of close personal relationships, including work on commitment to relationships, relationships between networks and close personal relationships, gender issues in the structure of marriage, and domestic violence. His current work is focused on two areas: gender and commitment, and domestic violence.

Krzysztof Kaniasty is an Associate Professor in the Department of Psychology at Indiana University of Pennsylvania. His specialization is social/community psychology. His research interests concentrate on social support exchanges in the context of stressful life events at both individual and community levels.

Douglas T. Kenrick is Professor of Social and Environmental Psychology at Arizona State University. He has conducted research on interpersonal attraction, person–environment interactions, altruism, aggression and mate selection across human cultures. His main theoretical interest is in integrating new developments in evolutionary theory with the traditional cognitive and socialization models of social psychology.

Renate Klein is an instructor in family studies at the University of Maine. She received her training in psychology at the University of Marburg, Germany, where she worked on altruism, personal relationships and the psychology of justice. In 1992 she came to the USA with a fellowship from the German Science Foundation to conduct research on conflict in couples' strategic preferences, the role of third parties, and the analysis of common ground and understanding between partners.

Archie B. Kwan is a doctoral student in applied psychology at the Ontario Institute for Studies in Education, University of Toronto, Canada, whose research focuses on cultural differences in children's interpersonal relationships.

Brent Mallinckrodt is Associate Professor and Director of Training in the Counseling Psychology Program at the University of Oregon. He received his PhD in 1986 in counseling psychology from the University of Maryland. His research interests include the psychotherapy relationship as a means of facilitating client change, the capacity for intimacy and emotional awareness, and attachment processes in adult relationships—especially the psychotherapy relationship. His own attachments include his wife and the mountains and sea coast near Eugene, Oregon.

Sandra Metts (PhD, University of Iowa, 1983) is a professor in the Department of Communication at Illinois State University where she teaches interpersonal communication, intercultural communication, language, and research methods. Her research interests focus on the management of problematic social and relational episodes including embarrassment, relationship disengagement, deception, social support and sexual communication. Recent books include *Self-Disclosure* (with Val Derlega, Sandra Petronio and Stephen Margulis) and *Facework* (with William Cupach). Her work appears in a variety of journals, as well as in edited volumes. She serves currently as the Chair of the Interpersonal Communication Division of the International Communication Association, as the Associate Editor of *Personal Relationships* and Editor of *Communication Reports*.

Robert M. Milardo is Associate Professor of Family Relationships at the University of Maine. He received his MS in social psychology from Connecticut College and his PhD in human development and family studies from the Pennsylvania State University in 1980. With a long-standing interest in developing models of social structure and their connections to the development of personal relationship, he edited *Families and Social Networks* (1988) and is currently the Editor of the *Journal of Marriage and the Family*.

Fran Norris is an Associate Professor and Director of Graduate Studies in the Department of Psychology at Georgia State University. Her specialization is community psychology. Her research has focused on the psychosocial consequences of natural disasters, crime and other seriously stressful life events.

Malcolm R. Parks (PhD, Michigan State University, 1976) is Associate Professor of Speech Communication at the University of Washington. His primary research interest focuses on the development of interpersonal relationships and personal networks. He has conducted studies on the development of work relationships, client relationships, friendships, dating relationships, marital relationships and computer-mediated relationships. His secondary research interests include communicative competence, deception and minor league ice hockey.

Samantha E. Poisson, is a doctoral student in applied psychology at the Ontario Institute for Studies in Education, University of Toronto, Canada, whose research focuses on cultural differences in children's interpersonal relationships.

Karen Rook (PhD, UCLA, 1980) is a professor of Psychology and Social Behavior in the School of Social Ecology at the University of California, Irvine. Her research examines the implications of social network involvement for emotional and physical health, especially in later life. Much of her work has focused on social networks as a source of stress as well as support, companionship and control. Additional research has investigated the causes and consequences of loneliness. A central interest throughout her work is the application of research on interpersonal processes to clinical and community interventions.

Caryl E. Rusbult is a professor in the Department of Psychology, University of North Carolina at Chapel Hill. Her research concerns commitment processes in close relationships, including the specific relationship maintenance mechanisms by which committed individuals sustain long-term involvements (e.g., accommodative behavior, derogation of tempting alternatives).

Maria von Salisch studied psychology in New York, Hamburg, San Francisco and Berlin, taking her PhD from the Freie Universität Berlin in 1989 where she is now an Assistant Professor. She published a book on children's friendship in German and is co-editor with Ann Elisabeth Auhagen of *The Diversity of Human Relationships* (Cambridge University Press, 1996). Her research interests are peer relationships and emotional development in the context of close personal relationships, especially negotiation of anger and shame.

Barbara R. Sarason is Research Professor of Psychology at the University of Washington, has worked extensively in the research areas of stress and coping and social support, and has published more than 100 articles and book chapters in the areas of social support, stress, and coping, promotion of prosocial behavior, and cultural influences on relationships. She is co-editor of four volumes on social support, the most recent of which are *Handbook of Social Support and the Family, Sourcebook of Theory and Research on Social Support and Personality*, and *Cognitive Interference: Theories, Methods, and Findings*.

Irwin G. Sarason is Professor of Psychology at the University of Washington and has published more than 200 articles in the areas of anxiety, stress, social support and health promotion. He is co-editor of five volumes on social support, the most recent of which are *Handbook of Social Support and the Family* and *Sourcebook of Theory and Research on Social Support and Personality*; the *Stress and Emotion* series; and *Cognitive Interference: Theories, Methods, and Findings*.

Barry H. Schneider is Associate Professor of Applied Psychology at the Ontario Institute for Studies in Education, University of Toronto. His research interests include social skills inteventions, peer relations of gifted children, the life-course of children's friendship, and cultural differences in children's friendship.

Andrea Smith is a doctoral student in applied psychology at the Ontario Institute for Studies in Education, University of Toronto, whose research focuses on cultural differences in children's interpersonal relationships.

Lisa M. Tillmann-Healy is a doctoral student in the Department of Communication at the University of South Florida. Her areas of emphasis include close relationships, interpretive and qualitative methodology, and health communication.

Edison J. Trickett is Professor of Psychology at the University of Maryland and is currently serving as Special Assistant on Sociocultural Processes in Mental Health at the National Institute of Mental Health. He received his PhD from Ohio State University, conducted postdoctoral research at Stanford University in the Rudolf Moos Social Ecology Laboratory, and taught at Yale University before joining the faculty at Maryland. His career interests have focused on the development of an ecological framework for research and intervention in community psychology. He has served as President of Division 27 of the American Psychological Association, the Society for Community Research and Action, is a recipient of that Division's award for distinguished contribution to theory and research in community psychology, and is currently Editor of the field's official journal, the *American Journal of Community Psychology*. His current research focuses on the experience and adaptation of refugee and immigrant adolescents to high school.

Melanie R. Trost is an Assistant Professor of Communication at Arizona State University. Her research investigates the evolutionary bases of interpersonal processes, such as flirting, rejecting flirtation, expressing and quelling jealousy, and selecting a mate. Her other research in the area of social influence includes the cognitive processing of minority group influence messages and the development of a scale to measure individual differences in preference for consistency.

Joseph Veroff is a social psychologist who holds a joint appointment at the University of Michigan as Professor in Psychology and Research Scientist at the Survey Research Center. With a BA from Wesleyan University in 1950 and a PhD from the University of Michigan in 1955, he was first immersed in research on individual motivations, but soon became involved in social psychology as he focused on the problem of well-being and help-seeking in the American population. Discovering in *Americans View Their Mental Health* (1960) and in *The Inner American* (1981) that for most people the bases of general well-being centered on how well a person's marriage fared, in 1986 he turned to the study of marital well-being and stability. Since that time he has been helping direct a longitudinal study of 373 newlyweds, the results of which figure in the chapter he has co-authored in this volume. He is in the 42nd year of his own marriage to Joanne Bennet Veroff.

Kathy Werking received her doctorate from Purdue University in 1992. She is an Assistant Professor at the University of Louisville, Kentucky. Her research interests include cross-sex friendship and the management of friendship after divorce.

Lee West is a doctoral candidate in the Communication Studies department at the University of Iowa. Her research interests include how social expectations organize and are reinstantiated through naturally occurring conversations, specifically in the (re)production of class, gender and race in both everyday talk and the discourse of academe. She is a co-author of a chapter on cross-sex friendship.

Amy M. Young is currently a PhD candidate in personality psychology at the University of Michigan. She received her Bachelor's degree from Earlham College in human development and social relations and her Master's degree in psychology from the University of Michigan. Her current research focuses on the impact of relationship dynamics on self-descriptions, and feminism and marital relationships.

Preface

The 1st Edition of this *Handbook*, in 1988, opened with remarks on the astonishing growth of the field in the preceding 10 years and drew the analogy to buying a house in a neighborhood that suddenly becomes fashionable. The Preface for that edition noted that many disciplines of academic life were now attending to the issues of personal relationships, from developmental and social psychology through sociology to communication and family studies to community and clinical psychology. The growth and excitement were both remarkable in those days, yet how little we knew or could predict what would follow! Whatever growth there was between 1978 and 1988 has probably tripled in the subsequent 10 years and organizations at that time yet unborn, such as the International Network on Personal Relationships, now have over 1250 members. Many disciplines to which the research in relationships was somewhat tangential have now begun to see its critical relevance to their other concerns, such as organizational psychology, group psychology, psychotherapy, gender studies, leisure studies and computer studies. The central truth that the dynamics of personal relationships are one key basis of social life has taken some time to filter down, yet it remains a central truth, to whose elucidation this edition of the *Handbook* further contributes.

The Preface to the 1st Edition made the claim (p. xv) that

> The field of research in personal relationships is *inherently and necessarily* a cross-disciplinary enterprise. It can grow in scholarship and application only if the different disciplines continue to feed one another with their insights and their own special contributions . . . [It] is not created nor sustained by the efforts of only one section of the community of scholars alone, but instead feeds and grows from the interaction of many different schools of thought, all of which need to be informed about the work of the others.

There is still some way to go before the validity of that claim is established beyond dispute, but a notable feature of the present edition of the *Handbook* is the number of cross-references to significant work from disciplines different from the authors' own and the signs that there is beginning to be established a canon of work from different places and areas of scholarship to which all personal relationships researchers refer, irrespective of original discipline.

While it is almost impossible to mark out the different contributions in order for presentation in sequence in a handbook, the order chosen here is to begin with the early point of the life cycle (*Developmental Psychology, Section I*), move on to the principles of individual psychological processes in social settings (*Social Psychology, Section II*), follow with the analysis of the communication that occurs between interacting adults (*Communication, Section III*), and thence proceed to the wider communities in which relationships operate both at the level of families and networks (*Family Studies and Sociology, Section IV*) and the level of community at large, in particular the disruptions and disturbances to health upon which relationships impinge (*Clinical and Community Psychology, Section V*).

Once more, the *Handbook of Personal Relationships* seeks to be not a compendium of past achievements but a source of inspiration for future researchers and theorists. As such it provides a whetstone for the cutting edge of future research and a stimulus for dismissal of complacency, even about the good work that has already been carried out. Authors were specifically requested to challenge rather than merely to report, to be selective and guiding rather than merely comprehensive, and to indicate future lines of promise rather than merely to applaud the accomplishments of the past. The contents of this *Handbook* thus provide readers with an implicit map of the future of the field but do not, of course, stand alone in their topography. Since 1988 some 30 or 40 other books have provided detailed or sketched maps of particular parts of the territory, or added together into series that have mapped the whole. No single volume can now do justice to the range and complexity of the field and its ramifications, so the chapters in this volume are necessarily selective and were chosen for their theoretical radiations and their illustration of principles that are of more general use than their particularities might immediately suggest. As in the 1st Edition, the coverage here is extensive but cannot be regarded as complete—the more so as the field continues its rapid expansion. Nevertheless, the present mapping of the research terrain is likely to serve scholars, as did the 1st Edition, with many new and exciting directions for their work and to provide the academic leadership from which the field can yield its greatest harvests.

Steve Duck

Introduction

Sewing the Field: the Tapestry of Relationships in Life and Research*

Steve Duck, Lee West
University of Iowa, IA, USA
and
Linda K. Acitelli
University of Houston, TX, USA

The question "What is a personal relationship?" was offered at the start of this decade as the central issue facing the field (Duck, 1990) and although reactions have been slow, attention is now turning to this matter quite noticeably (Shotter, 1992; Berscheid, 1994; Kelley, 1994; Duck, 1994a). The purpose of this essay is to extend that question by asking, "Whose personal relationship is the personal relationship literature talking about—the researcher's or that of the ordinary person going about a real life?". Three interwoven strategic threads form the basis for addressing this question: (a) the tacit representation of real life relationships reflected in researchers' theories and terminologies of relationships in different disciplines; (b); the nature of the "person" reflected in research practices, theories, and presumptions, and (c) the growing need to synthesize existing research from those different disciplines (based, as each always is, on somewhat different underlying presumptions and patterns of thought).

Our main thesis is that there is a discrepancy between personal relationships in lived experiences and personal relationships as represented in abstractions based on the kinds of research presently carried out. We believe that to lose sight of everyday lived experience is to lose sight of the purpose of research on personal

* We are grateful to Julia T. Wood, Kathryn Dindia and Leslie A. Baxter for their helpful comments on previous drafts of this chapter.

Handbook of Personal Relationships, 2nd edn. Edited by Steve Duck.
© 1997 John Wiley & Sons Ltd.

relationships and to overlook the importance of "context" in modifying and influencing the ways in which relat*ing* is carried out (Duck, 1993; 1994a). A weak view of "context" is that it is the momentary backdrop against which actions are carried out (such as place, environment, or situation; Argyle, Furnham, & Graham, 1981)—rather like a scenic backdrop in a stage play or as a black backcloth can give a portrait photograph a different "feel" from a white one. A stronger view is that place, time, ritual, ceremony, celebration, and other temporal contexts render different the experiences of relaters on those occasions or in those places (Werner et al., 1993). The strongest view is that context is like the water in which fishes swim, and which covers everything that is done there, such that relationships are steeped in such cultural attitudinal, societal, normative, conversational and dialectical contexts (Allan, 1993; Baxter & Montgomery, 1996).

This chapter expounds some of the implications of exploring "context" while also arguing that whatever messy parts of real life and social context are stripped away to provide realism in experiments or conceptual clarity for theory must later be consciously and explicitly reconnected to the explanation of the stripped-down processes (Acitelli, 1995). Our thesis then translates into four main sections of this chapter: (a) the paradigmatic "close relationship" in research (too often focused on openly conducted romantic relationships between able-bodied heterosexuals in their twenties) is essentially context-free; (b) "relationships" are misleadingly treated as the product or sum of two pre-formed contained minds; (c) consequently there is insufficient attention paid to the association of public/societal influence on apparently private and individual behavior; (d) therefore there is too little depiction of the effects of context as modifiers of processes or behavior in relationships. We will review each of these prevalent points and explore other assumptions that could usefully guide research. While such a position may lead some to argue for an ethnographic or anthropological approach (e.g., Berscheid, 1995), our thesis is that no single approach will be "better" for all purposes than any other. Rather, we urge relationship researchers to engage in a conversation with "natives" and also with researchers from different disciplines to produce a whole picture through common and shared effort, rather than struggling against other disciplines and approaches to establish a disciplinary hierarchy. We thus highlight the value of regarding participants, researchers, and scholars in other disciplines as colleagues in a complex conversational exercise rather than as competitors.

CHOICE AND TOPICS OF STUDY IN RELATIONSHIPS

Historically, relationship research sought to focus on deterministic predictability, explanation, and control—and this is presented as a primary purpose of much research even today (Aronson, Wilson & Akert, 1994; Berscheid, 1986, 1994). By contrast, our "take" on relationship life is that it is characteristically uncertain, nonetheless. Part of the reason why human beings (both research participants and research conductors) prefer prediction and control is to reduce the sensation of chaos that is otherwise ubiquitous. One pervasive human characteristic is to develop categories and labels that imply stasis and fixity (Duck, 1994a). The fluid and uncertain quality of relationships is absent from much theory, and indeed it is the (real or imagined) theoretical certainties and continuities that have been the bedrock of scholarly thinking about relationships.

We do not deny the value of such research certainties but instead we see many of them as *created* or *imagined by* scholars as a result of selections made from the phenomenal pool of uncertainty; continuities are retrospectively *made into* predictable patterns from the many different sequences possible from a given starting point—whether by relaters or by researchers (Duck, 1994a). The kinds of predictabilities and certainties chosen by everyday relaters on the one hand and researchers on the other are determined by the different projects, needs and audiences for whom each set of persons creates those categories at a given moment. In the case of social scientists, their method encourages researchers to isolate particular aspects of relationships from others in order to study them more effectively, and the consequence is that certain occurrences in relationships are given priority by such methods. The nature of everyday relationships, with all their tedium and repetitious boredom, has been allowed to be represented by researchers' local and focused enthusiasms. These enthusiasms essentially lead to the endorsement of the caricature that relationships are composed of all (and only) those exciting and dramatic things to which researchers have so far given their attention—as if everyday life were like the news headlines—or that they *are essentially* orderly. Relatively large amounts of research, for example, have focused on the rational side of relationships (Andersen, 1993; Berger, 1988, 1993; Berscheid, 1994; Fehr, 1993; Fincham & Bradbury, 1987; Fletcher & Fitness, 1993; Honeycutt, 1993; Kelley et al., 1983) compared to the rare and very recent efforts devoted to the apparently irrational or emotional (Fitness & Strongman, 1991) aspects such as shame and anger (Retzinger, 1995), or daily hassles (Bolger & Kelleher, 1993), or the dark side of relationships (Cupach & Spitzberg, 1994; Duck, 1994b). For a related set of reasons, the embarrassing and dark sides of relationships have received very little attention likewise in theories of close relationships that are nevertheless presented as general theories (for exceptions see Bowen & Michal-Johnson, 1995; Cupach & Spitzberg, 1994; Duck, 1994b; Duck & Wood, 1995; Roloff & Cloven, 1994).

In addition, sharp distinctions between light and dark are often made when the dark side is discussed. While researchers have attended assiduously to the negative side of such special behaviors as caring (Stein, 1993; Wood, 1994) or social support (La Gaipa, 1990; Rook, 1984), they are notoriously reluctant to accept that *all* relationships have simultaneously both bonds and binds (Wiseman, 1986), all have darkness and light in them (Duck, 1994b), and all have hassles and irritations that have to be not merely experienced but managed in daily life (Bolger & Kelleher, 1993). Some dialectical theorists argue that it is the simultaneity of contradictory needs which characterize experience in relationships (Altman, Vinsel & Brown, 1981; Baxter, 1988, 1993; Conville, 1988; Baxter &

Montgomery, this volume). Whether or not one accepts that argument, a number of scholars have noted that relational experiences can be described in different ways from different vantage points (Duck & Sants, 1983; Surra & Ridley, 1991) and that relational "facts" are actually someone's interpretations instead. For instance, as the passage of time adds a new vantage point, so a seeming negative aspect of a relationship can be transformed into a positive or neutral feature (e.g., the case where something negative like a conflict can be resolved in ways that advance the relationship; Cate & Lloyd, 1985; Wood et al., 1994), or a seeming positive feature can be reconstrued as a negative one (e.g., when a trait like "reliability" can be reconstrued as "boringness"; Felmlee, 1995), depending on the reporter's present state of mind. Yet very little research indeed assumes that both the good and bad are present simultaneously in the same relationship or are defined as such at a particular moment or circumstance (Duck, 1994a,b; Duck & Wood, 1995) and that relationships offer opportunities and challenges for partners to manage the tension between these fluid aspects of human engagement.

Furthermore, in real life, particular parts of relationships and relationship roles are variably foregrounded from time to time, and the relationship is not one consistent experience all the time, as measures defining the closeness of a relationship imply. Thus, people in life and in research studies are made to choose particular roles or aspects of the relationship as foci on different occasions. For example, central to the understanding of personal relationships and social support is the issue of how particular circumstances *warrant* different psychological reconstructions of the relationship between people. A sudden disaster warrants and evokes different facets of relational obligations and duties (see Kaniasty & Norris, this volume) from those regarded as "normal" at other times. Thus, whereas friends are normally valorized for doing such paradigmatically friendly things as confiding in one another, disclosing, talking, having fun together, and showing intimacy (Davis & Todd, 1985), the occurrence of a disaster may warrant switches from confiding to physical support, from playfulness to emotional assistance, and from intimate disclosure to self-sacrifice and perhaps physical effort. In the mundane exigencies of everyday life, choices about emphasis or switching of appropriateness are clearly a common experience: friends do not sit and confide intensely all day long, day after day. Rather, they play (Baxter, 1992), chat (Duck et al., 1991), have small talks (Spencer, 1994), argue (Wood, 1995), go shopping or play sports or have coffee or mend cars (Wood, 1993) . . . and so on.

Equally, the everyday conduct of relationships can involve momentary choices between relationships, between different distributions of time with different partners, and even strains on loyalties to different persons who may make simultaneous, competing demands on one's relational resources or provisions (Baxter et al., in press). A person may be faced with conflicts between or among different relationships—to spend time with spouse or with kids alone, with friends or with co-workers, with partner or with family, staying longer at a work social event or going home to play with the kids, in fulfilling obligations to parents or to neighbors and so on. In real life everyday relationships, a person's commitments to a particular relationship can be assessed as much by the relative distribution of time *between* relationships as by the balance between internal reward and cost systems *within* relationships.

To recognize such continuous changes in relational emphases is to require a different underlying view of relationships that sees them as multiplex, variable, subject to recharacterization, describable in many ways simultaneously, open-ended, to some extent contentious, and certainly the kind of conceptual entity that can be the subject of disputes about their "true nature" on occasion. Such tensions and choices may be viewed as "descriptive" or "rhetorical" (as may their management). That is to say, partners have choices about the language in which to characterize a relational act at a given point in time—and even which relational act is the focus of attention—and to do so they probably decontextualize it from the processes that swarmed around it at the time. Any person's selection of a description for features of a relationship at a particular time is a rhetorical act, not a simple descriptive one; that is to say, people describe relationships—or anything else—in a way that is consistent with a particular world-view and purpose, on a particular occasion, for a particular audience, or in a particular context (Duck, Pond & Leatham, 1994).

Equally, researchers have similar kinds of descriptive and rhetorical choices available to them. It is therefore important if we are to describe relationships usefully—let alone explain them—that researchers keep reminding themselves to return that which they took away in order to create a better experiment or a more focused study for a particular purpose on a particular occasion. Having, for good reasons, focused on a single process or the interaction of just two processes by momentarily removing them from their active sites and contexts of operation, any explainer of those processes has to remember to reinsert the previously removed parts of the picture.

This is particularly important when one acknowledges that relationships are depicted in research at the moment of measurement. This risks depicting relationship processes themselves in a form generalized from that moment so that relationships are then discussed as entities characterized totally by that measurement. Yet in treating relationships as cross-sections, unities, states, plateaux or turning points on a graph, researchers may overlook the *simultaneous* presence and intersection of a number of features and options or the pressures of real alternatives to the path actually taken. For example, turning points are choices between actual alternative options: to understand the choice one has to understand the psychological and social context of alternatives in which it was made (Duck, 1994a; Dixson & Duck, 1993). It is also necessary to portray the rhetorical context in which the choice was described, and to depict not only the outcome but the processes and dynamics surrounding it.

Yet often the rhetorical choices made by researchers are concealed in the discourse of objective description (Bazerman, 1987). "Description" sounds misleadingly neutral and shrouds the motives and skills of the "describer", yet scientific description, too, is carried out in particular ways within a rhetorical context (Nelson, Megill & McCloskey, 1987). We all—relaters and researchers alike—make choices about what to notice and how to describe it. For example, psychological researchers typically choose to study cognition, and more particularly rationality, as objectively determinable and as privileged over irrationality, chaos and emotionality (Fletcher & Fitness, 1993). In such a view, humans are cast as "naive scientists" where other views may position them as spirited collaborators and improvisational (co)performers of life (Harré, 1995; Shotter, 1992, 1993). Some scholars represent humans as energetic interpreters constructing narratives about their lives that "position" them in certain ways relative to other people (Harré, 1995), or erecting thriving and seething systems of personal meaning that relationships can bring into harmonious concord (Shotter, 1992, 1994). The former approach to cognition tends to regard "communication" as the simple transmission of fixed messages from one person to another (Duck, 1994a). Yet much communication is concerned with the *adapting* of messages to people and to circumstances, or with the rhetorical context in which someone might select a message or convey an evaluation or present an argument and viewpoint (Bryant, 1953). People—in relationships and in research—have choices about the words used to convey information or to describe their relationship as well as about the slant to be given to information selected from the pool of all that could be said. In exercising such choices people do relational work as much as they do it with messages themselves (see, for example, Hopper, 1993, on the rhetoric of the divorce process).

The prevailing research view represents relationships too simplistically because it omits the variety that persons face as they conduct relationships in a daily life that incorporates unpredictabilities and switches of emphasis—omitting not only the variety of experience but also the variety of descriptions that can be used to characterize that experience in different circumstances (Duck, 1994a). The risk is that, in a quest to impose their own kinds of selective order, theorists will falsely suggest a unity of experience in relationships that underplays the seething variability and frequent internal complexity or difficulty of management and description inherent in relationships as experienced (Duck & Wood, 1995). As a telling example, researchers typically determine *a priori* the nature of a relevant relationship based on social norms associated with relational labels, and so it is assumed *by definition* that friendship will exclude sexual activity. In real life, however, Ramey (1976) and others found this to be untrue (see also Nardi & Sherrod, 1994). In fact, Bradac (1983) identified the hybrid relationship "flovers" (friends who are lovers), and West, Anderson & Duck (1995) argue that the nature of the cross-sex friendship is contingent on the emphasis placed by the relational partners in a particular time or setting, and also on the difficulty of describing the relationship in terms outsiders will understand (Werking, this volume).

The social label that is ascribed to a relationship in part preordains a listener's expectations about the processes and sets limits to its features or to its "fuzziness" by establishing a prototype (Fehr, 1993). When researchers listen, they may hear such prototypes without the original fuzziness or may eliminate the fuzziness or disregard its importance. Hence research places less emphasis on the change, variabilities, struggles and tensions in relationships as lived experiences where partners decide how to define the bounds of their relationship's social labels and more emphasis on order and predictability. It is also therefore easy to reify networks and relationships by treating them as constants when in fact they change as folks get sick, die, get well, move to new addresses, develop other relationships, get promoted at work and do other things that people continuously do as life goes on (Wellman, 1985). Thus, one living element of relationships is that they constantly present people with interpersonal dilemmas, choices and changes in personnel, as well as with choices in descriptions of those events (Duck, 1994a; Duck & Wood, 1995; Stein, 1993; Wood, 1994).

Perhaps such dilemmas could easily be the grist for the insecurely attached person's everyday relational mill (Latty-Mann & Davis, 1996; Zeifman & Hazan, this volume), just as they may be grounds for the everyday arguments or conflicts within the couple. In real life, persons occasionally question the nature of their relationships, see partners as *simultaneously* "good" and "bad", or reflect negatively on each other without actually leaving the relationship (Duck & Wood, 1995; Felmlee, 1995). In addition, partners can feel good about a relationship sometimes and not at other times, can quarrel and make up (i.e., cycle through different feelings and characterizations of "the same" relationship) or can have good days and bad days *in the same relationship* (Barbee, 1990)—which is of no particular consequence, perhaps, unless a researcher measures the relationship only once and treats that measure as the complete story about the relationship, or has no interest in describing its variablities and variances (Duck, 1994a). However, if relationships are truly dynamic and multiplex, yet are represented in research as unitary states or social structures, then the experiential and often uneven process of relating is lost in the research process itself and it needs to be regained. Thus, we believe a fundamental need in future PR research is full and responsive recognition of the fact that relationships are not well represented by unitary labels that obscure their seething processes or imply a calm uniformity. We now review some sources and solutions for this problem.

PARADIGMS OF RELATING

Paradigm Relating: True Love Never Did Run Smoothly

In the periodic lamentations about the deficiencies of research on relationships, perhaps the simplest, most superficial, yet most frequent, observation is that research is implicitly or explicitly restricted to openly conducted, able-bodied, heterosexual romantic (or potentially romantic) relationships, particularly those of our obligingly captive sophomores. Naturally, the scientific method makes it harder to study "minority" or special relationships because they are more difficult to find and therefore expensive and complicated to study (Lyons & Meade, 1995; Wood & Duck, 1995). Likewise, the effects of constraints on "illicit" romantic relationships such as affairs (Duck, 1977) are rarely incorporated into theories of "close relationships", neither are the impacts of social norms about interracial romances (Gaines, 1995a; Gaines & Ickes, this volume) or the practical difficulties for gay and lesbian couples to obtain support for their relationships from family and community (Huston & Schwartz, 1995). Thus, theories limiting "close relationships" only to "openly-conducted socially approved romantic heterosexual relationships" are highly questionable informants about subtler (and often more painful) social processes in personal relationships for many social groups and relationship forms (Wood & Duck, 1995).

In addition, most relationships do not develop in intimacy (Delia, 1980). All the same, prominent theories "of relationship processes" are in fact tacitly theories of relationship *development* (e.g., Kelley et al., 1983; Murstein, 1986; Rusbult, 1987; Rusbult & Buunk, 1993) that lay out the conditions for growth (or decline) and have less to say about functioning, but non-developing, relationships that make up so much lived experience. Do relationships with parents, children, siblings, family, neighbors, colleagues and so forth really *develop*? If so, do the profiles created to explain romantic relationships apply equally well to them? In theories of romantic development, the role of family and friends is instrumental in challenging or supporting the development of a heterosexual romantic relationship (Driscoll, Davis & Lipetz, 1972). Research even on same-sex friendship assumes that sort of relationship is *normatively* supported by culture, family and other friends tacitly, unannounced and without fuss, yet Werking (this volume) indicates that cross-sex non-romantic friendships are often seriously questioned or challenged by such people. Huston & Schwartz (1995) show that gay and lesbian partners experience extra social burdens in carrying out their relationships in a living context where other people's reactions are extremely substantial. Further, Weston (1991) argues that "blood family" is often replaced for homosexuals by "families of choice". Because homosexuals often are not "out" to family, or may be estranged from their families specifically because of their homosexuality, the "blood family" can function very differently for gays and lesbians. Not only are gays and lesbians less likely to tell their parents and siblings of developing relationships, they are less likely to talk of *developed* intimate relationships (Huston & Schwartz, 1995). In examining the relationship between families of origin and lesbian couples, Murphy (1989) reports that even when parents of lesbians are aware of their daughter's significant romantic relationship, they often deny the bond or connection (e.g. by inviting just the daughter for holidays).

Such observations indicate not only the value of studying such processes in diverse or non-normative populations, as is usually proclaimed at this point in a review, but also the importance of studying the taken-for-granted operation of those same processes in *normative* relationships where they are hardly ever explored and are instead taken for granted (Duck & Wood, 1995; Wood & Duck, 1995). The key implication, however, is not that researchers may too easily forget that "relationship processes" are unlikely to be exhaustively represented by the activities of teenage heterosexual romantic couples. We all get reminded of that point often enough in the "limitations" sections of journal papers. Who could ever forget, even if the observation is subsequently more honored in the breach?

Rather, the key point is that even in such a restricted population, researchers have a very poor understanding of the variabilities that characterize conduct of these relationships in different contexts, moods, environments or circumstances, since even these captive subjects are usually studied in one-shot measurements or very restricted contexts. Claims to have general theories of personal relationships are suspect not only to the degree that they depend on such a limited sampling of human beings but also to the degree that they additionally depend on a limited sampling of the experiences of those limited samples of human beings. Those who advocate cumulative science could, after all, find out all there is to know about sophomores instead of complaining that they are "not representative" (of something no-one can describe because no-one has done the necessary work to depict that which should be represented).

Relationship Partners: More than Independent Contained Minds?

Implicit understandings of relationships, like any theory, contain a number of important assumptions, some explicated and some held implicit because they are taken for granted or shared within the researchers' discourse community (Duck, 1994a). In the discourse of relationship researchers, an important unspoken assumption concerns the nature of personhood or agency, yet models of relating implicitly contain representations of varying degrees of human agency. As a simple but powerful instance, the early research on attraction (e.g., Berscheid & Walster, 1969) used the metaphor of magnetism, which actually implicitly denies active human agency. Instead it focuses research strongly on empirical efforts to locate the list of inherent individual characteristics that propel people towards one another *involuntarily* (Berscheid & Walster, 1978). Implicit in, and ultimately unexplained by, this powerful metaphor is the notion that the pre-existing *characteristics* of a person, rather than behavior or social contexts, result in liking. The metaphor further implicitly represents liking as a *response* (or an "attitude" as Berscheid & Walster, 1969 defined it), something in a person's head. The metaphor therefore draws attention away from agents' behavior expressed or performed in a dynamic social context at a particular moment (McCall, 1988), or from the use of economic resources available to the partners for the conduct of their relationship (Allan, 1995; Wellman, 1985) or from sets of cultural beliefs and norms that influence individual cognitions and practice (Allan, 1993). The magnetic metaphor thus entails an implicit notion that the agency of a person is subordinate to uncontrollable forces (magnetism, attraction)—that the characteristics themselves *determine* attraction (see Aronson, Wilson & Akert, 1994, for a recent instance of this style of interpretation).

A later-generation assumption is that relationships are formed "between" (or else "contain") two separate autonomous beings who think for themselves, make attributions, have personalities, beliefs and values, and act strictly as individuals however close they become (see Andersen, 1993; Dindia, this volume, for review and critique).

> "Within that framework of understanding, interpersonal actions are undertaken as individual enactments of wants and needs, consonant with the unique qualities and objectives of the actor. Although those enactments may be adapted to the perceived qualities, needs and objectives of other participants, and to situational factors relevant to the task, the starting point for analysis is an assumption of independent selfhood as the basis for perception, action and interpretation" (Fitch, in prepatation).

This set of assumptions warrants the study of "closeness" as a discrete topic in which scientists attempt to depict the extent to which two such separate entities can become intertwined (Berscheid, Snyder & Omoto, 1989; Kelley et al., 1983). The assumption of "contained minds" also lies behind research presuming that relationships are operated by autonomous, intact, self-contained planners who set strategic goals and then bring them about—to a greater or lesser extent—by operating forcefully on the world of other autonomous, intact, self-contained minds (Berger, 1988, 1993). The assumption also authorizes casting of relationships as transactions between intact selves for social profit, implicit in all exchange-based models or investment models (see Rusbult & Arriaga, this volume), where individuals carefully compose calculations of value and self-interest.

The simplicity of these assumptions is appealing to some. Both implicitly and explicitly several lines of research suggest that relationships work best when they support a particular (pre-existing) conceptualization of one's self. For example, one of Weiss's (1974) provisions of relationships was "personality support", and Byrne's (1971) work on the reinforcing effect of similarity of attitudes indicates the value of the consistency of others' beliefs with an observer's belief system. Even recent work offering an attachment process model of partner selection (Latty-Mann & Davis, 1996) suggests that partners are attracted to one another as a function of their respective attachment profiles. All three models (similarity, complementarity, attachment) have the same basic assumption: that partners provide for one another that which is required by the partner's pre-existing personality composition.

However, the idea is too simple. Latty-Mann & Davis (1996) go on to note that the process of acquaintance is different from the simple expression of preferences during initial attraction—a point suggesting change in persons at different points of the relational process. Different aspects of others can become important as the relationship proceeds, the important final element being the negotiation of role matching and behavioral intersections that are workable in the relationship (cf. Murstein, 1987)—a point suggesting change in persons as relationships are constructed together. For one thing, persons have been shown to become more similar to one another over time, not only to start out being attracted to pre-existing similarity (Newcomb, 1961; Blankenship et al., 1984)—a point stressing change in persons over time together. Also, a person's needs, roles, intimacy requirements and general identity change in response to various experiences and reorganization of self across the life cycle (Prager, 1995)—a point noting change in persons as they age. Research on various nodes of life transition (such as transition to parenthood or retirement) are the most obvious examples of this point (Hansson & Carpenter, 1994). In such discussion then, the evidence is that relationships are not simply monolithic *containers* of invariant persons (Baxter & Montgomery, 1996)—the most common expression of which view is found in phrases about people *in* relationships. Relationships do not simply surround, encase or enclose the two individuals who are "in" them. It is misleading to describe development of *relationships,* rather than of partners, and to assess the changes in closeness of the relationship rather than the changes occurring in the persons themselves as they alter their view of themselves together (Conville, 1988).

Some models of personal relationships do emphasize personal growth and change, but do so by representing relationship-making as the construction of a third entity by two sovereign, contained, intact selves that are then modified by interdependence. Aron & Aron (1995; see also chapter in this volume) argue that personal relationships are a mechanism for "self" to expand in the sense of "taking the other into the self". Several first-generation stage models argued likewise for progressive invasion of self by the partner in the relationship (Kerckhoff & Davis, 1962; Duck & Craig, 1978). The assumption underlying this research is that a relationship is owned by the relational partners and is constructed by the merging of the two people who incorporate and develop one another's range of experiences, emotions and psychological preparations for the future through progressively revealed and integrated knowledge.

As an extension of such approaches, Uncertainty Reduction Theory (Berger & Calabrese, 1975; Berger & Bradac, 1982) derives increased liking, intimate information, non-verbal affiliative expressiveness and verbal communication from the acquisition of knowledge of another's pre-existing characteristics. Acquaintance is then the process of uncovering more of these characteristics and making sense of them. A similar underlying representation is found in the metaphors exploring the deliberate gradual revelation, peeling off, or disclosing of personal characteristics that extends to ones not superficially apparent in interaction, such as intimate private thoughts, past experiences and personal feelings. Such self-disclosure could be considered as the act of putting one's personal qualities into the relational chemistry, and several theories position the behaviors of self-disclosure as central for relational development. According to the original onion-skin metaphor in social penetration theory (Altman & Taylor, 1973), relational closeness is demonstrated by increased breadth and depth of self-disclosures about one's inner self, with relational distance or decline associated with the reverse. Altman, Vinsel & Brown (1981) later revised this notion to incorporate dialectics in which progressive, uninterrupted openness is not defined as the path toward intimacy. Further, placing more emphasis instead on the interactive dynamics of self-disclosure, Dindia (1994) argued that self-disclosure involves an intrapersonal–interpersonal dialectical process. Drawing on social welfare and psychological literature which describes the disclosures of stigmatized identities, Dindia (1994) offers a model of a cyclical process of intrapersonal and interpersonal self disclosure; "Self-disclosure is a dialectical process that occurs both within and between persons" (Dindia, 1994, p. 56). Similarly, emphasizing not the characteristics themselves but the process of interpreting them, Harré (1995) argues that the intended *action* of a discloser achieves its force as an *act* in a relationship only from the response of the perceiver, so that intent in the discloser may differ from the interpretation of the perceiver and affect the partners in the relationship differently.

Different in these approaches are the implicit models of human agency (person as a bundle of magnetisms, as layers of skins concealing an inner core, as a site of contest for dialectical forces, as a sense-maker). The differences focus on the extent to which the revealed self is seen either as formed and stable (but revealed in layers) or as continually open-ended, unstable and changing (Dindia, this volume; Duck, 1994a). Thus, to challenge the prevalent conceptualization of self-disclosure as based in Jourard's (1971) definition of "making yourself manifest . . . showing yourself so others can perceive you" (p. 19) is also to challenge a position that makes self-disclosure the province of the person and not of the relationship. Some scholars (e.g., Dindia, 1994; Spencer, 1994) have claimed, for example, that the behavior of talking with another about self is not an unveiling but a negotiation and construction of an identity (Baxter & Montgomery, 1996; Brown & Rogers, 1991; West, 1995). Similar to Mead's (1934) theory of self, West (1995) argued for a conceptual difference between self and identity: *self* was posited as emerging as a subjective and immediate experience (Mead's *I*), while *identity* (Mead's *Me*) is the objective awareness of self. The actions and interactions of self are christened as an identity in dialogue with others. Hence, what occurs in the sharing of self's thoughts, actions and biography with another is *construction* of an identity for self, not merely the *presentation* of an already formed self. Rather than presenting or revealing a prefabricated identity, the process of disclosure is actually the process of talking an identity into existence within the relationship at a particular context and point in time (West, 1995; see also Dindia, 1994 and this volume).

Yet if one treats identity as constructed in relationships, then one must at least concede that several different types of identity are simultaneously undergoing work there: (1) the selves of the partners in the relationship (i.e., the type of persons the partners are); (2) the selves of the persons in relationship to one another (i.e., the type of partner one is for a specific other person); (3) the social identity of the type of relationship that the partners are enacting (i.e., the socially recognized category of relationship, such as casual dating or serious dating). By ignoring multiple forms of identity that are open-ended or changing simultaneously during relational process, researchers obscure the impact of social contexts on these changes. For example, in treating relationships as self-contained products of individuals, action or thought that are separate from the evolving social context, researchers run the risk of overlooking changes in the surrounding standards of judgment about acceptable conduct for relationships (Prusank,

Duran & DeLillo, 1993). Yet individuals are constantly exposed to such standards through the cultural products of media and so forth (Kidd, 1975; McCall, 1988). They also encounter such standards through the choices of network members, who do not judge the appropriateness of a relationship solely by its own internal standards but perforce attach them to judgments of quality and warrants provided by the culture of the moment.

Society and Culture as Permanent Relational Houseguests

The nature and range of acceptable variation of relationships are to some extent themselves shaped by social and cultural schemata about relationship types (Andersen, 1993). In some cultures, for example, "a friend" is the loyal helpmeet who is willing to die for another (e.g., in Ancient Classical Greece this was a common theme), while in others "a friend" is only ever instantiated by a person from another distant village on the grounds that no-one at all is ever to be trusted, so the role of friend is symbolic and vacuous anyway (La Gaipa, 1981) and may as well be filled by someone you don't have to meet all that often. The incorporation of such schemata into a person's ways of conducting relationships indicates an important sense in which society pre-exists individuals and changes or develops independently of such persons and their uncertain lives, or else a sense in which "society" is a monolith that merely attaches to, bonds with or afflicts individuals, rather than intersects with it (Hinde, 1979). In this view, the fixed entity that operates on other fluid entities is the culture and the society that operates on both relationships and the individuals "in" them. However, even those who assume that society pre-exists the individual (e.g., Mead, 1934) do not assume that society and individual are independent. More recent theorists (e.g., Ginsburg, 1988) stress the social significance of the formulation of lines of action in ways that are consistent with expectations for partners. They also note that the apparently neutral interpretation of others' actions by reference to their assigned improvisational role in the drama in fact reflects a context of social expectation (Fitch, in prep.; Ginsburg, 1988; Argyle & Henderson, 1984). Such a context of expectations imbues even research interpretation of actions in subtle ways.

In research on relationships, such a point is reflected in the built-in assumptions about what can be taken as normal experience, what sorts of relationship types and forms are acceptable, or what may be taken as the right and proper expression of emotion. In using particular measures of relationships, researchers, of course, encode those assumptions into research. For example, in a Western culture we dress in black to express grief, but in an eastern culture the appropriate color is white; Western research accepts as "understandable" that romantic partners will display affection by holding hands—and may even use that as an operational measure of closeness in research (Rubin, 1973)—while an Eastern culture condemns such behavior as altogether inappropriate in public, so its occurrence at all would show not simple affection but defiance of norms also.

Similarly, connected to a view of personhood as sculpted by society is a related assumption about the "proper" relationship between such persons; whether, for example, it is one that assumes equality or one that assumes hierarchy, one that assumes merit in independence and individualism or one that sees individualism as selfish and prefers a collectivist style of involvement in group structure (Gudykunst, 1992). Furthermore, as Fitch (in preparation) notes, "Relevant to conceptualizations of both personhood and relationships are premises about communication itself: the circumstances under which particular forms and patterns of speaking are appropriate, and what connection exists among ways of speaking, enactments of identity, and formation of relationships". Such a position alerts us to the interpretive contexts provided by assumptions about relationships that infuse their daily conduct and to the essence of "communication" as beyond simple message sending or transmission of content. In particular the view challenges the prevailing assumption that relationships are containers which *encounter* other monolithic container entities, such as social networks, which respond/interact/relate to a *couple* (Klein & Milardo, 1993), instead of to relational partners as separate individuals (Bendtschneider & Duck, 1993). In other words the social network is typically marked as a boundary to the relationship (Baxter & Widenmann, 1993), or as an organized and functionally autonomous social unit entirely containing other persons who are separate from the relationship (for a critique, see Wellman, 1985; Milardo & Wellman, 1992). Little attention is paid to the fact that each person "in" the target dyadic relationship is simultaneously constituting a relationship with each other person "in" the network, often several relationships simultaneously.

In addition, public and private life are not separated by the front door, but are lived out within the same moment. Similarity, for example, is both a cognitive and a social construct; however, researchers rarely focus on both aspects simultaneously (Duck, 1994a). Relational researchers often will refer to the importance of similarity as a mechanism for relational development (Byrne, 1971; Berscheid & Walster, 1978), even though not all similar people can meet and build on the fertility of that similarity in the real social world. A major move in this line of inquiry was when researchers pointed out that functional proximity preceded similarity as an important influence on relational initiation (Festinger, Schachter & Back, 1950). Yet proximity is not merely physical presence in the social context (Kerckhoff, 1974; Murstein, 1971) but functions socially as well (Allan, 1993). We are "closer" to those of similar social standing. Socio-economic positioning plays an enormous role in the range of people who are considered "available" for relationships (Kerckhoff, 1974; Whitbeck & Hoyt, 1994). It could be argued, therefore, that socio-economic standing is largely presumed under the rubric "psychological similarity", typically elaborated on as attitudes, values and beliefs. Duck (1994a) laments that similarity has been interpreted as a cognitive, not as a social, construct and as a state, not as an open-ended process of continually perceived and/or reconstructed correspondence. The opportunity to consider as a partner someone who is similar or dissimilar is (at least initially) as much a matter of conformity (conscious or not) to demographics as it is a result of any "actual" psychological similarity which may or may not exist between interactants. Indeed, social structure itself determines the factors that are deemed to be bases for judgments of similarity in the first place (e.g., in the USA, "race" is emphasized as an issue, but in some cultures, caste is emphasized as an issue, or class is emphasized as an issue, or religion is an issue that precludes or disparages certain sorts of relationship candidates and approves or prescribes certain others). In other words, even psychological similarity between individuals is not an individually isolated phenomenon but one that occurs in a social context: social stratification sorts people in ways that affect the probability that they will have certain kinds of similarity (such as socioeconomic, racial, religious or political values) and the value of the similarity is determined or constrained by the social context.

Even if relationships were established between two initially independent and individual minds or bundles of cognitions and attributions, they are conducted in a context that "takes a view" about the ways in which independent entities are "supposed" to progress in "building" a relationship (Allan, 1993). The path of a relationship is ultimately a narrative imposed on a number of events and occurrences perceived within a particular social context as a reasonable path. For instance, "We met and fell in love and got married" is more acceptable in North America than "I ate some ground almond paste and the relationship just developed from there" or "We sacrificed some sheep and therefore we became closer" or "Our parents picked our partners from a catalogue and naturally we got married the next day". In short, cultural contexts provide individuals not only with views of how relationships are supposed to develop, but also with vocabularies for representing relationship growth. "We fell in love" is a common, and therefore privileged, discursive explanation in most Western cultures; "It is a good match for both families" is more acceptable in many other parts of the world. Thus, the arbiter for acceptability of matters of relationship identity and form or individual identity and form will ultimately also be some reference group outside of the relationship or individual alone (Simmel, 1950). The identity of a person in a relationship and of relationships themselves will thus ultimately be influenced by reference to social communities rather than by self and relationship alone. Attempts to identify relationship change or self transformation by looking only inside the relationship or the individual partners are therefore incomplete and limiting because they overlook such important social, sociological and assumptive contexts. Relevant also are the nature of human experience in general and social contexts in particular (Klein & Johnson, this volume; Milardo & Wellman, 1992).

In living their lives, individuals do not perceive themselves as responding to some social dictates in creating their relationship, but see themselves as sources of relational choice and embodiment. In a sense they *are* personally responsible for reproducing that social form. Yet they not only produce their relationship in their behaviors but also thereby *re*produce it and perpetuate the social form, its emotional tone, and its familiar topics and styles. In talking, the partners continuously recreate, revitalize and re-enact their conceptualization of the relationship itself (Berger & Kellner, 1964), just as their talk uses categories and constructs to represent their own patterned ways of imposing a personal order on the world and stabilizing the fluidity and chaos that the world would otherwise project. Because talk reifies the personal orders of the speakers, which are to some extent reflections of social order, the terms with which speakers describe and conceive their relationship place those relationships in the *moral* context of the larger social order that is implicit in other sorts of orders (Shotter, 1992). In focusing so exclusively on the psychological facet of relating as an individual internalized and cognitive activity, researchers run the risk of overlooking the extent to which actions have a social interpretation and force that carries moral and evaluative weight.

Context as Modifier of Relationship Experiences

One way to look at context is as a shared meaning system. Personal relationship research involves multiple meaning systems (acknowledged or not): cultural meanings, social meanings, familial meanings, symbolic meanings generally, the meaning systems constructed between two people, and the meaning systems that researchers themselves bring to their enterprise of observation. These meanings co-exist at any given point as society pours into relationships and relationships into society.

Yet one very often encounters the term "the relationship" used as if there is only one appropriate way to represent it, and hence that "a relationship is a relationship is a relationship" to all people equivalently, or to both partners identically, or to each person consistently at all times. All the same, views of the ideal way to conduct relationship in a given culture change across time quite dramatically (e.g., between even the 1950s and 1990s; Prusank, Duran & DeLillo, 1993). Furthermore, a specific counter-example of experiential uniformity within a type of relationship may be found in the cross-sex friendship literature (Werking, this volume). Furthermore, men and women describe their experiences of cross-sex friendship differently. Men report experiencing high levels of emotional support and women report either receiving significantly less emotional support (Wood, 1993) or talking about their relationships in different ways (Acitelli, 1988). The reported differences are specifically tied to gender: thus the experience of many aspects of relationships is a gendered social phenomenon. Investigation of relationships thus involves not merely identifying relationship behaviors but locating relationship behaviors in their social contexts (Wood, 1995).

Scholars have too often emphasized behavior itself to the neglect of the contextual and economic influences on relationship behavior provided by various social conditions and expectations (Allan, 1993; Duck, 1993). Focus on behaviors leads to schemes for differentiating relationships from one another (e.g., Hinde's, 1981, distinction between reciprocity and complementarity in relationships or between multiplexity and simplicity) that assume, essentially, that context-free qualities of context-free activities can define relationships. In fact, friendships are never "just behaviors" but are acts conducted in a "place" at a time (Werner, et al., 1993) and the notion of "place" has ramifications that affect the style and range of behaviors of friendship that will be enacted (Allan, 1995). For instance, those people or social groups who do not have the money to entertain at home or who have small inconvenient homes—or no homes at all—are more likely to conduct their relationships in a "place" that reflects those economic conditions. Such places also happen to limit the financial resources required of the respective partners—for example, the British pub, where "reciprocity" extends to the cost of a round of drinks rather than an elaborate meal which may be the reciprocated entertainment within the home for those who can afford it (Allan, 1995).

Other forms of overemphasis on abstracted behaviors and neglect of context are noted by Hendrick & Hendrick (1993), who observed that it is more likely that researchers would focus on the different types of love as absolute and relatively constant rather than on the variety of ways in which love could be expressed in different contexts or to different audiences (e.g., to a researcher, in writing, to parents, to a priest or to a sexual partner). Research could also explore the various manners in which the same person can express different sorts of love to the same partner as a function of place, context or perceived appropriateness to situation—e.g., in proposing marriage, on honeymoon, during a request for support (Duck, 1994).

The construction of form for a relationship is a matter of coordination of one's own behavior, not only with that of the partner but also with the network and the wider social group (Milardo, 1984; Parks & Eggert, 1991; Milardo & Wellman, 1992). All these constructions are essentially manipulations of meaning systems that involve the sharing and coordination of meaning—or rather more particularly, the coordination of meanings embodies *expectations* for one's own and others' behavior.

A problem in conventional views of relationship form as the product of two individuals alone has been the assumption of simple communality of expectations—that is, the assumption that the meanings associated with particular acts are commonly shared, uniformly agreed in particular cultures of study, and removable from contexts as "absolute" examples of behaviors that are always typical of a given sort of relationship (see, for example, Davis & Todd, 1985). By contrast, we are pointing to the fundamental negotiability of meanings for acts as a function of different reference groups and individual action, as well as being a function of the audience to whom a describer addresses the description of relational actions. In other words, for partners in a relationship to share meaning, they must be able to *evaluate* various "acts" and "responses" as equivalent and connected—for example, people have to *agree* that a particular act of payment of money is "about" the acquisition of specific goods or services for it to count as an exchange: if one party thinks the money is a gift and the goods are a loan then the transaction could be denied as an instance of exchange (indeed several law suits have resulted from such claims; Walker & Walker, 1972). In important ways, the development of relationships involves the negotiation of the meaning—and hence the personal value—of acts; many exchanges defined in terms of their commonly shared evaluations are unlikely to be adequately pre-dictive of specific behavior in a particular relationship (Duck, 1994a). Rather, researchers need to do more exploration of the manners in which partners negotiate such meanings between themselves—not just limited to clarifying the differences between a compliment vs. sexual proposition, or an insult vs. teasing, but the manners in which partner negotiate any intimacy in interactions as a general principle of communication in relationships (e.g., Harris & Sadeghi, 1987). In the process of negotiating the meaning of acts within a relationship, partners develop a specifically interpersonal set of meanings that go beyond the socially agreed culturally common set of meanings (Montgomery, 1988; Wood, 1995). They may even negotiate unique shared understandings of their relation-ships (Acitelli, 1993). Thus the identity of a relationship, of people as partners and even of themselves as individuals, is established rhetorically in the context of, and under the guidance or influence of, exterior social entities such as net-works and cultures.

Problematically, if one treats information or cognition as an objective and neutral text rather than as something shaped by contexts and by the rhetorical needs of the moment and of the audience, then it is hard to recognize that some aspects of relationships are inherently lop-sided—and indeed all relationships may have lop-sided aspects. One partner in a relationship can often understand the other person better than the reverse (Acitelli, 1993; gives the examples of a parent-and-child and Duck, 1994a, the confidence-trickster-and-dupe). Partners can have conflicting views of each other, of themselves and of their shared relationship (Acitelli & Young, 1996; Bernard, 1972; Fitzpatrick & Best, 1979). Furthermore, one person can understand the relationship itself better than the other partner does (Acitelli, 1993). For instance, it is easy to accept the point that a parent–child relationship is lop-sided in terms of understanding: for the most part, the parent understands the child better than vice versa and a piece of information, or a fragment of speech, or an idea, or a bit of communication means different things to the two partners, even though it is in some sense objectively the same piece of information (Duck, 1994a). Yet the same point could be extended to all relationships: to the extent that each person interprets informa-tion and cognition in accordance with a personal meaning system (Andersen, 1993), any piece of information can mean something different to two persons unless they negotiate or create agreement on meaning, whether actively between themselves or passively by adopting a cultural interpretation. The relational art is to create a symbiosis and ultimately a fusion of personal meaning systems so that interpretations of information, self-disclosure, historical context and so forth have roughly similar meanings for all parties in a relationship (Planalp & Garvin-Doxas, 1994). For example, Acitelli's (1988, 1993) work implies that social cogni-tive rationality (accuracy) is not as relevant to relationships as is the manner in which partners think about their relationship—that an argument is less significant to a relationship than the *perception* of there having been one. Our contention is that the experience called a relationship is not so much the sum of two minds as their mutual recognition and imperfect interpretation and understanding. To the degree that research objectifies "information" and separates it from personal and interpersonal meaning systems by depicting it as the same for all persons, it misses this important point about relationship processes.

PUTTING RELATIONSHIP RESEARCH BACK TOGETHER

By removing such relationship experiences from the concrete activities of everyday life, scholars risk traducing the ever-present need of choice between alternative activities or descriptions of activities that could realistically have been chosen instead. The intrusive permeation of a living social context, the chatter of playfulness, the not-so-small-talk that weaves lives together, or the live murmur of human interaction and the complexities of personal interpretations, are not merely busy; they are occasions for selection of response, action, emotion, description, attribution and reaction to context. We stress that, in real life, relating occurs in social contexts that are themselves experienced as dynamic processes, not as static structures, and that choice is a key aspect—and a dynamic aspect— of lived relational experience. Thus we recommend that relationship researchers ask individuals about their relationships while taking into account their social context; ask those partners *in depth* about their relationship in a search for narrative themes and take across time assessments of what people are actually *doing* in relationships.

Therefore, we need an approach to research that transcends disciplinary boundaries. Such boundaries can limit the kinds of observations made as well as the interpretation applied to them. One considerable change in research on relationships in the last 15 years has been the willingness of different scholars to read and attend to the work of other disciplines, but there is still some way to go. We have become used to relying on the sociologist to incorporate the social structural forces, power issues and network effects, the communication researcher to analyse the talk or the context and interpretation of messages and symbols, and the psychologist to explore individual differences, personality and attributional propensities. This is now the time for the next step. Instead of depending on various researchers from different disciplines to work on separate pieces of the puzzle, or to point to different textures of the pieces, we challenge researchers from different disciplines to go beyond the compilation of a composite picture from the separate pieces. Researchers from different disciplines might talk to one another before the pieces are ever constructed and so develop methods that take a pragmatic rather than a discipline-oriented approach that reflects real life experience in all its complexity. We could talk amongst ourselves about the kinds of questions, the kinds of assumptions, the kinds of data that we need in order to answer our fundamental common research concerns and what are the best ways to ensure that, in gathering them, we do not traduce the phenomena we seek to explain. This is preferable to total immersion in a disciplinary world view (Acitelli, 1995) or to claims that one discipline—even if it is not the author's own—might have the whole supply of magic bullets (Berscheid, 1995).

We have attempted in this Introduction to integrate the needs for such a proposal with a revised view of the nature of relationships themselves. Our alternative view of relationships is encapsulated by John Lennon's observation that "Life is what happens to you while you're busy making other plans" (or rather that real life relationships are what happen to real people while relationship researchers are busy making other models!). We three authors assume that human beings all live in an uncertain world. Even close relationships can break up; one partner can become momentarily disaffected with the other; surprising turns of events can accelerate or impede intimacy growth; people, networks and relationships change in both predictable and unpredictable ways; chance events exert an influence on the course of relationships (Perlman, 1986). This fact of life has received too little emphasis in recent relationship research, where the implicit theory depicts relationships as monolithic entities passing along charted pathways and having a constant identity. In each case the metaphorical model of relationship development is of a unit that travels through space and time, by means of stages of growth, witnessing and suffering the effects of external stimuli but still successfully surviving as more or less the same recognizable entity throughout (e.g., as *movement* of an entity that can be charted on a graph; Huston et al., 1981; Surra, Arizzi & Asmussen, 1988). Whereas studies of child development focus on internal and individual qualitative change (Bigelow & La Gaipa, 1980; Beinstein-Miller, 1993; Pettit & Mize, 1993), many studies of relationship development are more likely to focus on incremental (i.e., quantitative) change (where relationships reach greater levels of intimacy, or more closeness, or exhibit more disclosure; e.g., Honeycutt, 1993). Although there exist several different approaches, the very common pathway metaphors for relationship development (e.g., Surra, Arizzi & Asmussen, 1988) necessarily carry their own implications about the internal consistency of a relationship as it moves through time or up the incremental ladder. For instance, Wood (1993, 1995) carefully reviews and critiques models that place "bonding" on top of a hierarchy. This metaphor necessarily implies, perhaps unintentionally, that it is the path that changes or the ladder that reaches some high point and the relationship which moves along it or up it or that relationship change is characterized by positional or incremental change of the relationship itself along some trajectories (Duck, 1994a). Models using this idea necessarily place less emphasis on interior change or transformation within relationships and more on interior stability and the influence of exterior events on the relationship as it moves forward or backward, and therefore assess change quantitatively, not by emphasizing the dynamics working within it or interconnecting and reconnecting the two persons with the outside world (Conville, 1988). Other comparable models emphasize the stabilities in relationships, not the fluctuations within them, on the progression of a relationship through alphabetical stages (Levinger, 1980), not on the perpetual interior confusions and ups-and-downs that characterizes relationships. Representations of relationships as stages, monolithic depictions of relationships moving along pathways, and the implication that a relationship is an integrity all foster the general view that even if relationships seem like uncertain unfinished processes to the participants, they are nevertheless objectified containers and "things" to outside observers. Recognition of this paradox is perhaps the first step to resolving it.

The Paradoxes of Scientific Observation

Whereas some researchers have noted that there are "insider" and "outsider" ways to look at relationships (Olson, 1977; Duck & Sants, 1983; Surra & Ridley, 1991; Wood & Cox, 1993), less often is it noted that the outsider position is not simply outside the experience of the insiders, but that it typically imports other consequential elements to its depiction of those inside phenomena. For example, the outsider position presents only one cross-section in time, whereas the insider position is enriched by many cross-sections in time because partners rely on memory as well as any particular observation (Dixson & Duck, 1993). Also the outsider position necessarily "stabilizes" the interior dynamics of the participants by recording their momentary position rather than their fluctuations.

While the limits of the outsider perspective are clear, although under-reported in scientific articles, the insiders' view is also imperfect. For example, insiders can become enmeshed in their experience and thus not see a full picture of what is happening in their relating. Outsiders, particularly researchers with complex understandings of particular stratified processes, may have theoretical and critical lenses that allow them to notice and comprehend things that insiders do not even see. A position that claims that outsiders are objective and detached can go too far, but also one can go too far in honoring the native's perspective. Natives have information to give, insights to offer, experiences to report in depth, but they may also experience a reality that is partial, flawed and incomplete in ways that are different from but no less so than the "realities" of researchers. For example, Wood et al. (1994) focused on partners' perceptions of their relationships, yet noticed that one couple construed the man's dominance as valuable in that he could "educate" her and "improve" her because she was "dumb". As we remarked above in connection with moral orders, to buy into such an account is to make a moral judgment, just as it is if one declines to buy into it. Without discarding the partners' perceptions of the relationship, one could argue that there are other interpretations that are not seen by the insiders, although one is then faced not with outright acceptance of the insiders' or of the outsiders' view but with establishing a conversation between the two sorts of views (Wood & Cox, 1993). Our argument here is for such a conversation between researchers and participants and not the outright preference of one set of views over the other. In the unfolding of the sustained knowledge of the different sets of parties in the research enterprise, this conversation promises to be particularly lively.

Because of this paradoxical aspect of the process of observation, the issue is how to "get inside" (as well as outside) a relationship and to reassemble the model of the interior as we describe the exterior. For example, perhaps the cross-sectional outsider position adopted by most social scientific research on relationships will necessarily make relationships processes into monochromatic objects, and our goal in future must be to color them in.

One force operating to render relationships as monochromatic monoliths is methodological. Statistical methods are premised on locating probabilities, bounded by variances that constitute "error". Further, research designs often allow only for one-shot data collection, with research findings then used to generalize beyond that moment, and represent the relationship (e.g., its intimacy) *in toto*. Even if data collection occurred more than once, force-fit answers to questionnaires could still limit participants' ability to explain the nuances of giving the same answer (for example a "2" on a Likert scale of intimacy) at two different points of data collection. What occurs is a "glossing of difference": participants speak as clearly as possible to their general feeling of the relationship rather than the specific moment (yet in real life break-up of relationships, individuals may be guided by the fear that to give voice to specific dissatisfaction can make it real; Duck 1982). Researchers must compare and connect the insider and outsider perspectives: gathering of questionnaire data should be supplemented by dialog between researcher and participant about those data.

In the future, research needs to look within individual relationships on several occasions in order to depict patterns, rather than presume a fixed pattern of experience in the relationship on the basis of one point of measurement, as is presently implicit in many of our methods. Where Hinde (1981) called for more description of relationships (using an ethological analogy), we call for more work on the variabilities perceived by relationship partners such as the contradictions and uncertainties with which partners must cope (Baxter & Montgomery, 1996; Duck, 1994b; Duck & Wood, 1995), variations in expectations about the relationship (Miell, 1987), and the changing or varied patterns of talk in and about relationships (Acitelli, 1988, 1993; Duck et al., 1991). Here we place less emphasis (but still place some emphasis) on external, behaviorally-based description alone. By analogy, if a researcher adopts metaphors that focus on monolithic stasis, it is like assuming that the real point about boiling water is the particular mark it reaches on the thermometer, not the interior ebullience and structural change that takes place in the fluid mechanics of its constitution, or that "good sex" is a check-mark in a diary rather than something energetic, diachronic and composed of complex actions. We suggest, in keeping with our arguments about representations that have integrity, that "external" observation must in the future be more consistently combined with "internal" observations gathered over a long enough time period to display internal variabilities. Researchers must also replace the simple emphasis on "reliability" (which deliberately seeks to strip out variability) and instead recall what it is that reliability leaves out of our understanding of relationships.

As relationship researchers we should ask ourselves what our research designs would look like if we were to investigate *relating* rather than *relationships*? A shift in focusing from the noun to the verb could be profitable in our quest to see how behaviors construct (over and over again) the loose definition of partners, friends and family. The answers to such questions are to be found partly in this volume and partly in the future of the field of research on personal relationships and their conduct.

Section I

Developmental Psychology

Section Editor: Rosemary S.L. Mills
University of Manitoba, Winnipeg, Manitoba, Canada

The Developmental Section is concerned not with the way specific relationships develop but rather with the way we learn to relate to other people. A basic premise guiding theory and research in this area is that the most formative learning experiences are relationship experiences. The manner in which we relate to other people is largely determined by the relationships in which we have participated. Attempts to understand the nature of the learning processes have gradually been moving beyond separate accounts of specific types of relationships (parent–child, peer, sibling) to include the identification of linkages across different relationships (as predicted by Dunn, 1988a, in the First Edition of this *Handbook*). This development, in turn, has stimulated new ideas about how relationship learning occurs. The chapters in this section explore both these themes.

In their contribution, entitled "The Influence of Significant Others on Learning About Relationships", Ross Parke & Robin O'Neil review recent research on each of the major subsystems in the family (parent–child, marital, sib–sib), showing how it has gone beyond description to explanation. They distinguish between an initial phase focusing on description of the influences on children's relationship learning, and a second phase involving an effort to identify the processes through which learning occurs. Research in the first phase has raised awareness of the range of different ways in which family subsystems influence relationship learning. For example, we are now more cognizant of the important indirect role parents play in their children's social development by arranging opportunities for social interaction, the possible direct impact that marital discord may have on children, and the indirect influence that parent–sibling interactions may have on children's relationships with their siblings. Research in the second phase reveals a good deal of convergence on two basic sets of mediating processes: affect management skills (encoding and decoding of emotion, emotional understanding, emotional regulation) and cognitive representational processes (representations, attributions and beliefs). Parke & O'Neil conclude by outlining a comprehensive model specifying the linkages among the major family subsystems and setting out a research agenda to guide the study of these linkages and the way they combine to influence children's relationship learning.

Maria von Salisch takes up the theme of mediating processes in her chapter, entitled "Emotional Processes in Children's Relationships with Siblings and Friends". There has been a relative neglect of emotional processes until recently. It is difficult to overestimate their importance, however, given the highly emotional nature of social relationships. It is by experiencing the emotions elicited by interaction with others that we acquire the affect management skills and difficulties that characterize our style of relating to others. Conflicts seem to provide a prime medium in which such learning occurs. But as von Salisch points out, any interaction that involves the sharing of emotions ("emotion talk"), whether it is a conflict situation or not and whether the emotion is positive or negative, provides an important opportunity for learning. In her review, therefore, she focuses on three types of emotional processes in friendship and sibling relationships: the sharing of positive emotions, the sharing of negative emotions elicited by third parties, and the expression and regulation of anger in conflicts between children. As with family subsystems, it appears that the knowledge base in these areas is more descriptive than explanatory. We do not yet have a very good understanding of the way in which emotional sharing contributes to children's relationship learning.

The self-evaluative emotions (pride, embarrassment, shame, guilt) also may play an important mediating role in relationship learning. In her chapter, entitled "The Self and Relationship Development", Karen Caplovitz Barrett argues that these emotions are particularly relevant to relationship learning. They are both social and self-conscious in nature, and thus are essentially emotions about the "self-in-relationship". As such, they play a central role in relationship learning. They are concerned with meeting or failing to meet social standards, and hence serve to help children interact appropriately and develop and maintain positive relationships with others. Without a sense of guilt and the self-evaluation it entails, for example, we might not take responsibility for our actions or try to repair the harm we do to others. At the same time, these emotions are themselves socially constructed, in the sense that socialization experiences (particularly relationship experiences) have a significant impact on their development. For example, discipline strategies that highlight standards without impairing the parent–child relationship may be the ones most likely to arouse optimal levels of guilt and shame—levels high enough to motivate socially appropriate behavior but not so high as to interfere with it.

Other mediating processes are considered by Patricia Crittenden in her contribution entitled "The Effect of Early Relationship Experiences on Relationships in Adulthood". In this chapter, Crittenden tackles the complex issue of how our early relationship experiences affect us later in life. She presents a dynamic-maturational model of relationship patterning and discusses its fit with several major models of adult relationships. Crittenden's model is an account of the mental processing of information about relationship concerns and the organization of interpersonal strategies for managing these concerns. The model begins with two important assumptions: that relationships serve important functions, and that the brain has evolved to promote the processing of information relevant to these functions. In a synthesis of social learning, cognitive-developmental and information-processing theories, Crittenden proposes that relationship experiences lead to the development of internal representational models of relationships that vary along two dimensions: source of information considered most predictive (cognitive or affective) and degree of information integation. These representations are viewed as dynamic processes whose aim is to maintain a balance among sources of information and response strategies. Because of the way the brain has evolved, early conditions are disproportionately important to the interpretation of present conditions. As a result, despite the repeated modification of our mental models by maturation and experience, residues of our very early experiences can still be found in the functional organization of our behavior as adults.

Finally, the generalizability of relationship processes is taken up by Barry Schneider, Andrea Smith, Samantha Poisson & Archie Kwan in their contribution, entitled "Cultural Dimensions of Children's Peer Relations". The examination of cultural differences, by revealing what is universal across cultures and what is sensitive to cultural influences, provides clues about the determinants of relationship processes. In a review of studies of peer relations in different cultures and subcultures, Schneider, Smith, Poisson & Kwan describe evidence for both similarities and differences in such social behaviors as cooperativeness, aggression, assertiveness and shyness. They show how the findings mirror the social, economic and spiritual characteristics of the cultures, and suggest that the dimension of individualism vs. collectivism is useful in describing the sorts of differences that exist. But they also argue that conceptual and methodological advances are needed in order to move beyond the level of global description. Much more elaborated conceptions of individualism and collectivism, along with improved methods and measures, would permit a more fine-grained approach to the study of cultural differences.

The contributions to this section show that the study of relationship learning has moved beyond the dyadic level to the examination of systems of influence from the level of the family to that of the culture. They also describe advances that have taken place in the study of the processes and mechanisms involved in relationship learning. Emotional processes are assuming more importance now than they have before, the importance of self processes is noted, and the issue of mediating processes in general is highlighted. In reviewing these developments, the authors have made conceptual contributions in all these areas and set an agenda for the next phase of research on relationship learning that encourages us to examine the interconnections within and between systems of influence, to explore the affective and cognitive processes mediating this learning, and to study the dynamic developmental pathways that this learning takes.

Chapter 1

The Influence of Significant Others on Learning about Relationships

Ross D. Parke
and
Robin O'Neil
University of California, Riverside, CA, USA

INTRODUCTION AND ASSUMPTIONS

A major issue that has intrigued theorists over the past century concerns the ways children develop the knowledge and skills necessary to manage relationships with others. Freud viewed relationships among family members, especially the mother–child relationship, as critical for later social and personality development. In the modern era Bowlby, in his classic fusion of psychoanalytic and ethological theories, has continued the focus on early family relationships as the foundation for later relationships both inside and outside the family. Our goal in this chapter is to briefly review the major issues that guide current research in this domain and to set an agenda for future research in this area.

Two phases of research activity can be distinguished. In the first phase, research focused on description of the impact that patterns of family interaction have on children's developing relationships. In the more recent phase, the focus is on the processes and pathways that account for the linkages noted in Phase I research.

Certain assumptions guide our review. First, we build upon and extend the conceptualization of links among family relationships set forth in Dunn (1988a) by conceptualizing the family as a social system (Hinde & Stevenson-Hinde, 1988; Minuchin, 1985). According to this viewpoint, multiple subsystems of fam-

Handbook of Personal Relationships, 2nd edn. Edited by Steve Duck.
© 1997 John Wiley & Sons Ltd.

ily members need to be considered, including parent–child relationships, the marital relationship and sibling relationships. It is assumed that these subsystems are interdependent and one goal of research is to explore the mutual influences among these subsystems. Implicit in the notion of family subsystems is the notion that different levels of organization within the family need to be recognized, including dyadic, triadic and family levels of analysis. Second, it is important to distinguish between various ways in which family members influence each other. Research has traditionally focused on face-to-face interaction, such as parent–child, husband–wife, or sib–sib exchanges (Maccoby & Martin, 1983). More recently, the impact of witnessing the interaction between other individuals (e.g., parents or siblings) on children's developing relationships has received attention (Cummings & Cummings, 1988; Cummings & Davies, 1994). Third, family management of opportunities to learn and experience social relationships is emerging as a new way in which families influence children's learning about social relationships (Parke & Bhavnagri, 1989; Ladd, LeSieur & Profilet, 1993). Fourth, we recognize that families are embedded in a variety of external social systems including neighborhoods and communities which, in turn, influence the functioning of the family unit (Bronfenbrenner, 1979, 1989). Fifth, relationship learning changes across time as well as context. As Elder and other life course theorists have noted, historical contexts need to be considered in light of rapid shifts in family organization and structure, the changing nature of family–work relationships and the reliance on outside agencies for child care (Elder, Modell & Parke, 1993). Sixth, developmental shifts in the way that significant others influence learning about relationships need to be recognized. Although the traditional focus of research has been on infancy and childhood, recent research on adolescence is providing a corrective to the developmental profile. Finally, adults' development as well as children's development is recognized as important in understanding the emergence of relationships within and beyond the family. The timing of adult entry into various roles, and the impact of normative and nonnormative transitions are recognized as playing an influential part in both adults' and children's relationships (Baltes, 1987; Parke, 1988).

Parent–Child Relationships

Consistent with a family systems viewpoint, recent research has focused on a variety of subsystems, including parent–child, marital and sib–sib systems. In this section we consider the parent–child subsystem and the relation between parent–child interaction patterns and children's social relationships.

In the first set of studies we consider, the question that is being addressed is whether the style of parent–child interaction is related to children's peer relationships. Two research traditions can be distinguished. First, in the attachment tradition, the focus has been on the impact of early infant–parent attachment on social adaptation in the peer group. This literature suggests that a secure early attachment is associated with better peer relationships in preschool (Sroufe & Fleeson, 1986), childhood (Cohn, 1990) and adolescence (Elicker, Egeland &

Sroufe, 1992) (for review of this work, see Sroufe, Carlson & Shulman, 1993). Since research in the attachment tradition is reviewed elsewhere in this volume (Crittenden & Koback), our focus will be limited to research in the second tradition. The second tradition is illustrated by studies of the relations between particular styles of childrearing or parent–child interaction and children's social competence with peers. This research has progressed through several phases over the last decade. In the first phase, studies were designed to demonstrate that variations in patterns of parent–child interaction were, in fact, related to peer outcomes. The aim of these studies was a careful description of the specific types of parent–child interaction that, in turn, would be most predictive of variations in peer outcomes. More recently a second phase of research has begun, namely the search for mediating processes that, in turn, can account for the observed relations between the two systems.

PHASE I: PARENT–CHILD INTERACTION AND PEER COMPETENCE

The first phase of this research is based on the assumption that face-to-face interaction may provide the opportunity to learn, rehearse and refine social skills that are common to successful social interaction with peers. Research in this tradition has yielded several conclusions. First, the nature of the style of the interaction between parent and child is linked to peer outcomes. Consistent with Baumrind's (1973) early classic studies which found that authoritative parenting was related to positive peer outcomes, more recent studies have confirmed that parents who are responsive, warm and engaging are more likely to have children who are more accepted by their peers (Attili, 1989; Hinde & Tamplin, 1983; Putallaz, 1987). Moreover, recent evidence suggests that high levels of positive synchrony and low levels of non-synchrony in patterns of mother–child interaction are related to school adjustment rated by teachers, peers and observers (Harrist et al., 1994). In contrast, parents who are hostile and over-controlling have children who experience more difficulty with age-mates (Barth & Parke, 1993; MacDonald & Parke, 1984; Pettit, Dodge & Brown, 1988). High levels of negative synchrony between mother and child are, in turn, associated with poor school and peer adjustment (Harrist et al., 1994). Moreover, these findings are evident in the preschool period (MacDonald, 1987; Pettit, Dodge & Brown, 1988, Harrist et al., 1994) as well as middle childhood (Dishion, 1990, 1992; Henggeler et al., 1991).

Family interaction patterns not only relate to concurrent peer relationships, but cross-time relationships as well. In their study of third-grade children, Henggeler et al. (1991) found that children of fathers who were responsive to their children's requests became more popular over the school year than children of less responsive fathers. Similarly, Barth & Parke (1993) found that parents being better able to sustain their children in play predicted better subsequent adaptation to kindergarten.

Not only are differences in interactive style associated with children's social competence, but the nature of the emotional displays during parent–child interaction are important as well. The affective quality of the interactions of popular children and their parents differs from the interactions of rejected children and their parents. Consistently higher levels of positive affect have been found in both parents and children in popular dyads than in the rejected dyads (Burks, C᠎᠎᠎ & Pᵃ᠎ke, 1987; Parke et al., 1988, 1989).

ly Carson & Parke (in press) found that reciprocal negative affect ᠎he part of both parents and children tended to predict low peer ᠎s sharing and more aggressive behaviors, while exchanges of re᠎ ᐟe affect predicted high peer acceptance. The results for the reci᠎ tive affect were particularly strong for fathers, which suggest that ᠎ particularly salient role in how children learn to manage negative e context of social interactions. Similar evidence based on home f a relation between peer acceptance and the type of affective ᠎ibited during the course of parent–child interaction comes from a y Boyum & Parke (1995). The affective expressions of mothers, ldren were scored during a family dinner. Children whose fathers directed more anger toward them were less well accepted by their peers.

In summary, both the style of parent–child interaction as well as the affective quality of the relationship, especially fathers' emotional displays, are important correlates of children's success in developing relationships with others.

Parental Instruction, Advice Giving and Consultation

Learning about relationships through interaction with parents can be viewed as an indirect pathway since the goal is often not explicitly to influence children's social relationships with extrafamilial partners such as peers. In contrast, parents may influence children's relationships directly in their role as a direct instructor, educator or advisor. In this role, parents may explicitly set out to educate their children concerning appropriate ways of initiating and maintaining social relationships.

Several recent studies have examined these issues. In a study of parental supervision (Bhavnagri & Parke, 1985, 1991) it was found that children exhibited more cooperation and turn-taking, and had longer play bouts, when assisted by an adult than when playing without assistance. However, adult assistance enhanced the quality of play for younger (2–$3\frac{1}{2}$ years of age) more than older ($3\frac{1}{2}$–6 years of age) children. This suggests that parental facilitation may be more important for younger children who are beginning to acquire social skills than for older children. While both fathers and mothers were effective facilitators of their children's play with peers, under natural conditions mothers are more likely to play this supervisory/facilitory role than fathers (Ladd & Golter, 1988; Bhavnagri & Parke, 1991).

The quality of parental interventions is important as well. In an Australian study, Finnie & Russell (1988) examined the nature of maternal interventions aimed at assisting their child join two children playing among 4- and 5-year-olds of varying sociometric statuses. Mothers of well accepted children used more skillful strategies (e.g., verbal coaching, positive discipline), whereas mothers of poorly accepted children used less effective tactics (e.g., avoidance; talking exclusively to one child; poorly-assertive discipline). It is unclear whether these differences in maternal strategies may, in fact, have contributed to the emergence of differences in children's sociometric status, or whether mothers are merely responding to previously established patterns of behavior.

As children develop, the forms of management shift from direct involvement or supervision of the ongoing activities of children and their peers to a less public form of management, involving advice or consultation concerning appropriate ways of handling peer problems. This form of direct parental management has been termed *consultation* (Ladd, LeSieur & Profilet, 1993) or *decontextualized discussion* (Lollis, Ross & Tate, 1992). Interestingly, this role has received surprisingly little attention, in view of the extensive literature on coaching as a strategy to aid children with social skills deficits (Ladd, 1981).

Cohen (1989), in a study of third-graders and their mothers, found that some forms of consulting were associated with positive outcomes, whereas other forms were linked with poor social relationships. When mothers were supportive but non-interfering, the outcomes were positive. On the other hand, mothers who were too highly involved (e.g., interfering) had children who were socially withdrawn. Direction of effects, of course, are difficult to determine and perhaps the overly involved mothers were simply being responsive to their children's poor social abilities. Alternatively, high levels of control may inhibit children's efforts to develop their own strategies for dealing with peer relations (Cohen, 1989).

In a later study, Russell & Finnie (1990) found that the quality of advice that mothers provided their children prior to entry into an ongoing play dyad varied as a function of children's sociometric status. Mothers of well accepted children were more specific and helpful in the quality of advice that they provided. In contrast, mothers of poorly accepted children provided relatively ineffective kinds of verbal guidance, such as "have fun", or "stay out of trouble."

Earlier work focused on structured opportunities to provide advice. Do parents provide this kind of guidance under everyday conditions? This issue of naturally occurring advice was recently addressed in a study of preschoolers (Laird et al., 1994). About half of the mothers of the preschoolers in the study reported that they frequently engage in conversations with their children about peer relationships. Rates of conversation about peers were related to both peer and teacher ratings of social competence. Advice giving was a unique predictor of peer-rated competence even after controlling for the amount of conversation. Finally, the extent to which the child initiated the conversation was a further positive predictor of peer-rated competence. Although it is based on self-reports, this work extends prior work by demonstrating the impact of maternal advice giving in ecologically valid contexts.

These studies suggest that direct parental influence in the form of supervision and advice-giving can significantly increase the interactive competence of young children and illustrates the utility of examining direct parental strategies as a way of teaching children about social relationships.

PHASE II RESEARCH: PROCESSES MEDIATING THE RELATIONS BETWEEN PARENT–CHILD INTERACTION AND PEER OUTCOMES

A variety of processes have been hypothesized as mediators between parent–child interaction and peer outcomes. These include emotion encoding and decoding skills, emotional regulatory skills, cognitive representations, attributions and beliefs, and problem-solving skills (Ladd, 1992; Parke et al., 1994). It is assumed that these abilities or beliefs are acquired in the course of parent–child interchanges over the course of development and, in turn, guide the nature of children's behavior with their peers, and that these styles of interacting with peers may, in turn, determine children's level of acceptance by their peers. In this chapter we focus on two sets of processes that seem particularly promising candidates for mediator status: affect management skills and cognitive representational processes.

Affect Management Skills

Children learn more than specific affective expressions, such as anger or sadness or joy in the family. They learn a cluster of processes associated with the understanding and regulation of affective displays which we term "affect management skills" (Parke et al., 1992). It is assumed that these skills are acquired during the course of parent–child interaction which, in turn, are available to the child for use in other relationships. Moreover, it is assumed that these skills play a mediating role between family and peer relationships. Three aspects of this issue are examined, namely (1) encoding and decoding of emotion, (2) cognitive understanding of causes and consequences of emotion, and (3) emotional regulation.

The Relation Between Emotional Encoding and Decoding Abilities and Sociometric Status

One set of skills that are of relevance to successful peer interaction and may, in part, be acquired in the context of parent–child play, especially arousing physical play, is the ability to clearly encode emotional signals and to decode others' emotional states. Through physically playful interaction with their parents, especially fathers, children may be learning how to use emotional signals to regulate the social behavior of others. In addition, they may learn to accurately decode the social and emotional signals of other social partners.

Several studies (Beitel & Parke, 1985; Field & Walden, 1982; for a review, see Hubbard & Coie, 1994) have found positive relationships between emotional decoding ability and children's peer status. This evidence suggests that one component of peer acceptance may be a child's ability to correctly identify the emotional states of other children.

Emotional encoding is linked with children's social status as well. Others (Buck, 1975) have found positive relationships between children's ability to encode emotional expressions and children's popularity with peers. Carson & Parke (1995) extended earlier work by examining how sociometric status is related to emotional production and recognition skills within the family. Regardless of their sociometric status, children and their parents, are able to produce emotional expressions that are recognized by each other. However, some families may utilize idiosyncratic affect cues that are not recognizable in interactions outside the family. Their communications may reflect a "familycentric" bias. In support of this possibility, Carson & Parke found that undergraduates were better able to recognize the facial expressions of popular children than those of rejected children. There were no status differences in the recognition of the facial expressions posed by parents. This suggests that the emotional production skills of popular children are different than those of rejected children, because rejected children's facial expressions are not as well recognized outside the family. These studies provide support for the links between children's emotional encoding and decoding skills and children's sociometric status. Our recent work suggests that parent–child play is important in the development of emotional encoding and decoding skills which, in turn, contribute to children's social acceptance.

The Relation of Emotional Understanding to Peer Competence

In order to develop a more comprehensive model of the role of affect in the emergence of peer competence, we recently examined other aspects of this issue. Successful peer interaction requires not only the ability to recognize and produce emotions, but also requires a social understanding of emotion-related experiences, of the meaning of emotions, of the cause of emotions, and of the responses appropriate to others' emotions. Cassidy et al. (1992) evaluated this hypothesized role of emotional understanding in a study of 5- and 6-year-old children. Based on interviews with the children about their understanding of emotions, they found that a higher level of peer acceptance was associated with greater: (1) ability to identify emotions, (2) acknowledgement of experiencing emotion, (3) ability to describe appropriate causes of emotions, and (4) expectations that they and their parents would respond appropriately to the display of emotions. Other evidence is consistent with this work. Denham et al. (1990) found that children's understanding of the type of emotion that would be elicited by different situations was positively related to peer likability. These findings confirm the findings of other research that suggests connections between other components of social understanding and peer relations (Asher & Renshaw, 1981; Dodge et al., 1986; Hart, Ladd & Burleson, 1990). The next step, of course, is to determine how variations in family interaction may, in fact, contribute to individual differences in children's cognitive understanding of emotions (see Cassidy et al., 1992).

Emotional Regulation

An interesting body of research is emerging that suggests that parental support and acceptance of children's emotions is related to children's ability to manage emotions in a constructive fashion. Several recent theorists have suggested that these emotional competence skills are, in turn, linked to social competence with peers (Denham, 1993; Eisenberg & Fabes, 1992; Parke et al., 1992; Parke, 1994). Parental comforting of children when they experience negative emotion has been linked with constructive anger reactions (Eisenberg & Fabes, 1994). Similarly, several studies have suggested that parental willingness to discuss emotions with their children is related to children's awareness and understanding of others' emotions (Denham, Cook & Zoller, 1992; Dunn & Brown, 1994; Dunn, Brown & Beardsall, 1991). Similarly, Eisenberg et al. (1991) found that parental emphasis on direct problem-solving was associated with sons' sympathy, whereas restrictiveness in regard to expressing one's own negative emotions was associated with sons' physiological and facial indicators of personal distress. This pattern of findings is consistent with recent work by Gottman, Katz & Hooven (1995) on parents' emotion philosophy or meta emotion. By "meta emotion" these researchers refer to parents' emotions about their own and their children's emotions and "meta cognitive structure" refers to an organized set of thoughts, a philosophy and an approach to one's own emotions and to one's children's emotions. Hooven & Katz (1994), in a longitudinal analysis, found that fathers' acceptance and assistance with children's sadness and anger at 5 years of age was related to their children's social competence with peers at 8 years of age. Moreover, fathers' assistance with anger predicted academic achievement. Gender of child influenced these relationships. When fathers help daughters with sadness the daughters are rated as more competent by their teachers. When fathers help their daughters regulate anger, girls are rated as more socially competent by their teachers, show higher academic achievement and their dyadic interaction with a best friend is less negative. Fathers who are more accepting of their sons' anger and assist their boys in regulating anger have sons who are less aggressive. Finally, Roberts & Strayer (1987) demonstrated a link between parental acceptance of moderate levels of emotion and children's social competence. A self-report measure of the extent to which "father encourages emotional expression" was related to competence in an inverted U-shaped fashion, indicating that moderate levels of responsiveness to upset were associated with higher levels of competence. Maternal self-reports of encouragement of emotional expression were not related to child competence, perhaps due to the more limited variability in the maternal reports. These data are consistent with earlier theoretical views that suggest that learning to manage moderate levels of negative affect is a skill that is important for management of social relationships (Sroufe, 1979). Moreover, this work highlights the importance of fathers in learning about relationships, especially in learning the emotional regulatory aspects of relationships. Fathers provide a unique opportunity to teach children about emotion in the context of relationships due to the wide range of intensity of affect that fathers display and the unpredictable character of their playful exchanges with their children (Parke, 1995, 1996).

Together, these studies suggest that various aspects of emotional development—encoding, decoding, cognitive understanding and emotional regulation—play an important role in accounting for variations in peer competence. Our argument is that these aspects of emotion may be learned in the context of family interaction and serve as mediators between the parents and peers. Accumulating support for this view suggests that this is a plausible direction for future research.

Cognitive Representational Models: Another Possible Mediator between Parents and Peers

One of the major problems facing the area of family–peer relationships is how children transfer the strategies that they acquire in the family context to their peer relationships. A variety of theories assume that individuals process internal mental representations that guide their social behavior. Attachment theorists offer working model notions (Bowlby, 1969, 1973, 1980; Bretherton & Waters, 1985), whereas social and cognitive psychologists have provided an account involving scripts or cognitive maps that could serve as a guide for social action (Baldwin, 1992; Bugenthal, 1991; Nelson, 1986; Schank & Abelson, 1977).

Researchers within the attachment tradition have examined attachment-related representations and found support for Bowlby's argument that representations vary as a function of child–parent attachment history (Bretherton & Waters, 1985; Cassidy, 1988; Main, Kaplan & Cassidy, 1985). For example, children who had been securely attached infants were more likely to represent their family in their drawings in a coherent manner, with a balance between individuality and connection, than were children who had been insecurely attached.

Research in a social interactional tradition reveals links between parent- and child-cognitive representations of social relationships. Burks & Parke (in press) found some evidence for similarities between children and mothers in their goals, attributions and anticipated consequences when they responded to a series of hypothetical social dilemmas. These studies suggest that children may learn cognitive representational schemes through their family relationships, although the precise mechanisms through which these schema are acquired is not yet specified.

Next, we turn to an examination of the evidence in support of the general hypothesis that parents of children of different sociometric status differ in terms of their cognitive models of social relationships. Several aspects of cognitive models including attributions, perceptions, values, goals and strategies have been explored (for recent reviews, see Mills & Rubin, 1993; Grusec, Hastings & Mammone, 1994). Several recent studies will illustrate this line of research. Pettit, Dodge & Brown (1988) found that mothers' attributional biases concerning their children's behavior (e.g., the extent to which they view an ambiguous provocation as hostile or benign) and the endorsement of aggression as a solution to interpersonal problems were related to children's interpersonal problem-solving skill that, in turn, was related to their social competence. Other evidence suggests that parents hold different patterns of beliefs about problematic social behaviors such as aggression and withdrawal and that these patterns are associated with their children's membership in various sociometric status groups (Rubin & Mills, 1990). In this study, parents were concerned about both types of problematic behavior, but expressed more negative emotions, such as anger and disappointment, in the case of aggression. Few mothers or fathers made trait attributions to explain aggressive or withdrawn behavior, but instead attributed these behaviors to temporary or changeable conditions, such as "age or age-related factors". Strategies for dealing with these two types of behavior differed as well; the modal strategies were moderate power for dealing with aggression and low power for social withdrawal. This work is important because it suggests that parents do, in fact, have sets of beliefs concerning children's social behavior that may, in part, govern their behavior (Goodnow & Collins, 1991; Parke, 1978).

Recently, MacKinnon-Lewis and her colleagues (1994) found that mothers' and sons' hostile attributions were significantly related to the coerciveness of their interactions. Moreover, mothers' attributions were related to reports of their children's aggression in their classrooms. Similarly , Rubin, Mills & Rose-Krasnor (1989) found a link between mothers' beliefs and their preschoolers' social problem-solving behavior in the classroom. Mothers who placed higher values on such skills as making friends, sharing with others, and leading or influencing other children had children who were more assertive, prosocial and competent social problem-solvers. Additionally, the degree to which mothers viewed social behavior as externally caused or controllable was associated with higher levels of social competence among their children. In related work, Spitzer et al. (1992) assessed perceptions of *parental influence* (e.g., how much influence parents feel they have regarding their children's social behavior) as well as perceptions of *parental efficacy* (e.g., how easy or hard they found it to help their children's social behavior). Parents, especially mothers, who were high in both perceptions of influence and efficacy had children who were higher in their levels of social acceptance as rated by peers and teachers. Few effects were evident for father perceptions.

Recently, we have explored the links between parent- and child-cognitive representations of social relationships (Spitzer & Parke, 1994). In this study, parents and their children responded to a series of vignettes reflecting interpersonal dilemmas by indicating how they might react in each situation. Open-ended responses were coded for goals, causes, strategies and advice. We found that the cognitive representations of social behavior of both fathers and mothers were related to their children's representations. This confirms earlier work that showed that maternal and child representations are linked (Burks & Parke, in press), and provides the first evidence that fathers' representational models are linked to children's models of social relationships. Moreover, both mothers' and fathers' cognitive models of relationships appear to be linked to children's social acceptance. Mothers who are low in their use of relational and prosocial strategies have children with high levels of peer-nominated aggression. Similarly, mothers who provide specific and socially-skilled advice have more popular children. Fathers' strategies that are rated high on confrontation and instrumental qualities are associated with low teacher ratings of children's prosocial behavior and high teacher ratings of physical and verbal aggression, avoidance and being disliked. Fathers with relational goals have children who are less often nominated as aggressive by their peers and rated by teachers as more liked and less disliked.

Together, this set of studies suggests that cognitive models of relationships may be transmitted across generations and these models, in turn, may serve as mediators between family contexts and children's relationships with others outside of the family.

BEYOND PARENT–CHILD INTERACTION: PARENTS AS MANAGERS OF CHILDREN'S SOCIAL RELATIONSHIPS

Parents influence their children's social relationships not only through their direct interactions with their children. Parents function as managers of their children's social lives (Hartup, 1979; Parke, 1978) and serve as regulators of opportunities for social contact with extra-familial social partners.

Parental Monitoring

One way in which parents can affect their children's social relationships is through monitoring of their children's social activities. This form of management is particularly evident as children move into pre-adolescence and adolescence and is associated with the relative shift in importance of family and peers as sources of influence on social relationships. Monitoring refers to a range of activities, including the supervision of children's choice of social settings, activities and friends. These studies indicate that parents of delinquent and antisocial children engage in less monitoring and supervision of their children's activities, especially with regard to children's use of evening time, than parents of non-delinquent children (Belson, 1975; Patterson & Stouthamer-Loeber, 1984; Pulkkinen, 1981). Others (Gold, 1963) found that parents of delinquents perceive themselves as less in control of their sons' choice of friends. Dishion (1990, 1992) has confirmed these earlier findings. Low parental supervision and monitoring (e.g., knowing their child's whereabouts and setting clear rules for behavior) were positively linked with peer rejection. As will be argued below, it is unlikely that parental discipline, interaction and monitoring are independent. In support of this view, Dishion found that *both* inconsistent, negative and punitive discipline and low monitoring were related to emergence of antisocial behavior, which, in turn, was linked with rejection by peers. Consistent with this study is the work of Steinberg (1986), who found that children in Grades 6–9, especially girls who are on their own after school, are more susceptible to peer pressure to engage in antisocial activity (e.g., vandalism, cheating, stealing) than are their adult-supervised peers. Any adolescent who indicated that at least one adult was present in the after-school setting (regardless of whether there was face-to-face contact with the adult) was categorized as supervised. In addition, Steinberg found that children of parents who were high in their use of authoritative parenting practices (Baumrind, 1978) were less susceptible to peer pressure in the absence of monitoring, whereas children of parents who were low in authoritative child-rearing were more susceptible to peer pressure in non-supervised contexts. The importance of monitoring varies with other aspects of the family environment, including child-rearing practices. Nor are the effects of monitoring limited to a reduction in the negative aspects of peer relations. As Krappmann (1986) found in Germany, preadolescents of parents who were well informed about their children's peer relationships and activities had closer, more stable and less problem-ridden peer relationships. Isolation of other conditions or variables that alter the impact of monitoring would be worthwhile. Developmental shifts may be important, because younger children are less likely to be left unsupervised than older children; moreover, it is likely that direct supervision is more common among younger children, whereas distal supervision is more evident among adolescents.

Parental Participation in Children's Organized Activities

In addition to choosing a neighborhood as a way of increasing access to children, parents influence their children's social behavior by functioning as an interface between children and institutional settings, such as child-oriented clubs and organizations (e.g., Brownies, Cub Scouts, etc.). These mediational activities are important because they permit the child access to a wider range of social activities and opportunities to practice developing social skills that may, in turn, contribute to their social development.

There are clear sex-of-parent differences in these activities. Mothers communicate more frequently with child-care staff than fathers (Joffe, 1977) and have more frequent contact with teachers in elementary schools (Lightfoot, 1978) than fathers. In addition, Bhavnagri (1987) found that mothers and fathers differ in their views of the importance of preschool as an opportunity to learn social skills. Although both mothers and fathers indicated that the learning of social skills was an important factor in their choice of a preschool and an important goal of the preschool experience for their children, mothers' ratings of these factors were higher than fathers'. Together these findings suggest not only that mothers are more involved in the interface between the family and social institutions, but also that mothers view these settings as being more important for the development of social relationships than fathers.

Moreover, there are clear social-class variations in this activity. O'Donnell & Stueve (1983), in a study of children between 5 and 14 years of age, found marked social-class differences both in children's utilization of community organizations and in the level of maternal participation. Working-class children were only half as likely to participate in activities as were their middle-class peers, and working-class children were more likely to use facilities on an occasional rather than a regular basis. Middle-class mothers were more likely to sign their children up for specific programs, whereas working-class mothers were less likely to involve their children in planned activities. The level of maternal participation varied by social class, with better educated and economically advantaged mothers participating more heavily than working-class mothers.

Unfortunately, we know relatively little about how these opportunities for participation relate to children's social behavior with their peers. One exception is Bryant (1985), who found that participation in formally sponsored organizations with unstructured activities was associated with greater social perspective-taking skill among 10-year-old children, but had little effect on 7-year-olds. In light of the importance of this skill for successful peer interaction (Hartup, 1983), this finding assumes particular significance. Moreover, it suggests that activities that "allow the child to experience autonomy, control and mastery of the content of the activity are related to expressions of enhanced social-emotional functioning on the part of the child" (Bryant, 1985, p. 65). In support of this argument, Ladd & Price (1986) found that children who were exposed to a higher number of unstructured peer activities (e.g., church, school, going to the swimming pool or library) were less anxious and had fewer absences at the beginning of kindergarten.

Although we have limited understanding of how these activities differ as a function of children's age, it appears that there is an increase with age in participation in sponsored organizations with structured activities (e.g., clubs, Brownies, organized sports), with participation most prevalent among pre-adolescent children (Bryant, 1985; O'Donnell & Stueve, 1983). Finally, more attention to the ways in which fathers participate in these types of activities is needed, especially in light of their shifting roles (Parke, 1995, 1996).

Parent as Social Initiator and Arranger

Parents play an important role in the facilitation of their children's peer relationships by initiating contact between their own children and potential play partners, especially among younger children (Bhavnagri, 1987). Ladd and his colleagues suggest that parents' role as arranger may play a facilitory part in the development of their children's friendships. Ladd & Golter (1988) found that children of parents who tended to arrange peer contacts had a larger range of playmates and more frequent play companions outside of school than children of parents who were less active in initiating peer contacts. When children entered kindergarten, boys but not girls with parents who initiated peer contacts were better liked and less rejected by their classmates than were boys with non-initiating parents. Other evidence (Ladd et al., 1988) suggests that parents' peer management (initiating peer contacts; purchasing toys for social applications) of younger preschool children prior to enrollment in preschool was, in turn, linked to the time that children spent in peers' homes. Ladd & Hart (1991) found that parents who arranged a larger number of peer informal play contacts tended to have children with a larger range of playmates. In addition, these investigators found a positive relationship between the number of child initiations and the size of the playmate network. Moreover, these investigators confirmed earlier findings (Ladd & Golter, 1988) of a positive relationship between parents' initiations and higher levels of peer acceptance among boys, but not girls. Finally, parents who frequently initiated informal peer play opportunities tended to have children who were more prosocial toward peers and spent less time in onlooking and unoccupied behaviors.

Children's own initiation activity has been linked with measures of social competence. Children who initiated a larger number of peer contacts outside of school tended to be better liked by their peers in preschool settings. The Ladd & Hart (1991) study serves as a corrective to the view that initiation activity is only a parental activity, and reminds us that variations in the level of activity played by children in organizing their own social contacts is an important correlate of their social competence. Finally, Krappmann (1986) reported that the quality of peer relationships of 10–12-year-old children in a German sample was related to parental management activity. Specifically, children of parents who played an active role in stimulating and arranging peer contacts on behalf of their children had more stable and closer peer relationships than children of less active parents.

Future research should detail how parent- and child-initiated activities shift over the course of development. It is clear that parental initiating is important but over time it decreases and the factors that govern this decrease are important issues to explore. Moreover, it is critical to understand when parental initiation activity can, in fact, be beneficial and when it is detrimental to children's emerging social competence. Younger children may learn through observation of their parents how to initiate social contacts. On the other hand, as the child grows older, social competence may, in fact, be negatively affected if insufficient independence in organizing their social contacts is not permitted. At the least, a child may regard it as inappropriate for a parent to continue to initiate on their behalf beyond a certain age and parental micromanagment may be viewed as interfering rather than helpful and a potential source of embarrassment for the child.

Together these studies provide evidence of the possible facilitory role of parents in the development of social competence with peers. Little is known, however, about the possible determinants of parental utilization of neighborhood social resources, including other children as playmates. More work is needed on the determinants of parental initiating and arranging activities.

Adult Social Networks as a Source of Potential Peer Contacts for Children

In addition to the role played by parents in arranging children's access to other children, parents' own social networks of other adults, as well as the child members of parental social networks, provide a source of possible play partners for children. Cochran & Brassard (1979) suggested several ways in which these two sets of relationships may be related. First, the child is exposed to a wider or narrower band of possible social interactive partners by exposure to the members of the parent's social network. Second, the extent to which the child has access to the social interactions of his or her parents and members of their social network may determine how well the child may acquire particular styles of social interaction. Third, in view of the social support function of social networks, parents in supportive social networks may be more likely to have positive relationships with their children which, in turn, may positively affect the child's social adjustment both within and outside the family.

Cochran and his co-workers (Cochran & Davila, 1992; Cochran et al., 1990) have provided support for the first issue, namely, that there is overlap between parental and child social networks. Specifically, these investigators found that 30–44% of 6-year-old children's social networks were also included in the mothers' networks. In other words, children often listed other children as play partners who were children of their mothers' friends. Finally, the overlap was higher in the case of relatives than non-relatives but both kin and non-kin adult networks provided sources of peer play partners for young children. Other evidence from Sweden (Tietjen, 1985) suggests that there is overlap in the social networks of parents and children. However, in this case, there was overlap only between mothers and their 8–9-year-old daughters; no relations were evident in the case of mothers and sons. In light of the failure to find gender differences in network overlap across generations in other studies (e.g., Cochran et al., 1990), this issue merits further examination, especially the potential role of culture in accounting for these findings.

Several other studies suggest that the quality of adult social networks do, in fact, relate to children's social behavior. In an Australian study, Hormel, Burns & Goodnow (1987) found positive relations between the number of "dependable" friends that parents report and 11-year-old children's self-rated happiness, the number of regular playmates, and maternal ratings of children's social skills. Second, parents' affiliation with various types of formal community organizations was related to children's happiness, school adjustment and social skills. Unfortunately, the reliance on self-reports limits the value of these findings, but they do support the importance of parental, or at least maternal, social networks as a factor in potentially affecting children's social relationships. Recently, in a recent study in our laboratory, Lee & Welsh (1995) extended this work by showing a relation between parents' enjoyment of friends in their network and independent peer ratings. The more parents enjoyed their friends, the less the children were disliked and perceived as aggressive. Moreover, the more contact that parents had with relatives, the less disliked children were by their peers. Finally, these investigators found that maternal and paternal social networks have distinctive links to children's social relationships. Fathers who rated their networks as less enjoyable had children who were more aggressive and more disliked by peers, whereas the less contact that mothers had with their friends, the higher teachers rated their children on avoidance of interaction with other children.

Oliveri & Reiss (1987) found distinctive patterns of relations between maternal and paternal networks and the networks of adolescent children as well. The structural aspects (size, density) of networks were more closely related to maternal than paternal network qualities. This finding is consistent with prior work that suggests that mothers function as social arrangers and "kin keepers" more than fathers (Ladd & Golter, 1988; Tinsley & Parke, 1984). In contrast, the relationship aspects of adolescent social networks (positive sentiment between individuals; help received from network members) more closely resembled these aspects of fathers' social network characteristics. This supports the view that fathers may, in fact, play an important role in the regulation of emotion—a central ingredient in the maintenance of close personal relationships (Parke et al., 1992). A variety of mechanisms are probably involved in accounting for these patterns including the increased availability of social initiation and maintenance strategies.

CONTRIBUTIONS OF THE MARITAL DYAD TO CHILDREN'S UNDERSTANDING OF CLOSE RELATIONSHIPS

In the preceding section, parents were conceptualized as active influences, both directly and indirectly, on the development of children's social competence and understanding of relationships. Considerable evidence emerged in support of the parent–child relationship as a primary socializing influence on children's social development, in general, and on the development of specific relationship skills. However, children's experiences in families extend beyond their interactions with parents. As outlined in Dunn (1988a), evidence is beginning to emerge that suggests that children's understanding of relationships also is shaped through their active participation in other family subsystems (e.g., child–sibling) as well as through exposure to the interactions of other dyadic subsystems (e.g., parent–parent) or participation in triadic relationships (e.g., child–sib–parent, child–parent–parent).

Influence of Marital Satisfaction and Discord on Child Outcomes: Phase I Research

Several decades of investigation have amassed considerable evidence indicating that dimensions of marital functioning are related to aspects of children's longterm overall adjustment and immediate coping responses in the face of interparental conflict. Although the size of the associations are not always large (Erel & Burman, 1995; Jouriles, Bourg & Farris, 1991), a range of studies link marital discord and conflict to outcomes in children that are likely to impair the quality of interpersonal relationships, including antisocial behavior (Rutter, 1971), internalizing and externalizing behavior problems (Johnson & O'Leary, 1987; Katz & Gottman, 1993; Katz & Kahen, 1993; Peterson & Zill, 1986; Porter & O'Leary, 1980), and changes in cognitions, emotions and physiology in response to exposure to marital conflict (Cummings, 1987; Cummings et al., 1989; El-Sheikh, Cummings & Goetsch, 1989; Gottman & Katz, 1989). Although less empirical work has been directed specifically toward examination of the "carryover" of exposure to marital conflict to the quality of children's relationships with significant others such as peers and siblings, a body of literature is beginning to emerge that indicates that exposure to marital discord is associated with poor social competence and problematic peer relationships (Cummings, Iannotti & Zahn-Waxler, 1985; Emery & O'Leary, 1984; Erel & Burman, 1995; Katz & Gottman, 1991, 1993; Long et al., 1987).

Mechanisms Linking Marital Discord to Children's Adjustment: Phase II Research

Until recently, theoretical frameworks typically conceptualized marital discord as an indirect influence on children's adjustment that operated through its effect on family functioning and the quality of parenting (Fauber & Long, 1991). Factors that include affective changes in the quality of the parent–child relationship, lack of emotional availability, and adoption of less optimal parenting styles (Easterbrooks, 1987) have each been implicated as potential mechanisms through which marital discord disrupts parenting processes. In a recent investigation, for example, Katz & Kahen (1993) found that when parents used a mutually hostile pattern of conflict resolution, fathers were more likely to be intrusive and children were more likely to express anger during a parent–child interaction task. In addition, fathers' intrusiveness predicted more negative peer play and more aggressive play with a best friend. Interestingly, this study also suggests that an individual parent's style of handling conflict may be related to the quality of their *partner's* relationships with children in the family. When fathers were angry and withdrawn in a conflict resolution task, mothers were more critical and intrusive during interactions with their child. Maternal criticism and intrusiveness, in turn, was associated with unresponsiveness or "tuning out" by the child during mother–child interactions and higher levels of teacher-rated internalizing symptoms. Similarly, Cowan et al. (1994) examined the influence of marital quality on children's social adaptation to kindergarten, with results suggesting evidence of both direct and indirect links to children's social adjustment. Interestingly, internalizing difficulties (e.g., shy/withdrawn qualities) were predicted by the influences of marital functioning on parenting quality, whereas externalizing difficulties (e.g., aggressive/antisocial qualities) were predicted directly by qualities of marital interaction.

Family systems theory suggests that not only does marital discord interfere with dimensions of the mother–child or father–child relationship, it also may impair qualities of the mother–father–child triadic relationship by interfering with the effectiveness of how the mother and father work together with the child. In a study that examined the contribution of marital adjustment to the effectiveness of joint mother–father supportiveness, Westerman & Schonholtz (1993) found that fathers', but not mothers', reports of marital disharmony and disaffection were significantly related to the effectiveness of joint parental support toward their children's problem-solving efforts. Joint parental support was, in turn, related to fathers' and teachers' reports of children's behavior problems.

Despite considerable progress in elucidating specific parenting processes that are impaired by interparental conflict, a number of systematic investigations suggest that parental conflict also is associated with behavior problems independent of its influence on the parent–child relationship (Jenkins & Smith, 1991; Peterson & Zill, 1986). Recently, models that restrict their conceptualization of the influence of marital discord on children's adjustment as primarily *indirect* have been challenged on a number of conceptual and methodological grounds (Davies & Cummings, 1994; Emery, Fincham & Cummings, 1992; Grych & Fincham, 1990), stimulating considerable empirical interest in the examination of the *direct effects* of exposure to marital distress on children's adjustment. Accordingly, in the last 5 years, the focus of attention has turned to elucidating specific processes by which the marital relationship itself directly influences children's immediate functioning and long-term adjustment. A parallel research trajectory over the last several years has been movement away from studies that focus on global measures of marital satisfaction or adjustment to studies that focus on more specific aspects of marital interaction, particularly aspects of marital conflict, in order to identify the dimensions of the marital relationship that are most likely to influence children's immediate cognitive, emotional and physiological functioning. These immediate responses or "microprocesses", in turn, have been hypothesized to be critical links to children's long-term social adjustment in the face of interparental conflict (Fincham, 1994; Davies & Cummings, 1994; Grych & Fincham, 1990).

Although the investigation of these questions is considered by Fincham (in press) to be underdeveloped at this point, a number of promising directions appear destined to shed considerable light on processes by which exposure to marital conflict may influence children's interpersonal competence, social adjustment and interpersonal understanding. Analog studies, for example, have become a useful experimental methodology for systematically varying dimensions of interadult conflict in order to assess their influence on the immediate cognitive and emotional functioning of children. Such studies have begun to show that the form of expression of marital conflict plays a critical role in how children react. A recent review of the literature (Davies & Cummings, 1994) indicated that several aspects of parental conflict appear to be relatively consistently associated with poor outcomes for children. More frequent interparental conflict and more intense or violent forms of conflict have been found to be particularly disturbing to children and likely to be associated with externalizing and internalizing difficulties. Grych, Seid & Fincham (1991), for example, found that children who were exposed to an audiotaped analog of marital interaction responded with distress, shame and self-blame to intensely angry adult exchanges.

Davies & Cummings' (1994) review also indicated that conflict which was child-related in content was more likely than conflict involving other content to be associated with behavior problems in children. For example, in an analog study conducted by Grych & Fincham (1993), when the content of the conflict was child-related, children reported greater shame, responsibility, self blame and fear of being drawn into the conflict.

The findings from a number of studies also suggest that resolution of conflict, even when it was not viewed by the child, reduces children's negative reactions to exposure to interadult anger and conflict. Exposure to unresolved conflict, for example, has been found to be associated with negative affect and poor coping responses in children (Cummings et al., 1991). In addition, recent work suggests that the manner in which conflict is resolved may also influence children's adjustment. Katz & Gottman (1993), for example, found that couples who exhibited a hostile style of resolving conflict had children who tended to be described by teachers as exhibiting antisocial characteristics. When husbands were angry and emotionally distant while resolving marital conflict, children were described by teachers as anxious and socially withdrawn.

Conflict is inevitable in most parental relationships and is not detrimental to family relationships and children's functioning under all circumstances. In particular, as recent work suggests, disagreements that are extremely intense and involve threat to the child are likely to be more disturbing to the child. In contrast, when conflict is expressed constructively (Easterbrooks, Cummings & Emde, 1994), is moderate in degree (Montemayor, 1983), is expressed in the context of a warm and supportive family environment (Niemi, 1988) and shows evidence of resolution, children may learn valuable lessons regarding how to negotiate conflict and resolve disagreements (Davies & Cummings, 1994; Grych & Fincham, 1993).

Less well understood at this point in time are the specific emotional regulatory and cognitive-processing mechanisms through which exposure to interparental conflict is "carried over" into children's understanding of close relationships and social competence with others. Two recent conceptual frameworks have emerged, however, that reflect promising new paradigms from which to examine these "carry-over" questions. Using a cognitive-conceptual model derived from the stress and coping field (Lazarus & Folkman, 1984), Grych & Fincham (1990) focus on the cognitive and affective meaning that exposure to conflict has for the child. They suggest that certain dimensions of interparental conflict (e.g., intensity and content of conflict) and contextual factors (e.g., family emotional climate, past history) are used by the child to appraise or interpret the personal relevance of interadult conflict. In this model, three appraisals influence the child's coping responses to interparental conflict, including the level of perceived threat to the child, the child's perceived coping efficacy, and causal attributions and ascription of blame made by the child. Over time, a family environment that is characterized by high interparental conflict may play a role in the development of children's cognitive models of familial and extrafamilial relationships by exposing children to hostile and negative interpretations of interpersonal experiences and social situations (Davies & Cummings, 1994) and by undermining the child's sense of efficacy in regard to how to cope in social situations with peers and significant others. Further, children who are exposed to chronic levels of intense, unresolved conflict also may feel the threat of imminent separation which may influence children's responses in the face of conflict. Katz & Gottman (1993) and others have suggested that in extremely conflict-ridden marriages, children's externalizing behaviors may be an attempt to divert attention on to themselves and away from marital problems in order to circumvent divorce or separation.

Although little empirical work has examined these links, some evidence exists to suggest that the quality of the marital relationship may shape the cognitive dimensions of the family climate. Parents who report more satisfaction with their marriages have been found to speak in longer utterances to their children and to encourage more cognitive participation by the child in family conversations (Pratt et al., 1992). A number of studies suggest that spouses in discordant marriages are more likely than those in happy marriages to focus on negative aspects of interactions with their partners, to overlook positive behaviors, and to attribute their partners' behaviors to hostile intentions (Bradbury & Fincham, 1989; Markman et al., 1984; Markman & Kraft, 1989). Children who are exposed to marital discord may develop similar attribution processes in response to interactions with significant others. A number of researchers also have suggested that modeling of negative behavior patterns that children observe when exposed to marital conflict may be an important mechanism through which non-adaptive interaction styles are transmitted to children (Easterbrooks & Emde, 1988; Katz & Gottman, 1993).

In a model that builds on the cognitive-contextual framework of Grych & Fincham (1990), Davies & Cummings (1994) downplay cognitive factors and emphasize the primacy of emotions as organizers of interpersonal experience. In an extension of the literature linking attachment security in the parent–child relationship and quality of emotional functioning (see prior section), they propose that emotional security also derives from the quality of the marital relationship. They posit that the emotion-laden quality of marital conflict contributes to emotionality playing a primary role relative to cognitive processes in determining how children react to interparent conflict. They hypothesize that some forms of conflict are more likely than others to threaten the emotional security of the child and interfere with the ability to cope effectively with ongoing stresses and challenges. More specifically, they propose that several interrelated processes account for the impact of emotional security on children's functioning. First, emotional security affects the ability of the child to regulate his or her own emotions. Second, emotional security influences the child's motivation to intervene to regulate the behavior of their parents. Third, they postulate that emotional security affects the cognitive appraisals and internal representations of family relationships that are made by children.

Evidence that supports the role that chronic, intense marital conflict plays in undermining children's emotional regulatory abilities is beginning to emerge. Gottman & Katz (1989), for example, used structural equation modeling to examine a sophisticated set of relationships between chronic marital stress and children's social competence with peers. Specifically, they hypothesized that chronic marital tension might influence children by activating physiological processes and generating in the child a "flooding" of sadness and anger in response to the conflict. Activation of the autonomic system and chronic emotional flooding, in turn, was hypothesized to interfere with the development of emotion regulation skills and promote avoidance of high level interaction styles with others. In a test of this hypothesis, Gottman & Katz (1989) found that maritally distressed couples employed a parenting style that was cold, unresponsive, angry and low in limit-setting and structuring. Children who were exposed to this style of parenting exhibited high levels of stress hormones and displayed more anger and non-compliance. In addition, these children tended to play at low levels with peers and displayed more negative peer interactions. Not all problematic marriages are similar, however. Some problematic marriages are likely to be characterized by lower levels of openly expressed anger and hostility and higher levels of active withdrawal from interaction. The findings from other recent work suggests that children in marriages characterized by withdrawal rather than interaction accompanied by anger react differently (Katz & Gottman, 1993). These authors argue that withdrawal may be even more stressful for children than an angry but engaged marital relationship.

Although more work is clearly needed before conclusions regarding the mechanisms through which interparental conflict influences children's understanding of relationships, a number of potential mechanisms have been suggested and the challenge of future work lies in applying these models to future empirical investigations of the links between children's exposure to interparental interaction and the development of their own relationship skills.

CONTRIBUTION OF SIBLINGS TO CHILDREN'S UNDERSTANDING OF CLOSE RELATIONSHIPS

Rich and extensive descriptions of the normative patterns that characterize sibling relationships over the course of development (Buhrmester & Furman, 1990;

Dunn, 1983, 1988a) suggest that, in addition to parents, siblings may play a critical role in the development of children's understanding of interpersonal relationships. A number of studies indicate that most children are likely to spend more time in direct interaction with siblings than parents and significant others (Dunn, 1984) and that interactions with siblings provide a context for the expression of a range of positive social behaviors including friendly, cooperative exchanges, joint fantasy play, shared humor and discussions about feelings, as well as numerous conflictual encounters and experiences with conflict resolution (Dunn & Munn, 1985). Further, this rich array of interactions between siblings have been found to be typified by greater emotional intensity than the behavioral exchanges that characterize other relationships (Katz, Kramer & Gottman, 1992).

Sibling relationships have been hypothesized to contribute to children's understanding of relationships in a number of significant ways. A social learning framework analogous to the one posited to explain parental contributions to the development of children's social competence (Parke et al., 1988) predicts that through their interactions with siblings, children develop specific interaction patterns and social understanding skills that generalize to relationships with other children (McCoy, Brody & Stoneman, 1994; Stocker & Dunn, 1990). In addition, relationships with siblings also may provide a context in which children can practise the skills and interaction styles that have been learned from parents or others (McCoy, Brody & Stoneman, 1994). Older siblings function as tutors, managers or supervisors of their younger brother's or sister's behavior during social interactions (Edwards & Whiting, 1993) and may function as gatekeepers who extend or limit opportunities to interact with other children outside the family (Weisner, 1987). Also paralleling the indirect influence that the observation of parent–parent interaction has on what children learn about relationships, a second important avenue of influence on children's developing understanding of relationships is children's observation of parents interacting with siblings. These interactions have been hypothesized to serve as an important context in which children deal with issues of differential treatment and learn about complex social emotions such as rivalry and jealousy. In the following sections we examine in more depth the avenues through which siblings are thought to influence children's learning about relationships, and extend the discussion to include a number of promising recent directions.

Siblings as Socializing Influences: Phase I Research

Children's experiences with siblings provide a context in which interaction patterns and social understanding skills may generalize to relationships with other children (McCoy, Brody & Stoneman, 1994). According to Stocker & Dunn (1990), interactions with siblings provide a setting in which children "develop social understanding skills which may enable them to form particularly close relationships with a child of their choice, a close friend". We begin, again, with an examination of descriptive studies that address the question of whether systematic links exist between sib–sib relationships and other relationships that children develop. In general, there appears to be a mixed body of evidence in support of links between sib–sib patterns of interaction and interaction styles that develop in the context of friendships and more general peer relationships. The pattern of findings from the small, but growing, number of studies provide a modest and somewhat inconsistent picture of the connections between children's patterns of interacting with siblings and patterns of interacting with peers. Some studies report modest evidence of a straightforward "carry-over" of interaction styles between children's relationships with siblings and peers. Berndt & Bulleit (1985) examined behaviors of preschoolers at home with siblings and at school with peers. Children who initiated more aggression with siblings were more likely to initiate aggression in the classroom. Children who engaged in more onlooker/unoccupied play with siblings spent more time in this form of play at school. In a study of older children, Hetherington (1988) found that when children's relationships with their siblings were described as hostile and alienated as opposed to warm and companionate, they evidenced poorer peer relationships and other behavior problems. Others report little evidence of a carry-over effect between siblings and peers. Abramovitch et al. (1986), for example, found little evidence that patterns of sibling interaction were related to the interaction styles of children with a friend. Similarly, Brody, Stoneman and colleagues (1982, 1985) found that the roles that are adopted by older siblings in interactions with their younger siblings are qualitatively different from the roles characterizing interactions with a friend. Older siblings are more likely to assume dominant roles such as managers of activities and teachers during the course of their interactions with siblings, whereas the same children were more likely to adopt an equalitarian style during interactions with friends. Mischel (1984) and others (Putallaz & Sheppard, 1992) have posited that children with adequate social skills exhibit cross-situational specificity by adapting to the specific demands of each social relationship—behaving in a more reciprocal, equalitarian manner with classmates and in a more asymmetric, hierarchical fashion with siblings. In contrast, among children who lack social competence, deficits in social skills such as heightened aggressiveness and inability to initiate interaction will generalize across sibling and peer contexts.

Other recent studies continue to show only modest evidence of "carry-over" of interaction styles between children's relationships, and suggest that birth order effects and other processes need to be considered. For example, in a study that focused on 7–9-year-old firstborns and their younger sibs, Stocker & Dunn (1990) found that mothers who reported a positive relationship between the target child and his or her younger sibling, also described the child's relationship with a friend as more positive. However, children who were rated as more controlling and competitive with younger sibs were reported to have more positive friendships. In contrast, Stocker & Mantz-Simmons (cited in Dunn, 1993) reported that 7- and 8-year-old children, most of whom were laterborn, who were controlling with their siblings, were more controlling and less positive in interactions with friends. Differences in the meaning of control and competition for the target children as a function of the age of their sibling may help reconcile these findings. It has been suggested that when a child controls or manages the behavior of a younger sibling this may be appropriate, socially competent behavior that reflects sensitivity to the specific demands of the relationship—a characteristic that may carry over to other relationships. However, when a younger sibling is controlling and competitive in interactions with an older sibling, this may reflect a confrontational behavioral style or personality trait that carries over in a negative way to relationships with friends and peers. More work is clearly needed to examine the role that birth order plays in moderating the links between children's relationships.

Finally, the sibling relationship may play a role in compensating for other problematic relationships by providing an alternative context for experiencing satisfying social relationships and protecting children from the development of adjustment difficulties. East & Rook (1992) found that children who were socially isolated in their peer relationships were buffered from adjustment problems when they reported positive relationships with a favorite sibling. Similarly, Stocker (1994) reported support for the compensatory role of at least one positive relationship (either sibling, friend or mother) as protection from the development of behavioral conduct difficulties. Other work (Stocker & Mantz-Simmons, cited in Dunn, 1993) indicates that children who are cooperative with siblings may be more likely to report lower levels of companionship with friends, which may reflect lower motivation on the part of the child or the parent to seek out relationships beyond the family when sibling relationships are satisfying. A similar pattern of results were reported by Mendelson & Aboud (1991) and suggested that the ability of a good sibling relationship to compensate for friendships may be greatest among same-sex siblings.

Because a system of multiple family relationships typically antedates children's significant relationships outside the family, frameworks for studying the links between children's significant relationships have tended to emphasize the carry-over from parental and sibling relationships to relationships with friends and peers. One recent study, however, examined the role that positive relationships with peers play in children's adaptation to the birth of a new sibling (Kramer & Gottman, 1992). The findings from this study indicated that children who displayed a more positive interaction style with a best friend and who were better able to manage conflict and negative affect, behaved more positively toward their new sibling at both 6 months and 14 months. Further, the results of path analyses led Kramer & Gottman to speculate that management of conflict, a skill that is particularly useful when interacting with siblings, may be more likely to be learned in interactions with peers than in direct interactions with parents.

Mechanisms that Explain Links between Sibling Relationships and Children's Relationships outside the Family: Moving toward Phase II Research

Although these studies present only a modest pattern of evidence in support of the generalization of links between sibling subsystems and children's styles of

interacting in other significant relationships, this work sets the scene for important future work that will shed light on the contexts under which strong, weak
or compensatory connections might be expected between relationship systems,
as well as the processes through which children's experiences with siblings are
translated into relationship skills that are used in other relationships. The findings
from existing studies suggest, for example, that greater generalization of hostile,
aggressive interaction styles in both sibling and peer systems may emerge when
children lack adequate relationship skills (Putallaz & Sheppard, 1992) or when
children are experiencing stressful, negative family relationships (Dunn, 1993). In
contrast, under other circumstances, the associations between sibling relationships and relationships outside the family may be moderated by a number of
features that uniquely characterize each relationship. Dunn (1993) has pointed
out, for example, that friendship involves a mutual and reciprocated relationship
with another individual, whereas siblings do not necessarily feel this way about
one another. She also notes that in contrast to sib–sib relationships, friend and
peer relationships represent a more unique combination of backgrounds, experiences and temperaments that may generate interaction styles that are the result
of two unique individuals' approach to relationships. Further, there appear to be
different role expectations for sib and friend relationships that may differentially
influence interaction styles. For example, some evidence suggests that what is
considered a moral transgression when committed by a sibling may not be viewed
by such if committed by a friend (Slomowski & Killen, 1992) and that reason and
negotiation appear to be more common in peer interactions than sibling interactions (Raffaelli, 1991; reported in Dunn, 1993). Finally, a number of factors such
as birth order and birth spacing appear to play an important role in determining
the relative level of competency and the balance between leader/follower roles in
sibling relationships, which may influence the extent of correspondence expected
between sibling and peer relationship styles (Abramovitch et al., 1986; Stoneman,
Brody & MacKinnon, 1985). The challenge of future work will be to examine
more systematically the moderating and mediating influences of these factors in
order to better unravel normative patterns of associations between sibling and
peer relationships.

Siblings as Managers of Children's Social Lives

Just as parents function as managers of children's social lives, siblings in many
cultures perform similar management functions in relation to their younger siblings. Cross-cultural work indicates that in both African and Polynesian cultures
children, especially girls, become involved in sibling caretaking activities at a
relatively early age (Ervin-Tripp, 1989; Weisner, 1987). Relatively little is known,
however, about the caregiving role of siblings in contemporary Euro-American
families. Whiting & Whiting's (1975) study of patterns of sibling interaction in
New England families suggests that formal caregiving responsibilities may not
be as common in American culture as in other cultures. However, Bryant (1989)
suggests that although parents may not formally assign caretaking duties to
children, children frequently voluntarily assume the roles of caretaker, tutor and

teacher of younger siblings and make unique contributions to the socialization of young children. Most work examining these roles has focused on the influence that instruction from older siblings may have on children's cognitive development (see for example, Ellis & Rogoff, 1982; Stewart, 1983), and has only infrequently focused on children's social development. Although some work exists which suggests that children actively request advice from their older siblings (Handel, 1986) and that siblings are viewed as sources of counsel and support (Werner & Smith, 1977), relatively little is known about the role that siblings play as supervisors, managers or advisors of children's social lives and the influence that this may have on the development of children's knowledge of relationships. Given the amount of time that most children spend in the company of siblings, this is an area that clearly is ripe for future empirical investigation.

BEYOND THE SIBLING DYAD—CHILDREN'S OBSERVATIONS OF PARENTAL INTERACTIONS WITH SIBLINGS

Not only are children active participants in relationships, but they also spend time observing the interactions of other family subsystems, and these experiences appear to provide an important indirect avenue for learning about relationships. Just as children have been found to be particularly attentive to affectively-charged interactions between parents, a number of studies indicate that children attend to the interactions that occur between parents and siblings (Dunn & Munn, 1985; Kendrick & Dunn, 1982). Again, paralleling findings that focus on children's responses to parent–parent interaction, children appear to be particularly attentive to parent–sibling interactions that involve the expression of affect (e.g., disputes or games) and actively attempt to intervene in these interactions in order to draw attention to themselves (Dunn & Shatz, 1989). Further, as family systems theory predicts, the birth of a sibling has been linked to changes in the relationship between mother (or father) and the firstborn child, with changes being moderated by the quality of the parent–child relationship and gender of the firstborn child (Dunn & Kendrick, 1981; Howe & Ross, 1990). Specifically, in the Dunn & Kendrick (1981) study, in families with firstborn girls, if the mother–daughter relationship was particularly positive before the birth of the sibling, a more hostile relationship was likely to develop between the firstborn daughter and her sibling. In contrast, when mother and daughter had a more conflictual relationship, siblings were more likely to have a close, friendly relationship with one another one year later. Interestingly, just as the negative impact of marital conflict appears to be ameliorated when parents have conversations with the child regarding the conflict (Cummings, Simpson & Wilson, 1993), evidence also suggests that parental management strategies are likely to moderate the child's reaction to a new sibling, perhaps be actively influencing the child's attribution processes. In an examination of mothers' strategies for helping children process information about a new sibling, Dunn & Kendrick (1982) found that if mother used conversation to help the child think of his/her infant sibling in more positive way (for example, by focusing on the infant as an individual with needs and feelings), the child reacted in a more positive way. These findings suggest that close monitoring and sensitivity to relative differences in relationships begin to emerge early in children's significant relationships, and social comparison and cognitive-attributional processes may play an important role in how information about relationships is processed. However, the findings from these studies suggest, once again, that "carry-over" or generalization of positive dimensions of one relationship to other significant relationships may be too simple a mechanism to explain links between relationships. Several other principles seem relevant. First, social comparison processes appear to be operating that foster in children an understanding of the uniqueness of relationships and that may give children opportunities to learn about complex emotions such as jealousy and rivalry. Second, from an early age, children appear to take an active role in the construction of their relationships and may actively seek out positive relationships as alternatives to problematic or negative relationships.

More fruitful investigation of the links between relationships, as well as better understanding of the processes through which children come to understand the uniqueness of specific social relationships, may come with movement from a socialization framework to a relationships framework. Dunn (1993) points out that one disadvantage of a socialization approach is that it examines when and how social competence and social understanding are generalized from parent–child relationships to other relationships, but it does not adequately take into account the fact that even when a child acquires social competencies through interactions in one relationship, he/she may not be motivated to apply these skills in another relationship. In contrast, a relationships perspective takes into account the fact that each relationship reflects a unique set of demands and rewards as well as different challenges to a child's socio-cognitive abilities. This may lead to the generation of questions concerning the unique aspects of child (e.g., temperament, attachment security, self-confidence), the relationship partner, the dynamic of the relationship itself, and the broader social ecology (e.g., family stress, life transitions) which may contribute to a child being motivated or disinclined to behave in a socially competent manner. As Dunn points out, the goal is to specify "for *which* children, at *which* stages of development, *which* dimensions of particular relationships are likely to show associations with other relationships".

PUTTING THE PIECES TOGETHER: TOWARD A MULTIPLE SOURCES MODEL OF RELATIONSHIP LEARNING

Our family systems viewpoint argues for the construction of a comprehensive model in which the contribution of parent–child, parent–parent and sibling relationships are all recognized. Figure 1.1 outlines a comprehensive model of how children learn about social relationships from significant family members. To date, few studies have simultaneously addressed how these subsystems combine to produce their impact on children's relationship learning (for recent exceptions, see Katz, Kramer & Gottman, 1992; McCoy, Brody & Stoneman, 1994). Little is known about the relative weighting of parent–child relationships vs. other family relationships. Neither do we understand how the impact of these different relationships changes as the child develops. The most crucial issue remains; namely, the specification of the pathways through which these different relationships exert their influence. It is evident from our model that multiple pathways are possible and there is support for both direct and mediated effects. As noted earlier, marital relationships exert both direct (e.g., witnessed) and indirect effects (e.g., marital relationships influence parent–child patterns). Similarly, parent–child relationships could influence marital relationships. For example, a disciplinary encounter with a difficult-to-control child could, in turn, trigger a marital conflict due to disagreement about the child's misbehavior or management of the child, the carry-over of negative mood or the alignment of parent and child against a third party. Less is known about the impact of parent–child relationships on marital interactions than the reverse effects.

Moreover, recent research has begun to identify individual differences across families or family typologies (Filsinger, 1991; Bell & Bell, 1989) as well as at the level of family subsystems, such as marital dyads (Gottman, 1994). As a next step,

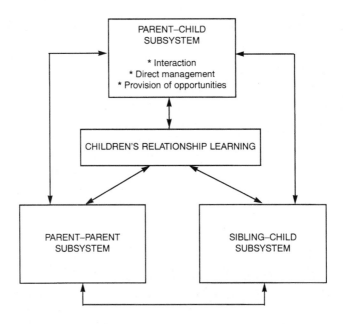

Figure 1.1 Model indicating the hypothesized relations among family subsystems and children's relationship learning

can we characterize families usefully in terms of the relative importance of various subsystems? Some families may invest heavily in directly parenting their children, but tend to protect their children from their marital problems. Earlier evidence suggests that exposure to marital conflict is higher for boys than girls (Hetherington, Hagan & Anderson, 1989; Emery, 1988, 1993; Cummings & Davies, 1994). Similarly, some families may encourage close sib–sib relationships, while others tend to encourage sibs to form separate social spheres. In turn, this kind of social arrangement will result in different types of relationship learning.

Do all combinations produce equally socially competent children or are some ingredients in this mix more important than others? Do different combinations produce different, but equally well adjusted children in terms of their social relationships? Can children in a family with a poor marriage compensate by investing "relationship energy" into another subsystem such as the sib–sib or parent–child systems? Studies of divorce (Hetherington, Hagan & Anderson, 1989) suggest that a close sib–sib relationship can help buffer children during a stressful divorce.

CONCLUSIONS AND UNRESOLVED ISSUES

This chapter reflects considerable progress in our understanding of how children learn about social relationships. However, progress is clearly uneven across the significant family subsystems that we have examined. Much more is known about the impact of the parent–child relationship than other relationships, such as the marital and sibling relationships, on children's relationship learning. Similarly, our understanding of the ways in which the subsystems are linked and how they operate together to produce their effects remain understudied.

The multidirectionality of influence is often included in our models but less often empirically evaluated. This concept of multidirectionality can take several forms. Within the family itself, the interplay among the subsystems needs more attention. As noted above, the mutual influence of parenting and marriage or sibling relationships needs more attention, instead of assuming that the direction of influence is usually singular (e.g., from marital interaction to parenting). Even when these subsystem links are more clearly understood, the assumption remains that the direction of influence flows from the family to extra-familial relationships. Although there is considerable evidence that extra-familial social friends and social networks have an impact on parent–child relationships (Belsky, 1984; Cochran & Davila, 1992), we rarely explore this issue with children. What is the impact of children's extra-familial relationships with friends, peers and relatives on their family relationships? As has been found in several studies, children's relationships with peers/friends can influence their adjustment to a new sibling (Kramer & Gottman, 1992) and their relationships with their parents (Repetti, 1993).

Distinctions need to be made between short-term and long-term opportunities for learning about relationships. The vast majority of research has focused on long-term models in which the effects of stable family influences (e.g., interaction style, management style, disciplinary views, marital satisfaction) are addressed and their relationships to some relatively enduring aspect of the child's relationship with other children is measured. In contrast, little attention has been devoted to short-term effects of fluctuations in either family functioning or peer relationships on peer experiences or the child's relationships in the family. The Repetti (1993) study is a good example of the impact of short-term shifts in the quality of peer relationships on subsequent experiences with family members. On the family side, what is the impact of being involved in an argument with a sibling or parent prior to going to school on subsequent peer relationships? Events in which the target child is directly involved (e.g., argument with a friend, conflict with sibling) and events that are witnessed (e.g., watch a friend receive an injury or an insult at school, witness mother–father or parent–sibling conflict) are both worth examination.

It is also important to distinguish between micro and macro level changes. In the Repetti work, for example, short-term (micro) shifts were studied, but less is known about the long-term impact of these repeated micro events on changes in relationships. Do these repeated school-based negative events lead to a change in the nature of parent–child relationships? To take a further example, does a child who develops a close friendship relationship, but who has a poor relationship with her parents, over time develop a better parent–child relationship?

Another issue that needs attention is the specification of the conditions under which children learn similar rather than complementary lessons about relationships from significant others. The bulk of the evidence suggests that most children learn to adopt similar styles and models of relationships. However, there is other evidence from adults that suggests that they compensate for their earlier, often poor, relationships by developing a very different approach to relationships. Involved fathers, for example, often reports that their own fathers were uninvolved and their current views of father–child relationships are in response to their own relationship history (Parke, 1996). The factors that promote similarity vs. compensatory relationships are not well understood.

A variety of temporary stressors of moderate duration merit exploration as well. The impact of divorce, parental job loss or residential relocation may affect the quality of children's peer relationships. For example, Hetherington, Cox & Cox (1979) found a significant deleterious impact of divorce on the peer relationships of preschool-age children, especially boys. Similarly, Ladd et al. (1988) found that families with two incomes and relatively stable residences (fewer moves) tended to have larger peer networks. More work on the impact of different types of family stress is needed, and Patterson and her colleagues (Patterson et al., 1992; Patterson, Vaden & Kupersmidt, 1991) have made substantial progress along these lines, especially concerning the impact of family socioeconomic circumstances on children's peer relationships.

Sixth, a developmental analysis of these issues is clearly needed. As other research suggests (Grotevant & Cooper, 1986; Krappman, 1989) the direction of influence between parent and child is more balanced across development, as issues of autonomy become of more central importance to the child and adolescent. Even fundamental descriptive data concerning the ways in which different interactive strategies or managerial processes shift across development are lacking at this point. More importantly, the ways in which the family strategies (e.g., as interactive partner, manager or direct tutor) relate to social relational competence at different points in the child's development merit investigation.

Seventh, how do parents of different ages manage their children's social relationships? Recent data suggests that late-time fathers, who began their child-rearing in their mid-30s, have different styles of interaction than early-time fathers and are less physical and more cognitively oriented in their interaction styles (Parke & Neville, 1995). How do these differences alter children's social relationships? Similarly, late-time mothers are more likely to continue employment outside the home than early-time mothers (Daniels & Weingarten, 1982). How is their greater use of day care likely to alter children's social relationships?

Eighth, a major concern is our limited understanding of the generalizability of the processes that have been discussed. Little is known about how variations in ethnicity, race and class influence how families teach their children about social relationships. Variations across ethnic lines represent important opportunities not only to explore the universality of processes and mechanisms, but they also provide naturally occurring variations in the relative salience of certain key determinants such as interactive style or emotional expressiveness. As we become aware of our own cultural diversity, it becomes important that we begin to make a serious commitment to an exploration of this diversity—both theoretically and through systematic empirical inquiry. The search for a balance between processes that are universal and processes that are unique to particular cultural, racial or ethnic group represents an important challenge for the future.

The range of influence agents that play a role in shaping children's social relationships needs to be expanded. Grandparents and other extended kin provide models and guidelines about social relationships and their contribution needs more attention in future research (Smith, 1995; Tinsley & Parke, 1984).

In sum, families play an important role in children's relationship learning, but only by focusing on the interplay among the subsystems are we going to advance our understanding of this issue.

Chapter 2

Emotional Processes in Children's Relationships with Siblings and Friends

Maria von Salisch
Freie Universität Berlin, Germany

Children's relationships with other children are often intensely emotional. Even a cursory glance at infants' delight when imitating their siblings' gestures, at preschoolers' serious faces when fighting over a toy, or at children's exuberant movements when engaged in high-spirited horseplay reveals how deeply emotional children's relationships with their companions can be. Other examples come easily to mind, such as primary school children gossiping over the "disgusting" characteristics of specific classmates or preadolescent chums discussing incidents which caused embarrassment to themselves or others. Indeed, one could make the point that the intensity (intense vs. weak), the variability (restricted to few vs. ranging freely across the whole range of emotions), and the social desirability (little vs. much) of the emotions expressed, as well as the ability to share, negotiate and resolve (conflicting) feelings, are indicators of the quality of children's relationships with other children. Failure to study the emotional processes involved in these relationships would mean missing a good part of children's experience in them.

Studying children's emotional development without embedding it in their interpersonal relationships would be equally deficient, for the following reasons. (1) From the first day of life children are social beings who orient to other people. The emotions communicated through face, voice, gestures and movements play an important role in the development of the infant's self (Stern, 1986) as well as in the establishment of attachment relationships. (2) Emotions can be defined as "processes of establishing, maintaining or disrupting the relations between the person and the internal or external environment, when such relations are signifi-

Handbook of Personal Relationships, 2nd edn. Edited by Steve Duck.
© 1997 John Wiley & Sons Ltd.

cant to the individual" (Campos, Campos & Barrett, 1989). Since interpersonal relationships are important to most people, many emotions arise in the context of relationships (Scherer, Wallbott & Summerfield, 1986), particularly in those with close associates. In his classic treatise on anger, Averill (1982) concluded that among adults anger was elicited in more than half of the cases by a "loved one" or by "someone you know well and like". (3) Emotion regulation takes place not only within the individual but also in interpersonal relationships. People influence each other in the perception and experience of their feelings. Processes such as emotion socialization or social support are unthinkable without (close) interpersonal relationships. (4) In face-to-face interactions people shape each other's behavior and attitudes, often without being aware that they are doing so. Simple reinforcement (Malatesta & Haviland, 1982; Patterson & Cobb, 1971), as well as more complex phenomena such as attunement (Stern, 1986), responsivity or empathy, can be understood only in the context of interactions with long-term relationship partners, such as family members and friends.

Emotional processes in friendships and sibling relationships play an important role in social and emotional development, because not only mothers and fathers but also siblings, peers and friends play an active part in children's growing up. Many of the regulatory processes which have been described between parents and children are likely to take place between siblings as well: older siblings are likely to selectively reinforce their baby siblings' smiles and other signs of enjoyment (Malatesta & Haviland, 1982), are likely to be sources of social referencing (Sorce et al., 1985) when parents are not available and can comfort their younger siblings when they are sad or upset over their mother's absence (Teti & Ablard, 1989). There is, however, an important difference between parent–child and child–child relationships: relationships between children, who are not too far apart in age, are characterized by symmetrical reciprocity (Youniss, 1980). Due to the reciprocal nature of these relationships, children will face unique challenges about the expression and regulation of emotion within these relationships (Brown & Dunn, 1991). No mother, for example, would seriously "dare" her child to jump from a wall in order to show that he is not afraid of heights, whereas peers might do so. Other implications of reciprocal relationships for children's emotional development will be discussed below.

These and other considerations speak to the need for a systematic investigation of the emotional processes involved not only in children's relationships with their parents but also in those with other children. What such investigation requires is a change in perspective, that is, a reconceptualization of the emotional mechanisms underlying some of the phenomena in children's relationship research which have been described in the past. The following overview will focus on two relationships, those of children with their siblings and those of children with their friends. Siblings and friends are both peers insofar as they are members of the same generation (von Salisch, 1996), but they differ from "ordinary" peer relationships in that children spend much time in them, they are maintained over longer periods of time and the children know each other well (Krappmann, 1996; Bukowsky & Hoza, 1989). These kinds of emotional processes will be considered:

children's sharing of positive emotions (e.g., enjoyment, humor or amusement) and their sharing of negative emotions that are elicited by, or directed at, third parties (e.g., sadness, anxiety, shame or anger). Sharing these emotions can be explicit and verbal, as when children discuss emotionally arousing incidents, or implicit and non-verbal, as when they giggle together. Sharing one's emotions is important to study because it means expressing and often validating these feelings, which implies a common evaluation of the circumstances which have elicited them. This may be significant not only for the adaptation of the individual child but also for the quality of the dyadic relationship. A further section will focus on the communication of anger occurring in the context of conflicts with siblings or friends. In each of these sections, the importance of studying these three emotional processes will be discussed and their development over the course of childhood and preadolescence will be described. Emphasis will be placed on the similarities between the processes of relating to siblings and to friends, leaving differences between these relationships for exploration in future studies.

SHARING POSITIVE EMOTIONS

Although conflict and negative emotions have been studied the most, there is no denying that children's relationships consistently include the sharing of happiness or enjoyment (Parke, 1994). In fact, Hartup (1983) considers the peer context as a unique opportunity for children to develop competencies in reciprocating positive emotions. Children's shared mirth can be as loud as toddlers' uproarious laughter at another child's burp or as quiet as the amused glances preadolescent friends exchange when a disliked classmate commits a faux pas. Smiling and laughing have probably developed from distinct phylogenetic origins; precursors of the relevant muscle movements can be identified in monkeys and apes (van Hooff, 1972).

Significance

One of the precursors of laughter in apes is the play face, and this is the context in which smiling and laughing can most often be observed in human infants. Malatesta & Haviland (1982) counted up to 12 smiles when they observed mothers and their infants of 3 and 6 months during 6 minutes of free play and a reunion. There is no reason to believe that it would be any fewer if the babies were playing with a friendly older sibling. Stern (1986) suggested that the exchange of emotions in repetitive play with caretakers and other people provides infants of about 2–7 months with numerous opportunities to experience the patterned quality of their inner feelings. This helps the infants to distinguish between the self and the other person and contributes to the establishment of their core self. Between 8 and 18 months the non-verbal sharing of enjoyment—

for example, over a new accomplishment of the child—is considered an indicator of attunement between two separate and mutually responsive selves. Attunement represents a new quality of closeness in the relationship, because it involves sharing not only one's focus of attention but also one's intentions and (underlying) affective states. At about 1 year of age children demonstrate social referencing, that is, children's watchful glances at mothers, fathers or substitute caretakers in the face of potential danger (Sorce et al., 1985). Also in later years, younger siblings are known to cast an apprehensive eye on their older siblings when confronted with an ambiguous situation, such as an adult who comes to visit once a year. In each of these cases, a reassuring smile informs the child that there is no risk, that everything is okay.

As everybody knows, sharing a smile with a congenial companion is more rewarding than smiling for oneself, and there are numerous research findings which attest to the social facilitation of smiles and laughter (e.g. Chapman, 1976; Bainum, Lounsbury & Pollio, 1984). Smiling the particularly cordial Duchenne smile (Ekman, Davidson & Friesen, 1990), which produces crows' feet and wrinkles aroung the eyes, creates emotional resonance in the interaction partner; he or she is induced to join with the same cordial type of smile, especially if it is a close friend (von Salisch, 1989). The contagious nature of smiles and laughter implies that their exchange can escalate to spirals of ever deeper and almost unstoppable cathartic laughter which in the end is deeply relaxing (Ruch, 1993). When analyzed in more depth, sharing positive emotions involves the communication and mutual validation of an (implicit) evaluation of the self, the interaction partner or other circumstances as delightful, amusing or relieving. Experiencing and acknowledging commonality makes the people involved feel good and strengthens their emotional bond, especially when it has a positive overtone. Their motivation to maintain the relationship is increased (Oatley, 1992).

Sharing their good feelings should also help children to cope with the frustrations they encounter while growing up. Be it rules and restrictions by parents, teachers or institutions, be it other children making fun of them, or be it their own lack of skills—all this causes expected frustrations. The intensity of children's gleeful laughter when an adult behaves like a fool certainly speaks for children's many frustrations. Being able to appreciate the absurdity of situations one cannot change (Lefcourt & Martin, 1986) and having a companion who concurs with this evaluation should help children to master these frustrations (McGhee, 1979).

Development

Infancy and Preschool Period

The exchange of smiles starts very early in life. Social smiles at specific persons first appear around the second month and laughter can first be heard around the fourth month of life (Campos et al., 1983). Toddlers who meet in play groups greet each other with the exchange of obvious signs of enjoyment, such as smiles or laughter (Ross & Goldman, 1976). When language begins to develop in the second year of life, these exchanges become more verbal and sometimes even take on a humorous quality. With the parallel advance of symbol formation, object play, and pretend play children begin to enjoy incongruous situations. Later in the second year, most children make their first jokes about misnaming objects or persons. Distorting the reality in these fantasies can be an amusing game with siblings or friends, especially when the word play centers around forbidden topics, such as farts or stinky diapers (Dunn, 1988b). Starting at about 3 years of age, children are able to come up with jokes about more complex concepts, such as ritual insults about gender. In addition, repetitive rhymes, nonsense and taboo words, as well as sexual innuendos, are all considered to be funny by preschoolers. Exciting activities and vigorous physical play can also elicit children's smiles and laughter. By about 7 years of age, children start to appreciate puns, riddles and jokes which involve double meanings. When confronted about their risqué content they can always pretend that the serious meaning was intended (McGhee, 1979). An observation study of the smiles and laughter of 3–5-year-olds in a nursery school confirms that children's humor becomes ever more verbal and more contrived. An increasing number of laughs and smiles are produced and responded to in the context of silly situations or clowning behavior (Bainum, Lounsbury & Pollio, 1984). The ability to share humor and to amuse one another seems to be one of the components indicating a growing intimacy in children's relationships with one another (Dunn & Brown, 1991; Chapman, Smith & Foot, 1980). Therefore, it is no surprise that previously unacquainted preschoolers who manage to establish positive reciprocity are more likely to become friends than their less congenial agemates (Gottman, 1983). Among peers and siblings there are marked differences in the ability to hit this enjoyable and joyful tone: Judy Dunn (1993) reports that the amount of humor shared among preschool siblings varies between an average of 0–7 jokes per hour of home observation.

Middle Childhood

These differences between sibling pairs are to some extent preserved into the school years; correlations assessing the stability of positive sibling behaviors ranged between 0.42 and 0.60 in three studies spanning 3 and 4 years respectively (Dunn, 1993; Brody, Stoneman & McCoy, 1994). When longer time-spans were assessed the results became more muddled, partly because of intervening life events and partly because different positive behaviors were aggregated into a compound variable indicating a positive relationship (e.g., Dunn, Slomkowski & Beardsall, 1994). Sharing excitement or happiness in jokes or silliness plays an important role in the friendships of school-age children. In a recent survey in Germany, over 90% of the children reported that they "fooled around" with their friends; indeed, this ability seemed to be a central category in their evaluation of their friendships. In a confirmatory factor analysis, Oswald et al. (1994) identified this component as the "fun factor" in children's friendships. Foot, Chapman & Smith (1977) likewise observed that 7- and 8-year-old friends smiled, laughed, touched and talked more when watching a funny film than did previously unacquainted children.

Preadolescence

Tiffany Field and her co-workers (1992) corroborate that the behavior of preadolescent best friends in a "free talk" situation in the laboratory seems to be more relaxed, more playful and more positive in affect than the behavior of acquainted children. In a field study of adolescent humor, Sanford & Eder (1984) observed that adolescents in grades six to eight tended to share practical jokes, funny stories or humorous behavior with their close friends, often with the intention of conveying peer norms or exploring sensitive issues, such as romantic relationships, body functions or sexuality, which were usually not discussed directly. A self-report study indicates that fifth- and sixth-graders take advantage of numerous opportunities to exchange humor; preferred occasions are during meals or while shopping, conversing or talking on the telephone (Zarbatany, Hartmann & Rankin, 1990). That many preadolescents and adolescents make use of these opportunities is suggested by a diary study by Larson & Richards (1991) which showed that, in the company of friends, adolescents' self-rated affect grew more positive between grades five and nine. When in the company of family members, affect ratings generally became more negative over these 4 years. Whether family members were parents or siblings is not clear from the report.

These studies provide a patchwork of findings which suggest that the sharing of positive emotions is an important feature of children's relationships with their siblings and friends. Studies of the antecedents suggest that a positive sibling relationship is promoted by a facilitating father (Volling & Belsky, 1992), a positive relationship between the parents (Brody et al., 1994), family cohesion and family expressiveness (MacKinnon, 1989), and a non-active temperament in the younger or in both siblings (Stoneman & Brody, 1993). What is missing are studies charting children's humorous exchanges at different stages of development in more detail. Including verbal and non-verbal components is important, because there are at least 18 different types of smiles, only two of which indicate felt enjoyment of the person showing it (Ekman, 1985). In order to gain a more complete understanding of the sharing of humor, amusement and other positive emotions, self-report data must be validated by observations and vice versa. To explore the implications that these joyful and enjoyable exchanges have for children's coping and health may be just as worthwhile as the examination of the concomitants of negative peer interactions has proven in the past (e.g., Gottman & Katz, 1989).

SHARING NEGATIVE EMOTIONS (DIRECTED AT THIRD PARTIES)

Everybody, including children, at times feels sad or hurt, anxious or fearful, embarrassed or ashamed. Although the antecedents of children's emotions have not been charted as carefully as those of adults (e.g., Scherer, 1988), there is every reason to believe that their structural features are the same. For example, just like adults, children often report that sadness was elicited by loss of control over something important to them (e.g., Fabes et al., 1988). Even though the abstract features of the eliciting situations may be similar for children and adults, however, the concrete contents of the emotion antecedents are likely to vary. Only in children, for example, is fear elicited by monsters and other creatures of the dark. The specific contents of the situational elicitors of emotions among children and adolescents need to be described with respect to both their normative development and their interindividual variations.

Significance

Studies of adolescents and adults indicate that when they have feelings of anger, anxiety and shame they communicate them between 64% to 78% of the time, often to more than one person (Rimé et al., 1992). Saarni (1995) reports that 20–42% of the children in middle childhood consider social support to be the best strategy for coping with aversive emotions, especially with sadness and fear. Sharing negative emotions with others provides the individual with an opportunity to clarify ambiguous emotional sensations, to cognitively articulate, label and formulate often diffuse feelings, to redefine challenged concepts of self and others, to garner social support in coping with these often overwhelming emotions and to tap into the culture's concepts for defining and managing their emotional experiences (Rimé et al., 1992). Sharing their fortunes and misfortunes with non-judgmental and trustworthy confidants helps children to develop a rich and realistic understanding of themselves and their peers, and contributes to their interpersonal sensitivity (Youniss, 1980). In addition, it most likely keeps their relationships intense and lively, because emotions are usually elicited by something that is important to them (Campos, Campos & Barrett, 1989). Having someone with whom to share distress, anxiety, sadness and disappointment in a satisfying way assists children and adolescents in their adjustment (Buhrmester, 1990) and in their coping with the tasks of social development, such as gaining acceptance in their peer group, finding a close same-sex friend or dealing with the complexities of sexual and romantic relationships (Buhrmester & Furman, 1986). In addition, exploring negative, ambivalent or conflicting feelings in the face of normative and non-normative life events may contribute to children's adjustment to these disruptions in their lives, because it gives them on the most basic level the feeling that they are not alone with their problems and that others experience similar feelings. Older siblings and friends may also provide advice or help in the practical implementation of plans designed to overcome the current difficulties (Ladd, 1990; Berndt, 1989; Kramer & Gottman, 1992; Garmezy & Rutter, 1983). On a more general level, when negative emotions are acknowledged and validated by the friend or sibling, it implies a similar view of the events which instigated them. The experience of shared meaning is likely to relieve the individual (he or she feels "understood") and to deepen their relationship (Duck, 1994a).

Compared to parents, children are at a particular advantage when it comes to understanding the emotions of a fellow child, even in their early years. Because children are on a similar developmental level of understanding themselves and "the world", the meanings which one child attaches to events may be immediately "available" to the other. Or as Judy Dunn put it: "Since what distresses, pains or excites a sibling is very close to what distresses, pains or excites the child, the child is likely to be far better placed to understand and find remedies for a sibling's distress than for the distress of an adult" (1983; p. 793). This argument can easily be extended to close friends, who seek each other out, spend much time together, and tend to know each other quite well (Ladd & Emerson, 1984; Diaz & Berndt, 1982). In addition, children often have a better understanding of the peer context which elicited the emotion than adults. From this perspective, sharing negative emotions becomes akin to the relationship provisions of intimacy and nurturance (Furman & Robbins, 1985). Breadth and depth of shared emotions as well as the ability to "work them through" should be a hallmark of warm and intimate relationships. Not being able to share most of these feelings may in the long run contribute to psychological maladjustment. Experiencing criticism or rejection when trying to share their negative emotions should "add insult to injury"; that is, it should maintain or intensify not only the existing aversive emotions, but should add the feeling of being misunderstood and rebuffed. The implications for children's and adolescents' self-esteem are obvious, but need to be established in empirical studies. This calls for studies charting the emotional exchanges that make up what psychologists call "social support" in more detail and explore the long-term ramifications for the participants.

Development

The Preschool Period

At 18–24 months most children utter their first emotion words and begin to talk about feelings and other inner states. Starting at about 3 years of age, children increasingly talk with their older siblings about feelings, mostly in the context of play or humor. While mothers tend to discuss the child's feelings in the context of controlling the child, older siblings prefer to talk about their own feelings, which tend to arise from their own immediate needs. The reciprocal sibling relationship makes fewer "allowances", but rather challenges the child to decenter and attend to the feelings of the other child. The results are not always peaceful: more negative *and* more positive emotional expressions can be observed between siblings than between mothers and children (Brown & Dunn, 1992). In addition, there are marked differences between sibling pairs in how often they discuss their feelings: in one sample the number of turns ranged from none to as many as 32 conversational turns of emotion talk per hour of home observation (Dunn, 1993). Some preschoolers indicated that they would share their bad dreams, fights or worries with their siblings and sought contact with them when they were sad or unhappy, especially when their parents were unavailable (Zelkowitz, 1989).

Another perhaps more circumstantial way in which feelings are communicated is through enactment in joint pretend play (Howes, Unger & Matheson, 1992). After a little "framing" both children slip into a shared fantasy world. Children as young as 18 months were able to participate in these delightful and challenging plays—provided that they had a friendly older sibling who set up the game and steered them through the rough spots. Between 24 and 30 months, younger siblings made increasingly active contributions to the shared pretend play and became less compliant in following their older siblings' directions. For one-quarter to one-third of the preschool sibling pairs, joint pretend play was a riveting activity, sometimes extending over more than 140 conversational turns (Dunn, 1993).

Children set off into shared fantasy worlds not only with their siblings but also with some of their friends. For Gottman (1986), coordinating fantasy play, self-exploration and managing conflicts are the most important social processes among preschool friends. Gottman (1986) describes how preschool boys use fantasy play in order to master their fears. He details how the two boys start off by discussing poison, then move on to the danger of rattlesnakes and finally explore the power of sharks, realizing that they are up against no small foe. After considering climbing a tree, shooting the creature, or transforming it into metal, they finally conclude that it can only be contained by an even more powerful metaphor—concrete. In another study, Kramer & Gottman (1992) suggest that fantasy play with their "best friends" can help young children cope with their real-life fears and worries, in this case the birth of a younger brother or sister. Preschoolers who were better able to "manage" their conflicts with their friends, who were able to achieve a higher quality of play and sustain longer episodes of fantasy play—often about the new baby—had a more positive and affectionate relationship with their younger sibling, when he or she was 6 and 14 months old.

Middle Childhood and Preadolescence

Gottman & Mettetal (1986) make the point that the most salient social process in middle childhood is gossip which evaluates the qualities of other children in a negative way. Friends can be overheard to share their anger and contempt at some classmate's characteristic or behavior. Agreeing about the evaluations implied in these emotions not only builds solidarity among the friends but also helps the children in their efforts at managing emotions which do not adhere to the rather strict standards of the peer society. Under the disguise of discussing a peer's "disgusting" behavior they can also explore their own unacceptable emotions. Peer acceptance may thus stimulate children in middle childhood to regulate the display of disruptive emotions, such as anger (von Salisch, 1995), anxiety (Harris, 1989) or fear (Altshuler & Ruble, 1989).

Around the age of 10, friendships among children often attain a new quality of sharing and intimacy (Sullivan, 1953). In Selman's (1980) stage model, children around this age start to conceptualize friendship as a framework for reciprocal intimate disclosure which is to be preserved for mutual and long-term benefits. Sharing secrets, which includes disclosing feelings which are not socially desirable, presupposes that the friend is trustworthy and will not tell the damaging information to other people. A questionnaire study by Buhrmester and Furman (1987) with children in second, fifth and eighth grades concluded that there is a steep increase in the intimacy ratings of the "best" friendship in fifth grade, especially among the girls. As many authors have noted, preadolescent close friendships thrive on the discussion of problems and preoccupations, many of which involve the sharing of embarrassment, anxiety and other negative emotions (e.g., Hirsch & Dubois, 1989). In Gottman & Mettetal's model, (1986) the accompanying processes of self-exploration and help in sorting out these feelings are the most salient processes in the friendships of preadolescents and adolescents.

Siblings may not be on the forefront of emotional support, but in 60–95% of families with a school-age child they figure among the top ten providers of social support (Bryant, 1985; Reid et al., 1989), especially when assistance is needed in regard to parents or finances (O'Brien, 1991). In Buhrmester & Furman's (1987) study, the ratings of self-disclosure towards the "best" friend soon surpass those towards the "favorite" sibling, which stay about the same over the whole time. Indeed, between grades three and twelve the degree of intimacy, affection and companionship in the sibling relationship actually decreases on average (Buhrmester & Furman, 1990). There are, of course, large individual differences in the warmth and closeness of the sibling relationship, larger perhaps than in voluntary friendships. Over the 7 years between preschool and preadolescence, the stability of warmth and closeness in the sibling relationship was about $r = 0.35$. Affectionate and intimate attitudes and behaviors were reported more frequently when the siblings were two sisters, when the family belonged to the middle class, and—perhaps surprisingly—when mothers indicated that the family had experienced some adversity, such as accidents, illnesses or peer problems (Dunn, Slomkowski & Beardsall, 1994). In this sample, very few parents experienced serious marital problems, but other studies report contradictory findings. Whereas Hetherington (1988) observed increased levels of sibling conflict in families with marital disharmony or difficult step-parent relationships, Jenkins (1992) reported that siblings may provide considerable support for each other.

Specifying the circumstances under which siblings (and perhaps friends) can help each other come to terms with children's ever more frequent experience of marital conflict, separation and divorce seems to be a worthwhile topic for further study.

Not all friendships are equally intimate. About 33% of the male adolescents interviewed by Youniss & Smollar (1985) reported no "best friendship" involving trust, intimacy and conflict resolution by "talking it over". Children who were low-accepted by their peers were more lonely and tended to engage less often in intimate exchanges about problems, secrets or "things that make one friend sad or mad" with the friend (Parker & Asher, 1993). Having a sibling may help some of these rejected or neglected children, particularly those who are isolated from their peers. High levels of support from a sibling helped to lower the high levels of anxiety and immaturity in these children (East & Rook, 1992). Whether siblings' assistance may also result in higher levels of peer acceptance should be explored in longitudinal studies.

ANGER IN CONFLICTS BETWEEN CHILDREN

Anger, anxiety, shame and contempt are not only aroused by children and adults outside the dyad but also by the relationship partners; that is, by the friends and siblings themselves. This can lead to disagreements between them. Since the 1970s, conflicts between unrelated peers have received much scientific attention, for the most part in research on social and cognitive development in the tradition of Piaget (1932/1986). Reviews of this literature can be found in Shantz (1987), Shantz & Hobart (1989) and in various chapters in the Shantz & Hartup volume (1992). In recent years the literature on conflicts between siblings has burgeoned. Interest in disagreements between siblings is not only motivated by social cognitive concerns (Dunn, 1988b), but also comes from the clinical side, because sibling discord is one of the most common and most persistent child-related problems parents complain about (Clifford, 1959; Kelly & Main, 1979). In a number of recent studies it has been found that amount and intensity of sibling conflict is influenced by child characteristics such as temperament, or rather by the temperamental match between the siblings (Munn & Dunn, 1989; Stocker, Dunn & Plomin, 1989; Brody, Stoneman & Burke, 1987; Stoneman & Brody, 1993), as well as by family variables, such as the quality of the parents' marital relationship (MacKinnon, 1989; Hetherington, 1988), family harmony and family cohesiveness (Brody et al., 1992), and differential or unresponsive treatment by one or both of the parents (e.g., Volling & Belsky, 1992; Brody, Stoneman & Burke, 1987; Stocker, Dunn & Plomin, 1989; Stocker & McHale, 1992; Bryant & Crockenberg, 1980; Furman & Buhrmester, 1985). In one study, the firstborn's security of attachment to his or her mother in infancy made an additional significant contribution in explaining the frequency of sibling conflicts 5 years later; that is, when the child was 6 years old and the younger sibling was a toddler or preschooler (Volling & Belsky, 1992). Vandell & Bailey (1992) provide an excellent review of these and other studies of family influences on sibling conflict.

In very few studies has there been an attempt to determine what emotions are associated with children's disagreements. As Shantz noted almost 10 years ago, which emotions precede and co-occur with claims and counterclaims is an almost uncharted territory, a proverbial blank spot on the map of scientific research (Shantz, 1987). Whether an assertion is made in a whiny or in a firm voice, whether the opposition to an initial claim is accompanied by surprise, fear or anger, whether in the course of the negotiation excitement prevails, or whether the end is marked by one party withdrawing in a huff or by the exchange of smiles—all this throws light on the nature of disagreements and their resolutions. "Everyday" quarrels and bickering may be differentiated from "all-out" confrontations, and hostile jibes from "friendly" provocations, because the emotions expressed through face, voice, words and gestures contextualize the conflict and elucidate its meaning.

In the following paragraphs, I will examine the expression and regulation of anger in disagreements between siblings and friends in three phases of their conflicts; that is, at the outset, during the course of the negotiation and at the outcome. This requires bringing together the literature on anger regulation, which focuses on individuals, with the "dyadic" research on conflict. Anger is likely to be present at the beginning of the disagreement, because if no one is angry or upset at the other there would be no reason to oppose the other. However, not every experience of anger leads to overt confrontation (Fabes & Eisenberg, 1992; Rotenberg, 1985); in a recent diary study 40% of the school-age children indicated that at least once over a 1-week period they had felt intense anger but had not communicated this feeling to the person who had instigated it (von Salisch, 1993). It is also conceivable to have disagreements in which conflicting goals are pursued in "cold blood"; that is, without overt or covert emotions. Expressing anger has an effect on the negotiation of the divergent viewpoints. Vandell & Bailey (1992) argue among other things that high amounts of affect are a hallmark of destructive conflicts. Although extreme expressions of anger or distress are likely to make the negotiation more difficult, if not impossible, in the short run, and may increase the risk of escalation, their long-term effects are less clear. In some relationships (and cultures) conflicts have to be brought to a head before they can be resolved, even if this involves a shouting match. Tolerance for intense expression of anger varies, of course, between individuals, dyads and relationships. The other extreme, not feeling or not expressing anger when unjustly attacked, is also not conducive to relationships (Eisenberg et al., 1994) because it implies withdrawal in the face of opposition or a tendency to give in to the demands of the other child. (Children are rather hard on peers who do not stand up for their own rights; they call them "whimps".) Optimal for conflict resolution in the short run seems to be a "medium" level of anger, that is enough to bring forward arguments (Dunn & Brown, 1994), to underline assertions and to resist illegitimate requests, but not to the extent that it prevents negotiation.

Being "a little" angry can, in addition, help children put forward their complaint when their friend or sibling is physically stronger or otherwise more powerful. Finally, one can ask what effect the expression and regulation of anger have on the immediate and the long-term outcomes of the conflict. This question becomes very relevant for children's relationships with their siblings and friends when put in the following way: under what conditions do children feel that a conflict was constructive in the sense that they have "learned a lesson" from it? (Shantz, 1993).

Significance

Anger at another person is usually aroused when expectancies are violated (Oatley, 1992) or when a goal-directed activity is frustrated and the other person is held responsible for it (Lazarus, 1991). The experience of anger gives the child an opportunity to learn about her wishes and preferences, expectancies and vulnerabilities. The confrontation of divergent viewpoints is—in the best and theoretical case—followed by an exchange about the ideas and motives underlying the child's angry feelings at her friend or sibling. Negotiating the child's anger helps this friend or sibling to gain a better understanding of her preferences and expectancies, attitudes and limitations, sensitive spots and strong points; in short, to develop sensitivity for the friend or sibling (Youniss, 1980; Rizzo, 1989). On a more general plane, talking about the "cause" of the angry feelings offers children a chance to change their construction of meaning, not only about the angry child, but also about the self and perhaps about the relationship. Conflict discussions may transform the participants' social roles *vis-à-vis* one another and may deepen their friendships (Whitesell & Harter, 1994; Selman, 1980, stage 3).

In the families of preschool children, discussing emotions seems to promote children's cognitive-emotional development. Children who talked more often about (conflicting) feelings with family members, and who used arguments in conflicts with their siblings, tended to score higher on measures of affective perspective-taking (Dunn et al., 1991; Slomkowski & Dunn, 1992; Howe, 1991). These children were better able to understand what a puppet would feel in an emotion-eliciting situation, such as going to the dentist, even when these feelings did not match their own feelings in the same situation. Emotion knowledge of this type seems to be a strong predictor of acceptance in the preschool peer group (Denham et al., 1990). In middle childhood the negotiation of conflicts among peers is believed to stimulate moral development (Piaget, 1932/1986) and eventually to result in the development of shared norms and values that apply to both children equally (Youniss, 1980; Keller, 1987).

These are, of course, ideal outcomes. It is evident that it may be difficult to discuss a peer's angry feelings, and that anxiety or defensiveness may prevail when one is the target of these sentiments. Negotiations between children may go awry; that is, they may end in physical harm or escalate into cycles of mutual retaliation and coercion (Patterson & Cobb, 1971; Herzberger & Hall, 1993). Another possibility is "premature" submission, in which one child yields to force or gives in against his or her own wishes. A third possible "derailment" involves the use of hostility or denigration when presenting one's case or when opposing the argument of the other. Denigrating the other child time and again causes psychological harm in the "victim", because it is likely to engender not only a model of the relationship partner as hostile, but also a model of the self as vulnerable, inadequate and ultimately worthless. When this happens over and over again, most friends will end their friendship (Selman, 1980), but in a sibling relationship there is no "escape". When older sisters of about 10 years of age displayed anger or disparagement at their later-born sisters in a teaching situation, the later-borns tended to reciprocate with anger, disparagement, competitive statements and the refusal to help or share with the older sister, leading to a vicious cycle of mutual competition and devaluation (Bryant & Crockenberg, 1980; Stoneman & Brody, 1993). A consequence of a multitude of such interactions may be a tendency to depreciate the self, which was found primarily among younger siblings (Minnett, Vandell & Santrock, 1983). Perhaps this is because in early and middle childhood older siblings have more power to define the situation and the relationship than do younger ones (Buhrmester & Furman, 1986). A study showing significant correlations between an older sibling's hostile comments and the younger sibling's tendency to internalize problems 2 years later (Dunn et al., 1994) fits this picture. It should be noted, however, that these findings are correlational and need to be replicated with a larger and more representative sample. What is also needed is a study tracing the development of the cognitive, expressive and interactive aspects of contempt and denigration in the context of children's relationships with parents and peers.

Development

The Preschool Years

On the basis of mothers' diaries, Goodenough (1931) reports that children of 2 and 3 years of age start to become angry when they encounter difficulties in their play with other children. Anger tantrums were more likely when the children were in bad health, when they had gone without a meal for some time, when they were tired, and when they had a larger number of older siblings. Dunn & Munn (1986) corroborate from family observations that an average of eight conflicts per hour take place between preschool siblings. About half of these sibling conflicts revolve around rights, possessions and property; about every tenth disagreement is marked by intense anger and distress (Dunn & Munn, 1987). Similar findings emerge from the obervations of Fabes and his co-workers (1988) in a nursery school serving children of $3\frac{1}{2}$–$5\frac{1}{2}$ years of age. These authors concluded that anger is almost always elicited in social situations, most of which involve other children. In about half of the cases, anger was aroused in the context of disagreements over material goods or possessions, and a further 28% were associated with physical confrontations, such as being pushed by another child. When asked to explain their peer's angry feelings, preschoolers referred in about 50% of the cases to the fact that the child's goals had been blocked. Adult and child attributions regarding the causes of children's anger were the same in more than 90% of the cases. When friends had shown ambiguous behavior, preschoolers were less likely to react with anger than when non-friends had behaved in an ambiguous way. Friends, so it seems, tend to receive the benefit of the doubt (Fabes et al., 1993). That anger and conflict behavior is embedded in specific relationships is also supported by Dunn & Munn's (1986) observation of siblings: the more anger and distress the toddler-age younger siblings showed during conflicts with their older brothers or sisters, the less likely they were to share, help, comfort or cooperate with this sibling in other situations or engage in pretend play with him or her, when they were 33 months old (Dunn & Brown, 1994). At this age, Dunn (1993) reports 0–56 episodes of sibling conflict per hour of observation. How many of these were accompanied by expressions of anger is not clear from the report.

There are two studies which detail what happens when preschoolers show facial expressions of anger, disgust or contempt (or threat) in the course of conflict negotiations in laboratory or closed-field situations. Matsumoto et al. (1986) report that preschoolers' expression of these negative emotions (as well as the expression of unfelt smiles or no emotions) made it more likely that their friends and partners would stalemate, betray or default in their next move during a simplified Prisoner's Dilemma game. Only the expression of felt (Duchenne) smiles raised the probability of a moral solution, and if this was reached, both children seemed to be so relieved or so satisfied that the display of anger or disgust was less likely in the next move. Even if the expression of these negative emotions does not further moral solutions, it may nevertheless help children in getting (or keeping) what they want. This is the result of Linda Camras' (1977) experiment in which two unacquainted preschoolers had a single gerbil to play with. When players showed one of those facial expressions which ethologists call "threat faces", their partners were likely to wait longer before renewing their request for the animal. Lowering their brows, wrinkling their noses, or making a pouting mouth thus helped the children to keep the cuddly beast.

In a study of preschoolers in an open-field situation, i.e., during free-play in a nursery school, Fabes, Eisenberg and their coworkers observed that children had quite different ways of dealing with their anger. Whereas boys tended to vent their anger (Fabes & Eisenberg, 1992), to show more intense irritation or to retaliate with physical means (Eisenberg et al., 1994), girls tended to put up more active resistance (Fabes & Eisenberg, 1992) or to object verbally to the other child's offensive behavior (Eisenberg et al., 1994). Children's ways of regulating their anger during the peer provocation were associated with their ways of coping with other problems, their temperament, their social competence (as judged by their teachers) and, last but not least, their sociometric status among their peers (Fabes & Eisenberg, 1992; Eisenberg et al., 1994). For example, verbal objections, i.e., negotiating the incident, were positively correlated with constructive coping and not very intense emotional reactions in other situations, as judged by mothers and school personnel alike. When the anger was instigated by a friend, children generally became less aroused, which made it perhaps possible to approach the incident in a more reflective way (Fabes et al., 1993). Hartup et al. (1988), who also observed preschoolers' conflicts during free play, corroborate the lower affective intensity of mutual friends' quarrels, although these authors do not specify *which* emotions they coded. Whereas non-friends tended to break up their play at the end of the confrontations, mutual friends were likely to remain in physical proximity or even to continue their play. Although children were not observed or asked about their emotions at this point in time, common sense suggests that the friends were probably no longer angry at each other.

Middle Childhood

From observation in a first-grade classroom, Rizzo (1989) concludes that two-thirds of the conflicts between friends are caused by "normal" disagreements over the course of play and one-third by the violation of friendship expectations. When school children report what makes them angry, teasing and name-calling, provocations and ostracism are each mentioned by over 20% of the girls, whereas the boys' list is topped by scuffles and physical assaults (Petillon, 1993; Shantz, 1993). Conflicts between siblings in middle childhood are motivated by some of the same topics, such as teasing and getting even, but also by control over resources, which is of course highly relevant in the family context, because there is so much to share (Prochanska & Prochanska, 1985). Psychotherapists Bank & Kahn (1982) suggest that beyond the sometimes rather trivial issues on the surface there may be at least two further layers of sibling conflict, one the never-ending struggle for status in the family and the other an undercurrent of resentment which may have built up over some years of mutual "warfare". What a sibling's behavior "means" is more likely to have become set and hence to resist change, when siblings have adopted opposing social roles towards each other. It may therefore come as a no surprise that quarreling, antagonism and competition seem to be more pervasive between siblings than between friends (Rotenberg, 1985), especially when they are close in age (Furman & Buhrmester, 1985). Siblings' perceptions of the amount of conflict between them are highly correlated ($r = 0.66$; Brody, Stoneman & McCay, 1994).

During the primary school years children acquire an increasingly sophisticated understanding of other peoples' motives, even when something as provocative as the destruction of their own property is involved: whereas first-graders only considered the perpetrator's (malevolent) intentions, third- and fifth-graders were also able to take prosocial motives and unavoidable accidents into account (Olthof, Ferguson & Luiten, 1989). Friendship seems to play a minor role in these attributions. When aggressive boys were the victim of a peer's ambiguous action, they were more likely to attribute hostile motives to the provocateur than their non-aggressive agemates (see also Dodge, 1986). But neither aggressive nor non-aggressive boys were influenced by the presence or absence of friendship between themselves and the perpetrator (Sancilio, Plumert & Hartup, 1989). The attribution of a peer's malevolent intentions seems to go along with the report of more intense feelings of anger and a greater risk for aggressive retaliation, at least among "normal" black boys (Graham, Hudley & Williams, 1992). The studies described here all used hypothetical stories to elicit the children's attributions. In order to advance our knowledge, it is necessary to place children's attributions in the context of their relationships to specific friends (e.g. Whitesell & Harter, 1994) or siblings (e.g., Herzberger & Hall, 1993), and to study the attribution processes during the many provocations children encounter in daily life.

When observing conflicts between peers, Shantz & Shantz (1985) concluded that aggression was rather seldom used: only 5% of the disagreements involved physical attacks and only 4% were accompanied by verbal derogations. Studies of the development of anger regulation likewise conclude that overt aggression decreases over the school years, particularly among girls, whereas indirect forms of retaliation increase (Rotenberg, 1985). By the end of their primary school years, children have a much wider repertoire of strategies for dealing with disruptive emotions, such that they are now better able to distance themselves physically or psychologically from their fear, distress (Harris, 1989), or anger (von Salisch, 1995). Over the years, children are also believed to acquire a more elaborate understanding of the temporal, interpersonal and management aspects of conflict and emotional disequilibrium (Selman & Demorest, 1987; Saarni, 1995). Whether they make use of these growing abilities depends, of course, on the concrete circumstances. The more the sibling relationship is characterized, for example, by conflict, the more likely children are to hit and yell at their siblings, to slam the door or to think denigrating thoughts about them (e.g., "She is so stupid that it is not worth my while to be mad at her") (Callondann, 1995). In divorced families, older boys were much more likely to make negative or demeaning remarks or facial expressions, or to grab, hit or push their younger sibling during a board game, than any other group of older children coming from divorced or married families (MacKinnon, 1989).

Board games like Parchesi challenge children's anger regulation skills because of the many frustrations built into them. For the researcher, these games present an excellent opportunity to study children's negotiation of their angry feelings in a closed-field, but not too contrived setting. That angry feelings are aroused and lead to debate is likely when, for example, two "best friends" are taught different rules for a board game. When Hartup et al. (1993) did just this, they observed that 9- and 10-year-old pairs of friends tended to disagree more frequently and at greater length than pairs of non-friends. Compared to non-friends' disagreements, friends' conflicts were more intense during their peak periods; unfortunately, the authors did not specify which emotions the children displayed "in the heat of the battle". Hartup and his colleagues interpret these findings, which contradict the stereotype children hold, that friendships are characterized by a particular harmony (Berndt & Perry, 1986), by pointing out that friends know each other better and are more secure in their relationship than non-friends. This gives friends the freedom to challenge each other's point of view and to disagree with enthusiasm.

That close (female) friends tend to be more outspoken in a conflict is corroborated by von Salisch (1991), who observed close and casual pairs of friends while cooperating on a computer game with a built-in defect. An analysis of the 11-year-olds' facial expressions revealed that close female friends showed significantly more of the cordial Duchenne smiles, than did casual female friends or close male friends. Close female friends also displayed Duchenne smiles more frequently in combination with reproaches, as if they wanted to signal to their girl-friend, "Your move was not okay, but we are still friends". That girls tend to deal with the relationship aspect of the friendship was also found by Miller, Danaher & Forbes (1986), who observed that girls tended to ameliorate conflicts by expressing their anger in indirect ways, such as suggesting compromises, changing the topic of conversation, or negotiating the point of contention. Hartup and co-workers' (1993) found that girls, especially female friends, tended to bolster their assertions with rationales, whereas male friends tended to insist on their point of view without arguments. This result can be interpreted as evidence for a stronger relationship orientation among female than among male friends.

Preadolescence

When Raffaelli (1990) asked 112 youngsters in grades five to eight about their conflicts with friends and siblings, 23% said they never argued with their friends and 6% said thay never argued with their siblings. Whereas disagreements with friends revolved most often around physical attacks and relationship themes, such as betrayal, neglect (girls only) or untrustworthiness (boys only) (see also Youniss & Smollar, 1985), sibling discord was most often elicited by questions of property rights and by verbal abuse. Even though preadolescent siblings indicated that they quarrelled "habitually", 66% of them reported that they felt angry during these conflicts, while only 13% reacted with indifference (Raffaelli, 1990). Because preadolescent siblings have known each other for a long time and the actions of one are in many ways predictable for the other, one might expect habituation to have occurred. Nevertheless, their conflicts tend to arouse angry feelings. When living together, one sibling's actions often have immediate consequences for the other, and siblings who do not defend their rights will soon find themselves at a disadvantage. Siblings' angry reactions thus further children's awareness of their respective wishes, characteristics and attitudes. This is true for the child who has become angry as well as for the target of his or her wrath. Shantz & Hobart (1989) link this process to the development of individuation.

Unfortunately, there are no studies of preadolescent siblings' anger-arousing attributions. About friends, there is only a study by Whitesell & Harter (1994), who investigated differences in the attribution of blame, the violation of expectancy, initial and subsequent feelings, as well as strategies for coping when an insult was received from a specific friend as opposed to a neutral classmate. Findings confirmed the prediction that children interpreted the insults received from a friend with more benevolence, highlighting their own contribution to it, or calling it a "misunderstanding", than they did insults received from a neutral classmate. When the friend had called them names, preadolescents (especially girls) reported not more intensive feelings of anger, but stronger feelings of sadness, distress and hurt. The youngsters indicated that they would avoid the insulting classmate in the future, but opted for "talking it over" and "working things out" with the friend. These findings support the conclusion that attributions, ensuing emotions and coping strategies are embedded in specific relationships. The same behavioral act of name-calling acquires a somewhat different meaning according to whether it takes place in the context of an established mutual friendship or in a more "normal" peer relationship.

Sibling conflicts tend to be brief: 42% of sibling arguments are settled within 5 minutes and a further 46% are resolved within an hour. This may be explained in part by the fact that parents intervened to stop the disagreement in 27% of the conflicts between siblings (compared to 9% of the conflicts between friends). In a further 34% of sibling arguments, the siblings disengaged and in an additional 30% one sibling gave in to the other. A compromise was reached in only 9% of the disagreements between the siblings (compared to 13% of those between friends). About half (54%) of the conflicts between friends ended with both parties going their own way, especially among the girls. Although 49% of the siblings and 34% of the friends did not report any reparative actions after the quarrel, there was a substantive minority of friends and siblings (about 25%) who indicated that one of them says "I am sorry" (Raffaelli, 1990). These self-reported differences between siblings and friends should be supplemented by observational data, especially on the emotional concomitants of these conflicts.

Self-report data by Buhrmester & Furman (1990) suggest that conflicts with older siblings become less frequent during the years of preadolescence and adolescence, when interaction rates between siblings generally decrease (Larson & Richards, 1991). Behind these cross-sectional group means, however, individual differences tend to disappear. Whereas some sibling pairs develop a more distant relationship, others may enjoy the increasingly egalitarian and supportive aspects of the relationship (Buhrmester & Furman, 1990). That the sibling relationship is still full of sensitive areas is evident from Goodnow & Warton (1992), who describe the many ways siblings can think of to hurt their siblings' feelings.

CONCLUSION

In this chapter I have reviewed research on three types of emotional processes in children's friendships and sibling relationships; namely their sharing of enjoyment, amusement and humor, their sharing of negative emotions elicited by third

parties, and the negotiation of anger-provoking conflicts within these relationships. Communication of positive and negative emotions (directed at events
outside the dyad) implies shared evaluations of persons or circumstances. Emotional sharing may be a key process in children's social and emotional development as well as in the establishment and maintenance of their relationships. The
emotional processes occurring in children's conflicts start out not from the con-
cordance but from the divergence of the viewpoints of the participants. They
have to do with the negotiation and ultimately with the outcome of the disagreement, also on an emotional plane. As many theorists have pointed out, the ability
to engage in and to resolve interpersonal conflicts stimulates individual children's
development and marks the quality of their relationships. The three emotional
processes outlined in this chapter can be subsumed under the heading of "emotion talk"; that is, the communication of internal states which are highly relevant
to the person who feels them but may not be obvious to the other person. As the
well known German feminist (and socialist) Rosa Luxemburg put it (admittedly
in another context): "Sometimes there is nothing so revolutionary as talking
about what is".

Chapter 3

The Self and Relationship Development

Karen Caplovitz Barrett
Colorado State University, Fort Collins, CO, USA

PROLOGUE

The topic of this chapter is the self and relationship development. In order to cover this topic thoroughly, one would need an entire, very large book. I have elected to discuss general issues regarding the self and social relationships that should apply to most age groups, but then to focus the review of empirical literature primarily on toddlerhood, the first period of development during which the development of self is widely believed to be a prominent influence on other domains of development. The other major time period during which self development is seen as a major influence is adolescence. Some of what is discussed in this chapter should pertain to that period as well; however, the "self" of toddlerhood is very different from the "self" of adolescence, so some ideas may not apply.

Attachment is an important topic that is extremely relevant to this chapter, in that it is believed to involve the development of working models of self and relationships. However, given that another chapter of this volume (Zerfman & Hazau) is devoted to attachment relationships, that topic will receive only cursory attention here.

Finally, this chapter will emphasize *affective* aspects of the self, given that whenever the self is involved in significant relationships with the animate and/or inanimate environment, emotion processes result (e.g., see Barrett, 1995; Barrett & Campos, 1987; Higgins, 1989). In particular, the relevance of the "social" or "self-conscious" emotions for the development of self and relationships will be emphasized, including the issue of how Erikson's "developmental crises" might relate to cultural differences in individualism vs. interdependence.

Handbook of Personal Relationships, 2nd edn. Edited by Steve Duck.
© 1997 John Wiley & Sons Ltd.

Many chapters on "self" would begin by defining "the self". Like many other current writers, however, I do not believe that "the self" is a single entity (e.g., see Fogel, 1995; Hermans, Kempen & van Loon, 1992; Kagan, 1991; Lewis, 1991b; Neisser, 1991) that is amenable to a unitary definition.

Some define the "selves" as differing primarily in level—with "level" defined primarily in terms of changes in self-understanding that are permitted by changes in cognitive abilities with development (e.g., Case, 1991; Lewis, 1991b). Few would question the assumption that changes in cognitive abilities allow for more complexity in conceptions of self. However, in this chapter, I will focus on interesting new developments that suggest the need for a concept of "self in relationships"—that suggest that the traditional dichotomization into self vs. other may be misleading.

The chapter will begin by noting that self in opposition to other is a Western phenomenon, and is overstated even in Western societies. Then, I will provide some evidence that self and relationships with others develop in tandem, as a function of one another, and that a crucial aspect of the self is the self-in-relationship. Third, I will suggest that "self-conscious" or "social" emotions, such as shame and pride, play an important role in the development of self-in-relationship. Finally, I will briefly outline an approach that incorporates these ideas.

INDEPENDENCE VS. INTERDEPENDENCE

The growth of cross-cultural research, the increased "cross-talk" among the disciplines of psychology, anthropology and sociology, and the growth of a new discipline of "cultural psychology" have all contributed to increased awareness by Americans that many assumptions about self and other that we take for granted are not shared by many other cultures. Examination of views of self and other in cultures characterized by differences in "collectivism" vs. "individualism" has suggested that the isolated, autonomous, independent self is not universally constructed (Sampson, 1988). On the contrary; in some cultures (and to some degree in our own, especially for females), the "true self" is an interdependent self. In fact, "standing out" as different from others is considered damaging to the self in such cultures (see also Markus & Kitayama, 1994).

The distinction at issue has been variously labeled "self-contained individualism vs. ensembled individualism" (Sampson, 1988), "individualism vs. collectivism" (e.g., J. Miller, 1995), "independence vs. interdependence" (Markus & Kitayama, 1994), and "agency vs. communion" (Bakan, 1966). Most researchers agree that although one can classify cultures as more interdependent or more independent, most countries show a mix of the two tendencies (but see Sampson, 1988).

The basic idea behind these distinctions is that "self" is defined differently in different cultures. In some cultures, such as the USA and Canada and much of Europe, the person is defined as a bounded individual entity who chooses and controls his/her interactions and relationships with others, and who has (and conceptualizes) a set of definable attributes that distinguish him/her from others. The self is this distinctive set of characteristics and/or the person's concept of them. The goal of the person is to distinguish him/herself from others as a unique individual, to achieve as much as he/she can as an individual, and to be autonomous relative to others.

Although interpersonal relationships are valued, they are seen as "healthy" only to the extent that each individual's needs are met, each person is free to pursue personal interests, each person freely commits to the relationship, and each person is valued for his/her "true inner self", rather than for the self that the other would like him/her to be. One should help others, but one is justified in expecting reciprocity (R. Miller, 1995); it is "against human nature" to be happy in a "one-sided" relationship in which one partner gives more than the other. Moreover, it is important, in relating to others, to "maintain appropriate boundaries". One feels pride (which is a positive experience) when one excels, especially in comparison to esteemed others, and anger when others do not allow one to pursue one's own goals.

In contrast, in other cultures such as Japan, China, India and much of of Africa and Latin America, the person is defined more in terms of duties, roles, and responsibilities toward others. The self *is* these roles and relationships; there is no separate bounded self. A person feels joy when fulfilling responsibilities or duties and negative emotion when "standing out" as different (Markus & Kitayama, 1994). "Amae", an emotion one experiences in Japan when one is in a dependent relationship with another (such as a parent) and one wants that person's indulgence, is considered reasonable and expectable, even in older children and adults. An Indian emotion, "lajya", whose closest translation into English is "shame", is viewed as positive, and is purposefully displayed as a show of civility and commitment to maintaining harmony. In short, it feels good to be in harmony with one's group and to fulfill one's duties and obligations to those group members. The bounded, insular, "self-actualizing" person is an enigma or at least an immoral person; the happy, well-adjusted person is interdependent with a group and makes group members happy through his/her behavior (see Markus & Kitayama, 1994; Sampson, 1988).

Sampson (1988) points out that within our own culture, subcultures may show an interdependent view of self. Mexican-Americans, African-Americans, Chinese-, Japanese- or Korean-Americans all may be socialized in more interdependent-oriented homes. Moreover, females typically are socialized to be more interdependent than are males. In fact, the notion of agency vs. communion (Bakan, 1966) is virtually the same as that of "masculinity" (agency) vs. "femininity" (communion) as discussed by others (see Spence & Helmreich, 1978).

Thus, the emphasis of the majority culture on individual growth and achievement, and the majority culture's view of mental health may conflict with the values of many subcultures. "Codependency", which is considered unhealthy in the American majority culture, may be viewed by other cultures and subcultures as a reasonable pattern of relating to others, as may well-defined roles and status differences. Many assumptions about mental health, self-esteem, and relation-ships can be seen to be culture-bound. If a child is socialized to be interde-pendent, what happens to Erikson's (1963) "normative" developmental crisis of autonomy vs. shame and doubt? Similarly, the developmental task of distinguish-ing self vs. other seems predicated on an *individualistic* self; to an interdependent self, the self is defined in relationship to others. It is highly likely that although some cultures emphasize the individualistic self and some the interdependent self, both aspects of self develop in both cultures. However, given that most of our literature is written by Western authors, it may be that an undue emphasis has been placed on the individualistic self and therefore on the development of self as the development of the ability to distinguish self from others. I will now discuss evidence that more attention to the self-in-relationships is needed, even in research regarding Western cultures.

SELF VS. OTHER

Most treatments of the development of the self during infancy and toddlerhood propose that this development involves distinguishing self from other. This is a proposal upon which quite disparate theoretical approaches are in agreement (although specifics vary), including Mahler's theory (Mahler, 1958; 1968), Piaget's theory (e.g., Piaget, 1952), and Martin Hoffman's theory (Hoffman, 1976), among many others. The basic idea is that newborn infants act upon a world without distinguishing their actions and/or needs and desires from that world.

For most psychoanalytic theories, the social world is emphasized; the baby and caregiver are at first fused, only later to be distinguished. For Piaget, the inani-mate world is emphasized, with the baby unaware that the object world is sepa-rate from its own actions; however, the social world should be unknown as well. Another basic assumption of all of these approaches is that in order to "develop a self" one must distinguish it from other people and things.

In recent years, however, several separate lines of work have independently suggested that this view that development of self vs. other should be reevaluated. First, a burgeoning literature on the capabilities of young babies has suggested that even the earliest self is a *relational* self; young babies are receptive *and responsive* to social stimulation, and are capable of modifying their own behavior so as to change social stimuluation (e.g., DeCasper & Fifer, 1980).

Second, research on self-development during infancy and toddlerhood has suggested that the tendency to engage in other-oriented responses such as empathy, altruism and coordinated action are related to the development of self-recognition/self-consciousness (e.g., Asendorpf & Baudonniere, 1993; Johnson, 1982). Although some would interpret this as support for the idea that what is developing is a sense of self vs. other (e.g., Johnson, 1982; Lewis, 1991b), these other-oriented responses, especially empathy, would seem to involve a feeling of connectedness with and similarity to others. Perhaps these other-oriented responses involve differentiation of other from self, followed by higher level integration, but if so, the higher level integration seems to develop remarkably quickly. Alternatively, perhaps a self that is developing during infancy and toddlerhood is, at its very core, an interpersonal self (see also Neisser, 1991).

And, third, research on self-regulation has suggested that others' regulation of the baby's state is by no means antithetical to the development of self-regulation (Kopp, 1982), compliance with parental demands is not necessarily antithetical to "internalized" self-regulation (Kochanska & Aksan, 1995), and self-assertion in toddlers is associated with child-rearing approaches that should promote close relationships (Crockenberg & Litman, 1990).

I will first briefly discuss the literature regarding each of these three topics in turn. Then, I will discuss how "social" emotions contribute to the development of the self-in-relationships, followed by a brief discussion of what I believe "self" and "relationship" entail during the first 3 or so years of life.

Young Babies' Responsiveness to Social Stimuli

Over the past two decades, a wealth of information on the young baby has been obtained. Research has laid to rest the depiction of the young infant as a disorganized and inept being who is insulated from the world by an "absolute stimulus barrier" (e.g., Mahler, 1958; Sroufe, 1979). Current evidence suggests that the newborn is an active organism who is "built" to interact with others. Days or even hours after birth, the baby will suck with a particular rhythm in order to hear its mother's voice (DeCasper & Fifer, 1980), can discriminate its mother's personal odors from those of other lactating women (MacFarlane, 1975), and will cry when other neonates cry (Sagi & Hoffman, 1976). Infants' visual responses to other people are limited by the poor acuity of the neonate. However, by about 7 weeks of age, when acuity has made some improvement, infants look at the facial features of people, and make eye contact with a person who is talking to them (Haith, Bergman & Moore, 1977).

By 3 months of age, babies interact smoothly when face-to-face with a parent, but show gaze aversion, increased heart rate, and decreased smiling when that same parent becomes unresponsive (e.g., Cohn & Elmore, 1988; Field et al., 1986; Fogel et al., 1982; Mayes & Carter, 1990; Murray & Trevarthen, 1985; Stack & Muir, 1990). But infants are not only perceptive about their parents; by 4 months, infants look more at a male when hearing a male voice and at a female when hearing a female voice *even when those persons are unfamiliar.*

Moreover, babies soon become responsive to the meaning of others' emotions. By about 7 months, babies match emotion information across perceptual modalities (Walker, 1982) and by 10 months, use another's emotion communication to guide their reactions toward ambiguous events (e.g., Sorce et al., 1985). From 8 to 10 months of age, infants increasingly "share" their smiles with their mothers, smiling and then turning to their mothers, and doing so much more frequently if their mothers are responsive. Moreover, there is evidence that such affect sharing is purposeful (Jones & Hong, 1995). In short, throughout infancy, babies are responsive to other people. Moreover, infants seem quickly to develop expectations that others will be responsive to them, that others can provide information to them about the affective significance of events around them, and that their own emotions are of interest to others. Many of these findings call into question theoretical notions of a "normal autistic phase" during early infancy, during which time the baby lacks awareness of others (Mahler, 1958), and these findings and others suggest that the baby begins with a propensity for interacting with others and never loses that inclination.

Neither is the self *merged* with others; the young baby can tell when the parent is unresponsive and can tell males from females; the older baby can relate others' reactions to its own responses to novel events, and seems to understand when the caregiver is receptive to its affect sharing. The baby develops in a social world, and its sense of self, other and relationships grow together.

Self Development and Other-oriented Attributes during Toddlerhood

Not only does the infant relate to others and regulate its own behavior in response to the behavior of others; the ability to respond appropriately to others and the self develop together. A small but consistent pattern is emerging from studies relating toddlers' level of self development and their ability to relate to others. Twelve- to 36-month-olds who have been classified as having secure attachment relationships with their parents are more advanced in their level of agency (acting on self, mother and dolls), than are those classified as insecurely attached (Pipp, Easterbrooks & Harmon, 1992). Moreover, securely attached 18–36-month-olds show more advanced featural self-recognition than do those classified as insecurely attached (Pipp, Easterbrooks & Harmon, 1992). Thus, toddlers who are more advanced in their senses of self and agency seem to have better relationships with their parents.

Similarly, toddlers who have more advanced knowledge of their appearance and/or agency seem to relate better to peers. Toddlers who recognize themselves in a mirror and/or in pictures are more likely to help others who appear to be hurt (Johnson, 1982), to show empathy for others (Bischof-Kohler, 1988, cited in Asendorpf & Baudonniere, 1993; Bischof-Kohler, 1991; Zahn-Waxler et al., 1992) and to show coordinated imitation of peers (Asendorpf & Baudonniere, 1993). Finally, toddlers who show a higher level of agent use in pretend play are better able to engage in cooperative problem-solving with peers (Brownell & Carriger, 1990). In several of these studies, the effects of age were controlled, and age did not account for the relation of self development measures to other-oriented measures (although, in the Zahn-Waxler et al. study, effects were found at 24 months but not at 18 months).

All of these findings suggest that, at least during toddlerhood, self development and other-orientation go hand-in-hand. Does this mean that, given our individualistic society, the way to relate well to others is to see self and other as distinctly different and separate entities (and to relate to others as such)? Or, is it possible that rather than or in addition to developing individualistic selves, toddlers, even in American culture, establish interdependent or interpersonal selves? These findings suggest an important direction for future research—delving into whether an interdependent self is an important aspect of self during early development in American cultures, and, if so, just what the development of an interdependent self is like in our country. Research also is needed regarding how our culture's socialization patterns affect the development of an interdependent self as well as children's social relationships.

Other-regulation, Self-regulation, Internalization, and Socialization

It has long been assumed that children must learn to regulate their behavior according to societal standards, and that until such "self-regulation" is possible, parents and other socializing agents must regulate children's behavior. According to traditional Western theories, children "internalize" the standards that socializing agents convey. According to Freudian theory, the child introjects the parent and parental "shoulds and shouldn'ts" to form a superego, in connection with the resolution of the Oedipus conflict, when the child is 5 or 6 years of age. Until the Oedipus complex is resolved and the superego established, the child is dependent on others in order to determine how to behave; only after the superego is established can the child be truly moral, because only then does the child regulate his/her own behavior (Freud, 1923/1961).

Traditional Social Learning Theory, although of course not proposing a superego, suggested also that the child must internalize the parents' rules and behavior in order to demonstrate self-regulation (e.g., see Aronfreed, 1968). Both Freudian and traditional Social Learning Theory approaches seem to suggest that (1) the child is more moral once the regulation comes from within, and (2) that once rules are internalized, the child does not rely on others to determine how to act. Freudian theory very explicitly indicates an age at which the standards are introjected, as though after that age, others are rather irrelevant; children govern their own behavior.

Even some current views seem to adhere to the belief that self-regulated behavior is a desired end-state that children achieve with development (although, as we shall see, they operationalize "self-regulation" in ways that do not preclude others' involvement). For example, in a recent review article on "conscience" development, Kochanska (1993) states:

> The gradual developmental shift from external to internal regulation that results in
> a child's ability to conform to societal standards of conduct and to restrain antisocial

or destructive impulses, even in the absence of surveillance, is the essence and hallmark of successful socialization (Kochanska, 1993; pp. 325–326).

This approach implies that a well-socialized child need not heed the directives, or specific, current needs and desires of other people in determining how to behave, unless those directives, needs or desires directly bear on a known rule. It suggests that Gilligan's (1977) "morality of care" is irrelevant to socially appropriate behavior. It also implies that once one has internalized societal standards, one no longer looks to others for guidance; and it implies that the child who is "high in self-monitoring" or who cares deeply about others' reactions and opinions is less self-regulated than one who is such a principled person that she/he must act in accordance with those principles even if many people will suffer because of the principled action.

In majority-culture American society, many of these beliefs may seem reasonable; the self independently acting in a principled way may seem the epitome of the self-regulated, moral person. However, this may not be at all true for many subcultures in the USA and many other cultures. Moreover, as any parent or developmentalist knows, even "good" children do not stop requiring others' directives once they have internalized societal rules. In fact, adults need others' guidance as well.

Current researchers interested in self-regulation or "conscience" are now attempting to distinguish the type of compliance that seems to involve self-regulation (or internalization) from the type of compliance that seems guided only by others' behavior (e.g., see Kochanska & Aksan, 1995; Kopp & Wyer, 1991). It seems clear to such researchers that there is a great deal of difference between complying because situational demands require compliance, and doing so because one *wants* to behave appropriately ("committed compliance": Kochanska & Aksan, 1995). Moreover, a growing body of research connects such desire to behave appropriately with a positive interaction pattern between parents and children.

Baumrind's (1971) seminal study on childrearing styles that predict later "instrumental competence" was one of the first to highlight the importance of a positive emotional climate in the family for the fostering of socially desirable behavior. The primary characteristics that distinguished her "authoritarian" parents from her "authoritative" parents was the mutually loving and respectful interaction pattern between parent and child. Also, as is well-known, authoritative parenting was associated with the most socially desirable child behavior.

Since that study, a consistent pattern has been found for the parenting style associated with long-term compliance, "early internalization", self-regulation or "impulse control". In short, research suggests that a warm, reciprocal relationship, in which children and parents seem to "meet minds" and interact harmoniously, is associated with self-regulated/compliant behavior. One of the first studies that directly addressed the importance of relationship quality to children's likelihood of complying with socializing agents was Londerville & Main's (1981), which indicated that securely attached children were more willing to comply (and less defiant).

More specific information about the *interaction* patterns associated with children's willingness to comply was provided by subsequent studies. Maccoby (see Maccoby & Martin, 1983; Parpal & Maccoby, 1985), for example, found that children were more willing to comply with their mothers' requests after those mothers were (by instruction) responsive to their children's interests, and Rocissano, Slade & Lynch (1987) found that toddlers who engaged in "synchronous" interactions with their mothers were more compliant to those mothers. Moreover, mothers who were less directive during compliance tasks, and who reported themselves as encouraging independence in their children, had 2-year olds who were more compliant in still another study (Silverman & Ragusa, 1990). Children whose parents are more responsive to them are not only more compliant, however; they also show more self-assertion (Crockenberg & Litman, 1990; Kuczynski et al., 1987; Matas, Arend & Sroufe, 1978) but not more defiance (Crockenberg & Litman, 1990).

Moreover, there is evidence (in addition to the work on attachment) that the reason that children willingly comply with responsive parents is that they have a more positive relationship with those parents. Kochanska & Aksan (1995) found that concurrent, zero-order correlations revealed positive relations between "committed compliance" and gentle control and guidance, social exchange (as a maternal control strategy), and mother–child mutually positive affect; as well as between a measure of internalization and both social exchange and mutually positive affect. Zero-order correlations also revealed *negative* relations between negative control and both committed compliance and internalization. However, examination of the relation between affect and maternal control strategies at home and the child's committed compliance 1–3 weeks later in the laboratory revealed that only mutually positive affect positively predicted later committed compliance. Maternal negative control, on the other hand, was negatively associated with later committed compliance. Moreover, mutually positive affect during one laboratory situation also was positively correlated with the child's committed compliance in the other laboratory situation; whereas, none of the maternal control variables was significantly correlated with committed compliance in the other situation.

Finally, hierarchical regression revealed that a score derived from principal components analysis, involving shared positive affect and child cooperation, significantly predicted children's internalization, even after variance associated with child age and sex was accounted for. These findings suggest that the positive relationship between parent and child may be the most important factor in ensuring that the child will willingly commit to parental rules, and a negative relationship in ensuring that she/he will not. Thus, positive relationships with others are crucial in fostering *self*-regulation. Again, relationship development and self-development are positively related.

THE "SOCIAL/SELF-CONSCIOUS" EMOTIONS DURING TODDLERHOOD AND THE DEVELOPMENT OF SELF-IN-RELATIONSHIPS

Self-regulation does not just involve "cold" awareness of how to behave and ability to control behavior. It also involves *caring* about behaving appropriately. In recent years, this emotional side of self-regulation has once again become the target of investigation. Although the connection between guilt and internalization was discussed by Freud (1923/1961) and others many decades ago, until remarkably recently, shame received virtually no attention, and empirical research on the early development of guilt, shame and related emotions was almost non-existent.

Now, a growing empirical literature suggests that shame, pride, embarrassment and guilt have their origins in toddlerhood (see Barrett, Zahn-Waxler & Cole, 1993; Lewis, Alessandri & Sullivan, 1992; Lewis et al., 1989; Stipek, Recchia, & McClintic, 1992), and are particularly relevant to a discussion of self, other and relationships for at least three, interrelated reasons: (1) they are frequently referred to as "social emotions", and yet also frequently are referred to as "self-conscious" emotions, (2) they both affect and are affected by the development of self, and (3) they affect and are affected by relationships with others. Also of interest in the present context is that the cultures that Benedict (1946) considered "shame" cultures are interdependent or collectivistic cultures, and those that she considered "guilt" cultures are characterized predominantly by independence, suggesting that the relative emphasis of a culture on the "self side" of self-in-relationship may promote more of one type of social emotion (guilt) and emphasis on the "relationship side" of self-in-relationship may promote more of another social emotion (shame). Regardless of which social emotion is emphasized, however, what emerges is a view of the baby as developing more and more complex views of self *in relationships* with the animate and inanimate environment because of the development of these emotions, and developing more complex versions of these emotions because of the development of the self-in-relationship.

Social and/or Self-conscious Emotions?

Pride, embarrassment, shame and guilt often are referred to as "social" or "interpersonal" emotions (see Barrett, 1995; Baumeister, Stillwell & Heatherton, 1995; Jones, Kugler & Adams, 1995), and also often are referred to as "self-conscious" emotions (e.g., see Lewis et al., 1989; Tangney & Fischer, 1995). Although if self is opposed to other, it would seem perplexing that both descriptors could apply; careful examination of these emotions suggests that both descriptors are apt.

It is beyond the scope of this chapter to review all of the major theoretical approaches to these emotions. However, most theories and self-report data suggest that in all of these emotions, the self is implicated. In embarrassment, the person/self (or presentation of self) seems to be on display (see Buss, 1980; Edelmann, 1987; M. Lewis, 1995; Miller, 1994); in shame, more central self-attributes or the entire self seem exposed, scrutinized or negatively evaluated (see Barrett & Campos, 1987; Buss, 1980; Edelmann, 1987; H. Lewis, 1971; M. Lewis, 1991). In guilt, the person feels responsible for something she/he did that was inconsistent with his/her own standards (Barrett & Campos, 1987; H. Lewis, 1971; Tangney, 1995). In pride, the person feels that she/he has accomplished something significant or met social standards (e.g., M. Lewis et al., 1989; Stipek, Recchia & McClintic, 1992).

Moreover, there is evidence that the development of self-recognition in a mirror is related to the development of embarrassment (M. Lewis et al., 1989; Pipp et al., in press; but see also Schneider-Rosen & Cicchetti, 1991, for contrary findings with lower SES children). Many theorists postulate that self-recognition is a prerequisite to "true" shame and/or pride and/or guilt as well (e.g., Buss, 1980; M. Lewis, 1991a; Mascolo & Fischer, 1995; Stipek, 1995), although an empirical basis for this claim is lacking. Given that virtually all characterizations of these emotions include self-evaluation as a component, and most developmental theories assume that ability to evaluate the self or at least see the self as an object is therefore required for these emotions, it seems reasonable to consider these emotions to involve self-consciousness.

Yet these emotions are also intrinsically social. First, these emotions are almost invariably connected with (real or imagined) interaction with a person. Guilt is aroused when someone perceives him/herself to have harmed a person— usually another, but potentially the self taken as an object (see Barrett, 1995; Baumeister, Stilisell & Heatherton, 1995). Moreover, there is some evidence that more guilt is experienced when a loved and/or esteemed other is harmed than when a stranger is harmed, and that one is more likely to try purposefully to make *loved ones, rather than strangers* feel guilty (Baumeister, Stilisell & Heatherton, 1995).

Shame typically involves the perception that *someone* finds one wanting or deficient (Barrett & Campos, 1987; H. Lewis, 1971; Stipek, Reccia & McClintic, 1992); an observing other is perceived, even if only in one's mind. The traditional approach to shame claims that, unlike guilt, which involves internalized moral standards, shame is experienced *when one is caught* by someone while committing (or with evidence that one has committed) a wrongdoing (e.g., Benedict, 1946; Erikson, 1963). In fact, this public/private distinction still is evident in some current theories (e.g., see Buss, 1980; Hogan & Cheek, 1983). Most current theorists, however, would argue that shame may be experienced even when no-one else is present physically (e.g., Barrett & Campos, 1987; Creighton, 1990; H. Lewis, 1971, 1987; Stipek, 1983; Wurmser, 1987). Still, the *sense* of being observed seems to be present during the experience of shame (see H. Lewis, 1971; Ferguson, Stegge & Damhuis, 1991). Embarrassment, too, seems to involve exposure in the face of real or perceived others and/or evaluation by real or perceived others (see Buss, 1980; Edelmann, 1987; M. Lewis, 1995; Miller, 1994).

Another way in which these emotions are social is that socialization centrally influences the development of these emotions. In fact, it seems accurate to characterize social emotions as social *constructions*. If humans did not live in social groups, there would be no need for the social emotions. The central concern of the person experiencing social emotions is meeting or failing to meet societal standards; these emotions serve to highlight and enforce such standards (e.g., see Ausubel, 1955; Barrett & Campos, 1987; Baumeister et al., 1995; Lindsay-Hartz, De Rivera & Mascolo, 1995). Moreover, social emotions also highlight the importance of and/or repair social relationships (Barrett & Campos; 1987; Baumeister, Stilisell & Heatherton, 1995; Lindsay-Hartz, De Rivera & Mascolo, 1995).

The behavior-regulatory functions of shame and guilt are social as well. Shame serves to distance the experiencing individual from important others, especially others who can evaluate or are evaluating one. In particular, in shame, activated behaviors are aimed at removing the *face* from exposure to others' evaluation. The shameful person avoids looking at others, hides his face, slumps his body, lowers his head and/or removes himself from contact with others (e.g., see Barrett, 1995; H. Lewis, 1971; M. Lewis, 1991a; Tangney, 1995). These same be-haviors serve social regulatory/social communication functions. The gaze aversion, slumping, hiding, and social withdrawal behaviors communicate deference and submission to others, and indicate that one feels "small", "low" or unworthy, in comparison to those others.

Guilt serves different functions that also are quite social. Guilt-relevant behaviors are aimed at repairing the damage caused by the person's wrongdoing and/or at confessing, both of which also help repair the person's relationship with the person who was harmed (e.g., see Barrett, 1995; Baumeister et al., 1995; Ferguson, Stegge & Damhuis, 1991). Finally, like shame, guilt highlights the importance of social standards.

Shame, Guilt, and the Development of Self

One type of adaptive function of social emotions that has been virtually unstudied is the role of these emotions in the development of the self. As has been mentioned, many theorists believe that shame and guilt become possible only *after* the child has objective awareness of self. It is my position that shame and guilt are also highly important influences on the *development* of such aware-ness (see also Barrett, 1995).

The shame experience *highlights* the self as others see one (or as one must appear to others). It causes one to step back from the self as agent and to evaluate that self and, thus, helps one elaborate and/or modify one's view of self. More-over, as an affective experience, it draws the person's attention to the *significance* of the experience.

It seems likely that most of a child's earliest experiences of shame occur in the presence of a caregiver with whom the child has a history of interactions. I find Bowlby's (1980) notion of a "working model" of self and other quite useful in conceptualizing the sense of self during infancy and toddlerhood and how shame might impact its development. According to Bowlby (1980), a child's interactions with a caregiver help shape "working models" of self and other. To the extent that the parent is responsive to the baby, the baby develops a view of that parent as responsive *and* a reciprocal view of self as worthy of being responded to. To the extent that caregivers show that they love the baby, the baby develops a notion of the caregivers as loving and the self as lovable. Such working models need not be cognitively elaborate and may at first involve "procedural" knowledge, such as expectancies that the child's actions will bring desired outcomes via the parent and that the parent will provide what is needed. Later, as the child's cognitive sophistication and interaction history become richer, the working models should become more elaborate and sophisticated, including both procedural and declarative knowledge (see Schachter & Tulving, 1994).

To the extent that the child views him/herself as competent in obtaining satisfaction from the caregiver and, in the shame-inducing situation, finds herself incompetent to obtain satisfaction (the caregiver actually may attempt to *prevent* the child from obtaining a desired end such as a china figurine), modification of the model is needed. Moreover, the painful nature of the shame experience motivates such modification by bringing the discrepancy into vivid awareness.

The child's initial revision may be to indicate that the caregiver is not so wonderful after all, or the child is not so wonderful after all, or both. To the extent that shame is infrequent, however, and the caregiver–child relationship is good in general, the shame may serve to highlight the contexts in which child or mom is "not wonderful", underscoring the standards being conveyed and/or the child's specific deficits. Moreover, the pain of shame should help discourage future violations of those standards, which should help the child form a working model of herself as a "good child". On the other hand, to the extent that shame experiences are very frequent, the child may come to view him/herself as incompetent and/or bad, and to become a shame-prone (and potentially, a depression-prone) individual. As further development of a sense of self occurs, the shame experience may induce the child to compare the other's beliefs about her to her own beliefs. This may further elaborate the child's beliefs and feelings about herself.

Guilt is most likely to influence the development of self as agent. To the extent that *guilt* rather than shame is more frequently experienced in the context of standard violations, the focus should be on the harmful *act* (and the child's responsibility for that act), rather than on a globally bad self (see H. Lewis, 1971; M. Lewis, 1991a). Thus, the child's power to harm others should be highlighted and, to the extent that reparation occurs and leads to positive outcomes, the power of the child to help others should be highlighted as well. Therefore, whereas frequent shame experiences should cause the child to view himself as bad, frequent guilt experiences should help the child see that he has the power to control his behavior—and that he can derive pleasure from helping others and discomfort from hurting others. In fact, there is some evidence that more frequent experience, according to maternal report, with engaging in destructive behavior (breaking toys) or behavior that is discrepant from parents' "ought expectancies" is associated with display of more guilt-relevant behavior (Barrett, Zahn-Waxler & Cole, 1993; Ferguson & Stegge, 1995). This would also explain why many studies have revealed *positive* correlations between aggression and prosocial behavior (see D. Barrett & Yarrow, 1977; Friedrich & Stein, 1973; Murphy, 1937; Muste & Sharpe, 1947; Yarrow & Waxler, 1976; but for opposite findings see D. Barrett, 1979; Harris & Siebel, 1975; Rutherford & Mussen, 1968).

Relationships and the Development of Self-consciousness and Self-regulation

It was mentioned earlier that shame, guilt and pride can be viewed as social emotions because they are centrally concerned with social standards, they help to enforce such standards, they impact social behavior, and they help to repair relationships that have been damaged by infractions of standards. By helping children to behave according to social standards, moreover, they help children interact "appropriately" with others, increasing the likelihood that positive relationships will be built with others. Not only do these emotions help children in forming and maintaining relationships, however; the formation of relationships may affect the development of these emotions.

If the person is a self-contained individual, who is primarily concerned with actualizing his/her own goals and self, then why should that person adhere to societal standards? In many cases, such standards are *contrary* to purely selfish interests. The child wants the toy that the other child has, for example; why shouldn't she/he just take it? An important question is just how social goals become significant goals for the individual. Significance is the crucial feature distinguishing emotion-inducing "appreciations" or "appraisals" from ordinary cognitive processes. A person can be aware that the light is red and she is not supposed to walk across the street, for example, but unless abiding by that law is a significant goal for her, she should not experience guilt (nor shame) when she crosses anyway.

Cultures differ greatly with respect to whether or not *many* particular behaviors are pre- or proscribed, as well as which standards are held to be crucially important (Shweder, Mahapatra & Miller, 1987), which suggests that most standards are largely arbitrary and socialized by the culture. How do such standards gain significance for the individual—how does the individual come to see them as important to him/herself and his/her well-being? I have suggested that both the establishment of standards as goals and the endowment of such goals with significance begin in conjunction with the baby's interactions with parents and other loved ones (Barrett, 1995).

The infant's close, extended contact with the parent enables that parent to be the first, and arguably the most important, socializing agent for the infant, and all of the many types of interactions of a parent with a baby are relevant to the development of guilt and shame. The most basic way in which parent–infant interactions help establish societal standards as goals and endow those goals with significance is through the effect of such interactions on the nature of the important parent–infant relationship. The nature of the relationship that forms should affect the child's desire to accept and heed the parents' standards—the child's belief that if the parent deems them significant, they probably are significant. In addition, the parent–child relationship should affect the child's tendency to care about hurting others, both because he has learned to care about someone (the parent) and because a nurturant parent, with whom the baby would be most likely to form a positive relationship, would model caring behavior. Consistent with these ideas are the data, reviewed earlier, suggesting that toddlers who have positive interactions and relationships with their parents are more likely to show long-term compliance with their parents' requests and internalization. Also consistent with this idea are data indicating that children of more nurturant parents show greater empathy (e.g., Barnett, 1987).

In most discussions of socialization influences on the development of guilt, reparation, or self-regulation, emphasis is not placed on the overall relationship between parent and child, but rather on discipline strategies (e.g., Hoffman, 1984; Power & Chapieski, 1986; Schneider & Larzelere, 1988; Zahn-Waxler, Radke-Yarrow & King, 1979). The assumption in much of this literature seems to be that discipline is important because it teaches a child to obey standards, even in the face of other desires, by teaching socially valued behavior and/or punishing socially undesirable behavior (e.g., see Hoffman, 1984).

Interestingly, however, those discipline strategies that are associated with long-term manifestation of appropriate behavior tend to be those which *highlight the significance* of appropriate behavior, and do so in a way *that does not impair the parent–child relationship*. Research with infants and toddlers has suggested that usage, at high levels, of techniques that threaten the parent–child relationship are ineffective in promoting self-regulation on a long-term basis. High usage of physical punishment is associated with lower "impulse control" and shorter latency to recurrence of misbehavior (Power & Chapieski, 1986; Schneider & Larzelere, 1988), and high usage of unexplained prohibitions is associated with lower levels of reparation for misdeeds (Zahn-Waxler, Radke-Yarrow & King, 1979). Moreover, although high usage of love withdrawal is associated with greater immediate reparation, it is not associated with later reparation (Zahn-Waxler, Radke-Yarrow & King, 1979) and is associated with *shorter* latency to recurrence of misbehavior (Schneider & Larzelere, 1988).

On the other hand, when some of the same techniques are used at lower levels, and in a manner that is less threatening to the parent–child relationship, they may be more effective. Use of corporal punishment at low (but non-zero) levels is not associated with poorer impulse control, and actually is associated with *longer* delay in recurrence of misbehavior when combined with inductive explanations (Power & Chapieski, 1986; Schneider & Larzelere, 1988; see also Hoffman, 1970 regarding older children). It seems quite possible that when such punishment does not occur sufficiently frequently and/or intensely that it impairs the parent–child bond, and it is accompanied by clear indication of which behaviors were unacceptable, it serves to highlight the significance of those particular acts.

The technique that has been associated with the greatest tendency for toddlers to make reparation for wrongdoings, both concurrently and on a long-term basis, is high usage of emotion-laden explanations—particularly those that include statements about general standards for behavior (Zahn-Waxler, Radke-Yarrow & King, 1979). This set of techniques highlights the significance of the misbehavior and/or the standards, while also making clear just what the standard is. Moreover, it does so in a way that is not likely to threaten the parent–child relationship—that is not excessively harsh and authoritarian. A particular version of this technique, induction (noting the consequences of misbehavior for others), has been associated with internalization and "guilt" in older children (however, the latter was not clearly distinguished from shame: see Hoffman, 1970). This type of discipline has also been studied as part of a general style of parenting (authoritative/reciprocal) in which the child is listened to, valued and reasoned with, and yet standards that parents believe in are highlighted and adhered to. This style, in turn, has been associated with long-term manifestation of socially valued behaviors in older children (see Baumrind, 1967, 1971; Maccoby & Martin, 1983). Thus, evidence suggests that a positive, mutual relationship with parents or caregivers forms the foundation for the development of self-regulation and reparation (which, as mentioned earlier, is a guilt-relevant behavior). It seems likely that children care about the rules and standards because they care about the persons imposing those standards; the rules and standards thus become significant to the child, and emotions like guilt and shame are aroused when these rules are violated. Obviously, this proposal is quite speculative at present; much more research is needed on the connection between the parent–child relationship and the development of the social/self-conscious emotions.

THE SELF IN RELATIONSHIPS

All of the information presented thus far suggests that the early development of the self is intimately intertwined with the development of relationships. Although we can not, at present, rule out the possibility that the self vs. other dichotomy is appropriate in individualistic societies, there seems to be enough reason to question this idea to warrant careful investigation of an interpersonal self or self-in-relationships.

An interpersonal self (or interpersonal selves) would seem important to the functioning of all societies; without a sense of connectedness with others, there would seem to be no real motivation to follow societal rules whose main benefit is to others (unless others are constantly monitoring and punishing "inappropriate" behavior). It seems plausible that, even in our predominantly individualistic culture, interdependent, interpersonal selves develop. Mainstream American culture allows one to experience pride as a positive emotion, yet even it negatively sanctions boastfulness and tactlessness following one's accomplishments. Even in mainstream American culture, toddlers show apparent embarrassment when simply asked to dance in front of others; according to Lewis (1995) and Darwin (1872/1965), this suggests that simple exposure to the gaze of others seems sufficient to trigger embarrassment.

The person we are constantly changes as we relate to the world around us, and our relationships with others and with the world change as our sense of self does. We do learn about ourselves through our relationships with others, and, in fact, *are* different people when interacting with different others (see Fogel, in press; Hermans, Kempen & van Loon, 1992). Some would propose that we do not even have an identity that is separate from our relationships with others (Fogel, 1995).

Perhaps the extent to which people have views of themselves that can be separated from their relationships changes with development. Perhaps the need for autonomy shown by toddlers in our culture is a result of socialization to create a sense of agency and autonomy in the context of an interdependent self. The toddler may already feel connected with others, but may have a new ability to be sufficiently autonomous to truly help or challenge those others. Much more research is needed regarding the origins of the interpersonal self in our society. Study of cultures and subcultures in which the interpersonal self is emphasized may give us a basis for studying the development of this self in our own society. Does the development of self foster the development of relationships? Does the development of relationships foster the development of self? Perhaps these are two sides of the same question. This is certainly an issue worth studying more in the future.

ACKNOWLEDGEMENTS

I would like to thank Rosemary S.L. Mills, as well as David MacPhee and the other members of the "Development of the Self in the Social Context" research cognate, for their comments on a previous version of this chapter.

Chapter 4

The Effect of Early Relationship Experiences on Relationships in Adulthood

Patricia M. Crittenden
Family Relations Institute, Miami, FL, USA

Half of all marriages fail. A larger proportion of love affairs fail. In most cases, the separating parties come to believe that they misjudged their partner, that their initial belief that the partner had exceedingly desirable qualities was in error. Indeed, they often come to believe that the partner actually has exceedingly undesirable characteristics and, sometimes, that the partner actively deceived them. How were they (and how are we) deluded?

In this paper, I review several bodies of knowledge to construct a model of how we learn to differentiate reality from appearance, to accept certain probabilities of error and refuse others and, on these bases, to establish relationships with a greater or lesser probability of satisfaction. The underlying construct is that of information processing. I choose this because all action, whether reflexive, habitual or thoughtfully considered, depends on the perception and interpretation of information. Thus, the adaptiveness of human behavior is constrained by the quality of information underlying it.

I argue that, as a species, we have evolved to perceive and interpret information in particular ways and that, as individuals, we have learned to modify these in ways that reflect our unique circumstances. It is on the outcome of these two levels of modification of information that we organize our behavior with regard to others. I use these propositions to guide a selective review of the literature on mental functioning, development, and relationships to make several points:

1. There are universal principles that can describe the patterning of relationships and these principles operate in a probabilistic manner.

Handbook of Personal Relationships, 2nd edn. Edited by Steve Duck.
© 1997 John Wiley & Sons Ltd.

2. A typology of relationships can be described that reflects these principles and that is functionally, developmentally and clinically meaningful.
3. Underlying the principles are the *evolutionary* issues of safety and reproduction and the *functional* issues of predicting and promoting these.
4. Relationships are central to both protection and reproduction.
5. Much of our brain evolution and mental development is organized around predicting with greater accuracy and promoting with greater skill conditions that are safe and favor reproduction.
6. Because safe conditions and opportunities to reproduce are not always discernible, the issue of appearance and reality is central to relationships. I propose that false information regarding safety and the opportunity to reproduce is central to failed relationships.

To construct this thesis, I first consider the function of relationships and the importance of false information to safety and reproduction. I then consider several models of child and adult relationships and offer a model that is both synthesized from these and tied to the functional principles that I propose. I then offer evidence that adult relationships are tied to early relationship experiences in which children learn what is safe and dangerous, what information best identifies safe and dangerous circumstances, and when and how to use falsified behavior to protect oneself. I conclude with a short discussion of the clinical applications of my perspective and a discussion of the need for empirical research to test the theory offered.

WHAT ARE THE PRINCIPLES THAT REGULATE RELATIONSHIPS?

Although relationships accomplish many functions, two are essential to the survival of the human species. These are protection and reproduction. Reproduction formed the basis of Freud's psychoanalytic theory, whereas protection formed the basis of Bowlby's attachment theory. Protection and reproduction also form the base of Maslow's hierarchy of human needs. I propose that together these two "ultimate" functions explain basic aspects of human motivation, behavior and relationship.

Protection by adult caregivers is essential to the survival of immature humans (Bowlby, 1969/82). Even in adulthood, however, relationships serve a protective function. This function is fulfilled physically when we seek our spouse during real dangers (for example, an attack) and when the risk of danger is higher (for example, when we sleep). It is fulfilled psychologically when our spouse's support enables us to venture into new activities and roles (for example, parenthood or a challenging job) that, in turn, promote the protection of ourselves, our partners and our progeny. Adult relationships also enable us to reproduce successfully, that is, with the maximum assurance that our progeny will be genetically fit and well protected.

Knowing when one is safe and with whom one can reproduce is important. Indeed, it is so important that one could argue that a major outcome of brain evolution is to promote transformations of sensory stimuli into meaningful information about safety and reproduction. I offer three sorts of transformations, each of which is vulnerable to predictable sorts of error.

Cognition and the Midbrain

Animals as evolved as reptiles have a midbrain, one function of which is to attribute causal meaning to sensory information. Such sensorimotor learning operates in accordance with the principles of learning theory (Ornstein & Thompson, 1984). When motor activity yields desirable outcomes, it is maintained or repeated. When undesirable outcomes ensue, behavior is modified or inhibited. Functionally, it is as though predictable, temporally ordered patterns were used to add causal meaning to sensory information. I call this transformation of sensory stimuli "cognitive" information.

Such information has tremendous protective value. With sensorimotor learning, individuals can adapt to the unique dangerous and safe aspects of their environments. Because such learning is preconscious, it is rapid and efficient; it is also prone to certain types of error. Specifically, causation may be attributed when there is no causal relation. That is, if something dangerous happens, preceding events or conditions may be treated in the future as though they caused the untoward outcome. In addition, in species capable of expectation, behavior that precedes an expected danger that does not occur may come to be treated as protective, i.e., it will be exhibited as though it caused safety. Although repetitions of the preceding events could be used to demonstrate the lack of causal relation, such repetitions are likely to be avoided if the event is dangerous. Indeed, the more dangerous the outcome, the more diligently the organism will avoid repetition.

Single-trial learning is especially likely to reflect erroneous causal attributions and to occur in the context of extreme danger (Gustavson et al., 1974). Such superstitious learning may become part of a person's behavioral repertoire and be exhibited as inhibitions and compulsions that can no longer be explained. Thus, I argue that the preconscious, protective function of the midbrain consists of organizing information temporally in ways that add causal meaning to sensory stimuli. That meaning may be in error and uncorrected error is most likely when conditions are very dangerous.

A second important function of the midbrain is to regulate sexual behavior. Because this is not relevant until puberty, I delay discussion of this function.

Affect and the Limbic System

The limbic system has evolved in mammalian species to respond to contextual stimuli by generating feelings of unfocused anxiety (MacLean, 1990). These feelings motivate the organism to flight (if possible) or prepare it to fight (Selye, 1976). The eliciting stimuli include darkness, sudden loud noises, entrapping conditions, etc., as well as being alone (Bowlby, 1973; Seligman, 1971; LeDoux, 1986). None of these conditions is itself dangerous, but all are associated with increased probability of danger. Having another person present, especially a stronger, wiser and more experienced person who is intensely interested in our welfare, both makes us feel less anxious and also is a substantial protective advantage (Bowlby, 1973). Put another way, the limbic system transforms sensory stimuli into affective information that enables us to prepare for dangers that we have not yet experienced, thus reducing the risk of injury or death during the first opportunity for experiential learning. Sometimes, however, feelings of anxiety are elicited when there is no danger. Similarly, feelings of comfort may be experienced in spite of imminent danger. Finally, unconditioned feelings may be generalized to associated conditions. This is particularly likely when there are multiple unconditioned elicitors of anxiety. I refer to this transformed information about context as "affect".

The Cortex

The cortex receives both "raw" sensory stimulation and transformed, meaningful cognitive and affective information. If the various bits of information are consistent, responding proceeds rapidly and unimpeded. If, however, the information is discrepant (for example, one feels anxious although previous experience indicates no danger), the mind has the opportunity to become alert and to attempt to resolve the discrepancy (Lashley, 1985/60). Three points are important. First, because transformed information is vulnerable to different sources of error, identification of discrepancy enables the mind to correct erroneous information generated by the lower brain. Second, the cortex matures over the course of childhood. Thus, with maturation it becomes better able to identify and resolve discrepancies (Piaget, 1952). Third, if the potential danger is very great, the mind will take protective action rather than run the definitive test to verify the information. Thus, I argue that the mind will choose safety over truth under conditions of threat.

HOW ARE THESE PRINCIPLES TRANSFORMED INTO INTERPERSONAL STRATEGIES OVER THE COURSE OF DEVELOPMENT?

Learning to Use One's Mind

Infants are born ready to transform and integrate information in sensorimotor ways. In addition, infants' affective reflexes provide others with information about infants' well-being. Through interaction, infants learn to attribute meaning to information (Vygotskii, 1987). There are only three patterns of response that caregivers can give to infants' affective behavior (Crittenden, 1995). Caregivers can respond predictably in ways that increase infants' comfort. Such infants are on a schedule of predictable reinforcement of their affective signals. They learn to make cognitive meaning of the relation between their behavior and their caregivers' responses and to associate feelings with meaningful changes in state. Their interpersonal strategy becomes one of open and direct communication of feelings to increase the probability of desired caregiving. In attachment terms (Ainsworth, 1979; Ainsworth et al., 1978), they are securely attached Type B[1] infants (see Figure 4.1, B1–4).

Other caregivers respond negatively to infants' affective signals (by shouting, shaking the baby, turning away, etc.). Because such babies are on a schedule of predictable punishment of affective signals, they learn to inhibit display of affect. Thus, they make cognitive meaning of the relation between their behavior and their caregivers', but learn that their feelings are both in error and also misleading. Consequently, they tend to attend to cognitive information and to disregard affect; this decreases the probability of punitive outcomes. In attachment terms, they are avoidantly attached (Type A). Nevertheless, most caregivers of Type A children are caring and protective; they simply dislike displays of negative affect. Their infants correctly learn that things work out best if they act as though there were no problem. However, some parents of avoidant babies are themselves a source of danger to the babies (Crittenden, 1988). Some are neglectful; when their infants inhibit affective signals, they respond even less to infant needs. Others are violent; display of infant affect increases the probability of danger (see Figure 4.1, A1–2).

The third group of caregivers is inconsistent. Their infants are on a schedule of unpredictable, intermittent reinforcement of affective signals. With sensorimotor intelligence, Type C babies are unable to organize their behavior to change the contingencies on parental behavior. Nevertheless, their reinforcement schedule ensures that fear, anger and desire for comfort will be displayed at high intensity and frequency, for long durations, in spite of punishment, reinforcement of incompatible behavior or attempts at extinction. Type C infants can make no meaning of information, are affectively aroused, and are considered ambivalently attached (see Figure 4.1, C1–2).

These three patterns, plus a combination A/C pattern (Crittenden, 1985), can be applied to essentially all infants. Nevertheless, even in infancy, there is wide variation in infants' developing personality. It is proposed here that essential mental transformations of information are universal to humans and that the A, B, C and A/C strategies reflect all possible integrations of the mental functions with

---

[1] As Bartholomew has pointed out, there are many attachment typologies (Bartholomew, 1994). The ABC "Types" used here refer to how cognitive and affective information is managed rather than to specific patterns of behavior, e.g. avoidance, resistance. Such patterns are age-specific, whereas the patterns of processing information are relevant throughout the life-span.

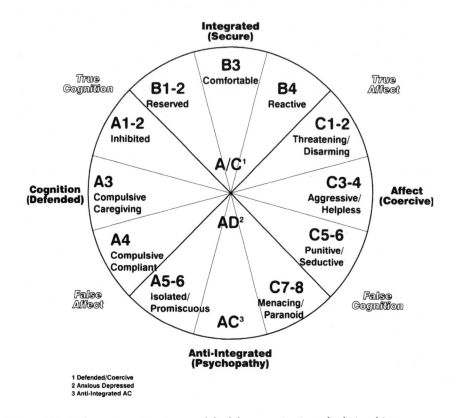

Figure 4.1 A dynamic-maturation model of the organization of relationships

experience. Personality, on the other hand, includes a second interaction, the interaction of strategies with unique, heritable (but non-essential) characteristics (Crittenden, 1995; Tooby & Cosmides, 1990). Personality, thus, varies more greatly than strategies.

The Preschool Years

With preoperational intelligence, children use information in more sophisticated ways and organize their behavior in more complex patterns. Linguistic communication becomes increasingly important and is used to communicate about past and future. As a consequence, internal representational models come to exist in both sensorimotor "procedural" form and, increasingly, in verbal forms that can be discussed with caregivers.

In addition, preschool-aged children use coy behavior to (1) disarm parental aggression (with the non-verbal signals of exposing the [vulnerable] belly and neck and displaying the "no weapons", empty-hands gesture), and (2) elicit parental nurturance (with little, non-threatening glances, an open-mouthed, no-teeth "smile", and a supplicating posture) (Crittenden, 1992, 1995; Eibl-Eibesfeldt, 1979). Together these changes enable many children to modify or change their strategy, i.e., quality of attachment.

Children who are Type B/secure in the preschool years learn to use language to express feelings and intentions and to negotiate and compromise with caregivers about plans (Marvin, 1977). They are balanced with regard to use of affect and cognition. This pattern is consistent with Baumrind's pattern of authoritative parents and competent children (Baumrind, 1971) and with Erikson's issue of autonomy (Erikson, 1950).

Type A infants discover that caregivers use false affect; that is, they express positive affect to conceal negative feelings, especially anger and fear (Crittenden, 1981). Type A/defended children learn to do the same because positive affect elicits the caregiving that they desire. Children with unresponsive parents use false bright affect and entertaining/caregiving behavior to attract attention (Figure 4.1, A3). This increases the probability of parental protection. Children with dangerously hostile caregivers learn to comply with parental demands, to falsify affective displays in parent-pleasing ways, and to be vigilantly alert; they are compulsively compliant (Figure 4.1, A4) (Crittenden & DiLalla, 1988). Thus, Type A children learn that there are predictable relations between events (even falsified events) that can be relied on whereas others' affect can deceive. Furthermore, Type A children learn to regulate parental behavior by creating the appearance of happiness to defend against feelings of anger, fear and desire for comfort. When parents are dissatisfied, such children feel responsibility and shame. This strategy is consistent with, but more elaborated than, Baumrind's pattern of authoritarian parents and socially ineffective children (Baumrind, 1971). It also fits Erikson's notion of preschool-aged children developing feelings of shame (Erikson, 1950).

Type C children show the most dramatic change in behavior. With coy behavior and preoperational intelligence, they organize a coercive strategy of (1) splitting the display of mixed feelings of anger, fear and desire for comfort into aggressiveness and disarmingly coy behavior; (2) exaggerating the display of one while inhibiting the display of the other; and (3) alternating the displays in concert with changes in adults' angry and placating behavior (Crittenden, 1992). For example, a little boy wants candy in a supermarket. He whines, cries and then screams in a rapidly escalating tantrum. As long as his parent placates him, he maintains his angry demands. But when his parent becomes fed up and angry, he switches to disarmingly submissive behavior; he looks sweetly innocent, incapable of anger and in need of nurturance. The parent soothes him. He needs more; he feigns helplessness until the parent gets fed up. Then he meets parental anger with his own anger and his parent, fearing another tantrum, placates him. And so on, in a coercive strategy that transforms parental unpredictability into child moodiness, volatility and unpredictability. Although all children learn the coercive strategy, children of inconsistent parents use it as their primary means of managing the parent–child relationship (see Figure 4.1, C1–2). This pattern is consistent with Baumrind's pattern of permissive parents and immature, anti-social children (Baumrind, 1971) and Erikson's notion of doubt (Erikson, 1950).

The coercive strategy functions to keep parents' attention on the child. Of course, it is also constraining and entrapping for parents. Many overcome the strategy by tricking children regarding the parents' future behavior, i.e., regarding their intentions. For example, they lead children to expect that they are not leaving and then, when the children are not looking, they sneak out. Such parents falsify cognitive information. Because preschool-aged children gauge reality on the basis of appearances (Piaget, 1952), they cannot discern the deception. Children who are repeatedly tricked in this way come to distrust cognitive information.

To conclude, with new cortical potential for organizing information, pre-school-aged children organize relationships in more differentiated ways than in infancy. These reflect both extensions of the infant patterns (Egeland & Farber, 1984; Greenberg, Speltz & DeKlyen, 1993; Stevenson-Hinde & Shouldice, 1995) and in some cases changes in strategy (Crittenden, 1992). Thus there is evidence of both continuity and change in children's strategies (Fagot & Paris, 1966; Teti et al., 1995; Vaughn, Egeland & Sroufe, 1979). Furthermore, there is clearer differentiation of normative and atypical[2] patterns. Each of the strategies has a normative form; in addition, the A and C strategies have subpatterns (i.e., Figure 4.1, A3–4 and C3–4) associated with both child behavior disorders and homes that are dangerous (Crittenden & Claussen, 1994; Erickson, Sroufe & Egeland, 1985; Lyons-Ruth, 1992; Teti et al., 1995).

The School Years

The school years are notable for three processes. First, school-aged children spend increasing amounts of time away from their parents and without adult supervision; consequently, they must depend upon their representations of reality and of others' behavior to assess danger and to regulate their own behavior in ways that promote both safety and exploration. Mentally, they become able to integrate diverse sorts of information and to represent diversity in behavior. This enables them to construct internal representational models that are more accurate and flexible because they are differentiated (by person and context) and conditional (as if–then structures.)

Second, school-aged children refine the three basic strategies and subpatterns to create a wider array of ways to manage relationships. For example, among

---

[2] Selecting terminology is difficult. Clinical terminology uses the terms adaptive/maladaptive and functional/dysfunctional to refer to behavior that I have referred to as normative and atypical. In evolutionary terms, all of the strategies and behavior patterns are adaptive and functional, *given the constraints of actual environmental conditions*. The maladaptation occurs when strategies learned in one context are applied without modification to another in which they do not achieve their function.

coercive-disarming children, there is a differentiation of silly, clown-like children from persuasive charmers, whiny blamers, submissive victims and coyly seductive clingers. Among defended children, some develop a public-pleasing, positive presentation that enables them to become socially popular with many children (although, possibly, intimate best friends with none), whereas others become increasingly isolated and lonely. Each new subpattern maximizes some aspect of the underlying strategy in an interaction of person and environment. Although these subpatterns are only sketched here, the important issue is the process of differentiation rather than the details of its outcome (Sroufe, Egeland & Kreutzer, 1990).

Third, school-aged children learn to deceive others with regard to their intentions. Put another way, they learn to use false cognitive information to cause others to lower their guard against the child's planned treachery. Among coercive-aggressive children, this results in a subgroup of punitive children (C5) who are obsessed with revenge. The pattern is well exemplified by gang-style vendettas and bully–victim relationships (Smith et al., 1994). Children who are frequently victimized reflect an obsession with rescue (C4).

Adolescence

Adolescence culminates in both mental (cortical) and sexual maturity. The mind becomes capable of sophisticated integrations of information. One function of the mature mind is to identify and correct distortions to create increasingly accurate representations of reality. Having a variety of sources of information permits the mind to perform a multi-method experiment on the nature of reality. In this experiment, errors generated at earlier developmental periods can be corrected. This, of course, increases the probability of revised internal representational models that reflect greater flexibility and complexity of behavior than at younger ages. If, however, danger is perceived as imminent and disguised, the mind may defend the self by presuming the environment to be pervasively malevolent. In this case, false affect may be integrated with false cognition to yield a representation of omnipresent danger. Individuals who hold such representations become exquisitely alert to treachery and constantly prepared to defend themselves. Some cower with paranoia, whereas others menace those who might harm them (see Figure 4.1, C7–8, AC). Because the best defense is often offense, such individuals become psychopathically dangerous to others.

Sexual maturity activates the second essential motivation of any species, i.e., reproduction. During adolescence and into early adulthood, humans seek partners who function not only as attachment figures but also as reproductive mates. This double function may explain the intensity of these relationships. It also explains some of the relation between early relationship experience with parents and relationship patterns among adults. Adolescents integrate genetically biased patterns of sexual behavior into their existing internal representational models of self and other behavior. In particular, coy behavior is transformed into flirtatious behavior that can be used to negotiate relationships and false positive affect is transformed into promiscuous (A5–6) invitations to intimacy.

This completes the components of a two-dimensional dynamic-maturational model of both the mental processing of information about safety and danger and also the organization of relationships (see Figure 4.1). One dimension is the source of information, i.e., cognitive or affective information, including both true and false information. The second dimension is extent of integration of the two sorts of information. Four major patterns are defined by these dimensions: balanced (B), defended (A), coercive (C), and coercive/defended (A/C, and AC).

There are three important points about this model. First, it is specifically hypothesized that individuals who have experienced danger, especially danger from caregivers, learn to emphasize the most predictive information and to ignore and/or falsify the least predictive information. Second, the meanings that individuals attribute to information are probabilistic; they do not define how things actually are in all cases, but rather how they might be. Because few things are certain, humans must decide how much certainty is needed before action is taken. The *perception* of danger is critical to making this decision. Third, the more eminent and threatening the danger is perceived to be, the more unreliable information will be distrusted and distorted.

Estimates of the probability of danger, however, are vulnerable to specifiable distortions of reasoning, including representativeness, availability, and adjustment and anchoring (Tversky & Kahneman, 1982). By increasing perceived probability, these distortions function to maximize safety. Thus, under dangerous circumstances, humans tend to choose safety over truth. Put concretely, a child who has experienced violence is more likely to perceive danger in neutral stimuli than a child growing up under safer conditions (Dodge & Frame, 1982; Rieder & Cicchetti, 1989).

Selecting a Partner

Selecting a partner is the focus of much adolescent activity. Adolescents advertize themselves in ways they hope will attract desirable partners. The advertisements, however, are not always accurate (Goffman, 1959). For example, flirtatious behavior that becomes seductive may exaggerate interest while underlying anger and fear are hidden. How can one tell? Some people are what they seem whereas others are not. Hypocrisy becomes a cardinal crime for adolescents who want a world in which everyone (else!) displays only accurately predictive information.

What is being predicted is less clear. Although there is a substantial literature on the tendency of males to seek mates with reproductive/nurturant value and females to seek mates with the resources and power to protect and nurture children (Buss, 1994), it is unlikely that these motivations are the sole motivations for adult partnerships. At a minimum, attachment must be considered. Adults desire partners who enable them to feel safe. The conditions that elicit this feeling are, of course, tied to each person's unique history of attachment relationships. Some adults prefer predictable, emotionally cool partners, some prefer those who are affectively intense and unpredictable in ways that keep the relationship lively, and others desire a balance between these. Meeting both attachment and reproductive goals can create conflict. For example, males' efforts to gain "reproductive" status may require reducing attention to family members. This creates opportunity for low status, but sweet-talking males with time on their hands to captivate the mates of high status males with too little time for tenderness. In other words, both the motivations underlying relationships and the strategies used to achieve them may be complex. Moreover, they may involve inconsistencies whose resolution elicits change in relationships, strategies and/or partners.

Adolescents scan potential mates for signs of their suitability. Is the potential mate trustworthy? Protective? A reliable parent for one's progeny? Does he only boast of power or is he powerful? Will she satisfy the insecure boy's desire to feel powerful? Does she really enjoy sex? Will she be faithful? It is not easy to know. As most adolescents discover, appearances can be deceiving. Not surprisingly, sincerity becomes highly valued, even more than beauty, strength, power and the other evolutionarily advantageous traits (Harrison & Saeed, 1977).

Relationships are tried out. Most fail, but in the process much is learned about appearance and reality, the process of discerning the difference, and the risks of mistaking them. Will the charming boy really be devoted to his girlfriend? Is jealousy a sign of commitment or a warning of violence to come? Is the quiet boy really uncaring? Can he be counted on to do as he promises? What about the seductive girl? Will she be loving and devoted (i.e., submissive) or is she really angry and dangerous? Can one sleep safely with her? Is promiscuity a sign of ready intimacy or of someone so isolated and fearful of intimacy, even when physically close, that there may be no other way for them to reproduce? Adolescents must learn to discriminate real predictive information from information that is too good to be true. Indeed, as astute shoppers and evolutionary biologists have discovered, the less one has to offer, the more one must promise (Margulis & Sagan, 1991; Tooke & Camire, 1991; Trivers, 1985).

It's tricky and apparently many of us aren't so good at it. This has implications for the many women who are battered by spouses and lovers, for the men who are killed or injured by attacking partners, for the half of adults who will divorce, for all those who live in embattled disharmony or silent separateness, and for all the children of these troubled adult relationships. Relationships are essential for reproduction and they greatly promote personal survival and the survival of children. For all of us, however, relationships represent both our haven of safety and the ultimate danger. Being able to tell these apart is very important.

Who will make errors? Ironically, it may be those who skew their processing of information specifically to prevent errors. If, in our prior experience, errors of judgment or action have been minor, and temporary setbacks allowed us to learn new discriminations, to revise representational models and to reorganize our behavior more adaptively, then risk can be accepted fairly often. If, on the other hand, risk has been associated with dangerous outcomes, then we must learn to identify the signals of risk, to construct representational models that maximize the avoidance of risk, and to behave in ways that preclude risk. Much less can be ventured in such circumstances and much less will be learned.

What kind of errors will be made? Most models of personality or relationship are silent on this issue, but jails, child protection services and mental hospitals are clear. Repeatedly, those who have experienced the most treachery in the past select partners who will be the most treacherous (Cowan & Kinder, 1985). Often this is true even when adults are aware of the problem and actively seek a partner who is completely unlike their previous partner. If my model is correct, choosing the opposite pattern is both very probable and also very dangerous because the new partner is likely to falsify the very information that is most trusted. Indeed, data suggest that, although Type B secure/balanced individuals are most likely to select a similar partner, Types A and C are equally likely to select the same or the opposite pattern (Crittenden, Partridge & Claussen, 1991). When partners' strategies are organized in opposite ways, there is risk that selecting an "opposite" partner will result in severe disappointments, unnecessary provocation when strategies misfire and, potentially, violence. However, nothing is simple. Choosing a partner with an opposite strategy also gives the dyad the advantages of both sorts of truth. It may work—sometimes in exciting and creative ways (Crittenden, in press).

HOW DO THESE PRINCIPLES AFFECT THE PATTERNING OF RELATIONSHIPS?

Many researchers have created models of human personality and/or relationship. I have already referenced two for which there are substantial empirical data in childhood. Baumrind's model of three types of parental styles with matching types of child functioning is quite similar to Ainsworth's model of secure, avoidant and ambivalent attachment. The constructs emphasized by Baumrind and Ainsworth are different, but compatible. Moreover, the two approaches would cluster dyads similarly. I have tried in the discussion above to tie the models together with the glue of evolutionary biology, social learning theory, cognitive development theory (both Piagetian and Vygotskiian), and information processing theory. In this section, I attempt to relate this developmental model to several well-known models of adult relationship. I discuss three: Gottman's empirical model, Satir's clinical model, and Olson's more theoretical circumplex model. These are selected because they reflect three academic disciplines, have substantial empirical evidence and focus on dyads, individuals, and families, respectively.

Gottman's Empirical Model

Gottman's analyses of spousal interaction have yielded three patterns of stable marriages: validating, volatile and conflict-avoiding (Gottman, 1993). These are highly analogous to the attachment Types B, C and A, respectively. Gottman also found two unstable patterns that often result in divorce or separation; these are best described as negative extensions of the volatile and conflict-avoiding patterns: hostile and hostile-detached, respectively.

Gottman's empirically-based conceptualization fits quite closely the developmental theory offered here in which the more extreme edges of the A and C patterns become progressively more distorted. There are some important differences, however. In the model offered here, false information is considered critical to understanding the meaning of dyadic communications; Gottman addresses only displayed (and, presumably, true) affect. Second, the patterns presented here reflect the outcome of a developmental process; this process, although not necessarily linear, is helpful in understanding the learning history and motivation behind apparently "dysfunctional" behavior. Finally, Gottman studied patterns that can be discerned in a single session of interaction. The perspective being offered here suggests that these interactions form larger patterns that function to promote protection and reproduction, given conditions as they are represented in each partner's mind. Discerning the two-sided, threatening-disarming coercive strategy, in particular, may require a larger timeframe than an interaction. Nevertheless, Gottman's model, unlike most other models, does not make the implicit presumption that all marriages occur under favorable circumstances, or that the validating/Type B pattern is necessarily best for everyone. If Gottman's model were expanded to address the situation of couples with histories of danger before and during marriage, then the interactive effects of development, maturation, information processing and current conditions to patterns of relationship might become clearer. In addition, application of the study of the physiological correlates of affect (Levenson, Carstensen & Gottman, 1994) to false affect might help to identify the internal process underlying the patterns.

Satir's Clinical Model

Satir's "model" is less formal than those of the other theorists considered here (Satir, 1972). On the other hand, it has the detail and complexity typical of real people that are often missing from highly structured models. Of particular interest are Satir's four patterns of communication: blaming, placating, distracting and computing; the physical stances that she associates with these patterns are highly consistent with the non-verbal behaviors that I have found in preschool-age threatening, disarming and defended children, respectively. Satir proposes that the blaming and placating patterns are frequently found together in parent–child and spousal dyads, whereas the computing pattern is affectively distancing. This is compatible with my notion of the coercive strategy of threats and bribes (with humor or incompetence functioning as distractors in a coercive-disarming pattern) and of the defended strategy as a cognitive pattern of inhibition of affect. It is also consistent with Gottman's observations of couples' interactions. In addition, Satir touches on physiological functioning, non-verbal communication, strategies and deceptive information. Satir seems to have discovered intuitively most of the components of the integrated theory that I offer, even though the components are less fully articulated than in later models.

Olson's Theoretical Circumplex Model

Olson's model is the most abstract and best organized of the three models. Olson proposes that families vary on two dimensions, cohesion and adaptation, and that being extreme on either dimension creates risk (Olson, 1989). Thus, both disengaged and enmeshed families show risk with regard to cohesion, whereas both rigid and chaotic families show risk with regard to adaptation. It is noteworthy that the disengaged/rigid combination is similar to the attachment Type A, the enmeshed/chaotic combination to Type C, and the less frequent disengaged/chaotic and enmeshed/rigid combinations similar to Type A/C. Olson conceptualizes balanced families as most adaptive and families who are extreme on both dimensions as dysfunctional. The organization is quite similar to my proposed two-dimensional model in which both balance and flexibility are desirable. Unlike my model, however, Olson does not consider the family/environment interactions that might give rise to extreme patterns that are adaptive, given their context. Finally, viewed from the family level, Gottman, Satir and Olson appear to cluster families similarly and in ways that are compatible with Baumrind and Ainsworth.

A Dynamic-maturational Model

This review of models of relationship suggests general agreement on the major dimensions differentiating relationships. The models described here, as well as other empirical data and models (e.g., Block & Block, 1980; Caspi, Bem & Elder, 1989; Caspi & Silva, 1995; Hazan & Shaver, 1987; Pulkkinen, 1996), all identify well-functioning relationships as having both warmth/closeness (affect) and predictable structure (cognition). Bartholomew's two-dimension, four-type model represents an exception (Bartholomew, 1994). Although its origins are in the attachment typology, its categories are based on appearances, such that, on the self-model dimension, true and false positive models are grouped together and, on the models-of-others dimension, false models are not considered at all. Moreover, Bartholomew's construct of self models specifically refers to models that are not reflective of feedback from real relationships. Such a non-interactive stance seems both simplistic and in conflict with developmental and systemic approaches. More similar is Patterson's social-interactional model (Patterson,

1982). The process that Patterson describes from early childhood to early adulthood is compatible with that offered here, as is the bi-directional approach to effects within families. Missing from Patterson's model are the notion that coercion includes disarming behavior and the underlying perspective of organization around predicting and preventing danger. These notions are not, however, incompatible with Patterson's thinking.

My second dimension of integration enters several of the models as the notion of balance or ego resiliency. There is less agreement on the pattern of organization and little attention to the evaluative aspect of the models (i.e., defining a "good" relationship). In addition, most models do not explain pathological behavior well or the complexity of relations among relationships (within families, across the life span, or cross-generationally).

One advantage of the conceptualization that I offer is that it accounts for deception (false information) with regard to both feelings and intentions in ways that (1) reflect familiar patterns of pathological behavior and (2) suggest the contexts in which these patterns represent successful adaptations. Because it was constructed from a developmental perspective, it encourages open-ended consideration of the issue of change and continuity. Furthermore, it focuses on the two functional issues of protection and reproduction, thus, creating a relatively unbiased, culture-free, non-pejorative means of evaluating relationship strategies.

Finally, the model that I propose is probabilistic rather than deterministic. Organisms use strategies that have probabilities of achieving their function. When the function is not fulfilled, when the organism changes as a function of maturation, or when the environment changes, both the behaviors used to implement strategies and the strategies themselves may change. This creates both continuity and change, such that early relationships have a clear effect on the organization of later relationships without the effect necessarily being linear or accounting for all of the variance. With a wider range of variation in patterns, more reliable and valid assessment procedures, and acceptance of the meshing of opposite patterns (i.e., Type A with Type C), the amount of variance accounted for should increase, but is still unlikely to be fully predictive. Chance occurrences, unique genetic influences, changing environmental conditions (not tied to individuals' functioning), and maturation all influence the development of relationships in dynamic (but lawful) ways.

HOW DO CHILDHOOD EXPERIENCES IN RELATIONSHIPS AFFECT THE QUALITY OF LATER RELATIONSHIPS?

A central issue in the study of development and psychopathology has been the extent to which early experience in relationships affects the quality of later relationships. This can be approached in several ways. The least complex is to ask if early experience with troubled relationships has predictable and detrimental outcomes at later ages. Another approach is to ask whether patterning of early relationships is tied predictably to patterning later in life. Finally, one can ask whether parents' patterns are predictive of children's patterns.

Negative Relationship Events in Early Life

There are many studies demonstrating that poor family relationships in childhood are related to less optimal outcomes later in life. For example, families with high conflict have adolescents with higher anxiety, depression and stress-related psychosomatic symptoms in adolescence (Mechanic & Hansell, 1989). Similarly, children, especially girls, whose parents divorced are likely to marry at younger ages, have children at younger ages, and have more children out of wedlock (McLanahan & Bumpass, 1988). There are similar outcomes for children whose parents engaged in spousal violence (Seltzer & Kalmuss, 1988); moreover, in some cases, parental violence results in adolescent violence to the parents (Peek, Fischer & Kidwell, 1985). Viewing relationships from children's contributions produces similar findings: children showing anti-social behavior in childhood disproportionately experience alcoholism, divorce, mental illness, criminality, family violence, and welfare dependency (Caspi, Elder & Bem, 1987; Farrington, 1983; Robins & Ratcliff, 1979). A pervasive hypothesis is that experiencing abuse as a child leads to being abusive as an adult. Nevertheless, it is clear that most abused children do not abuse their own children (Starr, 1979). Although Emery's (1988) conclusion is that most families have multiple problems and the causal relations among these are unclear, it appears that whenever safety or reproduction are threatened, the risk of undesirable outcomes is increased.

Patterning of Relationships

The broad empirical base of studies of infant attachment have made clear the relation between anxious attachment in infancy and undesirable outcomes later (Ainsworth, 1985). These include reduced problem-solving competence (Matas, Arhend & Sroufe, 1978), increased tantruming, aggression and ignoring of mothers (Sroufe, 1982), greater emotional dependance and need for attention (Sroufe, Fox & Pancake, 1983), and greater risk for attentional disorders (Jacobvitz & Sroufe, 1987).

Findings of continuity are not limited to studies of attachment. There are a number of studies that compare patterns of parental behavior with children's resulting behavior and personality. An early study of character development found that parents who were (1) consistent, warm and predictable had well-adjusted, rational and altruistic children; whereas those who were (2) inconsistent had expedient, manipulative children; (3) consistently autocratic parents had conforming children; and (4) rejecting and inconsistent parents had amoral children (Peck & Havighurst, 1960). Again, these findings are consistent with the Types B, C, A and A/C, respectively, as well as with Baumrind's patterns in adolescence when the mixed rejecting/neglecting pattern is added (Baumrind, 1991). The power of the combination of negative styles (i.e., A/C styled patterns) to leave children unprepared for reciprocal, supportive relationships has been replicated in the literature on conduct-disordered and delinquent boys (Patterson, DeBaryshe & Ramsey, 1989), child maltreatment (Crittenden, 1985, 1988), and bi-polar depression (Radke-Yarrow et al., 1985).

Thus, there is strong evidence that patterns of parental behavior have predictable effects on later child functioning when child outcomes are clustered functionally. That is, everyone finds that (1) predictable parental harshness yields conforming, rule-abiding, inhibited children and adolescents, whereas (2) inconsistent, permissive parenting yields acting out, hyperactive, conduct-disordered children, and (3) children who experience both conditions become antisocial in ways that may become dangerous. Nevertheless, there are three important limitations to these studies. First, they do not account for all the variance; not all children show the predicted problems. Second, they do not clarify which behavior, within a functional class, will be shown by a given child. Finally, they do not explain the motivation or internal process for either parents or children. Because it is clear that the patterns, especially the less desirable patterns, are very difficult to change, understanding the motivation and process behind the patterns is very important.

Child and Parent Patterns

A number of investigations using the attachment model have explored the direct effect of parents' pattern of attachment on children's pattern of attachment. Many have found evidence of continuity from adulthood to childhood in the next generation (Benoit & Parker, 1994; Crittenden, 1985; Crittenden, Partridge & Claussen, 1991; Fonagy et al., in press; Grossmann et al., 1988; Main, Kaplan & Cassidy, 1985). Based on van IJzendoorn's meta-analysis of 18 samples, approximately 22% of the variance in infant pattern could be accounted for by parental Adult Attachment Interview patterns (van IJzendoorn, 1995). Nevertheless, there are reasons for caution in interpreting these data. First, the proportion of variance accounted for by the continuity hypothesis is meaningful, but insufficient to preclude additional hypotheses. For example, my colleagues and I point to the "opposites" effect, i.e., children having the opposite pattern from adults (Crittenden, Partridge & Claussen, 1991). Second, the Adult Attachment Interview (Main & Goldwyn, in preparation) is not a measure of adult attachments; to the contrary, it was *constructed* to match the known patterns of adults' children. A true assessment of adult relationships with partners, parents or children might yield a different pattern of relations with child attachment. Third, the Main & Goldwyn attachment classificatory system in adulthood is based directly on the infancy system and does not reflect changes in the organization of attachment that may occur after infancy. Further exploration of the nature of relationships after infancy, and especially after puberty, is needed. In particular, I recommend attending to the possibility of increasing complexity in organization and the use of various sorts of deception (of both self and others). Finally, the Adult Attachment Interview assesses verbal responses to an interview, whereas children experience the effects of parental behavior; the relation between what parents believe and remember and what they do may not be exact. In conclusion, there is good reason to believe that parents' management of relationships affects children's strategies for managing relationships, but the scope of the relation is probably more complex than a simple linear effect of continuity.

HOW CAN THIS THEORY INFORM CLINICAL INTERVENTION?

Troubled relationships usually involve both distorted patterns of behavior and shattered expectations. Behavioral therapies that change behavior by changing eliciting and reinforcing conditions are often used to modify interactive patterns. Such interventions are, however, quite fragile. In fact, the recommended method of testing such an intervention, the ABAB design, is itself proof that the change is in contexts and not in individuals or relationships. Interventions are needed that change the participants in enduring ways.

Changing expectations, i.e., internal representational models, may help to accomplish this. Many therapies, including in particular the cognitive therapies, attempt to identify and change generalized belief and value systems. A risk is that the client will emerge from therapy well adjusted to current circumstances, i.e., with reasonably accurate internal representations models of self and other, only to find that new life changes unsettle the balance and problems reappear. On the other hand, if internal representational models are framed as working approximations of an ever-changing reality, and if clients are taught how to perceive new and important information and how to use it to reorganize both models and behavior, they may learn mental processes of assimilation and accommodation that will promote an evolving, synergetic balance between self and environment. Such a balance, one that is constantly being remade, may promote both enduring relationships and also safety and opportunity to reproduce in changing circumstances. The focus must, however, be on the process of opening models to new information and change rather than on correcting their content[3].

Changing strategies requires that one know the goal or function of the strategy. This chapter has focused on the functions of protection and reproduction as

---

[3] The attachment literature often refers to "working" models, i.e., models used to make predictions. I have avoided that term and used the more generic term "internal representational" models because most models, including very distorted models, are working models (Crittenden, 1990). Greater concerns in evaluating models are their openness to new information and the biases that operate in the transformation of the information to knowledge.

central to intimate relationships. Framing relationship disorders as attempts to maximize protection and reproductive opportunities, given the prior experience of the individual, can focus therapists on demonstrating to clients that historical conditions are no longer applicable and why, therefore, new strategies are needed. Diagnostically, knowledge of the strategies and of false affect and cognition can enable therapists to interpret accurately the presence of fear, anger and desire for comfort, even when these are not overtly apparent. Cognitive-behavioral therapies accomplish some of this, but do not adequately account for the evolved function of affect: indeed, they are often too rational, even about affect.

Clinically, troubled couples and parent–child dyads need to understand one another's strategies, to develop compassion for the conditions that elicited partners' strategies, and to behave in ways that create comfort and the opportunity to relinquish the strategy. This does not mean behaving in ways that thwart the strategy. Finally, adults who have repeatedly engaged in destructive relationships could be helped by understanding the two sides of the coercive pattern and the tendency of Type A and C adults to be attracted to one another. In both cases, appearances are deceiving. When adults better understand both their own strategy and the strategies of those whom they are likely to attract, they become better able to make balanced decisions about relationships. This is especially true if they learn to recognize the ways in which they distort information. It is important, however, for therapists to realize that these distortions and the strategies serve a purpose. If that purpose remains valid, the distortions and strategies will be maintained.

AN OVERVIEW OF A THEORY OF RELATIONSHIP AND CONTINUITY IN RELATIONSHIP

In this paper I offer a theory regarding the development of relationships. Of course, there are already many such theories and typologies. One might wonder if yet another is needed. I propose that further theory development may be valuable if the theory: (1) explains commonalities among a variety of empirically, clinically and theoretically derived theories; (2) offers a simple structure while, nevertheless, accounting for wide variation in human behavior; (3) is developmental in nature such that it not only accounts for incremental change over time, but also accounts for periods of rapid maturational change; (4) is framed in terms of processes rather than traits, events or conditions; (5) is interactional in accounting for human evolution, genetic variation, child-rearing contexts and cultural variations; (6) addresses the development of both typical and atypical personalities; and (7) has implications for parenting, under both normative and risk conditions, and for treatment under conditions of maladaptation. I am proposing, in other words, a theory that is both familiar in that it is drawn from existing research and theory and novel in that it integrates these in new ways that have implications for further research and for practical applications.

The theory that I offer proposes a model of human adaptation with two dimensions, source of information (i.e., cognition and affect) and degree of integration. These two dimensions interact around the functions of protection and reproduction. Evolved brain structures function to transform sensory stimulation into meaningful cognitive information about behavior and affective information about contexts, whereas experiential learning enables organisms to adapt these to unique life circumstances. The process of learning occurs in the context of relationships, and its outcomes, internal representational models and patterns of behavior are repeatedly modified, both by maturation and by change in circumstances. The modifications, however, are biased by innate and universal tendencies of mental functioning. These biases make early conditions disproportionately important to interpretation of present conditions and present conditions disproportionately important to current modeling and behavior. As a consequence, internal representational models become emergent phenomena to be assessed as processes rather than static conditions that can be defined finitely; indeed, models should be evaluated in terms of openness to discrepant information. Viewed this way, security is not a state; it is a process in which minor adjustments to internal representational models and behavioral strategies are constantly being made to maintain a dynamic balance between self and context.

Thus, the overall model is one of dynamic balance among sources of information and response strategies that, when adaptive, maximizes the flexibility of human response, thus promoting protection and reproduction under varying conditions. In addition, the model differentiates behavior from the functions that it serves, thus permitting wide variation in behavior as a consequence of variation in both heritable characteristics and environmental contexts. Three basic relationship strategies are proposed: balanced, defended and coercive, together with a fourth, defended/coercive. As with all systems theories, functional organization and not specific behaviors is the central focus. Various levels of analysis, including genes, neurological structures, mental structures (e.g., internal representational models), behavior, individuals, dyads, families and contexts are integrated into a hierarchy of interrelated systems. Finally, an important contribution of the model is to include the notion of false information, thus addressing both normative problems of whom to trust and with whom to form enduring relationships and also issues of psychopathology. Of course, full integration of these ideas cannot be accomplished in a chapter.

Nevertheless, something can be said that may be useful to all the relationships that end in disappointment. If the perspective offered here reflects a somewhat more accurate representation of human relationships than the models from which it has been derived, then we might conclude that individuals using coercive or defended strategies are more likely to delude both themselves and their partners. They are also more likely to misconstrue information and to do so in ways that heighten their perception of danger. If this is accurate, they would also be likely to respond in protective ways to the perceived threat. Finally, they, more than individuals using a balanced strategy, would desire to achieve a state of unchanging safety. Thus, they would expect their partners to remain the same and they would fail to adjust to change until the evidence of change was too discrepant to ignore. The change when noticed might well be perceived as alarming and elicit protective efforts to regain the prior balance. However, nothing stays the same and nothing goes backwards. Put in the abstract language of theory, healthy couples and healthy parent–child relationships are more "open" to new information and change than models in less healthy relationships. Thus, the "openness" of mental functioning may be critical to behavioral harmony and ultimate adaptiveness.

I cannot prove all (or maybe even any) of these assertions. That was never the goal. Instead, the goal was to use the existing literature to generate an integrative theory regarding the effect of early relationships on later relationships. I have tried to make the theory that I offer internally consistent and testable. Hopefully, enough empirical support has been offered to suggest the plausibility of the theory and enough applications suggested to indicate the importance of empirical testing and refinement of the theory.

Chapter 5

Cultural Dimensions of Children's Peer Relations

Barry H. Schneider, Andrea Smith, Samantha E. Poisson
and
Archie B. Kwan
University of Toronto, Canada

Sweeping political changes in most parts of the world have led to an increase in contacts among people of different cultural backgrounds. Due to emigration, immigration and urbanization, large subcultures of different ethnocultural origin co-exist more than ever before within many major Western societies. As members of these subcultures negotiate their relations with the "host" culture, they are compelled to re-examine the basic features of interpersonal relationships in their culture of origin. Although the first generation of immigrants may maintain the ways of the original country to a considerable degree, their children grow up faced with constant comparisons and choices between the relationship styles of the "old" and "new" countries.

Ironically, their cousins who remained at "home" may well be confronting many of the same comparisons and choices. Many cross-cultural differences in interpersonal relationships reflect differences in economic activity and political ideology (Schneider, 1993; Whiting & Edwards, 1988). In societies where hunting and gathering is a major economic activity, children are found to be competitive (Barry, Child & Bacon, 1959; Whiting & Edwards, 1988). In sharp contrast, during the communist era, children reared in places where collective economic activity was fully implemented displayed high levels of collectivist orientation to interpersonal relations (Ekblad, 1984; Hollos, 1980). We do not really know at this point how quickly or how completely changes in economic and political reality are translated into changes in the ways people relate to each other. Many formerly closed societies, once dominated by a single ideology, are becoming more open and complex.

Handbook of Personal Relationships, 2nd edn. Edited by Steve Duck.
© 1997 John Wiley & Sons Ltd.

No known lexicon for describing cultural variation is adequate to conceptualize these more complex cultures in any systematic way. The dichotomy between collectivism/individualism has long been seen as the most fundamental dimension of variation among cultures (Kim, 1994; Triandis, 1986). In a collectivistic society, a greater portion of a person's identity is related to his or her membership in the larger group. Many theorists believe that the interpersonal relationships of individuals within a society relate to the degree of individualism or collectivism that characterizes the culture (e.g., Gudykunst & Ting-Toomey, 1988). The collectivism or individualism of a society as a whole is thought to have a profound influence on interpersonal relationships at a small-group or dyadic level. For example, the continuation of a long-term friendship or romantic relationship is typically seen in the literature on adult relationships as depending on individual satisfaction and commitment (see Rusbult & Buunk, 1993). Some theorists have observed that individuals in collectivistic societies do not feel totally free to initiate and terminate relationships according to their individual "calculations" (Lin & Rusbult, 1995), but must take into account the expectations of third parties (Hsu, 1981). This might conceivably contribute to the longevity of relationships in collectivistic societies. Furthermore, Dion & Dion (1988) suggest that in individualistic societies, there may be a certain ambivalence toward interpersonal relationships because commitment to them may be seen as compromising one's own autonomy. Some examples of the implications of individualism/collectivism for children's relationships appear later in this chapter.

Most immigrants move from a collectivistic society to a more individualistic one (Triandis et al., 1988). With the decline of communism, moreover, most of the sweeping sociopolitical changes of our decade also appear to involve a transition from collectivism to individualism at a broad cultural level. This distinction between collectivism and individualism, however, tends to oversimplify matters. Within one society, subgroups may vary enormously in terms of collectivism/individualism. For example, those urban Koreans most involved in their nation's trend toward industrialization are known to be highly individualistic, in contrast with the collectivistic national norm (Cha, 1994). Societies may be collectivistic in some respects and individualistic in others. Indians, whether living in India or abroad, have been found to combine a collectivistic orientation to family contexts with an individualistic orientation towards interpersonal relationships and economic activity (Sinha & Tripathi, 1994). Phillipsen (1987) very aptly described the dynamic interplay of individualism and collectivism within cultures, without denying the utility of this fundamental dichotomy:

The reality of a culture as experienced by those who live it moves along an axis with two poles at the opposite extremes, one exerting a pull toward the communal, the other toward the individual, as the dominant themes and warrants of human thought, speech, and action. Locating a culture on this axis reveals a partial truth about it, a kind of cultural snapshot, but in order to perceive a culture fully, one must also know the culture's direction of movement along the axis and the relative strength of the competing forces pushing it one way or another (p. 245).

Phillipsen asserts that the interplay of these forces at the community level in Western societies over the past four centuries has had a profound influence on the beliefs, values and ideals of members of Western civilizations and on their communicative conduct. Based on literary sources, he documents a progressive shift in the center of moral gravity from the public to the intimate as the standard and the setting for interpersonal interchange. According to his analysis, honor has been replaced by dignity as the most sovereign of motives. Since individuals in contemporary Western society have relatively little need to be concerned about the evaluation of their speech by peer groups, there is less time spent on forethought and editing and, concomitantly, more time spent talking. The empirical basis for these interesting contentions is not clearly established. Furthermore, they may not fully reflect the cultural heterogeneity of contemporary Western societies.

The collectivism or individualism of a society is known to affect both adult and child cultures within it. Perhaps the best-known documentation of this is Bronfenbrenner's (1970) striking comparison of children's lives in the USA and the Soviet Union during the 1960s. His account depicted a marked collectivism in the USSR, which was propagated as if it were a religion. Collective ideology dictated the rituals of children's groups and permeated the lives of almost all the adults. Within the same culture, however, it is entirely possible that the differences in socialization and acculturation experienced from one generation to the next may be reflected in variations in the degree of their individualism or collectivism. Recent research on relationships in Russia suggests that many of the parents and grandparents observed by Bronfenbrenner may not have subscribed fully to the collectivism that pervaded the era (Goodwin & Emelyanova, 1995).

In most modern societies, children attend schools and other institutions which have as one of their goals the instilling of the collectivistic or individualistic values. These values may be mixed; they may also differ from those to which adults are expected to adhere. In individualistic North America, for instance, children are expected to identify at least to some degree with their schools, sports teams and scout troops. There may, thus, be less latitude for true individualism for American school children than for their parents.

Despite the enormous scope of recent sociopolitical changes, it would be naive to expect any immediate or radical transformations in culturally-ingrained styles of relating. Even after the collective economic or political organization that may have given rise to their relationship patterns has changed, individuals remain likely to follow the ingrained patterns that constitute their basic understanding of the rules of relationships. Furthermore, there are important cross-cultural differences in relationship styles, some of which will be detailed below. These differences must be understood within the context of the many features of social relations that are universal. Several theorists have emphasized that the value of cross-cultural research is not only in discovering differences among cultures, but also in learning about commonalities that are possibly inherent to our species (Segall, 1979).

This chapter is a selective review of theory and research pertaining to cultural influences on children's peer relations. It draws primarily from two bodies of literature. In the first, cultures are regarded as more or less distinct entities. Features of one culture, such as economic activity, religious belief or ideology, are compared with parallel features of other cultures and these cross-cultural differences are considered as potential sources of differences in interpersonal relations. This deductive style of inquiry may been seen as a far superior basis for the development of a theory of cultural variation in social relations than the hitherto casual comparison of cultures that has often been carried out. In order to use this method optimally, a broad sampling of cultures should be selected for comparison, all of which vary along a particular dimension of interest. For example, one might compare a selection of cultures ranging from very low to very high in deference toward authority figures. Unfortunately, this approach is the exception rather than the rule, probably because of the extensive resources and contacts required to carry out a rigorous study of many different cultures. This method is far more advanced in its application to social relations of adults, but it has been used in some studies conducted with children. Two countries—China and Italy—in which there have been several studies conducted with children which are considered below as examples of this approach. As is the case in much cross-cultural research, the choice of these two societies is somewhat fortuitous, in that they are the cultures with which the authors are most familiar. Nevertheless, comparison of the marked differences between these two cultures in terms of degree of overall collectivism/individualism, the priorities established for peer relations in each, and the demands for deference to authority may contribute substantially to the development of theories of cultural difference in peer relations. Despite the pronounced differences between Italy and China, however, the consequences of non-conformity in both cultures take the form of some degree of rejection. Similarities such as these, found within very disparate cultures, demonstrate the importance of theories that can account simultaneously for similarities as well as differences among cultures.

The second body of literature reviewed in this chapter is concerned with relations between members of different subcultures within the same larger culture. Two sets of studies will be reviewed: those that have investigated the sociopolitical context of peer relations among aboriginal children in North America, and those that constitute the substantial literature on inter-ethnic and inter-racial friendship in North America and the UK. The studies conducted with indigenous peoples provide valuable descriptions of the changes in interpersonal relationships that may occur when the values of minority cultures, which are often collectivistic, interact with the individualism of the majority culture. As noted above, this interaction occurs frequently in many Western countries today. The studies on inter-racial and inter-ethnic friendship illuminate the saliency of culture in determining children's preference for relationship partners. This phenomenon has been widely studied, perhaps because of the world-wide media coverage of the events leading to the racial desegregation of the American schools. For this reason, that data base consists of considerably more studies than the others reviewed in this chapter.

The Peer Relations of Chinese Children

The peer relations of Chinese children are influenced by a complex network of age-old traditions and philosophies that assign meaning to social behavior. Much of the literature on Chinese society, philosophy and family life consists of the work of sociologists, cultural anthropologists and social psychologists. It draws upon historical and literary writings (Chao, 1983), ethnographic fieldwork (Wolf, 1970), theoretical discourse (King & Bond, 1985) and personal narratives (Li, 1985). Recently, psychologists have begun to explore the social behavior of Chinese people empirically. For the most part, these sources suggest that the social behavior of the Chinese differs from those of individuals living in the West. According to Triandis (1986), China and most Western countries such as the USA occupy opposite ends of the collectivism–individualism dimension, with Chinese society ranking high in collectivism. This polarity has been used frequently to explain the differences in social behavior between these societies. In China, the individual is seen as existing within and being defined by an interactive social context (Bond & Hwang, 1986).

The collectivist nature of Chinese culture is seen as providing a structure for social behavior, in which interactions between individuals reflect the needs and expectations of the group. Yang (1981) suggests that the Chinese govern their social behavior according to the anticipated reactions of others. In this regard, Toupin (1980) states that rejection of verbal aggression, avoidance of direct expression of feelings and avoidance of confrontations are highly valued in Chinese society. The Chinese concept of "face" is inconsistent with direct confrontations between individuals (Chiu, Tsang & Yang, 1988). The importance of conflict resolution through mediation and bargaining is reflected in China's non-adversarial or inquisitorial procedural model of community justice (Cloke, 1987; Leung, 1987). The avoidance of conflict, and the rapid resolution of conflict should it occur, serve to preserve the interpersonal relationships that are assigned high priority in the Confucian value system. This value system also emphasizes cooperativeness and altruism.

At the core, Buddhism, Taoism and Confucianism are seen as dominating and guiding social relationships among the Chinese (Chao, 1983; Cryderman, 1992; Ryan, 1985). Buddhist, Taoist and Confucian principles combine to elevate the importance of harmony, social obligations and interrelationships in Chinese culture (Shenkar & Ronen, 1987). In particular, Buddhism represents the "self" or ego as composed of many social components that pertain to family, extended family, community and country (Ryan, 1985). Taoism promotes the rejection of self-assertiveness and competitiveness (Ryan, 1985). This rejection may influence children's moral and ethical conduct by discouraging behaviors that further their own interests at the expense of others. Confucian beliefs are guided by four fundamental principles: self-cultivation, maintaining a harmonious relationship with the family, taking responsibility in community affairs, and serving the country (Kong, 1985).

In Confucian precepts, the process of self-cultivation involves the perfection of interpersonal skills and the acceptance of a role in, and moral obligations to, the community (Kong, 1985; Shenkar & Ronen, 1987). Self-cultivation governs relationships and defines the responsibilities of each family member. Through self-cultivation, harmonious relationships within the family can be achieved and role conflicts within the family are avoided. Accordingly, the Chinese extended family has clear role differentiation and structure (Tsui & Schultz, 1988). The Chinese people believe that their family structure provides for continuity in society because it links successive generations with their ancestors, and thereby assigns to every individual a role in history (Kong, 1985).

Child-rearing Practices

Traditional child-rearing values and practices in China strongly reflect Confucian principles. Chinese parents are expected to emphasize proper conduct in the socialization of their children. The Chinese parenting style is largely authoritarian. Lin & Fu (1990) compared child-rearing practices among Chinese (Taiwanese), immigrant Chinese (American) and Caucasian-American parents. Parents completed a Likert-type scale regarding their control, encouragement of independence, expression of affection, and emphasis on achievement. The Chinese parents were more controlling, but, at the same time, they emphasized independence and achievement more than did Caucasian-American parents. These patterns were somewhat stronger for Chinese parents in Taiwan than among immigrant Chinese parents. These findings have been confirmed by other studies (e.g., Rosenthal & Feldman, 1990). The Chinese responses to control and achievement are consistent with more traditional Confucian values. Chen & Uttal (1988) suggest that although the Chinese value system encourages deference to the group, it also promotes a belief in personal control and in the fulfilment of internal goals. From this perspective, personal control requires independence. Lin & Fu (1990) speculate that the findings with regard to parental encouragement of autonomy could also indicate that traditional values of interdependence are declining. However, an intergenerational comparison by Ho & Kang (1984) suggests that child-rearing attitudes and practices have remained relatively stable among Chinese parents.

This stability has been confirmed in other research. Child-rearing studies in which Chinese and Western parents are compared tend to indicate that traditional values and practices rooted in Confucian principles have been retained among the immigrant group even within an external host culture (Lin & Fu, 1990). For example, Kelley & Tseng (1992) found that first-generation Chinese immigrant mothers tended to express more concern for their child's physical needs whereas American mothers of the majority culture expressed more concern for their child's psychological needs. Consistent with traditional practices, the immigrant mothers reported using more physical control over their children and more harsh scolding, and were less nurturant and less responsive than were their American counterparts. In conclusion, we might speculate that Chinese children are prepared by their parents for peer relations that conform closely to a cultural mould that emphasizes the continuity of relationships and the minimization of conflict. Higher levels of power assertions are used by parents to regulate their children's peer relations in light of the expectations of tradition and of society.

Empirical Studies of Children's Peer Relations

The literature on peer relations of Chinese children is limited and fragmented, although some important research in this domain has emerged in the past few years. Domino & Hannah (1987) examined parallels between cultural value systems and the content of children's stories. They compared the themes of stories told by Chinese and American children between 11 and 13 years of age. The researchers provided story stems that referred to rule-breaking behavior. It was found that Chinese children tended to be more socially oriented than their American counterparts. The Chinese children's stories focused on peer pressure, shame and group unity to correct deviant behavior. Furthermore, Chinese stories tended to include more authority figures, such as police and adults, than American stories. Consistent with Taoist principles, Chinese children emphasized greater moral and ethical conduct than their American peers. Thus, Chinese children seem to internalize the expectations of adult society with regard to their peer relations.

Chu (1979) explored the difference between Chinese and American second-graders on dimensions of conformity and imitation. Using a series of ambiguous perceptual tasks, Chu (1979) found that Chinese children were more conforming and more socially dependent than American children. In particular, Chinese children were more likely to imitate a socially popular and high-achieving child than their American counterparts. These findings may reflect the mutually interdependent nature of Chinese society and the traditional deference to authority figures.

Orlick, Zhou & Partington (1990) conducted an observational study of cooperation and conflict among 5-year-olds in China and Canada. Eighty-five percent of the behaviors of Chinese children were classified as co-operative. Chinese kindergartners engaged in many more helping and sharing activities than Canadian children of the same age. In sharp contrast, 78% of the behaviors of Canadian children involved conflict. Orlick, Zhou & Partington (1990) attributed the findings to differences in socialization processes in Canada and China. In particular, Chinese kindergartners engaged in more helping and sharing activities than was evident in Canadian settings.

Another study focusing on kindergarten children in Canada and China is that of Chen & Rubin (1992). Using self-report scales and sociometric measures, they found that Chinese children were less accepting of one another than their Canadian peers. In some respects, these are surprising findings, given the collectivist nature of Chinese society. However, Chen & Rubin (1992) suggested that Chinese children may be less accepting and prosocial because they tend to form small well defined "cliques".

There were also many similarities between the two cultures. Children's peer acceptance in both the Chinese and Canadian samples was positively correlated with children's ability to produce numerous alternative problem-solving strategies, with the quality of parental relationship, and with the socio-economic status of the parents. In another study, Chen, Rubin & Li (1994) explored in greater depth the social behaviors that were correlates of peer acceptance and rejection among 7–10-year old Chinese children. Consistent with studies of Western cultures, they found that sociable and prosocial behavior was positively related to social adjustment, while aggressive behavior was positively associated with maladjustment in Chinese children.

Chen, Rubin & Sun (1992) found that, whereas shy and sensitive Canadian children (aged 7–9 years) were likely to be rejected by their peers, among 7–10-year old Chinese children shyness and sensitivity were positively correlated with peer acceptance. Chen, Rubin & Li (1994) found that shyness-sensitivity in 8- and 10-year old Chinese children was positively and concurrently related not only to peer acceptance but also to teacher-assessed competence, leadership and academic achievement. However, by the age of 12, shyness-sensitivity was positively correlated with peer rejection.

Taken together, these findings suggest that, during early and middle childhood at least, there are cultural differences in the meanings assigned to certain social behaviors. It is difficult to determine the specific cultural factors contributing to these differences. Chen, Rubin & Li (1994) suggest that shy-inhibited 8- and 10-year-olds may be perceived by their peers as soft-spoken, well mannered and achieving in academic subjects. In the Chinese culture, these characteristics are seen as being virtues. However, by the age of 12, Chinese children are faced with different expectations. For example, high-school selection procedures in China place high levels of academic and achievement pressure on the 11–13 age group (Dong, Yang & Ollendick, 1994). The educational system may reflect the cultural expectation that children attain substantially more independence, responsibility and control by late childhood. Moreover, Chen, Rubin & Li (1994) suggest that successful social interaction requires greater degrees of assertiveness and interpersonal maturity in older children. While these expectations are also found in Western cultures, differences in the shyness-sensitivity dimension raises the possibility that there is a later age for the developmental shift in the Chinese sample. Therefore, by the age of 12, Chinese children are expected to function with greater autonomy in the fulfilment of culturally defined goals. This has broader implications for cross-cultural research on children's peer relations. The effects of collectivism/individualism may be more evident at particular ages or stages, and may be reflected in ages at which important transitions in the expectations of groups or individuals take place. This can only be confirmed in a systematic way by researchers who use cross-sectional and cohort sequential designs.

Ho & Chiu (1994) speculate that, in a changing China, the expectations for collectivistic behaviors may be required more consistently in relationships based on blood and marriage; although the expectations for collectivism in other relationships have by no means been abandoned. As Chinese society changes and more voluntary and instrumental relationships gain prominence (Ho & Chiu, 1994), the nature of Chinese collectivism may be changing. Hopefully, researchers will capture these changes in their longitudinal studies.

Some changes in the traditional pattern of collectivism may also emerge as result of the current metamorphosis of China's economic system, in which private enterprise is a growing feature. This places a premium on individual initiative and individual educational attainment. Chinese people are well known for the prominence of educational attainment in their hierarchy of values (Stevenson et al., 1991). Sociometric studies in the USA have revealed that elementary school children of the majority Anglo-American culture assign high social status to peers who do well in academic subjects (see Coie, 1985). This respect for academic achievement may be even more evident in China and among overseas Chinese. The intensity of the emphasis on academic prowess by the Chinese indicates that failure to consider its impact on social relations may lead to a very incomplete picture of Chinese peer relations. Udvari et al. (1995) studied the influence of various types of competitiveness and competition domains on children's evaluations of their peers' social status. Their study was conducted in a Toronto elementary school with a large East-Asian enrollment. In the sociometric choice nominations made *by* Chinese youngsters (i.e., nominations by Chinese pupils of all their classmates), children who were competitive *in academic tasks* were well liked, whereas children who were competitive in *physical or athletic activities* were disliked. This was very different from the data obtained from pupils who were not of Asian origin. In the non-Asians' nominations, pupils who were competitive in athletic pursuits were chosen more frequently as work or play partners. Competition in the academic domain was unrelated to peer acceptance. These important distinctions would not have emerged if Udvari and his colleagues had failed to consider the East Asian origin of a substantial part of their Canadian sample, and the potential importance of Chinese values to these participants.

Peer Relations in the Shadow of the Italian Family

The study of children's peer relations in Italy is of interest for reasons diametrically opposite to those that might lead the scholar to peruse the literature on children's social interaction in China and other East Asian countries. In sharp contrast to China, the personal identity of Italians is not intertwined with a sense of belonging to a larger collective unit. It has been well documented that there are strong cultural rules for interpersonal relationships in Italy, but it is abundantly clear that there is one set of rules for the family, clan or immediate neighbourhood and another for less proximate relationships (Banfield, 1963; Lanaro, 1992). From all available sources, conflict occurs regularly within the interpersonal relationships of Italian adults and children both inside and outside their families (Argyle et al., 1986; Genta et al., 1996). Accordingly, Italians should have relatively little need to suppress the expression of anger in relationships, and little worry about loss of face in the presence of a stranger or authority figure as a result of such expression.

Studies conducted in small Italian towns have documented the importance of the extended family to Italians (Banfield, 1963; Lanaro, 1992). Young & Ferguson (1981) found that, in Calabria, many parents regarded peer relations as an unnecessary distraction for their adolescent sons; responses of this type were unknown, however, among parents of Calabrian origin living in Rome or Boston. While Italy has undergone marked economic progress and urbanization since the Second World War, it is commonly held that the primary loyalty to one's extended family, clan or immediate neighbours is still a core feature of the Italian value structure (Keefe, 1977; Moss, 1981; New, 1988; Paci, 1982; Saraceno, 1981; Siebert, 1984). Thus, there is an interesting difference between Italy and the English-speaking countries in that children's peer relations seem to be much less of a priority for Italian families than for those in English-speaking countries.

Argyle et al. (1986) found that Italian adults were quite flexible in their expectations for interpersonal relationships with non-kin. As already mentioned, there was no sharp rule against the expression of conflict. Respondents in the UK and Hong Kong had clearly defined rules for behavior within relationships, but adults in Italy indicated fewer strict rules for relationships, and were inconsistent among themselves about what rules there were. Argyle and his colleagues discuss this phenomenon as an Italian ambivalence towards interpersonal relationships, but one could easily interpret it in a more positive light as a manifestation of *flexibility*. Perhaps the combination of this flexibility, the tolerance for conflict and the lesser investment in peer relations combine to explain Schneider & Fonzi's (1995) finding that a higher proportion of friendships remained intact over a school year among Italian 8-year-olds than among English-speaking Canadian boys and girls of the same age.

If ambivalence—or flexibility—extends to children's peer relations in larger groups, one might expect weak and inconsistent findings regarding the correlates of children's peer acceptance among Italian children. If the rules for children's behavior in peer contacts are as flexible as those for adult non-kin relationships appear to be, then perhaps no specific behavior should lead to rejection by the majority of a child's peers. One might also speculate that if conflict is a normal and expected feature of relationships, there would be relatively little reason for Italian children to reject classmates who are aggressive.

Relevant data are available from major urban settings regarding the behavioral correlates of peer status in Italian preschools (Fonzi, Tomada & Ciucci, 1994) and Grade-2 classrooms (Attili, Vermigli & Schneider, in press). These studies were conducted with large samples, using measures very similar to those used in most American studies. The results indicate that both the pattern and strength of the behavioral correlates of peer acceptance in Italy are very similar to those of most other countries, with correlations every bit as strong as those found in studies conducted in North America with both preschoolers and elementary school-age children. These data, combined with those from other countries, help establish that many aspects of peer acceptance in children's groups are more or less invariate across cultures, despite plausible reasons for cross-cultural differences. Aggressive/disruptive behavior is associated with rejection by peers, prosocial behavior is linked with their acceptance. Italian and North American data, among others, indicate that social withdrawal is also a correlate of rejection in the elementary school years. This does not apply to Chinese youngsters, as noted earlier, but the implications of withdrawal seem to change in China from preadolescence on. Whiting & Edwards (1988) emphasize the value of research that demonstrates *similarities* in social behavior in cultures that have little contact with each other. Such similarities may help us learn about "scripts" that children follow universally in relating to others at various stages of development. The growing cross-cultural literature on patterns of peer acceptance and rejection may eventually be more useful in this way than in underscoring any cross-cultural differences that emerge from disparities among the features of various cultures.

CULTURES IN CONTACT

The examples of China and Italy are useful in understanding the interplay between the economic and social structure of a society and the peer relations of its children. The second part of this chapter is devoted to the peer relations of children of different cultural origin within a larger heterogeneous culture.

Indigenous Peoples in North America

The indigenous peoples of North America, more than most other groups, have undergone rapid social, economic and political upheaval. As recently as 200 years ago, the indigenous peoples of North America lived free from European involvement, and adhered to their own values and social structure. Today, we are shocked by disturbing statistics about high rates of suicide (Cooper et al., 1992), drug abuse (e.g., Swaim et al., 1993) and alcohol abuse (Beauvais, 1992). The low rates of social interaction observed among aboriginal children and their lack of assertiveness can be interpreted in several ways. They may be a feature of children's lives in these cultures, which is only problematic when interpreted according to the majority culture's view that it is healthy for children to interact socially with both peers and adults. However, it is also possible to interpret their reticent ways in large groups as a symptom of more general social malaise. In any event, this mode of relating may serve as a handicap in transactions with members of the dominant culture.

It is difficult to identify a cohesive value system common to the aboriginal people of North America because of the sheer number of distinct groups within that classification, each of which adheres to its own specific values and beliefs. However, there are some common aboriginal values that can help provide a framework for viewing peer relations among the indigenous peoples. Many aboriginal people believe that there exists an Almighty, a supernatural spirit, whose form can be perceived in the life-power and light of the sun or the strength and fertility of the earth. This spirit, which is conceptualized differently by the various groups, is omnipotent. Maintaining a positive relationship with it is critical. According to Hay (1977), the Ojibwa of Wisconsin value emotional restraint, especially with regard to anger, for fear that the *pawaganak*, or supernatural beings, will look unfavourably upon them if they express themselves. They believe that the expression of anger can result in the imposition of death or illness by the supernatural beings. Another core belief of the aboriginal groups is that animals and plants are not very different from humans, since all are dependent on the life-giving powers and the spirits. Therefore, all should be respected and not dominated. Harmony with the land and with each other, tolerance and non-competitiveness are predominant values. The kinship structure is more egalitarian than in Euro-American families, with clear expectations for kinship, loyalty and cooperation (Watson, 1989). Therefore one could expect aboriginal children to be more altruistic and cooperative than their Euro-American counterparts.

The economic activities common among traditional aboriginal groups also have implications for peer relations. Some aboriginals engage in hunting and gathering in areas of limited food resources and low population density. Berry & Annis (1974) argue that in general, this pattern may result in less sociocultural stratification and more emphasis on self-reliance and independence. Other aboriginals live where food resources are more abundant and engage in agriculture, which tends to result in more stratification, with more emphasis on obedience, compliance and responsibility (Berry & Annis, 1974).

These traditional aboriginal values interact almost everywhere with those of the surrounding majority culture. Contemporary aboriginal populations are under pressure to alter their beliefs to accommodate the values of Euro-Americans and Euro-Canadians. For many Native Americans, the incongruities between the traditional value system and the highly individualistic values of the majority culture have been costly. Although it is possible to draw parallels between many of these traditional beliefs and the social reticence known to characterize aboriginal children, this should not be considered the only explanation. Kleinfeld (1973) found that Inuit and Indian children in Alaskan villages felt that they were better off being silent because they believed that, if they spoke, white classmates and teachers would laugh at them.

Values in the Interpersonal Domain

Powless & Elliot (1993) conducted a study of the social skills of aboriginal preschoolers. They compared 50 preschool children from the Oneida Reservation near Green Bay, Wisconsin, to 50 Caucasian preschoolers from Madison, Wisconsin. The Native American preschoolers and the Caucasian preschoolers were matched for gender and age. The researchers were interested in the frequency of utilization of social skills, as defined by the Social Skills Rating System (SSRS) and as measured by parent and teacher ratings using the SSRS. Five out of six of the teachers of the Native American preschoolers were Native American and all 10 of the preschool teachers of Caucasian children were Caucasian. The SSRS measures three positive aspects of social behavior (cooperation, assertion and self-control) and one domain of problem behavior (interfering behavior). A comparison of the reports of the parents and teachers of the two groups indicated that the Native American children were reported to have exhibited those social skills that the SSRS identified as positive less frequently than were Caucasian preschoolers. The difference was significant for all three positive scales; however, the largest difference between Caucasian preschoolers and Native American preschoolers was in the assertion domain, according to both teacher and parent ratings. There was no significant difference between the groups for the Interfering Behavior subscale. Although generalization of these findings could be problematic because the study was conducted close to a major American city, the passiveness of aboriginal children has been corroborated by many other researchers in several parts of the continent. With regard to assertive behavior, Philips (1972) studied the use of speech in the classroom by Native Americans and found that verbally-initiating responses depended greatly upon the participant structure of the activity. In general, being verbally assertive is not as highly valued a social skill among Native Americans as it is among Caucasian Americans. Non-verbal differences in communication style were reported by Greenbaum (1985), who videotaped the classroom interactions of Choctaw Indians and Anglo-Europeans in Florida. The aboriginal pupils spoke less often, used shorter utterances, and gazed more often at their peers while the teacher was talking.

The results obtained by Powless & Elliott might be misinterpreted if one assumed that more frequent social interaction in public is necessarily an indication of social competence. Asher, Markell & Hymel (1981) have addressed this issue, arguing that low rates of interaction alone are not enough to conclude that children are lacking in social competence. It is important to look not only at the quantity of social interactions, but also at their quality. These remarks may apply to cultural as well as individual differences.

Acceptance by the peer group may be less important to aboriginal children than their Euro-American counterparts. Withycombe (1973) studied the peer acceptance and self-concept of Paiute Indians in Arizona and their non-aboriginal classmates. She found that popularity was more highly valued in the Anglo-American group, although there was a significant correlation between social status and self-concept in the aboriginal group as well. Furthermore, aboriginal children were relatively inaccurate in estimating their own social status among their classmates. It is not surprising that children who are less concerned about social status are less proficient at its evaluation. As discussed above, the indigenous children's lower priorities for social competence may reflect the values of their cultures, and may be troublesome only for outsiders. However, social rejection must cause some distress to the aboriginal children themselves because social status is related to the children's self-concepts to some degree.

Attributes of Social Power

Weisfeld, Weisfeld & Callaghan (1984) examined peer- and self-appraisals of 67 Hopi and 144 Afro-American school children. These two groups were selected specifically because of their cultural differences. The Hopi, from north-east Arizona, are noted for their non-violence and punishment of violent or aggressive behavior. In fact, their full name means "the little people of peace" (p. 69). As of 1984, there were approximately 6000 Hopi. They are a matrilineal culture; land and homes are owned by the women and passed down from mothers to daughters. They are also a collectivistic culture, with little value being placed on individual achievements and interests. Peacefulness and egalitarianism are Hopi ideals, and decisions are usually based on unanimous consent. In contrast, the Afro-American children in the study were from a Chicago private school. Because large American cities such as Chicago are known for high rates of crime and violence, it can be assumed that this group was more tolerant of violent or aggressive behavior than the Hopi group.

Weisfeld, Weisfeld & Callaghan noted significant differences in the spontaneous social play of the two groups. The Afro-American children played in sex-segregated groups, with the boys playing softball and football and the girls jumping rope. In contrast, the Hopi boys and girls played a modified version of basketball together. Instead of dividing up into two teams to compete against one another, the object was to play as one team and get as many baskets as possible. There were also marked differences in the rate of conflict observed. The Afro-American children fought at a rate of once per hour per 70 individuals. In contrast, the Hopi children engaged in only one act of aggression in all the many hours of observations. This was a shoving match between two boys, which was quickly broken up by the other Hopi children. Unfortunately, the researchers did not publish any gender-specific information, neither did they indicate which behaviors constituted a fight in their coding system.

This study also incorporated a peer-report measure in which children were asked to nominate the members of their classes who corresponded best to certain characteristics. Respondents were permitted to nominate themselves (this is quite common, but not always permitted in research of this type). The self-nominations can be seen as an indication of either the respondents' self-concept or their willingness to ascribe positive or negative characteristics to themselves; the latter may reflect cultural norms. The Hopi children chose themselves infrequently and the Afro-Americans chose themselves very frequently on items such as who is the best athlete, best looking, the smartest, and the nicest person in the class. According to Weisfeld, Weisfeld & Callaghan, as Hopi children grow older, they become more self-effacing. The researchers propose that a possible explanation for the Hopis' greater modesty rests with the collectivist nature of the Hopi culture. It could become a liability in situations where the Hopi interact with members of the majority culture that rewards assertion.

The Weisfeld, Weisfeld & Callaghan (1984) study also sheds some light on the difficulty of conducting cross-cultural studies on peer relations as a result of the differences in meaning a word or phrase may have from one culture to another. In a post-questionnaire conversations with the subjects, it was discovered that the notion of acting grown-up meant very different things to the two populations. The Hopi children understood it to mean performing useful labor, whereas African-American participants may have understood it to mean wearing make-up, using profanity and insulting people. Bennett & Berry (1992) explored the Native American meaning of the word competence among a group of Native Americans from Big Trout Lake, Ontario. They discovered that the meaning of competence for this particular native group was highly related to notions of respect, paying attention and listening. Although this research did not involve a comparison group, we doubt that a Caucasian or Afro-American population would generate similar associations. Semantic differences need to be explored fully before one assumes that a specific question or item has a similar meaning across different cultures. This has not been done in many if not most studies. Therefore, there may be similar problems in many other studies that remain undetected and unreported.

Cooperation and Competition

Miller & Thomas (1972) conducted a study of the cooperative and competitive behaviors of native and non-native school children ranging in age from 7 to 10 years. The researchers compared 48 Blackfoot natives in Alberta, Canada, to 48 non-natives; each group comprised equal numbers of boys and girls. Cooperative and competitive behaviors were measured using the Madsen Cooperation Board, an 18-inch-square board with eyelets in the corners. Cords are strung through the eyelets and converge in the middle, attached to a pen. A piece of paper is placed on the board underneath the pen. On the paper are four small circles. The object is to pass the pen through the circles. The four players are most successful if they cooperatively move the pen. Two different reinforcement conditions were studied. On the first three trials players were reinforced as a group (group reward condition). That is, the subjects received one candy each as soon as the pen passed through all four circles. On trials 4–6, players were individually rewarded (individual reward condition). A candy was given to a player as soon as the pen passed through his/her own circle. The native youngsters, especially the boys, worked cooperatively even when it was not in their interest to do so, illustrating very clearly the survival of the Native American collectivistic orientation of the children in this group.

In an extensive field study, Condon (1990) investigated the impact rapid social change has had upon adolescent aggression and conflict management in an Inuit community. Located on the western coast of Victoria Island in Canada, Holman Island is populated primarily by descendants of the Copper Inuit. During three separate field trips, Condon used a combination of research techniques, including structured and unstructured interviews, participant observations and the investigation of pertinent police and court records. During his first field trip to Holman in 1983, children and adolescents comprised 55% of the island's population of approximately 340 people. Based on his study, Condon proposed a model of how changes in social, economic and demographic structures have affected adolescent peer relations. According to Condon, population concentration, population growth, increased financial security and exposure to Euro-Canadian values through schooling, radio and television have resulted in a significant delay in social maturity and a striking increase in adolescent autonomy. As a result of these two factors, peer relations among Holman adolescents have changed markedly. Prior to contact with whites, indigenous peoples relied heavily on intergenerational and family relationships as mechanisms of socialization. However, according to Condon, the significance of these mechanisms has been substantially reduced and the importance of peers as a socializing factor has increased. When the adolescents of Holman are not in school, they are "hanging out" with their peers, usually passing their time in economically non-productive activities. Parental contact has diminished. The peer group has become an important context for reinforcement and thus socialization. Condon documents the rise during the last 10 years of social problems such as vandalism, spousal abuse and increased conflict, and points to alcohol abuse as the culprit. Of the 20 incidents of alcohol-related violence recorded during the third field study, 14 of them were committed by teenagers and young adults under the age of 30. Condon suggests that alcohol abuse, drug use, crime and suicide are responses to frustration resulting from promised job satisfaction and financial well-being that never materializes. He notes that these activities are increasing in frequency as frustration grows.

Most studies indicate that Native American children are cooperative and collectivistic, but more attention needs to be directed at determining whether these characteristics have persisted despite the rapid changes in the social world of the indigenous peoples. One might also wonder whether their recent group assertiveness in demanding adjudication of land claims, their own judicial system, etc., may be reflected eventually in more assertiveness at the individual level. There are some indications that this kind of change is already under way. Crago, Annahatak & Ningiuruvik (1993) conducted a longitudinal study of the interactions of children and their caretakers in the Kangirsuk and Quaqtaq Inuit communities of Northern Quebec. They found that older women were quite traditional in their expectations for children and in their parenting. Younger mothers were unaware of some traditional customs, and disdainful of others. The younger mothers engaged their children in question-and-answer routines in the hope that their children would not be withdrawn and unexpressive in school.

Inter-ethnic and Inter-racial Friendship

The demise of racial segregation in American schools and the entrance of non-traditional immigrants to urban North American schools have aroused concern about relations among various ethnic and racial groups. Some studies in this area have investigated context variables such as teacher expectations, school climate or streaming by academic ability. Others have dealt with subject variables such as racism, prejudice, self-identity and self-esteem, or with relationship variables, such as inter-ethnic or inter-racial friendship. It is important to clarify some of the terminology used in this area, which can be misunderstood very easily. Prejudice refers to a stable pattern of evaluating members of another ethnic group in a negative way and behaving in a negative way toward them (Aboud, 1988). Prejudice depends on being able to identify oneself as a member of one's own ethnic group, which even 4- and 5-year olds can do. Aboud (1988) reviews the theoretical perspectives on the origins of children's prejudice. According to social reflection theories, children become prejudiced because they learn that different ethnic groups are valued differently in society as a whole, or by their parents in particular. Other, more psychodynamic, approaches contend that prejudice emerges in situations where parents or other authority figures punish any attempt by the child at expressing hostility. Members of lower-status ethnic groups become the targets of the displaced hostility. In cognitive-developmental theories, prejudice can be seen as a reflection of the egocentrism of the young child.

Aboud (1988) provides a useful compendium of research on prejudice, including studies that are useful in validating the theories discussed in the preceding paragraph. The following section pertains to studies on the *extent* and *quality* of the friendships between members of differing racial and cultural groups. As will be discussed later, the failure to form friendships outside one's own group may or may not be an indication of prejudice, since it may or may not relate to the attribution of negative characteristics to members of other groups and may or may not entail behaving in a negative way toward them. This research is interesting because it helps portray the extent of the meaningful interpersonal relationships between members of different cultural groups in multicultural societies where there is ample opportunity for such relationships to develop. Studies in this area are summarized in Tables 5.1–5.3.

Subject Characteristics

Children come into contact with others who may differ from them in a variety of characteristics, such as race/ethnicity, gender and grade/age. These variables are often used as a basis for choice or rejection of friends. Given that similarity is a basis for interpersonal attraction (Hallinan & Williams, 1987), many authors theorized that children will overwhelmingly choose friends from their own ethnic or racial group. This expectation has been borne out for students in the majority group in many of the studies listed in Table 5.1 (Braha & Rutter, 1980; Clark &

Table 5.1 Studies investigating subject characteristics in cross-ethnic/cross-race friendship

Study and location	N	Race/Ethnicity		Age/Grade (y) (Gr.)	Measure of friendship
Studies conducted primarily with younger subjects (aged 4–11)					
Cross-sectional studies					
Durojaiye (1969) UK	[1]312	203 109	White Black	8–11 y	Sociometric
Braha & Rutter (1980) UK	120	42 78	White Non-white	4–10 y	Sociometric
Davey & Mullin (1982) UK	3953	2584 731 638	White West Indian Asian	7–10 y	Sociometric
Denscombe (1983) UK	107	40 18 38 8 2 1	White Sikh Hindu Muslim West Indian Mixed	7–11 y	Sociometric
Howes & Wu (1990) USA	210	*128 *33 *37 *12	Euro-American Spanish-American Afro-American Asian-American	Kindergarten & Gr. 3	Sociometric Observation
Longitudinal studies (follow-up information in parentheses)					
Singleton & Asher (1979) USA	[2]227 (154)	48(38) 179(116)	Black White	Gr. 3 (6)	Sociometric
Tuma & Hallinan (1979) USA	*445		Black Non-Black	Gr. 4–6 (to end of school year)	Sociometric
Denscombe et al., 1986 UK	54(50)	27 11 12 3 1	White Hindu Sikh Muslim Buddhist	7–11 y (+6 months)	Sociometric Observation
Studies conducted primarily with older subjects (aged 7–20)					
Cross-sectional studies					
Lundberg & Dickson (1952) USA	1360		Jewish Non-Jewish White Japanese Negro Chinese	13–20 y	Sociometric

Table 5.1 (*continued*)

Study and location	N	Race/Ethnicity		Age/Grade (y) (Gr.)	Measure of friendship
St. John (1964) USA	*929	166 *763	Black White	High school Juniors	Sociometric
Rowley (1968) UK	1747	1109 358 245 35	British Indian West Indian European	7–15 y	Sociometric
Jelinek & Brittan (1975) UK	4300	2093 469 133 816 256 221 95 217	British Indian Pakistani West Indian Kenyan Asian Cypriot Italian Other	8–14+ y	Sociometric
Ziegler (1980) Canada	153	51 51 51	Anglo Chinese Italian	12–15 y	Observation
Clark & Ayers (1988, 1992) USA	136	44 92	Non-White White	Gr. 7–8	Sociometric
DuBois & Hirsch (1990) USA	292	216 76	White Black	Gr. 7–9	Sociometric
Longitudinal studies (follow-up information in parentheses)					
Zisman & Wilson (1992) USA	208	81 89 n/a n/a n/a	Black White Hispanic Asian Other	Gr. 8 (9)	Observation

Sample sizes were based on the number of subjects actually completing the sociometric measures, i.e. excluding missing data where reported.
*Estimates based on information in the original articles where precise subject information was not reported.
[1] A leadership substudy was carried out with 83 white and 55 black students, 10–11 years old. All subjects were retested 6 weeks later to check the accuracy of their responses.
[2] An additional group of 153 white and 52 black Grade 3 students were used in the last year of the study for time-lag comparison purposes.

Table 5.2 Studies investigating contextual characteristics in relation to cross-group friendship

Study and location	N	Race/Ethnicity	Age/Grade (y) (Gr.)	Measure of friendship
Studies conducted primarily with younger subjects (grades 4–7)				
Longitudinal studies				
Hallinan (1982) USA	*482	*239 Black *243 White	Gr. 4–7 (to end of school year)	Sociometric
[1]Hallinan & Sorensen (1985); Hallinan & Smith (1985); Hallinan & Teixeira (1987a, 1987b); Hallinan & Williams (1987) USA	1477	658 Black 697 White 75 Asian 47 Chicano	Gr. 4–7 (to end of school year)	Sociometric
Studies conducted primarily with older subjects (Grade 6 to high school seniors)				
Cross-sectional studies				
Damico & Sparks (1986) USA	677	White Black	Gr. 6–8	Student report of verbal interaction
Hallinan & Williams (1989) USA	[2]58 000	Black White	High school sophomores & seniors	Sociometric
Eshel & Kurman (1990) Israel	613	296 Ashkenazi Jewish 317 Sephardi Jewish	Gr. 6–8	Sociometric
Longitudinal studies				
Schofield & Sagar (1977) USA	*800	Black White	Gr. 7–8 (+5 months)	Observation

Sample sizes were based on the number of subjects actually completing the sociometric measures, i.e. excluding missing data where reported.
* Estimates based on information in the original articles where precise subject information was not reported.
[1] This group of studies focused on a subset of the 1477 students from a longitudinal study. In some of the studies the Asian and Chicano students were excluded.
[2] Only a subsample of the 58 000 students was used in the analyses.

Ayers, 1992; Denscombe et al., 1986; Durojaiye, 1969; Howes & Wu, 1990; Rowley 1968) . In all of the preceding studies, majority students showed a higher preference for friends from their own ethnic or racial group than did minority students. In contrast, St. John (1964), Jelinek & Brittan (1975) and Hallinan

Table 5.3 Studies investigating the effects of cooperative learning groups on cross-group friendship

Study and location	N	Race/Ethnicity	Age/Grade (y) (Gr.)	Measure of friendship
Weigel, Wiser & Cook (1975) USA	324	231 White 54 Black 39 Mexican-American	Gr. 7 & 10	Sociometric
Slavin (1979) USA	294	170 White 124 Black	Gr. 7–8	Sociometric
Hansell & Slavin (1981) USA	402	245 White 157 Black	Gr. 7–8	Sociometric
Ziegler (1981) Canada	146	64 Anglo-Canadian 21 Italian-Canadian 18 Chinese-Canadian 12 Greek-Canadian 11 West Indian-Canadian 20 Other	Gr. 5–6	Sociometric
Hansell (1984) USA	¹317	168 White 149 Black	Gr. 5–6	Sociometric

Sample sizes were based on the number of subjects actually completing the sociometric measures, i.e. excluding missing data where reported.
¹ Sixteen subjects did not complete the post-test sociometric questionnaire.

(1982) all found in-group preference to be highest in minority group students. There is no apparent reason why in some studies the majority group was more ethnocentric and in other studies the minority groups were more ethnocentric. Nevertheless, the incidence of cross-race or cross-ethnic friendship choice was much lower than would be expected if race or ethnicity were not a determining factor. Although the relative rarity of cross-ethnic/cross-race friendship can be seen as a reflection of ethnic/racial prejudice in children, many researchers do not see it that way, and do not regard it as inherently problematic (e.g., Denscombe et al., 1986).

Age/Grade

Multiple age groups participated in most of the studies in Table 5.1. Rowley (1968) found a slight increase, while Hallinan & Teixeira (1987a) and Jelinek & Brittan (1975) found a significant increase in own-group preference with increasing age. Lundberg & Dickson (1952) found an increase in own-group preference with age only for the majority group, while Hallinan & Teixeira (1987b) found this for the minority group. In contrast, Braha & Rutter (1980), Davey & Mullin (1982) and Denscombe et al. (1986) found no consistent age effect on friendship choice across racial and ethnic lines. Although the findings of the various studies were not consistent, the trend was in the expected direction, with increasing ethnocentricity with increasing age. The high degree of own-group preference, even in very young children (Braha & Rutter, 1980; Jelinek & Brittan, 1975; Rowley, 1968), has surprised many researchers.

Gender

Hallinan & Williams (1989) postulated that ". . . the pervasiveness of the negative effect of gender on youth's friendships makes it likely that it transcends race and other background characteristics" (p. 68). Cross-gender friendship in general is rare during the elementary school years, but it does occur. The results summarized in Table 5.1 concerning the effect of gender on cross-race friendship choice revealed inconsistent gender effects and a gender × race interaction. Friendships that crossed racial/ethnic barriers were usually same-gender (Hallinan & Teixeira, 1987a, 1987b). Cross-gender friendships were usually from the choosing subject's own ethnic group (Jelinek & Brittan, 1975). Some studies showed less ethnocentrism in males than in females (Lundberg & Dickson, 1952; Schofield & Sagar, 1977) while others showed more male ethnocentrism (Denscombe et al., 1986). Hallinan & Teixeira (1987a, 1987b) found that black females had more cross-race friends than black males while white males had more cross-race friends than white females, though neither finding was statistically significant. St. John (1964) and Howes & Wu (1990), unlike the others, found no major gender differences in inter-racial friendship choices. These studies led to the tentative conclusion that cross-sex, cross-race friendships are fairly rare and that white females are the least likely to form friendships with members of other races (Hallinan & Teixeira, 1987b).

Contextual Characteristics

Some sociologists, social psychologists and school administrators believe that simply placing members of different races or ethnic groups in the same school or class will lead to cross-ethnic/cross-race acceptance and friendship formation (Hallinan & Teixeira, 1987a). Their beliefs have not always been confirmed and sometimes mere proximity has served only to increase tension and hostility (Amir, 1969). The contextual characteristics of the schools, such as ability grouping, can act as a barrier to inter-ethnic/inter-racial friendships by limiting the opportunities for different ethnic/racial groups to interact with each other. The studies in Table 5.2 examined school organizational variables that may influence cross-ethnic/cross-race friendship choice, acceptance, communication and aggregation.

The effect of the racial composition of the classroom or school on friendship choice varies considerably. Hallinan & Smith (1985) found that the numerical minority group had more cross-race friendships than the majority group. Hallinan & Teixeira (1987b) found that racial composition had no effect on the cross-race friendships of blacks but that whites were more likely to choose a black classmate as best friend the more blacks there were in the classroom.

Denscombe (1983) found that whites showed a higher degree of in-group preference in a school with a higher ratio of minorities to whites than they did in other schools.

Ability Grouping

Being in the same ability group for instruction had a significant positive effect on whites' choice of blacks in both studies by Hallinan & Teixeira (1987a, 1987b). One of their reports indicates a slight negative effect on blacks' choice of whites (Hallinan & Teixeira, 1987a), while the other indicates no significant effect on the cross-race friendships of blacks (Hallinan & Teixeira, 1987b). Damico & Sparks (1986) found that whites talked with significantly greater frequency to blacks in the school without ability grouping than in the school where ability grouping was employed. Grouping blacks and whites together for instruction affected white students' inter-racial friendships more than it did that of black students. Hallinan & Teixeira (1987b) suggested that structural constraints on cross-race friendships influence whites more than blacks.

Classroom Climate

In classes in which marks were emphasized, whites were significantly less likely to choose blacks as friends but there was no effect on blacks' choice of whites (Hallinan & Teixeira, 1987b). Where there was an emphasis on basic skills and mastery of the curriculum, whites were less likely to choose blacks but blacks were more likely to choose whites (Hallinan & Teixeira, 1987b). When student initiative and enjoyment of learning were stressed, blacks were more likely to choose whites as best friend and there was a weak positive effect on the inter-racial choice of whites (Hallinan & Teixeira 1987b). The less competitive the classroom was academically, the more likely blacks were to choose whites as best friends. Hallinan & Williams (1987) concluded that the inter-racial friendships of blacks displayed greater responsiveness than those of whites to classroom climates that influence the status hierarchy.

Cooperative Learning

According to Allport (1954), "equal status contact between majority and minority groups in the pursuit of common goals" (p. 281) is a prerequisite for mutual acceptance. Table 5.3 lists studies on the effects of cooperative learning groups on inter-ethnic/inter-racial friendship choice. These groups contained a mixture of ethnic/racial groups and academic abilities. Students were encouraged to tutor and quiz each other in order to help each other learn the material. They were rewarded as a group for their achievement. All students in the group had an equal chance of contributing points to the group's score (Slavin, 1979). Slavin (1979) found a statistically significant effect for cooperative learning in terms of both the number and proportion of cross-race friends chosen. Ziegler (1981) found a significant increase in casual cross-ethnic friendship for the cooperative learning group in comparison to the control group, which received regular classroom instruction. No effect of the treatment on close other-race friendships was evidenced until 10 weeks after the experiment ended. Cooperative groups had positive effects on students' interaction with others of a different race.

It is fairly clear from the studies reviewed that children are quite ethnocentric in their choice of friends. This ethnocentrism tends to increase with age. The pattern of in-group preference exists regardless of the publication date of the study, country and division of groups by ethnicity or race. Whether the relatively low incidence of cross-race and cross-ethnic friendship is undesirable depends on one's values and the motives behind the choices. Preference for one's ethnic or racial group does not necessarily mean a rejection of the out-group (Braha & Rutter, 1980; Denscombe, 1983). In Durojaiye's (1969) study, when children were asked why they chose the friends they did, none mentioned race as a reason for their choice. However, it is possible that the children were aware of the reasons for their choice at only at a subconscious level, or did not wish to divulge that race or ethnicity played a role in their choices. Denscombe (1983) pointed out that the existence of even a small number of friendships across ethnic lines could be interpreted as an absence of prejudice, despite the more general trend for friends to be selected within one's own group, since even these few choices would indicate children's willingness to form friendships based on personal characteristics rather than ethnicity. On the other hand, it could be argued that if personal factors were a more important determinant of choice than ethnicity, there should be more out-group friendships among children, since no one group of people has a monopoly on desirable characteristics. Whether society or schools should be disturbed by the findings depends on one's view of race/ethnic relations. Lundberg & Dickson (1952) believed that "a certain amount of ethnocentrism is a normal and necessary ingredient of all group life." and it is "therefore, not in itself necessarily to be regarded as a problem" (p. 34). Others, of course, may be alarmed by ethnic/racial exclusivity and therefore view the findings with apprehension.

In summary, it is safe to conclude that, in Western societies where subcultures interact, ethnicity or race is a very important factor in the choice of children's friendships although, as we have seen, there are a number of important variables moderating this general trend.

GENERAL CONCLUSION

As the examples presented above illustrate, many aspects of children's peer relations mirror the social, economic and spiritual characteristics of their cultural background. Important cultural differences have been found in children's cooperativeness, aggression, assertiveness and shyness, as well as some similarities. The dimension of individualism/collectivism, long considered the most important element in classifying cultures, still appears somewhat useful in describing these cross-cultural differences. However, the complex structures of nations and peoples require that we elaborate extensively on earlier conceptions of individualism and collectivism, adding qualifiers and new parameters in order to portray differences within cultures among social contexts, generations, socio-economic classes and ethnic subgroups.

In accepting these challenges, researchers will have to bring new creativity to their methods and measures. Cross-cultural research has been widely criticized for the widespread use of measures that are not culturally sensitive, samples that are small and not representative of distinctions *within* cultures, such as socio-economic status and ethnicity, failure to consider developmental differences, and over-reliance on single sources of information (see Schneider, 1993). These flaws are problematic enough if one's goal is to compare two cultures that one believes are very distinct and very homogenous. The repercussions of these shortcomings are greater if one attempts to conduct research that reflects the diversity that exists within many major cultures and the transitions that many of them are undergoing.

As societies undergo rapid change, many of the findings regarding cross-cultural differences in children's social behavior may become outdated. Within the same culture, children reaching the same age at different times may find themselves in very different family, school and peer contexts. While even cross-sectional designs are not used frequently enough in cross-cultural research, it would be very useful to see cohort-sequential designs, which would better portray both developmental differences and era effects. Given the many obstacles to conducting cross-cultural research, this is probably too much to ask. Although there have been few attempts at comparing styles of social interaction before and after rapid socio-political change, some of the profound transformations in social systems have inspired some *post hoc* studies. For example, Krappmann (1995) compared the quality of elementary-school children's friendships in West and East Berlin after the unification of that city. Goodwin (1995) discussed individual differences in self-disclosure as a function of the increased latitude for self-expression in Russia after the disintegration of the Soviet empire. There have been also been recent studies on parents' beliefs and values regarding child-rearing in China (Ruan & Matsumura, 1991), Iran (Tashakkori & Thompson, 1988) and Russia (Goodwin & Emelyanova, 1995). In each case, the research was inspired by the researcher's understanding of connections between societal change and interpersonal interactions.

While children's peer relations have been studied in many different cultures, the methods used in these studies are usually very similar, and, with very few exceptions, are adaptations of techniques developed in the USA. Without this similarity of method, cross-cultural comparisons of results would be even more complex. Furthermore, American researchers have invested the most energy in this field, and have developed the most sophisticated tools. There is no clear reason to believe that the dimensions of peer relations contained in the American instruments are not valid in other cultures, but it is irresponsible to assume they are valid without demonstrating this. One cannot rule out the possibility that aspects of peer relations considered important in some cultures are being under-represented or mismeasured in some way.

Most peer relations research in America and elsewhere has focused on large groups such as classrooms and schools. As more attention is now being devoted to relationships at the dyadic level, especially relations between friends (see Schneider, Wiener & Murphy, 1994), it will be useful in future studies to identify patterns of cultural similarity and difference in the ways in which children relate to friends. This knowledge can help refine theory with regard to the influence of culture on behavior in relationships. It may enable us to distinguish between those aspects of child development that may emerge as species-related and universal and those that are sensitive to cultural differences. There may be important practical implications as well. Collett (1971) reported a successful intervention in which Englishmen were taught to understand the social behavior patterns of Arabs. Similar interventions with children may be useful in reducing friction among the cultural groups that interact more and more in schools and neighborhoods around the globe. Knowledge about cultural dimensions of children's social behavior could also inform practitioners contemplating interventions with children of different cultural origins. For example, many standard social skills programs used in the English-speaking countries may target and attempt to modify behaviors that are regarded as socially competent in other countries or communities. Some of these programs seek to modify social withdrawal which, as we have seen, may be normative and even valued by peers and parents in East Asian societies (Kashiwagi & Azuma, 1977). Other social skills interventions focus on the control of anger. These would probably be helpful in most cultures, but could, for example, be less meaningful when implemented with Hispanic children without an understanding of the complex dynamics relating to the expression of anger in many parts of Latin America (Arce & Torres-Matrullo, 1982; Guarnacria, delaCancela & Carrillo, 1989). Educators who do not understand cultural norms for children's social behavior may misinterpret the intentions of their pupils and make erroneous inferences about their adjustment. Such misinterpretations are often implicated in portrayals of the alienation of aboriginal children in American schools (e.g. Gallimore, Boggs & Jordan, 1974). Providing educators with information about the cultural origins of their charges could enhance the schooling experience of all participants.

Section II

Social Psychology

Section Editor: William Ickes
University of Texas, Arlington, TX, USA

The lack of theoretical diversity in the first wave of social psychological research on personal relationships made the area an easy target for critics. The problem was not a matter of there being no theory at all, as the more misguided of the critics wanted to suggest. Rather, the problem was that a single theoretical perspective—exchange theory—seemed to dominate the work in this newly emerging area. Blau's (1964) exchange theory, the prototype of this research tradition, was an extension into the interpersonal realm of ideas that could be found in Heider's (1958) balance theory. Analogizing from the individual's need for cognitive balance and harmony, Blau focused on the need of relationship partners to achieve a mutually acceptable balance of their respective costs and rewards.

Exchange theory, begat of balance theory, itself begat equity theory (Adams, 1965; Homans, 1961, 1974; Hatfield, Walster & Berscheid, 1978), the different versions of which aspired to be more precise about the intuitive formulas people use to calculate the returns on their relational investments. Equity theory, in turn, begat interdependence theory (Kelley & Thibaut, 1978), which was premised on the assumption that not all relationships reflected a mutual desire for equity and fair exchange. Acknowledging both the diversity and complexity of personal relationships, interdependence theory assumed that the motives of relationship partners can clash as well as converge, leading to a variety of outcomes such as aggression, altruism, competition, capitulation, cooperation, intransigence, etc. (see Rusbult & Arriaga, this volume). In this manner, theory about the subjective harmony or dissonance of a single individual's attitudes, motives, values or goals was extended and transformed into theory about the intersubjective harmony or dissonance of the attitudes, motives, values or goals of relationship members.

Although the issues invoked by exchange-based theories were clearly of central importance to the study of personal relationships, all of the theories of interpersonal harmony/disharmony tended to overlook a fundamental question:

what are the origins of the conflicting (or complementary) attitudes, motives, values or goals that generate interpersonal tensions (or symbioses)? The need to answer this question provided the impetus for new theoretical approaches that focused less on the dynamics of the conflicts/symbioses that occur within relationships (i.e., how they play out, how they are resolved) than on the etiology of these conflicts/symbioses (i.e., how and why they emerge in the first place). In consequence, there are at least two major themes evident in current social psychological theory about personal relationships: (1) the traditional theme of how individual motives conflict, converge and resolve into various individual and joint outcomes within the context of interdependent relationships; and (2) the newer but yet more "precursory" theme of the origins of the personal dispositions that cause such conflicts/symbioses to arise in the first place.

Both of these themes are evident in the set of chapters that compose Section II of the second edition of the *Handbook of Personal Relationships*. The precursory theme of the origins of the dispositions that lead to conflicts or symbioses in personal relationships is developed in Kenrick & Trost's chapter on evolutionary approaches to relationships (Chapter 6), in Zeifman & Hazan's chapter on the processes underlying adult attachment formation (Chapter 7), and in Gaines & Ickes' chapter on interracial relationships (Chapter 8). The traditional theme of how individual motives conflict, converge and resolve into various individual and joint outcomes is developed from two distinctly different theoretical perspectives: the perspective of interdependence theory (Rusbult & Arriaga, Chapter 9) and the perspective of self-expansion theory (Aron & Aron, Chapter 10). This same theme is also developed from a data-analytic perspective in Gonzalez & Griffin's chapter on "the statistics of interdependence" (Chapter 11).

The evolutionary origins of the personal dispositions that lead to conflicts or symbioses in close relationships is the topic of Chapter 6. In this chapter, Kenrick & Trost apply the basic assumptions and principles of evolutionary psychology to the study of human relationships. The authors begin with the premise that cooperative human relationships are generally adaptive in helping to ensure the inclusive fitness of individuals and their kin. They are careful to qualify this generalization, however, by describing how differences in the evolutionary "payoffs" for the individuals in potential or actual relationships may underlie a range of more competitive and/or conflictive phenomena. These phenomena include jealousy, intrasexual competition, deceptive mating strategies and family violence. Kenrick & Trost conclude that "the evolutionary perspective provides a comprehensive model of relationships", one in which even apparently anomalous behaviors can be interpreted and explained.

Chapter 7, by Zeifman & Hazan, concerns the convergence of individual needs and motives across time that enables adults to develop and maintain romantic relationships. Using Bowlby's (1969, 1973, 1980) ethological attachment theory as their guiding framework, the authors outline a normative model of adult attachment formation. While acknowledging some obvious differences between infant–caregiver attachment and attachment in adult romantic pairs (e.g., attachment bonds in adult romantic partners are typically reciprocal, rather than complementary; adult attachments can serve the function of sexual reproduction), Zeifman & Hazan argue convincingly that the stages in which adult attachment occurs (attraction and flirting, falling in love, loving, life as usual) are analogous to Bowlby's four phases of infant–caregiver attachment (pre-attachment, attachment-in-the-making, clear-cut attachment, goal-corrected partnership). In particular, they suggest that the needs and emotions evoked in each stage of adult romantic attachment parallel those evoked at the corresponding stage of infant–caregiver interaction, and that the complementary fulfillment of both partners' needs at each stage enables their relationship to form, strengthen and continue.

The topic of Chapter 8 is the origins of the differences between the perspectives of "insiders" and "outsiders" on interracial relationships. In this chapter, Gaines & Ickes examine the evolutionary, perceptual-cognitive, and sociohistorical influences that combine to make the perspective of outside observers of interracial relationships different from that of the relationship members themselves. The authors argue that tension between these two perspectives takes characteristically different forms in different types of interracial relationships (i.e., male–male and female–female friendships, heterosexual and homosexual romantic relationships). It is therefore important for the members of these relationships to understand the specific tensions involved in each case so that they can anticipate and attempt to resolve them—no easy task in the face of anti-"race-mixing" mindsets that have proved to be extremely resistant to change.

Chapter 9 addresses and updates the more traditional theme in theorizing about personal relationships: the theme of how individual motives conflict, converge and resolve into various individual and joint outcomes within the context of these relationships. Rusbult & Arriaga's comprehensive review of the work on interdependence theory provides both a cogent summary of the theory itself and an informative tour of the different lines of research it has inspired. Their chapter focuses on how relationship members perceive and act within the constraints of the interdependence structures that are the elemental features of their social experience. More specifically, it examines how individual motives, features of the situation, and features of the relationship itself define interdependence structures which, as their implications are perceived, can transform the motivation of one or both partners in ways that can precipitate a wide variety of individual and joint outcomes (altruism, competition, intransigence, etc.).

The upper limit of interdependence—the blurring of the boundaries between self and partner—is the topic of Chapter 10. In this chapter, Aron & Aron outline their model of self-expansion motivation, which is based on the notion that "people seek to expand themselves" (e.g., in their physical and social influence, in their knowledge and insight, and in their sense of identity and belongingness) through their relationships with others. The authors argue that the desire for self-expansion is a fundamental motive that is expressed not only in individual exploration, competence and efficacy, as various other theorists have noted (e.g., Bandura, 1977; Deci, 1975; Gecas, 1989; White, 1959), but through participation in relationships as well. The research they describe helps to document two basic processes suggested by the self-expansion model: "first, that relationship satisfaction is increased through the association of the relationship with self-expansion and, second, that the relationship means cognitively that each partner has included the other in his or her self". The model is shown to have a special utility in accounting for certain phenomena, such as the motivation for unrequited love and the effects on the self of falling in love, which other theories have rarely addressed.

The "statistics of interdependence" is the topic of Chapter 11 by Gonzalez & Griffin. In this chapter, the authors criticize the "ritualistic mutilation of dyadic data" by generations of researchers. Because of the problems inherent in analyzing such data, researchers have for decades attempted to circumvent these problems rather than to confront them directly and—ideally—solve them. The tricks they have resorted to include "(a) averaging interdependence away by creating a sample of 'independent' dyad mean scores, (b) partialling interdependence out and thereby creating a sample of 'independent' individual scores, and (c) dropping one dyad member's scores and thus creating a truncated sample of 'independent' individual scores". Drawing on the work of earlier statisticians (e.g., Fisher, 1925; Haggard, 1958; Kenny & La Voie, 1985) for their inspiration, Gonzalez & Griffin describe an ingenious family of statistical techniques that are based on the intraclass correlation and the pairwise method for computing it. These techniques enable individual-level and dyad-level covariances to be modeled as latent variables in different types of dyadic designs. Both univariate and multivariate applications of these techniques are presented and discussed in a style that is refreshingly "user-friendly". Researchers who want to analyze their dyadic data appropriately should start by reading—or re-reading—this chapter.

The chapters in this section of the *Handbook of Personal Relationships* illustrate the two major traditions of social-psychological theory about personal relationships. It should be noted, however, that many other theoretical and quasi-theoretical traditions have recently developed within this broad, interdisciplinary field of study. These include taxonomic models of different types of personal relationships, stage and developmental theories concerning the changes in relationships across time, process theories that focus on specific relational phenomena or outcomes, and so on. Any complaints critics may have had 30 years ago about the absence of, or lack of diversity in, theories about personal relationships are simply no longer valid on this eve of the next millennium, as the chapters in this and the remaining sections of the *Handbook* should make clear.

Chapter 6

Evolutionary Approaches to Relationships

Douglas T. Kenrick
and
Melanie R. Trost
Arizona State University, Tempe, AZ, USA

Evolutionary theory is arguably the most powerful set of ideas in the life sciences. No natural scientist studying the wing of a bat or the flipper of a seal or the long neck of a giraffe would ignore Darwin's theory of evolution by natural selection. Likewise for the behaviors of bats or seals or giraffes—obviously the unique bodies of these animals evolved to do something, and evolutionary theory helps to understand the co-evolution of physical morphology and behavior. Neither would many disagree that an evolutionary perspective is essential to understand the human body, with its upright posture, prehensile grasping hands and large brain capable of producing complex language. Yet many social scientists have not yet realized that an evolutionary perspective is just as essential for a full understanding of human behavior. Just as bats are designed to survive by flying through the night sky, seals by swimming through the ocean depths and giraffes by walking through the African plains, so human beings are designed to behave in certain ways in certain environments. To a large extent, humans are designed to live in social groups with other humans, and an evolutionary perspective can enhance our understanding of every aspect of personal relationships considered in this volume—including love, interdependence, social support, parent–child relationships and family conflicts. Indeed, an evolutionary perspective can help us see how all of these different aspects of human relationships are connected with one another and, at the next level, how they are connected with the evolved design of the human body and brain, and ultimately with the fundamental principles that underlie the design of all living creatures.

Handbook of Personal Relationships, 2nd edn. Edited by Steve Duck.
© 1997 John Wiley & Sons Ltd.

BASIC ASSUMPTIONS OF EVOLUTIONARY PSYCHOLOGY

Evolutionary explanations of life begin with Darwin's (1859) set of simple assumptions:

1. Organisms reproduce very rapidly, so by normal processes of geometric multiplication, even slowly reproducing animals such as elephants could cover the globe in a few centuries, if unrestrained. Any given species would therefore rapidly exhaust the limited resources available to it, if not for the fact that other animals are also competing for those same resources.
2. Animals vary in ways that influence their ability to survive in competition with members of their own and other species (some giraffes have longer necks, some have shorter necks).
3. Those organisms whose genetic traits provide an advantage in access to resources will survive longer and be more successful in mating. As a result, their genes will increase in the population relative to less well-adapted competitors.

(Of course, the population growth of even relatively well-adapted animals is still limited by resource availability, competition with members of other species, predators, parasites, and so on.) These processes of random variation and selective retention form the basis of natural selection. Analogous to the artificial selection exercised by animal breeders, as in selecting for short hair or a peaceful disposition in a dog, the forces of nature select certain characteristics over others.

As Darwin (1872) spelled out in his classic work on emotion, the process of natural selection also applies to behavior. Snarling communicates an intention to attack, and animals who recognize the signal and avoid a snarling adversary save themselves costly and bloody encounters. The abilities to both transmit and receive emotional communications are thus selected. Although the pioneering textbooks in social psychology were written from a Darwinian perspective (James, 1890; McDougall, 1908), later behavioral scientists largely ignored the implications of natural selection for humans. During the 1970s, however, stimulated in part by Wilson's *Sociobiology* (1975), social scientists began to incorporate evolutionary theory into their models of human social behavior.

Misunderstandings of the relationship between genetic predispositions and psychological development have led to misguided controversies about the extent to which human behavior is controlled by genes vs. cultural environment, or by genes vs. rational thought. The human capacities to create culture and to engage in complex cognition are themselves made possible by our genetic predispositions. These predispositions influence the choice of certain cultural practices over others and the inclination to attend to, think about and remember certain features of the environment (Lumsden & Wilson, 1981; Tooby & Cosmides, 1992). Genetic predispositions unfold in interaction with experience, resulting in cognitive and behavioral mechanisms that are themselves triggered by, and attuned to, events in the social and physical environment (Buss, 1995; Crawford & Anderson, 1989). Language provides a clear example. As Pinker (1994) notes, language is undoubtedly a species-specific evolved feature of humans: there are brain mechanisms dedicated to its production and understanding; the level of linguistic complexity is the same in all human groups; children acquire it with little effort; sign language shows some of the same deep structure as spoken language; and so on. However, the specific language that a child learns is determined by environmental inputs. No set of genes determines whether a child will say: "Come vanno le cose, signore?" "Hoe gaat het met je, mijnheer?" or "How's it going, man?".

Depending partly on environmental inputs, genetic predispositions may unfold very differently for different members of a species. Within one fish species, for instance, some males grow into large territorial animals that attract harems, others grow into small animals that look like females and attempt to "sneak-copulate", and still others begin life as females and only turn into males when a large territorial male dies (e.g., Gross, 1984; Warner, 1984). Hence evolutionary theory does not posit static immutable genes working *against* the environment. It proposes a set of general principles that shape the behavioral and cognitive mechanisms underlying human behavior across cultures, some of which may be shared with other species by common ancestry or ecological demands. These general principles may sometimes produce incredibly flexible mechanisms and may sometimes produce more rigid mechanisms. Even so, evolutionary theorists assume that to ignore the general principles underlying the evolutionary design of a behavior is to be blind to the ultimate causal mechanisms underlying that behavior.

SOME IMPORTANT GENERAL PRINCIPLES

In this section, we consider several general principles that have been used to generate evolutionary hypotheses about behavior. Before beginning, it is important to distinguish between ultimate and proximate levels of explanation. A *proximate explanation* considers behavior in terms of immediate determinants, such as the current environment or internal hormonal states. Laboratory experimenters tend to consider proximate causes—events in the immediate environment such as an aggressive prime or a confederate's remark. *Ultimate explanations* consider behavior in terms of more enduring background factors, such as the cultural norms that make a remark an insult, individual differences that make some people more prone to take offense, or an evolutionary past in which males were more concerned than females with challenges to their dominance. Evolutionary theorists are not unconcerned with proximate explanations, they are simply less likely to be satisfied without asking "why" a particular event might or might not elicit a particular response in a particular setting.

Reproduction, Kin Selection and Inclusive Fitness

The name of the evolutionary game is gene replication. Gene replication is accomplished directly via the production of offspring, hence evolutionary theorists have taken a strong interest in sexuality and heterosexual relationships. However, gene replication can be accomplished indirectly by helping those who share copies of one's genes. Thus, the theory applies not only to sexual behavior, but to mate attraction and selection, mate retention and kin relationships as well. Even foregoing the opportunity to reproduce directly may increase the "ultimate payoff"—more copies of one's genes. For instance, under conditions of resource scarcity and low survival rates for hatchlings, male birds may fare better by helping their brothers raise a clutch than by mating on their own (Trivers, 1985). Hatchlings receiving the extra resources provided by a helper are more likely to survive than birds raised with only two parents. Because brothers share half of their genes, the net benefit to both is greater if they cooperate than if they go it alone. This is an example of the general process of *kin selection*, which involves sacrificing direct reproductive opportunities to favor the survival and reproduction of relatives. The kin selection model helps explain the widespread occurrence of altruistic and cooperative behavior in animals. It has replaced the "red in tooth and claw" view of evolution as a process that exclusively involves survival by individual competition.

Before notions such as kin selection were developed, evolutionary biologists evaluated an animal's reproductive potential in terms of individual "fitness". This concept was sometimes operationally defined as the number of offspring that were successfully raised to reproductive age. At its base, however, fitness in an evolutionary sense meant not simply to survive but to successfully reproduce one's genes. *Inclusive fitness* is simply the logical extension of this notion, referring to the net number of one's genes passed on to future generations, a number that includes not only the individuals' direct contribution via personal offspring, but also their indirect contribution to the survival and reproduction of relatives who share copies of their genes (Hamilton, 1964).

Sexual Selection

As we just noted, a characteristic can be naturally selected because it provides a survival advantage to the individual or to kin. Darwin believed, however, that features such as peacocks' feathers or large horns on male mammals were selected through a process of *sexual selection*. Sexual selection occurs when a trait provides an advantage in attracting mates, even though it may hinder individual survival. There are two forms of sexual selection—*intersexual choice*, in which a trait gains an advantage because (like the feathers on a male bird) it is attractive to the opposite sex, and *intrasexual competition*, in which a trait gains an advantage because (like the horns on a male mammal) it helps an individual compete with same-sex rivals. Modern evolutionary theorists believe that sexual selection is just a special case of natural selection, in which the culling force is other members of one's species. The same sex provides obstacles to stop one another from mating; the opposite sex provides tests that must be passed before mating.

Parental Investment

Darwin noted that, when it comes to sexual selection, females are more likely to be the selectors, and males are more likely to be banging their heads against one another to win the females' attention. Trivers (1972) developed Darwin's insight into the theory of *differential parental investment*. According to this theory, the sex with the initially higher investment in the offspring has more to lose from a poor mating choice and will demand more before agreeing to mate. In general, females have a higher initial investment and should be more selective about choosing mates. There are, however, species in which males make the larger investment (e.g., by caring for the eggs and young offspring, as in seahorses), and in those species males tend to be more selective about their mates (Daly & Wilson, 1983; Trivers, 1985). In mammals, however, the normal discrepancy between males and females is especially pronounced, because females carry the young inside their bodies and nurse them after birth. Male mammals can reproduce with little cost, and frequently the male's direct input does not go beyond a single act of copulation. In such species, males tend to be non-selective about their mates, whereas females demand evidence of superior genetic potential before mating and will often mate only with males who have demonstrated superior capabilities. Humans also sometimes have sexual relations within less committed relationships, in the typical mammalian mode. Under those circumstances, an evolutionary perspective would predict typical mammalian differences—females high and males low in selectivity (Kenrick et al., 1990).

Unlike most mammals, however, humans tend to form long-term pair-bonds. Human males, therefore, often invest resources such as effort, time, money and emotional support in their offspring. Under those circumstances, men's selectivity is expected to approach that of women. However, to the extent that men and women make different contributions to the offspring, they should select partners along somewhat different dimensions. Women contribute their bodies, through internal gestation and nursing. Men would therefore be expected to value indications of fertility, including a healthy appearance and a waist–hip ratio characteristic of youthful sexual maturity (Singh, 1993). On the other hand, men primarily contribute their genes and indirect resources such as money and shelter. Presumably, women could appraise a man's genetic potential from physical attractiveness and his position in a dominance hierarchy (Thornhill & Gangestad, 1994; Sadalla, Kenrick & Vershure, 1987). His ability to provide resources could be gauged indirectly by his ambition and directly by his social status and acquired wealth (Buss & Barnes, 1986; Daly & Wilson, 1983; Symons, 1979). Even with these differential tendencies, humans cooperate in raising their offspring. Hence, a number of characteristics should be (and are) desired by both sexes, such as agreeableness, kindness and faithfulness (Buss, 1989; Kenrick et al., 1993).

Frequency-dependent Strategies and Individual Differences

A trait's fitness value depends on its distribution in the population. A frequency-dependent strategy is one that may or may not enhance fitness, depending on the number of others who possess it. To illustrate this dynamic process, theorists often use the analogy of a population of hawks and doves (e.g., Dawkins, 1976). If most birds in a population played a meek and non-competitive "dove" strategy and ran from conflict, any bird that used an alternative, aggressive "hawk" strategy, fighting for resources, would quickly benefit by easily driving doves away from their resources. Given this advantage, any genetic tendency toward "hawkishness" would increase in the population. If the majority of the population became vicious hawks, however, and were constantly tearing at one another over every scrap of food, the alternative dove strategy of "eat quickly and run" would have an advantage over the "stand and fight" approach. Once doves again gained the majority, however, hawkishness would be less dangerous, and would again increase. In nature, predator–prey relationships tend to remain in a similar state of dynamic equilibrium, with increases in either population quickly becoming self-limiting. This same analogy also applies within a species, where different forms designed to play different strategies are maintained in stable equilibrium. This dynamic equilibrium notion has been suggested as one explanation of the persistent co-existence of antisocial and well-socialized human populations (Kenrick & Brown, 1995; Kenrick, Dantchik & MacFarlane, 1983; Mealey, 1995). The marginal benefits of antisocial behavior decrease as the frequency of anti-social individuals in the population increases.

In line with the notion of differential parental investment, the biggest difference within a species is often related to sex, with females and males adopting different mating strategies. However, there is also evidence of individual differences in mating strategies within each sex for humans, as for other animals. For instance, Gangestad & Simpson (1990) considered differences in *sociosexual orientation* among females. Women adopting a "restricted strategy" prefer exclusive sexual relations within a long-lasting relationship. Other women are more inclined to have multiple partners, and may be willing to have sexual relations with relative strangers. Restricted women appear to place more value on characteristics indicative of fidelity and long-term investment; unrestricted women appear to place more value on physical attractiveness, which may indicate good "genetic potential" (Buss & Schmitt, 1993; Thornhill & Gangestad, 1994).

Evolutionary Hypotheses are Subject to the Same Standards of Empirical Evidence as Any Other Hypotheses

The principles described above have been tested in a number of studies of animal behavior, and several of them (such as kin selection and differential parental investment) are very well-established (Alcock, 1993; Daly & Wilson, 1983; Trivers, 1985; Wilson, 1975). Nevertheless, their application to any given instance of human behavior may or may not be appropriate. There is nothing any less refutable about a hypothesis derived from evolutionary principles than there is about a hypothesis derived from principles of information processing or classical conditioning. Some derivations are astute, others are stretched, and others are dead wrong. Consequently, some derivations receive empirical support, and some are refuted (Buss, 1995; Buss & Kenrick, in press; Kenrick, 1994). As we will describe below, evolutionary principles have proven fruitful in explaining gender differences in sexual behavior, mate preferences and aggressive behavior. In some cases, findings seem to refute alternative explanations from traditional social science models; in other cases, traditional models and evolutionary hypotheses have been used to complement one another. In other areas, such as kinship and friendship, there have been fewer tests of evolutionary hypotheses, and their utility remains to be seen.

THE ADAPTIVE FUNCTIONS OF RELATIONSHIPS

From an evolutionary perspective, the primary question about a physical or behavioral characteristic is: "What was it designed to do?" In discussing the functional design of human cognitive and behavioral mechanisms, evolutionary theorists often discuss the environment of evolutionary adaptedness (EEA). Although the distribution of alternative genes can change in a few generations, it is assumed that the redesign of a functional feature (such as the development of a giraffe's neck) will take, at a minimum, thousands of years (Lumsden & Wilson, 1981). There is thus considerable "lag time" in evolution, and any evolved human cognitive mechanisms were designed not for life on the freeways or malls of modern Los Angeles, but for co-existence in small hunter-gatherer groups. The hunting and gathering lifestyle set the stage for human social arrangements for well over a million years, as agriculture was only introduced within the last few thousand years (and then only for a minority of our ancestors), and large urban centers only began to predominate within the past few hundred years. Hence, evolutionary psychologists assume that the human mind was constructed for life in a small group of closely related individuals, in which there was a well-established dominance hierarchy, division of labor by sex (females devoting more time to parenting and gathering, males more to hunting), marriage to someone from a very similar background (usually a cousin from a neighboring group), and so on (Lumsden & Wilson, 1981; Tooby & Cosmides, 1992). Hunter-gatherers everywhere shared some very similar problems as a function of that lifestyle and, as a consequence, evolutionary theorists expect to find a number of human universals beneath the surface diversity of modern cultures (Brown, 1991). Undoubtedly there are psychologically important differences across cultures, and modern life has introduced many new problems for the human mind. However, there is an assumption that we can better understand how humans respond to contemporary cultural variations if we consider the social arrangements within which our ancestors evolved. Evolutionary theorists also assume that modern cultures are not randomly created, but include many customs and institutions actively constructed by organisms designed for a prehistoric lifestyle (Lumsden & Wilson, 1981; Kenrick, 1987; Tooby & Cosmides, 1992). In the following sections, we consider some of the functions that relationships might have served in the human environment of evolutionary adaptedness.

Romantic Relationships

The primary adaptive functions of romantic relationships are assumed to be sexual reproduction and bonding for the care of offspring (Kenrick & Trost, 1987; Mellen, 1981; Morris, 1972). Romantic relationships also provide secondary adaptive benefits such as mutual sharing, social support and protection. The joint investment in offspring should facilitate such sharing, moving couples into a strong, communal mode with little accounting of individual contributions or resources. Therefore, men and women should have some shared goals, such as finding a cooperative and compatible partner or ensuring the survival of the offspring.

   In line with our earlier discussion, however, men and women are also assumed to have some different goals in romantic relationships (Buss, 1995; Kenrick & Trost, 1987, 1989). For instance, women ought to be concerned that the man contributes his part (i.e., resources) to the child-rearing responsibility. A woman should thus be concerned if her partner is possibly squandering resources on outside mating opportunities. Men should be more concerned with ensuring paternal certainty; that is, that the offspring in whom he is investing are indeed his (obviously, maternal certainty is not an issue for women). In addition, a man is more likely to be concerned with gaining access to additional mates, a goal that is not as beneficial for a woman.

Kin Relationships

Relationships with close relatives primarily serve the ultimate goal of gene replication. By helping one's kin, one helps one's own genes. From an evolutionary perspective, one would expect to find, among close relatives, a higher prevalence of Clark & Mills' (1979) communal relationships than tit-for-tat exchange relationships. In fact, explicit accounting of exchanged rewards should diminish as an inverse function to r (an index of relatedness, which would be 0.5 for a woman and her sister, 0.25 for a woman and her mother's sister, 0.125 for a woman and her first cousin, and so on). It is expected that one's willingness to benefit one's kin is also a function of their future reproductive potential (Burnstein, Crandall & Kitayama, 1994). So, whereas a 40-year-old woman has the same degree of relatedness to her 17-year-old daughter and her 70-year-old mother, she would be expected to feel more positively about investing resources in her daughter (whose reproductive potential is quite high) than in her 70-year-old mother (who, although she may still be capable of providing the indirect benefits of grandmothering to the kin group, has a relatively low reproductive potential).

Friendships

Evolutionary theorists have devoted some attention to reciprocal alliances between non-relatives. Vampire bats, for instance, will often share their nightly take of blood with others. Research on this sharing indicates that it occurs between relatives, or between individuals who have forged a reciprocal exchange relationship (Wilkinson, 1988, 1990). The same sort of arrangement is found in hunter-gatherer groups (Hill & Hurtado, 1989). In traditional hunter-gatherer societies, the likelihood of capturing game may be quite low on any given occasion for any given individual. If one individual catches a large fish or a deer, however, it is often too much to consume alone, and will rot if not shared. By sharing, the individual helps the other members of the group survive, and accrues credit for the future when his or her own luck may be down.

In most traditional societies even today, one's best friends are usually related in some way (Moghaddam, Taylor & Wright, 1994). Even in modern urban societies, most women list a close relative when asked to name someone with whom they are intimate. In hunter-gatherer societies like those in which our ancestors evolved, individuals were all closely related. Thus, the immediate selfish obstacles to reciprocal sharing in humans were diminished by potential kin selection. It would be expected, however, that our ancestors would have benefited from sensitivity to differences between close and distant relatives, and that reciprocal alliances with more distant relatives would involve more direct accounting. In addition to the benefits of trading resources, friendships would have served other functions for our ancestors. In chimpanzees, friends protect one another and also form mating alliances (deWaal, 1989). Although the most dominant male in a group can monopolize the mating attention of the females, he can be toppled by an alliance of less dominant males. In humans, of course, one's social position is also often related to "who one knows", and cooperative alliances often involve large groups of individuals.

Dominance Hierarchies

In addition to cooperating to survive, group members also sometimes compete with one another. Dominance hierarchies serve to reduce continual competition in stable groups—once everyone knows who can defeat whom, there is less need to struggle over every new resource. When a new member is introduced into an existing group, there is often a period of conflict until a new hierarchy is established (e.g., deWaal, 1989). In addition to reducing conflict, male dominance hierarchies also define the most desirable mates for females to choose from.

Thus, male mammals tend to be more concerned than females with their status within dominance hierarchies. Note that there is no assumption of altruism here; animals do not take their place within a hierarchy to reduce conflict or to help the other sex make mating decisions. They jockey for the best available position, and will occasionally re-challenge those just above them in line. However, it is in their best interest to recognize those who are far above them in order to avoid unnecessary and costly competition with them. Thus, the group-stabilizing consequences of dominance hiearchies are indirect byproducts of individual selfishness.

Ultimate Goals Are Not Necessarily Conscious or "Rational"

It is important to note that evolutionary psychologists do not assume that people, or other organisms, are conscious of the ultimate goals of their behavior. A woman, for instance, does not have to be aware of choosing a dominant man for his genetic potential. In fact, evolutionary theorists have considered a variety of circumstances under which "self-deception" about one's ulterior motives would be adaptive (e.g., Lockard & Paulhus, 1988; Trivers, 1985). Just because humans are capable of some degree of self-awareness, it is not any more necessary to assume that humans are fully aware of the ultimate motivations underlying their behaviors than it is to assume that caterpillars or planarians are.

It is also important to note that the evolved mechanisms are not designed to confer omniscience about the adaptive consequences of every choice. Rather, they are blindly calibrated to the average consequences of a given behavior for our ancestors. A good example is the human preference for sugar, which assisted our ancestors in identifying ripe fruit (Lumsden & Wilson, 1981). This preference was helpful for millions of years and is still strong, even in those who are safe from starvation within modern society and those who have stored several months' worth of calories in the form of fat. In the same way, the comment "Our romance is based on a shared interest in Beethoven, and we have no interest in reproducing" may reflect on the depth of human self-aware-ness, but it does not negate the evolutionary significance of the mate choice mechanisms.

EMPIRICAL FINDINGS FROM EVOLUTIONARY PSYCHOLOGY

Evolutionary hypotheses have generated a number of empirical findings in recent years. We first review findings on universals in interpersonal communication. Next we consider findings on sexuality, mating and mate preferences, many of which follow directly from evolutionary models of sexual selection and parental investment. These same models have led to predictions regarding intrasexual competition, jealousy and deception, discussions of which are followed by a review of evolution-inspired research on aggression and child abuse. Finally, we consider the less extensive literatures on kinship and friendship.

Universals in Communication

The first research in the field of evolutionary psychology was conducted by Charles Darwin (1872), who surveyed early anthropologists and missionaries for evidence of universals in emotional expression. His conclusion that certain aspects of human emotional expression are universal has received corroboration from a series of studies by Ekman and his colleagues (e.g. Ekman, 1992; Ekman & Friesen, 1971; Ekman et al., 1987). In general, they have found that expressions indicating basic emotional states such as anger and happiness are recognized world-wide; and, although they can be suppressed in public or partially masked when necessary, the expressions do not appear to depend on shared cultural exposure.

Eibl-Eibesfeldt unobtrusively filmed women's responses to flirtation across a wide range of Western and non-Western cultures, and found certain universalities in the sequences of their movements. The patterns were too subtle to have been trained, and they agreed in microscopic detail from Samoa to Papua, France, Japan, Africa and in South American Indian tribes (Eibl-Eibesfeldt, 1975). Women's flirtation gestures include "proceptive" cues (Beach, 1976; Perper & Weis, 1987), such as smiling and maintaining mutual gaze a bit longer than usual, that invite advances from selected men (Givens, 1978; Moore, 1985).

Sexuality

Because of inherent differences in parental investment, males and females face a different matrix of costs and benefits in casual sexual relationships. A male faces an opportunity to replicate genes with relatively low cost. A female faces the danger of impregnation by a male who has made little commitment to invest in the offspring. If she has an existing partner there is much less marginal genetic gain from an additional partner, and the danger of abandonment or intense jealousy from her current partner can be extremely costly.

There is abundant evidence that women are less eager than are men to engage in promiscuous sex. Clark & Hatfield (1989) had confederates approach opposite-sex students with one of three invitations, to: "Go out tonight?" "Come over to my apartment?" or "Go to bed with me?". Approximately half of the women said yes to the date, but only 3% were receptive to going to the man's apartment and not one said yes to the invitation to go to bed. When men were approached with the same questions, about half of them also responded favorably to the confederate's invitation for a date, almost 70% were willing to go to her apartment, and over 70% were willing to go to bed with her. Buss & Schmitt (1993) also found that college men desired to have sex much sooner in a relationship than did women.

Besides being more willing to have sex, men also want to have sex with more partners than do women. Buss & Schmitt (1993) asked college students how many sexual partners they would ideally like to have during the rest of their lives. Men wanted, on average, over 18 sex partners in their lifetimes, whereas women desired, on average, fewer than five. Consistent findings are also found in research on erotica, with males generally indicating more interest in erotica and more fantasies involving strangers (Ellis & Symons, 1990; Kenrick et al., 1980). Men have somewhat more extramarital affairs than women. If not for the scarcity of willing women, the sex difference in partners would likely be even more pronounced, as indicated by the very large difference in sexual experience between male and female homosexuals (Daly & Wilson, 1983; Symons, 1979).

Men are also less selective about casual sexual partners. Kenrick et al. (1990) asked male and female college students about their minimum criteria in a member of the opposite sex for a date, a sexual partner, a steady dating relationship or a marriage. The two sexes differed most noticeably in their criteria for a sexual partner, with males willing to have sex with someone who did not meet their minimum criteria for a date.

Are these gender differences simply a reflection of an American or Western "double standard" of sexual behavior for men and women? Although there are clear cross-cultural variations in the norms involving premarital and extramarital sex, early anthropological reports of societies in which women were as interested in casual sex as men do not bear up under examination (Freeman, 1983). In reviewing the cross-cultural data on gender differences in sexuality, anthropologist Donald Symons concludes: "Everywhere sex is understood to be something females have that males want" (1979, p. 253). One of the unfortunate consequences of the inherent gender differences in selectivity for sexual partners is that males are much more likely to be the perpetrators, and females to be the victims, of sexual harassment (Studd & Gattiker, 1991). As noted by Clark & Hatfield (1989), males are likely to be receptive to, or at worst flattered by, sexual advances, whereas females are more likely to respond with some degree of aversion.

Love and Marriage

Anthropologists have observed cultural variations in mating relationships: some societies allow polyandry, some allow polygyny but not polyandry, and some allow only monogamy. However, the mix of possibilities is neither random nor arbitrary. First, all human societies have some form of marriage (Daly & Wilson, 1983). This is only surprising when one notes that pair-bonding is relatively rare among other mammals. If human mating patterns were completely arbitrary, one would see whole societies in which people were completely promiscuous, as in the Bonobo chimp, or arena mating patterns such as those found in the Uganda

kob (in which females select highly dominant males, but males make no investment in the offspring beyond insemination). On the other hand, pair-bonding is
more commonly found in bird species that, like ours, have helpless offspring who
require intensive parental care. Evolutionary theorists have argued that forming
a strong bond serves the same function in humans as it does in birds—to ensure
cooperation in caring for their helpless offspring (e.g., Kenrick & Trost, 1987;
Mellen, 1981).

If humans are designed to bond together to facilitate caring for their young,
one would assume romantic love to be a universal feature of our species. That
assumption was seemingly contradicted by social scientists' common wisdom that
romantic love is a recent phenomenon, traceable to the idle, courtly classes of
Medieval Europe (e.g., Stone, 1988). In a recent review of reports from 166
societies, however, Jankowiak & Fischer (1992) found only one in which the
anthropologist explicitly stated that there was no romantic love (and the supple-
mentary evidence was insufficient to confirm or deny the report). There was
evidence of sexual affairs in another 18 cultures, but ethnographers had not asked
about romantic love, and Jankowiak & Fischer were unable to establish that the
participants felt love. For the remaining 147 cultures, however, they found clear,
positive evidence of romantic love.

Although romantic love is a prevalent human bonding pattern, most societies
do not require that it occur within a monogamous relationship. Daly & Wilson
(1983) reviewed evidence from 849 cultures and found that only 137 were supposedly "strictly" monogamous—although even in those societies men were likely to
engage in more extra-pair copulations than were women. Most (708) cultures
allowed polygyny (one man with several wives), whereas only four allowed
polyandry (one woman with several husbands). Moreover, whenever polyandry
was allowed, so was polygyny. For instance, Pahari brothers in India pool resources to secure a wife, whom they share. If they accumulate more wealth,
however, they add wives. The tendency toward polygyny over polyandry is
consistent with the parental investment model. Women select men for their
resources, and men with great wealth or power, such as Roman emperors, can
attract multiple women because the benefits of sharing a wealthy husband may
outweigh the advantages of having a poorer man all to oneself (Betzig, 1992).
However, the reverse is not true. Because men select women for direct reproductive potential, a man sharing a woman, even a very desirable one, suffers a
disadvantage over a man having a less attractive woman to himself. Also, a
woman married to multiple husbands gains resources, but does not increase her
own reproductive output substantially enough to compensate for the additional
costs, such as male jealousy (Daly & Wilson, 1983, 1988a).

Mate Selection Criteria

Studies of characteristics requested and offered in singles' advertisements support predictions from the parental investment model—men seek youth and at-

tractiveness in partners, and promise economic and emotional resources; women are more likely to seek resources and offer attractiveness (e.g., Harrison & Saeed, 1977; Rajecki, Bledsoe & Rasmussen, 1991; Thiessen, Young & Burroughs, 1993; Wiederman, 1993). Although one could argue that such criteria reflect norms of American society, an extensive cross-cultural study of marriage preferences (Buss, 1989) indicated that men in diverse cultures place greater value than do women on youth and beauty in potential spouses, whereas women place greater value on characteristics associated with resource potential. There is also substantial cross-cultural agreement in judgments of female attractiveness, which cannot be explained by exposure to Western standards of beauty through the media (Cunningham et al., 1995).

Age Preferences in Mates

Researchers studying singles' advertisements have been struck by a consistent contradiction to the powerful similarity–attraction principle: women generally prefer older men and men prefer younger women (Harrison & Saeed, 1977; Bolig, Stein & McKenry, 1984; Cameron, Oskamp & Sparks, 1977). Explanations for this irregularity typically rely upon the influence of cultural norms (Brehm, 1985; Cameron, Oskamp & Sparks, 1977; Deutsch, Zalenski & Clark, 1986; Presser, 1975), such as the "norm" specifying that a husband should be older and taller so as to appear "mentally and physically superior" to his wife (Presser, 1975). An alternative evolutionary explanation focuses on inherent sex differences in resources that men and women bring to relationships (e.g., Buss, 1989; Symons, 1979). Men's indirect resources (e.g., food, money, protection, security) may actually increase over the lifespan, whereas the direct reproductive potential contributed by women decreases as they age, and ends with menopause around age 50.

Although both perspectives could predict the average 2–3-year difference in desired ages across all advertisers, their predictions differ if the preferences are broken down across the lifespan. A societal norm should operate the same for everyone in that society, regardless of age. This slavish desire to do what is regarded as societally "normal" should be most pronounced among younger people, who are especially sensitive to gender-role norms (Deutsch et al., 1986). In fact, the difference in ages should be most pronounced among teenage males, who are most concerned with gender-role-appropriate behavior. An evolutionary perspective, however, suggests that the reproductive value of men and women, not societal norms, underlies gender differences in age preference. Female fertility peaks around age 24, and then declines more rapidly than does male fertility. In fact, men can father children until very late in life. Therefore, a man's preferred age for a partner should, as he ages, get progressively younger than his own age. For a man in his forties, a woman of similar age would have few reproductive years left, but a younger woman would have many.

According to this view, teenage males should also be concerned with their partner's reproductive capabilities. A similarly-aged female would maximize the remaining reproductive years, but her fertility is lower. Contrary to the normative account, this reproductive exchange emphasis would predict that young males should not discriminate against women who are actually a few years older than they. Women, on the other hand, are looking for signs of status and wealth. Even though older males may lose physical resources (such as health and sexual arousability), they may gain indirect resources and social status. In fact, Leonard (1989) argues that a woman can optimize her reproductive potential by choosing a man 10 years older than herself: he will have more resources and status than a similarly-aged male, but will not be so old as to die while the children are young. If age preferences are tied to reproductive mechanisms, any gender differences should exist across cultures, as women in all societies experience child-bearing and menopause.

Kenrick & Keefe (1992) conducted a series of archival analyses of age preferences in mates, and found results consistent with an evolutionary life-history model. Women's preferences, even when broken down by decade, were surprisingly consistent: women of all ages specified men who were, on average, a few years younger to approximately 5 years older. When men's preferences were broken down by decade, however, they did not reflect the supposed normative pressure to marry someone several years younger. Men in their twenties were equally attracted to older and younger women, and older males expressed increasingly divergent age preferences. Men in their fifties and sixties showed a strong interest in younger partners. This same sex-differentiated pattern was found in singles advertisements from different regions of the USA (even those placed by "relatively wealthy" East Coast men and women) and in advertisements in Holland, Germany and India. It was also found in marriage records from a Philippine island during the early years of this century (Kenrick & Keefe, 1992), as well as records from several traditional African cultures (Broude, 1992; Harpending, 1992). The body of evidence makes it difficult to argue that these preferences are due to the arbitrary norms of modern American society.

Even more problematic for a normative explanation are the preferences of younger men. Not only are men in their twenties interested in both younger and older women, but adolescent males (aged 12–18) indicated a range of ages extending much further above than below their own age (Kenrick et al., 1996). Moreover, their "ideal" partner was several years older than their own age. The norm to prefer slightly younger women is obviously not shaping their preferences; but they are perfectly consistent with the reproductive exchange model, as the most fertile females will be older, not younger, than a teenage male.

Intrasexual Competition

As described earlier, human evolution is also subject to intrasexual selection—competition among members of the same sex for mating opportunities (Darwin, 1859). Within most species, intrasexual competition occurs mainly among males, manifested as (1) aggressive behaviors designed to limit other males' access to females; (2) competition to range more widely in search of females; or (3) competition in courtship for females (Trivers, 1985). Intrasexual selection plays out somewhat differently for humans because both men and women contribute substantial resources to their offspring. Human males, for instance, do not typically engage in direct combat for access to females, as do elephant seals or bighorn sheep; neither do they display anything similar to the bright plumage of the peacock in order to entice discriminating women. In addition, an ill-fated mating is disproportionately costly for women, so women should be just as eager to attract a man who is willing and able to invest in the offspring as men should be to attract a healthy and fertile woman.

Human intrasexual competition is more likely to be waged by both men and women through differential skills at (1) locating mates; (2) demonstrating interest or availability; (3) acquiring resources desired by the opposite sex; or (4) altering appearance to look more attractive (Buss, 1988a). The most effective tactics for mate attraction should emphasize the characteristics most valued by the opposite sex. Buss asked subjects to describe the behaviors that people use to make themselves attractive to the opposite sex. Men and women expressed a high degree of similarity not only in their alluring behaviors but also in the rated effectiveness of those behaviors. For instance, having a good sense of humor and being sympathetic, well-mannered and well-groomed were the most effective behaviors for both sexes. Buss also found results consistent with the predictions of a resource exchange perspective. Men were significantly more likely to engage in tactics related to the display of resources (e.g., flashing money to impress a partner), tactics that were also judged to be more effective than a woman's displaying resources. Women, on the other hand, were more likely to engage in tactics related to enhancing their appearance (e.g., wearing flattering make-up or dieting), tactics that were also judged to be more effective than men doing the same. In general, tactics of intrasexual competition are closely linked to characteristics desired in long-term partners (Buss & Barnes, 1986; Kenrick et al., 1990, 1993).

Jealousy

Selecting an appropriate mate is an essential element in successful reproduction. However, maintaining that relationship was also important to our ancestors, as a child with two devoted parents would be more likely to reach adulthood than a child with only one. Although we tend to associate jealousy with a variety of negative personal characteristics (cf., White & Mullen, 1989), it may also have had an adaptive function as a mate retention mechanism (Buss, 1988b; Daly & Wilson, 1983). Jealousy is both a pervasive (Buunk & Hupka, 1987) and potentially lethal reaction (Daly, Wilson & Weghorst, 1982). Women and men from Hungary, Ireland, Mexico, The Netherlands, the Soviet Union, and the USA all express strong, negative reactions to thoughts that their partner might flirt or have sex with another (Buunk & Hupka, 1987). In addition, anthropological evidence indicates that jealous outbursts result in wife-beating and spousal homicide across a wide variety of cultures (Buss, 1994; Daly, Wilson & Weghorst, 1982). Although jealousy is usually described as undesirable, its adaptiveness for our ancestors may have contributed to its widespread occurrence.

Both sexes can gain genetic fitness if their jealousy prevents a partner from being successfully courted by a rival: women can prevent the loss of resources required to raise children and men can avoid threats to paternal certainty. Because fertilization occurs inside the woman's body, men risk investing valuable resources in another man's offspring, and any behaviors reducing this possibility would have been selected (Daly, Wilson & Weghorst, 1982). Ancestral women were always certain of their genetic relatedness to their offspring, but had difficulty raising their highly dependent children without support. Women who could defend against threats to their relationship would thus be better able to raise their offspring to adulthood (Daly, Wilson & Weghorst, 1982). So, both men and women lose when a relationship is torn apart, and jealousy may be one of the psychological mechanisms that activates mate-guarding strategies (Buss, 1994).

Given the differences in the relational threats experienced by men and women, the circumstances that elicit jealousy should differ between the sexes. Even though both men and women report similar *levels* of jealousy (Wiederman & Allgeier, 1993), men report more intense jealousy to a scenario describing their partners' sexual indiscretions (exaggerating concerns about paternity); and women report more jealousy to a scenario describing their partners' emotional attachment to a rival (which could cause the man to redirect his resources). This pattern was found not only in the USA (Buss et al., 1992; Wiederman & Allgeier, 1993), but also in Holland and Germany (Buunk et al., in press). Moreover, the sex differences were most dramatic when imagining an infidelity before it had occurred (Wiederman & Allgeier, 1993). Once an infidelity *has* occurred, it may be most adaptive to end the tainted relationship and find a new, potentially monogamous partner, especially for men. Cross-cultural evidence indicates that wives' infidelity is cited more frequently as a cause for divorce than husbands' infidelity (Betzig, 1989), even though men are more likely to have extra-marital relationships. Moreover, consistent with the general tendency for men to be more violent, men are significantly more likely to murder their partners during a jealous rage than are women (Daly, Wilson & Weghorst, 1982). Assuming that a couple's offspring were conceived before an infidelity occurred, this tendency to flee an unfaithful partner might be attenuated in couples who have children because, for most of our evolutionary history, children with both parents would have had a survival advantage over single-parent children.

Deceptive Strategies in Mating and Acquiring Resources

Animals have evolved a variety of elaborate systems of deception (Trivers, 1985). These mechanisms tend to take the form of either deceiving predators or deceiving competitors for valued resources, such as food or mates. As an example of a physical characteristic designed to deceive predators, the brightly colored bands of the non-poisonous shovelnose snake mimic those of the highly poisonous coral snake. Another approach to avoiding predators is to develop deceptive behavioral strategies. For example, female pronghorn antelope routinely distance themselves from their fawns, presumably to decrease predation by coyotes (Byers & Byers, 1983). Deceiving the competition to gain access to valued resources, such as food or the opposite sex, can also enhance genetic fitness. For instance, male scorpionflies mimic female courtship behaviors in order to lure other males into handing over their nuptial gift of food, intended to woo a real female. This single act has the double benefit of disadvantaging the competitor while increasing the deceptive male's likelihood of attracting a mate (cf. Trivers, 1985). As these examples illustrate, successful deceit can provide a survival advantage.

Although modern humans may not need to "change our stripes" to repel predators, our mating strategies often involve deceiving both competitors and potential partners (Tooke & Camire, 1991). Moreover, the types of deception exhibited in intrasexual competition and intersexual relations take a familiar pattern: men and women deceive others about those characteristics that are most desired by the opposite sex. Women tend to enhance their bodily appearance through behaviors such as wearing perfume, suntanning, and walking with a greater swing than normal when around men. Men exaggerate their dominance or resources (e.g., wearing expensive "label" clothing they cannot really afford or misleading the partner about their career) and exaggerate their commitment (e.g., their sincerity, trust, vulnerability and kindness). Men also engage in more intrasexual deception to create the illusion that they are more desirable to women than their competitors. For example, in their interactions with other men, men tend to elaborate on their superiority (e.g., intelligence, toughness), and to exaggerate their level of sexual activity, sexual intensity and sexual popularity. Moreover, women use relatively passive deceptive techniques whereas men use active deception, in line with the notion that female choice limits male reproductive success and escalates the intensity of male–male competition.

Because hunter-gatherer groups were highly interdependent, the ability to detect violations of reciprocity in social exchange would be highly adaptive (Axelrod & Hamilton, 1981). Cosmides & Tooby (1989) argue that we may have evolved "social contract algorithms" allowing quick and effective detection of cheating. In line with this reasoning, Cosmides & Tooby (1989) found that students had great difficulty with an exercise in formal logic (called the Wason task) unless the content of the problem related to a standard social contract (costs vs. benefits). When the problem was framed in terms of "looking for a cheater", people easily solved the traditionally difficult logical problem. Cosmides & Tooby (1989) argue that, rather than having a brain that operates as a "general-purpose learning mechanism", the human brain is equipped with specialized algorithms that facilitate reasoning about social exchange problems with very little learning.

Violence in Relationships

Criminologists have frequently noted the high prevalence of homicide among family members. Gelles & Straus (1985) observed that: "With the exception of the police and the military, the family is perhaps the most violent social group, and the home the most violent social setting, in our society" (p. 88). Indeed, one of the classic studies of homicide found that almost one-quarter of victims were "relatives" (Wolfgang, 1958). From the standpoint of models of kin selection and inclusive fitness, family violence seemed to pose a puzzle for evolutionary views of human behavior. However, a closer examination of the classic statistics indicated that most homicide victims labeled as "relatives" were not blood relatives, but spouses (Daly & Wilson, 1988b; Kenrick, Dantchik & MacFarlane, 1983). Many were also step-relatives, who do not share common genes but may compete for common resources. Children living with a step- or foster-parent in two samples were 70–100 times more likely to be fatally abused than children living with both natural parents (Daly & Wilson, 1988b; Daly & Wilson, 1994). Relatives also spend more time together, providing more opportunities for conflict; however, the risk of homicide for unrelated co-residents is 11 times greater than the risk for related co-residents (Daly & Wilson, 1988b).

Daly & Wilson (1988a, 1989) have criticized prevailing cultural determinist explanations of homicide. The prominent criminologist Marvin Wolfgang, for instance, attributed the enormous gender difference in homicide he found to the "theme of masculinity in American culture" and the cultural expectation that females not engage in violence. Indeed, an examination of homicide statistics from the FBI's uniform crime reports indicates that, every year and despite changes in the overall rate of homicide, men commit over 80% of all homicides. However, to attribute any phenomenon to a particular culture requires cross-cultural comparisons (Daly & Wilson, 1989; Kenrick & Trost, 1993). In the case of homicide, Daly & Wilson note that the same gender difference appeared in every culture for which they found records and during every period of history they examined. In fact, the gender difference is somewhat less pronounced in American society than in other cultures—men never commit less than 80% of homicides in any society, and often commit closer to 100%. The universality of the gender difference fits with the parental investment and sexual selection models. Given that humans are mildly polygynous and that women select high-status men, it follows that men should be more competitive with one another everywhere. Further, male violence is particularly pronounced among males who are young, unmated and resource-poor (Wilson & Daly, 1985). Homicide case reports show that male–male violence is most often precipitated by an encounter between acquaintances, one of whom challenges the other's position in the local dominance hierarchy by attempting to humiliate him (Wilson & Daly, 1985).

Examination of spousal homicides reveals that they tend to occur when the reproductive interests of men and women conflict. As we noted above, men, not women, face the danger of cuckoldry. Consequently, jealousy is the predominant reason for a man to kill a woman across cultures (Daly & Wilson, 1988a; 1988b). When a woman kills a man, she is less likely to be jealous of another woman and more likely to be protecting herself from the man's jealous threats (Daly & Wilson, 1988a). Daly & Wilson (1994) also found that, in the rare instances in which a father kills his own children, it is likely to be accompanied by suicide and/ or uxoricide (wife-killing). Step-fathers who kill children are unlikely to commit suicide or kill their wives, but they are more likely to be brutal (beating the child to death). The authors suggest that step-fathers' murders seem to reflect feelings of antipathy towards their victims, whereas killings by genetic fathers indicate very different underlying motivations (accompanying suicide notes, for instance, often claim the motivation to "rescue" the children from a hopeless situation). Thus, the differential prevalence of step-parental murder, and the different means used, suggest different underlying conflicts that are consistent with inclusive fitness theory.

Rather than viewing homicide in terms of individual psychopathology, evolutionary theorists view it as the tip of the iceberg, revealing evolved coercive impulses in genetically important situations. Presumably, all humans possess the same cognitive mechanisms designed to elicit competitiveness and hostility in situations where survival or reproductive interests are challenged. Kenrick & Sheets (1994) asked people if they had ever had a homicidal fantasy, and if so, who and what caused it. Most men (75%) and women (62%) reported having had at least one homicidal fantasy. Men's fantasies were more frequent, longer and more detailed. Only 13% of the respondents had lived with a step-parent, and of those who had lived with a step-parent for over 6 years, 59% had at least one fantasy about killing that parent (compared to 25% for natural fathers and 31% for natural mothers). Thus, per unit of time spent together, homicidal fantasies were more likely to be provoked by step-parents, providing a complement to the statistics on step-parental abuse of children (Daly & Wilson, 1988b; Lenington, 1981).

Kinship, Friendship and Altruism

Although there has been less work conducted on kinship, the theory of inclusive fitness leads to a number of predictions about the preferential treatment of relatives. Rushton (1989a) reviewed human and animal evidence linking genetic similarity with altruism, family relations and friendship. Experimental research suggests that animals can recognize their kin, and are likely to treat them preferentially (Greenberg, 1979; Holmes & Sherman, 1983). For instance, rhesus monkeys are promiscuous, and it would be difficult for a male to know which offspring are his own. Nevertheless, blood tests matching adult males with the troop's young show that males treat their own offspring better than others (Suomi, 1982). Because of random variation and overlap between parents' genes, it is possible for children to have more genetic similarity to one parent than to another (Rushton, 1989a). There is evidence that human children who share more genes with their parents are perceived to be more similar to the parent than children who share fewer genes; to be seen as "taking after" the genetically-related parent more than the other. When a child dies, parents who perceive that the child "takes after" their side grieve more for the loss (Littlefield & Rushton, 1986). Compared with dizygotic twins, monozygotic twins are more altruistic, and more affectionate, towards one another (Segal, 1988). Finally, there is evidence that people choose friends who are genetically similar to them, and that the similarity cannot be fully explained as due to the tendency to choose friends who look like oneself (Rushton, 1989b).

Burnstein, Crandall & Kitayama (1994) asked people about their inclination to help others who varied in genetic relatedness, age and health. People were more inclined to help someone with whom they were more related (e.g., a nephew before a cousin of the same age). Most interestingly, helping genetic kin increased markedly in life-or-death situations and was linked to their reproductive capability. In everyday situations, people did the socially appropriate behavior—helping a grandmother in preference to a teenage sister, or a sick relative in preference to a healthy one. In life-or-death situations, however, helping was more likely to be directed towards those who would pass on shared genes—the teenage sister in preference to grandmother, and the healthy relative in preference to the sick one. These experimental findings, which indicate that kinship has a strong influence on life-or-death helping, are corroborated by studies of actual disasters, in which kin are helped first (e.g., Form & Nosow, 1958).

Shared genetic interests also influence the stability of romantic relationships. For instance, marriages with children from former unions have elevated divorce rates, but marriages in which the couple shares children are less likely to end in divorce (Daly & Wilson, 1988b). The importance of shared genetic interests is underlined by the fact that sharing children increases marital stability even though it decreases marital satisfaction.

The Cohesiveness of the Evolutionary Approach

The evolutionary approach is appealing for its intellectual cohesiveness and comprehensiveness. Although we have ranged over a wide variety of topics, from jealousy and violence through parenting and love, they are all closely connected. Figure 6.1 depicts some central connections between the concepts we have addressed in this chapter.

The basic concepts of evolutionary psychology can be used to generate empirical questions about many of the topics discussed in this *Handbook*. Consider, for instance, community psychology and social support. An evolutionary perspective could make predictions about the role of kinship networks in social support. As people are more likely to help kin in highly threatening situations, it might be hypothesized that, controlling for degree of stress, psychological disorder might be lower for those surrounded by kin as opposed to non-kin. Depression has

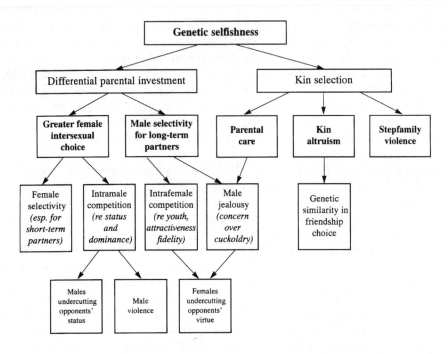

Figure 6.1 Interrelationships between general evolutionary assumptions about relationships. The theory of evolution by natural selection assumes competition between different genes. A number of general principles (such as kin selection and differential parental investment) flow indirectly from that central assumption. Various features of human relationships can in turn be derived from those general principles. This diagram is intended merely to illustrate the cohesiveness of the framework, and not exhaustively list the connections between different processes

increased dramatically during this century. Is its incidence inversely related to the decrease in contact with kin that accompanies urbanization and the modern work environment? If so, depression would be less prevalent in those who have maintained close relationships with kin. Interesting questions can also be asked about evolutionarily important issues in life stress. For instance, the most stressful life events include events such as divorce, death of a spouse and loss of a job (Holmes & Rahe, 1967), events that are directly connected to reproductive ability. Evolutionary hypotheses could be generated about the influence of gender, kinship networks and the stage of life cycle on the stressfulness of these events. For example, Thornhill & Thornhill (1989) review evidence and theory on psychological distress from an evolutionary perspective.

Likewise, we might ask about the role of kinship and shared reproductive interests in Aron & Aron's (see chapter in this volume) measures of overlap between self and others, or the effect of concerns about "face" in dominance hierarchies. For example, Wilson & Daly (1985) noted that "saving face" was a central concern in homicides committed by young males, and Hogan (1982) considered evolutionary constraints on self-presentation in social groups. Several chapters in this volume consider issues of development and aging. The evolutionary life history perspective assumes changes in reproductive behaviors at different ages that interact with variations in the social and physical environment (Belsky, Steinberg & Draper, 1991; Kenrick & Keefe, 1992). For instance, we noted that some fish change from a small drab male into a large colorful male if a territory becomes available, and even a female in a harem may change sex if the male dies. Do analogous processes apply to humans? For instance, is the onset of puberty influenced by the availability of attractive members of the opposite sex (signalled by a favorable sex ratio or feedback from the opposite sex about a preadolescent's relative attractiveness)? Is the onset of menopause influenced by the existence of nearby healthy children and grandchildren? These questions are not necessarily meant to be exhaustive and, as noted above, empirical research may indicate that they are ill-conceived. However, all living beings, including contemporary humans, are conglomerations of mechanisms designed by millions of years of natural selection. Our task is to identify those mechanisms and how they interact with the social and physical environment. Humans are in many ways unique as a species, but so are kinkajous, vampire bats and carpenter ants. An evolutionary perspective does not suggest that we ignore the unique adaptations of our species, only that we consider how they may be elucidated by the light of the most powerful set of principles applying to all living things.

An evolutionary perspective is completely compatible with an interest in cultural determinants of behavior (e.g., Barkow, Cosmides & Tooby, 1992; Lumsden & Wilson, 1981). However, researchers considering culture should also consider regularities across cultures, in addition to some of the seemingly bizarre differences between "us" and "them". Emerging evidence of cross-cultural universals, such as those regarding love and marriage, flirtation, aggression and mate criteria, suggest that underneath the surface variability there may be a similar core to human nature. Even cross-cultural differences, as in the case of marriage patterns, may reflect flexible underlying mechanisms. For instance, in cultures where there is a reasonable degree of promiscuity, paternal certainty is more problematic than in cultures with stronger norms of monogamy. In those cultures, maternal uncles may show relatively more interest in their sisters' children and relatively less interest in their wives' children (Daly & Wilson, 1983). This response makes sense from an evolutionary perspective because maternal uncles can be certain they share genes with their sisters' children. Considering culture through an evolutionary lens goes beyond cross-cultural universals, then, to consider how cultural practices reflect an interaction between ecological demands and the evolved cognitive and emotional mechanisms of our species.

EVOLUTIONARY PSYCHOLOGY AND EXISTING MODELS OF RELATIONSHIPS

Just as an evolutionary perspective can enrich, and be enriched by, existing empirical evidence on relationships, it can also enrich, and be enriched by, existing theoretical perspectives. For example, traditional social psychological models of relationships have emphasized: (1) the importance of self-evaluation in perceptions of a "fair exchange", (people desire partners who match or exceed their own "market value"), and (2) the importance of considering the phase of a relationship in partner evaluation (relationship expectations depend on the level of commitment). An evolutionary perspective sharpens predictions about how processes of self-evaluation and social exchange will be influenced by not only the level of investment in the relationship but also by the sex of the partner. We noted that men have less to lose from engaging in a casual sexual relationship. Hence, they should be less demanding in their criteria for casual sexual partners, and their criteria should be less tied to their own market value. Women, on the other hand, still risk impregnation in even a casual sexual relationship. They should remain very selective and concerned that the partner matches their own self-appraised "market value". Kenrick et al. (1993) examined subjects' self-ratings and their mate criteria for dating partners, one-night stands, and long-term partners and found clear support for these predictions. For committed, long-term relationships, women and men were equally selective and they both demanded partners matched to their own social value. Women considering partners for one-night stands showed the same self-calibrated standards. Men considering one-night stands, however, were not only willing to accept less desirable partners, but also showed less linkage between their criteria for casual sexual partners and their own self-evaluations.

These findings indicate how evolutionary and traditional social psychological perspectives can complement one another and lead to a more complex understanding of human behavior. Social psychological research on relationship phases was useful in extending previous evolutionary models; in turn, the evolutionary perspective focused attention on important gender differences in the content of the social exchange. The evolutionary perspective is, in essence, a social exchange model, but it differs from other models by making specific assumptions about the contents of social exchange, and rejecting the implicit assumption that what is valued depends arbitrarily on culture.

Cognitive approaches to social behavior can also be enhanced by an evolutionary perspective (Kenrick, Sadalla & Keefe, in press). Rather than assuming general cognitive processes that apply across judgment domains, an evolutionary perspective assumes adaptive, domain-specific mechanisms designed to deal effectively with issues important to survival and reproduction (Tooby & Cosmides, 1992). Consider one simple example. Previous research indicated perceptual "contrast effects" on a wide range of judgment tasks, including judgments of attractiveness (Kenrick & Gutierres, 1980): an average-looking stranger is rated as less attractive if judged after gorgeous people, and more attractive if rated after unattractive people. Interestingly, men in long-term relationships who looked at attractive female centerfolds not only rated their current partners as less attractive but also rated themselves as less in love with those partners. Women exposed to attractive male centerfolds showed a similar tendency, but it was much weaker (Kenrick, Gutierres & Goldberg, 1989). From an evolutionary perspective, the sex difference could reflect the gender difference in valuing signs of physical attractiveness; women being less likely to value a sexy, youthful body (as displayed in centerfolds) and more likely to value social dominance (which is not as apparent in centerfolds). A follow-up study varied both the physical attractiveness and social dominance of opposite sex targets (Kenrick et al., 1994). Men again rated themselves as less committed to their partners after viewing attractive women, whereas women who viewed attractive men showed no decrement in their relational commitment. Women's commitment was undermined by exposure to a series of highly dominant men, however. Hence, even ongoing cognition can be affected by the limits of evolutionarily adaptive mechanisms.

Adaptively "Irrational" Mate Preferences

Researchers using an evolutionary framework are often confronted with questions stemming from false assumptions (cf., Buss, 1995; Kenrick, 1994; Kenrick & Trost, 1987; Tooby & Cosmides, 1992). However, one recurring question is still unanswered: what about homosexuality? Homosexuality results in a failure to reproduce, making it appear to be genetically maladaptive. However, the involvement of genetic proclivities, hormones and neural structures contribute further to the puzzling biological status of homosexuality (e.g. Bailey & Pillard, 1991; Whitam, Diamond & Martin, 1993; Ellis & Ames, 1987; LeVay, 1993). A variety of hypotheses have addressed the potential adaptiveness of homosexuality (c.f., Kenrick et al., 1995), and it is premature to assume that it is either solely a result of environmental influences or uninformative about evolved adaptive mechanisms.

Bailey et al. (1994) suggested that homosexual preference might actually be informative about heterosexual mechanisms. They found that homosexual women, like heterosexual women, were relatively uninterested in casual sex (c.f., Buss & Schmitt, 1993; Kenrick et al., 1990, 1993). Obviously, this avoidance is not due to a conscious analysis of the relative costs of pregnancy, or lesbians would be more favorable toward casual sex than heterosexual women. Bailey et al. also found gay men to be as interested in physical attractiveness as heterosexual men, suggesting that heterosexual men's interest in attractiveness may not simply be a byproduct of media emphasis on female beauty. In general, Bailey et al. found the biological sex differences to be stronger than the effects of sexual orientation. In addition, the life-span pattern of age preferences in homosexual males is exactly the same as that shown by heterosexual males: young males want slightly older or younger partners, whereas older males prefer increasingly younger partners (Kenrick et al., 1995). These findings are difficult to explain in terms of either market-based rationality or cultural norms. Older homosexual males are not desirable to their preferred partners, for instance. Moreover, if media projections of the ideal member of the opposite sex determine preferences, homosexual men should, like heterosexual women, prefer relatively older partners. Instead, these data are more consistent with the notion that sexual attraction, like other adaptative systems, is a multi-faceted set of proximate mechanisms, each under the control of independent developmental processes (e.g., Buss, 1995; Tooby & Cosmides, 1992).

Modern evolutionary theorists assume that natural selection operates on specific environmentally triggered mechanisms, rather than producing individuals designed to think, feel and act in ways that are "generally adaptive". A generally adaptive organism is somehow presumed to be omniscient: to have prior knowledge about the particular genetic advantages likely to be gained from using each mechanism in each particular set of circumstances. The fallacy of that assumption can be demonstrated by considering a few mechanisms that appear to have evolved because of their past adaptive consequences. We have already mentioned the evolved preference for sweet tastes which, in the modern environment of abundant sugary foods, can lead to obesity and diabetes. However, this preference was selected under circumstances where it had, on average, a positive effect on survival. In the arena of sexual attraction, Shepher (1971) found that unrelated children raised in the same family-like kibbutz pods later showed a surprising lack of sexual and romantic attraction. Shepher argued that the unusual conditions of raising children together triggered a mechanism designed to dampen romantic attraction between siblings (thereby decreasing the danger of recessive gene combinations from incest). Again, the incest mechanism seems somewhat "irrational" when considered in isolation and in a novel, modern context.

From the modularity perspective, it becomes easier to understand how homosexual and heterosexual men can be alike in so many ways. By analogy, consider the case of vision, where we do not simply have a mechanism for "seeing" in general but a number of different structures for analyzing color, shape, movement, depth and other complex features of visual stimuli (Livingstone & Hubel, 1988). Given the central importance of reproduction to evolution, it would be surprising if the human brain had a single mechanism that controlled "reproducing like a male" VS. "reproducing like a female". Reproduction involves a series of very different tasks, including choosing a mate (weighing the relative importance of physical health, status, beauty and faithfulness), evaluating one's ability to attract a mate, making oneself attractive to a potential mate, competing with members of one's own sex for that mate, establishing an ongoing relationship, and so on (Buss, 1995; Kenrick & Trost, 1989). If these different processes, like the processes underlying vision or language, are controlled by independent mechanisms, we would not expect a change in one mechanism to be accompanied by reversals in all related mechanisms. If there is a biological mechanism that controls direction of sexual preference, it need not be accompanied by a complete reversal of other biological sex-typing mechanisms. Homosexual males clearly do not develop physically feminine secondary sex characteristics, such as wider hips and breasts, for instance. Hence, any biological mechanism involved in homosexual choice reflects not a global change in the "general" reproductive biology of the organism, but a much narrower change in one or a few specific cognitive mechanisms. Considered more broadly, this line of research suggests that even behaviors that seem anomalous may lead to interesting insights when considered in light of the emerging interdisciplinary synthesis of cognitive science and evolutionary biology.

CONCLUSION

The evolutionary perspective provides a comprehensive model of relationships, with the potential for elucidating and integrating all areas of relationship research. Beyond that, the model connects our work with cognitive science, anthropology and other areas of social science, as well as ecology, genetics, zoology and other sciences concerned with living organisms.

Chapter 7

A Process Model of Adult Attachment Formation

Debra Zeifman
and
Cindy Hazan
Cornell University, Ithaca, NY, USA

Imagine that while dining out one evening, you were to observe the interactions of three different couples. One couple (A) is standing at the bar talking. Each person seems intensely interested in and enthusiastic about everything the other has to say. Their animated conversation is interrupted by frequent laughter and seemingly awkward silences. The man reaches for his drink and "accidentally" brushes his arm against the woman's; their eyes meet briefly, they smile at each other, and then the woman looks down at her drink and begins stirring it. Across the room, a second couple (B) is seated at a corner table. They seem oblivious to the banter and bustle of activity around them. Their eyes are locked in mutual gaze, and their hands mingle playfully atop the table. They are speaking in hushed tones and appear to be totally absorbed in each other. They seem not to notice or care that the soup the waiter had placed in front of them is getting cold. Nearby, a third couple (C) sit across from each other studying their menus. After ordering, they speak in normal tones about the day's events. When their food arrives, they begin eating immediately and heartily. They seem very much at ease with one another.

It doesn't take a trained eye to notice such differences in the way couples interact, nor does it take any knowledge of the empirical literature on personal relationships to interpret these differences. Couple A is obviously engaged in a flirtation, from which one might infer that they just met. Couple B appear to be in love, and have probably been dating for several months. Couple C is an established pair whose comfort with each other suggests that they have been together for years. Their relationship may well have begun with a flirtation, like

Handbook of Personal Relationships, 2nd edn. Edited by Steve Duck.
© 1997 John Wiley & Sons Ltd.

that of couple A, and probably passed through a period during which their behavior toward each other resembled couple B's. What may not be so obvious is that this couple, who on the surface appear to be the least emotionally engaged, would likely be the most profoundly emotionally affected by a prolonged or permanent separation.

The fact that we can infer something about the length and nature of relationships from observed differences in couple interactions does not explain why such differences exist or why predictable changes occur. The meaning and function of such differences require explanation. Our primary goal in this chapter is to outline a normative model of adult attachment formation, using Bowlby's (1969/ 1982, 1973, 1980) ethological attachment theory as a guiding framework. In recent years, attachment-theoretical approaches to research on adult romantic relationships have proliferated (e.g., Bartholomew & Horowitz, 1991; Collins & Read, 1990; Feeney & Noller, 1990; Hazan & Shaver, 1987, 1990, 1993a,b; Hazan & Zeifman, 1994; Kirkpatrick & Davis, 1993; Kirkpatrick & Hazan, 1994; Kobak & Hazan, 1991; Mikulincer & Nachsohn, 1991; Parkes, Stevenson-Hinde & Marris, 1991; Simpson, 1990). The findings have enhanced our understanding of the ways in which people differ with respect to their relationship-related thoughts, feelings and behaviors (for a review, see Shaver & Hazan, 1993). However, virtually all of the work to date has focused on individual differences to the near-exclusion of normative processes. Moreover, adult attachment research typically presumes that romantic relationships are, by definition, attachment relationships. This assumption is based on Bowlby's (1979) claim that attachment behavior characterizes humans "from the cradle to the grave" and that, in adulthood, attachments take the form of pair-bonds—i.e., romantic or sexual relationships.

The tendency to presume that two individuals who are romantically involved are also attached to each other is understandable but, when we began to investigate the processes by which primary attachments are transferred from parents to romantic partners, we found that in adulthood, as in infancy, attachments take time to develop. Infants arrive into the world prepared to form attachments, but the emotional bond between infants and their particular caregivers requires months of interactions to become established. The same appears to be true of adult romantic attachments. However, the evolution of an adult flirtation into an attachment bond may be less pre-determined than the attachment of an infant to his or her caregiver. Not every romantic or sexual involvement develops into an enduring emotional bond. Research on adult attachment phenomena should ideally be grounded in an understanding of how adult attachments develop, and anchored to some index of the existence of an attachment bond. Independent of this more practical research concern, adult attachment formation processes are interesting and important in their own right.

The details of our model of adult attachment formation will be explicated in the pages that follow. The major components are: (1) the behaviors associated with attraction and infatuation can be viewed as species-typical programs designed to facilitate attachment formation; (2) these observed behaviors, as well as the associated underlying processes and mechanisms, evolved because attachment bonds serve unique and essential functions in human adaptation and survival at all ages; (3) the processes of attachment formation evident in adult couples are similar in important respects to the processes of attachment formation in infancy.

ETHOLOGICAL ATTACHMENT THEORY

Attachment theory (Bowlby, 1969/1982, 1973, 1980, 1988a) grew out of the following observations: infants and young children manifest profound and lasting distress if separated from their primary caregivers—even when their nutritional and hygienic needs are being met by surrogates—and reactions to such separations take the form of a predictable and universal sequence of stages. The first stage, *protest*, is characterized by obsessive search for the absent caregiver, disrupted sleeping and eating, inconsolable crying, and resistance to others' offers of comfort. This stage is reliably followed by *despair*, a period of passivity, lethargy and depressed mood. The duration of the reactions and the timing of the transition from the first stage to the second has been found to vary as a function of age and other individual difference factors, but their appearance and ordering is invariant across individuals, with one exception: infants younger than 7 months of age show little distress and accept surrogate caregiving without protest.

Initially, only the first two stages—protest and despair—were identified. Eventually, the youngsters resumed their normal, pre-separation activities and appeared to be fully recovered. It was only when they were reunited with their caregivers that the third stage became evident. Rather than exhibiting the expected response to reunion, these children ignored their primary caregivers and avoided contact with them. Their behavior suggested that a kind of emotional *detachment* had taken place. The reunions provided evidence of long-term effects of even brief separations. So did the fact that, when previously separated youngsters were visited by hospital staff several months after returning home, they exhibited an exaggerated fear response to what they thought signalled another separation.

Bowlby documented additional evidence that protracted separations can result in long-term deleterious effects on psychological development. Retrospective examination of the life histories of 44 juvenile delinquents revealed that a disproportionate number of them suffered episodes of maternal separation during infancy and early childhood (Bowlby, 1944). Attachment disruption qualified as a significant developmental risk factor, but the total absence of an attachment appeared to be even more costly. Abandoned infants reared in institutions, where basic nutritional and hygienic needs were met collectively by nursing staff, failed to thrive and often suffered alarming health decrements (Robertson, 1953; Spitz, 1946).

The search for an explanation of the reactions to and long-term effects of separation led Bowlby to examine the work of ethologists such as Lorenz and

Harlow. Based on careful observation and experimental manipulation, ethologists had demonstrated that the young of many altricial species possess an innate
tendency to become attached to a caregiver. In species who bear immature
young, the establishment of a strong and enduring bond between infant and
caregiver is adaptive in that it greatly enhances the infant's chances for survival.
Bowlby concluded that in our own altricial species, unlearned behaviors such as
clinging, sucking, smiling and crying serve to promote contact with a caregiver
and ensure that an attachment bond develops and that the infant receives the
care it requires in order to survive.

The reactions to separation from an attachment figure—protest, despair and
detachment—were thus comprehensible in terms of evolution and adaptation.
Were the infant to be accidentally separated from its mother in the environment
in which humans evolved, there would be a tremendous risk of death by starvation and predation. First the infant would let out a stream of loud calls in an
attempt to attract and guide the attention of its mother. But cries would only be
adaptive if the mother was nearby, and reunion imminent. Because continued
loud protests might attract predators, silent despair eventually becomes the more
adaptive response. Finally, when little hope of the mother's return remains,
survival depends on the youngster's being able to emotionally detach, fend for
itself or establish a new attachment.

Whereas the work of ethologists was helpful in explaining the importance of
attachment bonds and providing support for the notion that the tendency to
develop emotional bonds is a species-typical behavior, it was control systems
theory (Miller, Gallanter & Pribram, 1960) that Bowlby found useful in explaining the dynamics of attachment behavior and in identifying the features that
distinguish attachment bonds from other types of social relationships. All normal
human infants exhibit a common pattern of behavior in relation to their primary
caregiver: they tend to seek and maintain relatively close proximity to this person, retreat to her or him for comfort and reassurance in the face of perceived or
real danger, be distressed by and resist separations and, in this person's presence
(and in the absence of threat), engage in exploration and play.

From this universally observed dynamic, Bowlby postulated the existence of
an inborn behavioral system similar to the physiological systems that serve to
maintain set-goals for various body functions (e.g., temperature regulation, blood
pressure). The set-goal of the attachment system is a sufficient degree of physical
proximity to the attachment figure to ensure safety—a goal that would necessarily vary as a function of endogenous (e.g., state, age) and exogenous (e.g.,
novelty, threat) factors.

Implicit in the dynamic functioning of the attachment system are the features
or relational components that distinguish attachment bonds from other types of
social relationships. Specifically, the defining features of attachment are:
proximity-seeking (the tendency to seek and maintain relatively close proximity);
safe haven (the tendency to seek comfort and reassurance, especially in the face
of perceived or real threat); *separation distress* (the tendency to resist and be
distressed by separations); and *secure base* (the tendency to derive security from

and be emboldened by the availability of the attachment figure, which facilitates such non-attachment activities as exploration and play). A relationship in which these four components are present qualifies as an attachment bond.

Of course, infants do not emerge from the womb emotionally bonded to any particular individual. Whereas the attachment system itself—with its inherent dynamic and relational components—is hypothesized to be innate, the target of attachment behavior (i.e., the attachment figure) must be "selected". Attachment to a specific caregiver develops gradually over the course of the first years of life. Although the processes by which one individual comes to assume this position of lasting and pervasive influence is a continuous one, four relatively distinct phases can be discerned (Bowlby, 1969).

At birth, infants are prepared in a variety of ways to engage in social interaction (e.g., Trevarthan, 1979) and, when distressed, will seek and accept comfort indiscriminately. Bowlby called this the *pre-attachment* phase. Gradually, and beginning at around 3–4 months of age, the infant comes to preferentially direct signals (bids for interaction and contact) toward familiar adults, and especially the primary caregiver. This phase of differential signalling is referred to as *attachment-in-the-making*. A major transformation occurs around the age of 6 or 7 months. Infants not only become capable of self-produced locomotion but also begin to exhibit two new fears: strangers are treated with increasing caution and sometimes alarm, and separations from the primary caregiver are vociferously resisted.

Separation distress/protest has traditionally been considered the marker of an attachment (Ainsworth et al., 1978; Bowlby, 1969; Sroufe & Waters, 1977), and the associated phase is accordingly labeled *clear-cut attachment*. Another transformation in the attachment relationship occurs sometime during the second year of life. Increased representational and other cognitive capacities make brief separations more tolerable and delays in caregiver availability more understandable. In addition, children of this age show decreasing interest in their primary caregivers (and less frequent need for contact comfort), and increasing interest in exploratory activities and affiliative contact with peers. This final phase in infant-caregiver attachment formation is referred to as *goal-corrected partnership*.

ADULT ATTACHMENT

Bowlby believed that adults retain a strong tendency toward forming enduring emotional attachments. Whereas the infant becomes attached to a parent, prototypical adult attachments are formed with an opposite-sex peer. Weiss (1973, 1982, 1988) was the first to investigate adult attachment phenomena and, like Bowlby, he began with the responses of individuals to separation and loss. In his seminal work, Weiss noted that the ways in which his divorced and widowed subjects responded to separation were remarkably similar to the way children respond to separations from attachment figures. Initial reactions tended to be characterized by heightened arousal and anxiety. Subjects reported disruptions in their normal patterns of sleeping and eating, and also engaged in what could be seen as search behavior. For example, widows and widowers hallucinated their lost spouses; newly-divorced or separated individuals experienced a compulsion to reconnect with their former partners. Eventually, both separated and bereaved subjects grew listless and exhibited signs of depression. In time, most recovered through a process of gradual emotional detachment from the former beloved. As Weiss has argued, the sequence of reactions closely resembles the protest–despair–detachment pattern that Bowlby observed among infants and children (see also Lofland, 1982).

From an evolutionary perspective, attachment bonds between procreative partners are not as essential for individual survival as those between caregiver and infant. Nevertheless, they would have greatly enhanced the survival of off-spring. The trend among mammals (and primates in particular) to bear increasingly immature offspring and nurse them for several years imposed a heavy metabolic cost and increased predation risk for a female parenting on her own. As this burden raised the incidence of infant mortality, parental partnership and male parental care became necessary adaptations. Several authors have suggested that male–female romantic/sexual emotions were exploited for the purpose of keeping parents together in order to care for their offspring (Eibl-Eibesfeldt, 1975; Short, 1979).

Traditionally, the bond between adult partners has been viewed as having the primary purpose of shared parental caregiving. However, for the bond to serve that purpose effectively, it would have to precede the birth of offspring and be relatively enduring. The human female shows no outward signs of fertility, and may be sexually receptive at any point in her menstrual cycle. To ensure paternity, the human male would have had to guard his mate constantly until conception, which he could not reliably detect until months after it had occurred. In order to provide care for offspring, the male would have to remain during the lengthy gestation period. These facts all suggest that the attachment bond between adult lovers needed to be enduring and somewhat independent of offspring.

The similarities between infant–caregiver and pair-bond relationships are not limited to their adaptive significance. Both engage the emotion we call love, and are subserved by many of the same physiological and neurobiological mechanisms. In addition, there are many similarities in the conspicuous behavior of adult lovers and mother–infant pairs (Shaver, Hazan & Bradshaw, 1988). These two types of relationships are also widely perceived as the "closest" (Berscheid & Graziano, 1979) and both allow for the expression of behaviors that are non-normative in other social relationships, such as prolonged ventral–ventral contact and protracted mutual gazing (Hazan & Zeifman, 1994). Attachment relationships are a distinct subset of social relationships, distinguished by their characteristic features (e.g., separation distress) as well as their enduring and intimate nature.

Although there are many similarities between infant–caregiver dyads and romantic pairs, there are also several noteworthy differences. The attachment bond between infant and caregiver is complementary; the infant solicits comfort, and the caregiver provides it. Attachment bonds betweeen adult lovers are typically reciprocal, with both partners giving as well as receiving care. In addition, adult attachments also serve the function of sexual reproduction. Adult attachment bonds thus involve the integration of three behavioral systems: attachment, parenting and sexual mating (Shaver, Hazan & Bradshaw, 1988).

From a psychological perspective, it is not unexpected that these systems would become integrated to some extent in adulthood. Many studies have demonstrated the importance of mother–infant attachment for the possible development of normal parenting and sexual behavior. Studies of isolation-reared monkeys who did not form an attachment during infancy provide an example of the subsequent adult effects of infant attachment deprivation (Harlow & Harlow, 1965, 1962). Although these monkeys were rehabilitated in their affiliative relations with peers, they exhibited grossly dysfunctional parenting and sexual behaviors. Likewise, Lorenz's experimental subjects showed enduring effects of early attachment experiences (Lorenz, 1970). Ducklings who imprinted on him during infancy persisted in their attempts to mate with him when they reached sexual maturity. Such findings suggest that attachment experiences in infancy can influence adult parenting behavior as well as sexual mate choice.

In sum, there is ample evidence that infant-caregiver and adult pair-bond relationships are characterized by similar dynamics, have many features in common, and serve a similar function. Therefore, we postulate that both types of relationships are regulated by the same behavioral system—the attachment system. If this is the case, the processes by which attachment bonds are formed would likely be similar as well. As noted earlier, in tracking the development of attachment bonds during infancy, Bowlby identified four phases (although he acknowledged that the boundaries between phases are "fuzzy"). We propose a parallel four-phase process model to integrate and explain the behavior and phenomenology of adult romantic relationship development (a model explicated below and summarized in Table 7.1). Our focus will be normative processes, acknowledging in advance that each relationship is unique and idiosyncratic, and reserving a discussion of individual differences for later.

Pre-attachment: Attraction and Flirting

The distinguishing features of the pre-attachment phase during infancy are a readiness for and inherent interest in social interaction, and relatively indiscriminant social signalling. This combination of preparedness for certain types of social exchange and fairly promiscuous but distinctive signalling resembles adult flirting. Eibl-Eibesfeldt (1989) called this unique and distinctive pattern of behavior the "proceptive program". The defining characteristics of the program are: establishing eye contact and holding the gaze briefly; talking incon-

Table 7.1 A process model of adult attachment formation

Phase	Non-attached		Attached	
Attachment component*	Pre-attachment	Attachment-in-the-making	Clear-cut attachment	Goal-corrected partnership
	Proximity seeking	Safe haven	Separation distress	Secure base
Physical contact	Incidental/ "accidental"	Frequent, prolonged, arousing, "parental"	Frequent, less prolonged, comforting	Less frequent, deliberate, context-specific
Eye contact	"Stolen" glances, intermittent gazing	Frequent, protracted mutual gazing	Frequent, less pro-tracted mutual gazing	Less frequent, context-specific mutual gazing
Conversational content	Emotionally neutral, superficial, self-enhancing	Care-eliciting, emotional disclosure	Less emotional, care-eliciting, more mundane	Predominantly mundane
Voice quality	Animated, higher pitched, emotionally aroused	Hushed tones, whispers, soothing	Context-specific soothing, more normal tones and pitch	Predominantly normal
Eating/sleeping	Normal	Decreased	Near-normal	Normal
Mental representation of other	Generalized "template", expectations	Under construction	Begining to stabilize	Well-established, easily conjured-up
Neurochemistry/hormones	Pheromonal cues, PEA	PEA, oxytocin	(PEA), oxytocin, opioids	Oxytocin, opioids
Reactions to termination	None, minor disappointment	Lethargy, mild depression	Anxiety, disruption of activities	Extreme anxiety, pervasive physical and psychological disorganization

* Entries on this row represent the component of attachment that is added during each phase, such that all four components are present by the final phase.

sequentially but animatedly (by reason of vocal inflection, exclamation, exaggeration, laughing, heightened pitch and volume, and accelerated speed); progressively rotating to an *en-face* position; being brushed or lightly touched, as if inadvertently, without recoiling; and synchronizing postures, gestures and facial expressions. Typically, flirtatious displays are ambiguous, and hence deniable (Denzin, 1970), and their composition and meaning may vary as a function of gender (Montgomery, 1986).

Adult flirtations involve an exaggerated sense of excitement and regard for the other. Even relatively trivial information is met with great enthusiasm. This sends the message of interest and, by highlighting the emotional content of speech and gesture, may also serve to facilitate conversational synchronization. Flirtatious interactions are emotionally charged and have an arousing effect on the individuals involved.

However, unlike mother–infant pairs, lovers are not given to one another by birthright, and certainly their relationship begins on more precarious terms and with more limited intimacy. In contrast to the protracted gazing present almost from birth in caregiver–infant pairs (Stern, 1977), adult flirtations often begin with an accidental "catch of the eyes", and then a turning away, or with a seemingly "accidental" touch. Any presumption of intimacy is unwarranted at this stage and would likely be met with distancing by the receiving party. For example, premature self-disclosure of highly personal information places a developing relationship in jeopardy (Berg, 1984; Taylor, Altman & Wheeler, 1972). Disclosures designed to elicit care or emotional support would also violate social norms and likely pre-empt further progress of the pair. Rather, disclosures at this point are generally limited to superficial, often self-enhancing information (Altman & Taylor, 1973). Flirting, like the indiscriminant signalling of a young infant in the first months of life, is not restricted to one partner. Rather, it signifies a general readiness for social engagement. As such, the only component of attachment present during this phase is a strong motivation for *proximity seeking*.

Is there any reason to believe that a typical flirtation involves the attachment system at all? Isn't it more likely that the excitement and arousal are due to activation of the sexual mating system? We readily acknowledge that the sexual system is implicated in flirtatious behavior. As we have argued elsewhere (Hazan & Zeifman, 1994), sexual attraction is probably what fuels the proximity seeking that could eventually lead to attachment formation. However, there is evidence that flirting individuals are also responsive to attachment-relevant cues.

As noted earlier, infants come equipped with an attachment behavioral system, but the target of their attachment behaviors—the individual who will become their preferred partner—has to be selected. How does an infant "decide" whom to become attached to? Familiarity and responsiveness are the key factors (Ainsworth et al., 1978). Likewise, these factors play a major role in adult mate selection (Aron et al., 1989; Zajonc, 1968). When flirtations are initiated with more than immediate sexual gratification as the goal and, more specifically, with the hope or possibility that such engagement might lead to a lasting association, attachment-relevant cues like warmth, responsiveness and reciprocal liking are particularly important (Aron et al., 1989; Backman, 1959; Curtis & Miller, 1986). Sexual attraction ensures that we will seek and maintain proximity to individuals to whom we might become attached, but their attachment-worthiness is a consideration in and has an effect on the sexual attraction itself.

Attachment-in-the-making: Falling in Love

Sometime between 2 and 3 months of age, the indiscriminant signalling of infants becomes more selective. They begin to preferentially direct social signals (cries, smiles, gaze and vocalizations) toward the person who has been their primary caregiver. The interactions of mother–infant dyads during this phase begin to have the appearance of synchrony and attunement. Increasingly, they engage in intimate verbal exchanges, close bodily contact, and prolonged mutual gazing. The same behaviors are characteristic of two adults who are "falling in love".

Attachment-in-the-making is similar to the pre-attachment phase in the sense that social exchanges tend to be arousing. However, the arousal that accompanies infatuation is protracted and extends beyond the interaction. For example, adults in love experience sleeplessness and reduced food intake and, paradoxically, unbounded energy (Tennov, 1979). Liebowitz (1983) has hypothesized that this phase is mediated by the neurochemical phenylethylamine (PEA), similar in its effects to the amphetamines. In addition to stimulating increased arousal, amphetamines are known to act as mild hallucinogens, perhaps helping to account for the idealization known to accompany infatuation (Brehm, 1988; Tennov, 1979).

While couples who are in love find each other's presence stimulating, they also begin during this phase to find it comforting to be together, an effect that may be due in part to concomitant neurochemical and hormonal changes. The chemical basis for the desire to remain in close physical contact with the partner (i.e., cuddle), may be the same for mother–infant pairs and lovers. Oxytocin, a substance released during suckling–nursing interactions, and thought to induce maternal caregiving, is also released at sexual climax and has been implicated in the cuddling that often follows sexual intercourse (i.e., "afterplay") (Carter, 1992). Cuddling, or "contact comfort" as was demonstrated by Harlow, is central in establishing emotional bonds.

In the adult case, the trend toward increasingly comforting interactions is not limited to physical contact. Changes in voice quality can be noted, including soothing whispers and reassuring "babytalk". Further, whereas in the pre-attachment stage, self-disclosures may be limited to positive or neutral facts, as couples fall in love they begin to exchange more personal information, including stories of painful experiences, fears, family secrets and detailed accounts of previous relationships (Altman & Taylor, 1973). The exchange of this type of information constitutes a test of commitment, as well as a bid for acceptance and care. Hence, couples begin to serve as sources of mutual emotional support and their relationship takes on an additional feature of attachment—namely, *safe haven*.

A couple in love engages in the kinds of behaviors that, in infancy, are known to facilitate attachment formation. Prolonged mutual gazing, protracted mutually ventral contact, nuzzling and cuddling are typical and distinguishing features of infant–caregiver exchanges; significantly, they are also typical of lovers' exchanges, but not of friendships or other social bonds. There appears to be a need during the falling-in-love phase to maintain nearly continuous physical contact. It is also noteworthy that adults who are falling in love engage in physical contact that is "reassuring" in nature—as evidenced by "parental" gestures such as hand-holding or placing an arm around the other's shoulder or waist. These behaviors can be contrasted with the less intimate and arousal-inducing touches that typify flirtations or purely sexual encounters. We suspect that the prolonged mutual gazing typical of this phase facilitates the development of a mental representation of the partner—or what Bowlby (1979) referred to as an internal working model.

If a relationship ends during this phase (which, according to Liebowitz, is mediated by endogenous amphetamines), the individuals will probably experience feelings that are the opposite of energized, including perhaps even mild sadness or depression, but they are unlikely to experience the intense anxiety or severe disruption of daily functioning characteristic of attachment dissolution. Needs for emotional support (safe haven) can be almost as easily satisfied by family and friends, and stimulation can be found elsewhere.

In comparing the data on premarital break-ups in college samples with the data on divorce and widowhood, our expectations are confirmed. College students who end brief love affairs report experiencing a period of disappointment and depression, but rarely suffer from debilitating anxiety (e.g., Hill, Rubin & Peplau, 1976). The strategies for coping with premarital break-ups also tell us something about what has been lost; individuals increase time spent with friends, and often immediately begin dating someone else. These strategies differ markedly from those that Weiss (1975) documented for individuals who have lost a marriage partner. Recent widows and widowers can hardly imagine dating, and newly divorced individuals are often unsuccessful in their initial attempts. In these cases, the company of strangers and friends cannot replace the needs fulfilled by an attachment figure.

Clear-cut Attachment: Loving

At what point does a relationship partner become an attachment figure? The answer may lie in the sorts of changes that occur as couples make the transition from being in love to loving each other. In the course of a developing romantic relationship, several predictable changes occur. As couple members become increasingly familiar with each other, simply being together is no longer as arousal-inducing. Idealization, which is so common among new couples, is eventually replaced by a more realistic view of partners' imperfections and limitations (Hatfield, Traupmann & Sprecher, 1984). The frequency of sexual activity declines (Fisher, 1992; Traupmann & Hatfield, 1981), and the importance of emotional supportiveness and nurturance relative to sexual satisfaction increases (Kotler, 1985; Reedy, Birren & Schaie, 1981). Couples spend less and less time locked in mutual gaze and, having already shared the intimate details of their lives, begin to spend their time together discussing decreasingly personal and less relationship-focused issues (Brehm, 1992). When they talk to each other, they spend less time whispering and more time speaking in normal tones. In contrast to the diminished interest in food and sleep that dominated their first days and weeks together, they now relish shared meals and long hours of joint slumber.

What explains these predictable changes, and how do they relate to attachment? Recall the 7-month transition in infancy—a qualitative shift between simply enjoying social closeness and needing the closeness of a specific individual. Although infants of this age typically approach (seek proximity to) as well as solicit and accept care from a number of familiar people (i.e., use them as havens of safety), displays of separation protest and distress are usually exclusively directed toward the primary caregiver. The main function of an attachment bond is to provide a sense of security. Thus, it follows that individuals would experience feelings of anxiety and distress in the absence of their primary source of comfort and security.

The separation distress reactions of infants have been related to a class of brain chemicals known as the endogenous opioids. Panksepp (Panksepp, Siviy & Normansell, 1985) noted that separation distress reactions are similar to the drug withdrawal reactions of narcotics addicts. Both "withdrawal" syndromes are characterized by tearfulness and distress vocalizations, anxiety and trembling, stereotypies (e.g., rocking) and other self-soothing behaviors. Based on these similarities, Panksepp began an exploration of the role of endogenous opioids in infant attachment formation. In diverse species, opioid administration ameliorates the disorganizing effects of separation, whereas opioid blockage exacerbates it (Panksepp, Siviy & Normansell, 1985). These findings have led to the conclusion that opioids are implicated in the formation of attachment bonds.

According to Liebowitz's model, the shift from the amphetamine-like rush of the initial stages of a romance to the calm and contentment of a more established pair reflects a change in neurochemistry (Liebowitz, 1983). As noted earlier, PEA is one source of the feelings of boundless energy and invincibility that individuals often experience when they are in love. If things "go right", Liebowitz predicted, the amphetamine-like feelings mediated by PEA gradually give way to the contentment and subjective sense of well-being associated with endogenous opioids.

In addition to alleviating anxiety, opioids are powerful conditioning agents. Through classical conditioning, stimuli paired with opioid drugs rapidly become associated with their calming effects, and become strongly preferred. Moreover, such preferences are extremely difficult to extinguish. A typical intimate encounter between romantic partners involves an initial increase in stimulation and arousal, followed by relief, satisfaction and calm. The similarity in symptoms of an addict being weaned from a narcotic drug and a person suffering from a broken heart lends further support to the hypothesis of opioid involvement in the formation of affectional bonds. It also suggests that attachment may be defined as the conditioning of an individual's opioid system to the stimulus of a particular other. As such, separation distress would be an appropriate marker of attachment formation.

If attachment involves conditioning of the opioid system, such effects would be expected to result from repeated anxiety- and/or tension-alleviating interactions. Exchanges of this type are a common feature of both parent–child and adult romantic relationships. When a parent comforts a crying infant, the parent becomes associated (in the infant's mind) with the alleviation of distress. Similarly, a lover comes to be associated with stress reduction, including the alleviation of tension following sexual climax. In summary, relationships that develop into attachment bonds are hypothesized to be those in which heightened physiological arousal is repeatedly attenuated by the partner.

Liebowitz's description of the phenomenology of the attraction and attachment phases leads to predictions about the sensations that would be experienced were a relationship to end during each of these two phases. Because PEA is a stimulant, withdrawal would resemble caffeine withdrawal. Break-ups during the PEA-mediated phase of arousal and excitement would therefore lead to mild depression and lethargy. Former partners might, for example, eat and/or sleep more than usual, and be generally less active. If, on the other hand, the break-up occurred during the opioid-mediated phase (i.e., after an attachment had formed), the resulting symptoms would likely be quite different. Dissolution would be expected to cause heightened anxiety and even panic, increased activity, dysregulation of bodily functions, such as reduced appetite and insomnia.

Bowlby claimed that relationships characterized by the four defining features of attachment would tend to be those between children and their parents, and between adult romantic partners. We developed measures of these components of attachment and administered them to a large group of individuals representing the age range from late adolescence to late adulthood (Hazan & Zeifman, 1994). We found that full-blown attachments—that is, relationships in which all four components were present—were almost exclusively limited to bonds with parents or sexual partners. In addition, we found that adults who either had no partner or who had been with their partners for less than 2 years reported experiencing separation distress only in relation to their parents—and, interestingly, not in relation to best friends, siblings, or others with whom they probably also have close relationships.

Pending the results of our ongoing research, we suggest that separation distress is as plausible and reasonable a criterion of attachment formation in adulthood as it is in infancy. However, documenting adult separation distress, except in such extreme circumstances as divorce and death, is far more challenging than documenting it during infancy, when the attachment figure's mere departure from a room reliably elicits heart-wrenching cries (Ainsworth et al., 1978). Adults are more adept at regulating and inhibiting negative emotional reactions, and more capable of employing cognitive strategies to cope with otherwise painful and disruptive experiences. Nevertheless, studies of the prolonged involuntary separations associated with military service and work-related travel provide evidence that adults, like infants and children, are distressed and disrupted by separations from their attachment figures (Vormbrock, 1993).

Goal-corrected Partnership: Life as Usual

Couples eventually resume their pre-romance activities. Friendships, work and other real-world obligations that are often neglected by individuals in the midst of a courtship gradually reassume their status in the hierarchy of commitments. In a sense, life-as-usual returns.

This transformation parallels one that occurs sometime between the second and third years of life in the way infants (now toddlers) relate to their primary caregivers. The frequency of attachment behaviors decreases and the need for close physical contact is somewhat attenuated. The reliability of the caregiver is well established, and the resulting confidence and security provide support for non-attachment activities. The child exhibits increased interest in exploratory activity, especially social contact with peers. The final component of attachment—secure base—is now in place.

For adult pairs, there is a noticeable decrease in the frequency and duration of mutual gazing and physical contact—of the sexual as well as the parental variety. Also, there is a reorientation of attention and stimulation-seeking to sources outside the relationship. Conversations reflect an outward focus, in contrast to the personal, partner- and relationship-focused exchanges which dominate earlier phases. At this point, the strong emotional connection between partners is not readily apparent, but beneath the surface there may be a profound interdependence—a phenomenon described by Berscheid (1983).

Hofer (1984) has proposed that this deeper interdependence involves the co-regulation of physiological systems. In essence, each partner comes to serve as one of the external cues or stimuli that provide regulatory input to internal systems (just as light–dark cycles influence sleep). Hofer refers to this physiological interdependence as "entrainment". The removal of the cues explain in part the disorganization that accompanies bereavement.

Examples of entrainment abound in the animal and human infant literatures. For example, in one monogamous species of bird, the ring dove, elaborate interwoven behavioral and physiological changes associated with pair-bonding have been elucidated (Silver, 1978). The male sings, and the female's ovaries begin to develop; "she" displays signs of receptivity, and "he" begins to gather materials and build a nest for them. The relationship between human infants and their caregivers are also characterized by a high degree of physiological interdependence. For example, when a human infant cries, the temperature of the mother's breasts rises (Vuorenkowski et al., 1969); as the infant suckles, milk is let down (Brake, Shair & Hofer, 1988).

Entrainment in human pair-bonds has not been as thoroughly investigated, although a few examples can be found in the literature. For instance, women ovulate more regularly if they are in a sexual relationship than if they have only sporadic sexual contact, or are celibate (Cutler et al., 1985; Veith et al., 1983). Likewise, they are more likely to continue having menstrual periods in their middle years, that is to reach menopause later, if they engage in regular sexual activity (Cutler et al., 1986). Clearly, entrainment of the type described by Hofer does exist in human pair-bonds. Systematic study may reveal other physiological co-adjustments between couples that could help to explain the devastating and pervasive effects of separation and attachment loss.

Another telling sign of couples' dependence on each other as stimuli is the tendency among grieving individuals to report hallucinations and illusions of the bereavement object following death (Lindemann, 1942). This may be a remnant of a mechanism whereby the image is used to derive security during periods of separation. Mourners sometimes express the fear that the image, the face, of the loved one will be forgotten; hallucinations are a meager attempt to hold the image "on line".

INDIVIDUAL DIFFERENCES IN ATTACHMENT

Up to this point, we have said little about individual differences in attachment, except to note that they have been the focus of most adult attachment research to date. The same can be said about infant attachment research. In the first empirical tests of Bowlby's theory, Ainsworth identified three major patterns of individual differences (Ainsworth et al., 1978). Hazan & Shaver (1987; 1990) documented three analogous patterns of adult romantic attachment. The *secure* pattern is characterized by the enjoyment of closeness with partners, and confidence that partners will be reliable and responsive. In contrast, *ambivalent* attachment involves a strong desire for closeness coupled with a lack of confidence in partner responsiveness. This tension between desire and doubt leads to frequent and intense feelings of anger and fear. The *avoidant* pattern is also based on a lack of confidence in partners, but results in avoidance rather than intensified approach. In both infancy and adulthood, the normative pattern is secure attachment (Campos et al., 1983; Shaver & Hazan, 1988).

The present model summarizes attachment formation processes and phases from a normative perspective. We would predict some variations in the processes, and perhaps even the phases, as a result of individual differences in attachment, and there is empirical evidence to support such predictions. For example, we found attachment style differences in the types of physical contact that individuals seek and enjoy or try to avoid (Hazan, Zeifman & Middleton,

1994). Avoidant adults reported enjoying purely sexual contact (e.g., oral and anal sex) but found more emotionally intimate contact (e.g., kissing, cuddling, nuzzling) to be aversive. Ambivalents reported the opposite pattern of preferences, and viewed sexual activity primarily as a means for gratifying intimacy and comfort needs. The secure group found pleasure in both types of physical contact, especially within the context of an ongoing relationship (as opposed to one-night stands, for example).

The physical contact preferences associated with each attachment style may help to explain their relative rates of success when it comes to establishing an enduring relationship. The secures, who are relatively more successful and significantly less likely to experience relationship dissolution (Hazan & Shaver, 1987; Kirkpatrick & Hazan, 1994), engage in the kinds of physical contact necessary to satisfy their own and their partners' attachment (and sexual) needs. Avoidants, in contrast, have an expressed aversion to the type of contact thought to foster an attachment. The preferences of ambivalents suggest that they have somewhat excessive attachment needs and a marked lack of interest in sex, both of which could jeopardize their relationships. Thus, insecure attachment—through its effects on physical contact—appears to interfere with attachment formation.

The effects of attachment style differences are not limited to the arena of physical contact. Existing evidence suggests not only that attachment style influences behavior in several domains relevant to our process model, but that the pattern of influences is consistent across domains. In general, avoidants distance themselves from their partners and ambivalents make inappropriate and premature bids for intimacy. These patterns are revealed in such relevant behaviors as the frequency and selectiveness of self-disclosures (Mikulincer & Nachshon, 1991), the tendency to solicit comfort from a partner in response to stress (Simpson & Gangestad, 1992), and willingness to engage in uncommitted sex (Brennan, Shaver & Tobey, 1991; Simpson, 1990). Such findings, together with our normative model, suggest that avoidant adults might be reluctant to engage in the kinds of behavior that facilitate attachment formation, whereas ambivalents might attempt to rush the process and, in doing so, behave in ways that violate norms governing each phase. In both cases, the probability that a stable bond will develop is reduced.

Despite individual differences and their effects on relationship processes, insecure attachment does not preclude the development of strong and enduring emotional bonds. Just as infants who are abused or neglected nevertheless become attached to their caregivers (Crittenden, 1988), so too adults in dysfunctional relationships become attached to their partners. As Bowlby argued, attachment motivation is sufficiently powerful across the life span that attachment bonds can develop even under grossly non-optimal circumstances.

CONCLUSIONS AND FUTURE DIRECTIONS

We have presented a four-phase normative model of adult attachment formation. At this point, we are hypothesizing an invariant sequence of phases, as well as coherence of features within each phase. For instance, a certain level of self-disclosure would coincide with a corresponding level of eye contact; intimate physical contact would accompany a correspondingly intimate degree of psychological closeness, and so on. However, the timing of progress from one phase to the next would vary widely as a function of individual differences—e.g., in age, attachment style, gender, culture, values.

We are currently testing several different components and implications of the model. An overarching goal is to identify an index of the existence of an adult attachment bond. As we have argued, during the transition from non-attached to attached, a shift occurs in the balance of the arousal-inducing and arousal-moderating effects of the partner's presence. At the same time that the partner's presence becomes more calming than exciting, his or her absence elicits anxiety and distress. Thus, separation distress—the marker of attachment in infancy—is the prime candidate for an index of adult attachment.

Documenting adult separation distress has proved challenging. Unlike infants, adults are adept at inhibiting expressions of negative affect. Furthermore, they can utilize cognitive strategies to cope with separations and regulate their own negative emotional responses. While reactions to such extreme circumstances as death of or separation from a partner provide unmistakable evidence of separation distress, documenting the negative effects of temporary or short-term separations requires examination of more subtle indices, such as disruptions in routine patterns of sleep, activity and food intake.

We began with a description of three hypothetical couples whose interactions revealed differences in the nature of their respective relationships. Our goal was to move beyond observables to the underlying function and meaning of the differences. Doing so has required that we draw on work from a number of different disciplines and sub-areas within our own discipline of psychology. By adopting a comparative and multidisciplinary approach, we have elucidated several important but unexplored issues. With a full appreciation for the challenges that lie ahead, we invite the next generation of attachment researchers to join us in exploring this uncharted territory.

ACKNOWLEDGEMENTS

We thank Richard L. Canfield, Francesco Del Vecchio, Steve Duck, William Ickes, Elizabeth Leff, and David Sbarra for their helpful comments on earlier drafts of this chapter.

Chapter 8

Perspectives on Interracial Relationships

Stanley O. Gaines Jr
Pomona College, Claremont, CA, USA
and
William Ickes
University of Texas, Arlington, TX, USA

Because interracial relationships are different from other kinds of relationships, they warrant a special accounting. Providing such an accounting—or, at least, a first approximation of one—is the major goal of this chapter. Starting from the premise that interracial relationships are different from other types of interethnic relationships, we will explore the nature of these differences and their implications for the perceptions by "outsiders" and "insiders" of various subtypes of interracial relationships (same-sex vs. mixed-sex, romantic vs. platonic).

We begin by reviewing evidence that interracial relationships are indeed different from other kinds of relationships. We then examine interracial relationships from two general perspectives: (1) the "outside" perspective of individuals who are observers of these relationships, and (2) the "inside" perspective of individuals who are the members of these relationships. To help illustrate and explain the processes that are presumed to underlie each of these perspectives, a number of relevant theoretical principles from the field of social psychology are invoked. Our discussion of these issues leads us to examine six types of interracial relationships (i.e., male–male friendships, female–female friendships, male–female friendships, male–female romantic relationships, male–male romantic relationships, and female–female romantic relationships) in terms of the two contrasting perspectives. From the tensions implicated by the interplay of the "outside" and "inside" perspectives, dynamic elements characteristic of each of these six types of interracial relationships are then proposed.

Handbook of Personal Relationships, 2nd edn. Edited by Steve Duck.
© 1997 John Wiley & Sons Ltd.

INTERRACIAL RELATIONSHIPS ARE DIFFERENT FROM OTHER KINDS OF RELATIONSHIPS

Evidence that interracial relationships are indeed different from other kinds of relationships is not hard to find. Two types of evidence are especially relevant: (1) the statistical infrequency of interracial relationships, and (2) evidence that interracial relationships are different in distinctive ways from the larger class of interethnic relationships.

Interracial Relationships are Statistically Infrequent

Interracial relationships are statistically infrequent, occurring much less often than actuarial projections would predict. Even in this ostensibly post-civil rights era, interracial friendships remain the exception rather than the norm (Blieszner & Adams, 1992; Furman, 1985; Todd et al., 1992), as do interracial marriages (Levinger & Rands, 1985; Todd et al., 1992; Zweigenhaft & Domhoff, 1991). Statistics regarding the incidence of interracial friendships and dating relationships are, of course, substantially harder to find than are corresponding statistics regarding interracial marriages (see Zweigenhaft & Domhoff, 1991). However, if we assume that marital relationships are the most intimate (and, by extension, the most difficult to establish and maintain; Levinger & Rands, 1985) of all interracial relationships, we may regard the incidence of interracial marriages as a lower limit on the incidence of interracial relationships as a whole.

As of March 1993, interracial couples composed 2.2% of all married couples (US Bureau of the Census, 1994). Among interracial couples in 1993, 20.3% consisted of Black/White pairs. Furthermore, among Black/White pairs, 75% consisted of Black male/White female pairs. Interestingly, Latinas/os and Asian-Americans are much more likely to marry Anglos than are African-Americans (Sanjek, 1994). Also, persons of color rarely marry other persons of color who do not share the same ethnicity.

How do individuals decide which ingroups and outgroups are to be regarded as essential to their self-concept and self-esteem? Clearly, society provides us (via socializing agents such as parents, teachers, religious leaders and media figures) with the relevant information (Allport, 1954/1979); we are not born knowing which ingroup–outgroup distinctions are supposed to be most important. In the USA, the enslavement of African-Americans until the Civil War, the seizure of land previously settled by Native Americans and Latinas/os during the colonial era, and the incarceration of Asian Americans during World War II (especially those of known or suspected Japanese ancestry) all serve as vivid historical reminders that, as Cornel West (1993) put it, "Race matters".

Interracial Relationships are Different from Other Interethnic Relationships

Further evidence for the distinctiveness of interracial relationships is that they represent a distinct subset within the larger class of *interethnic relationships*. A comparison of interracial and interreligious marriages is informative because both represent different types of interethnic marriages (i.e., marriages involving persons from dissimilar racial, language, religious, and/or national groups; Ho, 1984; Yinger, 1994). Nevertheless, the relatively low rates of interracial marriage contrast sharply with those of interreligious marriages in the USA (Ho, 1984; Levinger & Rands, 1985). If Ho's (1984) estimate of interethnic marriages accounting for one-third of all marriages in the USA is correct, then even after taking marriages among "White ethnics" into consideration, interreligious marriages greatly outnumber (and are greatly more probable than) interracial marriages. Thus, Allport's (1954/1979) assessment that racial differences were markedly more salient than religious differences in American society is just is true at the close of this century as it was during the middle portion.

Of course, the categories of interracial and interreligious marriage are not mutually exclusive. For instance, Black Protestant/White Jewish marriages would qualify as interracial *and* interreligious (see Zweigenhaft & Domhoff, 1991). Nevertheless, the fact that interracial marriages are so infrequent and improbable in comparison to interreligious marriages is *prima facie* evidence for important differences between the two. It is important to note, however, that any consideration of such differences must begin with the recognition of a fundamental similarity: both interracial and interreligious marriages involve at least one partner who is stigmatized by society. Goffman (1963) classified stigmas pertaining to (1) race/ethnicity, (2) nation of origin, and (3) religion as "*tribal stigmas* ... that can be transmitted through lineages and equally contaminate all members of a family" (p. 49, italics added). Thus, marriages involving persons from different racial groups as well as persons from different religious groups both have the potential to draw unwanted attention toward the "stigmatized" (i.e., racial or religious minority) partner, toward the "normal" (i.e., racial or religious majority) partner, and toward their offspring as well.

Given that both interracial and interreligious marriages are stigmatized, what factors might account for the contrasting trends in their statistical infrequency? Levinger & Rands (1985) have suggested the following answers:

> An explanation may invoke slow-changing norms concerning race and fast-changing norms for religion. Racial discrimination, even though it has lessened greatly in the legal system, strongly resists change. Not only do people remain suspicious of others who look different physically, but racial differences are linked historically to differences in social class, residence, education, and economic opportunities and resources. One's racial features are determined genetically and do not change over time. In contrast, one's religious affiliation is independent of one's genetic features and is susceptible to alteration. Although some persons hold their religious beliefs

throughout their lifetime, others hold them so weakly that they may undergo dramatic change.

Given the fixity of race and the plasticity of religion, intermarrying racially versus religiously has quite different implications: interracial partners retain their public skin differences, whereas interreligious partners either can privately de-emphasize their religious beliefs or change toward a common orientation. Further, whereas the offspring of interracial unions are marked visibly by their parents' genetic makeup, children from interreligious marriages can develop their personal faith in their own unique fashion (pp. 315–316).

Levinger & Rands (1985) propose that the greater stigmatization of interracial vs. interreligious marriages derives from a number of interrelated factors. These include (1) *xenophobia*—being "suspicious of others who look different physically", (2) *negative social stereotyping* based on historical linkages "to differences in social class, residence, education, and economic opportunities and resources"; and (3) the origin of interracial differences in *genetic factors* which, unlike the different beliefs that underlie religious differences, are highly visible and cannot be readily altered or ignored. We suggest that Levinger & Rands' (1985) analysis neatly captures the essential features of what we term the "outsiders' perspective" on interracial relationships in general, including—but not limited to—interracial marriages. We further suggest that although this perspective is crucial to understanding interracial relationships, the understanding it provides is necessarily incomplete. A more complete understanding requires that the "outsiders' perspective" be complemented with an "insiders' perspective" that represents the view of an interracial relationship that is held by its members. Moreover, because the dynamic tensions between these two perspectives can influence the nature and course of interracial relationships, the interaction of these two perspectives must be considered as well.

Why should the insider–outsider difference regarding interracial relationships matter to relationship researchers? As Duck (1990) has noted, relationship researchers commonly assume that one "true" account of relationship processes is to be found and that they (rather than the relationship members) are uniquely equipped to construct that account. Such a rationale implies that when—as often happens—the insiders construct accounts of their shared lives that are at odds with relationship researchers' accounts of those same relationships, the outsiders (i.e., relationship researchers) are likely to privilege their own accounts over those of the relationship members (Olson, 1977; see also Duck, 1990; Duck & Sants, 1983; Kelley, 1979; Surra & Ridley, 1991). Such a danger is real even when researchers and their participants belong to the same racial group (usually Anglos), and becomes all the more imminent when at least one of the members of each dyad belongs to a racial group that is dissimilar to that of the researchers.

How does the elucidation of this insider/outsider difference in perspective help us to comprehend interracial relationship processes in particular? Furthermore, what does an examination of the tension between the two perspectives add to our ability to comprehend and explain interracial relationships? In answering these questions, we note that (a) acknowledging the insider–outsider difference allows us to make explicit and to critically evaluate the oft-implicit, oft-unscrutinized theories characterizing outsiders' accounts of such seemingly anomalous relationships; and (b) examining the potential impact of the tension between insider and outsider accounts upon the relational lives of insiders allows us to identify the overt and covert behavioral strategies that insiders employ in order to minimize that tension. Accordingly, in the remaining sections of this chapter we consider both the perspectives of the "outsiders" and the "insiders" regarding interracial relationships. We then examine some implications of the tension between these two perspectives for the various subtypes of interracial relationships.

THE "OUTSIDERS' PERSPECTIVE" ON INTERRACIAL RELATIONSHIPS

Levinger & Rands' (1985) analysis suggests that both genetic and environmental (i.e., social learning) factors contribute to the "outsiders' perspective", and thus in combination help explain the low incidence of interracial marriage. Unfortunately, a comprehensive review of all the genetic and social-learning factors that might be implicated by such an analysis is beyond the scope of this chapter. Our more modest goal, therefore, is to suggest that *genetic predispositions* provide a deep-rooted and essentially non-cognitive basis for the "outsiders' view" of interracial relationships, a view which—in humans, at least—is further modified, refined and complicated by a *cognitive overlay* that derives from a variety of perceptual and cognitive inputs. In discussing both the genetic predispositions and the cognitive overlay that presumably define the "outsider's view" of interracial relationships, we offer a few illustrative examples instead of an exhaustive list of all of the potentially relevant factors.

Xenophobia as an Unlearned Genetic Predisposition

Writing within an evolutionary framework, Rajecki (1985) proposed that *xenophobia* is a genetically determined phenomenon that explains human as well as infrahuman patterns of within-group cooperation and between-group competition. Rajecki's (1985) evolutionary approach provides a relatively non-cognitive account of what he assumes to be primary, deep-rooted reactions to interracial relationships.

To ensure both their personal survival and the survival of their genes in subsequent generations, humans—like other social animals—must be able to position themselves within status hierarchies. Ingroups such as family, tribe and nation provide individuals with unique niches within the prevailing social order. By maintaining harmonious relations with ingroup members, toward whom individuals adopt either a dominant or a submissive stance, individuals attempt to ensure that their physical and social environments will remain relatively stable and, thus, conducive to their survival as well as the survival of their progeny (Krebs & Miller, 1985).

Whereas interactions with ingroup members tend to promote social stability, interactions with outgroup members may portend social change. With social change comes an implicit or explicit threat to individuals' sense of security. Especially when tangible resources are scarce, outgroup members may serve as visible reminders that individuals' control over their own physical and social environments, and hence over their own survival (and the survival of their offspring), is tenuous at best. According to Rajecki (1985), xenophobia is evoked as an unlearned, genetically-based predisposition when an outgroup member intentionally or unintentionally enters territory demarcated by the ingroup in question. If the outgroup member is outnumbered by the ingroup members, the ingroup members generally will retaliate against the interloper (see also Krebs & Miller, 1985).

Why do ingroup members experience the xenophobia that leads them to retaliate against interlopers (i.e., outgroup members) who are in the minority? Rajecki (1985) proposed that when a pre-existing group is left to its own devices, each member of the ingroup is given the opportunity to mate and thus contribute to the "blood line" of the species. In order to minimize within-group conflict vis-á-vis acquisition of tangible resources that are crucial to the survival of individual ingroup members (e.g., food), and to the survival of the ingroup's genes from generation to generation (e.g., sex), ingroup members collectively construct dominance hierarchies in which each individual is granted at least minimal access to tangible resources—including opportunities to mate. Once an outgroup member of the same species, biological sex and approximate age as one or more of the ingroup members actually infiltrates the group, direct ingroup–outgroup competition ensues:

> ... The [key idea is] that more or less amicable relations between group members are due to their mutual control and predictability. ... [W]hen [an individual] encounters and confronts a stranger of the same age and sex, it neither knows for certain what behavior to expect nor what dominance relationship exists between itself and the other. Assuming that the sheer ambiguity is intolerable and further that most gregarious organisms continuously strive for dominance and exercise it when they have it, the issue of the status relationship between the two strangers should not remain unsettled for long. If the two remain in contact, attempts to establish predictability and control should be made manifest quickly, and perhaps dramatically (p. 17).

According to Rajecki's account of xenophobia, retaliation toward an outgroup member becomes more likely to the extent that, relative to ingroup members, the outgroup member is: (a) physically dissimilar (physical dissimilarity being a probable marker of genetic dissimilarity); (b) unfamiliar and behaviorally unpredictable (thus heightening anxiety and uncertainty about the dominance relationship that might exist); and (c) in a numerical minority (outnumbered). Because inclusive genetic fitness should be enhanced for ingroup members who retaliate against outgroup members when these conditions are met, evidence for outgroup retaliation of this type should be—and is—evident across a wide range of species (for a review, see Rajecki, 1985).

Interestingly, some of the most consistent and compelling evidence for this account comes from field studies of non-human primate species, including free-ranging Barbary macaques (Deag, 1977), pigtail macaques (Bernstein, 1969), mangabeys (Bernstein, 1971) and rhesus monkeys (Bernstein, 1964). For example, when outgroup members were introduced into natural ingroups of rhesus monkeys:

> [E]xcept for some infant strangers, all the rest of the introduced animals were met with intense aggression that included threats, chases, and direct physical attacks . . . Overall, aggression in natural groups such as these increased over baseline by from 42% to 82% as a consequence of the release of strangers in the vicinity. Of the 18 strangers released in the study (again, excluding infants) 100% were either killed or driven completely away! (Rajecki, 1985, p. 20).

Rajecki's account of xenophobic aggression toward physically dissimilar outgroup members might provide at least a partial explanation of some of more tragic and brutal instances of interracial violence in the history of the USA (Allport, 1954/1979; Du Bois, 1986; Rosenblatt, Karis & Powell, 1995). For example, a once-common lynching scenario in Southern states involved one or more young White males overhearing a rumor (whether verified or not) that a young Black male had entered a predominantly White community and made unwanted sexual advances toward a young White female. Such a scenario often ended with a mob of angry White men accosting the Black man, hanging him, and then mutilating his genitals as the final symbolic act of retaliation.

Rajecki's (1985) view of xenophobia as a biologically adaptive response to strangers of the same species conforms to commonly-held beliefs that ingroup–outgroup bias, overt prejudice and the miscegenation taboo are inevitable aspects of the human condition (Gaines & Reed, 1994, 1995). Returning to our original theme of interracial relationships, this view of xenophobia is also consistent with the relatively low incidence of relationships among those persons who phenotypically are most dissimilar (and, thus, likely to share the fewest number of genes), namely Blacks and Whites (Todd et al., 1992). An important irony should be noted, however. Given that (a) many, if not most, persons designated as Black have one or more White ancestors (Allport, 1954/1979; Porterfield, 1978; Zack, 1993) and (b) the genes responsible for group differences in physical features such as eye color, hair texture and skin pigmentation collectively represent no more than 5% of humans' genetic inheritance (Allport, 1954/1979), Rajecki's (1985) account implies that xenophobia leads individuals to ignore the overwhelming genetic similarities in favor of the relatively few genetic differences among human beings.

Perceptual and Cognitive Aspects of the "Outsiders' Perspective"

If xenophobia is an unlearned, reflexive response to the intrusion of outgroup members, interracial relationships may not even be recognized as such by fellow ingroup members who are "outsiders" with respect to those relationships. The prepotent response of these observers may simply be to view the outgroup member as an unwelcome intruder and to "help" the intruded-upon ingroup member drive the intruder off! Recognizing that a genuine relationship exists between their fellow in-group member and the outgroup member may be beyond the capacity of many infrahuman species, but it is an insight that humans will usually—though not always—achieve. When such insight *is* achieved, interracial relationships will typically present fellow ingroup members with a puzzling attributional problem. Why, given the influence of xenophobia and the psychological barriers created by various perceptual and cognitive processes (some of which are described below), should such a relationship form at all? And why, once it has formed, should such a relationship persist?

The "outsider" may be resistant to even recognizing that an interracial relationship exists because a number of perceptual and cognitive processes militate against such a conclusion. In the following section, some representative examples of these processes are briefly discussed. They include (a) similarity as a Gestalt organizing principle in perception, (b) the cognitive linkage of racial markers with negative characteristics, (c) the implications of such linkages for Heiderian models of the interracial relationship as cognitively and affectively imbalanced, and (d) the attributional consequences for the "outsider" of perceiving such imbalance.

Similarity as a Perceptual Organizing Principle

According to principles of Gestalt psychology (Köhler, 1947), individuals tend to perceive objects that share salient surface characteristics as "belonging" together, in what Heider (1958) termed a *unit relation*. Although Gestalt psychology initially was applied to object perception, the principle of sensory organization may be applied to person perception as well (Fiske & Taylor, 1984). Thus, persons whose skin pigmentation is similar are more likely to be perceived by outsiders as a social unit (as friends, dating partners, etc.) than are persons whose skin pigmentation is dissimilar (see Rosenblatt, Karis & Powell, 1995). Moreover, given that racial segregation persists across a variety of societal institutions (e.g., religious, educational, social) throughout the USA (National Research Council, 1989; Pinkney, 1993), the Black person who befriends a White person in a predominantly White setting or the White person who marries a Black person in a predominantly Black setting is likely to be regarded as a social anomaly.

Particularly when the target person is Black, the stigmatization that accompanies "standing out" by being conspicuously different from others (Goffman, 1963) may isolate an outgroup member perceptually and discourage the perception that he or she is a member of an interracial relationship. A double standard seems to be at work here, such that the question is not whether a White person "belongs" with a Black partner but whether a Black person "belongs" with a White partner. Thus, even though perceptual similarity may function as a general organizing principle, the fact that Blacks are singled out (at least by White perceivers; Stephan, 1985) as the targets who "don't belong" suggests that the perceptual process is accompanied by a cognitive bias that implicates more than the response of retinal cells to dissimilarities in skin color. Clearly, some degree of accompanying cognitive bias is required for such a non-random tendency to be expressed so often.

Linkage of Racial Markers with Negative Characteristics

The negative stereotyping of the outgroup member can clearly add this type of cognitive overlay to the outside observer's more reflexive xenophobic response. In some instances, racial markers such as skin color may be associated with negative characteristics because a genuine association exists (e.g., African-Americans having a slave ancestry and a higher rate of out-of-wedlock births than their European-American counterparts). In other instances, however, the association of racial markers with negative characteristics may be spurious. For example, although Kelly's (1955) psychology of personal constructs did not address race *per se*, a construct referring to a racial marker (e.g., the Black/White dichotomy) may be cognitively linked with a host of other dichotomies in a way that can lend to negative stereotyping (e.g., evil/virtuous, unenlightened/ enlightened, dirty/clean). To the extent that individuals fail to acknowledge physical or social objects that contradict such global categorization (e.g., black *and* virtuous, white *and* dirty), these linkages can provide one source of societal stereotypes. Similarly, through a process characterized as "illusory correlation" (Chapman & Chapman, 1969; Hamilton & Rose, 1980), negative behaviors or characteristics that are distinctive by virtue of their low frequency of occurrence in the general population can be spuriously linked with outgroup members who are also distinctive by virtue of their minority status.

Cognitive and Affective Imbalance

The association of racial markers with negative characteristics has direct implications for the outsider's reaction to an interracial relationship when it becomes one of the sentiment relations in a Heiderian (1958) p–o–x triad (i.e., one person's (p) feelings toward the other (o) person, the person's feelings toward an impersonal entity (x), and the other person's feelings toward the impersonal entity). Heider's (1958) balance theory proposed that such triads are cognitive structures that are evaluated with respect to their logical consistency, with inconsistency being experienced as psychologically aversive. Regarding the consistency of sentiment relations (i.e., feelings directed toward a particular person, place, or thing) within the context of p–o–x triads representing interracial or interethnic encounters, several propositions can be derived. For example, consistent with Rajecki's (1985) view of xenophobia, (1) individuals should tend to dislike persons who are dissimilar to themselves, and (2) individuals should tend to dislike persons who are unfamiliar. From the perspective of the outside observer of an interracial relationship, the ingroup member's apparent unit relation with the outgroup member sets the stage for considerable cognitive inconsistency, being inconsistent not only with the logic of both of the above propositions but also by virtue of linking the fellow ingroup member with an outgroup member whose racial markers are associated with negative characteristics. Thus, in addition to being a threat to the inclusive fitness of the ingroup as a potential competitor for their physical resources and opportunities to reproduce, the intruding outgroup member is a threat to the ingroup's cognitive consistency (i.e., "peace of mind") as well.

Outsiders who can apply p–o–x reasoning to interracial relationships are capable of generating a wider and more sophisticated range of reactions to them than outsiders who cannot. Their options can therefore extend beyond the simple, reflexive xenophobic reaction (i.e., to retaliate against—and either repel or destroy—the outgroup member) to include many additional options. For example, they can (1) deny that the unit relation (i.e., the interracial relationship) really exists; (2) acknowledge the unit relation but view it as momentary, transient, unstable; (3) redefine the ingroup in such a way that it can include the outgroup member; or (4) deny that the particular outgroup member involved in the interracial relationship has the negative characteristics that have been linked to the outgroup's racial markers. They can also (5) acknowledge the unit relation, but attempt to set limits on its strength and implications:

> The relations between sentiment and spatial or interaction closeness underlies the concept known as "social distance". By *social distance* is meant the degree of interpersonal closeness one accepts. For example, one might not mind living in the same city with a particular person, race, or class but would object to being neighbors. Or, one might accept neighborhood association, but resist membership in the same club. Acceptance of the marriage relation represents a minimal degree of social distance, community ostracism the other extreme (Heider, 1958, p. 191, italics ours).

Application of Kelley's (1972) Augmentation Principle

In cases in which the outsider cannot readily deny or minimize the unit relation (i.e., the interracial relationship), the outsider is confronted with a puzzling attributional problem. Why, given the influence of xenophobia and the psychological barriers created by various perceptual and cognitive processes of the types we have just described, should such a relationship form at all? And why, once it has formed, should such a relationship persist?

Responses to this attributional problem should vary greatly, depending on such factors as the outsider's intelligence, level of cognitive development, level of motivation (and patience) to solve the problem, willingness to accept a "satisficing" solution (Kahneman, Slovik & Tversky, 1982; Nisbett & Ross, 1980) to it, and so on. In response to such factors, some observers of the interracial relationship will not attempt to solve the attributional problem the relationship poses, reverting instead to either a primitive xenophobic response or to a minimally-effortful attempt to simply restore cognitive balance (e.g., by denying that the interracial relationship exists at all). However, more motivated and cognitively sophisticated outsiders will attempt to account for the interracial relationship, and their typical response will be to invoke Kelley's (1972) *augmentation principle* to assist them in this regard.

Given the various factors ("instinctual", perceptual and cognitive) that militate against the interracial relationship having been formed at all, the logical inference of the outside observer must be that some other factor(s) augmented the participants' desire to form the relationship to such an extent that this desire overrode the "natural" barriers to such a relationship. The observer's need to postulate the existence and operation of such augmenting factors should be greater to the extent that the barriers to the relationship itself are great—and the barriers to interracial relationships can be great indeed. They include not only the "instinctual", perceptual and cognitive reactions we have described above, but can include intense societal sanctions (verbal and physical attacks, ostracism, loss of employment, incarceration, etc.) as well. A reasonable inference for the outsider to make, then, is that if something holds an interracial pair together, "it must be something strong".

What is that *something* that causes an interracial relationship to form, and continues to hold its members together? In the lyric by John Sebastian quoted above, the singer's complete response was "I don't know what it is, but it must be something strong". And, just as in the lyric, outside observers are not always able to specify the augmenting factor(s) that would help them account for the interracial relationship, but can only assume that such factors must exist. In many cases, however, additional cues to the nature of the augmenting factor(s) are available in the subtype of interracial relationship that they are attempting to "explain". By using these cues to refine their inferences, outside observers can logically (though not always accurately) identify at least one augmenting factor that might account for the interracial relationship in question.

Once again, conditional elements such as the observer's intelligence, cognitive resources, motivation, etc., will combine to determine the cognitive sophistication of the inference that is made. The simplest, least effortful, least sophisticated inference would likely be the ascription of a generic disposition to the renegade ingroup member (e.g., "He's a nigger lover"). Such an inference might reflect the upper limit of cognitive sophistication for a group of men with limited educations who are wearing white hoods and are "cognitively busy" (Gilbert, Pelham & Krull, 1988) with the competing demands of trying to smash the victim's windows and set fire to a cross in his front yard.

On the other hand, for outside observers with more cognitive resources to invest, more differentiated inferences about the augmenting factor(s) that underlie the interracial relationship are often suggested by whether the relationship (1) involves same-sex or mixed-sex members, and (2) appears to be romantic or platonic. For example, to account for heterosexual interracial relationships, out-side observers are likely to infer that the major augmenting factor is either an unusually powerful sexual attraction or the lure of "forbidden fruit". They are likely to make a similar inference in the case of homosexual interracial relation-ships if the corresponding sexual orientation of one or both members is known. However, because augmenting factors that might underlie interracial platonic relationships are not as readily "available" (Kahneman, Slovik & Tversky, 1982; Nisbett & Ross, 1980), these relationships present a greater puzzle to the outside observer, who may be likely to infer a sexual motive in *any* mixed-sex interracial relationship—even when no such motive exists.

Of course, given more extensive information about the respective histories, personal dispositions and current circumstances of the members of an interracial relationship, the outside observer is in a position to make an even more refined inference about why the relationship exists and "what's in it?" for each of the members (see Triandis, 1987). We will return to the attributional puzzles posed by the different subtypes of interracial relationships in the final section of this chapter, after first considering the insiders' view of interracial relationships and how this view contrasts with that of outsiders.

THE "INSIDERS' PERSPECTIVE" ON INTERRACIAL RELATIONSHIPS

Some attribution theorists have rightly criticized personality theorists in general (Ross, 1977) and Freudian psychoanalytic theorists in particular (Nisbett & Ross, 1980) for tending to privilege their status as outsiders (instead of privileging their subjects' status as insiders) when attempting to account for their subjects' behavior (see Harvey, Ickes & Kidd, 1976). It is therefore ironic that both attribution theorists and personality theorists have tended to depict the sexual motive as being the major factor accounting for interracial romantic relation-ships—as if (a) no factor other than sex could explain the formation and persist-ence of *interracial* romantic relationships, and (b) any number of factors other than sex could explain the formation and persistence of *intraracial* romantic relationships (see Aldridge, 1978, 1991). All too often, the untested assumption that the partners in interracial relationships harbor an irrational yearning for "forbidden fruit" has been treated as incontestable within the social science literature (Aldridge, 1978; Davidson, 1992; Hernton, 1965/1988; Kouri & Lasswell, 1993; Porterfield, 1978; Rosenblatt, Karis & Powell, 1995; Spick-ard, 1989; Staples, 1994). Another judgment commonly expressed by outside observers—whether they are lay observers or social scientists—is that interracial relationships are highly volatile and unstable in comparison to intraracial relationships.

Rarely, however, do outside observers—even social scientists—check to see if

these attributions are shared by "insiders"—the members of interracial relationships (Olson, 1977; see also Duck, 1990, 1994a; Duck & Sants, 1983; Kelley, 1979;
Surra & Ridley, 1991). Rarely are the partners in interracial relationships (and,
within families, their offspring as well) given the opportunity to describe their
social-psychological experiences *in their own words* (for exceptions, see
Funderberg, 1994; Terkel, 1991). Is it any wonder, then, that the relationship
processes between persons from different racial backgrounds often are depicted
and interpreted in unflattering terms?

For example, would insiders agree with outsiders that xenophobia is the
primary barrier to interracial relationship development? Until the abolition of
anti-miscegenation laws by the US Supreme Court in 1967, individual states
(especially in the South) singled out Black–White marriages as being illegal, and
penalized offenders most severely, particularly when the groom was Black and
the bride was White (Porterfield, 1978; Spickard, 1989). For decades (and, in
some instances, centuries), state legislation stoked the fires of racial animosity
more directly than did those presumably innate tendencies that were used to
justify such legislation. As Allport (1954/1979) observed near the beginning of
the modern Civil Rights Movement, only after anti-miscegenation laws were
overturned would social scientists be able to determine whether interracial marriages were held in check by xenophobia *per se*. In contrast to the consistent
xenophobia implied by the outsiders' perspective, the overturning of state anti-
miscegenation statutes was followed by a dramatic increase in the frequency of
interracial marriages (with the notable exception of Black–White marriages;
Sanjek, 1994).

As this example suggests, an insiders' perspective that calls attention to such
societal barriers to the formation and maintenance of interracial relationships
can provide a valuable complement to the perspective of outside observers
(Duck, 1994a; McCall & Simmons, 1991; Surra & Ridley, 1991). It enables researchers to gain the kinds of insights that, in many cases, can only be found in
relationship members' accounts of their own experiences. With regard to interracial relationships, the "insiders' perspective" could potentially clarify whether
partners' stated motives for entering, maintaining or even leaving such relationships are as simplistic as the "outsiders' perspective" traditionally has maintained. Consider, for example, the following e-mail conversation among
individuals subscribing to an Internet newsgroup devoted to intercultural
couples:[1]

> ... I agree with you here. "Other races are exciting" sounds like conditioning to me.
> (Of course, a given person could find his *own* race "exotic and exciting" if he
> happened to have grown up differently.) (B. Saunders, April 25, 1995, personal
> communication.)

---

[1] All references to electronic mail correspondence as "personal communications" are in accordance
with recommendations set forth in the *Publication Manual of the American Psychological Association*, 4th edn (Washington, DC: APA, 1994).

This was the point I made about, after being married to a black woman for nearly nine years, I "see" her more than I "see" myself (because I only "see" myself when passing a mirror). Although I am white, being with anyone who was not black would have that "exotic and exciting" sort of thing about it—regardless if she was white or something other than black or white (C. Henry-Cotran, April 27, 1995, personal communication).

Exactly the way I feel. My wife is Chinese—at this point, any non-Asian woman would seem more "exotic" than another Asian women—but even a near-lookalike for my wife would seem awfully strange. Then again, I'm not after "exotic and strange"—if anything, I find my wife more attractive after [more than 13] years than I did when I first met her. After all this time, racial differences are not what registers when I see her—I see *Alice,* accept no substitutes (D. Crom, April 30, 1995, personal communication).

As these examples illustrate, the "insiders' perspective" on interracial relationships may assign little weight or credence to the desire for "forbidden fruit" *per se.* Are there, then, other motives that might explain the incidence of romantic interracial relationships *from the perspective of individuals within those relationships?* One possibility is that certain differences between the partners may be valued because they help to satisfy the partners' motives for self-expansion, novelty and sensation-seeking in areas that may include—but are in no way limited to—their sexuality. A second possibility is that the psychological similarity between the partners might be valued—despite their physical and cultural differences—because it helps to satisfy the partners' motive to have a congenial, supportive relationship with a compatible partner (Rosenblatt, Karis & Powell, 1995).

Valued Differences Contributing to Novelty and Self-expansion

Cultural differences between the partners might help to satisfy their *needs for self-expansion* (see the chapter by Aron & Aron in this volume). Through their interracial relationship, both partners can gain direct access to another culture or subculture—the one that shaped their partner's attitudes, values, habits, speech, dress, food preferences and esthetic sensibilities. Because the potential for self-expansion is great in interracial relationships, realizing this potential is likely to be one of the motives that underlie such relationships.

A related motive is the *need for novelty* (Berlyne, 1960). Interracial relationships are particularly likely to offer surprises—elements of novelty that may be highly valued by the partners (though this same novelty may be relatively unacknowledged and unappreciated by the outside observers). For example, a European-American man whose cultural heritage emphasizes individualism might find it stimulating to meet an African-American woman whose cultural heritage emphasizes collectivism (Penn, Gaines & Phillips, 1993; Phillips, Penn & Gaines, 1993). Part of the budding attraction between such culturally disparate persons might be due to precisely that disparity, which represents an opportunity for exploring value orientations other than one's own. Because people with a *high sensation-seeking motive* should be especially likely to value such novelty (again, including but not limited to having a novel sexual partner), we might expect them to find their participation in such relationships to be significantly above an actuarial baseline.

Valued Similarities Contributing to Compatibility and Rapport

On the other hand, perhaps it is the *similarity* between interracial partners' personal and social characteristics that, *despite their phenotypic differences*, serves as the basis for their mutual attraction. If so, interracial relationships would resemble intraracial relationships (whether romantic or platonic) in terms of factors underlying attraction (Byrne, 1971; see also Berscheid, 1985). The uncertainty that interracial partners themselves experience regarding these competing versions of the "insiders' perspective" is manifested in the following e-mail conversation:

> I think my husband and I have much more in common mentally and personality-wise than my co-worker and her spouse. So maybe people [like my co-worker and her husband] are looking for more external similarities such as race, religion, etc. While . . . people [like my husband and I] are more into inner compatibilities, so that the externals are not so important (D. Smith, April 28, 1995, personal communication, brackets ours).

> The difficulty is, what constitutes opposites? As you note . . . is it the visible externals or the interior emotional/intellectual viewpoint that is opposite, or alike? (R. Brown, April 29, 1995, personal communication).

> Yep, I share lots of political/social opinions with my white [significant other]. However, we are of different race, religion and (in some ways) cultural background. So are we similar or different? (J. Starkey, April 30, 1995, personal communication).

A key point to be made here is that the association between physical and psychological attributes, no matter how absurd the physical indicator (e.g., number of bumps on one's head, body size, cranial size), has enjoyed a long, if not particularly honorable, history in psychology (White & Parham, 1990). Throughout most of the twentieth century, scores of mainstream psychologists have earnestly believed (but have never demonstrated) that the same gene(s) responsible for skin pigmentation, eye color and hair texture somehow are responsible for intellectual capacity and personality endowment (Du Bois, 1947/1965; Fairchild, 1991; Howitt & Owusu-Bempah, 1994; van Dijk, 1993; Yee, Fairchild, Weizmann, & Wyatt, 1993). Even some scholars within the relatively new field of Black psychology have contended that racial differences in personality are due in part to unspecified "biogenetic" factors (Penn, Gaines & Phillips, 1993; Phillips, Penn & Gaines, 1993). With regard to interracial relationships, many psychologists and other relationship researchers have been so willing to accept such assertions as a matter of faith that they have not stopped to ask whether the members of interracial relationships evaluate their own points of "similarity"and "difference" using equally crude criteria.

Research Bearing on the "Insiders' Perspective"

Unfortunately, there is relatively little available research that bears directly on the "insiders' perspective". However, a number of findings provide at least indirect support for the conclusion that interracial relationships may be less "deviant" or "unstable" than the "outsiders' perspective" might suggest. For example, divorce rates for interracial couples do not appear to be as deviant from intraracial divorce rates as one might assume (Aldridge, 1978; Durodoye, 1994; Ho, 1990). And even if we were to accept the premise that interracial couples are particularly at risk for divorce, a primary reason may be that spouses in interracial marriages are more likely to be in their second or subsequent marriages (Aldridge, 1978; Durodoye, 1994)—a factor which itself is associated with a greater likelihood of divorce (Cherlin, 1989).

Moreover, when social scientists do make the effort to collect information from African-American as well as Anglo participants, a common result is that the ingroup–outgroup bias that usually is presumed to determine the outcome of interracial encounters (Duckitt, 1994; Stephan, 1985) simply is not as pronounced (especially among African-Americans) as attribution theory would lead one to believe (see Ickes, 1984; Korolewicz & Korolewicz, 1985; McClelland & Auster, 1990; Tucker & Mitchell-Kernan, 1995; but see also Todd et al., 1992). In addition, ever since Gunnar Myrdal's classic *An American Dilemma* (1944) was published, African-Americans in particular have proven less preoccupied with the issue of interracial intimacy than most Anglos (whether social scientists or laypersons) have tended to expect (Allport, 1954/1979; Hernton, 1965/1988; National Research Council, 1989; Rosenblatt, Karis & Powell, 1995). Finally, the USA historically has recorded some of the lowest rates of Black–White intermarriage in the Western world (Pettigrew, 1987), thus indicating that the supposedly "universal" phenomenon of ingroup–outgroup bias in reality is historically and situationally based (Gaines & Reed, 1994, 1995; Penn, Gaines & Phillips, 1993; Phillips, Penn & Gaines, 1993).

As might be expected, the study of interracial relationships is not well differentiated by subtype. For example, *male–male* or *female–female friendships* between African-Americans and Anglos have rarely been examined in the personal relationship literature (for an exception, see Messner, 1992). And judging from the available social-psychological literature, the phrase *interracial male–female friendships,* when applied to pairings of African-Americans and Anglos, would seem to be a contradiction in terms. Because the socio-economic disparity between Black males and White females is generally smaller than that between White males and Black females (French, 1985; Hernton, 1965/1988), we might expect that Black male–White female friendships would be more likely to develop than would be White male–Black female friendships. However, societal taboos against any type of Black male–White female relationship often lead White parents to express unusually strong disapproval of their daughters' friendships with Black males (Essed, 1991; Hernton, 1965/1988; Rosenblatt, Karis & Powell, 1995; Zweigenhaft & Domhoff, 1991).

Male–female romantic relationships between African-Americans and Anglos are the only cross-race romantic relationships to receive at least minimal attention in the social science literature—interracial *same-sex romantic relationships* (gay or lesbian) have essentially been ignored (see Huston & Schwartz, 1995). Porterfield's (1978) qualitative and quantitative research on 40 interracial married couples was crucial in challenging stereotypes regarding interracial romantic relationships as motivated primarily by dysfunctional and/or dishonorable motives. It revealed that interracial couples—like intraracial couples—usually marry because the partners are in love and hope to spend the rest of their lives together (see also Aldridge, 1978; Davidson, 1992; Hernton, 1965/1988; Kouri & Lasswell, 1993; Spickard, 1989; Staples, 1994). Complementary findings indicate that socio-emotional intimacy in these relationships not only is high but involves reciprocity of affection *and* respect (thus resembling male–female romantic relationships in general; Gaines et al. (1996); see also Porterfield, 1978; Rosenblatt, Karis & Powell, 1995). Moreover, preliminary data from an ongoing study of cultural value orientations and socio-emotional intimacy among interethnic married/cohabiting couples (Gaines, Rios et al., 1995) indicates that reciprocity of affection and respect is rooted in partners' shared orientations toward the welfare of their communities (i.e., *collectivism*; Gaines, Marelich et al., 1995; Triandis, 1990) and toward the welfare of each other (i.e., *romanticism*; see Doherty et al., 1994; Sprecher et al., 1994).

Theoretical Approaches Conducive to the "Insiders' Perspective"

Despite the lack of emphasis on the "insiders' perspective" in the research conducted to date, there is reason to hope that it will be better represented in future research. We suggest that a number of theoretical approaches may be particularly conducive to studying interracial relationships from the "insiders' perspective". Consider, as just three possible examples, how research on the contact hypothesis, filter theory, and social identity theory could be reframed for this purpose. All three approaches are unbiased in the sense that they view interracial relationships as non-deviant. In addition, they tend to privilege the relationship partners themselves (instead of objective or subjective observers) as the ultimate "experts" on the dynamics of interracial relationships.

The Contact Hypothesis

One approach that seems applicable to friendships as well as to romantic relationships is Allport's (1954/1979) *contact hypothesis*, which proposes that the social distance between African-Americans and Anglos should decrease as a function of societal dismantling of social, political, educational and economic barriers to integration (Gudykunst, 1992; Hernton, 1965/1988; Sigelman & Welch, 1994). To better capture the perspective of "insiders", research on the contact hypothesis might be reframed so that the members of different types of interracial relationships can report on whether and how such barriers are perceived as being obstacles to the formation and persistence of their relationships. Such research might help to explain why the rate of increase in interracial relationships lags far behind other indicators of societal change, such as desegregation in schools, neighborhoods and businesses (see also Brewer & Miller, 1987; Katz & Taylor, 1987; Pettigrew, 1987; Taylor & Katz, 1987). It might also help to explain why the rates of Latino–Anglo and Asian-American–Anglo marriages have risen dramatically since the 1960s, whereas the rate of African-American–Anglo marriages (which traditionally were the primary target of state anti-miscegenation laws; Spickard, 1989) has remained static (Johnson, 1992; Sanjek, 1994; Spigner, 1994).

Filter Theory

According to filter theory (Kerckhoff & Davis, 1962), mate selection (and, by extension, friendship selection) proceeds in two stages. In the first stage, potential partners limit their field of eligibles by pairing off on the basis of those external characteristics that are meaningful to them as individuals (e.g., race might be the determining factor for some persons, whereas socio-economic status might be the determining factor for others). In the second stage, partners pair off on the basis of those internal characteristics that matter to them individually (e.g., liberalism might be the determining factor for some persons whereas religiosity might be the determining factor for others). Thus, filter theory allows for the possibility that partners will choose each other on the basis of internal as well as external characteristics other than race. However, it is unclear whether real-life partners actually choose each other in the linear sequence that filter theory implies (Huston & Ashmore, 1986; Kephart & Jedlicka, 1988). Research seeking the "insiders' perspective" on this question could help to clarify the extent to which the members of interracial relationships considered race as a filter in their selection of a partner, and—if they did—how soon it was considered (early, later) and what type of valence (positive, neutral, negative) and priority weight (high, moderate, low) it was assigned.

Social Identity Theory

The question of which external characteristics and which internal characteristics ultimately serve as the bases for interracial attraction is particularly relevant to Tajfel's (1979) social identity theory, which is based on the assumption that self-esteem is a manifestation of both personal and social identities (Brown, 1986; Phinney, 1995; Taylor & Moghaddam, 1994). The theory postulates that self-esteem is not simply a byproduct of *intrapersonal* attributes, but also reflects a multitude of *interpersonal* attributes (all of which are defined jointly by self and others). From this standpoint, asking "insiders" to report on how their interracial relationship affects their self-perceived identity (and *vice versa*) could offer important insights about the formation, maintenance, internal dynamics and dissolution of these relationships (see also Penn, Gaines & Phillips, 1993; Phillips, Penn & Gaines, 1993).

RESOLVING THE TENSIONS BETWEEN "INSIDE" AND "OUTSIDE" VIEWS OF INTERRACIAL RELATIONSHIPS

The likely positivity/negativity of outsiders' attributions regarding interracial pairs as a function of the pair's level of involvement and gender composition suggests the sophistication that insiders must have in order to navigate through potentially treacherous social situations relatively unscathed. We hypothesize that outsiders generally will assume that an interracial same-sex pair is platonic, and thus will react to the pair with moderately positive affect and benign attributions about the reasons for their relationship, unless the partners make it known that they are gay or lesbian, in which case outsiders' attributions will become markedly negative (Frable, Blackstone & Scherbaum, 1990; Goffman, 1963). We further hypothesize that outsiders generally will assume that an interracial opposite-sex pair is romantically involved, and thus will react to the pair negatively, with accompanying disparaging attributions, unless the partners make it known that they are not married or dating, in which case outsiders' negative feelings and attributions will become somewhat attenuated.

In addition, a couple of more subtle interaction effects are proposed. First, regarding same-sex interracial relationships, outsiders' change from positive to negative reactions when a romantic involvement is attributed is likely to be greater when the partners are gay men (e.g., Black male/White male) than when they are lesbians (e.g., Black female/White female). Second, regarding opposite-sex interracial relationships, outsiders' change from negative to more positive attributions when a platonic interest is attributed is likely to be greater when pairing is between White males and women of color (e.g., White male/Black female) than when pairing is between men of color and White women (e.g., Black male/White female). Both of these more subtle interaction effects are consistent with the notion that Black male sexuality—whether real or imagined—poses the greatest threat to outsiders' sensibilities.

In each of the six subtypes of interracial relationships that we have considered, the members are likely to have an "insider" view of themselves and their relationships that differs dramatically from the "outsider" view that is imposed (or, perhaps more accurately, superimposed) by both lay and scientific psychology. That is, "insiders" are aware of many factors (e.g., seeing each other as individuals rather than as representatives of outgroups, being more aware of complementary and non-complementary attitudes, values, interests and personality traits) affecting their relationships that "outsiders" frequently do not take into account. Porterfield's (1978) study of 40 Black–White married couples provides considerable support for the ability of insiders to identify those psychological dimensions along which they and their partners are most similar or dissimilar.

At the same time, however, the relationship members as "insiders" are not immune to the implications of the ways in which their relationships are viewed from the "outside". On any given day, virtually all interracial pairs—whether same-sex or mixed-sex, romantic or platonic—may be subjected to a variety of stares, disapproving murmurs, or even verbal and/or physical attacks (Hernton, 1965/1988; Simpson & Yinger, 1985). Such unrestrained reactions by outsiders serve as constant reminders to insiders that, regardless of their implicit or explicit commitment to each other (Johnson, 1991a,b; Levinger, 1991; Rusbult, 1991), outsiders often take it upon themselves to challenge that commitment.

To some extent, outsiders might have a valid point regarding the potential for miscommunication and subsequent undermining of commitment in interracial relationships (see Andersen, 1993). Even though no single racial or ethnic group can claim sole ownership of any particular cultural value orientation (Gaines, 1995), it nonetheless is possible that, in some interracial relationships, the partners do not embrace a given cultural value orientation to the same degree. For example, a highly individualistic Anglo might be chagrined to find that his or her Latina/o partner equates individualism with selfishness (see Gaines, 1995; Mirande, 1977). Or, a highly familistic Asian-American might feel disillusioned upon discovering that his or her African-American partner views traditional nuclear families as relics of a bygone era (see Fine et al., 1992; Staples & Mirande, 1980).

Ironically, however, even when partners in interracial relationships are virtually identical in their expressed cultural value orientations, they still might find themselves ostracized by outsiders who ostensibly share the cultural value orientation in question (Penn, Gaines & Phillips, 1993; Phillips, Penn & Gaines, 1993). For instance, even though collectivism frequently is identified as part and parcel of a Afrocentric world view (Asante, 1987; Fine, Schwebel, & James-Myers, 1987; Gaines, 1994; Kambon & Hopkins, 1993; White & Parham, 1990), some Afrocentrists (e.g., Kambon & Hopkins, 1993) contend that any heterosexual interracial relationship is "odious", no matter how strongly the partners share collectivistic beliefs. Similarly, some Afrocentrists (e.g., Asante, 1987) argue that any homosexual interracial relationship is "misguided", regardless of how deeply the partners are committed to collectivism as a predominant cultural value orientation. This is not to say that all (or even most) Afrocentrists are xenophobic (for an excellent counter-example, see Parham, 1993). We simply wish to point out that although it is easy to understand how outsiders can construe differences between partners' endorsement of specific cultural value orientations as "proof" that interracial relationships are prone to conflict, even the lack of such differences cannot alter the anti-"race-mixing" mindset of certain outsiders. "Damned if we do, damned if we don't" might be the conclusion of some insiders.

If either of the partners in an interracial relationship has engaged in re-fencing (i.e., maintaining negative outgroup stereotypes despite positive interactions with one or more members of that outgroup; Allport, 1954/1979), the insiders themselves might end up espousing the same racist views that certain outsiders (e.g., neo-Nazis, Black separatists) have endorsed all along (Porterfield, 1978). As we mentioned earlier, some insiders might believe the sexual myths concerning, say, the presumed submissiveness of Asian-American women or the hypersexuality of African-American men. It is not difficult to imagine the disappointment or even outrage that an Asian-American woman or an African-American man might feel if her or his interracial relationship partner were to reveal that part of the impetus for the relationship derived from the partner's internalized stereotypes rather than from a genuine appreciation of the individual's unique qualities.

For partners in interracial relationships, the task of resolving "insider" and "outsider" perspectives is not easy. On the one hand, the "insider" view is legitimate in its own right and should be regarded as such by laypersons and social scientists alike (Olson, 1977; see also Duck, 1990, 1994a; McCall & Simmons, 1991; Surra & Ridley, 1991). On the other hand, social perceivers' reactions to interracial pairs as social units always threatens to impinge upon their jointly constructed lives. Furthermore, even "subjective" outsiders such as family and friends—normally the network of individuals whose counsel is sought in times of need (see Johnson et al., 1992)—often are just as skeptical as "objective" outsiders (e.g., passers-by, academicians). The resulting dilemma faced by partners in interracial relationships is essentially the social equivalent of the "double consciousness" or "two souls" of African-Americans that W. E. B. Du Bois (1903/1969; see also Early, 1993; Gaines & Reed, 1994, 1995; Jones, 1987; Walters, 1993) described so eloquently as an individual-level phenomenon (Rosenblatt, Karis & Powell, 1995).

How do partners in interracial relationships deal with this double consciousness or discrepancy between the "insider" and "outsider" perspectives, feeling that they are—at the same time—not only members of a viable, rewarding relationship but also people who are stigmatized and even scorned by outsiders for their membership in that relationship? This task might be easiest for partners in the male–male and female–female friendships, but only in those cases in which the partners are not presumed by most outsiders to be sexually attracted to each other (i.e., when they pose the least threat to outsiders' sensibilities). Thus, partners in same-sex interracial friendships might be in the best position to react to outsiders' attempts at ingroup–outgroup polarization (e.g., taunting the partners as "traitors" to their respective races) by shrugging off such unsolicited commentary and rededicating themselves to their friendship.

The task of resolving the insider/outsider discrepancy is considerably more difficult for partners in male–female interracial friendships and romantic relationships. To many (if not most) outside observers, both types of male–female relationship will be presumed—through invocation of the augmentation principle—to be sexual rather than platonic in nature (see Gaines, 1994; Rubin, 1985).

Given what many regard as a deep-rooted, biologically based taboo against miscegenation, the antipathy of outsiders toward partners in interracial mixed-sex relationships may be intense, immediate and unthinking. Thus, whereas epithets such as "nigger" and "nigger-lover" occasionally may be hurled at partners in same-sex interracial friendships, such slurs are likely to be experienced more frequently and virulently by partners in male–female interracial relationships (especially by women in those relationships; Porterfield, 1978). Unlike same-sex interracial friendships, male–female interracial relationships often trigger outrage in outsiders who feel that potential mates have been stolen from their grasp by disliked outgroup members (rather than simply other ingroup competitors; Allport, 1954/1979).

In the face of such daily challenges to their right to be together, partners in male–female interracial relationships must do more than simply proclaim anew their commitment to each other. Instead, in public settings they might deem it necessary to try to reduce outsiders' anxieties by placing greater physical and psychological distance between each other than normally would be expected of a heterosexual romantic couple. This strategy might be relatively effective for platonic male–female interracial pairs (who, after all, are simply letting outside observers know they are "just friends"). However, for romantic male–female interracial pairs, such a strategy may prove counter-effective in that the partners are, in effect, forced to deny publicly the love that they share privately. Alternatively, then, partners in romantic male–female interracial relationships might opt to return the stares that they receive and thus place outsiders (rather than allow themselves to be placed) on the defensive—a risky tactic that could backfire and result in an even more hostile outsider response (Hernton, 1965/1988).

Perhaps the most vexing dilemma of resolving the insider/outsider dilemma involves partners in male–male and female–female romantic relationships. These individuals are vulnerable to being doubly stigmatized, in that both the interracial and the sexual aspect of their relationship is repugnant to most outsiders. Because theirs is a visible stigma (Frable, Blackstone & Scherbaum, 1990), members of racial minorities typically cannot avoid being discredited by majority (i.e., White) observers on the basis of their phenotype (Goffman, 1963). Thus, members of racial minorities (as well as their Anglo relationship partners) cannot escape being tagged and, perhaps, targeted by hostile observers for the interracial aspect of their relationship. However, gay and lesbian partners in interracial relationships have to decide whether they also want to be vulnerable to the hostility that might be evoked by the sexual aspect of their relationship as well. Because their sexual preference, unlike their race, is not betrayed by their skin color or hair texture but potentially can be betrayed by their overt behavior, partners in gay or lesbian relationships might try to mask or conceals signs of their sexual orientation when in public. Male partners in gay interracial relationships might be particularly sensitive to the dangers of "coming out" in public settings because society places enormous importance upon male heterosexuality as normative (Huston & Schwartz, 1995).

The path of least resistance for same-sex romantic interracial partners might be to display a socially acceptable degree of physical and psychological distance

between each other (like male–female romantic and platonic interracial partners). Another response might be to exercise extreme caution in selecting the
neighborhoods in which they live and the social settings in which they express
their sexuality (a strategy that also is adopted by many interracial married couples; see Porterfield, 1978). This latter approach might be especially useful in
avoiding sexual epithets like "fag" or "dyke" along with racial epithets like
"nigger" and "nigger-lover".

Above all else, though, all interracial pairs will find it difficult to minimize the
ubiquity of the "outsiders' perspective" and the many ways that it impinges on
their interpersonal lives. Therefore, partners in interracial relationships might, in
relatively supportive social contexts, find it useful to discuss racism, sexism and
homophobia openly and condition themselves to anticipate outsiders' physical
and psychological attacks, as well as to practice those responses that were most
successful at lessening danger in the past and/or promise to be most successful in
the future. Such proactive strategies illustrate perhaps the most important point
in this chapter, namely, that just as individuals of color must acknowledge the
potential for insider–outsider conflict and prepare themselves mentally and
physically to minimize that conflict, so too must partners in interracial relationships (whether Anglos or persons of color) anticipate insider–outsider conflict
and respond accordingly. Unfortunately, society has not changed sufficiently
to avoid stigmatizing or persecuting interracial pairs, making it necessary for
those pairs to shield themselves from recurring assaults upon their minds and
bodies.

In a qualitative study of 21 married/cohabiting couples, Rosenblatt, Karis and
Powell (1995) concluded that many interracial couples continually remind themselves that they are "right" and racist elements in society are "wrong". African-
American partners in particular are likely to perceive current overt or covert
racist behaviors toward them as members of interracial couples as entirely consistent with past as well as present racist behaviors toward them as individuals
(see also Goffman, 1963). Although European-American partners are not as
likely to have experienced past racism as individuals, they nonetheless are especially likely to have rejected racist ideology prior to entering interracial unions.
Moreover, for those unions that produce offspring, parents typically make considerable efforts to buffer their children against the behaviors of individual racists
as well as the negative messages from media and other societal institutions.
Rather than allow themselves or their children to internalize racist messages,
partners in interracial relationships frequently learn to anticipate and respond to
verbal and physical assaults so as to defuse conflicts and thus place the onus of
change upon hostile outsiders (if not society as a whole).

FINAL THOUGHTS

Social myths encourage us to believe that American culture is either a true
"melting pot" in which racial and cultural differences are completely assimilated
or a "colorful mosaic" in which these differences are both recognized and valued.

Members of interracial relationships know better. They know that they do not fit within the mainstream of society and, hence, that they may experience profound loneliness even when in each other's company. In order to let other interracial pairs know that they are not alone, some partners in interracial relationships share their trials and tribulations with others via social support groups, magazines devoted specifically to interracial couples and their progeny, and electronic mail newsgroups (Gaines, Rios et al., 1995). Further research on interracial relationships could benefit greatly from examining these and other broadly cast social networks that often help sustain interracial pairs even when more tightly knit social networks of family and friends fail to do so.

But we cannot afford to be naive. The lasting strength of societal taboos in keeping many persons of African descent from establishing relationships with persons of European descent should not be underestimated—whatever the biological, psychological, and sociological origins of these taboos might be. What is most amazing, perhaps, is the fact that any of us manage to cross the color line and maintain such relationships (not to mention our sanity) in the process.

Chapter 9

Interdependence Theory

Caryl E. Rusbult
and
Ximena B. Arriaga
University of North Carolina, Chapel Hill, NC, USA

Interdependence is defined as the manner in which—as well as the degree to which—interacting individuals act upon or influence one another's experiences, in reference to the fact that the preferences, motives and behavior of the individual are relevant to those of the interaction partner. Interdependence is an elemental feature of social experience, in that: (a) interdependence structure constitutes an interpersonal reality with fundamental consequences for the interactants, defining the opportunities and constraints that characterize interaction; (b) individual-level dispositions, relationship-specific motives and social norms emerge as a consequence of adaptation to frequently encountered interdependence situations and, as such, reflect the situations from which those phenomena emerged; and (c) internal events such as cognition and affect frequently are oriented toward apprehending the meaning of interdependence situations, toward identifying appropriate action in such situations. Thus, experience in a relationship is inseparable from the fabric of interdependence characterizing the relationship.

Interdependence theory is a comprehensive model for understanding interdependence structure and processes. Thibaut & Kelley introduced their model for analyzing interdependence structure in *The Social Psychology of Groups* (Thibaut & Kelley, 1959), developing an analysis framework that was later expanded to deal with informational interdependence (Kelley & Thibaut, 1969). Their framework was enlarged in *Interpersonal Relations: A Theory of Interdependence* (Kelley & Thibaut, 1978). This chapter outlines the basic concepts of interdependence theory, citing illustrative empirical evidence where appropriate. In particular, we will discuss: (a) the evaluation of interactions and relationships;

Handbook of Personal Relationships, 2nd edn. Edited by Steve Duck.
© 1997 John Wiley & Sons Ltd.

(b) the structure of outcome interdependence, including a taxonomy by which all interdependence patterns can be analyzed in terms of degree of dependence, mutuality of dependence, correspondence of outcomes and basis for dependence; (c) transformation of motivation, including the primary types of transformational activity; (d) habitual transformational tendencies, including dispositions, relationship-specific motives and social norms; and (e) cognition, affect and self-presentation.

EVALUATING INTERACTIONS AND RELATIONSHIPS

Fundamentals of Interaction

Interdependence theory identifies *interaction* as a core feature of all interpersonal relationships. Interacting individuals engage in independent or shared activities, they speak to one another, and they create products for one another—they affect one another's preferences and options. Interaction yields outcomes for interacting individuals. Outcomes can be described in terms of overall "goodness", or can be conceptualized in terms of rewards and costs. The term "reward" refers to the positive consequences of interaction (e.g., contentment, joy, success) whereas the term "cost" refers to the negative consequences of interaction (e.g., pain, frustration, anger).

Individuals are assumed to be goal-oriented, implicitly seeking to obtain good outcomes and avoid bad outcomes. Does this mean that individuals myopically pursue self-interest? No. Although it is assumed that humans prefer patterns of interaction that yield desirable outcomes, preferences are only partially determined by immediate outcomes. Preferences are also shaped by that which "seems right" in light of the broader considerations that are at stake in interaction—considerations such as the well-being of an interaction partner or the impact of current choices on long-term goals. At the same time, the theory asserts that departures from self-interest tend to be highly contingent—the preferences that come to "make sense" in light of broader concerns depend on the specifics of the particular situation encountered with a given partner. More generally, it is important to note that, although interdependence theory frequently is presented as a theory of self-interested behavior, the heart of the theory concerns interdependence—its structures, patterns and effects on human experience.

Are preferences shaped by *nurture* or *nature*? Some interpersonal preferences are assumed to be learned, whereas others are largely guided by biological make-up; most preferences presumably reflect a combination of influences. Interdependence theory does not seek to identify a single preference-defining "engine" that drives social behavior (e.g., reproduction, attachment concerns; Bowlby, 1969; Maslow, 1968; Wilson, 1975). The theory is less concerned with categorizing the specific types of variable that shape preferences, and is more concerned with how individuals address existing patterns of interdependence—that is, the theory examines how the structure of interpersonal situations influences interaction-relevant preferences, motives and behavior.

Matrix Representation of Interaction Outcomes

Interdependence theory employs the *outcome matrix* as a tool in analyzing interaction. This is not to say that humans experience interaction as an analysis of 2 × 2 options and outcomes; the matrix is a theoretical tool, not a literal portrayal of lay cognition. Any interpersonal situation can be represented in matrix form, and a single, abstract pattern may represent a rather large class of concrete situations with dissimilar superficial features—the importance of the matrix lies not in the concrete behaviors and outcomes that are depicted, but in the patterns the matrix representation reveals. The columns in a matrix represent person A's behavioral options and the rows represent person B's options. Each cell in the matrix is associated with two outcome values, representing the joint occurrence of A's and B's behavior; the two values in each cell represent the impact of each joint event on each individual.

For example, Figure 9.1 depicts a possible interaction for Andy and Betty. Neither Andy nor Betty has done any housecleaning for two weeks. Neither partner likes housecleaning, but neither finds their current sordid circumstances to be congenial. If both Andy and Betty clean the house, both enjoy the moderate pleasure of an improved environment (4 and 4). Of course, both individuals would prefer that the partner clean the house (8), but each is irritated by the prospect of cleaning the house while the partner takes a free ride (−4). The cooperative choice would be to commence cleaning. At the same time, both

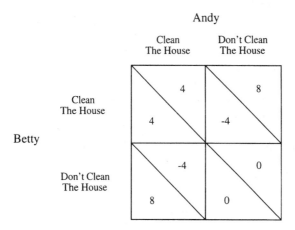

Figure 9.1 The outcome matrix: matrix representation of outcomes resulting from joint decisions to clean the house or not clean the house (a prisoner's dilemma pattern of interdependence)

Andy and Betty dislike housecleaning, so each individual feels tempted to "defect" and let the partner do the cleaning. If both Andy and Betty defect and pursue their immediate self-interest by failing to clean the house, both suffer poor outcomes (0 and 0).

Of course, interaction situations frequently are more intricate than symmetrical 2 × 2 matrices: The partners may possess more than two behavioral options, each individual may possess unique options not shared by the partner, and the partners may hold differing preferences for specific joint events. Interaction may involve more than two individuals, requiring the addition of a dimension to the matrix for each interacting partner. Also, the behavioral repertoires of the individuals may change over time, their preferences may change, and behaviors enacted on earlier occasions may modify either the range of options or the preferences attached to the options on future occasions. In essence, the matrix is a "snapshot" of an interdependence situation as it exists at one time. Although this simple tool ignores the dynamic continuity of actions and reactions in ongoing relationships, the static quality of the matrix allows for a rich analysis of the abstract qualities representing classes of interdependence pattern.

Standards for Evaluating Interactions and Relationships

Two standards are relevant to understanding how individuals gauge the adequacy of obtained outcomes. *Comparison level* (CL) refers to the quality of outcomes an individual has come to expect. CL is influenced by previous experiences in relationships and by social comparison (Festinger, 1954). *Comparison level for alternatives* (CL-alt) refers to the lowest level of outcomes an individual finds acceptable in light of outcomes obtainable elsewhere. CL-alt is influenced not only by the attractiveness of specific alternative relationships, but also by the desirability of the field of eligibles and the option of non-involvement. CL influences feelings of satisfaction, whereas CL-alt affects dependence.

Satisfaction level refers to the degree to which a relationship is experienced as gratifying. Individuals experience greater satisfaction when obtained outcomes exceed CL; outcomes falling short of CL are dissatisfying. Diverse literatures support the assertion that satisfaction is influenced not only by the objective quality of outcomes but also by subjective standards: individuals are happier with close partners to the extent that the partner is closer to the individual's ideal (Sabatelli, 1984; Sternberg & Barnes, 1985; Wetzel & Insko, 1982). Also, research on relative deprivation demonstrates that individuals feel dissatisfied when conditions compare unfavorably to their internal standards (Crosby, 1976), and research on self-discrepancy processes demonstrates that affective states are predictable on the basis of deviations from both ideal conditions and normatively prescribed conditions (Higgins, 1989). In addition, the J-curve model of protest suggests that dissatisfaction and revolution are more intense under conditions of rising expectations—for example, when prolonged economic growth is followed by a precipitous downturn in prosperity (Davies, 1962).

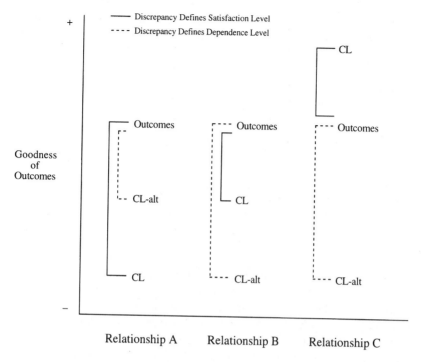

Figure 9.2 Satisfaction and dependence as a function of goodness of outcomes, comparison level (CL), and comparison level for alternatives (CL-alt): three illustrative patterns

Dependence level refers to the degree to which an individual relies on a partner for the fulfillment of important needs (i.e., the individual "needs" a relationship). To the extent that obtained outcomes exceed CL-alt the individual is increasingly dependent and increasingly likely to persist in a relationship; when outcomes fall below CL-alt the individual is more independent and more inclined to abandon a partner for the best alternative. Indeed, the literature demonstrates that dependence on a relationship is lower—and the probabililty of voluntary break-up is greater—among individuals who experience poor outcomes in the current relationship and perceive their alternatives to be attractive (Drigotas & Rusbult, 1992; Felmlee, Sprecher & Bassin, 1990; Rusbult, 1983; Simpson, 1987).

Satisfaction with a relationship ("am I happy?") and dependence on a relationship ("shall I stay?") to some degree are independent. Figure 9.2 displays three relationships with equivalent outcomes. In relationship A obtained outcomes are greater than CL-alt, which in turn is greater than CL. Because outcomes exceed expectations, the individual will feel satisfied; because outcomes do not greatly exceed CL-alt, the individual is only moderately dependent. In relationship B outcomes exceed CL, which in turn exceeds CL-alt. An individual will experience relationship B as moderately satisfying, and at the same time is highly dependent. In contrast, relationship C is one in which CL exceeds the individual's outcomes as well as CL-alt. This configuration of outcomes and standards is termed a *non-voluntary relationship*, in that the individual is dependent yet dissatisfied.

Non-voluntary involvement is tragically illustrated by the plight of the abused woman (Gelles, 1979; Strube, 1988). Whereas some researchers have attempted to explain why an abused woman might remain with a battering partner by reference to her personal dispositions (e.g., low self-esteem, learned helplessness), the decision to remain may be governed in part by dependence. Although the abused woman's outcomes are poor, her alternatives—especially her economic alternatives—may be even worse (Rusbult & Martz, 1995; Strube & Barbour, 1983). Thus, abused individuals do not necessarily remain with their partners because they are governed by "distorted" dispositions—sometimes abused individuals remain because they are dependent and have nowhere else to go.

Implications for Long-term Interdependence

Although we have described CL and CL-alt as static phenomena, over the course of an ongoing relationship these standards may change. Given that CL-alt influences the decision to persist in a relationship, high CL-alt stands as a threat to long-term involvement. Among individuals whose relationships persist, perceived quality of alternatives has been shown to decline over time (Rusbult, 1983). This decline in attractiveness of alternatives may occur because (1) alternatives "take themselves out of the running" when they become aware of an individual's involvement, or because (2) involved individuals behave in such a manner as to "drive away" tempting alternatives (e.g., wearing a wedding ring; Kelley, 1983a; Leik & Leik, 1976). In addition, involved individuals cognitively derogate tempting alternatives, presumably as a means of protecting the ongoing relationship from threat (Johnson & Rusbult, 1989; Kanter, 1968; Simpson, Gangestad & Lerma, 1990).

CL and satisfaction level, too, are likely to change over time. Given that CL is shaped partly by outcomes experienced in the current relationship, "the more satisfactory [a] relationship has been found to be, the higher will be the comparison level" (Thibaut & Kelley, 1959, p. 95). This rise in CL yields a corresponding decline in feelings of satisfaction. Additional forces toward dissatisfaction derive from (1) satiation and declining marginal utility (Brickman, Dunkel-Schetter & Abbey, 1987; Frijda, 1988; Solomon, 1980), and (2) the greater salience and potency of negative outcomes in relation to positive outcomes (Kahneman & Tversky, 1979; Schwarz, 1990; Taylor, 1991). Indeed, the literature reveals that over time, the subjective costs of involvement increase and satisfaction level declines (Campbell, Converse & Rodgers, 1976; Huston, McHale & Crouter, 1986; Rusbult, 1983; Weiss, 1980). Thus, partners may come to take one another for granted over the course of an ongoing relationship. How do partners stave off pressures toward negativity? The extant literature identifies several countervailing forces toward "positive illusion" (Taylor & Brown, 1988), including downward social comparison (Buunk & Van Yperen, 1991), tendencies toward perceived superiority (Van Lange & Rusbult, 1995), and the inclination to cognitively transform a partner's faults into virtues (Murray & Holmes, 1993).

STRUCTURE OF OUTCOME INTERDEPENDENCE: THE FUNDAMENTAL PROPERTIES OF INTERDEPENDENCE

The utility of the matrix representation resides in the fact that this analytic tool provides a basis for exploring the *structure of outcome interdependence*. Just as the Lewinian life space served as a tool for understanding individual experience (Lewin, 1936), the matrix is a tool for understanding interpersonal experience, providing a means of conceptualizing situations so as to identify their structural features. Given that the pattern of outcomes in a matrix reflects the structure of interdependence for a given interaction, it is useful to comment on the derivation of the numeric depictions of preferences that are displayed in matrices.

> The numbers entered in the outcome matrix are usually scaled from CL-alt as the zero point. The entries in the matrix indicate the degree to which each person is dependent on the dyad, and the pattern of entries thus represents their pattern of interdependence (Kelley & Thibaut, 1978, p. 10).

Scaling matrix values relative to CL or CL-alt does not alter the *pattern* of outcomes inherent in a matrix representation; CL and CL-alt affect the experiences of satisfaction and dependence, but such judgments are independent of the interdependence pattern implicit in an interaction.

All patterns of interdependence stem from three sources of control over the individual's outcomes (Cook, 1993): *reflexive control* (RC, or "actor control") reflects the degree to which the individual controls the quality of his or her outcomes (i.e., a main effect of Person A's actions); *fate control* (FC, or "partner control") reflects the degree to which the individual's outcomes are influenced by the actions of the partner (i.e., a main effect of B's actions); and *behavior control* (BC, or "dyadic control") reflects the degree to which the individual's outcomes are jointly influenced by his or her own actions in concert with the partner's actions (i.e., an interaction of A's and B's actions).

Kelley & Thibaut (1978) present a logical analysis of the domain of 2×2 matrices—an analysis in which all possible patterns of interdependence are examined, based on the relative contributions to each individual's outcomes of reflexive control, fate control and behavior control. This analysis yields a comprehensive typology of the domain of interdependence patterns, demonstrating that the patterns differ with respect to four properties—degree of dependence, mutuality of dependence, correspondence of outcomes, and basis of dependence. Indeed, these four properties align well with the properties that have been identified using inductive empirical techniques (Wish, Deutsch & Kaplan, 1976).

Degree of Dependence

Degree of dependence refers to the extent to which each individual's outcomes are influenced by the partner's actions and by the partners' joint actions. To the degree that Mary has little control over her outcomes and John has greater control over her outcomes, Mary is more *dependent* (i.e., her RC is low and John's FC and BC over her outcomes are high); to the degree that Mary has greater control over her outcomes and John has little control over her outcomes, Mary is more *independent* (i.e., her RC is high and John has little FC or BC over her outcomes). This definition expands on the definition based on CL-alt: individuals are dependent when they cannot unilaterally guarantee themselves good outcomes—either in an alternative relationship or through independent action—and accordingly rely on the partner for the fulfillment of important needs. For example, if Mary is John's main source of companionship—and if Mary unilaterally can accord or deny John companionship—John is dependent and "needs" his relationship with Mary.

Is level of dependence a psychologically meaningful feature of interdependence? As suggested earlier, dependence exerts profound effects on a variety of interpersonal phenomena. For example, to the extent that an individual is highly dependent on a close partner, the individual is "tied" to the relationship and becomes increasingly unlikely to end it (Felmlee, Sprecher & Bassin, 1990; Rusbult, 1980; Simpson, 1987). It has been suggested that feelings of commitment—including long-term orientation and intentions to persist—emerge out of the experience of dependence upon a relationship (Rusbult, 1983; Rusbult & Buunk, 1993). Dependence and commitment promote a variety of behaviors that are oriented toward sustaining a relationship, including: (1) derogation of tempting alternatives (Johnson & Rusbult, 1989; Simpson, Gangestad & Lerma, 1990); (2) constructive conflict resolution, including accommodating rather than retaliating when a partner behaves poorly (Rusbult et al., 1991); (3) willingness to sacrifice, or to forego direct self-interest so as to promote the well-being of a partner (Van Lange et al., 1995); and (4) the emergence of cognitive maneuvers that support the decision to persist, including the inclination to perceive one's relationship as better than (and not as bad as) other relationships (Buunk & VanYperen, 1991; Murray & Holmes, 1993; Van Lange & Rusbult, 1995).

Dependence also has its "down side": dependent individuals experience greater distress when the continuation of a relationship is threatened—for example, they experience jealousy and feel threatened by the partner's alternatives (Buunk, 1991; Strachan & Dutton, 1992; White & Mullen, 1989). Also, research on "entrapment" reveals that when dependence is strengthened through increases in the costs of ending an involvement—for example, through committing resources to a previously chosen course of action—persistence at a course of action is more likely, even when that course of action is costly or ineffective (Becker, 1960; Blau, 1967; Brockner & Rubin, 1985; Staw, 1976; Teger, 1980).

It is instructive to note that dependence is the converse of power (Huston, 1983). Dependence is greater to the degree that a partner can bring about a wide range of outcomes for the individual. A partner's power is limited by (1) the individual's ability to obtain good outcomes elsewhere (i.e., the individual's CL-alt defines a lower limit on the partner's usable power), and (2) the degree to which utilizing power harms the partner (i.e., the partner is unlikely to use available power if doing so yields poor outcomes for the self; Molm, 1985). Low-power individuals attend to relevant information in a more careful and differentiated manner; high-power individuals engage in "quick and dirty" processing of information (Fiske, 1993; Johnson & Ewens, 1971). In addition, in non-close relationships, powerholders tend to distance themselves from low-power targets (Kipnis et al., 1976).

Mutuality of Dependence

Mutuality of dependence refers to the degree to which partners are mutually rather than unilaterally dependent upon one another for attaining desirable outcomes. When just one individual is dependent, a relationship involves *unilateral dependence*; when both individuals are dependent, a relationship involves *mutual dependence*. It is instructive to discuss this property not only in terms of symmetric vs. asymmetric dependence, but also in terms of symmetric vs. asymmetric power: John's power is relatively greater than Mary's to the degree that (1) John possesses the power to provide (or not provide) Mary with outcomes of higher quality than Mary can provide for John, (2) John has the power to provide (or not provide) Mary with outcomes of poorer quality than Mary can provide for John, and (3) John has more attractive alternatives than does Mary (i.e., John has a higher CL-alt).

Is mutuality of dependence a psychologically meaningful feature of interdependence? Mutuality yields benefits that parallel those accruing from balance of power. Given that mutually dependent partners possess equal levels of control over one another's outcomes, there is reduced potential for exploitation. Indeed, research on the "principle of least interest" demonstrates that the partner receiving higher outcomes tends to exhibit enhanced dependence and reduced ability to control relationship events (Scanzoni & Scanzoni, 1981; Sprecher, 1985; Waller, 1938). Also, because mutually dependent partners are equally motivated to behave in such a manner as to sustain their relationship, there is less potential for negative emotions that undermine relationships—emotions such as insecurity or the sense of unwanted responsibility. Indeed, research has demonstrated that greater mutuality of dependence is associated with enhanced stability and superior couple functioning (Courtright, Millar & Rogers-Millar, 1979; Rusbult, Verette & Drigotas, 1995; Stafford & Canary, 1991).

Patterns of non-mutuality may originate in broad features of the environment, such as the field of eligibles. Imbalanced sex ratios—circumstances in which the ratio of men to women in the "mating market" deviates from 1.0—have been shown to

> dramatically influence the gender roles of men and women, shape the forms taken by relationships between men and women, and in turn produce changes in family structures and stimulate new kinds of association structures along gender lines (Secord, 1983, p. 525).

A high sex ratio (i.e., more men than women) is associated with valuing young women, norms of commitment, traditional division of labor and sexual morality; a low sex ratio (i.e., more women than men) is associated with sexual libertarianism, brief liaisons and tendencies for women to establish themselves as independent persons (Guttentag & Secord, 1983).

It is easy to imagine that differential dependence would typically lead to abuse, in that low-power individuals can do little but appease high-power individuals, who possess the wherewithal to use (or abuse) their power as they wish. Indeed, when partners' preferences are incompatible, non-mutuality is associated with suspicion and insecurity, abuse of power and avoidance of interaction (Tjosvold, 1981). However, under conditions of moderate to high compatibility of preferences, greater relative power activates norms of social responsibility. For example, dependence can enhance the probability of receiving help (Berkowitz & Daniels, 1963). Moreover, in situations of non-mutual dependence, low-power partners may develop tactics for inducing formal agreements through which exploitation is curtailed or prevented (Thibaut & Faucheux, 1965; Thibaut & Gruder, 1969). Given non-mutual resources, partners frequently adopt a "contributions" rule, whereby the advantaged individual contributes a greater share to promoting the partners' joint well-being (Murningham & King, 1992).

Correspondence of Outcomes

Correspondence of outcomes refers to the extent to which partners similarly evaluate the joint behavioral events available in their relationship—the degree to which events are mutually beneficial and mutually aversive (i.e., partners' evaluations of the "cells" in their full matrix are positively correlated). Correspondence does *not* imply similarity in the desirability of discrete behaviors. Partners may have correspondent preferences involving enactment of the same behavior (e.g., both John and Mary enjoy playing golf together), but they might also have correspondent preferences involving the enactment of different behaviors (e.g., a mutually congenial division of labor wherein John prepares meals and Mary cleans the house). Degree of correspondence defines a continuum ranging from perfectly correspondent outcomes (i.e., situations of pure coordination) through moderately correspondent outcomes (i.e., mixed-motive situations), to perfectly non-correspondent outcomes (i.e., zero-sum situations).

Why does correspondence influence the course of interaction? First, given that this property identifies the possibilities for congenial vs. conflictual interaction, degree of correspondence exerts reliable effects on cognitive and perceptual processes, determining whether interacting individuals feel that they are working with one another or against one another, whether their relationship is experienced as one of congeniality or war. Relationships characterized by non-correspondence are stormy, with partners developing suspicious, distrustful or even hostile attitudes toward one another (Blumstein & Schwartz, 1983; Gottman, 1979; Ickes, 1985; Surra & Longstreth, 1990).

Second, correspondence is relevant to ease of decision-making, in that decision difficulty is greatest under conditions of intermediate correspondence. Decisions are easy in correspondent situations, in that the obviously "rational" choice is to act in such a manner as to maximize both one's own and a partner's outcomes ("what's good for me is good for you"); decisions are easy in non-correspondent situations, in that the "rational" choice is to pursue self-interest (e.g., partners seldom worry about whether to compete in a tennis game). Moderately correspondent situations are maximally ambiguous with respect to the appropriateness of cooperation vs. competition (Blumstein & Schwartz, 1983).

Third, correspondence sets the stage for the elicitation of key motives, constraining the ability to act on the basis of some motives and providing opportunities for expressing others (Peterson, 1983). Given that it is not possible for both partners to achieve good outcomes in perfectly non-correspondent situations, as correspondence level decreases, competitive motives are activated; as correspondence increases, cooperative motives are activated (Kelley & Grzelak, 1972). Situations of moderate correspondence are highly ambiguous, and therefore activate a wider range of motives, including both (1) fear, derived from the possibililty that a partner may not cooperate, and (2) greed, derived from the temptation to "defect" in response to a partner's cooperation (Rapoport, 1966).

Basis for Dependence

Basis for dependence concerns the degree to which dependence rests on individual vs. joint control—that is, whether an individual's dependence derives from the partner's actions (FC) or from the partners' joint actions (BC). In general, situations of high fate control are governed by exchange, whereas situations of high behavior control are governed by coordination. Thus, relationships with high fate control are experienced as other-controlled ("my well-being is in my partner's hands"), whereas relationships with high behavior control are experienced as jointly-controlled ("together, my partner and I control what will transpire").

Achieving good outcomes in situations involving high fate control requires extended time orientation, in combination with norms of reciprocity ("I'll scratch your back this time if you'll scratch mine next time"; Axelrod, 1984). Given that the possibility of freeloading is a chronic problem in such situations, it goes without saying that high fate control frequently engenders threats, promises or other forms of agreement that enhance the predictability of interaction (Orbell, Van de Kragt & Dawes, 1988). Situations of high behavior control are less complex, in that they do not necessarily require long-term strategies—problems of behavior control frequently can be resolved "here and now".

Transition Lists and Interdependence

Kelley (1984c) expanded the analysis of interdependence through the use of *transition lists*—a "set of lists, each of which specifies each person's options. . . . and the consequences for each person of each combination of their respective selections among their options" (p. 960). The transition list overcomes several limitations inherent in the static outcome matrix by specifying how current actions enlarge or constrain subsequent outcomes or options, thereby addressing the sequential and temporal features of interdependence. This means of representing interdependence structure allows us to conceptualize interaction in terms of both (1) patterns of outcome interdependence and (2) changes in patterns. In addition to characterizing *outcome control*, the transition list also characterizes *transition control*, or control over movement from one situation to another.

Figure 9.3 displays an interdependence situation involving Anne and Bob

| | | | Consequences | | |
| | | | Outcomes | | Transition |
List	Option sets	Option pairs	Anne	Bob	(next list)
L	(A_1/A_2)	A_1 and B_1	+5	+10	M
	(B_1/B_2)	A_1 and B_2	+5	+5	L
		A_2 and B_1	0	+10	M
		A_2 and B_2	0	+5	L
M	$(A_1/A_2/A_3)$	A_1 and B_3	+5	-20	M
	(B_3/B_4)	A_1 and B_4	+5	-20	M
		A_2 and B_3	0	-20	M
		A_2 and B_4	0	-20	M
		A_3 and B_3	-5	0	L
		A_3 and B_4	-5	0	L

Figure 9.3 The transition list: Anne can rescue Bob from the consequences of an unwise action

(Kelley, 1984c). List L represents the partners' initial options (A_1 vs. A_2 for Anne, B_1 vs. B_2 for Bob) and the consequences of their actions. Outcome control in list L involves bilateral reflexive control—each individual's outcomes are controlled by the individual's own actions (+5 vs. 0 for Anne, +10 vs. +5 for Bob). In addition to representing the information traditionally displayed in a matrix, list L represents the future situations that will come to pass as a consequence of each set of joint actions. In list L, transition control rests in Bob's hands—B_2 leaves the two in the "safe" list L, whereas B_1 moves the partners to the "perilous" list M. If Bob pursues his self-interest in list L by enacting B_1, yielding outcomes for Bob of +10 (rather than +5 for B_2), the partners move to a situation in which all of Bob's outcomes are poor (−20 or 0). Also, in list M outcome control and transition control shift to Anne's hands. Rescuing Bob from list M requires an heroic act: by enacting A_3 and suffering poor outcomes (−5) Anne (1) ensures that Bob receives less than catastrophic outcomes (0 rather than −20) and (2) restores both partners to the safer list L. Thus, this pair of lists represents the results of an unwise act by Bob and the possibility of heroic rescue by Anne. Despite its simplicity, this example conveys the sophistication of the transition list representation, illustrating (1) how immediate choices influence the options, situations, and outcomes that unfold in the future, and (2) how patterns of outcome control and transition control may shift over the course of extended interaction.

Parallel to the bases of outcome control, transition control differs in (1) reflexive control, or the degree to which the individual controls transitions across situations, (2) fate control, or the degree to which the partner controls transitions, and (3) behavior control, or the degree to which control is joint. Preferences and choices frequently are influenced by the desire to enhance transition control. For example, John may control a conversation so as to avoid discussing the division of household labor, thereby reducing the odds that he and Mary will adopt a new, less congenial arrangement. In fact, partner conflict may center on issues of transition control ("you *always* say 'let's discuss it later'!").

Implications for Long-term Interdependence

Long-term partners exert considerable influence on one another's lives. Through their actions individuals not only (1) modify the immediate options available to their partners, but also (2) modify the options and outcomes available to themselves and partners in future interactions (Miller, Berg & Archer, 1983; Snyder, Tanke & Berscheid, 1977; Swann & Predmore, 1985; Wegner, Erber & Raymond, 1991). Through an extended process of behavioral confirmation (Snyder, 1984), partners can shape one another's dispositions: the individual (1) holds expectations about the partner and (2) behaves in an expectation-consistent manner, thereby (3) eliciting expectation-consistent behavior from the partner, and in the long run (4) partially shaping the partner's dispositions. Depending on the nature of the individual's expectations, such influence can be constructive or destructive.

Interdependent partner-enhancement refers to circumstances in which the individual's beliefs about and behavior toward the partner are congruent with the partner's ideal self, thereby eliciting behavior that is congruent with the partner's ideal self. Through deliberate choice or as an automatic consequence of John's expectations about Mary, John constrains opportunities for undesirable experiences and provides opportunities for the expression of Mary's best self. Over time, this process should lead Mary to become closer to the person she ideally would like to be. Based on empirical evidence employing both self-reports and friends' reports of changes in the self over the course of ongoing relationships, interdependent partner-enhancement has been shown to be associated with superior couple functioning and with greater odds of persistence (Drigotas et al., 1995).

TRANSFORMATION OF MOTIVATION

Given Matrix vs. Effective Matrix

Why do different individuals react in different ways to the same situation? If behavior were determined by simple self-interest, all individuals should react identically to a given situation (barring perceptual bias, random error and the like). The distinction between the given matrix and the effective matrix provides a partial answer to this question. The *given matrix* reflects the structure of interdependence based upon direct, self-interested preferences. Given matrix outcomes are "gut level" preferences:

> The outcome in each cell of the matrix. . . . is *given* for the relationship by virtue of the specifications of the social and physical environment and the relevant properties of the two persons (Kelley & Thibaut, 1978, pp. 16–17).

Behavioral choices frequently reflect more than the pursuit of immediate self-interest. Preferences are also shaped by broader concerns, including strategic considerations, desire to affect both one's own and a partner's outcomes, or long-term goals. A process termed *transformation of motivation* accounts for the fact that individuals often respond in ways that depart from "gut level" given matrix preferences, instead behaving in such a manner as to promote broader interaction goals.

> Transformation generally requires freeing behavior from control by the proximal situation and thereby enabling it to be responsive to more distal features, including the partner's outcomes. . . . and one's remote outcomes (Kelley, 1984a, p. 104).

The preferences resulting from the transformation process are represented in the *effective matrix*, which summarizes the reconceptualized preferences that directly guide behavior.

The Process of Transformation of Motivation

How does transformation of motivation come about? A schematic representation of this process is displayed in Figure 9.4. Given that humans are social animals, human intelligence is highly interpersonal in character (Cosmides & Tooby, 1989)—humans can identify key features of situations insofar as such features are relevant to personal well-being, recognizing that some situations "look like" previously-encountered situations. Thus, individuals respond to situations as instances of general patterns rather than perceiving and responding to each situation "*de novo*" (Kelley, 1984a). The transformation process begins when the individual "reads" the given matrix situation as either (1) a novel, unfamiliar situation or as (2) a situation similar to previous interactions sharing the same structure.

Given that the successes and failures of previous interactions direct behavior in current situations, the transformation process is partially shaped by categorizing the given situation as one pattern rather than another. When the perceived pattern is an "easy" one for which no broader considerations are relevant, the individual responds on the basis of immediate, given matrix preferences. But when the given pattern involves more complex constraints or opportunities, further events ensue. The contingencies of the given matrix may activate dispositions, motives or norms. These distal variables color the proximal events accom-

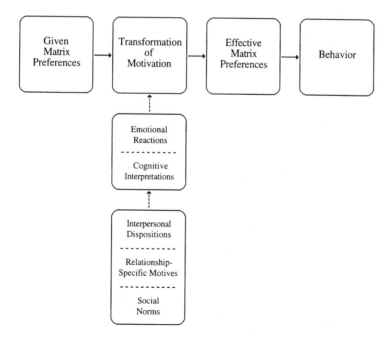

Figure 9.4 The proximal and distal determinants of transformation of motivation

panying an interaction by influencing event-specific cognition and emotion, leading the individual toward one of several possible transformations (e.g., desire to maximize joint outcomes). The resulting transformation process in turn yields a new set of preferences, and it is these new preferences—represented in the effective matrix—that direct behavior.

Does the transformation process necessarily involve elaborate mental activity? Through adaptation to repeatedly encountered patterns, individuals develop habitual tendencies to react to specific patterns in specific ways, such that the transformation process occurs quite rapidly, with little or no conscious thought. At critical choice points individuals may continue to engage in transformation-relevant information-seeking and rational decision-making, but just as often, habits reflecting prior adaptation may automatically guide behavior (Scott, Fuhrman & Wyer, 1991). Novel patterns involving mixed-motive structures tend to yield more deliberate processing of transformation-relevant information. Such complex patterns may induce a "piece-meal" analysis similar to that involved in reacting to novel information (Neuberg & Fiske, 1987).

Functional Value of the Transformation of Motivation

Why does the transformation of motivation occur, especially in light of the fact that such preference shifts frequently involve foregoing immediate self-interest? First, sometimes it is beneficial to behave in ways other than that which is dictated by immediate self-interest, in that behavior guided by the transformation process yields superior outcomes even in the short run. For example, in situations involving moderate non-correspondence, if both partners act on the basis of immediate self-interest, both suffer poor outcomes; if both partners engage in prosocial transformation, both receive better outcomes.

Second, as the transformation process becomes relatively more automatic, interactions shaped by such transformations tend to proceed in a smooth and predictable manner—that is, the transformation process provides a clear basis for choice, thereby reducing uncertainty. For example, in patterns of interdependence characterized by high levels of fate or behavior control with little reflexive control, self-interest provides no clear choice of action. In situations of this sort, the transformed, effective matrix may reveal a "desirable" course of action, where no such clarity existed in the given matrix.

And third, sometimes, departing from immediate self-interest facilitates coordination. For example, research on conflicted interaction reveals that in reacting to a partner's potentially destructive act, if the individual follows gut-level impulses and responds in a destructive manner, couple conflict escalates (Gottman, Markman & Notarius, 1977; Margolin & Wampold, 1981). If the individual instead seeks to maximize both own outcomes *and* those of the partner, the odds of escalating conflict are reduced. Such behavior not only (1) provides fairly good outcomes for both parties in the short run, but also (2) allows partners to avoid the costs of conflict, (3) minimizes the odds that the partner will behave destructively, (4) promotes the individual's long-term well-being by increasing the probability that the partner will reciprocate this cooperative act, and (5) communicates to the partner that the individual is trustworthy (i.e., cooperatively oriented). Thus, departing from direct self-interest not only solves the problem at hand, but also promotes long-term coordination and harmony (Axelrod, 1984).

Types of Transformations

That transformation of motivation occurs in everyday interaction belies the simple-minded notion that behavior is governed by direct self-interest. But exactly what does transformation of motivation entail? Three types of transformation can be identified. *Outcome transformations* are based on degree of concern with own outcomes in relation to a partners' outcomes. That is, transformations can be expressed in terms of the "weights" individuals assign to their own and partners' outcomes, as represented in Figure 9.5 (Griesinger & Livingston, 1973).

The simplest way in which to approach interaction is to act upon direct self-interest by maximizing one's own outcomes (i.e., MaxOwn, or individualism; see Figure 9.5); no transformation is involved, in that this orientation is consistent with preferences in the given matrix. However, individuals frequently seek to promote good outcomes for themselves *and* their partners (i.e., MaxJoint, or cooperation). Also, individuals may engage in transformations that are completely other-oriented (i.e., MaxOther, or altruism), especially with close partners or with individuals who desperately need assistance. Another prosocial transformation—one typically motivated by justice concerns—involves attempts to ensure that partners obtain equal outcomes (i.e., MinDiff; this does not follow from Figure 9.5 because it does not involve maximizing own or partner's outcomes—the goal is equality, not outcome maximization).

Sometimes individuals seek good outcomes *in relation to* others (i.e., MaxRel, or competition)—a transformation that necessarily involves social comparison (e.g., siblings competing for parental attention). Other transformations are possible, including assigning negative weights to the partner's outcomes (i.e., MinOther, or aggression), to one's own outcomes (i.e., MinOwn, or self-abnegation), or to both individuals' outcomes (i.e., MinJoint, or intransigence). Although such negative transformations can be observed in reaction to specific patterns, tendencies of this sort are rare. Finally, more complex transformations are possible, including MaxiMin (i.e., enhancing the well-being of the person with the poorest outcomes) or MinCost (i.e., avoiding the most aversive outcome for oneself).

Transpositional transformations take account of the microtemporal features of interdependence. This type of transformation entails reconceptualizing the situation so as to employ pre-emptive action; the partner who acts second is confronted with the decision to match or not match the "initiator's" choice. For

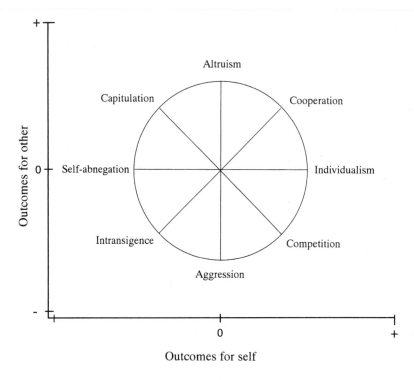

Figure 9.5 A typology of outcome transformations

example, John and Mary may be working on tasks for which each needs the other's help. If John acts first, and helps Mary, the decision confronting Mary is whether to reciprocate by helping John. Transpositional transformations are particularly relevant to situations involving high behavior control, where matching frequently yields coordination. Alternating interdependence situations provide good opportunities for coordination, in that (1) the partner who acts first does so in recognition of how the partner is likely to respond, and (2) the partner who acts second does so in full knowledge of the initiator's choice. Often, the "dilemma" in such situations centers *not* on which of several possible responses to enact, but on whether to be the first or the second to act.

Sequential transformations take account of the macrotemporal implications of interdependence, involving successive choices over the course of extended interaction. For example, individuals may adopt strategies such as tit-for-tat ("I'll cooperate as long as you do"; Axelrod, 1984) or may develop a pattern of turn-taking ("Let's do it your way this time, my way next time"). Sequential transformations typically are responsive to the partner's probable transformation. For example, the individual who approaches a situation cooperatively may change this strategy if the partner is consistently selfish. Sequential transformations may also serve communicative purposes. For example, individuals may enact prosocial choices as a means of expressing their loyalty, or may behave destructively in response to a hostile partner as a means of signaling the boundaries of willingness to accommodate.

Empirical Demonstrations of Transformation of Motivation

It is not easy to document the transformation process, in that the transformation of motivation is quite routine and may occur in a relatively automatic manner. Nevertheless, existing research provides evidence that is consistent with the transformation concept. For example, subjects behaving in accord with the given matrix exhibit shorter response latencies than do those who transform that pattern: individualists (who respond based on self-interest) exhibit shorter latencies when allocating funds to themselves and others than do competitors (who enact MaxRel transformation) or cooperators (who enact MaxJoint or MinDiff transformation; Dehue, McClintock & Liebrand, 1993). Also, subjects in games research (1) describe transformation-relevant reasons for their choices (e.g., "to help the partner obtain more points"), (2) assign different meaning to identical situations depending on the transformation applied to the situation, (3) engage in transformation-relevant information-seeking, and (4) exhibit more prosocial choices when interacting for extended periods of time (Pruitt & Kimmel, 1977).

It might be argued that the motives governing deviations from self-interest are thoroughly defined by the nature of a given relationship. For example, close partners might automatically take one another's interests into account; in intimate relationships, self-interest and partner-interest could be inextricably merged (Aron & Aron, 1986; Clark, Mills & Powell, 1986). However, even close partners distinguish between personal well-being and partner well-being. In describing previous conflicts, the responses subjects actually enact (effective matrix) are considerably more constructive than are the responses they entertained prior to acting (given matrix; Yovetich & Rusbult, 1994). Also, when the concerns that normally influence behavior—concern for the partner's feelings, the future of the relationship, or public image—are eliminated, and subjects report how they "earnestly wish to behave", their preferences are less constructive than are those of subjects operating on the basis of normal social concern (Rusbult et al., 1991). Moreover, in reacting to a partner's destructive acts, behavior is more constructive given plentiful response time; when time for transformational activity is limited, prosocial behavior is less probable (Yovetich & Rusbult, 1994).

Implications for Long-term Interdependence

Individuals frequently act on the basis of broader goals rather than in the service of immediate self-interest. At the same time, departures from self-interest tend to be highly contingent, applying to specific situations and specific partners (Huston & Vangelisti, 1991; Miller & Kenny, 1986):

> The advantages of acting in ways other than those indicated by short-term self-interest are gained only under certain circumstances. . . . in all cases they are conditional (Kelley, 1984b, p. 4).

The several types of transformational activity flow from different determinants (i.e., relative concern for own vs. partner well-being; micro- and macro-temporal possibilities), and are relevant to different interdependence domains. Outcome transformations are relevant to a variety of situations, including both single-choice interactions (e.g., interactions with strangers) and "never-ending" relationships (e.g., interactions with one's mother). Transpositional transformations are relevant only to alternating choice situations, and sequential transformations are relevant only to situations involving repeated interaction.

In recognition of the diverse features of interdependence that may affect motivation and behavior, it is instructive to address the issue of *altruistic motivation* (Kelley & Thibaut, 1985). Interdependence theory has been criticized for "sanctioning selfishness" (Wallach & Wallach, 1983). This critique is misplaced, in that behavior is shaped by concerns extending beyond immediate self-interest, including such determinants as fairness considerations or desire to enhance the well-being of a partner. Also, although the theory suggests that prosocial tendencies reflect adaptation, this is not to argue against the existence of altruistic motives. Repeatedly experiencing situations in which prosocial acts yield good consequences may give rise to relatively more stable prosocial tendencies, but the fact that adaptation underlies such tendencies is not to suggest that self-interest mediates current behavior. This logic places interdependence theory "inside the head" of the individual, suggesting that (1) we are aware of prior adaptations, (2) prior adaptations are labeled as "self-interested", and (3) current prosocial acts are interpreted as parallel self-interested adaptations. Once a transformational tendency is established, such a motive may achieve considerable autonomy, taking on value and acquiring the power to guide behavior in its own right. More generally, it is unfortunate that this debate frequently decays into an exercise in categorization, pitting (1) selfish behavior, or acts including any taint of self-interest, against (2) altruistic behavior, or acts that are completely free of such contamination (Batson, 1987). Such an exercise ignores the multifaceted nature of motivation, in that frequently the "smart" thing to do is also the "good" thing to do—the existence of self-interest does not preclude genuinely altruistic impulses.

HABITUAL TRANSFORMATIONAL TENDENCIES: INTERPERSONAL DISPOSITIONS, RELATIONSHIP-SPECIFIC MOTIVES, AND SOCIAL NORMS

When individuals initially encounter specific interdependence patterns, such patterns are experienced as unique events—as specific "problems and opportunities" to which the individual must react. In reacting to such situations, the individual may (1) behave in an impulsive manner or (2) deliberately review the options, consider the consequences, and consciously decide how to behave. If the reaction to a given pattern yields poor outcomes, the individual will behave differently in future situations with similar patterns; if the reaction yields good outcomes, the individual will react similarly in future situations with similar patterns (i.e., win–stay, lose–change). Over time, some patterns will be regularly encountered and a stable orientation to those patterns may emerge—for example, individuals may develop tendencies to forego self-interest in non-corre-spondent situations with a specific partner.

Interpersonal orientations are pattern-contingent "solutions" to repeatedly-encountered situations—solutions that on average yield desirable outcomes. Typically, stable orientations do not operate as a function of conscious calculation. Individuals sometimes studiously decide how to behave, but just as often such "decisions" are the automatic product of established habits. Once a stable orientation is established, the individual routinely engages in the activities that are set into motion by the orientation, only occasionally (if ever) being aware of such habitual processes, and only occasionally (if ever) experiencing the behavior as antithetical to self-interest. As illustrated in Figure 9.4, interpersonal orientations exert their effects by (1) coloring cognitive activities and emotional experiences, and (2) giving rise to stable, pattern-contingent transformational tendencies.

Interpersonal Dispositions

Interpersonal dispositions are person-specific inclinations to respond to particular interdependence patterns in a specific manner across numerous partners (Kelley, 1983b). How do dispositions emerge? Over the course of development different individuals experience different interdependence histories, undergoing different experiences with parents and siblings, and confronting different opportunities and constraints in peer interaction. As a result of their unique histories individuals acquire dispositions, reflected in the manner in which they approach specific interdependence patterns—they develop tendencies to perceive patterns in predictable ways, and to apply transformations to those patterns with greater or lesser probability (Halberstadt, 1986; Reis, Senchak & Solomon, 1985).

It is instructive to illustrate this process using the example of attachment style (Bowlby, 1969; Hazan & Shaver, 1994). From the outset, it is important to note that dependence is dangerous, in that dependence reflects a partner's ability to provide one with exceptionally good *or* exceptionally poor outcomes (e.g., affirmation vs. betrayal; Reis & Shaver, 1988). Individuals develop avoidant styles as a consequence of seeking intimacy and repeatedly experiencing rejection or betrayal. Accordingly, avoidant individuals come to perceive intimacy situations as dangerous, and "solve" such dilemmas by exploiting their partners or by avoiding intimacy patterns. Just as competitors elicit competition from others and "create" a distrustful world for themselves (Kelley & Stahelski, 1970), avoidant individuals elicit avoidance, and thus create a cold and barren world (Simpson, Rholes & Nelligan, 1992). In contrast, secure individuals experience interdependence histories in which attempts at intimacy yield good outcomes. Accordingly, secure individuals perceive intimacy situations as safe, behave in a trusting manner, and create opportunities for partners to safely seek intimacy in return. Presumably, anxious-ambivalent individuals experience inconsistent intimacy histories and therefore come to behave in an erratic manner, alternating between (1) desperately grasping at that which they most desire (i.e., intimacy, closeness) and (2) cautiously avoiding the risks of dependence.

The functioning of dispositions is also illustrated in research on social value orientations (Messick & McClintock, 1968). When presented with opportunities to distribute outcomes to themselves and others, some subjects consistently select options in which own outcomes are greatest (individualism), whereas others are oriented toward distributions of the MaxJoint (cooperation) or MaxRel variety (competition; Liebrand & Van Run, 1985). Social value orientations (1) influence behavior in a variety of situations, (2) are associated with distinct patterns of belief regarding others' orientations, and (3) are reflected in the probability with which sequential transformations are applied to given patterns (McClintock & Liebrand, 1988). For example, prosocials approach interaction cooperatively, and continue to do so as long as the partner behaves cooperatively in return. Individualists are susceptible to the temptation to exploit a partner's cooperation, but cooperate when it is advantageous to do so. Competitors are unwilling to cooperate even when doing so would maximize their outcomes. The orientations embodied in such dispositions exert their effects by shaping the emotions and cognitions accompanying a given pattern. For example, competitive individuals perceive a wide range of patterns as competitive, believe that others are competitive, and interpret cooperative acts as "stupid" or "sneaky". Given that interaction partners frequently compete in response to competition from others, the competitive individual's assumptions about others' goals and motives are more likely to be confirmed than disconfirmed (Kelley & Stahelski, 1970; Snyder, 1984).

Relationship-specific Motives

Relationship-specific motives are inclinations to respond to particular patterns in a specific manner within the context of a given relationship (Holmes, 1981). Relationship-specific motives are especially evident in situations involving dilemmas between personal well-being and the well-being of the partner or relationship. Holmes & Rempel (1989) term such patterns "diagnostic situations", in reference to the fact that behavior in such situations is diagnostic of the individual's motives. One important motive concerns trust, which reflects a partner's confidence in the individual's benevolent intentions (Rempel, Holmes & Zanna, 1985). When an individual enacts prosocial behavior in a diagnostic situation, departing from direct self-interest for the good of the relationship, such behavior communicates concern for the partner's well-being. Such behavior should (1) increase the partner's trust in the individual's benevolent intentions, (2) strengthen the partner's commitment, and (3) increase the odds that the partner will exhibit prosocial transformation in the future. For example, given that John trusts Mary, he experiences more benign emotions and forms more benevolent interpretations of Mary's actions, which in turn enhances his tendencies toward prosocial transformation of motivation and prosocial behavior.

Commitment is another important relationship-specific motive (Johnson, 1989; Levinger, 1979; Rusbult, 1980). Commitment emerges as a consequence of dependence upon a partner, and includes long-term orientation and the sense of being "linked" to a relationship. Commitment is strengthened when satisfaction level is high (e.g., the individual loves the partner), when the quality of available alternatives is poor (e.g., alternative partners are unappealing), and when invest-ment size is large (e.g., important resources are linked to a relationship). Com-mitment is the strongest predictor of voluntary decisions to persist (Rusbult, 1983), and promotes prosocial maintenance behaviors such as derogation of alternatives (Johnson & Rusbult, 1989), accommodation (Rusbult et al., 1991), willingness to sacrifice (Van Lange et al., 1995), and perceived superiority (Rusbult, Van Lange et al., 1995). Commitment colors emotional reactions to specific interdependence patterns (e.g., feeling affection rather than anger when a partner is neglectful) and gives rise to patterns of thought that support the decision to persist (e.g., derogation of alternatives). In turn, such benevolent thoughts and feelings promote prosocial transformation, especially in situations of moderate correspondence (e.g., accommodating rather than retaliating when a partner behaves badly; Rusbult & Buunk, 1993).

Social Norms

Social norms are rule-based inclinations to respond to particular interdepend-ence patterns in a specific manner, either with people in general (e.g., never be the first to "defect") or in the context of a given relationship (e.g., never betray your best friend; Campbell, 1975; Simon, 1990). Norms are manifested in (1) observed regularity of behavior, (2) attempting to regain control by appealing to the norm in situations where regularity has been interrupted, and (3) feeling guilty about having violated the norm (Thibaut & Kelley, 1959). For example, most societies develop rules regarding the expression of anger; such rules help groups avoid the chaos that would ensue if individuals were freely to give rein to hostile emotions. Likewise, etiquette and everyday rules of civility regulate behavior so as to yield more harmonious interaction—"manners" represent effi-cient solutions to everyday interdependence dilemmas. For example, in the ab-sence of normative prescriptions, Mary might feel irritated when John offers his mother the front seat of the car when driving to a restaurant. But in light of norms regarding suitable behavior toward one's elders, the potential for conflict in such situations is reduced.

Long-term partners may develop relationship-specific rules to solve problems of interdependence. For example, although the temptation to become involved with alternatives can be acute, the costs of doing so can be equally acute. Therefore, most couples either comply with existing norms or develop their own norms to govern such behavior and minimize the negative impact of extrarelationship involvements. Such norms typically specify the circumstances under which extrarelationship involvement is acceptable (e.g., marriage primacy), as well as the conditions under which such behavior is unacceptable (e.g., high visibility). Couples who adhere to the "ground rules" of their marriage tend to exhibit lower levels of jealousy regarding a spouse's infidelity (Buunk, 1987).

In like manner, partners frequently adopt rules governing the distribution of resources in their relationship (Mikula, 1983; Walster, Berscheid & Walster, 1976). Allocation rules minimize conflict and enhance couple functioning. Thus, it is not surprising that (1) partners adhere to distribution rules such as equity, equality, or need, and that (2) individuals experience discomfort when normative standards are violated. Also, allocation rules frequently are relationship-specific. For example, in parent–child or other "communal" relationships, the norms guiding behavior are need-based rather than contributions-based (Clark & Mills, 1979; Deutsch, 1975). Moreover, rules governing conflict resolution frequently center as much on the procedure by which conflicts should be resolved as on the outcome distribution *per se* (Lind & Tyler, 1988; Thibaut & Walker, 1975).

Implications for Long-term Interdependence

Over the course of extended interaction partners are interdependent not only (1) in the patterns of interdependence that are implicit in given matrix preferences, but also at a "higher level" (2) in the transformations the partners routinely apply to given patterns. When John's orientations lead him toward prosocial transformation, Mary's options and outcomes are enhanced; when John is inclined toward self-centered or antisocial behavior, Mary's options and outcomes are degraded. Thus, just as we can characterize outcome interdependence in terms of control, dependence and correspondence, we can characterize the interdependence of interpersonal orientations in a parallel manner.

To the extent that a partner's transformational tendencies are firmly established, the individual's transformational task is simplified. For example, in some respects it is easier to be involved with a partner who is reliably self-centered than to be involved with a partner who is *un*reliably prosocial, in that the tasks of prediction and coordination are more difficult in the latter instance. Moreover, to the extent that partners possess knowledge of one another's orientations, uncertainty is reduced and the odds of achieving congenial and mutually gratifying outcomes are enhanced. Given that such knowledge rests on abilities and traits such as empathy and perspective-taking, long-term functioning should be enhanced to the extent that one or both partners excel at the sorts of social-cognitive and social-emotional dispositions that increase sensitivity and awareness of a partner's preferences and motives (Davis & Oathout, 1987; Ickes, Stinson et al., 1990; Rusbult et al., 1991).

COGNITIVE INTERPRETATIONS, EMOTIONAL REACTIONS, AND SELF-PRESENTATION

Meaning Analysis: Cognitive Interpretations and Emotional Reactions

As displayed in Figure 9.4, (1) proximal mental events such as cognitions and emotions represent the individual's internal construal of the meaning of a given pattern, and (2) proximal mental events are colored by the orientations that have developed over the course of repeated exposure to specific instances of general patterns. Kelley (1984a) used the phrase *interest-relevant situation* in reference to the fact that interdependence situations have implications for the individual's personal well-being. No two situations are identical, but the properties characterizing situations possess sufficient regularity that classifications are possible. Scanning a situation for its meaning plays a critical role in adaptation, in that such activity provides the material for

> marking and recording the pattern (and type of pattern) of the interest-relevant features of each just-experienced situation and of identifying and orienting oneself to each forthcoming situation in terms of its pattern of such features (Kelley, 1984a, p. 91).

Meaning analysis involves reflecting on a given situation, noting its interest-relevant features and discerning its broader implications (Frijda, 1988; Mandler, 1975). Meaning analysis is oriented toward rendering the social world predictable, and therefore controllable. As Fiske (1992) suggests, "thinking is for doing"; we suggest that "feeling is for doing" as well. Cognitions and emotions prompt and direct action in such a manner as to adapt to interdependence patterns that will be encountered in the immediate or more distant future. In particular, cognitions and emotions guide interaction via their role in (1) interpreting the direct significance and broader implications of an event, (2) relating the implications of this knowledge to one's own needs and preferences, and (3) directing reactions to the event. Retrospectively, internal events denote a change in the individual's welfare and serve as summaries of the causal factors that are relevant to that event. Prospectively, internal events prompt and direct behavior with respect to the particular causal structure inherent in a given event.

Cognitive interpretations are relevant to interaction in at least three ways. First, individuals scan situations for their interest-relevant features; responding effectively depends on correctly detecting key properties of the situation at hand (Kelley, 1984a). Second, individuals form inferences regarding the motives underlying behavior, attending in particular to departures from given matrix preferences—deviations from self-centered choice reveal the individual's unique goals and motives (Holmes, 1981). In early stages of involvement expectations are "probabilistic" in that they are based on assumptions about how the average person would react; in later stages individuals also employ "idiographic" expectations based on knowledge of how the partner has behaved across a variety of situations (Kelley, 1991). Third, cognition is central to understanding behavior in novel situations for which stable tendencies have not yet emerged. Individuals are able to engage in "informed" transformation to the extent that they can predict the partner's preferences, motives and behavior. Such prediction involves abstracting general "rules" from knowledge of a partner's behavior in previous situations (Weiner, 1986). More generally, cognition is shaped by the interpersonal orientations embodied in dispositions (e.g., anxious-ambivalent individuals interpret a busy partner's neglect as rejection), relationship-specific motives (e.g., committed individuals are inclined to ignore a partner's rude remark by attributing it to work-related stress), and social norms (e.g., in conflict situations, obeying the injunction to "count to ten" before reacting yields calm and cooperative behavior).

Emotional reactions, too, guide the course of interaction. Prevailing conceptualizations suggest that emotions signal (1) interruptions to the flow of interaction (Berscheid, 1983) or (2) changes in action readiness caused by appraising events as relevant to personal well-being (Frijda, 1988; Kelley, 1984a). The prototype approach asserts that emotion prototypes are formed as a result of repeated experience with particular interaction patterns (Shaver et al., 1987). Emotions vividly and efficiently "summarize" the meaning of a pattern, directing attention to key features and identifying the interest-relevant aspects of the situation. Moreover, emotions are colored by dispositions, motives and norms. For example, attraction to an alternative partner is likely to arouse guilt among committed individuals and among individuals who adhere to the normative prescription that adultery is wrong. In turn, feelings of guilt lead the individual to respond effectively, behaving in a cool manner so as to "drive away the alternative" or cognitively derogating the alternative so as to eliminate the temptation.

Self-presentation

Just as individuals examine one another's behavior for information regarding preferences and motives, they attempt to communicate their own preferences and motives via *self-presentation* (Baumeister, 1982; DePaulo, 1992; Leary & Kowalski, 1990). Sometimes individuals engage in deceptive self-presentation and sometimes self-presentation is oriented toward making true motives and preferences evident. In either event, self-presentation has the goal of shaping or controlling observers' emotions, cognitions, preferences, motives or behavior.

Much self-presentational activity involves creating a context in which departures from self-interest are highlighted—revealing one's given matrix preferences so as to make higher-order motives apparent. For example, while serving dinner John may comment on the techniques involved in making fresh pasta vs. fresh bread, thereby hinting at the effort involved in preparing the meal. Individuals may also distort given matrix patterns, manipulating the context within which their actions are judged. For example, when Bobby ends up with a black eye as a consequence of a fight he initiated, he must decide whether to confess to his mother that he started the fight (a given matrix representation that would elicit anger) or to "reconstruct" the situation by telling his mother that he was the hapless victim of a bully's violent eruption (a representation that would elicit sympathy).

Thus, self-presentation involves conveying disparities between situational demands and behavioral choices, thereby presenting one's preferences and motives in the desired light. Ultimately, the possibilities for conveying self-relevant information are limited by the inherent qualities of a given interdependence pattern. For example, it is difficult to convey considerateness in a perfectly correspondent situation (i.e., "considerate" behavior aligns with self-interest; Jones & Davis, 1965).

Implications for Long-term Interdependence

Cognition, emotion and self-presentation are exceptionally important in the context of ongoing relationships. To the extent that partners form benign interpretations of one anothers' actions, couple interaction becomes more congenial and the quality of couple functioning is enhanced (Baldwin, 1992; Bradbury & Fincham, 1990; Fletcher & Fincham, 1991). Why so? Evaluations of interaction in part are attribution-mediated—that is, experiences are evaluated not only in terms of the direct outcomes experienced in interaction, but also in terms of the orientations that are revealed as a result of interaction (e.g., commitment, self-centeredness; Kelley, 1984b). Such congenial (or in other cases, conflictual) experiences with a partner exert effects on partners' long-term beliefs about their involvement.

Attribution-mediated evaluation is central to the development of trust, in that trust emerges as a consequence of observing the partner engage in prosocial behavior, even when doing so is antithetical to the partner's immediate self-interest (Holmes & Rempel, 1989). Trust represents the individual's inference that the partner's motives are benevolent, and reflects conviction that the partner can be relied upon to behave in such a manner as to promote one's well-being. In turn, trust reduces the risks associated with increasing dependence, and enhances the individual's willingness to enact reciprocal prosocial departures from self-interest (Wieselquist et al., 1995). Thus, while relationship-specific motives color the emotions and cognitions partners experience over the course of interaction, these affective and cognitive processes also reaffirm relationship-specific motives, and consequently play a central role in accounting for growth and vitality in an ongoing relationship.

DIRECTIONS FOR FUTURE WORK AND CONCLUSIONS

Directions for Future Work

It is important to comment on some of the strengths and limitations of interdependence theory as it is currently conceptualized. First, Kelley & Thibaut's (1978) comprehensive analysis of the domain of interdependence patterns provides the field with a much-needed typology of interpersonal situations. Attempts to understand social phenomena should begin with an analysis of the structure of the situation in which the phenomenon emerges and is sustained, thereby enlarging our knowledge of the constraints and opportunities that are inherent in a given domain, including (1) possibilities for coordination and conflict, (2) issues of control, power, and dependence, (3) opportunities for the expression of key values and motives, and (4) internal psychological processes that are likely to be operative.

The concept of transformation of motivation stands as a second notable strength of the theory, illuminating the significance of departures from direct self-interest. If behavior frequently deviates from self-interest, why should we attend to given matrix preferences? First, the given pattern ultimately "makes itself known". For example, imagine that John and Mary disagree about the desirability of bearing children. The partners may develop a seemingly congenial solution to this impasse—Mary may exhibit prosocial transformation, becoming pregnant even though she does not wish to have children. But this decision is unlikely to be cost-free—the underlying non-correspondence is an undeniable *reality* that will exert its effects, in that the given matrix has implications for broader interdependence processes such as dependence and power, guilt and resentment. Second, the essential meaning of interpersonal phenomena resides in the disparity between self-interested given matrix preferences and transformed effective matrix preferences. One of the more informative features of Mary's decision to become pregnant centers on the benevolent, prosocial *meaning* of the decision. Such meaning is evident only when one recognizes the possibility of alternative transformations of the given matrix "raw material".

A third strength of the theory lies in its potential for integrating such diverse sub-fields as prosocial behavior, bargaining and intergroup behavior. Across sub-fields, researchers tend to employ differing methodologies (e.g., experimental games, coding of videotaped interaction), although they frequently examine common properties of interdependence. Unfortunately, at present there is little integration across sub-fields—for example, textbooks devote separate chapters to specific domains of behavior, as though the superficial character of a behavior necessarily defined the essential meaning of the behavior. Interdependence theory has clear potential for eliminating such artificial distinctions, via its emphasis on the fundamental properties that define interdependence phenomena.

What are the primary limitations of the theory as it is currently conceptualized and employed? One limitation centers on the proximal mechanisms by which transformation of motivation comes about. Kelley's (1984a) discussion of the role played by affect takes important steps toward analyzing the internal events accompanying transformation of motivation. At the same time, a good deal remains to be accomplished—both theoretically and empirically—in understanding the role of cognition and emotion in accounting for transformation of motivation, and in determining how interpretations of past experiences influence current cognitive and affective states (Duck & Miell, 1986).

A second limitation concerns the distal mechanisms accounting for stable transformation tendencies. Earlier, we noted that stable orientations can best be understood as adaptations to the interdependence patterns that are encountered over the course of interaction. Our model was based on Kelley's (1983b) analysis of the origins of "dispositions"—an analysis which did not differentiate among types of disposition. To identify potentially important types of "disposition" we distinguished among dispositions, relationship-specific motives and social norms. At present these distinctions are somewhat *ad hoc*, but it might be useful to pursue this task in a systematic manner, attempting to analyze important differences among the several embodiments of stable transformation tendencies.

A third limitation of interdependence theory centers on the fact that the theory has been under-utilized in the study of interaction and relationships. Why so? First, for the past few decades, the prevailing orientation in the social sciences has centered on the study of internal events. Such an orientation makes it easy to (unwisely) ignore the broader context in which such events emerge and function. Second, the theory is "difficult"—it includes quantitative representations of interdependence patterns, processes are described using mathematical formulae, transition lists are difficult to follow . . . the theory cannot easily be communicated in a soundbite. And third, the theory's key constructs were not developed hand in hand with operational definitions. Translation of abstract concepts into specific empirical procedures is left to the researcher—a task which can be daunting. It is to be hoped that increasing numbers of scientists will adopt the interdependence approach over the coming decade, and that this orientation will become an increasingly "accessible" means of understanding interpersonal phenomena.

CONCLUSION

Interdependence theory presents a logical taxonomy of interdependence patterns, thus offering a conceptual framework in which all possible forms of interdependence can be analyzed using four key properties—degree of dependence, mutuality of dependence, correspondence of outcomes, and basis for dependence. By extending the traditional matrix representation through the use of transition lists, we are able to understand important temporal and sequential features of interdependence. Via the concept of transformation of motivation, the theory explains how behavior is shaped by broader concerns, such as long-term goals or strategic considerations. In addition to identifying the themes and properties that define the interpersonal world, the theory also discusses the process of adaptation to repeatedly encountered patterns of interdependence; we have examined the embodiment of such habitual tendencies in dispositions, relationship-specific motives and norms. The theory also provides a framework for understanding social-cognitive phenomena such as attribution, emotion and self-presentation. Our hope is that this chapter helps to convey the comprehensiveness of interdependence theory, as well as its status as a truly *social* account of the nature and consequences of interdependence.

ACKNOWLEDGEMENT

Preparation of this chapter was supported in part by a grant to the first author from the National Science Foundation (No. BNS-9023817).

Chapter 10

Self-expansion Motivation and Including Other in the Self

Arthur Aron
and
Elaine N. Aron
State University of New York at Stony Brook, NY, USA

In this chapter we examine thinking and research relevant to what has come to be known as the self-expansion model of motivation and cognition in close relationships. We begin with an explanation of the key elements of the model, followed by a comment on the utility of a model of this kind in terms of the role of metaphor in science. The second and third sections of the chapter consider in some detail two key processes suggested by the model, discussing the theoretical foundation and research relevant to each. These two processes are, first, that relationship satisfaction is increased through the association of the relationship with self-expansion and, second, that the relationship means cognitively that each partner has included the other in his or her self. The fourth section considers more briefly some implications of the model for three other relationship-relevant issues: selectivity in attraction, motivations for unrequited love, and the effects on the self of falling in love. We conclude with a brief consideration of other relationship-relevant ramifications of the model.

THE SELF-EXPANSION MODEL

The self-expansion model proposes that a central human motivation is self-expansion and that one way people seek such expansion is through close relationships in which each includes the other in the self.

Handbook of Personal Relationships, 2nd edn. Edited by Steve Duck.
© 1997 John Wiley & Sons Ltd.

Self-expansion Motivation

The original formulation of the self-expansion model (Aron & Aron, 1986) arose directly from an examination of motivation. We began with the question of why people enter and maintain close relationships, which required thinking long and hard about why people do anything, assuming that their basic motivations also influence their desires regarding relationships. We realize that social animals such as primates may simply have a predilection, genetic or cultural, for a social rather than solitary life. Yet there is something different about humans in the way they elaborate everything, be it eating, sex, communication or social relationships.

It seemed that one way of understanding much of human motivation, including the elaboration of biological drives, is to say that people seek to expand themselves. At least four areas of expansion seem to interest humans in varying degrees (according to temperament, experience, subculture, and so forth):

1. Physical and social influence (through territoriality, power relationships, possessions, etc.).
2. Cognitive complexity (differentiation, the discovery of linkages, and general knowledge, insight, and wisdom).
3. Social and bodily identity (by identifying with other individuals, groups such as family or nation, and nonhumans ranging from animals to gods).
4. Their awareness of their position in the universe (that unique human interest in metaphysics, the meaning of life, ritual, religion, mythology, etc.).

Most of the time this self-expansion serves the cause of individual exploration, competence, and efficacy (e.g., Bandura, 1977; Deci, 1975; Gecas, 1989; White, 1959). But there are seeming exceptions, as when parents sacrifice opportunities to experience personal self-efficacy for the sake of their offspring. However, if one emphasizes *perceived* self-efficacy, which we do, and assumes that a self can be expanded to include another, which the research discussed below suggests, then one can imagine someone experiencing a very self-expanding efficacy through another's accomplishments, as demonstrated, for example, by Tesser's (1988) work on "reflection". This is one more example of the elaboration of a biological "given", parental self-sacrifice, but an important one because it allows for sacrifice of the self not merely for the sake of an offspring but for the sake of other relationship partners and for the group and the culture.

There are, of course, specialties or preferences for modes of expansion, and these may also change over the course of a day or a lifetime. There are exceptions to expansion motivation as well, when individuals seem to evidence little desire to expand, explore or even think due to extensive experiences of failure or punishment for their efforts. We have also emphasized (Aron & Aron, 1986) that there is a correspondingly strong desire to integrate expansion experiences and make sense of them, a desire for wholeness or coherence which sometimes pre-empts the desire for expansion until it is satisfied to some degree. But expansion and integration are two steps in a general pattern of movement towards self-expansion (much as Piaget, 1952, 1963, saw the growth of intelligence as involving steps of accommodating to new experience alternating with the assimilation of the new experiences into existing schemata). Finally, once one has integrated new material into the self, there is a motivation to resist de-expansion or de-integration of self, a motive consistent with processes described by Greenwald (1980) and Swann (1983).

Including Each Other in Each Other's Self

Having assumed a general motivation to expand the self, we then proposed that the desire to enter and maintain a particular relationship can be seen as one especially satisfying, useful and human means to this self-expansion. Cognitively, the self is expanded through including the other in the self, a process which in a close relationship becomes mutual, so that each person is including the other in his or her self.

People seek relationships in order to gain what they anticipate as self-expansion. When faced with a potential relationship, one compares one's self as it is prior to the relationship—lacking the other's perspectives, resources, identities and so forth—to the self as prospectively imagined after it has entered the relationship, a self now with full access both to self's own perspectives and so forth *plus* the other's perspectives and so forth. Metaphorically, I will have the use of all my house plus gain the use of all of yours. Thus, before one enters a relationship the motive of self-expansion may have a decidedly self-centered air to it. But after entering the relationship, the effect of including each other in each other's self is an overlapping of selves. Now I must protect and maintain my house *and* your house, as *both* are "mine" (as both are now "yours"). This post-inclusion, larger self creates (and explains) the remarkably unselfish nature of close relationships.

Self-expansion Processes as Metaphors

We have come to think of an important aspect of any theory to be the metaphors or analogies it embodies (Lakoff, 1987; Lakoff & Turner, 1989; Langer, 1948; also see Duck, 1994a, for a review of the literature on the metaphors or lay theories; Kovecses, 1986, 1991), employed by those in close relationships, as well as a discussion of some of the metaphors currently used in close relationships research). Metaphor maps onto confusing phenomena or the "target domain" a schema that is already familiar from the "source domain", generally a bodily experience (Lakoff, 1987). The better the theory's metaphor, the more a phenomenon's intricacies are captured in it. Much of a theory's heuristic value comes from the richness of the parallels between its guiding metaphor and the target phenomenon. In addition to the parallels that are consciously recognized, the metaphor in a model often engenders creative new ideas by opening us up to semi-conscious images that we otherwise would not have considered as aspects of the phenomenon. (For example, to speak of "branches of science" might also activate connections to science's growth, pruning, fruit, roots and so forth.) Further, when theories or metaphors already explored in other fields, such as market exchanges as a metaphor in economics, are applied to a new field, such as the study of close relationships, all insights already gained in the original application of the metaphor can be tested in the new field.

All metaphors, however, have limits (Duck, 1994a). The images they generate direct attention in one direction, tending to close off interest in another. They may mislead as well as lead, be aesthetically jarring rather than pleasing. For example, theories with metaphors rooted in economic exchange will capture important aspects of relationships, yet will also have their limits in that they connote materialism or self-centeredness. They direct attention away from, for example, intimacy. Another example, attachment theory, has its own inherent limits because its core metaphor is parent and child, and one of its images is the primate infant clinging to its mother. The metaphor of attachment directs attention away from, for example, sexuality and adult cognitive processes.

A reason for the growing interest in the self-expansion model seems to be that it captures new aspects of the target domain of close relationships, perhaps because its metaphors are so close to basic bodily experiences and images of expansion and merger. For example, a sense of expansion in the heart or chest is a common bodily experience associated with deeply felt positive experiences, such as when people first fall in love, or looking at their sleeping child. A bodily experience of having the other included in the self can occur when one's own muscles move while watching a beloved partner perform, or when one receives news that would please or upset the other were she or he there, and one feels the physical signs of joy or grief that the other would feel. Most striking, perhaps, are descriptions of losing a partner being like having a part of one's body ripped out or die. Indeed, the common term for the end of a close relationship, "break up", seems to refer to the end of a physical oneness.

Obviously an emphasis on self, expansion and inclusion directs attention away from important other aspects of relationships, but for now we leave that to other models and metaphors to correct. A greater concern for communicating about this relatively new model of self-expansion is that metaphors have different associations and emotional connotations for different people. When metaphors become the framework for research models, the associations they engender tend, over time, to become shared by all those working in the field. For example, whereas the general public may associate learning theory with metal Skinner boxes and callous treatment of animals, psychologists have more neutral or positive images of the theory as useful and enlightening. However, with a new model—one that is neither shared nor borrowed from another field—personal connotations constitute more of a difficulty. In the case of our model, we have found that self-expansion connotes for some people the acquiring of scarce resources (food, space, money, attention) at the expense of others. For others, ourselves included, self-expansion primarily connotes a broadened identity or awareness, so that expansion can be virtually unlimited and usually leads to greater altruism, not less. We hope that in time the latter connotations will be the more universally shared meaning of the metaphor.

Likewise, the metaphor of including each other in each other's self is one that can connote for some a loss of individual identity, following the issues raised, for example, by family systems theorists (e.g., Olson, Russell, & Sprenkle, 1983). Such a loss of individual identity would seem to be an appropriate description of the situation for a relationship partner whose individual identity has not been well developed—this kind of analysis is suggested by Erikson's (1950) model. (An analogy might be the unequal merging of my one goldfish with your aquarium of twenty specimens, so that the result would feel to me like your aquarium, not mine or ours.) But when each partner's identity is well developed, our assumption is that individual identity is *not* lost, but rather is enriched and expanded, by each including aspects of the other into her or his self. Indeed, there is some evidence that this latter understanding corresponds to the way most individuals understand this metaphor (Aron, Aron & Smollan, 1992).

THE FIRST OF THE TWO KEY PROCESSES: INCREASED RELATIONSHIP SATISFACTION THROUGH ASSOCIATING THE RELATIONSHIP WITH SELF-EXPANSION

The Autonomous Desirability of Whatever Is Associated with Expansion and the Decline of Relationship Satisfaction over Time

If a basic human motive is self-expansion, then situations and persons present during, or associated with, self-expansion experiences should—through classical conditioning—become secondarily reinforcing or desirable in themselves (Dollard & Miller, 1950). In the case of human relationships, when two people first enter a relationship, typically there is an initial, exhilarating period in which the couple spends hours talking, engaging in intense risk-taking and self-disclosure. The partners are expanding their selves at a rapid rate by virtue of the intense exchange. Once the two know each other fairly well, however, opportunities for further rapid expansion of this sort inevitably decrease. For a time, satisfaction may remain through the association of the other and of the relationship with the just-completed period of breathtakingly rapid self-expansion. But once self-expansion slows to the point it becomes negligible or non-existent, there is little emotion, or perhaps boredom. Hence we see the well documented typical decline in relationship satisfaction after the "honeymoon period" in a romantic relationship which is maintained over subsequent years (e.g., Blood & Wolfe, 1960; Glenn, 1990; Locke & Wallace, 1959; Rollins & Feldman, 1970; Tucker & Aron, 1993).

The major theoretical approaches to close relationships (interdependence, attachment, symbolic interaction, family systems theories) say surprisingly little about the reasons for the decline in relationship satisfaction. They seem to assume that a relationship will be satisfying so long as one sees one's own outcomes as interdependent on the other's, investments are high, alternatives low, the partners have secure attachment styles, adequate non-conflictual role enactment is achieved, meaning is shared, individual personal growth is supported, and so forth.

Those who have commented most on the decline are those who have applied learning theories to marital relationships (e.g., Huesmann, 1980; Jacobson & Margolin, 1979). They see such a decline as a special case of habituation— adaptation to a stimulus through repeated exposure (Peeke & Herz, 1973)— which occurs at every level, neuron to whole organism. Formerly valued reinforcement becomes less intensely rewarding as it becomes predictable or familiar. An ongoing relationship is almost by definition repetitious in some ways, increasingly predictable and therefore subject to becoming less reinforcing. Plutchik's (1967) model also makes "lack of novelty" a prominent force for marital instability. Cognitive theories have redefined habituation as a loss of informational uncertainty for decision-making processes. Too much uncertainty is over-arousing, aversive, and its loss is desired. This is the main emphasis of Berger's (1988) application of uncertainty reduction theory to personal relationships. But too little uncertainty leaves one under-aroused, which is also aversive. Berger also makes the same point—emphasizing a kind of dialectical relationship between levels of predictability sufficiently high for comfortable interpersonal coordination, but with levels of novelty (perhaps in less central relationship domains) sufficient to maintain some level of excitement. Altman, Vinsel & Brown (1981) also proposed a similar dialectical relation between what they described as "stability" and "change".

Uncertainty undoubtedly stimulates some of the arousal surrounding the initial phase of a relationship.

> Since uncertainties must either be reduced or not, it is inevitable that these cumulative probabilities will eventually stabilize, making nearly inevitable the end of the romantic phase of the relationship (Livingston, 1980, pp. 145–146).

Other psychological explanations have expanded in particular ways on the habituation notion. For example, Aronson & Linder (1965) argued that satisfaction declines in long-term relationships because we habituate to the other's positive evaluation of self, so that the net gain in self-esteem that other can provide decreases over time. Another habituation-type explanation comes from psychodynamic theories of idealization, which discuss the decline in terms of increasing familiarity, making it more difficult to project an all-loving parent

(Bergler, 1946), ego-ideal (Reik, 1944), or anima/animus (Jung, 1925/1959) onto the other in the relationship.

The Self-expansion View of the Decline in Satisfaction

The self-expansion model builds on the basic habituation idea by specifying what about the other and the relationship become decreasingly novel (the loss of new information to be included in the self) and why habituation leads to dissatisfaction (the decline in the highly desired rapid rate of self-expansion, in this case associated with the relationship). Thus, the model provides a more precise and motivationally-based explanation for the role of habituation in relationships. Further, it has made an important and successful prediction: after the initial relationship period, increased time spent together, which ought to increase habituation and decrease satisfaction, will *increase* satisfaction if the time is spent doing self-expanding activities together. The reason is that once the other is familiar (so that further inclusion of other is not a major source of new expansion), then if the couple engages together in self-expanding activities (which are now activities other than getting to know each other), the highly desired self-expansion experience remains associated with the relationship.

The self-expansion model is still consistent with the more elaborated versions of the habituation idea just discussed. For example, idealization is made possible, Aron & Aron (1986) argued, because a particular other is seen as offering a potential for very great expansion (see also Brehm, 1988, who expressed a similar view). We would emphasize, however, that the self-expansion model implies limits to the idealization and self-esteem explanations. When couples engage in self-expanding activities together, while this enhances relationship satisfaction, it probably does not usually make the other highly idealized again or provide new gains in self-esteem, suggesting that simple association of the relationship with self-expansion is the basis of or acts in addition to these other processes during the original attraction process.

Because of the theoretical importance of the hypothesized consequences of sharing exciting activities, we will discuss this process in some detail.

The Effect of Shared Participation in Activities that Are Associated with Self-Expansion: the General Principle

Studies consistently find wide variation in marital satisfaction, even after the initial phase, with some couples even reporting very high levels of passionate love after 25 or more years of marriage (Traupmann & Hatfield, 1981; Tucker & Aron, 1993). As we read the literature, it seems that at least some among the more satisfied couples have found ways to associate their relationship with self-expansion by participating in more expanding activities together.

North American couples clearly consider spending time together, regardless of the type of activity, to be an important maintenance strategy (Baxter & Dindia, 1990; Dindia & Baxter, 1987). Further, intuition suggests that couples often do adopt this strategy of engaging jointly in expanding activities—traditionally they build a home and a family (although in US culture these goals are not always shared or central, or may be a source of stress and too much expansion, as suggested by the apparently negative typical impact of the birth of the first child; e.g., Tucker & Aron, 1993). Other examples are causes taken on jointly, businesses run together, and shared professional or recreational activities. Presumably, these shared self-expanding experiences provide relationship satisfaction because the experience or feeling of self-expansion becomes associated with the partner and the relationship, an idea borrowed from learning theory. If self-expanding activities are reinforcing, then through stimulus generalization, when couples engage in such activities together, they experience reinforcement of both the behaviors involved in that activity and also the behavior of staying near the other and any other behaviors that maintain the relationship. The point is that the self-expansion model contributes an explanation for why certain kinds of activities would be especially rewarding: They arise as a result of or are associated with expansion of the self.

What distinguishes an activity that is self-expanding? We think that there are two key aspects, novelty and arousal. Participating in a novel activity expands the self by providing new information and experiences. In general, novel experiences are also arousing (Berlyne, 1960), but arousing experiences that are not novel, such as physical exertion or high sensory stimulation loads, are probably also self-expanding to some extent, in that high but tolerable arousal of any kind seems to create a sense of alert expansion and competence. In terms of how self-expanding activities are recognized, we have assumed that the most likely ordinary-language label is "exciting", since this term covers both arousal and novelty. And, as noted in the research below, it is precisely novel and/or arousing activities that couples report when asked about the kinds of exciting activities in which they engage.

Survey Studies Linking Shared Expanding Activities with Satisfaction

There is substantial evidence that, in general, time spent together is correlated with marital satisfaction. For example, significant associations were found in five separate US studies conducted in the last 30 years employing probability samples (Kilbourne, Howell & England, 1990; Kingston & Nock, 1987; Orden & Bradburn, 1968; Orthner, 1975; White, 1983). None of these studies on time together and marital satisfaction looked specifically at participation in activities that would be classified as self-expanding. However, findings regarding different categories of activities suggest that the important ones may be those that are self-expanding. Several studies (Holman & Jacquart, 1988; Kingston & Nock, 1987; Orden & Bradburn, 1968; Orthner, 1975) reported substantially stronger correlations with marital satisfaction for activities that were intensely interactive vs. passive, parallel, or merely in the company of others. Hill (1988), in finding a strong overall link between shared activities and marital stability, reported the strongest effects for shared "recreational activities", all of which were comparatively active or involved some novelty (such as "outdoor activities, active sports, card games, and travel", p. 447).

There are also some correlational data focusing directly on the link between "exciting" activities and satisfaction. McKenna (1989), in a study of respondents to a questionnaire printed in a newspaper, found a strong positive correlation ($r = 0.52$) between scores on a standard marital satisfaction scale and responses to the item "How exciting are the things you do together with your partner?" Further, the link between satisfaction and exciting activities was mediated by reported boredom with the relationship. Finally, there was a clear interaction between exciting activities and length of marriage in predicting marital satisfaction, such that those together more than 3 years had a correlation of 0.27, while those together a longer period had a correlation of 0.62. This interaction is important theoretically since in the early phases the relationship's development by itself should provide the partners all the self-expansion each needs or can tolerate. Thus, it is only after this initial phase that one would expect any substantial impact from participating together in self-expanding activities.

In another study (McNeal & Aron, 1995), members of dating and married couples attending night classes completed a standard relationship satisfaction scale and responded to an extensive rating of the activities in which they had participated with their partner in the last 30 days. Over all subjects, there was a moderate correlation of 0.29 between number of exciting activities engaged in with partner and relationship satisfaction. However, once again there was the interaction such that the correlation for married couples was 0.48; for dating couples, 0.08. Also once again, the exciting-activities–satisfaction link was clearly mediated by reported relationship boredom. All of the above results remained essentially unchanged when controlling for overall number of activities (of all kinds) participated in with partner. This study also included some items assessing opportunities to participate in shared exciting activities with the partner. Analyses of the pattern of results involving these measures was consistent with the hypothesized causal direction of exciting activities affecting satisfaction (and inconsistent with the reverse).

Finally, this study provided an indication of the types of shared activities perceived to be exciting. Consistent with our association of self-expansion with arousal and novelty, the exciting activities tend to be of two types—those with high levels of physical activity (e.g., bicycling, dancing, riding horses, roller skating, hiking) and those emphasizing newness or exoticness (e.g., attending musical concerts and plays; studying nature and bird-watching).

Studies of Arousal/Unusualness and Attraction

Another relevant line of research focuses on the link between initial attraction to a potential romantic partner and arousal, or being together under unusual or challenging circumstances (Aron, 1970). Research in this area has mainly been inspired by a study (Dutton & Aron, 1974) in which subjects met an attractive confederate in a novel and arousing vs. a more common and non-arousing situation (a suspension bridge vs. a footbridge). The results were that there was greater attraction in the novel/arousing situation. A number of further experiments have examined the connection between arousal and romantic attraction (Allen et al., 1989; Dutton & Aron, 1989; Riordan & Tedeschi, 1983; White, Fishbein & Rutstein, 1981; White & Kight, 1984), generally with subjects meeting an attractive stranger in arousing vs. non-arousing circumstances and a measure being taken of their attraction to the stranger. The arousing situations have included humorous or violent films and physical exertion. In most studies, romantic attraction is significantly greater under arousal conditions. Further, Aron et al. (1989) found that one-third to two-thirds of college students' accounts of falling in love included prominent mentions of circumstances that could be coded as either "arousing" or "unusual".

Researchers have suggested a variety of processes underlying the arousal/attraction connection: (1) misattribution of the arousal from its true source to the attractive stranger (Dutton & Aron, 1974, 1989; White, Fishbein & Rutstein, 1981; White & Kight, 1984), (2) the object of attraction being associated with a decrease of aversive overarousal (Kenrick & Cialdini, 1977; Riordan & Tedeschi, 1983); and (3) arousal facilitating the most available response in a person's hierarchy (Allen et al., 1989). The self-expansion model argues that arousal is associated with the highly desired state of self-expansion, as are attractive others, and in this case all three are present at once and so all these elements are associated with each other. Further, the model suggests that even if the experience is not highly arousing but is nevertheless novel, the effect should still occur. (This latter idea, though not yet tested directly in the experimental research, is consistent with the studies examining reports of falling-in-love experiences.)

Experimental Studies with Ongoing Relationships

Reissman, Aron & Bergen (1993) randomly assigned volunteer married couples to one of three groups. Those in the first group, the Exciting Activities Group, were instructed to spend $1\frac{1}{2}$ hours each week, over a period of 10 weeks, doing one activity from a list of activities both partners had rated as exciting on independently completed prestudy questionnaires. Couples in the second group, the Pleasant Activities Group, were assigned activities both had rated as pleasant. A third group of couples served as a waiting-list, no-activity control group. The Exciting Activities Group, compared to the Pleasant Activity Group, showed a significantly greater increase, of moderate effect size, in relationship satisfaction over the 10 weeks. There was no significant difference for the other planned orthogonal contrast, comparing the control group that spent no extra time together to the two experimental groups taken together. In other words, just spending time together did not increase satisfaction. But doing something exciting, and therefore presumably self-expanding, did increase satisfaction.

Because there are other possible interpretations of the Reissman et al. findings, Norman & Aron (1995) developed a laboratory paradigm for studying the phenomenon. The paradigm enables various aspects of the situation to be systematically manipulated, thereby permitting tests of potential mediating mechanisms. The approach is basically an extension of the arousal-and-romantic-attraction paradigm (e.g., Dutton & Aron, 1974). In the Norman & Aron paradigm, couples in ongoing relationships participate in what they believe is a laboratory evaluation that involves completing some questionnaires, taking part together in a task in which their interaction is videotaped, and then completing more questionnaires. In actuality, the questionnaires are pretest and post-test measures of relationship satisfaction and the task is the experimentally manipulated independent variable of arousal and novelty.

In the first study to use this approach, the experimental task was manipulated to be either arousing and novel or to be sedate and boring. The results were consistent with predictions—significantly greater increases in satisfaction for the arousing/novel-activities group—and this increase was significantly greater for those who had been together a longer period of time. Subsequent studies (which are now in progress) use this paradigm to sort out systematically the possible alternative explanations for the effect, such as reattribution of arousal, cooperation, success, negative effects of boredom, and so forth.

THE SECOND OF THE TWO KEY PROCESSES: PERSONAL RELATIONSHIPS AS INCLUDING EACH OTHER IN EACH OTHER'S SELF

Related Theorizing

The notion that in a relationship each is included in each other's self is consistent with a wide variety of current social psychological ideas about relationships. For example, Reis & Shaver (1988) identified intimacy as mainly a process of an escalating reciprocity of self-disclosure in which each individual feels his or her innermost self validated, understood and cared for by the other. Wegner (1980) suggested that empathy may "stem in part from a basic confusion between ourselves and others" (p. 133), which he proposed may arise from an initial lack of differentiation between self and caregiver in infancy (Hoffman, 1976). Indeed, perhaps the most prominent idea in social psychology directly related to the present theme is the "unit relation", a fundamental concept in Heider's (1958) influential cognitive account of interpersonal relations. This idea is also related to

Ickes et al.'s (1988) idea of "intersubjectivity"—which Ickes and his colleagues made vivid by citing Merleau-Ponty's (1945) description of a close relationship as a "double being" and Schutz's (1970) reference to two people "living in each other's subjective contexts of meaning" (p. 167).

Several currently active lines of theory-based social psychology research focus on closely related themes. For example, in a series of experimental and correlational studies, Tesser (1988) has shown that a relationship partner's achievement, so long as it is not in a domain that threatens the self by creating a negative social comparison, is "reflected" by the self (i.e., the self feels pride in the achievement as if it were the self's). Another relevant line of work focuses on what is called "fraternal relative deprivation" (Runciman, 1966), in which the relative disadvantage of the group to which self belongs affects the self as if it were the self's own deprivation. Yet another example is work arising from social identity theory (Tajfel & Turner, 1979), which posits that our identity is structured from membership in various social groups. In a related line of thinking, Brewer (1991) presents arguments and evidence that people seek an optimal level of distinctiveness from others: they identify with groups to some extent, but are uncomfortable when too closely identified with that group (though the seeking of differentiation from one group typically involves identification with a different group).

In the field of marketing, Belk (1988) has proposed a notion of ownership in which "we regard our possessions as part of ourselves" (p. 139), an idea that has been the subject of considerable theoretical discussion and several studies. For example, Sivadas & Machleit (1994) found that items measuring an object's "incorporation into self" (items such as "helps me achieve my identity" and "is part of who I am") form a separate factor from items assessing the object's importance or relevance to the self. Ahuvia (1993) has attempted to integrate Belk's self-extension approach with the self-expansion model and has proposed that processes hypothesized in the domain of personal relationships also apply to relations to physical objects and experiences. In a series of interviews, Ahuvia showed that people sometimes describe their "love" of things in much the same way as they describe their love of relationship partners, that they often consider this "real" love, and that they treat these love objects as very much a part of their identity. At the same time, as with human relationships, there is often a sense of autonomous value to the object and even a sense of being controlled by or at the mercy of the object. These ideas about including the owned object in the self are also related to the notion of relationship as each "possessing" the other (e.g., Reik, 1944).

The notion of relationship as an overlap of selves has been popular more generally among psychologists and sociologists, starting at least with James (1890/1948). For example, Bakan (1966) wrote about "communion" in the context of his expansion on Buber's (1937) "I–Thou" relationship. Jung (1925/1959) emphasized the role of relationship partners as providing or developing otherwise unavailable aspects of the psyche, so leading to greater wholeness. Maslow took it for granted that "beloved people can be incorporated into the self" (1967,

p. 103). And from a symbolic interactionist perspective, McCall (1974) described "attachment" as "incorporation of . . . [the other's] actions and reactions . . . into the content of one's various conceptions of the self" (p. 219).

Research on the Perception of Including Other in the Self

One line of relevant research focuses on the extent to which people *view* relationships as connected or overlapping selves. In one recent study, Sedikides, Olsen & Reis (1993) found that people spontaneously encode information about other people in terms of their relationships with each other, grouping them together by their relationships. This suggests that cognitive representations of other individuals are in a sense overlapped or at least tied together as a function of these others being perceived as being in close relationships with each other.

Focusing on the issue of the perceived overlap of one's self with a relationship partner, Aron, Aron & Smollan (1992) asked subjects to describe their closest relationship using the Inclusion of Other in the Self (IOS) Scale (see Figure 10.1), which consists of a series of overlapping circles from which one is asked to select the pair that best describes one's relationship with a particular person. The scale appears to have levels of reliability, as well as of discriminant, convergent and predictive validity, that match or exceed other measures of closeness—measures which are typically more complex and lengthy. (For example, the correlation between a score on this test and whether the subject remained in a romantic relationship 3 months later was 0.46.) Further, most measures of closeness seem to fall into one of two factors: they measure either *feelings of closeness* or *behaviors associated with closeness*. The IOS Scale, however, loads, to some extent, on both of these factors. This suggests that the IOS Scale may be tapping the core meaning of closeness and not merely a particular aspect of it.

Agnew, Van Lange & Rusbult (1995), in a study of dating couples, found that scores on the IOS Scale correlated highly with a variety of relationship measures,

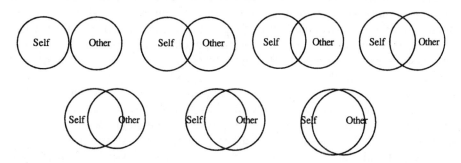

Figure 10.1 The Inclusion of Other in the Self (IOS) Scale. Respondents are instructed to select the picture that best describes their relationship. From Aron, Aron & Smollan, 1992, reproduced with permission

such as satisfaction, commitment, investment in the relationship, and centrality of the relationship. Most interesting, the IOS Scale correlated moderately with proportion of first-person plural pronouns ("we" and "us") the dating partners used when speaking about their relationship, a finding that Agnew et al. took as an indication of what they called "cognitive interdependence."

Finally, Pipp et al. (1985) also used overlapping circle diagrams as part of a measure of closeness. They had adolescents draw a picture of two circles, one representing the self and one a parent, "in relation to each other as you believe best illustrates your relationship with that parent . . ." (p. 993). Among other findings, Pipp et al. reported that perceived closeness and the amount of overlap of the circles were both strongly related to scale ratings of love and friendship.

Research on Including Other's Perspective in the Self

A significant body of social psychology research over the last 25 years has focused on differences in actor vs. observer perspectives in attributional processes, beginning with the pioneering work of Jones & Nisbett (1971). In the context of the self-expansion model, to the extent a particular person is included in the self, the difference between self's and that particular person's perspective should be reduced. Several studies support this conclusion. Using methods adapted from the original Jones & Nisbett (1971) work, Nisbett et al. (1973, Study 3) found that the longer people had been in a relationship with a close friend the less willing they were to make dispositional attributions about the friend. Similarly, Goldberg (1981b) found that subjects made fewer dispositional attributions for people they have spent more time with, compared to people they have spent less time with.

Other research has followed this same theme of examining actor–observer differences in attribution but using different approaches. Prentice (1990) had subjects describe various persons in specific situations and found least overlap between situations for descriptions of self, next least for a familiar other, and most for an unfamiliar other. This finding suggests that people are making situational attributions for self and those close to self but regard less familiar others in terms that are not differentiated by situation. Using yet another approach, Sande, Goethals & Radloff (1988) found that self, and then liked friends, and then disliked friends, were progressively less likely to be attributed *both* poles of pairs of opposite traits (for example, "serious–carefree"). The point here is that for self—and those liked by self—behaviors can vary, even to the extent of representing opposites, according to the situation. But for those distant from self, a single-sided trait description (that is, a dispositional attribution) is quite adequate. Aron et al. (1991, introduction to Study 2) replicated Sande, Goethals & Radloff's (1988) procedure, but compared different degrees of *closeness* (as opposed to liking vs. disliking). They found choices of both traits were most frequent for self, next for best friend, and least for a friendly acquaintance.

Yet another approach relevant to including the other's perspective in the self is based on an adaptation of a research paradigm developed by Lord (1980, 1987). Lord presented subjects with a series of concrete nouns, for each of which they were instructed to form as vivid and interesting a mental image as possible of a target person *interacting* with whatever the noun referred to. The target person was sometimes self and sometimes someone else, such as Johnny Carson. On a free recall task afterwards, Lord found *fewer* words were recalled which were imaged with self than which were imaged with the other target person. He interpreted these results in terms of a figure–ground difference between one's experience of self and other when acting in the world. Because self, being ground, is less vivid than other, imaging things interacting with the self is less enhancing to memory than imaging them interacting with someone other than self.

From the perspective of the self-expansion model, if this figure–ground difference represents a different way of understanding and appreciating the world, then if other is included in one's inner world, other should become more like ground and less like figure—that is, more like the self. Based on this reasoning, Aron et al. (1991, Experiment 2) replicated Lord's procedures, again using as target persons self and a prominent entertainment personality, but also added a third target, a close other, the subject's mother. Consistent with predictions, recall was greatest for words imaged with the entertainment personality and much less for both those imaged with self and those imaged with mother. This result was also replicated in a new sample, substituting friend of mother for the entertainment personality (to deal with the possibility that entertainment personalities are simply especially vivid images). In the replication, subjects were also asked to rate their similarity, closeness and familiarity with their mother. The difference of recall for words imaged with mother's friend minus recall for words imaged with mother (presumably indicating the degree to which other is included in the self) correlated 0.56 with ratings of closeness to mother, but only 0.13 with similarity and 0.16 with familiarity.

Research on Processing Information about Other as if Other Were One's Self

Another influential general body of research in social cognition has focused on the unique role of self-representations, going back to the pioneering articles by Markus (1977) and Rogers, Kuiper & Kirker (1977). For example, consider the issue of self-relevant information processing (the so-called "self-reference effect", that information processing and memory is enhanced for information related to the self). If, in a close relationship, each includes other in the self, then any advantage for self-relevant information over other-relevant information should be lessened when other is in a close relationship with self—a pattern supported by several studies. In one such study, Bower & Gilligan (1979) found little difference in incidental memory for adjectives which subjects had earlier judged for their relevance to their own life or their mother's life. In another study, Keenan & Baillet (1980) had subjects indicate whether trait adjectives were true of a particular person. The persons were self, best friend, parent, friend, teacher, favorite TV character, and the US President. They found a clear linear trend from self through President for time to make decision and number of adjectives recognized later. Similarly, Prentice (1990) showed that both the content and organization of self-descriptions and other-descriptions tended to follow a pattern in which familiar others were intermediate between self and unfamiliar others.

A related approach focuses on the idea that if being in a close relationship means other is included in the self, then, to the extent one is in a close relationships with a person, there should be a tendency to confuse traits of self with traits of that person. To test this idea, Aron et al. (1991, Experiment 3) had married subjects first rate a series of trait adjectives for their descriptiveness of themselves and their spouse. After a distracting intermediate task they made a series of "me"–"not-me" reaction time choices to these trait words. The prediction was that there would be most confusion—and thus longer response latencies—for trait words that were different between self and spouse (that is, the confusion is hypothesized to arise because one is asked here to rate these traits as true or false for *self*; but if other is part of self, when self and other differ on a trait, the difference is a discrepancy between two parts of "self"). The results were as predicted—longer response times when the trait was different between self and spouse. The same pattern was obtained in a follow-up study. Also, in the follow-up study, subjects completed the IOS Scale, which correlated 0.59 with the difference between the average response time to spouse-different words minus the average response time to spouse-similar words.

Smith & Henry (1996) have successfully applied this method to demonstrate that even members of ingroups with which we only moderately identify are included in the self. In their study subjects were consistently faster at deciding whether a trait was true or false of self when the trait had been previously rated as similarly true or false of a typical ingroup person (students with like majors) as compared to the situation when the trait had been rated differently than self. However, decision time was unrelated to whether the trait had been rated as similarly true or false to a typical outgroup member (students with different majors).

Finally, Omoto & Gunn (1994), found a self–other confusion effect for episodic memory. In their study, subjects paired with friends vs. subjects paired with strangers were more likely to mix up whether they or their partner had earlier solved particular anagram tasks. Although the focus of their study was on other issues, these data would seem to suggest that in a personal relationship identities are sufficiently intermixed that we can actually confuse biographical memories of self and other.

SOME ADDITIONAL IMPLICATIONS OF THE SELF-EXPANSION MODEL RELEVANT TO RELATIONSHIPS

In this section we consider the implications of the self-expansion model for three other relationship-relevant issues: selectivity in initial attraction, motivations for unrequited love, and the effects of falling in love on the self.

Initial Attraction

Presuming that self-expansion is a major motivator in general, then it is reasonable to suppose that, other things being equal, when selecting among potential close relationship partners, one will be most attracted to the person who offers the greatest potential for self-expansion via a relationship with that person. Thus, following a kind of value-expectancy approach, we have reasoned that attraction to a particular other should be affected by two key factors:

1. The perceived degree of potential expansion of self that is possible through a close relationship with a particular other.
2. The perceived probability of actually obtaining that expansion with the other—that is, the probability that one could actually form and maintain a close relationship with this particular other.

The first factor can be summarized as "desirability" (or reward value); the second, as "probability" (or likelihood of achieving that reward value). As noted, this analysis is basically an application of classic value-expectancy analysis (e.g., Rotter, 1954) to our notion that relationships provide rewards by enhancing self through including other in self.

The delineation of these two factors has been useful (Aron & Aron, 1986) in making sense of long-standing findings in the attraction literature that had previously seemed paradoxical. For example, based on the extensive work of Byrne (1971) and others (e.g., Newcomb, 1956), a fundamental tenet of the social psychology of attraction had been that similarity leads to attraction. However, Walster & Walster (1963) found that under conditions in which self is led to believe that other likes self, there is actually a preference for dissimilar partners. In the same vein, Jones, Bell & Aronson (1972) found that when self is led to believe other likes self, the preference for those with similar attitudes is eliminated.

Although this exception to the general rule that similars attract was long known, there was no general explanation for it: Murstein's (1971) commentary on the attraction literature at that time did hint at a process similar to that described here, but it was not elaborated in any detail. Applying the self-expansion model of attraction, these results make sense. Perceived similarity serves as an indication that a relationship could develop and be maintained. But if, as in the studies just cited, the probability of forming a relationship is made highly likely by knowing other likes self, then further probability information (provided by similarity information) adds no incremental benefit. Rather, it is now dissimilarity that enhances attraction, by increasing the potential for self-expansion—the more different a person is, the more new perspectives the person can add to the self.

Using a variety of methods and samples, researchers (Aron et al., 1989; Aron & Rodriguez, 1992; Sprecher et al., 1994) have consistently found the same two near-universal precursors to falling in love—physical and personal attractiveness and discovering other likes the self. These precursors, which are consistent with the self-expansion model (i.e., they represent desirability and probability), are also consistent with other theoretical perspectives. However, an important contribution of the self-expansion model is its metaphor of expansion, which does seem to explain well the counter-intuitive appeal of opposites in combination with similarity.

Unrequited Love

Thinking about unrequited love in the context of the self-expansion framework, Aron, Aron & Allen (1995) postulated a three-factor motivational model for unrequited love. The first two factors are the same as in the general attraction model: desirability (perceived potential expansion of self through a close relationship with this particular person) and probability (perceived probability of forming and maintaining a close relationship with this person). Desirability is probably the main element, in the sense that if a relationship with other is seen as extremely valuable, then one might be attracted even if the probability is low. It is a bit like betting on the lottery—small odds but big winnings. An emphasis on probability suggests a second way that unrequited love might arise: sometimes individuals may initially feel quite certain that their love is reciprocated but then later discover it is not; however, by then they are already in love with the other.

A third path to this state is more specifically inspired by the self-expansion model, and involves wanting the expansion associated with enacting the culturally scripted role of lover, but *not* necessarily wanting a relationship. When this factor of desiring the state of being in love is foremost, unrequited love can be highly rewarding, but only from the viewpoint of self-expansion.

To test this three-factor motivational model, Aron et al. (1995) developed a psychometrically adequate questionnaire measure of the three key motivational variables, then administered this questionnaire to a new large sample. The first and most important prediction in this research was that each of these three motivational factors would significantly and independently predict the intensity of unrequited love. This prediction was supported.

This same research also examined a set of subsidiary hypotheses having to do with the interaction of the different motivational factors with attachment styles (Hazan & Shaver, 1987). In the context of the self-expansion model, we interpreted the attachment-theory work as suggesting that early experiences shape one of the more important channels through which people seek to expand—through relationships. Those who were regularly successful in their early attempts to expand through interpersonal closeness become "securely attached", those who were regularly unsuccessful become "avoidants", and those who had inconsistent experiences become "anxious/ambivalents". Two key predictions, which were supported, were (1) that there would be an interaction in which desirability was most important in predicting intensity for anxious ambivalents compared to its importance among the other two styles, and (2) that the desirability of the state of unrequited love would be most important for avoidants, compared to its importance for the other two styles. (A third prediction, which did not reach significance, was that probability would be most important for the secures.)

Effect of a Close Relationship on Expanding the Self

Yet another implication of the model is that developing a relationship expands the self by including other in the self (as well as in other ways associated with being in a relationship). If in a close relationship other is included in the self, then when one enters a close relationship the self should be expanded to include aspects of the other.

In one relevant study, Sedikides (personal communication, October, 1992) collected self-descriptions of subjects who were or were not currently in a close relationship. These self-descriptions were analyzed to determine the number of different domains of the self they included. Consistent with this prediction (based on the self-expansion model), Sedikides found that the self-descriptions of people in relationships included terms representing significantly more domains of the self.

Following up on this idea, in a longitudinal study Aron, Paris & Aron (1995) tested 325 students five times, once every $2\frac{1}{2}$ weeks over a 10-week period. At each testing, the subjects listed as many self-descriptive words or phrases as came to mind during a 3-minute period in response to the question, "Who are you today?" and answered a number of other questions which included items indicating whether the subject had fallen in love since the last testing. As predicted, there was significantly greater increase in the diversity of self-content domains in the self-descriptions from before to after falling in love than was found for average changes from before to after other testing sessions, when compared to typical testing-to-testing changes for subjects who did not fall in love. A second study, with a new sample of 529 subjects, assessed the subjects' self-esteem and self-efficacy every $2\frac{1}{2}$ weeks. As predicted, there was a significantly greater increase in these variables from before to after falling in love than was found for average changes from before to after other testing sessions, when compared to typical testing-to-testing changes for subjects who did not fall in love. In both of these studies, the effects on the self were maintained when measures of mood change were controlled statistically.

ADDITIONAL IMPLICATIONS AND CONCLUSION

The self-expansion model offers ways of looking at relationship phenomena that have only begun to be examined with the lines of research discussed here. For example, the model has implications for break-ups and loss: the degree of psychological distress should be predictable from the degree of previously existing overlap of self and other. Similarly, commitment may be enhanced by fear of de-expansion (or experienced de-expansion when some moves toward separation are tried), a process related to Rusbult's (1983) investment model of commitment. That is, one can consider inclusion of each other in each other's self an investment that would be lost in a relationship break-up. Another set of implications relates to effects on relationships of the interaction between self-expansion processes and *individual differences* in such variables as boredom susceptibility and desired level of arousal, or *situational differences* such as degree of expansion experienced in other domains of life, or whether there needs to be the predicted alternations in expansion and integration. Another potentially fruitful application would be to other types of relationships, such as therapist–client. Yet another is the possibility of applying findings in this area to other areas of social psychology such as intergroup relations, altruism or aggression.

On the other hand, even in the areas in which there have been a number of relevant studies, in most cases data are preliminary in the sense that some alternative explanations have not been ruled out and only limited populations have been studied. Perhaps what we have at this point can best be described as a demonstration of the potential of the model's metaphors for inspiring an interest in relationship phenomena that might not otherwise have become the subject of systematic research attention—phenomena such as participation in exciting activities and self-other confusions. And we hope that the model's metaphors will serve to continue to generate ways of thinking about relationships that do not entirely overlap with those embedded in other relationship models.

Chapter 11

On the Statistics of Interdependence: Treating Dyadic Data with Respect

Richard Gonzalez
University of Washington, Seattle, WA, USA
and
Dale Griffin
University of Sussex, Brighton, UK

"The time has come," the Walrus said,
   "To talk of many things:
Of shoes—and ships—and sealing wax—
   Of cabbages—and kings . . ." (Lewis Carroll, *Through the Looking Glass*).

Dyadic relationships form the core element of our social lives. They also form the core unit of study by relationship researchers. Then why (to paraphrase Woody Allen) do so many analyses in this area focus on only one consenting adult at a time? The reason, we suspect, has to do with the rather austere authority figures of our early professional development: statistics professors who conveyed the cherished assumption of independent sampling. However, when we collect data in which the sample units do not arrive one at a time, as in the idealized world of independence, but instead arrive two at a time, as in the real world of dyadic interdependence, we are faced with a frustrating dilemma. How do we capture the psychology of interdependence with the statistics of independence?

Unfortunately for the development of interpersonal relationships theory, the patterns laid down during the imprinting period of graduate statistics classes tend to dominate the rest of one's professional life. Interdependence in one's data is typically viewed as a nuisance and so dyadic researchers have developed strate-

Handbook of Personal Relationships, 2nd edn. Edited by Steve Duck.
© 1997 John Wiley & Sons Ltd.

gies to sweep interdependence under the statistical rug. These strategies include (1) averaging interdependence away by creating a sample of "independent" dyad mean scores, (2) partialling interdependence out and thereby creating a sample of "independent" individual scores, and (3) dropping one dyad member's scores and thus creating a truncated sample of "independent" individual scores. This ritual mutilation of dyadic data comes at a high cost: important information about the similarity or dissimilarity between dyad members is lost.

In this chapter, we review some recent developments in dyadic data analysis that are aimed at making the statistics of interdependence as accessible as the statistics of independence (see Kenny, 1988, for a similar analysis from a slightly different perspective). These techniques give researchers the ability to study interdependence directly; they view interdependence as an opportunity to ask novel research questions, not as a problem to avoid. We focus on correlational methods and their underlying models because these represent the areas of greatest confusion among researchers. The techniques we will describe should help to prevent four particular errors of interpretation that haunt dyadic data analysis: the assumed independence error, the deletion error, the cross-level or ecological error, and the levels of analysis error. We first discuss these four common errors in the analysis of dyadic data and then present a general framework that can handle many data analysis issues that occur when subsets of subjects are interdependent.

Four Common Errors

We consider the problems and opportunities of dyadic data analysis in light of a specific example. Stinson & Ickes (1992) had pairs of male students interact in an unstructured "waiting room" situation. These interactions, some between friends and some between strangers, were videotaped and coded on a number of dimensions including the frequency of verbalizations and the frequency of gazes. How should researchers evaluate the strength of the linear relation between speaking and gazing in the context of individuals interacting in dyads? We point out four errors that researchers should avoid when evaluating the strength of relation between two variables in the context of dyads.[1]

First, researchers must avoid the *assumed independence error*, which consists of correlating the $2N$ interdependent data points as if they were independent (where N represents the number of dyads). To do this would invalidate the statistical test of the correlation, which depends primarily on the appropriate sample size. One remedy is to adjust the significance test to take into account the degree and type of interdependence in the sample. This approach is described in more detail later in the chapter.

---

[1] These errors were not made by Stinson & Ickes, who used these data to answer different research questions than those being addressed here.

Second, researchers should not create independent data by throwing out half their sample, an error that we call the *deletion error*. Although in some situations this may not bias the actual correlation obtained, it is a waste of power to drop subjects. The deletion error also prevents the researcher from assessing the type and degree of interdependence in dyads. We view the assessment of interdependence as an opportunity to examine interesting theoretical questions, not as a statistical nuisance that needs to be eliminated.

Third, researchers must avoid the tendency to generalize from one level of aggregation to another, the *cross-level error*. In particular, researchers should not attempt to circumvent the independence problem by creating dyadic averages on each variable and then interpreting the correlation between averages as an index of the correlation for these individuals (Robinson, 1950, 1957). Depending on the degree of interdependence within dyads on each variable, the correlation between dyadic averages can be quite different from the correlation computed for individual scores. This will be discussed in more detail below.

Finally, researchers must avoid a common interpretational fallacy, the *levels of analysis error*. That is, they must avoid interpreting the correlation between dyad means as indicating "dyad-level processes" and similarly avoid interpreting the correlation between individual scores as indicating "individual-level processes". Instead, they must appreciate the fact that both of these correlations contain a *mix* of dyad-level and individual-level information. Separating the dyad-level and individual-level correlations requires an approach that explicitly identifies and models the degree of interdependence within and between variables at each level of analysis.

Identifying common errors is useful only to the extent that sensible alternatives are available. Having pointed out errors to avoid, we now turn to a technique that helps researchers avoid these errors. This technique, which we call the *pairwise method*, is simple to use, produces Pearson-type correlations that are familiar to researchers, and permits relatively straightforward significance tests that adjust for the observed degree of interdependence within the dyads. The primary advantage of the pairwise method, however, is that it offers researchers a general framework in which to think about psychological processes in dyads. Within the pairwise approach, researchers can (1) ask questions at both the dyad-level and the individual-level simultaneously, (2) use data from both members of the dyad, and (3) test the significance of an observed correlation or regression slope in a manner that appropriately adjusts for the degree of interdependence in the dyad members' responses.

ASSESSING INTERDEPENDENCE ON A SINGLE VARIABLE

In this and the next few sections we deal with the problem of assessing interdependence in a dyad for a single dependent variable (i.e., univariate interdependence). In each case, we illustrate the concepts using data from Stinson & Ickes

(1992). In the case of strangers, the dyadic partners were randomly assigned by the experimenter, so we can assume that individuals start off no more similar to their partners than they are to any other person in the sample. However, if interaction leads to interdependence—so that the dyads are no longer simply the "sum of their individual parts"—then interaction should generally lead to individuals becoming more similar to their partners than to the other people in the sample.[2]

There is a fundamental dimension on which both types of dyads in the Stinson & Ickes study (i.e., male friends and male strangers) differ from other kinds of dyads that researchers may study. In some dyads, such as heterosexual couples, the dyad members are *distinguishable* because sex can be used to differentiate the members within the dyads. That is, when computing a correlation, the researcher "knows whose score to put in column X and whose score to put in column Y" by virtue of the individual's sex. In this example, we are using sex as the variable to distinguish the dyad members, but the general point is that in the distinguishable case *some* meaningful variable can be use to distinguish the two dyad members. However, with same-sex platonic friends or homosexual couples, the dyad members are *exchangeable* because they are not readily distinguished on the basis of sex or any other non-arbitrary variable (i.e., the researcher does not know whose score to put in column X and whose score to put in column Y). When the dyad members are distinguishable it is possible for the scores of the members within each category to have different means, different variances and different covariances. When the dyad members are exchangeable, however, their scores have the same mean, the same variance, and the same distribution because there is no meaningful way to divide them into distinct categories.

How do we assess the degree of interdependence in the distinguishable case? That is, on a single variable, how similar are the two distinguishable dyad members? Most readers will realize that the standard interclass, or Pearson product moment correlation, can be used to assess interdependence when the two individuals in each dyad are distinguishable. The interclass correlation assesses "relative similarity"—for example, whether a woman who receives a high score on a variable *relative to other women* tends to be paired with a man who receives a high score on that variable *relative to other men*. Because it assesses relative—rather than absolute—similarity, mean group differences do not affect the interclass correlation. This is an important point because the interclass correlation in this context cannot be interpreted as a measure of absolute similarity, or agreement, between the dyad members (Robinson, 1957).

How do we assess the degree of interdependence in the exchangeable case? In

---

[2] Note that when dyadic sorting is non-random, as in the case of heterosexual romantic relationships or male friends as in the Stinson & Ickes (1992) study, this inference is not so straightforward. Similarity within dyads may indicate interdependence arising through interaction, but it may also be an artifact of sorting due to common interests, common abilities or common status. In such cases, all the statistics presented here will still be appropriate, but their interpretation may be different depending on whether there was random or non-random pairing.

this situation the researcher cannot meaningfully distinguish the dyad members so the interclass correlation cannot be computed. However, it is possible to compute the intraclass correlation. The assumption of equal variance is guaranteed in this case because there is no meaningful way to separate the two members; they are both sampled from the same distribution. In the exchangeable case it is not possible to examine relative similarity but it is possible to examine absolute similarity.

It is also possible to measure absolute similarity in the distinguishable case when it can be assumed that the two groups come from populations with equal variances. This similarity measure is the intraclass correlation with mean differences partialled out. This index of interdependence generally yields a value that is very similar to the interclass correlation, but unlike the interclass correlation it can be used as the basis for the more complex measures that are introduced later.

We have argued that the intraclass correlation and the partial intraclass correlation can be useful in assessing intra-dyadic similarity. There have been several treatments in the literature on computing and testing the intraclass correlation (Kenny, 1988; Shrout & Fleiss, 1979); these treatments presented the intraclass correlation in the context of analysis of variance (ANOVA). The ANOVA framework does not always make concepts transparent to the researcher who (understandably) tends to be more interested in answering research questions than in learning statistical theory. We present a different framework, a correlational approach based on the pairwise coding of data that, we hope, makes the relevant concepts more intuitive to the researcher. The advantage of the pairwise approach will become obvious when we generalize the univariate situation to the multivariate case. The complicated analysis problem of multivariate dyadic data will be seen as relatively simple when we apply the techniques developed in the next section. Another benefit of the approach used here is that significance tests are straightforward to derive (which is not necessarily the case in the ANOVA framework).

The Pairwise Intraclass Correlation as a Measure of Interdependence

Exchangeable Case

A useful measure of intra-dyadic similarity for a single variable is the *pairwise intraclass correlation* (Donner & Koval, 1980; Fisher, 1925). The pairwise intraclass correlation is so named because each possible within-group pair of scores is used to compute the correlation. For example, with individuals Adam and Amos in the first dyad, there are two possible pairings: Adam in column one and Amos in column two; or Amos in column one and Adam in column two. With three exchangeable dyads (Adam and Amos, Bob and Bill, and Colin and Chris) the pairwise set-up consists of the scores on X of Adam, Amos, Bob, Bill, Colin,

Table 11.1 Symbolic representation for the pairwise data setup in the exchangeable case. The first subscript represents the dyad and the second subscript represents the individual. Categorization of individuals as 1 or 2 is arbitrary

Dyad #	Variable	
	X	X'
1	X_{11}	X_{12}
	X_{12}	X_{11}
2	X_{21}	X_{22}
	X_{22}	X_{21}
3	X_{31}	X_{32}
	X_{32}	X_{31}
4	X_{41}	X_{42}
	X_{42}	X_{41}

Chris in the first column (denoted X) and the scores on X of Amos, Adam, Bill, Bob, Chris, and Colin in the second column (denoted X'). Note that each pairing occurs twice, but in opposite orders (Adam in column 1 with Amos adjacent in column 2, then Amos in column 1 and Adam adjacent in column 2, etc.). Thus with $N = 3$ dyads, each column contains $2N = 6$ scores because each member is represented in both columns. This coding is represented symbolically in Table 11.1. The two columns (i.e., variables X and X') are then correlated using the usual product–moment correlation. This correlation is denoted $r_{xx'}$, and is called the *pairwise intraclass correlation*. The correlation $r_{xx'}$ indexes the absolute similarity between two exchangeable partners in a dyad. In other words, $r_{xx'}$ is the intraclass correlation of one person's score with his or her partner's score. It is important to point out that the intraclass correlation, unlike the usual Pearson correlation carries a "variance accounted for" interpretation in the $r_{xx'}$ form, that is, there is no need to square the intraclass correlation (see, e.g., Haggard, 1958).

It is important to remember that the correlation $r_{xx'}$ is computed over all $2N$ pairs. However, because the correlation $r_{xx'}$ is based on $2N$ pairs rather than on N dyads as in the usual case, the test of significance needs to be adjusted, i.e., a researcher cannot use the p-value printed by standard statistical packages. The sample value $r_{xx'}$ can be tested against the null hypothesis that $\rho_{xx'} = 0$ using the asymptotic test[3]

$$Z = r_{xx'}\sqrt{N} \tag{1}$$

---

[3] To simplify matters, we have chosen to present large sample asymptotic significance tests throughout this chapter, unless a well-known and easily accessible "small sample" test was available. For most applications of these tests, "large sample" refers to approximately 30–40 (or more) dyads. We also present a null hypothesis approach rather than a confidence interval approach because the former is relatively simple in the pairwise domain. Readers interested in the relevant standard errors to compute confidence intervals can consult the more technical papers we cite.

where N is the number of dyads and Z is normally distributed. The observed Z can be compared to critical values found in standard tables. Thus for most applications where the researcher sets the Type I error rate at $\alpha = 0.05$ (two-tailed), the critical value for Z will be 1.96. An observed Z greater than or equal to 1.96 leads to a rejection of the null hypothesis that $\rho_{xx'} = 0$.

The pairwise intraclass correlation indexes the similarity of individuals within dyads, and so is closely related to other methods of estimating the intraclass correlation, such as the ANOVA estimator (Fisher, 1925; Haggard, 1958). However, the pairwise method has several important advantages in the present situation. Most important, it is calculated in the same manner as the usual Pearson correlation: the two "reverse-coded" columns are correlated in the usual manner, thus offering ease of computation, flexibility in the use of existing computer packages, and an intuitive link to general correlational methods. As we will show, it also has certain statistical properties that make it ideal to serve as the basis for more complicated statistics of interdependence. Moreover, the same pairwise method used to compute the intraclass correlations within a single variable can be used to compute the "cross intraclass correlation" across different variables, an important index that is discussed below.

Distinguishable Case

The calculation of the *partial pairwise intraclass correlation* in the distinguishable case follows the same general pattern. However, in the distinguishable case the pairwise correlation model requires one extra piece of information: a grouping code indexing the dyad member. This extra information is needed because each dyad member is distinguishable according to some theoretically meaningful variable, and this raises the possibility of mean differences between the classes that will bias the value of $r_{xx'}$. Therefore, it is necessary to create an extra column of data to partial out mean class differences. This first column (labeled "C") consists of binary codes representing the "class" variable, e.g., the sex of the subject. For instance, if the researcher decided to code wives as "1" and husbands as "2", the first column would consist of "1" in the first row and "2" in the second row, and this pattern would be repeated for each of the N dyads in the sample, yielding $2N$ binary codes.

The second column (labeled X) consists of the scores on the variable of interest corresponding to the class code in column one. So, for example, adjacent to the first "1" in column one (representing the female member of the first dyad) the first woman's score would be placed. Below that, adjacent to the first "2" in column one (representing the male member of the first dyad) the first man's score would be placed. This pattern would then continue for the N dyads in the sample, again yielding a total of $2N$ scores. Column three is created by the pairwise reversal of column two. For example, adjacent to each person's score in column two is placed his or her partner's score in column three. Again, this pairwise "reversed" column of scores on X is referred to as X'. This coding is represented symbolically in Table 11.2.

Table 11.2 Symbolic representation for the pairwise data setup in the distinguishable case. The first subscript represents the dyad and the second subscript represents the individual. Categorization of individuals as 1 or 2 is based on the class variable C

Dyad #	Variable		
	C	X	X′
1	1	X_{11}	X_{12}
	2	X_{12}	X_{11}
2	1	X_{21}	X_{22}
	2	X_{22}	X_{21}
3	1	X_{31}	X_{32}
	2	X_{32}	X_{31}
4	1	X_{41}	X_{42}
	2	X_{42}	X_{41}

The sample estimate of the partial pairwise intraclass correlation is simply the Pearson correlation between X and X' partialling out variable C. The partial pairwise intraclass correlation is denoted $r_{xx'.c}$. This correlation can be computed with standard statistical packages (e.g., the partial correlation routine in either SAS or SPSS). For completeness we present the formula for the partial correlation

$$r_{xx'.c} = \frac{r_{xx'} - r_{cx}r_{cx'}}{\sqrt{\left(1 - r_{cx}^2\right)\left(1 - r_{cx'}^2\right)}}$$

The sample value $r_{xx'.c}$ can be tested against the null hypothesis that $\rho_{xx'.c} = 0$ using the large sample, asymptotic test

$$Z = r_{xx'.c}\sqrt{N}$$

where Z is normally distributed and can be compared to critical values found in standard tables. Note that the equality of variance assumption applies in the distinguishable case. For instance, the population variance for the men on variable X is assumed to be equivalent to the population variance for the women on variable X. Standard tests for the equality of two dependent variances can be used to determine if this assumption is valid (e.g., Kenny, 1979). See Gonzalez & Griffin (1995b) for advice about dealing with situations where the between-group variances are different.

Examples of the Pairwise Intraclass Correlation

In this section we present examples of the pairwise intraclass and partial pairwise intraclass correlations.

Exchangeable Case: Pairwise Intraclass Correlation

From the Stinson & Ickes data, we selected three variables on which to measure dyadic interdependence: gazes, verbalizations and gestures. Our example focuses on the 24 dyads of same-sex strangers. Each variable was coded in the pairwise fashion, creating a total of six columns of data for the three variables (e.g., the $2N$ gaze scores in column 1, and the $2N$ gaze scores in reversed order in column 2, and so on). The resulting value $r_{xx'}$ for the frequency of gazes was 0.57; for the frequency of verbalizations, 0.84; and for the frequency of gestures, 0.27 (i.e., 57%, 84% and 27% of the variance in each variable, respectively, was shared between dyad members). These values of $r_{xx'}$ suggest that dyad members were quite similar on the frequency of their gazes and the frequency of their verbalizations, but it appears that the similarity between dyad members in the frequency of their gestures was low.

A direct application of Equation 1 yields significance tests for these three sample $r_{xx'}$ values against the null hypothesis that $\rho_{xx'} = 0$. In this example there were $N = 24$ dyads (thus 48 individuals). The corresponding values of Z were 4.12 for gaze, 2.79 for verbalization, and 1.11 for gestures. Thus, using a two-tailed $\alpha = 0.05$, the dyadic similarity was significantly different from zero for gazes and verbalizations, but not for gestures.

Distinguishable Case: Partial Pairwise Intraclass Correlation

Consider the following example from a study of distinguishable dyads. Sandra Murray (1995) collected self-evaluations and partner-evaluations from both members of 163 heterosexual couples who were dating exclusively. A comparison of the men's and women's variances on these two variables revealed that, in each case, the between-group differences were very small (i.e., the men and women had approximately equal variance), justifying the use of pooled variances in the partial pairwise intraclass correlation. The partial pairwise correlation for self-evaluations was 0.218, which is significant $Z = 0.218\sqrt{163} = 2.78$) and the partial pairwise correlation for partner-evaluations was 0.365, also significant ($Z = 4.65$). Thus the partners resembled each other on each of the two variables. It is interesting to note that the interclass correlation between self-evaluation and partner-evaluation for the men was 0.46, and the same interclass correlation for the women was 0.55, which was not statistically different (Z difference = 1.08).

Now that we have introduced the pairwise method of computing the intraclass correlation in the dyadic case, we will use this technique as a building block for more complicated correlational methods. In the remainder of the chapter we present methods for examining dyadic correlations between two variables, methods for separating individual and dyadic effects, and methods for testing actor–partner effects in dyadic research. We take each topic in turn.

OVERALL CORRELATION AND THE CROSS INTRACLASS CORRELATION

Consider the situation where the researcher has two variables, X and Y, measured on each member of the dyad. For instance, suppose a trust scale and a satisfaction with relationship scale are given to each member of N dyads. There are two natural questions the researcher might ask: is an individual's trust associated with his or her satisfaction? and is an individual's trust associated with his or her partner's satisfaction?

To answer these questions, the researcher might compute two Pearson correlations: (1) a correlation between X and Y, which we call the *overall correlation* (e.g., individual's trust associated with satisfaction), and (2) a correlation between an individual's X and his or her partner's Y, which we call the *cross intraclass correlation* (e.g., individual's trust associated with partner's satisfaction). The values of these two correlations serve as estimates of the underlying linear association. Unfortunately, the tests of significance for these two correlations given by most statistical packages will be incorrect. They commit the assumed independence error because the standard test assumes there are $2N$ independent subjects, yet the data may not obey independence. This violation of independence can obviously have a dramatic effect on the result of a significance test (e.g., Kenny & Judd, 1986).

Pairwise Approach for the Exchangeable Case

Fortunately, a straightforward solution for the test of significance for both the overall correlation and the cross intraclass correlation can be found by using a generalization of the pairwise approach developed in the previous section. We first consider the case for exchangeable dyad members and then the case for distinguishable dyad members. The pairwise coding is done on each variable X and Y separately. That is, the $2N$ scores for X, the $2N$ scores for X that have been "reverse coded" (denoted X', as previously shown in Table 11.1), the $2N$ scores for Y, and the $2N$ scores for Y' are entered into four columns. This creates a total of four variables, X, X' Y, and Y', which are shown symbolically in Table 11.3. In this framework there are six possible correlations, which are depicted in Figure 11.1. Figure 11.1 shows that the pairwise intraclass correlations for X and Y are given by $r_{xx'}$ and $r_{yy'}$, respectively; the overall correlation is given by r_{xy}; and the cross intraclass correlation is given by $r_{xy'}$. Note that in this framework $r_{xy'} = r_{x'y}$ and $r_{xy} = r_{x'y'}$.

Given the four basic correlations found in Figure 11.1 it is possible to compute tests of significance for r_{xy} and $r_{xy'}$ that take into account the degree of interdependence. For details regarding the derivation of these tests and supporting simulations, see Griffin & Gonzalez (1995a). Under the null hypothesis that $\rho_{xy} = 0$, the approximate large-sample variance of r_{xy} is $\dfrac{1}{N_1^*}$, where

Table 11.3 Symbolic representation for the pairwise data setup for two variables in the exchangeable case. The first subscript represents the dyad and the second subscript represents the individual. Categorization of individuals as 1 or 2 is arbitrary

Dyad #	Variable			
	X	X'	Y	Y'
1	X_{11}	X_{12}	Y_{11}	Y_{12}
	X_{12}	X_{11}	Y_{12}	Y_{11}
2	X_{21}	X_{22}	Y_{21}	Y_{22}
	X_{22}	X_{21}	Y_{22}	Y_{21}
3	X_{31}	X_{32}	Y_{31}	Y_{32}
	X_{32}	X_{31}	Y_{32}	Y_{31}
4	X_{41}	X_{42}	Y_{41}	Y_{42}
	X_{42}	X_{41}	Y_{42}	Y_{41}

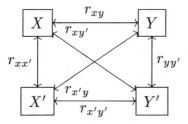

Figure 11.1 All possible pairwise correlations between variables X, Y, and their corresponding "reverse codes"

$$N_1^* = \frac{2N}{1 + r_{xx'}r_{yy'} + r_{xy'}^2}$$

Thus the overall correlation r_{xy} can be tested using a Z test where

$$Z = r_{xy}\sqrt{N_1^*} \qquad (2)$$

Intuitively, N_1^* can be thought of as the "effective sample size" for r_{xy} adjusted for dependent observations (see Rosner, 1982, and Eliasziw & Donner, 1991, for the development of this intuition).

The formula for the effective sample size N_1^* illustrates that a common practice used by some researchers may be flawed. Some researchers follow the practice of first testing the intraclass correlations, and if both intraclass correlations are close to zero, proceed as though the data were independent. The problem with this practice is that there is another source of dependence relevant to the standard error of r_{xy}: the cross intraclass correlation $r_{xy'}$. Only when all three sources of dependence are zero can the data be treated as independent. The Z test in

Equation 2 is useful because it can be applied regardless of the values for the three sources of interdependence.

The correlation between an individual's score on variable X and his or her dyad partner's score on variable Y (i.e., the variable Y') is the cross intraclass correlation. The cross intraclass correlation $r_{xy'}$ assesses the strength of the relationship between two variables measured on different dyadic partners. Under the null hypothesis that $\rho_{xy'} = 0$, the asymptotic variance of $r_{xy'}$ is $\dfrac{1}{N_2^*}$, where

$$N_2^* = \frac{2N}{1 + r_{xx'}r_{yy'} + r_{xy}^2}.$$

The cross intraclass correlation $r_{xy'}$ can be tested using a Z test, where

$$Z = r_{xy'}\sqrt{N_2^*}$$

Like N_1^*, N_2^* can be thought of as the "effective sample size" for $r_{xy'}$ adjusted for dependent observations.

An Example of the Exchangeable Case

Consider the 24 same-sex, stranger dyads studied by Stinson & Ickes. Researchers might be interested in the following questions. Over all individuals, were the three variables (frequency of gazes, frequency of verbalizations, and frequency of gestures) significantly related to each other? Examination of the boxed values in Table 11.4 reveals that all three overall correlations are positive and moderately large: the overall correlation between verbalization frequency and gaze frequency was 0.386, the overall correlation between verbalization frequency and gesture frequency was 0.449, and the overall correlation between gaze frequency and gesture frequency was 0.474. Recall that the significance test of the overall correlation r_{xy} depends on the effective sample size N_1^*. Between verbalizations and gazes, $N_1^* = \dfrac{48}{1 + (0.841)(0.570) + 0.471^2} = 28.22$; between verbalizations and gestures $N_1^* = 33.81$; and between gazes and gestures $N_1^* = 38.88$. The resulting

Table 11.4 Pairwise correlation matrix for randomly sampled, same-sex strangers (Stinson & Ickes, 1992). Pairwise intraclass correlations are typed in bold. Verb = frequency of verbalizations. Gaze = frequency of gazes. Gest = frequency of gestures

	Verb	Verb'	Gaze	Gaze'	Gest	Gest'
Verb	1.000					
Verb'	**0.841**	1.000				
Gaze	0.386	0.471	1.000			
Gaze'	0.471	0.386	**0.570**	1.000		
Gest	0.449	0.479	0.474	0.325	1.000	
Gest'	0.479	0.449	0.325	0.474	**0.226**	1.000

significance tests were $Z = 0.386\sqrt{28.22} = 2.05$, $p < 0.05$; $Z = 2.61$, $p < 0.05$; and $Z = 2.96$, $p < 0.05$, respectively. All three overall correlations were significantly positive.

We now turn to the assessment of the cross intraclass correlation $r_{xy'}$. Is an individual's score on one variable related to his partner's score on a second variable? The cross intraclass correlation $r_{xy'}$ between verbalizations and gazes was 0.471. The effective sample size was $N_2^* = \dfrac{48}{1 + (0.841)(0.570) + 0.386^2} = 29.48$, and the resulting Z was $0.471\sqrt{29.48} = 2.56$, $p < 0.05$. The correlation $r_{xy'}$ between verbalization frequency and gesture frequency was 0.479. Testing $r_{xy'}$ against its standard error (with $N_2^* = 34.49$) yielded an observed $Z = 2.82$, $p < 0.01$. Similarly, the cross intraclass correlation $r_{xy'}$ between gaze frequency and gesture frequency was 0.325. Testing $r_{xy'}$ against its standard error (with $N_2^* = 35.46$) yielded an observed $Z = 1.94$, $p < 0.10$. The significant, positive values for $r_{xy'}$ indicate that individuals who speak frequently are associated with partners (in this case strangers) who gaze and gesture frequently; individuals who gaze frequently are moderately associated with partners who gesture frequently.

Pairwise Approach for the Distinguishable Case

The computational setup for the overall and the cross intraclass correlations in the distinguishable case parallels the setup in the exchangeable case. As with the pairwise intraclass correlation, the distinguishable case is treated differently than the exchangeable case only in terms of the coding variable that is partialled out. The basic data arrangement is shown in Table 11.5, which is similar to Table 11.3

Table 11.5 Symbolic representation for the pairwise data setup for two variables in the distinguishable case. The first subscript represents the dyad and the second subscript represents the individual. Categorization of individuals as 1 or 2 is based on the class variable C. The primes denote the reverse coding described in the text

Dyad #		Variable			
	C	X	X'	Y	Y'
1	1	X_{11}	X_{12}	Y_{11}	Y_{12}
	2	X_{12}	X_{11}	Y_{12}	Y_{11}
2	1	X_{21}	X_{22}	Y_{21}	Y_{22}
	2	X_{22}	X_{21}	Y_{22}	Y_{21}
3	1	X_{31}	X_{32}	Y_{31}	Y_{32}
	2	X_{32}	X_{31}	Y_{32}	Y_{31}
4	1	X_{41}	X_{42}	Y_{41}	Y_{42}
	2	X_{42}	X_{41}	Y_{42}	Y_{41}

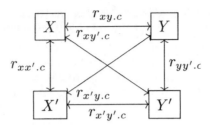

Figure 11.2 All possible pairwise correlations between variables X, Y and their corresponding "reverse codes" in the distinguishable case. Variable C has been partialled out from all correlations

for the exchangeable case except for the extra column representing the categorization of individuals within the dyad. The coding variable C is partialled from all correlations. Figure 11.2 shows the possible correlations between the four variables, using a ".c" in the subscript to denote that variable C has been partialled out. The standard formula for the partial correlation is used. Therefore, the partial overall correlation $r_{xy.c}$ is computed according to the formula

$$
r_{xy.c} = \frac{r_{xy} - r_{cx}r_{cy}}{\sqrt{\left(1 - r_{cx}^{2}\right)\left(1 - r_{cy}^{2}\right)}}
\tag{3}
$$

and the partial cross intraclass correlation $r_{xy'.c}$ is computed as

$$
r_{xy'.c} = \frac{r_{xy'} - r_{cx}r_{cy'}}{\sqrt{\left(1 - r_{cx}^{2}\right)\left(1 - r_{cy'}^{2}\right)}}
\tag{4}
$$

These partial correlations can be computed in standard statistical packages such as *SAS* or *SPSS*. Note that the partial pairwise intraclass correlations for X and Y are denoted by $r_{xx'.c}$ and $r_{yy'.c}$, respectively; the partial overall correlation is denoted by $r_{xy.c}$; and the partial cross intraclass correlation is denoted by $r_{xy'.c}$.

Unlike the exchangeable case, there are three assumptions that need to be checked before proceeding: (1) equality of variance between the two classes on each variable (e.g., the variance for men on X needs to equal the variance for women on X, and the variance for men on Y needs to equal the variance for women on Y); (2) equality of covariances between the two variables across classes (e.g., the covariance between X and Y for men needs to equal the covariance between X and Y for women); and (3) equality of cross covariances between the two variables (e.g., the covariance between the women's X and the men's Y needs to equal the covariance between the men's X and the women's Y). The reason these assumptions were not made in the exchangeable case was because the individuals could not be meaningfully separated into two classes (e.g., men vs. women) and the data were therefore combined. However, in the distinguishable case the individuals can be separated into two classes; consequently, the equivalence of the variance and covariances must be checked before the data from the two groups are pooled for the partial overall and partial cross intraclass correlations. Recall that the equality-of-variance assumption was also made for the partial pairwise intraclass case. Griffin & Gonzalez (1995a) discuss the details for testing these assumptions. In general, when these assumptions are met the computation of the relevant correlations will be more efficient and the corresponding tests more powerful compared to the usual strategy of analyzing data for the members of each class separately. There are also substantive reasons for making these assumptions (see Griffin & Gonzalez, 1995a).

Given the four basic correlations found in Figure 11.2 it is possible to compute tests of significance for $r_{xy.c}$ and $r_{xy'.c}$ that take into account the degree of interdependence. For details regarding the derivation of these tests, supporting simulations, and a discussion of how to perform the tests using strandard structural equations modelling programs see Griffin & Gonzalez (1995a). Under the null hypothesis that $\rho_{xy.c} = 0$, the approximate large-sample variance of $r_{xy.c}$ is $\frac{1}{N_1^*}$, where

$$N_1^* = \frac{2N}{1 + r_{xx'.c}r_{yy'.c} + r_{xy.c}^2} \tag{5}$$

Thus the partial overall correlation $r_{xy.c}$ can be tested using a Z test where

$$Z = r_{ry.c}\sqrt{N_1^*}$$

The partial cross intraclass correlation assesses the strength of the relationship between two variables measured on different dyadic partners partialling out mean differences between the two partners. Under the null hypothesis that $\rho_{xy'.c} = 0$, the asymptotic variance of $r_{xy'.c}$ is $\frac{1}{N_2^*}$, where

$$N_2^* = \frac{2N}{1 + r_{xx'.c}r_{yy'.c} + r_{xy.c}^2} \tag{6}$$

The partial cross intraclass correlation $r_{xy'.c}$ can be tested using a Z test, where

$$Z = r_{xy'.c}\sqrt{N_2^*}$$

An Example of the Distinguishable Case

Recall that Murray (1995) found that for the 163 couples the correlation between self and partner evaluations for the men was 0.46, and the correlation between the same two variables was 0.55 for the women, which was not statistically significant. The correlation between the women's self-evaluation and the men's partner-evaluation was 0.37, and the correlation between the men's self-evaluation and the women's partner-evaluation was 0.41. Further, the variances for the men were similar to the variances for the women (on each variable). Thus the necessary conditions for computing the overall partial and the cross intraclass correlation are met for these data.

The partial overall correlation (with sex partialled out) between self-evaluations and partner-evaluations is 0.501. That is, controlling for sex differences, it appears that each individual's self-evaluations was correlated with his or her evaluation of the partner. This result, along with the previously-reported partial intraclass correlations of 0.218 for self-evaluations and 0.364 for partner-evaluations, gives an $N_1^* = \dfrac{163*2}{1 + 0.218*0.364 + 0.392^2} = 264.39$, a straightforward application of Equation 5. The Z value for this overall correlation $r_{xy.c}$ was $0.501*\sqrt{264.39} = 8.15, p < 0.001$.

The partial cross intraclass correlation between one person's self-evaluations and the other's partner-evaluation was 0.392. That is, controlling for sex differences, it appears that an individual's self-evaluation was moderately correlated with his or her partner's evaluation of the individual. The partial cross intraclass correlation can be tested using the effective sample size given by substituting sample size N, the two partial pairwise intraclass correlations, and the partial overall correlation into Equation 6, which for this sample was 244.30. The Z value for this sample $r_{xy'.c}$ was $0.392*\sqrt{244.30} = 6.13, p < 0.001$.

A LATENT VARIABLE MODEL FOR SEPARATING INDIVIDUAL AND DYADIC EFFECTS

We now apply the pairwise framework to address levels of analysis problem present in dyadic research. A researcher studying dyads can ask questions at either the level of the individual, the level of the dyad, or both (Kenny & La Voie, 1985). To make this issue concrete we refer to the Stinson & Ickes (1992) study. A researcher can ask the question, "Do *individuals* who gesture more also verbalize more?" A researcher can also ask the question, "Are *dyads* where both individuals gesture more also the dyads where both individuals verbalize more?" The two questions differ in their level of analysis: individuals or dyads.

Both levels of analysis can be informative, and focusing on only one level is wasteful of information that might be theoretically interesting. Further, it is possible to find situations in which the direction of the relationship between two variables differs in sign across the two levels. For instance, imagine that trust and satisfaction scales are taken from married couples. Each partner answers both scales so there are a total of four observations per couple: two trust scores and two satisfaction scores. It is plausible that the relationship between trust and satisfaction at the dyad-level is positive (more trusting dyads are more satisfied with the relationship) whereas at the individual-level the relationship between trust and satisfaction could be negative (the individual within a dyad who is relatively more trusting could be relatively less satisfied because his or her trust is not reciprocated). Thus, it is possible to find associations in different directions (positive or negative) at the different levels of analysis. Such patterns are interesting from the perspective of both theory development and theory testing because a complete theory of dyadic interaction must address both levels of analysis.

The problem of separating the individual-level analysis from the dyad-level analysis has bothered methodologists for a long time. Robinson (1950) pointed out that the correlation between two aggregated variables (e.g., mean educational attainment and mean income correlated *across* states) is not equivalent to the correlation between the same two variables measured on individuals (e.g., educational attainment and average income *within* a state). In sociology, the cross-level error, or the erroneous generalization from one level to another, is termed the "ecological correlation fallacy" (Hauser, 1974; Robinson, 1950). The need for statistical techniques that permit analysis at different levels ("multi-level analysis") has led to a cottage industry of different viewpoints and statistical programs (see Bock, 1989; Bryk & Raudenbush, 1992; Goldstein, 1987; Goldstein & McDonald, 1988; Kreft, de Leeuw & van der Leeden, 1994).

In this section we show how different levels of analysis can be incorporated into the pairwise approach. Our own work has been greatly influenced by Kenny & La Voie (1985), who proposed a group correlation model to decompose individual-level and group-level effects. Kenny & La Voie derived their group correlation model in the context of ANOVA. We present the pairwise version of Kenny & La Voie's group correlation model. We call it the *pairwise latent variable model*. The ingredients for this model again depend on whether the dyad members are exchangeable or distinguishable.

Pairwise Latent Variable Model for the Exchangeable Case

Figure 11.3 shows a simple latent variable model for the exchangeable dyadic design. In this model, each measured variable is coded in a pairwise fashion so that the variables X and X' (and, by the same logic, Y and Y') are identical except for order. The variance of a given observed variable is assumed to result from two different latent (not measured) sources: a dyadic component representing the portion of that variable that is shared between dyadic partners and an individual component representing the portion of that variable that is unshared or unique.

As Figure 11.3 illustrates, there are two levels at which the variables can be related. The shared dyadic variance of X and Y can be related through the dyadic correlation r_d. The unique individual variance of X and Y can be related through the individual-level correlation r_i. The model depicted in Figure 11.3 permits simultaneous estimation and testing of r_d and r_i.

The individual-level correlation, r_i, and the latent dyad-level correlation, r_d, can be computed as follows:

$$r_i = \frac{r_{xy} - r_{xy'}}{\sqrt{1 - r_{xx'}}\sqrt{1 - r_{yy'}}} \tag{7}$$

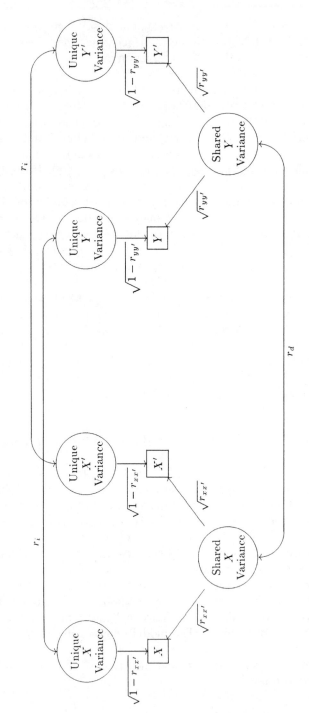

Figure 11.3 A latent variable model separating individual-level (unique) and dyad-level (shared) effects

and

$$r_{\mathrm{d}} = \frac{r_{xy'}}{\sqrt{r_{xx'}}\,\sqrt{r_{yy'}}}. \tag{8}$$

Note that both r_i and r_{d} are computed from the four basic correlations shown in Figure 11.1. The numerator of the individual-level correlation r_i is the difference between the observed correlation r_{xy}, which combines dyad-level and individual-level effects, and the cross intraclass correlation $r_{xy'}$, which contains only dyad-level effects. Thus r_i is a measure of the individual-level relation uncontaminated by dyad-level effects. The numerator of the dyad-level correlation r_{d} is simply the pairwise cross intraclass correlation $r_{xy'}$, and in this model corresponds to the direct measure of the dyad-level relations. The denominators, too, are conceptually straightforward: they correct the scale of the correlations for the fact that only "part" of each observed variable is being correlated. When the individual components of variables X and Y are correlated, the denominator adjusts for the proportions of variance in the observed X and Y that correspond to the *non-shared* effects ($\sqrt{1-r_{xx'}}$ and $\sqrt{1-r_{yy'}}$, respectively). Similarly, when the *dyadic* components of the variables X and Y are correlated, the denominator adjusts for the proportions of variance in the observed X and Y that correspond to the shared dyadic effects ($\sqrt{r_{xx'}}$ and $\sqrt{r_{yy'}}$, respectively). Note that r_{d} can be interpreted as $r_{xy'}$ that has been disattenuated (i.e., divided by the intraclass correlations representing the proportion of dyadic variance). The pairwise latent variable model is equivalent to the maximum likelihood group-level correlation suggested by Gollob (1991).

Testing the Underlying Correlations r_i and r_d in the Exchangeable Case

For the special case of dyads, r_i can be computed either by Equation 7 or by correlating the deviation scores on X and on Y. That is, the dyad mean on X is subtracted from each X score and the dyad mean on Y is subtracted from each Y score, and then the $2N$ deviations on X are correlated with the $2N$ deviations on Y. For dyads, Equation 7 and the deviation method yield identical values for r_i, which can be tested using the usual Pearson correlation table (or the associated t-test formula) with $N-1$ degrees of freedom (Kenny & La Voie, 1985).

Note that when either of the intraclass correlations $r_{xx'}$ or $r_{yy'}$ (or both) are small, r_{d} will tend be large and may even exceed 1.0. Because the dyadic model is based on the assumption of dyadic similarity, the model should only be tested when *both* intraclass correlations are significantly positive. In general, the practice of restricting the application of this model to cases when both intraclass correlations are significantly positive should reduce the occurrence of out-of-bounds values for r_{d}. A significance test for r_{d} is reported in Griffin & Gonzalez (in press). Interestingly, the p-value associated with r_{d} is identical to the p-value associated with $r_{xy'}$. Therefore, when both intraclass correlations are significant, implying significant dyad-level variance in both X and Y, we recommend interpreting $r_{xy'}$ as the raw-score version of r_d. Note that r_d is a disattenuated version of $r_{xy'}$.

The Mean-Level Correlation

It may appear that the correlation between the means of each dyad on the two variables should yield an estimate of the dyad-level correlation. Contrary to this intuition, the "mean-level" correlation (which we denote r_m) reflects both individual and dyad-level effects and can best be thought of as a "total" correlation. The mean-level correlation r_m should not be used as an index of dyad-level relations because it can be significantly positive or negative even when $r_d = 0$. According to the model in Figure 11.3, a positive dyad-level correlation exists only when the tendency of *both* dyad members to be high on X is matched by the tendency of *both* dyad members to be high on Y. However, this is only one of several circumstances that can lead to a positive value of r_m, indicating that a high *average* value on X is matched with a high *average* value on Y. For example, a positive mean-level correlation will result when the tendency of one member to be extremely high on X is matched with the tendency of that member to be extremely high on Y-regardless of the score of his or her dyadic partner on either variable. See Griffin & Gonzalez (in press) for a more systematic treatment of r_m.

Example for the Exchangeable Case

We continue using the Stinson & Ickes (1992) data to illustrate the exchangeable case. Having determined that there was dyad-level variance—as indexed by the pairwise intraclass correlation—in at least two of the three variables of interest, we calculate and test r_d and r_i. In the case of verbalizations and gazes,

$$r_d = \frac{0.471}{\sqrt{(0.841)(0.570)}} = 0.680.$$ The observed Z and p-value for r_d was identical to

that found for $r_{xy'}$ (i.e,. $Z = 2.56$, $p < 0.01$). The latent dyad-level correlation (r_d) between gaze frequency and gesture frequency was 0.906, $Z = 1.94$, $p < 0.1$, just shy of statistical significance. The dyad-level correlation (r_d) between verbalization frequency and gesture frequency was 1.10, which is "out of bounds". Such out-of-bounds values are most likely to occur when the intraclass correlation for one or both of the variables is marginal or non-significant (as in the case of gestures). In sum, the significant, positive values for $r_{xy'}$ (and r_d) indicate that dyads in which both members speak frequently are also dyads in which both members look at each other frequently and gesture to each other frequently.

Were the three variables related at the level of *individuals* within dyads? The computation of the individual-level correlation, r_i, between verbalizations and

gazes is straightforward: $\dfrac{r_{xy} - r_{xy'}}{\sqrt{1-r_{xx'}}\sqrt{1-r_{yy'}}} = \dfrac{0.386 - 0.471}{\sqrt{(1-0.941)(1-0.570)}} = -0.325.$ In contrast to the positive dyad-level correlation between verbalization and gaze (0.680), the individual-level correlation is negative. That is, the dyad member who speaks *more* often tends to be the dyad member who looks at the other *less* often (or, to turn the relation around—the dyad member who listens more often looks at the other more often). This negative individual-level correlation emerges despite the fact that dyads in which there is frequent speaking also tend to be dyads in which there is frequent gazing. However, the individual-level correlation is also only marginally statistically significant (just as were the dyad-level correlations reported above),

$$t_{N-1} = \frac{r_i \sqrt{N-1}}{\sqrt{1-r_i^2}}$$

$$= \frac{-0.325\sqrt{23}}{\sqrt{1-0.325^2}}$$

$$= 1.65,$$

$p < 0.10$. Note that this significance test relies on the usual formula for testing a correlation, except that in this case the degrees of freedom are $N-1$ (rather than $N-2$). The individual-level correlations for the other pairs of variables were relatively small and non-significant. For verbalizations and gestures $r_i = -0.086$, and for gestures and gazes $r_i = 0.258$. All three values of r_i were markedly discrepant from the corresponding values of r_d and $r_{xy'}$, underlining the importance of separating the dyad-level and individual-level relations.

Recall that all three overall correlations were moderate and positive. However, the overall correlation represents a combination of underlying dyadic and individual-level correlations. A more detailed picture of the social interactions that occurred in this study emerges when the two levels are decomposed. Verbalizations and gazes were negatively related at the individual level, but positively correlated at the dyad level. Verbalizations and gestures were unrelated at the individual level, but positively correlated at the dyad level. Finally, gazes and gestures were positively correlated at both the individual and dyadic levels.

Pairwise Latent Variable Model for the Distinguishable Case

The pairwise latent variable model for the distinguishable case is similar to the model for the exchangeable case except that the "class" or grouping variable C needs to be partialled out of the four variables X, X', Y and Y. Thus the corresponding model is identical to the model depicted in Figure 11.3 for the exchangeable case, except that all observed correlations are partial correlations (with the grouping variable C being the control variable). In this chapter we simply sketch the pairwise latent variable model for the distinguishable case and refer interested readers to Griffin & Gonzalez (1995a) for more detail.

The formula for the partial individual-level correlation r_i can be expressed in terms of the observed partial correlations given in Figure 11.2:

$$r_i = \frac{r_{xy.c} - r_{xy'.c}}{\sqrt{1 - r_{xx'.c}}\sqrt{1 - r_{yy'.c}}}$$

Note that because the individual-level correlation r_i uses the correlations $r_{xy.c}$ and $r_{xy'.c}$ in its computation, the assumptions needed for computing the partial overall and partial cross intraclass correlations apply to r_i as well. The implication of these assumptions is that the individual-level relationship is required to be the same for each level of the category variable (e.g., r_i for husbands equals r_i for wives).

The sample r_i can be tested against the null value of 0 using the standard t-test for a correlation. In the distinguishable case, the test has $N - 2$ degrees of freedom (one degree of freedom less than the r_i for the exchangeable case to account for partialling out the binary class variable C). For the Murray data sample r_i between the self-evaluation and the partner's evaluation was 0.155, yielding an observed $t = 2.00$, $p < 0.05$.

The partial dyad-level correlation r_d can also be expressed in terms of the observed correlations given in Figure 11.2:

$$r_d = \frac{r_{xy'.c}}{\sqrt{r_{xx'.c}}\sqrt{r_{yy'.c}}}. \tag{9}$$

Again, the estimation of r_d for the pairwise model requires an assumption that the partial cross intraclass correlations are equal at each level of the class variable. For instance, the population correlation between the husband's self-evaluation and the wife's partner-evaluation is assumed to equal the population correlation between the wife's self-evaluation and the husband's partner-evaluation. If this assumption is plausible given the sample data, then the partial cross intraclass correlation can be used as the raw-score version of the dyad-level correlation (i.e., not disattenuated by the partial intraclass correlations). If this assumption appears to be violated, then a more general model can be estimated using a structural equations approach (see Griffin & Gonzalez, 1995a).

For the Murray data, the equality of partial cross intraclass correlations appears to hold ($r_{xy'.c} = 0.41$ for the men and $r_{xy'.c} = 0.37$ for the women; the difference was not statistically significant). Also, recall that the partial intraclass correlation for self-evaluation was 0.22 and for partner-evaluation was 0.364. Even though both of these values are statistically different from zero, they are still relatively small and we anticipate this could produce an out-of-bounds value for r_d. The dyad-level correlation r_d for the Murray data turned out to be out-of-bounds, $r_d = 1.39$, making it difficult to interpret as a correlation. Fortunately, because the partial intraclass correlations were significant we can interpret $r_{xy'.c}$ as the raw-score estimate of r_d (i.e., the dyad-level correlation that has not been disattenuated by the partial intraclass correlations), which was 0.392. The Z test for this sample $r_{xy'.c}$ was 6.13, as we saw before.

STRUCTURAL MODELS IN DYADIC RESEARCH

Researchers often wish to go beyond calculating the strength of the linear relation between variables. Most commonly, they wish to go beyond the correlational index and estimate parameters in a structural model in which one or more independent variables determine the value of a dependent variable. There are several ways that this can be accomplished with dyadic data. We will briefly outline some of these models, focusing on examples of their use rather than on detailed computational descriptions.

Regression Models for Dyadic and Individual Effects

The correlational methods for separating dyadic and individual-level effects presented above can be extended to cases with multiple predictor variables. Although such analyses are straightforward for the individual level of analysis, their application to the dyadic level of analysis are more complex. The individual-level analysis is simple because the interdependence between dyadic partners has been "partialled out" of the individual-level correlations, and so the individual-level correlations can be entered as input to standard multiple regression routines or structural equation modelling programs, allowing complete estimation and significance testing through standard programs. The dyad-level correlations, in contrast, measure only interdependent information and therefore violate the independence assumption that is essential to standard regression routines. Thus, even though the dyad-level correlations can also be entered as input to multiple regression routines, the resulting significance tests are not appropriate.

Consider again the results of Stinson & Ickes' (1992) study. In our earlier analysis of the dyad-level and individual-level correlations, we assessed whether the three relevant variables were interrelated at the dyadic level of analysis, at the individual level of analysis, or at both levels of analysis. As an extension of these correlational analyses, we have formulated the model illustrated in Figure 11.4. Such a model allows the estimation of the partial, or unique, effect of each predictor with the other held constant. This path diagram implies that gesture frequency and gaze frequency are both causes of verbalization frequency. Given that our goal in this paper is to illustrate the application of several statistical models, we do not provide psychological motivation for the particular examples we selected. For a possible psychological theory that relates the three variables, see Duncan & Fiske (1977).

The multiple regression model must be estimated separately for the two levels of analysis. Turning first to the individual level, we know that the individual-level correlation between the two predictors (gestures and gazes) is 0.258. This remains unchanged in the regression model, and because it is rather small, we will expect little change between the zero-order correlations and the standardized partial regression coefficient. When the three individual-level correlations (and the appropriate N, see below) are entered into a multiple regression program that

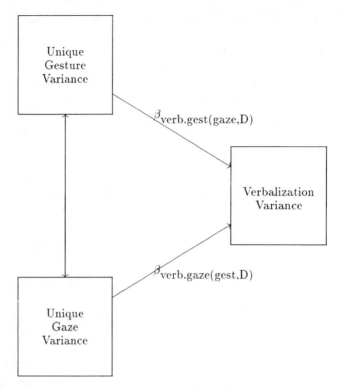

Figure 11.4 Representation for the regression between individual-level effects. All input correlations are the individual-level rs. The variable D represents a set of $N - 1$ dummy codes. We follow the standard notation in the regression literature: the variable to the left of the dot is the dependent variable, the variable(s) to the right of the dot are the predictors, and the variable(s) in the parentheses are variables that have been controlled for, i.e., entered in a previous step

accepts correlations as input (such as the REGRESSION command in *SPSS*; see Table 11.6 for example code), we find that the standardized coefficient for predicting verbalizations from gazes is −0.324 (virtually identical to the individual-level correlation). The coefficient for predicting verbalizations from gestures is −0.002, again virtually the same as the comparable individual-level correlation. These two standardized regression coefficients are denoted $\beta_{verb.gaze(gest)}$ and $\beta_{verb.gest(gaze)}$, respectively.

For this individual-level analysis, the appropriate significance test depends on the number of subjects. However, because the individual-level correlations are actually derived from one score for each dyad, the appropriate N to enter into the multiple regression routine is the number of dyads, *not* the number of subjects. In this case, the correct "sample size" to enter in the multiple regression routine is 24. At this sample size, neither coefficient is significant, although the regression coefficient for gazes is marginal ($t = 1.52$, $p < 0.15$). A method equivalent to that

Table 11.6 Example SPSS code for executing the regression model described in the text. The input correlations are the individual-level correlations r_i between all possible pairs of gesture, gaze, and verbalization frequency

```
matrix data variables = gest gaze verb
   /contents = corr
   /n = 24
begin data
    1
   0.258      1
  -0.086    -0.3251
end data
regression matrix in (*)
   /noorigin
   /dependent = verb
   /method = enter gest gaze
```

described here is to create $N - 1$ dummy codes that represent the dyads, and run the regression of verbalization on the dummy codes, the gesture variable, and the gaze variable. The β's for the gesture and gaze predictors are the standardized coefficients at the individual-level.

The analysis is more complicated for the dyad-level portion of the analysis because of the sample size problem caused by interdependence. That is, each dyadic correlation is based on a different "effective sample size" depending on the degree of dyadic interdependence in the two relevant variables. Two possible, but inexact, solutions to this problem come to mind. First, because each dyadic correlation will be associated with an effective sample size of at least N, the number of dyads, this could be entered into the program as a conservative estimate of sample size. Second, one could use the smallest effective sample size associated with any of the dyad-level correlations in the model. In our example, we will use the second strategy, entering the smallest effective sample size, 29.5 (rounded down to 29), and the three cross intraclass correlations into the *SPSS* multiple regression routine. All possible cross intraclass correlations between the relevant variables (i.e., the raw-score index of the dyad-level correlations) are submitted as input to the regression procedure. In this case, the cross intraclass correlation between the predictors is again moderate, 0.325, indicating that the standardized coefficients will not be much different than the corresponding zero-order correlations. In fact, both standardized regression coefficients remain significant when the two predictors are entered together. The coefficient for gestures is somewhat reduced (0.364, $p < 0.05$, compared to the cross intraclass correlation of 0.479), as is the coefficient for gazes (0.352, $p < 0.05$, compared to 0.471).

It is possible to use this approach for either exchangeable or distinguishable dyads. However, for distinguishable dyads it is also possible to use structural equation modeling, which will yield exact significance tests in the distinguishable case. In such a case, the covariance matrix is entered directly into a structural equation modeling program such as *LISREL* or *EQS*, following the general procedures outlined in Griffin & Gonzalez (1995a). Note again that it is not appropriate to enter the pre-computed dyadic correlations into a structural equation modeling program and obtain significance tests, because the sample size will not be correct.

A Regression Model for Separating Actor and Partner Effects

Earlier we noted that the overall correlation in a dyadic design can be decomposed into underlying correlations representing the dyadic-level and individual-level relations. It is these correlations that were entered into the multiple regression models discussed in the preceding section. However, this particular decomposition is only one of a number of possible models that can be applied in this situation. Another useful way to model the social interaction within a dyad is as a combination of two paths linking X and Y: an actor effect, which represents the extent to which a dyad member's (the "actor") standing on variable X determines that actor's standing on variable Y, and a partner effect, which represents the extent to which the partner's standing on X determines the actor's standing on Y.

In the Stinson & Ickes example, we might ask: "What predicts an individual's verbalization frequency?" An example of an actor–partner model for this situation is now given. An individual actor's speech frequency might be caused by the joint effect of the individual's own gazes and his or her partner's gazes. Following this structural model, which is illustrated in Figure 11.5, leads to the interpretation of the pairwise r_{xy} as the "actor correlation" and the pairwise $r_{xy'}$ as the "partner correlation". To obtain the actor and partner effects in the exchangeable case, it is necessary to partial out the shared component of the actor and partner variance—which means partialling out $r_{xx'}$, the pairwise intraclass correlation on X. The comparison of this model (depicted in Figure 11.5) with the decomposition presented earlier in this chapter (Figure 11.3) illustrates the importance of a theoretical model in guiding and formulating how an analysis should be conducted. Under different models the same correlations r_{xy} and $r_{xy'}$ carry different interpretations.

The actor–partner regression model (introduced in its most general form by Kenny, 1995) can easily be estimated using the pairwise method. The dependent variable of interest (Y) is simply regressed on the X and X' columns, following the same pairwise data setup we have used throughout this chapter. Either the raw regression coefficients or the standardized regression coefficients can be read from the program output and tested for significance using the relevant test from Griffin & Gonzalez (1995b). Like the tests for the pairwise model given earlier, the significance tests for the actor and partner regression coefficients are made up of the four pairwise correlations: $r_{xx'}$, $r_{yy'}$, r_{xy}, and $r_{xy'}$. We will not go through the

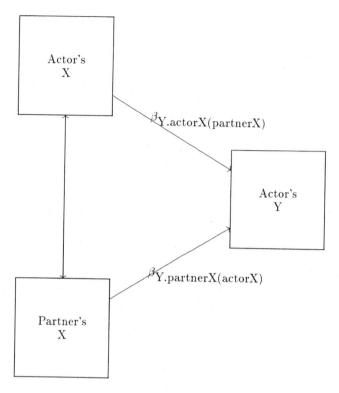

Figure 11.5 Representation of the actor–partner regression model

computational details here, but simply present examples and discuss their interpretation. The technical details are given in Griffin & Gonzalez (1995b).

For the Stinson & Ickes data that we have been using throughout this chapter, the actor correlation r_{xy} between gaze and verbalization was 0.386. In the context of the model shown in Figure 11.5, the standardized regression coefficient was 0.173 ($Z = 0.97$). This standardized regression coefficient is interpreted as the influence on an actor's frequency of verbalization given one standard deviation change on the actor's frequency of gaze, holding constant the partner's frequency of gaze. In this case, the actor effect was not statistically significant. Similarly, the partner correlation $r_{xy'}$ between gaze and verbalization was 0.471. The standardized regression coefficient was 0.372 ($Z = 2.09$). In other words, the influence on the actor's frequency of verbalization given one standard deviation change on the partner's frequency of gaze, holding constant the actor's frequency of gaze, was statistically significant. The partner's gaze frequency was a more powerful predictor of the actor's verbalization frequency than the actor's own gaze frequency. For one possible theoretical analysis of these results see Duncan & Fiske (1977).

A more complicated form of the actor–partner regression model is used for analyzing data from distinguishable dyads, because when there are two different types of dyad members it is usually of interest to examine whether the actor effects and the partner effects vary across the two types of individuals. For example, consider the model presented in Figure 11.6, adapted from Murray, Holmes & Griffin's (1996) study of married couples. In this model, a woman's image of her partner is determined by two causes: her own self-image (the "projection" path labeled *a*, which is an actor effect) and her partner's self-reported self-image (the "matching" path labeled *b*, which is a partner effect). A man's image of his partner is similarly determined by an actor effect (*d*) and a partner effect (*c*).

In such a model, it is of central interest to test whether the actor (projection) paths are equal across sexes, and whether the partner (matching) paths are equal across sexes. This can be most easily done using structural equation modeling, as in the Murray, Holmes & Griffin study, where the fit of the model is compared when the relevant values are set equal and when they are free to vary. If both the actor and the partner effects are equal across the two classes, then *a* and *d* can be pooled and *b* and *c* can be pooled. In a simple model such as this, the pooled structural equation model is essentially equivalent to carrying out the pairwise regression model adjusted for distinguishable dyads, because there the parameters are also averaged across the two types of people. The structural modeling

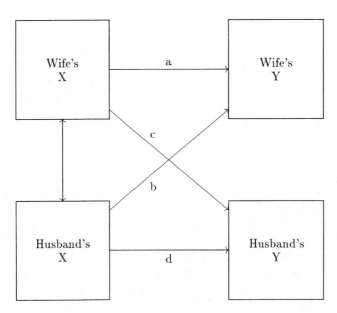

Figure 11.6 Representation of the actor–partner regression model for testing differences in regression coefficients between two classes

approach can be extended to estimate much more complex models, as illustrated in the Murray, Holmes & Griffin paper.

In the Murray, Holmes & Griffin example, the tests revealed that both the actor and partner effects were equal across husbands and wives. Furthermore, both the actor and partner effects were highly significant and almost equal in magnitude (standardized regression coefficients = 0.315 and 0.304, respectively).

The actor–partner regressions are interpreted quite differently than the regressions based on the dyadic or individual-level correlations. The actor–partner models are simple bivariate regressions, and are used to answer whether an actor's score on an outcome variable is determined by that actor's score on a predictor variable or by his or her partner's score on the predictor variable. These models provide estimates that are corrected for interdependence, but they do not specifically model the interdependence itself. The dyadic-level regressions, in contrast, can be bivariate or multiple regressions, but they explicitly model the interdependence within dyads and answer questions at different levels of analysis. Finally, the individual-level regressions may be bivariate or multiple regressions, and they answer whether the unique or unshared qualities of an individual on the outcome variable are determined by some combination of his or her unique qualities on the predictor variables.

EXCHANGEABLE AND DISTINGUISHABLE DYADS IN THE SAME DESIGN: A SPECIAL ACTOR–PARTNER EFFECT

A special case of the actor–partner model is the Kraemer–Jacklin method (Kraemer & Jacklin, 1979). As Kenny (1995) has pointed out, this is a model for analyzing "mixed" dyads. This is applicable when some dyads are made up of distinguishable members and others are made up of exchangeable members. The classic use of the Kraemer–Jacklin method is to examine whether sex differences in mixed-sex dyads arise from direct (actor) effects or indirect (partner) effects. For example, are men in heterosexual couples more aggressive than their partners because they are men (the actor effect) or because they are paired with women (the partner effect)? In the terminology used by Kenny (1995), is the effect of sex on aggression due to an actor effect or a partner effect? This question cannot be answered in a design where all the dyads contain both men and women—instead it requires a mixed design where some dyads contain a man and a woman, some contain two men, and some contain two women. This design allows the researcher to separate the effect of being a man from the effect of being paired with a woman. Mendoza & Graziano (1982) presented an extension of the Kraemer–Jacklin model to multivariate data. This method used contrasts to test the hypotheses assumed within the model.

The basic Kraemer & Jacklin (1979) design can also be handled by the pairwise regression model. In the classic balanced design (using sex differences as an example), k dyads are male–male, k dyads are female–female, and $2k$ dyads are mixed sex, where $k = 1/4N$ (other divisions are possible, but this offers the greatest power because it yields an orthogonal test of the actor and partner hypotheses, see Kenny, 1995). One column codes the sex of the subject and a second column codes the sex of the partner. Two more columns of data are used to code the dependent variable, one coding the outcome variable for the subject and the other coding the outcome variable for the partner.

In the original Kraemer & Jacklin example, there were 12 male–male, 12 female–female and 21 mixed dyads. The outcome variable was frequency of offering one's partner a toy. In the columns representing subject sex and partner sex, it is convenient to code boys −1 and girls +1 (although the codes could be reversed without loss of generality). When the outcome variable is regressed upon these two pairwise variables, the actor effect is simply the partial regression coefficient for the subject sex column and the partner effect is the partial regression coefficient for the partner sex column. Again, these coefficients are tested by a formula based on the four pairwise correlations $r_{xx'}$, $r_{xy'}$, r_{xy} and $r_{xy'}$ (Griffin & Gonzalez, 1995b). In a perfectly balanced design, such as the one described in the preceding paragraph, the actor and partner effects are orthogonal, so that $r_{xx'} = 0$. This restriction simplifies the hypothesis testing phase. However, in the original Kraemer & Jacklin study, the design was not orthogonal because there are 21 rather than 24 mixed dyads.

In this example, the unstandardized coefficient for the actor effect is one-half the mean difference between toy offers made *by* girls vs. boys. The partner effect represents one-half the mean difference between toy offers made *to* girls vs. boys. (Actually, the means are slightly adjusted for the fact that there is an unbalanced design, but the principle is the same). The raw-score coefficients in this case are 0.29 for the actor effect (indicating girls were more likely to offer toys) and 0.48 for the actor effect, indicating that girls were more likely to be offered toys. Both of these values are identical to the estimates from the original method proposed by Kraemer & Jacklin, which involves a much more tedious method of estimation. The Z tests for the two effects were 1.1 (ns) and 1.80 (marginally significant), both very similar to the values obtained by the original method. For more details about the pairwise formulation of the Kraemer & Jacklin method, along with derivations and supporting simulations, see Griffin & Gonzalez (1995b).

CONCLUSION

"But wait a bit," the Oysters cried,
   "Before we have our chat;
For some of us are out of breath
   And all of us are fat!" (Lewis Carroll, *Through the Looking Glass*).

We have given various examples of research questions that can be answered using the pairwise approach. Our approach differs from those that have been suggested by others. The usual approach to dealing with interdependence has been to define new estimators for a variety of special cases. Some of these estimators have not been readily accessible and have been difficult to implement. In contrast, our approach is to alter the way the data are arranged in the data matrix and then use well-known estimators (such as the Pearson correlation, the partial correlation, correction for disattenuation, regression slopes). The pairwise approach is relatively easy to implement and, as demonstrated here, quite general in the range of possible research questions that it permits.

However, statistics should not be used in a vacuum. The use of statistics in research should be guided by the substantive theory relevant to the particular domain, the measurement concerns, and the design issues (Gonzalez, 1995). The pairwise technique provides one piece of the puzzle. The other pieces, equally as important, are also necessary for full advancement of a research area. For instance, researchers should develop paradigms that permit the possibility for interdependence to emerge (see, for example, the paradigm described by Ickes et al., 1986, 1990). Then, armed with statistics for interdependence, relationship researchers can ask new research questions, develop new theory, grapple with measurement issues, and construct new paradigms and research designs. In fact, our own interest in studying the statistics of interdependence grew out of an eagerness to return to research questions that were important during the early stages of our field, which in our opinion have not been adequately resolved.

One of the central phenomena of interest in the history of social psychology was the nature and character of the "group mind". At the turn of the century, French sociologists such as Tarde and Le Bon were fascinated by the difference between the irrational crowd and the rational individual. To them, the crowd was an entity in itself, something more than the sum of its individual parts. However, the phenomenology of the crowd was not amenable to controlled, experimental research and soon dropped out of favor as a topic for research. Later, in the 1930s and 1940s, the group again became the focus of an influential school of researchers in social psychology: the Group Dynamics researchers. Once again, however, this group-based approach to social psychology was soon left behind, in part because of statistical design considerations. In particular, the realization that statistical dependency among group members' scores made the analysis of group data more complicated than individual data led to the virtual abandonment of experimental group research in favor of the use of confederates, paper-and-pencil descriptions, audiotapes, and similar individual-focused methods (Steiner, 1974, 1986).

It is our contention that with the introduction of conceptually and computationally straightforward techniques for assessing and separating group- and individual-level effects, we can return to the classic questions that fascinated earlier generations. Some of these questions have been addressed in recent years because of the availability of models developed by David Kenny and his colleagues (Kenny, 1990; Kenny, 1995; Kenny & La Voie, 1984, 1985; see Kenny & Albright, 1987 for an applied example). Our own work on the pairwise framework has been greatly influenced by the models of Kenny and his colleagues. We can imagine few questions more central to social psychology than those pertaining to when—or whether—groups act as more than the sum of their parts. A good place to start addressing these questions is with the simplest possible group structure: the dyad. (We are currently generalizing the pairwise method presented here to groups of arbitrary size, Gonzalez & Griffin, 1995a.) We hope that the techniques presented in this chapter for dyadic data will provide tools that will be useful in asking and, we hope, answering, stimulating theoretical questions about dyads and the individuals that comprise them.

ACKNOWLEDGEMENTS

This research was supported by a grant from the National Science Foundation (Gonzalez) and by a grant from the Social Sciences and Humanities Research Council of Canada (Griffin). We thank Bill Ickes for supplying data and for his general support of our efforts. We also thank Sandra Murray for supplying data.

Section III

Communication

Section Editor: Kathryn Dindia
University of Wisconsin, Milwaukee, WI, USA

Duck, West & Acitelli open the 2nd edition of the *Handbook on Personal Relationships* asking whether personal relationships researchers are studying ordinary persons' relationships. They argue that there is a discrepancy between ordinary persons' relationships and personal relationships as represented in personal relationships research. Specifically, they present four criticisms of personal relationships research. First, they argue that personal relationships research is limited to heterosexual romantic relationships of college students and this leaves out the vast majority of personal relationships. Second, they argue that researchers treat relationships as static, monolithic containers of two pre-formed, intact, stable, independent selves, whereas real persons' relationships are dynamic processes involving change and individuals in relationships are open-ended, unstable and changing and are constructed in relationships. Third, they argue that personal relationships researchers have ignored the fact that real relationships are conducted in social and cultural contexts that impose a view on what is normal and acceptable and that these cultural and social views affect both partners' perceptions of their relationships and researchers' perceptions of relationships. Fourth, they argue that relationships do not exist in a vacuum but take place in a social, cultural and economic context which influences relating and relationships, and that this too has been ignored by personal relationships researchers. These four themes are elaborated in the various chapters in this section of the *Handbook*.

Bochner, Ellis & Tillman address an aspect of real persons relationships that has been largely overlooked in the personal relationships literature, the stories people tell about their relationships. Their chapter focuses on narrative modes of investigating and representing interpersonal relationships. Specifically, they argue that we create and understand our relationships in the form of stories and we reveal our understandings of our relationships to others by telling them our relationship stories. Relationships are given shape and meaning by the stories that form and inform their enactments (Bochner, Ellis & Tillman, this volume). The authors discuss canonical and popular stories and their influence on personal stories. They review three narrative approaches to personal relationships: accounts, storied lives and evocative narratives. In sum, these authors argue persuasively for a narrative approach, rather than the traditional social scientific approach, to personal relationships.

Rather than updating the article on relational dialectics published in the 1988 edition of the *Handbook* (Baxter, 1988), Baxter & Montgomery present a new and original discussion of this perspective. In particular, they discuss the commonly shared assumptions of a dialectical perspective, major scholarly research programs emerging from a dialectical perspective, and directions for future research based on Bakhtin's dialogic perspective. Dialectical perspectives, by definition, address several of the criticisms presented by Duck, West & Acitelli in the opening chapter to the *Handbook*. According to a dialectical perspective, relationships are not static but rather dynamic, involving contradiction, change, interdependence and contextual embeddedness. Further, from a dialogic view, individuals are not contained, pre-formed, intact, stable and sovereign selves, rather individuals are fluid, social, open-ended, unstable and changing. Selves are constructed in relationships. To a lesser degree Baxter & Montgomery also address Duck, West & Acitelli's third and fourth criticisms, arguing that relationships exist in social and cultural contexts that affect the experience and meaning of dialectical contradictions in relationships.

Parks specifically addresses Duck, West & Acitelli's fourth criticism, that no relationship exists in a vacuum, by discussing the social networks in which relationships are situated. Parks argues that relationships and networks are connected from relationship beginning to end. To develop his argument, Parks first discusses the dimensions of relationship development and deterioration, and second discusses the features of communication networks that are most relevant for relationships. Parks then reviews the research linking the development of personal relationships with the partners' surrounding social networks and advances a theoretic perspective for understanding these linkages. The social contextual perspective advocated by Parks fills a theoretic void in the interpersonal communication literature by explaining how personal relationships are situated in the larger social network and how participants' social networks affect and are affected by the process of relationship development and deterioration.

Metts discusses the role of facework in personal relationships. Metts argues that one of the most pervasive yet seldom studied aspects of personal relationships is the degree to which partners enhance, preserve or diminish each other's desired identity, or face. Metts demonstrates in this chapter the utility of a face perspective for the study of personal relationships. Metts begins the chapter with a discussion of "face" and "facework", based on the writings of Goffman, and illustrates the contribution of Goffman's perspective to personal relationships by discussing the management of relational transgressions, the management of conflict, and the management of a couple's joint identity in public. Metts then moves to a discussion of face and facework as elaborated by Brown & Levinson in politeness theory, and illustrates the contributions of this perspective to the study of personal relationships by discussing the role of positive politeness in the provision of social support and relationship disengagement. In particular, Metts's chapter addresses Duck, West & Acitelli's second criticism, in that it clearly indicates that partners' identities (and couples' joint identity) are not pre-formed and stable but are greatly affected by partners' facework.

Werking goes beyond the tradition of studying heterosexual romantic relationships by discussing cross-sex friendship. Werking conducts a critical examination of the existing cross-sex friendship literature and, in particular, addresses the ideological assumptions underlying research conducted in the area of cross-sex friendship. Werking argues that the selection of research topics in the area of cross-sex friendship reflects an ideological stance and that existing studies privilege an individualistic and heterosexist view of cross-sex friendship. Although her observations and recommendations are directed toward the cross-sex friendship literature, they are useful to the larger audience of personal relationships researchers in general because the ideological assumptions she speaks of are found in all areas of personal relationships research.

Finally, in the last chapter in this section of the *Handbook*, I address the issue of self-disclosure from a transactional/dialectical perspective. Primarily, I elaborate on the second of Duck, West & Acitelli's criticisms, that relationships are not static containers of two stable individuals. I do this in reference to the phenomenon of self-disclosure. In particular I argue that self-disclosure is not a dichotomous event (either a person has disclosed or has not disclosed; either a person is out of the closet or is not out of the closet). Rather, in real relationships self-disclosure is an ongoing process that is inherently dialectical in nature. Individuals in relationships disclose on the same topics over time, revealing, then concealing, then revealing. . . . Full or total disclosure is impossible from a transactional/dialectical perspective because individuals are always changing. In particular, the ongoing processes of individual identity and relationship development mutually affect and are affected by the ongoing process of self-disclosure.

Duck, West & Acitelli conclude their opening chapter to the *Handbook* by urging personal relationships researchers to investigate "relating" rather than "relationships", to shift from focusing on the noun to the verb, and to focus on how individuals continually construct relationships and how relationships continually construct individuals. The chapters in this section of the *Handbook* respond to this call, elaborating the processes, contexts, meanings and interdependencies of relating. These chapters begin to address the criticisms posed by Duck, West & Acitelli. However, much is left to the future and we hope that the chapters in this section of the *Handbook* have provided useful guidelines for making future personal relationships research true to the nature of real persons' relationships. Individuals and relationships are processes and therefore always unfinished business (Duck, 1990). So is personal relationships theory and research.

Chapter 12

Relationships as Stories

Arthur P. Bochner, Carolyn Ellis
and
Lisa M. Tillmann-Healy
University of South Florida, Tampa, FL, USA

We are born into a world of stories. Our births mark the beginning of a distinctive story in which each of us assumes a leading part. Our deaths end our unique stories, which live on in the minds and hearts of our survivors. Between birth and death, we rely on stories circulating through our culture to make sense of our everyday lives and guide our actions. Much of who we are and what we do originates in the tales passed down to us and the stories we take on as our own. As Robert Coles (1989, p. 24) says: "Few would deny that we all have stories in us which are a compelling part of our psychological and ideological make-up". Barbara Myerhoff (1978, p. 272) refers to human beings as "*Homo narrans*", a term that places narrative and storytelling at the core of human existence. Undoubtedly narrative plays a crucial role in understanding and organizing human experience.

Nevertheless social scientists are just beginning to appreciate the profound significance of narrative in the lived experience of personal relationships. The first edition of the *Handbook of Personal Relationships* (Duck, 1988a) gave no systematic attention to the connections between narrative and relationship development. Accounts written in diaries were discussed briefly by Harvey and his associates (Harvey, Hendrick & Tucker, 1988) in a chapter on "self-report methods". The authors emphasized subjective thoughts and feelings associated with personal relationships and complained that "[s]ocial science has formalized the process of researching personal relationships but often without 'touching' us in the process" (Harvey, Hendrick & Tucker, 1988, p. 113). In a chapter on "rules, scripts and prototypes", Ginsburg (1988) also mentioned the potential significance of studying accounts, calling attention to the "words and phrases" (but not the stories) interactants use to justify their involvement in personal relationships.

Handbook of Personal Relationships, 2nd edn. Edited by Steve Duck.
© 1997 John Wiley & Sons Ltd.

The terms "narrative" and "storytelling", however, were not included in the index of the *Handbook* (Duck, 1988a).

TOWARD MEANING

Over the past 10 years, interest in narrative among other social scientists has mushroomed. Scholars in several disciplines have inaugurated new journals promoting the narrative study of lives (Josselson & Lieblich, 1993; McCabe, 1993), encouraged storied versions of interpersonal events (Denzin & Lincoln, 1994; Harvey, 1996), and published an extensive corpus of books and monographs reflecting a shift from analytic to narrative modes of investigating and representing interpersonal life (see Baumeister & Newman, 1994; Bochner, 1994; Bochner & Ellis, 1992, 1995, Bochner & Waugh, 1995; Brody, 1987; Butler & Rosenblum, 1991; Bruner, 1986, 1990; Coles, 1989; Denzin 1989a, 1989b, 1993; Ellis, 1993, 1995a, 1995b, 1996; Fisher, 1987; Frank, 1991, 1993; Gergen, 1992; Gergen & Gergen, 1986, 1987; Harvey, Flanery & Morgan, 1986; Harvey, Weber & Orbuch, 1990; Kerby, 1991; Linden, 1993; Maines, 1993; McIntyre, 1981; Mishler, 1986, 1995; Mukaia, 1989; Paget, 1993; Parry, 1991; Parry & Doan, 1994; Polkinghorne, 1988; Ronai, 1992, 1994; Richardson, 1990; Riessman, 1990, 1992; Rosaldo, 1984; Rosenwald & Ochberg, 1992; Sarbin, 1986; Stone, 1988; Swados, 1991; Yalom, 1989; Yalom & Elkin, 1974; Zola, 1982a, 1982b). Collectively, these works underscore the significance of narrative as both a way of knowing about and a way of participating in the social world. The turn toward narrative promoted by these works coincides with two related developments influencing research on personal relationships: (1) the turn away from orthodox approaches to scientific representation; and (2) the turn toward interpretive perspectives that focus on human sense-making.

The Crisis of Representation

Postmodernist and poststructuralist writers have seriously challenged some of our most venerable assumptions about scientific knowledge and truth (Denzin, 1992; Dickens & Fontana, 1991; Foucault, 1970; Kuhn, 1970; Lyotard, 1984; Rorty, 1979; Rosenau, 1992). In particular, these writers have impeached the theory of language on which orthodox approaches to scientific inquiry are based. The correspondence theory of knowledge, which is the foundation of scientific method, attributes significance to language scientifically only insofar as language can achieve its denotative and referential function of describing objects in a world *out there*, apart from and independent of language users (Bochner & Waugh, 1995; Rorty, 1967, 1982, 1989). Accordingly, the language used in scientific theories implicitly assumes that words represent *the* world, rather than specifying *a* world, and can denote what is *out there* in the world apart from, or prior to, the interpretations of language users. Conforming to this view, orthodox communication theory, for example, treats messages and meanings as "things" or "objects" that are merely *transferred* from one person to another, reducing what is problematic in communicative experience to metaphors such as *information processing*, *social exchange*, *transmission* or *attributional errors*. Communication thus becomes a kind of *external object*, a commodity to be packaged and exchanged (Bochner & Waugh, 1995).

The history and philosophy of science since Kuhn (1970) shows that we should understand language as not simply a tool for mirroring what is discoverable about reality, but as an ongoing and constitutive part of reality (Bochner & Waugh, 1995). The assumption that language is a neutral medium of communication has been displaced by a deeper understanding of the ways we use language to deal with the world (Kerby, 1991). What we can say in language about the world inevitably involves the indistinguishable provocations of the world *and* the interventions of language by which we make claims about it (Bochner & Waugh, 1995; Rorty, 1982). The world we seek to describe as social scientists does not exist in the form of the sentences we write when theorizing about it (Rorty, 1989).

As the model of language underlying social science research practices necessarily shifts from the presumption of neutral description to engaged communication, from language as a tool to language as a means of coping, the focus of social science research shifts accordingly from the goal of describing a pre-existing world of stable objects to the goals of understanding how, as social scientists, we are part of the world we investigate and the ways we use language to make and change it (Bochner & Waugh, 1995; Steier, 1991). Our focus becomes showing how meaning is performed and negotiated by speakers and interpreters (Bochner & Waugh, 1995), a decidedly narrative endeavor. Although academic disciplines deeply entrenched in the correspondence theory of knowledge, such as mainstream psychology and sociology, have been slow to respond to the challenges of postmodernism, a new generation of social scientists who understand and appreciate language as a way of dealing with the world are drawn increasingly to a narrative approach to inquiry.

The Interpretive Turn

Interpretive approaches to social science focusing on human sense-making have gained wider acceptance and legitimation. If language cannot be differentiated from the world and we cannot remove language from our lives, then our understanding of the empirical world and our hope for coping with the world must originate in something other than modes of representation presumed to mirror the world. By showing that all knowledge claims rely on contingencies of language and, however "objective" or "scientific", inevitably involve "attaching significance" by interpreting (Gergen, 1973, 1982; Maturana, 1991; Rabinow & Sullivan, 1987; Schutz, 1971; Steedman, 1991; Taylor, 1977), writers championing the causes of phenomenology (Berger & Luckmann, 1966; Schutz, 1971), hermeneutics (Bleicher, 1980; Gadamer, 1989; Taylor, 1977), social construction

(Gergen, 1973; Gergen & Davis, 1985; Shotter & Gergen, 1989), sociology of knowledge (Berger and Luckmann, 1966), and interpretive interactionism (Denzin, 1989a, 1989b) gradually inspired a wider acceptance of alternative ways of understanding the empirical world and displaying its possible meanings. Particularly in the human disciplines, where we are inside what we are studying, there is only and always interpretation (Denzin, 1993; Taylor, 1977).

As attention turned toward what it means to live in a mediated world, writers across the divides of the human sciences concentrated on the issue of how people use language to make sense of their lived experiences. Geertz (1973, p. 5) portrays anthropology as "not an experimental science in search of law, but an interpretive one in search of meaning". Defining psychology as an interpretive discipline, Bruner (1990, p. 2) refers to meaning as "the central concept of psychology". Harvey and his associates (Harvey et al., 1992; Weber & Harvey, 1994) suggest that persons are "inexorably driven to search for meaning", and successful coping with stressful turning points in life is dependent on one's ability to construct meanings. Bochner (1994) argues that displaying how people do things together in the process of "making meanings" should be a central focus in the study of interpersonal communication; and Duck & Pittman (1994, p. 683) maintain that "the construction of relationships is part of a wider tendency to co-construct meaning with others . . .".

MEANINGS THROUGH STORIES

The interpretive turn in social science research shifts the focus of inquiry from objects to meanings (Rabinow & Sullivan, 1987). Of particular interest is the interactive and conversational work of constructing meanings, the process of making sense of experiences by situating them in an intelligible frame. "The primary human mechanism for attaching meaning to human experiences", writes Brody (1987, p. 5), "is to tell stories about them". Narrative—the stories people tell about their lives—is both a means of "knowing" and a way of "telling" about the social world (Richardson, 1990). By framing our experiences in the form of stories, we investigate what they mean to us, and we make what we understand about our experiences accessible to others by telling them our stories. As Stone (1988, p. 244) concluded at the end of her detailed study of family stories, "Our meanings are almost always inseparable from stories, in all realms of life".

Storytelling is not only the way we understand our relationships, but also the means by which our relationships are fashioned. A personal relationship, in this sense, is a work of art, something made rather than given (Weinstein, 1988). Co-created by the joint actions of two people, a personal relationship lives as a contingent sequence of intertwined experiences given shape and meaning by the stories that form and inform its enactments. To have or be in a relationship is to have or be in a story and, usually, to want to tell about it. When we tell others about our relationships, we portray events in the form and language of stories:

who did what to whom, where, when and why. These "acts of meaning", as Bruner (1990) calls them, give content to our relationships. Through the signifying practices of narration, the abstract construct we refer to as "relationship" assumes concrete meaning and value. Thus, a personal relationship may be construed as the conversational work through which two people negotiate, co-construct and story the meanings and values of essentially incomplete experiences (Duck, 1994a). All couples face the sense-making problem of transforming vague experiences into stories.

The precise connection between experience and story is hotly contested among narrative theorists. Is life narratively structured or is human narration an *ad hoc* grafting of story onto experience? Some writers allege that humans impose narrative structures on their experiences. Louis Mink (1969–1970), for example, argues that life is not lived as a story. Instead, stories are projected onto experience after the fact. Accordingly, the meanings of experience are not given by or inherent in the experience itself. As Hayden White (1980, p. 8) observes: "It is because real events do not offer themselves as stories that their narrativization is so difficult". When we form stories out of lived events, we give them structure and meaning which, as Shotter (1987, p. 235) suggests, "they do not in themselves possess but which none the less they will afford or allow".

Other writers, however, dispute the idea that stories arbitrarily impose a narrative structure on memories. They argue that experience seems to call forth narration, not only because humans feel a need to tell stories about their lives but also because "consciousness is itself an incipient story" (Crites, 1971, p. 297). Storytelling is a direct and obvious form of recollecting memories because the modalities of experience are temporal and the images preserved in memory are cinematic, transient episodes that gain significance and continuity by being situated in a story (Crites, 1971). Alasdair McIntyre (1981, p. 197) opposes the idea that experience can be severed from narrative because ". . . we all live out narratives in our lives and . . . we understand our lives in terms of the narratives that we live out . . .". McIntyre's sentiments are echoed by Kerby (1991, p. 42), who argues that "our unexamined life is already a quasi-narrative, and that lived time is already a drama of sorts". Accordingly, the prenarrative level of experience constitutes what Ricoeur (1983) called "a demand for narrative". Life anticipates narrative.

The dispute over the connection between lives and stories about them revolves mainly around the question of whether stories falsify experience. What is the truth value of a story that depicts meanings attached to one's lived experiences? To say that stories are imposed on experience is to suggest that narrative gives experience a structure it does not have, that stories fictionalize life. Shotter (1987) expresses this point of view when he laments the distortions introduced by plot structures of stories. Stories can have the effect of giving a determinate ordering to indeterminate and incomplete experiences. Because stories about relationships are based on details that often are vague and uncertain, that is, open to many interpretations, Shotter (1987) seeks an alternative to narratives that would be more grounded in facts and less prone to distortion. The alternative he chooses is a lexicon of tropes along the lines advanced by Barthes' *A Lover's Discourse* (1983), because Barthes' "dictionary" does not promote the illusion of completeness or order implied by many stories.

Shotter's (1987) concern about the distortions of narratives, however, runs the risk of limiting the ground claimed by narrative to that of a mirrored retrieval of the past. He is correct to say that narratives cannot depict the way things are or were, and this is precisely the point. Narrative truth seeks to keep the past alive in the present; through narrative we learn to understand the meanings and significance of the past as incomplete, tentative and revisable according to contingencies of present life circumstances. The factual distortions that may arise from contingencies of narrative emplotment are worrisome only if one sees narrative interpretation as a neutral attempt to mirror the facts of one's life, to recover already constituted meanings. But it is not the "facts" themselves that one tries to redeem through narrative tellings, but rather an articulation of the significance and meaning of one's experiences; it is within the frame of a story that "facts" gain their importance. Life stories are thus based on "facts" but not determined by them. "Facts" achieve significance and intelligibility contextually by being articulated within a temporal frame that considers what came before and what comes after. Stories that address the meanings of a life always seek a way of extending them into the future (Rosenwald, 1992).

The kind of truth narratives seek is not akin to correspondence with prior meanings assumed to be constituted in prenarrative experience. Scholars need not assume that narratives aim to represent lives correctly, only that narrators believe they are doing so. One narrative interpretation of events can be judged against another, but there is no standard by which to measure any narrative against the meaning of events themselves because the meaning of prenarrative experience is constituted in its narrative expression. Life and narrative are inextricably and dialectically connected. Life both anticipates telling and draws meaning from it. Narrative is both about living and part of it.

To eschew human storytelling because of its possible distortions is to miss or ignore the interpretive importance of narrative for understanding and accepting life's contingencies. We are not scientists seeking laws that govern our behavior; we are storytellers seeking meanings that help us cope with our circumstances. Our stories must be adequate for the situations with which we must deal. Even if we wanted to, we could not turn off our narrative sensibilities. As adults we have lost any semblance of narrative innocence by being socialized into a narrative realm of consciousness. We use language, and we have seen, heard, read and interpreted stories; we are already embedded in a story, and we are committed to a life imbued with meaning (Kerby, 1991). We tell our stories in a particular style, for a particular purpose, at a particular time. Often our purpose is to foster a story of the past that helps us function effectively in the present. Our tellings rework, refigure and remake our past in accordance with a future onto which we project our possibilities. Thus narrative truth is pragmatic truth (Spence, 1982). The question is not whether narratives convey the way things actually were, but rather what narratives do, what consequences they have, to what uses they can be put.

NARRATIVE AND TIME

A relationship is an historical process; time is the medium of relationship; change its constant. The dynamic, temporal qualities of relationships are, at once, the most obvious and most frustrating aspects of relationship life with which researchers must cope. It is one thing to say that relationships are developmental, that they evolve over time. It is considerably more difficult, however, to know how to incorporate time meaningfully in research on relationships. Narrative is the way people express a continuity of experience over time (Crites, 1971, 1986). Moreover, to the extent we, as social scientists, seek to represent relationship life as dynamic process, we must use the resources of narrative to express the movement and modalities of change over time. We must not only understand how couples use narrative as a means of coping with contingencies of time and order, but we also must use it ourselves as a form of writing that expresses the ebb and flow of lives lived together over time. As Crites (1971, pp. 303, 306) tells it:

> Narrative alone can contain the full temporality of experience in a unity of form . . . Only narrative form can contain the tensions, the surprises, the disappointments and reversals and achievements of actual temporal experience.

Personal relationships are lived within the tensions constituted by memories of the past and anticipations of the future. Our personal identities seem largely contingent on how well we can bridge the remembered past with the anticipated future to provide a continuity of meaningful experience across time. The narrative challenge to which many stories are put is a desire for a continuity of experience over time (Crites, 1986). The stories we tell are remembrances of the past situated in connection to the present moment in which they are recollected and projected toward an anticipated but uncertain future. "The present of things past and the present of things future", says Crites (1971, p. 302), "are the tension of every moment of experience, both united in that present and qualitatively differentiated by it". Thus, our storied accounts of past lived experiences appropriate the past in the interest of the future (Crites, 1986). It is not uncommon to recognize the changes and revisions we make as we edit the stories we tell about our past, in part because the moment of telling has changed and in part because our vision of the future has been altered. Storytelling thus promotes "a continuous life of experience", forging coherence from the stream of experience flowing across the temporal coordinates of one's life.

CANONICAL, POPULAR AND PERSONAL STORIES

Narrative interpretation is a method of negotiating and renegotiating meanings in a world of others. Any storied account of an event is subject to the evaluation of others—its audience—and thus must draw on situated narrative conventions and cultural typifications to achieve intelligibility. Models of intelligibility endemic to our culture constrain both how we tell our stories and what stories we can tell. In particular, narratives that become culturally "normative" function to legitimate dominant forms of understanding and organizing reality and subsequently operate as a form of social control (Langellier & Peterson, 1993).

Canonical forms are stories that represent the generally accepted version in a particular culture, the "right story" which, on the whole, is taken for granted as the way things are supposed to work (Bruner, 1990; Yerby, Buerkel-Rothfuss & Bochner, 1995). Elizabeth Stone (1988, p. 50) suggests that families have a special interest in promoting canonical tales:

> The fact is that the family, any family, has a major stake in perpetuating itself, and in order to do so it must unrelentingly push the institutions that preserve it—the institution of marriage especially, but also the institution of heterosexual romantic love, which, if all goes the way the family would have it go, culminates in marriage, children, and enhanced family stability.

Canonical stories express the boundaries of acceptable relationship and family practices against which alternative stories are judged. When a person's actions deviate from the canonical story, the person may feel a strong need to explain, justify, excuse or legitimize these actions (Scott & Lyman, 1968). For example, Riessman (1990) observes that individuals whose marriages end in divorce go to great lengths to explain why they are divorced; the canonical story sets the expectation, after all, that married persons will live "happily ever after", together until death. As Riessman (1990) notes, the divorced person typically feels the need to convince other people that it was right to leave the marriage, because in our culture it is taken for granted that marriage is "a desired and honored state; one cannot walk away from it lightly" (Riessman, 1990, p. 78). On such painful occasions, the work of narrative accounts is not only to provide a meaningful defense and justification for one's actions, but also to provide a means for surviving separation and loss (Harvey, Flanery & Morgan, 1986; Weber, Harvey & Stanley, 1987; Weiss, 1975). These accounts respond to the canonical stories against which they must be measured. Gay and lesbian families, interracial marriages, single-parent families, families with adopted children, and childless couples, to name a few notable cases, are recognizable examples of relationship stories lived out against a background of "official" canonical stories, that silence, closet or otherwise marginalize these forms of lived relationship life.

Many of the stories that are crucial to the development of interpersonal relationships emphasize personal troubles and existential dilemmas (Denzin, 1989a, 1989b). Our storytelling is an effort to make sense of epiphanies, what Denzin (1993) refers to as "existential turning points", which may include such personal traumas as incest, alcoholism, family violence, unexpected death, chronic illness, abortion, adultery and betrayal. Tales about such experiences emphasize both the crisis and the recovery. Denzin (1991, 1993, 1995) sees these existential narratives as stories embedded in meaning systems made available or forced upon us by our culture and its textual representations. These personal narratives are drawn from popular forms of communication—music, television and film—that shape the meaning and values we attach not only to epiphanies but also to the quotidian experiences of romance, love, intimacy and sexuality.

Portraying humans as voyeurs adrift in a sea of visual and aural symbols, Denzin (1991, 1993, 1995) argues that the images and meanings that flow through cinema, television and music teach us ways of seeing, feeling, talking and thinking. Thus, we live in a second-hand world of consciousness (Mills, 1963) mediated, commodified and dispatched by mass communications. Accordingly, stories transmitted by popular culture are received passively and eventually become part of what we take for granted in performing our relationships. Thus, many of the meanings we think we make and live ourselves may actually be chosen for us, not by us. Our dreams and crises are screened for us by the cinematic world through which our consciousness is mediated. As a consequence, writes Denzin (1993, p. 5), "we become storied versions of somebody else's version of who we should be".

Although Denzin's argument exaggerates the degree to which our own experiences are manipulated and replaced by the fictions staged by popular culture, the attention he draws to the ways everyday social life interacts with the productions of popular culture raises important issues for narrative research. Undoubtedly, we need to study the ways in which cinema and personal relationships interact with and mutually inform each other. In Denzin's terms, we need to become "the projectors that screen for ourselves the very histories we come to call our own" (1993, p. 10); hidden assumptions become exposed when we are able to retell the course by which our stories were secured, the stories about our stories (Rosenwald, 1992). If we are to become authors rather than carriers of our own stories, we need to better understand why we talk the way we do about our crises and their resolutions, as well as what options exist for reframing or inventing new terms for understanding and articulating the meanings of these epiphanies.

Human beings are not condemned entirely to live out the stories passed on through cultural productions and family traditions. Often we seek to define ourselves and our lives by stories of our own making, stories that conflict with or deviate from the expected, usual or conventional. Much of the work of personal narrative involves mitigating the constraints of canonical and cultural conventions. As Bruner (1990, p. 68) indicates, the power of narrative rests not only on an ability to understand what is culturally canonical but also "to account for deviations that can be incorporated in narrative". Many personal narratives attempt to authorize and/or legitimate marginalized, exceptional or particular experiences. These narratives function as oppositional stories that seek to reform or transform canonical ones. Personal and relational development are facilitated not by strict compliance of stories to conventions but by the tensions and conflicts between them (Rosenwald, 1992). If our stories did not thwart or contest received and canonical stories, we would have no expectation of change, no account for conflict, no reason for diversity, no real demand to account for our actions, no sense of agency. We would be locked forever within the walls of normative stories.

One problem with Denzin's cultural production thesis is simply that stories are underdetermined by narrative conventions. Social actors continually remake and remystify the meanings of their social worlds despite, or perhaps because of, the power culture brandishes against them. It is precisely the workings of these meaning-centered negotiations between people and cultural productions that is missed, slighted or overlooked by an insistence on the imperial control of culture (Sherwood, Smith & Alexander, 1993). When we look at how people articulate and use personal narratives, we learn that cultural forces are not sovereign in the realm of human subjectivity (Rosenwald, 1992). Culture may establish the routine parameters of experience but it does not fill in all permutations. Humans have a dazzling capacity to conceive optional ways of reforming or reframing the meaning of their actions (Bruner, 1990). Moreover, socialization is rarely successful in consigning human desire to the demands of culture. As Rosenwald points out, there is always an uncomfortable tension between restless desire and stabilizing conventions (Rosenwald, 1992). Culture's grip is not unbreakable. Surely, we reap certain rewards by abiding by rules and conventions, but just as surely we may recognize, however momentarily, the potential tyranny and numbing effect of blindly succumbing to them. Regarding family stories, Stone (1988, p. 195) acknowledges that often we learn that they are "... not at all what we wanted, but a burden we either live with uncomfortably or struggle later on to get rid of".

Many people come to a decisive moment in their lives when they feel a need to take charge of their stories, subverting the constraints of received and inherited stories by "drawing alternatives out of the vast realm of unremembered, neglected, minimized, and even repudiated events" (Parry, 1991, p. 53). This point may be particularly significant for the course of a personal relationship because, as Parry observes, in deconstructing and re-forming received stories we learn to see our own stories as connected to the stories of significant others:

> while each of us is the central character in our own stories, we are also characters in the stories of all those others with whom we are connected, whether by marriage, family, friendship, or simply by being an inhabitant of the earth [Parry's emphasis] (Parry, 1991, p. 45).

This feature gives personal narratives a relational quality.

We expect other people involved in our lives to play certain roles and be certain characters within the plot of our lives. Other people also have a place for us in their stories; they assume we will play certain parts in their stories. Who we are in their stories and who they are in ours presumably are meshed. When they are not meshed, we introduce the possibility of confusion, misunderstanding, mystification or betrayal (Goffman, 1959, 1967; Laing, 1969). Normally, some degree of mutuality and agreement on the script is expected; the supportive roles we play in one another's stories help us maintain a stake in each other's lives— albeit a fragile one. In examining any particular relationship between people, one can ask: "Who is he expected to be as a character in her story? What role does she want him to play in hers?"

Within a marriage, however, it may be necessary to do more than simply coordinate individual stories. Usually, there is a desire for a collective story, "our story", the couple's story (Parry, 1991). The two stories of the individuals may be retained, but there is a need, if not a demand, to underscore the couple's togetherness by negotiating a co-authored or co-constructed story (Bochner & Ellis, 1995; Ellis & Bochner, 1992) that can become a shared story of their life together. The two individuals become characters in a single story of "us" rather than merely role players in each other's separate stories which may, of course, still be retained.

Bochner & Ellis (1992; 1995) conceive *narrative co-construction* as an active method to create stories that address turning points in relationships. They provide procedures for comparing and synthesizing partner's perceptions, expectations and aspirations for a given relationship. These procedures can function effectively both in therapeutic and research situations, encouraging each member of a family or relationship to have a voice and play a part in plotting the course of their relationship.

NARRATIVES OF PERSONAL RELATIONSHIPS

All research on personal relationships can be considered narrative insofar as it tries to make sense of relationship life by placing it within an intelligible frame of reference. We may call what we do "theorizing", but the theories we spin are never free from interpretations that rely on certain conventions for turning "knowing" into "telling" (White, 1980). And no matter how hard we try to make our tellings neutral and data-based, our research promotes a normative plotline that risks turning "is" into "ought" (Montgomery, 1988). Social science research consists of hundreds of studies of attraction, courtship, love, marriage, parenting and family life that, taken collectively, advances a story line, whether intentional or not, about the "natural" course of personal relationships. These studies provide a discourse on personal relationships that may unwittingly pass on the logic of the culture, both the culture of causal social scientists (Shotter, 1987) and the larger interests of the society in which social science is deeply entrenched (Gergen, 1973, 1982; Lannamann, 1991). In our view, there has been far too little interest in examining closely the attitudes and values our research transmits to the public, but for our purposes here we need only make the point that social science is itself a canonical discourse on relationship life that promotes ways of thinking and talking about this subject.

Narrative approaches to personal relationships show how people breach canonical conventions and expectations, how they cope with exceptional, difficult and transformative relationship crises, how they invent new ways of speaking when old ways fail them, how they make the absurd sensible and the disastrous manageable, and how they turn calamities into gifts. What is special and important about a storied approach to personal relationships, and what may make it so appallingly difficult to digest for more orthodox relationship researchers, is its oppositional stance. Stories activate subjectivity and compel emotional response; stories long to be used rather than analyzed, to be told and retold rather than theorized and settled, to offer lessons for further conversation rather than truths without any rivals; and stories promise the companionship of intimate detail as a substitute for the loneliness of abstracted facts. Thus, stories not only breach ordinary and canonical inscriptions about living, but ideally they challenge norms of writing and research, forcing us to reconsider the goals of our research, the forms we use for expressing relationship experience, and the divisions we accept and enforce that separate literature from social science. Below we briefly review three narrative approaches to personal relationships: (1) accounts; (2) storied lives; and (3) evocative narratives. Collectively these approaches represent an attempt to use personal narratives to show, tell, and analyze the lived experiences of personal relationships.

Accounts

Scott & Lyman (1968) introduced the term "account" into sociological research to emphasize how talk is used to repair and/or restore order when relational expectations have been violated. Inspired by accounts of loss presented in Weiss' (1975) landmark work on marital separation, Harvey and his associates (see, e.g., Harvey, Agostinelli & Weber, 1989; Harvey, Orbuch & Weber, 1990, 1992; Harvey et al., 1992; Harvey, Weber & Orbuch, 1990; Harvey, Wells & Alvarez, 1978; Harvey & Uematsu, 1995) broadened the concept of account beyond its earlier microsociological application. They developed a storied version of the account-making process and initiated a program of research on relationship loss that focuses on empirical analyses of the motivations, content and functions of accounts. Although they grant that accounts apply to positive as well as negative experiences, Harvey and his associates centered their research on account-making as a narrative strategy for working through relationship loss (Weber & Harvey, 1994).

Using interviews, diaries, archival materials and other non-reactive procedures for producing accounts, Harvey and his colleagues portray how people deal effectively with different kinds of losses in their lives, ranging from separation and divorce to death of a spouse and loss of home and possessions in natural disasters (Harvey & Uematsu, 1995; Weber & Harvey, 1994). Although important qualitative differences distinguish relationship breakups from death of a spouse, these researchers emphasize needs that cut across different forms of loss: the need to construct meanings, to reach completion, and to learn a lesson that can be passed on to successive generations. In their view, the grieving process associated with loss involves both the subjective process of chronicling, confirming and translating strong emotions and memories into symbolic images accessible for communication with others *and* the opportunity to confide the story of loss to others on a personal level. Recovery from loss appears to be contingent on both the private experience of formulating an account and the public experience of disclosing it to others (Weber & Harvey, 1994; Harvey & Uematsu, 1995). Their discussion of the private and public levels of account-making may leave the impression that accounts are formulated privately, then disclosed publicly, although the process undoubtedly is more reflexive and interactive; that is, the formulation of one's story may be significantly influenced by the activity of telling it to others. After telling a story to a confidant, one may be inspired to rethink its meanings and to search for different and more satisfying ways of communicating the story to others.

Until recently most research on accounts has relied on data-reduction techniques and conventional styles of reporting. Individual cases have rarely, if ever, been presented in their entirety or in a comprehensive, evocative style. Instead, case materials have been conventionally summarized or cut down to snippets to illustrate conceptual arguments. Recently, Harvey & Uematsu (1995) have shown interest in the merits of presenting more extended narrations of accounts of loss (Uematsu, 1996).

Storied Lives

Rosenwald & Ochberg (1992) have developed a critical–cultural perspective for investigating the stories people tell about their lives. While conceding that

> all stories are told and that all self-understanding takes place within the narrative frame each culture provides its members (Rosenwald & Ochberg, 1992, p. 2),

these writers are concerned, nonetheless, with the tensions between personal narratives and the conventions from which they achieve intelligibility. Storied lives become interesting when they push beyond conventions and canonical forms and thus become a site for critique and innovation. The stories people tell contribute significantly to the identities they create, perform and live. Stories also provide access to interpretations and critical evaluations of cultural conditions that constrain and may oppress the way people live and what they can tell. Narrating one's life history provides opportunities for self-renewal over time as a person objectifies life experiences in stories, evaluates their successive accounts, and generates new cycles of lived experience and new accounts of it. Storied lives often take on a relational focus, first because the story defines who one is in relation to others, and second because self-accounts normally attempt to achieve harmony with accounts that significant others give of the narrator and of themselves (Rosenwald & Ochberg, 1992).

Three essays published in *Storied Lives* (Rosenwald & Ochberg, 1992) are relevant to the study of personal relationships, particularly from a critical–

cultural perspective. Rosenberg, Rosenberg & Farrell (1992) use marital conversations with a single family, initially contacted in the early 1970s and interviewed again in 1984, to interrogate Berger & Kellner's (1964) contention that the family is where people turn for a sense of self and satisfaction. They present vignettes from the 1984 interviews in which the family discussed their changes over the 12 years and each family member individually narrated an account of family and personal history. Although the narratives show the family trying hard to interpret troubling events in ways that protect the esteem of the family, their stories also present a painful and complicated portrayal of the ideological intricacies with which marital and family conversation must cope. The family conversation painfully reveals "ambivalence and confusion about how merged they sometimes feel with an entangling familial mass of emotion, beliefs and values" (Rosenberg, Rosenberg & Farrell, 1992, p. 50). While the authors seem too intent on tearing down the wall of security promoted by Berger & Kellner's (1964) romanticized ideal of family stability, the accounts they analyze show that relationships can never totally satiate desire. The irony promoted by cycles of mismatched expectations and unequal power among family members is that

> each needs the other to liberate him or her by granting a self that feels fulfilling, yet each resents and fights the possibility of the other's owning his or her life in this way (Rosenberg, Rosenberg & Farrell, 1992, p. 58).

Addressing the question of what cultural forces inspire such high expectations for the experience of parenting, Walkover (1992) discusses accounts provided by interviews with 15 young couples unable to conceive. These couples struggle with a split consciousness in which, on the one hand, parenting is viewed as an experience that provides "a richness and depth otherwise unattainable" while, on the other hand, child-rearing is considered potentially restricting, oppressive and alienating (Walkover, 1992, p. 180). In terms of their marriage, these couples see the transition to parenting as an inspiration for deeper love, but also as "a wedge that could drive them apart" (Walkover, 1992, p. 180). Moreover, the cultural discourse of reproduction encourages couples to personalize their ambivalence and remain unconscious of the moral impositions of cultural definitions of the meaning of parenting. The anxieties they express in their stories revolve around hidden moral assumptions, both about the importance of conceiving children and about the proper ways of raising them. The insidious cultural rhetoric on which their expectations are grounded promotes moral expectations that parents should care "perfectly" for their children and should consider a child's actions as a reflection exclusively on the parent(s) (Walkover, 1992).

Riessman (1992) analyzes the story of Tess, a 23-year-old white woman who justifies her decision to divorce her husband on the grounds of marital rape. Attempting "to heal wounds that only narrative can heal" (Riessman, 1992, p. 247), Tess creates a heroic portrait of her painful life as a victim of her husband's sexual abuse. Her narrative reveals the power of language to make a difference in a person's life. Applying "marital rape" as a metaphor for expressing her husband's savage behavior, Tess is able to escape a violent and abusive marriage and offer publicly acceptable terms for ending it. The vocabulary of sexual abuse—a relatively new public discourse—offers Tess an intelligible means of interpreting and communicating her story in ways previously unavailable to women.

Evocative Narrative

Whereas research on accounts and storied lives tends to conform to rational/ analytical conventions of social science reporting, evocative narratives break away from these traditions. In evocative narratives, the author often writes in the first person, making herself the object of research and thus breaching the separation of researcher and subjects (Jackson, 1989); the story usually focuses on a single case and thus breaches the traditional concerns of research from generalization across cases to generalization within a case (Geertz, 1973); the mode of storytelling is more akin to the novel or biography and thus fractures the boundaries that normally separate social science from literature; the disclosure of hidden details of private life highlights emotional experience and thus challenges the rational actor model of social performance that dominates social science; and the episodic portrayal of the ebb and flow of relationship experience dramatizes the motion of connected lives across the curve of time, and thus resists the standard practice of portraying a relationship as a snapshot.

Space permits only a selected review of the wide range of evocative narratives relevant to the study of personal relationships. Below we discuss four recent works that display distinctly different styles of expressing lived experiences in personal relationships. The four we have chosen focus on the course of a single relationship over an extended period of time ranging from several months to 9 years.

Patrimony is the "true story" of novelist Philip Roth's (1991) intimate bond with his elderly father during the last few months of his father's life. Forced to reassess his appraisal of his father in light of the father's old age and chronic illness, Roth achieves an empathic understanding that reframes his father's most offensive characteristics as merely what it took to survive for 86 years. Told in the first person, this unmistakably autobiographical account plunges readers into the emotional trauma many people experience when they become parents to their parents. Recognizing that "if not in my books or in my life, at least in my dream I would live perennially as his little son, just as he would remain alive there not only as my father but as *the* father sitting in judgment of what I do" (pp. 237–238), Roth nevertheless musters the courage to take charge of the man who had terrorized him as a boy, ushering in "the end of one era, the dawn of another" (p. 83). Roth's narrative paints a rare portrait of an ambivalent son trying to "do it right" for his father, coming to grips with "the overpowering force of bloodbonds", the workings of a mind seeking to detach itself from "the agonizing isolation of a man at the edge of oblivion" in order to find comfort as a member of a clan, and the dissonance arising from the necessity of uniting into a single father the fierce and vigorous father of his childhood and the fragile and stricken father of the present moment.

In *Cancer in Two Voices*, Sandra Butler & Barbara Rosenblum (1991) use journal entries and personal letters to tell their story of what it was like to live with terminal cancer and what it was like to be the partner who survives. Beginning to write within a few days of Barbara's diagnosis of advanced breast cancer, Butler & Rosenblum define their narrative as "a story of loss and the gifts it brings" (p. 1). In Barbara's voice we hear a candid assessment of what she did to mobilize the help and love of her friends to help her cope with the fear of this scary disease; of her feelings about the war being waged inside her body; of her growing recognition that the cancer spreading inside her was *hers* not theirs, and that ultimately she would have to fight it alone; of how she and Sandra "closed ranks" to face their crisis together; of how her friend of so many words silently withdrew as they became trapped in their own terror and were unable to reach each other; of what it was like to face the "if only" days after mastectomy and to want desperately to squeeze life out of every minute of the day; of the changing images of her concept of a future and the meanings of money, sexuality and love; of the ironies of being kept alive with poisons that cause fatigue and depression; of her hope for miracles and the aloneness of one who faces death squarely within a finite body that is changing radically every day; and finally, of being too weak to speak or interact or care.

In Sandy's voice, we hear her tell of a fear of losing herself in her partner's needs; of trying to stay calm in the face of her partner's terror; of sometimes being angry at Barbara for getting cancer and ruining their lives together, then wanting to protect her from the cancer; of her growing feelings of disengagement and loneliness; of beginning to imagine a life without the person she wanted to grow old with; of their fight for meaning and for maintaining connection; of her longing for the way things used to be; of how Barbara's body became *the* body in their lives and how she became only an extension of Barbara's physical capacities; and then, at the end, of the guilt of survival and comparison.

Written with an ethnographer's commitment to tell a story that coheres with details of memories, field notes and systematic introspection (Ellis, 1991), *Final Negotiations* presents Carolyn Ellis's (1995a) detailed personal account of her 9-year intimate relationship with Gene Weinstein, a sociologist 20 years older than she, who died of emphysema in 1985. Told through her perceptions and emphasizing her feelings and coping strategies, Carolyn takes the measure of herself as a sociologist and as a romantic partner caught in the grip of attachment and loss, as she and Gene wage their insatiable appetite for life against the relentless progression of his disease. In *Final Negotiations* conversation is shown not only as the means for endowing a relationship with meaning but also as a writing method for bringing the flux and flow of connected lives to life with immediacy and vitality. Splicing concrete, ethnographic details regarding the entrapment of chronic illness onto the liberating effects of a relationship devoted to conversation and negotiation at all costs, Carolyn reminds us how untidy, ambiguous and menacing relationships can be. Offering her work as "comfort and companionship [and] . . . when your time comes . . . a point of comparison" (p. 335), she uses literary strategies of writing to make the reader a participant in emotional episodes of jealousy, rage, depression, embarrassment, fear and pain, as she and Gene negotiate a balance between hovering and making space, denial and acceptance, arguing and making up, and feeling and blocking out pain.

Dan Franck's *Separation* (Franck, 1993) is a daily chronicle of a man's obsessive attempt to understand and prevent the dissolution of his marriage. Using a third-person narrative style, the main character, presumably Dan, keeps detailed notes of his conversations with friends and records, in micro-detail, observations of his wife's behavior in his presence as she enters into a relationship with another man. Written "to purge himself, to give some direction to his excavation of his own feelings, and perhaps to win her back" (pp. 58–59), *Separation* is not only about the demise of a relationship but part of it: "his children and his wife were like characters getting ready to walk out of his book" (p. 52). Chilling in his anguished yet coolly detached observations of betrayal, mistrust and obsession, the main character highlights in astonishing detail the observable nuances of relational performances—what happens when one person decides to give up the act while the other plays on. *Separation* delivers a believably stark account of the frightening consequences of asymmetrical attachment—"a meadow turned to weeds"—and shows convincingly that no matter how deep one's longing, the loving course of a relationship must be jointly authored.

These four books, and other works of the same genre (see Frank, 1991; Haskell, 1990; Kiesinger, 1995; Mairs, 1989; Mukaia, 1989; Ronai, 1992, 1994; Swados, 1991; Yalom, 1989; Zola, 1982a) should appeal to students of personal relationships who prefer experience-near depictions of relationship life and are willing to abandon established conventions of social science writing that promote the illusion of distance and detachment. As evocative narratives, these "true" accounts provoke emotional absorption; they invite readers to connect their own experiences to those of the author; they inspire serious attention to matters of choice and commitment and arouse understanding of life's contingencies and uncertainty; they mention the unmentionables of everyday life, revealing the flaws and warts of human character as well as human decency and virtue; they reach our minds and our hearts, showing us that our intellects can never be fully cut off from our emotions; they display life's details, reminding readers of past experiences and shaping future dreams and expectations; and they make it clear that the most compelling issues of relationship life are moral questions, struggles to decide the right way to act in concert with others (Coles, 1989).

CONCLUSION

We can do nothing to prevent the entropic march of time. Personal relationships change over time and so must the study of personal relationships. As scholars approaching the next generation of work on personal relationships, we face vexing questions about the inspiration, purposes and significance of our work. What Richardson (1994) said about much of academic sociology applies—our work is under-read; undergraduates find many of our publications boring; graduate students often say our scholarship is dry and inaccessible; seasoned scholars confess they don't finish half of what they start reading; and the public hardly knows we exist. Should we care? Can we do anything about it?

Narrative inquiry is not necessarily a solution, but it is clearly an alternative. To embrace narrative inquiry is to desire works that may be more author-centered and, at the same time, more inviting to readers. Narratives ask readers to feel their "truth" and thus to become fully engaged—morally, aesthetically, emotionally and intellectually. If we can accept this vision of our work, one that opens the study of personal relationships to the storied particulars of lived experience in their diverse moral, cultural, emotional and intellectual dimensions, we may be able to touch people where they live and make our work linger in their minds. Whether we trust stories or not, they remain one of the few human resources capable of telling us what we do not hear and showing us what we fail to see.

Chapter 13

Rethinking Communication in Personal Relationships from a Dialectical Perspective

Leslie A. Baxter
University of Iowa, Iowa City, IA, USA
and
Barbara M. Montgomery
Millersville University, Millersville, PA, USA

A dialectical perspective on communication in personal relationships was presented in the 1988 edition of this *Handbook* (Baxter, 1988). Since then, substantial empirical and theoretical work has appeared in which the term "dialectical" has been invoked. Rather than simply updating the 1988 chapter, we think it is more useful to offer a fresh articulation of this perspective, organized around three themes: (1) the commonly shared assumptions of a dialectical perspective; (2) major scholarly research programs emanating from a dialectical perspective; and (3) directions for future research. Our motive for addressing "shared assumptions" is to advance criteria by which a perspective can rightfully be described as dialectical; our observation is that the term "dialectical" has been invoked too loosely by some to describe work that is not fully dialectical in nature. Our motives for summarizing the major scholarly research programs are twofold: first, we want to give the reader bibliographic guidance to the major programmatic approaches that adopt a dialectical perspective; and second, we want to emphasize that each of the major dialectical scholars contributes something unique to the study of communication in personal relationships. Several excellent pieces of dialectically-oriented research have been conducted outside the framework of the research programs which we will be summarizing, and we refer the reader elsewhere for more comprehensive reviews of this work (Baxter & Montgomery, 1996; Werner & Baxter, 1994). We reserve the bulk of

Handbook of Personal Relationships, 2nd edn. Edited by Steve Duck.
© 1997 John Wiley & Sons Ltd.

the chapter to a discussion of directions for future research based on our reading of the dialogic perspective articulated by the Russian scholar Mikhail Bakhtin.

SHARED ASSUMPTIONS OF A DIALECTICAL PERSPECTIVE

Dialectics is not a theory in the traditional sense. It lacks the structural intricacies of formal theories of prediction and explanation; it offers no extensive hierarchical array of axiomatic or propositional arguments. It does not represent a single, unitary statement of generalizable predictions. Dialectics describes, instead, a small set of conceptual assumptions. Those assumptions, which revolve around the notions of contradiction, change, praxis and totality, constitute what is better thought of as a meta-theoretical perspective (Benson, 1977; Buss, 1979; Cornforth, 1968; Murphy, 1971; Rawlins, 1989; Rychlak, 1976).

Contradiction

From a dialectical perspective, contradictions are inherent in social life and are the basic "drivers" of change and vitality in any social system. The term "contradiction" holds a technical meaning to dialectical theorists and refers to "the dynamic interplay between unified opposites".

In general terms, tendencies or features of a phenomenon are "opposites" if they are incompatible and mutually negate one another. Not all oppositions are alike, however. A logically defined, or "negative", opposition takes the form "X and not X". That is, an opposition consists of some feature and its absence, for instance, stable vs. not stable, autonomous vs. not autonomous, and loving vs. not loving are logically defined contradictions in personal relationships. By contrast, functionally-defined, or "positive", oppositions take the form "X and Y", where both "X" and "Y" are distinct features that function in incompatible ways such that each negates the other. Examples include stable vs. fluid, autonomous vs. connected, and loving vs. hateful. In practice, functionally defined oppositions are easier than logically defined contradictions to study simply because both oppositional poles are more explicitly referenced phenomena (Adler, 1927, 1952; Altman, Vinsel & Brown, 1981; Georgoudi, 1983; Israel, 1979).

But functionally defined oppositions have their own complications. First, because the researcher does not have the luxury of logical negation (i.e., "X" and "not X") as the basis of defining an opposition, he or she bears the burden of demonstrating that "X" and "Y" are functionally opposite. That is, that the totality of one precludes the other. What constitutes a functional opposition in one context, culture or time period might not generalize to another.

A second complication of functionally defined oppositions is that they are likely to be more complicated than a simple binary pair; that is, many oppositions, not just one, are likely to exist in relation to a given feature. For example, the researcher interested in examining the feature of "certainty" from a dialectical perspective might identify several dialectical oppositions that co-exist: certainty–unpredictability, certainty–novelty, certainty–mystery, certainty–excitement, etc. The complete dialectical understanding of "certainty" rests on the researcher's ability to understand the complexity of multiple oppositions of which "certainty" is an element.

Opposition is a necessary but not sufficient condition for contradiction. In addition, the opposites must simultaneously be unified or interdependent with one another, a concept often referred to as "the unity of opposites". Dialectical unity can occur in two basic ways (Altman, Vinsel & Brown, 1981). First, each oppositional tendency presupposes the existence of the other for its very meaning; this is a unity of identity. The concept of "certainty", for example, is meaningful only because we have an understanding of its logical and/or functional opposites; without knowledge of "uncertainty", "chaos", "unpredictability" and so forth, the concept of "certainty" would be meaningless.

Second, the oppositional tendencies are unified as interdependent parts of a larger whole; this is interdependent unity. For example, in the context of personal relationships, individual autonomy and relational connection are unified opposites. The two tendencies form a functional opposition in that the total autonomy of parties precludes their relational connection, just as total connection between parties precludes their individual autonomy. However, individual autonomy and relational connection form an interdependent unity, as well. Connection with others is necessary in the construction of a person's identity as an autonomous individual (e.g., Askham, 1976; Mead, 1934; Zicklin, 1969), just as the ever-changing nature of a relational connection is predicated on the existence of the parties' unique identities (e.g., Askham, 1976; Karpel, 1976; Kernberg, 1974; L'Abate & L'Abate, 1979; Ryder & Bartle, 1991). Thus, in a contradiction, opposites negate one another at the same time that they are interdependent or unified with one another. Unity is the basis of the "both/and" quality of contradictions.

Third, a requisite condition for a contradiction is dynamic interplay or tension between the unified opposites. Within the dialectical perspective, the concept of tension carries no negative connotations; instead, the term simply refers to the ongoing, ever-changing interaction between unified oppositions. This interplay is what distinguishes a dialectical perspective from a dualistic one. It is easy to confuse dialectics with dualism, because both perspectives emphasize the presence of opposites. In dualism, however, opposites are conceived as more or less static and isolated phenomena that co-exist in parallel fashion. For example, research exists on self-disclosure and on its binary opposite, privacy regulation. However, this research is dualistic so long as each phenomenon is conceived to be definitionally, developmentally and practically independent. By contrast, a dialectical perspective emphasizes how parties manage the simultaneous but ever-changing exigence for both disclosure and privacy in their relationships and, especially, how the "both/and"-ness of disclosure and privacy is patterned through their mutual influence across the developmental course of a relationship. In short, dualism emphasizes opposites in parallel, whereas dialectics emphasizes the interplay of opposites.

Dialectical Change

The interplay of unified opposites means that all social systems experience the dynamic tension between stability and change. Although all dialectical approaches presume that change is an inherent feature of dialectical contradiction, differences of emphasis can be identified with respect to two underlying issues related to change: (1) the position taken with respect to causation, that is, the relative weighting given to Aristotle's "efficient cause" and "formal cause"; and (2) whether change is regarded as fundamentally indeterminate or teleological.

Aristotle's "efficient cause" refers to linear antecedent-consequent relations, that is, the familiar cause–effect relation, whether this relation is one-way (X is a cause of Y) or reciprocal (X and Y cause and are caused by one another) (Rychlak, 1988). By contrast, Aristotle's "formal cause" refers to the patterned relations among phenomena, that is, the "pattern, shape, outline, or recognizable organization in the flow of events or in the way that objects are constituted" (Rychlak, 1988, pp. 5–6). Unlike an emphasis on one-way or reciprocal cause–effect relations, formal cause focuses on how phenomena mutually define one another in patterned ways, how events flow and unfold over time, and how patterns shift and change; from the perspective of formal cause, none of the component phenomena is "caused" by any prior occurrence of another phenomena. Dialectical theorists differ in their emphasis on efficient causation and formal causation, as we illustrate later in the chapter.

A second issue around which dialectical theorists differ is whether the change process is presumed to be fundamentally indeterminate or teleological in nature. A teleological approach to change presumes that change is the servant of ideal end-states or goals; phenomena are more or less "pulled" toward an ideal outcome. By contrast, indeterminacy presumes that change is not directed toward some necessary or ideal end-state; rather, change involves ongoing quantitative and qualitative shifts that simply move a system to a different place. Some dialectical theorists endorse a teleological view of change in which contradictions are transcended in a thesis–antithesis–synthesis dynamic. At a given point in time, one pole or aspect of a given contradiction is dominant (the so-called "thesis"), which in turn sets in motion a qualitative change that leads to the salience at a second point in time of the opposing aspect or pole (the so-called "antithesis"), after which a transformative change occurs in which the original opposition of poles is somehow transcended, such that the contradiction no longer exists (the so-called "synthesis").

Other dialectical theorists reject the teleological goal of transcendent change or synthesis, endorsing instead a model of indeterminacy in which two opposing tendencies simply continue their ongoing interplay (Rychlak, 1976). This indeterminate interplay of opposites can involve both cyclical change and linear change. That is, change can be characterized by a repeating pattern (cyclical) and/or a series of changes representing progression from one state to another (linear). Cyclical change occurs when the interplay of oppositions takes on a back-and-forth flavor, with relationship parties emphasizing first one oppositional tendency and then the other in an ongoing ebb and flow pattern. Visually and theoretically, such an ebb-and-flow pattern would look like repeating sine waves; in actuality, the cycles are characterized by varying amplitudes and rhythms through time, rather than by the uniformity and regularity of sine waves (Altman, Vinsel & Brown, 1981). In contrast, linear change involves a series of non-repeating changes in which the system never returns to a previous state. Further, these two types of change can be combined into linear, cyclic change, or what Werner & Baxter (1994) refer to as spiraling change. Strictly speaking, cyclicity assumes that phenomena recur in identical form. A spiral, by contrast, involves recurrence but recognizes that phenomena never repeat in identical form; a spiral thus combines elements of both cyclical change (recurrence) and linear change (the absence of identical repetition). Because cyclicity in its strict sense is counter to most conceptualizations of social interaction, spiraling change is probably a more accurate characterization of indeterminate change.

The ebb-and-flow nature of indeterminate, spiraling change often leads people mistakenly to conclude that a teleological goal of homeostasis or equilibrium "drives" this form of dialectical change (e.g., Stafford, 1994). Just the opposite is the case. What propels a spiral to shift toward the other pole(s) is not homeostasis but neglect of that pole. As Bopp & Weeks (1984) observed, the concept of homeostatic equilibrium privileges permanence and stability, thereby ignoring the pervasive dialectic tension between stability and change. Attempts to categorize dialectics as an equilibrium theory fail to recognize its core presumption that spiraling is "driven" by the nature of contradiction, which assumes that some aspect of the opposition is *always* left wanting.

Praxis

The third tenet of dialectics is that people are at once both actors and objects of their own actions, a quality dialectical theorists have termed "praxis" (e.g., Benson, 1977; Israel, 1979; Rawlins, 1989). People function proactively by making communicative choices. Simultaneously, however, they are reactive, because their actions become reified in a variety of normative and institutionalized practices that establish the boundaries of subsequent communicative choices. People are actors in giving communicative life to the contradictions that organize their social life, but these contradictions, in turn, affect their subsequent communicative actions. Every interaction event is a unique moment at the same time that each is informed by the history of prior interaction events and informs future events.

Praxis is an abstract and empty construct without consideration of the concrete practices by which social actors produce the future out of the past in their everyday lives. Dialectical theorists situate praxis in various domains of social life, depending on their particular interests. Marxist dialectical materialists, for example, center their study of contradiction in the material resources of production and consumption by the proletariat and bourgeoisie classes in capitalist societies. By contrast, dialectical theorists who study communication in relationships situate the interplay of opposing tendencies in the symbolic, not material, practices of relationship parties. They emphasize communication as a symbolic resource through which meanings are produced and reproduced. Through their jointly enacted communicative choices, relationship parties react to dialectical exigencies that have been produced from their past interactional history together. At the same time, the communicative choices of the moment alter the dialectical circumstances that the pair will face in future interactions together. Many possible patterns of dialectical change result from a pair's communicative choices (Baxter, 1988; Baxter & Montgomery, 1996), and we will return to this point later.

Totality

The fourth and final core concept of dialectics is "totality"; that is, the assumption that phenomena can be understood only in relation to other phenomena (Benson, 1977; Israel, 1979; Mirkovic, 1980; Rawlins, 1989). From a dialectical perspective, the notion of totality does not mean "completeness" in the sense of producing a total portrait of a phenomenon; the world is an unfinalizable process in which we can point, at best, to fleeting and fluid patterns of the moment. Totality, from a dialectical perspective, is a way to think about the world as a process of relations or interdependencies. On its face, the concept of totality appears to be the same as any number of other theoretical orientations that emphasize such holistic notions as contextuality or relatedness. Put simply, dialectics is one form of holism but not all holistic theories are dialectical; the criterion that distinguishes dialectical holism from other holistic perspectives is the focus on contradictions as the unit of analysis. Dialectical totality, in turn, implicates three issues: where contradictions are located, interdependencies among contradictions, and contextualization of contradictory interplay.

The Location of Contradictions

The first important implication of the dialectical emphasis on the whole is that the tension of opposing dialectical forces is conceptually located *within* the interpersonal relationship, not necessarily as antagonisms *between* individual partners.

That is, dialectical attention is directed away from the individual as the unit of analysis and toward the dilemmas and tensions that inhere in relating. Dialectical tensions are played out, relational force against relational force rather than relational partner against relational partner (Montgomery, 1993). As people come together in any social union, they create a host of dialectical forces. Although partners are aware of many of the dialectical dilemmas they face (e.g., Baxter, 1990), a dialectical tension does not need to be consciously felt or expressed. Dialectical interplay may work "backstage" beyond partners' mindful awareness, nonetheless contributing to relational change.

Dialectical tension is thus jointly "owned" by the relationship parties by the very fact of their partnership. But joint ownership does not translate to perfect synchrony in the parties' perceptions; often there is little commonality in partners' experiences of relational contradictions. As Giddens (1979) has noted, dialectical interplay may surface as interpersonal conflict between parties if they are "out of sync" in their momentary experience of a contradiction, such that one person aligns his or her interests with one pole and the other person aligns his or her interests with the other pole. For example, a relationship party may want greater independence from their partner, whereas the partner wants to maintain or increase interdependence between the two of them. Mao (1965, p. 48) refers to this asynchrony as antagonistic struggle. Thus, interpersonal conflict is not the equivalent of dialectical tension although, under special circumstances, dialectical tension may be manifested in interpersonal conflict between the parties.

Interdependencies among Contradictions

A system usually contains not one but many contradictions; Cornforth (1968, p. 111) describes this as the "knot of contradictions" that co-exist and change in relation to one another over time. In analytically disentangling this dialectical "knot", dialectical theorists have introduced two basic distinctions in types of contradictions. The first, between principal and secondary contradictions, hierarchically organizes contradictions with respect to their impact on or centrality to the dialectical knot. Primary contradictions are those which are more central or salient to a dialectical system at a given point in time. For example, the interplay between autonomy and interdependence has often been identified by dialectical theorists as the most central of all relational contradictions, organizing the pattern of interdependencies among such secondary contradictions as openness and closedness (e.g., Baxter, 1988).

The second distinction is between internal contradictions and external contradictions (Ball, 1979; Cornforth, 1968; Israel, 1979; Mao, 1965; Riegel, 1976). As the term "internal" might suggest, an internal contradiction is constituted within the boundaries of the system under study, whereas an external contradiction is constituted at the nexus of the system with the larger system in which it is embedded. Within the context of personal relationships, internal contradictions are those oppositional forces that function within the boundaries of the dyad and which are inherent to dyadic relating; for example, how the partners can be open and expressive at the same time that they sustain privacy and protectiveness. By contrast, external contradictions are those inherent oppositional forces that operate at the nexus of the dyad and its external environment; for instance, how partners can both conform to society's conventions for relating at the same time that they construct a unique relational bond. External contradictions underscore that relationships are inherently social entities. That is, couples and society sustain a relationship, and in so doing they engage inherent contradictions of such relationships. From a dialectical perspective, internal and external contradictions are presumed to interrelate in dynamic ways. For example, society's conventions for self-disclosure in relationships no doubt are associated with a given couple's experience of their internal dilemma between openness and closedness.

Contextualization of Contradictory Interplay

As Mao (1965) observed, the fact of contradiction is universal but the particulars of the contradicting process vary from one context to another. Dialectical scholars are thus obliged to study contradictions *in situ* at both universal and particular levels, in contrast to efforts which might seek to reduce contradictions to abstractions stripped of their localized particularities. Social phenomena encompass concrete environmental, situational and interpersonal factors which are integrally related with issues of praxis and the nature of dialectical change.

MAJOR DIALECTICAL RESEARCH PROGRAMS IN THE STUDY OF COMMUNICATION IN PERSONAL RELATIONSHIPS

A number of perspectives on communication in personal relationships echo with dialectical reverberations, some quite strongly (e.g., Altman, 1993; Conville, 1991; Rawlins, 1992), and others more faintly (e.g., Billig, 1987; Shotter, 1993). We cannot provide an exhaustive summary of this work here (see Baxter & Montgomery, 1996), but we hope to give a flavor of the contributions currently being made to a dialectical understanding of communication in personal relationships.

Bochner's Work on the Dialectics of Family Systems

Bochner (1984) articulated an early dialectical framework for understanding communication in personal relationships, which has been developed more recently in studies of family systems (Bochner & Eisenberg, 1987; Cissna, Cox & Bochner, 1990; Ellis & Bochner, 1992; Yerby, Buerkel-Rothfuss & Bochner, 1990). Bochner and his colleagues emphasize three particular functional contradictions in social interaction: (1) how partners are both expressive, revealing and vulnerable (open) and, simultaneously, discrete, concealing and protective (closed) with each other; (2) how family members sustain unique individual identities and behave independently (differentiation), while at the same time they share a family identity and behave in interdependent ways (integration); and (3) how the family system manages to be both stable (stability) yet adaptive to fluctuating demands placed on it (change).

Bochner is interested in formal cause, not efficient cause, and he argues that scholars should not "confuse predictive efficiency with an understanding of developmental processes" (Bochner, 1984, p. 580). He suggests that the contradictions that organize social life are ongoing throughout a relationship's life cycle, a position that implies indeterminate change rather than teleological change. He also calls for developing a research language of process and change that would recognize incremental variations but also temporally complex "turning points" and momentum reversals. In his recent work (e.g., Ellis & Bochner, 1992), Bochner has emphasized the "lived experience" of contradictory dilemmas as they are concretely and subjectively felt by relationship parties. Bochner's empirically oriented work is interpretive and particularly emphasizes the study of narratives (Bochner, 1994).

The work of Bochner and his colleagues builds productively on a tradition of dialectical approaches to family systems that goes back as much as three decades. Family therapists, for example, have long been intrigued by contradictions, paradox, disequilibrium and inconsistencies (e.g., Haley, 1963; Selvini-Palazzoli et al., 1978; Watzlawick, Weakland & Fisch, 1974). In addition, the conceptual ground in family studies was fertile for nurturing the seeds of dialectics in the 1970s and 1980s, and many dialectical perspectives were produced (e.g., Bopp & Weeks, 1984; Hoffman, 1981; Kempler, 1981; Minuchen, 1974; Wynne, 1984).

Altman's Transactional World View

Over the past 20 years, Irwin Altman and his colleagues have contributed significantly to scholarly discourse about such topics as relationship development (Altman & Taylor, 1973; Altman, Vinsel & Brown, 1981), privacy regulation (Altman, 1977), cross-cultural relationship rituals and practices (Altman et al., 1992; Werner et al., 1993), and social psychological implications of the home environment (Altman & Gauvain, 1981). This body of work stems from a particular theoretical perspective, which Altman (1990, 1993) refers to as "a transactional world view". Altman uniquely couples transactionalism with dialectics to explore phenomena particularly salient to personal relationships. The mainstay of this work is a holistic integration of interpersonal processes (e.g., intimacy, self-disclosure), physical and social environments (e.g., the home; the culture) and temporal qualities (e.g., pace and rhythm of change) to understand social phenomena. Transactional dialectics thus gives particular emphasis to dialectical totality. Phenomena are not viewed in antecedent-consequent relations, but instead are seen as embedded in a continuing and dynamic process of patterned interplay. Altman and his colleagues contend that these coherent patterns of change and fluidity (i.e., formal causation) maintain a "transactional unity" among the elements of processes, environments and time.

Altman and his colleagues view dialectical contradiction as an intrinsic aspect of social existence. They have focused especially on the functional oppositions of openness and closedness, stability and change (Altman, Vinsel & Brown, 1981), and individuality and communality (Altman & Gauvain, 1981) as specific manifestations of social dialectics. Some of their work examines these basic contradictions with the individual as the unit of analysis; for example, how individuals both open themselves up to interaction with others yet maintain a boundary of privacy (e.g., Altman, Vinsel & Brown, 1981). Other work examines larger social units, including couples, families, neighborhoods and cultures; for example, how couples within different cultures are integrated into the social networks of their families and friends while, at the same time, are differentiated as separate social entities.

Temporally-oriented descriptions of change are paramount in Altman's work. He and his colleagues view the focus on change "as a necessary antidote to the proliferation of social psychological approaches that emphasized stability, consistency, or homeostasis as relational goals to the exclusion of needs for change, growth, and movement" (Brown, Altman & Werner, 1992, p. 510). Collaborations with Werner and others (Werner, Altman & Oxley, 1985; Werner et al., 1987, 1988) have produced a conceptual framework of temporal qualities like pace, rhythm and duration, which have been used to describe the changing qualities of relationships, home environments and cultural practices.

One of the strongest themes in the Altman et al. work is its multi-method orientation. Multiple sources of data (e.g., interviews, observations, archival data) are emphasized in order to represent different perspectives on events. "Methodological eclecticism" is valued with respect to research designs, procedures and measures.

Rawlins' View of Friendship over the Life Course

Like Altman, Rawlins (1983a, 1983b, 1989, 1992, 1994a; Rawlins & Holl, 1987, 1988) stresses totality by incorporating dialectics into what could be called a transactional view, although Rawlins limits his study to platonic friendships. To Rawlins (1992, p. 273), "A dialectical perspective calls for investigating and situating enactment of friendships in their concrete social conditions over time". The concrete social conditions of friendships which are most salient in Rawlins' studies are work, marriage, family, retirement and personal crisis. Time, for Rawlins, is defined predominantly by the life stages of childhood, adolescence, young adulthood, adulthood and later adulthood.

Rawlins has relied on the interpretive analysis of interviews with people of all ages to gain a dialectical perspective on a number of functionally defined contradictions, which he calls the "pulse" of friendships. He identifies two fundamental types. "Contextual dialectics" represent contradictions in culture-based notions, norms and expectations that frame the way any particular friendship is experienced or enacted. These include the tension between public and private enactments of friendship and the tension between abstract ideals and actual realities of friendship. "Interactional dialectics" represent the contradictions involved as friends manage and sustain their relationship on an ongoing, everyday basis. These "communicative predicaments of friendships" include the dialectics of exercising the freedoms to be independent and dependent, caring for a friend as a means-to-an-end (instrumentality) and as an end-in-itself (affection), offering evaluative judgements and offering unconditional acceptance, and, finally, being open and expressive and also being strategic and protective. While Rawlins focuses most on these six contextual and interactional contradictions, he has introduced others through his analyses, like the tension between historical perspectives and present experiences, a dialectic found to be particularly evident in adolescents' interactions with parents and friends (e.g., Rawlins & Holl, 1988).

Rawlins implicates both efficient cause and formal cause in his elucidation of dialectical change. Much of his empirical work seeks to describe the complex, patterned interplay among contradictions indicative of formal causation. However, in total, his extensive analyses construct an argument for efficient cause in that variations in the manifestations of dialectical tensions are due to types and degrees of friendship, cultural constraints and individual characteristics, especially age and gender. Indeed, change and flux are represented most strongly in the transitions between life stages and not in day-to-day interaction. Rawlins appears to suggest that an individual's age is the antecedent causal variable that results in particular manifestations of given contradictions. Thus, both adolescents and older persons experience the dialectical interplay of independence and interdependence, but these two developmental stages lead people to experience this interplay differently.

Rawlins recognizes both teleological change and indeterminate change. Teleological change, or what Rawlins (1989) calls the "dialectic of transcendence", occurs when friends resolve contradictions and, in so doing, create new ones through the process of thesis–antithesis–synthesis. Rawlins also evokes a kind of indeterminate change when he talks about the "dialectic of encapsulation", which represents relatively closed, regulated and narrowly circumscribed change. While Rawlins' (1989) conceptual discussion of encapsulation focuses most on patterns that reflect the selecting and sustaining of a dominant polarity over a secondary one, his descriptive data about actual behavioral practices emphasize indeterminate changes represented in cycles and spirals between fairly equally weighted polarities (Rawlins,1983a, 1983b, 1992).

Conville's Relational Transitions Model

Conville (1983; 1988; 1991) integrates dialectical notions into a structural approach to understand the development of personal relationships. Specifically,

Conville argues that during the process of resolving dialectical contradictions, partners are "out of kilter". This imbalance propels relationships through transitions, which link the times when partners are "in kilter", i.e., feel comfortable, occupy complementary roles and coordinate their actions. Moreover, these periods of "in kilter" security are but one phase of a recursive process, driven by dialectical oppositions. Security is followed sequentially by the phases of disintegration, alienation and resynthesis to a new pattern of security.

These teleologically defined, relational transitions occur throughout the relationship course, which Conville likens to a spiral or helix. He stresses that the helix represents the recurrence of "second-order" or qualitative changes, which result in the restructuring of the social realities of a relationship, creating new grounds for relating. Conville contrasts this with first-order change, which is change within the context of the given grounds for interaction. For instance, partners deciding to spend more (or less) time together is a first-order change; partners redefining a relationship from "a romantic fling" to "a long-term romance" is a second-order change. According to Conville, partners can cycle through the second-order change process of security–disintegration–alienation–resynthesis many times over the course of their relationship's history, qualitatively transforming the definition of their relationship with the completion of each four-period cycle. In this way, Conville's model underscores the functionality of relationship crisis, which signifies the disintegration of an old relational state and the partners' alienation from it which, in turn, provides a catalyst for resynthesis and the emergence of a secure, new relational state.

Conville's conception of contradiction stresses efficient causation. The structural constraint of sequenced episodes leading, always, from security to disintegration, to alienation, to resynthesis and to a new security, represents the assumption of standard, directional changes in relating. Additionally, Conville defines two "meta-dialectics" in this sequence, formed in the juxtapositions of security–alienation and of disintegration–resynthesis. These primary contradictions set the relational stage for the playing out of the secondary contradictions associated with the themes of time (i.e., past–future), intimacy (i.e., close–distant) and affect (i.e., positive–negative).

Conville has applied his structural model to understand a variety of relationship case studies, ranging from the friendship of Helen Keller and Anne Sullivan to the romantic and marital relationships of ordinary persons. His method is a form of interpretive structural analysis.

Baxter's and Montgomery's Dialectical Work

Until recently, each of us has contributed independently to the literature on dialectics in personal relationships. Baxter's work has involved both quantitative and qualitative studies of contradictions in friendships (Bridge & Baxter, 1992), romantic relationships (e.g., Baxter, 1988, 1990; Baxter & Widenmann, 1993), marital couples (Baxter & Simon, 1993; Braithwaite & Baxter, 1995), and families (Baxter & Clark, 1995). Six internal and external contradictions have received attention in this work: the internal contradictions of autonomy–connection, predictability–novelty, and openness–closedness; and the external contradictions of separation–integration, conventionality–uniqueness, and revelation–non-revelation (Baxter, 1993, 1994). Montgomery's work (1984, 1992, 1993) has been characterized by its theoretical orientation, building up on the work of Bateson (1972, 1979) in articulating the ongoing flux of both internal and external contradictions experienced by relationship parties. We have both emphasized the praxis of contradiction; that is, how contradictions are created and sustained through communicative practices.

Most recently, however, we have collaborated in an articulation of ways to rethink the dialectical study of communication in personal relationships (Baxter & Montgomery, 1996). This recent articulation reflects a shift in our previous dialectical work and raises new possibilities for the dialectically-oriented work of others. In particular, we have been influenced by one specific variant of dialectical thinking, Bakhtin's dialogism. Despite variability in recent understandings of dialogism, scholarly opinion seems to be coalescing on the centrality of the "dialogue" to Bakhtin's lifelong intellectual work (Clark & Holquist, 1984; Holquist, 1990; Morson & Emerson, 1990; Todorov, 1984). Bakhtin was critical of the "monologization" of the human experience that he perceived in the dominant linguistic, literary, philosophical and political theories of his time. His intellectual project was a critique of theories that reduced the unfinalizable, open and heterogeneous nature of social life to determinate, closed, totalizing concepts (Bakhtin, 1965/1984, 1981, 1984, 1986; Voloshinov/Bakhtin, 1973[1]). To Bakhtin, social life was a "dialogue", not a "monologue". The essence of dialogue is a simultaneous differentiation from, yet fusion with, another. To enact dialogue, the parties need to fuse their perspectives while maintaining the uniqueness of their individual perspectives; the parties form a unity in conversation but only through two clearly differentiated voices. Dialogue, unlike monologue, is multivocal; that is, it is characterized by the presence of at least two distinct voices. Just as a dialogue is invoked by and also invokes unity and difference, Bakhtin (1981, p. 272) regarded all social processes as the product of "a contradiction-ridden, tension-filled unity of two embattled tendencies", the centripetal (i.e., forces of unity) and the centrifugal (i.e., forces of difference).

The implications of Bakhtin's work are substantial for moving dialectical work beyond efforts to date, which have tended to emphasize the task of identifying and categorizing binary contradictions in a variety of kinds of relationships. Page limitations do not permit a comprehensive discussion of the implications of

---

[1] Some scholars believe that Bakhtin, not Voloshinov, wrote *Marxism and the Philosophy of Language*. The most recent discussion of Bakhtin authorship is Bocharov (1994). We will refer to "Voloshinov/Bakhtin" throughout.

dialogically-oriented dialectics, but we can sample some of of the more interesting and significant ones in the space that remains (for a more complete discussion, see Baxter & Montgomery, 1996).

SOME IMPLICATIONS OF DIALOGIC DIALECTICS FOR FUTURE RESEARCH

Rethinking the Sovereign Self

A dialogic perspective is predicated on a view of the self as social, in contrast to existing dialectically-oriented research (including much of our own prior work) which is predicated largely on the notion of a contained, sovereign self. To argue that the self is social is to say that communication precedes and is the foundation for psychological or mental states. Further, communication is essential not only for the acquisition of mental states but also in the lifelong enterprise of sustaining and changing them. This is not a new idea, and many have creatively explored its relational implications (e.g., Buber, 1965; Mead, 1934; Sullivan, 1953; Vygotsky, 1986). Few, however, have accorded it as unqualified a rendering as Bakhtin, who saw the boundaries of our selves reaching far beyond the casings of our brains and bodies, encompassing *all* those with whom we interact. As Bakhtin indicated, "I become myself only . . . through another and with another's help" (in Todorov, 1984, p. 96). This dialogic self is one that is much more of the moment and fluid than more traditional notions, which assume kinds of stable "mental reservoirs" from which all actions spring.

A view of the self as social challenges us to rethink two contradictions that have garnered much attention among dialectical scholars: openness–closedness (e.g., the tension between disclosive expression and its opposites) and autonomy–connection (e.g., the tension between interdependence with another and independence from another).

Rethinking the Openness–Closedness Contradiction

Existing work tends to view the self as pre-formed and intact before relating; the process of interacting in relationships, thus, is one of revealing the sovereign self. From the perspective that presumes a sovereign self, relationships are problematic because of the risk and danger entailed in revelation. Self-disclosure is "owned" by the sovereign self and functions as an "access gate" that opens or closes one's self-territory to another's gaze. The theme of risk and danger appears throughout the dialectical work, especially in discussions of the openness–closedness contradiction. For example, Rawlins (1983b) refers to the dilemma between candor and discretion, with vulnerability serving as the arbiter of just how disclosive a person will be with another. Other dialectically-oriented scholars have similarly framed openness and closedness in terms of the vulnerabilities of disclosure (e.g., Altman, Vinsel & Brown, 1981; Baxter, 1988; Dindia, 1994).

By contrast, a dialogic perspective shifts emphasis from the revelation of sovereign self to the emergent co-construction of self. Self-disclosure is not a decision made by a contained self but a kind of utterance that gives voice to self-as-becoming. From a Bakhtinian perspective, an utterance is more complex than the individuated act of an autonomous speaker. As Voloshinov/Bakhtin (1973, p. 86) put it:

> . . . word is a two-sided act. It is determined equally by whose word it is and for whom it is meant. As word, it is precisely the product of the reciprocal relationship between speaker and listener, addresser and addressee. Each and every word expresses the "one" in relation to the "other" . . . A word is a bridge thrown between myself and another.

This relational view of a "word", including words about the self, discourages the limiting juxtaposition of openness–closedness as it is currently conceptualized around the assumption of a contained, already defined, self. Rather, understanding communication that is relevant to the continually emerging and social self requires focusing on three additional contradictions (Bakhtin, 1986): the contradiction between *the said and the unsaid*, or the dialectical interplay between meaning encoded in verbalized language and meaning carried in the context; the contradiction between *freedom and constraint*, or the dialectical interplay between the "given" that is inherited by any interaction and the "new" that is created in any interaction; and the contradiction between *inner speech and outer speech*, or the dialectical interplay between personal meaning and social meaning, out of which individual consciousness constantly re-emerges. From a dialogic perspective, then, it is too simplistic to ask whether a person is open or closed with respect to his or her "true self". Such a question ignores the complexity of contradictions underlying any utterance. A dialogically-based dialectics, thus, requires scholars to rethink the openness–closedness dialectic, complicating it with a multivocal set of contradictions that center around the process of co-constructing self-as-becoming.

Rethinking the Autonomy–Connection Contradiction

Just as the openness–closedness contradiction in existing dialectical research is conceived from the perspective of a sovereign self, so is the autonomy–connection contradiction. Rawlins (1983a), for example, discusses this contradiction as a matter of individual rights and responsibilities; the contained self grants to himself or herself the right of freedom of action, but the contained self also assumes a responsibility to be there when called on to fulfill the other's needs. Other dialectical scholars similarly conceptualize the autonomy–connection dialectic as an individually-centered tension between the desire to be autonomous or independent and the desire to be interdependent with another (e.g., Altman et al.,

1988; Baxter, 1988; Bochner, 1984). From the perspective of a sovereign self, interdependence is something the individual trades off against individual independence; independence is sacrificed to achieve interdependence. The social-exchange logic that undergirds this conception of the autonomy–connection dialectic is clear: sovereign selves enter relationships with their respective reward–cost structures as guides, and they experience both costs and rewards in independence (the loss of other's assistance and freedom of action, respectively) and both costs and rewards in interdependence (loss of freedom of action and reliance on other's assistance, respectively).

A dialogic perspective offers an alternative conception of autonomy and connection and so challenges the social exchange simplicities. A relationship is conceived as a dialogue, and as such, implicates both the differentiation and fusion of relationship parties. Just as a dialogue is the ongoing, joint coordination of two distinct voices, a relationship is an improvised, fluid boundary of unity and difference. An individual relationship party does not "negotiate away" his or her independence in the other's dependence. Instead, relating is a joint dialogue of the two parties in which both connectedness and autonomy are inherent. Party B has a relational interest not only in Party A's responsibility for interdependence but a relational interest, as well, in Party A's independence, and *vice versa*. Both differentiation (autonomy or independence of the parties) and unity (connectedness or interdependence of the parties) are critical to relationship vitality and inherent in the very process of relating. Thus, from the perspective of a social self, the autonomy–connection contradiction is not centered in the individual but in the relationship between parties.

Rethinking Binary Contradictions

Existing dialectically-oriented scholarship has tended to conceive of contradictions as binary oppositions, for example, independence–interdependence, openness–closedness, and so forth. By contrast, a dialogic dialectics urges a more complex view in which multiple voices of opposition function at once, a phenomenon we call "multivocal contradiction".

By way of illustrating the implications of a shift from binary to multivocal contradictions, let us again reconsider the autonomy–connection contradiction. Existing dialectical work tends to conceive this contradiction narrowly in terms of behavioral independence and interdependence. From a dialogic perspective, this single binary pair is too limiting. The relationship dialogue is about unity and difference in many simultaneous manifestations including, but not limited to, behavioral independence–interdependence. For example, relationship partners can grapple with tensions between autonomy and co-dependence, autonomy and domination, autonomy and dependence, and autonomy and intimacy and many of these struggles can be engaged simultaneously. Additionally, partners can engage these struggles relative to many different levels of social existence implicated in personal relationships, including values, attitudes, beliefs, and ideal and actual behavioral practices (see, e.g., Duck, 1994a; Wood et al., 1994).

The multivocality of autonomy–connection becomes even more complex when we recognize that relationship parties are situated locally. Bakhtin (1981) refers to this situatedness as a "chronotope", that is, a time–space location, observing that "every entry into the sphere of meaning is accomplished only through the gates of the chronotope" (p. 258). Relationship parties are always relating from the time–space horizons of the moment, which hold the potential for multiple meanings of autonomy and connection. Goldsmith (1990), for example, found five qualitatively different meanings of "connection" and "autonomy" for parties reporting on the different developmental moments of their respective romantic relationships. Similarly, Stamp & Banski (1992) have reported qualitative shifts in what married partners mean by connection and autonomy upon the birth of the first child. Masheter's work with post-divorce couples has found that the connection–autonomy contradiction takes on a different meaning to partners before and after the divorce (Masheter, 1991, 1994; Masheter & Harris, 1986). In short, the autonomy–connection contradiction has multiple radiants of meaning which are dynamically chronotopic. By limiting this and other contradictions to single radiants anchored at either end by polar opposites, dialectical scholars have operated as if contradictions were simple binary pairs rather than complex webs of oppositions, all of whose elements are in simultaneous interplay with one another.

Rethinking Relationship Development

Linear progress is the dominant conception of relationship development in existing research and theory. That is, relationships are thought to move in a unidirectional manner from states of less to more on several key dimensions: less to more interdependence, less to more openness, less to more certainty, and so forth. Once some teleological end-state is achieved (typically marriage), the relationship shifts to homeostatic maintenance. Relationship deterioration and break-up is envisioned as the reverse developmental course: that is, moreness to lessness on the key underlying dimensions. In the Baxter (1988) *Handbook* essay, the process of contradictory change was rendered compatible with the dominant view of relationship development in that the essay discussed a movement from autonomy to connection, to a synthesis of autonomy with connection, to the return of autonomy in break-up. By contrast, a dialogic perspective views relationship change as an indeterminate process with no clear end-states and no necessary paths of change. Relationship change involves both centripetal and centrifugal movement, rather than centripetal unidirectionality alone. Relationships move both "upwards" and "downwards", both "toward" and "away from", both "forwards" and "backwards". However, in this approach terms such as "upwards" and "downwards" are stripped of their connotations of progress and regression, respectively. Relationship change is conceived as dialogically complex, that is, simultaneously characterized as both independent and interdependent, both intimate and non-intimate, both open and closed, both certain and uncertain, both separated from the social order and integrated with the social order, and so forth. The ongoing interplay of contradictory forces opens up the playing field of change to encompass more than bidirectional movement; the very nature of the playing field is likely to change in qualitative ways which allow the relationship parties to change in new directions that are emergent in dialogic interplay. Thus, dialogic change is conceived as multivocal, both quantitatively and qualitatively.

A dialogic perspective adds a different perspective to the scholarly conversation on relationship beginnings, middles and endings. From the monologic stance of progress, a relationship begins when parties shift from strangers to acquaintances and ends when the parties cease to function interdependently. From a dialogic perspective, a relationship begins with the interplay of contradictory voices representing different forces that must be addressed by virtue of the two people being together. A relationship ends in dialogic silence when contradictions are no longer present. As Masheter's (1991, 1994; Masheter & Harris, 1986) work demonstrates, this does not occur at traditional ending markers like divorce, because "ex's" usually continue to grapple with a host of dialectical tensions around such themes as autonomy and connection and openness and closedness. Thus, a relationship is constituted solely in and through the dialogues of its multivocal contradictions.

The reconceptualization of relationship "middles" is predicated on the notion that a relationship is not teleologically oriented toward some idealized destination or outcome. Such relationship types as acquaintance, friendship and romantic attachment are not viewed as less developed "way-stations" along the road of courtship; rather, these types stand conceptually on their own ground (Delia, 1980). Acquaintanceship, for example, is not merely an undeveloped relationship but rather a relationship form in its own right that should be studied for its dialogic complexities. In abandoning the notion of some idealized destination for relationships, a dialogic perspective positions scholars to be more responsive to what Stacey (1990) has called the postmodern relationships that characterize late twentieth century Western culture, relationships that are "inhabite[d] uneasily and reconstitute[d] frequently in response to changing personal and occupational circumstances" (p. 17). Bridge & Baxter (1992) join Stacey in suggesting the prevalence in modern society of "blended relationships", that is, those that cross the boundary between role-based and personally-based elements. Blended relationships, such as friendships at work and mentor–protegé relationships, are not easily understood from the traditional monologue of developmental progress. Rather than marginalizing these relationships that are simultaneously impersonal and personal in structure, a dialogic perspective would have us examine them each in its own right for its dialogic complexities.

The progress orientation of existing research and theory on relationship "middles" emphasizes homeostatic equilibrium once the relationship's destination is reached. Dialogic dialectics positions us to view differently the "maintenance" of relationships (Montgomery, 1993). Because there is no destination in a dialogic system, there is no homeostatic goal whose steady state is sought through adaptive change. Relationships are not homeostatically organized around a stable point of "equilibrium", neither are they developmental organisms whose evolution is marked by progressive "moreness". Thus, the very concept of "relationship maintenance" is seen to privilege one pole only of the ongoing and ever-present dialectic between stability and change. For these reasons, we prefer to think of partners "sustaining" a relationship rather than "maintaining" it. Relationships are sustained to the extent that dialogic complexity is given voice.

In short, a dialogic perspective conceives of relationship development as fundamentally indeterminate, slippery and fuzzy. Relationship parties are forever improvising their relationship, forever coordinating the multiple centripetal and centrifugal voices of contradiction. Instead of envisioning relationship development as a linear musical scale that progresses from lower to higher notes of intimacy, relationship change is more like a jazz improvisation of competing, yet coordinated, musical sounds.

Rethinking Praxis

The indeterminacy that characterizes relationship change is a direct result of the many praxical possibilities that can be enacted by relationship parties at any given moment. Relationship change thus can be envisioned as a tree with many branches, each of which fans out in a dense array and which changes over time. The path of change for a given relationship can follow any of multiple branching possibilities. To date, dialectically-oriented research has largely been in the business of documenting that contradictions exist and cataloguing them (for a more detailed review, see Werner & Baxter, 1994). Study of praxis, that is, the joint actions of relationship parties in response to the dialectical exigencies of the moment, has received fairly limited attention by researchers.

We have recently modified the list of praxis possibilities originally articulated in the 1988 *Handbook* chapter. Instead of six basic praxical actions, we now envision at least eight and are confident that this expanded list is far from exhaustive (Baxter & Montgomery, 1996). The praxis patterns are not equally functional. A functional praxis response is one which celebrates the richness and diversity afforded by the oppositions of a contradiction. Pearce (1989, p. 199) captures this spirit of celebration in his call for the development of "substantive irony", that is, learning to live on "friendly terms" with paradox, contradiction and multivocality.

Two patterns are characterized by limited functionality, although they might appear with some frequency in relational life. The praxis pattern of *Denial* is characterized by discourse in which the parties basically seek to extinguish the contradictory nature of their relationship, e.g., the couple who says they want to be together 24 hours a day or the pair who says they are always totally open with each other. The second praxis pattern is *Disorientation*. This praxis pattern involves a fatalistic attitude in which contradictions are recognized as inevitable but negative. The relationship parties view their relationship as disorienting, that is, plagued with nihilistic ambiguities and uncertainties.

The remaining six praxis patterns display greater functionality than either denial or disorientation. They all show recognition of contradiction and involve proactive response patterns of one kind or another:

1. *Spiraling alternation* is characterized by a back-and-forth quality in which the relationship parties privilege different oppositional polarities at different times.
2. *Segmentation* is a response in which the relationship parties develop dialogic specializations, with certain topics or activities privileging one oppositional polarity and other topics or activities privileging other oppositional polarities. As relationship parties shift from one topic or activity to another, different opposing themes are privileged.
3. *Balance* involves an effort to respond to all oppositions at one point in time through compromise. Each oppositional exigence is responded to only partially, given the nature of compromise.
4. *Integration* is a response in which the relationship parties manage to celebrate simultaneously and fully all polarities of a contradiction. Several scholars have suggested that rituals illustrate integration because they can hold all sides to a contradiction at once (see Werner & Baxter, 1994, for a more extensive discussion of rituals as dialectical).
5. *Recallibration* is characterized by a transformation in the form of the opposition such that the initially experienced polarities are no longer oppositional to one another. Different from the teleologically oriented dialectical concept of transcendence as a permanent resolution of a contradiction through synthesis, recallibration is a practice that only transcends the form in which a given opposition is expressed but without resolving the underlying contradiction.
6. *Reaffirmation*. This praxis pattern, like disorientation, involves an acceptance by the parties that contradictory polarities cannot be reconciled. However, unlike disorientation, reaffirmation celebrates the richness afforded by each polarity and tolerates the tension posed by their unity.

Some scholarly work has been done on dialectical praxis (e.g., Altman et al., 1992; Baxter, 1988, 1990; Baxter & Simon, 1993; Baxter & Widenmann, 1993; Braithwaite & Baxter, 1995; Conville, 1991; Rawlins, 1992; Van Lear, 1991; Werner et al., 1993). Relationship parties appear to respond most typically to dialectical exigencies by invoking a spiraling pattern, in which one oppositional polarity is privileged and then another oppositional polarity is privileged in a waxing-and-waning pattern across time and across various topic or activity domains. Additionally, various communication rituals provide occasions where multiple oppositions can be symbolically voiced simultaneously. In short, existing dialectical work suggests that spiraling alternation, segmentation and integration dominate the praxis of relating.

Although this research is insightful, it focuses on the molar level of analysis, failing to inform us about situated praxis, that is, meaning that is constructed in the moment-to-moment discourse between interlocutors (for a notable exception, see Van Lear, 1991). A finer-grained dialogic perspective would complement this molar-level work with information about the subtle nuances of contradiction in enacted talk. As Bakhtin (1981, p. 272) observed:

> Every concrete utterance of a speaking subject serves as a point where centrifugal as well as centripetal forces are brought to bear. The processes of centralization and decentralization, of unification and disunification, intersect in the utterance.

Bakhtin was critical of the dialectical tradition of Hegel and Marx because it was insufficiently grounded in the concrete practices of everyday sociality. As he argued, "Take a dialogue and remove the voices, remove the intonations, carve out abstract concepts and judgments from living words and responses, cram everything into one abstract consciousness—and that's how you get dialectics" (Bakhtin, 1986, p. 147). Sensitive to Bakhtin's critique, we call here for a dialectical approach that takes seriously and elevates centrally the details of enacted dialogue in relationships.

Rethinking Dyadic Boundaries

With some exceptions (e.g., Baxter, 1993; Brown, Altman & Werner, 1992; Hinde, 1979, 1987; Montgomery, 1992; Rawlins, 1989, 1992; Werner et al., 1993), dialectical theorists have tended to view the personal relationship in a socio-cultural vacuum. Thus, internal contradictions (i.e., those located within the boundary of the dyad) have received disproportionate attention in comparison to external contradictions (i.e., those located between the dyad and the larger social system). However, if one takes the dialectical principle of totality seriously, as Bakhtin urges with his emphasis on the chronotopic nature of social life, then our ability to understand even internal contradictions is limited until we incorporate information about the social context in which parties live their relationship. Relationship parties are always positioned concretely; they are embodied in real persons who are feminine or not, Euro-American or not, economically privileged or not, socialized in a dysfunctional family or not, and so forth. The relationship created between people exists in a socio-cultural milieu that is characterized by its own "interpersonal ideology", that is, widely recognized, legitimated and prescribed beliefs about what a relationship is and how people ought to conduct their interpersonal lives (Fitch, 1994). There are no "clean slates" in relationships; no relationship "starts fresh". Instead, all relationships, as a social birthright, are heirs to the living history of social existence; at the same time, they are the guardians, the wards and the executors of that dynamic social estate. Partners relate or act into a relational context that is partly created in their acting and is partly the product of all other relationships in history. Any particular partners—by the way they interact with each other, their family, friends, neighbors, acquaintances, and even strangers—add to that history by reinforcing or modifying its patterns.

How relationship parties are chronotopically positioned affects the exigencies of contradictions in a number of ways. First, the very construction of "opposition" is acomplished socially and culturally. For example, the interplay between autonomy and connection among Euro-Americans who are socialized to believe in individualism no doubt differs from the autonomy–connection interplay among Japanese socialized to a sociocentric conception of personhood (e.g., Rosenberger, 1989). A similar, though not quite so pronounced, difference emerges when comparing Anglos to Hispanics and African-Americans (see Wood, 1995). These examples argue for a mindful consideration of cultural and social context in identifying contradiction. Second, relationship parties who are socially and culturally positioned with vested interests in different polarities of a given contradiction are likely to enact antagonistic struggles in the dialogue of their relationship. For example, to the extent that feminine socialization and masculine socialization are implicated in connection and autonomy, respectively, opposite-sex relations in American society are chronotopically predisposed to experience an antagonistic enactment of the autonomy–connection contradiction. Finally, chronotopic positioning undoubtedly affects praxis, as well. The range of praxical options that a couple perceives as viable, for example, is greatly affected by the ideology of relating that pervades the culture and the particular position of their relationship in the social matrix. To date, dialectically-oriented scholars have not taken as seriously as they must the socio-cultural chronotopes in which relationships are embedded.

Rethinking Scholarly Inquiry

A dialogic view of dialectics extends to the process of inquiry with the warrants that theory and method are inextricably linked (Duck & Montgomery, 1991) and that inquiry is a kind of social interaction just as much as is relational communication. To the extent that we recognize and encourage a dialogic view of communication in personal relationships, we must also do so with regard to inquiry about communication in personal relationships.

Unlike some dialectical scholars, we do not limit dialectical inquiry to interpretive approaches. Neither are we advocates of exclusive reliance on traditional, quantitatively oriented approaches. Rather, a dialogic view of inquiry is necessarily multivocal, respecting the internal integrity of all approaches to research. Dialogic inquiry is not merely a plurality of voices engaged in parallel scholarship. Dialogic inquiry assumes that understanding emerges from the active interchange among incommensurate views. We disagree with those who have offered critiques of pluralistic approaches based on the expectation that all participants in the dialogue will adopt the same evaluative criteria (e.g., Bostrom & Donohew, 1992; Burleson, 1991; Fitzpatrick, 1993; Miller, 1989). Instead, we agree with Pearce (1989) that the value of engaging incommensurate approaches depends partly on a kind of social eloquence rather than rhetorical eloquence. That is, the point of the dialogue is not to persuade, and it is not to produce coherence or convergence into a single point of view. Rather, the point is to elaborate the potential for coordination, a process Pearce describes as a kind of interaction that brings about an event that participants interpret as meaningful from their own, particular perspectives. Such coordination in the inquiry process does not require consensus. Approached eloquently, however, it does require recognition and appreciation of different viewpoints. Dialogic inquiry will be most fruitful when scholars collaborate to produce research in much the same way that people who mean different things can collaborate to produce a conversation. Collaborators do not necessarily have to agree; they do have to forge a relationship to produce something that works. Contradictory tensions between rigor and imagination, precision and richness, prediction and contingency, and creativity and verification push researchers to try different methods and to see different things in their data (see Guba, 1990). These tensions will not be escaped or transcended, neither are they necessarily negative outcomes or restraints on the productivity of ideas and understanding.

Beyond these meta-methodological issues, the study of relational interaction from a dialogic perspective must be attentive to its basic assumptions. The particular methods of choice are not as important as that the methods acknowledge that the "text" of any communication event emerges from the interaction of multiple voices, and that these voices are not uniquely identified with individuals but with the relationship between individuals (McNamee, 1988). Dialectics does not pit self-contained individual against self-contained individual. Certainly, antagonistic contradictions do occur from time to time in the form of interpersonal conflict, but users of methods of study must distinguish many more than two voices expressing the tensions of relating. Researchers must listen for those voices as they emanate between relational partners and also from the cracking, disjointed articulations of a single partner describing his or her contradictory experiences of the relationship. Such contradictory experiences are multivocal, not binary, involving complex webs of oppositions all of which are unified and negated through time and space.

In arguing for multivocality in a number of ways—multiple perspectives in dialogue, multiple voices relating, multiple times and socio-cultural locations of relating, multiple voices in research—dialogic inquiry challenges the "sacred cows" of agreement and consistency that have long driven the research enterprise. If one accepts a view of the world as dialogic, then such an outcome is inevitable. Problematic, for example, are the efforts in which researchers simply average the disparate scores of relationship parties in an effort to derive a single, unitary index of the phenomenon under investigation. Problematic as well are the efforts in which researchers privilege the outsider perspective as closer to objective truth instead of recognizing it as merely an alternative voice to those of the insiders. And the efforts in which researchers sustain universalizing generalizations are challenged, as well. The shift to multivocal inquiry is admittedly disconcerting. However, as Bakhtin (1986, p. 7) stated, "[M]eaning only reveals its depth once it has encountered and come into contact with another, foreign meaning".

CONCLUSION

Our purpose in this chapter has been to describe key concepts in, and approaches to, a dialectical perspective on social interaction in relationships. Taking a traditional scholarly approach to this explicative task, we have enumerated key assumptions like contradiction, change, praxis and totality. We also have described the conceptual and methodological implications for understanding and studying such notions as the social self, relationship change and dyadic interaction and for viewing them as relationally situated. Finally, we have given examples of inquiry conducted from a dialectical perspective to illustrate the perspective's range of application. It would be inaccurate for us to claim that all of these concepts are unique to a dialectical perspective. Although an emphasis on contradiction as the key unit of analysis uniquely characterizes a dialectical approach, some aspects of other concepts we have examined (e.g., the social self, indeterminacy of change, totality) can be identified as well in other scholarship on personal relationships (e.g., Bateson, 1972, 1979; Duck, 1994a; Pearce, 1989; Gergen, 1994). In short, a dialectical perspective is both similar to and different from these other perspectives. A dialectical perspective thus joins the scholarly dialogue on personal relationships in its simultaneous unity with, and differentiation from, other scholarly voices.

Slighted in this scholarly rendering, however, is the spirit of a dialectical perspective. Partly because of the norms of scholarship and partly because of our own styles, we have found it far easier to present the digitized version of dialectics on these printed pages than the analogic vision. But that vision is every bit as important to grasp, for it extends understanding of a dialectical perspective beyond *what* assumptions and questions are central to *how* those are integrated into a dialectical view of relationships.

The spirit of dialectics is marked by a healthy dose of *irony*, a sense that things are both what they seem to be and something else as well. Irony entertains both belief and doubt, both hope and despair, both seriousness and play, and in these kinds of complexities it hints at the very nature of social dialectics. *Creativity* is another hallmark. As Bakhtin (1986, p. 120) observed, "it is much easier to study the given in what is created . . . than to study what is created". Dialectics demands that we reach beyond our "ready-made" vocabularies of generalized central tendencies to appreciate the uniqueness of each communicative moment. *Inclusiveness* is key as well. Dialectical approaches respect different meaning systems, are attuned to their distinct voices, and so represent a multivocal social reality. Lastly, we wish to stress the sense of *fluidity* and *unfinalizability* that characterizes dialectical approaches. All is becoming, but never becomes.

We like the metaphor of the jazz ensemble to convey the dialectical spirit. Jazz is musically identified by its inclusiveness and its improvisation; collaboration of unique, sometimes discordant, instrumental voices happens in the service of spontaneous creativity. The musical score and deep structures of jazz provide just enough guidance to allow for that collaboration, but an accompanying irreverence for the music as written allows for the synergy of collaborative improvisation. These same themes of mutivocal collaboration, respect for difference, and creativity of the interactive moment characterize our notion of relational dialectics.

Chapter 14

Communication Networks and Relationship Life Cycles

Malcolm R. Parks
University of Washington, Seattle, WA, USA

Cynthia and John have just met at a social event sponsored by John's employer. Both are unattached and enjoying the unfolding conversation. We wonder, as perhaps they do, whether this conversation will mark the beginning of a romantic relationship. As scholars, of course, we also wonder how best to understand why John and Cynthia may have one relational future rather than another. Surely their individual needs and desires will matter. So, too, will the fact that they come from the same ethnic group and social class. But individual characteristics and societal categories are not sufficient. We must look at the interaction itself. But even that is not enough. We must look as well at the broader social context in which individual actions and relationships are woven together. It also may be important, for example, that Cynthia came to the party with Claire, who is John's co-worker and friend. It may be very important that Claire introduced them or that John is friendly with Claire's new husband. Whether Cynthia introduces John to her other friends or to her mother may make a difference later on.

These possibilities point to the fact that the way a given personal relationship changes over time will be intertwined with what happens in the participants' other relationships. To create a theory to account for these connections, we must first address two more basic questions. What is it that changes as a relationship develops or deteriorates? What are the features of communication networks that are most relevant for the particular dyads within them? After addressing these questions I will review previous research linking the developmental paths of personal relationships with the dynamics of the participants' surrounding social networks and then articulate a theoretic perspective for understanding these linkages.

Handbook of Personal Relationships, 2nd edn. Edited by Steve Duck.
© 1997 John Wiley & Sons Ltd.

CONCEPTUALIZING RELATIONSHIPS AND NETWORKS

The Relationship Life Cycle

Relationships exist in the structure and content of communication over time. While there are certainly cognitive, affective and structural concomitances, relationships live in the communication between the participants. This is not to say that relationships are merely "undigested interactions" (Duck, 1988b) or that what people think and feel does not matter. Rather, I emphasize the generative nature of communication. Interaction both stimulates changes in cognition and affect and is the medium through which those changes become real for the self and others.

The first task of a theory of relational life cycles is to identify the dimensions along which interaction changes as relationships develop and deteriorate. Many approaches commonly found in the literature on personal relationships fail to do this. Measuring the simple longevity of a relationship, for example, reveals nothing about the changes going on inside it. Categorizing relationships in terms of broad social labels (e.g., casual friend, friend, close friend) also does little to elucidate the underlying dimensions of the relational life cycle. Conceptualizing the relational life cycle in terms of single indicators such as satisfaction, attraction or closeness suffers from the same problem. We must look more specifically at what changes when a relationship develops or deteriorates. I believe that a useful working definition of the relational life cycle would include at least six factors: (1) interdependence, (2) breadth or variety of interaction, (3) depth or intimacy of interaction, (4) commitment, (5) predictability and understanding, and (6) code change and coordination.

Interdependence

Interdependence has long been recognized as a defining feature of the developmental process (e.g., Kelley et al., 1983; Levinger & Snoek, 1972). I interpret interdependence generously to include three specific types of mutual influence. The first is true interdependence or mutual behavioral control. It represents the degree to which each person's outcomes are influenced by the way their overt actions and internal states fit with the other's (Kelley & Thibaut, 1978). For example, John and Cynthia would be interdependent in this way if each person's desire to see a particular movie varied with the other person's desire to see the same movie. Another kind of interdependence takes the form of simple mutual dependence. John's enjoyment of a movie may depend on how much Cynthia likes it, although Cynthia may find it possible to enjoy a movie regardless of how John reacts to it. On the other hand, Cynthia's tastes in music may be much more dependent on John's preferences than his are upon hers. Although no one of these strands of dependency is binding, together they form a complex pattern of mutual dependencies that bind the couple together. A third form of interdependence is reflected in the degree to which each person's utterances in a sequence depend on the other's. The way relational partners introduce, develop and retire topics, as well as the ways in which they negotiate identity claims, may involve considerable collaboration. Conversational interdependence is worth distinguishing because it focuses us on the give and take of ongoing conversation, on its true communicative character, in a way that outcome-based definitions do not. As the degree of mutual influence represented by these three types of interdependence increases, a relationship develops. As they decrease, the relationship deteriorates.

Variety or Breadth of Interaction

As relationships develop, the "breadth" or "richness" of interaction increases (Altman & Taylor, 1973). As they deteriorate, breadth decreases. Three aspects of variety or breadth warrant delineation. At the broadest level we may think of breadth as the variety of behaviors or resources exchanged. The exchange matrix expands with development and contracts with deterioration. In Hays's (1984) study of same-sex friendships, for example, friends who grew closer over a 3-month period displayed a greater variety of behaviors across a greater range of categories (i.e., task sharing, assistance, expressing emotion, mutual disclosure) than friends whose relationship stagnated or terminated. Breadth may also be conceptualized in terms of the variety of conversational topics. Taylor (1968), for example, tracked the number of different topics new college room-mates discussed during their first 3 months and found increases in both non-intimate and intimate topics. Finally, breadth may be conceptualized in terms of the variety of communicative channels or contexts used. For instance, personal relationships started in computer-mediated channels such as the Internet often expand over time to incorporate other channels including face-to-face contact (Parks & Floyd, 1996).

Depth or Intimacy of Interaction

The depth or intimacy dimension of the relational life cycle has most often been associated with self-disclosure and intimacy. While early approaches focused only on the simple revelation of personal information (e.g., Jourard, 1971), more recent approaches have emphasized the process-oriented, communicative aspects of this dimension. Intimacy is defined as a "process in which one person expresses important self-relevant feelings and information to another, and as a result of the other's response comes to feel known, validated, and cared for" (Clark & Reis, 1988, p. 628). Although the communicative turn represented by this definition is laudable, limiting the conceptualization of depth to this sort of positive affective intimacy makes it difficult to apply it to a wide range of relationships. I favor a more general approach in which depth is conceptualized in terms of the subjective importance participants place on the topics they discuss and the behaviors they exchange. This definition would cover intimacy, but would also include depth in the sense of two business associates working on larger projects or taking greater risks together.

Commitment

Commitment is the expectation that a relationship will continue into the future. This expectation may be based on the feeling that one wants the relationship to continue, that it ought to continue, or that it has to continue. Johnson (1991a, 1991b) refers to these as personal commitment, moral commitment, and structural commitment. Johnson's tripartite model parallels two other approaches to commitment: Levinger's (1965, 1991) cohesiveness model and Rusbult's (1980, 1991) investment model. These models differ in how they categorize concepts, in the importance they place on moral factors, and in how explicitly they focus on the dyadic level. All three, however, share the view that commitment is a psychological state rooted in private judgments. They ignore the communicative nature of commitment. Yet what one's partner has said or not said about commitment is obviously important. Although some of the basic options for expressing commitment have been identified (Knapp & Taylor, 1994), we know little about how commitment is expressed or inferred in an ongoing way in different kinds of relationships. Put another way, the level of commitment people actually feel or think that their partners feel is highly contingent upon a whole set of factors having to do with the interactive dance of expression, with explicitness, with timing and with mutual revelation.

Predictability and Understanding

Participants in a relationship must have some understanding and agreement about what behaviors are desirable, acceptable, what responses each is likely to have, and how each person's actions fit into larger relational sequences. They must become experts on one another (Planalp & Garvin-Doxas, 1994). Of course, uncertainty is never fully eliminated and our desire for novelty may sometimes cause us to increase rather than decrease relational uncertainty (Altman, Vinsel & Brown, 1981; Baxter, 1993; Baxter & Montgomery, this volume). Nonetheless, the requirements for coordinated interaction will always impose the need to manage uncertainty and create understanding. The management of uncertainty therefore figures prominently in nearly every major theoretical perspective on the relational life cycle. It plays the title role in uncertainty reduction theory (Berger & Calabrese, 1975). It plays less explicit, but no less important, roles in social exchange models such as social penetration theory and interdependence theory (Altman & Taylor, 1973; Kelley & Thibaut, 1978).

Communicative Code Change

Developing relationships create their own linguistic forms and cultural codes. I believe that three particular changes occur in communication codes as a relationship develops. The first of these is code specialization. Specialized language in the form of personal idioms, for example, both affirms the relational bond and increases the efficiency of communication. Research on personal idioms has consistently shown their use and variety to be related to perceptions of satisfaction and closeness (Bell, Buerkel-Rothfuss & Gore, 1987; Bell & Healey, 1992; Bruess & Pearson, 1993). Less research has been conducted on the two other ways codes change as relationships develop. One of these is code abbreviation. As a relationship develops the participants may no longer need to elaborate as much (Bernstein, 1964). Their conversation is marked by rapid topic shifts, incomplete expressions and frequent gaps in content (Hornstein, 1985). The other change is code substitution. Interaction that once required considerable verbal coordination now requires less and may often be managed with non-verbal communication. Non-verbal communication substitutes for verbal communication. Owing to a lack of research, we can only hypothesize what happens to these changes as relationships deteriorate. I believe that sharp reductions in the use of positive personal idioms are one of the harbingers of relational trouble. The ability to rely on less elaborated messages and on non-verbal messages should also be compromised as interactions become less coordinated and partners make contrasting assumptions.

The relational life cycle, then, may be defined in terms of changes along six dimensions: interdependence, breadth, depth, commitment, predictability and communication code use. Three aspects of this conceptualization warrant further mention. First, while it is generally presumed that increases along these dimensions are associated with increases in affect, there is no assumption that deterioration necessarily weakens affect or that the affects must be positive. We could, for example, use these dimensions to describe the development of a bitter rivalry. Second, this conceptualization encompasses the concept of relational maintenance which, after all, usually centers on each sustaining a given level of development (Dindia & Canary, 1993). Finally, although the dimensions of change are continuous, change is rarely smooth or linear. There will be considerable, perhaps constant, fluctuation. Indeed, even the perception of stability may be a relational achievement (Duck, 1994a). There may be sharp breaks in which major changes in several dimensions occur at the same time. People may experience these abrupt shifts as "turning points" and scholars may use them to mark the boundaries of different relational stages (e.g., Baxter & Bullis, 1986; Knapp & Vangelisti, 1992).

Communication Networks

No relationship exists in a vacuum. John and Cynthia, our couple from the introduction, for example, each have friends, co-workers, kin and so on. Together these social contacts form a network. Although the idea of looking at sets of relationships as networks has a rich interdisciplinary history, the application of network concepts to the dyadic life cycle is a comparatively recent phenomenon.

Understanding how this network becomes involved in the relational life cycle requires us first to specify who is counted as a network member and then to identify specific network dimensions for scrutiny.

Because people typically maintain networks containing several hundred contacts (Killworth, Bernard & McCarty, 1984), researchers have always sampled members using one of two basic approaches. The first and most common approach is to sample people who are psychologically significant for the subject. Subjects may be asked to list people who are important to them or to whom they feel close (e.g., Johnson & Milardo, 1984; Parks, Stan & Eggert, 1983). Sometimes researchers define particular social roles, such as friend or parent, as important on *a priori* grounds (e.g., Lewis, 1973). Another variation is to ask subjects to list confidants, sources of personal favors, or other people who serve particular functions (e.g., Fischer, 1982). The second approach is to sample members in terms of some prespecified rate or level of interaction they have with one another. When direct observation is not possible, subjects may be asked to create a record of their interactions with a log or diary or to respond to retrospective questions about their interactions within some specified period of time. In one study, for example, subjects were telephoned seven times during a 3-week period and were asked on each occasion to list the people with whom they had interacted voluntarily for 5-minutes or more during the previous 24 hours (Milardo, 1989). The first approach yields what is referred to as the "psychological network", while the second yields an "interactive network" (Milardo, 1988, 1989).

These approaches yield quite different network rosters. When Milardo (1989) compared the psychological and interactive networks of spouses, for example, he found that only 25% of the peple listed appeared in both networks. The relative merits of each approach have been the subject of considerable discussion elsewhere (Milardo, 1988, 1989; Surra & Milardo, 1991).

Four more general points, however, have been largely overlooked. First, neither approach yields the total network. Second, these are not mutually exclusive approaches. Fischer and his colleagues (1977, p. 45), for example, combined the two approaches by asking men to name "the three men who are your closest friends and whom you see the most often". Burt (1983) advocated identifying network members through a set of questions that captured both psychological importance and interactive frequency. Third, interactive and psychological networks are not so much different networks as different sectors within the same overall network. People will appear in one and not the other only when there is a large disparity between their stated importance to the focal person and their frequency of communication with the focal person. Finally, the choice of sampling procedure depends upon the research questions being asked. If one is interested in the effects of opposition or support from network members, for example, it may be more useful to look at the reactions of significant others because their support or opposition may have a greater impact than that of less important network members. On the other hand, if one is interested in structural effects such as access to alternative partners, it may be more useful to look at a broader interactive network because it better captures the everyday structure of the network.

Our present concern is with those aspects of network structure and content that are most intertwined with the dyadic life cycle. These include: (1) network distance, (2) network overlap, (3) cross-network contact, (4) cross-network density, (5) the partners' attraction to network members, and (6) support for the relationship from network members.

Network Distance

Everyone is linked directly to a set of people who are in turn linked to others, who are linked to still others, and so on. Everyone is thus connected indirectly to everyone else. As we know from the "small world" studies, five to ten links are usually all that are needed to connect any two randomly selected persons (e.g., Milgram, 1967). The distance between any two unacquainted persons is determined by the number of links separating them. This characteristic has been variously referred to as "reachability" (e.g., Mitchell, 1969), "network proximity" (Parks & Eggert, 1991) and "distance" (e.g., Surra & Milardo, 1991). Whatever term is used, the network distance between unacquainted persons should be closely related to their likelihood of initiating a relationship.

Network Overlap

Several important network characteristics are related to the more general concept of density—the extent to which network members are connected to each other. The overall density of the relational partners' network, however, will be less important than the density of specific local sectors or structures. If we think from the standpoint of a particular couple, say John and Cynthia, it quickly becomes apparent that we are most interested in the density of those sectors where Cynthia and John's individual networks come into contact with one another. One measure of this is network overlap—the number or proportion of people that are common members of the relational partners' individual networks. It is a measure of the extent to which partners have formed a joint network.

Cross-network Contact

Cross-network contact represents the degree to which each partner knows and communicates with members of the other's network. It is conceptually equivalent to network overlap when only the interactive network is considered. When the psychological network is considered, contact and overlap will differ. John and Cynthia, for instance, may both name Claire as a close friend (overlap) or perhaps only Cynthia will list her and John will be asked to report how often he communicates with her (contact). Sampling networks according to the type or importance of relationships preserves the subtle, but potentially important, distinction between "our friend" and "your friend with whom I have contact".

Cross-network Density

A broader measure of density is what I call cross-network density—the extent to which members of each partner's network know and communicate with members of the other partner's network. In traditional network analytic terms this measure would represent a special kind of "clustering" between members of the partners' separate networks (Barnes, 1969). This dimension has not been assessed in research on the relational life cycle, presumably because a rigorous measure of cross-network density would require contacting all network members.

The difficulties of contacting network members are illustrated in a study by Kim & Stiff (1991). First, they found that perhaps as many as 20% of the couples in their sample where lost because one or both members refused to give access to network members. Even with a reduced sample, however, data collection must have been a daunting task because nearly 1000 network members were named by approximately 75 couples. A more practical, but still useful, measure can be obtained by having the focal partners estimate the level of cross-contact between the members of their individual networks. In one prototype, for example, we asked dating partners to create a grid in which one person's contacts were listed along the rows and the other's were listed in the columns. They were then asked to determine jointly if each possible combination of people had ever met and, if they had, how often they communicated with each other.

Attraction to Partner's Network

People in relationships often come to see one another not simply as individuals, but as part of a social package. The course of any one relationship may thus be greatly influenced by each participant's attraction or repulsion for the partner's friends, family, work associates and so on. Attraction may be based on the positive attributes of network members as individuals or on their value as a social links to other people and resources. Patterns of attraction have long been the subject of sociometric analysis (e.g., Cartwright & Harary, 1956; Davis, 1970), but less attention has been devoted to the role of attraction to network members in the development of dyadic relationships and still less has focused on the actual communication of attraction or repulsion. Yet the way in which partners talk about their feelings toward the members of one another's network may well have an impact on the development of relationships that goes well beyond the feelings themselves.

Support from Network Members

Although there is a voluminous literature on social support, most of it has dealt with support for individuals rather than for relationships. The two types of support need not be the same. Supporting Cynthia as an individual does not necessarily mean that one is also supporting her relationship with John. Indeed, some network members may believe that the best way to support Cynthia as a person is to oppose her relationship with John. We know remarkably little about how people actually express support for relationships. Presumably networks act as "buffers" from stress and "channels" for resources at the relational level just as they do at the individual level (Gottlieb, 1983). But relationships may be supported or opposed by network members in many other ways, including the symbolic reinforcement conveyed both explicitly through verbal comments and implicitly through devices such joint invitations (Lewis, 1973; Parks & Eggert, 1991).

Research to date has generally focused on the perceived supportiveness of network members. Concentration on global perceptions, however, may blind us to the more strategic process through which partners and network members negotiate what is known, presented, and expressed about the relationship.

CONNECTING RELATIONSHIPS AND NETWORKS

We are now in a position to explore how the private world of relationships becomes intertwined with the broader, more public world of the participants' social networks. Relationships and networks are connected from start to finish, so I will look across three general phases of the relational life cycle: initiation; development and maintenance; deterioration and termination.

Initiation and Before

If we want to understand how a relationship comes into being, we need to examine the conditions just prior to its formation. Some of these conditions exist in the inner qualities of the prospective partners. Others emanate from cultural and group norms. Still others reside in the physical context. The importance of physical proximity, for instance, is well recognized (e.g., Festinger, Schachter & Back, 1950). Some physical settings are simply more conducive to relationships than others (e.g., Werner et al., 1992).

When we think of relationship initiation from a network perspective, however, a new set of factors becomes apparent. As a case in point, consider the following account of how Julie met her future husband, Barry (Seattle Times, 1994):

> My husband and I met at my best friend's wedding. I was her maid of honor and he was her photographer. When I first saw him I thought he was the handsomest man I had ever seen. After that night I had to think of a way to see him again, so I took my nephew in for pictures. My future husband asked me out a few weeks later.

This account obviously notes psychological factors such as Julie's strong physical attraction. Perhaps the physical and cultural context of the wedding itself also helped put romance in the air. But let's back up. Imagine that we could take a movie showing Julie and Barry's network in the months prior to the wedding. They already have an indirect relationship because each has a connection with the bride. Suppose we back up the movie still further and ask how Barry was selected as the photographer in the first place. We do not know, but it is probable that Barry had been recommended by someone who was close to the bride and perhaps knew Julie. As we move backward, then, we find a trail of indirect linkages between Julie and Barry long before they met. If we now move forward again, we would see Barry and Julie coming ever closer as their network distance shrinks. They are carried toward one another on the social plates of their networks by forces quite beyond their intention and control. This line of thinking points to social proximity effects in relationship formation.

Social Proximity Effects

As the number of links separating any two people decreases, their probability of meeting increases (Parks, 1995; Parks & Eggert, 1991). Social proximity is not the same thing as physical proximity. One is likely to encounter only a few of the many potential partners with which one shares a given geographic space. Two people can be physically proximal, but socially distal (as in the case of neighbors who do not speak to one another). Conversely, people can be widely dispersed in a geographic sense, but relationally linked. Indeed historical changes in organizational structure and technology have made it possible for many urbanites to create personal networks that are only vaguely tied to a particular geographic locale (Wellman, 1979; Wellman, Carrington & Hall, 1988).

No one has yet tested the social proximity hypothesis directly. Doing so would require measuring changes over time in the network structure for a large set of people. Nonetheless, the hypothesis is consistent with the structure of friendship choices in sociograms (e.g., Davis, 1970). A person who is a friend of one person is far more likely than not to be listed as a friend of that person's friends as well. Evidence from our studies of same-sex friendships and premarital romantic relationships is also consistent with the social proximity hypothesis (Parks, 1995; Parks & Eggert, 1991). In a series of large data sets collected in the mid-1980s we asked respondents to obtain a list of their partner's 12 closest kin and non-kin contacts. Respondents were then asked to indicate how many of these people they had met prior to meeting their friend or romantic partner for the first time. If the social proximity hypothesis is correct, most of our respondents should have reported that they had such prior contacts. And indeed they did. Two thirds (66.3%) of the nearly 900 respondents reported that they had met at least one member of their partner's network of close social network prior to first meeting their partner.

Although this result is consistent with the social proximity hypothesis, the precise extent of the effect remains unclear. Because it is based only on the partner's current network rather than the network the partner had at the time of the first meeting, our estimate of the social proximity effect may be biased. If changes in the network between the first meeting and the time of data collection favored retaining people who knew the subject, as we would predict they would, reports of prior contact would be inflated. On the other hand, there are also good reasons to think that the 66% figure is probably an underestimate. Our method only counted the subject's contacts with members of the partner's network and not the partner's prior contacts with the subject's own network. Also, we only examined the closest 12 in a network of direct contacts that probably contains several hundred members (Killworth, Bernard & McCarty, 1984).

Beyond the need for more direct, comprehensive data on the social proximity hypothesis itself, several related areas call for attention. In our samples there was substantial variation in the number of people with whom the subject had prior contact. While there were no significant sex differences, other individual differences may come into play and influence factors like network size or the willingness to reach out to new people and new situations. We found no age differences, but our samples were limited to high school and college students. Previous researchers have found age-related changes in the number and complexity of friendships across the adult lifespan (e.g., Blieszner & Adams, 1992) but have not examined differences in the sources of new friends or in patterns of initiation. Still, the school years are marked by easy access to a large number of potential friends and lovers within a relatively contained environment. Few environments in later life, save perhaps retirement communities, are likely to offer such easy access. Without such access, people may become even more dependent on common acquaintances and group ties. Finally, social proximity effects may vary according the type of relationship being examined. We found, for example, that prospective romantic partners had almost twice as much prior contact with members of each other's close networks as did prospective friends (Parks & Eggert, 1991).

Third Party Effects

While much of what leads up to the initiation of personal relationships is impersonal and structural, social networks also reflect the active choices and actions of individuals. Network members directly influence the initiation and early development of personal relationships in at least four ways.

Network members sometimes act as passive reference points for the judgments prospective partners make about one another. The process may be entirely visual, as in the case of one of our respondents who saw her future boyfriend talking with some people with whom she had played volleyball. The fact that she liked them contributed to her positive appraisal of him. The use of network members as reference points also emerges in the talk between between prospective relational partners. Conversation analysts, for instance, suggest that interaction between previously unacquainted individuals is guided by "membership devices" that locate the participants in groups—such as place of residence, job or academic major (Maynard & Zimmerman, 1984; Sacks, 1972). I would go one step further to suggest that these linguistic locators often include searches for common acquaintances. One is thus judged by whom one knows.

Network members may also an active role in the initiation and early development of others' relationships. Although the activities of "third-party helpers" beg for additional research, the broad outlines of their activities emerged in a study of third-party help in dating relationships by Parks & Barnes (1988). These researchers found that the friends of prospective romantic partners employed three general strategies on their behalf. One of these involved direct initiations in which the third party introduced prospective partners, arranged for them to meet "by accident", or organized a blind or double date. A second general strategy involved a wide range of behaviors that functioned as attraction manipulations. Examples included telling one prospective partner positive things about the other and downplaying negative features, telling one of the other's interest in him or her, and emphasizing how much the prospective partners had in common or would like each other. In addition network members did a variety of things that might be called direct assistance. These included relaying information back and forth between the prospective partners, providing one with information about how to contact the other, and coaching one person on what to say (and not say) to the other.

Third-party help is so common that it is almost normative. Nearly two-thirds (64%) of those who had started a romantic relationship in the previous year reported that they had received help from network members (Parks & Barnes, 1988). Moreover, they generally believed that this help had been important in the initiation of their relationship. This belief was supported by the finding that unattached people who did not receive third-party help dated less often during the previous year than those who did. Finally, it is worth noting that third-party helpers were most often acting in collusion with one or both recipients. In 80% of the cases at least one of the recipients was aware of the helper's activity and in about 64% of the cases at least one of the recipients had asked or "hinted" for help.

Before turning to the development and maintenance of intepersonal relationships, it is worth pausing to appreciate just how different a social contextual view of relationship initiation really is. The vast bulk of previous research on personal relationships has either not addressed the process of initiation or has failed to recognize the crucial role of social context (Parks, 1995). The actual process of initiation can not be triggered merely by providing subjects with written descriptions or pictures of other people (e.g., Byrne, 1971, 1992; Snyder, Berscheid & Glick, 1985). Neither can it be adequately modeled by procedures in which previously unacquainted individuals are paired by the researcher in the laboratory (e.g., Cappella & Palmer, 1990; Cramer et al., 1985; Sunnafrank, 1984; Van Lear, 1987). At best such procedures create involuntary relationships that are disconnected from the subject's life world and that have no consequences for it (Parks, 1995). It is not surprising that psychological factors and processes are highlighted by such procedures. They may be so socially stripped that only these factors remain. To understand how actual relationships form, we must study the process *in situ*, in a context of existing relationships, commitments, network structures and opportunities.

Development and Maintenance

More network factors come into play as personal relationships move beyond their early stages. Structural factors like the degree of network overlap and cross-network contact, and density, become important. Support from and attraction to network members also influence and are influenced by development and maintenance. Indeed, the various life cycle factors and network factors outlined earlier define a complex matrix of possible links between networks and dyads. Not all of these have been examined, of course, and so the discussion below is meant not only to summarize existing research, but also to point to new areas for research.

Structural Factors in Development and Maintenance

Only two structural factors have been examined systematically. One of these is *network overlap*, the degree to which partners interact with the same people or name the same people as significant contacts. As romantic couples move toward marriage, they also develop a shared network (Krain,1977). Milardo (1982), for example, found that about 30% of the network members of casually dating couples were shared, while almost 77% of the network members of engaged couples were shared. Both cross-sectional and longitudinal analyses revealed positive associations between network overlap and courtship stage, a global measure of relational development. Kim & Stiff (1991) measured relational development with an index composed of items tapping intimacy, predictability (uncertainty reduction) and commitment in heterosexual relationships. As predicted, this index of development correlated positively with the proportion of overlapping members in the partners' combined network. Studies of network overlap in marriage are not generally centered around developmental issues, but do generally show that network overlap and marital satisfaction are positively related (Julien & Markman, 1991).

Additional research is needed to evaluate the generality of the link between development and overlap. We not know if overlap plays a greater role in some dimensions of development than others. Though we would expect network overlap to operate in similar ways across different types of relationships, the research to date has been limited to premarital romantic relationships.

More research has focused on the connection between relational development and *cross-network contact*. One measure of cross-network contact is the number or proportion of people one has met in the partner's network. This measure is positively related to a number of developmental indicators in romantic relationships, including measures of intimacy or love, closeness, predictability and commitment (Eggert & Parks, 1987; Parks, Stan & Eggert, 1983). It is also positively related to commitment in same-sex friendships among high school students, although it does not appear to be related to other developmental indicators such as intimacy and predictability (Eggert & Parks, 1987). Another measure of cross-network contact is the frequency of communication with the known members of the partner's network. This, too, has been positively associated with a variety of developmental factors in romantic relationships. Increases in feelings of love, closeness, predictability and commitment go hand in hand with increases in the frequency of communication with the partner's friends and family (Parks, Stan & Eggert, 1983). Together, these results suggest that cross-network contact is indeed related to relationship development, although it appears to be more strongly related to commitment than to the other dimensions examined to date. It is not yet clear why this should be, or why cross-network contact appears to be more strongly related to development in dating relationships than in same-sex friendships.

Much less attention has been devoted to *cross-network density*, even though it is often implicated in theoretic discussions of development (e.g., Lewis, 1973; Milardo & Lewis, 1985; Parks, 1995; Surra & Milardo, 1991). The only data currently available on cross-network density come from Kim & Stiff's (1991) study of heterosexual relationships. These researchers found that couples who scored higher on a global measure of development also had a greater number of contacts between the members of their individual networks. Kim & Stiff's study is also notable because it is the only study to have gathered data directly from network members themselves.

Content Factors in Development and Maintenance

The information or content that flows through the network structure is, of course, at least as important as the structure itself. This content includes both discourse and perceptions among network members. Sometimes it is as generic as the extent to which members of a pair mention their activities with other network members or share news of other network members. Unfortunately, actual discourse about network members is rarely studied. Instead researchers have focused on perceptions of attraction and support.

To put it simply, attraction rubs off. That is, *attraction to members of the partner's network* and attraction to the partner should be related. Liking the partner's family and friends should lead to greater liking for the partner. By the same token, increases in attraction to the partner should render his or her family and friends more attractive. This connection is uniformly supported in the research to date. Studies of heterosexual romantic relationships among both high school and college students report a strong positive relationship between how attracted partners are to the members of each other's networks and how intimate, close and committed they feel toward each other (Eggert & Parks, 1987; Parks, Stan & Eggert, 1983). Similar findings emerge from studies of same-sex friendship. Here, too, those who are more attracted to one another's network members are also report greater intimacy, closeness and commitment (Eggert & Parks, 1987).

One need not, of course, like all network members equally. In a study of young adult friendships, for example, we found that 82% of the subjects could think of at least one close friend who had a close friend who was disliked by the subject (Parks & Riveland, 1987). Although subjects typically reported having regular contact with the disliked person, most did little to resolve the imbalance. Instead they avoided the topic when communicating with their friend or used cognitive coping strategies, such as trying to think about the disliked person's positive qualities or trying not to think about the disliked person at all. Much more remains to be learned about the choice of coping strategies, about the consequences of strategy choices, and about the factors that influence the level of imbalance that people are willing to tolerate. Many of the coping strategies reported in our exploratory study allow friends to think that network members like one another more than they actually do. Identifying the factors that influence how accurately people judge liking among network members is an obvious research priority.

The *perceived supportiveness of network members* also exerts a powerful role in the development of personal relationships. In two-earner families, for example, the best predictor of a father's involvement with childcare tasks is the extent to which his friends and other non-kin contacts support his father–child relationship (Cochran et al., 1990). As children form their own relationships, support from network members becomes important for them as well. Although there appears to be a gap in the research on network support in children's relationships, the importance of network support has been solidly established in research on adolescents. Among high school students, for instance, the perceived supportiveness of network members has been linked to the development of both same-sex friendships and opposite-sex dating relationships. Subjects who perceive that the members of both their network and their partner's network support their relationship report higher levels of intimacy and commitment (Eggert & Parks, 1987; Parks & Eggert, 1991). Similar patterns hold for the development of romantic relationships and mate selection among young adults. The importance of parental support has long been recognized, not only in courtship but also in marital adjustment (e.g., Burgess & Cottrell, 1939; Locke, 1951). More recent research has systematically documented the positive link between support from the partners' networks and the development of intimacy and commitment in premarital romantic relationships (Krain, 1977; Leslie, 1983; Leslie, Johnson, & Houston, 1986; Lewis, 1973; Parks et al., 1983). In doing so, it has consistently rejected the notion that opposition from network members can intensify feelings of attachment. While this "Romeo and Juliet effect" (Driscoll, Davis & Lipetz, 1972) is deeply embedded in romantic mythology, it has little empirical basis.

Several distinct subprocesses are probably reflected in these findings. Some relationships may not be revealed to network members until the participants believe they will be supported (Baxter & Widenmann, 1993; Parks et al., 1983). Once the relationship is public, partners may lobby network members for support by providing reassurance, minimizing the partner's failings, highlighting the partner's good qualities, and strategically arranging social events to place the relationship in the best light. In one study approximately 85% of dating partners reported using such strategies with their parents (Leslie et al., 1986). As I noted in the previous section on initiation, network members also have their own strategies should they wish to support the relationship. In addition, relational partners may simply withdraw from unsupportive network members. Knowing this, network members may express more support once it appears that the partners are committed to the relationship (Driscoll, Davis & Lipetz, 1972; Johnson & Milardo, 1984; Leslie et al., 1986).

Several other aspects of the role of network support remain unresolved. We have no data on either how accurately relational partners perceive the level of support from network members or how accurately network members judge the level of development in other members' dyadic relationships. Considerable inaccuracy should be expected, given the many strategic manipulations of information alluded to above. In addition we know little about how the impact of support or opposition might vary across sources and relationship types. In adolescent romantic relationships, for example, support from the partner's network appears to be more strongly correlated with intimacy and commitment than support from the subject's own network. In adolescent friendships, however, the source of support does not seem to matter as much and, if anything, support from the subject's own network is a stronger correlate of development (Eggert & Parks, 1987; Parks & Eggert, 1991).

Deterioration and Beyond

As the social fabric weaving partners' networks together unravels, so does their personal relationship. The deterioration of personal relationships, like their initiation and development, is accompanied by changes in the structure and content of network relations. These changes flow both ways. Partners may seek to redefine their networks as their relationship deteriorates, or changes in network structure and content may disrupt an otherwise viable relationship.

Structural Factors in Deterioration

Rifts in the shared network are particularly common as personal relationships deteriorate. *Network overlap* may fall as the partners shift their interaction from shared to unshared relationships. Once the problems in the dyad become apparent, network members may withdraw either because of negative judgments or because they fear adverse impacts on their own relationships (Goode, 1956; Spanier & Casto, 1979). Alternatively, relationships may be stressed if social or environmental conditions isolate them or tear away their shared network. Whatever the direction of causal influence, reductions in network overlap should be associated with instability and deterioration. Milardo (1982), for example, found that both the size of the shared network and the amount of communication with it declined over time in deteriorating premarital romances. More generally, divorce rates tend to be higher in cultures where the spouses maintain comparatively separate networks (Ackerman, 1963; Zelditch, 1964).

Deterioration is also associated with reductions in both *cross-network contact* and *cross-network density*. That is, in deteriorating relationships there will be less contact with the members of the partner's network and the members of both partners' separate networks will have less contact with each other. Several different longitudinal studies support these predictions. Premarital romances, for example, are more likely to deteriorate over time when the partners have less contact with each other's friends and family (Parks & Adelman, 1983). Same-sex friendships are more likely to terminate if they are set in loosely knit networks rather than tightly knit networks (Salzinger, 1982). Cross-network density seems to be important in a variety of settings and relationships, as Hammer (1980) found in her study of relationships in a factory, a church group, and a doughnut shop. Relationships in each of these settings were more likely to be terminated when the partner's networks were comparatively unconnected.

Whether pulled or pushed, the parting of networks also marks a return to earlier network patterns. After marital separation, for instance, people typically focus more of their network activity with same-sex friends, drop contacts with the ex-spouse's friends and relatives, and generally develop a less densely interconnected network (Rands, 1988).

In many cases, however, images of relationships ending or networks fully separating are misleading. Most divorced parents who remain in the same geographic area, for example, continue to interact with each other directly (Ahrons & Rodgers, 1987). Their relationship is redefined rather than terminated. Even when former relational partners do not maintain direct contact, their *network distance* may not be very large. Ex-spouses who never speak may continue to be indirectly connected through children, friends and relatives. Indeed, they may be quite strategic about maintaining such indirect linkages. We interviewed one recently divorced man, for example, who said he stayed in a carpool largely because one of the other riders could tell him what his ex-wife was up to. Systematic research on the use of networks to monitor former partners is essential not only for theoretical reasons, but also because ex-spouses so often react negatively, even violently, to what they learn about one another's activities.

Content Factors in Deterioration

Just as attraction to the partner's network may bring relational partners closer, repulsion may drive them apart. This may happen gradually or quite suddenly, as in the case of romantic partners reacting negatively when they reveal a previously hidden relationship to disapproving family and friends. Unfortunately there is no systematic research backing the obvious prediction that reductions in *attraction to the partner's network* should be associated with the subsequent deterioration of the relationship. As this research is conducted, it may be important to examine changes in attraction to specific members of the partner's network as well as to the partner's network as a whole. We might also find wide differences in expectations regarding attraction both at the individual level and across relationships types.

More research has been devoted to the *perceived supportiveness of network members*. Several studies, for example, have shown that dating relationships are more likely to dissolve when the participants believe that their friends and family are unsupportive (Johnson & Milardo, 1984; Lewis, 1973; Parks & Adelman, 1983). This effect also appears in marriage. Compared to those who remain married, those who divorce typically report far higher levels of family opposition before and during the marriage (Thornes & Collard, 1979).

These findings no doubt summarize a much more complex communication process that unfolds as relational partners and network members negotiate and renegotiate their stance on the relationship. Nearly everyone occasionally reveals relational complaints to network members. When people who are satisfied with their relationship discuss their complaints with confidants, they typically co-construct a conversation that supports both the expression of complaints and the maintenance of the relationship (Julien, Begin & Chartrand, 1995; Oliker, 1989). The conversations of dissatisfied individuals with their confidants, however, do not show this delicate patterning of complaint and maintenance talk. Talk no longer contextualizes the expression of problems within general support for the relationship. Complaints are now treated as signs of deeper problems and the relationship is "spoiled" (McCall, 1982) in the eyes of network members. This in turn may trigger alliances which, while they may be supportive of the complaining partner as an individual, have the ultimate effect of undermining the relationship still further (Goldsmith & Parks, 1990).

THEORIZING ABOUT RELATIONSHIPS AND NETWORKS

The belief that personal relationships are purely private entities is a myth. As the research reviewed here demonstrates, personal relationships derive their life course not only from the character of their participants, but also from the larger social networks in which they are situated. From beginning to end, personal relationships are continuously embedded in the social context created by interactions with other network members and through which individual desires are enacted and cultural values are realized.

No one explanatory principle is sufficient to account for the linkages between personal relationships and their surrounding networks. Moreover, networks are not merely sources of influence, but are also resources that participants actively manipulate. Theory must therefore include processes that shape relationships in response to both structural imperatives and individual choices. Doing this brings us to several microprocesses that function to tie together the fates of relationships and networks. These may be grouped into two broader theoretical categories that I refer to as uncertainty management and network structuring.

Uncertainty Management

Efforts to manage uncertainty are represented in several of the microprocesses that link the relational life cycle to networks. For example, people in close relationships generally expect to meet their partner's other close associates. Meeting the partner's friends, family or close work associates satisfies a widely held social expectation and thus contributes to the management of uncertainty. Failing to meet them may raise doubts about the partner's feelings or one's own desirability and thus retard or reverse the development of the relationship (Parks & Adelman, 1983). According to theories of cognitive balance in social relations (e.g., Cartwright & Harary, 1956; Newcomb, 1961), we also generally expect to like the people our partner likes. Attraction to the partner should create a cognitive strain toward liking the members of the partner's network. Similarly, attraction to members of the partner's network should create a cognitive strain toward liking the partner more. Imbalances in feelings for the partner and members of his or her network can create uncertainty which may lead to either an attenuation of the relationship with the partner or coping strategies that have the effect of denying or concealing the imbalance (Parks, 1995; Parks & Riveland, 1987).

Linkages with network members open vast trade routes of information about the partner and the relationship. Even without explicit discussion, the relationships of network members create reference points against which partners evaluate their own relationship. Married couples, for instance, commonly compare their marriage to the marriages of their friends (Titus, 1980). Discussion with network members provides information about the past behaviors of the partner, ready-made explanations for his or her behavior as well as one's own, and opportunities to compare one's own judgments to those of others. Exchanges with network members yield information that goes beyond what can be learned from the partner directly. Perhaps this is why the frequency of communication with members of the partner's network is a better predictor of uncertainty in romantic couples than is the amount of communication directly with the partner (Parks & Adelman, 1983).

Some of the most important information exchanged with network members deals with whether network members support or oppose the participants' relationship. Almost without exception, research on friendship, premarital romantic relationships and marriage reveals positive associations between relational development and support received from network members. Indeed, support is so important that it is the subject of considerable strategic activity by partners and network members alike. Participants and network members conspire to conceal, reveal and distort information that may be challenging to their larger interests.

Because their interests often do not coincide, the interactive dance between participants and network members typically unfolds as a series of signals, interpretive offers and inferred responses.

Network Structuring

We may describe the social location of people relative to one another in terms of their structural positions in a larger network. Several measures of relative structural position are especially important for the life cycle of any given dyad within this larger network. These include distance, overlap, cross-network contact, cross-network density and cross-network linkage. These factors are important not only because they contribute to the management of uncertainty, but also because they both represent and influence participants' broader relational behavior.

One reason for this is that the opportunity for any two individuals to interact is in large part a function of network structuring. Even before they meet for the first time, prospective partners may be carried toward one another by the physical and social structures they inhabit. The research on third parties demonstrates that people actively manipulate the network to create opportunities to interact with prospective partners. Once their relationship is established, relational participants realign the structure of their networks so that their opportunities to interact are maximized. They may, for instance, be drawn toward a shared network because a shared network gives them chances to be together that they would not otherwise have. If nothing else, the intertwining of network structure should be associated with development and stability because it reduces the number of conflicting demands on the dyadic partners' time and energy. On the other side of the relational life cycle, people may actively manipulate their network structures so as to minimize their time together when they feel their relationship is deteriorating. They develop independent relationships, spend less time with shared network members, and increase network distance by forcing the partner to gain information through intermediaries. These changes, of course, need not be deliberate. They could be unintended consequences of other actions, such as moving from one part of town to another, or they could result from larger social changes over which the individual has no control. Either way, changes in the network structure surrounding a relationship affect it because they alter the participants' opportunities to interact with each other.

Network structure also regulates both the desirability and availability of alternative partners. Although the notion of networks as barriers to dissolution has been around for some time (e.g., Levinger, 1979), there are probably more effects than have been previously recognized. For one thing, being embedded in a shared network or a heavily cross-linked network with a relational partner reinforces the desirability of the present relationship. This network may provide resources or other attractions that would not otherwise be available. Supportive network members are unlikely to introduce the participants to alternative partners. Simply being embedded in a shared, cross-linked network makes it more difficult to both meet and spend time with alternative partners of all kinds. Once a relationship has ended, the structure of the individual's network may make it easier or harder to find new partners. It has been hypothesized, for example, that divorced people's access to alternative partners is enhanced when their networks are predominantly composed of friends and reduced when kin make up the bulk of their networks (Milardo, 1987).

Looking Ahead

Some personal relationships never really get started. Some flower. Others wilt. Still others descend into hells of abuse. Whatever their path, all relationships change over time as the result of changes in individual abilities and wishes, changes in the external conditions impinging upon them, or both. There is no steady state. Understanding how relationships change over time is essential not only on general scientific grounds, but also because the social and individual consequences of disordered relationships are so high. To develop such an understanding, I believe we must ask at least four basic questions: What are the central dimensions of the relational life cycle? What aspects of social networks are most relevant for the relational life cycle? How are social networks linked to the relational life cycle? And, why?

The answers to these questions comprise a social contextual theory of the relational life cycle. Like all scientific theory, it is best viewed as work-in-progress. Indeed one of the primary functions of theory is to point out how much you do not know. Although they have not been brought together as I have done here, there is considerable agreement about the salient dimensions of the relational life cycle. Theoretical statements typically incorporate all of most of the dimensions of interdependence, breadth, depth, commitment, predictability and verbal and non-verbal code change (e.g., Altman & Taylor, 1973; Berger & Calabrese, 1975; Kelley et al., 1983). Yet our understanding of these dimensions is limited by our tendency to think of them in purely psychological terms. Thus, we know more about how psychological factors like satisfaction and perceived investment are related to psychological judgments of commitment than we do about how people actually express commitment to one another. We know more about uncertainty as a psychological state than we do about the actual communicative sequences people use to regulate their uncertainty.

Equally large gaps and opportunities exist in our knowledge of social networks. There is little question that both structural and content features are important. The findings to date justify attention to structural factors like overlap and content factors like support. Yet the importance of other factors, like network distance and attraction, is only beginning to be explored. Some, like cross-network density, have almost no research history. Although summary measures of content factors like attraction and support are useful, future theory may best be served by greater attention to the communicative dance through which relational partners and network members reveal, conceal and distort their judgments. It is here that the real relationship between dyad and network is worked out.

The nascent status of social contextual theory is even more apparent when we bring the dimensions of the relational life cycle together with the salient network dimensions. Relatively few of the specific links between the six life cycle dimensions and the six life cycle dimensions I have identified here have been investigated. Most investigators have relied on global indices or limited measures of relational stages instead of specific measures of life cycle dimensions. In addition to studies investigating the links between specific dimensions of the life cycle and networks, future theory development would benefit from research on an expanded range of relationships. Most research to date has focused on romantic relationships and same-sex friendships among young adults. Yet the theoretic mechanisms that tie networks to the relational life cycle are in no way limited to these relationships. They should also emerge in work relationships, intercultural relationships, and relationships among older adults.

Even though much remains to be done, the social contextual perspective has already added already important new dimensions to our understanding of personal relationships. Models that incorporate network factors have been shown to do a better job of predicting relational events than models that are restricted to purely individual and dyadic factors (Parks & Eggert, 1991). While most theories of personal relationships are not triggered until prospective partners meet for the first time, the social contextual perspective offers an account of the forces that bring people into contact with each other. Perhaps most important, the social contextual perspective is unique in that it provides theoretic transport between the macro- and micro-levels of analysis. It is a vehicle for situating our understanding of individuals and relationships within larger structural and cultural processes.

Chapter 15

Face and Facework: Implications for the Study of Personal Relationships

Sandra Metts
Illinois State University, Normal, IL, USA

Although there are many features of interactions that contribute to the quality and stability of personal relationships, one of the most pervasive yet little studied features is the degree to which partners enhance, preserve or diminish each other's desired identity, or face. Indeed, even when relational deterioration appears to stem from such common issues as money management or sexual problems, closer analysis often reveals that the struggle occurs within a subtext of face concerns. That is, the conversations of troubled relationships tend to exhibit a prevailing lack of protection for and validation of one or both partners' desired identity. In the absence of such confirmation, one or both partners may avoid the aversive state of disconfirmation by withdrawing from problem-solving interactions or may engage in such interactions from a defensive posture. Ultimately, attempts to solve problems are cosmetic and unsatisfying. Conversely, the conversations of healthy relationships are marked by the ability and willingness to protect and validate the assertion of both partners' desired identities. In the presence of such confirmation, problems are resolved at the level of issues, leaving intact the integrity of each partner's desired identity.

The purpose of this chapter is to demonstrate the utility of a face perspective for the study of personal relationships. Because the terms *face* and *facework* have entered the common vernacular and scholarly writing with varying degrees of precision, this chapter begins with a discussion of face and facework based on the original writings of Goffman (1959, 1967). The contribution of this approach to personal relationships is illustrated with several common relationship stressors, with particular emphasis on complaints and conflict. The chapter then moves to

Handbook of Personal Relationships, 2nd edn. Edited by Steve Duck.
© 1997 John Wiley & Sons Ltd.

a discussion of face and facework as elaborated by Brown & Levinson (1987) in politeness theory. The contributions of this tradition to the study of close relationships is illustrated with two problematic episodes, provision of social support and relationship disengagement. The chapter concludes with a brief discussion of possible avenues for future research.

FACE AND FACEWORK

Goffman's Model

Goffman (1967) employed the term *face* to refer to the situated public identities, or positive social values, that a person claims during an interaction. Ordinarily, face is granted and sustained as a routine and unnoticed consequence of interaction. However, in some instances, face concerns are the substance of the interaction. These occasions are personally relevant because people are emotionally invested in their face. When an interaction goes better than expected and face is enhanced, interactants feel positive emotions (e.g., pride); when an interaction goes worse than expected and face is diminished or lost, interactants feel negative emotions (e.g., embarrassment or shame). According to Goffman, "poise" is the ability to control emotional reactions and continue to interact even when one's face has been questioned by others as inappropriate or undeserved ("be in wrong face") or when one has no sense of the type of identity that should be projected in a situation ("out of face").

Facework refers to a variety of communicative devices available to interactants for preventing face loss (both their own and others'), restoring face if lost, and facilitating the maintenance of poise in the advent of disrupted interactions (Goffman, 1967). "Avoidant facework" includes such practices as steering a conversation away from topics that would be embarrassing to self or other, pretending not to hear a belch or burp, or ignoring a rude comment. It also includes "disclaimers", statements used to preface remarks that could reflect negatively on a speaker (e.g., "I could be wrong, but . . ." or "Some of my best friends are Catholic, but . . .") (Hewitt & Stokes, 1975). Goffman also comments on more sophisticated strategies, or "tact", whereby people give options to the recipient of a message so that he or she is able to avoid face threats in giving a response. Goffman uses the example of social etiquette, which advises "against asking for New Year's Eve dates too early in the season, lest the girl find it difficult to provide a gentle excuse for refusing" (1967, p. 29). More recent illustrations might be found in the prevailing norm of indirectness in early stages of courtship. For example, scripted routines such as flirting afford both sender and receiver the opportunity to negotiate, with a minimum of face threat to both parties, whether affiliative communication actions will constitute signs of sexual intent or signs of conversational friendliness.

"Corrective facework" functions to restore face and re-engage routine interaction after a person's face has been lost or put in jeopardy. Typically, a ritualized sequence of four moves—challenge, offering, acceptance and thanks—suffices to restore the social order. The remedial interchange begins when a challenge (sometimes called a reproach) calls attention to some action that is inappropriate or inconsistent with a proffered identity. It may be verbalized (e.g., "You're late again"), or be nonverbally expressed (e.g., indications of surprise, an awkward silence, looking angry or hurt). An offering is the attempt to repair face damage by expressing regret or providing an explanation. The most deferential and self-deprecating offering is an apology; it not only acknowledges the severity of an offense, but also assumes responsibility for the act, disparages the "bad self" who did the act, offers atonement or restitution, and promises more appropriate behavior in the future (e.g., "I'm so sorry I'm late. I know how important it is to you that we get to the Jones' dinner party on time. I was terribly careless but I promise this won't happen again"). An excuse is a type of offering that provides an account for an offensive action by minimizing responsibility for the act (e.g., "I know I'm late and that getting to the Jones' on time is important, but I got caught in a meeting and it went on much later than I expected"). A justification is also an account, but focuses more on minimizing the severity of the offensive act than the person's responsibility (e.g., "I know I'm late, but we still have plenty of time to get to the Jones' if we hurry; no harm done"). Offerings may also consist of the expression of appropriate emotions such as embarrassment, shame or guilt without an accompanying account. Writings subsequent to Goffman (e.g., Cupach & Metts, 1994; McLaughlin, Cody & O'Hair, 1983; Scott & Lyman, 1968; Semin & Manstead, 1983; Schonbach, 1980) provide more detailed typologies of offerings including, for example, humor, offers of restitution, expressions of empathy and support, denials and refusals to provide an account.

Goffman (1967) contends that in most cases both avoidant and corrective facework are done in a cooperative manner. That is, people are reluctant to challenge another person's role performance and are willing to support a person's effort to maintain poise when their face has been threatened. If an offense has been committed, people readily offer an apology or account and expect that it will be accepted graciously. Such cooperation, according to Goffman, is the logical consequence of social and personal interests. As a general social maxim, it is rational for people to support the role performances of others because such support is likely to be reciprocated. If all interactants are willing and able to cooperate in the maintenance of face, interactions go smoothly. If persons are not willing or able to do so, then interaction breaks down and everyone feels awkward and unpoised. Even persons who have not themselves lost face will typically feel embarrassed for the person who has lost face (Cupach & Metts, 1990). In addition, individuals are motivated by more personal concerns including, for example, the desire to present self as an honorable and compassionate person, out of a sense of moral obligation, and because he/she feels an emotional attachment to the face of the other person.

On occasion, however, facework is not done cooperatively, but aggressively. In such circumstances, a person attempts to protect, enhance or restore his or her face at the expense of another's face. Success is determined not only by introducing favorable information about oneself and unfavorable information about the other person, but also by being better at the game of verbal dueling and "one-up-manship". Goffman does not elaborate on why supposedly rational people would be inclined to engage in aggressive facework, but several motivations can be inferred from his broader discussion. People might use aggressive facework when the speech event (e.g., bargaining) legitimizes it (see Wilson, 1992), when initial offerings for an offense (e.g., an apology) are rebuked, or when the role performance of another person is somehow counterfeit and must be stopped (see also Gross & Stone, 1964). In addition, Goffman notes that some individuals are simply less responsive to the affective consequences of face loss. He refers to persons who can witness another person's loss of face without emotional response as "heartless", and those who can experience their own face loss without emotional reaction as "shameless".

Perhaps because Goffman's notions of face and facework were conceived initially as a mechanism to explain the ritual order of social interaction, the applicability of his model to personal relationships has not been widely investigated. Its most systematic application to date lies in the research generated by politeness theory (Penman, 1994) and in integrative reviews of research from a face perspective (e.g., Cupach & Metts, 1994). Before moving to that literature, however, it is worth affirming that Goffman's original notions of face and facework have much to tell us about interaction patterns in personal relationships.

Goffman makes an observation about public interactions that is particularly relevant to interactions in personal relationships. He says that ordinarily the maintenance of face is a "condition" of interaction, not its "objective" (Goffman, 1967, p. 12). By this he means that the logical utility of reciprocal face support provides a structuring mechanism for interactions that allow people to meet their goals and accomplish their tasks in ways that are consistent with face. It is only when the mechanism breaks down by accident or by design that face maintenance becomes the explicit objective. This principle holds true in close relationships as well. Face maintenance is not typically the explicit objective of intimate interactions. Problems are negotiated and annoyances are voiced in ways that do not undermine the other's identity as a valued and competent relational partner. However, when this identity is seriously threatened by a person's own inappropriate behavior or by a challenge from his or her partner, then facework must be skillfully employed to repair the damage. Three examples of situations that hold the potential to seriously threaten face will be discussed briefly. These include the management of relational transgressions, the management of conflict, and the management of a couple's "joint identity" in public.

Relational transgressions are violations of cultural or idiosyncratic rules that a couple considers fundamental to the conduct of their relationship (Metts, 1994). When a violation is admitted or discovered, the couple is faced with the difficult task of managing not only the transgressor's loss of face but the collateral damage to the partner's face as well. Because the transgressor acted in a manner that

undermined his or her own role performance as a trustworthy, honorable partner, he or she has impaired partner's ability to act in a loving and trusting manner.
Thus, facework is necessary at two levels, one to restore the interaction and a
second to restore the legitimacy of role performance as a relational partner. In
such cases we would expect highly elaborated, cooperative and partner-centered
facework. The research on relationship repair episodes prompted by one partner's relational transgression (e.g., infidelity, deception, betrayal) supports this
assumption. Regardless of the type of offense, an apology (i.e., admitting culpa-
bility, chastising self and promising better performance in the future) is the type
of facework most likely to appease partner and restore relational harmony
(Hupka, Jung and Silverthorn, 1987; Metts, 1994, Metts & Mongeau, 1994;
Ohbuchi, Kameda & Agarie, 1989). In addition, when an apology is reinforced by
nonverbal impression management tactics (e.g., "I acted guilty and ashamed")
the combination is even more predictive of satisfaction with the confrontation
episode and the likelihood that relationship stability will be restored (Aune,
Metts & Ebesu, 1991).

While an apology seems to be a necessary condition for successfully managing
the initial trauma of a relational transgression, it is not a sufficient condition. The
apology expresses the willingness to present self as a remorseful person, but it
does not provide an explanation for the cause of the untoward behavior or its
meaning to the relationship. Accounts serve this purpose. Excuses (acknowledging the seriousness of the offense but providing extenuating circumstances) are
generally preferred over justifications (accepting responsibility but minimizing
the seriousness of the event), perhaps because justifications tend to negate a
partner's assessment of the act as important (Metts, 1994). However, when the
transgression involves a real or potential infidelity, justifications are preferred
over excuses and more strongly associated with commitment (Hupka, Jung &
Silveithorn, 1987; Metts, 1994). Apparently, when a transgression includes a third
party who could threaten the viability of a relationship, assurances that the event
did not entail emotional involvement are necessary in order to provide a sincerity
condition for the apology (Metts, 1994).

This research suggests that, in general, the remedial interchange can be used
successfully to manage potential relationship damage stemming from a partner's
inappropriate behavior. However, the success of this process is influenced significantly by variations in the tone, directness and degree of face threat implied in
the initial reproach. As Schonbach & Kleibaumhuter (1990) have demonstrated,
when a reproach entails a severe threat to a person's sense of personal control or
self-esteem, it not only "strengthens an actor's tendency to refute the opponent's
charge or justify his or her behavior during the failure event, but also markedly
weakens the actor's readiness to offer some concessions" (p. 241). The research
on complaints and conflict in personal relationships provides ample evidence of
this pattern, particularly in unhappy couples. For example, complaint sequences
of dissatisfied couples, compared to satisfied couples, are more likely to originate
with complaints about a partner's personal characteristics rather than, for exam-

ple, behavior (Alberts, 1988). These reproaches tend to be met with denials of the legitimacy of the complaint (Alberts & Driscoll, 1992), and/or counter-complaints (Alberts, 1988; Gottman, 1979).

It is no surprise that such complaint sequences routinely escalate into conflict that is characterized by aggressive facework. Indeed, the dysfunctional conflict patterns described by Gottman (1994) as the "Four Horsemen of the Apocalypse" might well be read as variations on the theme of aggressive facework. The first horseman, "criticism", is defined as "attacking someone's personality or character—rather than a specific behavior—usually with blame" (p. 73). The second, "contempt", is defined as the "intention to insult and psychologically abuse your partner . . . lobbing insults right into the heart of your partner's sense of self" (p. 79). These strategies can be viewed as complaints and/or counter-complaints with increasingly strong attacks on partner's face. The third horseman is labeled "defensiveness" and defined as a response mode characterized by unwillingness "to take responsibility for setting things right" (p. 84) (e.g., denying responsibility, cross-complaining, yes-butting). This pattern reflects a heightened sensitivity to protect one's own face, to the point of refusing to offer even the semblance of an account. Finally, "stonewalling" is characterized by communicative withdrawal, lack of engagement and passivity. According to Gottman, "it conveys disapproval, icy distance and smugness" (p. 94). At one level, stonewalling represents an unwillingness to engage in the remedial interchange; apologies are no longer offered or accepted with sincerity, and accounts are perfunctory or not offered. At a deeper level, however, it may also indicate that remediation is not even necessary because partners no longer have an emotional attachment to aspects of face that are linked to the relationship.

Satisfied couples are able to keep these "horsemen" at bay by instituting regulatory rules that engage a more formal, public level of interaction during conflict. Jones & Gallois (1989) identified 45 rules that a sample of married couples believed to be important during conflict. Factor analysis using ratings of importance yielded five factors, three of which are remarkably similar to Goffman's notion of facework: consideration (e.g., not saying hurtful things), conflict resolution (e.g., willing to say you are sorry), and positivity (e.g., being positive and supportive). In a study using the same items, Honeycutt, Woods & Fontenot (1993) obtained a slightly different factor structure, but an underlying theme of regulating face threat still emerged. The primary factor, labeled "positive understanding", included such face-supportive rules as being able to say you are sorry, giving praise to the other, listening to the other, acknowledging the other, and seeing the other's point of view. Not only was the positive understanding rule cluster the dominant factor (accounting for 44% of the variance), it was also the only factor associated with relationship quality after controlling for multicollinearity among the rule dimensions. These findings seem to indicate that satisfied couples recognize the need to make one's own face vulnerable at the service of partner's face. This is evidenced in the high cost to speaker's face implicit in such rules as being willing to apologize, to listen, and to give praise even during the emotionally charged exchanges characteristic of conflict. Less satisfied couples may not recognize the collateral damage that accrues to the relationship when protecting one's own face results in the destruction of partner's face. The problem, of course, is that interaction behaviors are strongly contingent; it is fairly easy to grant face to partner when partner is also granting face, but increasingly difficult to do so when partner threatens face. Thus, regulative rules are only effective to the extent that both partners endorse and follow the rules.

In addition to providing insight into the way couples manage face in the private domains of relational transgressions and conflict, Goffman also provides insight into why face support from a partner is particularly salient in public forums. According to Goffman (1959), couples, families and even co-workers form a "joint identity", or linking of individual identities. This connection implies that members will support each other's role performance because they are a "team" and the loss of face by any member discredits the role performance of the entire team. The greater the importance of the team to the individual, the greater the effort expended to maintain its public performance. When intimate couples constitute the team, the public performance of their relationship is generally characterized by mutual signs of respect, caring and commitment, although of course these signs may be tacit or manifested in good-natured teasing and other rituals. Their joint identity implies an emotional attachment to the face of partner similar to the emotional attachment felt to one's own face.

As a general rule, couples and families adhere to the norm of public face support: partners create idiomatic devices to communicate criticism while in public (Hopper, Knapp & Scott, 1981), married couples confirm and support their partner's public recounting of their relationship stories (Dickson, 1995), and family secrets are kept at home (Vangelisti, 1994). Indeed, as with most ordinary interactions, face maintenance is automatic and non-remarkable. However, when violations do occur, they are likely to be relationally consequential. First, the information that intimates have about each other tends to be quite personal and perhaps inconsistent with more public images. Revealing such information can undermine role performance in uniquely devastating ways. Second, couples generally operate under the assumption that mutual face support is motivated by high regard for the public image of their relationship and by emotional investment in each other's face. Repeated and intentional violations of the norms of public face support may be interpreted by the couple (and even by observers in the social network) as lack of regard for the relationship and/or lack of emotional investment in partner.

In a study of the nature and consequences of public embarrassment of romantic partners, Petronio, Olson & Dollar (1988) found that public embarrassment was likely to take the form of revealing relational secrets (e.g., sexual behaviors, relational problems, intimate feelings) or acting in ways that discredited the joint identity of the couple (e.g., explicit sexual advances in public, openly flirting with other people, intentional inattentiveness). The frequency of these behaviors was negatively associated with length of relationship, quality of the relationship, and satisfaction with relational communication. Similarly, Argyle & Henderson

(1984) found among the rule violations most likely to lead to the end of a friendship several that constitute public disregard for the other's face: not keeping confidences, criticizing you in public, not showing you positive regard, and not standing up for you in your absence.

Politeness Theory

Brown & Levinson (1987) were less interested in the corrective function of facework and more interested in the preventive function. In this regard, their conceptualization of facework is similar to Goffman's notion of avoidant facework. However, they extend Goffman's model by arguing that face concerns are motivated by two fundamental human needs, autonomy and validation. These motivate two types of face needs: negative face needs and positive face needs. Negative face needs refer to an individual's desire to be free of imposition and restraint, to have free access to his or her own territory and possessions, and to have control over the use of his or her time, space and resources. To show regard for another person's negative face is to avoid imposing on their time or resources, to protect their privacy, to avoid intruding, and generally to promote their autonomy and independence. Goffman's discussion of tact is implicitly a discussion of how people show regard for the negative face of others.

Positive face, on the other hand, is more akin to Goffman's notion that people value the attributes they claim during an interaction. Brown & Levinson (1987) define positive face needs as the desire to have the attributes or qualities that one values appreciated and approved of by people who are relevant to those attributes or qualities. To have regard for others' positive face is to show approval of their personality, attributes, accomplishments, appearance and so forth, as well as to show that they are considered likeable and worthy to be a friend and companion. Although Brown & Levinson do not distinguish between being valued and being liked, subsequent scholars have explored the possibility that these are distinguishable needs. Lim & Bowers (1991) and Lim (1990, 1994) argue that positive face should be divided into two types of face: (a) "fellowship face", defined as the desire to be included and to be viewed as a worthy companion, and (b) "competence face", defined as the desire to be respected for admirable traits (e.g., knowledgeable, intelligent, experienced, accomplished, and so forth).

Showing regard for the face needs of another person is often more complicated than it appears. First, although some messages threaten only one type of face need (e.g., a request threatens primarily negative face whereas a criticism threatens primarily positive face), other actions tend to threaten *both* negative and positive face (e.g., interruptions, threats, strong expressions of emotion and requests for personal information). Interruptions, for example, might signal disregard or disagreement with a speaker's comments (threat to positive face), and signal that the speaker should stop talking and become a listener (threat to negative face). Requests for personal information not only constrain a person to answer when they may not otherwise have raised an issue (threat to negative face), but may also force revelation of information detrimental to their projected image (threat to positive face). This particular dilemma seems to be at the core of the prevailing preference among daters to assess the risk of HIV infection in a potential sexual partner through indirect and inferential strategies rather than by direct, specific and face-threatening questions about sexual history and drug use (Cline, Johnson & Freeman, 1992).

A second, and in some ways more frustrating, complication for persons in close relationships is the fact that attempts to enhance one type of face can threaten the other. Because negative face is satisfied largely through deference and avoiding behaviors, whereas positive face is satisfied largely through connection and approaching behaviors, a tension exists between the two types of face needs (Brown & Levinson, 1987, p. 74). Thus, a person who intends to show respect for another's privacy by leaving them alone may inadvertently send signs of disregard for their positive face. Likewise, a person who intends to show regard for another's positive face through frequent contact, signs of affection and gifts may impose serious threat to the other person's negative face by making them feel obligated. In fact, a characteristic plateau in many developing relationships is reached when partners realize that the rewards for positive face gained from partner's attention and solicitous behaviors are no longer significantly greater than the loss of autonomy necessitated by relationship obligations. The resolution of this tension determines whether the relationship continues to escalate or moves to termination (Eidelson, 1980).

A third complication identified by Brown & Levinson (1987) is that during the process of attending to the negative and/or positive face of a hearer, speakers can threaten their own negative and/or positive face. Brown & Levinson provide examples such as giving thanks or accepting offers (which validate the other person's positive face but humble the speaker and incur a debt). Similarly, apologies, confessions and emotional expressions (1987, p. 68) may address the positive face of an offended person, but potentially threaten the speaker's own positive face. An interesting illustration of this phenomenon is available in the analysis of the simple phrase "I love you" when uttered for the first time in dating relationships. Owen (1988) analyzed the naturally occurring conversations of couples where "I love you" was said for the first time. Often, the initial expression was met with "I love you too" and the positive face of the expresser was confirmed. Sometimes, however, the initial expression was met with "pseudo-reciprocation" in comments such as "Well, I like you too", resulting in the positive face of the expresser being compromised. On occasion, the initial expression was met with "refutation" in comments such as "You can't be in love; we've only known each other for three weeks". In these instances, the expresser's positive face is discredited, and perhaps even his or her negative face in the implicit injunction not to feel love, let alone proclaim it outloud.

Fortunately, languages provide members of a culture with mechanisms (verbal and non-verbal) for managing the threats to positive and negative face that are endemic to social interaction (Brown & Levinson, 1987). We routinely need to ask favors, borrow resources, express displeasure with someone's actions or personality, and so forth. Although speakers may sometimes choose not to do the face-threatening act (FTA), they sacrifice the chance to attain their goals in making that decision. Speakers may sometimes choose to do the FTA with no attention at all to face concerns, but in so doing, risk the consequences of having issued an unredressed face threat. More often, people will choose a middle ground between these extremes. They might do the FTA but do it "off record" through hinting and innuendo. This strategy will only work to the degree that the other person successfully infers the intention of the speaker. The most efficient and still face-saving strategy is to go on record with the FTA but employ politeness to minimize its severity. Positive politeness is manifested in such communicative acts as claiming common ground (e.g., similar attitudes, opinions, empathy, etc.), indicating that the listener is admirable, attending to the listener's needs, exaggerating approval, including listener in activities, seeking agreement and avoiding disagreement, joking, and giving gifts. Negative politeness is manifested in such communicative acts as providing a listener with options, hedging while making a request, avoiding the use of coercion, showing deference, apologizing, offering to be in debt in return, and being vague or ambiguous. The five suprastrategies for doing FTAs are presented in Figure 15.1.

According to Brown & Levinson, as the seriousness or "weightiness" of an FTA increases, a speaker will be more likely to use higher numbered strategies. That is, if the threat is not at all consequential, a person might well do it with little or no face redress (e.g., "Can I have a quarter?"), but do more elaborate facework if the threat is greater (e.g., "I hate to bother you, but I don't have time to get to the bank until after class; if you happen to have a little extra cash, could you possibly loan me $5.00 until tomorrow?"). What is important in determining the seriousness of an FTA, however, is not merely the nature of the act itself, but

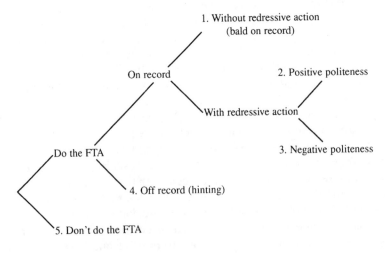

Figure 15.1 Strategies for doing FTAs

also the context in which the act occurs. For example, the request for $5.00 in the previous example might be made bald on record ("Give me $5.00") if a husband were asking his wife for cash in order to tip a server in a restaurant after dinner. Brown & Levinson formalize these contextual features as a set of three sociological variables: (1) the *social distance* between the interactants (i.e., familiarity, closeness, interdependence); (2) the *power* of the hearer relative to the speaker (i.e., authorized or unauthorized ability to assert one's will over the other); and (3) the *ranking* of the face threat (i.e., the cultural and personal estimate of how much threat an act entails). The ranking of threats to negative face depends on the type of goods or services required (e.g., asking to borrow a quarter vs. $5.00), whether a legitimate obligation to comply exists (e.g., terms of employment), and whether possible enjoyment might be associated with performing the act. The ranking of threats to positive face depends on the discrepancy between a person's desired image in a given context (e.g., successful, beautiful, generous, intelligent, good parent, sensual, likeable, etc.) and the image conveyed in the FTA.

One particular element in Brown & Levinson's model that has generated considerable discussion among scholars attempting to apply it to personal relationships is the position of privilege afforded negative politeness. According to the model, negative politeness is more face-redressive (numbered higher on the hierarchy) than positive politeness. In fact, the only strategies more face-preserving than negative politeness are hinting or not doing the FTA. Brown & Levinson argue this position from a pan-cultural view of the importance of autonomy over validation. They claim that, in general, trying to minimize a face threat by telling someone we share common ground with them, or care about or admire them, is less redressive than being deferential, offering to incur a reciprocal obligation, and allowing the person maximum freedom in deciding how they will respond to the threat. According to Brown & Levinson, in most cultures, it is presumptuous to think our signs of inclusion and validation are as important to another person as his or her autonomy. Thus, threats to negative face are the more egregious offense and negative politeness is the more redressive action.

However, one of the defining characteristics of personal relationships is that partners expect increased interdependence to result in some loss of autonomy. Much as Brown & Levinson argue that "terms of employment" constitute a legitimate obligation that lessens the degree of threat to negative face, it might be argued that "terms of commitment" constitute a legitimate obligation in personal relationships—at least for relatively routine impositions ("Will you make dinner tonight?", "Can you get the kids after work?", etc.). Additionally, because "pleasure in performing an act" lessens the threat in being asked to perform it, we might assume that the negative face threat in many requests made of a partner is mitigated by the pleasure felt in making partner happy or helping partner in some way (e.g., "I know you're trying to finish that project so I'll get dinner tonight"). Roloff (1987) suggests that intimates are not only expected to comply with requests from their partners, but to identify needs and fulfill them without being asked.

While partners may expect increased interdependence to result in some loss of autonomy, they do not expect it to result in loss of positive regard. Rather, they expect interdependence to afford increased opportunity for assurances of liking and inclusion from a valued significant other. Thus, threats to positive face in a personal relationship may be more highly ranked than in a social relationship because it is *not* presumptuous to think our expressions of regard matter, and because we have unique knowledge about traits, competencies and qualities our partner would like to have valued. In general, then, threats to positive face should be the more egregious offense in personal relationships. In addition, when threats to negative face exceed some level of absolute magnitude, legitimate obligation or vicarious pleasure, impositions on negative face eventually implicate positive face as well if partner begins to feel exploited (i.e., under-valued). Thus, although the communication of intimates shows a general tendency to make direct (unredressed) impositions on negative face (Roloff et al., 1988), this does not mean that intimates are less polite to each other than to strangers. Studies that have manipulated levels of intimacy between a speaker and the target of a request find that intimates employ more overall politeness when making a request than do strangers (Baxter, 1984; Roloff & Janiszewski, 1989). Studies that have also manipulated the severity of face threat represented by a request find that intimates use more positive politeness in situations of greater negative face threat than do strangers (Leichty & Applegate, 1991; Lim & Bowers, 1991). Two situations are used here to illustrate the importance of positive politeness in attenuating potential damage to face in personal relationships: social support and relationship termination.

Providing social support to someone in need is both gratifying and problematic (Goldsmith, 1992, 1994). Each supportive interaction has the potential to restore an identity damaged by failure, loss or rejection. However, it also has the potential to exacerbate a situation and do more harm than good (La Gaipa, 1990). Although a number of scholars have suggested that advice and problem-solving support is best tempered with messages that validate feelings (e.g., Burleson, 1994), the most systematic analysis of social support from a politeness perspective is offered by Goldsmith (1992, 1994). Goldsmith notes that the support provider may feel constrained by having to give support (negative face), and may feel diminished if his/her efforts seem not to be effective or appreciated (positive face). Likewise, the support seeker may feel his/her positive face diminished by his/her own admissions of need, failure or distress unless the support provider is able to confirm a more competent image.

As Barnes & Duck (1994) point out, most of these face dilemmas are regulated and diffused through the everyday communication of relationship partners. They argue that routine interactions allow partners to *detect* changes in mood or behavior that might warn them of possible problems before they become crises, to *ventilate* routine frustration and stress before it intensifies, and to *distract* partners, at least temporarily, from the strain of problems and other sources of stress. However, on any given occasion, when a particular event necessitates more focused supportive efforts, politeness, especially positive politeness, appears to be a key element in the success of the episode. In a study of comforting messages in close friendships, Goldsmith (1994) asked respondents to assess the degree of face threat in three types of social support messages given in response to a friend's experience of rejection (unwanted relationship termination) or failure (doing poorly on an exam). Each supportive message was accompanied by either positive politeness or negative politeness. She found, as expected, main effects for the type of supportive message. Advice posed the greatest threat to both positive face and negative face, whereas offers to help posed the least threat to positive face, and expressions of concern posed the least threat to negative face. However, when support messages were accompanied by positive politeness, the threat to face was moderated. In fact, ratings of how helpful a message was perceived to be revealed that advice with positive politeness was significantly more helpful than advice given bald-on-record and even advice given with negative politeness. Offers to help accompanied by positive politeness were also perceived to be more helpful than offers made bald-on-record or with negative politeness. Goldsmith speculates that positive politeness emerged as the more effective facework strategy because it not only mitigates the loss of autonomy and privacy implied by seeking support (i.e., negative face), but also "constructs an image of the friend as likeable and accepted following a breach in face created by the support seeker's disclosure of a failure or rejection" (pp. 41–42). Negative politeness may serve to mitigate the loss of autonomy and privacy, but does not additionally validate the positive face needs of the support seeker.

Although greatly simplified, an analogue between Goldsmith's description of how face support operates in comforting situations and how it could, ideally, operate in disengagement episodes can be drawn. The difference, of course, is that the person who terminates the relationship is the proximate, not distant, cause for the partner's loss of positive and negative face. As a consequence, the person who terminates a relationship, particularly when it is a unilateral decision, incurs an obligation to redress the positive face and negative face of partner, even though the attempt may place his or her own positive face and negative face in jeopardy.

The recognition that disengaging partners manage identities and provide accounts to the social network has been carefully explored (Harvey, Weber & Orbuch 1990). Much less attention has been given to the fact that partners also manage identities in their interactions with one another during the disengaging episode(s). Implicit in the various typologies of disengagement strategies that have been offered, however, is the tension between asserting one's need to be independent of partner (asserting own negative face needs) while not making partner feel diminished (avoiding threat to partner's positive face needs). For example, Cody and his colleagues (e.g., Cody, 1982; Banks et al., 1987) have proposed five general categories of disengagement strategies: (1) avoidance ("I didn't say anything to the partner. I avoided contact with him/her as much as possible"); (2) negative identity management ("I told him/her that I was going to date other people and that I thought he/she should date others also"); (3) justification ("I fully explained why I felt dissatisfied with the relationship, that it hasn't been growing and that I believe we will both be happier if we don't date anymore"); (4) de-escalation ("I told him/her that I need to be honest and suggested that we break it off for a while and see what happens"); and (5) positive tone ("I told him/her that I was very, very sorry about breaking off the relationship"). Each of these strategies communicates some element of concern for one's own or partner's face. Avoidance, for example, may entail threat to the disengager's negative face if he or she alters typical social habits, avoids certain places or people, and even hesitates to answer the telephone in order to avoid contact with the partner. However, by avoiding a disengagement episode, the disengager also protects his or her negative face (will not have to explain feelings or resist reconciliation attempts by partner) and his or her positive face (avoids possible accusations or recriminations from partner). Negative identity management illustrates a willingness to meet face-to-face, but is still an assertion of the disengager's own negative face needs and the imposition of this decision on the negative face needs of partner. Justification illustrates the willingness to provide an account and to show concern for both one's own and partner's positive face (i.e., we are both important enough to deserve happiness). De-escalation shows more concerted effort to redress one's own positive face (as an honest or caring individual), partner's positive face (this doesn't necessarily mean rejection), one's own negative face (temporary autonomy), and partner's negative face (the option of re-engagement is possible). Finally positive tone strategies are essentially apologies; they do little to redress negative face needs of either person, but do a great deal to enhance the worthiness of partner's positive face through the disengager's expression of remorse.

Baxter and her colleagues (e.g., Baxter, 1982; Wilmot, Carbaugh & Baxter, 1985) created a similar list of strategies. These include withdrawal, pseudo-de-escalation and mutual pseudo-de-escalation (false declaration of desire to retain some level of relationship); cost escalation (making the cost of staying in a relationship high by rude or hostile actions); fading away (partners share an implicit understanding that the relationship is over); *fait accompli* (simple and direct statement that the relationship is over); state-of-the-relationship talk (decision to leave is couched in the appearance of a discussion of the relationship's problems); attributional conflict (agreeing to break up but arguing over the reasons and placing blame); and negotiated farewell (sensemaking session without blame). In a summary of this research program, Baxter (1985) organized these strategies along three dimensions: direct–indirect, unilateral–bilateral, and other-orientation–self-orientation. According to Baxter (1985), direct strategies are explicit statements of one's desire to exit the relationship, whereas indirect strategies attempt to achieve termination without an explicit statement of the goal. Unilateral strategies represent one party's intent to disengage, whereas bilateral strategies represent a fairly equal or mutual desire by both partners to disengage. Other-oriented strategies are those which avoid hurting, embarrassing or manipulating the other person in the break-up, whereas self-oriented strategies "display primarily expedience for self at the other party's cost" (Baxter, 1985, p. 247). In general, greater face threat for partner and less face threat for the disengager is associated with direct, unilateral and self-oriented strategies. Less face threat for partner and greater face threat for disengager is associated with indirect, bilateral and other-oriented strategies.

Although these typologies were not generated from a facework perspective, politeness theory provides a coherent framework for integrating a number of findings (for details see Metts, 1992; Cupach & Metts, 1994). Politeness theory would predict that as the severity of a threat increases, the degree of politeness should increase. In the context of disengagement, this would mean that as the significance of the termination increased (e.g., breaking up a highly developed and committed relationship compared to a more casual involvement), the degree of elaborated and other-oriented politeness would also increase. To the extent that it does not, disengaged couples would report greater dissatisfaction with the process. This prediction is supported by the literature. In relatively low levels of threat (e.g., relationships of low interdependence and short duration), a minimal level of face redress is expected—minimal to the extent that the disengager is at least willing to provide a "face-to-face accounting" (Baxter, 1987), even if it is not marked by elaborated facework. When avoidance strategies such as withdrawal are used, the break-up is particularly unsatisfying for both the disengager and the partner, even in low-level relationships (e.g., Metts, Cupach & Bejlovec, 1989; Wilmot, Carbangh & Baxter, 1985). This lack of satisfaction can be traced, at least in part, to the ambiguity of not knowing whether one should continue to act as though he or she is still in a relationship (negative face is constrained for both), the unsettling sense of the disengager that he or she was not willing to "face the music" and state the desire to disengage (diminished positive face), and the perception of the partner that he or she was not significant enough to merit an accounting or an apology (diminished positive face). In relatively higher levels of threat (relationships of higher interdependence and longer duration) strategies that directly address both the positive and negative face of partner should be even more important. De-escalation, pseudo-de-escalation, and mutual pseudo-de-escalation attempt to compensate for loss of positive face implied in the disengager's decision to scale down the relationship by expressing continued desire to be in a relationship, to be friends, and to be affiliated. Positive tone strategies present the disengager as a person keenly aware of the seriousness of the act and remorseful over the role he or she is playing. Banks et al. (1987) found that disengagers were more likely to use positive tone, de-escalation or justification when network overlap was high, the relationship was intimate, and post-disengagement friendship was desired. Metts, Cupach & Bejlovec (1989) found that when an initiator used positive tone strategies, the couple was more likely to remain friends after the break-up, underscoring again the important role of positive politeness in the conduct of personal relationships.

FUTURE DIRECTIONS

Additional research is necessary before a full understanding of the role of facework in close relationships is realized. To date, the research tends to be of two kinds. One type is the "reading" of existing research from a facework perspective (e.g., Cupach & Metts, 1994). A second approach is to test the components of a facework theory, such as politeness, through a manipulation of relevant variables (e.g., distance and degree of imposition or severity of reproach) in a scenario or role play experiment. While both of these methods are useful, several additional research programs must be undertaken if we are to develop a comprehensive picture of the role of facework in close relationships.

First, it is essential to study facework processes as they are enacted in the everyday talk of ongoing personal relationships. Granted, close relationships emerge from the larger culture and thereby organize themselves within certain normative constraints. Thus, the basic principles of facework should be evident in couples' communication. However, intimacy, interdependence and emotional investment reframe the notions of what counts as a face threat, what exacerbates severity, what constitutes legitimate explanations for face violations, and what counts as appropriate types and degrees of facework. The relative importance of positive face compared to negative face, for example, appears to be an important distinction between personal relationships and social relationships. Yet we know little about the mechanisms partners routinely use to avoid threats to positive face, to repair threats to positive face, and to enhance positive face. Idiomatic expressions, terms of endearment, and even unsolicited offers to help may function as positive politeness within the familiar context of personal relationships. It is doubtful that scenario studies will reveal these nuances. Patient analysis of couples interacting is likely to be the more informative approach.

This is not to suggest that linguistic features can or should be counted. Researchers who have attempted to use Brown & Levinson's exemplars as a classification system for coding politeness in discourse (e.g., Craig, Tracy & Spisak, 1986; Tracy, 1990; Wood & Kroger, 1994), argue that the exemplars are difficult to use because they do not constitute equivalent or mutually exclusive categories. The exemplars include, for example, large units of speech and other actions (e.g., show interest in the speaker), sentences (e.g., an apology), and individual words (e.g., in-group markers such as "we" or hesitations such as "well . . ."). In addition, some tactics are face-relevant because of their content, and others are face-relevant because of their form (e.g., indirectness). However, Brown & Levinson (1987) claim that politeness theory was never intended to be a mechanism for quantitative research and does not lend itself easily to that endeavor. They view facework as a kind of "speech act" that is performed in both the content and structure of messages, through a variety of techniques, with its ultimate effect residing in the interpretation of the interactants in a given context. Thus, messages that contain politeness features may be used to perform actions other than face redress, and messages that seem to contain no explicit politeness marker are nonetheless understood as polite by the people who share intimate knowledge of each other and their interaction practices. Therefore, the researcher interested in the role of politeness in personal relationships will need to enlist the help of the persons in those relationships in order to isolate interaction patterns that represent both speakers' intentions to protect or repair face and listeners' interpretations of these patterns as polite in particular contexts.

A related area for future research is to find patterns of face threat and face support within personal relationships that distinguish satisfied couples from dissatisfied couples. The extant literature reviewed previously indicates a strong association between face issues and relational satisfaction. It is time to identify more precisely what those issues are. Several possibilities present themselves. Perhaps threats to negative face are non-problematic so long as they are "equitable" between partners. However, when one partner endures significantly more imposition relative to his or her partner, politeness, even in great measure, may no longer suffice. For positive face, however, more complicated patterns might be associated with satisfaction: e.g., (1) frequency of positive face threat, (2) the domain of positive face threat, (3) the proportion of positive face support relative to positive face threat, and/or (4) both partners' willingness to threaten their own positive face through concessions and apologies when appropriate. Of course the challenge of this pursuit is to untangle the reciprocal influence of face-relevant actions on satisfaction from the influence of satisfaction on face-relevant actions (Fincham, 1992).

Finally, research would also profit from a more complete understanding of individual differences in face needs and facework competence. To date, efforts to create a measure of individual predispositions toward negative and positive face needs have met with only limited success (e.g., Cupach & Metts, 1993; Metts, Backaus & Kazoleas, 1995). However, it seems self-evident that some people need a great deal of autonomy whereas others need much less. Some people seem to have "thin skins" when it comes to criticism and others seem less sensitive to threats to positive face. The process of developing and maintaining a relationship is no doubt partly constituted in the communicative practices that reveal these individual differences and help partners to accommodate to them. To the degree that partners are willing and able to meet each other's particular face needs, even when they do not have similar face needs, we should expect that individual differences are not a problem. However, to the extent that differences in face needs cannot be accommodated, for example, when one spouse has a high need for positive face but the other is not willing or able to offer the desired level of positive face support, then individual differences may become important. This same argument is inherent in the theory of interpersonal needs proposed by Schutz (1958). Indeed, the similarity between the needs of inclusion and affection and positive face, and the similarity between the need for control and negative face, suggest that the two lines of research could be mutually informative.

CONCLUSION

This chapter has attempted to illustrate the utility of facework for the study of personal relationships. For the most part, at least in satisfied couples, it recedes into the background of ordinary conversation. Care is taken, more or less consciously, to support the public identity of the relationship and the privately negotiated identities of the partners. Face threats are avoided through redressive actions and face damage is repaired through corrective sequences. However, when face issues become salient, even mundane relationship processes can become infused with escalating aggressive facework. Penman (1994) makes the observation that "the concepts of negotiating individual identity and relationship definition are remarkably similar to those of positive and negative face, respectively" (pp. 16–17). Although Brown & Levinson (1987) might not be entirely satisfied with this comparison, it does point out the inherently relational quality of facework. Although studying facework in personal relationships is admittedly a difficult undertaking, its contribution to the goal of understanding relationship processes make it an effort worth expending.

Chapter 16

Cross-sex Friendship Research as Ideological Practice

Kathy J. Werking
University of Louisville, Louisville, KY, USA

... in describing a given system, the scientist makes many choices. He chooses his words, and he decides which parts of the system he will describe first; he even decides into what parts he will divide the system to describe it. These decisions will affect the description as a whole in the sense that they will affect the map upon which the typological relationships between the elementary messages of description are represented (Bateson, 1991, p. 62: gendered language in original).

INTRODUCTION

Scholars make choices as they reconcile various quandaries posed throughout the research process. These choices, as described by Bateson (1991), profoundly influence the resulting descriptions of the chosen phenomena. However, by and large, the discussion in scholarly circles regarding our research decisions centers on issues of epistemology rather than ideology. Specifically, we enter lively and useful debates about theory, methodologies and data analysis. Yet our research decisions are permeated with ideological assumptions. In other words, these decisions are not neutral, rather they reflect assumptions about what constitutes knowledge and what form of knowing will be privileged at particular historical moments.

Lannamann (1991) acknowledges the link between epistemology and ideology when he contends:

To develop or maintain an epistemological stance is a social act like any other. It is subject to the same constraints, limitations and contradictions as other social actions. An epistemology, then, is never neutral in terms of power or privilege. The

Handbook of Personal Relationships, 2nd edn. Edited by Steve Duck.
© 1997 John Wiley & Sons Ltd.

choice of whose punctuation of power will become the influential myth in a dyad or society is never arbitrary. The choice follows from particular historical developments and social contingencies. Thus, to reduce power to an epistemological stance is to define away the importance of ideology in the study of interpersonal communication. (p. 186)

As scholars interested in increasing our understanding of relationships, we must move beyond discussions about research findings and appropriate methodologies and begin a self-conscious examination of the latent ideological content of our work. The risk of neglecting the ideological underpinnings of research in the field of personal relationships is that scholars may perpetuate and reify particular ways of knowing, elevating them to the status of natural fact rather than acknowledging them as culturally constructed patterns of thought (Lannamann, 1991).

A critical examination of the existing cross-sex friendship literature is necessary and timely because the study of friendship between women and men is attracting research interest, and scholars of cross-sex friendships are debating epistemological issues. I have donned the role of "devils advocate" in the spirit of invoking conversation of an ideological nature among such scholars. It is through this form of conversation and reflection that we gain new understandings regarding how we conduct research and what we do with the products of our research.

My overarching goal in this chapter is to address the ideological assumptions underlying research conducted in the area of cross-sex friendship, my chosen area of research. First, I argue that the selection of research topics reflects an ideological stance. I do this by tracing the history of cross-sex friendship research. Next, I contend that existing studies privilege an individualistic, heterosexist view of cross-sex friendship. In supporting this rather thick contention, I address each adjective in the above statement individually and provide illustrations of each adjective's presence in the existing cross-sex friendship literature. Throughout my discussion, I propose alternative ways of knowing that might be employed in the study of cross-sex friendship, sketching possible research projects for the future.

My observations and recommendations in this chapter are directed toward the cross-sex friendship literature specifically; however, I believe my comments will be useful to a larger audience of relational researchers, for many of the issues I raise in this chapter are found in other areas of research on personal relationships as well. For example, Rawlins (1992) critiques the social scientific literature on friendship in general for its lack of dyadic analysis and neglect of larger cultural contexts. Similarly, Duck (1993b) argues that relationship researchers need to expand their focus to sustained consideration of the social context in which relationships are developed, sustained, and dissolved. Finally, several contributors to a special section on the study of personal relationships published in the *Journal of Social and Personal Relationships* (1995) advance suggestions similar to those included in this chapter, such as an increased emphasis on talk, context and diversity in the types of relationships studied.

A HISTORY OF CROSS-SEX FRIENDSHIP RESEARCH

The story of research into cross-sex friendship is brief because this form of man–woman relationship has been largely ignored by scholars. The first empirical study was conducted by Booth & Hess (1974). This study emphasized the structural opportunities and normative constraints affecting the formation of cross-sex friendships of middle-aged and elderly persons.

The next study to include cross-sex friendship in its analysis was published 6 years later (Block, 1980). Several empirical studies on cross-sex friendship were published during the early 1980s. These inquiries focused on the affective qualities of cross-sex friendship, examining the relationship along a variety of dimensions, such as intimacy (Rose, 1985; Sapadin, 1988), stability (Davis & Todd, 1985), satisfaction (Argyle & Furnham, 1983) and self-disclosure (Hacker, 1981).

In general, one goal of these studies was the comparison of the above qualities with those found in same-sex friendship. A second goal was the comparison of men and women's perceptions of their cross-sex and same-sex friendships. The studies published during the 1980s are closely modeled by research conducted in the 1990s because, in general, researchers continue to focus on affective qualities, comparing these qualities across friendship type and assessing women and men's perceptions of these qualities in their cross-sex and same-sex friendships (e.g., Monsour, 1992). The following review of the cross-sex friendship literature reflects these research foci.

Structural Opportunities for the Development of Cross-sex Friendship

Booth & Hess (1974) investigated the opportunities for cross-sex friendship development using a sample of middle-aged and elderly persons. First, their findings suggest that education and social class influence the experience of cross-sex friendship. Specifically, white-collar workers were more likely to have cross-sex friends than were blue-collar workers. In addition, married persons in their sample reported less frequent interaction with cross-sex friends than with their same-sex friends and a reduction in the amount of affect in their cross-sex friendships. Age was also a factor in the development of cross-sex friendship for, with increasing age, persons experienced a decline in the number of cross-sex friendships. In this study, sex appeared to interact with age because older females reported fewer numbers of cross-sex friends than did their male counterparts. Sex appears to be a prime determinant of the number of cross-sex friends, because Booth & Hess found the number of cross-sex friendships reported by men in their sample was significantly higher than the number reported by the participating women.

The influence of age, sex and marital status has also been documented in more recent studies. There appears to be a curvilinear relationship between age and occurrence of cross-sex friendship. Cross-sex friendship in childhood and preadolescence is rare (Gottman, 1986; Maccoby, 1988). The number of cross-sex friendships rises during adolescence, but does not match the number of reported same-sex friendships (Kon & Losenkov, 1978). It appears that late adolescence and early adulthood are prime developmental periods for cross-sex friendship occurrence. For example, Rose (1985) found all of her undergraduate participants experienced cross-sex friendship. Werking (1994a) reported the number of reported friendships was highest during the high school and college years.

The number of cross-sex friends, however, decreases after early adulthood. Utilizing samples of persons in their mid-20s to mid-40s, Werking (1992; 1995), reported a decline in cross-sex friendship opportunities as persons married and raised families. The studies of Chown (1981) and Adams (1985) revealed that older participants report lower numbers of cross-sex friends and that age affects the number of cross-sex friends for women more than for men. The interaction of age and gender is also supported in other studies (Bell, 1981; Block, 1980; Rubin, 1985; Rose, 1985) which consistently found that men report a higher occurrence of cross-sex friends than do women.

The influence of marital status on the development of cross-sex friendship has also been evident in several studies. Specifically, Rose (1985) reported that 47% of the married women and 33% of the married men in her sample said they had no cross-sex friendships. This contrasts with the numbers reported by the single participants. All of the single undergraduates and male graduate students and 73% of the single female graduate students said they were involved in at least one cross-sex friendship. Likewise, Block (1980) reported that only 6% of his married participants named a cross-sex friend in his survey, and 78% of the men and 84% of the women in Rubin's (1985) sample of married or cohabitating persons said they did not have a cross-sex friend. Finally, Werking (1994a) found persons not involved in a cross-sex friendship cited marriage as a significant obstacle to the development of such a friendship.

In sum, the influence of age, sex and marital status on the formation of cross-sex friendship is consistently documented in the existing literature. First, older adults are less likely to have a cross-sex friend than are young adults. Second, men are more likely to experience cross-sex friendship than are women. Lastly, unmarried persons are more apt to develop cross-sex friendships than married persons.

The Affective Qualities of Cross-sex Friendship

The findings of studies investigating the affective dimensions of cross-sex friendships have centered on comparing same-sex and cross-sex friendship along these dimensions and comparing women and men's perceptions of the levels of affect achieved in their cross-sex friendships. I will first review the studies comparing cross-sex and same-sex friendship.

Researchers have measured a variety of affective qualities by surveying participants about their cross-sex and same-sex friendships. The measured qualities include goodness and enjoyableness (Bukowski, Nappi & Hoza, 1987), intimacy (Aukett, Richie & Mill, 1988; Davis & Todd, 1985; Monsour, 1992; Rose, 1985; Sapadin, 1988), stability and supportiveness (Davis & Todd, 1985), loyalty (Rose, 1985), satisfaction (Argyle & Furnham, 1983) and self-disclosure (Hacker, 1981). Taken together, the above studies reveal several significant differences between the participants' perceptions of their same-sex and cross-sex friendships. For example, cross-sex friendships were less intimate and stable (Davis & Todd, 1985), less supportive (Rose, 1985), and less satisfying (Argyle & Furnham, 1983) than same-sex friendships. Hacker (1981) found that levels of self-disclosure were reduced in cross-sex friendship. Rose (1985) stated that cross-sex friends experienced less common interests, affection, acceptance and communication while developing and sustaining their friendship than did same-sex friends.

Despite the many differences between the two friendship types, similarities are also found in existing studies. Specifically, Davis & Todd (1985) found no differences between cross-sex and same-sex friendship in the reported levels of trust, respect, acceptance, spontaneity and enjoyment. Similarly, cross-sex and same-sex friends were nearly identical in the meanings they assigned to intimacy in their friendships (Monsour, 1992). Finally, Werking (1992) obtained similar descriptions of persons' ideal same-sex and cross-sex friendships.

Researchers have also been interested in assessing the mediating influence of biological sex on the reported affective character of cross-sex and same-sex friendships. Similar to the above comparative studies, significant differences between men and women's perceptions were discovered by several researchers. Men and women, however, also shared similar perceptions in a number of studies.

Overall, women tend to assign less intimacy to their cross-sex friendships than do men (Rose, 1985; Rubin, 1985). For example, Rubin (1985) reported that approximately two-thirds of the women named by a man as a close friend did not agree with the man that they had a friendship. Women are also more apt to discuss their personal problems with their female friends than with their male friends (Aukett, Richie & Mill, 1988). In comparison, men typically state their friendships with their woman friends exhibit more caring and acceptance (Sapadin, 1988), security (Furman, 1986) and emotional support (Aukett, Richie & Mill, 1988) than their friendships with men.

Despite these differences, women and men also share many similarities in their descriptions of their friendships with one another. For both sexes, cross-sex friendship provides new understandings and perspectives of the other sex (Sapadin, 1988; Werking, 1992). Existing studies also found correspondence between men and women's reported amounts of intimacy and enjoyment (Monsour, 1992; Sapadin, 1988; Werking, 1995) and in the functions of help, availability and recognition in cross-sex friendship (Rose, 1985). Gaines (1994) reported that men and women give as well as receive ample amounts of affection and respect in their cross-sex friendships and did not frequently engage in respect-denying behaviors with their cross-sex friends. Finally, both men and women tend to keep their friendships and sexual relationships as separate relationships (Sapadin, 1988; Werking, 1995).

Recent research has begun to expand its scope from the traditional focus on the affective qualities of cross-sex friendship to the study of other aspects of cross-sex friendship. Monsour, Betty & Kurzweil (1993) examined interpersonal perception in the context of cross-sex friendships and found cross-sex friends tend to agree with one another regarding the intimacy in their friendship and the importance of the friendship. Werking (1994b) examined the talk and activities of close adult cross-sex friends. From this study, it appears close cross-sex friends spend most of their time together talking with one another about personal issues. The majority of these conversations tended to take place face-to-face between the friends rather than in a group setting. The participants also reported eating meals together, watching television, visiting friends and shopping.

While researchers have been interested in why or how cross-sex friendships begin (e.g. Rose, 1985), Werking (1994c) researched the reasons why cross-sex friendships terminate and the strategies by which persons dissolve such friendships. Physical separation as a result of attending different colleges, moving to other geographical locations, and changing jobs or class schedules was by far the most frequently mentioned reason for cross-sex friendship termination. This reason is not unique to cross-sex friendship; however, it is interesting to note the next two most frequently mentioned reasons centered around the management of romance and sexuality; issues that tend to be particular to cross-sex friendship. Taken together, 48% of the sample stated their close cross-sex friendships ended because a romantic relationship between the two friends was not successful, one or both of the friends became romantically involved with another person, or one of the friends wanted a romantic relationship with their friend but the desire was not reciprocated. This study also explored the ways persons end their close cross-sex friendships and found 38% of the sample said their friendships simply faded away. Other people stated they simply cut off contact with their friend (23%) or intentionally avoided their friend (17%).

Theorizing about Cross-sex Friendship

Just as empirical research on cross-sex friendship has been limited in scope, theoretical work on the topic has been sparse. Rawlins (1982) published the first theoretical essay on cross-sex friendship, outlining a typology of man–woman relationship definitions. This typology consisted of five categories: (1) *friendship*, an affectionate and personal relationship lacking expressed sexuality; (2) *platonic love*, a relationship of deep intimacy and high emotional commitment without sexual activity; (3) *friendship-love*, an ambiguous relationship involving degrees of friendship as well as a potential for transition to a romantic relationship; (4) *physical love*, a relationship based primarily on sexual relations rather than emotional involvement; and (5) *romantic love*, an exclusive emotional and physical relationship.

In this article, Rawlins (1982) described the challenges facing cross-sex friends as they manage the internal dynamics of romance, sexuality and sex role socialization. Rawlins also addressed the external dynamics of creating a viable public image of cross-sex friendship so that outsiders to the relationship perceive the relationship as a "friendship" rather than as a "romantic relationship".

The notion of "challenge" was further elaborated by O'Meara (1989). O'Meara identified four challenges, or potential difficulties, facing women and men as they forge friendships with one another. These challenges were: (1) reconciling ways of practicing friendship, because women and men typically enact same-sex friendship differently; (2) overcoming culturally embedded power differentials between men and women; (3) negotiating the issue of romance and sexuality within the context of friendship; and (4) creating an image of cross-sex friendship that is considered legitimate by friends, family, romantic partners and co-workers. In a response to data suggesting that structural and normative barriers exist which prevent opportunities for men and women to interact in environments conducive to the development of friendships, O'Meara (1994) added another challenge, the cross-sex friendship opportunity challenge.

Lastly, my own work (Werking, 1992, 1995) has extended the work of Rawlins and O'Meara as I have proposed a theoretical model of cross-sex friendship which weaves together the cultural and relational contexts in which cross-sex friendship is enacted. Specifically, my work has focused on the inherent tensions created between widely accepted cultural models of man–woman romantic relationships and the everyday practice of friendship between men and women. These tensions are a result of a "clash of relational ideologies". Primarily, current cultural models of woman–man relationships adhere to an ideology of heterosexual romance which may or may not include equality, is passionate in nature, and has a goal of marriage. In contrast, the ideology of friendship is based on equality, affection, communion, and is an end unto itself (Badhwar, 1987). Men and women engaged in friendship must, therefore, manage the disparities between these ideologies as they co-create their friendships. The model proposes that this management takes place simultaneously inside the friendship as friends create relational definitions and outside the friendship as the friends address the perceptions of friends, family, co-workers and romantic partners.

Although the number of published articles on cross-sex friendship has risen substantially in recent years, we still cannot claim that interest in cross-sex friendship is high. Further, few empirical studies have tested the theoretical propositions described above (see Monsour, 1994). Why have there been so few studies of cross-sex friendship? In response to this question, one could argue that friendship between women and men does not occur frequently enough to warrant research attention. This argument pales, however, on close scrutiny of the numbers of cross-sex friendships reported in existing studies.

Indeed, Wright (1989) averaged across the non-college samples of four studies conducted in the past 20 years (Bell, 1981; Block, 1980; Booth & Hess, 1974; Rubin, 1985) and found 40% of the men and 30% of the women reported close cross-sex friendship. Further, Sapadin (1988) found 89% of her sample of professional men and women reported engaging in cross-sex friendship. In college, the frequency of cross-sex friendship appears to be even higher, as all of the undergraduate and male graduate students and 73% of the female graduate students participating in Rose's (1985) study claimed at least one close cross-sex friendship outside of their romantic relationships. It appears, then, that women and men have been developing friendships with one another on a fairly frequent basis for quite some time. To understand the lack of research in this area, I contend that we need to investigate the deeply embedded cultural beliefs about woman–man relationships. Our choices of research topics arise within specific historical and cultural circumstances which legitimate certain areas of inquiry and overshadow other areas.

CULTURAL BELIEFS ABOUT HETEROSEXUAL RELATIONSHIPS

Heterosexism is an organizing principle in American society. This ideology assumes heterosexuality is the norm and, as such, idealizes heterosexual romantic relationships. This type of relationship is widely recognized as the primary basis for marriage, therefore women and men are encouraged to establish romantic relationships with one another. Messages regarding the importance, establishment and sustenance of these relationships are provided to members of the culture by important social institutions such as the media, family, friends and the legal and educational system. In essence, heterosexual romanticism is the reigning ideology for woman–man relationships (Brain, 1976). Consequently, this ideology provides an interpretive framework for our thoughts, feelings, and behaviors in regard to personal bonds between men and women. Romantic relationships between women and men appear to be the "natural" form of male–female bond.

Because it seems natural, the ideology of heterosexual romanticism structures the possibilities for non-romantic forms of cross-sex bonds, as the legitimacy of alternative forms may be denied or questioned (Laws & Schwartz, 1981). One such alternative form of man–woman relation is platonic friendship. Cross-sex friendship shares many similarities with romantic heterosexual relationships. For example, both relationships are voluntary in nature, involve feelings of affection and love, and require a substantial amount of emotional commitment if either type of relationship is to survive (Rawlins, 1993).

There are, however, important differences between ideal cross-sex friendships and ideal romantic heterosexual relationships. First, cross-sex friendship does not usually entail a strong sexual dimension (Rawlins, 1982; Werking, 1992). Second, the goal of cross-sex friendship is not marriage. In this regard cross-sex friendship stands in opposition to the dominant romantic ideology. Finally, cross-sex friendship is a relationship among equals. It is a relationship in which men and women hold equivalent rights and responsibilities as they relate to one another as persons qua persons rather than role occupants (Paine, 1974).

In contrast, researchers have constructed paradigm cases of romantic heterosexual love relationships and identified asymmetrical eligibilities as a characteristic of romantic relationships (Davis & Todd, 1985; Roberts, 1982). Asymmetrical eligibilities means that both relational partners do not have equivalent rights and responsibilities in romantic relationships. The presence of asymmetrical eligibilities, therefore, implies the possibility of an imbalance of power within romantic relationships. Several scholars of heterosexual romantic relationships (e.g., Argyle & Furnham, 1983; Cates & Lloyd, 1992) note that this imbalance of power underlies struggles with issues of dependency, control and the management of relational resources in heterosexual romantic relationships.

Due to American society's preoccupation with heterosexual dating and marital relationships, we lack a cultural conversation about friendship between women and men. The media remain silent regarding cross-sex friendship, as portrayals of authentic cross-sex friendships are rarely seen in television sitcoms, film and the popular literature (Werking, 1995). Typically, when cross-sex friendship does appear in the media, it is sexualized because the plot often centers around what I call the "will they or won't they?" dilemma.

Further, in our everyday lives, the viability of cross-sex friendship is questioned as cross-sex friends report receiving numerous and persistent questions regarding the nature of their relationship from friends, co-workers, family and romantic partners (Swain, 1992; Werking, 1992). Cross-sex friends themselves recognize the deviant nature of their relationship when they label their relationship as "weird", "abnormal" or "unusual" (Werking, 1992).

Finally, researchers have not contributed to a conversation about cross-sex friendship. Instead, studies of heterosexual dating and marital relationships have dominated the personal relationship literature since the inception of the field (Blieszner & Adams, 1992; Hendrick & Hendrick, 1992). These types of studies are useful and needed as they provide insight into a form of heterosexual relationship that is important in people's lives. However, by maintaining an almost exclusive focus on this form of heterosexual bond, researchers have mirrored cultural beliefs about woman–man relationships rather than exposing these beliefs and presenting alternative forms of relating. We have to ponder, therefore, the degree to which we have reproduced the romantic heterosexual ideology in our work.

IDEOLOGICAL ASSUMPTIONS UNDERPINNING THE STUDY OF CROSS-SEX FRIENDSHIP

In addition to reflecting on our selection of research topics, we must also explore how we investigate our chosen topics. I now turn to two ideological stances enacted in existing cross-sex friendship studies. First, I discuss the ideology of individualism in cross-sex friendship studies. Second, I discuss the heterosexist nature of existing cross-sex friendship studies.

In many ways it is paradoxical that cross-sex friendship researchers tend to focus on the individual, because friendships are developed and maintained by the continual shared negotiation of a relational definition by *both* partners (see Duck, West & Acitelli, this volume). Nevertheless, individualism, the notion that persons are self-contained beings acting in the world, is deeply ingrained in American society (Bellah et al., 1985) and in research on relationships (Duck, 1994a; Gottman, 1982). From this perspective, individuals are "lifted" out of their social, historical and cultural contexts and the locus of personhood is placed squarely with the individual rather than located in interactions with other humans.

The ideology of individualism is clearly evidenced in the cross-sex friendship literature in four ways: (1) the variables of interest are viewed as properties of individuals and not of relationships because the unit of analysis is typically the individual rather than the dyad or social group; (2) studies center on persons' subjective appraisals of the cross-sex friendships rather than their concrete friendship practices; (3) research is not embedded in the history of the studied relationships; and (4) research is acultural in nature. I will discuss each of these issues below.

The Individual as the Unit of Analysis

One consequence of employing individualism in our research is that the popular research concepts of gender, role, attitude, trait and cognitions are conceptualized as possessions of individuals (Haley, 1963; Lannamann, 1992) rather than the creation of ongoing social processes. For example, research assessing the role of gender (I use this example because of the large proportion of cross-sex friendship research concerned with this issue) in the development and maintenance of cross-sex friendship has conceptualized gender as a static individual characteristic brought to cross-sex friendships. Wright (1989) described this particular conceptualization of gender as the "dispositional approach" and, on reviewing the extant literature, asserted "the friendship research exploring gender differences in general has overwhelmingly favored the dispositional approach" (p. 198).

One outcome of employing an individualistic perspective when studying gender and cross-sex friendship is the perpetuation of the belief that, through the socialization process, men and women have internalized culturally determined, and qualitatively different, "core" gender identities which remain intact over time and across a variety of interpersonal situations (Risman & Schwartz, 1989; West & Zimmerman, 1987). Thus, the distinction between biological sex and gender has been demolished as researchers assume biological sex and its attendant cultural norms determine gender orientation. This assumption is clearly evident as writers often interchange the biologically-based terms "males and females" (or "men and women") with "gender" (see Wood, 1993, for a clear distinction between biological sex and gender).

Relational scholars (e.g., Deaux & Major, 1987; Risman & Schwartz, 1989) are questioning the individualistic approach to gender and are advancing alternative constructions. Specifically, these scholars conceptualize gender as an emergent property of social relationships and their structural contexts (West & Fenstermaker, 1995). From this perspective, relationships are the *producers* of gendered identities as well as the *products* of gender-linked behaviors.

Although scholars are taking note of the work cited above, alternative forms of constructing gender have not appeared in the cross-sex friendship literature. Instead, cross-sex friendship researchers continue to equate biological sex with gender (but see Lin & Rusbult, 1995). Scholars simply ask respondents to check whether they are male or female on their surveys and then treat "gender" as an independent variable in their analyses. Further, in scholars' articulation of research goals and discussion of findings, claims are advanced regarding the influence of *gender*, rather than biological sex, on cross-sex friendship (e.g., Monsour, 1992; Rose, 1985; Sapadin, 1988; Werking, 1994).

An alternative to this approach, one that relates to the propositions advanced by West and others, is to view gender not exclusively as an independent variable in our studies, but as a dependent variable as well. In this way, researchers could assess how particular gender orientations are produced, maintained and altered during the course of relationships. Specifically, cross-sex friendship scholars could examine how gender fluctuates as a function of relationship context and begin to answer the questions: does the gender orientation of a person depend on the gender orientation of the person with whom they are interacting?; how does gender orientation change over time in response to relationship experiences?; and is gender-linked behavior dependent on the type of relationship in which interaction takes place? My work suggests that the gender-linked practices of men and women are connected to whether or not the relationship is defined as romantic or platonic in nature (Werking, 1992, 1995). Specifically, behaviors which defy gender role stereotypes are possible and even facilitated in relationships where sex-typed gender identity is heightened, such as in same-sex friendship and romantic heterosexual relationships, or diminished, such as in cross-sex friendships. For example, men participating in my studies reported enacting a feminine type of friendship with their woman friends while simultaneously exhibiting normative male friendship behaviors in their same-sex friendships and in their romantic relationships with women.

Individuals as Subjective Entities

In addition to conceptualizing social properties as the possessions of individuals, cross-sex friendship researchers have pictured individuals as subjective entities because cross-sex friendship researchers have based their studies solely on persons' perceptions of interaction rather than investigating the interaction itself. These studies, therefore, underscore only one aspect of the complex processes surrounding interaction: the ability of humans to interpret the world around them. What is left out of this subjectivist stance is consideration of the concrete practices of cross-sex friends and the material conditions (the ideologically created context involving systems of language, meaning, and power relations) within which interaction takes place (Lannamann, 1991). For example, how do cross-sex friends talk about their friendship with outsiders when the friends are questioned about the nature of their relationship? Why do these inquiries arise? What language resources do the friends and the outsiders employ in these instances? What do cross-sex friends say to one another about such inquiries?

Furthermore, even though researchers are interested in investigating the friendship relationship, they have relied on the reports of only one party in deriving their conclusions. The use of the perceptions of one relational partner has been lamented in the larger literature on personal relationships as well (Duck, 1990, 1994a). With few exceptions, the studies of cross-sex friendship generalize from one partner's perspective to the other partner's perspective and to the relationship they negotiate together. The possibilities of discrepancies in reports is rarely addressed (for exceptions, see Monsour, Betty & Kurzweil, 1993; Werking, 1992), although extensive evidence for differential perceptions of shared relationships has been presented (Thompson & Walker, 1982). In neglecting both insiders' views of a relationship, researchers transform what originally was a single respondent's "perceptions of the relationship" to a summary description of "what is the relationship". In other words, one person's construction of the relationship becomes the objective report of the "reality" of the relationship. By neglecting the other's perceptions of the relationship, researchers risk limited and one-sided views of complex relational phenomena (Larson, 1974).

In short, cross-sex friendship scholars have not examined first-hand the *interaction* of cross-sex friends and the conditions under which these interactions take place. Instead, we have limited our analyses to our participants' *perceptions* of their relationships, because we have confined our data collection methods to surveys and interviews. Typically, surveys gather cross-sex friends' perceptions of predetermined global relationship qualities, such as the amount of intimacy, loyalty or companionship found in their friendships, through the use of Likert-type items. Interview studies are not as common as surveys in the cross-sex friendship literature. Interview studies encompass a wide range, varying from interviews consisting of two open-ended questions (Rose, 1985) to in-depth interviews with participants about their cross-sex friendships specifically (Werking, 1992, 1995) or about their friendships in general (Bell, 1981; Block, 1980; Rawlins, 1981, 1992; Rubin, 1985). Interviews may be designed to gather in-depth information about cross-sex friendship. Nevertheless, like surveys, data gleaned from interviews are participants' descriptions of their cross-sex friendship experiences rather then segments of their actual friendship interactions.

Why might it be important for researchers to focus on the actual interaction of cross-sex friends? First, a focus on interaction necessitates a focus on the dyad rather than the individual, because by definition interaction takes place between two individuals. Second, researchers can examine specific cross-sex friendship interactions which may lead to the participants' assessments of relational qualities, such as affection, frustration and companionship. If our participants say they are (dis)satisfied with their cross-sex friendship, how is this (dis)satisfaction conveyed in their talk with one another (Duck, 1994a)? Third, through the analysis of interaction, researchers may investigate language-in-use and, therefore, analyze the ideological forces which shape the ways in which man–woman relationships are negotiated through talk.

Next, I present a segment of tape-recorded conversation between two cross-sex friends. I will use this excerpt to demonstrate the usefulness of examining the interaction of cross-sex friends in two ways: the window it affords into relationship negotiation and into the cultural/ideological context within which cross-sex friendship interactions take place.

I have been collecting the conversations of cross-sex friends by audio-taperecording 15–20-minute conversations. The following is an excerpt from a conversation between Mary, 25, and John, 24. Mary and John are Caucasian, heterosexual college students. Both friends are involved in romantic relationships with other people. Mary and John have been close friends for $3\frac{1}{2}$ years. In this excerpt, John and Mary are discussing how other people perceive their relationship:

M: I can think of numerous specific examples of people comin' up to me and sayin', you know, "So what's up with you and John?" But . . .

J: Well, even at the bar the other night, when that girl thought I was hittin' on you and I smiled and I told I wasn't, that you and I are . . . it's the way that I say that, you know, people say I don't get defensive or anything, I just sort of smile . . .

M: Yeah! (Laughing)

J: . . . because, I don't know. I don't deny it totally, it's not like I want to deny 'cause then I would be like saying, "She's not my friend", you know . . . 'Cause, you know, you're my best friend. In a way it's way beyond hittin' on you.

M: Right. Right!

J: So when people say that, I just sorta smile 'cause they are trivializing what it is. So, I guess that makes it harder for people to believe that there's not anything going on because I don't deny it.

M: Yeah. I follow that exactly because I suppose if both of us were like, "No way!", you know, then they'd believe us. I don't know, I guess, you know, I'm very fond of you and that's what people see when I say, "Oh, you know, we're just friends or whatever". I guess they see that, you know, 'cause people read what you're, not only what the words are, but the message behind the words.

J: Yeah.

M: So, I guess if I didn't really care about you or whatever and I went like, "Naw", then it would be different.

J: I agree. When people ask me about you, I know I get that little, my eyes sort of (pause) they light up.

M: (Laughs)

J: You know, 'cause when I think about you, we really have fun, we laugh. You know, all we do is fun things and, you know, yeah, I can't say anything hostile or . . . I light up and people probably read that the wrong way.

M: Um hm. Then I guess it's actually *our* fault, you can't fault people for seeing that . . .

In the above excerpt, we witness Mary and John conversationally struggle with the dilemma of being friends. On one hand, being friends necessitates feelings of caring and affection between John and Mary. Demonstrating these friendship qualities publicly, however, may be misinterpreted by others since outsiders to the friendship may overlay a romantic template on affectionate behaviors. This interpretation of Mary and John's relationship is expressed in the phrases John and Mary use to describe the reactions of others, such as, "What's up?", "hittin' on you", "not anything going on", and "read that the wrong way". From their conversation, it is apparent Mary and John do not want a romantic reading of their relationship because it is the "wrong" reading. Further, they feel this read- ing "trivializes" the relationship because their relationship is "way beyond hittin' on you".

In addition to functioning as a means to reveal their feelings about the misperceptions of others, this conversation is also a sense-making experience (Duck, 1994a) for Mary and John because they attempt to explain to one another what their relationship means to them. In articulating their feelings toward one another, they use the words "fond", and "fun" and the phrase, "my eyes light up". They also cite the relational category of "best friends" to make sense of their experiences. Thus, this conversation provides information to researchers about feelings the friends have for one another and the specific ways these feelings are communicated to one another.

The ongoing negotiation of cross-sex friendship is a highly collaborative activ- ity and is achieved through talk. In order to understand this activity, researchers should observe, tape-record and transcribe the interaction of cross-sex friends. Through these activities, researchers may then witness for themselves cross-sex friends' affection for one another, their enjoyment of one another, and the enmeshment of their lives as they talk about themselves, friends, family, future plans, past events and work with one another; not to a third party. As Duck (1994a) notes:

> . . . persons symbolize their relationship with others in many different ways through talking. That fact helps each person (and could help researchers) to discover some- thing useful and important about the partner, the partner's vision and the partners' attitudes toward one another. Talk provides them with evidence about the way in

which another constructs the relationship and, more importantly, the frameworks of comprehension within which the other does so (p. 149).

Acultural

John and Mary's conversation may also be used as a way for researchers to examine the cultural context within which this interaction takes place. It is important for researchers to consider seriously the link between what occurs between cross-sex friends and their cultural and social contexts, yet, due to our focus on individuals, this type of analysis is rarely undertaken (e.g., Davis & Todd, 1985; Mahoney & Heretick, 1979; Sapadin, 1988). Several commentaries have been written about the potential influence of the cultural context on the nature of cross-sex friendship (e.g., O'Meara, 1989; Rawlins, 1982), however extended analyses of cultural texts and the symbol systems available to participants for describing their experiences have not been undertaken.

Typically, when "cultural norms" or "sex roles" are offered as explanation of findings, researchers do not provide specifics on the nature of these norms and roles. For example, Hacker (1981) explains her finding of perceptions of lesser intimacy in cross-sex friendship for women than for men by simply pointing to "social norms" regulating the relationship between men and women friends (p. 398). Hacker (1981) does not offer an explanation regarding the specific ways these norms regulate man–woman friendships. Similarly, the Bukowski, Nappi & Hoza (1987) finding that men report greater intimacy in their cross-sex friendship than in their same-sex friendships is explained by "cultural proscriptions" in regards to intimacy among males (p. 602).

Researchers need to consider seriously the connection between cross-sex friendship and the embracing culture, because the available tools for the conduct of relationships, language and metaphor, are informed by cultural ideologies (Duck, 1994a). The prevailing heterosexual romantic ideology I described earlier in the chapter constrains the daily interactions of cross-sex friends, because it structures the possibilities for friendship (O'Meara, 1994) and brings to the fore specific issues in cross-sex friendship. These issues include the degree to which the friendship incorporates expressions of romance and sexuality, if the man and woman are heterosexuals, or the extent to which outsiders to the friendship will accept the relationship as a "friendship" rather than a "romance".

Furthermore, the symbol systems utilized by cross-sex friends to address these and other issues are infused with a heterosexual romantic ideology, so that terms such as "just friends" are used to describe cross-sex friendship. Friends also struggle to create new ways of expressing their feelings for one another so that these expressions will not be misinterpreted as romantic in nature. Cross-sex friends particularly struggle to find substitutes for, or clarify their use of, "love" as an expression of feeling (Werking, 1995).

Clearly, in their conversation, Mary and John interactively reproduce the prevailing heterosexual romantic ideology. The ideology is reflected in their description of the misperceptions of others. Interestingly, Mary and John take responsibility for the misperceptions of outsiders by saying, "It's actually our fault, you can't fault people for seeing that". The ideology leaks into their own perceptions of their relationship as well because they "trivialize" their relationship by using the phrase "just friends", implying they too consider their friendship as "less than" a romantic relationship.

Studying the actual interactions of cross-sex friends is only one way researchers might tap into the cultural context in which cross-sex friendship is enacted. I focus on this method because it is under-utilized by cross-sex friendship researchers. Interviews, surveys and textual analysis of media images of cross-sex friendship would also reveal relevant information. Whatever the methodology of choice, our understanding of the challenges, tensions and rewards associated with cross-sex friendship will be enriched by a description of the cultural contexts in which the studied friendships take place.

Acontextual

The social network of cross-sex friends also influences the character of cross-sex friendship (Parks, this volume). Nevertheless, cross-sex friendship researchers have just begun to chart the linkages between cross-sex friendship and other social relationships. For example, cross-sex friends' perceptions of the social network subsuming their dyad have been collected in only a handful of studies. In these studies, the marital relationship has been linked to participation in cross-sex friendship. Booth & Hess (1974) and Rose (1985) limited their documentation of this link to an analysis of the influence of marriage on the number of cross-sex friends. Other work has tapped into the connections between romantic relationships, same-sex friendships, family relations and cross-sex friendship. (Werking, 1992; 1995). For example, I (Werking, 1992) interviewed pairs of cross-sex friends about times when their romantic relationships with third parties influenced their friendships. This study revealed that the cross-sex friendships were often reconstructed during these times, either by not spending as much time with one another or by including the romantic partner in friendship activities in order to reduce the romantic partner's insecurity about the cross-sex friendship. Ironically, the cross-sex friendship was viewed as more stable and beneficial than the romantic relationship by nearly all of the participants. This example also illustrates the overlap between cultural ideologies and the nature of social relationships at a personal level, because my participants reported privileging their romantic relationships over their cross-sex friendships while simultaneously describing their cross-sex friendships as more stable and beneficial. Work of this type is in its initial stages and future research is needed prior to claiming understanding of the connections between cross-sex friendship and cross-sex friends' third-party involvements, such as same-sex friendships, work relationships, family relationships and romantic relationships.

Ahistorical

I have argued that individualism is evidenced in the cross-sex friendship research in the conceptualization of research concepts, in the choice of the unit of analysis, and in the lack of focus on the cultural and social contexts of cross-sex friendship. A final consequence of individual-centered relationship research is that cross-sex friendship researchers rarely consider the studied relationships' histories.

The majority of existing cross-sex friendship researchers utilize the survey method. These surveys typically obtain minimal information about the friendships described by research participants. In general, the respondents' sex and age, the type of friendship (best, close, casual, etc.) and the length of friendship appear to be the only background information of interest. Because the type of information gathered through the use of surveys is abstract in nature, so too are the claims researchers may legitimately make regarding their results. In contrast to the survey method, interviews can provide detailed descriptions of the historical patterning of interactions within the studied friendships. Nevertheless, cross-sex friendship researchers do not necessarily choose to exercise this capacity (e.g., Hacker, 1981; Rose, 1985; Sapadin, 1988).

An alternative to ahistorical research is grounding research in the participants' relationships and examining their patterns of development and interaction. This perspective views relationships as co-constructed patterns of interaction which are built up over time (Bateson, 1978). These patterns compose a relational context which is in "continuous and reverberating motion" (Gergen, 1980, p. 243), unfolding as interactants choose and revise courses of action in tandem. Furthermore, the relationship and the acts of the partners are intertwined because the relationship is constituted by the partners' actions and, in turn, shapes their practices. A backwards look at these patterns thus reveals to the researcher the premises for interpreting the actions occurring within the relationship.

Only two interview studies (Rawlins, 1981; Werking, 1992), however, have grounded the analysis of the participants' descriptions of their close cross-sex friendships in the historical context of the studied relationship. Each of these researchers constructed "friendship histories" prior to interpreting their participants' descriptions of their friendships. A friendship history is in essence a story of the friendship as told to the researcher by *both* members of a friendship. This story consists of key relational events and themes, such as the friends' meeting, celebrations, special nicknames, and disagreements. Constructing such a history aids researchers' interpretations of the participants' responses to questions. For example, instances of physical contact between cross-sex friends may be interpreted by a researcher as being romantic and/or sexual in nature unless the researcher considered how touching has been interpreted by the friends in the past and how the relationship has been defined by the friends.

In sum, by lifting individuals' assessments of their cross-sex friendships out of the relational context, researchers have lost the ability to answer such questions as: how did these assessments arise in a particular form? or what led a participant to check off "very satisfied" rather than "somewhat satisfied" in response to the question, "How satisfied are you with your friendship with X?". Behind participants' responses are specific experiences and practices which remain unexamined by researchers.

Further, without historical information about the cross-sex friendships, to what do we anchor our participants' descriptions? How can we "interpret" their interpretations? Actions are accorded particular meanings because they are enacted in a particular context. By peeling the context from respondents' actions, cross-sex friendship researchers risk imposing researcher-owned categories of description on their participants' responses rather than participant-owned categories.

"Decentering" the individual in cross-sex friendship necessitates a profound shift in research practices (Lannamann, 1992) because it involves shifting our focus to interaction as it takes place within particular historical, relational and cultural contexts. Such a shift reverberates through the questions we ask to the methods we choose for data collection to the ways in which we analyze our data.

THE IDEOLOGY OF HETEROSEXISM

The ideology of individualism has partly shaped what we know about cross-sex friendship. I now revisit a second organizing principle for cross-sex friendship research, the ideology of heterosexuality. I argued earlier in this chapter that heterosexism informs scholars' decisions about what constitutes viable research topics and is practiced in the everyday interactions of cross-sex friends. Unfortunately, heterosexism also undergirds many of the existing cross-sex friendship studies.

First, scholars often assume the participants in studies are heterosexual men and women, or specifically sample only heterosexual men and women (e.g., Swain, 1992; Werking, 1994) and thus neglect other forms of cross-sex friendship, such as friendships between gay men and lesbians. A recent literature review (Werking, 1995) uncovered no empirical studies of friendship between the gay and lesbian community and a limited number of studies investigating friendships between gay men and straight women (Malone, 1980; Nardi, 1992; Whitney, 1990).

Second, researchers exhibit a heterosexist ideology when we assume that issues of romance and sexuality constitute ongoing concerns only in cross-sex friendships between heterosexual persons, rather than acknowledging that these issues may be raised in varying degrees in same-sex friendships between homosexual and/or heterosexual persons (Nardi, 1992; Rawlins, 1994b) or between cross-sex friends where one or both friends are homosexual. The danger in making this assumption is that researchers fall into dichotomous ways of thinking about sexual orientation. The scant research conducted into the friendships between gay men and heterosexual women questions this assumption. For example, the research of Malone (1980) and Whitney (1990) paradoxically reveals that, although many of their participants viewed their friendship as a safe haven from the perils of sexual and romantic relationships initially, sexual attraction and activity between the friends existed. The participants in both studies further reported sexuality threatened their friendships and summoned feelings of frustration and anxiety.

Dichotomous thinking about sexual orientation may also be challenged by friendship between lesbians and gays. While studies have not yet been conducted in this area, an interesting collection of essays written by persons engaged in friendship highlights the close and complex relationships between gays and lesbians (Nestle & Preston, 1994). These writings uncover the sensual nature of gay–lesbian friendship and, in this way, further undermine the heterosexist assumption that expressed or unexpressed sexual attraction occurs only between heterosexual men and women.

There is much to be learned about cross-sex friendship in the homosexual community as well as cross-sex friendship between homosexual/heterosexual women and men. Such study is worthwhile because ignoring the various forms of cross-sex friendship limits our knowledge of the diversity of norms, rules and societal contexts within which men and women forge friendships (Duck, 1994a).

Lastly, romance and sexuality are important topics for study in the area of cross-sex friendship because these issues have been defined culturally as central to man–woman relations. Many participants in our studies reflect this centrality as they report these issues are important to them in their everyday experiences in forging cross-sex friendships (e.g., Bell, 1981; Furman, 1986; Rubin, 1985). Cross-sex friendship scholars, however, should be cautious not to let investigation of sexual issues overshadow studies into other dimensions of the cross-sex friendship experience. Let us look beyond the issue of sex and pursue studies about other important cross-sex friendship dynamics, such as what cross-sex friends do and say with one another. And let us be cautious not to investigate these dynamics only as they occur between heterosexual persons, but as they are practiced between persons of differing sexual orientations.

CONCLUSION

The narratives told by research participants about cross-sex friendship are constructed within specific historical, cultural and social configurations. So, too, are the texts produced by researchers. Both types of narratives are constrained by interrelated complexes of ideological forces. Through our research practices ideologies gain their power because these practices reaffirm and reify ideological assumptions. In this chapter, I have problematized what appears to be rarely questioned ways of thinking about and researching cross-sex friendship. Specifically, I have addressed the latent individualism and heterosexism evident in the cross-sex friendship literature and charted the ways these ideological themes position our research. Such questioning is needed because the debate over the theoretical and methodological approaches (in short, the stories we construct about cross-sex friendship) is constricted unless issues of ideology are addressed. As Shotter (1993) states:

> Stories may tell us what in certain particular circumstances we should do to fit our actions into a particular order, but their danger is, that by revealing in their telling only a selection of the possibilities open to us, they can so easily conceal from us what the range of possibilities is (p. 147).

Cross-sex friendship provides a unique opportunity to assess the interplay between cultural ideals and norms regarding woman–man relationships, unique relational patterns of interaction, and subjective individual experiences. Let us approach this opportunity thoughtfully and creatively so that our research is emancipatory rather than repressive in nature.

Chapter 17

Self-disclosure, Self-identity, and Relationship Development: a Transactional/Dialectical Perspective

Kathryn Dindia
University of Wisconsin Milwaukee, WI, USA

Personal relationships theory and research are plagued by static approaches to a dynamic phenomenon. Self-disclosure (SD) plays a vital role in relationship development and maintenance (c.f., Derlega et al., 1993) but is currently conceived of and studied as a static phenomenon. Theory and research on SD in personal relationships treats SD as a single, dichotomous act of revelation (i.e., either a person has or has not self-disclosed). However, SD is not a one-time event; it is a dynamic process. *In real-life relationships, topics are not either disclosed or not disclosed but are part of the ongoing process of SD.* Some topics are perpetually "on the agenda" and are repeatedly discussed in relationships, such as one's view of self, partner or the relationship, one's view of how one's children are turning out, one's career, and so on. Similarly, Spencer (1994) argued that family members discuss the same topics repeatedly over time, each time disclosing at some more explicit level of detail or making more clear their particular intentions and desires with regard to the topic. Because individuals and relationships are not static entities but are themselves processes that are continually evolving, one can never fully reveal oneself. *SD is a life-long/ relationship-long process*, a process that changes as individuals and relationships change. Therefore, when personal relationships researchers conceive of and

Handbook of Personal Relationships, 2nd edn. Edited by Steve Duck.
© 1997 John Wiley & Sons Ltd.

study SD as a single dichotomous act of revelation, they miss crucial information about the structure and function of SD in individual lives and personal relationships.

Transactional (Pearce & Sharp, 1973) and dialectical perspectives (Altman, Vinsel & Brown, 1981; Baxter, 1988; Baxter & Montgomery, this volume; Rawlins, 1983b) view SD as a process, but so far haven't followed through in studying it as such. A review of the literature on SD in personal relationships indicates that SD has been and continues to be primarily studied as a personality trait, a relationship characteristic or a static event, rather than a dynamic process.

The purpose of this chapter is to argue that SD is a transactional process that is inherently dialectical in nature. I will review evidence from research on the disclosure of stigmatized identities which supports the conceptualization of SD as a transactional/dialectical process. By examining research on SD of stigmatized identities, I hope to demonstrate the utility of conceptualizing and studying SD as a transactional/dialectical process.

DEFINITION OF SELF-DISCLOSURE

SD has been defined in a number of ways. A typical definition of SD is what individuals verbally reveal about themselves (including thoughts, feelings and experiences) to others (Derlega et al., 1993). Although some limit the definition of SD to the disclosure of private or intimate information, generally intimacy or depth of SD is considered the primary dimension of SD. However, in this chapter I focus on the disclosure of intimate, private or risky information. The disclosure of superficial, public or non-intimate information about self is crucial in the beginning stages of relationship development; as stated by Derlega et al. (1993), "It is hard to imagine how a relationship might get started without such self-disclosure" (p. 2). Similarly, "catching up" or debriefing your partner about what happened during the day is an important relational maintenance strategy which is positively related to marital satisfaction (Vangelisti & Banski, 1993). However, this type of disclosure, while important, is qualitatively different from and serves different functions from the disclosure of private, intimate, or risky information. As stated by Goodstein & Reinecker:

> While some information about one's self is rather public . . . there is other information about one's self that is rather private or intimate and is disclosed under special circumstances. This private, intimate information about the self ought to be the focus of both research and theorizing about SD. If this is not done, the term "SD" becomes vague and general . . . losing any special meaning (Goodstein & Reinecker, 1974, p. 51).

Of course, this definition of SD ignores the fact that intimacy can be assessed from different perspectives, that what is intimate differs from person to person, and that discloser, recipient and observer may perceive the intimacy of SD differently (Chelune, 1979; Spencer, 1993a).

Similarly, I realize that the disclosure of intimate information is not a common, everyday occurrence, at least for most of us (it has been argued that disclosure of stigmatized identities is an everyday issue for those who are stigmatized; Mazanec, 1995). Pearce & Sharp (1973) stated that relatively few communication transactions involve high levels of disclosure and subsequent empirical research supports this generalization (Dindia, Fitzpatrick & Kenny, 1989; Duck et al., 1991; Van Lear, 1987). However, though intimate SD may occur infrequently, it has important ramifications for individual identity and relationship development.

PERSPECTIVES ON SELF-DISCLOSURE IN PERSONAL RELATIONSHIPS LITERATURE

Self-disclosure as a Stable Characteristic of Individuals and Relationships

Early theory and research on SD viewed SD as a personality trait, an enduring characteristic or attribute of an individual. An individual's "ability", or "willingness" to self-disclose was studied (Cline, 1983a). This was accomplished by having subjects complete self-report measures which assessed SD as a personality trait (i.e., questionnaires that ask individuals how much they disclose to strangers, friends, etc., such as the Jourard Self-disclosure Questionnaire (JSDQ); Jourard, 1971a). Studies cast within this perspective attempted to identify high and low disclosers and correlate individual differences in SD with demographic and biological characteristics (sex, age, race, religion, birth order), sociocultural differences and other personality traits (Archer, 1979). However, the results of these studies have been inconsistent, and the magnitude of individual differences in SD have been generally small (Archer, 1979). For example, a recent meta-analysis of sex differences in SD from 205 studies (Dindia & Allen, 1992) found that sex differences in SD are small ($d = 0.20$) and that a number of variables moderate the effect of sex on SD.

Closely aligned with the perspective of SD as a characteristic of individuals is the perspective of SD as a characteristic of relationships. Here, characteristics of the relationship (e.g., relationship status, length of relationship, relational satisfaction) are used to predict SD (and *vice versa*). An example is Fitzpatrick's (1987) typological approach to marital interaction. Fitzpatrick describes three types of couples, traditionals, independents and separates, arguing that there are similarities within and differences between different types of couples in the degree to which couples self-disclose and value SD. Although the unit of analysis is the dyad instead of the individual, this perspective, like the personality trait perspective, views SD (and relationships) as a static phenomenon.

Self-disclosure as an Action or Event

The view of SD as a personality trait gradually has been replaced by the view of SD as an action, message, behavior or event (Cline, 1983a). For example, SD has been defined as "the act of making yourself manifest" (Jourard, 1971a, p. 19). From this "communication-as-action" perspective, communication is viewed as something one person does or gives to somebody else (Stewart, 1995). Research from this perspective focuses on individual messages or behaviors. The unit of analysis is the message, and typical research variables include intimacy, amount, valence, accuracy, clarity and flexibility of SD (Cline, 1982). Research cast from this perspective attempts to identify the causes and effects of SD and studies SD as the independent or dependent variable (Pearce & Sharp, 1973). Often the independent variables used to predict SD are characteristics of the individual (e.g., sex of subject), the target (e.g., partner sex), or the relationship (e.g., couple type). Thus, SD is viewed as an action which is determined by a stable characteristic of a person or relationship. Although viewing SD as an event is significantly different from viewing it as an individual or relationship characteristic, both perspectives view SD as a static phenomenon.

Self-disclosure as a Transactional Process

Pearce & Sharp (1973) criticized the view of SD as a personality trait or an event predicted by personality traits and argued that SD is a transactional process:

> It is what happens when communicators transact with each other, rather than characteristics of either or both in other contexts, which provides an understanding of self-disclosing communication (Pearce & Sharp, 1973, p. 413).

Similarly, Gilbert & Horenstein (1975) argued that SD should not be categorized into "those who do" and "those who do not".

To say that SD is a transactional process is to apply several axioms or principles to SD. First, a transactional perspective implies that SD is a dynamic, continuous and circular process, rather than a single event (Barlund, 1970; Berlo, 1960). You cannot identify the "act" of SD, its beginning and end, its cause and effect, its stimulus and response, the actor (discloser) and acted upon (disclosee) (Barlund, 1970; Berlo, 1960; Pearce & Sharp, 1973; Stewart, 1995). Similarly, as a relationship develops, the intimacy level of SD does not necessarily increase in a linear fashion. Developing or continuing relationships might exhibit cycles of openness and closedness; some relationships might not progress toward increased openness at all (Altman, Vinsel & Brown, 1981).

Second, SD is contextualized, and the context influences the process of SD (Pearce & Sharp, 1973). In particular, SD occurs in the context of individual lives and personal relationships and should be studied as such. From a transactional perspective, it makes no sense to study SD between strangers (the "stranger-on-the-train" phenomenon). According to a transactional perspective, communication is contextualized within the life-span; one cannot understand communication without first discovering the developmental process of which communication is part (Nussbaum, 1989). When applied to SD, this means that if one is interested in SD, one would be interested in explaining the process by which SD developed, not only within the relationship but also within the life-span that contextualizes the relationship.

Third, all the elements in the process of SD are interdependent; each affects all of the others (Berlo, 1960). The processes of self-identity/human development and relationship identity/development are interdependent with the process of revealing self. Who we are as individuals as well as who we are in relationship to each other emerges out of SD, and *vice versa.*

In contrast to the action view, which treats people as if they had set identities (Stewart, 1995), the transactional view argues that individuals are not intact, contained, whole, formed, static selves who reveal themselves to others. Identity is continually open-ended, unstable and changing (Duck, West & Acitelli, this volume):

> What occurs in the sharing of self's thoughts, actions and biography with another is *construction* of an identity for self, not merely the *presentation* of an already formed self. Rather than presenting or revealing a prefabricated identity, the process of disclosure is actually the process of talking an identity into existence within the relationship at a particular context and point in time (p. 12).

Similarly, relationships are not intact, contained, formed, static phenomena (Duck, 1994a). Who "we" are affects and is affected by the process of SD. SD and relationship identity/development are "mutually transformative" (Derlega et al., 1993); SD transforms the nature of the relationship and the relationship transforms the meaning and consequences of SD.

Although SD and relationship development are *mutually* transformative, theory and research on SD in personal relationships typically focuses on the one-way effect of SD on the relationship. SD is viewed a major factor in the development, maintenance and deterioration of relationships (Derlega et al., 1993). According to uncertainty reduction theory (Berger & Bradac, 1982), through SD we obtain predictive and explanatory knowledge about another. This acquisition of information (or reduction in uncertainty) facilitates relationship development. Similarly, through SD we acquire mutual knowledge, or knowledge that two people share, know they share, and use in interacting with one another (Planalp & Garvin-Doxas, 1994).

However, SD in which the speaker reveals information about him- or herself is not the only type of SD that functions to develop relationships. SD in which the speaker reveals thoughts and feelings about his or her partner and the relationship also affects relationship development. As a relationship becomes established, not only how the speaker feels about him- or herself but also how the speaker feels about the partner and the relationship become part of an individual's self-concept (Fitzpatrick, 1987). Thus, disclosing how one feels about the partner and the relationship constitutes SD. Similarly, as a relationship develops, not only how the speaker feels about him- or herself but also how he or she feels about the relationship is disclosed. As stated by Fitzpatrick (1987), "Individuals in ongoing relationships may discuss their emotional reactions to one another, and these reactions may become a major part of the relationship" (p. 140).

SD of thoughts and feelings about the partner and the relationship functions to negotiate relationships. Archer (1987) argued that disclosure is used in its most social form to represent and negotiate the terms of relationships with others (e.g., "I've always thought of us as a two-career family. What will happen to us if you quit the firm?"). Research by Tolhuizen (1989) provides evidence that SD is used to negotiate the relationship. Seriously dating college students were instructed to describe the things they said and/or actions they took to change their relationship from one of casual dating to one of serious and exclusive dating. Twenty-nine percent of the subjects reported *relationship negotiation*, defined as initiating or engaging in a direct discussion about the relationship, about feelings in the relationship, and what is desired for the future of the relationship, as a strategy to intensify dating relationships. In contrast, only 15% reported SD in which the content of the information is about the self (e.g., "I told my partner a great deal about myself—more than I had told anyone before") as a strategy to intensify the relationship (Tolhuizen, 1989).

SD also affects relationship development through the *relational message* that is communicated when an individual self-discloses. Watzlawick, Beavin & Jackson (1967) distinguished between the content aspect of communication and the relationship aspect. The content aspect is the literal message; in the case of SD, the content of the message refers to the self (or to feelings about one's partner or the relationship). The relationship aspect says something about the relationship between participants. All communication has both a content and a relationship aspect; one cannot self-disclose without simultaneously offering a definition of the relationship.

Cline (1982, 1983a, 1983b) viewed SD as relational communication. According to Cline (1982), SD functions to define the relationship; "Rather than 'telling you who I am', when I engage in SD, I am . . . defining who 'we' are" (Cline, 1982, p. 2). Similarly, Derlega et al., (1993) state that recipients of SD not only respond to the content of the information disclosed but also to what the SD says about the relationship, implications for the future of the relationship, and so on.

SD as relational communication is conceptualized as the system of behaviors and perceptions that function to define where partners stand in relation to each other. As such, SD consists of proposed relational definitions, responses to those proposals, and perceptions of those proposals and responses (Cline, 1983b). In particular, SD constitutes a proposal about the closeness of the relationship. For example, by disclosing intimate information about myself to you I propose a definition of our relationship as intimate. If you respond to my SD with acceptance and support, you accept my definition of our relationship. If you respond to my SD with rejection, you are rejecting my definition of the relationship and countering with a definition of the relationship as unintimate.

Cline (1983b) argues that research on both reciprocity of SD and SD and relationship development provides empirical support for SD as relational communication. Cline argues that an implicit negotiation process is involved in reciprocity of SD, although she admits that the reciprocity research cannot provide direct evidence of this. Cline also cites research on relationship development, which consistently supports the existence of a positive linear relationship between the amount and intimacy of SD and the stage of relationship (Taylor & Altman, 1987), as support for SD as relational communication.

More persuasive is the results of a study by Miell & Duck (1986) on the strategies individuals used to develop friendships and restrict the development of friendships. Research participants indicated what they judged to be appropriate behaviors when interacting with someone they just met and when interacting with a close friend. They also indicated strategies they would use to restrict a relationship's development and intensify a relationship's development. The results of the study were that several of the behaviors appropriate between strangers (including superficial SD) were listed as strategies to restrict the development of a relationship. Similarly, several of the behaviors appropriate between close friends (including intimate SD) were listed as strategies used to intensify a friendship. Thus, superficial SD communicates the relational message, "we are strangers"; intimate SD communicates the relational message, "we are friends".

Although some have argued that the role of SD in relationship development has been overrated (Bochner, 1982), I would argue the opposite. Research on SD and personal relationships has focused on SD in which the content of the information is about the self. SD of thoughts and feelings regarding the partner and the relationship, as well as SD as relational communication, have been virtually ignored in the personal relationships literature.

Although others since Pearce & Sharp have argued that SD is a transactional process, theory and research on SD in personal relationships has been relatively unaffected by this view and predominantly reflects a static, linear, one-way, cause–effect view of SD. For example, three types of *effects* have been consistently studied in the literature on SD and relationships: reciprocity of SD, SD and liking, and SD and relationship development (Berg & Derlega, 1987). Research on reciprocity of SD typically examines the effect of one person's SD on another person's SD rather than viewing SD as *mutually* interdependent (Dindia, 1994). Research on SD and liking has studied three effects: (1) do we like others who disclose to us?; (2) do we disclose more to people we like?; and (3) do we like people as a result of disclosing to them? (Collins & Miller, 1994). SD is the independent variable for the first and third effects; SD is the dependent variable for the second effect. Research on SD and relationship development examines the one-way effect of SD on relationship development. Longitudinal studies of SD and relationship development are rare (Taylor & Altman, 1987); typically, cross-sectional comparisons of SD are made between relationships at different stages of development, with SD treated as the independent variable and relationship development as the dependent variable (for a review of this research, see Taylor & Altman, 1987).

There is some research on SD in personal relationships that begins to examine the process of SD. Time-series analysis of conversational sequences (Dindia, 1982, 1984; Spencer, 1993c) and ethnography of natural conversation (Spencer, 1993b) have been used to examine short conversational sequences centering around SD. In particular, these studies focus on the comments occurring directly before and after SD. However, these studies implicitly assume that SD is a one-time event occurring within the confines of a single conversation, typically within a single utterance. Research by Van Lear (1987) examines the process of SD across six conversations between zero-history dyads. This study identifies patterns of SD across conversations, including changes in levels of SD and reciprocity of SD. However, all of these studies make the "act" the unit of analysis.

Self-disclosure as a Dialectical Process

Relational dialectics shares many of the assumptions of a transactional perspective (i.e., process, interdependence, contextual embeddedness; see Baxter & Montgomery, this volume, for elaboration of these assumptions from a dialectical perspective) but adds the unique and fundamental assumption of a dialectical perspective, contradiction. According to a dialectical perspective, relationships are viewed as involving contradictory and opposing forces (Baxter, 1988; Baxter & Montgomery, this volume; Montgomery, 1993).

Several theorists have posited openness–closedness as a dialectical tension in relationships (c.f., Altman, Vinsel & Brown, 1981; Baxter, 1988; Rawlins, 1983b). According to this perspective, individuals continually face the contradictory impulses to be open and expressive vs. protective of self and/or other. Self-disclosure is necessary to achieve intimacy but SD opens areas of vulnerability. To avoid hurting each other, people must undertake protective measures (Rawlins, 1983b). Thus, the contradictory tension between information openness and information closedness requires decisions to reveal or conceal personal information (Rawlins, 1983b).

Although a number of theorists and researchers have recently argued that SD is a dialectical process, there is little research examining SD from a dialectical perspective; in addition, some of the research that does exist still studies SD as a static phenomenon (e.g., Baxter & Simon, 1993). However, some research on SD in personal relationships examines SD from a dialectical perspective. For instance, Rawlins' (1983b) research on the dialectics of SD in friendships elaborates and illustrates the contradictory impulses between expressiveness and protectiveness in conversations between friends. Rawlins' definition of SD included revealing personal aspects of oneself to another as well as commenting about another's individual qualities. Rawlins interviewed 10 pairs of close friends, eliciting their subjective interpretation of their ongoing interaction, and then conducted an interpretative analysis of the transcribed interviews. Rawlins found two conversational dilemmas resulting from the contradictory impulses to be open and expressive vs. protective of self and/or of other. In deciding whether to disclose information regarding self, an individual confronts the contradictory dilemma of protecting self by restricting personal disclosure and of striving to be open by confiding in other. Disclosing personal information to another makes one susceptible to being hurt by the other. The decision to self-disclose will be a function of at least two things: an individual's need to be open about a given issue, and the individual's trust of the partner's discretion (his/her ability to keep a secret and exercise restraint regarding self's sensitivities). The decision to reveal or conceal involves assessing what will be gained or lost by either choice (Rawlins, 1983b).

In deciding whether to disclose information regarding the partner, an individual confronts the contradictory dilemma of protecting partner by restricting negative feedback and of striving to be open and honest to build trust in the relationship. The decision to disclose information regarding other will be a function of the self's need to be open and honest about a given issue and the amount of restraint appropriate to the topic. An individual develops an awareness of topics which make the other vulnerable to hurt or anger. In particular, *"Self must determine whether telling the truth is worth causing the other pain and breaching the other's trust in self's protective inclinations"* [original emphasis] (Rawlins, 1983b, p. 10).

Privacy Regulation as a Dialectical Strategy

Several scholars (Altman, 1975; Derlega & Chaikin, 1977; Petronio, 1988, 1991) view SD as a privacy regulation mechanism. Altman (1975) defined privacy as:

> . . . an interpersonal boundary process by which a person or group regulates interaction with others. By altering the degree of openness of the self to others, a hypothetical personal boundary is more or less receptive to social interaction with others. Privacy is, therefore, a dynamic process involving selective control over a self-boundary either by an individual or by a group (p. 6).

Communication Boundary Management Theory (CBMT) (Petronio, 1988, 1991) extends Altman's privacy regulation theory and more specifically relates it to SD. CBMT argues that individuals manage their communication boundaries in balancing the need for disclosure with the need for privacy. The basic thesis of CBMT is that revealing private information is risky because one is potentially vulnerable when revealing aspects of the self. Receiving private information from another may also result in the need to protect oneself. To manage both disclosing and receiving private information, individuals erect a metaphoric boundary as a means of protection and to reduce the possibility of being rejected or getting hurt (Petronio, 1991).

Three assumptions underlie CBMT. First, individuals erect boundaries to control autonomy and vulnerability when disclosing and receiving private information. Second, because disclosing and receiving private information is risky and may cause potential vulnerability, partners regulate their communication boundaries strategically to minimize risks. Third, decision-making rules are used to determine when, with whom, and how much private information is disclosed, as well as how to respond to the disclosure (Petronio, 1991).

Privacy regulation and communication boundary management have been proposed as theories of SD. However, I view privacy regulation/communication boundary management as strategic responses to the dialectical tension of the need to reveal and conceal. By regulating privacy (or managing communication boundaries), individuals employ a strategy designed to satisfy the oppositional forces of openness–closedness. By setting a hypothetical boundary individuals designate some things as appropriate for disclosure and some things as inappropriate for disclosure. This strategy is similar to Baxter's (1988) "segmentation" strategy, which differentiates topic domains into those for which SD is regarded as appropriate and those for which SD is regarded as inappropriate (i.e., taboo topics). In studying the existence of and response to dialectical tensions in relationships, Baxter (1990) found that the most dominant strategy reported for the openness–closedness contradiction was segmentation. The difference between Baxter's segmentation strategy and privacy regulation viewed as a dialectical strategy is that segmentation is conceived of as a static strategy whereas privacy regulation is conceived of as a fluid process.

DISCLOSURE OF STIGMATIZED IDENTITIES

Theory and research on disclosure of stigmatized identities, such as sexual abuse, homosexuality, HIV antibodies, and AIDS (c.f., Goffman, 1974, Limandri, 1989, Sorenson and Snow, 1991), illustrates the principles of SD from a transactional/dialectical perspective. Although this research lies outside the field of personal relationships, it provides examples for personal relationships researchers of how SD can be conceptualized and studied as a process.

The process perspective is not evident in all of the literature on disclosure of stigmatized identities. Some of the research on disclosure of stigmatized identities invokes the "SD as action or event" perspective. For example, several researchers have examined the strategies used to disclose stigmatized identities and the outcomes of such disclosure (c.f., Edgar, 1994). Others have assessed how, when, where, why and to whom gays and lesbians disclose their sexual orientation (Wells & Kline, 1987). The research I will review conceives of and studies disclosure of stigmatized identities as a transactional/dialectical process.

The term "stigma" refers to a stable characteristic of an individual that is perceived as damaging to the individual's image or reputation. Stigmas include, but are not limited to, physical disability, membership in some stigmatized group, character defects, which are manifested by some discrediting event in the person's past or present, and disease. Goffman (1974) differentiated those who are stigmatized into the "discredited" and the "discreditable". The discredited is one whose stigma is already known about or is immediately perceivable by others. The problem for the discredited is managing tension generated during mixed social contacts (i.e., contacts with "normals"). The discreditable is one whose stigma is not known about or immediately perceivable by others. Thus, the major problem for the discreditable is information control, or the management of undisclosed discrediting information about self:

> To display or not to display; to tell or not to tell; to let on or not to let on; to lie or not to lie; and in each case, to whom, how, when, and where (Goffman, 1974, p. 42).

Theory and research on the disclosure of stigmatized identities is not limited to disclosure of homosexuality, sexual abuse, AIDS, etc., but is generalizable to SD of intimate, negative and risky information in general. As Goffman pointed out, the problem of stigma control is not a case of a few who are stigmatized and the majority who are not:

> Stigma management is a general feature of society, a process occurring wherever there are identity norms. The same features are involved whether a major differentness is at question, of the kind traditionally defined as stigmatic, or a picayune differentness, of which the ashamed person is ashamed to be ashamed (Goffman, 1974, p. 130).

All people suffer some discrepancy between their virtual identity and their actual identity and thus are faced with the problem of identity management and must make decisions regarding SD (Goffman, 1974).

Research on the disclosure of stigmatized identities employs interview and observational methods to elicit conversational sequences of SD that extend across a particular conversation to multiple conversations and sometimes to the life-long process of SD. Limandri (1989) studied the process of disclosure of stigmatizing identities from the perspective of the discloser. Limandri conducted a qualitative analysis of 29 interviews of disclosure of women's abuse, AIDS or HIV antibodies, and herpes. Limandri found that SD is a process, not an event:

> On the surface, disclosure seemed to be a dichotomous variable composed of disclosure or concealment. However, with further examination of the interviews, there appeared to be smaller categories of disclosure. . . . there seemed to be an unlayering process to disclosure (Limandri, 1989, p. 73).

Similarly, MacFarlane & Krebs (1986) described the process of children's disclosure of sexual abuse as the "no-maybe-sometimes-yes" syndrome. They frequently observed children who initially said "no" without any qualifications to an inquiry of abuse, who later acknowledged that "maybe it happened sometimes", and who finally fully revealed sexual abuse.

SD of stigmatized identities often involves a process of "testing the waters" in which the discloser tests the reaction of the recipient before self-disclosing in more detail (Miell, 1984). Limandri (1989) found that disclosure of stigmatizing conditions usually begins with a small revelation to test the environment. MacFarlane & Krebs (1986) state that children frequently tell what happened to them in small pieces, saving the worst part until they see how the recipient reacts to the things they disclose first. Spencer & Derlega (1995) report that because many people are afraid of those who are HIV-positive, disclosure of HIV antibodies requires the discloser to investigate the attitudes of a potential recipient before disclosing HIV-status. Spencer & Derlega provide the following example from one of their study respondents:

> I was dating someone not too long ago, went out, was asked out. I didn't tell them right at that point. The way I handled it on the first date, I steered the conversation around to AIDS-related topics; because of my own volunteer work, I was able to do that—start talking about them and seeing what their reaction was. Were they going to try to change the subject, were they uncomfortable, or were they comfortable and compassionate with the whole thing? That was it for the first time, and the second time I brought it up again. I brought up that a former lover of mine had recently tested positive, which he had. Which sort of puts it into their mind that I probably would be, too, and if they were horrified, well that was it and I wouldn't see them again. If that went fine, then the next time it was, "Yes, I have tested positive myself". . . . But that's the way I do it; just sort of a gradual thing, test the waters a bit, not just jump right in it, telling them and scaring them to death (p. 4).

However, SD doesn't necessarily move from non-disclosure to disclosure in a linear fashion. In studying the process of disclosure of stigmatized, identities, Limandri (1989) found that some would conceal for a while, disclose, then retract back into concealment:

> This [deciding whether to tell or to conceal] is not a simple decision or a decision that is made only once, but rather the process simulated a swinging gate or valve that could be completely open, completely closed, or partially open. . . . disclosure occurs many more times than once, . . . people can retract their disclosure at times, and . . . the process can expand and contract over time" (Limandri, 1989, p. 76).

Summit (1983), in discussing child sexual abuse, states that whatever a child says about sexual abuse, she or he is likely to reverse it. Summit refers to disclosure–retraction as being the "normal" course of children's disclosure of sexual abuse.

Sorenson & Snow (1991) studied 630 cases of alleged child sexual abuse in which the authors had been involved as therapists and/or evaluators. Qualitative analysis of clinical notes, conversations, audio- and videotapes, and reports revealed four progressive phases to the process of children's disclosure of sexual abuse: denial, disclosure (which contains two sub-phases, tentative disclosure and active disclosure), recant, and reaffirm. *Denial* is defined as the child's initial statement to any individual that he or she had not been sexually abused. *Tentative disclosure* refers to the child's partial, vague or vacillating acknowledgment of sexual abuse. *Active disclosure* refers to a personal admission by the child of having been sexually abused. *Recant* refers to the child's retraction of a previous allegation of abuse. *Reaffirm* is defined as the child's reassertion of the validity of a previous assertion of sexual abuse that had been recanted. According to this model, children typically begin by denying that they have been sexually abused and this is followed by tentative then active disclosure. Some children recant and later reaffirm sexual abuse.

Sorensen & Snow (1991) tested their model of the disclosure process in a qualitative analysis of 116 case studies involving sexually abused children of 3–17 years of age who were eventually confirmed as credible victims. The results were that 72% of the children initially denied having been sexually abused. Denial was most common when (1) children were initially questioned by a concerned parent or adult authority figure, and (2) children were identified as potential victims and initially questioned in a formal investigative interview. Tentative disclosure was the common middle stage for the majority of these children (78%) with only 7% of the children who denied moving directly to active disclosure. Active disclosure, a detailed, coherent, first-person account of the abuse, was eventually made by 96% of the children (including children who originally did not deny having been sexually abused). In approximately 22% of these cases, children recanted their allegations; of those who recanted, 92% reaffirmed their allegations of abuse over time. The results of these studies provide evidence that SD does not necessarily move from non-disclosure to disclosure in a linear fashion and instead indicates that individuals may reveal then conceal then reveal in a circular manner.

A central aspect of a transactional process of SD is that it takes place over time. Sorenson & Snow (1991) found that the time-frame involved in the progression through the stages of SD (denial, tentative disclosure, active disclosure, recant, full disclosure) was unique to each case. Some children moved from denial to tentative disclosure to active disclosure in a single session; others took several months to reach the active phase.

The process of SD of stigmatized identities is ongoing and continues throughout the life-span of individuals and relationships. You can never fully reveal yourself (e.g., you are never totally out of the closet). Research on disclosure of stigmatizing identities has found that disclosure of stigmatizing identities continued as long as the person had the stigmatized condition (Limandri, 1989). Similarly, "coming out" is a lifelong process for gays and lesbians (Herdt & Boxer, 1992; Mazanec, 1995).

Although there is no research which examines SD over the life-span, there is research which examines the role of SD in the development of a stigmatized identity. Goffman (1974) referred to the similar "moral career" of persons who have a particular stigma, arguing that these people tend to have similar learning experiences regarding their stigma and go through similar changes in self concept; thus, they go through a similar sequence of personal adjustments. For Goffman, in the first phase of this process the stigmatized person learns and incorporates the standpoint of society regarding the particular stigma. In the second phase, the person learns that he/she possesses a particular stigma and the consequences of possessing it. Learning to "pass" or conceal the stigma constitutes the third phase in the socialization of the stigmatized person. In the fourth phase, the stigmatized individual "can come to feel that he should be above passing, that if he accepts himself and respects himself he will feel no need to conceal his failing" (Goffman, 1974, p. 101). It is here that SD fits into the moral career.

Similarly, SD is conceived as one of the phases in the "coming out" process. Coming out, in popular American culture, refers to public disclosure of a gay or bisexual identity. However, in the scholarly literature, coming out refers to the larger developmental process of acquiring a gay identity, of which disclosure of gay identity is only a part (Paradis, 1991). A number of models of coming out have been advanced (c.f., Berzon, 1992; Cass, 1979; Coleman, 1982; Mazanec, 1995; Plummer, 1975). In these various models, disclosure of gay identity is typically a stage of the coming out process. For example, Coleman (1982) describes a five-stage model; "coming out" is the second stage, during which individuals begin the process of SD to others. Berzon (1992) describes a turning point process in which disclosure to a non-gay person is the third turning point and disclosure to family, friends and co-workers is the seventh and final turning point.

Disclosure of stigmatized identity is typically viewed as a developmental task in the process of gay identity development (Coleman, 1982). Wells & Kline (1987) state that "prerequisite to the emergence of a positive homosexual identity is the communication of one's sexual orientation to significant others". According to this perspective, SD to accepting individuals is paramount in affecting positive identity development (Wells & Kline, 1987). The function of SD is self-acceptance:

> Recognizing the need for external validation, individuals risk disclosure to others in hopes that they will not be rejected. This is a very critical point, for the confidants' reaction can have a powerful impact. If negative, it can confirm all the old negative impressions and can put a seal on a previous low self-concept. If positive, the reactions can start to counteract some of the old perceived negative feelings, permitting individuals to begin to accept their sexual feelings and increase their self-esteem (Coleman, 1982, p. 34).

Although the term "dialectics" is not used in the literature on the disclosure of stigmatized identities, these researchers are positing disclosure of stigmatizing identities as a dialectical process. In particular, the circular nature of SD is hypothesized to be the result of the dialectical tension between the need to reveal and the need to conceal. Limandri, in the study of disclosure of women's abuse, AIDS/HIV and herpes, states that informants in her sample "were confronted with the need to tell or to conceal" (1989, p. 76). Similarly, Gershman (1983) described the "catch 22" of disclosure of homosexuality: one experiences anxiety in disclosing one's true feelings, yet failure to disclose engenders the anxiety of not being oneself. Gard (1990) argued that disclosure of HIV infection to parents may also involve a similar catch 22.

According to Limandri (1989), the dialectical process of disclosure of stigmatized identities is due to the fact that stigmatizing conditions contribute to feelings of shame and the wish to conceal or hide; however, those who experience such conditions often need to confide in others and seek help from professionals. Marks et al. explain:

> One may feel the need to inform a significant other for purposes of support but may fear rejection from that person. Similarly, one may feel an ethical obligation to inform medical providers (e.g., dentists) but may simultaneously fear that disclosure will result in refusal of services (Marks et al., 1992, p. 300).

Research on the disclosure of stigmatized identities also provides evidence of privacy regulation/communication boundary management as strategic responses to the dialectical nature of SD. Because disclosing stigmatized identities is risky and may cause potential vulnerability, partners regulate their communication boundaries strategically to minimize risks. Decision rules are used to determine to whom, how much, when, where and why to disclose. For example, Limandri (1989) found that her subjects considered the costs and rewards of disclosing their stigma. Specifically, to decide whether to disclose, subjects tried to anticipate how the other person would respond. If the anticipated response was negative, the discloser might decide not to risk SD. Similarly, Marks et al. (1992) argued that disclosure of HIV infection is a reasoned action that follows from the perceived social, psychological and material consequences of informing others. People with a stigma evaluate the consequences of informing a particular target person before a disclosure is made. Further, the factors considered in deciding whether to disclose to a particular person (e.g., a parent) differ from the factors considered in deciding whether to disclose to another target (e.g., a sexual partner). Siegel & Krauss (1991) found four considerations that influenced whom individuals told they were HIV positive: (1) fear of rejection; (2) the wish to avoid the pity of others; (3) the wish to spare loved ones emotional pain; and (4) concerns about discrimination.

CONCLUSION

SD is not a dichotomous event defined by whether the person has disclosed (e.g., is out of the closet) or has not disclosed (e.g., is not out of the closet). Instead, SD is an ongoing process that is extended in time and is open-ended, not only across the course of an interaction or series of interactions, but also across the lives of individuals as their identities develop/unfold, and across the life of a relationship as it evolves. The process of SD is circular; SD does not necessarily move from non-disclosure to disclosure in a linear fashion. The end state of this process is not full disclosure. Although some theorists argue that the ideal end state is full disclosure (e.g., it is often argued in the gay literature that you should come out of the closet; similarly, Jourard (1971a) argued that to be healthy one must disclose oneself), this is not realistic given the inherent risk involved in the disclosure of intimate information. Additionally, full disclosure (or total concealment) is impossible from a dialectical perspective (see Baxter & Montgomery, this volume). SD is contextual and is embedded in the larger processes of self-identity/human development and relationship identity/development. The process of SD is interdependent with processes of self-identity and relationship development. Who we are as individuals as well as who we are in relationship to each other affect and are affected by SD. Finally, the process of SD is inherently dialectical; disclosure is governed by the dialectical tension between the need to reveal and the need to conceal. Privacy regulation or communication boundary management is the fluid mechanism for responding to this dialectical tension.

The transactional/dialectical perspective on SD has important ramifications for theory and research on SD in personal relationships. SD can no longer be conceptualized as a one-time event. Personal relationships researchers need to examine the ongoing conversational patterns of SD over time within real-life relationships. Hopefully, by reviewing research on disclosure of stigmatized identities, personal relationships researchers will see how SD can be conceived of and studied as a process.

ACKNOWLEDGEMENTS

The author would like to thank Steve Duck, Robert McPhee and Jack Johnson for their feedback on earlier drafts of this chapter.

Section IV

Family Studies and Sociology

Section Editor: Robert M. Milardo
University of Maine, Orono, ME, USA

Although the field of family studies has a long and rich academic history, it has only recently seen the development of a more specialized focus on the character of particular relationships. The nature of these relationships may take many forms but typically involves individuals who view themselves as a unit with a long-term commitment to continue their relationship. Traditionally, at least in Western societies, families are defined in terms of two parents living together with responsibility for rearing their children. In fact, these so-called nuclear families are unique in many respects. For instance, in the USA the Bureau of the Census reported in 1992 that married couples living together with one or more children represented only 26% of all American families. Single parent families, childless couples, lesbian or gay male couples with or without children are all represented in the broad mix of relations we may usefully refer to as families.

The six chapters that compose this section examine relations between adult family members and their connections with two key social environments in which family relations are embedded: work and relations with kin and friends. Joe Veroff, Amy Young & Heather Coon author the first chapter on early marriage. They frame their work in a perennial question, one that has inspired family scholars since Ernest Burgess' work on marriage in the 1930s. How do young relationships become enduring relationships? Fortunately several longitudinal studies following couples through their early years of marriage are currently ongoing, and consequently provide an enriched source of material. The Veroff group examine how partners manage two broad sets of tasks, one concerning relations with external environments, and one concerning internal environments. They address questions regarding how partners begin to blend their networks of kith and kin, the demands of work and the commitments of parenthood. They then move into the arena of couple dynamics and the fault lines where conflicts so frequently emerge, with issues about creating a balance of responsibility for household labor and a comfortable level of mutual gratification. In their analysis, these authors are as much interested in establishing an understanding of the pattern of successful entry into early marriage as they are in understanding the potential variability in that pattern. Hence they examine how African-American and white non-Hispanic couples differ by virtue of their different cultural experiences. In doing so, they reiterate an important theme echoed in later chapters, that social positions imply differential access to primary resources, like wealth and education, that in turn become important foundations for negotiations in marriage.

Terry Cooney in her contribution turns to relationships between parents and their adult children. She begins with relations among parents and adolescents and argues quite reasonably that the task of growth in adolescence is not simply a matter of separation and individuation from parents but rather is far more richly textured. Here we find as well that the growth needs of parents are themselves influenced by those of the adolescent child and require a transformation of parental responsibilities that allow for their own separation and development as well as those of their children. The process of individual development is thus recast in terms of the modification of a relational bond. Separation is not an individual developmental task but a relational task requiring that parent and child come to view one another anew. The chapter continues these themes in an analysis of relations among adult children and parents, in addition to considering this study within a wider system of family relationships. Undoubtedly relations between adult children and parents are influenced by their relations with spouses, in-laws and siblings. In her own work, Cooney finds significant links between the expression of conflict among parents and reduced closeness reported by adult children, particularly with fathers.

The theme of conflict is advanced further in a chapter by Renate Klein & Michael Johnson. Here the authors draw on a wide variety of theory and research ranging from studies of organizational bargaining and strategic choice to important theoretical advances in the analysis of family violence and wife-battering. An informative introduction defines key concepts and proceeds to analyze individual and situational factors that influence strategic choice. Three patterns of action common to close relationships are examined in depth: the demand/withdrawal pattern in asymmetrical conflict, negative reciprocity and physical violence. Throughout, Klein & Johnson are careful to integrate their analysis of strategic choice with contemporary feminist analyses of gender and the asymmetries that result from the situated construction of gender. They explore, for example, how heterosexual relationships, and especially marriage, are assembled in ways that benefit husbands and disadvantage wives, which in turn result in distinct preferences for actions in conflict episodes. Their analysis is both provocative as it is penetrating.

Few areas in family studies have engendered more attention of late than the intersection of work and family. Ann Crouter & Heather Helms-Erikson examine the complexity of dual-earner families where wives and husbands each bring to the family their own work-related experiences. In doing so they wisely acknowledge that marital events must be understood in terms of the systematic differences in the circumstances of employment for men and women, circumstances that result from the gender stratification of work. Men and women generally work in distinctly different occupational sectors, with different opportunities for advancement, authority, job complexity, prestige and pay. These variations in inequality become an appropriate backstage for the latest generation of research on work and family. Then too, in dual-earner families the implications of one spouse's experiences of work can be understood best relative to the other partner's work experience. From this distinctly dyadic perspective, Crouter & Helms-Erikson address three dimensions of wage labor and their implications for marital relationships. They examine spouses' access to work-related resources such as income and occupational prestige as these factors influence, for example, marital power or husband's contributions to household labor. They examine job complexity and the extent to which work encourages adults to value self-direction for themselves and others, and how this complexity influences the construction of stimulating home environments. Finally, they examine how the daily experience of work-related tensions spills over into home life. Their perspective is fresh and insightful, drawing on a rich array of contemporary theory and research in an area of central concern to any student of family relationships, and perhaps equally of concern to spouses and their children.

Graham Allan and I examine the social context in which marriages develop. We review nearly four decades of research addressing how the configuration of spouses' networks of personal associates influences the character of their marriages. We begin with an analysis of Elizabeth Bott's early hypotheses linking network configuration with the organization of conjugal roles (i.e., spouses' joint or separate participation in household labor, child care and leisure pursuits). We critique the empirical studies directly testing her hypotheses as well as the literature on non-human primates which is directly relevant to the linkage of network properties and relational (dyadic) outcomes. This analysis leads us to reframe Bott's original hypotheses into more general sociological terms by specifying how the structure of a network can be conceptualized in terms of the pattern of ties linking members, how the predictive power of this structural configuration is apt to be linked to the value consensus among members, and how configuration influences the conduct of a marriage. For instance, where network members know and interact with one another, a condition we refer to as structural interdependence, optimal conditions exist for the development, maintenance and enforcement of a consistent set of normative beliefs and expectations, and any deviations from those beliefs are most visible. Structure is thereby closely tied to the development of norms, the flow of information between members, and the sanctioning of individual behavior. Where networks are highly structured, spouses, like all other structurally equivalent members, will experience considerable influence to act in accord with those norms. We end the chapter by noting the considerable challenges that yet remain in the development of network theory, especially with regard to the very definition of a network and its membership.

The final contribution to this section is a chapter by Victoria Bedford & Rosemary Blieszner. They begin with a focus on relationships among family members where at least one member is old and how these bonds, most notable for their sheer longevity, are typically arranged. Some elderly families are composed of multiple generations, including children and grandchildren, while others live within families of single generations. Nearly one-third of all White Americans and nearly one-half of Black Americans live without surviving children, for example. Bedford & Blieszner then turn to several primary features of the family relationships of the elderly, including their ascribed or non-voluntary status, persistence over time, their largely symbolic status, instability as the pool of constituents and the resources they offer one another declines during the course of old age, and finally their integration in a system of relations that span multiple generations with corresponding variety in the types of familial roles and normative expectations that each implies. This analysis extends the focus on marriage and friendship, which so typically defines the current study of personal relationships, into areas more germane to the actual experiences of the elderly, and in this way enriches the full domain of inquiry.

Taken together the six chapters in this section span a variety of theory and research, perhaps sharpening our understanding as well as designs for future developments.

Chapter 18

The Early Years of Marriage

Joseph Veroff, Amy M. Young
and
Heather M. Coon
University of Michigan, Ann Arbor, MI, USA

The study of the early years of marriage has largely focused on how the two partners in a couple confront the tasks and problems in blending their lives. Couples commonly experience an erosion of their well-being in the initial years (Markman & Halweg, 1993), and for a third of all new marriages this erosion leads to divorce in the first 5 years (National Center for Health Statistics, 1991). Most family researchers have sought to illuminate why some couples remain relatively satisfied while others find it difficult to maintain commitments to each other. These researchers have further assumed that even if divorce does not occur in the early years, reactions in early marriage set the style of adaptation that will characterize the trajectory of the marriage well into the future. Then too, because many marriages are not faring well as we approach the twenty-first century, there is more than theoretical interest in understanding the dynamics of early marriage.

We examine situational circumstances as well as behaviors and attitudes that contribute to the stability of early marriages and to the sense of marital well-being in individual partners. Because the study of early marriage has focused more on problems inevitably confronting couples than on theoretical questions about interpersonal dynamics, we organize our chapter around critical problems of adaptation in marriage that have been highlighted in social research. These problems have been of interest to both sociologically- and psychologically-minded family researchers. From the sociological emphases in the literature, the identified problems boil down to three: how couples weave their social networks (particularly their families of origin) into the fabric of their marriages; how couples negotiate the world of work and react to each other's com-

Handbook of Personal Relationships, 2nd edn. Edited by Steve Duck.
© 1997 John Wiley & Sons Ltd.

mitments to work and earning money; and how couples react to becoming a family of procreation with the introduction of children into their lives. These are not totally independent externally demanding tasks, but they can be differentiated.

From the psychological emphases in the literature, we identify four major tasks that describe how couples must regulate their patterns of interaction with one another. Two tasks deal with the more overt activities of the couple: how to divide the labor of the household and how to manage inevitable conflicts. Two additional tasks deal with the covert meaning of their interactions: how couples develop a sense of being a collaborative unit, and how they promote the gratification of each other's affectional and esteem needs. Again, these tasks are interrelated but distinct.

The sections of this chapter are organized around the three external tasks (networks, work demands, demands of parenthood) and the four interactive tasks (dividing household labor, managing conflict, developing a collaborative unit, and promoting gratification of affectional and esteem needs). Because these tasks are not entirely differentiated from one another, with the interactive tasks often embedded in the external tasks (e.g., the need to divide household tasks often flows out of work demands, or the need to manage conflict is stimulated by the birth of a child or the provocation of networks), discussion of one task is often relevant to discussion of the other tasks. Nevertheless, each task is presented separately. For each, we will highlight major conclusions drawn about factors that affect how that task is negotiated, and the theoretical concepts that have been useful in understanding these factors. Furthermore, we identify how the tasks are different for men and women, and for different ethnic/class groups. At the end of the chapter we draw conclusions about the relative importance of outside vs. inside factors in affecting early marriage, as well as how outside and inside factors are interconnected. In addition we bring together the findings about gender and ethnicity differences to make some general observations about how these factors affect early marital adaptation.

It is important to note that while we have attempted to draw strictly from research on the early years of marriage, for some marital processes it has not always been possible to do so because of the paucity of research. Although some marital issues change over the course of marriage, while others remain relatively consistent, certain marital processes may be only prominent during the early years of marriage when the partners are adjusting to their lives together. Thus, it is arguable whether general research findings on marital issues are applicable to the early years of marriage. Although we feel comfortable with this assumption, future research needs to address the extent to which processes of adaptation in early years of marriage are distinct from processes discovered about the later years. In order to allow our readers to make their own judgments, throughout this chapter we note when we are referring to data that specifically address the early years of marriage.

OUTSIDE FACTORS AFFECTING EARLY MARRIAGE

Social Network

During courtship, planning and arranging the wedding, and thinking through goals after the honeymoon, a couple's friends and family are very much part of the couple's lives (Surra & Milardo, 1991). The newlywed couple is traditionally permitted only a minimum period of withdrawal from its social networks in courtship and early marriage, a time unencumbered with social obligations. Slater (1963) and Johnson & Milardo (1984) argue that withdrawal, when it occurs, is selective, for the couple needs to construct a joint network and clarify where circles of associates and kin should overlap and where they should be separate (for empirical work describing these processes, see Milardo, 1982, Milardo, Johnson & Huston, 1983, and Parks & Eggert, 1991). These negotiated networks in early marriage are important for they help define the norms of the marriage and lay the foundation for whether support experienced during difficult periods the couple may face will have positive or negative consequences.

Tallman (1994) has studied the role socialization implicit in the models for marriage that newlywed couples get from their families of origin. For newlyweds, the strains in the marriages of their parents can be particularly important in providing positive or negative models for the development of any trust that the couple has for one another. Tallman found that judgments about the family of origin affect the couple's expectations and trust, which in turn have an impact on what couples disagree about and how serious those disagreements are in the initial months of marriage. Thus, ongoing and past behaviors observed within families of origin or even in married friends (Oliker, 1989), serve as models for marriage that individual spouses use to shape their newly formed marital dyads.

The implicit models spouses act upon vary in their permeability with some family systems having more closed boundaries to any newcomer, and others having more open boundaries (McGoldrick, 1980). The husband's family and the wife's family, as well as married friends, offer a variety of norms for how husbands and wives are to behave or what they should feel. One important task for newlywed couples is to learn to be selective within their networks about which norms will be primary, and which will be inappropriate. To date, few researchers have explored these adaptive and creative processes.

Social networks are significantly involved in the variables found to be predictive of marital instability (Veroff, Douvan & Hatchett; 1995). Using a representative urban sample of newlyweds, henceforth to be called the EYM (Early Years of Marriage) sample, Veroff, Douvan & Hatchett found that interferences felt from friends and family in the couples' lives in the first 2 years of marriage were associated with marital instability 2 years later. On the positive side, feelings of closeness with family were predictive of relative stability among African-American couples, but were not significantly related to marital stability among white couples. Moreover, Timmer, Veroff & Hatchett (in press) found in the EYM study that various measures of a spouse's closeness with in-laws are positively associated with feelings of marital well-being, although measures of a spouse's closeness to his/her own family are less uniformly tied to feeling happy about that spouse's marriage. While these results from the EYM study cannot establish for a fact what the direction of causality is (unstable marriages can induce interferences from the network; stable marriages can promote closeness with in-laws), being longitudinal in its method, the results do support the interpretation that networks can affect the quality of the marital relationship.

Timmer and her colleagues may not have found a direct positive relationship between one's marital well-being and closeness to one's own family because: (1) some wives and husbands in the early years of marriage who feel particularly close to their own families may be just the ones that are having difficulties adjusting to the transition; and (2) extremely close ties can be signs of enmeshment in one's family of origin, which can preclude making strong commitments to new partners (Bott, 1971; Blood, 1969). Timmer, Veroff & Hatchett (in press) found that African-American women are particularly involved with their families of origin; they see their families of origin more than their husbands do, and more than white wives or husbands do. However, this strong connection is not correlated with strong feelings of support from family members that would help these women transact rough times in their marriage. Thus, one must distinguish between the kind of closeness with families that can be supportive of marriage bonds in the early years of marriage, and the kind of closeness that may be so strong that it prevents the formation of a strong new bond between spouses and the new family they are creating. Burger & Milardo (1995), for example, find in a sample of young married couples that the impact of strong connections on their marriages with perceived networks was generally positive for husbands and negative for wives. Furthermore, the particular identity of the family member determined whether there was a positive or negative effect of being particularly close to a member of a family.

Family closeness is not the only network variable that may play a significant role in affecting marital well-being in the early years. Vangelisti & Huston (1994) examined satisfaction with one's network as part of another longitudinal study of newlyweds, henceforth called the PAIR project (Project on Processes of Adaptation in Intimate Relationships) (Huston, McHale & Crouter, 1986). Vangelisti & Huston found that satisfaction with network ties was correlated with the overall marital well-being of wives but not husbands when they were first married. Furthermore, network satisfaction did not affect the way wives feel about their marriage as the years progressed. These results suggest that network satisfaction plays only a minor direct role as a contributor to marital well-being in early marriage and only with women in the newlywed stage.

Work Demands

Most newly married couples must financially support themselves, and working can affect couples' marriages in many ways. Satisfactions and stresses experienced at work have reverberations in the marriage. In addition, many couples today must deal with the additional challenge of being a dual-earner couple, and the employment of women outside the home has led to significant differences from traditional power dynamics within the marriage. Furthermore, the attitudes of both spouses regarding their roles as providers can have a significant impact on their marriage.

Crouter & Helms-Erikson (this volume) provide a detailed overview of the effects of work on marriage. One of the major phenomena they cite is that stress and bad moods at work spill over to the marriage, following people home and affecting relationships with their spouse and family (Bolger et al., 1989). Unemployment has also been shown to have negative spillover (Vinokur & Van Ryn, 1993). Although the studies summarized by Crouter & Helms-Erikson do not focus on the early years of marriage specifically, data from the EYM study indirectly support the spillover phenomenon for the early years. By the seventh year of marriage, Veroff (1994) found in the EYM study that spouses who were satisfied with their marital relationship were particularly happily married when they had outside satisfactions, including their jobs. These results were statistically significant for most working spouses, but were not for African-American working women. This pattern of results corroborates other research cited by Crouter & Helms-Erikson that indicates that the work–marriage spillover effect is less apparent for some women, but consistently present for men. It is also interesting to note that the EYM study found spillover not with regard to stress, but with regard to satisfaction, which has not been generally examined in work–family spillover research. Gratification at work thus potentially has positive consequences for a marriage, and *vice versa*, for some people.

Aside from spillover, some theorists have argued that the fact that a wife works may have another type of consequence for marriage. By working a woman increases her overall power within the household because she contributes more resources than she would if she were not employed, and the power gained should be proportional to the income and prestige associated with the job. However, women's employment has not resulted in a redistribution of power within the couple in a clear and straightforward manner (Hochschild, 1989; Kompter, 1989; Crouter & Helms-Erikson, this volume). Issues of power are never clear-cut, because there are so many different bases of power. Nevertheless, Sexton & Perlman (1989) found that dual-career couples were more likely to try to influence each other than single-career couples. At least at one level, therefore, wives in dual-career families were exhibiting more overt attempts to exert power than were women in single-career families.

The fact that wives work outside the home can have effects on power dynamics in another sense. Working can help engender interests outside the relationship. Kurdek (in press) suggests from a longitudinal study of early marriage that when wives value autonomy (e.g, having interests outside the relationship), they are less involved in being the traditional relationship repairers and in performing the roles of traditional nurturing. Kurdek finds that such values predict marital dissatisfaction over time for both husbands and wives. If the mere fact of working makes women value their autonomy more, then Kurdek's results can be read to mean that working women are less dependent on and less committed to their relationships, all other things being equal.

Furthermore, the power that women experience in being employed may be subtly transmitted in their interactions with their husbands. Ruvolo & Veroff (1994), using EYM data, measured the discrepancies between ideal characteristics wives would like their husbands to have and their appraisals of what their husbands were actually like. The researchers found that these discrepancies are correlated 2 years later with lower marital quality for both husbands and wives, but only if the women were employed. Ruvolo & Veroff interpret the findings to signify that, compared to full-time housewives, employed wives can more easily attend to the dissatisfactions with their husbands and communicate them to their husbands. The researchers argue that in being employed, women develop a sense of their own worth, which permits them to take their criticism of their husbands more seriously.

Finally, as Crouter & Helms-Erikson (this volume) suggest, husbands' and wives' attitudes about their own roles as providers are related to their marital satisfaction. For instance, men who value the idea of being the main providers (or "breadwinners") tend to be very satisfied with their marriages if they do not participate in household work, while men who are ambivalent about being a main provider but at the same time do a lot of housework are less satisfied with their marriage (Perry-Jenkins & Crouter, 1990). It is important realize that couples may continually redefine what it means for husbands and wives to be workers and providers, and these definitions may be particularly salient to young, newly-married couples as they integrate their work and family lives, and compare their integrations with those from their valued networks.

The Transition to Parenthood

An exciting and challenging transition faced by many newly-married couples is the birth of a child. Children not only require extensive attention but often they create disequilibrium within the couple as spouses learn to balance new responsibilities and attempt to maintain old ones. Changes in perceptions of one's own identity, as well as changes in couples' interactions and patterns of conflict, often lead to a drop in marital harmony that can indeed have long-term consequences. The division of labor often has to be reconsidered, both with and without the benefit of a parental leave from work. Revisions in household assignments require new collaborative agreements if transitions are to be handled smoothly. In juggling new and old tasks, adapting to disruptions in sleep and sexual patterns, couples must develop new ways to regulate their feelings, reapportion their time, and satisfy their esteem and relational needs. Outlined below is a discussion of these new demands as they have been highlighted in research about the transition to parenthood.

Dealing with Negative Affect Emerging from Conflict

The transition to parenthood involves a great change in the interaction patterns of the couple, creates conflict and thus induces a need to regulate affect. Positive affective interactions between spouses decrease after the birth of a child (Belsky, Spanier & Rovine, 1983; McHale & Huston, 1985) and levels of conflict increase (Cowan et al., 1991). These changes occur generally over the first years of marriage, but to a greater extent among new parents compared to childless couples. Although White & Booth (1985b) find the opposite effect (fewer conflicts in new parents), they did not control for length of marriage. With the increasing level of conflict in the transition to parenthood, a major task for many couples is how to deal with this new level of tension between them. Cowan et al. (1991) indicate that many new parents are at a loss for dealing with conflict at this point in their lives, and this difficulty affects the entire family unit. Cowan et al. propose that the solution involves learning how to regulate affect. Couples who do learn to regulate affect are thought to become secure models of attachment for their children (Cowan & Cowan, 1994).

Reapportionment of Time

In general, household division of labor after the birth of a child has been characterized as more traditional, with women assuming more of the burden for cooking and cleaning (Belsky, Lang & Rovine, 1985; McHale & Huston, 1985). However, more recent work by Cowan & Cowan (1988) suggests that the division of labor, and men's and women's roles, become both more traditional and more non-traditional, depending on the time of assessment relative to the birth of the child and the questions asked. In their longitudinal study, there was no general shift from one person to another in responsibility for household tasks; however, there was more role specialization, with each parent assuming more responsibility for certain tasks.

Cowan & Cowan (1988) also measured the level of spousal satisfaction with the division of labor. First, men's level of involvement in household tasks positively affected wives' satisfaction with the chores each was doing. However, husbands were doing less collaboration than their wives expected (Belsky, Ward & Rovine, 1986). Finally, for both spouses, satisfaction with the labor arrangements was related to self-esteem, parenting stress and marital quality after childbirth. Negotiating the division of labor is not a trivial affair. In several studies, spouses reported that the division of family labor after the birth of a child was the issue most likely to cause arguments (Belsky, Ward & Rovine, 1986; Cowan et al., 1991).

In addition to reapportionment of household responsibilities, parenthood requires a reapportionment of leisure and sexual activities. It is quite easy to understand why parents of newborns have to alter their leisure activities and put constraints on their sexual lives. In fact, Belsky, Spanier & Rovine (1983) found a significant decrease in joint leisure activities of spouses for the third trimester of pregnancy, and through three months post-partum, with a leveling off at this lower level after that. McHale & Huston (1985) in the PAIR study observed a change in the kind of leisure activities in which the spouses engaged; they became more child-centered. It follows that with less joint leisure time and more child-centered leisure, there would be less time for sex.

Gratifying Self and Relational Needs

Being constantly responsible for another person brings many frustrations along with the gratifications. Parents are often called upon to make their own needs subservient to their infants' and therefore the parents experience frustration. With parenthood, wives and husbands see themselves less as lovers and more as partners (Belsky, Spanier & Rovine, 1983; Belsky, Long & Rovine, 1985; Cowan et al., 1991). In addition, women's focus back to the home gives them a reduced sense of being workers or students. Coping with these psychological changes is one of the main difficulties that couples face in the transition to parenthood; they affect a person's whole sense of identity. Further, men and women change differently (Cowan et al., 1991), and depending on the directions each goes in, the changes can be bases for either couple estrangement or couple development. Generally, negative changes are experienced first by women. Men seem to experience change only after women. Perhaps because women are more relationship-oriented, they "pass on" the negativity they feel to their husbands.

While most of the results reported above document the difficulties associated with the transition to parenthood, it should be pointed out that the actual differences found between parents and non-parents were modest (Belsky & Pensky, 1988). In addition, marriages that were doing better before the child was born continue to look the same relative to other marriages after the birth of a child (Belsky, Spanier & Rovine, 1983; Belsky, Ward & Rovine, 1986; Cowan & Cowan, 1988; Cowan et al., 1991; McHale & Huston, 1985). Cowan et al. (1991) speculate that declines in marital satisfaction during the transition to parenthood will widen already existing differences between partners.

Furthermore, having and raising a child remain important sources of fulfillment for most couples. Thus, the increased stress associated with child-raising may not necessarily mean that there is a decrease in overall life satisfaction as people become parents, whatever challenges it may bring for marital functioning. In fact, parenthood may actually bring an increase in life satisfaction because parents see themselves as achieving important goals in their lives. When asked how their lives are changed by having children (Veroff, Douvan & Kulka, 1981), many parents answer in terms of the new meaning they find in their lives. Depner (1978) found that a measure of value fulfillment through parenthood related significantly to overall life satisfaction, while a measure of parental satisfaction did not. Depner's results suggest that the goals of being parents can play an important part in well-being independent of the dissatisfactions attendant to the role discovered in early marriage.

We should note the special case of step-parenting in its effects on early years of marriage. In our own society, due to the increasing permissibility of bearing children out of wedlock and the high divorce and remarriage rate, many couples come into marriage with children already born, either to the couple or to one or the other of the spouses from previous relationships or marriages. To these couples, parenthood is a given at the onset of marriage, and they need to deal immediately with the issues of these external matters as a part of becoming married (Coleman & Ganong, 1994).

By and large, step-parenthood decreases the stability and satisfaction of second marriages (White & Booth, 1985a). However, Kurdek (1989) suggests that among newlyweds who have both been married before, the presence of stepchildren has a positive association with reported marital quality. Thus the effects of stepchildren on the early years of a marriage are indeed complex, although most of the evidence points to the disruptive effects they have.

We should also note the not so uncommon case of entering a first marriage with a child of one's own conceived before marriage. Sutherland (1990) has shown that newlyweds who had never previously married but who enter marriage with a child (whether or not the child is from the from another relationship or the couple's own) find marriage more difficult than either having no children at entry or experiencing the transition to parenthood during the early years. In Sutherland's study, using the EYM data, couples who had experienced premarital children or pregnancies were especially economically disadvantaged and suffered the most inadequate network supports in the first year of marriage. This was true for both White couples and African-American couples. When income and education were controlled, the negative relationship between premarital pregnancy/ birth and marital stability disappeared. Interestingly, White women who married the father of their premaritally conceived or delivered child indicated the greatest marital happiness in the first year.

INTERNAL FACTORS AFFECTING EARLY MARRIAGE

All the external factors affecting early marriage we have discussed reverberate in the psychological responses of the couples. Networks, jobs and having children are structural phenomena that couples adapt to more or less by finding a compatible way of regulating their lives, relations and the demands of others. We limit ourselves to discussing four broad issues. Two are quite salient to the couple's own conscious appraisal of their lives and include the division of labor in the household and the management of conflict. Two represent more non-conscious processes and include how couples define their collaborative working unit and how spouses satisfy each other's esteem and relational needs.

Division of Labor in the Household

Each couple would like to seek out the optimal division of labor in the household so that the work gets done efficiently and well. Changing gender roles in our society, however, have complicated what had been the traditionally simple set of expectations in modern industrial America: men should work outside the home for money and women should do the inside household work. The division of household labor is affected in many ways by who works outside the home and how spouses perceive their role as providers.

Equity with regard to household labor is difficult for most couples to achieve. The clearest finding in many studies is that regardless of any advances in equality that women have made in the workplace, within the home women continue to carry the burden of the workload (Hochschild, 1989). Furthermore, the work that women do out of the home does not influence the amount that husbands do within the home (Pleck, 1985; Baxter, 1992). Thus, for women, work outside of the home simply means more work rather than an exchange of outside-the-home labor for inside-the-home labor. Interestingly, this is not the case for husbands. The more work that they perform outside the home, the less work they perform within the home (Baxter, 1992). However, some data suggest that among many African-American couples, for whom the dual-earner norm has been prevalent for decades, there has been some movement towards egalitarian roles in the household and with some success. For example, it has been estimated that African-American wives perform 60% of the household work (Wilson 1990), whereas white wives perform 70% (Berk, 1985; Demo & Acock, 1993).

Regardless of behaviors, attitudes about household work at least are changing, although the traditional attitudes are hard to erase. With these changing norms for husband and wives, newly-married couples have a greater task before them and it becomes exaggerated during the transition to parenthood, as noted in our discussion of parenthood demands. Child care can clearly be seen as an interruption of individual pursuits (Crawford & Huston, 1993), and thus the allocation of household labors can be a source of considerable negotiation during the transition to parenthood.

The division of labor in the household thus requires more negotiating within the couple than it once did. Conflicts about household labor are the most common source of tension reported by newlyweds (Tallman, 1994). How then do couples negotiate the allocation of tasks? Many researchers have noted that this negotiation depends on the power distribution within the couple (Ross, 1987; Hartmann, 1981). According to this argument, men's and women's relative earning power outside the home provides the leverage in negotiating the allocation of household labor. However, research on power distribution and household labor fails to provide conclusive support for this claim (Crouter & Helms-Erikson, this volume).

Dissatisfaction with the distribution of household labor is related to incongruencies between gender role attitudes and actual division of labor. McHale & Crouter (1992) have found that newly-married women rated their marriage more negatively if they had traditional household roles and egalitarian attitudes. Men, on the other hand, rated their marriage negatively if they had traditional attitudes but egalitarian roles. Thus, not all women are unhappy with the unequal distribution of household labor, and not all men are unhappy about equality in household labor. Although both partners agree that this inequality exists, they do not always view this differential as unfair (Thompson, 1990). It is only when wives expect their husbands to share the housework equally that they become unhappy. Thus, women's expectations about men's involvement, and the meanings that they attribute to their contributions to household labor, play a significant moderating role in the relationship between division of labor and marital and personal well-being (Pina & Bengston, 1993).

There is, no doubt, some resistance by many men to changing their participation in household labor. In fact, one study suggests that the optimization of marital happiness, especially for men, occurs when women profess traditional household attitudes. Vangelisti & Huston (1994) have shown that more traditional ways of dealing with household tasks increases men's loving feelings towards their wives in the PAIR sample, which is heavily working-class. These positive feelings then have positive repercussions on their wives' feelings about their marriages. Tallman & Riley (1995), in an analysis of feelings about and actual participation in household labor in their sample of newlyweds in Washington State, speak of a cultural lag that reinforces both men and women seeing the traditional division of labor with regard to household chores as more comfortable. Orbuch & Custer's (1995) analysis of the EYM data indicates that White males whose wives work felt particularly distressed if they were sharing in household chores.

The pattern of results in the Orbuch & Custer analysis was not true for the African-American males. It is important to realize that for African-American couples the expectation that wives work has been more normative for a longer period of time. This suggests that as it becomes more common for women to work, "traditional" gender expectations about the division of labor in the household will erode. If this trend continues, in the twenty-first century young dual-earner couples will gravitate more easily to an equitable division of labor. Already some couples are willing and perhaps eager to take on "peer marriages" (Schwartz, 1994), sharing equally in household responsibilities among other things. Schwartz finds that there are potential costs to such an arrangement, but argues that the collaboration involved in such marriages undergirds a solid marital structure with intense personal fulfillment.

Managing Conflict

All married couples find themselves engaged in some kind of conflict throughout their marriage. However, conflict does not necessarily lead to marital distress and destruction. Instead, conflict can intensify spouses' intimacy (Miller et al., 1986) and can be indicative of positive functioning (Markman, 1991). Although newlyweds may experience an initial "honeymoon" phase with few conflicts, they have to learn continuously how to manage the conflicts that occur, a task that began in courtship. The processes of conflict management may be more critical for marital satisfaction than the actual conflict, although successful management should reduce the sheer number of conflicts (Klein & Johnson, this volume).

Several approaches of marital conflict management have been extensively studied: *constructive engagement*, characterized by open, direct communication; *destructive engagement*—"attacks" toward a partner involving criticism and hostility; and *avoidance* (withdrawal), evidenced by ignoring or denying the problem (Miller et al., 1986; Raush et al., 1974). Raush et al. (1974) demonstrated that compatibility of conflict styles is critical to marital harmony for newlyweds. Generally, constructive engagement in conflict leads to new understandings of the relationship. In contrast, avoidance tends to stifle relationship growth. However, Raush and his colleagues also showed that conflict avoidance within the context of a bond of mutual affection does not necessarily steer couples to an unhappy marriage, especially if it is normative for the couple. This suggests that it is not conflict behaviors *per se* that lead to distress but rather how spouses think about them.

Crohan (1988, 1992) studied the moderating role of conflict beliefs in the relationship between conflict behaviors and marital satisfaction with the EYM sample. She found that one configuration of conflict styles was especially important to well-being. Marriages where both partners believe disagreements can be settled through discussion had higher levels of marital happiness than marriages where both spouses believe that disagreements cannot always be solved, and where the spouses disagreed about their beliefs. Moreover, modererately attacking (but not severely attacking) behaviors were positively related to marital well-being among spouses who believe disagreements are healthy. Such was not the case for spouses who did not hold these beliefs.

In examining the aforementioned results separately for African-Americans and Whites, Crohan (1988) pointed to patterns that may be different for African-American newlyweds. Most notably, African-American women were more likely than White women to believe that disagreements can always be settled, that people should try to control their anger, and that conflict should be avoided. Furthermore, avoiding conflict had more negative consequences for the well-being of White couples than African-American couples.

Some sex differences were observed in Crohan's analysis as well. Men and women did not, in general, hold different beliefs about conflict. However, the use of constructive engagement was more important for the well-being of men than it was for women. Women who believed in confronting conflicts reported being happier when negative behaviors were exhibited in a conflict resolution task; such was not the case for men. Women used constructive behaviors less frequently than men did, and these behaviors did not predict happiness as well for women as they did for men.

In addition to conflict beliefs, the attributions that spouses make about each other during fights are related to the successful management of conflict. Fincham

& Bradbury (1987, 1993) find that dissatisfied spouses compared with satisfied spouses make negative attributions about their partner's behavior. When conflicts occur, distressed spouses tend to view their partners as selfishly motivated and behaving with negative intent. This suggests that attributions about conflict can exert some causal influence on judgments of relationship quality.

There is no single ideal style of conflict management. Instead, couples can confront conflict in different ways and still maintain high levels of marital satisfaction. Conflict beliefs and attributions regarding negative behavior play central roles in successful conflict resolution.

Nevertheless, there are certain behaviors that occur in the context of conflict that are in themselves indicative of marital distress and dissatisfaction. One pattern identified by a number of researchers (Christensen & Heavey, 1990; Gottman & Krokoff, 1989; Gray-Little & Burks, 1983; Heavey, Lane, & Christensen, 1993; Markman, 1994) is male withdrawal from conflict in conjunction with demanding behaviors by females (i.e., emotional engagement in the conversation, blaming, and pressures for change). Couples with these highly stereotypic interactions were found to be most at risk for marital dissatisfaction. Heavey, Lane & Christensen (1993) found that this conflict pattern was most likely to occur when couples were discussing issues in the husband's behavior that the wife wanted to change. In contrast, when couples discussed behaviors that the husband wanted to change, there was no distinction in the roles each spouse took in conflict management. Heavey, Lane & Christensen hypothesize that men's higher status in society allows them generally to structure the relationship more to their liking and that, as a result, they have less need to change what is happening in a marriage. Conflicts are thus usually about wives' complaints, which induce the stereotyped and often dysfunctional conflict management styles.

Negativity also plays a central role in managing conflict. Gottman (1979) found that the proportion of positive behaviors exhibited during conflict resolution was less indicative of relationship distress than was the proportion of negative behaviors. Over time negativity becomes a good predictor of marital dissatisfaction. Huston & Chorost (in press) support macroanalytically what Gottman found microanalytically. In their PAIR project, Huston & Chorost found that negativity had adverse effects on marital satisfaction because the marriage becomes less affectionate in the early years. However, negativity does not always sharply affect marital quality. Affective expression, the level of affection spouses express toward each other, and substantial effort on relationship maintenance buffer the effect of negativity on women's marital quality. Huston & Chorost found that when husbands exhibit high levels of affective expression toward their wives, their negativity is less associated with a drop in wives' satisfaction over time. However, no such buffering occurs when examining the effects of wives' negativity on husbands' satisfaction. Because women's affective expression is more taken for granted by men than men's affective expression is by women, women's affective expression may not serve any buffering function for men.

So how can this pattern of negativity and withdrawal be reversed? Markman (1994) and his colleagues (Markman et al., 1993) have developed interventions to predict and prevent "erosion" in couples' satisfaction and, like Cowan & Cowan (1994), state that affective regulation is a key to understanding how conflict can be managed. Spouses need to support one another during conflict resolution by validating each other and summarizing each other's distress rather than by cross-complaining and summarizing one's own position. Support during conflict management occurs more often in non-distressed couples than in distressed couples, perhaps because support prevents withdrawal/avoidance in conflicts and prevents the escalation of conflict. Cutrona (1994) has presented experimental evidence for this effect in young married couples. The results of the Huston & Chorost (in press) study would suggest that support from men can be found simply in expressing positive feelings towards their wives in the context of conflict, but support from women in ongoing conflict interactions may have to go beyond simple expression of feelings towards their husbands and entail complex affirmation of their husbands' ideas and positions.

In summary, learning to manage conflict and avoiding certain patterns of conflict behavior in the early years of marriage may be critical for the long-term survival of the marriage. Markman (1991) suggests that expressing conflict may be related to dissatisfaction in the early years of marriage as couples struggle to determine their conflict style, but ultimately, expressing conflict early on seems to be positively related to satisfaction with marriage, especially if it occurs in the context of general support or with a clear problem-solving orientation (Conger, 1994).

Defining the Collaborative Unit

Getting married is a public commitment. The new legal status emerging from that commitment enjoins a man and a woman to shift their focus of concerns from themselves as individuals to the collective. For partners who already thought of themselves as a collective, especially among those who had cohabited, this is a minor transition. For others who had not psychologically emphasized being a couple, it is a major transition. Living together in marriage is supposed to require each partner to coordinate with his/her spouse's concerns. Money, work, eating, housework, sexual needs and leisure activities are now to be transacted in a collaborative system. How seriously individuals take these implicit rules for collaboration that becoming married brings, and how far partners go in enacting ideals of collaboration, are questions that couples face when first married. Should spouses give up their private life space entirely to the collective life space or reserve a large territory of their private space? This question defines a major task for the early years of marriage, one that can be assessed only indirectly. A couple's success at this task is related to their shared perceptions of marriage and of each other (see Berger & Kellner, 1964).

Whether partners share attitudes and values can affect the ease of collaboration in marriage. Creamer & Campbell (1988) have found that well adjusted couples describe themselves as being more similar in beliefs and preferences than do poorly adjusted couples. Such findings do not implicate collaboration directly, but only suggest that similarity between spouses can pave the way for greater collaboration. More direct evidence comes in Kurdek's (1993) 5-year longitudinal study of newlyweds, which finds that discrepancies in husbands' and wives' perceptions of the reasons for entering the marital union are good predictors of marital dissolution. Having similar motives for marriage helps the couple collaborate and regulate each others' lives without elaborate discussion or working through conflicts about goals and means for arriving at goals. The Cowans and their colleagues (1991) also found that smaller discrepancies in partners' relationship values were predictive of how well they dealt with the transition to parenthood. Again, shared meaning, more covert than overt, helps regulate how a couple together might approach a momentous event in their lives.

Tallman, Burke & Gecas (in press) likewise reason that early marriage represents a negotiation of roles based on the individual socialization experiences of each partner and the resources they bring to marriage. A collective identity is required. Veroff et al., (1993) also show that a jointly derived positive reconstruction of the couple's courtship in a narrative of their relationship is predictive of their happiness. These findings and others (Veroff, Douvan & Hatchett, 1995; Acitelli and Veroff, 1995) about joint narratives suggest that a collaborative orientation to their affective life is important to couples' well-being in early marriage.

The importance of collaboration in early marriage can also be found in Aron, Aron & Smollan's (1992) work on the degree to which the self and other are perceived as being connected or merged in good relationships. They use a series of two circles that are depicted as being non-overlapping at one extreme, and almost completely overlapping at the other extreme. Men and women are asked to pick the two circles that best describes their marital relationship. These authors find that selecting the two circles that depict more perceived merging rather than independence is correlated with happier marriages, a result that was repeated by Veroff (1994). There is a hint in Aron, Aron & Smollan's work that over-merging may be a problem for women, who interpret the extreme of the perceptual measure used by the researchers (highly overlapping circles) as representing a submergence of self, which can be negatively experienced. For those women, over-emphasis on collaboration disrupt their ideals for marriage, and may mean subjugating their wishes to a husband who is seen by some to have more power in the unit.

With that note of caution, that collaboration can mean an unequal submergence of the self on women's part, we would still suggest that embracing marriage in the early years as a collaborative enterprise can subtly set that stage for a strong sense of well-being and commitment to the marriage. Collaboration is difficult to teach but may be subtly generated when partners have similar goals and values as well as a commitment to the collective rather than to individual needs. The transition to parenthood may be the severest test of the collaborative capacity of the couple in the early years.

Gratifying Each Other's Affectional and Esteem Needs

There is considerable evidence for a general proposition that to find marriage satisfying, partners have to learn to balance their needs for relating affectionately to each other with their needs for appreciation of their individual worth, to balance giving and receiving love, to accommodate to one another without losing a sense of self. Such positions are explicit in various dialectical theories (e.g., May, 1973; Veroff & Veroff, 1980) and can be found implicitly in Askham's (1986) views of social identity in marriage, Rusbult & Buunk's (1993) application of theories of interdependence to relationships, Fromm's (1956) views of the nature of love, and Malley's (1989) application of Bakan's (1966) dualistic theory of agency and communion to marriage. Two themes run through these theoretical views. First, for gratifying relationships, couples need to accommodate to one another. Second, couples need to feel affirmed as individuals. Such affirmation and accommodation may be difficult to achieve as couples adjust to the inevitable flaws that crop up when two people, however well-intentioned they may be, stake out their lives together. Under what conditions do affirmation by and accommodation to one's spouse take place in a gratifying way?

It is suggested that men and women will attempt to maintain illusions to accommodate to difficulties in the way their spouse acts towards them. Murray & Holmes (in press) find that young married couples project their ideals onto their partners, over and above any tendencies they may have to see people in a "pollyanna" way. These evaluations are more positive than their partners' own view of themselves. This type of illusion seems to have positive consequences for their partners, perhaps helping to maintain both affectional and esteem needs and inoculating them against life's inevitable difficulties.

It has also been found that happily married couples partially maintain their idealization of each other by attributing partners' negative behaviors to situational forces, rather than to anything dispositional about the partner (Bradbury & Fincham, 1990). Kayser's (1993) remarkable retrospective study of how men and women retell the stories of their disaffection in marriage indicates the implications of focusing on the negative features of one's spouse. Doing so can contribute to further hurt, alienation and anger during conflicts, which in turn create a spiraling, potentially unchangeable disaffection process. In contrast, Murray & Holmes (in press) present evidence that couples can fend off doubts raised about each other by turning apparent flaws into virtues and highlighting something positive in spite of a flaw. Again, these processes are cognitive construals that help maintain affirming attitudes towards one's partner. Such affirmation can positively influence one's partner who, in turn, may reduce the frequency of the negative behaviors that originally induced the concerns.

Veroff, Douvan & Hatchett (1995) have found that communicating affirmation of one's partner is a central subtle process that undergirds stable marriages in the early years. Does a husband believe his wife makes him feel good about having his own ideas and ways of doing things? Or, does a wife think her husband feels especially caring towards her and makes her life especially interesting and exciting? Positive answers to these questions make up a scale of "affective affirmation", which in the EYM study has been a strong correlate of marital stability and well-being. A surprising finding was that affective affirmation by wives was especially important for men, which is interpreted to mean that men's affirmation through their spouse may be the major or only source of affirmation they experience, while women may more readily find affirmation through friends and other family members.

Among White males in our society, one strong basis of affirmation seems to occur by establishing a particularly satisfying sexual relationship with their wives. Veroff et al. (in press) examined the bases of especially happy marriages among couples in their third year of marriage who were very committed to the marriage, and found that sexual satisfaction in White men is a clear marker of these happy marriages. From these results one might infer that White men feel particularly affirmed in their marriages if they can give and receive sexual pleasure. These results were not apparent among African-American couples. White males evidently have considerable self-esteem tied up in their sexual lives in marriage.

Affirmation processes take many forms and seem to be different for men and women. For women, the expression of affection, rather than sexual gratification, seems to be paramount for maintaining good feelings about marriage. Newly-married husbands' affection expressed towards their wives may serve as cushion for the bad effects that nasty encounters have on their wives' evaluation of their marriage (Huston & Chorost, in press).

Once discrepancies between marital expectations and reality are found, another process that can help preserve the partner's feelings in a relationship is to accommodate to what is actually present in the relationship. Rusbult & Buunk (1993), conceptualizing accommodation in a theory of interdependence and commitment, highlight a number of strategies that spouses use: downplaying alternative partners' attractiveness, focusing on comparisons to other marriages where things appear worse, being willing to sacrifice, and establishing rules controlling extradyadic involvement.

A different kind of accommodation is to change oneself in the direction of the goals set by one's partner. Using EYM data, Ruvolo (1990) designed such a measure, and Veroff, Douvan & Hatchett (1995) found that measure in men *negatively* related to marital stability. Evidently, men may accommodate in the sense of changing to please their wives only in faltering marriages; women may accommodate as part of their expected way of operating in marriage, whether the relationship is good or bad.

This differential basis of accommodation in men and women undoubtedly reflects the societally supported greater power that men have in the commitment process in marriage. It is perceived, at least within the dominant culture, that most men can initiate alternative relationships if a marriage goes sour and that men generally have fewer risks with regard to employment and less responsibility for children if the relationship were to dissolve. Among African-American couples the picture may be different. Ending a marriage may be an easier alternative for women, because African-American women have had many models of women who are self-reliant economically and have turned easily to family for assistance with children.

SOME GENERAL OBSERVATIONS

We have organized our thinking about early marriage into external factors and internal factors, and along the way we have suggested how these categories affect each other. We have not specified any ordering of the importance of these sets of factors in couples' experience, either within or across these broad categories. Our guess is that within certain ethnic groups and socio-economic statuses some categories are dominant over others.

One way to focus on factors that determine marital quality and stability in the early years is through the ethnicity lens. Veroff, Douvan & Hatchett (1995) present a wealth of data to capture many kinds of determinants of stability. One clear finding is that factors "outside the couple" seem to govern the stability of African-American couples more than they do White couples, and that internal determinants seem to govern the stability of White couples more than African-American couples. For example, husbands' concern about financial security is related to marital instability among African-American couples but not White couples, and a sense of closeness to family and friends is also more important in the African-American couples. In contrast, factors of sexual life and interpersonal perceptions are more prominent in understanding well-being among White couples than among African-American couples. Thus, a couple's position in the larger society can determine what factors will take over as primary for understanding their marriage relationship. Different social positions imply different access to resources, which becomes the basis for role negotiation in marriage (Tallman, Burke & Gecas, in press). This might be particularly so in the early years as couples establish themselves in the economic structure. We suggest that a young married person of a non-dominant social or ethnic group in our society is more conscious of the salience of power in society and focuses on external regulations of married life (i.e., work demands, parenting and networks). These factors should be the prime regulators of the adaptation that couples from minority groups or lower status groups experience. In contrast, a person from a dominant social group may tend to focus on the internal workings of the marriage. We suggest that this interpretation may also be useful in comparing marriages from different class positions, but it is particularly useful in thinking about African-Americans who, in addition to being generally lower in economic status, have been disadvantaged for so many years in accessing the resources of the society, because of institutional racism.

Gender is another important lens for viewing the determinants of marital quality. Women and men may ask different questions as they evaluate their marriages because their assumptions about their lives and their selves are so different (Lykes, 1985). Women as a group have also been deprived of power in society. That fact alone could determine how men and women look at their marriages, particularly the power inherent in their relationships with their partners. Kompter (1989), however, has suggested that the amount of power that women have in marriage is not just related to whether they work and how much money they earn in relation to their husbands. She argues that there may be latent power and invisible power in the marital relationship, both of which favor men. Latent power is the ability of husbands to keep their wives silent about their desires. Invisible power comes in perceptual biases that permit men to exaggerate the amount of effort they expend towards the household or towards meeting their wives' affectional needs (for a more detailed examination of feminist views of marital power, see Osmond & Thorne, 1993).

Because of their long history of competing relatively well compared to their husbands in the economic arena, African-American women may experience more overt power in their marriages than their White counterparts. However, they still may be overshadowed by their husbands with regard to latent power. To the degree that African-American men have been deprived of a dignified position in the economic structure, and to the degree that their wives have been able to gain some access to steady work, African-American men may be especially eager to hold on to the latent and invisible power afforded them in our society. We should at least be aware that the dynamics of power differential for husbands and wives in their marriages may be different for African-American couples than for White couples.

In addition to considerations of power, we should also consider the differential meanings social relationships have for men and women and specifically the role that marriage plays for self-definition in the matrix of other relationships. The intimate social support provided in marriage is typically more critical for men than women; women tend to be more generally relationship-minded than men, making their friends, family of origin, and family of procreation all important facets of their selves (Antonucci, 1994). Women more than men rely on and invest in relationships in addition to marriage for defining themselves. These networks of relationships are engaged by women to compensate for their reduced power in marriage and in society at large, at least compared to men. For women marriage may be important, but it is only one of many supports available to them (Argyle & Furnham, 1983; Oliker, 1989; Fowers, 1991). However, for men the marital bond is the major relationship in their lives. Therefore, compared to women, the intimacy of marriage through love and sex becomes the critical basis of support for men's self-definition.

Women are still more aware than men about problems in their relationships

(Markman & Kraft, 1989; Notarius & Pellegrini, 1987), but in one sense men are more love-dependent on marriage than women. The pattern may be especially striking for African-American men in the early years of their marriage. Among African-American men there may be some special sensitivity to being accepted as men by their wives. Deprived of status in the outside, they may be particularly eager to seek status in the *inner* dynamics of their marriage. Some of the results from the EYM study support this hypothesis, especially showing that affective affirmation is so critical to the marital well-being of African-American men.

Although different groups may emphasize either the external or the internal factors that we have selected to review for this chapter, it is the case that all groups are affected by both external and internal factors determining how couples adapt to the early years of marriage. Furthermore, external and internal factors clearly interact, and in the approach we have taken it is hard to assert simply that external factors or internal factors shape the nature of marital well-being in the early years. Networks matter; work matters; becoming parents matters, but each of these external contexts implicate the internal dynamics of a marriage. These include arranging the division of labor in the home, managing conflicts, building collaborative efforts as a couple, and gratifying each others' relational and esteem needs. We particularly highlighted how gender differences in external factors affect the way couples consider internal aspects of their marriage. We have also examined differences between African-American couples and White couples in their access to external power in the society and how that might shape their differential reactions to internal issues in marriage. We have relied heavily on the EYM study which permits comparisons of these groups. As more data accumulate about gender and ethnicity effects among African-American couples and among couples from other ethnic groups, researchers will be in a better position to spell out more fully the complexity that a contextual approach to the study of marriage in the early years engenders.

Chapter 19

Parent–Child Relations across Adulthood

Teresa M. Cooney
University of Delaware, Newark, DE, USA

The bulk of the parent–child relationship today is situated in the adult years for both generations; with average life expectancy currently exceeding 75 years, we are expected to live over 40 years as adults with at least one surviving parent (Watkins, Menken & Bongaarts, 1987). Yet much of research and theorizing about normative parent–child relationships focuses on the relationship as it exists early in the child's life. Then, as noted by Hagestad (1981), researchers "seem to drop the relationship and not pick it up again until parents are old and the children are middle-aged (p. 33.)". At that point, research attends primarily to the relationship during non-normative crises, as evidenced by the voluminous caregiving literature (Zarit & Eggebeen, 1995). In contrast, little attention is paid to the relationship between adult daughters and mothers in the absence of maternal frailty and ill-health (Barnett et al., 1991). Consideration of adult males in their roles and relationships as sons is even more limited (Barnett, Marshall & Pleck, 1992).

This chapter presents an overview of the literature from the past 10–15 years that deals with adult child–parent relationships in the absence of caregiving during crises. It begins with an overview and critique of a few of the recent, popular frameworks for conceptualizing young adult child–parent relationships. Next, the chapter considers some of the processes involved in the transformation of parent–child relationships between adolescence and later adulthood. Current, popular views on mid- to later-life parent–child relationships are described next, followed by a final section identifying key challenges for researchers working in this area today.

Handbook of Personal Relationships, 2nd edn. Edited by Steve Duck.
© 1997 John Wiley & Sons Ltd.

THE YOUNG ADULT YEARS

Whereas in later adulthood, researchers study parent–child relationships prima-rily for their inherent interest in interpersonal relationships and family life (Fischer, 1986; Hagestad, 1984; Rossi & Rossi, 1990), in late adolescence and early adulthood parent–child bonds are viewed almost exclusively in terms of their implications for individual development—and then for the younger genera-tion only. With this in mind, two dramatically different views of parent–child relationships as they pertain to individual development during late adolescence and early adulthood are presented below.

Detachment from Parents: Separation–Individuation Theories

The central task of adolescence, according to the "new" developmental psychol-ogy (Josselson, 1988), is the formation of a unique identity distinct from that of one's parents. Separation and individuation from parents are viewed as key prerequisites to identity formation. Supposedly, physical and emotional detach-ment from their parents contributes to adolescents' ability to clearly differentiate between self and other. To theorists who support such notions, "separation of the self out of the more or less enmeshed child–parent web is what adolescence is all about" (Josselson, 1988, p. 94).

Measuring Adolescent Separation–Individuation

One widely used empirical formulation based on this separation–individuation theory of parent–child relations is Hoffman's (1984; Hoffman & Weiss, 1987) Psychological Separation Inventory (PSI). This inventory assesses the degree to which late adolescents have separated and individuated from their parents in four domains originally laid out by Blos (1979) as central to the adolescent separa-tion–individuation process. Specifically, emotional independence emphasizes "freedom from an excessive need for approval, closeness, togetherness and emo-tional support" (Hoffman, 1984, p. 171) from parents. Attitudinal independence addresses value and attitudinal differences between oneself and one's parents. Conflictual independence denotes the absence of negative feelings toward par-ents, such as mistrust, inhibition and anger. Finally, functional independence, refers to managing the practical matters of one's day-to-day personal life without parental involvement (Hoffman, 1984).

In developing the PSI, Hoffman recommended that the measure be applied separately to mother–child and father–child relationships. In so doing, Hoffman recognizes the uniqueness of relationships with mothers vs. fathers and, as a consequence, the distinctiveness of the separation process in relation to each parent. Lopez, Campbell & Watkins (1986, 1989) demonstrate the reality of this distinction for adolescents by reporting greater independence from fathers than mothers for adolescents with divorced as well as married parents.

Sex Differences in Adolescent Separation–Individuation

Not only is the sex of the parent potentially important in examining levels of adolescent separation, but so too is the sex of the younger generation. Studies comparing average PSI scores for males and females note lower levels of separation from parents for daughters than sons, at least on some of the four dimensions (Lapsley, Rice & Shadid, 1989; Lopez, Campbell & Watkins, 1986). Subscale scores on various PSI dimensions also correlate negatively with young women's college adjustment (Kenny & Donaldson, 1992; Lopez, Campbell & Watkins, 1986). This finding is critical given that, theoretically, greater separation–individuation is equated with healthy development and positive functioning among youth, and perhaps healthy marriages and adult relationships as well.

While findings inconsistent with the theory are more often found for females than males, Hoffman (1984) reports significant negative associations between attitudinal independence and personal adjustment for both sexes, as do Lapsley and associates (1989). Hoffman (1984) provides *post hoc* speculation that attitudinal similarity may reflect internalization of the parental objects by the youth, which could be positive for the adolescent if it promotes higher quality parent–child relations and subsequently better personal adjustment. This reasoning is noteworthy because it conflicts with most of the separation–individuation literature that largely dismisses parental input in the adolescent's individuation experience.

Limitations of Separation–Individuation Theories

Despite their popularity, separation–individuation theories present several problems. One criticism is that the separation–individuation process is discussed in an extremely individualistic fashion although it actually involves modifications in a relational bond. To illustrate, Hoffman's PSI appears to have no parallel "parent measure" of adolescent–parent separation. Without parental reports of the process, it is difficult to understand the relational interplay that this process involves. Moreover, separation–individuation is viewed as a personal characteristic of the adolescent, rather than as a property of a given relationship, even though Hoffman requires that relations with each parent be assessed separately. Finally, in largely overlooking the parents' contribution to separation–individuation, this perspective fails to address what role behaviors are expected of parents during the process. The relationship of the parents' own development to this process also is totally ignored. Indeed, Youniss (1983) notes that in the conventional view of adolescent development, the process is totally self-instigated and self-guided on the part of the adolescent.

When the interplay of the adolescent's and the parents' development has been recognized, the discussion has been based on anecdotal impressions or small case-study approaches (Colarusso & Nemiroff, 1982; Farrell & Rosenberg, 1981; Kidwell et al., 1983). Kidwell et al. (1983) claim, for example, that the parents' development contributes to changes in relations with their developing adolescents, without explicitly examining the impact of parental development on the relationship or *vice versa*. Colarusso & Nemiroff (1982) more specifically argue that parental (in this case paternal) support and encouragement of adolescent independence may be instrumental in the parents' own successful resolution of the generativity–stagnation task (Erikson, 1968) in mid- to late-adulthood. Still, they too present no data to support their claim.

One published study that links parent and adolescent development is a cross-sectional investigation of early adolescents and their parents by Silverberg & Steinberg (1987). They report significant correlations between various measures of parents' development and well-being at mid-life and their offsprings' levels of independence, as well as parent–adolescent conflict. Greater emotional autonomy among adolescent boys is associated with both heightened levels of mid-life concerns among fathers and reduced life satisfaction. For mothers, reduced life satisfaction is linked to greater conflict with adolescents of both sexes. While the authors recognize that these associations may be bidirectional, they primarily cast their findings in terms of psychoanalytic theory that claims that mid-life reappraisal, self-questioning and doubt (elements of what Silverberg & Steinberg refer to as mid-life concerns), may be triggered by the increasing independence and identity formation of adolescent offspring, which includes de-idealization of parents, questioning of parental choices and views and so on. Thus, a bias reflected in this literature is that the adolescent is the driving force behind parent–child relationship changes.

Finally, severe criticism of this perspective deals with its perceived lack of applicability and validity for female development (Gilligan, 1982; Josselson, 1988). As noted, several studies have reported sex differences in measures of separation–individuation from parents. In response, critics have charged that to merely interpret these sex differences as illustrative of females' more problematic or stalled development is invalid because male and female development may not necessarily proceed along the same track. Indeed, as Josselson (1988) notes, several perspectives suggest that, unlike the male developmental trajectory that is characterized by increasing levels of autonomy and self-attainment, "female development proceeds on an interpersonal track (p. 99)" and is embedded "in the context of ongoing connection (p. 95)". Therefore, adolescence, at least for females, requires a rebalancing of an enhanced need for autonomy and self-expression and continued need for relationship.

In sum, conventional approaches to adolescent development, such as Hoffman's (1984), assume "that the adolescent develops as an individual precisely by moving outside the relation with parents" (Youniss, 1983, p. 95). Speaking of the fate of the parent–child relationship during this period, Josselson (1988) contends that to developmentalists like Blos (1967, 1979) Mahler (1968) and Anna Freud (1969), "Once it has served its presumed developmental function, the relationship that it was separated from has no further interest (p. 94)". Gaining attention and popularity, however, is an emergent school of thought grounded largely in feminist revisions of development. In this view, adolescent individuation occurs within an ongoing relationship with parents, where parent–child relations, for both sexes and generations, are merely transformed during the transition to adulthood and thereafter, rather than being totally eliminated. Conceptualizations of this type are considered next.

Bringing Parents Back In: New Views on Parent–Adolescent Relations

Recent conceptualizations of parent–child relations in late adolescence and early adulthood emphasize an ongoing connection between the generations. Although this position holds that the parent–child relationship remains intact during this period, it is not viewed as static. Supposedly, as offspring confront their increasing need for individuality, they revise their connections to their parents. Through the rebalancing of individuality and connectedness, truly individuated relations are achieved (Cooper, Grotevant & Condon, 1983).

Adolescent individuation, according to Cooper and associates (1983), is not an absolute psychological characteristic achieved by an individual (as Hoffman and others seem to assume), but instead applies to specific relational contexts. For example, the level of individuation an adolescent has achieved may vary in regard to each parent. For this reason, I refer to these theories as *contextual theories*, whereas those reviewed in the former section will be called theories of *absolute separation–individuation*.

The process of individuation within a context of connection entails four distinct sets of behaviors (Grotevant & Cooper, 1982). Two of these—the adolescent's ability to recognize differences between self and other (labeled separateness), and the ability to assert one's own point of view—comprise the individuation component. The connection aspect of the process involves permeability—the ability to be open and responsive to another's point of view—and mutuality—which is demonstrating respect for alternate viewpoints (Cooper, Grotevant & Condon, 1983). The individuation part of the process largely involves the relinquishment of over-identification with parental beliefs and recognition of one's own uniqueness, whereas the connection aspect involves the maintenance of relationships despite recognized differences.

A unique aspect of these contextual perspectives, in contrast to views of absolute individuation–separation, is that connection to parents is considered beneficial, if not necessary, to the individuation process. Bell & Bell (1983) contend that the maintenance of parental bonds is necessary for adolescents to obtain validation of their new, unique selves in the process of individuation. Family bonds also provide adolescents a secure base from which to explore the world and the divergent views it holds en route to achieving an individuated identity (Cooper, Grotevant & Condon, 1983).

Assessing Relationship Transformations of Parents and Offspring

The transformation of parent–child relations during late adolescence is discussed in terms of achieving more peer-like ties based on interdependence and interrelatedness instead of dependence, submission and rebellion (Josselson, 1988).

White, Speisman & Costos (1983) provide a framework for viewing this relationship transformation, using adolescent individuation as an initial stage in a series of six stages involving relational changes for both generations. Theoretically, the end goal of this process is a symmetrical relationship based on mutuality and a broadened sense of perspective-taking between the generations. Yet White, Speisman & Costos (1983) report that most offspring in their 20s do not achieve the final stage characterized by "full peer-like mutuality" in relation to their parents—in this case their mothers.

Still, their framework is appealing because it considers individuation in the context of relationships and it specifies changes that both generations must make in this process. Both generations, for example, are expected to increasingly recognize the other as individuated persons apart from their respective family roles. Although not articulated by White, Speisman & Costos (1983), it is likely that the individuation process of adolescence also entails some redefining of self by the parents. Colarusso & Nemiroff (1982) mention identity changes fathers must make as their offspring move through adolescence—shifting from role of protector and caretaker to one of interested facilitator of the child's development.

In recognizing the interactive, reciprocal nature of parent–child relationships, the contextual theories (in contrast to the absolute separation–individuation theories) present the possibility that individuation from parents may be initiated and directed by alterations in the behavior and thinking of both generations. Parents may either consciously or inadvertently control the pace of the individuation process, perhaps in response to their own developmental needs. Extending Bengtson & Kuypers' (1971) concept of the developmental stake, parents may try to block the younger generation's attempts at individuation as a means of maintaining a sense of continuity and generativity in their own lives.

How parents approach their children's individuation process also may depend on family situations and structure. Greene & Boxer (1986) speculate that the developmental stake posed by Bengtson & Kuypers (1971) may have different meaning, for example, as a result of family size and birth order. The developmental press may be less urgent for parents in larger families or in reference to the youngest child, therefore the psychological need to maximize closeness to and similarity with a particular child—and perhaps to stall or interfere with individuation—may be attenuated (Greene & Boxer, 1986). Regardless of the scenario one draws, the key point is that contextual theories of parent–young adult relations recognize the possibility of parental influence on parent–child relationship transformations in early adulthood, although the data at hand may not address it.

Sex Differences in Applying the Contextual Perspective

Employing their six-stage model, White, Spiesman & Costos (1983) find greater progression through the stages of parent–child relationship transformation for females than males. This finding may demonstrate valid sex differences in relational maturation in young adulthood or it could be an artifact of the research method. Males might have shown greater progression in this process than females if relations with fathers rather than mothers had been considered, as others (Youniss & Ketterlinus, 1987) report greater differentiation favoring relations with mothers over fathers by daughters than sons. Also, because White's model emphasizes relatedness in the form of verbal sharing and expressivity, females may actually be favored in scoring over males, given that feminine socialization is verbally-oriented, with an emphasis on talk about relational issues and feelings (Wood, 1993). Thus, whereas absolute separation–individuation frameworks may have an underlying male bias, these contextual perspectives may be biased in favor of female socialization.

Strengths and Limitations of Contextual Perspectives

Frameworks like that posed by White, Speisman & Costos (1983) are appealing because they conceptualize the process of adolescent individuation within a dynamic, bidirectional parent–child relationship. They also appear more grounded in reality than do absolute separation–individuation theories; that is, rather than disregarding the actual way in which parents and children are known to live and interact in adolescence and adulthood (Youniss, 1983), the contextual theories support the empirical findings showing interdependence between parents and offspring across adulthood (Cooney & Uhlenberg, 1992; Eggebeen & Hogan, 1990; Spitze & Logan, 1992).

Although these frameworks demonstrate strong theoretical promise, their empirical application to date remains limited. One problem is that the literature is based almost entirely on the perspective of the younger generation. If models such as this are to be relational in nature and sensitive to dyadic issues, more research is needed where multiple perspectives are gathered and analyzed. Such work will enhance our theoretical understanding of the relational changes each generation experiences during these middle years.

In summary, at least two schools of thought exist regarding parent–child relations in young adulthood. Absolute separation–individuation theories emphasize detachment and emancipation from parental influence and connections, whereas contextual theories recognize the ongoing relationships between parents and children and concentrate on the transformation of these bonds during the offspring's late adolescent and young adult years. The next section briefly describes how such relationship transformations are initiated and proceed in the middle years of family life.

PROCESSES OF RELATIONSHIP TRANSFORMATION IN ADULTHOOD

As offspring become more psychologically mature and complete the social transitions associated with adulthood in our culture (e.g. leaving home, completing school, getting married: see Hogan & Astone, 1986), they expect new rights within the family, particularly in relation to their parents. As argued, perhaps the most accurate description of what happens to parent–child ties at this point is movement of the child away from dependence on the parents to a situation of *interdependence* between the generations—an outcome quite different from the isolated independence posed in Hoffman's (1984) model. Viewed within a context of transformation, the parent–child relationship in early to mid-adulthood involves the "renegotiation of the interdependencies that bond and bind" (Greene & Boxer, 1986, p. 138) the two generations.

Central to this renegotiation process is the establishment of clear boundaries—recognized distinctions—between maturing children and their parents. The most obvious boundaries are physical, where adult children establish a residence apart from their parents. But other boundaries, such as psychological (e.g. value differences between parent and child) and behavioral ones (e.g. grandparents avoiding interference in the rearing of the grandchildren) are equally important to negotiate. Specific strategies for re-establishing boundaries between parents and children are discussed below.

Developing Privacy Rights

The development of privacy rights is central to the individuation process of adult offspring and involves behavioral changes by both parent and child (Petronio, 1994). Some of the issues that demand renegotiation in adulthood are the ownership of space, belongings and information. According to Petronio (1994), by regulating privacy, offspring and parents can more effectively coordinate separateness while maintaining closeness in their relationship—a view that is consistent with the contextual theories discussed earlier. Clearly, the issue of privacy is a salient one during young adulthood. A lack of privacy is one problem young adults anticipate when they consider residing with their parents (Shehan & Dwyer, 1989).

Most of the literature on privacy issues and boundary conflicts in the family during late adolescence and early adulthood (see Petronio, 1994) considers how parents deny maturing children adequate privacy by interfering in their lives (e.g. asking too many questions, demanding to know more than the child wants to share). Considered less often, except perhaps by clinicians, are situations where parents jeopardize boundaries by offering too much about their own personal lives to the child, or expecting their adult children's input on issues that may create stress for them.

Triangulation, as referred to by clinicians, is when parents over-extend their relationships with their children, expecting more peer-like interaction with them (e.g. getting advice and emotional support), at the cost of failing to meet the children's needs (see Fullinwider-Bush & Jacobvitz, 1993). Generally, triangulation involves daughters who are promoted to the level of a parental peer by their mothers. Such cases often involve high levels of interparental conflict

(Fullinwider-Bush & Jacobvitz, 1993), which may partially explain why one of the parents turns to the children for support, comfort and advice rather than to the more appropriate choice—the marital partner. The discussion of triangulation is relevant here because it suggests that while the development of mutual relationships between parents and adult offspring is important (White, Speisman & Costos, 1983), there are still boundary distinctions between the generations that need to be recognized for healthy individual development and interpersonal relationships. These boundaries pertain to issues that are of a personal nature to parents as well as their adult offspring.

Intrafamilial Strategies for Establishing Boundaries

Many of the strategies used to establish intergenerational boundaries revolve around the issue of how maturing offspring and their parents manage divergent viewpoints and lifestyles in relating to one another. One approach, represented by Hagestad's (1979) concept of demilitarized zones (DMZs), is that of avoidance, in which potentially conflictual topical areas are mutually and knowingly omitted from family discussions.

Boundary recognition is another less conflict-oriented strategy used to facilitate relationship maintenance between adult children and parents (Greene & Boxer, 1986). With boundary recognition, parents and children may disagree and differ in such things as behaviors, attitudes and values, yet these differences are openly accepted as a valid part of each person. Greene & Boxer (1986) theorize that as children mature, an increasing number of issues in their lives becomes protected from parental input and criticism as a result of this process. Their proposition is consistent with speculation raised by Shehan & Dwyer (1989) that children's autonomy from parents may be reflected in the number and/or proportion of personal decision areas that are not open to negotiation with parents.

Extrafamilial Influences on Boundary Establishment

The status and roles adult offspring possess outside the family are major determinants of the extent to which boundaries are recognized in the adult child–parent relationship. Boundary facilitators are status and role changes beyond the family of origin that promote increased recognition of intergenerational boundaries (Greene & Boxer, 1986) and which may result in greater mutual respect, understanding and other positive interpersonal factors. Young women's marriage, for example, is associated with increased emotional connectedness to their mothers (Frank, Avery & Laman, 1988), as is parenthood (Fischer, 1981). Yet some studies fail to find effects of children's marital and/or parental status on relations with parents (Barnett et al., 1991; Baruch & Barnett, 1983), and some even report negative outcomes as a result of these status transitions (Baruch & Barnett, 1983; Frank, Avery & Laman, 1988).

Research on fathers and children also links the assumption of adult roles by sons with enhanced father–son understanding and empathy, whereas fathers' increased understanding with daughters appears more closely linked to daughters' assuming non-traditional roles, particularly in the work sphere (Nydegger & Mitteness, 1991). Nydegger (1991) claims that the adoption of roles similar to those of one's parents fosters the development of "filial comprehending" by offspring, where they begin to view their parents as individuals rather than just parents. She proposes that this ability is one of two essential requirements of filial maturity—the other being filial distancing. This latter concept refers to the emotional distancing from parents that is necessary for maturing children to gain greater objectivity about themselves and their parents.

Attending to the dyadic nature of relationship transformations, Nydegger (1991) argues that a parallel process of parental maturity also occurs. This entails the need for parents to facilitate their children's development by encouraging their distancing efforts; moreover, by distancing themselves from their children, parents begin to reshape a self-definition based on something other than parenting, which is critical as the centrality of this part of their lives wanes. In addition, parents must comprehend how their children are developing within their own distinct social worlds if they wish to maintain close, positive relations with them and facilitate their development.

Intergenerational boundaries also are altered in response to the loss of extrafamilial social status or roles, as these transitions typically contribute to the weakening of parent–child boundaries (Greene & Boxer, 1986). When roles typically linked to adulthood are lost, the rights adult children have in relation to their parents seem threatened. For example, in a study of parents with co-resident adult offspring, Aquilino & Supple (1991) note greater relationship negativity and parental dissatisfaction with the situation when the offspring are unemployed, divorced or financially dependent. The process of boundary disruption is illustrated in Hetherington's (1989) work as well, as she finds that divorced women who reside with their parents feel "infantilized" by them, as evidenced by conflicts with their parents regarding their independence and social lives, and parenting of their own children (the grandchildren).

In sum, role and status markers outside the family drive role renegotiations inside the family (Greene & Boxer, 1986). Who has greater leverage in establishing relationship boundaries—the adult child or the parents—is determined by whether adult social roles are gained or lost by the offspring. These processes are key determinants of the nature of parent–child relationships that evolve in mid- to late-adulthood. Current conceptualizations of these relationships are considered next.

PARENT–CHILD RELATIONS IN THE MIDDLE YEARS

While much of the literature on parent–child relationships during mid to later life takes a more practical rather than theoretical approach to the issues under study

(Hagestad, 1982), a substantial body of work (Bengtson, Olander & Haddad, 1976; Bengtson & Roberts, 1991; Glass, Bengtson & Dunham, 1986; Roberts & Bengtson, 1990; Rossi & Rossi, 1990) has been grounded in the perspective known as family solidarity. Bengtson's notion of family solidarity is derived from Durkheim's (1893) conceptualization of mechanical solidarity at the societal level, which depicts individuals as similar and undifferentiated as a result of shared norms and values. As a result of such similarity, persons can supposedly occupy a number of positions and serve a wide variety of functions within a social system. Moreover, shared experiences and perspectives bond persons together.

Measurement of Family Solidarity

Just as Durkheim emphasized that societal cohesiveness is partly a result of similarity in norms, values and experiences, Bengtson, Olander & Haddad (1976) originally viewed family unity or cohesiveness—what they called solidarity—as primarily based on congruence in sentiment and attitudes, and association among family members. While the proposed number of dimensions that contribute to family solidarity has varied over time with the development of the concept, the latest conceptualization includes six constructs: intergenerational family structure, and associational, affectional, consensual, functional and normative solidarity (Bengtson & Schrader, 1982). Structure refers to the size, type and geographic distribution of the family. Associational, affectional and consensual solidarity refer to the degree to which family members interact, feel positively toward one another and agree on values and issues, respectively. Functional solidarity is the extent to which services and aid are exchanged between the generations, and normative solidarity pertains to expressed levels of familial obligation (Bengtson & Schrader, 1982). It is assumed that high levels of familial obligation, mutual assistance, association, consensus and positive regard are desirable, as they, along with heightened opportunities for interaction (an aspect of family structure), contribute to a higher-order construct of family solidarity.

How these observable dimensions contribute to a more abstract concept of family solidarity is still under study. Results from recent empirical tests of propositions dealing with family solidarity suggest that a simple linear addition of the various dimensions (especially association, affection and consensus) is not valid. For example, while Bengtson & Roberts (1991; Roberts & Bengtson, 1990) reveal significant connections between association and affect, neither they nor others (Atkinson, Kivett & Campbell, 1986) find significant associations between either of these dimensions and attitudinal consensus. In fact, Roberts & Bengtson (1990) reveal a negative (albeit insignificant) correlation between affect and consensus; thus, they suggest that consensus may contribute independently to the overall construct of solidarity. In terms of empirical verification, therefore, this model is early in its development and likely to face further refinement.

Criticism of the Solidarity Framework

Criticism of the solidarity perspective stands in juxtaposition to that of the absolute separation–individuation perspective of young adulthood. As noted, models like Hoffman's (1984) have been faulted for their narrow emphasis on separation and independence from parents, despite overwhelming empirical evidence of intergenerational interdependence in adulthood. In sharp contrast is Bengtson's view that interdependence and similarity between parent and child are what are valued in adulthood; virtually no mention is made of a need to maintain any independence within relationships after young adulthood, or whether too much attitudinal similarity or association, for example, may be maladaptive. This contrast in perspectives is strikingly evident in Table 1, where sample items used to assess four of the relational dimensions in Bengtson's model are shown along with sample items from the four dimensions of Hoffman's independence model. A key point to reiterate is that in the solidarity model it is high solidarity that is viewed positively, whereas in Hoffman's independence framework low levels of similarity and connection are valued.

The lack of attention to boundary maintenance and some degree of separateness in the solidarity literature is particularly interesting given the extensive discussion in the adolescent/young adulthood literature on the renegotiation of boundaries between adult children and parents. Indeed, Atkinson (1989) criticizes Bengtson's conceptualization for over-reliance on mechanical solidarity and

Table 19.1 Sample items used to assess parent–child relations in Bengtson's measure of family solidarity and Hoffman's psychological separation inventory

Bengtson's dimension	Sample items	Hoffman's dimension	Sample items
Functional solidarity	In the past month, how often have you turned to your mother/father for advice on child-rearing?	Functional independence	I ask for my mother's/ father's advice when I am planning my vacation time
Affectual solidarity	How is communication between yourself and your mother/father— how well can you exchange ideas and talk about things that really concern you?	Emotional independence	I sometimes call home just to hear my mother's/father's voice
Consensual/ attitudinal solidarity	In the past year, how often have you and your mother/father argued about politics and political candidates?	Attitudinal independence	My beliefs regarding national defense are similar to my mother's/ father's
Associational solidarity	How often do you do things together with this parent?	Conflictual independence	When I don't write my mother/father often enough I feel guilty

neglect of what Durkheim (1893) labeled organic solidarity. This latter form of solidarity results from differentiation between persons and the division of labor within a social system, with individuals becoming interdependent on one another in order to manage all of the functions of daily life.

Empirical findings indicate the value of both similarity and difference in the bonding of parents and adult children. In support of the similarity view, several studies indicate that when parents and children occupy similar social and family positions (e.g., spouse, parent, worker) they report stronger family ties. Yet, evidence conflicting with the similarity emphasis is presented by Bengtson himself, as his work with Roberts (Roberts & Bengtson, 1990) fails to find a link between attitude similarity and emotional closeness. In addition, studies like that of Aquilino & Supple (1991) reveal that excessive dependence and contact may contribute to strained intergenerational relationships. Thus, mixed evidence suggests that both similarity and difference are important to parent–adult child relationships, supporting Atkinson's (1989) view that organic solidarity deserves more attention in theorizing and research on intergenerational relationships in adulthood.

The concept of family solidarity also is criticized for downplaying the value of conflict and negotiation (Marshall, Matthews & Rosenthal, 1993) and considering only positive affect between adult children and parents. This practice, which is evident in the literature on middle-aged children and their parents more generally (Mancini & Blieszner, 1989), fails to address the multidimensional nature of familial affect, thereby overlooking the possibility that positive and negative affect and behavior may independently exist within a given relationship, each having its own set of predictors and outcomes. In addition, the potentially beneficial aspects of conflict, such as promoting positive family change (Petronio, 1994), are ignored. Finally, the lack of attention to conflict, or viewing it as merely the polar opposite of positive affect on a unidimensional scale, raises serious methodological consequences (Bengtson & Mangen, 1988; Landry & Martin, 1988).

In summary, a review of the recent literature on parent–child relations in adulthood reveals a need for a unified lifespan perspective for conceptualizing this relationship. While the domains of relevance to the relationship appear consistent across early and later adulthood (e.g. functional and affective issues), how researchers conceptualize relationship dynamics during these two life phases is dramatically different. It is possible that a need for distinctiveness and relative independence is a valid characterization of the relationship early in adulthood, whereas similarity and dependence predominate later in life. Indeed, Newman & Newman (1975) claim that strong individuation is necessary and may actually alienate adolescents from their parents, temporarily. Yet, after establishing a necessary level of individuation and autonomy young people are ready to rebuild connections with their families. The fact that adult offspring report an increase in the likelihood of receiving advice from their parents between their early and late 20s is one piece of empirical support for this notion (Cooney & Uhlenberg, 1992). It may be that establishing independence—in this case functional independence

(Hoffman, 1984)—is particularly critical early in adulthood, but once individuation is achieved offspring are more receptive to parental input in a context of mutuality and reciprocity. If this is the case, much more interdisciplinary psychosocial research is needed to explain how this dramatic shift in emphasis comes about and the role of each generation in the process. This problem clearly requires some added thought from researchers who assume a lifespan orientation, as do a few other theoretical and methodological issues discussed next.

ADULT CHILD–PARENT RELATIONSHIPS WITHIN A WIDER FAMILY SYSTEM

The study of parent–child relationships in adulthood is based almost exclusively on the perspective of only one member of the dyad. The problems inherent in this approach are somewhat avoided in the few well-known multi-generational studies that have been fielded in recent years (Bengtson & Mangen, 1988; Hagestad, 1984; Rossi & Rossi, 1990). Still, these and most studies generally fail to address how the adult child–parent relationship operates within the various relational subsystems of the larger family unit (Sprey, 1991). Little is known about how relations between adult children and parents are influenced by the involvement of each party in other relational sub-systems of the family, such as sibling, marital and other parent–child relationships.

When family scholars have examined the impact of other family subsystems on parent–child relations they have concentrated on the marital relationship of the parent generation. Belsky's 1984 model of the determinants of parenting is a popular example of this; he considers how the parents' marital relationship (along with such factors as work and personality) may influence children's development via its impact on parenting practices. Until very recently, research on adult child–parent relationships was primarily limited to examining how the parents' marital status (typically widowed vs. married) affected intergenerational relationships (Bulcroft & Bulcroft, 1991; Cooney, 1989; Cooney & Uhlenberg, 1992; Eggebeen, 1992). Only in the past few years have researchers linked parental marital interaction with adult child–parent relationships.

Recent studies fairly consistently document a significant connection between parental marital problems and reduced parent–child closeness, particularly with fathers (Cooney, 1994; Rossi & Rossi, 1990; Webster & Herzog, 1995). Webster & Herzog (1995) examined adults' ratings of their relations with parents along both positive and negative dimensions, and found that childhood family structure and marital problems were correlated with the positive but not the negative relationship dimensions. Parental divorce and marital conflict were predictive of lower scores on measures of feeling loved and listened to by one's father. Thus, past interparental conflict did not result in a negative, acrimonious bond with one's aging father, but instead led to somewhat empty, distant relations.

Cooney (1994) considered the interplay of relational subsystems in the family by analyzing the correlation between father–child and mother–child relationship quality for young adult offspring. Interestingly, in intact two-parent families, relationships with mothers vs. fathers were highly correlated for young adults of both sexes. Yet, relationships with fathers and mothers were not correlated in families where parents had divorced within the past 3 years. Cooney concludes that "parent–child relations in intact families appear to operate as a system of relationships—highly interdependent on one another—while those in divorced families exist virtually apart from each other (p. 52)."

Others have considered the interaction of family subsystems as they relate to individual outcomes. Hoffman & Weiss (1987) examined how the connection between interparental problems and daughter–mother relations affected the personal adjustment of college-aged females. Their rather complex findings showed that daughters who reported greater hostility and conflict with their mothers appeared to be less affected by their parents' marital problems than did young women reporting lower levels of conflict in relation to their mothers. Perhaps daughters in close, non-conflictual relationships with their mothers responded more empathically to parental marital problems because of the confiding their mothers were likely to be doing with them (Cooney et al., 1986). But when marital problems existed in a context of poor mother–child relations, perhaps these daughters distanced themselves from those problems. Additionally, the negative impact of parental marital problems may be more evident in offspring who are not also reacting to conflict in the parent–child relationship.

Despite these few examples that demonstrate increasing awareness of the need to consider the wider family system in work on adult child–parent relationships, much more attention is needed. Future studies should consider, for example, how the marital relations of adult offspring affect their relations with aging parents. Although past work has assessed how the adult child's marital status affects ties to aging parents (Baruch & Barnett, 1983; Fischer, 1981; Frank, Avery & Laman, 1988) little is known about how their marital quality may also influence these relationships. The interplay of the sibling and parent–child subsystems also requires further attention. In one of the few studies in the adult child–parent literature to consider sibling configurations, Barnett, Marshall & Pleck (1992) speculate that men's emotional connection to their parents may be enhanced when they have sisters. It is the consideration of these types of systemic interactions within the family that Sprey (1991) argues is necessary for a deeper understanding of multi-generational family life.

METHODOLOGICAL CONCERNS

A number of methodological limitations exist in the literature on adult parent–child relations, some of which have been discussed above. Very briefly, this section will identify issues of concern in the areas of sampling, units of observation and analyses, and data gathering and measurement.

Transformations in parent–child relations across adulthood and the inter-generational ties that exist during this period are certainly likely to vary for persons of different racial and economic groups, given subcultural variations in familial norms, family needs and resources. Indeed, several investigations reveal differences in patterns of intergenerational exchange based on race, ethnicity and social class (Cooney & Uhlenberg, 1992; Eggebeen & Hogan, 1990; Spitze & Logan, 1992). Yet, studies consist primarily of White, middle-class samples. This is especially the case in research on young adulthood, where data are drawn heavily from college students (Boxer, Cook & Cohler, 1986; Frank, Avery & Laman, 1988; Hoffman, 1984). The process of young adults' identity achievement and expected changes in relation to parents and family, as posed by the new developmentalists, also may differ significantly for ethnic and racial groups, such as Mexican-Americans (Williams, 1990), who adhere to strong norms of fa-milism. Similarly, how parents figure into the process of identity achievement in young adulthood, and how family roles are renegotiated during this period, may differ in populations where the role of biological parents is less central in the lives of children, and the "parenting" role of extended kin and pseudo-kin is intensi-fied due to the absence of the father, and/or to problems with the parents, or their young age (Burton, 1992).

The widespread use of college student samples to study relations between young adults and their parents also may compromise the validity of findings on relationship transformations during early adulthood, because the college experi-ence may constitute a unique experience for youth (Murphey et al., 1963). In addition, young people who choose to attend college away from home may already differ systematically from those who continue to reside with their parents in terms of their progress on tasks of identity development and in relationships with their parents. Possible selection effects of this type also exist in some of the multigenerational studies, such of that of Rossi & Rossi (1990), where sampling was restricted to parents and adult children who resided in the same geographic region. Living in close geographic proximity to one's parents or children may be both a result of some unique relationship property and a predictor of other relationship dimensions.

The literature on parent–child relations between adults also is limited by its nearly exclusive focus on individuals as the unit of observation and analyses. Some of the conceptual problems with this emphasis were already discussed. Another issue in studies that include multiple generations in the family is that divergent perspectives may be given by different family members. To illustrate, Boxer, Cook & Cohler (1986) found little intergenerational agreement between grandfathers, fathers and sons concerning the topics that created conflict between them, how conflict was handled, and whether it was ever resolved. These findings raise the critical question of whether there are indeed "family experiences" or properties to be studied and understood. In addition, such findings present diffi-cult analytic choices such as how to handle divergent perspectives from family members.

Marshall, Matthews & Rosenthal (1993) encourage greater use of typologies in studying families to avoid the constraints introduced by quantitative methods that require observations to be statistically independent (an impossible requirement for data drawn from multiple individuals from the same family). Moreover, typologies may get at the deeper meaning or greater complexity of family relationships (something for which qualitative rather than quantitative methods are often favored) because they allow for the simultaneous consideration of more than one analytic construct or variable.

UNDERSTANDING GENDER IN ADULT CHILD–PARENT RELATIONS

Whether one assumes an individualistic or more relational approach to gathering data on adult children and their parents, it is increasingly evident that research questions and methods must be framed in terms of the gender of both the parent and the adult child. Indeed, in nearly all of the literature cited in this chapter, it was necessary to specify which parent–child relationships revealed particular effects, because findings that apply equally to mother–daughter, mother–son, father–daughter and father–son relations are rare.

Gender-sensitive research requires more than merely asking the same standardized questions in reference to the four possible dyads of parent and child. Such an approach can err in at least two ways. First, certain topics or questions about the parent–child relationship may possess a gender bias. Using items that only tap interpersonal sharing and expression of emotion to measure parent–child closeness and intimacy, for example, may force men's family experiences into what is actually a female model of interpersonal relationships (Boxer, Cook & Cohler, 1986; Wood, 1993). A typical result is that family relationships involving men end up looking deficient (Boxer, Cook & Cohler, 1986).

A second problem with applying the same questions across all four parent–child dyads is that specific dyads may fail to display quantitative differences on a particular question or item, yet the underlying relationship may actually be qualitatively different across dyads. Nydegger & Mitteness (1991) asked fathers about the degree of difficulty they experienced in raising their adult offspring. Although fathers reported no differences in level of difficulty based on the child's sex, raising sons and daughters posed qualitatively different struggles for them. Fathers reportedly had difficulty handling their sons' attempts at independence, whereas they found handling their daughters' emotional reactions to situations to be especially challenging (Nydegger & Mitteness, 1991).

It is unlikely that such sharp qualitative differences would have emerged from highly structured survey questions where no interviewer probing occurs. Thus, to better understand how male bonds are displayed in families (where female models of relationships have dominated) may require, at least initially, greater dependence on qualitative methods where the research subjects are granted more freedom to report on their social reality (Thompson, 1992). Once the relevant domains are identified, quantitative methods may be more appropriate.

Finally, to advance our understanding of gender in family relationships more studies must examine the role of socially constructed gender characteristics in parent–child relations, in addition to the role of the sex of the parent and child (Rossi & Rossi, 1990; Wood, 1993b). The value of such work is evident in the Rossis' research, where they find that expressivity, a gendered characteristic, explains more of the variance in parent–child intimacy and exchange than does sex. Highly expressive men are more intimate in relation to and involved with their parents (Rossi & Rossi, 1990). Apparently, a much deeper understanding of gender and its role in parent–child relations can be gained with approaches that go beyond simple comparisons of males and females.

SUMMARY

This chapter has reviewed the literature on parent–child relations across adulthood in an effort to demonstrate conceptual problems and methodological limitations that exist in this body of work. An apparent problem is the lack of a lifespan view of parent–child connections. The popular conceptualizations of the relationship in early adulthood emphasize independence and distinctiveness between the generations, whereas frameworks used to study the relationship in the middle and later years of adulthood focus heavily on interdependence and similarity. How parents and adult children make this relational shift, if indeed they do, is not clear from the theoretical or empirical literature. Finally, the need for dyadic studies that consider parent–adult child relations within a broader family system and diverse cultural contexts was identified, as was greater consideration of the meaning of gender within adult parent–child relations.

ACKNOWLEDGEMENT

Work on this chapter was supported by a First Award from the National Institute of Mental Health (#1 R29 MH46946).

Chapter 20

Strategies of Couple Conflict

Renate C.A. Klein
University of Maine, Orono, ME, USA
and
Michael P. Johnson
Pennsylvania State University, University Park, PA, USA

This chapter is about couple conflict in family relationships (for discussions of intergenerational conflict in families see Fincham & Osborne, 1993; Halpern, 1994; and Osborne & Fincham, 1994). Our focus is on conflict strategies and more specifically on an analysis of the factors that shape partners' choices among different strategies. The chapter is organized around the concept of strategic choice, which we borrow from negotiation research (Carnevale & Pruitt, 1992).

The chapter is composed of five sections. In the introduction we explicate the terms family, conflict, conflict strategies, and strategic choice. Second, we discuss individual and situational factors in strategic choice and focus on three response patterns in couple conflict that have received considerable attention recently: the demand/withdraw pattern in asymmetrical conflict; negative reciprocity; and physical violence. Third, we focus on the role of third parties in strategic choice, an important field that, we believe, will receive more attention in the future. The fourth part has a theoretical focus and presents a discussion of strategic choice from a situated sense-making perspective that takes into consideration the balance of interpersonal, social and economic power between partners. Finally, we briefly summarize the chapter and point to our main conclusion about the importance of social context in couple conflict.

Handbook of Personal Relationships, 2nd edn. Edited by Steve Duck.
© 1997 John Wiley & Sons Ltd.

INTRODUCTION OF CONCEPTS

Family

Although this chapter is about couple conflict in family relationships, we would like to be clear at the beginning that we intend to focus on couple conflict in "families", broadly defined. Recent debates in the field of family studies (Burr et al., 1987; Marks, 1987; Beutler et al., 1989a,b) have persuaded us and many other scholars that a narrow focus of the field on the traditional biological family is not conducive to the development of adequate theory. We find the arguments of Marks (1987) and Scanzoni et al. (1989) quite persuasive, that a broader focus on units that are organized around a sexual bond (Scanzoni et al., 1989) drawing upon broad theories of personal relationships (as exemplified in this volume) will be much more productive than would a narrower focus on the "traditional" family (cf. Bedford & Blieszner, this volume).

We think that such a broader concept of the family draws attention to the fact that similar conflict issues may play out differently in different family "types". For example, spouses in traditional, male-breadwinner families are likely to debate issues around household chores differently than spouses in "peer marriages" (Schwartz, 1994). Similarly, arguments over household chores may play out differently for lesbian than for gay male couples, because lesbian couples on average have a lower expendable household income than gay couples and are therefore less able to resolve chore conflicts by "expanding the pie" (Rubin, Pruitt & Kim, 1994), in this case, by buying more free time for both partners. In addition, because most domestic workers are female, for many lesbian couples hiring household help may take on an unwelcome ideological meaning: by hiring female domestic servants they contribute to women's confinement to low wage, part-time jobs (Patterson & Schwartz, 1994).

Conflict

While conflict can be perceived and defined in different ways (e.g., Baxter et al., 1993; Lloyd, 1987; Peterson, 1983) we are concerned with conflicts that arise when partners believe their needs and interests are incompatible. Similar notions of conflict have been adopted in a variety of disciplines. For example, Margolin (1988) defined marital conflict as the "incompatibilities or antagonisms of ideas, desires, and actions between the two partners" (p. 195). Similarly, in their discussion of social conflict, Rubin, Pruitt & Kim (1994) understand conflict as the "perceived divergence of interest, or a belief that the parties' current aspirations cannot be achieved simultaneously" (p. 5).

Conflict Strategies

We define conflict strategies as behaviors intended to manage or resolve conflict, which includes everything partners do and do not do in response to perceived or actual disagreement, from humorous and thoughtful discussions of each other's needs and interests to fierce and violent battles for power and control. Conflict strategies have been assessed through self-reports (e.g., Kurdek, 1994) and behavior observation (e.g., Gottman, 1979; Hahlweg et al., 1984; Prager, 1991), cross-sectionally and longitudinally (Gottman & Krokoff, 1989; Noller et al., 1994; McGonagle, Kessler & Gotlib, 1993; for a discussion of different methodologies see Bradbury & Karney, 1993, and Weiss & Heyman, 1990).

Many research areas are related to strategic choice but cannot be covered within a single chapter. The reader is referred to other sources on blue-collar and white-collar marriages (Krokoff, Gottman & Roy, 1988), influence and control tactics (Falbo & Peplau, 1980; Howard, Blumstein & Schwartz, 1986; Stets & Pirog-Good, 1990; Christopher & Frandsen, 1990), coping with unsettled disagreements (Bowman, 1990), relationship maintenance (Baxter & Dindia, 1990; Dindia & Canary, 1993; Stafford & Canary, 1991), and commitment processes (Johnson, 1991a; Rusbult et al., 1991).

Conflict strategies constitute the course of conflict over time (Lloyd & Cate, 1985). Although we know that some conflict strategies reduce conflict and strengthen the bond between partners, whereas other conflict strategies escalate conflict and antagonize partners (Jacobson & Holtzworth-Munroe, 1986; Markman & Hahlweg, 1993; Markman et al., 1993), we are still far from fully understanding partners' choices in couple conflict (Jacobson & Addis, 1993). Therefore, we organize our review of couples' conflict strategies around the concept of strategic choice.

Strategic Choice

We organize our discussion of conflict strategies around the concept of choice for two reasons. First, we do so because we believe that partners do have a choice in how they respond to conflict and are not confined to "inevitable" developments of their disagreements. This does not mean each partner is capable and free to act as he or she pleases, neither are we implying that each choice involves a careful analysis of the consequences of different strategies. Although some choices may be the result of informed foresight, other choices may be the result of guesswork, mindlessness or years of habit.

Second, the concept of strategic choice draws our attention to factors that may explain why partners choose one strategy rather than another. While there can be important internal or dispositional factors such as the effects of socialization, personality or temperament (Gilligan, 1982; Seltzer & Kalmuss, 1988; Smith, 1990), we will focus on situational factors in strategic choice, using "situational" in a broad sense. On a micro-level, situational factors may include the structure of conflict within the dyad and the behavior of one's partner. On a macro-level, situational factors may include structural arrangements of intimate relationships (e.g., marriage) or the influence of third parties. In short, we will examine to what extent partners' strategic choices are situationally constructed and review empirical evidence on the demand/withdraw pattern, negative reciprocity, and physical violence. In the theoretical section we will take a step back and discuss strategic choices in terms of "sense-making" and the subjective meaning imposed by partners on confusing interaction sequences (Duck, 1994a), and in terms of "differential advantage" and the constellation of power between self, partner and third parties at any given point in the relationship.

STRATEGIC CHOICES IN COUPLE CONFLICT

Dual-concern Model

Our concept of strategic choice is borrowed from negotiation research where it has been researched and represented in the heuristic framework of the dual-concern model (see Pruitt & Carnevale, 1993, for a detailed description). Developed from work on managerial decision-making (Blake & Mouton, 1964) the dual-concern model has been used increasingly to analyze strategic choice in couple and family conflict as well (Buunk, 1980, cited in Schaap, Buunk & Kerkstra, 1988; Fry, Firestone & Williams, 1983; Rahim, 1983; Syna, 1984; Galvin & Brommel, 1986; Levinger & Pietromonaco, 1989; Rinehart, 1992; Spitzberg, Canary & Cupach, 1994; Klein, 1995).

The dual-concern model distinguishes between four basic conflict strategies (Pruitt & Carnevale, 1993): *contending* (e.g., being competitive, aggressive); *problem-solving* (e.g., being cooperative, talking things through, being creative); *yielding* (e.g., being conciliatory, giving in); and *inaction* (e.g., being passive, avoiding confrontation). These strategies have been observed across a variety of settings (Putnam, 1994; van de Vliert, 1990) including couples' responses to conflict and disagreement (Kurdek, 1994).

The dual-concern model attributes strategic choices to the blend of partners' egoistic and altruistic motivations: concern about one's own interests and concern about the other's interests (see Figure 20.1). Contending is interpreted as evidence of high self-concern combined with low other-concern, whereas problem-solving is interpreted as evidence of high self-concern combined with high other-concern. Yielding indicates low self- and high other-concern, whereas inaction indicates low self- and low other-concern (for experimental evidence supporting these links, see Ben-Yoav & Pruitt, 1984a,b; Pruitt & Carnevale, 1993).

We present the dual-concern model in some depth for several reasons. First, because it parsimoniously relates a broad range of conflict strategies to few underlying factors (for alternative models see Kelley, 1979; Rusbult, 1987). Secondly, what makes the dual-concern notion appealing to conflict management is the idea that opponents are not limited to a zero-sum approach to conflict in which they can choose only between a self-serving and a self-sacrificing approach. Instead, opponents can approach conflict in a way that integrates the interests of both self and other to their mutual benefit. Finally, the dual-concern model provides a focal point from which to examine factors that may shape concern and strategic choice.

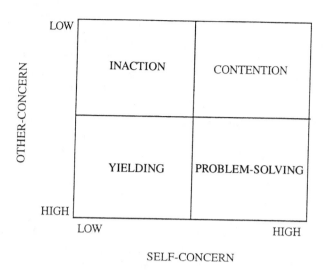

Figure 20.1 Dual concern model

Dispositional and Situational Factors in Concern

Feminist scholars such as Miller (1976) and Gilligan (1982) have argued that women tend to pursue a dual agenda in their social interactions, taking their own interests as well as those of the other party into consideration. More recent work locates evidence in support of such a dual agenda in "enabling" interaction styles (see Maccoby, 1990) or the "double-voice discourse" of young girls (Sheldon, 1992). Notions such as "double-voice discourse" or "self in relation to other" (Miller, 1976) capture the same idea as the combination of high self-concern and high other-concern in the dual-concern model: that it is possible to resolve interpersonal conflict constructively by attending to both sides simultaneously. For couple conflict in particular this would mean that, to the extent that women practice a dual agenda, they have the potential to be successful relationship diplomats and peace-makers. Yet, it is evidently not the case that relationships in which women are involved are automatically peaceful (e.g., Straus & Gelles, 1990). Women as peace-makers aside, it is important to realize that couple conflicts bear this contradiction: on the one side there is tremendous potential for constructive conflict management; on the other side couples are facing destructive negativity, deadlock and violence. This contradiction suggests that the course of conflict reflects complex constraints on strategic choice.

While dispositional constraints are important, such as a socialization-based preference for compromising strategies, situational constraints such as the behavior of the partner can be extremely powerful. Referring to social interaction in general, Maccoby (1990) had argued that women can realize a dual agenda most successfully when interacting with other women but not with men, while men can pursue a self-concerned agenda most successfully when interacting with women rather than with other men. The argument that the viability of self-concerned or dual-concerned strategies is contingent on the interaction partner implies that strategic choice to some extent is constructed situationally and arises from the constraints and options each partner encounters during a particular conflict (see Rubin, Pruitt & Kim, 1994, for the notion of feasible strategies). As observers of conflict we are prone to explain couples' strategic choices in dispositional terms and to underestimate the impact of situational factors (Ross, 1977). Consequently, we will focus on important situational constraints and options, beginning with the structure of conflict.

Conflict Structure and the Demand/Withdraw Pattern

The structure of conflict refers to the distinction between symmetrical and asymmetrical conflicts (Pruitt, 1991). In symmetrical conflicts opponents have incompatible interests but play similar roles. For instance, a young couple argues about how to spend the evening: he wants to spend it on his hobby, she wants to spend it together. In asymmetrical conflicts this issue takes on a different twist: one partner is now in the role of a complainant who wants to change the *status quo*, while the other partner is in the role of a respondent who is resisting change. Imagine the couple again after three years during which they ended up spending most of their evenings individually. When she raises the issue again, she is now in the complainant's position and needs to overcome years of habit. In contrast, he is now in the respondent's position and wants to maintain cherished habits. Even if we assume that with regard to spending their evenings both partners are self-concerned and try to advance their own interests, the asymmetry of the conflict suggests different strategic choices (Peirce, Pruitt & Czaja, 1991). If she wants to advance her interest in time together, she has to come forward and take an active approach, because otherwise things will remain the same (i.e., he will disappear into the den). If he wants to advance his interests in time spent on his hobby, he needs to remain as passive and withdrawn as possible because then things will remain the same (i.e., he will disappear into the den).

Such a conflict may result in what has been termed the "demand/withdraw" pattern, in which one partner "attempts to engage in a problem-solving discussion, often resorting to pressure and demands, while the other partner attempts to avoid or withdraw from the discussion" (Heavey, Layne & Christensen, 1993, p. 16). Observations that women seem to be more often in the role of the pursuer than men (Christensen, 1988; Heavey, Layne & Christensen, 1993) gave rise to different explanations of this gender pattern. One dispositional explanation emphasizes the differential socialization of men and women. According to this explanation, women engage in conflict because they have been socialized to take care of relationships (Rubin, 1983). An alternative dispositional explanation suggests that men try not to engage in conflict because they find the accompanying physiological arousal more aversive than women (Gottman & Levenson, 1986). However, dispositional explanations overlook potential situational constraints on strategic choice, such as the structure of the conflict (Christensen & Heavey, 1990), and neglect strategic aspects of gender differences in reactions to conflict.

With regard to strategic aspects of gender differences in conflict strategies, Sattell (1976), in response to the heavy socialization emphasis in the early litera- ture on "the inexpressive male", has explicated the strategic advantages to men of avoiding or withdrawing from conflict, because such a tactic serves to maintain the *status quo*. More recently, feminist scholars have moved away from a heavy emphasis on gender as socialized, to a more balanced focus on the situated construction of gender (West & Fenstermaker, 1993). To the extent that the roles of complainant and respondent are related to a gendered organization of partner- ship, marriage or family life, the gender difference in the demand/withdraw pattern could be constructed situationally.

In fact, several authors have argued that heterosexual relationships, most notably marriage, are set up in a way that benefits the husband and puts the wife at a disadvantage (e.g., Bernard, 1982; Delphy & Leonard, 1992; Jacobson, 1990). In heterosexual relationships, women seem to desire change more often than men (Gottman, 1994). For example, one study of couple conflict (Klein, 1995) found that in 70% of the couples the woman had confronted the issue first. To the extent that the male partner benefits from the arrangement, he should resist change. To the extent that the female partner is unsatisfied with the *status quo*, she should desire change and hence find herself more often in the complainant's role, facing the difficult task of bringing about change.

In a study to compare dispositional (i.e., gender socialization) and situational (i.e., conflict structure) constraints on strategic choice, Christensen & Heavey (1990) found no gender asymmetry in the demand/withdraw pattern when the husband was the complainant; however, when the wife was the complainant, there was a pronounced gender asymmetry, with the wife being in the demanding role more often than the husband. We wonder whether this finding, which was replicated by Heavey, Layne & Christensen (1993), reflects an interaction be- tween conflict structure and dual-concern thinking. A simple conflict structure explanation assumes that all respondents are alike and will stubbornly resist change. However, if we argue that women are more likely than men to entertain a dual-concern agenda, then a wife-respondent should be more likely to consider a husband-complainant, making excessive demanding by the husband unneces- sary. In contrast, the resistance of a husband-respondent would be amplified by a self-concern agenda, making withdrawal a top priority for the husband and forcing the wife into the demanding position.

Future observations of the demand/withdraw pattern in same-sex couples might shed some light on this issue. Assuming that women import the dual- concern agenda into lesbian relationships and men import the self-concern agenda into gay male relationships, we would suspect that lesbian couples would be less likely to get caught in the demand/withdraw pattern because the com- plainant would be likely to be interacting with a considerate respondent. In contrast, the demand/withdraw pattern would pose a serious threat to gay male couples because the complainant would more frequently be interacting with a stubborn respondent, resulting in a strong demand/withdraw asymmetry with the complainant forced to pursue vigorously.

We used the demand/withdraw pattern to illustrate our notion that strategic choice is situated in the complex web of partners' general orientations toward self and other and situation-specific constraints in asymmetrical conflict. The demand/withdraw pattern is important because it has been linked to destructive conflict-management and relationship distress (Schaap, Buunk & Kerkstra, 1988), and may be a precursor of eventual relationship dissolution. For instance, Gottman and his associates argue that withdrawal (or "stonewalling") is a sign of serious communication breakdown and foreshadows relationship dissolution (see Gottman, 1994, for details). Another pattern that has been linked to destructive conflict-management is "negative reciprocity", which we will discuss next.

Negative Reciprocity

Negative reciprocity has been termed a "hallmark of marital conflict" and denotes "the increased tendency to respond to a negative communication from the partner with one's own negative communication" (Epstein, Baucom & Rankin, 1993, p. 51; see also Margolin & Wampold, 1981; Revenstorf et al., 1984). Distressed couples reciprocate negative behavior more often than non-distressed couples (Gottman, Markman & Notarius, 1977) thus demonstrating how difficult it can be to back out of a spiral of angry accusations and sniping remarks (Rubin & Rubin, 1993). Nonetheless, non-distressed couples, although not immune to negative interaction cycles, are able to exit them more quickly than distressed couples, such as physically aggressive couples (Burman, Margolin & John, 1993).

In addition to these differences in negative reciprocity between distressed and non-distressed couples, research on heterosexual married couples suggests gender differences in the likelihood to reciprocate negative behavior. For instance, Gottman, Markman & Notarius (1977) found that non-distressed wives were least likely to reciprocate negative behavior and thus were instrumental in terminating a negative interaction cycle. Similarly, Notarius et al. (1989) report that distressed wives were least likely to respond with positive behavior. Although these findings suggest that women can be relationship "peace-makers", it is unclear under what conditions women's peace-making develops successfully.

Considering women's dual agenda we can argue that non-distressed wives are better able to integrate their husband's agenda and generate positive responses, whereas distressed wives are less able to do so, presumably because "genuine concern about the other party is enhanced by positive feelings and a perception of common group identity with that party" (Pruitt & Carnevale, 1993, p. 108), both of which may be questionable or even absent in distressed marriages.

Genuine concern, and its absence, may also influence how partners interpret a negative exchange. While both partners are more likely to reciprocate the other's negative behavior if they attribute it to negative intent (see Fincham, Bradbury & Scott, 1990; Noller & Ruzzene, 1991), concern for the other may encourage a partner to mistakenly assume a positive intention where there was none (giving the partner the benefit of the doubt), whereas the absence of such concern may encourage partners to mistakenly assume a negative intention (Gaelick, Bodenhausen & Wyer, 1985).

Although negative reciprocity is considered a destructive approach to conflict management, conflict engagement (which often includes negative remarks about the partner) can improve relationship satisfaction in the long run (Gottman & Krokoff, 1989). However, constructive conflict engagement is contingent on the cooperation of both partners (Gottman, 1994). This poses a very real dilemma to the partner who wants to engage in conflict in order to make changes in the relationship. To the extent that cooperation from the respondent in asymmetrical conflict is not very likely, partners who strongly desire change may find themselves caught between a rock and a hard place because the conflict engagement necessary to improve a relationship can contribute to its very decline.

Faced with the dilemma of trying to engage an unwilling partner to change a relationship he or she is not motivated to change, the complainant could consider two more options: not trying to change the relationship from within but instead leave it ("exit" in Hirschman's, 1970, terminology; see also Rusbult et al., 1991), or trying to increase the respondent's motivation to collaborate by threatening to leave. These options are generally not viable for a complainant who is very committed to the relationship, and here we find that it is often wives whose various commitments preclude both options, and deepen the dilemma (Oliker, 1989). Wives are in many ways more personally, morally and structurally committed to the relationship than are husbands (Johnson & Kapinus, 1995). Lennon & Rosenfield (1994) have recently demonstrated that women's economic dependence on a relationship (an aspect of structural commitment) inhibits the development of dissatisfaction with an inequitable division of labor, a dissatisfaction that can be nothing but painful when one is relatively powerless.

To sum up, we think that women are often cast into the role of pursuer as well as primary peacemaker because they more often desire change, while social and moral obligations, not to mention economic necessity, force them to change relationships from within. More generally, it appears to us that the social arrangements of intimate relationships exert a powerful influence on the strategic choices partners can make. Taking heterosexual marriage as an example, we wonder to what extent this institutionalized arrangement of male–female relations (Delphy & Leonard, 1992) shapes spouses' strategic choices, such as by putting women into the complainant's position, but generally providing little in the way of resources to bring about change.

As the final part in our discussion of situated constraints on partners' strategic choices we will now consider aggressive and physically violent conflict strategies.

Aggression and Physical Violence

It is unfortunately the case that responses to conflict sometimes involve the use of violence, a "resource" too often ignored in resource theories of power, which tend to draw upon an imagery of civilized exchange between relative equals, one of whom brings a bit more to the relationship than does the other, and thereby gets his or her way more often (Blood & Wolfe, 1960; Frieze & McHugh, 1992; McDonald, 1981; Sabatelli & Shehan, 1993). The authors of the National Family Violence Surveys (Straus & Gelles, 1990) have estimated that conflict strategies involve occasional violence in as many as 50% of American couples. In this connection, we would like to make a distinction between what we have elsewhere called "common couple violence" and "patriarchal terrorism" (Johnson, 1995).

Common couple violence is the occasional violence that arises out of strong reactions to the escalation of a particular disagreement. It is occasional in two senses: (1) it is situated in the interpersonal dynamics of a particular occasion rather than in a general pattern of power and control; and (2) it happens only occasionally in most families in which it occurs. Johnson (1995) has argued that this is the type of violence that is tapped by large sample survey research, and the type, therefore, which is the source of the much-quoted 50% estimate alluded to above. The violence identified in the National Family Violence Surveys occurs on average about once every two months, does not seem to escalate, involves both partners in two-thirds of the families in which it occurs, and is almost perfectly gender-balanced. This sort of violence is probably best explained by means of theories that focus on the interpersonal dynamics of escalation in conflict situations, on the privatized nature of family life that protects such incidents from public scrutiny, and on a normative context that may accept the "unfortunate" possibility or even likelihood that family conflict will occasionally erupt into "minor" violence.

For obvious ethical reasons, there is no research, at least to our knowledge, that documents the escalation of a heated argument into a physical fight. The escalation explanation implies that violence is a last resort response "at the end" of a sequence of increasingly hostile, aggressive and desperate exchanges. Minor physical violence, then, should be correlated with other instances of aggressive or desperate behavior. Moreover, those individuals should be more likely to resort to minor physical violence who lack alternative coping skills. In fact, Hammock & Richardson (1992) found moderate but consistent correlations between contentious and physically aggressive conflict strategies. Moreover, during marital interactions in the laboratory, husbands in physically violent relationships displayed more non-verbal signs of irritation and frustration as well as more attacking, defensive and patronizing behaviors than husbands from other distressed but not violent relationships (Margolin, John & Gleberman, 1988; Margolin, Burman & John, 1989). However, wives did not differ across relationships. Margolin, Burman & John (1989) also report that physically aggressive couples lack alternative problem-solving skills. Also, O'Leary & Vivian (1990) report that in abusive couples problem-solving is characterized by anger and the reciprocation of negative affect; and Murphy & O'Leary (1989; cited in O'Leary & Vivian, 1990) found that verbal abuse predicted the onset of the first instance of physical abuse. Taken together, these findings suggest that occasional violence could result from prolonged, unsuccessful attempts to resolve conflict.

There is another form of family violence that is embedded in a general pattern of power and control rooted in the patriarchal traditions of the family (Dobash & Dobash, 1992). This "patriarchal terrorism" is the sort of violence that is missed almost entirely by large sample surveys, with their 40% non-response rates (Johnson, 1995), but which shows up clearly in research that draws its data from agencies such as the police, the courts, hospitals and women's shelters. This violence happens frequently in those families in which it occurs (more than once a week on average for the women in shelters), it almost inevitably escalates, and it is initiated almost exclusively by men. The pattern is one of general power and control exercised by means of a variety of control tactics, ranging from economic control and purposeful social isolation to the use of sexual and non-sexual violence (Pence & Paymar, 1993). This sort of violence may not be so easily explained by general theories that focus on the interpersonal dynamics involved in attempts to resolve incompatibilities. The men involved have a need to exercise and to display control as a feature of "ownership" that may have little to do with particular incompatibilities or their partners' responses to them.

The analyses of physical violence in couple conflict serve as an unavoidable reminder of the central role of the cultural and social context in what at times may appear to be a very personal and private matter. Couple conflict can be private in the sense that it often occurs in the privacy of couples' homes and eludes public scrutiny. However, even if conflict occurs in the isolation of anonymous urban apartment blocks or remote rural homes, we think that, in a different sense, the enactment of conflict strategies is not isolated from the wider social context. For instance, norms that legitimize certain conflict strategies and outlaw others (Milardo & Klein, 1992) are likely to influence strategic choices of even geographically isolated couples. While the cultural and social context in which conflict strategies are enacted can be analyzed from various angles, we will in the next section focus on social context in terms of third parties, such as partners' kin and friends.

STRATEGIC CHOICE AND THIRD PARTIES

Although the term "third party" is most often used to denote a formal role, such as mediator, attorney, counselor or consultant, we use it in a broader sense that includes informal advice and intervention from friends, kin and other members of partners' social networks (Klein & Milardo, 1993). The following discussion will focus on how informal third parties can shape partners' strategic choices (for a discussion of formal third parties in family conflict, see Blades, 1985). This does not mean that third-party influence is unidirectional. To some extent partners grant influence to third parties by deciding with whom they will associate and whom they will ask for advice.

An important aspect of third parties, which we will mention only briefly, is the extent to which third parties are available to each partner. For example, is one partner cut off from his or her family, while the other is living amidst them? Do both partners, or just one of them, have close friends? We think it is important to consider the availability of third parties for each partner separately, not just for the couple as a whole, because separate third parties may exert different types of influence (e.g., partisan support; see Black, 1993) than joint third parties (Klein & Milardo, 1993, 1995).

In this section we will discuss primarily the different ways in which third parties can shape partners' strategic choices, such as by influencing partners' interpretations of the conflict, by providing approval or disapproval for strategic choices, and by providing or withholding necessary resources.

Conflict Interpretation

Several lines of research across different disciplines suggest that third parties can influence how opponents view the conflict (Black, 1993; Donohue, Lyles & Rogan, 1989; Mather & Yngvesson, 1981; Thomas, Schankster & Mathieu, 1994). For example, there is evidence that support and criticism by network members are related to the perceived legitimacy of partners' interests (Klein & Milardo, 1995).

The contribution of best friends to wives' "marriage work" (Oliker, 1989) illustrates the role of informal third parties in conflict interpretation. Marriage work denotes the active involvement of friends in efforts to "achieve or sustain the stability of a marriage or a sense of its adequacy" (Oliker, 1989, p. 123). Best friends helped with the marriage work in several ways. For example, they tried to make the wife see her husband in a rosier light, by generating positive feelings for him ("You know, he's probably feeling real insecure and angry", p. 125), ennobling him ("Doreen tells me, 'Jesse loves you'. And he's this and he's that. She tells me his fine points and puts me in good spirits about him", p. 126), and turning anger directed at the husband into a more "appropriate emotional response" (p. 126).

Anger is inappropriate because the purpose of marriage work is to sustain commitment to the marriage. With one exception, the third parties in Oliker's study helped women resolve "marital conflicts by capitulation or adaptation" (p. 129) rather than conflict engagement. Oliker mentions two reasons for this emphasis on unilateral accommodation. The first concerns the implications of wives' contentiousness on the level of marital interaction, "Taking combative stances after confirmatory discussions with friends, Nancy and others found they provoked husbands' rage and triggered a level of conflict they had not anticipated" (p. 132). The second concerns the implications of wives' contentiousness on the level of losing the economic support associated with marriage, "A majority of women stated flatly that their biggest problem if their marriage ended would be economic survival" (p. 139). Aware of the implications of contentious conflict strategies, third parties helped to interpret the conflict in terms that made accommodative strategies seem more appropriate. This marriage work, supported by best friends, illustrates again how strategic choices can be constrained by power differences between partners arising from the arrangement of intimate relationships.

Support for Strategic Choices

Third parties can also influence strategic choices by approving of and encouraging certain strategies. This type of third party influence is well documented in the realm of bargaining and negotiation, such as constituent pressure on negotiators to adopt a tough bargaining stance (Rubin & Brown, 1975). In a study of conflict strategies among young couples where partners were unmarried and the women, unlike those in Oliker's study, were not financially dependent on their partners, we found that those women who claimed support from their own network were less willing to compromise, and those women who claimed support from their partner's network were more willing to engage in contentious strategies (Klein & Milardo, 1995).

Another piece of evidence for the impact of approval by third parties comes from research on abusive peers (DeKeseredy, 1990a). Even if some forms of violence are detached from disagreements and are no longer conflict strategies in our definition (Johnson, 1995; Lloyd & Emery, 1994), we mention evidence on abusive peers because it is conceivable that aggressive and violent conflict strategies are shaped by third-party support. DeKeseredy (1990a) reviewed evidence suggesting that men who have frequent contact with abusive male friends are more likely to abuse their female partners than men who are not exposed to this contact (DeKeseredy, 1990b). The positive correlation between having abusive friends and being abusive, of course, can have different reasons. First of all, it is possible that abusive men prefer to associate with other abusive men and thus actively seek out peer approval of their strategic choices. Secondly, it is not clear to what extent abusive peers are influential because they model aggression and violence, because they approve of violent strategies, or because they fail to disapprove of them.

Nonetheless, the evidence on abusive peers illustrates how third parties can be implicated in partners' strategic choices. More specifically, it illustrates how third parties may contribute to the creation of aggressors. A related question is to what extent third parties contribute to the creation of victims (i.e. easy targets of abuse) by depriving one partner of the resources needed to prevent, avoid or retaliate against abuse.

Provision of Resources

Baumgartner (1993) cites several anthropological examples of how economic support (e.g., shelter) provided by a wife's family allows her to leave an abusive husband. The partisan support that grows out of strong ties between the wife and her family of origin in some cases includes retaliatory aggression against physical abuse by her husband (Baumgartner, 1993). Family also provide support through the provision of temporary housing. Kirkwood's (1993) study of women in the USA and UK who left their abusers found that over one-third of the group stayed with family or friends as one step in the process of escape (p. 93). Kirkwood and others have also argued for the central importance of the role of public agencies in providing information about available resources, temporary housing, and direct economic support during the transition from an abusive relationship to independence (Kirkwood, 1993, pp. 89–113; Dobash & Dobash, 1992).

TWO THEORETICAL PERSPECTIVES ON STRATEGIC CHOICE: SENSE-MAKING AND DIFFERENTIAL ADVANTAGE

This final section is guided by two questions about strategic choice: (1) Does our understanding of conflict strategies improve if we treat them as evidence of partners' sense-making activity?; (2) Does our understanding of conflict strategies improve if we treat them as evidence of differential advantage? Sense-making suggests that partners' strategic choices reflect the meaning they impose on interaction sequences (Duck, 1994a). Differential advantage suggests that partners' strategic choices reflect the specific constellation of interpersonal power that exists between partners at a given moment in their relationship (Gray-Little & Burks, 1983). In this section we weave the two questions together, as partners make sense of interaction within a context of power and utilize their resources in courses of action suggested by their interpretations (Noller, 1993).

Several authors across different disciplines have argued recently that the development of social relationships (Duck, 1994a), and more specifically the management of controversies and disagreements (Morley, 1992), can be understood as a process of continuous interpretation through which the protagonists make sense of each other and their relationship. Examples of sense-making (Duck, 1994a), or the construction of meaning, may be attributions of responsibility and blame (Fincham, Bradbury & Scott, 1990), relationship beliefs (Eidelson & Epstein, 1982), and account-making in relationships (Harvey, Weber & Orbuch, 1990).

A sense-making perspective can increase our understanding of conflict strategies in several ways. First, it draws attention to the processes through which partners interpret each other's behavior, such as attributions and accounts. Secondly, sense-making suggests that two partners can arrive at different interpretations, and thus draws attention to issues of perspective-taking and understanding (Acitelli, Douvan & Veroff, 1993). Finally, the notion of sense-making suggests that the course of conflict is contingent on any number of factors that influence the construction of meaning, such as cognitive factors in the processing of social relationships (see Miller & Read, 1991) or exposure to messages that influence the construction of meaning (see Fletcher & Kininmonth, 1991).

We think that a sense-making perspective can increase our understanding of strategic choice if we do not view the construction of meaning as an arbitrary, personal activity of equals who can construct and reconstruct meaning at will. We believe that we need to take into consideration that most strategic choices occur under conditions where one partner has some advantage over the other, whether it is temporary and minimal (e.g., asymmetrical conflict) or ongoing and profound (e.g., based upon differences in structural commitment to the relationship, or the threat and use of physical violence).

We use the term differential advantage rather than power in order to emphasize that the specific constellation of one's own interests, partner's behavior, age, third-party support, and additional resources, can change over time and benefit one partner today and the other tomorrow (Millar & Rogers, 1988). Although resources (Blood & Wolfe, 1960) and physical force (Frieze & McHugh, 1992) can freeze differential advantage into long-term, unequal power differences, this does not always happen. For instance, higher income does not always translate into more influence on decision-making (see Blumstein & Schwartz, 1991), neither does body strength always translate into getting one's way in a controversy. We use the term differential advantage to convey the idea that it is the specific constellation of self, partner, and third parties at a given point in time that shapes strategic choice, such as the structure of the conflict, the commitment to the relationship, third party support, and other resources.

Sense-making itself may be shaped by the particular constellation among partners and third parties, because when we talk about sense-making we can ask to whom things need to make sense and who is the audience for which we create meaning. If strategic choices need to make sense only to the self, then a partner has more freedom in constructing meaning than when strategic choices need to make sense to the partner or third parties. For example, if Melissa tries to make her partner take out the garbage every week, she can explain this to herself in whatever way pleases her most ("I enjoy making other people take out the garbage"). She probably has different explanations for her partner ("I always do the dishes, so you could take care of the garbage"), and maybe even for different third parties (for her mother: "You have to be tight with men, otherwise they dump all chores on you, like Daddy used to"; and for her female friends: "Jack and I really believe in equality in relationships, and we try to split household chores equally").

We need to consider the audience to which sense-making is directed. We need also to keep in mind that audiences are often more than passive recipients of sense-making. One's personal realities are socially constructed, in collaboration with a network of contemporaries, although both the individual and the network draw upon their personal and cultural stock of knowledge for the frameworks that help them to make sense of relationship events (Berger & Luckman, 1966; Schutz & Luckman, 1973). This network of friends, relatives, acquaintances and professionals with whom one consults regarding one's relationship can be quite active participants in the sense-making process (Johnson, 1982, pp. 64–73). Thus, while a batterer may insist that he hits his partner only because she asks for it, the counselor and support group at the local women's shelter may offer quite a different interpretive structure (Pence & Paymar, 1993). Kirkwood (1993, pp. 76–78) provides the following example: "One woman explained how, despite the loss of most friends and the accompanying sense of intense isolation, one friend in particular continued to maintain close contact. She planned meetings with this woman nearly every day, away from the apartment she shared with her abuser. Most of their meetings were spent with the friend simply listening to the woman, although at times, she would make pertinent comments on how an event might be related to specific feelings voiced by the woman. Over time, the woman began to trust this friend and, together, they explored her relationship and its impact".

Although the self as the audience of sense-making may allow considerable freedom, it can impose limits, such as when strategic choices are made in the service of saving face (Ting-Toomey et al., 1991) or preserving the integrity of the self (Bartky, 1990). The partner as the audience can impose other limits on sense-making. For example, partners can be unable to understand what we mean (Kelley, 1979; Noller & Ruzzene, 1991; Sillars, Folwell, Hill, Maki, Hurst & Casano, 1994) or unwilling to share in our experience (Harber & Pennebaker (1992). Partners and third parties as audiences can try to prescribe what they consider acceptable sense-making, for example by defining what are "rational" and "irrational" accounts for relationship problems. Partners and third parties can confront us with the limits of culturally acceptable accounts for strategic choices. A violent husband will find it easier to explain his wife-battering to his abusive peers than to the staff of the local women's shelter. More generally, it is easier to justify aggressive strategic choices to an audience who believe that escalation of conflict into physical violence is "normal" (Harris, Gergen & Lannamann, 1986), or that anger "triggers" violent outbursts (Averill, 1993; Tavris, 1982) than to an audience who objects to these beliefs.

Future research needs to examine to what extent sense-making and differential advantage explanations are useful in understanding either retrospective accounts of strategic choice or on-going strategic choices. A sense-making perspective may be particularly sensitive to the development of retrospective accounts of couple conflict (e.g., Buehlman, Gottman & Katz, 1992), whereas a differential advantage perspective may be sensitive to the development of ongoing choices in relationships. Of course, both aspects, sense-making and differential advantage, may work together so that partners make some choices based on differential advantage and then look back and interpret their choices in light of a comprehensive organizing scheme. Kirkwood (1993, p. 114), for example, speaks of the "long-term reconstruction of their identity and self-esteem . . . [and] continued recognition and rejection of the damaging messages about themselves instilled by their abusers" that is an important part of the process of healing that follows the end of an abusive relationship. This process is one example of the continued interpretation of one's biography that has long been a theme of phenomenological sociology (Travisano, 1970).

Hopper (1993) concluded from his study of divorce rhetoric that "divorce may be a more disorganized and more random unfolding of events" than we presume (p. 811). Prior to the divorce both spouses reported "similar feelings of indecision and ambivalence. They described pain, dissatisfaction, and feelings of being trapped; at the same time, they described good things that they did not want to forgo." (Hopper, 1993, p. 806). As soon as one spouse had announced the decision to divorce (which we might add could have been made on the basis of differential advantage), spouses were cast into the roles of initiator and non-initiator and from that point on their accounts differed systematically, with initiators' rhetoric drawing from the vocabulary of change and non-initiators' rhetoric drawing from the vocabulary of commitment. It is as if the declaration of initiator had flipped an ambivalent and disturbing—chaotic—experience into a coherent and meaningful one. Of course, these chaotic experiences are not interpreted in isolation. Such dramatic experiences cry out for interpretation (Berger, 1963, pp. 147–163) that is constructed in concert with others (Brown et al., 1976).

Future research needs to address under what conditions sense-making improves or impedes conflict management. For instance, from a sense-making perspective we would argue that distressed couples get caught in negative exchanges because they interpret each other's behaviors in consistently negative terms, whereas non-distressed couples are able to exit negative exchanges because they interpret each other's behaviors in positive terms (Fincham, Bradbury & Scott, 1990). Both negative–negative and negative–positive exchanges could be "reactive contingencies" (Jones & Gerard, 1967, pp. 505–513), in which the behavior of one partner can be predicted from the behavior of the other partner. However, the available evidence suggests that in non-distressed couples, one partner's behavior is not as contingent on the other's as in distressed couples (Gottman, 1994, pp. 63–64). We wonder whether these "unpredictable" couples move from a reactive to a "pseudocontingency" (in which partners' actions are not contingent on the other's behavior; Jones & Gerard, 1967, pp. 505–513) because they temporarily stop making sense of each other. The question is whether sense-making can backfire if partners impose meanings on each other's behaviors that lead them into deadlock, when they would be better off assuming occasional "senselessness" in their exchanges.

SUMMARY AND CONCLUSION

Many couple conflicts arise from incompatible goals and interests. To achieve their goals, partners engage in a variety of conflict-management strategies, ranging from problem-solving and compromise, to unilateral accommodation and the use of insults, threats and physical force. In this chapter we discussed factors that shape partners' choices among different strategies. Starting with the dual-concern model we explored how egoistic and altruistic motivations affect strategic choice. Using evidence on the demand/withdraw pattern we tried to show how strategic choices may result from interactions between individual motivations and features of partners' social contexts such as the structure of conflict.

We used evidence on negative reciprocity and physical violence among spouses to further illustrate how seemingly personal choices are made within the context of social constraints, such as women's economic dependence on marriage. A different aspect of the social context of partners' strategic choices are third parties, such as family, friends, and professionals who can influence couple conflict by interpreting the controversial issues, supporting strategic choices, and providing or withholding necessary resources. From a theoretical perspective the evidence on strategic choice in couple conflict speaks to the importance of partners' sense-making in the context of differential power and unequal resources.

We believe that the concept of strategic choice provides a fruitful starting point for our understanding of couples' conflict-management. However, we believe that strategic choices cannot be understood as individual phenomena. Rather, it is necessary to pay attention to the features of partners' social contexts that shape and constrain their options. In a similar vein, Rubin, Pruitt & Kim (1994) have argued that although concern motivates strategic choice, in order for strategies to be adopted, they need to be seen as feasible. We conclude from our review that the feasibility of conflict management options in couple conflict depends on several aspects of each partner's social context: the other partner, culturally available interpretation schemes, third parties, and the precise configuration of interpersonal, social and economic power.

Chapter 21

Work and Family from a Dyadic Perspective: Variations in Inequality

Ann C. Crouter
and
Heather Helms-Erikson
Pennsylvania State University, University Park, PA, USA

Employed men and women spend a large portion of their adult lives on the job. On work days, they head off to factories, mines, offices, hospitals, schools and stores where they become engaged in activities that often have profound effects on their own psychological development, as well as on their family roles and relationships (Crouter & McHale, 1993).

For dual-earner families, the work–family interface is particularly complex because there are two sets of workplace influences to consider: his and hers. Husbands and wives in dual-earner families each bring to the family their own work-related histories and current work experiences that must be understood in combination with those of their partner. Understanding the impact of work on family relationships in dual-earner families requires attention both to the separate, work-related experiences of each spouse and to the relative experiences of a wife and her husband (Brayfield, 1992). It requires conceptualizing the work–family interface from the perspective of the dyad.

A dyadic perspective on the impact of work on family relationships underscores differences in the circumstances of paid employment for men and women. The work world is highly stratified by gender. Men and women generally work in different occupations, with women clustered in a narrow range of jobs that are relatively poorly paid and offer few chances for advancement (England & McCreary, 1987). Even when men and women are found in the same occupation,

Handbook of Personal Relationships, 2nd edn. Edited by Steve Duck.
© 1997 John Wiley & Sons Ltd.

they tend to be clustered in different lines of work, or different types of firms, within that occupation (Bielby & Baron, 1984).

England & McCreary (1987) present four major factors underlying occupational segregation: gender role socialization in childhood and adolescence, leading to differential educational choices and career aspirations on the part of men and women; differences in the extent to which men and women invest in their own "human capital", such as education and job training; discrimination against women in hiring, placement, and promotion; and differences in the structured mobility ladders within occupations. One clear correlate of gender segregation in the workplace is income inequality; on average, employed women make 71 cents for every dollar earned by men (U.S. Bureau of the Census, 1992).

There are other important differences in the work-related experiences of wives and husbands, some of which stem from the fact that wives generally garner fewer resources from their jobs than do their husbands, and hence may have less bargaining power in the context of family decision-making. Women are more likely than men to leave a job and to move to a new location in response to a job opportunity for their spouse (Shihadeh, 1991). Women are more likely to take time off at the birth of a child (Ferber, O'Farrell & Allen, 1991) and to be absent from work when children are sick than are men (Fernandez, 1986). Even in Sweden, a country that has sought to promote equality between men and women, men are much less likely than women to take advantage of the generous parental leave benefits offered to new parents (Haas, 1992).

What does the fact that men and women have quite divergent occupational worlds mean for dual-earner couples? On average, husbands and wives have unequal access to work-related resources such as income and prestige. Other work conditions that are important influences on adults' psychosocial functioning—such as occupational self-direction, authority and job complexity—are also likely to be unequal, on average, for a given husband and wife in a dual-earner family. But the term "on average" masks considerable variability across families in the extent to which husbands and wives experience similar vs. different work worlds. In many families, the occupational conditions of husbands and wives are so different that Perry-Jenkins & Folk (1994) have argued that "social class" is more accurately conceptualized and measured as an individual-level variable than as a family-level condition; in other families, spouses' experiences on the job are quite similar.

The circumstances that give rise to systematic differences in husbands' and wives' work experiences—and the implications of these "variations in inequality" for family roles and relationships—deserve to be a focus of study for the next generation of research on work and family (Crouter & McHale, 1994a, 1994b). This area of study can be examined from several theoretical perspectives. A focus on within-couple variability in the experience of work is consistent with a feminist perspective on the family because it emphasizes that the family is not "a unitary whole.... (with) a single class position, standard of living, and set of interests" (Ferree, 1990, p. 867). It is also consistent with the notion of the family as "a non-shared environment". This construct has emerged from research in behavioral genetics to help to explain why siblings growing up "in the same family" are so different from one another (Dunn & Plomin, 1990), but it also nicely captures the dramatic differences in the work and family lives of many wives and husbands.

In this chapter, we consider three dimensions of work experience and their implications for relationships in dual-earner families. In reviewing the literature in each area, we take a dyadic perspective which recognizes that, in dual-earner families, the implications of one spouse's experiences at work can be understood only in relation to the partner's work experiences. The first dimension that we examine is spouses' access to work-related resources such as income and occupational prestige. In social exchange terms, a wife's resources, relative to those contributed by her husband, are one determinant of her power in the marriage. Most research in this area has focused on domestic work and has asked whether husbands are likely to perform a greater share of household work when their wives bring in a larger share of resources from work. Work status, income and prestige tell only part of the story, however; it is also important to understand how husbands and wives think and feel about work and family roles. The second occupational condition we consider is job complexity and the extent to which work encourages adults to value self-direction for themselves and others. There is a rich body of sociological literature that has demonstrated that adults are socialized by the work that they do (Kohn, 1977; Kohn & Schooler, 1983; Mortimer, Lorence & Kumka, 1986; Parcel & Menaghan, 1994). Men and women in jobs that offer opportunities to be self-directed and provide complex, challenging activities become intellectually better able to deal with complexity and more apt to create complex, stimulating environments for themselves and their children (Kohn & Schooler, 1983; Parcel & Menaghan, 1994). A dyadic perspective addresses the question: what implications does this process of work socialization have for families when husbands and wives have similar—or different—levels of access to complex, self-directed work? The third work condition of interest has to do with short-term work stressors and overloads, the daily work-related tensions and pressures that may spill over into family life. Here, a dyadic perspective draws attention to what we know about these processes for men and for women, and whether husbands and wives respond in the same way to their spouse's experience of day-to-day stress on the job.

HUSBAND–WIFE DIFFERENCES IN WORK-RELATED RESOURCES

We begin by considering the connections between husbands' and wives' access to work-related resources and their family roles and relationships. Most of the research in this area has focused on the division of housework, specifically the conditions under which men assume more responsibility for performing the household tasks that have been traditionally handled by women, such as cooking, cleaning and laundry. The other role that has received attention is that of provider or breadwinner. As we will show, this field has evolved in interesting directions, as studies have gradually taken more complex and differentiated approaches to the study of family roles.

Before considering how family roles may be affected by spouses' access to work-related resources, it is important to understand what we mean by the term "role". Peplau (1983) defines a role as a consistent pattern of individual activity composed of behavior, cognition and affect. This pattern of activity develops in the context of a relationship with one or more other people and is influenced not only by expectations of the individuals involved but also by cultural norms and partners' shared relationship goals.

All three components of roles—behavior, cognition and affect—must be considered in order to understand how the differential resources of wives and husbands are linked to how couples structure the homemaker and provider roles. Behavioral patterns refer to events and activities. Part of the provider role, for example, involves working at a paid job. Role behavior also refers to the distribution of activities between partners in a relationship, as in the way a husband and wife divide household tasks. The cognitive domain involves how spouses think about and ascribe meaning to their family roles. Wives and husbands, for example, develop notions of "fairness" that influence their level of involvement in family work (Thompson, 1991). Finally, affect accompanies roles. Emotional experiences are an important part of roles in close relationships, emerging not only as a response to behavior but also prompting behavior. These three components of roles (i.e., behavior, cognition and affect) provide a useful way to organize the literature on how husbands' and wives' differential work-related resources influence family roles.

Until recently, far more attention was given to the behavioral than to the cognitive and emotional components of family roles. For many years, researchers assumed that as women entered the paid labor force in greater numbers, men would respond by increasing their level of behavioral involvement in unpaid family work. This logic was consistent with the principles of social exchange theory; the assumption was that women would gain new resources through paid employment with which to bargain for greater assistance with family work. However, time diary studies conducted in the 1970s revealed that husbands did *not* participate in more housework and child care when their wives worked outside the home (Meissner et al., 1975; Robinson, 1977; Walker & Woods, 1976); men in dual-earner families performed proportionally more housework than their single-earner counterparts only because their wives decreased their level of involvement in housework when employed outside the home. More recent studies confirm this pattern; however, they also stress the *variability* across dual-earner families in the way wives and husbands divide family work (Ferree, 1991). Understanding the conditions under which wives and husbands divide housework more or less equally requires attention not only to spouses' work status, but to the absolute and relative levels of resources that each partner acquires on the job, as well as to partners' attitudes, cognitions and feelings about work and family roles.

Research addressing the effects of absolute earnings and occupational prestige on husbands' and wives' family work has yielded mixed findings. Results from several studies indicate that husbands' and wives' incomes are important determinants of the division of family work (Berk & Berk, 1978; Kamo, 1988; Maret & Finlay, 1984); yet other findings reveal weak or no effects for income on how family work is allocated between spouses (Berardo, Shehan & Leslie, 1987; Coverman & Sheley, 1986). Likewise, several researchers have found that spouses' job prestige is not related to spouses' division of labor (Coverman, 1985; Berardo, Shehan & Leslie, 1987), while others have found husbands' relative share of housework to be related to their job prestige (Berk & Berk, 1978).

A dyadic perspective on work-related resources draws attention to the "gap" in work-related resources of wives relative to their husbands and how these measures may interact with gender (Ericksen, Yancey & Ericksen, 1979; Ferree, 1988; Ross, 1987). For example, Ross (1987) demonstrated that the more husbands earn relative to their wives, the less the husbands proportionally contribute to family work. Similarly, McHale & Crouter (1992) found that greater income and prestige discrepancies favoring husbands were associated with a more traditional division of housework.

Brayfield's (1992) study of Canadian couples reveals the importance of considering both absolute *and* relative work-related resources. In her study, wives at all income levels were found to "benefit" from a relative income advantage over their husbands, meaning that the more income wives earned relative to their husbands, the fewer female-typed household tasks wives performed. Similarly, husbands performed fewer female-typed tasks when they earned more than their wives. For husbands, however, the effect of the relative income advantage depended on husbands' absolute income. At the lower end of the income distribution, the relative income advantage was strongly connected to husbands' performing fewer tasks. At the upper end, however, the association was attenuated. Brayfield speculates that the relative advantage in income did not "benefit" high-income men as much as low-income men because men at the upper end of the income distribution tend to be better educated and to favor a more egalitarian division of labor. Brayfield's interpretation of her results illustrates the importance of examining role-related attitudes and cognitions in conjunction with behavior, data that were not available in her data set.

In recent years, there has been a "very substantial and continuing transformation of sex role attitudes in the USA" (Thornton, 1989, p. 875); men and women have generally become more egalitarian in their attitudes and expectations about family roles (Thornton, 1989). Underlying this demographic shift is considerable variability in attitudes across individuals, as well as differences between families in husbands' and wives' level of consensus on sex role attitudes. The way wives and husbands think about and define their work and family roles plays an important part in whether and how wives utilize power obtained from job earnings and prestige. Furthermore, the convergence of behavior and attitudes around work and family roles is linked to partners' subjective evaluations of their marital relationships.

The distinction between role enactment (i.e., behavior) and cognitions or attitudes is apparent in research on the role of provider or breadwinner. As Hood (1986) explained: "Provider roles are determined not only by incomes but also by each spouse's expectations of the other as a provider as well as each spouse's role attachments—that is, the investment one has in one's present role" (p. 354). Although partners in dual-earner families both have incomes and thus can provide financial resources for the family, paid work often holds different meanings for husbands and wives. For example, even though most married women work outside the home and their earnings account for at least 30% of the family income on average, most wives are not assuming the provider role, neither are husbands relinquishing breadwinning or the psychological responsibility to provide (Haas, 1986; Hood, 1986).

Hood (1986) used qualitative interviews with husbands and wives in dual-earner families to identify three types of providers. Main/secondary providers view the husband as responsible for providing for the family and the wife as primarily responsible for homemaking; the wife's income is seen as helpful, rather than necessary. In contrast, co-providers acknowledge the importance of both spouses' incomes to the family's financial stability and see both partners as responsible for providing. Finally, ambivalent co-providers are dependent on both partners' incomes but are unwilling to acknowledge the importance of the wife's role as a provider. Hood (1986) offered a revealing quote from an ambivalent co-provider husband:

> Like now, we just use her paycheck to pay the house payments. So that's about all we do with hers . . . just pay the house payments. So that's a whole lot of money I don't have to worry about (p. 355).

Provider-role attitudes are linked to husbands' and wives' behavior in the home. Examining couples in which both husbands and wives worked full-time, Perry-Jenkins & Crouter (1990) found that husbands' provider-role attitudes were associated with their involvement in family work; husbands ascribing to a main/secondary provider orientation were less involved in traditionally feminine household tasks than either ambivalent co-providers or co-providers. Furthermore, involvement in household tasks had different implications for men's marital satisfaction depending upon their provider role attitudes. Husbands who reported the greatest marital satisfaction were main/secondary providers who performed relatively few household tasks and co-providers who shared household task more equally with their wives. The combination of being highly involved in housework, yet holding ambivalent coprovider attitudes, was linked to lower levels of marital satisfaction for husbands.

Ferree (1987) provides converging evidence for the importance of providing or breadwinning from the perspective of wives. She found that women who defined themselves as breadwinners thought their husbands should contribute more to family work. This finding was particularly true for working-class wives for whom earning money and assuming the breadwinner role led to a willingness to insist on more help with housework from husbands. Ferree suggests that it is not how much paid work wives perform, but rather what a wife's work means to the family that empowers wives to make greater demands on their husbands.

Thompson (1991) argues that the connections between spouses' paid work and family work cannot be understood without reference to their ideas about "fairness". Surprisingly, although most wives perform a greater proportion of household tasks than their husbands, only a small number of wives in dual-earner families view the division of family work as unfair (Thompson & Walker, 1989). Thompson suggests that husbands and wives assess fairness in their relationship based on how much each spouse values particular family chores, how well and how often they perform tasks as compared to other husbands and wives, and how well they can justify not performing certain tasks. Blair & Johnson (1992) note that the symbolic meaning of household tasks as an act of caring is an important correlate of fairness; women who feel that their contribution to housework is appreciated see the division of labor as more fair.

Concerns about lack of fairness can lead to low marital satisfaction and higher levels of conflict between spouses (Blair, 1993; Perry-Jenkins & Folk, 1994; Wilkie, Ratcliff & Ferree, 1992). For example, Wilkie, Ratcliff & Ferree (1992) found that it was not partners' differences in the amount of domestic or paid work that determined marital satisfaction; rather, it was their different expectations about and the meanings they ascribed to the division of paid and unpaid work that predicted marital satisfaction. Blair (1993) found that wives' assessment of inequity in their marriages was the strongest predictor of both husbands' and wives' perceptions of marital conflict, a theme echoed by Perry-Jenkins & Folk's (1994) analyses of middle-class wives' perceptions of fairness and their reports of marital conflict. Finally, McHale & Crouter (1992) found that wives with relatively non-traditional sex-role attitudes—who nonetheless were experiencing a more traditional division of family work—reported lower marital quality, less marital satisfaction and greater marital conflict, in comparison both to their own husbands and to other women. The same pattern held true for husbands who espoused traditional sex-role attitudes but were sharing family work more equally with their wives.

In sum, the relative and absolute resources that husbands and wives each bring from work to the family help to determine the way in which they divide family work. Earning similar or greater income than their husbands and achieving similar or greater occupational status helps wives to bargain for more involvement in housework on the part of their partners. But work-related resources reveal only a limited part of the picture. The division of labor also depends upon husbands' and wives' attitudes and cognitions about roles, including whether or not they have assumed the responsibility to be a provider or breadwinner. Finally, partners' feelings of dissatisfaction with the relationship are evoked when role behavior and attitudes are at odds and partners feel that their current arrangement is not fair.

SPOUSAL INEQUALITY IN WORK COMPLEXITY

We began our review by focusing on income and prestige because there is ample evidence that the extent of resources contributed to the family by wives vs. their husbands is linked to the division of family work and to relationship dynamics. A less obvious occupational "resource" has to do with the *nature* of the work that men and women perform, specifically the complexity of the work and the extent to which it offers the worker opportunities to be independent and self-directed. While considerable research has been conducted in this area, attention to the occupational complexity experienced by husbands and wives in the same family is rare (see Parcel & Menaghan, 1994).

The focus on occupational complexity and self-direction grew out of Kohn's classic study on social class in relation to parental values and child-rearing strategies (Kohn 1969, 1977; Kohn & Schooler, 1983). Basing his conclusions on a national survey of over 3000 employed men, Kohn argued that men in working-class jobs come to value conformity and obedience in their children because they recognize that these are the qualities needed to be successful in a working-class world, while their counterparts in middle-class occupations come to value self-direction and independence for the same reason. As Kohn explained in *Class and Conformity* (1977):

> Members of different social classes, by virtue of enjoying (or suffering) different conditions of life, come to see the world differently—to develop different conceptions of social reality, different aspirations and hopes and fears, different "conceptions of the desirable" (p. 7).

In later work, Kohn and his colleagues focused on three occupational conditions that determine how self-directed one can be in one's work and thus lie at the heart of what has come to be understood as social class: freedom from close supervision, a non-routinized flow of work, and substantively complex work. The substantive complexity of work has received the most attention and is most germane to the focus of this chapter.

Using 10-year longitudinal follow-up data on their national sample of employed men, Kohn and his colleagues demonstrated that having a job characterized by substantive complexity influences men's views of the world. That is, over time, men come to value self-direction for themselves and for others, and they become more "intellectually flexible", meaning that they are better able to manipulate ideas and to see multiple sides of an issue (Kohn & Schooler, 1983). Moreover, the substantive complexity of work, over time, promotes a more intellectual choice of leisure activities, "evidence that people generalize directly from job experience to the activities they perform in their leisure time" (Miller &

Kohn, 1983, p. 240). Kohn and his colleagues were able to use their longitudinal data to explore whether the causal arrow also runs the other way, that is from intellectual flexibility and the intellectuality of leisure to substantive complexity on the job. Indeed, these processes exist, but they are generally lagged rather than contemporaneous, meaning that, over time, men modify their jobs or leave them for other jobs that are more consistent with their intellectual functioning. Despite these selection effects, strong processes are apparent that indicate that jobs socialize people in ways that have implications for personality and behavior off the job.

Kohn and his colleagues did not take their line of reasoning in the direction of considering the implications of occupational self-direction for family relationships, but others have. Pioneers in this area are Parcel & Menaghan (1994) who have utilized the National Longitudinal Survey of Youth to explore, with longitudinal data, the implications of parental work conditions for the kinds of home environments that parents establish for their young children and, in turn, for children's psychological functioning. Parcel & Menaghan document that, controlling for education, age, intelligence, income and other potential confounding variables, mothers employed in jobs characterized by greater substantive complexity create more stimulating home environments for their children. Most interesting from a dyadic perspective, although father's job complexity in and of itself is not related to the home environment, are the positive effects of high maternal occupational complexity that are most apparent when the father in the family is employed in a job that is low on complexity. A theme in Parcel & Menaghan's research is that the effects of one parent's working conditions depend upon those of the other parent.

Parcel & Menaghan's work is rife with interesting interaction effects that illustrate the complexity of work–family linkages from a dyadic perspective. For example, in an examination of the correlates of problem behavior in young children, they report that the effect of a mother quitting work and becoming a homemaker depends to a large extent on the nature of the paid work that she was performing. Quitting work has the positive effect of reducing subsequent behavior problems in the child only if the mother's job had been characterized by low occupational complexity or very long hours. Similarly, mothers with higher levels of intellectual ability tended to have children with greater verbal facility, but this association was enhanced when mothers worked in jobs characterized by complexity. Parcel & Menaghan argue that complex jobs reinforce and strengthen mothers' intellectual skills in ways that pay off for their children's learning.

Occupational complexity is not always uniformly positive in its effects, however. Parcel & Menaghan, again demonstrating sensitivity to the importance of considering husband–wife combinations of work conditions, report that jobs high in complexity tend to absorb time and energy and that this can be problematic for children's psychosocial functioning under certain conditions: when parents have large numbers of children, when they are adjusting to a recent birth, or when both parents in the family face the demands of highly complex jobs.

Parcel & Menaghan's research indicates that "having a parent in a complex job can be a resource for children in that it sets a high level of expectation regarding self-direction and intellectual flexibility, qualities that should increase children's socioc-eonomic well-being as they mature" (1994, p. 14). The day-to-day experience of work socializes parents to have certain values regarding self-direction and either provides opportunities to practice intellectual and social skills that in turn can be applied to childrearing or impedes such opportunities and skills. But what of the marital relationship? Does the extent to which husbands and wives have access to complex and self-directed jobs have any implications for their marital relations?

Although few studies have explored the links between spouses' access to occupational self-direction and the marital relationship, there is ample evidence that this is an area well worth greater attention. Brayfield's (1992) analysis of Canadian data tested the idea, based on social exchange theory, that "husbands' and wives' employment characteristics influence the balance of power over the distribution of feminine-typed (household) tasks" (p. 20). Brayfield examined not only husbands' and wives' relative and absolute incomes, but also their levels of workplace authority, reasoning that, "Power on the job may influence power in the family" (p. 21). She found that women with greater workplace authority performed fewer household chores, especially if they had greater authority on their job than their husband had on his job. This effect was most pronounced for women at higher levels of authority.

The effects of relative access on the part of husbands and wives to jobs that encourage self-direction and provide complex, interesting work may be most apparent in situations in which the workplace—or the job—is undergoing a fundamental change in the way that it is organized. Crouter (1984a) conducted qualitative research in a manufacturing plant that was experimenting with "participative approaches to management". Blue collar workers on the factory floor were organized into work teams that were given an unusual level of responsibility for hiring and firing, quality control and inventory management. The manufacturing and assembly work was also reorganized so that teams were responsible for large, complex tasks, such as assembling an entire engine. Workers were paid on the basis of skill level, rather than seniority, and were encouraged to rotate through new tasks and to take training courses in order to master new skills quickly. The result of all of these changes was a push for self-directed, complex work at the blue collar level.

Open-ended interviews were conducted with men and women in a variety of types of work teams. The most striking comments related to the marital relationship came from women in blue collar manufacturing and assembly teams. They described a complex process in which the challenges of participative work had pushed them to develop new skills and abilities, a process they described as both stimulating and stressful. As a result of these experiences, they reported feeling a new sense of self-confidence and self-efficacy, as well as a strong feeling of loyalty and commitment to fellow team members. Several women noted, however, that their husbands resented their new skills and felt threatened by their new levels of self-confidence. These men worked in traditionally managed factories in the same community and were denied the same opportunities for personal growth. As one female worker explained:

> My husband got to the point where he didn't want to hear about my work. He's a little threatened by my learning new things . . . He felt like he was stupid and I was smart, and he wanted to keep up with me (Crouter, 1984a, p. 80).

Differences in husbands' and wives' feelings of self-esteem and competence may underlie power dynamics in the marriage. Kompter (1989) argued that gender differences in perceptions of self and spouse "may be regarded as invisible power mechanisms because they confirm and justify power inequality ideologically, unintentionally, and often unconsciously" (p. 207). In Kompter's semi-structured interviews with Dutch, dual-earner, working- and middle-class couples, wives expressed less self-esteem than did men and saw themselves as less competent than their husbands. Husbands saw themselves as more competent than their wives, particularly when their wives were homemakers. As Kompter explains:

> The husbands' greater self-esteem gave them greater marital bargaining power . . . The power effect is invisible because the apparent naturalness of the assumed differences in personality traits prevents wives and husbands from acknowledging it" (Kompter, 1989, p. 208).

Kompter's argument reveals why the husbands of blue collar women who were engaged in highly demanding participative work felt threatened. It also illuminates why male employees in the same factory never described their wives as feeling threatened by their access to complex, self-directed work; those wives probably saw their husbands' growing sense of competence and self-esteem as expected and natural. These findings underscore themes that emerged earlier in our review of the literature on husbands' and wives' differential access to work-related resources. Again we see that differences in spouses' access to complex, self-directed work must be examined in light of their cognitive interpretations of these differences. Moreover, these cognitive schemata are gendered. For many couples, it may be "natural" for husbands to have jobs that provide more opportunities to exercise self-direction than their wife's job provides; when the situation is reversed, however, and the wife is given an opportunity to develop on the job that exceeds that of her husband, the situation is seen as unusual and, sometimes, as a source of resentment.

THE IMPACT OF DAILY WORK STRESS ON HUSBANDS AND WIVES

Thus far, we have written about husbands' and wives' employment as if it were an emotionally neutral one. We have emphasized the importance of the differential resources garnered by husbands and wives through their jobs, and we have explored the psychological impact of substantively complex, self-directed work. Regardless of the kinds of jobs that men and women hold—and the resources they receive for performing that work—there is an emotional tone underlying the work experience that has implications for relationships in the family. Over the last decade, a small body of carefully conducted, methodologically sophisticated research has emerged that examines, on a day-to-day basis, whether—and how—fluctuations in stress and strain on the job affect interactions at home. None of these studies has examined this issue from the perspective of the husband–wife dyad, a focus that would require sensitivity to the combination of work-based stressors experienced by the two partners on a given day. But several studies have focused on how one partner's daily work stress is linked to the other partner's affect or behavior in the family, and the literature has consistently compared men's and women's emotional lives at work and at home, as well as the reactivity of men vs. women to short-term stressors.

With an interest in the contextual conditions surrounding family members' experience of emotions, Larson & Richards (1994) collected data on mothers, fathers and their adolescent offspring using the "experience sampling method", an approach in which family members carried electronic beepers throughout the day and were paged at random moments. When paged, they completed brief questionnaires about their activities, companions and emotional states. Larson & Richards' data on the contrasting moods of mothers and fathers at work and at home underscore how differently men and women perceive and experience these contexts. Employed wives recorded their most positive moods while at work; indeed, wives' emotions were generally more positive than were husbands' when they were paged on the job. Wives, however, experienced an emotional decline at home during the evening hours which were filled with housework and child care (see also Wells, 1988). Husbands, on the other hand, recorded their most negative emotions in the workplace; at home, their moods lightened, in part because non-work time provided a source of leisure for them. Even when men performed housework or child care, however, their moods during these tasks were more positive than was the case for their wives when they performed the same activities. Larson & Richards (1994) propose that housework and child care elicit a more positive reaction from husbands than wives because it is seen as *voluntary* work by husbands. Men get involved when they are "in the mood", and their efforts are noted and appreciated by wives (see also Thompson, 1991).

What are the kinds of events at work or at home that elicit emotional reactions? Bolger et al. (1989) asked 166 married couples to complete a daily diary for 42 consecutive days. The diary consisted of a short questionnaire about a variety of daily stressors , including the experience of "overloads" and "tensions or arguments" both at work and at home. In the analyses of these data, "day" was treated as the unit of analysis, and controls were entered to hold constant individual differences that were stable across days; thus, the analyses focused on intra-individual variability in the experience of stressors across days. Analyses of work-to-home spillover of stress revealed that, on days when husbands experienced an argument at work with a co-worker or supervisor, they came home and engaged in more arguments with their wives. The pattern was similar—although not statistically significant—when wives experienced arguments at work. On days when husbands experienced "overloads" at work (meaning having to do a lot of work), they performed less work at home; on those stressful days, their wives stepped in and performed more work at home. The parallel pattern did not occur, however; when wives experienced overloads at work they too performed less work at home, but their husbands did not step in and perform more. Bolger et al. (1989) summarize these data as follows:

> Thus, in terms of coping with a contagion of role overload from the workplace into the home, the most appropriate unit of analysis is clearly the marital dyad, with wives, in particular, acting as buffers for their husbands, protecting them from excessive accumulation of role demands (p. 181).

Bolger and his colleagues offer this finding as one possible explanation for the fact that marriage has been found to benefit the emotional health of men more than that of women (Kessler & McRae, 1982). Building on the argument we have developed in this chapter, we would argue that this "asymmetry in the buffering effect" (Bolger et al., 1989, p. 182) mirrors the power dynamic in the marriage. Future research should explore the hypothesis that wives are more likely to take on the buffering role—and husbands less likely to do so—when wives are disadvantaged, relative to their husbands, in the extent to which their work provides income and prestige, as well as substantive complexity, encouragement of self-direction and authority.

How are children influenced by daily fluctuations in their parents' experiences of stress and work? Bolger et al.'s study examined arguments with spouse and arguments with children separately and found no significant associations between work overload or work arguments and subsequent arguments with children. Parents may generally be able to buffer their children from these effects.

One of the mechanisms through which children may be buffered from the spillover of negative work experiences is emotional and behavioral withdrawal. Repetti & Wood (1994) examined this issue using an ingenious sampling strategy. To ensure that mothers' moods at the end of the work day were elicited by work experiences, and not by a long commute, errands or other intervening experiences, Repetti & Wood (1994) identified their sample through a work-site child care center; all mothers picked their children up immediately at the end of their work shift. Using mood data collected at the end of the work shift and self-report and observational data collected in the first minutes of the mother–child reunion at the day care center, Repetti & Wood found that mothers of preschoolers were much more likely to withdraw from their children, both emotionally and behaviorally, on days during which they had experienced either overloads or negative interpersonal interactions at work. Stress on the job generally was not followed by aversive mother–child interaction. Indeed, Repetti & Wood found some evidence in the observational component of their study that mothers were actually somewhat more patient with their children after high-stress work days, a pattern they interpret as part of emotional and behavioral withdrawal. The extent to which mothers were able to refrain from engaging in negative interaction depended, however, on the mother's own general level of psychosocial functioning. Mothers characterized as high on Type A behavior were less able to refrain from interacting negatively with their children than were mothers with low scores on that measure.

The finding that an inclination toward Type A behavior moderates the relationship between work stress and maternal negativity echoes an earlier study by Repetti (1994) of fathers who were employed as air traffic controllers, an occupation that is characterized by high day-to-day variability in stress. On high-stress days, traffic controllers were less engaged emotionally and behaviorally with their school-age children. Despite this pattern of withdrawal, however, the air traffic controllers also reported that they reacted more angrily and used more discipline on high-stress days. Repetti & Wood (1994) offer the hypothesis that "negative spillover responses occur primarily under background conditions of chronically high-stress, such as among mothers whose children are difficult to manage . . . or mothers who are high in Type A or depression . . . or fathers in very demanding occupations . . ." (p. 32).

In comparison to studies on spouses' access to work-related resources or to research on occupational complexity, the literature on short-term stress in relation to family interaction is notable for its focus on day-to-day variability. These labor-intensive studies generally involve small samples but precise temporal sequencing of the experience of a stressor at work and subsequent interaction in the home. They could benefit, however, from including spouses' attitudes and cognitions about work and family in their designs. Exploring the extent to which husbands and wives monitor their partner's level of strain at the end of the work day, how each responds behaviorally to the other's psychological state, and how each partner interprets the chain of events in terms of "fairness" (Thompson, 1991) would begin to integrate this domain of research with other relevant studies in the area of work and family.

CONCLUSIONS, CAVEATS AND NEW DIRECTIONS

The studies we have reviewed in this chapter focus on how spouses' work situations influence roles, relationships and daily activities in the family. Several themes cut across the three domains of literature we have reviewed. First, it is clear that family life in dual-earner families is linked in important ways not just to the husband's work situation, or to the wife's, but to the work pattern of both partners in combination.

Secondly, the gendered nature of the work–family interface is a theme that runs through all of this literature. Gender is not only an important determinant of occupation, and thus of income, prestige and access to self-directed, complex work, but it also underlies how men and women think and feel about work and family roles. Having similar or greater access to work-related resources in comparison to one's husband may give a woman the objective circumstances from which to argue for more equal roles in the home, but she is unlikely to do so unless she perceives her current situation as unfair (Thompson, 1991). Perceptual filters tend to operate in such a way as to advantage men (Kompter, 1989) who are seen as more competent and therefore perhaps as more deserving of special consideration at home after a stressful day at work (Bolger et al., 1989) or of appreciation when they make a contribution to housework or child care.

In this chapter, we have focused on three ways in which adults' work experiences influence their roles and relationships off the job. We would be remiss, however, if we did not underscore several caveats. First, the relationship between work and family is far more complex than our seemingly uni-directional focus implies. While there has been less research on the effects of family experiences on workers' lives on the job, such processes clearly exist (Barnett, 1994; Bolger et al., 1989; Crouter, 1984b); indeed, the connections between work and family are probably bi-directional in nature.

Secondly, conceptualizing this set of issues under the heading of "work and family" puts the emphasis on context and downplays the active role that the individual plays in making choices in such areas as education, career, workplace, marital partner, children and child-care arrangements. These choices are based in part on psychological predispositions: values, attitudes, preferences and skills (Vondracek, Lerner & Schulenberg, 1986). No sophisticated statistical model can completely remove the presence of these naturally occurring selection effects; neither is it necessarily desirable to do so because these variables are intertwined in the real world. Understanding the complexities of selection processes into— and out of—work and family roles is an important, but often overlooked, research area in its own right.

Not all selection effects occur at the level of the individual and his or her psychological predispositions. Structural inequalities in our society result in considerable variability across individuals—as a function of gender, social class, race, ethnicity and historical cohort—in the range of choices available; options are often constrained by discrimination and lack of access to opportunity. The review of the literature must be interpreted in light of these caveats.

In which directions should the field move over the next decade? First, researchers need to continue to broaden the populations they study in terms of gender, race, class and culture. In the research areas reviewed in this chapter, gender has been a central focus. Social class has received some attention, especially from researchers interested in occupational complexity and self-direction, as well as from scholars who are interested in whether men and women in working class and middle class families view breadwinning (Ferree, 1987) and men's and women's contributions to housework (Perry-Jenkins and Folk, 1994) differently. Race, however, has received somewhat less explicit attention in the work–family literature. This is somewhat surprising given that, historically, African-American women have been maintained a greater, and more continuous, level of participation in the paid labor force than have White women (Bose,

1987). There may be important differences as a function of race in how men and women conceptualize the provider role, the connections between providing and the division of household work, and perhaps in conceptions of fairness, making this an important area of future study.

Our selection of the husband–wife dyad as the lens through which to examine the work–family literature meant that we excluded research on single-parent families in this chapter. However, work and family issues may be at least as important to workers heading single-parent households as to employees in two-parent, dual-earner families (Perry-Jenkins & Gilman-Hanz, 1992). In addition, the transition from single-parent and household head to a first or second marriage offers researchers interested in the husband–wife dyad an opportunity to explore how the experience of heading a household and being a single parent influences men's and women's subsequent negotiation of work and family roles.

Another important direction involves integrating the work and family literature with the study of families and their socialization of children and adolescents. Much of the literature on child development has focused on the impact of maternal employment status (conceptualized all too often as maternal absence) on children's psychosocial adjustment, rather than on the connections between mothers' and fathers' ongoing daily experiences at work and their children's ongoing daily experiences at home (Crouter & McHale, 1993). Parcel & Menaghan's research (1994) is an exemplar of what can be done in this area. Their work, however, has focused exclusively on early childhood. The middle childhood and adolescent years are also deserving of attention because this is the developmental period during which children develop ideas and expectations about their own future work and family lives.

Our research group has begun to examine the implications of variations in role inequality of husbands and wives, both at work and at home, for their sons' and daughters' gender role socialization experiences in the family. We are beginning two new, five-year longitudinal studies, one of development in middle childhood (Crouter & McHale, 1994a) and one of adolescent development (Crouter & McHale, 1994b). Mirroring the complexity of family life, the two studies pay equal attention to the day-to-day experiences of husbands, wives, and two children in each family, as well as to their attitudes and cognitions about work and family roles. The focus on two children per family will enable us to make within-family comparisons of the daily family experiences of same-sex and opposite-sex sibling dyads. We will be asking, for example, whether daughters and sons *in the same family* receive more sex-typed, differential treatment when parents maintain a traditional division of labor than when their roles are more egalitarian (see Crouter, Manke & McHale, 1995). We are also interested in the conditions under which boys and girls view differential sibling treatment by parents as fair or unfair and the connections between these perceptions and children's long-term adjustment (see McHale & Crouter, in press).

A final area that is deserving of attention is the role of workplace friendships in the work–family interface. It is curious how little research has been done on relationships at work, given that they are a common and valued feature of many people's work experience (Marks, 1994). How might relationships at work make a difference in terms of family relationships? Riley's (1990) research on fathers' social networks provides one example. He argues that the geographic mobility associated with contemporary white collar work uproots men from kin-based social networks with the result that "non-kin allies"—friends, co-workers and neighbors—come to exert more influence on their behavior as fathers. The higher the proportion of non-kin allies in a father's social network, Riley reports, the more likely he is to be highly involved in child care; conversely, the higher the proportion of kin, particularly female kin, in his network, the less likely he is to become involved in parenting. Work plays two roles. First, it creates geographic mobility which affects the composition of the social network; secondly, it makes possible certain work-based friendships that in turn exert an effect on attitudes and behavior in the family domain. Additional work is needed that examines the separate and combined effects of husbands' and wives' work-based friendships on family roles, relationships and activities.

Work and family, as the two central arenas of adult life, are interconnected in complex and interesting ways. As researchers in the field of personal relationships become increasingly attuned to the importance of contextual influences on relationships, this area of research will receive even more attention. Given the increasing predominance of two-parent, dual-earner families as a context for contemporary marital and parent–child relationships, we urge the next generation of researchers to pay equal attention to the work and family experiences of both employed partners, singly and in combination, and to chart, with greater precision and across a broader array of relationship phenomena, the antecedents and consequences of variations in spousal inequality.

ACKNOWLEDGEMENTS

We are most appreciative of the advice and suggestions offered by Susan McHale and Maureen Perry-Jenkins throughout the preparation of the chapter, as well as the helpful feedback provided by Bob Milardo and Steve Duck.

Chapter 22

Social Networks and Marital Relationships

Robert M. Milardo
University of Maine, Orono, ME, USA
and
Graham Allan
University of Southampton, Hampshire, UK

The individual is not a separate unit, but a link, a meeting place of relationships of every kind (Carlo Levi, 1947, p. 259).

This chapter critically examines network theory, methodology and research as it relates to understanding the internal character of a marriage, or marriage-like relationship. We are concerned with questions about the influence of the personal associates of spouses or adult partners on the conduct of their relationship. Kin, friends, co-workers and the like may directly influence partners and their relationship through the provision of support, companionship or criticism. Network members may also collectively influence partners through their coordinated efforts, yielding a structural effect, as we term it.

In the following pages we critically review the theory and corresponding research linking a network's structure with the internal character of a relationship, a tradition of research that began with the publication of Elizabeth Bott's curious study of 20 London families in 1955. We continue with a critique of the structural perspective followed by a summary of advances in both the precise conceptualization of networks and their enumeration.

Handbook of Personal Relationships, 2nd edn. Edited by Steve Duck.
© 1997 John Wiley & Sons Ltd.

STRUCTURAL INFLUENCE: THEORY AND FINDINGS

Introduction

Elizabeth Bott (1955, 1971) was among the first to hypothesize a link between the structure of spouses' social networks and the internal character of their marriage. In Bott's case, the interest was in explaining conjugal roles. Through an extensive examination of the division of labor and leisure time amongst the couples included in her study, and of the social relationships they were involved in outside the household, Bott postulated that there was a link between the structure of their social networks and the conjugal role relationships they developed. In particular, she suggested that "the degree of segregation in the role-relationship of husband and wife varies directly with the connectedness of the family's social network" (1971, p. 60). Bott took "connectedness" to be "the extent to which the people known by a family know and meet one another independently of the family" (1971, p. 59). Since then the term "density" has replaced that of "connectedness" in the social network literature, but it essentially refers to the same structural property: the degree of linkage among the people in the network. Density is just one of many measures of a network's structural properties, though undoubtedly it is the most frequently used (and arguably over-used) in the social analysis of networks (Milardo, 1986; Scott, 1991; Surra, 1988).

In evaluating the adequacy of Bott's approach, it is useful to return to the concerns that initially led to the development of her hypotheses. Essentially Bott's "problem" was to uncover the features of a couple's social location that patterned and shaped the character of their marital relationship. Dissatisfied with the then standard attempts at doing this, for example through crude measurements of class position or geographical location, Bott interpreted the issue through a concern for what she termed the couple's "immediate social environment". In essence her argument was that an appropriate conceptualization and measurement of the immediate social environment would help explain the form that different marital relationships took. However, the concept of immediate social environment, theoretically suggestive as it was, was not readily operationalized. It needed further refining if it were to prove useful for empirical investigation. It was here that the leap to network analysis was made. By interpreting immediate social environment into the language of social networks, and consequently defining structural or configurational properties of networks as crucial variables, Bott was able to formulate her ideas in a testable format.

Undoubtedly this was an enormous advance on previous work. The use of the network conceptualization not only allowed a precision in the measurement of a couple's immediate social environment, but was also analytically persuasive in that, intuitively, network configuration did appear linked with patterns of informal social control, which in turn represented a mechanism for understanding why marital relationships might be differentially organized. What is important in this for the present purposes are the theoretical connections that this formulation entails between the concepts of "social location", "immediate social environ-ment", "network configuration" and "informal social control".

At its root, the link Bott drew between marital relationships and network configurations is premised on the idea that the character of informal control that shapes the organization of marital (and by implication, other types of) relation-ships is influenced by network properties. As came to be recognized clearly in the decade following the publication of Bott's research, network approaches allowed these patterns of informal control to be mapped in a more convincing fashion than the then dominant functionalist role theories managed (Epstein, 1969; Wellman, 1988). Rather than simply being norm-based, Bott, like other network analysts, showed how behavior was influenced by its relational context.

Reframing the Bott Hypothesis

Although research in this area generally refers to a uniform or singular "Bott hypothesis" (e.g., Hill, 1988; Morris, 1985), in fact two models linking network structure and conjugal roles are implicit in Bott's work and much of the research that followed. The two models differ in the specific mechanisms linking structure and conjugal roles and in terms of the mediating variables they call into question. In the first model, Bott hypothesized that highly interconnected networks would be more apt to share similar values and beliefs regarding conjugal roles relative to loosely connected networks. Bott hypothesized a direct path, with network structure determining the strength of normative influence. The specific norm of interest concerned the segregation of conjugal roles. Highly interconnected net-works should adopt a consistent gender-based ideology, with husbands and wives having very separate responsibilities for decision-making, household labor and child care, as well as separate personal associates and leisure interests. Loosely connected networks would be less predictable. Without the co-ordinated influ-ence of network members, pairs of spouses should be freer to adopt their own arrangement of roles and responsibilities and accordingly they might adopt sepa-rate or joint conjugal roles.

The strength of this first model rests on the recognition that marital outcomes (e.g., interactions between spouses and the outcomes of those interactions) could be affected by the ties linking network members (i.e., conditions existing apart from spouses' relationship to one another), with the vehicle of influence being a system of normative beliefs. This is an extraordinary contribution because it represents the first concrete attempt to define social structure in terms of the patterned interconnection of people, and subsequently to quantify the degree of structure (Mitchell, 1969). It contrasts sharply with traditional conceptualizations of social structure based on categorical memberships like sex, race or class, conceptualizations from which structure can be only inferred (Wellman, 1988). On the other hand, a sharp limitation of the model is a failure to explain why a network would subscribe to one belief, such as role segregation or patriarchal norms, rather than any other.

A second model inherent in Bott's work links structure and marital roles through a slightly different pathway. In this model the key norm is one concerning the exchange of mutual support, both instrumental and symbolic, presumably based upon a sense of felt obligation (Stein, 1993; Uehara, 1995). Members of interdependent networks will provide considerable aid to one another, a system of mutual exchange that is possible only to the extent that members know and interact with one another. In interdependent networks, mutual assistance among members is high and as a consequence spouses will have less need for one another's practical aid and companionship, and segregated marital roles emerge. In contrast, in more loosely structured networks, members are less likely to know one another and less likely to provide mutual aid, so spouses must rely more fully on one another, creating the conditions for joint conjugal roles to emerge. Joint conjugal roles were defined in terms of joint responsibility for household labor, child care, and the joint use of leisure time.

The Bott hypotheses have engendered considerable research interest, particularly because they offered non-intuitive explanations of marital action. However, as new research has been produced, Bott's hypotheses have not been widely supported. Of the 14 empirical tests of the Bott hypotheses we have identified, five were generally supportive and two provided mixed results (see Tables 22.1 and 22.2). Several studies reported modest positive associations between network connectedness and segregated marital roles (Blood, 1969; Hill, 1988; Morris, 1985; Nelson, 1966; Turner, 1967). For example, in Hill (1988) although high network density, as indicated by the proportion of kin living nearby, is associated with segregated roles ($R^2 = 2\%$), spouses' beliefs and parental status are far more robust predictors: those who believe in sharing roles do so ($R^2 = 16\%$), and those with young children do not ($R^2 = 15\%$). This finding is similar to Turner (1967) and Gordon & Downing (1978) in that couples who originate and reside in the same locality are more likely to report close-knit networks and segregated roles relative to couples who reside in areas far from their families of origin. Similarly, Richards (1980) reports that segregated roles increase with the degree of contact with kin.

What is unclear in these findings is whether kin have a distinctly different collective impact relative to spouses' friends, and whether this impact is purely a function of a network's structure. That is, rather than being a consequence of network structure, perhaps segregated roles are simply the result of the fact that some spouses have a life-long commitment to (or enmeshment with) kin and this precludes their developing a close marital bond with one another (Blood, 1969; Lee, 1979). Although this argument is conceivable, there is rather little evidence to support it.

Timmer et al. (in press), using single-item, global measures of closeness with kin, found among Black wives closeness with in-laws corresponds with greater marital happiness for both spouses, while similar associations for White couples were non-significant. Timmer et al. suggest these findings indicate that integration of spouses with their in-laws balances over-identification with families of origin. This explanation could explain the connection of closeness to in-laws and

Table 22.1 Research supporting the Bott Hypotheses

Citation	Sample	Network	Measure of interconnectedness	Role segregation	Findings
Nelson, 1966	$N = 131$ wives, urban Connecticut	4 Kin or friends visited most often	Cliques who interact minimum once weekly, with three or more partners	Attitudes toward marital roles	Clique members report less companionate marriage
Turner, 1967	$N = 115$ rural couples, UK	Kin and friends contacted minimum 1/2 weeks	Density of connections between households	Performance of domestic tasks, child-care, leisure	Density increases with role segregation
Blood, 1969	$N = 731$ Detroit wives	Kin	Percentage kin in neighborhood	Mean number of household tasks by husband or wife	Role segregation increases with number of kin in neighborhood, but also with lower support from kin
Morris, 1985	$N = 40$ working-class couples, Wales	Kin and friends	Pattern of interaction, group oriented or dyadic	Performance of domestic tasks, child-care	Role segregation associated with same-sex, high density networks
Hill, 1988	$N = 150$ working-class wives, Altoona, Pennsylvania	Kin	Percentage kin living in area (Altoona)	Performance of domestic tasks, child-care	Role segregation increases with percentage kin in area

Table 22.2 Research failing to support the Bott Hypotheses or showing mixed support

Citation	Sample	Network	Measure of interconnectedness	Role segregation	Findings
Udry & Hall, 1965	N = 43 middle class couples, California, plus interview with four best friends of each spouse	Four best friends with most contact in last year	Density	Performance of household tasks	No relationship of role segregation with density
Aldous & Straus, 1966	N = 391 wives, rural Minnesota	Eight women visited most often	Density	Performance of household tasks	Greater density in farm vs. town families
Wimberly, 1973	N = 40, middle-class Japanese couples	Largely friends	Degree of interaction among friends	Performance of domestic tasks, child-care, use of leisure time	No support, but little variation in connectedness. No couple had a joint conjugal marriage.
Hannan & Katsiaouni 1977	N = 408 Irish farm couples	Confidants of spouses	Network homogeneity; overlap	Performance of household tasks, child-care, decision-making	Greater overlap = less role segregation, shared household labor and decision-making. Homogeneous networks modestly correlated with shared household labor
Gordon & Downing, 1978	N = 686 wives, urban Ireland (Cork)	Six individuals or couples most frequently visited by wife	Density; overlap	Performance of domestic tasks, child-care, decision-making, leisure	Greater overlap = less role segregation. Role segregation increases with number of husband's kin in area (marginal significance)

Richards, 1980	N = 331 working-class wives, Boston 1958	Network involvement, combines nine questions on contact with kin and non-kin	Degree of interaction	Performance of household tasks, decision-making, leisure	Greater "network involvement" = less role segregation and greater joint leisure. Role segregation increases with kin contact
Rogler & Procidano, 1986	N = 200 Puerto Rican couples in New York City	Eight closest companions of same-sex	Density; composition	Performance of household tasks, decision-making, leisure	No association between network density and sharing household tasks, decision-making, or leisure
Chatterjee, 1977	N = 33 Indian couples	Kin, co-workers, neighbors	Density, overlap	Household and child-care tasks	Greater overlap and density, less role segregation
Goldenberg, 1984–5	N = 1170 societies	None identified	Residence patterns used as proxy. Patrilocal residence viewed as "connected", matrilocal as "dispersed"	Normative views of division of household labor	No difference in gender segregation of roles by residence patterns

marital quality for Black wives, but it does not explain why such an association fails to appear for White couples, neither is there any direct evidence for either race of the negative effects of over-identification with families of origin, so called enmeshment. In fact, wives' closeness to families of origin is unrelated to either spouses' reports of marital quality. Indeed, some research suggests a far more interesting pattern of interconnections based around gender and network composition, with higher levels of kinship solidarity having very different effects for wives and husbands.

Blood (1969), for example, reported that wives in kin-centered networks were less likely to discuss personal problems with their husbands and experienced lower levels of marital satisfaction. This intriguing finding could suggest the ill-effects of over-identification with kin, but it may as well suggest the effects of a non-responsive partner and troubled marriage. In more recent work, Burger & Milardo (1995) found the association of marital qualities and kinship ties varied by gender, type of kin, and whether integration with kin was evidenced by a simple enumeration of kin in a network, or by the frequency of interaction. Generally, global measures of the size of a kinship sector, or the perceived frequency of interaction with classes of kin (e.g., all in-laws) are inadequate because these measures obscure the profound effects of some kin relations, the apparent non-effects of others, and the completely contrasting effects of still others for wives and husbands. For instance, the presence of brothers-in-law in the networks of wives successfully predicts 52% of the variance in her own reports of marital conflict and 32% for her husband's (Burger & Milardo, 1995), whereas for husbands, contact with fathers is critical, being associated with his greater love of his partner, as well as lower levels of marital conflict reported by wives. The importance of husband's integration with kin is also evidenced in Cotton's studies of white Australian couples (Cotton, Autill & Cunningham, 1993; Cotton, 1995) and the Timmer et al. (in press) longitudinal study of early marriage, at least among African-American men. Neither study, however, differentiated between types of kin relationships.

Relations with friends, on the other hand, have distinctly different associations with marital outcomes. Whereas kin tend to provide a variety of supportive functions (Wellman & Wellman, 1992) and to be sources of criticism (Rook, 1992), friends are unique sources of companionship (Larson & Bradney, 1988; Wellman & Wellman, 1992), resource acquisition (Uehara, 1994) and social comparison (O'Connor, 1992; Oliker, 1989; Surra & Milardo, 1991), and they are rarely linked directly to spouses' kin (Wellman & Wellman, 1992). Not surprisingly, relations with friends show a different pattern of association with marital outcomes, compared to relations with kin. Cotton (1995) reported husbands whose wives were embedded in dense friendship networks experienced lower marital satisfaction. Similarly, in a sample of US couples, when wives report high frequencies of social contact with close friends, their husbands report high levels of conflict as well as ambivalence regarding their marriage, and lower love of their spouses (Burger & Milardo, 1995). It remains for future work to elucidate these potential sex differences and the causal pathways that produce them.

Few have directly questioned the relative influence of structure and composition, although Nelson (1966) examined whether segregated roles were the result of network structure or more simply a function of being integrated into traditional extended families. In this study, even wives with highly interconnected networks composed entirely of friends were more apt to favor traditional values (80%) than those with networks composed entirely of kin (56%), suggesting that network structure takes precedence over network composition. The measure of network structure he used is also unique. Rather than being based on proxy measures like the geographic dispersion of network members (e.g., Blood, 1969; Gordon & Downing, 1978; Hill, 1988), or the interconnectedness of households (Turner, 1967), Nelson used an index of clique structure, defined as a pool of network members who jointly and routinely interacted with one another. In many ways, clique structure is preferable to measures of density or geographic dispersion, because it is less influenced by overall network size (Kapferer, 1973; Milardo, 1986).

Least interesting are studies testing the Bott hypotheses that lack even remotely adequate measures of key variables like network connectedness or conjugal roles, or adequate variability in these key variables. For instance, in the 40 Japanese couples studied by Wimberly (1973), no couple reported a joint conjugal relationship; it is rather difficult to explain variation in a dependent variable where none exists. Goldenburg (1984–5) attempted to test the Bott hypothesis with data from 1170 societies in the Ethnographic Atlas. Without direct measures of spouses' networks, the author uses residence patterns as a proxy for network connectedness. Patrilocal residence patterns are viewed as representative of dense networks and matrilocal patterns of loose networks, an argument that requires a significant conceptual leap of faith.

With respect to the dynamics underlying the link between network attributes and marital roles, no study has yet examined whether network structure (e.g., density) is linked to the consistency of members' beliefs or sanctioning of members' actions, as Bott proposed, although several have examined the link between network support and conjugal roles, with mixed results. In Hill's (1988) study, there was a modest association between wives receiving support from parents and segregated roles ($r = 0.16$), whereas Blood (1969) reported that greater support for wives from kin parallelled shared conjugal roles: "Helpful (non-segregated) spouses tend to have helpful relatives" (p. 181).

In addition, several investigators have explored the connection of network structure to global measures of marital satisfaction and individual well-being. Generally, spouses with denser networks report greater well-being (Acock & Hurlbert, 1993; Cotton et al., 1993) and those with overlapping or shared networks report greater marital satisfaction (Ackerman, 1963; Cotton, 1995; Julien & Markman, 1991). Shared networks are thought to act as a stabilizing force by reinforcing a consistent set of group norms, underscoring the identity of partners as a couple and providing sources of social support and comparison (Healey & Bell, 1990; Milardo, 1982; Parks & Eggert, 1991; Stein et al., 1992). In an intriguing study that compared couples in terms of their relative configurations of shared and separate networks of kin and friends, Stein et al. (1992) found spouses with the highest reported marital satisfaction were those who maintained relatively balanced proportions of joint and separate networks of family and friends. Given the cross-sectional nature of this work, causal directions are not discernable and in fact Yi (1986) has argued persuasively that patterns of marital interaction, rather than resulting from network configuration, direct patterns of extrafamilial associations (cf. Wellman & Wellman, 1992).

Non-human Primates

Curiously, some of the finest work on the close relationship–network connection comes not from work on humans but on non-human primates. Maryanski & Ishii-Kuntz (1991) reviewed approximately 90 studies of 17 species of Old World primates, including three species of apes. Many primate species are well studied with observational data on entire communities, which contain both identifiable networks and mating pairs. Sentiments, of course, are difficult to determine. Nonetheless, the strength of relational ties between individuals can be defined in terms of observable features such as interaction frequency, physical contact and proximity (including mutual grooming, food sharing, cooperative alliances, mutual aid and protection) and, for adults, relationship stability. Network density is defined in terms of the relative proportion of strong ties, as is occasionally the case in studies of humans (Marsden, 1990). For mating pairs, role segregation can be defined in terms of the amount of leisure time pairs spend with one another, the degree of father's participation in child care, the degree of shared family maintenance (e.g., defense against marauding intruders), and the relative dominance or status of partners. Pairs who share in three of the four domains are viewed as having joint conjugal roles.

Maryanski & Ishii-Kuntz argue the findings are generally supportive of Bott. Primates with highly segregated roles show close- or medium-knit networks, and two species with moderately segregated (gorillas) or joint roles (gibbons) show loose-knit networks. Among all species, close-knit networks are associated with greater support from network members—perhaps, as Bott suggested, accounting for the greater likelihood of segregated roles in conditions of high density. In addition, for monkeys and apes, dispersal from families of origin (natal units) is related to the prevalence of loose-knit networks, as is the case in much of the work on humans (Hannan & Katsiaouni, 1977; Hill, 1988; Turner, 1967).

In explaining the connection between the roles adopted by cohabiting partners and the structure of their networks, Maryanski & Ishii-Kuntz deviate from Bott's reliance on *normative influence* and instead focus on the particular *character of relationships* with network members, especially kin. They argue that most material and symbolic support flows through strong ties (Wellman & Wortley, 1990) and consequently such ties are highly valued and very costly to terminate. Strong ties require maintenance in that the potential receipt of support is balanced with an obligation to be supportive (Uehara, 1995), ensuring the stability of the tie.

Thus, time spent in maintaining strong ties is not available for initiating new ties, and indeed research on humans supports this argument (Salzinger, 1982).

Segregation of roles among cohabiting partners is possible because of the support available from network members and may be required to the extent that network members require reciprocal support, leaving partners with little time or need for one another. On the other hand, without the responsibility of maintaining strong ties or the availability of support derivative from them, joint roles among cohabiting pairs can flourish. Among gibbons, for example, "male and female roles almost fuse, seemingly because each partner has no enduring outside relationships. . . . For gibbons, a co-partnership in domestic activities may serve to reinforce bonds that endure for almost a lifetime. It would appear that the modern, mobile, middle-class family is but a less extreme variant of the gibbon nuclear family" [without the patriarchy] (Maryanski and Ishii-Kuntz, 1991, p. 418). Among human and non-human primates there appear to be inherent and fundamental properties of social networks and the relationships that compose them, properties that operate similarly across intelligent species.

Problems of Comparison

Examining the impact of different network configurations on the involvement of pairs of non-human primates is highly innovative, although in a number of respects methodologically less problematic than studying human couples. To begin with, the possibility of observation is made simpler because issues of access and privacy are of little consequence. Equally, the exchange basis of the various relationships involved, and how these change over time, can be measured through observation more straightforwardly than when intention and human agency are involved. In contrast, the different attempts there have been to test Bott's ideas on human relationships have been fraught with conceptual and methodological problems. Making sound comparisons between the research studies reported in the literature is extremely difficult because of the different ways in which the elements in Bott's hypotheses have been operationalized. Few studies provide more than basic descriptive information about the networks generated. Information on average size, composition or density is often omitted, so that reliable comparison and theorizing is severely hampered (see Tables 22.1 and 22.2).

Equally few of the studies report on the precise wording of the network-eliciting questions. As we shall discuss, this is important because different methods yield different constituencies, i.e. different types of questions generate different networks which may well have different structural characteristics and distinct influences (Milardo, 1992; Surra & Milardo, 1991; van der Poel, 1993). Moreover, some research, like Bott's, focuses on the couple's collective network, whereas other work relies on data from only one of the spouses, usually the wife. So, too, in their identification of network members, many studies limited the size of a network to the 6 or fewer close associates. Yet a variety of research demonstrates that approximately 30% of North Americans have more that 6 intimates in their networks (Milardo, 1992), even if it is accepted that it is appropriate to focus only on intimates. Severe limitations in the size of a network limit the variation in other structural features, and most likely produce over-estimates of other network properties, like density.

This in turn raises the issue of which structural properties of networks are most suitable for examining the impact of informal control on couples' norms and behavior. As we have seen, the measure Bott used was network density—the ratio of actual linkages in the network to all possible linkages—and it is this which has dominated most analyses of personal networks. However, it is only one of a number of possible ways of characterizing the structural properties of networks, and there is little debate in the literature about why theoretically it is the best for capturing the effective exercise of informal social control over the organization of marital relationships. It could well be that other measures, in unison or collectively, offer better possibilities for explaining the various empirical patterns which occur. As we have suggested, clique structure, as used by Nelson (1966) and Salzinger (1982), may be a more suitable measure than overall density. (For a discussion of different measures of network structure, see Milardo, 1986; Scott, 1991; Surra, 1988; and Wellman, 1988.)

Recasting the Bott Hypotheses

In considering the collective work on the network structure–conjugal role link, with human and non-human primates alike, the overall empirical support is less than clear-cut. We suspect this is the case for two reasons: (1) because of an inadequate specification of the underlying theoretical model; and (2) because conceptual definitions of networks have lagged behind advances in methodology.

We want to argue that Bott's model was mis-specified in two important ways. The first mis-specification concerns the confusion of network structure with the content of members' beliefs. Bott, as well as nearly all the work that was to follow, assumed that all dense networks would subscribe to traditional norms. This may have been the case in the working-class environs of mid-1950 London, where her study was conducted, but it is an unnecessary limitation to the model. Bott's basic argument, that network structure determines degree of influence, works regardless of the particular beliefs of members. Their impact should be evidenced equally in cases where they hold radical feminist views or traditional patriarchal views. The point is that if a network is structurally interdependent, the possibility of more concerted informal control operating among its members is greater than if it is not so. In short, the precise beliefs of network members is a variable and can not sensibly be assumed to take any particular form. In reframing the original model, we believe it will be useful to allow for variation by treating consensus of normative beliefs as a variable, as well as allowing for variation in content whereby network members may subscribe to a range of beliefs, including those that promote patriarchal norms and those that do not.

Second, while recognizing the greater informal social control likely to be exercised in highly interconnected networks (or clusters), it does not automatically follow that the higher the network density the greater the consensus over values is, as assumed in Bott's arguments. We suspect many people's networks are much like contemporary legislators, with a variety of interest groups holding different sets of values. This fracturing of networks into distinct subsets is dramatically illustrated in work on lesbian relationships. Among lesbian couples, networks are often fractured into those that know of and approve of the couple's sexual orientation and those that do not, sectors that are apt to share very different sets of values (Ulin & Milardo, 1992).

So, too, network members may differ in their beliefs across generations or social contexts (e.g., kin vs. non-kin, co-workers vs. close friends), and as a consequence form distinct sectors. To express this slightly differently, given the social and economic conditions of late modernity, individuals have a degree of freedom in the construction of their social identity (Allan, 1993). Writers like Goffman (1959) and Giddens (1991) have emphasized that the way we present ourselves depends on situational and contextual factors, as well as on more inherent personality or character traits. Thus we highlight certain aspects of self in one setting, but other aspects elsewhere. The extent to which we can do this successfully is likely to depend on how well "insulated" from each other the different settings are, and, as Goffman (1959) argued, on the willingness of those permitted into the "back region" to sustain and give credence to the performance.

While it can be argued that behaviorally different presentations of self are unlikely in the specific context of marital and domestic organization, such considerations nonetheless highlight the possibility that individuals have variant social identities within different segments of their overall network (Klein & Milardo, 1993). In such cases, as with the lesbian couples mentioned above, the informal control exercised by the network overall is unlikely to be acting uniformly or in concert. This in turn suggests that the structural influence of a network is only crudely assessed by measures of composition or overall density, and can be more sensitively assessed with measures of clique structure or the clustering of members into highly interconnected subsectors of the overall network (cf., Nelson, 1966; Salzinger, 1982). Clustering is far less sensitive to changes in the overall size of a network, relative to measures of density, and it may well be a keener index of other structural features, such as sex composition or proportional measures of kin and non-kin (Kapferer, 1973; Milardo, 1986).

This discussion leads us to several related hypotheses. Where networks are highly interdependent structurally, or where there are highly interdependent cliques, optimal conditions exist for the development, maintenance and enforcement of a consistent set of normative beliefs and expectations, and any deviations from those beliefs are most visible. Structure is thereby closely tied to the development of norms, the flow of information between members, and the sanctioning of individual behavior. Where networks are highly structured, spouses, like all other structurally equivalent members, will experience considerable influence to act in accord with those norms (Milardo & Klein, 1992). In contrast, among members of networks low in structural interdependence, the development, maintenance and sanctioning of common norms is inhibited and personal discretion over marital behavior is substantial. As Bott herself suggested, the development of industrial society fosters this within marriage, except possibly amongst those with the fewest resources whose poverty is likely to result in more restricted and more localized networks.

Defining and Enumerating Networks

What is not entirely clear is which types of network members are most likely to be influential or even how networks are best defined. How are the networks used in attempting to explain marital organization to be constructed? It is now widely recognized that the configurational properties of personal (or couple) networks are not immutable, given and ready to be recorded by the analyst, but depend entirely on what he or she takes to constitute a link. As Mitchell (1974, p. 292) indicated, "Any statement we may wish to make about the morphological features of a social network must be premised upon what links constituting the framework of the network are assumed to be" (see also Barnes, 1979; Scott, 1991). Whether researchers attempt to plot all those "known" or "known well" to the individuals concerned, whether they rely on their three (or six, or whatever) "closest", "most intimate" or "most significant" personal ties, or whether they attempt to specify different exchange bases of relationships, the resultant network is clearly a construction resulting from these decisions (cf. Campbell & Lee, 1991; Milardo, 1992; van der Poel, 1993). Consequently, in examining how network configuration impinges upon marital relationships, it is important to determine theoretically the appropriate criteria for the inclusion or exclusion of particular relationships within the analyzed network. In our view this issue has not been resolved at a theoretical level. Little heed has been paid to the definition of theoretically significant ties within the context of the informal social controls exercised over marriages.

A second issue here is the question of equivalence of relationships within the network that have been constructed. Aside from the theoretical void surrounding configurational decisions, there is the question of whether all ties within the network exert equivalent influence, depending only upon their configurational location. The argument of the original Bott approach is that configuration rules. What matters is the overall constellation of ties in the network irrespective of the strength or character of individual relationships within it. On *a priori* grounds, this might be questioned, because some relationships are likely to have a greater or lesser influence in terms of the informal control they can exert, independently of their structural location within the network.

More recent approaches have clearly recognized that relationships are not all the same (Burger & Milardo, 1995; Milardo & Wellman, 1992) and that the constructed network needs to incorporate in more detail the exchange basis, or other differential characteristics of relationships. As indicated earlier, different schemes of categorizing relationships have been developed in recent years. However, what remains under-developed is the theoretical rationale for adducing the relative influence of different categories of relationships, and different constellations of relationships within the constructed networks, in terms of their impact on marital (or other relational) conditions. The issue here is not whether we possess appropriate mathematical network tools and techniques for analyzing networks containing variable ties (and arguably we do), but rather whether from a sociological standpoint we have sufficient knowledge of theoretical principles and practices for analyzing the relative impact of these ties on behavior. As various commentators have indicated, there is quite a discrepancy between the complexity of mathematical and sociological theories invoked in network analyses (Emirbayer & Goodwin, 1994; Grannovetter, 1979; Scott, 1991; Wellman, 1988).

Expressed most simply, it is not clear how "additive" different types of relationships are within a constructed network. From the standpoint of sociological theorizing about informal social control, the relative pull or force of different types of relationships is, as yet, under-theorized. As a result there is little basis for determining which measures of structure and which corresponding mathematical principles are the most appropriate for assessing the collective impact of the detailed network configuration. It is worth adding here that this point remains true regardless of what form of relationship typology is drawn upon. Whether it be premised on exchange characteristics, measures of emotional closeness or social distance, or simply social categorizations such as kinship or friendship, the difficulty of calculating the cumulative impact of a given network configuration remains.

In attempting to address these issues we can usefully speak of two distinct networks: those with whom we interact routinely but may or may not consider close, and those we consider significant or especially close but may or may not interact with frequently. Earlier work suggests the two types of ties represent very different ways of conceptualizing networks that are distinct both theoretically and empirically (Milardo, 1992; Surra & Milardo, 1991).

Psychological networks are composed of people considered important or significant to respondents. These are "people to whom P is committed emotionally and psychologically, who provide P with a concept of self, and who can sustain or alter one's self definition through communication" (Surra & Milardo, 1991, p. 12). People become members through a history of direct interaction or indirectly through their association with others considered important (e.g., a parent of a fiancé), but once established such a relationship need *not* require frequent, recent or long interaction. In contrast, *interactive networks* are composed of the people with whom interactions occur routinely. Unlike the largely sentimental ties that comprise the psychological network, these are the kin, friends, co-workers and other personal associates with whom we routinely exchange aid, information, advice and, occasionally, criticism (Milardo, 1992).

In a direct comparison of the composition of psychological and interactive networks, Milardo (1989) required spouses to identify members of their psychological networks in face-to-face interviews, i.e., people who were believed to be providers of material or symbolic aid, important confidants or social companions. Members of the interactive network were identified via seven phone interviews on non-consecutive days. During each interview, a spouse was asked to identify the people with whom interactions occurred over the previous 24 hours.

We might expect the two types of networks to be reasonably similar; they are not. In a direct comparison the network types overlapped minimally. Spouses each identified an average of 39 network members. Seventy-five percent of these individuals were identified by one procedure but not the other. Moreover, there is no appreciable co-variation in the size of each network, or in the size of the psychological network and the frequency of interaction with members of the interactive network. Spouses with relatively large psychological networks are not necessarily socially active and those with modest psychological networks are not necessarily socially isolated (Milardo, 1989).

We examine interactive networks because we are interested in the potential for the contemporary exchange of normative influence. On the other hand, the significant others who compose psychological networks shape beliefs merely by the imagination and subsequent anticipation of their reactions (e.g., "If my father could only see me now. He'd . . ."). Their influence is not necessarily tied directly to contemporary interaction, but it is nonetheless current and potentially significant. It remains for future research to compare these two distinct types of networks in terms of their structural properties, and to delineate models for predicting their relative importance in predicting relational outcomes. In what domains are the interior furnishings of one's mind apt to be of consequence, compared to the daily enterprise of social conduct?

Issues for Future Research

As we have said, while there have been a good number of studies that have set out to test Bott's hypotheses, the empirical evidence generated has not been noticeably supportive. One response to this might be to reject her ideas and stop searching for correlations between network configuration and marital organization. We do not consider this to be appropriate. Bott's work remains one of the most insightful and suggestive studies conducted on any aspect of family life. Recently Gordon Marshall, writing from a British perspective, has gone even further in declaring: "Her purposes may have been purely exploratory, but to my mind at least, her achievement constitutes probably the most original piece of sociological research to have emerged during the postwar era" (1990, p. 237). Many of the empirical tests of Bott's ideas have used methods so different from hers that their adequacy as tests is called into question. Bott's fieldwork was both qualitative and intensive—between eight and 19 lengthy interviews were conducted with each couple. Restudies that rely on brief interviews with only one spouse and focus exclusively on a small number of network members may not be capable of capturing the holistic perspective that was central in Bott's analysis.

Yet questions clearly remain. In particular, there must be doubts about the extent to which purely configurational properties of a couple's network are of themselves capable of explaining conjugal role relationships, or indeed other social actions. In other areas of social inquiry that draw on network analysis, there does seem to have been a move away from claiming singular explanatory power for network analysis towards using it more descriptively, as one element within a broader explanation of behavior. For example, in studies of community ties, network analysis tends to be used as a tool for mapping out and contrasting the different structure of people's social universes, with these differences then being explained by other aspects of their economic and social location (e.g., see Allan, 1993; Wellman, 1985; Wellman, Carrington & Hall, 1988). Similarly, studies of the impact of marital separation and divorce (or other changes in personal circumstances) on patterns of social participation may be informed by a network perspective but still draw on extraneous factors to help account for these changes (see, for example, Rands, 1988).

So it can be argued that Bott's approach gave too high a priority to network configuration. In effect, what such an approach misses is any way of integrating wider contextual issues into the analysis. The effectiveness of informal control is likely to be influenced by aspects of network structure, but other features of the contexts shaping social action also need considering. Bott's notion of "immediate social environment" is particularly relevant here as this incorporates a broader field of relevance into the perspective. Translating this into network configuration made it more easily operationable, but arguably in the process rendered it too specific. In a sense it is this broader context that is missing from the central Bott equation of "configuration leads to content". Without some contextualizing, it is hard to see how action (i.e., content) can be properly understood or theorized. "Network analysis gains its purchase upon social structure only at the considerable cost of losing its conceptual grasp upon agency and process" (Emirbayer & Goodwin, 1994, pp. 1446–7). Our analysis of two such processes involving the creation and maintenance of beliefs and the exchange of support are attempts at better understanding how the links between network structure and relationship outcome are established.

The difficulty with this limitation, of course, is that it renders Bott's initial hypotheses somewhat less powerful than they otherwise are. In saying that network structure can be important but is only one of a number of factors that may influence people's role relationships, the taut elegance of Bott's approach is undermined. In the absence of clear confirmatory support for her argument, though, and in the light of the types of conceptual and methodological matters we have expressed in this chapter, this perhaps should not be of too much concern.

It would be curious indeed if the social and economic contexts in which marriages are constructed, for example whether or not wives were employed or the presence of children in the household, did not influence the role expectations spouses hold about one another, irrespective of network formation. This can be accepted without thereby saying that couples' immediate social environments are of no consequence, that different patterns of informal social control do not operate, or that network configuration is not an important influence. The task for the future is to develop more fully the theorization of the impact on conjugal role relationships of different network configurations in specific contexts, and then assess such theorizing using appropriate, rather than simply convenient, empirical measures.

Chapter 23

Personal Relationships in Later-life Families

Victoria Hilkevitch Bedford
University of Indianapolis, IN, USA
and
Rosemary Blieszner
Virginia Polytechnic Institute and State University, Blacksburg,
VA, USA

The field of family and aging now spans a broad array of issues, theories and applications from many disciplines (cf. Blieszner & Bedford, 1995). Focusing on dominant Western societies, we examine *relationships* among family members where at least one member is old. Because references to family in the personal relationship literature often do not apply to old members or relegate them to the family periphery, the first aim of this chapter is to arrive at a definition of family that includes old people, even the very old (85 years of age and more). To do this we review some demographic data that reveal the kinds of family relationships that are available to old people.

Next, we identify features of family relationships that are not typical of the kinds of relationships usually targeted in personal relations research, such as their ascribed (non-voluntary) status and their longevity. In a review of the available literature, we consider how such features affect the nature of family relationships.

TOWARD AN INCLUSIVE DEFINITION OF FAMILY

Among dominant Western societies, most old people are widows (i.e., single women) and most old people live alone. *Family* typically refers to the nuclear family, a household consisting of two adults engaged in an intimate heterosexual

Handbook of Personal Relationships, 2nd edn. Edited by Steve Duck.
© 1997 John Wiley & Sons Ltd.

relationship and their biological or adopted children (Aerts, 1993; Broderick, 1993). By this definition, the expression "family and aging" is a contradiction in terms. At best, the older family members are among the "incidental linkages of nuclear families to their kin" (Riley, 1983, p. 447). We suggest, instead, that *family* is more accurately and inclusively represented as a class of relationships that are determined by biology, adoption, marriage, and in some societies, social designation. Note that in this chapter the term marriage includes intimate relationships between gay or lesbian couples and between common-law heterosexual couples. *Marriage*, therefore, designates both legal marriage and marriage-like relationships.

Below we describe current and projected structures of families that include older adults, based on recent demographic data. Our purpose is to identify which family relationships are available to people generally, and to old people in particular.

Demographics of Family and Aging

Consideration of the age structure of Western society reveals that the modal relationship involves an adult child and an adult parent, not an immature child and a parent. In other words, people spend more time as adult children than as parents of young offspring. In further support of the relative infrequency of parent–dependent child relationships, evidence suggests that adults are having fewer children (Dwyer, 1995). Gerontologists have predicted, therefore, that kinship structure is tending towards "verticalization", wherein few members occupy any one generation, but many of these sparsely populated generations will survive into old and very old age (Hagestad, 1984; Bengtson, Rosenthal & Burton, 1990). This vertical family structure conjures up images of several generations of adults doting on one small child rather than a flock of children vying for the attention of one or two surviving grandparents.

Not everyone agrees with the verticalization of family prediction. Investigators of the families of very old persons have not found many generations living concurrently yet; many very old people have few family relationships available. Often they have survived even their own children, as well as their spouse and siblings. In a recent study of the very old, 32% of White and 45% of Black Americans either had no surviving children or never had children (Johnson & Barer, 1996); demographic studies forecasting to 2020 project even fewer children in future cohorts (Dwyer, 1995). Not surprisingly, few of the very old childless adults have grandchildren or great-grandchildren (6% of Whites and 18% of Blacks) (Johnson & Barer, 1996). Nonetheless, most old people (75%) have grandchildren and about 50% have great-grandchildren (Robertson, 1995).

Others have also challenged the notion that few family members will be found within any one generation. Today the members of the baby boom generation (born 1946–1964) are known for their large siblingships. Many of these siblings should be available to them when they begin to reach old age in 15 years. By 2020, baby boom elders will be more likely to have surviving children than previous elders were (Dwyer, 1995). Despite these inconsistencies in number of members within families, relationships between members of adult generations, rather than between adults and dependent children, are the modal family relationships. A comprehensive definition of family needs to account for these ties.

Another demographic trend that affects the definition of family is seen in the structure of the marital bond and its equivalent. People are living in marriages much longer now than in the past. Whereas long-term marriages endured for an average of 35 years in 1900, in the 1980s long-term marriages lasted an average of 47 years (Johnson, 1988). Still, this increase is not as great as gains in longevity would predict (Riley, 1983) due to the gender mortality gap (women lived 2–3 years longer than men in 1900 and 9 years longer in 1990) and the rising divorce rate (about 12% of marriages in 1900 and over 50% in 1990 ended in divorce) (Dwyer, 1995). Thus, an older man's family often includes a spouse (nearly half of men older than 85 years live with a spouse), whereas an older woman's family is frequently without a spouse (7–10% of women over age 85 live with a spouse) (Dwyer, 1995; Huyck, 1995). At the same time, a trend in developed countries reveals a tendency to avoid marriage altogether. The highest rate of never-married adults is in Sweden where, in 1985, 39% of men and 30% of women had never married at all (Kinsella, 1995).

Finally, a definition of family inclusive of older adults, who are often spouseless, demands that co-residence with family members cannot continue to be a criterion. Whereas in developing countries old people tend to live with others, the tendency is toward living alone in developed countries. Considerable evidence shows that old people prefer the latter living arrangement if they can afford it. This preference is not a rejection of family, but rather a relational style of "intimacy at a distance" (Gratton & Haber, 1993). The implication is that family relationships are enhanced rather than curtailed by separate household arrangements. In support of this position, a recent finding on a national probability sample of adults aged 18–80 years demonstrated that having an uncongenial household member takes a greater toll on one's well-being than living alone (Ross, 1995). No doubt, independent households in later life serve to manage potential family conflict.

An Inclusive Definition of Family

Having reviewed some trends and projections in family vital statistics, we can move on to consider other dimensions of a more suitable definition of family. Most attempts at including old people in a such definition rely on the anthropological practice of segregating them within the kinship system (Baum & Page, 1991; Johnson, 1993; Johnson & Barer, 1996; Riley, 1983). In other words, *family* refers to nuclear family, whereas *kin* refers to all other relatives. Although relationships with and by old people are taken into account using this dual family terminology, it contains the assumption of non-mutuality in the designation of one another: adult children belong to their parents' family, but their parents belong to adult children's kinship system, not to their family. The "modified extended family" concept (Litwak, 1960) includes the notion of linked households, but excludes intergenerational co-residential households, which constitute 18% of all American households of elders with a living child (Lawton, 1994).

In contrast, Riley's definition of family, "a continuing interplay among intertwined lives within the entire changing kinship structure", does not incorporate a household-related restriction (1983, p. 447). This definition improves on the one based on the kinship concept by not overtly segregating old people, but it excludes many family ties of aged persons that are activated only when needed or are based on the expectation that they could be activated, although they may rarely or never be so activated (Bedford, 1995; Johnson, 1993). These possibilities are included, however, in another description of family by Riley as "a matrix of latent relationships . . . relationships that are latent because they might or might not become close and significant during a lifetime . . . a latent web of continually shifting linkages that provide the *potential* for activating and intensifying close family relationships" (1983, p. 441).

Although Riley's conception of family encompasses potential family relationships, it still neglects two important aspects of old people's families. That is, 40–45% of the very old depict their family relationships as either devoid of contact while personally significant (15–20%) or virtually non-existent (attenuated) (25%) (Johnson, 1993). These relationships, too, must be accounted for within any definition of family.

Taking all of the above issues into consideration, we offer the following addition to our initial definition of family. A *family* is a set of relationships determined by biology, adoption, marriage and, in some societies, social designation and existing even in the absence of contact or affective involvement, and, in some cases, even after the death of certain members. This implies that the boundaries of a family cannot be described by an observer; one must ask the respondent because family, according to this definition, is subjective (see Duck, 1994a, for a discussion of subjective experience as the location of relationships). Having arrived at a definition of family that does not exclude elders, we next turn attention to special features of families that count old people among their members.

PERSONAL RELATIONSHIPS WITH FAMILY MEMBERS

Our proposed definition of family brings into focus a number of issues concerning the scope of personal relations scholarship. Most personal relations research examines active, ongoing, voluntary relationships, such as romantic and friendship affiliations. Further, these relationships have a course of development marked by periods of formation, maintenance and dissolution. The qualities of voluntary affiliations, high activity level and distinct stages of development are not nearly as salient to non-spousal family relationships, especially in old age. Yet, family relationships meet Hinde's (1979) criteria of personal relationships: ties between two or more people who are personally known to each other and who have had a period of intense interaction at some point in their history.

The study of family relationships, then, provides an opportunity to scrutinize a fuller range of the kinds of interactions that come under the rubric of personal relationships. Specifically, studying family relationships of old people gives attention to bonds that are (a) ascribed, or non-voluntary; (b) persistent, bounded only by birth and death (Riley, 1983); (c) primarily sentimental or symbolic, often in the absence of much face-to-face contact; (d) unstable, as the pool of potential resources diminishes during the course of old age (Johnson, 1993); (e) embedded within and influenced by a kinship system of relationships that span generations of members both living and dead; and (f) subsume a variety of role types (e.g., sibling, spouse, child), each with some unique norms and expectations. In the following sections we analyze each of these characteristics in turn.

Ascribed Status

Because family relations are usually assigned by birth, adoption or marriage (with the exception of spouses in non-arranged marriages, who are not included in this discussion of ascribed relationships), the objects of these relationships are not a matter of choice; they are "givens". As mentioned previously, one focus of personal relations research has been the formation of close ties, such as the role that attraction plays in the initiation process. The principles learned from such research might be applied usefully to voluntary aspects of family ties, but do not illuminate the meaning that ascribed status has for the nature and development of relationships.

It appears that the ascribed status of family ties provides a sense of security, allowing those in need of help to take it for granted that family members may be asked and are likely to respond with the desired assistance. Thus, family relationships need not be earned or won. This confidence explains a pattern rarely found in voluntary relationships, whereby intimacy is found when the need arises, even in the absence of seeking out or enjoying the person's company generally. The sense of security engendered by ascribed status also permits a greater ability to maintain active long-distance relationships with family members than with voluntary ties (Wellman & Wortley, 1989).

Persistence

The longevity of family relationships is remarkable. In Wellman & Wortley's (1989) study of 40-year-old Canadians living in East York, for instance, kin had known each other an average of 35 years, which was three times as long as for non-kin ties. Siblings usually share the longest-lived relationship of all. The significance of relationship persistence to the nature of the bond might be due to any of three influences: (a) simply the passage of time; (b) the formative nature of early experiences which largely occur with family members; and (c) the storehouse of joint experiences and knowledge of one another that accumulates over the years and that few others know.

Effects of the Passage of Time

Few relationship scholars consider the effect of the passage of time. One exception is the study of long-term friendship (e.g., Shea, Thompson & Blieszner, 1988; see also Duck, 1994a). An example of research on the effects of time is found in marriage, where persistence seems to predict marital stability. In other words, the longer a marriage has lasted, the more likely it will continue; most marriages break up during the first few years and the number of break-ups decreases as the length of marriage increases (Troll, 1985). Nonetheless, vulnerable periods occur throughout the course of marriage, such as when a couple's children reach adolescence (Huyck, 1995).

A potential source of knowledge about the influence of persistence on relationships is to study old people's marriages. Based upon reports from volunteers, old people (but husbands more than wives) rate their marriages as happy or very happy, and they report high marital satisfaction. Further, compared to younger people, old people are less likely to admit to experiencing negative feelings in their marriages, but they are also less likely to report as many positive interactions (Huyck, 1995). Also, in a study based on observational coding of a conflict resolution episode, older couples were less emotionally negative and more affectionate than middle-aged couples were (Carstensen, Gottman & Levenson, 1995). Of course, in all these investigations, age of partners co-varies with length of marriage and age marks other potential relational influences such as personality development (Gutmann, 1987; Helson & Moane, 1987; Helson & Wink, 1992), normative life events and, in the case of cross-sectional research, attrition of unhappy marriages due to divorce.

In a rare prospective study of very long-lived marriages (50–69 years in length), within-marriage change was charted (Weishaus & Field, 1988). Satisfaction and feelings of closeness increased over time for 47% of the women and 37% of the men, but this result was linked to more contact with children and less club and church activity, not to relationship longevity *per se*. Also, period effects and cohort specificity could not be ruled out. Finally, although the most common pattern of marital satisfaction was curvilinear (highest in early and late adulthood, lower in middle adulthood), diversity of reactions to marriage was the rule (see Huyck, 1995, for a review of this small literature).

Although studies of long-term marriage provide some evidence about the effects of persistence on close relationships, additional research is warranted. Specifically, investigations designed expressly to focus on relationship duration effects and studies of other long-enduring relationships, such as sibling ties, are needed to understand fully the unique importance of persistence in personal relationships.

Effects of Early Experiences

The effects of early experiences in family relationships on their later nature could be explained by both attachment and psychodynamic theories. According to attachment theory, internal working models of relationships with primary caregivers formed during infancy are subject to modification but tend to be quite stable (Levitt et al., 1994). The theory, however, postulates a shift in the attachment object in adolescence and young adulthood, so that the patterns of intimacy learned with the early attachment figures apply in adulthood to new relationships, usually with a romantic partner (Weiss, 1982). Because of this theoretically expected shift, adult attachment styles typically are not studied in connection with the family relationships in which they originally formed. One exception is the case of siblings, who sometimes function as attachment figures for infants (e.g., Stewart & Marvin, 1984). Results of a recent study indicated that attachment style contributed considerably to feelings of attachment for siblings in middle and old age (Bedford, 1993), signifying the utility of studying non-romantic attachment in adulthood.

The focus of psychodynamic theories on early experience has informed some family theories. Although usually employed in the context of clinical interventions, they can also be applied to study of the nature of later-life family relationships. Qualls (1995) explained that the way in which children's needs are met in the original family context has much to say about adult children's response to dependent parents' needs in adulthood. For example, when adult children use geographical or emotional withdrawal to regulate conflict resulting from unmet childhood needs, resumption of an active relationship for the sake of parent care might reactivate early feelings of distress and result in overt interpersonal conflict.

A few systematic studies of early experience effects in adult family relationships have appeared recently (e.g., Whitbeck, Simons & Conger, 1991). Results of one such study indicated that for three within-family generations of Swedish adults, the memory of parental preference toward a sibling compromised the level of warmth and affection between parent and child in each generation, although the association weakened in the oldest generations. It could not be determined whether the effect of early experiences weakened due to the distance in time from the event, or whether the early experience was never so intense for the older generation in the first place, based upon historical differences in family structure (Bedford, 1992).

Effects of Shared Experiences

Relationship persistence is often accompanied by an accumulation of shared experiences. This shared history has been invoked to help understand the frequent finding that sibling relationships seem to mellow in later life (Bedford, 1989; Gold, 1989). Accordingly, siblings might increasingly value their relationship over time, at least in part because they become a repository of shared family experiences, persons with whom to reminisce and affirm one's self-continuity over the years. For those whose parents are deceased, siblings are the only witnesses of early experiences in the immediate family.

Sentimental and Symbolic Ties

Sentimental Ties

Many family relationships of old people are emotionally important, despite little or no contact with individual members. These personal relationships are sustained by memories of intense interaction that occurred earlier in life. Adult siblings who are geographically distant often fall within this category (Bedford, 1989; Cicirelli, 1985). Johnson legitimized this kind of relationship in her study of the oldest old with her notion of "the family as a vessel of sentiment" (Johnson, 1993). Characterizing family rather than individual relationships, Johnson explained that in these families "no instrumental functions are performed, roles have become inactive and reciprocity is absent. Even when feelings of attachment persist, contacts are usually confined to intermittent letters and telephone calls. Thus most of the time, the family persists in the memories of surviving members" (1993, p. 326).

Recognizing purely sentimental family relationships is a significant change from the decades-old pattern of using frequency of contact with family members as a handy measure of the psychosocial importance of ties with relatives. Today much evidence supports the fact that rate of interaction among family members is not directly associated with the quality of the relationships, their meaning to the partners, or the level of satisfaction derived from them (e.g., Field & Minkler, 1993; Thompson & Walker, 1984). Johnson's (1993) findings illustrate that quite a few very old people derive considerable satisfaction from relationships that include very little contact or are devoid of it altogether. The question arises, then, under what circumstances does contact (or its lack) either enhance or interfere with satisfying family relationships in later life?

Lack of contact with a relative who is geographically distant, has limited financial resources, or suffers poor health might be easier to excuse than with one whose neglect appears to be volitional. Interestingly, deprivation of contact due to death is not always excused by the surviving relative. An initial grief response is frequently anger, sometimes directed at the deceased person (Kübler-Ross, 1969), even though death is not usually considered to be purposeful unless it was caused by suicide or an extremely unhealthy life style. Perhaps the underlying quality of the relationship plays a mediating role in the association between contact frequency and relationship satisfaction. For instance, limited contact would relate to positive feelings in a basically conflicted relationship when physical distance is used to manage tension (Weisner, 1982). As mentioned earlier, however, when frequent contact is again resumed, any problematic aspects of the relationship are often reactivated (Allan, 1977; Laverty, 1962).

Also, attributing negative motivation to a family member's contact is likely to interfere with deriving pleasure from visits. When there is no contact, this is not an issue; an old person does not have to worry, for instance, that the family member is in touch purely out of obligation, which is often assumed by old persons when they are ill (Field & Minkler, 1993). Lack of contact, thus, can potentiate the idealization of family relationships and the containment of difficult relationships within a manageable context.

Attenuated Ties

Relationships with deceased family members have not been studied, but Moss & Moss (1995) recommend this as a topic of future research. In support of this recommendation, Troll (1994) found that 59% of her sample of adults in their 80s named a deceased person as an attachment figure. It appears, then, that such relationships might be central to the lives of quite a few older adults. An important question is how such ties are sustained; possible means are through diary entries addressed to a deceased relative, plans to meet in a later life, and regular communications at the grave site of a relative. Also, nothing is known about the location of such ties within personal networks, or the network characteristics that support such ties. For instance, are continued ties with deceased family members most likely to be found among individuals whose active social needs are met? Or do they substitute for impoverished relationships or depleted social networks? Do they answer a need for immortality, providing hope that the survivor's memory will be sustained similarly?

Some old people have non-active ties with relatives that do not even engage the emotional life of the elders, namely, the "attenuated ties" identified by Johnson (1993). Typically, at least for very old persons, these relationships were broken off due to severe conflict or they resulted from the death of relatives who were subsequently forgotten. Sibling ties attenuated earlier in adulthood often prove to be latent and resume activity later, when life circumstances permit (Bank & Kahn, 1982).

Such a change is not likely to occur in late life when few years of existence remain, but nothing is known about the meaning of a lack of family ties in old age. Does such an absence serve some adaptive function for old people who must cope with multiple losses or neglect from family members? Does it reflect unresolved conflicts with family members? Do elders with no family ties have substitutions for family relations via fictive kin or friends? Nor is much known about the effect of an attenuated family on the well-being of old persons, except that they are likely to lack informal caregivers, should the need for care arise (Johnson & Troll, 1996).

One special case of attenuated ties with family members occurs among some Holocaust survivors who avoid conversation and thoughts about relatives who perished in the ordeal. Perhaps refraining from emotional engagement with the memories of these relatives is unconsciously motivated by a wish to keep them alive. Specifically, the lack of engagement actually helps to maintain ties with the dead. By avoiding overt references to the murdered relatives, the survivors avoid mourning their loss, which, in turn, maintains the illusion that the relatives are still alive. The price of the illusion, however, is buried memories and an incomplete family history to share with future generations (Shoshan, 1989). Whether this formulation has application to other attenuated ties in old age awaits further study.

Instability

The loss of family members, particularly through death, creates a situation of social instability in the lives of old people. Geographic mobility and death are the chief sources of family losses. Geographic distance can be bridged though technological means (telephone calls, travel) when financial and temporal resources are available and when health permits. Loss through death, of course, eliminates the possibility of any kind of interaction other than the symbolic form described earlier. Other losses result from functional causes, as when the family partner is no longer coherent or able to maintain one side of the partnership. Whatever the cause, these losses alter the interpersonal life of old individuals.

Whether relationship instability affects the quality of family ties in later life is another area deprived of direct research results. Nevertheless, a large literature on widowhood offers some insight into this question where one central loss has been experienced. An additional perspective on the effects of relationship instability can be gained from research on friendship in old age.

Widowhood as an Example of Instability

Relationship instability manifested in widowhood gives a fairly concrete picture of how loss affects other family relationships in old age. Widowhood is a common experience of older adults, especially women. Among adults aged 65 years and older, 70% of women but only 22% of men are widowed. Further, women are widowed for a longer period on average (15 years) than are men (6 years) (O'Bryant & Hansson, 1995).

Despite a vast literature on widowhood, the consequences of its anticipation for other relationships have not been investigated. Perhaps its near universality for women at least helps to account for women's greater involvement in friendship networks than men's (Blieszner & Adams, 1992) and the fact that married women, unlike their husbands, share confidences outside their marital relationship (Oliker, 1989). Although other reasons are usually given for such gender differences in social networks, anticipated widowhood would seem to be a sensible motive as well.

Research on adaptation after widowhood with respect to other relationships indicates that widows tend to preserve their independence from other family members, but to move geographically nearer to them. Sometimes, an adult child moves in with a widowed parent (O'Bryant & Hansson, 1995). After controlling for family size in longitudinal analyses of family interaction among widows, findings indicate that the number of family contacts increases for older widows, but does not change for widowers (Morgan, 1984). These patterns suggest that widowed persons are not seeking substitutes but are attempting to compensate for the spousal loss in some way with more access to other family members than they had prior to their widowhood.

Studies of remarried widowed persons compared with non-remarried widowed persons demonstrate many social and emotional advantages of remarriage. Apparently, for many bereaved elders the best adjustment to the loss of a marital partner is to remarry. These findings are consistent with Weiss's (1982) observation that one type of relationship cannot substitute effectively for another, although this might be more true for men than women. Despite increased contact with other family members, intimacy needs specifically met by a marital partner cannot be met by others, except perhaps in relationships between sisters (O'Bryant & Hansson, 1995). In fact, loneliness is the major affective problem of widowed persons. Children tend to provide financial aid when needed and to help more with household tasks than before their parent was widowed, but these services do not address their parent's loneliness. Nevertheless, widowed persons' typical stated reasons for wanting to remarry do not address alleviation of loneliness. Rather, widowers express the desire for a friend and confidant, whereas widows desire the prestige and status afforded them by their social circle when they are courted (O'Bryant & Hansson, 1995).

Adaptation to Instability

Matthews (1986) developed a typology of relational responses to friendship loss that might apply to family relationships as well. According to the typology, the effect of a friendship loss on people's lives depends on how they defined the relationship. For example, people who define a loss in terms of friendship generally, rather than in terms of a particular individual, might be able to substitute a new friend for the old one, thereby replenishing the pool of associates. At first glance, applying this friendship style to family ties reveals that many lost family relationships, such as those with a child, spouse (particularly for women, given the dearth of available men in later life), or sibling, have no literal replacement. Studies of childless older adults indicate, however, that a broader definition of family can open the possibilities for substitutions. Whereas attempts at vertical substitutions (up and down generational lines) limit the pool of eligible relatives, collateral substitutions, typical of those practiced by Blacks and Italians, provide more possibilities (Johnson & Barer, 1996). Cousins, nephews and nieces, for instance, can substitute for absent siblings and children in old age.

Another adaptation to friendship loss is to let circumstances dictate their substitution (Matthews, 1986). Thus, friends are where one finds them; when friends depart, those who inhabit one's life circumstances take their place. This coping style can be applied to family loss in terms of the adoption of fictive kin. In Johnson's sample, an aunt explained that her niece, whom she reared, is thus her daughter. Fictive kin are not necessarily relatives of a different degree; they need not be related at all. Particularly in Black communities, fictive kin can take the place of relatives who died, were never present, or were rarely needed earlier, as in the case of old people who never had children (Johnson & Barer, 1996).

Family Systems

Just as at other stages of the life course, family interactions in the later years take place within a system of interlocking relationships. The extended family system typically refers to the totality of kin relationships, synonymous with a social network of relatives. Following cybernetic principles, each member of the family and particular relationships between members cannot be regarded as independent units that function in isolation from one another (La Gaipa, 1981). One person's behavior is influenced, whether knowingly or unknowingly, by behaviors of others, within and across generations and households. In turn, each member's behaviors are responded to by others, resulting in complex feedback loops. Subjective family relationships with members living and dead play a major part in the family system. For instance, an unresolved rift with a parent who has since died will, inevitably but without awareness, be reflected in the adult child's relationship to his or her children. If the rift is unresolved, the next generation will likely be affected by it as well (Bozormenyi-Nagy & Spark, 1973).

Applications of Systems Theory

Clinicians have applied such principles to understanding problematic relationships between family members and psychological disorders of individuals. Qualls (1995) expanded this application to understanding issues involving old members of families. According to the systems formulation, presenting problems are symptoms of basic dysfunctional processes within the family. Typical symptoms in later-life families are cut-off relationships, in which one family member breaks off all contact with another; excessive disability in one member, usually an older one; and excessive conflict surrounding care of aged parents, whether between child and parent, or among siblings. Such symptoms are believed to channel attention away from more fundamental problems. Symptoms are difficult to alleviate, because doing so would enable the underlying problems involving other family members to erupt (Qualls, 1995). For example, in a sibling caregiver support group, some primary caregivers who felt they got no cooperation from their siblings learned that they (the caregivers) were actually pushing their siblings away in a last-ditch effort to finally win favored status from their parent, which they had coveted since childhood (Altschuler, Jacobs & Shiode, 1985). Thus, an unrecognized parent–child conflict, which might have had roots in the parent's original family, is manifested in sibling conflict over parent care.

The systems framework is usually used to understand the behaviors of whole families rather than personal relationships within the family (Sprey, 1991), in part because general systems are much simpler than highly complex, constantly changing, less organized family processes (Broderick, 1993). Recent examples include research on normative family processes, such as the division of parent care tasks among siblings (Matthews & Sprey, 1989) and assignment of the family kin keepers (Troll, 1996).

The systems model is also useful for identifying many family-level variables that might contribute to personal family relationships (La Gaipa, 1981). Properties of systems that might be applied to understanding older families are (a) their openness, referring to input to the family system from the environment and output from the family system to the environment; (b) their ongoing nature, suggesting that they are constantly in flux, responding to environmental pressures (e.g., income loss) and changes in family members (e.g., onset of illness or developmental transitions); (c) their goal-seeking, indicating the selection, rank ordering and pursuit of aims; and (d) their self-regulating nature, or responding appropriately with change (adaptation) or maintenance of stability (homeostasis) in order to preserve the integrity of the system when threatened (Broderick, 1993).

Effects of Systems Properties on Family Relationships

How do these general systems properties influence family relationships with and by old members? Openness and stability are two systemic properties that have particular relevance to relationships in later-life families. The openness of the system can be translated into the dimension of cohesiveness (see Olsen, Russell & Sprenkle's 1979 presentation of the circumplex model for a thorough discussion of this dimension). Cohesive or highly integrated families provide a sense of belonging and of integration with the family group, responding to the need for connection. An opposing need is the individual's desire to differentiate from the family unit and to forge a separate identity, which requires distancing from others while engaging in independent interests, ideas and relationships. The needs for connection and separateness do not present problems in family relationships when the relative strength of these opposing needs is similar for an interacting set of partners, because the shifting "relational distance" between them in response to one or the other need is mutually satisfying (Broderick, 1993). When relational distance needs conflict and a compromise cannot be negotiated, however, problems can emerge, such as the disenchantment evident in long-term marriages and the loneliness expressed by Swedish wives (Josselson, 1992). The concept of *intimacy at a distance*, referring to a pattern of living in a separate household but staying closely connected to family members, is an example of a satisfactory resolution of these opposing needs for "bonding and buffering" in relation to family members (Josselson, 1992). By maintaining separate households, old people protect their privacy and independence, meeting such personal needs as self-reflection (see Gratton & Haber, 1993).

Stability, or degree of adaptiveness to change by the family system, is another helpful concept for understanding relationships in later-life families. As the focus moves from the level of whole systems to subsystems to individuals, stability decreases. In other words, individuals and dyads change more easily than the family as a whole does. For instance, even if a family member dies or a couple divorces, family celebrations of holidays are not likely to be affected too much. The system is usually maintained by one or more kin keepers who host and organize such functions. As a testimony to the stability of the system, kin keepers who die or are no longer able to carry out their functions are invariably replaced by other family members, even in very loosely bonded families. In such families, though, the succession process is less smooth and the number of kin keepers participating is smaller than in more tightly bonded families (Troll, 1996).

Making decisions about goals and their relative priorities and executing them is a complex process that involves the relative power of family members, pragmatic needs, resources and other concerns. Family gerontologists have been criticized for ignoring the systems level when investigating the processes involved in care-giving (see Matthews & Sprey, 1989; Sprey, 1991). A recent attempt to analyze the decision to institutionalize a parent demonstrated rather dramatically the degree to which systemic as opposed to individual level factors accounted for the decision. Change in the health status of the frail family member was not a significant factor in the decision. Instead, a wide array of family variables contributed to the determination to use an institution: placement was more likely when there were more, not fewer, care-givers, when no spouse was present, and when the care-giver's subjective distress increased (Lieberman & Kramer, 1991).

Role Type

Effects of Role Types

Family role type appears to contribute some unique information about the ensuing relationship. Examples of types of family roles are mother, father, child, sister, brother, aunt, uncle, spouse, various in-laws. In the social support literature, relationship category is considered to be a property of personal relationships (e.g., Pierce, Sarason & Sarason, 1990; Sarason, Sarason & Pierce, 1994). No doubt this property subsumes many expectations of the role, expectations derived from personal experiences with someone in that role, the norms peculiar to one's own family system and the social norms of broader reference groups. Of interest here is whether a family role type has shared meaning (within or across cultures), what the nature of that shared meaning might be, and how that meaning affects the nature of family relationships in later life in addition to the other influences already discussed. See recent reviews of research on old age parent–child, sibling and marital and marital-like relationships in Blieszner & Bedford (1995) and Dykstra (1990) (for discussions of relationships with inlaws, see Kivett, 1989; Burger & Milardo, 1995)

Of particular concern to gerontologists are the functions various family role types provide old people. Empirical studies converge on the finding that, in general, some social support provisions cluster around certain role types. In other words, in most categories of network members, people provide a few specialized functions (Fehr & Perlman, 1985; Wellman & Wortley, 1989). Similarly, using a very large sample, Dykstra (1993) found among the Dutch that overlap among relationship categories occurs, but people in every category also provide some unique forms of social support. An important exception is parents and adult children who engage in exchanges of multiple provisions (Wellman & Wortley, 1989). Other inter- and intragenerational distinctions are discussed further in the next sections.

In a recent study by van Tilburg (1990), type of role relationship was not a good proxy for social support functions of relationships. This finding did not rule out the possibility that role type conveys other important information about social support, however. Those occupying various relationship categories might behave similarly, such as providing the same services, but the effect of these functions might be experienced quite differently, depending on who (in terms of role type) is carrying out the task (Pierce, Sarason & Sarason, 1990; Sarason, Sarason & Pierce, 1994). In fact, this expectation has been demonstrated in several studies. The same specific behaviors, for example, are differentially helpful to cancer patients, depending upon the source of the support given (Dakof & Taylor, 1990; Felton & Berry, 1992). Also, contact with family members of different role types appears to be differentially associated with the marital satisfaction of young middle adults. Further, the direction of the association might be different for husbands and wives. Wives' kin contacts, particularly with brothers-in-law, are associated with negative marital qualities, whereas husbands' contacts with kin, particularly fathers, are associated with positive marital qualities (Burger & Milardo, 1995).

Effects of Generational Categories

These investigations indicate, then, that role type differentiates relationships both according to some functions and according to the shared meanings individuals attribute to their actions. Role types fall into two broader categories, however, that also differentially affect family relationships. These categories are intergenerational (vertical) and intragenerational (horizontal) relationships. They are distinguished by generational membership within the family and, it is assumed, by cohort difference. The latter distinction, that familial generations occupy different generations in time, or cohorts, should not be taken for granted, however. One's sibling might be comparable in age to one's child and one's step-parent, aunt or uncle might be near one's own age. In the typical case, however, when cohort differences are much greater between generations than within generations, one important difference between inter- and intragenerational relationships is that the former involve individuals who have different historical backgrounds. Historical events experienced by different generations are likely to shape their expectations and outlooks differently (Hagestad, 1984). Thus, intergenerational partners are faced with divergent value systems, technological advances, interests and experiences. Apparently, outright conflict is avoided in families by steering clear of sensitive topics and by reciprocal socialization, or educating each about the other. Hagestad suggested that those who occupy both parent and child roles simultaneously in multigenerational families might play a special role in bridging intergenerational differences because of their personal insight into both positions. As such, they function as "brokers" of stability and change across generations (1984, p. 141).

Intragenerational relationships also have unique properties. Most noticeable is the status equivalence between these relatives compared to that of intergenerational relatives (Johnson & Barer, 1996). In Western societies, intragenerational ties are more voluntary than intergenerational ones. Therefore, when intragenerational ties are active, they are more likely than intergenerational ones to be based on affection (Leigh, 1982). A comparison of Black and White siblings in old age indicates important differences, however. For instance, value consensus is a key predictor of sibling association among Whites, whereas Blacks are more likely to associate with a sibling who is different—perhaps younger in age or less educated (Suggs, 1989). Another characteristic that differentiates collateral from intergenerational bonds is that collateral ties usually recruit more relatives. Strong sibling relationships lead to more ties with cousins, nieces and nephews who also occupy collateral family positions, whereas a vertical emphasis results in peripheral relations with collateral relatives. The result of having the wider pool of relatives that accompanies an emphasis on collateral ties is that old people in such families are likely to have their social support needs fully met, as seen in the Black community (Dilworth-Anderson, 1992). Nowhere is the difference between the emphasis on collateral and vertical ties more noticeable than in the family support systems of very old childless Blacks, who are relatively unaffected by the absence of children of their own, and very old childless Whites, whose family resources are greatly impoverished by having no children (Johnson & Barer, 1996).

SUMMARY AND CONCLUSION

In the first section of the chapter, we used demographic trends and projections to illustrate characteristics of families that include old people. We also evaluated various definitions of family, developing them to arrive eventually at one that incorporates elderly members and accounts for the structure and processes found when families have elderly members.

In the second section, we examined family relationships of old people in terms of a selection of features that tend to be invisible in the more commonly studied relationships of the personal relations field, namely, marriage and friendship. Thus, we identified six themes that typify family bonds generally, some of which are brought into sharper focus when older adults are involved. The literature on these themes was mined for their known effects on relationships, the effects, in sum, of ascribed rather than voluntary relationships, persistent interactions, sentimental or symbolic ties, unstable relationship resources, systemic functioning and varying role types.

The literature associated with these dimensions of family bonds is vast and we could provide only a few examples and brief summaries in this review. Readers should realize, nevertheless, that the family gerontology literature reveals a rich array of interaction patterns and outcomes that hold much promise for extending the findings from research on romantic and friendship relationships, and for a much fuller understanding of interpersonal life in general.

Not only does study of the family relationships with and by old people expand and sharpen the vision of personal relations study, this category of relationship experience is becoming increasingly normative in the lives of adults and it is enduring through ever longer periods of their lives. Demographic data suggest that most people's lives will be touched by increased involvements with older family members of the same or different generations. It makes no sense, therefore, to continue segregating the study of relationships with and by older adults in a separate research specialty; such relationships should be integrated within mainstream research on personal relationships.

It is also important to keep in mind that personal relations research has much to contribute to the understanding of older families which are, of course, composed of personal relationships, albeit highly interconnected ones. A constructive dialogue between the two sets of scholars holds much promise in unraveling many unsolved riddles about human relationships. One highly intriguing one, with significant practical implications, is how social support buffers stress. For instance, in research comparing spouses and siblings providing care for a frail old person, why was it found that only siblings suffered when the relationship was of poor quality, and why did siblings suffer more than spouses from lack of respite and from perceived conflict in their lives (Mui & Morrow-Howell, 1993)? Perhaps this example shows that family and aging scholars have contributed to the personal relationships literature in general by highlighting a previously hidden dimension of marriage. That is, the marital relationship *per se* can have a powerful buffering effect on stressful experiences, even when the marital partner himself or herself is a source of stress. In turn, perhaps personal relations scholars can glean new insights about the affective consequences to a relationship of having accumulated a vast store of social debt within it. Thus, reciprocal interplay between family gerontology and personal relations research has potential for greatly enhanced understanding of the functions and processes of personal relationships across the life course.

Section V

Clinical and Community Psychology

Section Editor: Barbara R. Sarason
University of Washington, Seattle, WA, USA

Personal relationships are not always benign and relational behavior may have a negative impact. Further, some individuals are so lacking in meaningful personal relationships that others, as clinicians or members of the community, may need to supply the resources and functions that positive personal relationships would ordinarily provide. This section shows some of the important intersections between the study of personal relationships and both community processes and clinical phenomena, including the etiology and treatment of maladaptive behavior. It is interesting and significant that such diverse phenomena as the immigrant experience, serious psychiatric disorders such as schizophrenia and major depressive episodes, physical health outcomes, natural disasters, and psychotherapy can all be fruitfully analyzed in terms of interpersonal and relational dynamics. The chapters in this section explore these dynamics in the light of recent research.

Nearly a decade ago, in the previous edition of this *Handbook*, two commonalities between clinical and community psychology and the study of personal relationships were evident: (1) a focus on the observation and measurement of interpersonal behaviors, and (2) an emphasis on the present rather than the past in understanding current problems. The importance of an individual's personal relationships was recognized in studying both the onset and development of clinical problems and how those working from either an individual or community perspective might design appropriate interventions for amelioration or prevention. As the chapters in this second edition of the *Handbook* show, these themes are still highly relevant. However, the level of sophistication in dealing with them empirically has increased greatly. Researchers have come to realize that personal interactions and personal relationships can be important change agents and that a variety of aspects of these relationships, including both their positive and negative qualities, need to be considered. Further, progress can be seen in the fact that researchers in the areas of community and clinical psychology are increasingly including personal relationship variables in their research designs, rather than merely paying them lip service. Further, they are working actively to develop and evaluate measures of a variety of aspects of these relationships and their connection to outcomes in a variety of situations.

One of the research areas that illustrates this change most clearly is that of social support. All the chapters in this section deal, with varying degrees of explicitness, with perceptions and provision of social support. In their chapter, Sarason, Sarason & Gurung review some of findings concerning the tie between social support and health. They point out a number of continuing problems in this field of research, including definitional and measurement issues as well as the sometimes negative consequences of attempted support provision. Evidence reviewed in this chapter indicates that one solution to some of the controversies, concerning not only connections between social support and health but the process by which they are achieved, lies in a study of the qualities of the personal relationships between the support providers and the support recipients. In their chapters, Trickett & Buchanan, and Kaniasty & Norris, respectively, deal with the role of support and personal relationships in assisting individuals in stressful situation. Hooley & Hiller, in the following chapter, deal with a very special type of stress, having a person with a severe mental disorder in the family. These authors highlight the role that personal relationship qualities can play in preventing relapse for the affected person as well as lessening feelings of stress of other family members. Heller & Rook, in their analysis of community level support, present a penetrating view of how specification of the processes involved in social ties can shed theoretical and practical light on the way to create effective support interventions on a community level. In the final chapter in this section, Mallinckrodt carefully delineates the role relationships play in individual and group psychotherapy both as direct therapeutic agents and in the enhancement of social competencies.

Sarason et al. point out the significance not only of the degree to which a person believes support to be available, but also of the characteristics of the relationship between the supporter or potential supporter and the intended recipient. A number of researchers have now pointed out that support may come at a price. The recipient may feel diminished by receiving help, guilty for causing others to be inconvenienced, or angry at the price exacted by expectations of the supporter concerning future behaviors of the support recipient. These authors also describe research findings showing that information about qualities of the relationship with the supporter add to the prediction of a variety of health and adjustment outcomes. They argue that the global measures of support generally used in the field are often relatively weak predictors of health outcome, because they call upon the respondent to give an overall or impressionistic view of the help to be available without taking into account the meaning transmitted to the recipient as a consequence of positive and negative aspects of his or her relationship with the support provider. In the same way, the messages conveyed implicitly by the potential recipient may alter the providers' implicit communications that accompany the support. Although support researchers are becoming cognizant of the importance of support definitions and measurement issues, the lack of basic theory in the social support field has represented an important obstacle to progress in understanding the support process. The inclusion of the personal relationship perspective, together with emphasis on cognitions and expectations of both the recipient or potential recipient and the support provider may be an important avenue to improving both theory and predictive efficacy.

In their chapter, Trickett and Buchanan are concerned with the role that relationships play when people make transitions in social and cultural contexts. They adopt an ecological perspective that heightens the importance of the context in which the transitions are taking place and the personal relationships that are involved. These questions are important because individuals' lives usually encompass a series of transitions that may produce at least temporary disequilibrium that has both social or ecological and interpersonal aspects. Transitions differ greatly in their adaptive requirements, but all require some changes in individuals' assumptions about the world, themselves and others. The stress produced by these changes may tax an individual's coping abilities. Thus, in this chapter the authors utilize a ecological or community perspective to clarify how personal relationships may impact adjustment in a wide variety of stressful transitions, including motherhood as an unmarried adolescent, school transitions for adolescents and becoming an immigrant to a country in which the cultural setting may differ widely from that the person has known. In each of these transitions, the authors point out how cultural and social context can shape the meaning and role of personal relationships. The inclusion of the immigrant experience, both in this chapter and in the Heller & Rook chapter in this section, illustrates a new and increasingly important focus within several fields of psychology, the role of cultural change as a stressor and the effects of differing cultural expectations in relationship satisfaction.

Just as relationships can provide support and enhanced coping in stressful situations affecting an individual, the adjustment of whole communities to overwhelming events such as natural disasters can be affected by the dynamics of social support. In their chapter, Kaniasty & Norris present an overview of what is known about who gets support and who is neglected when a community is hit by disaster. They point out that the image of widespread altruism following disasters and the participation in what has been called the post-disaster therapeutic community are not phenomena in which all community members participate equally. Apparent need, size of relationship network, race or ethnicity, economic status, age and even gender all play a role in determining both what types of support and how much support is offered. Further, the kind of help needed, for example help for illness or injury vs. property damage, also plays a role in the degree to which these variables predict who will receive the most help. Relationship-based support is often less available than usual because those in individuals' networks are likely to live close by and to be affected by the disaster as well. The limitations of well known principles of disaster response in predicting support received by any individual in the disaster area, as well as the findings of Kaniasty's & Norris's own research, not only point toward improved disaster response but to better reactions to other collective events that may impact large numbers of individuals. They also provide important theoretical clues for those interested in the support process.

In their chapter, Heller & Rook also deal with support interventions and the crucial knowledge gaps that exist concerning the ingredients that make a supportive intervention effective. They are particularly concerned with how community psychologists may provide guidance in the development of new or alternate supports for individuals and groups for whom indigenous support is either lacking in presence or in effectiveness. They, as do Sarason et al., and Kaniasty & Norris, point out the difficulties inherent in the various conceptualizations and definitions of support for social support theory and application. Just as Kaniasty & Norris found that different types of needed support provision were predicted by different sets of variables, Heller & Rook point out the various types of support provision that need to be considered in understanding how to build supportive interventions. They also highlight the role that social relationships play, not only in providing social support but also in enhanced coping efforts, in affect regulation in which negative emotions are not only diffused but positive affect is stimulated, and as a source of social control which may be helpful even if these actions are not perceived by the recipient as affirming. Taking all these effects into account, the Heller & Rook chapter provides an in-depth discussion of indigenous vs. grafted social ties as effective support provision. The effects of these different sources of support and the approaches to substitution of grafted ties if the the indigenous ties are lacking provide both theoretical and practical guidance concerning the role of relationships in support. Knowledge of the critical constituents of both forms of support and their effects can be helpful in formulating support efforts in a wide variety of situations. One situation in which Heller & Rook have particular current interest is in work with immigrants referred for clinical treatment of psychological disorders. Interventions with such individuals need to include efforts to overcome cultural stereotypes and concerns of both the client and those with whom they have meaningful relationships—family members and others within their ethnic community—because such stereotypes often prevent those with serious psychological problems from obtaining adequate clinical treatment.

In their chapter, Hooley & Hiller deal with a stressor very different from transitions and sudden environmental changes discussed in the preceding chapters. They focus on the stress of major mental disorders and their effects on family relationships. They point out that although there is still relatively little evidence concerning the role of psychosocial factors in the onset of mental disorders, the role of these risk factors in psychiatric relapse is becoming well documented. In the 1950s and 1960s many theorists, particularly those of a psychoanalytic or family systems persuasion, considered disturbed family relationships and intrafamilial transactions as probable causes of severe mental disorders, especially schizophrenia. This view, which often led to the blaming of family members by mental health professionals, was challenged and gradually replaced by genetic explanations. However, for some time afterwards, negative views of these earlier theories made suspect the study of relationships in families in which one member developed severe psychiatric symptomotology. Over the past three decades researchers have been measuring forms of family members' emotional expression in the home that might help account for increased likelihood of relapse, especially in individuals who had been discharged from a hospital with a diagnosis of schizophrenic disorder. This research, on what came to be called expressed emotion, has developed a solid body of work connecting relapse in patients with schizophrenic disorder with the presence in the living situation of at least one person who displayed behavior that met the expressed emotion criteria in the areas of criticism, hostility and/or emotional over-involvement. More recently these research efforts have suggested that family relationships characterized by high levels of expressed emotion also are associated with probability of relapse in major depression and bipolar disorder, dietary control in diabetic as well as obese patients, and anorexia. Another aspect of disturbed family communication, communication deviance, has been found to predict the onset of a serious disorder in two studies of children who already were thought to be vulnerable to disorder. Research on expressed emotion and communication deviance within family relationships has also led to intervention efforts focused on improving family–patient relationships and family communication skills, especially clarity of communication. Some of these programs have been quite successful, although success seems related to treating patient and family members together and focusing on problem-solving and on behavior, rather than on dynamic insight. The authors highlight how attention to the specifics of communication patterns and content, and other aspects of social interactions between patients with severe psychiatric disorders and their families and their recursive effects, can advance theory as well as intervention efforts.

In the final chapter in this section, Mallinckrodt focuses on one of the mainstays of clinical psychology, psychotherapy. He develops a social competencies interpersonal process model of psychotherapy that takes into account characteristics of both client and therapist as they contribute to the therapeutic outcome. This chapter is focused primarily on the interpersonal relationship processes as a vehicle for change in client symptoms and behaviors. From this purview client symptoms are viewed as interpersonal problems. Mallinckrodt believes that interpersonal behavior, in the case of the therapeutic setting primarily verbal behaviors, can be most fruitfully conceptualized by using some variation of the interpersonal circumplex model. He lays out clearly how a variety of aspects of relationships play a role in therapy. First, the relationship between therapist and client may be therapeutic in itself. The therapeutic relationship also may have an effect on the social competencies of the client as the therapist and client work at managing conflict and disappointment in the therapy sessions. Throughout the chapter Mallinckrodt emphasizes the dyadic nature of the therapeutic situation in individual psychotherapy. His discussion encompasses therapists' past personal experiences as well as supervisory experiences as contributors to the therapeutic relationship, not only in terms of transference and countertransference but also as determinants of the actual client–therapist relationship and the working alliance that is developed. Throughout the chapter he cites a variety of studies and theoretical positions regarding the role of relationships in therapy and evaluates the current status of each. Finally, the chapter examines these same ideas as they apply to group therapy and describes the roles of both therapist–client and group member relationships in the therapeutic process.

When viewed as a whole these chapters demonstrate the degree to which the study of personal relationships and interpersonal communication have become central in many aspects of theory and practice in clinical and community psychology. At the same time the state of knowledge in each of the areas covered—physical and mental health, transitions, disasters, and individual and community efforts at prevention and rehabilitation—demonstrates clearly the need for continued attention to, assessment of, and effective strategies for alteration of deficient personal relationship patterns.

Chapter 24

Close Personal Relationships and Health Outcomes: a Key to the Role of Social Support

Barbara R. Sarason
Irwin G. Sarason
and
Regan A.R. Gurung
University of Washington, Seattle, WA, USA

Social support has been found to be health-promoting, health-restoring and associated with a decrease in mortality risk. It appears to protect individuals from the negative effects of stress on health and adjustment. However, important questions regarding the social support–health connection remain to be answered, such as: What counts as social support? Is it important to specify the sources of social support? What role do close personal relationships play in the support process? Are various types of social support equally effective in relation to health outcomes? This chapter will argue that although the past two decades have greatly enhanced our confidence that a social support-health connection exists, and at least in some circumstances may be robust, we must turn back to a study of the role of close personal relationships in order to understand the social support process.

The field of social support rose to prominence both quickly and relatively recently. Although the topic first appeared in the research literature in the early 1970s, the total number of papers dealing with social support has now grown to well over 5000. Much has been learned in a little over two decades, but the issues raised above indicate that many questions of both theoretical and practical importance remain to be answered. This chapter reviews some of what we do know about social support and health and suggests how investigating their connection in terms of the role played by close personal relationships and the meaning of

Handbook of Personal Relationships, 2nd edn. Edited by Steve Duck.
© 1997 John Wiley & Sons Ltd.

these relationships to the individuals involved can contribute substantially to our understanding of the support process, as well as providing enhanced prediction of the effects of social support.

Those interested in social support and its effects might do well to remember that they are interested in *social* support and that the implications of the term "social" deserve careful assessment. In one of two papers generally recognized as seminal to the field, Cassel (1976) referred to the importance of "meaningful social contact" for health and focused on social support largely through its mediation of physiological processes. Because Cassel used both animal and human studies to draw these conclusions, his view of social contact was primarily concerned with its presence or absence rather than with aspects of the relationships on which the social contact might be based. Looking at Cassel's paper from a later perspective, we can argue that perhaps the word "meaningful" is key to the effects he described but that its conceptual and practical importance may have been ignored as the field has grown (see also Duck, 1994a). Because the most meaningful social contact for most people is provided by those they consider their intimates, a sharpening of many current definitions of social support might be desirable to take into account the qualities of the relationships involved in these social contacts and the way that meaningfulness is established and affects both relationship-based supportive behavior and its interpretation, Cobb (1976), in the second paper most often cited as seminal in the social support field, approached the topic from a different perspective. He focused on the information provided to the recipient of social support rather than on the general effects of social integration. In his view support consisted of one or more classes of information conveyed through social interactions: information that led the individual to believe that she or he was (a) cared for and loved, (b) esteemed and valued, and (c) belonged to a network of communication and mutual obligation in which others could be counted on for assistance if necessity arose. This information could serve to enhance the person's feelings of personal worthiness as someone who is worth caring about and, in addition, might decrease anxieties concerning personal coping efficacy by suggesting that if personal coping was inadequate, others' help would be forthcoming. Cobb was, at least by implication, focusing on the role of close relationships in providing support and the meaning of the relationship behaviors in communicating the qualities of the relationship.

Other early papers on social support also made the emphasis on close relationships even more explicit. When Henderson (1977), in his work on the role of social bonds, sought to measure social support, he designed a measure focused on each of two somewhat different types of interpersonal contacts (Henderson et al., 1980). One part of his measure, the Interview Schedule for Social Interactions, assessed casual social contacts that are part of most people's daily routine and presumably cause them to feel interconnected or embedded within the community. The second part focused on the presence of an intimate confiding relationship and the qualities of that relationship. Henderson argued that the two types of social contacts and the support they provided had different roles in individual adjustment. Brown & Harris (1978) focused their attention on social support in terms of the buffering or protective role of at least one close relationship and showed that the availability of one or more confidants was essential for mental health, at least when a person had experienced stressful life situations. Although both Henderson and Brown & Harris were influenced by John Bowlby's (1969, 1980a, 1980b) attachment theory and its role in mental health, most researchers in the field of social support did not begin to focus on Bowlby's ideas until much later. Despite the emphasis on relationship-based support by these pioneers, over time emphasis in the social support area turned away from a focus on close relationships and their effects. This came about in part because of the ways in which support was operationalized in a rapidly increasing range of assessment instruments. These efforts to quantify the support phenomenon, briefly reviewed later in this chapter, enhanced research efforts by providing convenient methods of assessment. However, they also distracted both theorists and applied researchers from some issues basic to understanding and utilizing social support.

Before reviewing what we now know about the role of close personal relationships in social support, and what pursuing this avenue further might yield in enhanced understanding of the support process and the mechanisms by which it affects health outcomes, we will first look at several related topics. These include: What are the primary definitions of social support on which the instruments currently used in support research are based? What assumptions concerning personal relationships, both their nature and how they function, are implicit in each of these definitions? What do we know about the relations between social support and health? Do these relations differ depending on the definitions of social support used? How might a consideration of findings resulting from different definitional bases of social support enhance, rather than confuse, our understanding of the support process? Do aspects of the person relate directly to these health outcomes or do they primarily function indirectly through their effects on the person's social support receipt or expectations? How might a consideration of close relationships, especially communication that establishes participants' views of relationship quality, enhance this theoretical picture as well as the practical applications of knowledge gained through social support research?

CONCEPTUALIZATIONS OF SOCIAL SUPPORT

In order to discuss the meaning of the social support and health findings to date, it is important to review how social support has been conceptualized. The origins of the idea can be traced to non-theoretical ideas about basic human requirements for association with others (Veiel & Baumann, 1992) and, as a result, early ideas concerning the support concept excluded concerns about mechanisms and processes. Early studies defined and measured social support by categorizing the individual as married or single, and roughly determining contact with others both in his or her daily contacts and through membership in voluntary groups. This apparent simplicity, reflected in several important early studies, provided considerable appeal to researchers in fields of epidemiology, psychology, psychiatry and sociology. As the social support research area developed further, several alternative approaches to measurement evolved. The measurement instruments that grew from these approaches can be grouped into three general categories: (1) network measures that assess embeddedness in a social group; (2) measures that assess the amount of support reported to have been received in a particular time period; and (3) measures that assess the person's perception of the degree of availability of support should it be needed. In addition, a related but somewhat different way of evaluating support provision is in terms of its functions. Advocates of this approach argued that support provided must be relevant to the type of stressor and the needs of the individual at a particular time. However, the question still arises, by whom is this relevance determined?

Despite the apparent differences in these conceptualizations, for many years support researchers tended to gloss over the possible implications of different approaches to assessment and have, with a few exceptions, ignored the issue of who determines supportiveness. As a result the support literature contains many (at least seemingly) contradictory findings. A number of researchers have tried to shed light on some of these contradictions. Cohen & Wills (1985) reviewed the support literature with a view to understanding when social support serves primarily as an aid to those exposed to stress, what is called the buffering hypothesis, and when it functions as an overall benefit regardless of the level of stress in the situation. Barrera (1986) developed measures of two distinct aspects of social support, perceptions of support and reported support receipt, and employed them jointly in research studies. Sarason et al. (1987b) carried out a series of studies utilizing measures based on different concepts of support. They demonstrated that measures based on different basic definitions do not produce highly correlated scores. However, they also found that measures, even those quite different in format, were reasonably well correlated if they were based on similar conceptualizations. The Sarason et al. results clearly suggested that implicit differences in the conception of the relational process concealed in these measurement approaches, rather than simply differences in the format alone, were responsible for the different associations among variables described by social support researchers. Dunkel-Schetter & Barrett (1990) provided a rationale for the lack of association or the inverse relationship found by a number of researchers between support receipt and perceptions of support availability. They suggested that others' views concerning the degree of stress to which the individual was exposed and the adequacy of the stressed individual's personal coping abilities, as well as his or her help-seeking behavior, might play important roles in explaining how much support was provided by others. Thus, those that appeared most needy received the most support. Another important focus that helped to clarify the lack of relationship between network measures and either perception of or receipt of support was the idea, to be discussed in detail later in the chapter, that social support may have negative consequences (Fisher, Nadler & Whitcher-Algana, 1982; Nadler, 1986), or at least that supportive behavior may not have the expected beneficial effect because of aspects of the personal relationships between supporters and the person supported (Coyne & DeLongis, 1986).

Although initially support researchers attempted to deal with contradictions in research findings by focusing on which view of social support was the most "correct" or useful one, investigators are beginning to adopt a more integrative view by trying to understand how each definitional approach might contribute to the overall understanding of the mechanisms and effects of social support as it impacts health and other aspects of the person. Not only could enhanced awareness of the definitional differences help to prevent creation of yet more conflicting research findings about social support, but widespread use of carefully chosen measures in combination might have important benefits. House and his colleagues (House, Landis & Umberson, 1988) recommended some time ago that if we are to understand more about the processes connecting support and health, all studies should contain measures derived from more than one of these basic perspectives in order to determine how they relate to each other and to various types of outcomes. Vaux has suggested that social support should be considered as a meta-construct that was not a definable and measurable entity but rather a general or global concept with many at least potentially measurable aspects (Vaux et al., 1986). This view also implies multiple measurements. However, despite such recommendations, many current papers still rely not only on single measures but the particular assessment tools are selected, without adequate consideration of the implications of the implicit representation of relationships that lies behind their choice.

In summary, current views of social support consider it a characteristic of the social environment, as a characteristic of an interactional context with emphasis on what is received from others, or as a stable meaning attached to behavior of others resulting from earlier experience and based on views of self and others developed as a partial consequence. Rarely, but with increasing frequency, support is considered from several of these viewpoints. Although this multifaceted view represents a theoretical advance it focuses only in an indirect way, if at all, on an important topic, the role of close personal relationships as key sources of support provision. Even beyond the identification of these specific relationships with respect to support, a further need is consideration of the way meaning is imbued to relationship behaviors as the relationships develop over time. At a more basic level, many of the contradictory findings in the social support literature may lie in researchers' lack of appreciation of discrepancies between what is measured and the implications of the social support construct. Just as relationships are processes, not states (Duck, 1994a; Duck & Sants, 1983), social support may be thought of as a process based on the meaning of close relationships and the behavior ensuing from those relationships. This process is not well captured in most currently used approaches to assessing social support.

SOCIAL SUPPORT AND HEALTH

Social support's linkage with health outcomes, both physical health and psychological health, is widely recognized in the scientific literature. A number of years ago, House and his colleagues pointed out the strength of the inverse health–social support association as rivaling the effects of such well-recognized health risk factors as cigarette smoking, blood pressure, blood lipids, obesity and low levels of physical activity (House, Landis & Umberson, 1988). At the same time that they argued that the social support–health relationship was well demonstrated and was sizeable enough to have important practical ramifications, they pointed out that knowledge was lacking concerning process or causative mechanisms that might account for this association. Although considerable time has passed since then, progress in this direction has been only tentative despite the continuing popularity of the social support topic with researchers.

Close examination of the social support and health literature reveals that for an adequate evaluation of the health–support link, additional specificity is needed not only in the definitions of social support but in definitions of health. Health can be thought of in terms of overall or disease-specific morbidity or mortality; it can also be considered in terms of other categories of health outcomes, such as physical health and psychosocial functioning. This latter category, sometimes referred to as emotional health, ranges from mental disorders such as depression to measures of psychological well-being. Rapidity of recovery, recovery quality, rate of disease progression, and prevention of illness and health promotion are other aspects of the health–social support relationship that merit consideration. In each of these areas data exist that connect health and social support. However, the quantity of data and consistency concerning the specifics of the health–support association vary depending on the aspect of health considered. We will next briefly review what is known about the relation of social support to some widely studied aspects of health and illness.

Mortality

One of the first findings that provided a basis for the health–social support connection stemmed from mortality data derived from a 9-year epidemiological study in Alameda County, California (Berkman, 1985; Berkman & Breslow, 1983; Berkman & Syme, 1979). In this study the social integration of healthy men and women was negatively related to later mortality for both sexes. The study did not assess social support directly but measured social integration by inquiring into several types of social connections: marriage, contact with family members and close friends, and memberships in religious and other voluntary organizations. The age-adjusted relative risk for both men and women who were weakly socially connected was more than twice as high as the risk for men and women with strong social connections. Not only was an effect found for overall mortality, but mortality differed between the two groups for many specific causes of death, including ischemic heart disease, cancer and circulatory and cerebrovascular disease. The associations found were robust and persisted even after a variety of health behaviors and habits were taken into account. However, because only extreme groups were used in assessing this relationship, it may be that the results overestimate the true size of the population risk. In a European-based longitudinal study, Orth-Gomer & Johnson (1987) also found social integration effects related to all-cause mortality for both men and women. In a recent review of longitudinal studies of mortality and social integration, Orth-Gomer (1994) concluded that most research demonstrated an inverse, graded relationship between mortality and levels of social activity, even after a variety of risk factors were controlled. These results suggest a non-specific main effect of social support rather than a buffering effect in which social support becomes protective only in the context of life stress.

Other studies have found that higher levels of social integration were associated with decreased all-cause mortality only for men. After a variety of control variables, including health status, were taken into account, only the increased mortality among men remained significant in the Tecumseh, Michigan, 10-year prospective community study, although without these controls women who had a low social integration score also appeared to be at increased risk (House, Robbins & Metzner, 1982). A study by Schoenbach et al. (1986) also found differences in mortality only for men. Although all cause mortality and social integration were significantly related only for men in these two studies, more fine-grained analyses of the results relating to specific disease–mortality associations showed effects for women. While in general the association between social integration and mortality seems to be weaker for women than for men, the social support–mortality risk association might be stronger in some age ranges than others. A pertinent fact may be that although women report receiving more emotional and health-related support from their children and friends than do men (Depner & Ingersoll-Dayton, 1988) and appear to use all types of support more than men do (Belle, 1987), they also are more likely than men to be support providers (Kessler, McLeod & Wethington, 1985; Flaherty & Richman, 1989). Thus, women may be more likely to be exposed to negative social outcomes regarding both themselves and others than is true for men (Shumaker & Hill, 1991). Women with larger networks may be more involved in dealing with the stresses of others and thus experience more stress than women with smaller networks or than men.

Social integration has been associated with mortality not only in general population studies but also for individuals who were ill when first studied. Ruberman et al. (1984) studied 2320 male survivors of myocardial infarctions. They found that life stress and social isolation, both alone and in combination, were significant predictors of mortality. Life stress was defined by subjects' reports concerning such problems as job difficulties, divorces and separations, accidents and criminal victimization. Social isolation was defined in terms of contacts with friends and relatives and membership in social, church and fraternal organizations. For men who were high in both life stress and social isolation, the risk of dying was four times greater than for men who were low in both life stress and social isolation.

Epidemiological studies of general populations have also examined the relationship between social integration and mortality in terms of the health consequences of the death of a spouse. While findings in this area tend to be inconsistent (Bowling, 1987; Ferraro, 1989), there seems to be agreement that the mortality risk for the survivor is increased in the first 6 months after bereavement and that the risk is greater for men than for women (Schwarzer & Leppin, 1992). Whether or not the risk decreases over time is unclear. Parkes and his co-workers found that excess mortality among widowers gradually decreased over time, so that 5 years after the wife's death there was no difference in mortality between widowers and a control group (Parkes, Benjamin & Fitzgerald, 1969). In contrast, in a mortality study of men over a 12-year period, there was no significant decline in the excess rate over time after death of a spouse (Helsing, Szklo & Comstock, 1981). In general, however, studies of the widowed have found that for both men and women there is a tendency for mortality rates to approach the normal age-adjusted rate as time passes after the bereavement. Although death of a spouse can be viewed in the context of severe life stress, it also makes sense to view it as representing a loss of a significant member, perhaps the *most* significant member, of one's social support network.

What can we conclude overall concerning the relationship between social support and mortality? In an effort to clarify this issue, Schwarzer & Leppin (1992) carried out a meta-analysis to assess the association between social integration, social support and mortality. They identified 18 data sets, containing a total of almost 11 000 subjects, that provided information about the association between these variables. Their meta-analysis showed a stable relationship between all-cause mortality and social integration with a correlation of −0.07. Schwarzer & Leppin point out that although this correlation may seem negligible, such small correlations may be important when matters of life and death are considered. They showed that, on the basis of their meta-analytic results, it could be predicted that if 107 of 200 persons with weak social embeddedness died in a specified time period, only 93 in a group of 200 persons with strong social embeddedness would be expected to die in the same time period. In addition, Schwarzer & Leppin also investigated mortality from specific causes in the same group of studies. They found the mortality data associated with some specific causes of death showed even stronger results. For example, almost twice as many single as married individuals died from coronary heart disease.

What does a review of studies of mortality and social support tell us about the aspects of social support that may play a role? The findings give a reasonably consistent message that in general, associations between all-cause mortality and social support measures other than social integration have not shown significance, although Blazer (1982) found that the perceived adequacy of support predicted decreased mortality in a sample of older adults while, in contrast, his measures of social integration did not show this difference.

Morbidity

A number of researchers (Cohen, 1988; Leppin & Schwarzer, 1991; House, Landis & Umberson, 1988) have argued that in contrast to their clear association with mortality, social relationships have an inconsistent association with physical health status. When individual studies are considered, the results linking social integration or any other aspect of social support and physical illness are relatively weak and contradictory. One solution suggested for dealing with the inconsistencies in the empirical findings concerning physical health and social support is recognition of the importance of assessing specific types of support and controlling for factors that might interact with social support to provide inconsistent outcomes (see, for example, Heitzmann & Kaplan, 1988; Vaux, 1988; Veiel, 1987). As we shall see, the evidence connecting social support and morbidity varies considerably, depending on the disorder studied.

Heart Disease

The strongest and most researched association between social support and a specific disease is that between cardiovascular function and social integration; at least 50 studies have now focused on this topic. The relationship between social support and cardiovascular function is important because cardiovascular disorders are the leading cause of death in the USA and also because support status has implications for both the development and the progression of coronary heart disease. Stroebe & Stroebe (in press) concluded from their review of the literature that evidence for a tie between coronary heart disease and social support is strongest for cross-sectional studies, but somewhat mixed for prospective studies. They found the most consistent evidence of the role of social support to concern recovery from heart disease or heart surgery. Eriksen (1994), in a recent review of research concluded that social support may affect both mortality and morbidity in connection with coronary heart disease.

In a frequently cited study of Japanese-American men, social integration was negatively associated with coronary heart disease (Reed et al., 1983). However, because of a somewhat problematic measure of social integration and, in addition, because of possible cultural differences between this group and other American subcultures, these results may not generalize. The association between heart disease and social integration, however, is in line with mortality data found in several epidemiological studies. Another type of social support definition was used by Seeman & Syme (1987), who studied coronary artery disease in men and women angiography patients. They found that people who felt loved had less atherosclerosis and, in addition, reported receiving more instrumental support than patients who felt less loved. However, in the same study, a measure of social integration was not related to degree of atherosclerosis. These findings again emphasize the importance of reporting the type of social support measure used in conjunction with either positive or negative results.

The results of available research, including those from a number of prospective studies, suggest that social support may produce its beneficial effect by moderating the potentially harmful effects of negative emotions and potentially harmful cardiovascular response to psychological challenge. However, because personality factors were not assessed and controlled in most of these studies, the social support variable may be a proxy for one or more personality variables. For example, Type A personality is a stable person characteristic known to be related to some types of heart disease (Friedman & Rosenman, 1974). The Type A–heart disease connection was supported in a study of perceived social support in a group of patients who were scheduled to undergo coronary angiography (Blumenthal et al., 1987). In this study perceived social support was inversely related to coronary artery disease only for Type A patients.

Another connection between social support and presence of coronary heart disease has been found in studies of stress in the workplace. Support, measured in terms of the degree of interaction with co-workers, has been shown to moderate or buffer effects of work stress (Johnson & Hall, 1994). For instance, women in the Framingham Heart Study who rated their supervisors to be more supportive also showed a lower rate of coronary heart disease (Haynes & Feinleib, 1980). However, such results may need to be interpreted with caution because they may reflect general job stress rather than simply level of supervisor support.

The linkage between social support and cardiovascular pathology illustrates the complexities involved in determining the relationship between psychosocial variables and physical functioning. In certain contexts social support may have direct effects on cardiovascular function, and in others it might contribute indirectly. For example, an association between social support and cardiovascular function could be due to social support's role in influencing diet and lifestyle. People high in social support may engage in better health practices generally. However, several studies have reported an association between social support and cardiovascular function even after controlling for at least some of these types of variables (Bland et al., 1991; Janes & Pawson, 1986; Stavig, Igra & Leonard, 1984).

Complications of Pregnancy

Emotional and tangible support perceptions have been found to act as stress buffers with respect to several types of complications of pregnancy. Norbeck & Tilden (1983) found a decrease in several categories of pregnancy complications to be associated with increased support perceptions although there was no difference in total number of birth complications. Social integration among Navajo women also was found to protect this group from pregnancy complications, although the effect was small (Boyce et al., 1986). The presence of a supportive figure during childbirth labor has been found by several researchers to both facilitate the labor process and to reduce the number of complications (Bertsch et al., 1990; Kennell et al., 1991). One finding of interest in terms of close relationships in the Bertsch et al. study was that the outcome was better if the companion was a *doula*, a woman who was trained to be supportive during the labor process but a stranger to the pregnant woman, than if the companion was the prospective mother's male partner. In this case the intimate tie seemed less important than the presence of a reassuring and presumably less anxious and upset stranger. These findings raise several questions concerning the mechanism that might be responsible for the health outcome of the support variable. It is possible that the supportive companion's primary effect may be to reduce maternal anxiety and thus not only reduce the mother's catecholamine levels, but also facilitate uterine contractions and uterine blood flow. While such effects are likely, they are far from proven to be responsible for the observed support–pregnancy outcome association.

Disease in General

Schwarzer & Leppin (1989, 1992) used a meta-analytic approach to investigate the general relationship of social support and disease and found a population effect size of the same magnitude (–0.07) as that produced in their meta-analysis of social support/social integration and mortality previously discussed. In addition to this overall support–disease relationship, they were able to investigate effect sizes for different definitions of support. Their results reinforced the conclusion that different definitions of social support may have different associations with health outcomes. The population effect sizes of the association between disease and social support defined as social integration, as functional support, and as satisfaction with support were –0.07, –0.08 and –0.25, respectively. These analyses suggest that satisfaction with the support provided or available is a more potent predictor of morbidity than either of the other support definitions. Schwarzer & Leppin also used a number of more specific disease categories in their analysis of the relation between social support/social integration and disease. Despite their derivation from individual studies that had generally produced significant results for disease-specific analyses, not all these more specific categories met meta-analytic statistical criteria and consequently social support–disease relationships for specific diseases could not be interpreted with confidence. However, two categories did meet these criteria: the severity of disease category and the category of all diseases except coronary heart disease. The effect sizes for these analyses were –0.08 and –0.13, respectively.

Schwarzer & Leppin also investigated gender differences in the relationships between types of social support and illness. For men, the association between illness and support was lower than that for women for all disease categories and did not vary by type of support measured. Thus, support made more difference for women than for men in relation to illness. However, within the women's group, the kind of predictor used made a difference. For women, the negative associations of illness with support satisfaction and with emotional support were each considerably stronger than the negative illness–network support association. This may suggest, as mentioned earlier, that during certain periods of the life span women may bear an increased load of support-giving that may outweigh the benefits of support receipt.

Disease Severity and Recovery

There is considerable evidence that social integration or social support can favorably effect the severity or the incapacities associated with chronic disease.

For example, appraisal of available social support was inversely related to emergency room visits for adults with chronic asthma (Janson, Ferketich & Benner, 1993). Family support appears to play a role in discouraging maladaptive behaviors among chronic pain patients (Jamison & Virts, 1990). Those who perceived their family relationships as supportive and low in conflict reported less pain intensity, less reliance on medication and greater activity levels than patients who described their families as disharmonious and unsupportive. Women with rheumatoid arthritis who were higher in social support and had large social networks reported better quality of life than women with lower support even when degree of disability was considered (Krol, Sanderman & Suurmeijer, 1993). In a study in which stressful life events were first taken into account, the effect of social support was still found to be beneficial for the long-term physical functioning of a large group of chronically ill patients (Sherbourne et al., 1992). Low levels of social support were particularly damaging for older subjects. In contrast to research findings such as these, other work suggests that social support does not affect physical health outcomes but rather has an effect only on life satisfaction or mental health (Sherbourne & Hays, 1990). Some researchers have argued that characteristics of the person rather than the situation underlie the observed relationship between social support and adjustment to illness (Roberts et al., 1994).

Not only may social support play a role in alleviating the effects of chronic disease, but it also can affect the recovery process. Social support has been associated with speed of recovery from surgery, both in terms of time in an intensive care unit and time spent in the hospital before discharge (Kulik & Mahler, 1989). Social support defined as support group participation has been shown to positively impact the survival of patients with metastic breast cancer (Spiegel et al., 1989). Post-operative recovery has been shown to be affected by the presence of a hospital roommate as well as by the roommate's personal characteristics (Kulik, Moore & Mahler, 1993). Affiliation with pre- and post-operative roommates played an important role in recovery and suggested the need to take into account the characteristics not only of the patient but also of key figures in her or his hospitalization experience.

Psychological Adjustment and Perceived Quality of Life

Social support is widely presumed to protect against anxiety and depression and to enhance perceived quality of life. Comprehensive views of the early work in the area of social support showed that support indicators are positively related to mental health in the normal population and also discriminate between normal population controls and psychiatric cases (for example, see House, 1981; Mitchell, Billings & Moos 1982; Turner, 1983). Because stress has been widely viewed as negatively impacting psychological adjustment, much of the earlier research focused on the possible role of social support as a moderator of stress. Wethington & Kessler (1986) presented evidence that the buffering effect of social support in relation to stressful events was a function of perceived support rather than of support receipt. Their results document "not only that perceptions of support availability are more important than actual support transactions but that the latter promotes psychological adjustment through the former, as much as by practical resolutions of situational demands" (p. 85). Turner (1992), concurring with and generalizing this view, believes that perceived support is the most consistently and strongly associated with various health outcomes. House (1981) also shares the view that social support is effective only to the degree that the recipient perceives it. One reason for the strong effects obtained in many studies concerning psychological health and quality of life may be that both types of measures rely on the individual's perceptions and thus may share a certain response bias. However, response bias alone cannot be an explanation for these associations, because in some cases the health outcomes are assessed by independent and non-questionnaire criteria, such as clinical diagnosis or reports of others concerning the individual's health status.

Depression

A considerable amount of research has focused on the association between low levels of social support and depression, often in clinically depressed individuals. In an effort to determine the generality of this type of association, Henderson (1992) searched the English-language literature for studies conducted on community or other untreated samples that dealt with social support and depression. He identified 35 studies, including nine that were longitudinal. Despite the varied social support definitions and assessment methods used, ranging from the intensive, theory-based Bedford College interview method (Brown & Harris, 1978) to a single questionnaire item concerning the presence or absence of a confidant (O'Neill, Lance & Freeman, 1986) to a brief postal questionnaire (Holahan & Moos, 1981), these studies were in agreement on two findings. First, there was an inverse relationship between social support and affective symptoms; second, when severe stress was present social support produced a buffering effect on depression. In addition, Henderson identified several studies in which lack of support was associated with depression whether or not severe life events had occurred. On the basis of his review Henderson concluded that a strong negative link between depression and social support exists. However, he pointed out that before suggesting that the relationship is causal we need to consider how potential third variables, such as personality, may affect both social relationships and vulnerability to depression. The studies also did not make clear what components of the social environment, if lacking, might increase the risk for depression and whether these components differed across the lifespan.

In addition to addressing the question of whether depression and lack of social support are related in untreated population samples, it is useful to think of depression as a process with relatively distinct stages over time when considering the impact of social support (Monroe & Johnson, 1992). These stages of clinically relevant depression extend from onset of depressed feelings, through a depressive episode, through recovery and possible relapse and recurrence. Social support may be relevant, not only for depression onset, but also at transitions across stages. However, research findings so far have generally not addressed the specific questions necessary to understand the role of social support throughout a depressive illness, or the process by which support is effective (Monroe & Depue, 1991).

Social Support and Well-being

Instead of a focus on negative affect and depression, some researchers have studied positive affect and well-being, states that may or may not be the other pole of negative affect. One question concerning the relationship of social support and well-being is whether prior social support predicts later well-being or whether well-being is predicted only in terms of current support. In a longitudinal study by Reis and his colleagues, quality and quantity of social interaction of college students predicted several types of students' health problems and infirmary visits several months later (Reis et al., 1985). The pattern was clearest for female students. Demakis and McAdams (1994) found that college students' perception of social support availability assessed at college entrance was directly related to their life satisfaction and feelings of personal well-being at the end of the first semester, but had no relation to end of the semester physical well-being. In a study of adults in the community, Winefield, Winefield & Tiggemann (1992) found that while psychological well-being was predicted by reported life stress, the addition of social support as a predictor doubled the variance accounted for. The support measure with the strongest association with well-being was the frequency of supportive behaviors toward the respondent by close family and friends.

PERSONALITY CHARACTERISTICS, SOCIAL SUPPORT AND HEALTH

Some researchers have suggested that the connections found between social support and health might be partially or primarily due to third variables, personality characteristics. There is a considerable literature linking personality and health, although little knowledge exists about the mechanisms involved. Several possibilities exist. It may be that personality characteristics are linked with physiological responses to stress. Another possibility is that personality characteristics are linked with certain response styles when social support is evaluated via a questionnaire. It may also be that certain personality characteristics are simply linked with the feeling of being supported, regardless of the objective characteristics of the situation. Still another option may be that certain personality characteristics engender or discourage the support of others through their effect on relationship formation or the quality of the relationships that exist. It is likely that each of these possibilities has some merit. In any case, it behooves researchers to

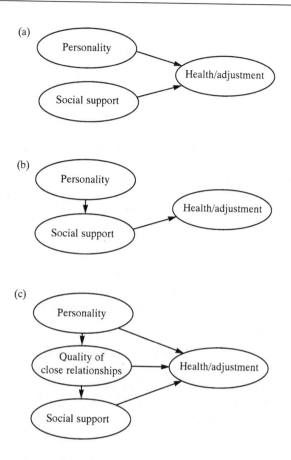

Figure 24.1 Alternative models relating personality, social support and health/adjustment outcomes

take personality characteristics into account when studying social support and health.

Several alternative models of the process by which personality and social support may influence health are shown in Figure 24.1. The first model (a) shows health and adjustment outcomes as a function of both personality variables and a supportive environment operating independently. The second model (b) suggests that social support is merely a mediator between personality and health and adjustment outcomes and plays no independent role in these outcomes. The third model (c) shows personality characteristics important both in direct effects on health and on the development and quality of close relationships. In this model, while personality characteristics and social support may contribute directly to health and adjustment outcomes, personality factors also contribute to close relationships and these relationships contribute directly to health and adjustment outcomes as well as to social support.

Much of the research in the social support-health area has utilized only the health-social support connection part of model (a) shown in Figure 24.1. Some researchers interested in personality variables have suggested that model (b) is the most appropriate. They concluded that when pertinent personality characteristics are taken into account, observed relationships between social support and health disappear. Thus, support may serve only as a mediating variable. For example, Henderson has suggested that perceptions of social support are actually a proxy for degree of neurosis (Henderson, Byrne & Duncan-Jones, 1981). This view is supported by findings in a study of the effects of perceived social support from friends, family and spouses on psychological adjustment of newly diagnosed breast cancer patients (Roberts et al., 1994). Overall, greater distress was associated with lower levels of social support only when personality characteristics of patients were ignored. When the individual difference characteristic of social desirability was taken into account the relationship between social support and adjustment was substantially weakened. This led these researchers to conclude that the degree of well-being patients described in this stressful situation was due to personality characteristics rather than directly to perceptions of social support. Researchers came to a similar conclusion in a prospective study of the effect of social relationships and personality on anxiety and depression experienced before and after a medical school entrance examination (Bolger & Eckenrode, 1991). After controlling for personality or prior mental health status, the apparent buffering effect of social relationships was concluded to be a spurious reflection of these variables. Despite this evidence for model (b), we believe that model (c) provides the greatest possibility for understanding the contributions of social support to health and adjustment. This view, discussed more in detail later in the chapter, emphasizes the meaningfulness of relationships and how that meaningfulness is communicated.

Personality Characteristics and Health

There is some evidence that an individual's perception of available social support is a stable personality characteristic in its own right (Lakey & Cassady, 1990; Sarason, Sarason & Shearin, 1986). For example, individuals' reports of their social support tend to be highly consistent, both when assessed longitudinally over relatively long time periods and before and after transitions. If social support plays an important role as a personality characteristic, its relationships to other personality characteristics also require investigation. We will review some of the characteristics the research literature suggests might be related to social support and outcome measures of interest.

Because of the persuasiveness of early research findings linking stress and illness, much of the initial work on moderators of stress focused either on personality characteristics or characteristics of the environment, prominent among which was social support. Stress has been linked to health primarily because of the stress-caused activation of the sympathetic and parasympathetic nervous system (Selye, 1956). Stress has also been linked to an increase in the likelihood of contracting infectious illnesses such as colds and flu and to a general suppression of cellular immune function (Glaser et al., 1987). However, people differ in the degree of upset they feel in stressful situations. These differing responses could be due to a variety of individual difference variables including temperamental characteristics and intellectual level, both of which contribute to coping efforts. Individual differences as well as potential environmental moderators play a role in the magnitude of the stress response. For example, some individuals show much larger habitual cardiovascular changes in response to psychological challenge than do others (Krantz & Manuck, 1984). These over-responders may be at higher risk both for long-term disease processes and for acute coronary events as well (Karmack & Jennings, 1994). An individual's response to stress may be due not only to physiological factors but also to the way the person evaluates both the situation and how he or she may deal with it (Lazarus & Folkman, 1984). Thus personality characteristics have been associated with the magnitude of the stress response.

How are personality variables related to the ability to deal with stress? Rather than considering the entire gamut of personality variables we will consider briefly those most often associated with the degree to which a person is able to deal with a stress experience. These personality variables, which may play important roles in an individual's support perceptions, fall into two major classes. One group includes aspects of personality that are often considered to be based on temperament and biologically determined patterns of response, for example, neuroticism and extraversion–introversion. Each of these variables relates to individuals' typical reactions to stress as well as to whether or not they tend to seek out situations that lead to physiological arousal or quiescence. A second group includes personality variables that have a strong cognitive component, for example such well-researched personality characteristics as locus of control, self-efficacy, hardiness, conscientiousness and dispositional optimism. However, a third group of less traditional personality variables is particularly relevant in the study of social support. These include characteristics that may be called schemas or working models concerning individuals' views of their personal worthiness and their expectations concerning the behavior of others towards them (Bowlby, 1980a, 1980b). More information is needed concerning the interrelationships of these three aspects of personality.

Temperamentally-based Personality Characteristics

Temperamental factors have been considered to be important in both vulnerability to stress and resiliency under stress. Extraversion–introversion, neuroticism, and the Type A personality pattern illustrate temperamental characteristics that quite likely intersect with social support.

The degree to which a person is extraverted or introverted is considered by some personality psychologists to be one of the basic aspects of personality (Costa & McCrae, 1988; Eysenck, 1967). Eysenck considers extraversion–

introversion, as well as neuroticism or, as he has more recently termed it, emotional stability, to be supertraits or underlying dimensions of personality. Extraversion–introversion and neuroticism are among the five superordinate factors, the "Big Five", believed by some psychologists to reflect the basic structure of personality (see, for example, Goldberg, 1981; John, 1990; McCrae & Costa, 1987). Extraverts, because they prefer to spend time with other people rather than being alone, are likely to have relatively sizeable social networks (Sarason et al., 1983). Eysenck conceives of extraversion as a biologically based trait related to preferred levels of external stimulation. He argues that introverts often find social interaction too physiologically stimulating, while extraverts are more comfortable with greater stimulation levels. Under stressful conditions extraverts are also more likely than introverts to seek out others to talk things over rather than withdrawing from social interaction; their accessing of social support may aid in stress reduction. For example, nurses high in extraversion required more work-related peer support than more introverted nurses to avoid emotional exhaustion or burnout (Eastburg et al., 1994). Although extraversion might be related to desired degree of social interaction with friends and other social contacts, it may be less relevant in family relationships. In a study of male college students in India, those high and low in extraversion differed in their self-described social adjustment but not on aspects of adjustment relating to physical and emotional health and family relationships (Chaudhary & Sinha, 1992). Extraversion has been linked to mental health and well-being over a wide age range from late adolescence to very old adults (Martin et al., 1992; Swindle, 1989). It has also been shown to be negatively related, over a 17-year period, to both physical and psychological symptoms in men who had entered a longitudinal study in good health (Spiro et al., 1990). Although response bias may be contribute to the positive relationship between health and extraversion, Cramer (1990) found that even after extraversion was controlled, the perceived adequacy of close attachments was still negatively associated with psychiatric illness. The connection between extraversion and health may not be direct, but rather extraversion may lead to larger or more frequently accessed social networks and consequently to the individual's perception of greater social resources.

Neuroticism can be defined as a broad dimension of personality characterized by the tendency to experience negative emotions and depression. Those high in neuroticism are likely to describe themselves as having a greater number of symptoms and symptoms of greater severity than those lower in this personality characteristic (Jorm et al., 1993; Lu, 1994). Watson & Clark (1984) have argued that neuroticism is one way of conceptualizing negative affect, and that it, together with many other commonly assessed personality characteristics, should be placed under the basic construct of a tendency toward negative affect. However it is defined, neuroticism or negative affect is related to symptom-reporting behavior, although whether this symptom-reporting behavior is related to actual health status is unclear and the research results have been conflicting. Watson & Pennebaker (1989) showed that, in a generally healthy sample, the disposition of negative affectivity was unrelated to biological markers of health such as blood pressure elevation or serum lipids although it was related to self-ratings of poor health. Costa & McCrae (1987) found neuroticism scores to be related to angina and chest pain, but unrelated to biologically identifiable events such as myocardial infarction or death from cardiac disease. It might be tempting to conclude that neuroticism is simply related to symptom reporting; however, perhaps counter-intuitively, health behaviors of those high in neuroticism are likely to be poorer than those low in this characteristic. Individuals who view life in a more negative frame are more likely to smoke, use drugs, and drink to excess than those low in neuroticism. These behaviors may be associated with poorer health outcomes as well as fewer positive social relationships (Friedman, 1992). Neuroticism, in women but not in men, has also been found to be more characteristic of the divorced than the currently married (Cramer, 1993). Thus it may be an indirect link to actual health outcomes through the mediator of social integration. Although neurotic individuals report more stressful events, events with greater negativity, and more physical symptoms, it is presently not justifiable to consider these reports simply as nuisance factors in understanding the connection between neuroticism and health because perceived health has been shown to predict mortality independent of biological risks (Adler & Matthews, 1994; Kaplan & Comacho, 1983). In addition, the neuroticism–health link is important because of its effect on the utilization of the health care system as well as the effects on individuals and their families (Weiner, 1991).

One of the earliest bodies of research linking a personality characteristic and health was research on Type A personality. Type A personality, which was originally conceived to include feelings of time pressure, anger and demandingness of others, and hostility, was considered to be a heart-attack-prone syndrome (Friedman & Rosenman, 1974). The driving, pressured quality of Type A is related to greater stress on the circulatory system, both directly through hostility and anger and indirectly through a consistently high stress level. More recently, after considerable research yielding contradictory findings about the relation between Type A and heart disease, the aspects of Type A personality that seem to be most related to heart attack proneness are hostility, anger, cynicism and suspiciousness of others (Barefoot et al., 1987). As in the case of neuroticism, Type A personality characteristics do not tend to be associated with high levels of social support. In view of their frequent negative attitude to other people, it would not be surprising if Type A individuals were relatively low in perceived support. Whether Type A personality should be classified as a temperamentally based or cognitively based characteristic is not clear, although as research on this characteristic has progressed the cognitive aspects of Type A have become more prominent.

Cognitively-based Personality Characteristics

In addition to the temperamental attributes described above, a group of cognitively-based personality variables characterized by particular expectations or schemas have been associated with positive coping and a decreased experience of stress. These cognitively associated variables include such traditional constructs as locus of control and self-efficacy, hardiness, conscientiousness, optimism and self-esteem. After reviewing these briefly, we will move on to more cognitively complex constructs such as working models and schemata.

Locus of control and self-efficacy, although somewhat different constructs, both relate to a person's perceptions of his or her relation to environmental outcomes. Locus of control was one of the early variables suggested as a moderator of stress (Lefcourt, 1981). People who have an internal locus of control believe that they can affect what happens to them. With respect to health that means that they see themselves as having an active role in preventing health problems and, if health problems do occur, of following whatever medical regimen is recommended. Self-efficacy is the individual's belief that he or she is able to influence environmental outcomes in a particular domain by personal action (Bandura, 1986). Like those high in locus of control, individuals high in self-efficacy are motivated to try to do something about problems in their environment and believe that they have the skills to improve the situation. The presence of such a belief, in itself, probably decreases health-injurious excitation levels as well as providing motivation for coping in a problem-oriented rather than an avoidant way. Bandura's view provides more of an action orientation than does locus of control, a more descriptive construct. For example, appropriate social support was found to enhance the feelings of mastery that cardiac patients develop in a rehabilitative conditioning program. Some of this social support appears to come from working-out with other patients and with staff in the program, so that exercise tends to become viewed as normative for patients recovering from a myocardial infarction (Dracup, 1994). When wives also participated with husbands who were recovering from myocardial infarctions, the wives' confidence that their husbands could do the exercises without harm increased and this increased confidence was related to better treadmill performance by husbands 6 months later (Taylor et al., 1985), presumably because the wives become more supportive of their husbands' exercise efforts.

An older construct, hardiness, first investigated by Kobasa (1979) as a characteristic that might affect vulnerability to work-related stress, appears somewhat similar to locus of control and self-efficacy. Although Kobasa conceived of hardiness as composed of several dimensions—commitment or involvement, control or the ability to influence one's environment, and challenge or the willingness to undertake activities that may provide opportunities to growth—later work suggests that health outcomes seem to be systematically associated with only some parts of the construct, either commitment and control variables (Hull, VanTreuren & Virnelli, 1987) or merely commitment (Cohen & Edwards, 1989).

Another health-related personality characteristic may be conscientiousness. Using data from a study begun by Terman in 1921 (Terman & Oden, 1947), Friedman and his co-workers found that conscientiousness measured in childhood was related to mortality. Those who were high in conscientiousness were likely to live longer (Friedman et al., 1993). Several explanations have been suggested for this relationship. Conscientiousness may be associated with better health habits, lower probability of drug and alcohol abuse, and higher likelihood of following medical regimens (Block, Block & Keyes, 1988; Conley, 1985; Tomlinson-Keasey & Little, 1990). It may also be related to better preparation for the unexpected in everyday life and consequently with a lower level of stress when life events are encountered. Perhaps underlying all these possibilities is the effect conscientiousness has on lessening psychophysical disruptions that weaken resistance to disease (Friedman, 1991).

A personality construct with some similarity to conscientiousness is ego control. Block & Block (1980) defined ego control as the degree of impulse control reflected in delay of gratification, inhibition of aggression and planfulness. Together with the allied construct of ego-resiliency, which refers to the ability to adapt to environmental demands by appropriately modifying the habitual level of ego control, level of ego control appears trait-like in that it is relatively consistent from childhood at least until adolescence. Low levels of ego control have been related to problem drinking and ego over-control to total abstinence from alcohol (Jones, 1971). Similar findings exist for use of illegal drugs (Shedler & Block, 1990). Work by Mischel (1974) and others suggests that, at least in young children, an appropriate degree of ego control is associated with children's use of certain adaptive cognitive coping mechanisms, for example self-distraction and self-distancing. Mischel also demonstrated that such cognitive techniques can be taught and that their acquisition can improve ego-control behavior. A related personality characteristic, ego strength, also has been shown to be associated with a healthy life style. Vaillant (1977, 1992) used the ego strength construct to successfully predict both mental and physical health outcomes over time. He demonstrated that male college undergraduates' ego strength, defined by the use of various defense or coping mechanisms, predicted the health and psychological adjustment of the same individuals when they were middle-aged. Vaillant suggested that choice of defense mechanisms at college age was associated not only with later level of alcohol and drug use and positive health behaviors, but also with the character and stability of close personal relationships.

Another personal characteristic, dispositional optimism (general positive expectations) has also been studied in relation to both mental and physical health outcomes. While related to self-efficacy, this construct also includes optimistic expectations, optimistic explanatory style, and high self-esteem (Scheier & Carver, 1992). Dispositional optimism has been related to active coping responses during stress as well as to more rapid recovery from bypass surgery (Aspinwall & Taylor, 1992; Scheier et al., 1989). Men who had a non-optimistic explanatory style as Harvard undergraduates have been found to have poorer physician-diagnosed health in mid-life than did comparable students with a more optimistic style even when initial health status was taken into account (Peterson, Seligman & Vaillant, 1988). In a group of elderly individuals, a non-optimistic style was associated with a lower level of immunocompetence, although not with current health status (Kamen-Siegel et al., 1991). Despite a variety of evidence for a positive association between dispositional optimism and health, optimism is not always associated with positive health outcomes. For instance, Friedman et al. (1993) found in their analysis of adult mortality and childhood personality characteristics that optimism was inversely related to health. They suggested that optimistic people may underestimate the danger of certain health risks and fail to practice positive health behaviors or to follow medical advice. Dispositional optimism would seem to share some characteristics with another personal characteristic, self-esteem. Self-esteem level may be positively related to health outcome through enhanced health behaviors and feelings of self-efficacy, but low self-esteem may also produce an increased vulnerability to stress. For example, low self-esteem was associated with more health problems, including backache, sore throat, and flu-like symptoms for workers who had experienced stress the prior day than for those who had not (DeLongis, Folkman & Lazarus, 1988). Students with low self-esteem were found to use the student health center more often than students with high self-esteem (Brown & McGill, 1989). Low self-esteem students also reported lower physical well-being after they experienced a positive life event. These findings suggest that aspects of the person affect the impact of both positive and negative events.

Social Support as a Personality Characteristic

Although traditional personality variables may play a role in a person's desire to build a personal network and his or her success in achieving one that is satisfactory and positive, another important individual difference variable, perhaps at a different level of analysis, lies in the customary way a person views him or herself, others and the qualities of relationships. Several researchers have argued that perceived social support, although presumably based at least in part on earlier experience, may be a stable characteristic of the person (Lakey & Cassady, 1990; Sarason, Pierce & Sarason, 1990; Sarason, Sarason & Shearin, 1986). While not denying that social support can be defined in other ways, these researchers have argued that understanding more about social support perceptions may be instructive in understanding processes involved in producing physical and mental health outcomes. From this viewpoint, perceived social support is an individual difference variable or aspect of personality that is reflected in working models based on early experience with others (Bartholomew & Horowitz, 1991), just as early childhood experience and parenting have been demonstrated to be related to later self-esteem and feelings of being loved (Harter, 1990). Working models can be thought of as a special class of schemata that encode both affective and cognitive information (West & Sheldon-Keller, 1994). Although some researchers, including Bowlby in his later work (1980a, 1980b), believe that working models may be subject to revision and adjustment in response to new attachment experiences, major changes are thought to be uncommon (West & Sheldon-Keller, 1994). The concept of attachment as it relates to adult relationship behavior has been investigated by several researchers (Hazan & Shaver, 1987; Kobak & Sceery, 1988; Main, Kaplan & Cassidy, 1985).

The focus on social support perception as a personal characteristic based on working models has both adherents and detractors. The adherents point to the importance of support perceptions in a variety of health outcomes as well as research findings that indicate that perceptions of support to a standard stimulus vary depending on predictable aspects of the person (Pierce, Sarason & Sarason, 1992). Those who oppose this emphasis on stable perceptions of support level as an individual characteristic decry what they call the psychologizing of social support. They argue that such a view should not be termed social because it is not a function of social network characteristics and interaction patterns but that the focus of social support research should be on supportive behavior (Gotlieb, 1985; Lieberman, 1986). Vaux (1988) in his description of social support as a meta-construct emphasizes that person variables are only one component of a triad that also includes actual support resources and supportive behaviors.

CLOSE RELATIONSHIPS AND HEALTH

Personality variables such as those mentioned in the previous sections may play a role in health outcomes by their direct association with such variables as physiological processes involved in response to stress and health-related behaviors. However, their role may be less direct as well. Henderson, for example, stresses that "it is not satisfactory to study the social or interpersonal environment without simultaneously bearing in mind the contribution made by that individual to the manner in which the environment operates" (1992, p. 90). Newcomb (1990), who views social support from an interactional perspective, has argued that it is a resource that evolves throughout life and is shaped in a reciprocal, bidirectional process between the individual and significant others. He contends that this process deserves much more research than it has received. Perceived levels of social support are joint products of personal characteristics and interactions with the social environment. Personality variables may play an important role, not only in the stressors individuals encounter but in the quantity and quality of individuals' social support networks and the frequency with which they receive support when needed, as well as the quality of that support. Further, close personal relationships are likely to be the source of most support received (Cutrona, 1986) as well as what is perceived to be available. If this is the case, then it would be helpful to assess aspects of close relationships and use this information to enhance prediction of health outcomes, as well as to increase understanding of the way in which support functions with respect to health. Close personal relationships can be considered to be a preferred subset of personal relationships that are characterized by intensity and intimacy, perhaps the adult equivalent of early attachment. It may be useful to take a functional view of attachment in adults as the achievement of felt security rather as a structurally determined set of behaviors (West & Sheldon-Keller, 1994).

This understanding of attachment is close to the definition of perceived support. In this view, working models relate to the quality of the relationship, whether the supporter will respond if needed, and whether the response will be sensitive to the needs of the person supported. Thus, an understanding of close relationships is particularly important to an understanding of perceived support. Perceived support and its associated working models are likely to be based to a significant degree on earlier life experiences especially those within the family. The work of Bowlby (1969, 1980a) and later researchers (Hazan & Shaver, 1987; Kobak & Sceery, 1988; Sroufe & Fleeson, 1986) suggests that the working models that people hold in regard to themselves and toward the behavior of others are a potent force in determining relationship behavior in adulthood. Baldwin et al. (1993) have viewed these working models in terms of the internalization of significant relationships, self-construals and scripts people form of their interactions with others.

One of the advantages that knowledge of close personal relationships brings to the study of social support lies in the likely possibility that social support may not be a unipolar construct (Coyne & Downey, 1991). Someone who is low on social support may have few supportive relationships. Another possibility is that he or she may have a number of relationships from which support is derived but these same relationships are also characterized by negativity and conflict (Coyne & Bolger, 1990; Wethington & Kessler, 1986). Several studies have found that the negative features of social relationships appear to be related more strongly than the positive features both to perceptions of social support (Rook, 1984; Sarason et al., 1993) and to symptoms, at least psychological symptoms (Fiore, Becker & Coppel, 1983; Pagel, Erdly & Becker, 1987). Conflict in interpersonal relationships is not necessarily at the opposite end of a continuum anchored on the other end by social support. Researchers need to take a more multidimensional approach to the study of personal relationships.

An example of how consideration of the quality of relationships can enhance understanding of results in the traditional social support health literature comes from a large epidemiological community study (Weissman, 1987). The study found that the risk of clinical depression was slightly lower in married people who could talk to their spouses than for people who were single, separated or divorced. However, those who were married and unable to talk to their spouses had an extraordinarily high risk for depression. It may be, however, that it is not simply the lack of a confiding relationship in itself that produces this result, but rather the effect of being in a "bad marriage" (Roy, 1978).

The protective effects of social support in stressful situations may relate not just to overall support but to support specific to the particular setting in which the stress occurs. Studies of work settings and stress, for example, often indicate that social support from those in the workplace is health-promoting because it reduces the effects of work-related stress, but that family and friend support is not particularly useful in this regard (Brand & Hirsch, 1990; House, 1981). Such findings also suggest the importance of knowing more about the specific relationships represented by scores on general measures of social support.

Researchers have responded to this need in a variety of ways. For example, Hirsch & Rapkin (1986) showed that the structural characteristics of married women's social networks predicted their adjustment after a divorce. Women with tight, interconnected networks in which they and their husbands had most social relationships in common prior to the divorce did less well than those with looser networks, in which some network members were connected to the woman alone and not to the spouse. Another approach that has also been shown to be useful is focused on perceived social support assessment that targets different relationship groups. Procidano & Heller (1983) developed a social support measure that differentiated family-based perceptions of support availability from friend-based perceptions. Particular types of personal relationships, such as family and friends, may vary widely with regard to their supportive features. Rook showed that at least for older adults, family and friends serve quite different support functions (Rook, 1987). While family members can be called upon to help (provide instrumental support) when needed, companionship provided by friends may be more effective in promoting happiness and emotional well-being. Thus friends, more than family members, may produce joy, an emotion linked to increased immunocompetence.

Pierce, Sarason & Sarason (1991, 1992) developed the Quality of Relationships Inventory (QRI), a measure of support, conflict and depth in a specific relationship. This measure can be used to assess these relationship variables for a variety of relationship types. Research with the QRI indicates that the scores of an individual show high specificity to the relationship that is being described. For example, subjects' QRIs for their mothers, but not their QRIs for their fathers, predicted behavior observed in a laboratory interaction of each subject and his or her mother (Sarason, Pierce & Sarason, 1995). QRI scores also predicted the degree of supportiveness students attributed to a written message that they believed was composed by their mothers, although the message was actually a standard one that each mother had copied in her own handwriting (Pierce, Sarason & Sarason, 1992). Thus, the results suggested that QRI scores relate to expectations concerning specific relationships and therefore may tap a distinctive working model concerning that relationship or that type of relationship (for instance, what is typical of friend behavior or of romantic partner behavior).

The development of the QRI provides an example of how the assessment of individual relationships may add to an understanding of the association between social support and various health outcomes. In two studies, QRI Support and QRI Conflict scores, completed by college students about their mothers, fathers, and siblings predicted whether or not the family member would engage in supportive behavior with respect to the student, in this case by returning mailed questionnaire materials that were part of students' research participation (Sarason et al., 1993; Zavislak & Sarason, 1992). This prediction was significantly better than prediction of questionnaire return based on the students' assessments of their overall perceptions of social support availability using the Social Support Questionnaire (SSQ; Sarason et al., 1983).

QRI scores for specific relationships (mother, father, romantic partner, friend) also enhanced prediction of a variety of measures of adjustment including depression, loneliness and anxiety (Aseron, Sarason & Sarason, 1992). Not only did aspects of these relationships predict additional variance after overall support perception was taken into account, but the types of relationship seemed to be associated differentially to the adjustment variables. For example, less positive romantic relationship and friend relationship qualities predicted loneliness, while less positive parental relationship quality was associated with depressed mood. This association between mother and father relationships and student depression was also observed in another study (Adams & Sarason, 1995). Support and conflict reported for the two parental relationships predicted depressed mood, but support and conflict for a best friend and romantic partner relationships did not.

Brock developed a method of using the Social Support Questionnaire to obtain information concerning support perceived to be available from specific categories of relationships (Brock et al., 1995). In this research each individual's nominations of supporters for each SSQ item were tabulated by relationship category. Categories for mother, father and friends were used for prediction. Brock found that even after a measure of general level of perceived support (the Social Provisions Scale; Cutrona & Russell, 1987) was taken into account, the relationship category support scores predicted additional variance for several adjustment outcomes. Further, when the perceived support was broken down into specific types of support provision, the difference in what aspects of support were expected from mother, father and friends was clearly defined.

While people have relatively well-formed expectations and attributions about available support in general, they also have specific expectations about the availability of support from particular significant people in their lives. While a person's global and relationship-specific expectations for social support may be related, they reflect different aspects of perceived support and each may play an important and unique role in coping, well-being and health. Perceived support grows out of a history of supportive experiences, especially with family members. The general expectations one has about the forthcomingness of others, in turn, influence whether and how an individual approaches others to form new potentially supportive relationships. Perceived support, as a working model of relationships, may be especially influential in the formative stages of a relationship before individuals have developed clear ideas about how they would like their relationship partner, as opposed to others in general, to respond in particular situations. As a relationship progresses and relationship-specific expectations develop, each person's global expectations may become less influential in the relationship.

CONCLUSION

The term social support has become an umbrella term that covers a variety of diverse phenomena. A large percentage of research studies on the topic deal with associations between assessed support and particular aspects of life, including health status, illness, recovery from illness and adjustment and psychological functioning. A review of this research leads to the conclusion that social support is a good thing to have. People with satisfying levels of support seem to cope better with stress, are healthier and recover from illness more quickly, and seem to be better adjusted. Thus, perceived social support functions in many ways as an individual difference variable. If it is a good thing to have and if it inheres within the individual, what aspect of support is doing the inhering? We think it is a set of working models of one's self as someone with certain competencies and characteristics that imply worthiness of the support and caring of others, expectations of the social forthcomingness of others, and the qualities of relationships expected with particular people. These working models lead a person to conclusions about the degree to which she or he is valued. These conclusions influence (1) the development of current relationships with others, (2) the acquisition of feelings of self-efficacy that are both generalized and related to specific tasks, (3) the perceived availability of social support, and (4) effectiveness in stress-coping and the ability to maintain a task focus.

It is now clear that social support is not simply membership in a social network, assistance that is exchanged among network numbers, or an appraisal of that assistance; neither is it only one's perception of what network members may potentially provide. Instead, social support reflects a complex set of interacting events and processes that include behavioral, cognitive and bodily components. Despite this complexity, one finding emerges consistently: the qualities of personal relationships, their meaning to the individuals involved, and how that meaning is communicated are active, crucial ingredients in the social support equation. An adequate understanding of social support processes must specify the role of these qualities of personal relationships in the provision, receipt, and appraisal of social support. As Heller & Swindle (1983) pointed out a number of years ago, social support is a process that involves an interaction among social structures, social relationships and personal attributes. It is now time for social support researchers not only to fully embrace that view in their empirical work but to move beyond it to include the contribution of the important positive and negative qualities of specific close relationships, as well as the meaningfulness of these relationships in the individual's life. Doing so should not only advance understanding of the social support and health connection, but should provide a way to move ahead in our understanding of the entire social support process, in part, at least, by increasing our understanding of the nature of the relationships represented implicitly or explicitly in our social support measurement tools.

Chapter 25

The Role of Personal Relationships in Transitions: Contributions of an Ecological Perspective

Edison J. Trickett
and
Rebecca M. Buchanan
University of Maryland, College Park, MD, USA

Transitions occur "whenever a person's position in the ecological environment is altered as a result of a change of role, setting, or both" (Bronfenbrenner, 1979, p. 26). Whether the impetus for this change in position originates primarily in the individual or in the environment, transitions demarcate periods of social and personal disequilibrium surrounding events which require change and adaptation beyond the ongoing changes of everyday life. This disequilibrium can take many forms depending on the nature of the specific transition. However, such times are of particular import because they typically represent both unusual opportunities for growth as well as points of potential vulnerability (Bronfenbrenner, 1979).

The direction and nature of the resolution of transition-induced disequilibrium are often influenced by the networks of personal relationships in which individuals are embedded. However, just as transitions vary enormously, the concept of personal relationships has become increasingly differentiated in the literature, implying a multiplicity of potential ways in which personal relationships can affect the negotiation of transitions. Further complicating the nature of the role of personal relationships in transitions are the influences, often neglected in the literature, of the larger social and cultural contexts in which the transitions occur.

Handbook of Personal Relationships, 2nd edn. Edited by Steve Duck.
© 1997 John Wiley & Sons Ltd.

The purpose of the present chapter is to deepen our conceptualization of this complex topic by examining the contributions of an ecological perspective to the study of the role of personal relationships in transitions. Ecology, by focusing on person–environment transactions, heightens an awareness of the importance of the context, conceptualized at multiple levels of analysis, surrounding transitions, personal relationships and their intersection. An ecological perspective asks what kinds of relationships are useful for facilitating what kinds of transitions within what social and cultural contexts. Simply by reframing the phenomenon in these terms, an ecological perspective promotes an increasingly refined and differentiated understanding of this topic.

THE CONCEPT OF TRANSITION

The defining characteristic of the transition concept involves its discrimination from everyday changes. For instance, Wapner (1981) defines a transition as a "perturbation to the person-in-environment system" (p. 26) which is so potent that ongoing modes of transaction with the environment no longer suffice. The resulting disequilibrium has both social/ecological and intrapersonal aspects. The social nature of transitions has been described by Wapner & Craig-Bray (1992) as occurring

> ... as part of the socialization process during which time the individual's social identity changes in keeping with assigned status, roles, classes, and other social labels. These transitions are easily detected by their objective, public character, often involving social institutions, and are represented by events such as entry to school, marriage, illness, and retirement. Subjective (intrapersonal) aspects of transitions, in contrast, emphasize the experiential nature of the event to the individual (p. 162).

In addition to such broad distinctions, the literature on transitions suggests that the concept encompasses enormous diversity in the substance of particular transitions as well as the adaptive requirements placed on participants. Transitions range in content from changing schools (Jason et al., 1992) to changing countries (Portes & Rumbaut, 1990), going from employment to unemployment (e.g., Kessler, Turner & House, 1988), from becoming a wife to becoming a widow (Silverman, 1988) and, ultimately, from life to death. In terms of their adaptive requirements, transitions range from those which are "limited both temporally and in their repercussions for individuals' lives" to those "really better viewed as markers or precipitants of the unfolding of major changes. ... which may engender new stresses and changes and demand adaptive efforts for some time to come" (Felner, Farber & Primavera, 1983, p. 290). They vary in the extent to which they involve normative changes, such as entering school, or non-normative ones, such as a forced relocation due to a flood (Kaniasty & Norris, this volume). Transitions also differ in terms of whether they are made with a cohort of one's peers or family or by the solitary individual without an accompanying social network. Finally, transitions occur at different points in the life cycle where individuals have differing skills and capacities to cope.

Each of these different kinds of transitions involves certain adaptive challenges, such as reordering one's assumptive world, shifting one's role definition and role behavior, and reconstructing one's social networks and social supports (Alvidrez & Weinstein, 1993). However, the range and diversity of transitions suggest that such seemingly similar general tasks should be linked to the specific situations and contexts within which they occur if we are to capture the richness of the phenomena subsumed under the transition concept. The ecological challenge is to specify the rich interdependence of transition and context.

THE CONCEPT OF PERSONAL RELATIONSHIPS

Within community psychology, personal relationships refer most often to one's social network, or relationships with the members of the different reference groups which compose the individual's social sphere. These relationships have been found to be of critical importance for the well-being of individuals experiencing stressors such as those associated with transitions. While this literature is reviewed elsewhere (e.g., Cohen & Syme, 1985; Sarason, Sarason & Pierce, 1990), it clearly shows the potential stress-buffering role which personal relationships play in coping with the disequilibrium created by a variety of transitions.

The concept of personal relationships, like transitions, has become increasingly differentiated in the literature. For instance, these relationships vary in terms of their salience at different times in the life cycle, such as the heightened importance of peers during adolescence (Berndt & Savin-Williams, 1993), type of support offered in the relationship, including both instrumental and emotional support, and the relationship's duration and degree of intimacy (for overviews, see Mitchell & Trickett, 1979; Barrera, 1986; Vaux, 1988; Jacobson, 1986). Further, they can be distinguished by the degree to which members of one's circle of friends themselves have "connections" or serve as "weak ties" (Granovetter, 1973) to other networks not immediately accessible to the individual. For example, a personal friend with family in a city where an individual is about to relocate may serve as a weak tie to those who can provide relevant information important to anticipatory coping efforts.

THE INTERSECTION OF TRANSITIONS AND PERSONAL RELATIONSHIPS: BEYOND THE SPECIFICITY MODEL

The above suggests that both transitions and personal relationships vary along a number of specifiable dimensions. It further suggests that in order to understand the role of personal relationships in transitions, it is useful to link the demands of the particular transition with the kind of support necessary for dealing with it. In the social support literature this perspective is perhaps best exemplified by the "specificity model" (Cutrona, 1990; Jacobson, 1986), in which the support relevant to coping with transitions is tied to the specific demands of different transitions themselves. Furthermore, various studies within this framework have suggested that not only are different types of support relevant to different types of transitions, but the same type of support may have differential impact at different points in the transition process. Similarly, the same type of support provided by different sources in the network may be experienced differently by the individual undergoing the transition (see Dunkel-Schetter & Wortman, 1982; Jacobson, 1986; Cutrona, 1990).

While the specificity model has generated support in the research literature, it has focused primarily on the specific transition and mode of support, with little or no attention paid to the impact of broader social and cultural contexts on the personal relationship-transition process and outcome (Jacobson, 1986). The present chapter attempts to move beyond this event-specific approach to assess the ways in which the social and cultural contexts surrounding transitions and personal relationships affect their process and outcome. That context, says Jacobson, includes:

> ... those ideas, beliefs, and values which people hold about persons and the social relationships in which they take part. Ideas about autonomy, dependency, and reciprocity, for example, shape the ways in which individuals define support, as well as give, get, accept, or reject it. Moreover, different communities (or cultures or sub-cultures) hold different ideas about the provision, receipt, and circumstances of support (p. 259).

As it forms the basis for an analysis of this type of context, we turn now to an overview of the ecological perspective.

ECOLOGY AND THE STUDY OF TRANSITIONS AND PERSONAL RELATIONSHIPS

Ecology generally focuses attention on the interdependence of people and their environments. Within psychology, varied ecological frameworks have been developed in the last 30 years for understanding the contexts of both behavior and person-in-context interactions. These perspective have varied in approach, with some defining the environment in terms of the perceptions of its members (e.g., Moos, 1979) and others in terms of the behavior settings it includes (e.g., Barker, 1968). Some focus on the environment's physical attributes (e.g., Stokols & Altman, 1987), others on how it reflects a developmental history of person–environment transactions (e.g., Lerner, 1991). Research derived from each of these perspectives substantiates the importance of contextual factors for understanding human behavior. Further, this work has shown that environmental influences span multiple levels of analysis, ranging from person-in-situation (e.g., Endler, Hunt & Rosenstein, 1962) to person-in-culture (e.g., Berry et al., 1992).

The present chapter draws most heavily on Bronfenbrenner's definition of the ecological environment (Bronfenbrenner, 1979) and the ecological analogy developed within community psychology by Kelly and his colleagues (Kelly, 1968, 1970, 1979, 1986; Trickett, Kelly & Todd, 1972; Trickett, 1984, 1986; Trickett & Birman, 1989; Kelly & Hess, 1986). Together, these perspectives provide a powerful heuristic for conceptualizing the role of personal relationships in transitions within social and cultural context.

Bronfenbrenner's rich perspective cannot be adequately portrayed here (see Bronfenbrenner, 1979; Bronfenbrenner & Weiss, 1983). However, his description of the ecological environment as a series of nested systems which exert both direct and indirect influence on the individual is central to understanding how context may influence the role of personal relationships in transitions. The smallest of these systems, the microsystem, is the person in a specific context such as the family or classroom. This implies that, even at the smallest level of analysis, individual behavior cannot be understood without simultaneous attention to the nature of context. The next largest system, the mesosystem, is composed of the interrelationships between different microsystems in which the individual participates. Since the relationships among different systems, such as the home and school, may exert influence on individual behavior in both systems, behavior in any one setting may reflect the demand characteristics of other settings involving the individual. The third nested system is the exosystem, composed of settings not containing the individual but which nevertheless exert influence, such as the impact of school board policies on children. Finally, the macrosytem highlights the role of culture which operates as an attribute of multiple levels of the ecological context as well as of individuals.

From this perspective, every transition is embedded or nested within a variety of systems ranging from macrosystem influences such as culture to the more immediate community and family contexts and their interdependence. Hence, the role of personal relationships in facilitating transitions may likewise be affected by factors operating at different levels of the ecological environment. For example, the transition to a new school may be affected by the family microsystem in terms of its cultural definition of support and the availability of kin to serve as resources; the potential mesosystem influences of home–school congruence in terms of the academic demands of school and family interaction patterns and learning styles; and exosystem policies governing how incoming classes are grouped and stratified.

Bronfenbrenner provides a persuasive approach to describing the ecological environment in terms of levels of analysis and their interdependence. His focus, however, is on their implications for the individual person. Kelly's ecological analogy, on the other hand, provides ideas for dissecting different aspects of the ecological contexts themselves. He draws on four ecological processes that field biologists have found useful in understanding the functioning and evolution of plant and animal communities over time; adaptation, cycling of resources, interdependence and succession. Each focuses attention on a different aspect of the ecological context.

Adaptation

In biological communities, the adaptation principle focuses attention on what the adaptive requirements are to survive in a particular environment. Applied to human communities, it focuses on those traditions, norms, processes, structures and policies which, taken together, constitute the environment which both constrains and promotes certain kinds of adaptations for individuals and groups (Trickett & Birman, 1989). With respect to transitions, it suggests the importance of assessing the adaptive requirements of different kinds of transitions, the constraints they impose, and the different kinds of personal resources available in the environment. It further implies that individual behavior be viewed in terms of the coping resources, cultural frames of reference and social resources the individual brings to the transition process.

The relationship of broad adaptive requirements of communities to individual behavior is beautifully captured in Stack's (1972) *All Our Kin*. Here the adaptive requirements faced by a poor Black community are met through the development and perpetuation of a particular set of cultural traditions, norms and processes. The concept of kin, less a biological than sociocultural bond among individuals, provides a unifying image for the intricate set of personal relationships characterized by mutual reciprocal obligations to give and receive. These relationships, necessitated by scarce resources and enriched by cultural tradition, provide an ongoing and dependable source of support around such tasks as the rearing of children. However, they constrain as well as facilitate by obligating those in the kinship network to give their resources freely to others. Thus, individuals with significant resources are constrained from leaving the community because their resources are needed to sustain the functioning of the overall kinship network.

Cycling of Resources

In biological communities, cycling of resources refers to the manner in which energy or nutrients relevant to the survival and evolution of the community are generated and cycled through the community. Applied to the social and cultural context of transitions, it advocates the analysis of the manifest and latent resources available for successfully negotiating the transition process. For example, transitions may be facilitated by the presence of social settings to develop friendships, the availability of a community of individuals from the same culture, or the access of newcomers to "weak ties" whose information is critical for adaptation. Where such structures or settings are absent, preventive interventions which facilitate the development of personal relationships may become resources, as shown by the varying kinds of programs for students transferring into new schools, outlined by Jason et al. (1992).

The cycling of resources principle also draws attention to how individuals define, develop, and call on personal relationships to function as resources during times of transition. This suggests examining what kinds of personal resources are currently available to the individual, what resources are needed, and how capable the individual is of developing and accessing such resources (see Gottlieb & Todd, 1979). As suggested by the prior discussion of *All Our Kin*, such questions must be considered within the cultural and subcultural contexts which affect the meaning and functions of personal relationships.

Interdependence

The interdependence principle asserts a fundamental assumption of systems theory also spelled out clearly by Bronfenbrenner; namely that parts of a system are interconnected, such that change in one part evokes changes in other parts of the system. This principle draws attention to how the changes accompanying transitions by individuals reverberate throughout the interpersonal system. It suggests that transitions such as having a child or leaving home for college carry implications for the ecology of interpersonal relationships surrounding the individual as well as for the individual him/herself. Thus, the concept of social support is not static but part of an interactive process of mutual influence which changes in configuration as individuals in the network assume new roles, settings or both. How support providers may themselves be affected by the transition of the individual constitutes an important question.

Succession

The final principle focuses on the time dimension of individuals and their ecological contexts, including culture, neighborhood, school and family. It includes both an historical appreciation of how they came to their current status and an anticipatory appreciation of what goals and aspirations they hope to achieve (see Trickett & Schmid, 1993). The succession principle thus draws attention to the changing nature of the cultures and contexts into which transitions are made and suggests that cultural and institutional history represent relevant aspects of the contexts within which transitions occur. It also suggests that research on transitions be viewed in a time and context-bound framework both in terms of findings and in terms of the phenomena themselves. The history of the integration of the public schools, for example, suggests that the tasks of school transition for both Black and White students in the early 1960s may differ from those of today, because both the larger societal context and the demographics of current public schools are vastly different.

At the individual level of analysis, the succession principle suggests the value of placing the individual's history and hopes within a sociocultural context. Here, the issue is how, over time, social and cultural factors have become part of the ways in which individuals make sense of their world. This sociocultural history helps form a perspective from which individuals perceive the transition situation and the personal resources relevant to it.

APPLICATION OF THE ECOLOGICAL PERSPECTIVE TO THE ROLE OF PERSONAL RELATIONSHIPS IN TRANSITIONS

Thus far, we have outlined aspects of an ecological perspective which can contribute to the study of the role of personal relationships in transitions. Demonstrating the full power of this framework, however, requires examination of several extended examples drawn from existing research. To further this end, we have selected three substantive areas which represent a wide range of transitions: one primarily involving a change in role (transition to adolescent motherhood); one primarily involving a change in setting (school transitions); and one involving a change in both role and setting (transition to a new country).

Within each of these areas a brief review of the existing literature on the role of personal relationships in the particular transition is presented first, followed by a research example which attends explicitly and in depth to the ecological context of a particular transition and the role of personal relationships in its negotiation. These examples each highlight different aspects of an ecological perspective, including the importance of conceptualizing this phenomenon in terms of different levels of analysis, the role of individual and group sociocultural history, and the interdependence between the context being exited and the context being entered.

The Role of Personal Relationships in the Transition to Adolescent Motherhood

The transition to adolescent motherhood is often seen as a transition into the role of becoming a parent, with an attendant need to develop child-rearing skills and relevant knowledge about developmental milestones and timetables (Halpern & Covey, 1983). However, an ecological perspective on this transition suggests the importance of other associated tasks, including decisions about whether and how to continue schooling, possible alterations in household living arrangements for the mother and child, and potential changes in the roles of the existing peer network in terms of their attitudes toward and information about the new role of the adolescent mother (Trent & Harlan, 1994; Wasserman, Brunelei & Rauh, 1990; Lin, 1986).

There is a significant literature on the role of personal relationships in making this transition. Empirical studies have documented the helpfulness of many different sources of social support for young women, including support from a male partner (Thompson & Peebles, 1992), family (Kissman & Shapiro, 1990), peers (Kissman & Shapiro, 1990), natural adult mentors (Rhodes, Ebert & Fischer, 1992), as well as social support generally (Unger & Wandersman, 1985; Colletta & Lee, 1983). The importance of this differentiated notion of social networks is confirmed by Boyce, Kay and Uitti (1988), who found that young women exhibiting the best adaptation to parenthood displayed a richer, more differentiated view of their social network and perceived individual network members to be more diverse in their capacity to provide broad, multi-faceted support. Interventions involving formal sources of support, such as a visiting caseworker or membership in a support group, have also been found helpful (Thompson & Peebles, 1992; Unger & Wandersman, 1985).

Benefits associated with social support range from lower levels of psychological distress (Thompson & Peebles, 1992) and depression (Thompson & Peebles, 1992; Rhodes, Ebert & Fischer, 1992) to improved well-being (Kissman & Shapiro, 1990), adjustment (Unger & Wandersman, 1985) and self-esteem (Rhodes, Ebert & Fischer, 1992). Furthermore, benefits may extend to the children as well, including improved child health and development (Unger & Wandersman, 1985).

These studies document both the importance of personal relationships and their relationship to various mental health-related outcomes for adolescent mothers. Further, the literature provides suggestions about important differentiations in sources of social support which are meaningful to these adolescents. For instance, Unger & Wandersman (1985) found that, while both partner and family support were related to greater life satisfaction, each was associated in a different way with parenting and concerns about daily living. Similarly, the importance of making differentiations based on cultural context has received limited support in the empirical literature through studies which document racial differences in both the level and type of family support arrangements provided for these adolescent mothers (Stiffman, 1991; Mayfield-Brown, 1989). However, while providing information with both descriptive and theoretical relevance about the role of personal relationships in the adaptation of adolescent mothers, the literature does not generally offer a complex portrait of the cultural and family dynamics surrounding this transition.

An exception can be found in an examination of the work of Burton and her colleagues (Burton, 1990, 1991; Burton & Dilworth-Anderson, 1991) which illustrates how cultural context, represented here by the set of extended family relationships found in the African-American communities she studied, shapes the meaning of transitions as well as defining the personal relationships relevant to their negotiation. Her work suggests that cultural norms regarding both the timing of family transitions and the expected roles of family members arise as groups apply their social resources to meet the adaptive requirements of their environments over time. Thus, this example illustrates the ways in which culture interacts simultaneously with multiple levels of the ecological environment

(Bronfenbrenner, 1979), including individuals, their extended families and their collective history, to influence the role of personal relationships in the transition represented by adolescent childbearing.

Burton's work throws into question the assumption that adolescent childbearing, within the context of a particular community of low-income African-American families, represents a transition to early parenting in the sense that it is commonly used in the literature. Rather than assuming that teenage childbearing represented a monolithic transition, Burton employed qualitative strategies to identify patterns of caregiving and support within families with an adolescent childbearing member. This approach uncovered 14 different patterns of subsequent childcare within the 48 families studied, suggesting that a similar event, adolescent childbearing, did not necessarily imply a similar transition for the adolescents. Furthermore, in keeping with the interdependence principle, it suggests the importance of considering the transition that adolescent childbearing potentially creates for other family members who may become very involved in childrearing.

In addition to shaping the meaning of the transition, the cultural context, as expressed by the set of extended family relationships, simultaneously defined the personal relationships relevant to its negotiation. In large part, the diversity and complexity of the patterns of caregiving that emerged reflect the variable family networks in which teenage parents are embedded. Adolescents defined their family networks as differing not only in who was in the network (e.g., friends, boyfriends and siblings) but how many generations of family were in it (e.g., two, three or four). The salience of personal relationships was contingent on the nature of the specific constellation of available network members. The roles of these network members, in turn, were constrained by the web of responsibilities entailed by their other personal relationships. Thus, the availability of personal relationships depended not only on the presence of supportive others, but also on the context of other relationships in which they functioned.

Burton's work beautifully illustrates the interdependence of the adolescent childbearer and the constellation of intertwined personal supports which serve as resources for dealing with the transition. In many instances, the presumed stress associated with this transition is minimized for the adolescent by other network members. As one adolescent mother commented, "Taking care of this baby is not as hard as people might think . . . You got to build a group of people who can help you" (Burton, in press, p. 92).

In addition to considering the effect of the adolescents' current social context, Burton's work also suggests ways in which a group's history is a relevant dimension of the ecological context. As suggested by the succession principle, the meaning of transitions and the relationships deemed relevant to their negotiation reflect not only current ecological conditions, but past ones as well. For instance, in an ethnographic study of rural low-income African-American families, Stack & Burton (1993) describe the emergence of strict family scripts which differ from mainstream norms regarding the sequence/timing of family transitions and the assignment of family tasks to members. Specifically, they observed a unique pattern which involved young adults having children and then migrating north to secure jobs in order to send money back home. Their young children were left behind in the south to be reared by grandparents or older aunts and uncles. After an extended period of time, the migrating adults return to the south and their now young adult children repeat the cycle.

This strategy emerged in response to the adaptive requirements of reproduction and economic survival, common to all families, faced by this group in the context of extreme local poverty. Poor in economic resources, the community successfully applied their familial resources, including an intense commitment by family members to the survival of future generations, to generate and cycle adequate resources through their community. For the strategy to succeed, family members had to coordinate their personal relationships closely in order to synchronize the multiple transitions involved, including transitions to early childbearing, subsequent migration and work, return to the south, and finally assumption of surrogate parenting responsibilities as grandparents.

Once established, patterns defining the meaning of particular transitions, as well as the relevant personal relationships, may become somewhat self-perpetuating as they create the conditions of future ecologies. For instance, returning to the more common urban patterns described by Burton, the timing of prior transitions in the family seemed to affect the supportive roles members assumed. Within maternal female lineage families in which two or more generations of females have been adolescent childbearers, the great-grandmother (ages 46–60), grandmother (27–38), and adolescent mother (13–18) are often "early occupants" of their respective roles. Given these early transitions to family roles, the great-grandmother typically emerges as the most responsible care provider and may provide economic and babysitting support for the grandmother, continue to parent the adolescent mother, while also assuming the role of surrogate parent to her great-grandchild (Burton, in press).

As the work of Burton and her colleagues demonstrates, the change in role brought on by an adolescent becoming a parent is best understood by a contextual analysis of the situation in which the transition occurs. While much research exists documenting the general importance of personal relationships in negotiating this transition, it is clear that the forms these relationships take and their success in serving as a stress buffer for the adolescent and as a positive force in the development of the child differ across culture and context.

The Role of Personal Relationships in School Transitions

School transitions typically involve changes from one educational setting to another. Research has examined the impact on adolescents of the transition into middle and junior high school (e.g., Hirsch & Dubois, 1992; Hirsch & Rapkin, 1987; Simmons, Carlton-Ford & Blyth, 1987; Feldlaufer, Midgley & Eccles, 1988; Fenzel & Blyth, 1986); Elias, Gara & Ubriaco, 1985; Seidman et al., 1994); high school (Barone, Aguirre-Deandreis & Trickett, 1991; Felner, Ginter &

Primavera, 1982; Felner & Adan, 1988); and from high school to college or the world of work (Barone et al., 1993; Terenzini et al., 1994; Compas et al., 1986).

While these studies have defined the adaptive tasks of such transitions in different ways depending on the developmental level of students and on the kinds of schools involved, Elias, Gara & Ubriaco (1985) have identified a general set of adaptive challenges facing adolescents during school transitions: (1) shifts in role definition and expected behaviors; (2) changes in membership in and positions within social networks; (3) reorganization of personal and social support resources; (4) restructuring the way one perceives one's world; (5) management of stress resulting from uncertainty about expectations and goals and one's ability to accomplish the transition tasks (pp. 112–113).

As this set of challenges suggests, successful negotiation of school transitions requires the mobilization of social support resources to buffer stress even as the transition potentially disrupts aspects of the social network. To date, studies have assessed the role of personal relationships in school transitions in terms of social support provided by family (e.g., Papini & Roggman, 1992; Lord, Eccles & McCarthy, 1994), peers (e.g., Hirsch & Dubois, 1992), or support more generally (Compas et al., 1986). Typical findings suggest, for instance, that close peer ties in the first semester of junior high school are a prospective predictor of classroom adjustment at the end of the first year in the new school (Hirsch & Dubois, 1992). Similarly, Compas et al. (1986) found that satisfaction with social support 3 months prior to the transition to college predicted lower levels of psychological and somatic symptoms at the hypothesized time of greatest vulnerability during this transition, 2 weeks after students arrived at college.

In addition to these studies of naturally occurring social support, many successful interventions have been developed based on the premise that interpersonal relationships can provide a supportive environment which can mediate the stresses associated with various school transitions. For instance, successful interventions for transfer students have included making use of in-school tutors and parents as resources (Jason et al., 1992) as well as "buddy system" approaches which pair new students with students already in the school (Allan & McKean, 1984). Interventions to facilitate the transition to junior high and high school have ranged from comprehensive restructuring of schools to increase access to emotional and instructional support from school staff and other students (Felner, Ginter & Primavera, 1982; Felner, Primavera & Cauce, 1981; Felner & Adan, 1988) to a creative drama prevention program intended to improve peer relations among entering junior high school students (Walsh-Bowers, 1992). At the college level, Gottlieb & Todd (1979) report on the formation and effects of support-oriented groups of incoming freshmen designed to help them identify transition-related issues and develop appropriate interpersonal resources for dealing with them.

While such studies document the general importance of personal relationships for students undergoing school transitions, the literature has failed to make central questions about the cultural and social context of these transitions, despite recurrent indications of their importance. For instance, the relationship of race, ethnicity and gender to school transitions has seldom been a central research focus. However, when these variables have been examined they have yielded intriguing findings. For instance, when Fenzel & Blyth (1986) identified a group of students who gained in indicants of good adjustment following the transition to junior high school, they found that the male "gainers" were more intimate with their same-school friends than were "decliners", whereas female "gainers" showed lower or equal levels of intimacy compared to female "decliners". This suggests that peer friendships may function differently for boys and girls in mediating the stress associated with school transitions.

Other important aspects of the ecological context for understanding the role of personal relationships in school transitions involve the structure and social climate of the contexts of exit and those of entry. In a direct test of the change in school ecologies related to transitions, Feldlaufer, Midgley & Eccles (1988) assessed student, teacher and observer perceptions of the classroom environment before and after the transition to junior high school. Based on these multiple sources and a large sample of classrooms, the authors found that the post-transition classes called for less cooperative interactions between students and that teachers were characterized as less caring, warm, friendly and supportive. Additional support for the potential importance of assessing the contexts of exit and entry can be found in studies which invoke post hoc ecological explanations for their findings. For instance, when Fenzel & Blyth (1986) found an unexpected overall positive adaptation to junior high, they speculated that this positive outcome might have resulted from an innovative team approach school staff used to aid the school transition, thus buffering its potential negative effects. Initial predictions of the effects of transition had not taken into account this aspect of local ecology.

These cases, and others like them, argue for more explicit assessments of the contexts of exit and the contexts of entry involved in various school transitions *a priori*. Such a stance would increase our understanding of such concepts as that of "developmental mismatch". This intriguing ecological notion, focusing on the degree of congruence between developmental stages of students and the structure of schools, has been suggested as an explanation for the decrements in performance and self-esteem found in many school transition studies (Eccles & Midgley, 1989, 1990; Simmons & Blyth, 1987; Seidman et al., 1994). However, because the design of these studies did not involve specific environmental assessment of local school ecology conceptually related to the mismatch, this intriguing concept remains elusive.

One investigation which did conduct a more explicit assessment of both the cultural and institutional contexts surrounding a school transition involved a qualitative study of the transition to college reported by Terenzini et al. (1994). One of the central questions of the study was, "Is the nature of the transition process different for different kinds of students? For similar students entering different kinds of institutions?" (Terenzini et al., 1994, p. 58). As such, it investigated issues raised earlier by the specificity model of social support.

To address these questions, the authors used a focus-group interview procedure with students entering four colleges which differed in size, racial/ethnic composition of the entering class, urban/rural location, and degree to which students were commuters or in residence. Subsequent analysis of the qualitative data focused on "the identification of themes that were common across campuses and subgroups of students, as well as on thematic differences distinctive to a campus setting or student subgroup" (Terenzini et al., 1994, p. 60). Selected findings highlight the importance of a contextual understanding of the role of personal relationships in school transitions.

Terenzini and colleagues (1994) found important differences in the meaning of the transition to college for different groups of students. For example, "the place of college in the life passage" was one of the general themes which cut across campuses and subgroups of students. However, within this theme important differences emerged between "traditional students" and "first generation students". For "traditional students", who were primarily White, college attendance represented "school as continuation" of an unbroken educational trajectory which was consistent with family and sociocultural expectations and tradition. Insofar as the transition represented a disjunction, it was primarily an interpersonal one and thus their major concern was with making new friends. For "first-generation" students, however, where attending college was not part of the family or sociocultural tradition, the transition was experienced as a major disjunction involving multiple academic, social and cultural aspects. Typically, these students were initially concerned with negotiating the academic transition, deferring other aspects of the transition until they felt they had their academic lives under control.

Given the different meanings of the college transition for different groups of students, it is not surprising that expressed social support needs also differed by group. While the need for "somebody to care" appeared to be a universal prerequisite for a successful transition, students differed in the types and sources of validation they sought. In keeping with their experience of the transition to college as primarily interpersonal, traditional students sought social validation through peer acceptance. They were less concerned with academic validation as they had already experienced academic encouragement and success in their prior educational settings and were further validated academically by being accepted by their moderately selective institutions. First-generation students, on the other hand, required more comprehensive validation from a variety of sources as they negotiated the multiple transitions represented by college attendance. They sought a series of in- and out-of-class experiences with family, peers, faculty members and staff to gain a feeling of acceptance in their new community, receive confirming signals that they could succeed in college and were worthy of a place there, and could have their previous work and life experiences acknowledged as legitimate forms of knowledge.

Cultural and institutional differences also interacted with the social context of students to affect the nature of their transition. For instance, the role of high school friends was affected by whether or not they were attending college themselves. Entering college with a small cohort of friends seemed to ease the initial transition to college because old relationships bridged the past and the present, albeit for a limited period of time. In contrast, high school friends who did not go on to college served to complicate and hinder the transition by functioning as "interpersonal anchors", tending to hold the student in the network of friends and pattern of activities and interests of the precollege years. The availability of support from peer relationships was also influenced by whether or not the transition took place in a residential context. For residential students, the transition often became a cooperative process in which classmates helped one another to meet and make new friends.

Similarly, the role of family support depended on both cultural and institutional influences. While the importance of family support cut across students, families differed both in their first-hand knowledge of the nature of the transition and in their expectations concerning change in their relationships with the student. For some students, particularly those residing at school, an important aspect of the transition entailed the development of greater personal independence and autonomy from family. This, in turn, required the renegotiation of their relationships with parents to one more closely resembling the equality of adults. Other students, particularly those from Black, Hispanic or Native-American families, were faced with the challenge of maintaining relationships with parents who were often fearful that children might metaphorically never return home due to the cultural disjunction the transition to college represented. Sensing such fears, "some of the students of these parents appeared to find their anxiety levels rising in ways and to degrees probably unimagined by most middle-class white students, faculty members, and administrators" (Terenzini et al., 1994, p. 66).

The work of Terenzini and his colleagues suggests that understanding the impact of the college transition on adolescents requires a contextual analysis of both settings involved in the transition and the ways in which these interact with students' cultural and social contexts. Specifically, the study highlights the impact of these contextual factors on the meaning of the transition to college for students, their social support needs, and the roles played by family and peers in students' adaptation. Such distinctions, made in a vivid and compelling way in this qualitative inquiry, are less likely to be present in the previously cited school transition literature.

While some of this omission may be due to real differences among school transitions depending, for instance, on developmental level, there are several aspects of this transition to college study which are quite relevant at earlier times. For example, the impact of cultural disjunctions on the expectations and hopes of students' social support networks for school performance and behavior is likely to be an important consideration prior to college attendance. Thus, this work provides a useful heuristic for understanding a variety of school transitions, insofar as each entails the interaction of school contexts of exit and entry with students' social and cultural contexts.

The Role of Personal Relationships in the Transition to a New Country

While adolescent childbearing represents primarily a change in role, and school transitions primarily a change in settings, the transition to a different country represents a change in both. Perhaps the most comprehensive transition of this kind involves immigration from one's country of origin to a country with different cultural and historical traditions. One central task of negotiating this transition has been defined as the process of acculturation, the changes in individuals resulting from first-hand contact between two distinct cultural groups. While earlier models conceptualized acculturation as assimilation to the host culture and loss of one's culture of origin (Stonequist, 1937), more recent multilevel models (Mendoza, 1984) propose that the basic acculturation task involves negotiating a general balance between the culture of origin and the host culture, rather than giving one up in favor of another. The individual, then, acquires or fails to acquire the customs of an alternate culture while retaining or failing to retain the norms of his or her native culture. By considering each of the cultures independently, a multilevel approach allows for the possibility that culture of entry may diverge, converge or conflict with culture of origin (Tyler, Susswell & Williams-McCoy, 1985). It further allows the possibility of a number of different resolutions of the basic acculturation task (e.g., Berry, 1994; Birman, 1994; Mendoza & Martinez, 1981; Szapocznik & Kurtines, 1980), ranging from biculturalism, where both cultures are retained, to marginality, in which neither culture is retained/acquired.

While the above outlines the broad task of acculturating to a new country, other more specific tasks can be inferred from the multiple dimensions along which the acculturation process is thought to proceed. Some tasks are behavioral (Szapocznik et al., 1978) including, for example, language use and familiarity (Marin et al., 1987; Cuellar, Harris & Jasso, 1980). Other tasks relate to reconciling values and maintaining a sense of identity throughout the transition (Szapocznik et al., 1978). Still other tasks may relate specifically to social interaction with members of the host culture (Marin et al., 1987; Cuellar, Harris & Jasso, 1980).

Given the range and scope of tasks subsumed under the acculturation concept, it is understandable that the interplay between personal relationships and acculturation is complex. On the one hand, acculturation theories posit that change occurs in the individual as the result of "sociocultural contact", suggesting that personal relationships instigate and shape the transition. For example, the literature suggests that relationships developed in a variety of life spheres, including school, family, employment and neighborhood, may influence the acculturation of individuals (Saravia-Shore & Arvizu, 1992). However, neither the specific ways in which this occurs nor the key relationships in the process have been clearly delineated.

On the other hand, it is clear that changes in the acculturating individual, in turn, affect his or her personal relationships. For instance, in the case of immigrant families, each family member must not only adapt as an individual, but must also maintain viable relationships with other family members, each of whom is also changing in response to still other relationships. The difficulties engendered by this situation have been documented by a number of studies which have linked the emergence of intergenerational differences in acculturation within immigrant families to family conflict (Szapocznik & Truss, 1978; Scopetta, King & Szapocznik, 1977; Buchanan, 1994).

Although limited, this literature nevertheless illustrates some of the complexity involved in disentangling the multiple roles of personal relationships in the transition to a new country. In keeping with the characterization of the transition to a new country as one which signals the beginning of a long series of changes occurring over an extended period of time, studies which explicitly link aspects of personal relationships to acculturation tasks as they unfold over time are most likely to be instructive. Given the centrality of culture to the nature of this transition, instructive studies must also attend to the ways in which culture affects the role of personal relationships in the transition.

The work of Aroian (1992) is exemplary in terms of the attention paid to issues highlighted by the "specificity model" and their interaction with the cultural attributes of the individuals providing and receiving social support. Specifically, this study provides an illustration of the various tasks associated with the resettlement process for a group of Polish immigrants. Different sources and types of support were sought by the immigrants, depending on the specific transition tasks they were facing and upon their own cultural characteristics relative to the cultural attributes of support providers. Furthermore, both the transition tasks and the cultural attributes of the immigrants changed over time, resulting in longitudinal changes in personal relationships.

For instance, Aroian (1992) found the variety of tasks associated with the resettlement process during the first 3 years were each associated with different personal relationships. Some of the tasks were best facilitated by personal relationships developed with Polish immigrants from earlier waves or with Americans of Polish descent who could serve as "culture brokers". Thus, participants reported that Polish immigrants from earlier waves, and Polish-Americans, were their major source of tangible assistance because they were already financially stable, were familiar with life in the USA, and yet were bilingual and able to communicate with recent arrivals.

In contrast, other tasks of this stage were best facilitated by personal relationships formed with other recent immigrants. Thus, participants' need for information about typical immigrant experience was best supplied by others undergoing the same process. Similarly, the need for emotional support and friendship was likewise provided by personal relationships with other immigrants, for reasons involving language and the belief that a shared heritage and current life circumstances provided a strong basis for a sense of belonging.

As these immigrants became more acculturated, however, both transition tasks and the role of personal relationships in confronting these tasks changed. Thus, by the time these immigrants had resided in the USA from 3–10 years, they no longer required significant tangible assistance, and informational needs "shifted from basic to more intricate knowledge, including subtle cultural differences in styles of social interaction and using English for more complex communication" (Aroian, 1992, p. 190). In addition to changing needs, the immigrants had also changed themselves and could, for example, converse in English. Thus, rather than relying exclusively on prior waves of immigrants or Polish-Americans, attention now turned to social relationships with Americans in order to "gain information about job opportunities, master nuances of the English language, and learn about American cultural practices" (p. 193). As the immigrants became increasingly acculturated to the US culture, relationships with Americans also evolved to include emotional as well as informational support.

These new relationships, however, did not displace prior relationships with other immigrants and Polish-Americans. In addition to providing a continuity of understanding, attachment and a sense of belonging, these ongoing relationships became an important source of support for maintaining immigrants' Polish heritage. For immigrants who had resided in the USA over 10 years, maintaining proficiency in the mother tongue and transmitting Polish culture and language to their children emerged as an important transition task. In this example, then, personal relationships ebb and flow as adaptive demands change and as the primary tasks associated with acculturation change over time.

CONCLUSION

The intent of the present chapter has been to bring an ecological perspective to bear on the role of personal relationships in transitions. We selected contrasting types of transitions to focus both on the range of experience subsumed by this concept and the importance of understanding the differing demands they place on participants. Further, within each of these types of transitions, we sought to highlight how they themselves are embedded in cultural and social contexts which shape the meaning and role of personal relationships in their negotiation. Our ecological framework directed attention to diverse aspects of these contexts, including influences occurring at different levels of analysis, the sociocultural histories and current realities facing individuals who occupy different places in the social order, and the interdependence between the contexts from which individuals come to the transition and those in which the transition occurs. Each was shown to be vital to understanding the role of personal relationships in transitions.

Our examination of the literature across these varied transitions, however, suggests that much of the current work is based on paradigms which minimize or ignore the importance of such factors. The ecological perspective we drew on represents our effort to provide a conceptual antidote to this situation. In searching for research examples, we were consistently drawn toward qualitative rather than quantitative work. In each of our examples, qualitative data enriched our understanding of the role of relationships in transitions in ways which highlight the importance of context and suggest directions for future research in this area.

Our affinity for selecting qualitative work does not reside in a context-free preference for one kind of understanding over another. Rather, it stems from a belief that at this historical moment investigations of the facilitative role of personal relationships in transitions can benefit from the heuristic contextual richness which good qualitative inquiry provides. The spirit of qualitative inquiry is the spirit of searching out the complexity of lives as they are led in different ecologies. By locating knowledge in a cultural and social context, qualitative work thus increases our appreciation of the ecological contexts and constraints we face in the real world of transitions and the role of relationships in their negotiation. Such a perspective opens a window to a diversity of possibilities for exploring the many ways in which transitions are facilitated by personal relationships.

Chapter 26

Social Support Dynamics in Adjustment to Disasters

Krzysztof Kaniasty
Indiana University of Pennsylvania, Indiana, PA, USA
and
Fran H. Norris
Georgia State University, Atlanta, GA, USA

Although systematic research on social support is relatively recent, the idea that morale and well-being are partly sustained through primary group ties has appeared in almost every psychological and sociological theory or doctrine. Across the years, since the original conceptualizations by Cassel (1976), Cobb (1976) and Weiss (1974), social support has been defined in a variety of ways. Most often it is referred to as those social interactions that provide individuals with *actual assistance* and *embed them* into a web of social relationships *perceived to be* loving, caring and readily available in times of need (see Barrera, 1986; Hobfoll & Stokes, 1988; I. Sarason, Sarason & Pierce, 1992). This general definition points to three major facets of social support: received support (actual receipt of help), social embeddedness (quantity and type of relationships with others) and perceived support (the belief that help would be available if needed).

The role of social support as a coping resource has been studied within the context of many stressful life events ranging from individual level stressors (e.g., bereavement, pregnancy, divorce or illness) to community-wide events (e.g., crowding, unemployment, disaster or war). Reviews of literature often note the limitations of supportive relationships in times of stress (e.g., Coyne, Wortman & Lehman, 1988; La Gaipa, 1990; Rook, 1992) but have generally concluded that social support is beneficial to psychological well-being and physical health (e.g., Cohen & Wills, 1985; Cutrona & Russell, 1990; Kessler & McLeod, 1985; Sarason & Sarason, this volume; Schwarzer & Leppin, 1991). The vast majority of studies that have provided evidence for such conclusions were based on two dominant

Handbook of Personal Relationships, 2nd edn. Edited by Steve Duck.
© 1997 John Wiley & Sons Ltd.

theoretical formulations, the stress buffer (interactive) model and the main effects (additive) model. Whereas these models are viable ways of describing how social support operates, they do not account for all possible relations between stress, social support and psychological functioning. A major conceptual problem with these two dominant hypotheses is that they consider stress a static phenomenon. The principal assumption of both models is that stress and social support are unrelated to each other. In fact, the link between stressor and social support, though often observed, has been largely ignored or considered a conceptual or methodological inconvenience (see Barrera, 1986; Thoits, 1982). However, both lay and empirical observations provide numerous examples of stressful life events changing the availability and quality of social ties. Whenever stressful circumstances meaningfully influence social support and personal relationships, buffering and main effects models offer quite limited grounds for explaining the dynamics of the stress process.

Disasters that are brought about by forces of nature (e.g., floods, hurricanes, earthquakes) or human agents (e.g., toxic contamination, nuclear power plant accidents, toxic spills) constitute a large set of stressful events that undeniably exert strong impact on social relationships. In this chapter, we will consider the role of social support and personal relationships in coping with disasters that impact entire communities. Although other catastrophic events are often referred to as disasters (e.g., transportation accidents, fires of public buildings, industrial accidents), our focus is on those events that simultaneously affect large groups of individuals in their own habitats and familiar surroundings. Disasters, such as floods, tornadoes or nuclear core meltdowns, are more than individual-level stressful events. They engulf whole communities. When disasters strike, the victims must cope with their threats and losses at a time when their social support networks are most likely to be disrupted and potentially unable to carry out their supportive roles. Victimization is shared, and the distinction between victim and supporter is more a matter of speech than reality. Recipients and providers are victims themselves and must rely on each other's coping efforts and reciprocity. Receiving and providing help evolves into a mutual struggle with shared misfortune. However, it is important to remember that the post-crisis exchanges of interpersonal concern and assistance take place in a context of pre-existing socio-political structures and ties, with established rules and norms of resource distribution that regulate the quality and quantity of supportive relations. The bottom line is that social support forces influencing the process of coping with disasters are dynamic reflections of transactions among characteristics of the individuals, the community and the stressor.

These relations are particularly complex in the context of disasters because very different, and at times conflicting, processes emerge. On one hand, disasters elicit an outpouring of immense mutual helping. On the other hand, disasters remove important others from victims' support networks through death and relocation, they disrupt day-to-day activities that maintain social ties, and they often overwhelm the available social resources. The defining manifestations of social support mentioned at the beginning of this chapter may prove useful in describing what might seem a paradox. It could be said that the instantaneous mobilization of help is in the domain of *received support*, whereas a lingering sense of deterioration and disruption is in the domains of *perceived support* and *sense of embeddedness*.

A conceptual framework depicted in Figure 26.1 will guide our review of the literature. The explicit premise of this model is that disaster exerts a direct adverse impact on psychological health (Direct Impact, path A). The stress that challenges victims of disasters is multifaceted. It often involves immediate trauma arising from exposure to death and injury (horror), extreme physical force (terror) and life-threatening situations. The stress of disasters entails destruction of goods and possessions of substantial monetary value as well as keepsakes of symbolic and emotional significance. Disasters may diminish victims' sense of self-esteem, feelings of security and beliefs in justice. Jointly or singularly, all these facets of disaster stress threaten and shatter valued resources needed to sustain physical and psychological health. Not surprisingly, then, research has documented reliable increases in physical and psychological symptomatology following disasters (for reviews see, e.g., Baum, 1987; Freedy, Kilpatrick & Resnick, 1993; Green & Solomon, 1995; Raphael & Wilson, 1993; Rubonis & Bickman, 1991). For most victims, these negative consequences will dissipate within a year or two (e.g., Phifer & Norris, 1989; Thompson, Norris & Hanacek, 1993) but for some victims, they may become more lasting (e.g., Gleser, Green & Winget, 1981; Green, 1995).

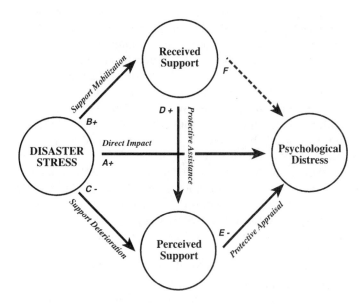

Figure 26.1 Social support dynamics in adjustment to disasters: social support deterioration deterrence model

To cope with disaster stress, victims need all the support they can get. Immediately after impact, most victims of disaster are provided with high levels of help. The process of *support mobilization* (Figure 26.1, path B) is governed, however, by various norms and rules of inclusion and exclusion. Most importantly, the initial rush of spontaneous helping inevitably ceases, long before the stress of disaster is over. It is at that time that victims discover that their losses and psychological trauma are accompanied by social disruption, interpersonal conflict and a depletion of available support. This process of *support deterioration* (path C), is one way through which disasters indirectly exert their detrimental impact on psychological well-being (paths C and E). Thus we must take both the mobilization and deterioration processes into account to understand psychological adaptation to disasters. However, adequately mobilized received support should be positively associated with perceptions of support availability (Protective Assistance, path D) and could serve to counter or reduce the deterioration in perceived support otherwise seen. Through this process of *deterioration deterrence* (paths B and D), the mobilization of received support indirectly affects mental health (paths B, D and E) by preserving perceptions of social support. Ultimately, the sense of being reliably connected to others, perceived social support, serves its usual protective role (Protective Appraisal, path E).

SOCIAL SUPPORT MOBILIZATION

Across a variety of life events, it is not uncommon to observe that stressors mobilize support networks to aid those affected. In essence, this is exactly what people expect from their personal relationships: when help is needed, supporters are supposed to provide it. Numerous studies document that stress, often considered as an index of need for support, is related to greater amounts of support actually received (e.g., Dunkel-Schetter, Folkman & Lazarus, 1987; Hobfoll & Lerman, 1989; Jackson, 1988; Joseph et al., 1993; Kaniasty & Norris, 1992). Thus, stressful life events may show a positive association with social support, most specifically with received support. Although the stress buffer model dismisses the potential of a causal link between life events and social support, the positive linkage between stress and support is not necessarily inconsistent with that model. A broad definition of stress-buffering as any condition that decreases the overall detrimental effect of stress would include the possibility that the effects of life stressors are suppressed, or counteracted, through an activation of social support networks (Barrera, 1988; Ensel & Lin, 1991; Wheaton, 1985). This conceptualization has often been called a *suppressor* or social support *mobilization* model.

Public responses following natural disasters provide excellent examples of support mobilization. High levels of mutual helping often vividly materialize in those contexts. Contrary to common beliefs about mass panic and chaotic disorganization, victims quickly tend to regain a collective sense of determination and rapidly immerse themselves in the process of aiding each other. This immediate phase has been referred to as the "altruistic or therapeutic community" or "post-disaster utopia" (see Barton, 1969; Frederick, 1980; Fritz, 1961; Giel, 1990). The most distinguishing features of this collective entity are heightened internal solidarity, disappearance of community conflicts, utopian mood, and an overall sense of altruism. Many observers have claimed that the experience of the same fate increases identification among victims and causes previous class, race, ethnic and social class barriers to disappear temporarily (see Eranen & Liebkind, 1993, p. 958).

Media accounts of post-disaster behavior provide an abundance of illustrations of such spontaneously occurring helping and concern for each other. In today's technological age of global communication, we are exposed to instant transmissions of unveiling horror, grief and heroism among victims of major disasters. In recent years, we have witnessed "live" the pain, determination and unselfishness of people struck by hurricanes (e.g. Charleston, September, 1989; South Miami, August, 1992), earthquakes (e.g. Northridge, January, 1994; Kobe, Japan, January, 1995) and floods (e.g. mid-west USA, July, 1993). Whereas mutual helping behavior is clearly abundant in the immediate aftermath of catastrophic events, expressions such as "altruistic community" may inadvertently create a false image that all victims are equally enveloped by these supportive efforts. Altruistic or therapeutic communities do develop, but they are not all-inclusive. Likewise, these instances of post-crisis benevolence may create a false image that these communities inevitably evolve. Although these images are heartwarming and reassuring, we cannot accept them uncritically. Important questions need to be addressed. What are the rules governing the development of altruistic communities? Do they develop in all contexts of collective disasters? How long do they last?

The Rule of Relative Needs

The altruistic community does not distribute aid randomly or equally. Priority is given to those victims who experience the greatest exposure to the disaster's destructive powers and, thus, assistance is generally allocated in accordance to the *rule of relative needs*. In the Fall of 1990, 1 year after Hurricane Hugo devastated large areas of North and South Carolina (September 22, 1989), we interviewed a total of 1000 persons—500 victims (i.e., respondents residing in two stricken cities, Charleston, SC. and Charlotte, NC.) and 500 non-victims (i.e., respondents residing in two "control" sites, Greenville, SC. and Savannah, GA). We asked all the respondents about the tangible, informational and emotional help they had received in the 2 months following the hurricane (see Norris & Kaniasty, 1992, for discussion of delayed self-reports in disaster research). Because we asked about *any* support received regardless of the reason (therefore not necessarily linked to the disaster experience) we were able to compare victims to non-victims on the amounts of support received during that timeframe (Kaniasty & Norris, 1995a). Disaster exposure, operationalized as *loss* (of property and belongings) and *harm* (injury or threat to life), was strongly associated with the amount of help received. The between-group differences were pervasive: disaster victims received much more help than non-victims, and high-impact victims generally received more support than low-impact victims. Drabek & Key (1984) also found the extent of damage to be associated with the amount of help received among victims of a destructive tornado in Topeka, Kansas, in 1966. Bolin (1982) likewise observed the rule of relative needs following devastating tornadoes in Vernon and Wichita Falls, Texas, in 1979. A similar allocation of support has been documented across many other stressful life events at both the individual and community levels (e.g., Dunkel-Schetter, Folkman & Lazarus, 1987; Hobfoll & Lerman, 1989; Jackson, 1988; Kaniasty & Norris, 1992).

Disaster victims primarily rely on their indigenous support networks. However, the quantity of help varies by donor. Not surprisingly, families usually are the most utilized source of support (Quarantellii, 1960; Smith, 1983; Solomon, 1986). Reliance on kin is found most often among victims who maintained relatively strong kin relationships prior to disaster (Drabek & Key, 1984). Non-kin informal networks, such as friends, neighbors and local religious congregations, also appear to play a vital role in assisting victims, particularly where kin ties are temporarily unavailable, weak or absent (Drabek & Key, 1984; Solomon, 1986; Perry, Hawkins & Neal, 1983). In the two tornado-stricken sites studied by Bolin (1982), 75% of the victims reported receiving aid from kin, 68% received help from friends and 48% received support from neighbors.

A similar hierarchy of support utilization has been observed in other disaster studies. Essentially, the most consistent finding is that victims are quite reticent in utilizing assistance from sources outside their immediate network and rely mainly on their families, relatives, friends and neighbors (see Solomon, 1986). In other words, the pattern of help utilization following disasters resembles a pyramid with its broad foundation being family and other primary support groups and its narrow top being aid provided by formal agencies. The pyramid analogy (see Wills & DePaulo, 1991) implies that the closer the source of support is to the victim, the greater will be the amounts of support he or she provides. In a study of 400 Floridians, whom we interviewed about 6 months after Hurricane Andrew, we asked about help received from different sources. Specifically, we assessed the support victims received from their family (those connected by blood or marriage), their friends (including neighbors, co-workers and others known from church or social organizations), and people outside their immediate circle (people not known personally, e.g., community leaders, voluntary organizations, professional service providers). In general, victims reported receiving substantial amounts of help from all three sources. However, within each type of support (tangible, informational and emotional) the rank order of the greatest reliance being on family, followed by friends, and then finally outsiders was preserved (Kaniasty & Norris, 1994). Moreover, this hierarchy emerged within each of the three ethnic groups studied (Blacks, Latinos and Whites).

The distribution of assistance within different sources of support is also guided by the rule of relative needs. Drabek & Key (1984) found that the extent of damages from the Topeka tornado was consistently associated with the amount of help received from a variety of donors including relatives, friends, religious organizations, Red Cross and other voluntary and governmental agencies. Similarly, in our study of victims of Hurricane Andrew (Kaniasty & Norris, 1994; Norris & Kearse, 1995), disaster impact predicted receiving help from each of the three sources. Nonetheless, the rule of relative needs is by no means always present. For example, in a study of elderly victims of widespread flooding that occurred in southeastern Kentucky in 1981 and 1984 (Kaniasty, Norris & Murrell, 1990), disaster losses significantly predicted help from non-kin sources (friends, neighbors, churches) but not from kin sources (immediate family and relatives), in spite of the fact that the kin sources were more relied on. This difference could reflect a generally greater tendency for non-kin networks to be mobilized by relative needs or losses, which seems especially appropriate in collective stress situations where many persons are simultaneously in need of assistance. On the other hand, help from immediate family and relatives may not always be guided by such a rule and, at times, could be allocated somewhat irrespectively of the extent of losses experienced (e.g., Bolin & Trainer, 1978).

Solomon (1986) suggested that ubiquitous reliance for help following a traumatic event on personal relationships rather than professional sources stems mainly from their status as non-professionals. Informal networks are less stigmatizing, less costly, more geographically accessible and more likely to assist early in the crisis. As members of communal relationships (Clark & Mills, 1979), the providers are motivated primarily by a concern of being responsive to the other person's needs. Providers tend to offer their help spontaneously rather than in response to requests by the victims (Bolin, 1982; Drabek & Key, 1984). "The interaction is voluntary, reciprocal, and mutually beneficial, since members have the opportunity to both give and receive esteem" (Solomon, 1986, pp. 240–41). In essence, these reciprocal exchanges of assistance represent best the manifestations of common purpose and fellowship in post-disaster altruistic communities. Altogether, the preference of disaster victims for help from close relationships is not unusual because, generally, the most frequent help-seeking and providing occurs within informal social networks (see Wills & DePaulo, 1991). Unfortunately, in the context of community-wide stressors the over-reliance on personal relationships might create an extra burden for those victims who are also the providers. The influx of additional communal obligations and responsibilities disrupts their own coping efforts, making them more vulnerable to post-disaster distress (Solomon et al., 1987; Thompson, Norris & Hanacek, 1993). Formal sources of support must tailor their services to be more readily available and genuinely intertwined within the indigenous community to take their "fair share" of the burden (see Hobfoll & de Vries, 1995; Solomon, 1986). Planning and outreach are essential.

Shelter and Hammers, How-to Tips, and Love and Compassion

According to leading models of stress (e.g., Hobfoll, 1988; Lazarus & Folkman, 1984), the efficacy of social support is determined by the extent to which it functions to promote preservation or recovery of important physical and psychological resources necessary for successful adaptation (see Hobfoll & Lilly, 1993). Social support research illustrates this role of support as "provider" of emotional comfort, material goods, self-esteem, information and opportunities for social interaction. To be effective in a variety of circumstances, informal support networks must provide those coping resources that are both most challenged by the stressful event and most needed for coping (Cutrona & Russell, 1990). Natural disasters are synonymous with destruction of the physical environment, loss of possessions and depletion of valuable assets. Thus, generally speaking, in the aftermath of natural disasters, tangible help may be the most uniquely relevant type of social support. Shelter is frequently the obvious priority. Victims also need assistance with cleaning their properties. They need tools, equipment and money. They need help with household chores such as cooking, grocery shopping and child care. Disaster studies attest to the foremost importance of victims' receiving tangible goods and services (Bolin, 1982; Bolin & Bolton, 1986; Cook & Bickman, 1990; Drabek & Key, 1984). Consequently, the rule of relative needs should be most predictive of tangible help because of its distinct relevance to victims' lives. Accordingly, in both the Hurricane Hugo and Hurricane Andrew studies, we found that disaster impact was most strongly associated with receiving help in the realm of tangible support.

Disaster victims require information and guidance as well. Victims' recovery depends on finding quick and practical solutions to many exacting predicaments. Victims must learn how to organize clean-up efforts and how to protect what is left of their property and belongings. They need to know where to turn for formal assistance and how to deal with local, governmental and insurance agencies involved in their recovery. For these reasons, we hypothesized and showed that informational support was also predicted by disaster impact following Hurricanes Hugo and Andrew.

The importance of tangible and informational support notwithstanding, being surrounded by those who are loving and understanding is undoubtedly critical for disaster victims. Survivors of catastrophic events may be exposed to violent and sudden deaths, often grotesque and indelible, may sustain severe physical harm or injuries, or experience profound threats to their lives and those of others (see Green, 1993). Even in less horrific circumstances, victims may experience substantial losses of material, symbolic and emotional significance. Personal relationships must provide a "trauma membrane" (Lindy & Grace, 1986, p. 156) to protect the victimized and promote their healing. "The best help was from those who could *listen* and just *spend time*", a victim reflected following the 1980 volcanic eruption of Mount St Helens, Washington (Murphy, 1986, p. 71). Thus, not at all surprisingly, supporters generally are quite aware of these needs, and emotional support appears to be the most frequently exchanged type of help in a variety of stressful upheavals (e.g., Dakof & Taylor, 1990; Dunkel-Schetter et al., 1992; Lehman, Ellard & Wortman, 1986). Similarly, in absolute terms, emotional support has been the most frequently exchanged type of help in our studies (Kaniasty & Norris, 1994, 1995a). However, in the case of Hurricane Hugo, victims were not as much different from non-victims in receiving emotional support as they were in receiving tangible and informational support. Furthermore, in the case of Hurricane Andrew, the rule of relative needs failed to apply to the allocation of emotional help. Across the two studies, analyses of the concomitants of support receipt indicated that emotional help was determined less by disaster impact and more by person characteristics than were tangible and informational help. Possibly, people desire emotional support at all times, whereas their need for tangible aid and advice is determined more by demands of the stressor. We have also speculated (Kaniasty & Norris, 1995a) that because emotional support is so frequently communicated through routine daily contacts (Leatham & Duck, 1990) it becomes a kind of "ubiquitous entity". People generally expect it, regardless of need. Consequently, its omnipresence could be assumed by people, even if it has not actually materialized. This suggestion implies a possibility of a response bias, especially on the part of low-impact victims and non-victims, manifested in inflated self-presentations (see Paulhus, 1991; Taylor & Brown, 1988). Or it could be that measures of emotional support evidence "ceiling effects". More research on these potential biases or measurement problems would be useful. On the other hand, emotional support may actually be less *uniquely* relevant to victims of disaster, whereas the other two domains of social support—tangible and informational support—are more closely matched to the ecological demands of the event. This issue bears some theoretical and practical importance because receipt of support should be most advantageous if the specific demands of the stressor and the actual support provisions are compatible with each other (see Dunkel-Schetter & Bennett, 1990; Kaniasty & Norris, 1992; Martin et al., 1994).

Beyond the Rule of Relative Needs

Besides relative need, what other factors affect the distribution of social support in post-disaster communities? Empirical and common observations alike suggest that irrespectively of needs, certain individuals may have a *relative advantage* in receiving support (see House, Umberson & Landis, 1988; Vaux, 1988). For example, people with larger support networks typically receive more support (Drabek & Key, 1984; Kaniasty & Norris, 1995a; Sarason et al., 1987a; Stokes & Wilson, 1984). Women usually receive more support than men, particularly in the domain of emotional support (Kaniasty & Norris, 1995a; Rosario et al., 1988; Stokes & Wilson, 1984).

Research on post-disaster helping behavior suggests that elderly, the poor, the less educated and ethnic minorities may experience a *pattern of neglect*. It appears that victims with higher socio-economic status (SES), as measured by income or education, generally receive more help from informal support networks whereas those of lower SES have to rely more on formal sources (Bolin, 1982; Drabek & Key, 1984). Our study of the Kentucky floods is a disheartening illustration of how scarcity of resources could result in a pattern of neglect

(Kaniasty, Norris & Murrell, 1990). The flood victims in that study were disadvantaged in many ways. These older adults, who averaged only 8 years of education, resided in an impoverished rural setting (Appalachia) characterized by poor housing and high unemployment (20% at the time the study was conducted). Moreover, unlike many more recent disasters, the Kentucky floods attracted little attention from the media and general public. Because the floods occurred in the midst of an ongoing panel study in the area, we were afforded pre- as well as post-disaster measures (see Norris, Phifer & Kaniasty, 1994; Phifer & Norris, 1989). Using a prospective design, still relatively rare in disaster research, we were able to examine how expectations of help in a hypothetical life crisis (i.e., pre-flood perceived support availability) fared during an actual emergency. The victims of Kentucky floods generally received little help. We found that pre-flood expectations of help in hypothetical life crisis were about three times higher than the amount of help actually received following the disaster. For example, only 24% received a "fair" or "great" amount of help from relatives outside the home, compared with 73% who had expected that much help prior to the flood. Similarly, 22% of the victims actually received a "fair" or "great" amount of help from their neighbors, compared with 73% who expected to receive that much support in a hypothetical emergency. These results were not congruent with the image of widespread altruism following disasters. We offered several explanations for these findings (see Kaniasty, Norris & Murrell, 1990) but the pattern of neglect seemed most viable. Apparently, these poor, rural and older victims were denied participation in a post-disaster therapeutic community.

Older age has been associated with unequal involvement in helping communities following other disasters. Accounting for the degree of damage, Drabek & Key (1984) found that, following the Topeka tornado, families headed by persons over 60 received aid far less frequently from all the sources than families headed by persons under 60. Similarly, age was inversely related to received support in the Hurricane Hugo study (Kaniasty & Norris, 1995a). In analyses that controlled for both the extent of loss or harm experienced and a host of other socio-demographic factors, older age was found to be consistently associated with less support received. However, the relative disadvantage of older people (main effect) was not augmented by the disaster (interaction). No interactions were significant when disaster exposure was operationalized in terms of tangible losses and damages. On the other hand, the interactions between age and disaster impact were significant when exposure was operationalized in terms of physical harm. However, the form of these interactions was such that older respondents received *more* help than equally threatened younger victims.

What do these age-related findings mean? Drabek & Key (1984) concluded that "elderly families simply did not participate as fully in the emergent post-disaster therapeutic community as did the younger victims" (p. 100). In fact, it was this situation that inspired Kilijanek & Drabek (1979) to coin the term "pattern of neglect". Although the data from the earlier Kentucky flooding study were consistent with this view, our more recent findings require a somewhat more complex interpretation that takes the nature of the exposure into account. With regard to property damage, older adults may sometimes suffer from a pattern of neglect; however, with regard to physical illness and injury there may actually be a *pattern of concern* that mobilizes support networks to provide more assistance to the elderly. Quite possibly, illness or physical complaints serve as powerful cues indicating a need for attention, concern, guidance and assistance (e.g., DiMatteo & Hays, 1981; Dunkel-Schetter, Folkman & Lazarus, 1987). Informal support networks may be especially attentive to health threats experienced by the elderly because of their assumed vulnerability in the physical health domain. Given that it is these same traumatic stressors (injury, life-threat) that have been shown to be most devastating to mental health (e.g., Green, 1993), older people may be fortuitously receiving the most psychologically relevant social support. This pattern of concern may explain why older adults are typically at *less* risk for poor psychological outcomes than middle-aged and younger victims (Green, 1995; Thompson, Norris & Hanacek, 1993).

In the Hurricane Hugo study, we also took a closer look at the role of race and socio-economic status (as indicated by educational level) in predicting received social support (Kaniasty & Norris, 1995a). In general, Blacks reported receiving less tangible help from their informal networks than Whites and persons with lower educational attainment received less emotional support than persons with more education. Moreover, race and education moderated the impact of disaster exposure on receipt of social support. That is, in the presence of disaster losses, Black victims consistently received less tangible, informational and emotional help than equally affected victims who were White. This pattern also emerged among victims with little education. Thus disaster exposure *sharpened their relative disadvantage*, resulting in a clear pattern of neglect.

These findings are important, and disheartening, because they are not limited only to Hurricane Hugo. Although the results from the Andrew study are a little more complicated because we included Latinos in the sample and assessed different sources of support, the general trend was, again, for Blacks to report receiving less help than equally affected Whites and Latinos, with the latter two groups reporting basically similar levels of aid (Kaniasty & Norris, 1994). Following their comprehensive examination of four natural disasters (tornado, flooding, hurricane and earthquake) that struck four culturally and ethnically diverse sites (Texas, Utah, Hawaii and California), Bolin & Bolton (1986) observed that poor families had the greatest difficulties securing adequate assistance. Therefore, their chances for speedy recovery could have been hampered by their limited involvement in the post-disaster helping community.

Why do some people receive less help? Why do those who are already marginalized by the society become even less visible in crisis and participate to a lesser extent in the emergent altruistic community? Is it because they are reluctant to seek help? Is it because they are less efficacious in mobilizing or utilizing available resources? These factors are of potential significance because, as found in the Andrew study, the strongest predictor of all types of help from all sources was help-seeking comfort. Simply, victims who held a favorable attitude toward seeking help received more of it (Kaniasty & Norris, 1994; Norris & Kearse,

1995). However, stopping here in answering these questions risks "blaming the victim". Quite possibly, the quantity of help received by minorities and lower socio-economic class persons could be a direct result of their restricted access to support resources. Support mobilization processes are highly influenced by larger social forces that operate behind the immediate characteristics of individuals and their environments (Eckenrode & Wethington, 1990). Socially and economically disadvantaged groups are frequently too overburdened to provide ample help to other members in time of additional need. Ability to develop and sustain thriving social resources may be hindered by their lower societal position (House, Umberson & Landis, 1988). Unemployment, poverty, prejudice and cultural and political marginalization affect the matrix of social relations. Lack of resources and opportunities to build strong networks augments the risk of further resource depletion (Eckenrode & Wethington, 1990; Hobfoll & Lilly, 1993). "In a sense, the poor in disaster are double victims: they are first of all victims of poverty and that, in turn, adds to the degree of 'victimization' in disasters" (Bolin, 1982, p. 247).

In sum, communities in the aftermath of disasters cannot escape the pre-existing societal conditions of inclusion and exclusion. Post-disaster helping communities, when they arise, are not ruled in the most egalitarian way. The often talked about altruism and fellowship that the public marshals in times of crisis should not obscure the fact that not all victims are fully participating in these emergent altruistic communities.

Another qualification to the commonly held image of the overarching post-crisis benevolence, altruism and solidarity relates to the question of whether altruistic communities develop in all contexts of collective disasters. The answer to this question appears to be "No". Besides the most salient distinction of origin—nature (God) vs. technology (human)—there are many important differences between natural and technological disasters (see Baum, Fleming & Davidson, 1983; Berren et al., 1989; Bolin, 1993). The impact of natural disasters is usually immediate, direct and clearly visible, whereas the impact of technological disasters is quite frequently slowly evolving, uncertain and not readily perceptible. Technological emergencies, such as nuclear power plant accidents, chemical or toxic waste spills "contaminate rather than merely damage" (Erikson, 1991, p .80). Cuthbertson & Nigg (1987) noted that because of their ambiguity and invisibility and the lack of a clearly identifiable low point ("worst is over"), post-disaster altruistic communities are unlikely to develop following technological emergencies. Evidence suggests that victims of such events do not receive the high levels of compassion and help routinely offered to victims of acts of nature (Bolin, 1993). Instead, the aftermath of technological events seems to be characterized by interpersonal conflict and erosion of social cohesion (see Baum, 1987; Bolin, 1993; Kroll-Smith & Couch, 1993), a point to which we will return later.

Finally, and most importantly, above all the qualifications, is the issue of persistence. This heightened level of helping and concern inevitably must cease "and in no case can it be expected to last the length of the recovery process"

(Bolin, 1982, p. 60). The initial and short-lived period of intense affiliation, heroic sacrifice, altruism and hopefulness, a stage at times somewhat ironically labeled a "honeymoon", will soon give way to a gradual disillusionment and realization of the harsh reality of grief, loss and destruction (see Frederick, 1980; Raphael & Wilson, 1993). Shortly after the attentive media and many of the considerate and generous outsiders leave for another crisis, the victims discover that the struggle to rebuild their physical and social environments has only just begun. It is then they will notice that the need for support far exceeds its availability. As a "rise and fall of utopia" (see Giel, 1990), disasters are vivid portrayals of how communal upheavals move from an initial abundance of mutual helping to an often inadvertent longer-term depletion of supportive resources.

SOCIAL SUPPORT DETERIORATION

If stressors can mobilize social support, they can also diminish it. Social support research shows that the stigma and uncertainty associated with many psychological conditions, diseases, disabilities and victimizations may transpire into victims' feelings of isolation or actual neglect. Social support networks may not recognize the need or see it as legitimate, may not know how to help, or may attempt to provide support but deliver it ineptly (e.g., Coyne, Wortman & Lehman, 1988; Dakof & Taylor, 1990; Dunkel-Schetter & Skokan, 1990; Eckenrode & Wethington, 1990; Rook, 1992; Shinn, Lehmann & Wong, 1984; Wortman & Dunkel-Schetter, 1979). Exchanging support in times of crisis is a complex and difficult process where good intentions and sincere concerns often blend with confusion, skepticism and psychological threats experienced by both recipients and providers. These impediments of the helping process may generate, at times rightly so, perceptions that support is not available or adequate. Additionally, certain characteristics of stressful life events may directly alter the actual and perceived availability of social support. Developmental transitions (e.g., graduation or retirement) or exit events (e.g., death or divorce) not only dissolve focal relationships but also transform existing patterns of daily interactions, and thus may undermine access to support providers. Potentially chronic stressors such as unemployment, crime, crowding, illness, marital difficulties, parenting strain or job stress can also result in diminished perceptions of available support (Atkinson, Liem & Liem, 1986; Bolger et al., 1996; Bolger & Zuckerman, 1994; Eckenrode & Wethington, 1990; Julien & Markman, 1991; Lane & Hobfoll, 1992; Lepore, Evans & Schneider, 1991; Quittner, Glueckauf & Jackson, 1990). The potential of stressful events to curtail social support is recognized by a *social support deterioration model* (Barrera, 1988; Ensel & Lin, 1991; Wheaton, 1985) that stipulates that the stressor-induced erosion of support is one way through which the stressor exerts its adverse effect on well-being.

As for disasters, accounts of lingering disruption of social structure and sense of community are at least as frequent as, or even more frequent than, accounts of instantaneous but ephemeral post-disaster altruistic communities. It appears that the gains of coping resources in the form of social bonding and mobilization of received support are routinely defeated by an accelerating cycle of losses that sweeps through disaster-stricken areas. According to Hobfoll's (1988) conservation of resources theory, resource loss is difficult to prevent and more powerful than resource gain. Although many disasters occur suddenly, the stress they inflict is not just acute. Like other major stressful events (see Pearlin, 1989), disasters evoke an array of secondary stressors that continuously challenge victims and strain their coping resources at a rate faster than the progress of recovery (Norris & Uhl, 1993; Riad & Norris, 1996). Often, the initial mobilization of social support may not be sufficient to conquer the creeping deterioration in social relationships.

Sense of Loss: a Collective Experience

Disasters diminish the sense of support because they disrupt the composition of social networks. At the extreme, disasters are "a blow to the tissues of social life that damages the bonds linking people together and impairs the prevailing sense of communality" (Erikson, 1976b, p. 302). Most tragically, disasters remove significant supporters from victims' networks through death. Temporary or permanent relocation is often necessary. Although victims frequently find shelter among people they know, love and can count on, the quality of their relationships with hosting families may eventually break down as conflicts emerge due to crowding and financial difficulties (Bolin, 1982, 1985a). Following large-scale disasters, many victims must rely on temporary housing that very seldom reflects pre-disaster personal relationships and neighborhood patterns (Bolin, 1985a; Bolin & Stanford, 1990; Erikson, 1976a; Gleser, Green & Winget, 1981; Riad & Norris, 1996). Some people move away and never come back, changing the structure of social relations permanently (Hutchins & Norris, 1989). The loss of important attachments is almost unavoidable.

Whereas the instant mobilization of helping behavior is a clear manifestation of received social support, the deterioration processes following disasters are more directly manifested in declining perceptions of social support availability. It has generally been assumed that, as the proportion of victims to non-victims within a community increases, the psychological and social consequences of the disaster also increase (Green, 1982). Disasters harm entire neighborhoods and communities. The likelihood is high that potential support providers are victims themselves and, as a result, the need for support across all affected frequently surpasses its availability. Thus the majority of victims often face the reality of their own interpersonal networks' deficiency to fulfill their supportive roles. To the extent perceptions of social support are environmentally based, people residing in disaster-stricken areas may have to "revise" their expectations about how much support is currently available.

The Kentucky floods study (Kaniasty, Norris & Murrell, 1990) provided a clear demonstration of disaster's potential to diminish perceived support. Controlling for pre-flood perceptions of social support, we found that the impact of disaster was associated with declines in expectations of support from both kin and non-kin sources. Similar declines in perceptions of social support have been documented by other studies. Solomon et al. (1993) showed that disaster victims, particularly single parents, experienced substantial losses in the access to emotional support. Examinations of Hurricane Hugo and Hurricane Andrew have also indicated that those events led to lower perceptions of social support availability (Norris & Kaniasty, 1996) or a general sense of loss of social support (Ironson et al., 1993). Possibly, these declines in perceived availability of support from personal relationships reflected the victims' "disappointments in the level of support provided by relatives and supposed friends" (Harvey et al., 1995; p. 319). However, the loss of perceived support is not just limited to *primary victims*, that is, those victims who are personally affected by disasters (see Bolin, 1985b). In the Kentucky floods study, *secondary victims*, that is, those who lived in the affected area but sustained no personal injuries or damages, reported analogous declines in their perceptions of social support. Accordingly, the decline in perceptions of help availability experienced by both primary and secondary victims could have reflected a veridical assessment of their personal networks' as well as the whole community's inability to provide support at that time. Thus, a disaster is more than an individual-level event; it is a community-level event with psychological and social consequences, even for those who incur no direct losses. In his powerful account of the Buffalo Creek dam collapse, Erikson (1976a) spoke of two facets of victimization, "individual trauma" and "collective trauma". Fortunately, not all collective crises are as horrifying as the Buffalo Creek tragedy, but still it can be said that in most disasters, whether small or great, annual or centennial, "the two traumas occur simultaneously, and are experienced as two halves of a continuous whole" (p. 154).

A communal dimension of the impact of disasters was also evidenced in the finding that both primary and secondary victims of the Kentucky floods experienced a post-disaster deterioration in their sense of social embeddedness. Residents of disaster-stricken areas often report decreased participation in social activities with relatives, friends, neighbors and community organizations (Bolin, 1985a, 1993; Hutchins & Norris, 1989; Solomon, 1986). Occasions for social interactions could be restricted because physical environments or settings instrumental for maintaining companionship are damaged or destroyed. Routine activities such as visiting, shopping, recreation and attending religious services are frequently curtailed and, with them, the day-to-day opportunities to convey and preserve the sense of support and feeling of being reliably attached to valued groups (see e.g., Leatham & Duck, 1990). Social activities may be disrupted not only as a direct consequence of disaster but also by the recovery efforts (Trainer & Bolin, 1976). Victims must prioritize the use of their resources and allocate their energies to the physical reconstruction process, often putting their "social life" on hold. According to Rook (1985), the companionship domain of social support embraces taking part in communal activities, sharing with others the moments of leisure, or just simply enjoying being together. It appears that victimized communities may be denied for a long time this particular aspect of social relationships. In fact, deviations in the patterns of social interactions may outlast the actual physical reconstruction of the community (Trainer & Bolin, 1976).

Interpersonal Weariness and Burden

Changes in social support are not only due to the physical parameters of a disastrous event such as the extent of destruction, forced relocation, or depletion of tangible resources like money or time. There are, undoubtedly, socio-psychological dynamics of the victimization experience that may also contribute to the diminished perceptions of social support. The initial frenzy of heroism, while distracting from preoccupation with trauma and potentially therapeutic, may inadvertently delay a personal resolution concerning the meaning of the experience (Jerusalem et al., 1995). Victims of stressful events that impact larger groups often subject themselves to "pressure cooker" (Hobfoll & London, 1986) or "stress contagion" phenomena (Riley & Eckenrode, 1986), whereby, para-doxically, social interactions and sharing of feelings and fears may exacerbate their symptoms of distress (see Hobfoll, Briggs & Wells, 1995). Being over-exposed to emotional disclosures about trauma can be psychologically threaten-ing. The supportive network may become saturated with stories of and feelings about the event. Consequently, victims and their supporters begin to minimize or downplay the importance of revealed emotions or may even escape interacting (Coyne, Wortman & Lehman, 1988; Silver, Wortman & Crofton, 1990). Pennebaker & Harber (1993) observed that some residents in areas struck by the Loma Prieta earthquake (San Francisco, October 1989) soon lost interest in hearing other victims' accounts and appeared to be "erecting barriers to prohibit others from bringing up the topic" (p. 133). Four weeks after the disaster, T-shirts surfaced that read "Thank you for not sharing your earthquake experience" (p. 133). Thus, another "social fence" (Platt, 1973) has been raised: whereas victims want and need to be listened to, they and others in their social environments may not necessarily wish to be the listeners. Lifton & Olson (1976) noted that as much as victims long for love and attention they may have real difficulties accepting genuine expressions of caring. With a grave sense of being betrayed and victim-ized by what was once assumed to be a benign and just world (see Janoff-Bulman, 1992), some supportive exchanges may be spoiled with suspicion and mistrust (Erikson, 1976a; Lifton & Olson, 1976; Murphy, 1986). Thus, even in the context of clearly devastating and unambiguous stressful events, the intricacies of helping processes may be overwhelmed with psychological defenses or prejudices that beget perceived or real neglect.

Families residing in areas affected by disasters are subjected to a number of secondary stressors in the form of the psychological problems of loved ones and interpersonal burdens. Under such circumstances, personal meanings attached to specific relationships—the building blocks of the global schemata of being sup-ported (Sarason, Sarason & Pierce, 1994)—could be undermined and may have to. be re-evaluated. McFarlane (1987) observed that among the families victimized by the Ash Wednesday bushfires (1983, Australia) psychological difficulties experienced by one of the members had a tendency to grate on others, augmenting the adverse effect of the disaster on the whole family (see also Solomon, 1986). A survivor of the Buffalo Creek flood said: "My kids seem to be doing all right, but when I go to pieces now they go to pieces too" (Lifton & Olson, 1976, p. 15). Loss of familiarity with physical and social environs, continuous tension, lack of personal resolution, disagreements about the meaning and consequence of the event may incite family or marital distress and disharmony (Bolin, 1982; Gleser, Green & Winget, 1981; Haas, Kates & Bowden, 1977; Harvey et al., 1995; Lifton & Olson, 1976; Smith, 1983; Solomon, 1986). Norris & Uhl (1993) showed that Hurricane Hugo led to increases in marital stress, parenting stress, and filial (caretaking) stress. In Buffalo Creek, "Wives and husbands discovered that they did not know how to nourish one another, make decisions, or even engage in satisfactory conversations when the community was no longer there to provide a context and set a rhythm" (Erikson, 1976b, p. 304). A few studies of post-disaster social functioning have reported increases in the number of divorces, annulments, alcohol-related disputes or domestic violence (e.g., Adams & Adams, 1984; Erikson, 1976a; Hall & Landreth, 1975).

Not all the evidence is consistent with concluding that disasters lead to elevated family stress. In an article entitled "Good news about disaster" Taylor (1977) stated that 6 months to a year after a tornado in Xenia, Ohio (1974), only 2% of the interviewed victims reported worsening relationships with close friends and family, whereas 27% claimed that such relationships improved. Moreover, according to 28% of the victims, their marital relationships became more satisfying following the tornado, whereas only 3% admitted to perceived declines. There was no overall change in the marriage or divorce rates after this disaster. Such contradictory findings remain the norm in disaster research and at present we know too little to integrate all conflicting results. There may be true community-level differences that cannot be empirically demonstrated because the predominant research strategy has been to study specific events in specific communities at particular points in time.

Toxic and Antagonistic Communities

Deterioration in social support and personal relationships is most evident following technological disasters. Because the parameters of the agent's impact are fuzzy, the very first issue faced by people residing in afflicted areas is to answer the question "Who are the true victims?" (Cuthbertson & Nigg, 1987). Residents, local authorities and those considered responsible for the hazard often bitterly debate the severity of the actual threat or the extent of harm. Residents of affected areas divide into antagonistic factions and those asserting to be victimized or wronged may be rejected, stigmatized and discriminated against. "People who claim to be contaminated are likely to be treated as contagious and routinely placed outside the boundaries of their emotional community" (Kroll-Smith & Couch, 1993, p. 83). Most naturally, those who perceive themselves as victimized and those who see no harm or deny it try to empower themselves by forming competing social circles that fuel the process of community polarization and interpersonal conflict. A resident of Centralia, Pennsylvania, a small mining community that after a lingering underground mine fire was finally deemed uninhabitable, vividly described such frictions: "The fire has split us up, it has torn us apart, you know—divided us. We're divided this and that way. We're worse than a pie cut into eight pieces" (Kroll-Smith & Couch, 1990, p. 5). The majority of residents of that community reported that interpersonal conflicts caused by the event were more stressful than the fire itself. In addition, technological disasters are frequently followed by lasting disputes and litigations concerning the alloca- tion of blame for the calamity. Such antagonisms further separate, fragment and politicize the community (Bolin, 1993). Not surprisingly then, victims of techno- logical catastrophes are found to experience greater levels of anger, alienation, suspicion and mistrust of others, loneliness and isolation (see Baum, 1987; Bromet, 1989; Cuthbertson & Nigg, 1987; Green, Lindy & Grace, 1994; Kroll- Smith & Couch, 1993). The overall post-disaster reality of persons affected by technological disasters is that of deterioration of social support and erosion of sense of community. The conflicted interpersonal dynamics observed in the aftermath of technological hazards may be "toxic" in their own way.

The distinction between technological and natural disasters has been fading. More and more, natural disasters are not perceived as politically neutral acts of nature or God. Rochford & Blocker (1991) have shown how a natural disaster such as flood can instigate collective protest and conflict because of the victims' appraisals of the event as *not* solely outside human control. When the search for the causal factor moves away from *nature* towards the *human* agent, community animosities and divisions become even more likely to surface. Advances in tech- nological control over the forces of nature may eventually change the way people assess and react collectively to so-called natural disasters:

> Indeed, the American experience of the past three decades seems to be one wherein God is losing ground very rapidly. Increasingly, disaster victims engage in a blame assignation process. And when a culprit has been identified, their interpretations of the event and its impacts on them and those involved in recovery may reflect processes that do not occur when they view their plight as 'God's doing' " (Drabek, 1986, p. 201).

Regardless of a disaster's origin, disaster-stricken communities may become contaminated by political confrontations at larger societal levels. As we men- tioned before, disasters vividly expose and augment pre-existing social inequali- ties along the lines of ethnicity, race and socio-economic status. Often forceful public emphasis on "getting back to the way things were before" cannot be a viable option for some of the victims because it would simply mean a "return" to their disadvantaged position. Bolin & Stanford (1990) reported that in some communities damaged by the Loma Prieta earthquake, the process of allocation of temporary housing to victims inspired allegations of racism, political and cultural discrimination, and further marginalization of minorities, elderly and the poor. This, in turn, led to organized demands for the improvement of political process and existing social arrangements. Bolin & Stanford concluded:

> The social, political, and economic disruption can provide opportunities for social change, particularly in instances where victims view the disaster as a vehicle to obtain social and economic resources historically denied them. These efforts at social change, because they typically challenge traditional patterns of power, privilege, and property, may be resisted, resulting in conflict" (p. 107).

Disasters may create opportunities for empowerment and social change but simultaneous pressures for political consensus and return to the *status quo* may antagonize communities even further (see Stallings, 1988).

Beyond the Buffering Hypothesis

Altogether the evidence gathered across variety of disasters suggests that a short-lived therapeutic phase of increased cohesion and helpfulness is overtaken by a protracted and diffused process of social support deterioration. Post-event declines in social support may be one of the reasons why stress-buffering properties of support are only sporadically found (e.g., Fleming et al., 1982; Cowan & Murphy, 1985). When present, stress-buffering properties are likely to be confined to specific subgroups, locales or contexts of mass disasters (e.g., Cook & Bickman, 1990; Ironson et al., 1993; Murphy, 1988; Solomon et al., 1993). For example, Solomon and her colleagues (Solomon et al., 1987) reported that the advantage of having social support in times of disaster was observed only for those victims with moderate, but not high, levels of support. This finding was interpreted as indicating that the additional demands placed on victims with more social support had overridden the expected benefits. Cook & Bickman (1990) also pointed out that buffering effects of social support may be overwhelmed by the force and scope of a "collective stress experience". Of course, these observations do not mean that having greater levels of perceived support is not related to better psychological outcomes among people subjected to disastrous events. In fact, almost all of the referenced studies in this section found that perceived availability of support was directly related to the victims' mental health outcomes, with higher levels of support being associated with better prognoses (see Figure 26.1, path E, Protective Appraisal). However, one critical issue has to be addressed: do declines in quality of personal relationships and social support following disasters matter for psychological health of disaster victims? In the case of collective stressors, the post-event declines in social support could contribute to the detrimental impact of stress rather than counteract (buffer) them. In other words, the disaster-induced erosion of social support could account for, or explain to some degree, the resulting impact the stressor has on psychological well-being. Consequently, a mediating model, not a moderating model (see Baron &

Kenny, 1986), may be more appropriate for describing the role of social support in the disaster recovery process.

We tested the mediating role of social support in the context of the Kentucky floods (Kaniasty & Norris, 1993). Our hypothesis was that an erosion of social support following disaster would account, to an extent, for the impact of disaster on victims' psychological well-being. Using a methodologically conservative design that controlled for prevent levels of functioning (symptoms and social support), we found that primary and secondary victims experienced the psychological consequence of flooding (i.e., an increase in depressive symptomatology) both directly, through immediate damage and exposure to trauma (see Figure 26.1, Path A, Direct Impact), and indirectly, through deterioration of perceived support and sense of embeddedness (Paths C and E). The evidence strongly indicated that post-disaster declines in perceived support were responsible for both the immediate and delayed mental health impact of disaster stress. The loss of social support has also been found to mediate the psychological consequences of Hurricanes Hugo and Andrew (Ironson et al., 1993; Norris & Kaniasty, 1996). In sum, deterioration of social support is a useful way of describing one possible pathway of how collective stress operates to affect psychological symptomatology. It also illustrates the value of conceptualizing the stress process in terms of resource loss (Hobfoll, 1988; Hobfoll & Lilly, 1993). Personal relationships and social support are critical assets whose loss in times of need adds to the catastrophe and is catastrophic in itself. Under the most tragic circumstances, the sense of being attached to others may be completely destroyed, and with it "the power it gave people to care for one another in moments of need, to console one another in moments of distress, and to protect one another in moments of danger" (Erikson, 1976b, p. 305).

SOCIAL SUPPORT DETERIORATION DETERRENCE

Is the deterioration of perceived support inevitable? This is an important question because it directly asks if participation in the emergent helping community protects victims against the deleterious impact of disaster stress. Our hypothesis is that the actual support mobilization following a stressful event acts to maintain or preserve perceptions of social support (see Figure 26.1, Path D, Protective Assistance). This simple statement has direct relevance for general social support theory. Over the years, most of the research on social support has concentrated on perceived support, leaving received support largely unexplored. In fact, the beneficial functions of social support have been most consistently shown to be contingent not so much upon the actual supportive exchanges (received support) as upon the mere perceptions that, if needed, support would be available (perceived support; see Barrera, 1986; Dunkel-Schetter & Bennett, 1990; Kessler & McLeod, 1985). Nevertheless, both theoretical (e.g., buffer hypothesis) and commonsense notions explaining ways in which perceived support operates to promote adaptive coping and psychological health have often assumed that some form of actual helping will materialize. Yet studies that examined the question of whether received support accounted for the relation between perceived support and well-being found no evidence of such a mediational role of actual support receipt (e.g., Lakey & Cassady, 1990; Wethington & Kessler, 1986).

However, a reverse causal process is plausible wherein receiving support may exert its beneficial effect on well-being through perceptions of social support availability (see Wethington & Kessler, 1986). To address this issue, we proposed a *social support deterioration deterrence model* (Kaniasty & Norris, 1995b; Norris & Kaniasty, 1996), that is, a conceptual variation of the already mentioned support-mobilization or stress-suppressor model. We believe that the most proximal consequence of receiving support in times of stress is the maintenance of perceptions of social support. Based on the findings of research reviewed in this chapter, the proposed model (see Figure 26.1) postulates that the stress of disaster and received support affect psychological distress in part through their influences on perceived support. First, we hypothesized that the disaster exposure has both a direct harmful effect on mental health (Path A, Direct Exposure) and an indirect effect through its adverse influence on perceived support (Path C, Support Deterioration). However, disasters also mobilize indigenous social networks to provide help to victims (Path B, Support Mobilization). Received support, in turn, should be positively associated with subsequent perceptions of support availability (Path D, Protective Assistance). We further hypothesized that perceived support would serve its usual protective role (Path E, Protective Appraisal): the higher the perceived support, the lower the distress. Because we predicted that the beneficial role of received support would be mediated through perceived support, we assumed there would be no direct effect of received support on distress (Path F).

Together, paths B and D form the *deterioration deterrence effect* that is the core hypothesis of the model. Whereas the direct effect of disaster on perceived support was expected to be negative in sign, this indirect path of deterioration deterrence was expected to be positive. If deterioration deterrence was complete, the values of the two effects would be roughly equivalent, resulting in the total effect of disaster stress on perceived support that would differ from 0 no more than could be expected by chance. However, we anticipated that the deterioration deterrence effect would reduce but not necessarily negate the deterioration effect (Path C). In other words, we expected to show that disasters decrease perceived support, but that effect would have been substantially worse if disasters had not also led to a mobilization of received support.

Our analyses (Norris & Kaniasty, 1996) of data collected 12 and 24 months following Hurricane Hugo and 6 and 28 months following Hurricane Andrew provided strong evidence for the hypothesized model. Most generally, perceived support mediated the long-term effects on psychological distress of both the disaster stress and post-disaster received support. More specifically, although disaster stress led to deterioration of perceived support, the *total* effects of disaster on perceived support were less severe than they might have been because the stress of disaster was positively associated with received support. Received support, in turn, was positively associated with ensuing beliefs regarding the perceived availability of support. Thus, post-event deterioration of social support is not inevitable. When victims receive high levels of help following a disaster, they appear to be protected against a salient erosion in their evaluations of support availability. Across two distinct events, we found significant and lasting effects of received support on perceptions of social support. Our tests have also convincingly showed that received support exerted its long-term beneficial effect on mental health through perceptions of support. This suggests, as predicted, that a preservation of perceived support via mobilization of received support strongly benefits the victims' psychological health. Thus, it is quite reasonable to assume that across a variety of other stressful events, received support exerts its helpful effects on well-being indirectly through perceived support.

Our findings were consistent with those of Drabek & Key's (1984) analysis of social functioning 3 years after the Topeka tornado. Controlling for the degree of damage, tornado victims who received help from friends or relatives, as compared to those who did not, reported being less alienated, healthier, happier in their marriages, and more involved in activities with friends, churches or social organizations. Bolin (1982) and Bolin & Bolton (1986) have also observed that primary group aid facilitated emotional recovery from various disasters. Altogether, the available evidence indicates that received support matters in the aftermath of disaster and is what it is usually intended to be—supportive!

Altruistic Community Revisited

Do these findings show, as some researchers have claimed, that disasters engender an all-inclusive therapeutic community that protects individuals from experiencing adverse psychological consequences? Let's review the arguments for and against this popular view. As we understand the literature, the distress mitigating function of the altruistic community has primarily been inferred from null findings; disasters sometimes have been found to have no adverse effects or almost always have been found to have modest, or time-limited, effects on psychological health. Thus it is not at all unusual for the post-disaster phase of altruism to serve as *the explanation* for why disasters caused little or no long-term negative consequences. Undoubtedly, in most cases, there will be a progressive return to equilibrium. The sense of diminished support and embeddedness will eventually dissipate and pre-event levels are likely to surface again (Kaniasty, Norris & Murrell, 1990). Quarantelli (1985) evoked an analogy of a "social sponge" to portray the victimized community's ability to withstand the enormous trauma and destruction and still be able to return to its usual state. Furthermore, he has argued that disasters may actually generate positive psychological effects, and there are studies that showed some traces of increased cohesion in some, but not all, personal relationships in disaster-stricken communities (e.g., Bolin, 1982; Drabek & Key, 1984; Fritz, 1961; Harvey et al., 1995; Taylor, 1977). Providing additional credence to this line of thinking are the often-heard testimonials of victims about how the disaster brought the community together and made it stronger than ever before.

On the other hand, there are reasons to retain a healthy skepticism about the validity of such overarching constructs when attempting to explain complex social phenomena. Altruistic or therapeutic communities do emerge in the aftermath of many collective catastrophes with their distinguishing characteristics of solidarity, togetherness and reciprocity. But their patterns of exceptions and limitations should not be ignored. Many victims are excluded from, or overlooked by, helping communities and recovery programs, whereas others have a clear advantage in securing post-disaster relief. Moreover, fellowship and consensus are infrequent features of the social milieu following technological hazards and disasters. Even in the best of circumstances, the intensified levels of mutual support and concern must inescapably end. And finally, as much as victims' testimonials conform to our optimistic and romantic ideals, it is very difficult to determine whether these claims are a reflection of actual gains or a reflection of coping mechanisms at work. Victims' ability to find the silver lining in, and grow from, traumatic experience is an important facet of the process of recovering from stressful events and requires more investigation (see Jerusalem et al., 1995; Lehman et al., 1993).

Possibly, the major problem with the therapeutic community concept as traditionally formulated is that it is not falsifiable. The very ability to test this hypothesis could be taken as evidence against it. If the altruistic community was truly all-encompassing, there would not be sufficient variability in received support to show its beneficial effect. All in all, the concept of altruistic community may be directly testable only in studies involving multiple communities, where support can be defined at the macro level. Such a test is possible, but it would be so difficult methodologically that no one has attempted it yet. These criticisms aside, at the core of the altruistic community formulation is a theoretically and practically significant question—Does receiving support matter? Our answer is "Yes".

CONCLUSIONS

Figure 26.2. depicts a schematic summary of our discussion of different processes linking the stress of disasters, social support and consequent psychological health (Kaniasty & Norris, 1995b). First of all, disasters exert a powerful direct effect on psychological distress (*direct impact*). Exposure to death, trauma, injury and destruction of material and symbolic possessions significantly harm psychological functioning of victims and, at times, may leave long-lasting scars. As in any other context of stress experience, pre-existing sociopsychological conditions and resources of the individuals will affect the extent of exposure to the stressor (*differential exposure*) and the extent of psychological distress (*differential vulnerability*). At their onset, many disasters mobilize social support networks (*support mobilization*) into a heroic and altruistic struggle to fulfill the immediate

Figure 26.2 A summary model: processes linking the stress of disasters, characteristics of the individuals and their communities, social supports and psychological health

needs and shield victims from the overwhelming sense of loss. However, the mobilization of support is a most *in*egalitarian process. Altruistic communities are governed by patterns of concern and neglect wherein the mobilization of support is influenced by victims' relative advantage or disadvantage (*rules of inclusion/exclusion*). At times, therapeutic communities may not evolve at all. Even if present, altruistic communities are ephemeral and the stress of disasters continues to persist well beyond the therapeutic phase of initial support mobilization. Consequently, victims of disasters often face the sad reality of a declining sense of social support (*support deterioration*) which happens, paradoxically, at the time when they need the protection of their personal relationships the most. Disasters severely curtail workings and capacity of indigenous support networks, making support exchanges difficult, strenuous or even impossible. The erosion of perceived social support and sense of belonging may inevitably contribute to poorer physical and mental health. Fortunately for many victims, the initial mobilization of received support may counteract this deterioration and preserve perceptions that their supportive nets are still in place (*protective assistance*). These beliefs of being reliably connected to others will hopefully guard them from experiencing more intense distress (*protective appraisal*).

While the processes we described may not fully generalize to other stressful events, especially those confined to lone individuals or small groups (e.g., bereavement, divorce, transportation disasters), we believe that these dynamics apply to many collective events (e.g., unemployment, epidemics, crime waves). By definition, community stressors impact great numbers of people simultaneously, many of whom are members of each other's support networks, and are mutually dependent on each other's coping efforts. Everybody is affected, thus distinctions between victims and supporters become inconsequential. These defining features of collective stress dramatically influence the availability and distribution of coping resources. We need to beware of being lulled into complacency by stories that inevitably appear in popular and professional literature or media about communities coming together to rebuild in the aftermath of a tragic event. Spontaneous mobilization of social support is a great asset but the emergent helping community is unlikely to fulfill all the needs and it may inadvertently leave many citizens without adequate assistance. The heartening examples of genuine solidarity and altruism that the public can marshal in times of communal catastrophes should not obscure the fact that the lasting deterioration of quality of personal relationships and other social ties is equally real. However, the challenge for researchers of social support and personal relationships is not only to describe and understand these complexities. A detailed analysis of dynamic transactions among individuals, their social networks, community resources and environmental pressures is necessary for the development of intervention programs that will prove useful to people who experience specific circumstances in particular contexts (see Milgram et al., 1995; Norris & Thompson, 1995). The ultimate task is to foster a mobilization of community support in times of stress that will be all-inclusive and powerful enough to conquer the spiral of losses. The only way to achieve such a goal is to capitalize on the proactive nature of social support and people's continuous need to seek and maintain supportive relationships, regardless of whether they are currently facing stress. Thus the process of helping people to help each other in times of crisis must begin long before the crisis strikes.

ACKNOWLEDGEMENTS

Preparation of this chapter was supported by Grant No. RO1MH51278 from the National Institute of Mental Health, Fran H. Norris, principal investigator. Research conducted by the authors was supported by NIMH Grants Nos. RO1MH40411, RO1MH45069 and RO1MH51115.

Chapter 27

Family Relationships and Major Mental Disorder: Risk Factors and Preventive Strategies

Jill M. Hooley

and

Jordan B. Hiller

Harvard University, Cambridge, MA, USA

No one, regardless of culture, income or privilege, is entirely immune from mental disorder. Schizophrenia, the most serious and complex form of psychopathology, has little respect for geographical, financial or social boundaries. With a prevalence of just under 1%, it currently affects the lives of more than two million Americans (American Psychiatric Association, 1994). Moreover, with lifetime prevalence estimates in North America averaging around 5% for major depression and 1% for bipolar disorder (see Smith & Weissman, 1992), countless more patients suffer from mood disorders. When the impact of these disorders on close family members is also considered, it is clear that many lives are fractured, either directly or indirectly, as a result of mental illness.

Understanding the etiology of major mental disorder has long been at the forefront of the clinical research agenda. Encouragingly, as investigators have risen to meet this challenge important ground has been gained. For example, much has been learned about the role of genetic factors in the development of schizophrenia (Kendler & Diehl, 1993). It is also becoming increasingly apparent that schizophrenia is a disorder characterized by abnormalities in a number of different brain areas, and that in all probability at least some of these deficits or abnormalities are present from birth (*inter alia*, Benes et al., 1991; Berquier & Ashton, 1991; Roberts, 1991; Weinberger, 1987). Although somewhat less is

Handbook of Personal Relationships, 2nd edn. Edited by Steve Duck.

understood about the etiology (or etiologies) of depression, genetic factors are again implicated, although more so for bipolar disorder than for unipolar depression (Bertelsen, Harvald & Hauge, 1977). It is also clear that at least some forms of depressive disorder involve abnormalities of one or more neuro-transmitter systems (e.g., Delgado et al., 1992). Whether these problems are primary or reflect as yet unexplored disturbances elsewhere, however, is unclear. Much has been learned, but many of the most important questions still remain unanswered.

The focus of this chapter is on the role of relationships in the prevention of major mental disorders. In the light of the current strong interest in the biological bases of mental illness, this might at first seem paradoxical. However, the notion that psychosocial factors play a role in schizophrenia is no longer an issue in much dispute, even within biological psychiatry. Realizing that much variance still remains to be explained, many of the most sophisticated biologically- and psychosocially-oriented researchers are looking toward each other with an eye to future collaborative endeavors. Indeed, as Reiss, Plomin and Hetherington (1991) have pointed out, ". . . a balanced image of the future contains a growing and equal partnership of the social sciences and molecular biology" (p. 290).

In the pages that follow we examine the characteristics of families and family relationships that have been empirically linked to the development and recur-rence of major forms of mental illness such as schizophrenia, bipolar disorder (manic depression) and major depressive disorder. While remaining cognizant of the biological underpinnings of these disorders, we will describe the psychosocial risk factors that have been identified thus far and review the evidence pertaining to these risk factors. Wherever possible, we consider the role of psychosocial risk factors in both the onset and the course of the disorder. However, because there is relatively little evidence with respect to the role of psychosocial factors in the onset of mental disorders, most of our discussion will center around their role in the return of symptoms and their importance with regard to the prevention or delay of psychiatric relapse. In keeping with our focus on prevention we will discuss results of treatment trials that have been designed to modify some of the family characteristics associated with high risk for relapse and look at the extent to which such endeavors have been successful. Finally, we will highlight some issues that remain unresolved and offer some suggestions for topics that warrant placement on the research agenda of the next decade. We begin, however, with a description of the theoretical model that guides much of the work we discuss, and which provides the conceptual framework for the integration of biological and environmental factors in psychopathology.

THE DIATHESIS-STRESS MODEL OF PSYCHOPATHOLOGY

The diathesis-stress (Meehl, 1962; Rosenthal, 1970) or stress-vulnerability model (Zubin & Spring, 1977) incorporates both biological and environmental factors into an integrated explanatory framework. Initially developed as a heuristic for understanding schizophrenia, this model has now become widely accepted as a theoretically appealing explanation for many different forms of psychopathology. Central to the model is the notion of an intrinsic vulnerability that mediates risk for the later development of a particular disorder. This vulnerability or trait-like deviation is most typically thought of as being inherited. It may, however, also be acquired by other means such as injury, illness, insult or possibly even a psychosocial event. By virtue of their placement on the vulnerability continuum, individuals are hypothesized to be at greater or lesser risk of developing psychopathology when exposed to environmental stressors. Thus, as indicated in Figure 27.1, very little stress may be needed to move a highly vulnerable individual from the "well" to the "ill" side of the line. In contrast, when intrinsic vulnerability is low, more extreme stress will be required.

Of course, this simple formulation, although appealing, is not without problems. Not the least of these is the ambiguity of the key terms. Vulnerability may take many forms and is not easily measured or quantified. How to operationalize a term such as stress also defies an easy answer. It is also the case that the vulnerability model, as Richters (1987) has pointed out, assigns a dual role to stress. Some environmental stressors might be implicated in the formation of a vulnerability, while others might serve as triggers and precipitate the actual onset of an episode of illness.

Clearly, the value of the vulnerability-stress model lies not in the precision of its elements but in its ability to provide a coherent conceptual framework to guide research. Although simple at first glance, the model has an intrinsic complexity and flexibility. It is for these reasons that it has been so remarkably successful, serving as a model of both onset and relapse.

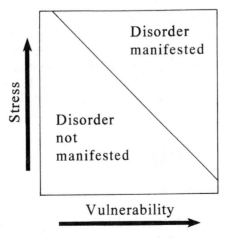

Figure 27.1 The diathesis–stress model of psychopathology

FAMILIES AS A SOURCE OF ENVIRONMENTAL STRESS

The study of the family interaction patterns associated with schizophrenia has a long and rather unfortunate history. Psychoanalytic thinkers and family systems theorists in the 1950s and 1960s observed discordant family relationships and disordered communication between schizophrenic patients and their parents, and they came to view pathological intrafamilial transactions as causal agents in the development of severe psychosis. Their ideas, which were neither suggested nor supported by solid empirical findings, were embraced by a generation of clinicians. One tragic consequence of this was that parents not only had to cope with the sadness and hardships associated with having a schizophrenic offspring, but many were also blamed by mental health professionals for the psychiatric problems that had occurred.

During the 1960s and 1970s, earlier assumptions about the etiological role of the family were severely challenged by growing evidence of the importance of genetic factors and by the success of psychotropic medications. Further problems for the familial causation model were posed by the general failure to demonstrate reliable group differences for almost all of the major theoretical concepts, and also by the poor effectiveness of the family-based treatments stemming from the models (Massie & Beels, 1972). In combination, these developments prompted clinicians and researchers to reconsider the nature and the role of family variables. Today, concepts such as marital schism and marital skew, and notions of the schizophrenogenic mother, no longer command serious empirical or clinical attention, and few mental health professionals now believe that families cause schizophrenia. The notion that pathological family interactions play a primary and causal role in schizophrenia has given way to more sophisticated multivariate models of influence. Moreover, with the advent of the diathesis-stress model it is also realized that levels of intrafamilial stress need not be unusual or extreme to take a toll on an individual with high intrinsic vulnerability. With that in mind we will now consider three family-based constructs that have been empirically linked to severe psychopathology in general, and to schizophrenia in particular. These constructs are *communication deviance* (CD), *expressed emotion* (EE), and *affective style* (AS). In the sections that follow we examine their predictive and concurrent validity. For the convenience of the reader, a summary of the constructs and the major findings associated with them is also provided (see Table 27.1).

FAMILY RISK FACTORS

Communication Deviance

Communication deviance, a measure that is concerned with the structure, clarity, and logical coherence of speech, is the only remaining survivor of the original family research tradition in schizophrenia. Noting the suggestions in the early

Table 27.1 Family risk indicators: a summary

Construct	Communication deviance (CD)	Expressed emotion (EE)	Affective style (AS)
First appearance	1963	1962	1981
What does it measure?	Fragmented, amorphous, or unclear communication	Emotional attitudes toward patients	Emotional verbal behavior toward patients
How is it measured?	Usually from a projective test administered individually to parents	From a semi-structured interview conducted with family members individually	From a direct interaction procedure between the patient and his/her parents
Major components	1. Misperceptions 2. "Failure to integrate" closure problems	1. Criticism 2. Emotional over-involvement 3. Hostility	1. Criticism 2. Guilt induction 3. Intrusiveness
Does it distinguish between parents of schizophrenic and parents of non-schizophrenic persons?	Yes	Unknown	Unknown
Does it predict relapse in: Schizophrenia Bipolar disorder Major depression	Unknown Unknown Unknown	Yes Yes Yes	Yes* Yes Unknown
Does it predict the onset of schizophrenia spectrum disorders?	Yes	Yes**	Yes

* Evidence is limited to one study with a highly selected sample. Results may not generalize to other samples.
** EE was predictive of onset individually, but it did not remain significant when the effects of CD and AS were controlled.

clinical literature that communication in the families of schizophrenic patients tended to be disordered (Lidz et al., 1958; Rosenbaum, 1961; Schaffer et al., 1962), Wynne & Singer attempted to quantify the degree of disorganization present in the communication of parents of schizophrenic patients (Singer & Wynne, 1965a,b; Wynne & Singer 1963a,b). A central hypothesis of this line of research was articulated by Wynne et al. in 1958:

> The fragmentation of experience, the identity diffusion, the disturbed modes of perception and communication, and certain other characteristics of the acute reactive schizophrenic's personality structure are to a significant extent derived, by processes of internalization, from characteristics of the family social organization ... Also internalized are the ways of thinking and of deriving meaning, the points of anxiety, and the irrationality, confusion, and ambiguity that were expressed in the shared mechanisms of the family social organization (p. 215).

Communication deviance has been measured in a number of different ways. In Singer & Wynne's initial work (1963a,b), CD was derived from Rorschach protocols obtained from relatives of schizophrenic patients. Nine categories or patterns of Rorschach responses were identified. All were thought to tap various "styles of handling attention and meaning", and were thought to distinguish the families of schizophrenic patients from the families of non-psychotic psychiatric controls. Singer & Wynne's scoring system was refined in a later replication (Wynne et al., 1977) and the number of overall categories of deviant speech reduced to three (although with a total of 41 subcategories). The principal forms of communication deviance included (1) closure problems, (2) disruptive communication behavior, and (3) peculiar language or logic.

Another scoring system for communication deviance was developed by Jones (1977), this time utilizing responses to the ambiguous picture stimuli of the Thematic Apperception Test (TAT) rather than Rorschach protocols. Applying 29 scoring codes to TAT protocols obtained from parents of schizophrenic, normal, borderline and neurotic offspring, Jones used factor analysis to derive six summary scores. The resulting summary scores included: (1) contorted/peculiar language, whereby the listener has difficulty following the stilted and long-winded speech of the storyteller; (2) misperceptions, where the speech reflects distortions of external reality; (3) "flighty" anxiousness, where the subject jumps from one idea to another, forgets task instructions, and interrupts his or her own sentences prematurely; (4) over-personalized closure problems, where the identification with the figures in the TAT card is so high that the listener has difficulty identifying the boundary between the story and the story teller; (5) faulty over-intellectualization, where the efforts of the storyteller are strained and over-intellectualized; and (6) "failure to integrate" closure problems, where the story omits major elements or figures in the TAT card and the listener has to struggle to reconcile the gap between an obviously complex card and an incomplete and abbreviated story (Jones, 1977). Jones's research indicated that scores on this latter factor and the misperceptions factor were higher in the parents of schizophrenic patients than they were in the parents of non-schizophrenic adolescents. Subsequent investigators have since used these two factors to classify TAT profiles as either high, intermediate or low in communication deviance (Miklowitz & Stackman, 1992).

When viewed through the lens of more current conceptualizations of communication (e.g., Duck, 1994a) it is clear that the construct of communication deviance fails to capture much of the complexity and sophistication of modern day communication theory. As Duck points out:

> Talking is not merely the conveyance of carefully wrapped packets of information ... Talk also serves many other purposes simultaneously, some strategic, (e.g., the denial of other counter positions; self-presentation; impression management, and so on), some individual (e.g., enacting, expressing, or making real an individual's particular goals in interaction; acknowledging others' beliefs and values), and some relational (e.g., allowing discussion about similarities; purveying disagreement; indicating affection; making relational propositions). (Duck, 1994a, pp. 13–14)

In other words, talk is more than speech, and communication is more than just talk. At the very least, communication both concerns and reflects such elements as the comprehension of symbols, family idiom, cultural values, coordination of speech acts, the pragmatics of communication and such stylistic issues as dysfluency, dominance and control among others. When viewed in this light, how a family member of a psychiatric patient talks about an ambiguous stimulus such as an ink blot or a TAT card is obviously but one thin slice of a very rich conceptual pie. Toward the end of this chapter we return to this issue and stress the advantages that will likely come from a more sophisticated approach to the nature of communication. Nonetheless, although it was based on notions of communication that characterized the 1950s, the construct of communication deviance has yielded some interesting empirical findings and it is to a discussion of these that we now turn.

Validation Studies

The most consistent finding in the CD literature is that parents of patients with schizophrenia can be reliably distinguished from parents of non-schizophrenic persons on the basis of their CD scores. Interestingly, this finding endures even when different measurement techniques are employed (*inter alia*, Hirsch & Leff, 1971; Jones, 1977; Singer & Wynne, 1965a, 1965b; Wynne et al., 1977; for a more detailed review, see also Miklowitz & Stackman, 1992). In these studies, parents of patients with schizophrenia showed the highest levels of CD, while the lowest CD scores were found in parents of normal offspring. Parents of children with other disorders, such as autism and "borderline schizophrenia" (which today might be most properly classified as paranoid or schizotypal personality disorder) typically fell between these two extremes.

It is important to note that although the parents of schizophrenic patients exhibit higher levels of communication deviance than do the parents of non-schizophrenic offspring, high levels of communication deviance are not limited to families containing a schizophrenic patient. Miklowitz et al. (1991) have studied both recent-onset schizophrenic patients and bipolar manic patients and their families. Interestingly, no differences were found between the levels of CD in the two groups of parents. These results suggest that high CD may be associated with thought disorder in general, rather than with schizophrenia in particular.

Expressed Emotion

Although it originated on the opposite side of the Atlantic, expressed emotion, the second psychosocial risk construct, also has a nearly 40-year history. In 1958 George Brown and his colleagues in London made the interesting empirical observation that schizophrenic patients who returned home from an inpatient hospitalization to live with either wives or parents had a higher rate of relapse than those patients who were discharged to live in lodgings, or with their siblings (Brown, Carstairs & Topping, 1958). Speculating that the emotional environment of the home might play a role in the outcome of schizophrenia, Brown and colleagues began a series of studies designed to elicit and measure the forms of emotional expression that might be involved (Brown, Birley & Wing, 1972; Brown et al., 1962; Brown & Rutter, 1966; Rutter & Brown, 1966).

Brown suspected that what might be important with regard to the outcome of schizophrenic patients was not the presence of markedly disturbed or pathological patient–family relationships (although those could certainly be found), but something much more ordinary and ubiquitous. Now, viewed through the frame of the diathesis-stress model this assumption makes perfect sense. At the time, however, Brown's hunch that researchers should focus on "the range of feelings and emotions to be found in ordinary families" (Brown, 1985, p. 22) represented a significant departure from earlier thinking about the nature of relationships within families containing a schizophrenic patient.

Expressed emotion is best thought of as a measure of family atmosphere. It is assessed using a semi-structured interview administered to relatives individually, typically during a hospitalization of the schizophrenic family member. The interview schedule used for this purpose is the Camberwell Family Interview (CFI; Brown & Rutter, 1966; Rutter & Brown, 1966; Vaughn & Leff, 1976b). This interview requires the relative to talk at some length about the patient's psychiatric history about the events preceding the patient's current hospitalization, and also about the patient's symptoms and day-to-day activities. The interview typically lasts between 1 and 2 hours.

EE scoring is performed by trained raters who listen to audiotapes of the interviews. The interviews are coded on three principal dimensions, each indexing a different aspect of the relatives' speech. Most important is the measure of criticism. This is a simple count of the number of critical comments made by the relative about the patient during the course of the interview. Criticism can be rated on the basis of the content of the remark (e.g., "I resent the fact that she doesn't lift a finger around the house") or on the basis of changes in voice tone (i.e., changes in the speed, pitch or inflection) that occur when the relative talks about the patient. Regardless of whether it is expressed directly in the content of the remark, or is inferred from changes in voice tone, criticism reflects clear-cut dislike or resentment about some aspect of a patient's behavior. If the relative of a schizophrenic patient makes six or more critical comments during the course of the CFI, he or she is classified as being high in expressed emotion.

The second component of the EE index is hostility. This is rated on a 0–3 scale and is a more extreme expression of negative feeling toward the patient. Whereas critical remarks concern something the patient does, hostile comments typically criticize the patient as a person (e.g., "She is a supreme con-artist") or convey rejection of the patient by the family member (e.g., "Sometimes I leave the house just to get away from him"). Any expression of hostility on the part of the relative results in a classification of high EE.

The third element of the EE index, termed emotional over-involvement (EOI), is conceptually a little different from both criticism and hostility. Emotional over-involvement reflects an over-protective or extremely dramatic attitude toward the patient's illness on the part of the relative. In other cases, EOI is indicated by extreme self-sacrifice or overly devoted behavior. Rated on a 0–5 scale, a rating of 3 (or, in some studies 4) is sufficient to warrant a relative being classified as high EE, even in the absence of any criticism or hostility. If none of the aforementioned conditions hold (i.e., the relative makes fewer than six critical remarks and shows neither hostility nor marked EOI), the family member is designated low EE. It should be noted that most studies have found that criticism makes the strongest contribution to EE classification. Moreover, it is rare for a relative to be classified as high EE on the basis of hostility without also meeting criteria for criticism.

The Predictive Validity of Expressed Emotion

Schizophrenia

The basic finding in EE research is as striking as it is robust: patients with schizophrenia who return from the hospital to live in a household with at least one high EE relative are at elevated risk for relapse in the following 9–12 months compared with patients discharged to live with low EE family members. The association between EE and relapse in schizophrenia has been replicated many times and in places as far afield as the UK, Australia, India and the USA (see Vaughn & Leff, 1976a; Vaughan et al., 1992a; Vaughn et al., 1984; Leff et al., 1987, respectively). A meta-analysis of the EE-relapse link for schizophrenia confirms the predictive power of EE. Combining the results of 23 studies, Butzlaff & Hooley (1995) found an unweighted mean effect-size r between 0.29 and 0.32 for the relationship of EE and relapse, which was highly statistically significant. The available literature thus clearly suggests that there is a reliable association between high family levels of expressed emotion and elevated risk of relapse in patients diagnosed with schizophrenic illness.

Other Disorders

In addition to being a valid predictor of outcome in patients with schizophrenia, expressed emotion has also been fruitfully examined in relation to a variety of other disorders. Associations between high EE family environments and relapse have been demonstrated in adults with major depression (Hooley, Orley & Teasdale, 1986; Vaughn & Leff, 1976a) and in bipolar patients experiencing a manic episode (Miklowitz et al., 1987, 1988). Interestingly, parental EE also predicts 1-year outcome in depressed children. Asarnow et al. (1993) found that a brief measure of EE (five-minute speech sample, or FMSS; Magaña et al., 1986) was significantly associated with the amount of depressive symptomatology shown by children 1 year after their hospital discharge.

There is also evidence linking high family levels of EE to poor outcomes in physical as well as mental disorders. Koenigsberg et al. (1993), for example, have shown that EE predicts poorer glycemic control in diabetic patients. Expressed emotion is also associated with poorer diet compliance in obese persons (Fischmann-Havstad & Marston, 1984; Flanagan & Wagner, 1991), and predicts dropping out of treatment in anorexic patients (Szmukler et al., 1985). Interestingly, the results of Butzlaff & Hooley's (1995) meta-analysis of the EE literature suggests that the effect-size of EE for non-schizophrenia-related conditions is even greater than it is for schizophrenia. EE is thus a construct of interest to researchers studying a wide range of psychopathological and non-psychopathological outcomes.

Affective Style

Affective style, the third and final family risk indicator, was developed at UCLA by Jeri Doane. It is a measure concerning the actual verbal behavior of the relative during an emotionally charged discussion with the patient (Doane et al., 1981). Thus, while expressed emotion can be viewed as a measure of the attitude of a relative toward an identified psychiatric patient, assessed in the *absence* of the patient in question, the measurement of affective style involves the patient and his or her family discussing a topic that has been a source of friction in the past. The discussion is recorded, and AS coding is then performed on verbatim transcripts.

The unit of analysis for AS coding consists of up to six consecutive lines of uninterrupted speech by a single speaker (Doane et al., 1981). Affective style codes are then assigned based on the content of the speech. Affective style codes include (1) support, (2) criticism, (3) guilt induction, and (4) intrusiveness. These are fully described in Table 27.2. Frequency counts of each type of code are

Table 27.2 Affective style codes: definitions and examples

Category	Definition	Example
Support	The parent conveys directly to the child that he feels genuine concern for the child himself or about the child's problems or behavior	I want you to know I care about you
Criticism		
Personal criticism	The criticism has one or more of the following qualities: unnecessary or overly harsh modifiers, references to broad classes of behavior, or reference to the child's character or nature	You have an ugly, arrogant attitude
Benign criticism	The criticism is circumscribed, matter-of-fact and directed toward specific incidents or sets of behaviors	You have a bad attitude about homework, John
Guilt induction	Statements that convey that the child is to blame or at fault for some negative event and that the parent has been distressed or upset about the event	You cause our family an awful lot of trouble
Intrusiveness	Intrusive statements imply knowledge of the child's thoughts, feeling states, or motives when in fact there is no apparent basis for such knowledge	
Critical intrusiveness	The intrusiveness contains a harsh, critical component	You enjoy being mean to others
Neutral intrusiveness	The intrusiveness has a neutral quality and refers to the child's emotional states, ideas or preferences	You say you're angry (at us), but I think you're really mad at yourself

Definitions and examples are taken from Doane et al., 1981.

made. In addition, families are also usually classified as either benign or negative in AS, based on the presence or absence of intrusive, critical and guilt-inducing statements.

Validity of AS

There are few relapse studies measuring AS. This is because AS has proved to be rather difficult to rate reliably. As a consequence, AS tends only to be used by the research group that developed it. However, the work of this group provides some evidence that AS predicts relapse in adult patients with schizophrenia (Doane et al., 1985, 1986). Unfortunately, the generalizability of these results is doubtful, because the families in this sample were selected on the basis of their high EE attitudes or by virtue of the presence of severe family stress or burden. Interestingly, however, AS has been found to predict relapse in recent-onset manic patients (Miklowitz et al., 1988). Like communication deviance and expressed emotion, AS thus appears to be a family risk indicator that is of interest with regard to more than one psychopathological condition.

ARE CD, EE AND AS MEASURES OF THE SAME UNDERLYING CONSTRUCT?

Our three familial risk factors were developed by different researchers, at different times, and in different geographical locations, yet they are similar in many respects. Their inherent similarity begs an important question: Are CD, EE and AS measures of a unitary latent construct, or do they instead tap unique aspects of family functioning that are of importance in the study of psychopathology? We address this question by exploring the concurrent validity of these three family constructs and examining the extent to which they are intercorrelated.

Expressed Emotion and Affective Style

Because EE measures emotional attitudes and AS measures emotionally salient verbal behavior, it is perhaps not surprising that, in general, sizeable and significant correlations between these two constructs have been obtained. High EE relatives have been shown to make more negative AS statements during direct interactions with their patient relatives in several different samples. These include a sample of behaviorally disturbed but non-psychotic adolescents (Valone et al., 1983), a relatively chronic sample of schizophrenic patients (Miklowitz et al., 1984), and a sample of recent-onset schizophrenic patients recruited in the UK (Strachan et al., 1986).

In families containing a manic patient, however, EE and AS appear to be uncorrelated. Moreover, Miklowitz and his colleagues (1987, 1988) found that both AS and EE were strong individual predictors of 9-month relapse rates, and that the prediction of relapse was even more accurate when EE and AS were considered jointly. Interestingly, however, the presence of both family risk factors was not associated with a greater risk of patient relapse than was the presence of either one alone. It was also the case that EE and AS predicted different courses of illness in these bipolar patients. Specifically, patients with high EE families tended to experience a remission of symptoms prior to a symptom exacerbation or relapse. Patients in negative AS environments, on the other hand, tended to have persisting symptoms throughout the follow-up period (Miklowitz et al., 1987). Although the sample size was small, and these findings await replication, it is possible that for bipolar patients EE and AS measure different aspects of the family environment and that these are associated with different courses of illness.

Communication Deviance and Expressed Emotion

To date, only two studies have directly addressed the relationship between EE and CD. Miklowitz et al. (1986) compared the CD and EE scores of three separate groups of relatives of schizophrenic patients recruited from Pittsburgh, Southern California, and London, UK. Higher levels of CD were found in families that were rated as high rather than low in EE. Subsequent analyses revealed that this effect was largely due to emotional over-involvement. Among high EE relatives, those who were considered emotionally over-involved had higher CD levels than those who were rated as high EE on the basis of criticism. Unfortunately, because outcome data were not available for these samples, the investigators were not able to assess the extent to which EE and CD predicted relapse, either separately or together.

Docherty (1995), studying parents of schizophrenia outpatients, measured EE with the CFI and CD with a new method using samples of conversational speech (Docherty, 1993). No significant differences in CD levels were detected between high EE and low EE parents. However, the fact that the CFI was not administered during an acute psychotic episode, as is customary, suggests that this negative result should be interpreted with caution, as does the small sample size of this study ($n = 19$).

Affective Style and Communication Deviance

Finally, we consider the relationship between AS and CD. These two constructs have been assessed together in only one sample, the UCLA high-risk sample of behaviorally disturbed non-psychotic adolescents (which will be described in greater detail below). In this study AS and CD were unrelated (Doane et al., 1981). Although both measures individually predicted the later development of schizophrenia spectrum disorders, prediction was greatly improved using both constructs together. This was true at both the 5-year (Doane et al., 1981) and the 15-year follow-up (Goldstein, 1987). Clearly, future data concerning the association between affective style and communication deviance in already diagnosed schizophrenic patients and in patients with mood disorders would greatly increase our understanding of the relation between these constructs.

Summary

In general, studies have demonstrated that EE and AS are perhaps more closely related to each other than they are to CD. This makes intuitive sense given that EE and AS are both considered to be measures of the family emotional environment, while CD is essentially a measure of a family member's ability to share a focus of attention and meaning with another person. Moreover, the demonstration that CD, EE and AS predict onset and/or relapse more accurately in combination than alone suggests that, although they are related, they are far from equivalent, with each measure contributing unique variance to the prediction of outcome. Insofar as all three variables are fundamentally limited measures of how people talk, however, we must acknowledge that they only convey a very small amount of information about relationships between patients and relatives. As we move toward the future, elements of relationships that are not captured by CD, EE or AS should become an increased focus of concern and investigation.

A FEW WORDS ABOUT CAUSALITY

In their initial enthusiasm about the empirical findings linking CD, EE and AS with various aspects of psychopathology, researchers generally assumed that these three constructs indexed environmental influences on the development and course of mental illness. Fitting neatly within the diathesis-stress framework, CD, EE and AS were seen as stressors in the family environment that increased the risk for onset or exacerbation of illness in vulnerable individuals. Although this model has a certain appeal, it is clear in hindsight that the findings do not support this causal hypothesis exclusively. The studies in this area are of course correlational rather than experimental. Short of the random assignment of newborns into homes that differ in terms of CD, EE and AS, there is no reliable method of conclusively demonstrating a causal connection between the risk factors we describe and the development of schizophrenia and mood disorders. Other models and mechanisms must therefore be entertained.

A full discussion of the models that have been proposed is beyond the scope of the current discussion, and this topic has been examined at length elsewhere (Hooley & Richters, 1995; Hooley, Rosen, & Richters, 1995; Miklowitz & Stackman, 1992; Nuechterlein, Snyder & Mintz, 1992). However, we wish to emphasize that there are plausible alternatives to the family-as-causal hypothesis that deserve consideration. In the case of EE and AS, it has been suggested that patients who are more severely ill, and therefore more likely to experience relapse, are inherently more difficult to deal with, and hence are more likely to elicit critical attitudes and behaviors from key relatives. In a slightly different vein, parental CD may reflect a genetically mediated vulnerability to develop thought disorder that is shared both by parents and their offspring, but which is expressed more severely in the latter. Increasingly, conscientious researchers will be obliged to use more precise and powerful designs in their efforts to untangle the causes and effects of family environment and psychopathology.

The question of causality is obviously of great importance to those who hope to apply our knowledge concerning family factors to the problem of primary and secondary prevention of psychopathology. But such intervention efforts cannot wait for the development of full and detailed statements about causal mechanisms. The preventive strategies and efforts that we describe below have indeed assumed that CD, EE and AS are psychosocial stressors that contribute to the development or persistence of psychopathology in vulnerable individuals. Although questions about the validity of this assumption remain, we nonetheless believe that efforts to develop psychosocially-based interventions are justified. In clinical psychology the need to provide help to patients and their families outweighs the need to know exactly how treatment works, at least initially. Concern for the mentally ill and for their families dictates that we must act even if we are not assured of success.

HIGH RISK STUDIES AND PROSPECTS FOR FAMILY-BASED PRIMARY PREVENTION

The diathesis-stress model leads quite naturally to a simple prescription for the primary prevention (i.e., prevention of onset) of psychopathology. First, we must identify individuals who are at high risk for the development of psychopathology due to the presence of a genetically mediated vulnerability and/or to unusually high amounts of psychosocial stress. In theory at least, it may then be possible to target these individuals for interventions that reduce the amount of stress to which they are exposed, thereby reducing their risk for relapse. Unfortunately, this is rather easier said than done. The problem, of course, lies in the identification of "high-risk" individuals. Current methods of detection have inadequate specificity—that is, they identify far too many false positives. As a result, we cast too wide a net when deciding who should receive preventive interventions. This problem sorely limits the practical feasibility of such a primary prevention program, and is the main reason why one has not yet been attempted.

Another vital issue regarding primary prevention is whether CD, EE, and AS actually predict the *onset* of psychopathological conditions in vulnerable individuals. Our assumption that family stressors contribute to the onset of illness requires that they should be present in the family prior to the development of the illness. One limitation of the studies described thus far is that family variables were assessed *after* patients had become ill. In order to learn more about the relation between family factors and the onset of psychopathology, an attempt must be made to determine if high levels of communication deviance, high expressed emotion, and negative affective style characterize the families of schizophrenic patients *before* the onset of illness and predict the *later* development of psychopathology.

Unfortunately, our discussion of this issue must be brief. This is because, to date, only the UCLA Family High Risk Project has measured familial risk factors such as communication deviance, expressed emotion and affective style *and* has also employed a prospective longitudinal design (see Goldstein, 1987). Goldstein and his colleagues recruited 64 families who presented to a university psychological clinic for help with a problem adolescent. These adolescents were deemed to be at risk for the development of schizophrenia due to their behavioral disturbance. At the time of the initial assessment all of the adolescents were mildly to moderately disturbed but were non-psychotic. Patients and families were then followed up, initially for 5 and subsequently for 15 years, and the predictive validity of the family variables examined.

Considered individually, all three of the familial risk factors were predictive of the later development of schizophrenia or schizophrenia-related disorders in this sample. Regardless of their initial presenting problem, adolescents whose families were classified as being high in CD, high in EE, or negative in AS at the time of entry into the study were significantly more likely to develop schizophrenia or personality disorders falling within the extended schizophrenia spectrum. However, when the three constructs were considered simultaneously in a log-linear analysis, CD and AS remained significant predictors of outcome, but EE was no longer predictive after the effects of the other two had been controlled. Moreover, the strength of the relationship between CD and onset was even greater when schizophrenia spectrum disorders in the subjects' siblings were also considered and the most severe offspring diagnosis was used as the dependent variable.

An alternative design addressing the issue of the role of family factors in the onset of psychopathology has been employed by Tienari's group in the Finnish Adoptive Family Study (Tienari et al., 1987, 1989, 1994). In an effort to segregate environmental and genetic contributions to the pathogenesis of schizophrenia, these investigators tracked down the adopted-away offspring of mothers with schizophrenia and performed a battery of assessments on the offspring and their biological and adoptive parents. While this study was not prospective (in that a majority of the offspring were already well into or past the age of greatest risk for onset of schizophrenia by the time of family assessment), we discuss it here because its methodology affords a rare opportunity to explore the dynamics of genetic influence, family factors and onset of schizophrenia.

The Finnish study is still in progress and the data concerning the communication deviance scores of biological and adoptive parents are not yet available. But there are some promising preliminary results concerning adoptive family mental health ratings, made on the basis of interviews with the whole family. Specifically, adopted offspring were more likely to develop various forms of psychopathology if their adoptive families were rated as disturbed (Tienari et al., 1989, 1994). This suggests that a healthy family environment may have a protective effect against the development of schizophrenia and related disorders in genetically vulnerable individuals. However, there is an equally plausible alternative explanation. In this study, as in the Goldstein (1987) study, the possibility that the mental disturbance of the adopted offspring resulted in disordered family functioning cannot be ruled out. A prospective longitudinal study on a subset of this sample is currently being conducted, which may ultimately help to resolve this issue.

In summary, evidence from the UCLA and Finnish studies indicates that family stressors may predate the onset of schizophrenia. While this suggests that family interventions for the primary prevention of psychopathology could theoretically be possible, such interventions will remain impractical until we can identify vulnerable individuals with a high degree of specificity. In all probability the developments necessary to do this lie many years ahead, if they are part of our future at all.

EFFORTS AT FAMILY-BASED SECONDARY PREVENTION

As just discussed, the main impediment in implementing interventions for primary prevention is the identification of individuals who are at risk for the onset of psychopathology. This problem is no longer relevant when we consider secondary prevention, or the prevention of relapse. Those at risk for relapse are of course those who have had prior episodes of mental illness.

Drawing inspiration mainly from the EE literature, several investigators have developed family intervention programs designed to reduce risk for relapse in schizophrenia by modifying those aspects of the patient–relative relationship thought to be central to the expressed emotion construct (Falloon et al., 1982; Goldstein et al., 1978; Hogarty et al., 1986; Köttgen et al., 1984; Leff et al., 1982, 1989; McFarlane et al., 1995a, 1995b; Tarrier et al., 1988b; Vaughan et al., 1992b; for a review see Lam, 1991). For practical purposes, what this entails is working with patients and their families to educate them about the illness, to facilitate the development of problem-solving skills, to improve coping skills, and to enhance communication skills. In some cases (e.g., Leff et al., 1982), however, decreasing the sheer amount of time that the patient and family members spend together is also a therapeutic goal.

In order to facilitate the comparison of intervention efforts, we will restrict our discussion to those studies where: (1) patients were randomly assigned to either family intervention or to a control treatment, usually consisting of routine outpatient care; and (2) patients were followed for at least 9–12 months after discharge. These criteria eliminate three studies (Goldstein et al., 1978; McFarlane et al., 1995a, 1995b), leaving us with seven to consider at the time of writing.

As is apparent from Figure 27.2, family intervention programs have been quite successful—at least with respect to patients' outcomes. For patients whose relatives receive family-based interventions, relapse rates hover around 10%. In contrast, the 9–12-month relapse rate of patients from control families tends to be closer to 50%. Two studies, however, did not demonstrate a significant reduction in relapse as a result of family-based intervention. As failure is sometimes more informative than success, we will briefly consider these two studies before discussing the effective ones.

The failure of Köttgen et al.'s (1984) intervention trial in Hamburg may be particularly telling, given that their treatment was quite different from those used in the more successful intervention programs. Instead of treating the entire family unit, this intervention consisted of separate therapy groups for patients and relatives, with the expressed goal of providing a peer support group for patients and a forum for airing relatives' pent-up frustrations. It is also worthwhile to note that the intervention had a psychodynamic orientation, with thera-

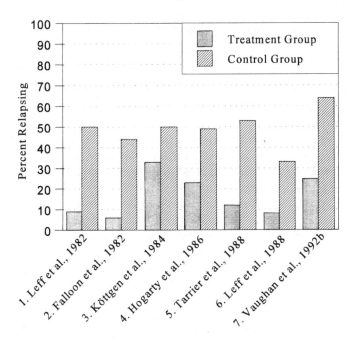

Figure 27.2 9–12 month relapse rates for family intervention studies. 1. Comparison groups consisted of routine clinical management (controls) vs. routine clinical management plus education, family therapy and a relatives' support group (experimental condition). 2. Patients in the control condition received individual treatment. The experimental group received behavioral family treatment. 3. Comparison groups consisted of routine clinical treatment (controls) vs. patients' and relatives' groups (experimental group). 4. A control group receiving routine outpatient treatment was compared with experimental groups receiving (a) family treatment, (b) social skills training for patients, or (c) family treatment and social skills training. The figure shows the result of the control vs. the family treatment only group. 5. High EE families received either routine treatment (control condition) or (a) enactive behavioral treatment, (b) symbolic behavioral treatment, or (c) education only. The comparison between the control group and the average of the two behavioral treatment groups is depicted in the figure. 6. Comparison groups consisted of education and family therapy (experimental group) vs. education and a relatives' support group (control group). 7. Control group received routine outpatient care. Treatment group received routine outpatient care plus relatives' counseling

pists adopting a group-analytic approach. Insight-oriented therapy may have been less helpful than the concrete problem-solving stance adopted by other programs. However, the methodological weaknesses of this study must temper conclusions that are drawn about the efficacy of the intervention (Vaughn, 1986). Specifically, the majority of patients in this sample did not live with their parents during the 9-month follow-up period. This may have had the effect of reducing the relapse rate in the control group, because vulnerable patients were removed from potentially stressful home environments. A possible beneficial effect of intervention in this study may therefore have been obscured. On the other hand, as shown in Figure 27.2, the relapse rate of the control group in the Köttgen et al. (1984) study is roughly comparable to that of the other intervention studies, rendering this argument less than compelling.

The other study that did not find a significant effect for intervention was the Australian study of Vaughan et al. (1992a,b). As a possible explanation of their negative result, the authors of this study pointed to the fact that, like Köttgen and colleagues (1984), they did not treat relatives and patients together. The intervention consisted of relatives' counseling only, and patients were excluded. While this may be a relevant consideration, it is also important to note that, with only 34 subjects, this investigation may have suffered from low power to reject the null hypothesis. Although the results of this study did not achieve significance at the 0.05 level, the findings are in the hypothesized direction: 7 out of 17 (41%) of the patients whose parents received counseling experienced a relapse within 9 months of discharge, while 11 out of 17 (65%) of the patients in the control group relapsed. The effect-size estimate for the observed relationship between treatment and nine-month outcome ($\phi = 0.24$) is certainly not negligible. A quick glance at Cohen's power tables (Cohen, 1988) indicates that this study had only an approximately 40% chance of rejecting a false null hypothesis at an alpha level of 0.05, given 34 subjects and assuming a medium-sized effect ($\phi \sim 0.30$). Thus, it would be inaccurate to conclude that Vaughan and associates' treatment program was ineffective. Clearly another trial of this intervention with a larger sample size is warranted.

Among the other intervention studies that were successful in reducing relapse, there is great heterogeneity, in terms of format, frequency, duration and theoretical orientation. However, these interventions do have several elements in common (see Lam, 1991). Successful intervention programs enlist families as partners in the treatment process, not regarding them as a cause of the patients' illness, but rather as the first line of defense against relapse. They all use conventional family therapy concepts, such as the importance of strengthening the marital dyad and maintaining appropriate interpersonal boundaries. Regardless of their stated theoretical orientation, all of the intervention programs use behavioral techniques to achieve their ends. Also, they share a problem-solving orientation, seeking to reduce affective valence and improve the clarity of communication between relatives and patients.

At this point, a word of caution about interpreting the results of family intervention is in order. Although there is much evidence that psychosocial family intervention can result in lower 9-month relapse rates, it does not seem that family-based treatments actually *prevent* schizophrenic relapse. Instead, available evidence suggests that relapse is merely delayed (Hogarty et al., 1986). For many of the intervention studies described above, 2-year follow-up assessments were conducted (Falloon et al., 1985; Hogarty, Anderson & Reiss, 1987; Leff et al., 1985, 1990; Tarrier et al., 1989). Two-year relapse rates were still generally lower in the groups that had received family intervention than they were in control groups. Nevertheless, relapses were uncomfortably common: usually 30–40% of patients in the experimental groups had experienced relapse by the 2-year mark. It is perhaps significant that the lowest 2-year relapse rate (17%) was obtained by Falloon and colleagues, the only research group that had notable clinical contact with families after 9 months. This suggests that sustained maintenance family treatment may prove to be more effective in reducing relapse than shorter-term interventions (see also McFarlane et al., 1995a).

The mechanism of psychosocial family intervention is presumed to be through change in the family emotional climate. By providing families with problem-solving skills, these interventions are thought to reduce the stress associated with affectively charged communication and conflict between relatives and patients, thereby reducing the risk of schizophrenic relapse. Accordingly, improvement in the emotional climate after family intervention has been demonstrated in several studies. When EE was assessed both before and after intervention, reductions were found in one or more components of EE (Leff et al., 1982, 1989; Tarrier et al., 1988b). Furthermore, no relapse had occurred by 9 months after discharge in *any* patient from these studies whose family EE status changed from high to low during the course of the intervention (see also Hogarty et al., 1986). However, the conclusion that the interventions caused the change in EE status is not necessarily warranted. Spontaneous reductions in EE have been documented (Brown, Birley & Wing, 1972; Tarrier et al., 1988b), perhaps owing to the fact that initial EE measurements made during a hospital admission tend to be higher than when the patient is in remission.

Less is known about changes in CD or AS following family intervention. The only study concerning AS has found reduction of negative AS in relatives of persons with schizophrenia after intervention (Doane et al., 1986). No investigators have examined CD in connection with family intervention, perhaps because there is no compelling evidence linking CD to the relapse process.

The success of family intervention in reducing schizophrenic relapse, and also the relatively recent demonstration that EE and AS predict relapse in manic bipolar patients (Miklowitz et al., 1988), have now inspired the development of a psychosocial family intervention for patients with bipolar disorder (Miklowitz & Goldstein, 1990). This intervention, consisting of education about bipolar disorder, communication skills training and problem-solving skills training, was closely modeled after the intervention for schizophrenic families developed by Falloon and colleagues (1982, 1985). Final results have not yet been published. However, preliminary results from nine patients appear most promising (Miklowitz & Goldstein, 1990).

WHERE DO WE GO FROM HERE?

The results of the family intervention studies are encouraging. Evidence suggests that interventions designed to reduce family levels of expressed emotion significantly reduce the patient's risk of relapse—at least in the short (9–12 months) term. This is a promising start, but much remains to be learned. In the section below we discuss some of the challenges that lie ahead and highlight some issues that will demand the attention of researchers in the coming decade.

Why Do Psychosocial Factors Predict Relapse?

Future developments in psychosocial treatments of schizophrenia and other major mental disorders will rely heavily on two issues. The first is the extent to which we comprehend the nature and origins of the family risk factors involved. The second involves an understanding of why and through what mechanism (or mechanisms) risk factors such as high CD, high EE and negative AS are associated with poor patient outcomes. At the heart of these issues are questions about causal paths of influence—not only causes of high-risk family styles but also causal explanations of the link between family factors and patient relapse. These are complex issues, and although we cannot hope to explore them thoroughly in the space allotted, we nevertheless feel obliged to offer a few observations about the nature and origins of high-risk family attitudes and behaviors, and also about the various causal hypotheses linking family factors to relapse.

It is reasonable to expect that the mechanisms through which high parental CD, high EE and negative AS are linked to patient psychopathology will not necessarily be the same. For example, the genetic load hypothesis is intuitively appealing in the case of CD. It would not be surprising if the subtle speech aberrations indexed by high communication deviance resulted at least in part from a genetically mediated predisposition to develop schizophrenia or bipolar disorder. Consistent with this is evidence suggesting that CD is correlated with attention- and information-processing deficits in relatives (Wagener et al., 1986), deficits that are themselves hypothesized to be vulnerability markers for schizophrenia (see Nuechterlein & Dawson, 1984). Therefore, high CD in first-degree relatives might serve to inform clinicians about the intrinsic vulnerability of patients, rather than about stress in their family environments. If this is the case, then psychosocial interventions aimed at reducing CD in relatives would likely prove ineffective. However, the hypothesis that CD is a psychosocial stressor contributing to the onset of psychiatric disorder is also plausible, and has not been ruled out (Miklowitz & Stackman, 1992). Further investigation testing these two competing models will undoubtedly yield valuable insights concerning the role of CD in future intervention efforts.

High levels of expressed emotion and negative affective style, on the other hand, may reflect problems in the relationship between the patient and his or her family member. Certainly, depressed patients with high EE spouses report higher levels of marital distress than depressed patients with low EE spouses (Hooley & Teasdale, 1989). Moreover, interactions between patients and their high EE relatives are characterized by more negative interactional behavior and by more frequent sequences of negative escalation than are interactions between patients and their low EE family members (Hahlweg et al., 1989; Hooley, 1986, 1990;

Kuipers et al., 1983). This is true not only of depressed patients, but also for schizophrenic patients and their relatives.

Precisely why high- and low EE relationships differ is obviously an important topic for investigation. Although EE does not appear to be correlated with any obvious clinical or demographic characteristics of patients, (e.g., Brown, Birley & Wing, 1972; Miklowitz, Goldstein & Falloon, 1983; Vaughn & Leff, 1976a; Vaughn et al., 1984), it is quite possible that specific individual symptoms or behaviors might serve as triggers for criticism from relatives (see Hooley, Rosen & Richters, 1995). Personality characteristics of the relatives themselves may also contribute to EE. Hooley & Hiller (1994) have recently demonstrated that, compared with low EE relatives, high EE relatives of schizophrenic patients score lower on those scales of the California Psychological Inventory (Gough, 1987) that measure tolerance, empathy, flexibility, psychological-mindedness and achievement via independence. It is therefore plausible to view high levels of EE as reflecting the interaction of both patient and relative factors, with less tolerant relatives being more likely to react to certain hard-to-manage patient behaviors with criticism and hostility. The resulting psychosocial stress may then contribute to and accelerate the relapse process in a vulnerable patient. In the case of schizophrenia this may occur through an increase in levels of psychophysiologic reactivity (Dawson & Nuechterlein, 1984; Nuechterlein & Dawson, 1984; Sturgeon et al., 1981, 1984; Tarrier, 1989; Tarrier et al., 1979, 1988a). In the case of depression, the possible mechanism is still unclear. Psychophysiological hypotheses cannot be ruled out. However, for both schizophrenia and mood disorders, other mechanisms also warrant consideration. Criticism from a close family member may constitute a chronic threat to a vulnerable patient's self-esteem. Alternatively, a critical or hostile spouse may fail to provide an adequate buffer against stressful life events (Leff & Vaughn, 1980, 1985; Ventura et al., 1989). These and other hypotheses concerning the precise mechanism of psychiatric relapse deserve thorough investigation in the coming years.

What Aspects of Our Interventions are Most Helpful?

Our review of the literature concerning families and major psychopathology underscores the importance of working with the family to decrease overall levels of tension and to improve the quality and clarity of the interactions between and among family members. Moreover, in many instances, the empirical findings indicate that the interaction difficulties do not just involve the specific family member who is high in EE or AS or CD, but the identified patient also. This emphasizes the importance of recognizing that the difficulties likely lie at the level of the *relationship*, rather than in the behavior of any particular family member. Interventions clearly need to be targeted accordingly.

More specifically, however, we can still say very little about *why* our family-based interventions work so well. What we do know, however, is that simply educating relatives about the patients' illness yields little direct clinical benefit to patients (Tarrier et al., 1988b). The results of Köttgen et al.'s (1984) intervention further suggest that psychodynamically-oriented interventions are probably less valuable than behaviorally-oriented ones. However, few other firm conclusions can be drawn at this time.

Another problem is that family-based interventions are labor-intensive and, at least in the short term, expensive. As we move into the era of managed health care, researchers and clinicians will be increasingly required to justify their intervention strategies and streamline their procedures. A thorough understanding of what factors are necessary to effect change in families and impact patients' relapse rates would not only improve the success of treatment efforts; it might also allow such treatments to be made more widely available to families in the broader community. In short, there is an evident and urgent need for future researchers to identify which elements of their interventions are the "active ingredients" that are essential for the reduction of risk for relapse.

But how might this be accomplished? Clearly the constructs and variables that characterize communication within families need to be articulated and defined. Although efforts to describe differences between families using such concepts as relational control (e.g., Wuerker, 1994) represent important steps in this regard, many valuable developments in communication studies or in the study of social and personal relationships may be going largely ignored by clinical researchers. We believe that psychopathologists have much to gain from collaborations with those who study the very constructs (e.g., communication, relationships) that are widely believed by clinicians to be the vehicles for therapeutic change (see, for example, the journals *Communication Monographs* and *Human Communication Research*; see also Baxter & Montgomery; Bochner, Ellis & Tillman; and Duck, West & Acitelli, all in this volume). Cross-fertilization of ideas across disciplines may teach us much about how to conceptualize, measure and modify the actions and transactions that characterize relationships involving psychiatric patients.

When Should We Intervene?

The simple answer here is probably the sooner the better. This is because EE levels appear to increase with time. Although the overwhelming majority of family members of recent-onset schizophrenic patients are low in EE, after 5 years of patient illness the opposite appears to be true (Hooley & Richters, 1995). This suggests that high levels of expressed emotion may be an almost inevitable consequence of continued exposure to chronic mental illness. If this is the case, and relatives become less tolerant as time goes on, then it is clear that families should be involved in treatment at the earliest possible stage. Moreover, these interventions should not only focus on helping patients cope with their disorder, but clinicians should also attempt to provide specific help for family members. In some cases this may mean involving relatives in individual as well as in family-based treatment.

The importance of early intervention becomes all the more crucial as evidence continues to grow about the role of kindling sensitivity in some forms of mental disorders. First noted by Post (Post & Kopanda, 1976; Post, Rubinow & Ballenger, 1984), kindling refers to a process through which a system shows an escalating response to a repetitive stimulus. Eventually, however, a point is reached whereby the stimulus is no longer necessary to trigger the response and the illness essentially takes on a life of its own. If vulnerability is thus conceptualized as a dynamic construct capable of changing as a consequence of prior episodes of psychopathology, then it becomes clear that a below-threshold stressor at one point in time may become an above-threshold stressor for the same individual at a later point in time. To the extent that this is true, early intervention is not only highly desirable, it is also an essential means of preventing increasing sensitivity to ambient stress.

A full appreciation of the way in which patient vulnerabilities and patient–family relationships may change as a consequence of the duration of the illness is thus fundamental to successful intervention. Treatment strategies aimed at modifying high-risk aspects of the family environment after the patient is first diagnosed may not necessarily be those strategies that are most effective for families of patients who have been ill for an extended period of time. Researchers and clinicians need to remain cognizant of the fact that levels of EE, AS and CD may change over the course of the patient's illness. Moreover, there is every reason to expect that these changes might also be accompanied by changes in the relationships between and among family members. In short, family dynamics are unlikely to be static. Duck (1990) views relationships as "unfinished business conducted through resolution of and dialog about personal, dyadic or relational dilemmas, through talk" (p. 9). The most effective intervention strategies of the future are likely to be those that acknowledge and respect both the complexity and changing nature of patient–family relationships, as well as those that acknowledge the differences in perspective that will inevitably occur among and between family members and that are, themselves, likely to vary across time.

How Can We Identify High-risk Families?

In a world where resources are limited, psychosocial interventions need to be offered to those patients and families who are most in need of assistance. Unfortunately, all three of the family risk factors discussed in this review are costly and time-consuming to measure. Less expensive and more widely accessible methods of identifying high–risk families are obviously needed.

We know of no short cuts to the reliable identification of relatives who are high on communication deviance, although this is a characteristic of families that experienced clinicians may be able to detect as they interact with family members (Docherty, 1993). Given the problems associated with achieving reliability in

AS ratings, we are also not optimistic that a more rapid AS assessment procedure will be forthcoming. However, there are currently several approaches that may be useful in the classification of families as high or low in expressed emotion.

The five-minute speech sample (FMSS) is a brief measure of expressed emotion developed by Magaña et al. (1986), based on procedures established by Gottschalk & Gleser (1969) and Gift, Cole & Wynne (1985). Rather than being interviewed in the conventional manner, the relative is simply asked to talk about the patient for 5 uninterrupted minutes. The speech sample is then coded for criticism and EOI, and the quality of the patient–relative relationship.

FMSS-EE ratings appear to correspond reasonably well with EE classifications derived in the conventional manner. Magaña et al. (1986) and Leeb et al. (1991) reported that approximately three-quarters of relatives classified as high- or low EE on the FMSS were also classified as high- or low EE using the CFI. Importantly, the FMSS appears to be a particularly reliable method for identifying high EE family members. Relatives classified as high EE according to the FMSS are almost always classified as high EE using the CFI. False positives are therefore rare. However, some relatives who are rated as high EE on the CFI are misclassified as low EE by the FMSS. False negatives notwithstanding, if the goal is to identify high-risk family settings, the FMSS is clearly a valuable first step. Clinical efforts expended on FMSS-classified high EE families are likely to be worth the investment.

Yet another way to identify patients at elevated risk of relapse may be to assess the quality of the patient–relative relationship. Hooley & Teasdale (1989) administered the Dyadic Adjustment Scale (DAS; Spanier, 1976) to a sample of depressed inpatients and their spouses. Not only were patients' self-reported levels of marital satisfaction correlated with the EE levels of their spouses, but patients' DAS ratings were also interchangeable with EE ratings as a significant predictor of 9-month relapse rates. Even more interestingly, patients' ratings of how critical their spouses were (rated on a 10-point Likert-type scale) explained even more of the variance in relapse than either EE, or EE and DAS combined. These findings clearly await replication and extension in depressed patients and in other diagnostic groups. However, the clinical utility of simply asking patients about the quality of their relationships and how critical they find their close relatives should probably not be dismissed too readily.

Finally, we mention that Hooley & Hiller (1994) have recently developed an EE screening scale based on a subset of items from the California Psychological Inventory (Gough, 1987). These items were strongly associated with high levels of expressed emotion in the derivation sample (relatives of patients with schizophrenia). This scale is now being validated in another sample of relatives. If scores on the screening scale prove to be predictive of relapse, and are also correlated with EE in the second sample, clinicians and researchers may be able to administer a brief self-report questionnaire to family members in order to identify patients at elevated risk of relapse.

What About Patients in Non-family Settings?

Not all psychiatric patients live in family settings. An important question therefore concerns the relevance of constructs such as high EE or negative As for
patients who do not currently reside with relatives. Although work in this area is
in its infancy, several groups of researchers are now extending the EE construct
to hospital settings and examining the attitudes of treatment staff toward the
patients with whom they work.

The evidence clearly suggests that high EE attitudes are not confined to the
relatives of psychiatrically ill patients. High EE has been found in psychiatric
staff working with patients in long-term treatment settings (Heinssen et al., 1994;
Moore, Ball & Kuipers, 1992). This suggests that rather than being a characteristic of the biological relatives of psychiatric patients, high EE may be a natural
response of some individuals to the challenges and frustrations of providing
long-term care for a psychiatrically impaired patient. Such findings also speak to
the difficulties inherent in trying to modify high EE family attitudes. Rather than
viewing high EE as something bad about families, we should perhaps recognize
that it is the norm (see Hooley, Rosen & Richters, 1995). We should also consider
that, when we attempt to intervene with high EE families, we are trying to instill
a level of tolerance for impaired functioning that is, in essence, somewhat unusual. If even those who are professionally trained to care for the mentally ill can
become high EE, family members should surely not be judged too harshly for the
negative attitudes that they may hold.

What More Can We Do?

The success of the psychosocial interventions described earlier gives us obvious
cause for optimism. But this is not a time to rest on laurels. All forms of intervention have their limitations and psychosocial treatments for the families of patients
with schizophrenia are no exception in this regard. While family intervention may
prevent or delay relapse or rehospitalization of patients with schizophrenia, it
would be quite wrong to equate lack of relapse with freedom from psychological
or psychiatric impairment. Many persons with schizophrenia experience debilitating "negative" symptoms, such as reduced emotional expression, social withdrawal and lack of interest in everyday activities. These symptoms often persist
long after an acute psychotic episode has ended. Moreover, these negative symptoms may themselves engender criticism and/or hostility from relatives. Thus, in
addition to reducing the quality of everyday life for patients, residual symptoms
may also contribute to the relapse process (Hooley, 1987; Hooley et al., 1987).
For these reasons, future intervention efforts should be aimed not only at reducing relapse rates, but also at improving patients' social adjustment and day-to-day
functioning.

Another issue concerns the way that psychosocial treatments are typically
allocated. In the treatment trials that have been conducted to date, psychosocial

interventions were most usually offered only to families containing a high EE relative. From a clinical perspective, this is an obvious and necessary first step, because of the increased risk for relapse that high EE family environments confer upon patients. However, from a practical perspective, what this translates into is that only relatives who were obviously troubled or frustrated by patients' behavior received attention.

But should attending to the "squeaky wheel" be done at the expense of low-EE family members? Patients in low EE families may be as psychiatrically impaired as those living in high EE families. And, even though patients' relapse rates may be lower in low EE as opposed to high EE homes, it would be naive to believe that low EE families cope with the stress of psychiatric illness in a close family member without any difficulty or hardship. In short, even though we may as yet know comparatively little about what low EE families may need in the way of assistance from mental health professionals, we should perhaps not immediately assume that they need nothing. Both researchers and clinicians need to pay attention to this issue. If we do otherwise, we run the risk of denying our very best treatment efforts to certain families simply because they suffer in silence.

Finally, it would behoove us to consider the way in which we conduct family-based interventions. Although the conventional model is to engage families in single-family treatment, extending relatives' social support networks through multiple-family treatment groups seems to be a valuable and cost-effective way of decreasing the sense of isolation experienced by many families of the mentally ill (McFarlane et al., 1995a,b). McFarlane and colleagues also report substantial reductions in 4-year relapse rates in patients whose families engage in multiple family treatment. There is thus every reason to believe that these relatively inexpensive forms of intervention may represent one model for the future.

CONCLUDING REMARKS

Our review of family risk factors in psychopathology has identified three variables, two of which can be considered particularly important. Communication deviance is a measure of a family member's inability to establish and maintain a shared focus of attention. It distinguishes between parents of individuals with schizophrenia and other parents, and it has been shown to predict the onset of schizophrenia and schizophrenia-related conditions in psychiatrically vulnerable adolescents. However, there is no evidence relating parental CD to increased risk for relapse in already diagnosed schizophrenic and manic patients.

Expressed emotion, on the other hand, while not obviously linked to the onset of major mental disorder, is clearly a valuable predictor of the course of illness. Patients with schizophrenia who return home from hospitalization to live with high EE family members are approximately twice as likely to experience relapse in the following 9–12 months compared with patients who return home to live in low EE family environments. For patients with mood disorders, the increased risk for relapse associated with high EE may be even greater.

Despite years of research, many important questions still remain. Although we can now say with some confidence that family factors are important with respect to the outcome of psychiatrically vulnerable patients, we can still say little about why this should be so. Understanding the mechanisms through which patient vulnerabilities interact with and perhaps even engender negative family attitudes or deviant communication styles is an inherently difficult task. It is also a task that calls for highly sophisticated longitudinal research strategies that hold the potential to untangle what are likely to be many and complex directions of influence. Yet longitudinal research is likely to be uninformative in the absence of conceptual or theoretical developments that guide the direction of study (see Duck, 1990), and advances in this area are solely needed. Almost 40 years has elapsed since the development of the two most important family based-concepts in psychopathology. In that time, much of the theoretical richness that characterized the early empirical work has been sacrificed in the service of methodological precision and scientific rigor. This is both inevitable and appropriate, and it has brought us a long way. Perhaps now, however, the time is right to look toward the flourishing fields of communication studies and social and personal relationships, as well as toward cognitive science and neuroscience for developments that may inform and enhance future theory and understanding of the family relationships of psychiatric patients. For the present, and perhaps also for the future, the prevention of the onset of psychopathology is an impossible goal. However, we can now delay relapse via family-based interventions. As our understanding grows of the mechanism through which the characteristics of relatives reflect and also interact with the biological and psychological vulnerabilities of patients, and as we learn more about the risks and resources provided by close relationships, there is every reason to hope that we will be able to do even more.

Chapter 28

Distinguishing the Theoretical Functions of Social Ties: Implications for Support Interventions

Kenneth Heller
Indiana University, Bloomington, IN, USA
and
Karen S. Rook
University of California, Irvine, CA, USA

The goal of this chapter is to foster a conceptual understanding of the processes by which supportive relationships operate. We believe that it is time to step back from arguments about micro-level facets of support processes (i.e., main vs. buffering effects, instrumental aid vs. emotional support, the potency of positive vs. negative aspects of social relationships) to a broader discussion of theoretical templates that can explain the diverse findings in the support intervention literature. Periodic calls have been issued for greater specification of the mechanisms by which supportive relationships influence health and well-being (Heller, 1990; Heller & Swindle, 1983; Rook & Dooley, 1985; Sarason, Sarason & Pierce, 1990; Thoits, 1985). Attacking the problem piecemeal, however, has had limited success in the absence of overarching theoretical constructs. For example, there is an active debate, currently about the differential impact of positive vs. negative elements of social relationships (Rook, 1992), but we suspect that this controversy, as well as others in the literature, will be better understood with an overarching view of social relationships that explains the conditions under which esteem-enhancement and esteem-denigration are differentially important.

We hope to shed light on possible intervention alternatives by discussing their theoretical foundations; specifically, the social provisions provided by interper-

Handbook of Personal Relationships, 2nd edn. Edited by Steve Duck.
© 1997 John Wiley & Sons Ltd.

sonal relationships. We believe that the social transactions through which basic interpersonal functions are expressed represent important building blocks of relationships and, by extension, important building blocks of support interventions. In addition, we are acutely sensitive to the problem that, while a great deal has been written in recent years about the health-protective effects of social relationships, the support intervention literature is amazingly silent in describing successful programs. For example, at the present time we do not know whether intentionally provided support can substitute for prior support deficiencies (Heller, Price & Hogg, 1990). Neither do we know why a number of well-designed support intervention studies have yielded null findings (Baumgarten et al., 1988; Heller et al., 1991). A crucial gap in knowledge exists about the effective ingredients in supportive interactions. It is difficult to draw definitive causal inferences from epidemiological studies because they are primarily correlational; better evidence would come from *theory-based*, randomized intervention trials (Cohen & Wills, 1985; Thoits, 1985). Thus, at this point, discussing theoretical foundations has the advantage of allowing us to step back to re-examine some of the basic assumptions upon which support interventions might be built.

In reviewing the literature on support interventions, Gottlieb (1992, p. 296) questioned whether the "voluminous literature on social support offers a theory or any scraps of a theory that might be called on in the planning and execution of interventions." He concluded that the literature provides only weak guidance for action because the contexts in which natural indigenous support occurs are considerably different from those involved in the development of new or "grafted" relationships (Gottlieb, 1988). This state of affairs also exists because theoretical propositions have not been adequately articulated, causing the boundaries of what constitutes a support intervention to be diffuse and ill-defined. Stated more boldly, support group and network interventions have "the status of a black box, appealing strongly to practitioners but leaving obscure the pathways to support afforded by different features of the natural and engineered social surround" (Gottlieb, 1988, p. 530).

We begin with some historical comments to note the particular American flavor of this field. The health protective effects of social ties have been noted in a number of other industrialized countries as well (Veiel & Baumann, 1992). For much of the world in which geographic dispersion of primary kin and friendship groups has not occurred, however, social ties are not conceptualized as so important to health as they are in this country.

REASONS FOR THE EXTRAORDINARY INTEREST IN SOCIAL SUPPORT

The interest in support interventions in the USA reflects, in part, the ambivalence with which social relations are viewed in society at large. On the one hand, this country was built upon the spirit of individualism and non-interference from others, with the typical response to group conflict being separation. So long as there was an open frontier, individuals or groups with social or religious views that differed from those of the majority were free to move and establish their own communities of like-minded citizens. The spirit of individual self-sufficiency still represents an important force in American life that is repeatedly celebrated in folk literature describing rags-to-riches stories of self-made men like Horatio Alger. (Self-sufficiency in women is treated more ambivalently in American folk legends.) The importance of self-sufficiency and the negative attitude toward help-seeking, particularly among men, also can be seen in the "autonomy–connectedness dialectic" (Wood, 1993b), in which men are described as preferring independence and emotional control, a view supported by research demonstrating that men often see help-seeking as a threat to their competence (DePaulo, 1982).

At the same time, sociological observers have noted a yearning for community among many citizens (Bellah et al., 1985; Bernard, 1973; Sarason, 1974). Sarason put the matter most poignantly when he stated:

> The community in which we live is a geo-political entity with which we feel little kinship ... We may wish it were otherwise, but we feel impotent to do anything ... We do not feel needed in our community and we rarely if ever seriously think about how we can contribute to the solution of its problems ... we yearn to be part of a larger network of relationships that would give greater expression to our needs for intimacy, diversity, usefulness and belongingness (Sarason, 1974, pp. 2–3).

Traditionally, sociologists believed that social anomie was the direct result of large-scale urbanization and that living close to a large number of people with whom one had no significant emotional ties fostered a spirit of competition and mutual exploitation (Nisbet, 1973; Wirth, 1964). Subsequent research discovered much greater complexity. Although instances of social disintegration could be found in large cities, primary group ties also flourished (Fischer, 1982; Wellman, 1979). City dwellers might come into daily contact with many strangers with whom personal contact might be guarded, but that did not necessarily mean that they had fewer friends or acquaintances (Fischer, 1982; Heller, 1989). Still, a basic theme in sociological commentary is the perception of a social rootlessness and disaffection with social and community institutions (Bellah et al., 1985; Homans, 1950; Reisman, 1950; but also see Baltzell, 1968; Reynolds & Norman, 1988).

One factor influencing the perception of social detachment is the decreased ability of local citizens in modern, globally-interdependent, technological societies to influence decisions affecting the quality of their lives (Heller, 1992; Littrell & Hobbs, 1989). Crucial decisions are often made by remote, outside actors such as large corporations and locally removed national and international political officials (Gamson, 1979). The lack of local decision-making structures not only increases the sense of political impotence but also provides few opportunities for relationship development outside of one's own immediate primary group. In addition, geographic dispersion and population mobility make American society particularly vulnerable to social disaffection compared with equally urbanized areas elsewhere in the world.

EARLY PSYCHOLOGICAL PERSPECTIVES ON THE EFFECTS OF SOCIAL TIES

The social facilitation and affiliation literatures of the 1960s anticipated the current debate concerning the positive vs. the negative effects of social relationships (Heller, 1979). Social facilitation theory posits that the presence of others functions as a source of arousal or drive when the individual anticipates that others will negatively evaluate his/her performance (Zajonc, 1965; Geen & Gange, 1977). Research that has tested this formulation has found that high drive (or anxiety) facilitates the performance of already learned, habitual behaviors but impedes learning in novel situations. Thus, the social facilitation literature pointed toward negative effects of social ties when confronting unanticipated stress, at least when social ties were operationalized as the mere presence of a non-interactive stranger. When others were seen as a source of negative evaluation or competition, anxiety typically increased.

The social affiliation literature seemed to produce the opposite finding—when given a choice, individuals anticipating stress preferred to have the company of others rather than to wait alone (Epley, 1974; Schachter, 1959). The research also found that affiliation under stress improved performance and lowered psychophysiological reactivity (Amoroso & Walters, 1969; Angermeier, Phelps & Reynolds, 1967), particularly if the significant other was known to the subject (Kissel, 1965). Several theoretical explanations were offered for the anxiety-reducing effect of affiliation, including boosting morale through downward social comparison (i.e., seeing oneself as better off than a less fortunate other), using others to determine the appropriate standards for one's own behavior, modeling the behavior of calm others and distracting one's attention from the anticipated stressor (Epley, 1974; Wills, 1981). Although a clear explanation for the anxiety-reducing effects of affiliation never emerged, these early lines of work were significant in highlighting both the positive (calming) and negative (anxiety-arousing) aspects of social relationships.

The Need to Specify Basic Theoretical Functions of Social Relationships

Despite the now widespread empirical confirmation of the importance of social relationships for both psychological well-being and physical health, surprisingly little agreement exists about how to conceptualize or assess the potent elements of these relationships. "Social support" is the most popular term, but its definition eludes consensus, referring at times to structural characteristics and/or functions of social relationships and at other times to personal interpretations or perceptions (Veiel & Baumann, 1992). Reflecting upon the diverse meanings of the term, Heller & Swindle (1983) suggested that "facets" of support, such as social connections, skills in accessing and maintaining social networks, support appraisals and support-seeking behaviors should be distinguished conceptually and empirically. This has rarely happened, however and the multiple meanings of the term have made it difficult to integrate diverse findings. Perhaps most striking is the lack of theoretical substance to the various definitions that have been proposed, contributing to the low level of explanatory power of the support construct. The literature is largely descriptive in nature, demonstrating repeatedly that various aspects of social relationships influence health outcomes, without providing much insight into why these effects occur.

Given the diverse forms that social relationships can take and the variety of ways that people can either help or hinder one another, perhaps it should not be too surprising that definitions of supportive relationships vary so greatly. But it makes little sense to develop programs to "increase support" without some sense of what aspects of social relationships tend to be health-protective, neutral, or perhaps even noxious.

FUNCTIONS SERVED BY SOCIAL RELATIONSHIPS: THE BUILDING BLOCKS OF SUPPORT INTERVENTIONS

Researchers increasingly agree on the value of distinguishing the important components of support and these generally conform to the facets described by Heller & Swindle (1983)—namely, network resources, perceived support or appraisals, and received support (Barrera, 1986; Vaux, 1988). But these refer to levels, or domains of analysis, rather than to the theoretical functions of relationships.

An early categorization of the theoretical functions of social relationships was offered by Weiss (1974), who argued that social relationships afford six basic "social provisions". These provisions included: *attachment*, a sense of security, closeness and comfort provided by others; *social integration* into a network of like-minded individuals; opportunities to provide *nurturance* to others; *reassurance of worth* provided by the reactions of others that affirm one's role performance; the establishment of *reliable alliances* for the provision of mutual assistance; and the opportunity to obtain *guidance* for dealing with various stressful events.

A similar set of functions was proposed by Vaux (1988), who distinguished between functions relevant to a stressful event and those relevant to non-stress-related social encounters. During a stressful event, significant others can provide direct assistance, guidance, diversion or emotional regulation. During normal social encounters, in contrast, others can provide intimacy, companionship and a sense of belonging, feedback that enhances esteem, opportunities for social role enactment and social comparison, and support for personal aspirations.

Some empirical research suggests that different functions such as these have distinctive effects. Cutrona & Russell and their colleagues have done considerable work linking the Weiss typology to various physical and mental health outcomes. They developed a "Social Provisions Inventory" to assess the six social provisions proposed by Weiss (Cutrona & Russell, 1987). In studies of young mothers and elderly adults, they found that some provisions were more likely to be available in kin relationships (guidance, attachment, nurturance and reliable alliance), whereas other provisions were more likely to be available in non-kin relationships (social integration and reassurance of worth) (Cutrona, 1986). Total scores on the Social Provisions Inventory significantly predicted older adults' physical health ratings at a 6-month follow-up, controlling for initial health status; reassurance of worth and the opportunity to provide nurturance exhibited the strongest predictive associations (Cutrona, Russell & Rose, 1986). Thus, older adults who felt that they were seen by their network members as competent and who had opportunities to provide support to others were more likely to maintain favorable views of their health than were older adults who had fewer of these provisions. In a study of spouses of cancer patients, the six provisions individually and collectively predicted better immune functioning, after controlling for life events and depression (Baron et al., 1990).

The finding that each of Weiss' social provisions predicted immune functioning would seem to question the importance of differentiating among them. While researchers can differentiate support provisions, ordinary citizens may have greater difficulty doing so. This difficulty arises, in part, from the fact that support providers often perform multiple social functions (Hirsch, 1980). Thus, for socially integrated individuals, health-protective social provisions are often bundled together within a given network member and duplicated to some extent across network members. For socially isolated individuals, however, this is unlikely to be the case. The relationships they do have may provide quite limited, specialized forms of support. Even if one or two associates do perform multiple social functions, the absence of a reservoir of potential support providers creates vulnerabilities. Thus, efforts to disentangle theoretically distinct support functions are apt to have greater yield and special importance in work that focuses on socially isolated individuals.

Thoits (1985) proposed a somewhat different list of relationship functions than Weiss and Vaux. The functions described by Thoits include: *social integration*; the *development and maintenance of identity and esteem*; *coping assistance*; *affect regulation*; and *social control*. We have listed these functions in Table 28.1, along with examples of behaviors that can lead to either positive or negative effects.

Some obvious similarities exist among the formulations offered by Weiss, Vaux and Thoits. For example, establishing reliable alliances for the provision of mutual assistance (Weiss) and obtaining guidance for dealing with stressful events (Vaux) can both be subsumed under Thoits' category of coping assistance. Providing security and comfort (Weiss) and opportunities for companionship

Table 28.1   Theoretical functions provided by social relationships

Social integration
   Positive —activities that stregthen identification with the social group
   Negative—activities that discourage group affiliation

Development and maintenance of identity and esteem
   Positive —successful role performances
              —positive esteem conveyed by network members
   Negative—failures in role performances
              —esteem denigration conveyed by network members

Affect regulation
   Positive —network activities that relieve distress or increase positive affect
   Negative—network activities that increase distress or serve as a basis for negative
              social comparisons

Coping assistance
   Positive —practical help with life tasks
              —activities that further individual competence
   Negative—expected network help is not forthcoming
              —help is provided in ways that undermine competence

Social control
   Positive —network member actions that reinforce socially approved behaviors
   Negative—network member actions that encourage social deviance or risky health
              practices

(Vaux) fit well in Thoits' category of affect regulation. We prefer Thoits' categorization because the functions can be distinguished cleanly, and so we will discuss these in depth. We recognize, however, that our decision is somewhat arbitrary and that other theorists might prefer a different system. Ultimately, the value of any categorization scheme rests in its utility, and our next task, accordingly, is to examine the predictive utility of differentiating social provisions. Because social provisions have been distinguished infrequently in empirical studies, the literature upon which we can draw is somewhat sparse. Nonetheless, we believe that the exercise may be useful as a guide to needed research, particularly research that can help inform the development of support interventions.

We recognize that a number of theorists have argued that the significance of support for well-being transcends specific social provisions, and resides more globally in relationships and how they are perceived and appraised (Baumeister & Leary, 1995; Sarason, Pierce & Sarason, 1990). We generally agree, but would add that relationships with network members emerge from, and are organized around, exchanges and activities that reflect the functions we will be discussing. Their differentiation is particularly important in constructing interventions to restore lost of missing social provisions. By describing a diverse set of theoretically distinct relationship functions, we hope to encourage attention to a broader array of plausible interventions than is typically considered in discussions of "support interventions".

Social Integration

Because of their orientation toward personal relationships, most support researchers tend to overlook the social structures that give rise to relationships. Families, workplaces, residential neighborhoods, religious and community organizations, and other settings and structures affect how relationships form and develop. Mechanic (1974) noted some time ago that the ability to cope with environmental demands depends on the efficacy of the solutions that culture provides and on the adequacy of the preparatory institutions to which an individual has been exposed. Culture also determines role availability and social opportunities, which vary according to an individual's ethnicity, social class, economic status, gender and age. All of these factors influence relationship formation and the benefits that can be extracted from social relationships (Heller, Price & Hogg, 1990; House, Umberson & Landis, 1988).

The typical method of assessing social integration is to examine the social ties and organization memberships that an individual maintains and the frequency of interaction with others. Measures might include the number of church and community group memberships, the number of family and friend ties, the frequency of participation in community activities, and the frequency of visiting with friends and family. Less socially integrated individuals have been found repeatedly to be at increased risk of mortality from all causes compared to more integrated individuals (Berkman & Syme, 1979; House Robbins & Metzner, 1982; Cohen, Kaplan & Manuck, 1994). In a prospective study of students preparing for a medical school entrance exam, Bolger & Eckenrode (1991) found that socially isolated individuals reported more anxiety than did more integrated individuals, after controlling for support appraisals, personality dispositions and prior coping responses. Because perceived support was unrelated to anxiety, the authors speculate that measures of social integration may tap social provisions of which individuals may be unaware and hence unlikely to report.

Intervention Implications

Unfortunately, we still lack evidence that increasing the social ties of isolated individuals lowers their health or mortality risk. Furthermore, the beneficial effects of social integration probably are not due to the sheer extensiveness of social networks, but rather to role relationships that are embedded in these network ties. Such role relationships provide meaning and purpose to life, and a sense of personal and group identity. For most people, social network participation almost always involves meaningful role activities, which makes it easy to overlook the benefits of these role activities in planning support interventions. We now know, for example, that helping lonely people acquire new friends may yield few discernable health benefits if the resulting activity fails to enhance social roles and identity functions (Heller et al., 1991; Rook, 1991).

The Development and Maintenance of Identity and Self-esteem

A major theme in the symbolic interactionist literature is that people develop their self-concepts by internalizing the appraisals of others. Although the belief that personal identity and self-esteem primarily have social origins has been difficult to verify (McNulty & Swann, 1994), evidence indicates that the appraisals of parents, teachers and peers influence children's self-concepts (Cole, 1991; Felson, 1989). Adults appear to be more impervious to these influences, however, (Kenny & DePaulo, 1993). Moreover, among adults, initial self-views partly determine how they will be perceived by others. McNulty & Swann (1994) demonstrated that causal processes can occur in both directions: self-views influence the appraisals of others, and the appraisals of others can influence self-views, although not necessarily in the same dyads at the same time.

Although the views of others may be an important determinant of self-esteem, we believe that the reciprocal chaining of personal accomplishment, recognition by others, and self-appraisal entails greater complexity than is recognized either by traditional symbolic interaction theory or its critics. The self-identity literature generally overlooks the fact that self-appraisals and the appraisals of significant others occur on an ongoing basis in the context of ordinary life experiences. As people interact, their behaviors are monitored and evaluated both by themselves and by others. Both more competent and less competent role performances receive note and become part of social appraisal and self-identity processes. Using the rules acquired through ordinary socialization, people regularly evaluate the adequacy of their social role performances. Thus, it is difficult to conceptualize self-perceptions that do not have a social basis. Once established, self-views may be difficult to change in further social interactions, but they nonetheless have a social origin.

Intervention Implications

Two practical implications flow from this argument. First, positive appraisals communicated by others during supportive encounters may do little to raise self-esteem if prior negative self-schemas are firmly entrenched, as in chronic depression, for example. Thus, although support has been found to ameliorate depressive symptoms, chronic depression might be more difficult to impact (Monroe & Johnson, 1992). Second, competent role performance may be an essential underpinning of positive self-esteem. Despite what others may tell us about how much we are valued, self-esteem may erode if, at the same time, we must confront role failures and/or daily reminders of diminished competence. In planning a support intervention we should not expect new supportive exchanges to overcome constant reminders of role failures; efforts to improve role competence may be a more productive avenue, where they are feasible.

Coping Assistance

Thoits (1986) suggests that it is useful to conceptualize support as help that significant others provide to supplement an individual's coping efforts. Coping typically refers to actions taken to prevent or alleviate the negative consequences of stressful events (Lazarus & Folkman, 1984). Significant others can participate in these stress management efforts in a number of ways by helping to alter a stressful situation, to change its meaning, or to modify the emotional reactions that are elicited. Thus, a wide variety of behaviors qualify as coping assistance. Examples include the help that significant others provide in anticipating problems and rehearsing effective solutions. Network members also provide help by offering advice about how to solve a problem or by intervening directly in problem resolution. Network members also can assist in the process of assimilating and reinterpreting stressful events in order to minimize their most noxious elements and can help stressed individuals deal with the negative emotions aroused by events.

Thoits (1986) further proposes that coping assistance is most likely to be effective when it comes from others who have faced or are facing similar stressors. Similarity enhances the likelihood that the individual will receive empathic understanding along with coping assistance. Empathy allows others to recognize and seek to address the full range of needs and threats experienced by the distressed person. In addition, empathic assistance overcomes some of the self-evaluative difficulties that can arise when people accept help from others. Individuals can accept help comfortably only as long as their self-esteem is not threatened by doing so. Non-empathic attempts to provide support may be motivated more by consideration of the helper's needs than the distressed individual's needs and, as a result, may prove ineffective or even harmful.

Coping assistance has received the greatest attention as an aid to adaption to life stress, but it may serve as well to facilitate the pursuit of personally valued life goals, outside of the context of stressful events. Ruehlman & Wolchik (1988) sought to bridge work on social support with research on personal strivings by arguing that network members, particularly intimate members, may facilitate the attainment of valued goals and thereby contribute to well-being. Social network members can affirm one's personal goals as worthwhile, can encourage goal-related activity and bolster motivation during setbacks and can assist directly with goal-relevant tasks (Ruehlman & Wolchik, 1988).

Intervention Implications

The preceding discussion implies that providing support can be a complicated matter. Help from others can strengthen personal coping and contribute to a sense of competence (Sarason, Pierce & Sarason, 1990). Yet, not all support transactions achieve these beneficial outcomes. Theory and research demonstrate very clearly that support sometimes undermines, rather than enhances, the recipient's sense of competence (e.g., Fisher, Nadler & Whitcher-

Alagna, 1982). It is not unusual, for example, for individuals who are recovering from a serious chronic illness to report that well-intentioned family members become over-protective and controlling in their efforts to provide support (e.g., Coyne, Wortman & Lehman, 1988; Peters-Golden, 1982). Moreover, the very structure of many support transactions can imply a hierarchy of ability between help providers and help recipients, leading the latter to experience an uncomfortable mixture of inferiority and indebtedness (Fisher et al., 1988). In addition, although support providers' actions often help to contain or reduce emotional distress, their actions can also increase distress, as will be discussed in the next section.

Affect Regulation

Stressful life events can provoke intense psychological distress by causing valued resources (personal, social or material) to be lost or threatened (Hobfoll, 1989). At such times, social support provided by members of one's social network may help to alleviate the depression, anxiety, anger and other forms of negative affect that stressful events arouse. This "palliative emotional support is aimed not at problematic events or appraisals of them but at their emotional consequences" (Vaux, 1988, p. 141). Emotion-focused social support, as distinct from problem-focused social support, thus is directly parallel to the emotion-focused form of coping that coping researchers have emphasized (Thoits, 1986).

Social network members may employ a variety of different strategies in seeking to reduce a friend's or family member's negative affect, including empathic listening, expressing concern, reinterpreting or relabeling the negative affect, diverting attention from the stressor, and reinforcing expressions of more positive affect (e.g., Thoits, 1986; Vaux, 1988). In addition, network members may offer a distressed person stimulants (e.g., coffee) or depressants (e.g., alcohol, tranquilizers) to counter the physiological distress that can accompany negative affect (Thoits, 1986). The effectiveness of such attempts at emotion regulation will depend on a variety of factors, including the extent of the support provider's prior experience with this kind of stressor and the support recipient's perceptions of the support provider's motives. Misery appears to love not just any company but miserable company, making those who have experienced similar life difficulties more capable of empathic understanding (Thoits, 1986). In addition, misery appears to love sincere company, leading others' attempts at emotion regulation to be more effective when they are perceived to be motivated by genuine caring rather than obligation or self-interest (Thoits, 1986; Wortman & Lehman, 1985). Network members' support gestures sometimes derive more from a desire to alleviate their own discomfort than to be responsive to the needs of the distressed person (e.g., Cialdini et al., 1987; Wortman & Lehman, 1985). Such self-interest may cause expressions of concern to "ring hollow" or, worse, may lead network members to disengage from or derogate the distressed person (Coyne, Ellard & Smith, 1990).

The role of social relationships in affect regulation is not limited to their potential for decreasing or increasing negative affect. Social relationships also influence well-being by stimulating positive affect. Friendships and family relationships provide opportunities for purely enjoyable interaction, such as shared leisure activities, humor and reminiscence. This "plain, unvarnished camaraderie—the joking, griping, teasing, story-swapping, interest-sharing, hobby-sharing, note-comparing, kind of interaction" lies at the heart of many close relationships (Wright, 1989, p. 218). Unlike interaction oriented toward problem-solving or goal attainment, these companionate activities are undertaken for their own sake (cf. Gordon & Gaitz, 1976). Novelty and spontaneity have been identified by some emotion theorists (e.g., Mandler, 1975) as necessary antecedent conditions for positive arousal and emotion, and it is just such attributes that characterize many forms of companionate activity (Blau, 1973; Hays, 1988). Shared leisure also allows people to transcend work and family problems or other concerns, even if only briefly. Leisure activities have been found to encourage a fluid, open state of mind that people find enjoyable and that helps them shift their attentions from worries and preoccupations to more pleasurable matters (Csiksentmihalyi, 1975; Larson, Mannell & Zuzanek, 1986). Moreover, the emotional benefits of companionship tend not to be diluted by the status asymmetries that inhere in exchanges of support between help-providers and help-recipients; companionate activities typically have an more egalitarian structure, making their contributions to affect regulation less complicated (Rook, 1990).

Intervention Implications

Thus, we believe that social relationships play dual roles in affect regulation by helping to diffuse negative affect and to stimulate positive affect. The former role has received a great deal of attention in the social support literature and provides a rationale for problem disclosure and empathic listening in many support interventions. The latter role has received less attention but represents a viable focus for support interventions, particularly those that seek to address enduring problems of loneliness and social isolation rather than acute life crises.

For example, Heller et al. (1991) sought to increase opportunities for emotional support and companionship among lonely older women living in a rural area through an intervention that paired participants with similar older women and encouraged them to maintain regular telephone contact. The intervention had only limited success but proved instructive about the special challenges that arise in seeking to nurture the development of companionship among lonely individuals. First, the women in this study were not introduced to each other through shared activities and collaborative projects that might have provided "grist" for their interactions and a non-threatening context in which they could evaluate each other's suitability as potential friends (Rook, 1991). Incorporating such interdependent activities warrants consideration as a component of interventions aimed at alleviating loneliness, as these activities are believed to reduce self-consciousness and awkwardness and to foster camaraderie. Second, subgroup analyses conducted by Heller et al. (1991) indicated that the loneliest women in their study derived the least benefit from the intervention. Very lonely individuals may have long-standing social skill deficits or social inhibitions that interfere with their efforts to establish and maintain friendships (Rook, 1991). Pilisuk & Minkler (1980) commented in this regard that "where the fact of belonging and interacting is in itself foreign . . . special difficulties [arise] in establishing trust levels that enable supportive interpersonal linkages to develop" (p. 106). When such special sensitivities exist in a target population, intervention planners must devise comfortable points of entree for participants' social engagement and may need to find ways to augment participants' social skills.

Social Control

Social relationships serve not only as sources of identity maintenance, coping assistance and affect regulation, but also as sources of control. The control, or regulatory, function of social relationships has been emphasized most often by sociologists (e.g., Durkheim, 1897/1951; Hughes & Gove, 1981; Umberson, 1987) who argue that individuals embedded in a cohesive network of social ties are likely to be deterred from engaging in risky or deviant behavior.

Social control theorists distinguish two basic mechanisms of social-network-based restraint. First, many close relationships, such as those involving marriage and parenting, entail enduring responsibilities or obligations (Umberson, 1987). Such responsibilities, or social role obligations, exert a stabilizing influence on behavior. Individuals who have significant responsibilities to others, as compared to those who lack such responsibilities, have greater motivation to discontinue unstable or risky behavior and to engage in more health-protective behavior (e.g., Hughes & Gove, 1981; Leventhal, Prohaska & Hirschman, 1985). This mechanism of social control is largely indirect (Umberson, 1987). Even without explicit feedback or sanctions directed toward shaping a focal person's behavior, the existence of significant role responsibilities and commitments would serve to encourage more stable functioning and better self-care. For example, the parent of a young child who reduces or refrains from substance use may be motivated to do so, in part, because of the need to carry out parental role responsibilities.

Social control also occurs through more direct means, such as explicitly urging someone to engage in sound health practices and to avoid unsound or risky practices (Hughes & Gove, 1981; Umberson, 1987). These attempts at social control may incorporate sanctions and persuasive appeals (Umberson, 1987). Thus, social control operates through network members' efforts to monitor, persuade, and reward or punish a focal person as well as through a focal person's self-restraint of risky behavior.

Findings consistent with the social control perspective have appeared in studies that have contrasted people with different living arrangements (Hughes & Gove, 1981), and marital and parental statuses (Umberson, 1987). For example, married individuals have been found to engage in fewer health-compromising behaviors than unmarried individuals (e.g., Umberson, 1987), presumably because spouses can readily monitor and influence the behavior of their partners.

Unlike social support theorists, who often argue that social support must be affirming in order to be helpful (e.g., Kahn, 1979), social control theorists argue that regulatory actions by others may be helpful even when they are not affirming. For example, intervening to stop a family member from excessive drinking may help to preserve his or her physical health but may arouse resentment as well. In this vein, Hughes & Gove (1981) hypothesized that others' social control attempts may provoke psychological distress even though they lead to less deviance and more stable functioning. "Constraint may be the source of considerable frustration; at the same time it tends to reduce the probability of problematic or maladaptive behaviors" (p. 71). This assumes, of course, that the norms of the social network converge with those of the broader society with respect to the desirability of specific behaviors. When norms diverge from prevailing societal norms, social networks may encourage rather than discourage maladaptive behavior (Hirschi, 1969; Jessor, Donovan & Costa, 1991; Wills, 1990).

Intervention Implications

Several practical implications follow from the recognition that informal social networks can operate as a source of social control. First, in some community interventions, participants may need a mix of both social support and social control. For example, psychiatrically impaired individuals may experience welcome relief from loneliness and anxiety through contact with others who can provide social support, but they also may benefit from contact with others who challenge (rather than affirm) unrealistic or delusional beliefs. Achieving a suitable balance of affirmation and challenge (or support and control) requires considerable sensitivity to participants' needs and vulnerabilities, particularly because social control attempts can provoke distress (e.g., Hughes & Gove, 1981) and could lead to program withdrawal or attrition.

A dialectic tension may exist between social support and social control in many social relationships, such that support can undermine the success of control attempts, and *vice versa* (Rook, 1990). Communication scholars have argued that this tension surfaces when an individual seeks to induce behavior change in a friend or family member without harming the relationship (e.g., Miller G.R., et al., 1988). Intense persuasive appeals that succeed at the expense of relational outcomes constitute "pyrrhic victories" (Dillard & Fitzpatrick, 1985). Yet, less intense persuasive appeals that evidence tact and sensitivity may contribute to relational solidarity but may fail to bring about the needed behavior change (Miller & Boster, 1987). When discouraging risky or health-compromising behavior represents a legitimate objective of a social network intervention, it will be important to consider how to achieve this "social control" objective without eroding the existing base of support in the network.

Distinguishing between indirect and direct social control reminds us, however, that appropriate behavior and self-care can be fostered not only through others' direct appeals and sanctions but also by increasing social role obligations. Providing people with the skills and opportunities to assume valued social roles may have a variety of psychological and behavioral benefits (Heller & Swindle, 1983), including possible reductions in unreliable or inappropriate behavior. Encouraging such self-regulation by increasing and rewarding an individual's network involvement and role responsibilities may avoid some of the interpersonal pitfalls that have been postulated to accompany direct forms of social control.

INDIGENOUS VS. GRAFTED SOCIAL TIES

The functions of social relationships that we have discussed have emerged from theoretical and empirical analyses of naturally occurring relationships, or indigenous social ties. Such social ties may differ in important respects from new ties that are forged through interventions, or grafted social ties (Gottlieb, 1981; Kiesler, 1985; Rook & Dooley, 1985). In this section, we examine several implications of this distinction.

Evidence for the Effects of Indigenous vs. Grafted Support

Most investigations of the association between social support and health outcomes (psychological well-being, morbidity, mortality) have examined the support that emanates naturally from members of informal social networks. This might be termed indigenous support. Evidence that indigenous social support appears to promote health and well-being is sometimes interpreted as indicating that social support obtained through interventions in which new social ties develop, or grafted support (Gottlieb, 1981), has similar health-promoting effects. Yet indigenous support may be effective precisely because of its naturalness (Gottlieb, 1981; Rook & Dooley, 1985). In fact, evidence for the benefits of social support appears to be stronger, on balance, for indigenous relationships than for grafted relationships. For example, studies of the role of social support in sustaining smokers' efforts to quit smoking (and to remain abstinent) have revealed fairly consistent evidence that naturally occurring support plays an important role in the health behavior change process; intervention-based support, in contrast, generally has been unsuccessful in facilitating this behavior change (Cohen et al., 1988).

Limitations of Indigenous Relationships as a Source of Support

The available empirical evidence that social support contributes to well-being appears to be more convincing for indigenous relationships than for grafted relationships, but this does not mean that indigenous relationships always function as an adequate source of support. Friends and family members sometimes fail to provide the support that a distressed person needs or may even add to the person's distress. The limitations of indigenous support arise from several factors.

First, stressors that directly affect a particular individual, such as unemployment or conjugal bereavement, often have effects that ripple through a social network, causing would-be supporters to experience distress themselves (Kessler & McLeod, 1984; Rook, Dooley & Catalano, 1991; Thompson & Vaux, 1986). Wives of unemployed men, for example, have been found to suffer from psychological distress of a magnitude comparable to that experienced by women who themselves have lost a job (e.g., Rook, Dooley & Catalano, 1991). Evidence of the adverse effects of indirectly experienced stressors, or "network events" (Kessler & McLeod, 1984; Kessler, McLeod & Wethington, 1985; Riley & Eckenrode, 1986), has emerged in a growing number of empirical studies (e.g, Atkinson, Liem & Liem, 1986; Dew, Bromet & Schulbert, 1987; Kessler & McLeod, 1984; Kessler, McLeod & Wethington, 1985; Riley & Eckenrode, 1986; Rook, Dooley & Catalano, 1991). Such "contagion of stress" can interfere with the ability of would-be supporters to provide effective social support (Riley & Eckenrode, 1986).

Second, network members who lack experience dealing with stress of the type experienced by a distraught family member or friend often find it difficult to mount an effective response (Wortman & Lehman, 1985). A growing body of evidence indicates that people often report confusion and uncertainty in attempting to respond supportively to network members who have suffered a serious stressful event that falls outside the realm of their own personal experience (e.g., Wortman & Lehman, 1985). For example, friends of parents with a terminally ill child in one study provided poignant accounts of their awkwardness in attempting to express their concern or to offer suitable assistance (Chesler & Barbarin, 1984). Moreover, even when would-be helpers have good ideas about how to provide aid or comfort to a distressed network member, anxiety appears to interfere with their ability to act effectively on their help-giving intentions, causing their gestures of support to be clumsier or less sensitive than desired (Lehman, Ellard & Wortman, 1986).

Misguided conceptions of how people should cope with life crises also can limit the quantity and quality of support that flows from a social network (Wortman & Silver, 1989). Widespread but unsubstantiated beliefs about the grieving process, for example, can lead people to withhold support from the bereaved or to disapprove of their coping efforts. Cancer patients and patients with other serious conditions similarly have reported that family members and friends often appear to shun discussion of the patients' fears and sorrows or to disapprove of the patients' pace and style of coping (Dunkel-Schetter, 1984; Manne & Zautra, 1989; Revenson et al., 1991).

A fourth factor that can constrain the support available from a social network stems from a tendency for people to become over-involved in a family member's recovery from an illness or other life crisis, such as a heart attack (e.g., Coyne &

Smith, 1991) or onset of mental illness (e.g., Vaughn & Leff, 1976a,b). This over-involvement is particularly likely to emerge in situations that require long-term caregiving and substantial realignment of familial roles. Support providers tend to feel responsible for alleviating their family member's distress or illness, experience a strong need for the family member to improve, become frustrated by lack of improvement, become critical or demanding of the family member, and suffer flagging morale that is communicated to the family member (Coyne, Wortman & Lehman, 1988). This sequence of events obviously has the potential to aggravate rather than alleviate the ill person's distress and to undermine the course of recovery.

Finally, although most of the limitations described thus far stem largely from good intentions gone awry, it is important to recognize that good intentions do not inevitably abound in informal social networks. Network members can add to a stressed person's emotional distress though actions that are plainly critical, competitive, exploitative, or otherwise motivated by self-interest (see review by Rook, 1992). Some empirical work, for example, has treated network conflict as a stressor in its own right that exacerbates the effects of other problems that a person may be experiencing (e.g., Kiecolt-Glaser, Dyer & Shuttleworth, 1988; Manne & Zautra, 1989; Okun, Melichar & Hill, 1990). Unpleasant interactions with network members generally occur less often than do supportive interactions, but they appear capable of provoking considerable distress when they do occur (Rook, 1992). The fact that naturally occurring social relationships sometimes fail to provide needed support, or worse, provoke conflict and distress, provides a rationale for interventions designed to improve these relationships or to develop new relationships that can serve as sources of support.

GENERAL CONSIDERATIONS IN PLANNING SUPPORT INTERVENTIONS

Our basic recommendation is that support interventions should be based upon knowledge of the functions served by social ties, coupled with an assessment of what is missing in the social life of targeted persons. While this might seem to be a reasonable strategy, we suspect that the planners of support interventions typically do not approach their task in this way. A common belief is that providing support means offering empathic understanding after listening to people talk about their problems. This interpretation of how support should be administered is probably borrowed from clinical practice and traditions associated with psychotherapeutic helping. We would argue, however, that the process of providing support is much more complex. It makes little sense to intervene without knowing what social functions are needed or considering whether the format for providing support might in itself cause additional problems.

Consider the research by Ireys et al. (1990) as an example of some of the difficulties encountered in designing a support intervention based on a problem-disclosure model of helping. The initial plan in this work was to develop a support program for mothers of children with serious chronic illnesses by training a group of lay helpers who were called "family advocates". The advocates were to function as empathic supporters who encouraged problem discussions. They were then to assist families in identifying and using available services to deal with these problems. The program was quickly changed, however, as it became apparent that a negative social comparison process was being engendered. The mothers interpreted the offered help as a sign of their own incompetence. They concluded that the advocates, who had similar problem children, were coping more effectively than they were because the advocates had been recruited by the project to provide help to others.

A major challenge, then, is to find ways to constitute support activities that avoid demeaning help recipients by casting them in the role of incompetent or ineffective copers. Within ongoing social relationships, exchanges of support involve reciprocal and interdependent helper and helpee roles. Understanding these features of indigenous support functions becomes important in deciding whether, and in what ways, gaps in indigenous support might be remedied.

Table 28.2 describes a set of important factors that should be assessed by planners of support interventions. We will illustrate how these factors might guide the planning of support interventions by describing a current project on which we are both collaborating. Because this work is just beginning, we have no data about the project's ultimate outcome, but we can share our thoughts about how the planned support interventions should be conceptualized and designed.

An In-progress Example

We are working in a populous county in California that has a large proportion of south-east Asian and Hispanic residents as part of its mental health catchment area. The Asian group, which is the initial focus of the research project, is primarily of Vietnamese background. Many of these individuals came to this country after America's withdrawal from military involvement in South Vietnam. Language and cultural differences have made it difficult to provide services to these groups. It has been estimated that 80% of Vietnamese families in the county continue to speak their native language at home, with 50% of the entire group being linguistically isolated, i.e., unable to conduct daily affairs outside of the Vietnamese-speaking community (I. Niem, personal communication).

A major goal of the project with which we are associated is to provide mental health services to individuals with chronic mental illness. The standard treatment for severe mental disorder at county and medical school facilities involves supervised administration of one of several anti-psychotic medications. One such drug, Clozopine, demonstrates a significant symptom improvement rate of approximately 70–80%. Unfortunately, about half of Asian mental patients terminate treatment prematurely, while the dropout rate for Caucasian patients is only about 18% (S.G. Potkin, personal communication).

Mental health personnel working with these patients believe that family influ-

Table 28.2   Factors to consider in planning support interventions

Orienting perspective: why is intervention being considered?
  What is the individual trying to accomplish?
  Can others help in reaching these goals?
  What stressors are impeding progress toward these goals?

Social integration
  What social ties exist?
  Are additional ties desired and/or would they be useful?
  Are there factors impeding the helpfulness of existing ties, such as:
    —network members' unfamiliarity with the impinging stressor
    —shared emotional impact of the stressful event on network members
    —network members' lack of skill or ability in maintaining supportive ties
    —a history of conflict and poor relationships with network members
  Can indigenous network members be helped to provide greater support, or are new
    "grafted" relationships needed?

Development and maintenance of identity and esteem
  Role availability
    Does the individual have the opportunity to engage in socially useful activities?
  Role competence
    Does the individual perform role activities in a competent manner?
    Are existing ties and participation in meaningful social roles a source of esteem and
      satisfaction?
    Do negative self-schemas prevent the individual from recognizing and obtaining
      gratification from competent role performances?

Affect regulation
  Network activities that relieve distress and/or increase positive affect
    Are there network members available for companionship, participation in
      pleasurable activities or respite from chronic stressors?

Coping assistance
  Does the individual need help in coping with impinging stressors, and if so, what
    type of help is needed?
    —aid in formulating or socially validating an effective action plan
    —practical help or material aid
    —affect regulation, ie, help in dealing with the emotional concomitants of stressful
      events
  Do cultural practices advocated by network members conflict with effective coping?

Social control
  Does the individual have social ties that encourage responsible self-care and
    discourage self-destructive or health-compromising behavior?
  Does the individual have access to social roles that require and reward stable,
    responsible behavior and that discourage unstable, risk-taking behavior?

ences contribute to the high termination rate among Vietnamese patients (I.
Niem, personal communication). Vietnamese family life is very close, and Vietnamese families believe that it is their responsibility to be intimately involved in
the treatment and care of needy family members. Yet, traditional views of mental
disorder held by these family members sometimes interfere with treatment. For
example, among the Vietnamese, mental disorder is thought to reflect badly on

the family name, jeopardizing the marriage prospects of family members. As a result, patients sometimes are hidden, and their disorder is not acknowledged. Furthermore, Western medical practices are not always understood or appreciated. For example "medicine" is viewed with suspicion if it produces negative side effects, yet such complications are extremely common to the various antipsychotic drugs. Similarly, the practice of drawing blood periodically to monitor medication dosages is not easily accepted. Empirical data are not yet available to confirm these hypotheses about the reasons for early termination from treatment, but the fact of early termination is well documented and is a cause for concern among treatment personnel.

What sort of education or support could be provided to Vietnamese psychiatric patients and their families to increase treatment compliance? Would family members benefit from an improved understanding of the nature of mental disorder and help in patient management? Research conducted with other populations suggests that they would (Mueser & Glynn, 1995; Norbeck et al., 1991), but observations from the county clinics indicate that very few Vietnamese families actually attend educational or therapeutic sessions. Thus, the task is to find ways to provide the needed support in a cultural and social context that families would accept.

To design such an intervention, we believe that we must first obtain a better understanding of the conduct of social relations in the local Vietnamese culture. In particular, we want to understand the typical stressors that impinge on the lives of patients and family members, their manner of coping with these stressors, and the support functions already provided by existing indigenous networks (see Table 28.1 for the list of theoretical functions and Table 28.2 for their intervention implications).

Following this outline, we would want to know the stressors experienced by Vietnamese patients and their families—for example, financial problems, difficulties in employment, acculturation strains, social isolation, strains associated with monitoring patient conduct, etc. We would want to assess how patients and family members view these problems and typically cope with them. It is also important to determine the goals toward which patients and family members are striving, and whether help can be provided in reaching these goals. For example, is job training for a family member or the patient a realistic goal, and are there barriers (e.g., language, education) that need to be overcome in order to reach that goal? If family caretakers report stress associated with constant supervision of patient behavior, would they accept respite care for the patient, and what conditions would make this a viable service (e.g., cost, care at home or in a supervised facility, the status and training of the respite care workers, etc.)

Table 28.2 lists a number of additional factors that should be assessed in planning an intervention. For example, in our project, it would be important to determine the extent of family isolation and whether having a mentally ill family member contributed significantly to that isolation. Furthermore, it would matter whether reduced social contact arose from the shame associated with having a mentally ill family member or from aspects of the patient's behavior that caused others to withdraw. It would also be important to assess the source of any criticism and conflict that might be occurring to know who should be included in the intervention. For example, other children in the family might resent the attention given to their psychiatrically ill sibling, and accuse their parents of favoring or indulging the patient. The content of the intervention also would vary as a function of the problems uncovered. If increased knowledge or attitude change were needed, intervention might emphasize discussions about the nature of mental illness and attempts to normalize or de-stigmatize the phenomenon. Such an educationally oriented program might be targeted to family members, patients, or members of the wider community. But an intervention also could be focused more directly on helping the patient achieve greater independence through skill training, better medication control, or reducing excessive caretaker concern and worry.

As Table 28.2 indicates, it also is important to consider the competencies, positive activities, and meaningful social roles that already exist, or that could be established, from which patients and family members might draw esteem and satisfaction. For example, it would not be unreasonable to consider whether a patient with creative talents might obtain full or part-time employment, or whether these talents might be used constructively in other ways. One tends not to think of competencies when thinking about mental patients, but should dormant talents exist, they could be a considerable source of esteem and satisfaction.

Increases in social competencies and useful social roles also can occur through increased participation in social and community organizations. It is important to assess the availability of such organizations and whether patients and/or family members could be linked to these indigenous resources. Family members might initially be reluctant to ask others for help but, as Silka & Tip (1994) note, south-east Asian culture emphasizes communal values and activities, so mutual aid organizations represent a culturally appropriate helping modality. This contrasts with a more Western psychotherapeutic practice of relying on helping strategies that target the individual in isolation from the broader community. They also note that, among south-east Asians, problems often are not conceptualized in intrapsychic terms, neither is recovery expected to occur by talking about problems to a person outside of the family. This underscores an alternative intervention strategy focused on the mastery of real-life problems (jobs, language training, etc.) and the competencies needed to overcome these external barriers.

CONCLUSION: REFLECTIONS ON THE SCOPE OF SUPPORT INTERVENTIONS

Some might argue that suggestions such as these, while good ideas, stretch the meaning of the term "support". After all, why should providing social skills training, or facilitating the acquisition of better English language skills, or helping an individual engage in productive, esteem-building activities fall within the "support" rubric? It is our view that some of the ambiguity in the field occurs, not only because support definitions are too broad, but because they are atheoretical. Objective markers of social integration (e.g., number of ties) or subjective perceptions of "supportiveness" miss the point if theoretical functions represented by these measures are ignored. Being embedded in a large social network can enhance a sense of self-worth and belonging, but it can also be a stifling experience that places family obligations above individual initiative and happiness. For example, reflecting the dialectic between support and social control noted earlier, it is very possible that the Vietnamese mental patients in our example do not need closer family ties, but less family interference or attempts to control their behavior.

We believe that the solution to these dilemmas is to articulate more clearly the specific goals to be accomplished by any planned intervention. For example, what is to be accomplished by introducing a friend or companion to an individual, and why is that sort of help needed? Thinking in this way moves our conception of "support" toward an emphasis on the functions of social encounters. This is what Heller, Price & Hogg (1990; p. 484) had in mind when they stated that an activity or relationship should be considered supportive "if it fosters the development of competence, esteem, and a sense of belonging through the actual or anticipated exchange of tangible or psychosocial resources". We concur with this definition but would extend it to include a focus on the social structures that are part of ongoing community life and that provide the foundation from which social relationships and support functions typically arise.

Chapter 29

Interpersonal Relationship Processes in Individual and Group Psychotherapy

Brent Mallinckrodt
University of Oregon, Eugene, OR, USA

Several graduate students were overheard discussing what noted psychologists believed about the secret to enduring happiness. One student, paraphrasing a quote attributed to Freud, stated that the founder of psychoanalysis maintained the secret of happiness "is to love and work well". A second student responded that Freud was on the right track, but she was convinced that he had confused the essential elements. A much more important secret to happiness, proclaimed this student, is knowing that "to love well is work!" In taking up the topic of psychotherapy this chapter will remain close to the wisdom expressed by my second student friend.

Much of what a therapist does can be described as assisting clients with the hard work of loving well. A large proportion of psychotherapy, sometimes indirectly and often directly, has the aim of improving clients' interpersonal functioning. Among these goals are: achieving healthy balance in ties with kin; recruiting and establishing a network of supportive friends; exploration of self-identity in transaction with others; expanding one's capacity for intimacy and mutuality; communicating emotional needs; developing satisfying close romantic attachments and fulfilling sexual relationships based on a partnership of mutual growth; learning to nurture healthy attachments in one's own children; and finally, managing conflict, disappointment and loss in any of these relationships.

The number of therapists who describe themselves as practicing a variant of "interpersonal" psychotherapy has grown rapidly in the past decade. This approach to individual and group therapy is the special focus of this chapter.

Handbook of Personal Relationships, 2nd edn. Edited by Steve Duck.
© 1997 John Wiley & Sons Ltd.

Because no formal, mutually agreed definition of interpersonal therapy exists, for the purpose of selecting research for this review I have adopted the following working definition:

> Interpersonal approaches to psychotherapy (a) aim to improve the client's functioning in current or prospective close personal relationships, and (b) make deliberate use of the psychotherapy relationship as a means of facilitating client change needed to achieve these goals.

Because clients seek therapy for many reasons other then improving their personal relationships, many presenting problems fall outside this definition (e.g. bereavement). In addition, not all approaches that improve interpersonal functioning make explicit use of the therapeutic relationship as a vehicle for facilitating change. Thus, a number of important approaches and theories of therapy fall outside this working definition of "interpersonal". All approaches that are included manifest two central themes following from the definition above, namely, that therapy is *about* relationships and that therapy *is* a relationship. The purpose of this chapter is to review major trends during the past 8 years in individual and group interpersonal therapy research and theory related to these two themes.

The beginnings of the interpersonal approach can be traced to psychodynamic theorists who broke with orthodox psychoanalysis by emphasizing the importance of interpersonal relationships for psychological development. Among these were Horney (1950) and Sullivan (1953). Sullivan's work has been particularly influential because it stressed the parent–child relationship as the foundation for later close personal relationships, and described established patterns of relating to others as essentially strategies for managing anxiety. Interpersonal psychotherapy was further advanced by a number of object relations theorists (for reviews, see Anchin & Kiesler, 1982; Greenberg & Mitchell, 1983). Many current interpersonal training texts still exhibit a strong psychodynamic and object relations influence (Klerman et al., 1984; Luborsky, 1984; Strupp & Binder, 1984). Others are more broadly eclectic, for example, incorporating family systems theory (Teyber, 1992) or cognitive theory (Safran & Segal, 1990).

Figure 29.1 presents a model intended to organize the large body of research that meets the inclusion criteria for this chapter. The "Social Competencies Interpersonal Process" (SCIP) model is my attempt to depict in a single organizing scheme linkages between several of the most influential developments in interpersonally oriented psychotherapy and research on close personal relationships. I am keenly aware of Duck's (1990) admonition that writers who propose such a "box and arrow" model must pay as much descriptive attention to the arrows as the boxes. In other words, the *processes* whereby the proposed constructs influence one another are at least as important as the static states depicted by the constructs alone. Research reviewed in this chapter is organized around the arrows depicted in Figure 29.1, which are given two-letter designations to indicate proposed causal links between elements of the model.

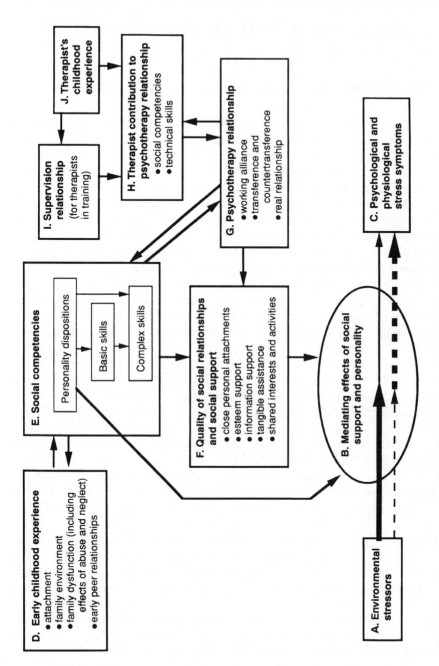

Figure 29.1 Social competencies interpersonal process model of psychotherapy

AN INTERPERSONAL VIEW OF WHAT CLIENTS BRING TO THERAPY

A Model of Stress and Coping

The SCIP model begins with the connection between environmental stressors (A) and the psychological and physiological symptoms of these accumulated stressors (C). Only two sets of the many possible mediating variables are included in the SCIP model, namely, the effects of social support and personality disposition. These mediating effects are shown with a circle in Figure 29.1 to depict a process rather than a static state. The heavy top arrow (A → C) is shown reduced in size as it passes through this mediating process to depict "buffering effects" of social support that ameliorate some of the detrimental effects of stressors. Also depicted are the effects of personality disposition that have similar beneficial effects. Because research suggests that well-intentioned offers of support may sometimes have harmful effects (Lehman, Ellard & Wortman, 1986), and some personality dispositions exacerbate the impact of a stressor, Figure 29.1 includes a second dashed A → C arrow that grows in width to depict mediating effects that tend to increase the impact of a stressor.

A high quality social network provides social support that mediates the impact of stressors (F → B). Research suggests that social support buffering effects are most likely to occur when a particular functional type of social support is well-matched to the coping demands of a particular stressor (Cohen & Wills, 1985; Cutrona & Russell, 1990). Following the Social Provisions model developed by Weiss (1974) and elaborated by Cutrona & Russell (1990), Figure 29.1 lists five functional types of social support (box F) that may have buffering effects. Personality variables, for example, cognitive appraisal (Lazarus & Folkman, 1984) also play an important role in determining the magnitude of psychological or physiological stress symptoms (E → B).

Personality, social support, and stressors interact in complex ways that can not be depicted by a single arrow in Figure 29.1. A circle is used for element B the SCIP model to indicate that personality variables interact with social support to produce mediating effects on the stressor–stress symptom relationship. The positive effects of these interactions are often noted, but it is important to also consider the negative effects of poor quality social relationships. An F → C arrow is not drawn directly from social relationships to stress symptoms because research suggests that the negative impact of factors such as relationship conflict are also mediated by personality dispositions. For example, attachment style in adult romantic relationships may influence relationship functioning (Carnelley, Pietromonaco & Jaffe, 1994) and may mediate levels of post-divorce distress (Berman, 1988).

Social Competencies as Determinants of Relationship Quality (E → F)

Because interpersonal therapists view the quality of social relationships as a focus for intervention, a major focus of research interest is the determinants of relationship quality, perhaps especially satisfaction with available social support. In early studies, social support was often characterized as exclusively a property of the environment—either more or less available. However, increasing evidence points to the importance of individual differences in one's ability to make use of available support. For example, Sarason, Sarason & Shearin (1986) found conversation partners who rated themselves higher in social support were rated by independent judges as more socially skilled and interpersonally attractive. In another study, persons who rated themselves higher in social support were rated by dyad partners as more socially skilled, and by trained raters as more skilled and attractive (Sarason et al., 1985). Thus, levels of social support may be determined, in part, by trait-like factors such as interpersonal attractiveness as well as individual differences in social skills.

The SCIP model proposed in Figure 29.1 uses the term "social competencies" to refer to all the factors within an individual that influence relationship quality. It may be useful to distinguish between three kinds of social competencies: basic skills, complex skills, and personality dispositions. Basic skills are behaviors such as maintaining appropriate eye contact, conversational topic-following, or sensitivity to non-verbal communication (Duck, 1991), that can be demonstrated during a relatively brief observing interval (e.g., less than 1 hour). Basic skills are integrated into more complex skills that can only be applied with observable results on a time scale of days and months in a relationship. Complex skills include the capacity for emotional intimacy, the ability to form romantic attachments or nurture and maintain a supportive friendship (Prager, 1995). Clearly, drawing a line at skills that could be fully demonstrated in less than 1 hour is somewhat arbitrary, but does have important implications for psychotherapists who, of course, generally work in 1-hour time units.

The third component of social competencies is personality disposition. These dispositions influence the acquisition of basic or complex skills, and influence the circumstances in which an acquired skill is used. For example, research suggests there are distinct enduring patterns of adult attachment in close personal relationships that may be based on childhood attachment to caregivers (Berman & Sperling, 1994; Hazan & Shaver, 1994a,b). Adult attachment style may be considered a personality disposition characterized by differing patterns in preferences for relationship intimacy and different approaches for maintaining these preferences. Personality dispositions also include cognitive "interpersonal schemas", composed of expectations about relationships and preferred modes of coping with threats to a particular relationship (Safran & Segal, 1990). Other personality dispositions that have been linked to the quality of social relationships are self-efficacy for social outcomes and "object relations" capacity (Mallinckrodt, McCreary & Robertson, 1995; Sherer & Adams, 1983).

Early Family Environment and Development of Social Competencies (D → E)

Many interpersonal therapists are strongly influenced by the notion that one's early family environment has an important influence on the development of social competencies and quality of adult relationships. Recent reviews of the growing number of studies in this area present convincing evidence that attachment relationships in infancy have a profound influence on the development of social competencies in children and the quality of their peer interactions (Coble, Gantt & Mallinckrodt, in press) and that childhood attachment to caregivers also has a strong influence on adult personal relationships (Hazan & Shaver, 1994a,b; Rothbard & Shaver, 1994). Memories of parental bonds have been associated with self-efficacy in social relationships (Mallinckrodt, 1992), social support (Flaherty & Richman, 1986; Mallinckrodt, 1992; Sarason, Sarason & Shearin, 1986), and capacity for intimacy, emotional self-awareness and social network size (Mallinckrodt, McCreary & Robertson, 1995).

Attachment theory holds that cognitive social schemas or "working models" of others as either generally benevolent and helpful or disappointing and harmful, and of the self as either the type of person worthy of comfort and care, or unworthy, form quite early in development and are based on the consistency of caregivers responsiveness to the emotional and physical needs of a young child, together with the internalized perceptions of the value with which the child is regarded. Working models become increasingly resistant to change as development proceeds, because new information that does not fit into existing structures is difficult to process and tends to be defensively excluded (Bowlby, 1969, 1973; Bretherton, 1985). Social competencies developed through the infant–caregiver attachment appear to have a strong influence on the child's first peer friendships. Research suggests that early peer relationships and developing social competencies are reciprocally related (D → E, E → D) in a manner that might be described as "the rich get richer, and the poor, poorer" (Coble, Gantt & Mallinckrodt, in press; Shulman, Elicker & Sroufe, 1994).

INDIVIDUAL PSYCHOTHERAPY

Client Symptoms Viewed as Interpersonal Problems

Psychotherapy begins with assessment of the client and the presenting problem for which help is sought. In other words, applying the framework of the SCIP model, how do deficits in social competencies influence the quality of a client's relationships, and how is the quality of a client's relationships related to the presenting problem that prompted the client to seek help? Analysis of the natural language persons use to describe their presenting problems suggests that their descriptions often contain two components, complaints about physiological *symptoms* such as anxiety, depression, insomnia or chronic fatigue, and descriptions of interpersonal *problems* such as struggles with intimacy, or painful conflict with others (Horowitz, 1979). Until recently, cataloging and describing symptoms has received much more research attention than methods of measuring and categorizing client interpersonal problems (Horowitz & Vitkus, 1986). The "Inventory of Interpersonal Problems" (IIP) is based on clients' natural language descriptions, and was developed to assess presenting problems in terms of difficulties in interpersonal relationships (Horowitz et al., 1988).

The IIP can be very useful for assessing how deficits in social competencies affect the quality of social relationships (E → F). Research suggests that clients at intake whose complaints are expressed more as interpersonal problems rather than psychological symptoms are judged more suitable for brief therapy and, if accepted for treatment, are less likely to prematurely end their therapy. Clients' self-reported improvement in interpersonal functioning (measured by changes in IIP scores) was also significantly correlated with therapists' ratings of improvement (Horowitz et al., 1988). Horowitz et al. (1988) found that some symptom clusters, such as the desire to be more assertive, were discussed often in therapy and showed marked improvement, whereas others, such as the desire to increase intimacy, although often discussed, showed little improvement in brief therapy. Research with the IIP also suggests that clients' ability to describe significant others clearly may be related to their interpersonal problems as well. Clients whose presenting problems contained a high proportion of interpersonal complaints, relative to psychological symptoms, provided the clearest and most specific descriptions of their parents, whereas clients with a high proportion of complaints of psychological symptoms tended to describe their parents in more vague, less specific terms (Horowitz, Rosenberg & Kalehzan, 1992).

Taken together, these studies provide support for the conventional wisdom that clients who tend to "somaticize" their interpersonal problems are poor candidates for brief therapy. Results suggest that this may be true, in part, because clients who express problems in terms of physical complaints lack important social competencies. These deficits may include complex skills such as the ability to think about and describe persons in clear conceptually rich terms that capture relationship nuances. Other research suggests that personality dispositions may also be associated with the inability to describe others clearly. Adults whose style of attachment in close relationships is detached and distant tend to describe themselves in vague terms, whereas those with enmeshed adult attachment styles describe themselves with personal schemas that contain contradictory elements (Horowitz, 1994; Horowitz, Rosenberg & Bartholomew, 1993). Underlying these deficits for clients with the most extreme tendencies to somaticize may also be deficits in basic skills, such as appropriate conversational topic-following and non-verbal behavior.

A second, independent line of research suggests that the interpersonal behavior of depressed persons may engender negative reactions in others that increases the likelihood of rejection by potential relationship partners (Coyne, Burchill & Stiles, 1990; Segrin, 1993). Taking these findings together with evidence of continuity of attachment patterns from early experience through adulthood, we see the beginnings of empirical support for causal linkages between early family experience, social competencies of all three types, and the quality of adult relationships (D → E → F).

Case Conceptualization

If the first step in psychotherapy, assessment, relates to questions of *what* are the client's problems, the next step, case conceptualization, relates to questions about *why* the problem has developed and *how* it is maintained. The interpersonal circumplex, or "Interpersonal Circle" model (Benjamin, 1994; Kiesler, 1983; Leary, 1957; Wiggins, 1982; among others) has become a remarkably useful tool in case conceptualization for psychotherapy researchers. In its simplest form the model postulates two dimensions of interpersonal behavior, one of *control* anchored by dominant vs. submissive behavior, and a dimension of *affiliation*, anchored by friendly vs. hostile behavior. (Note that "behavior" when used by psychotherapy researchers applying the circumplex model most often refers to *verbal* behavior.)

These two orthogonal dimensions form the axes of a two-dimensional interpersonal space. Elaborations of this basic model provide for intermediate combinations (e.g., friendly-submissive, friendly-dominant) that anchor the circumference of the circumplex (Horowitz, Rosenberg & Bartholomew, 1993; Kiesler, 1983). The rules of circumplex complementarity (Carson, 1969; Kiesler, 1983) hold that interacting dyad partners are motivated to conform to one another's self-presentation on both the control and affiliation dimensions in the following way: a verbal stimulus on the affiliation dimension pulls for a similar response on the affiliation dimension (i.e., friendly begets friendly, and hostile begets hostile), whereas a given stimulus on the control dimension pulls for a reciprocal response on that dimension (i.e., dominant begets submissive, and *vice versa*). Thus, applying these rules to the intermediate points on the Horowitz, Rosenberg & Bartholomew (1993) model, an "advise" stimulus is likely to be met with a "defer" response, and a "scold" stimulus is likely to be met with a "sulk" response. Departures from complementarity introduce tension into the relationship, for example, when a dominant stimulus is met with an equally dominant response, or when the offer of advice is met with a sullen sulk.

Reviewing the then available research, Orford (1986) concluded there was only mixed support for complementarity in interpersonal interactions. Contrary to the model's predictions, friendly-dominant responses tend to follow both friendly-dominant and hostile-submissive responses; and hostile-dominant behaviors are very often met with hostile-dominant responses. Orford stressed the role of contextual factors, such as the relative status and role of the dyad partners, as well as the setting in determining whether or not the rules of complementarity are accurate predictors of the transaction.

The interpersonal approach to case conceptualization (Horowitz & Vitkus, 1986) holds that some psychological problems tend to be self-perpetuating. For example, depression may involve a lack of assertiveness and pervasive sense of powerlessness. Some evidence suggests that the interpersonal behavior of depressed persons lies predominantly in the submissive half of the interpersonal circumplex (Schreiber, 1984, cited in Horowitz & Vitkus, 1986). Invoking the principles of complementarity, we can see that this behavior tends to invite strongly dominant responses from others who interact with depressed persons. Thus, depressed persons may unwittingly engage in interpersonal behavior that maintains their sense of helplessness (Horowitz & Vitkus, 1986).

Developments in the application of circumplex theory have been used to refine case conceptualization. Clients' difficulties in doing the hard work of "loving well" can be viewed as a lack of flexibility in their interpersonal responses. Sectors of the circumplex can be considered categories of social competencies. Thus, healthy interpersonal functioning can be defined as the ability to engage in behaviors in any sector of the circumplex that an ongoing interaction may require, whereas persons with interpersonal difficulties tend to behave in inflexible and extreme patterns (Wiggins, 1982). Van Denburg and Kiesler (1993) found some evidence to suggest that the behavior of normal volunteers became more extreme in the direction of their characteristic friendly-submissive pattern when exposed to a stressful interview, and also displayed less diversity of responses in other segments of the circumplex. Benjamin (1994), whose "Structural Analysis of Social Behavior" (SASB) model features three two-dimensional circumplex surfaces, argues that "flexibility appropriate to context" (p. 286) is the hallmark of healthy interpersonal functioning. Thus, an assessment of *context* and characteristic patterns of response are both necessary for case conceptualization. Research suggests conditions such as borderline or antisocial personality disorder can be diagnosed and differentiated according to predictable patterns in the inflexibility of a client's interpersonal functioning (Benjamin, 1993, 1994; Pincus & Wiggins, 1990).

Other approaches to case conceptualization do not rely on circumplex models, but are nevertheless also based on the notion that client dysfunction can be viewed from the perspective of maladaptive, inflexible patterns of interpersonal behavior. The Core Conflictual Relationship Theme (CCRT) is perhaps the best known of several methods that use client narrative descriptions of their relationships with significant others as base data (Crits-Christoph et al., 1987). In this method transcripts of "relationship episodes", in which the client describes a reasonably complete interaction with the significant other, are evaluated by trained judges. Episodes are scanned for the following patterns: (1) the client's wishes or needs from the relationship partner; (2) how the partner typically responds; (3) how the client responds to this response. The initial tests of the CCRT method showed that judges could reach a high level of consensus about what constituted an acceptable relationship episode from the stream of a client's ongoing session dialog, and judges could reach an acceptable level of consensus about reoccurring themes in the client's responses, especially to wishes that were not gratified (Crits-Christoph et al., 1987).

Some themes appear so frequently that a standard set of CCRT categories has been developed. For example, in one sequence of standard CCRT categories a client may (a) wish "to be independent", (b) perceive that others "are rejecting", and (c) respond by "feeling depressed". Research with a sample of over 30 clients seen in brief psychodynamically-oriented psychotherapy (Luborsky, Barber & Diguer, 1992) suggests that narratives describing interpersonal relationships occur frequently (a mean of four per session); episodes are introduced by specific semantic markers ("I'd like to tell you about Jill . . ."), the telling of a single narrative lasts about 4–6 minutes, about 30% of all narratives concern one's intimate relationship partner, an additional 25% are about a member of one's family, and significant symptom relief and positive outcome are associated with a decrease in the pervasiveness of a theme, that is, a theme that at first occurred in a high percentage of all narratives decreases in frequency over the course of therapy.

Concerning the narrative themes themselves, the most common wishes were "to be close and accepted", "to be loved and understood", or "to assert self and to be independent". Perhaps not surprisingly, the most common themes of responses from others to these wishes were negative in the sense that the original need is frustrated or wish not met (Luborsky & Crits-Christoph, 1990). In other studies clients have been found to tell a similarly high proportion of negative relationship narratives (73% of the total) to a person whom they knew was not a therapist (Luborsky & Crits-Christoph, 1990). Apparently, unmet needs in relationships are more memorable and salient for clients in their descriptions to both therapists and others, supporting the contention that relationships are best considered "unfinished business" (Duck, 1990).

Importance of the Psychotherapy Relationship and its Components

Emphasis on the psychotherapy relationship follows logically from decades of psychotherapy research pointing to the conclusion that approaches to therapy with widely differing techniques are essentially equally effective (Stiles, Shapiro & Elliott, 1986). This conclusion spurred researchers to find a generic ingredient, active across nearly every therapy, responsible for facilitating change (Frank, 1979). The leading contender, and reigning champion in terms of research interest, has been the psychotherapy relationship. When a client begins therapy and this relationship is initiated, the therapist becomes another member of the client's social network and thus a potential source of social support. Some writers stress the similarities of the therapy relationship to other close personal relationships (Derlega et al., 1991), while others point out differences such as the inherent power imbalance and expected asymmetry of self-disclosure (Kottler, Sexton & Winston, 1994). The SCIP model acknowledges that therapists often directly provide support to clients (G → F). However, in practice many therapists are cautious about relying too strongly on the direct provision of support as a means of facilitating change. Therapists are cautious about fostering client dependency and, particularly therapists with an interpersonal orientation, view their direct provision of support as, at best, a temporary measure that may be necessary to stabilize and support a client until the work of improving social competencies can begin.

Gelso and Carter (1985, 1994), drawing from a psychodynamic tradition, provided a framework for understanding how this work is accomplished by describing three components of the therapeutic relationship that apply across a broad range of approaches. These are: (1) *the working alliance*, a collaborative tie forged between client and therapist based on emotional bonds of trust and mutual regard, together with agreement about the goals of therapy and tasks needed to reach the goals; (2) the *transference–countertransference configuration*, involving misperception of one member of the dyad by the other, often stemming from unresolved conflicts in previous close relationships; and (3) *the real relationship*, the distortion-free perceptions of one another that occur in ongoing therapy, which are not necessarily tied to agreement about goals or tasks or the emotional bond the develops between the participants.

The last two components of this model have received far less research attention then the working alliance. A meta-analysis of outcome studies suggests that the quality of the working alliance, assessed as early as the third session, accounts for at least 25% of the variance in eventual psychotherapy outcome, and perhaps nearer to 40% (Horvath, 1994; Horvath & Symonds, 1991). With the working alliance emerging as such a potentially powerful influence on psychotherapy outcome, it is not surprising that researchers in the last decade have turned their attention to the client variables that influence development of a productive therapy relationship.

Social Competency Influence on the Therapy Relationship (E → G)

In the search for client pre-therapy characteristics that influence development of the working alliance, the interpersonal circumplex has been a useful tool. Client patterns of interpersonal behavior that lack flexibility and tend toward the extremes of intensity in the hostile half of the circumplex are associated with poor working alliances (Kiesler & Watkins, 1989). Clients' problems in the friendly-submissive quadrant of the circumplex were found to be related to the development of productive working alliances, whereas problems located in the hostile-dominant quadrant were associated with poor working alliances (Muran et al., 1994). Research has linked other client social competencies to the development of productive working alliances, including quality of clients' personal relationships (Kokotovic & Tracey, 1990; Moras & Strupp, 1982), quality of social support (Mallinckrodt, 1991), object relations capacity (Piper et al., 1991b), and relations with family members (Kokotovic & Tracey, 1990).

These studies suggest that client social competency deficits interfere with development of the working alliance. Psychodynamic theorists (cf. Strupp &

Binder, 1984) maintain that transference occurs when this interference takes the form of specific conflictual, unresolved patterns that originally developed in a client's close personal relationships, become ingrained, and are now imposed (largely outside the client's awareness) on the psychotherapy relationship. Working models generalized from a client's attachment relationships have been suggested as one source of transference misperceptions (Mallinckrodt, Coble & Gantt, 1995b). The small number of studies investigating transference has increased recently. For example, an intensive case study suggested that conflictual themes involving the therapist gradually converged over the course of therapy to become more and more similar to the problematic themes evident with significant others in the client's life (Crits-Christoph, Demorest & Connolly, 1990).

Specific object relations deficits (Piper et al., 1991b), as well as lack of parental emotional responsiveness (Mallinckrodt, 1991; Mallinckrodt, Coble & Gantt, 1995a) have been linked to poor working alliance. Bowlby (1988a,b), in some of his last writings about attachment theory, speculated that the generalized expectations about others and beliefs of self that form "working models" in early attachment experience may profoundly influence the therapeutic relationship—which, he pointed out, shares important similarities to the caregiver–infant attachment. Mallinckrodt, Gantt and Coble (1995) tested these ideas by developing an instrument to measure the client's attachment to the therapist. Subscales that emerged from a factor analysis appeared to parallel observed patterns of infant (Ainsworth et al., 1978) and adult attachment (Bartholomew & Horowitz, 1991). Attachments to the therapist marked by hostility or by a preoccupation with the therapist and the therapist's other clients, were associated with lower client social competencies, and poorer client-rated working alliance than secure attachments to the therapist. Thus, this research suggests that client attachment history and adult attachment style may have an important influence on the therapy relationship. However, other research suggests that client's attachment style in adult close relationships is not related to their perceptions of the working alliance, but *does* predict their therapists' ratings of the alliance (Dolan, Arnkoff & Glass, 1993).

The Psychotherapy Relationship as a Vehicle for Change (G → E)

Many interpersonal therapists use unfolding difficulties in the therapy relationship as data for assessment and case conceptualization. Further, interpersonal therapists base their interventions on the belief that the influence of social competencies and the therapy relationship is bi-directional, that is, the relationship itself can serve as an important means of effecting client change. Approaches that emphasize the importance of the therapy relationship can be classified according to the extent they hold that the struggle to establish a productive relationship is all that is needed to facilitate change—in essence, all the client's most important problems in outside relationships can be resolved in the crucible of negotiating an ongoing relationship with the therapist, vs. approaches that maintain an optimal relationship is necessary for administering other techniques but not sufficient in itself (Gaston, 1990).

The last 8 years have seen an increase in studies of how the psychotherapy relationship influences client social competencies. Central to many of these studies has been the notion of the therapist being "an authentic chameleon" (Lazarus, 1993, p. 404), that is, planfully offering relationship conditions needed to produce change for the particular client at this point in the therapy. Stage models of therapy hold that in successful cases, early in therapy interpersonal complementarity is important to promote development of the working alliance. However, in the middle stage the therapist must break the established pattern by behaving in non-complementary ways that will induce clients to change, since the rules of complementarity will compel clients to respond in complementary ways to the changed presentation offered by the therapist. The final stage is marked by a return to complementary behavior as the clients patterns change (Tasca & McMullen, 1992; Tracey, 1993).

Research support for this stage model has been mixed. For example, therapist complementarity in the early stages of therapy in the hostile half of the interpersonal circumplex only was associated with more positive ratings of the working alliance for clients, and therapist complementarity in all quadrants of the circle was related to their own positive ratings of the alliance (Kiesler & Watkins, 1989). Thus, early in therapy it may be important for therapists to meet a client's hostile verbal behavior with hostile (confrontational) responses. In contrast, Tasca & McMullen (1992) distinguished between friendly vs. the unfriendly complementary responses and found that unfriendly complementary responses predicted poor therapeutic outcome. The predicted high–low–high pattern of complementarity across stages of successful therapy was not evident. Other research suggests that therapist friendly responses are associated with success, regardless of whether they are complementary, and that when a client's hostility is met with therapist counter-hostility, poor outcome is the likely result regardless of complementarity (Henry, Schacht & Strupp, 1986, 1990). Tracy (1993) criticized complementarity research for ignoring moderating variables such as context, different meanings ascribed to a friendly or hostile behavior, differences between manifest and latent levels of communication, and individual differences. When these moderating variables were included, Tracey (1994) found stronger evidence for interpersonal complementarity in a study of conversations in non-client volunteers. However, because of conceptual confusion, measurement difficulties and lack of empirical support, research interest in the complementarity-stage model may have passed its peak (Claiborn, 1993; Friedlander, 1993).

In contrast, a relatively new approach that emphasizes attempts to repair the inevitable weakening and breaches in the client–therapist working alliance shows early promise of stimulating considerable research interest (Safran, 1993). From this perspective, threats to the continuity of the working relationship are inevitable because the therapist can not possibly respond to the client with accurate empathy at all times, or meet all the client's expectations for their work together. The experience of having emotional needs frustrated and of significant others failing to empathically understand, when it occurs chronically early in childhood, may lead to maladaptive patterns for some persons that are at the core of their interpersonal problems. After an initial disappointment, if continued efforts to elicit the needed emotional response are met with continued disappointment, children learn that relationships are not flexible or negotiable (Tronick, 1989).

Safran (1993) notes that the inevitable empathic failures of the therapist are likely to evoke a similar pattern of responses for the client that were adaptive at an early time in life with a unresponsive caregiver, but are now causing difficulty in relationships with persons that are potentially more responsive. Therapists provide a corrective emotional experience when they demonstrate to their clients, repeatedly, that the therapeutic relationship is flexible and its terms are negotiable to an important degree. As a therapist and client work at managing conflict and disappointment in their relationship, the client gains valuable social competencies that early developmental experience did not provide.

Although the concept of the therapy relationship providing a corrective emotional experience is not new (Alexander & French, 1946), Safran's notions provide an innovative formulation that has just begun to stimulate empirical interest. Research suggests that adults who recall their parents as emotionally unresponsive (Mallinckrodt, 1992), or who survived familial sexual abuse (Mallinckrodt, McCreary & Robertson, 1995), have a lower sense of their own self-efficacy for modifying personal relationships. Intensive case study suggests that clients respond to perceived empathic failures of their therapists with one of two distinct patterns, overtly aggressive accusatory statements or passive withdrawal. Preliminary findings suggest that if therapists respond at these junctures by shifting the focus from the topic at hand to a here-and-now exploration of the relationship and the client's feelings (usually negative) toward the therapist, positive changes may follow'(Safran, Muran & Wallner-Samstag, 1994). Among these beneficial outcomes are an exploration of maladaptive patterns in the client's generalized expectations about self–other interactions.

Some research (Kivlighan & Schmitz, 1992) has confirmed that therapists' increased focus on the here-and-now, as well as a willingness to challenge the client's viewpoint, distinguishes working alliances that begin poorly, but improve, from those that remain poor. Other findings suggest that therapist interpretations to clients that most accurately depicted the client's core conflictual themes lead to improved working alliances, whereas mis-matched (i.e., mistaken) interpretations result in deteriorating alliances (Crits-Christoph, Barber & Kurcias, 1993). These studies suggest specific techniques that therapists can employ to repair inevitable breakdowns in their working relationships with clients. The findings are also consistent with the notion that attempts to repair and build an alliance help clients acquire critical social competencies.

It should be emphasized that "social competencies" in the SCIP model is a construct that includes a broad array of components. Thus, depending on the clients' needs, interpersonal therapists may use the psychotherapy relationship to: (1) teach clients basic social skills within a single session; (2) help them develop more complex skills over the course of therapy, for example, conflict management or emotional intimacy; or (3) undertake to modify basic aspects of personality, such as attachment style or interpersonal schemas. Often these tasks involve more than simply facilitating clients' learning new skills (as the term "social competencies" might suggest). Instead, therapists frequently must struggle first to help clients relinquish maladaptive patterns that may have been a long-standing part of their interpersonal relationships.

Therapist's Contribution to the Psychotherapy Relationship (H → G, G → H)

A large body of research has accumulated investigating individual technical skills therapists employ to produce specific client reactions (for a summary of one of the most extensive lines of this research, see Hill, 1992). Less is known about skills needed to develop and maintain the psychotherapy relationship *per se*, but we have seen in the preceding section that therapist technical skills may be important, as well as the ability to tolerate—even encourage—the expression of clients' hostile feelings toward the therapist. The SCIP model proposes that technical skills must be viewed in connection with the therapist's general social competencies in relationships, which are no less important than the client's social competencies in determining the quality of the therapeutic relationship.

The model also accounts for two-way effects of this influence in which each new therapeutic relationship tests and modifies the therapist's technical skills and social competencies. For example, research suggests that novice therapists, relative to experts, are equally able to form the emotional bond component of the working alliance, but that increasing experience is needed to reach agreement about the tasks of therapy, and high levels of experience are needed to forge an agreement about therapeutic goals with clients (Mallinckrodt & Nelson, 1991). Using sequential analysis of discourse, Reandeau & Wampold (1991) found that the highest quality working alliances were characterized by therapist high-power statements followed by client low-power/high-involvement messages, whereas the lowest quality alliances were characterized by much lower frequency of client high-involvement responses to the therapist high-power statements. Thus, it appears that therapists must cultivate the social competencies needed to engage their clients at a high level in the relationship, particularly when the therapist uses high-power strategies.

In recent years studies of therapist technical skills have been numerous, but few have focused specifically on the skills needed to facilitate a productive therapeutic relationship, and fewer still have investigated the role of a therapist's generalized competencies for building and maintaining relationships. The coming decade may herald a shift in that direction. Two relatively new lines of research have begun to break this ground. These are represented as the last two elements of the SCIP model, namely, the role of the supervision relationship for the therapist-in-training, and the role of the therapist's own early developmental experiences.

Influence of the Clinical Supervision Relationship (I → H)

Through the focused work of a relatively small number of investigators, research has accumulated about the importance of the relationship between supervisor and supervisee in the acquisition of therapist technical skills (for a review see Holloway, 1992). Of special interest to researchers in the field of personal relationships may be the concept of "parallel process" in supervision (Mueller, 1982; Mueller & Kell, 1972). Through this process important features of the supervisor–therapist relationship are transferred to the therapist–client relationship and similarly, over time, aspects of the psychotherapy relationship become manifest in the supervision relationship. For example, a session in which a client expresses feelings of being overwhelmed and pleads for help from the therapist may be followed by the therapist pleading for direct advice from the supervisor about how to handle this difficult case! Because parallel process is believed to operate in the reverse direction, a supervisor who seems cold and unconcerned to the therapist may prompt the therapist to remain emotionally withdrawn from the client. Very few studies have probed for the existence of parallel process, but preliminary findings suggest that aspects of the supervision relationship are mirrored in the psychotherapy relationship, and *vice versa* (Friedlander, Siegel & Brenock, 1989). Due to the prevalence of peer supervision and other forms of collegial consultation, the operation of parallel process is probably not limited only to students in training.

Importance of the Therapist's Childhood Experience (J → H, J → I)

Among the other influences on the supervision relationship may be the therapist's own childhood developmental experiences with caregivers, and internalized working models of others. Pistole & Watkins (1995) draw parallels between the supervision relationship and the help-seeking and proximity maintenance features of early attachment, which ideally provide young children with a "secure base" and facilitate exploration of the physical environment (Bowlby, 1988a). Future studies are needed to investigate how the supervision relationship provides an environment for therapists' self-exploration and the acquisition of relationship facilitation skills that can be used to improve a their working relationships with clients.

The concept of countertransference implies that therapists' early experience also directly influences their psychotherapy relationships. Empirically, this construct has been difficult to study. Therapist countertransference involves misperception of a current relationship with the client that are based on the therapist's past unresolved conflicts. Therefore, any attempt to measure countertransference (or transference) necessarily involves the difficulty of comparing a person's subjective perceptions with some objective, non-distorted standard (Greenberg, 1994). Therapy analogue methods have been used to present samples of therapists with standardized client stimuli. Withdrawal of involvement in the relationship seems to be a common therapist marker of countertransference (Robbins & Jolkovski, 1987). Fortunately, from the standpoint of graduate training this withdrawal effect tends to be attenuated in therapists who are highly sensitive to their own affective reactions to clients. Recent preliminary studies of actual psychotherapy suggest that therapists' own family history may in fact have an indirect influence on therapy outcome, mediated by the interpersonal process in sessions, perhaps especially the tendency to "disaffiliate" from certain clients (Hillard, Henry & Strupp, 1995).

GROUP PSYCHOTHERAPY

Active Ingredients in Group Therapy Derived from Relationship Processes

The pre-eminent model in the past decade of group psychotherapy research was advanced by Yalom (1985, 1995) who described a taxonomy of 11 therapeutic factors, which in turn represents a synthesis and elaboration of models developed by previous theorists (cf. Bloch & Crouch, 1985). Yalom describes the workings of interpersonal process therapy groups that have as principle aims improving clients' personal relationships. Briefly, the therapeutic factors Yalom described are: (1) *instillation of hope*, often provided by therapist reassurance and testimonials from other group members; (2) *universality*, a sense of relief as others self-disclose their concerns and a client realizes that problems once thought to be unique are in fact fairly common; (3) *information*; (4) *altruism*, increased self-worth derived from opportunities to help other group members; (5) *corrective recapitulation of the primary family group*; (6) *socialization* and (7) *imitation*, twin processes through which clients observe therapists and fellow group members, and adopt the functional social skills they witness; (8) *interpersonal learning*, receiving feedback from others about the effects of one's behavior, attempting to modify the behavior, and receiving feedback about effects of the change, (9) *group cohesiveness*, the corollary to the therapeutic relationship in individual therapy—cohesiveness involves client attraction for the group and willingness to participate in its tasks; (10) *catharsis*, an affectively charged release, especially useful if experienced in the here-and-now of the group and combined with insight; (11) *existential factors*, Yalom's perspective that in effective groups clients often confront basic questions about their own mortality and search for meaning.

Although some of these ingredients are present in individual therapy, for example, therapists working individually instill hope and help clients gain insight, the presence of other clients in the therapy group affords unique avenues for change. Universality, for example, is probably much more potent in group than individual therapy. Therapeutic transference, in which feelings and perceptions appropriate to an earlier relationship are mistakenly projected on to the therapist in individual therapy, is given a much wider range of possible expressions in group therapy. One such possibility is for the co-therapists, who often are a male–female dyad, and the other group members to offer the symbolic roles of parents and siblings for a group therapy client. Thus, the group environment may be perceived by the client to recapitulate important features of the primary family group, and becomes a stage on which the client inevitably re-enacts the drama of these earlier conflicts.

Therapy Group as Social Microcosm

Central to interpersonal theory is the notion that any significant difficulties a client experiences in personal relationships outside the therapy group will sooner or later be evident in relations the client has with other group members or the therapists. This concept of the group representing a "social microcosm" is derived from the concept of transference in individual therapy and leads Yalom, among others, to stress the importance of a therapist facilitating here-and-now interactions between clients in an unstructured group climate. It may seem counter-intuitive that clients complaining of great suffering in relationships with others are encouraged after a very short time in the group to relinquish their propensity to dwell on these extra-group relationships. Yalom maintains that shyness, struggles for acceptance, aggression, dominance, reactions to authority, self-defeating attempts to meet interpersonal needs and many other presenting problems, all bloom in full flower if the client feels sufficient cohesion to stay in the group and the therapist focuses on the here-and-now interactions between members.

After clients' dysfunctional patterns of interacting emerge in the microcosm of the group, feedback from group members and the therapists provides a key impetus for change. Clients are encouraged in the group to give up the norm of polite social discourse that proscribes commentary on how the social behavior of others impacts them. For example, a statement like, "When your tone sounds so cold and dismissing to me, I am afraid to tell you anything further about myself" might elicit astonished gasps in a casual conversation, but would be considered quite appropriate in many therapy groups. Because group therapy clients receive more accurate and uncensored feedback about the impact of their communication on others, and feedback about how new patterns they adopt lead to new reactions, the group provides an "interpersonal laboratory" for learning not available in any other close personal relationship.

Unfortunately, popular misconceptions abound that therapy groups are a kind of interpersonal abattoir in which a client's defenses are ruthlessly stripped away and intimate self-disclosures are wrung sequentially from each client, who is then relentlessly confronted. Quite the contrary, most group therapy theorists emphasize that cohesion and consistent support are necessary preconditions for client change. Clients are encouraged to offer as feedback genuine perceptions uncensored by the norms of polite social communication. However, other powerful compensating group norms are encouraged. For example, clients are encouraged to offer feedback only after it has been solicited by the potential recipient. Feedback is shaped to conform to rather strict conventions, for example, the norm of personal ownership of a perception rather than global accusation (e.g., "I feel rejected and dismissed by the way you just responded to me" vs. "You are a cold unfeeling bastard!"). Similarly, although the deepening of intimately personal self-disclosure between relative strangers is accelerated far beyond the pace of accepted norms in everyday life, countervailing substitute norms are encouraged in the therapy group, for example strict rules about confidentiality, and the admonition that all self-disclosure should be voluntary and never coerced by the therapist or group peer pressure (Corey, 1994; Yalom, 1985, 1995).

Research on the Therapeutic Factors

Unfortunately, few studies have examined aspects of the interpersonal model of group therapy described above. As measurement methods of the therapeutic factors have developed, for example based on Q-sort technology (Rohrbaugh & Bartels, 1975; Freedman & Hurley, 1980) or coding of critical incidents (Bloch et al., 1979), studies of the therapeutic factors have recently begun to accumulate. Some support has been found for the idea that therapeutic factors evoking a client's least well-developed interpersonal skills are rated by that client as the most crucial catalysts of change. The specific factors most responsible for therapeutic change may depend on personality characteristics such as affiliative or dominant tendencies (Kivlighan & Goldfine, 1991; Kivlighan & Mullison, 1988) which can be measured with the Inventory of Interpersonal Problems. Several stage models of the developmental tasks of interpersonal therapy groups have been proposed (cf. MacKenzie & Livesley, 1983). It has been proposed that the importance of a therapeutic factor, for example universality, waxes and wanes as the group evolves (Yalom, 1985), but research findings on this point are mixed (Kivlighan & Goldfine, 1991; Kivlighan & Mullison, 1988).

A meta-analytic review of non-therapy group research suggested cohesion is composed of three relatively independent elements, interpersonal attraction to the group, pride in the group, and commitment to the group task (Mullen & Copper, 1994). Only the latter element seems to be associated with the quality of a non-therapy group's performance. Cohesion has been one of the most widely studied therapeutic factors. Despite serious problems with theoretical and operational definitions for the construct, a number of studies suggest that cohesion plays an important role in the effectiveness of group therapy (cf. Budman et al.,

1989). In their comprehensive review of group therapy research, Bednar & Kaul (1994) conclude that enough evidence now exists to support the conclusion that several therapeutic factors are related to positive group therapy outcomes. These include cohesion, interpersonal feedback, self-disclosure, leadership style, group structure and personal risk-taking. Unfortunately, the mechanisms by which the factors produce beneficial outcomes remain to be demonstrated.

Studies of the Group Social Microcosm

Relationship factors that may contribute to the creation of the social microcosm in group therapy have been the focus of an important strand of recent research. Group participants characterized differently along the two circumplex dimensions of dominant-submissive and withdrawn-affiliative were found to have different perceptions of the therapy group climate. Participants with self-rated interpersonal problems stemming from being too dominant tended to perceive the group as avoidant and anxious on a measure of group climate (Kivlighan & Angelone, 1992). Participants with self-rated problems stemming from being too cold and interpersonally distant tended to rate the group climate as less engaged, more anxious and conflictual than did participants who rated themselves as having fewer problems with affiliation. Other research (Kivlighan, Marsh-Angelone & Angelone, 1994) suggests that the same circumplex dimensions influence group members' perceptions of group leaders. In keeping with the social microcosm concept, perceptions of the same leaders or group environment appear to vary as a function of the filters used by a specific client to view their interpersonal world. Client interpersonal problems may have an especially potent influence on their perceptions.

The availability of social support in therapy groups is also an important part of the interpersonal model. Many groups are formed for the specific purpose of increasing social support. "Theme" groups of clients brought together with a similar concern, for example those coping with an eating disorder, appear to provide members with more of some specific types of support, for example tangible and information support, than general interpersonal process groups in which client problems are quite varied (Mallinckrodt, 1989). However, relief of symptoms in both interpersonal and theme groups was found to be more strongly associated with increases in social support from persons outside the group than to support provided by group members (Mallinckrodt, 1989). Support provided from group members is analogous to the G → F link in the SCIP model in which the therapist directly supports a client in individual therapy. Increased support provided by persons outside the group may be indicative of gains in social competencies represented by the E → F arrow in the SCIP model. These findings highlight the importance during the final stages of group therapy of applying the social competencies gained first in the "interpersonal laboratory" of the group to improve relationships with others in the client's wider social network.

FUTURE RESEARCH

Group Therapy

In this chapter I have tried to illustrate how findings from the study of personal relationships have great relevance for psychotherapists, for example, identification of competencies that are necessary for developing and maintaining intimate ties. Of course, there is much unrealized potential for further cross-disciplinary contributions. All of the links in the SCIP model require further study, but some areas may prove to be especially fruitful. Some of the techniques familiar to relationship researchers have only recently been applied to group therapy settings. For example, analysis of verbal discourse has been attempted to identify structure in patterns of therapy group communication (Lichtenberg & Knox, 1991). Although no significant patterns were uncovered in this study, the technique holds great promise. Coding models such as Benjamin's (1994) SASB could provide a useful illumination of group process, perhaps especially struggles for dominance and acceptance by group members or the structure of group leader's interventions.

Variables are much less likely to be directly manipulated in group psychotherapy research than in many of the other disciplines represented in this volume. However, approaches that use a combination of experimental and field-correlational methods also show great promise. For example, a study manipulating client delivery of positive and negative feedback to a fellow group member suggested that fear of causing harm to the recipient of the feedback was an important impediment to delivering it, but an even stronger dampening factor was the client's fear of rejection by other members of the group (Morran, Stockton & Bond, 1991). This study provides a good start, but we need to know more about the role of feedback in promoting interpersonal learning. It appears that the task of delivering corrective feedback is made more difficult by prevailing social norms. Much could be learned from a study of therapist attempts to foster clients' struggle to abandon some of these norms in group therapy. What substitute norms aid this process?

Perhaps more than any other, I believe the coming years will prove the social microcosm effect to be a fruitful avenue for researchers in the field of personal relationships to contribute to the study of group therapy. Much could be learned from a systematic comparison between a group therapy client's close relationships with persons outside the group and enacted relationships with fellow group members. What relationship patterns are most likely to be enacted, and enacted first, in the group micro-environment? After these studies are undertaken, then researchers could study whether the process works in reverse, as Yalom and others predict. Over time, are changes in interpersonal interaction patterns that are first attempted in the group eventually evident as changes in the client's outside close personal relationships? In short, how does group therapy change a client's social competencies and social network?

Individual Therapy

Turning now to research that could make a significant contribution to both individual and group therapy, more work needs to be done to establish the relative continuity of attachment patterns from infancy through adulthood, as scholars in the field of adult attachment have urged (Hazan & Shaver, 1994a,b). Such research need not involve a longitudinal study spanning more than two decades; instead, overlapping 5-year age spans, for example, could be studied in multiple cohorts with shorter longitudinal spans. Developmental studies are needed to establish how social competencies are acquired in childhood, how they affect contemporaneous relationships, and how the combination predicts future competencies and relationship quality. Another research area which may be fruitful in the next years is measurement of any of a broad range of individual difference variables (e.g. "big five" personality traits, capacity for intimacy, attachment patterns) investigated in connection with enacted social behavior, verbal discourse, any of the group therapeutic factors, or the quality of the psychotherapy relationship in individual therapy. This type of study can yield crucial information about person–environment interactions and the effectiveness of group therapy, as well as the development of the psychotherapy relationship in individual therapy. Are personality differences in fact partly responsible for observed differences in basic or complex social skills? If so, how "trainable" are these social skills and on what time scale? Of course, the contributions of personal relationship researchers are badly needed to continue documenting the social competencies needed for tasks such as recruiting social support, establishing mutually rewarding friendships, managing conflict, and maintaining intimacy—to name just a few.

The concept of transference, freed from its particular meaning for orthodox psychoanalytic theory, is believed by many interpersonal therapists to be a facet of all close personal relationships. To use pantheoretical terms, early developmental experience establishes a fundamental template for interpersonal interactions involving behavioral routines, expectations about relationships, and cognitive schemas (Safran, 1990). Although these schemas may have been adaptive early in life, they tend to become over-generalized, inflexible and maladaptive in adult relationships. These assumptions are at the core of interpersonal approaches to therapy, but they remain only weakly supported by empirical research, and require further investigation.

Another assumption of interpersonal therapists, that the therapeutic relationship provides the impetus that drives much (some claim most) of the client's change in therapy, needs further exploration. The heart of this assumption is that interpersonal therapy is effective because a productive therapy relationship demands the very same social competencies which—when lacking—contribute to the client's interpersonal problems. How then do the client's social competencies change over the course of therapy? How can therapists structure their relationships with clients to increase the pace of this change? (Here research on working alliance breaches offers an excellent starting point.) Most importantly, how can social competencies that are initially acquired in interactions with a therapist be generalized to other important relationships? Finally, the social competencies of therapists themselves must become a focus of more intensive study. For example, what influences therapist's skills for remaining engaged with a frequently hostile client, or for fostering the kind of astonishingly intimate relationship intended from the outset to ultimately make its continuation unnecessary?

CONCLUDING COMMENT

Note that all the studies I have suggested can be described as research on psychotherapy process. Despite a shift in emphasis toward process studies, unfortunately, the bulk of the research over the past 8 years can still be characterized as studies of outcome only. Research linking process with outcome remains minuscule by comparison. Desperately needed in the coming years are studies of interpersonal process to identify the "why", "how" and "with whom, under what conditions" explanations for therapy effectiveness. Bednar & Kaul (1994) stress that without these studies we run the risk of "scientific misattribution" (p. 632) for the causes of our therapeutic success. In other words, claiming that therapy works without being able to explain the mechanism of effect is tantamount to superstition.

Over a century ago, drinking a concoction that contained foxglove flowers, among other substances, sometimes relieved chest pain. Until digitalis was discovered to be the active ingredient, nobody could be sure why this mixture worked—and a great many unpalatable and medically useless substances were swallowed with the foxglove along the way. The complex interplay of process variables that may affect outcome in individual therapy and possible therapeutic factors in group therapy, presents researchers with something analogous to an enormous salad of herbal remedies, taken in one huge dose repeated weekly— with great variations in individual metabolism! In this review I hope I have given some glimpse of this complexity, and encouraged readers to participate in searching for the foxglove somewhere in the salad.

References

Abramovitch, R., Corter, C., Pepler, D.J. & Stanhope, L. (1986). Sibling and peer interaction: a final follow-up and a comparison. *Child Development*, **57**, 217–29.

Acitelli, L.K. (1988). When spouses talk to each other about their relationship. *Journal of Social and Personal Relationships*, **5**, 185–99.

Acitelli, L.K. (1993). You, me, and us: perspectives on relationship awareness. In S.W. Duck (Ed.), *Understanding Relationship Processes 1: Individuals in Relationships* (pp. 144–74). Newbury Park: Sage.

Acitelli, L.K. (1995). Disciplines at parallel play. *Journal of Social and Personal Relationships*, **12**, 589–96.

Acitelli, L.K. & Veroff, J. (1995). Taking a relationship perspective increases well-being (manuscript under review) ••.

Acitelli, L.K. & Young, A.M. (1996). Gender and thought in relationships. In G.J.O. Fletcher & J. Fitness (Eds), *Knowledge Structures and Interaction in Relationships*. Mahwah, NJ: Erlbaum.

Acitelli, L.K., Douvan, E. & Veroff, J. (1993). Perceptions of conflict in the first year of marriage: how important are similarity and understanding? *Journal of Social and Personal Relationships*, **10**, 5–19.

Ackerman, C. (1963). Affiliations: structural determination of differential divorce rates. *American Sociological Review*, **69**, 13–20.

Acock, A.C. & Hurlbert, J.S. (1993). Social networks, marital status, and well-being. *Social Networks*, **15**, 309–34.

Adams, B.J. & Sarason, B.R. (1995). Social support and depressed mood. Paper presented at the annual meeting of the American Psychological Association, New York, NY.

Adams, J.S. (1965). Inequity in social exchange. In L. Berkowitz (Ed.), *Advances in Experimental Social Psychology* (Vol. 2, pp. 267–99). New York: Academic Press.

Adams, P. & Adams, G. (1984). Mount St. Helens ashfall: evidence for a disaster stress reaction. *American Psychologist*, **39**, 252–60.

Adams, R.G. (1985). People would talk: normative barriers to cross-sex friendships for elderly women. *The Gerontologist*, **25**, 605–11.

Adler, M.J. (1927). *Dialectic*. New York: Harcourt.

Adler, M.J. (Ed.) (1952). *The Great Ideas: A Syntopicon of Great Books of the Western World*. Chicago: Encyclopedia Britannica.

Adler, N. & Matthews, K. (1994). Health psychology: why do some people get sick and some stay well? *Annual Review of Psychology*, **45**, 229–59.

Aerts, E. (1993). Bringing the institution back in. In P.A. Cowan, D. Field, D.A. Hansen,

A. Skolnick & G.E. Swanson, *Family, Self, and Society: Toward a New Agenda for Family Research* (pp. 3–41). Hillsdale, NJ: Erlbaum.

Agnew, C.R., Van Lange, P.A.M. & Rusbult, C.E. (1995). *Cognitive Interdependence: Commitment and the Mental Representation of Close Relationships.* Unpublished Manuscript, University of North Carolina, Chapel Hill.

Ahrons, C.R. & Rodgers, R.H. (1987). *Divorced Families: A Multidisciplinary Developmental View.* New York: W.W. Norton.

Ahuvia, A. (1993). I Love It! Towards a Unifying Theory of Love across Diverse Love Objects. Unpublished PhD Dissertation, Northwestern University.

Ainsworth, M.D.S. (1979). Infant–mother attachment. *American Psychologist*, **34**, 932–7.

Ainsworth, M.D.S. (1985). Patterns of infant–mother attachment: antecedents and effects on development. *Bulletin of the New York Academy of Medicine*, **61**, 771–91.

Ainsworth, M.D.S., Blehar, M.C., Waters, E. & Wall, S. (1978). *Patterns of Attachment: Assessed in the Strange Situation and at Home.* Hillsdale, NJ: Erlbaum.

Alberts, J.K. (1988). An analysis of couples conversational complaints. *Communication Monographs*, **55**, 184–97.

Alberts, J.K. & Driscoll, G. (1992). Containment versus escalation: the trajectory of couples' conversation complaints. *Western Journal of Communication*, **56**, 394–412.

Alcock, J. (1993). *Animal Behavior* (5th Edn). Sunderland, MA: Sinauer.

Aldons, J. & Straus, M.A. (1966). Social networks and conjugal roles: a test of Bott's hypothesis. *Social Forces*, **44**, 576–80.

Aldridge, D.P. (1978). Interracial marriages: empirical and theoretical considerations. *Journal of Black Studies*, **8**, 355–68.

Aldridge, D.P. (1991). *Focusing: Black Male–Female Relationships.* Chicago: Third World Press.

Alexander, F. & French, T.M. (1946). *Psychoanalytic Therapy: Principles and Application.* New York: Ronald.

Allan, G.A. (1977). Sibling solidarity. *Journal of Marriage and the Family*, **39**, 177–84.

Allan, G.A. (1993). Social structure and relationships. In S.W. Duck (Ed.), *Understanding Relationship Processes 3: Social Contexts of Relationships* (pp. 1–25). Newbury Park: Sage.

Allan, G.A. (1995). Friendship, class, status and identity. Paper presented to annual convention of the International Network on Personal Relationships, Williamsburg, VA, June.

Allan, J. & McKean, J. (1984). Transition to junior high school: strategies for change. *School Counselor*, **32**(1), 43–8.

Allen, J.B., Kenrick, D.T., Linder, D.E. & McCall, M.A. (1989). Arousal and attraction: a response-facilitation alternative to misattribution and negative-reinforcement models. *Journal of Personality and Social Psychology*, **57**, 261–70.

Allport, G.W. (1954/1979). *The Nature of Prejudice.* Cambridge, MA: Addison-Wesley.

Altman, I. (1975). *The Environment and Social Behavior: Privacy, Personal Space, Territory, and Crowding*, Wadsworth Publishing, Belmont, CA.

Altman, I. (1977). Research on environment and behavior: a personal statement of strategy. In D. Stokols (Ed.), *Psychological Perspectives on Environment and Behavior: Conceptual and Empirical Trends* (pp. 303–23). New York: Plenum.

Altman, I. (1990). Toward a transactional perspective: a personal journey. In I. Altman & K. Christensen (Eds), *Environment and Behavior Studies: Emergence of Intellectual Traditions* (pp. 225–56). New York: Plenum.

Altman, I. (1993). Dialectics, physical environments, and personal relationships. *Communication Monographs*, **60**, 26–34.

Altman, I. & Gauvain, M. (1981). A cross-cultural and dialectic analysis of homes. In L. Liben, A. Patterson & N. Newcombe (Eds), *Spatial Representation and Behavior Across the Life Span* (pp. 283–320). New York: Academic Press.

Altman, I. & Taylor, D. (1973). *Social Penetration: The Development of Interpersonal Relationships*. New York: Holt, Rinehart & Winston.

Altman, I., Brown, B., Staples, B. & Werner, C.M. (1992). A transactional approach to close relationships: courtship, weddings and placemaking. In B. Walsh, I. Craik & R. Price (Eds), *Person–Environment Psychology* (pp. 193–241). Hillsdale, NJ: Lawrence Erlbaum.

Altman, I., Vinsel, A. & Brown, B.B. (1981). Dialectic conceptions in social psychology: an application to social penetration and privacy regulation. In L. Berkowitz (Ed.), *Advances in Experimental Social Psychology* (Vol. 14, pp. 107–60). New York: Academic Press.

Altschuler, J.L. & Ruble, D.N. (1989). Developmental changes in children's awareness of strategies for coping with uncontrollable stress. *Child Development*, **60**, 1337–49.

Altschuler, J., Jacobs, S. & Shiode, D. (1985). Psychodynamic time-limited groups for adult children of aging parents. *American Journal of Orthopsychiatry*, **53**, 397–403.

Alvidrez, J. & Weinstein, R.S. (1993). The nature of "schooling" in school transitions: a critical re-examination. *Prevention in Human Services*, **10**(2), 7–26.

American Psychiatric Association (1994). *Diagnostic and Statistical Manual of Mental Disorders*, 4th Edn. Washington, DC: American Psychiatric Association.

Amir, Y. (1969). Contact hypothesis in ethnic relations. *Psychological Bulletin*, **71**, 319–42.

Amoroso, D.M. & Walters, R.H. (1969). Effects of anxiety and socially mediated anxiety reduction on paired-associate learning. *Journal of Personality and Social Psychology*, **11**, 388–96.

Anchin, J. & Kiesler, D.J. (Eds) (1982). *Handbook of Interpersonal Psychotherapy*. Elmsford, NY: Pergamon Press.

Andersen, P.A. (1993). Cognitive schemata in personal relationships. In S.W. Duck (Ed.), *Understanding Relationship Processes 1: Individuals in Relationships* (pp. 1–29). Newbury Park: Sage.

Angermeier, W.F., Phelps, J.B. & Reynolds, H.H. (1967). Verbal stress and heart-rate in humans exposed in groups. *Psychonomic Science*, **8**, 515–16.

Antonucci, T.C. (1994). A life-span view of women's social relations. In B.F. Turner & L.E. Troll (Eds) *Women Growing Older* (pp. 239–69). Thousand Oaks, CA: Sage.

Aquilino, W.S. & Supple, K.R. (1991). Parent–child relations and parent's satisfaction with living arrangements when adult children live at home. *Journal of Marriage and the Family*, **53**, 13–27.

Arce, A.A. & Torres-Matrullo, J. (1982). Application of cognitive-behavioral techniques in the treatment of Hispanic patients. *Psychiatric Quarterly*, **56**, 230–36.

Archer, R.L. (1979). Anatomical and psychological sex differences. In G.J. Chelune & Associates (Eds), *Self-disclosure: Origins, Patterns, and Implications of Openness in Interpersonal Relationships* (pp. 80–109). San Francisco: Jossey-Bass.

Archer, R.L. (1987). Commentary: self-disclosure, a very useful behavior. In V.J. Derlega & J.H. Berg (Eds), *Self-disclosure: Theory, Research, and Therapy*. New York: Plenum, pp. 329–42.

Argyle, M. & Furnham, A. (1983). Sources of satisfaction, and conflict in long-term relationships. *Journal of Marriage and the Family*, **48**, 849–55.

Argyle, M. & Henderson, M. (1984). The rules of friendship. *Journal of Social and Personal Relationships*, **1**, 211–37.

Argyle, M., Furnham, A. & Graham, J.A. (1981). *Social situations*. Cambridge, MA: Cambridge University Press.

Argyle, M., Henderson, M., Bond, M., Contarello, A. & Iizuka, Y. (1986). Cross-cultural variations in relationship rules. *International Journal of Psychology*, **21**, 287–315.

Aroian, K.J. (1992). Sources of social support and conflict for Polish immigrants. *Qualitative Health Research*, **2**(2), 178–207.

Aron, A. (1970). Relationship variables in human heterosexual attraction. Unpublished doctoral dissertation, University of Toronto.

Aron, A. & Aron, E.N. (1986). *Love and the Expansion of Self: Understanding Attraction and Satisfaction* (pp. 19–67). Washington: Hemisphere.

Aron, A. & Aron, E.N. (1995). Three suggestions for increased emphasis in the study of personal relationships. *Journal of Social and Personal Relationships*, **12**, 559–62.

Aron, A. & Rodriguez, G. (1992, July). Scenarios of falling in love among Mexican, Chinese, and Anglo-Americans. In A. Aron (Chair), Ethnic and cultural differences in love. Symposium conducted at the Sixth International Conference on Personal Relationships, Orono, ME.

Aron, A., Aron, E.N. & Allen, J. (1995). Motivations for unrequited love. Manuscript under review.

Aron, A., Aron, E.N. & Smollan, D. (1992). Inclusion of Other in the Self Scale and the structure of interpersonal closeness. *Journal of Personality and Social Psychology*, **63**, 596–612.

Aron, A., Aron, E.N., Tudor, M. & Nelson, G. (1991). Close relationships as including other in the self. *Journal of Personality and Social Psychology*, **60**, 241–53.

Aron, A., Dutton, D.G., Aron, E.N. & Iverson, A. (1989). Experiences of falling in love. *Journal of Social and Personal Relationships*, **6**, 243–57.

Aron, A., Paris, M. & Aron, E.N. (in press). Prospective studies of falling in love and self-concept change. *Journal of Personality and Social Psychology*.

Aronfreed, J. (1968). *Conduct and Conscience*. New York: Academic Press.

Aronson, E. & Linder, D. (1965). Gain and loss of esteem as determinants of interpersonal attraction. *Journal of Experimental Social Psychology*, **1**, 156–71.

Aronson, E., Wilson, T.D. & Akert, R.M. (1994). *Social Psychology: The Heart and the Mind*. New York: Harper Collins.

Asande, M.K. (1987). *The Afrocentric Idea*. Philadelphia: Temple University Press.

Asarnow, J.R., Goldstein, M.J., Tompson, M. & Guthrie, D. (1993). One-year outcomes of depressive disorders in child psychiatric in-patients: evaluation of the prognostic power of a brief measure of expressed emotion. *Journal of Child Psychology and Psychiatry and Allied Disciplines*, **34**, 129–37.

Asendorpf, J.B. & Baudonniere, P.M. (1993). Self-awareness and other awareness: mirror self-recognition and synchronic imitation among unfamiliar peers. *Developmental Psychology*, **29**, 88–93.

Aseron, R.G., Sarason, I.G. & Sarason, B.R. (1992). Social support and conflict: global and relationship-specific aspects. Paper presented at the annual meeting of the American Psychological Association, Washington, DC.

Asher, S.R. & Renshaw, P.D. (1981). Children without friends: social knowledge and social skill training. In S.R. Asher & J.M. Gottman (Eds), *The Development of Children's Friendships* (pp. 273–96). New York: Cambridge University Press.

Asher, S.R., Markell, R.A. & Hymel, S. (1981). Identifying children at risk in peer relations: a critique of the rate-of-interaction approach to assessment. *Child Development*, **52**, 1239–45.

Askham, J. (1976). Identity and stability within the marriage relationship. *Journal of Marriage and the Family*, **38**, 535–47.

Askham, J. (1986). *Identity and Stability in Marriage*. Cambridge, MA: Cambridge University Press.

Aspinwall, L.G. & Taylor, S.E. (1992). Modeling cognitive adaptation: a longitudinal investigation of the impact of individual differences and coping on college adjustment and performance. *Journal of Personality and Social Psychology*, **63**, 989–1003.

Atkinson, M.P. (1989). Conceptualizations of the parent–child relationship: solidarity, attachment, crescive bonds, and identity salience. In J.A. Mancini (Ed.), *Aging Parents and Adult Children* (pp. 81–97). Lexington, MA: Lexington Books.

Atkinson, M.P., Kivett, V.R. & Campbell, R.T. (1986). Intergenerational solidarity: an examination of a theoretical model. *Journal of Gerontology*, **41**, 408–16.

Atkinson, T., Liem, R. & Liem, J.H. (1986). The social costs of unemployment: implications for social support. *Journal of Health and Social Psychology*, **27**, 317–31.

Attili, G. (1989). Social competence versus emotional security: the link between home relationships and behavior problems at school. In B.H. Schneider, G. Attili, J. Nadel & R.P. Weissberg (Eds), *Social Competence in Developmental Perspective* (pp. 293–311). London: Kluwer.

Attili, G., Vermigli, P. & Schneider, B. (in press). Friendship patterns and peer relations of Italian schoolchildren in cross-cultural perspective. *International Journal of Behavioral Development*.

Aukett, R., Ritchie, J. & Mill, K. (1988). Gender differences in friendship patterns. *Sex Roles*, **19**, 57–66.

Aune, R.K., Metts, S. & Ebesu, A.S. (1991, November). Managing the outcomes of discovered deception. Paper presented at the Speech Communication Association Convention, Atlanta, GA.

Ausubel, D.P. (1955). Relationship between shame and guilt in the socialization process. *Psychological Review*, **62**, 378–90.

Averill, J. (1982). *Anger and Aggression. An Essay on Emotion.* Berlin: Springer.

Averill, J.R. (1993). Illusions of anger. In R.B. Felson & J.T. Tedeschi (Eds), *Aggression and Violence.* Washington DC: American Psychiatric Association.

Axelrod, R. (1984). *The Evolution of Cooperation.* New York: Basic Books.

Axelrod, R. & Hamilton, W.D. (1981). The evolution of cooperation. *Science*, **211**, 1390–96.

Backman, C.W. (1959). The effect of perceived liking on interpersonal attraction. *Human Relations*, **12**, 379–84.

Badhwar, N.K. (1987). Friends as ends in themselves. *Philosophy and Phenomenological Research*, **XLVIII**(1), 1–23.

Bailey, J.M. & Pillard, R.C. (1991). A genetic study of male sexual orientation. *Archives of General Psychiatry*, **48**, 1089–96.

Bailey, J.M., Gaulin, S., Agyei, Y. & Gladue, B.A. (1994). Effects of gender and sexual orientation on evolutionarily relevant aspects of human mating psychology. *Journal of Personality and Social Psychology*, **66**, 1074–80.

Bainum, C.K., Lounsbury, K. & Pollio, H. (1984). The development of laughing and smiling in nursery school children. *Child Development*, **55**, 1946–57.

Bakan, D. (1966). *The duality of human existence: isolation and commitment in Western man.* Boston: Beacon Press. .

Bakhtin, M.M. (1965/1984). *Rabelais and His World* (H. Iswolsky, Trans.). Bloomington: Indiana University Press.

Bakhtin, M.M. (1981). *The Dialogic Imagination: Four Essays by M.M. Bakhtin* (M. Holquist, Ed.; C. Emerson & M. Holquist, Trans.). Austin: University of Texas Press.

Bakhtin, M.M. (1984). *Problems of Dostoevsky's Poetics* (C. Emerson, Ed. and Trans.). Minneapolis: University of Minnesota Press (original work published 1929).

Bakhtin, M.M. (1986). *Speech Genres and Other Late Essays* (C. Emerson & M. Holquist, Eds; V. McGee, Trans.). Austin: University of Texas Press.

Baldwin, M.J. (1992). Relational schema and the processing of information. *Psychological Bulletin*, **112**, 461–84.

Baldwin, M.W., Fehr, B., Keedian, E., Seidel, M. & Thomson, D.W. (1993). An exploration of the relational schemata underlying attachment styles: self-report and lexical decision approaches. *Personality and Social Psychology Bulletin*, **19**, 746–54.

Ball, R. (1979). The dialectical method: its application to social theory. *Social Forces*, **57**, 785–98.

Baltes, P. (1987). Theoretical propositions of life span developmental psychology: on the dynamics between growth and decline. *Developmental Psychology*, **23**, 611–26.

Baltzell, L.D. (1968). *The Search for Community in Modern America.* New York: Harper & Row.

Bandura, A. (1977). Self-efficacy: toward a unifying theory of behavioral change. *Psychological Review*, **84**, 191–215.

Bandura, A. (1986). Social foundations of thought and action: a social cognitive theory. Englewood Cliffs, NJ: Prentice Hall.

Banfield, E.C. (1963). *Moral Basis of a Backward Society*. Glencoe, IL: Free. Press.

Bank, S. & Kahn, M.D. (1982). *The Sibling Bond*. New York: Basic Books.

Banks, S.P., Altendorf, D.M., Greene, J.O. & Cody, M.J. (1987). An examination of relationship disengagement: perceptions, breakup strategies and outcomes. *Western Journal of Speech Communication*, **51**, 19–41.

Barbee, A.P. (1990). Interactive coping: the cheering-up process in close relationships. In S.W. Duck with R. Cohen Silver (Eds), *Personal Relationships and Social Support*. London: Sage.

Barefoot, J.C., Peterson, B.L., Dahlstrom, W.G., Siegler, I.C., Anderson, N.B. & Williams, R.B. Jr (1987). Suspiciousness, health, and mortality: a follow-up study of 500 older adults. *Psychosomatic Medicine*, **49**, 450–57.

Barker, R.G. (1968). *Ecological Psychology*. Stanford, CA: Stanford University Press.

Barkow, J.H., Cosmides, L. & Tooby, J. (1992). *The Adapted Mind: Evolutionary Psychology and the Generation of Culture*. New York: Oxford University Press.

Barlund, D.C. (1970). A transactional model of communication. In J. Akin, A. Goldberg, G. Myers & J. Stewart (Eds), *Language Behavior: A Book of Readings in Communication* (pp. 43–6). The Hague: Mouton.

Barnes, J. (1979). Network analysis: orienting notion, rigorous technique or substantive field of study? In P.W. Holland & S. Leinhardt (Eds), *Perspectives on Social Network Research*. New York: Academic Press.

Barnes, J.A. (1969). Graph theory and social networks: a technical comment on connectedness and connectivity. *Sociology*, **3**, 215–32.

Barnes, M.K. & Duck, S.W. (1994). Everyday communicative contexts for social support. In B.R. Burleson, T.L. Albrecht & I.G. Sarason (Eds), *Communication of Social Support: Messages, Interactions, Relationships, and Community* (pp. 175–94). Thousand Oaks, CA: Sage.

Barnett, M.A. (1987). Empathy and related responses in children. In N. Eisenberg & J. Strayer (Eds), *Empathy and Its Development* (pp. 146–62). Cambridge, MA: Cambridge University Press.

Barnett, R. (1994). Home-to-work spillover revisited. *Journal of Marriage and the Family*, **56**, 647–56.

Barnett, R.C., Kibria, N., Baruch, G.K. & Pleck, J.H. (1991). Adult daughter–parent relationships and their associations with daughters' subjective well-being and psychological distress. *Journal of Marriage and the Family*, **53**, 29–42.

Barnett, R.C., Marshall, N.L. & Pleck, J.H. (1992). Adult son–parent relationships and their associations with sons' psychological distress. *Journal of Family Issues*, **13**, 505–25.

Baron, R.S., Cutrona, C.E., Hicklin, D., Russell, D.W. & Lubaroff, D.M. (1990). Social support and immune function among spouses of cancer patients. *Journal of Personality and Social Psychology*, **59**, 344–52.

Baron, R. & Kenny, D.A. (1986). The moderator–mediator variable distinction in social psychological research: conceptual, strategic, and statistical considerations. *Journal of Personality and Social Psychology*, **51**, 1173–82.

Barone, C., Aguirre-Deandreis, A.I. & Trickett, E.J. (1991). Means–ends problem-solving skills, life stress, and social support as mediators of adjustment in the normative transition to high school. *American Journal of Community Psychology*, **19**, 207–25.

Barone, C., Trickett, E.J., Schmid, K.D. & Leone, P.E. (1993). Transition tasks and resources: an ecological approach to life after high school. *Prevention in Human Services*, **10**(2), 179–204.

Barrera, M. Jr (1986). Distinctions between social support concepts, measures, and models. *American Journal of Community Psychology*, **14**, 413–45.

Barrera, M. Jr (1988). Models of social support and life stress: beyond the buffering hypothesis. In L.H. Cohen (Ed.), *Life Events and Psychological Functioning* (pp. 211–36). Beverly Hills: Sage.

Barrett, D.E. (1979). A naturalistic study of sex differences in children's aggression. *Merrill-Palmer Quarterly*, **25**, 193–203.

Barrett, D.E. & Yarrow, M.R. (1977). Prosocial behavior, social inferential ability, and assertiveness in children. *Child Development*, **48**, 475–81.

Barrett, K. (1995). A functionalist approach to shame and guilt. In J.P. Tangney & K.W. Fischer (Eds), *Self-conscious Emotions* (pp. 25–63). New York: Guilford.

Barrett, K.C. & Campos, J.J. (1987). Perspectives on emotional development. II. A functionalist approach to emotions. In J. Osofsky (Ed.), *Handbook of Infant Development* (2nd edn, pp. 555–78). New York: Wiley.

Barrett, K.C., Zahn-Waxler, C. & Cole, P.M. (1993). Avoiders versus amenders— implications for the investigation of guilt and shame during toddlerhood? *Cognition and Emotion*, **7**, 481–505.

Barry, H., Child, I.L. & Bacon, M.K. (1959). Relations of child training to subsistence economy. *American Anthropologist*, **61**, 51–63.

Barth, J.M. & Parke, R.D. (1993). Parent–child relationship influences on children's transition to school. *Merrill-Palmer Quarterly*, **39**, 173–95.

Barthes, R. (1983). *A Lover's Discourse*. New York: Hill & Wang.

Bartholomew, K. (1994). From childhood to adult relationships: attachment theory and research. In S. Duck (Ed.), *Learning about Relationships: Understanding Relationship Processes*, Vol. 2 (pp. 30–62). Newbury Park, CA: Sage.

Bartholomew, K. & Horowitz, L.M. (1991). Attachment styles among young adults: a test of a four category model. *Journal of Personality and Social Psychology*, **61**, 226–44.

Bartky, S.L. (1990). *Femininity and Domination*. New York: Routledge.

Barton, A.M. (1969). *Communities in Disaster*. Garden City, NJ: Doubleday.

Baruch, G. & Barnett, R.C. (1983). Adult daughters' relationships with their mothers. *Journal of Marriage and the Family*, **45**, 601–12.

Bateson, G. (1972). *Steps to an Ecology of Mind*. New York: Ballantine.

Bateson, G. (1978). The pattern which connects. *The Coevolutionary Quarterly*, **Summer**, 5–15.

Bateson, G. (1979). *Mind and Nature: a Necessary Unity*. New York: E.P. Dutton.

Bateson, G. (1991). Naven: Epilogue 1958. In R.E. Donaldson (Ed.), *A Sacred Unity: Further Steps to an Ecology of Mind* (pp. 49–69). New York: Harper Collins.

Batson, C.D. (1987). Prosocial motivation: is it ever truly altruistic? In L. Berkowitz (Ed.), *Advances in Experimental Social Psychology*, Vol. 20 (pp. 65–122). New York: Academic Press.

Baum, A. (1987). Toxins, technology, and natural disasters. In G. VandenBos & B. Bryant (Eds), *Cataclysms, Crises, and Catastrophes: Psychology in Action* (pp. 9–51). Washington, DC: American Psychiatric Association.

Baum, M. & Page, M. (1991). Caregiving and multigenerational families. *The Gerontologist*, **31**, 762–9.

Baum, A., Fleming, R. & Davidson, L. (1983). Natural disasters and technological catastrophe. *Environment and Behavior*, **15**, 333–54.

Baumeister, R.F. (1982). A self-presentational view of social phenomena. *Psychological Bulletin*, **91**, 3–26.

Baumeister, R.F. & Leary, M.R. (1995). The need to belong: desire for interpersonal attachments as a fundamental human motivation. *Psychological Bulletin*, **117**, 497–529.

Baumeister, R.F. & Newman, L. (1994). How stories make sense of personal experiences: motives that shape autobiographical narratives. *Personality and Social Psychology Bulletin*, **20**, 676–90.

Baumeister, R.F., Stillwell, A.M. & Heatherton, T.F. (1995). Interpersonal aspects of guilt:

evidence from narrative studies. In J.P. Tangney & K.W. Fischer (Eds), *Self-conscious Emotions* (pp. 255–73). New York: Guilford.

Baumgarten, M., Thomas, D., Poulin de Courval, L. & Infante-Rivard, C. (1988). Evaluation of a mutual help network for the elderly residents of planned housing. *Psychology and Aging*, **3**, 393–8.

Baumgartner, M.P. (1993). Violent networks: the origins and management of domestic conflict. In R.B. Felson & J.T. Tedeschi (Eds), *Aggression and Violence* (pp. 209–31). Washington, DC: American Psychiatric Association.

Baumrind, D. (1967). Child care practices anteceding three patterns of preschool behavior. *Genetic Psychology Monographs*, **75**, 43–88.

Baumrind, D. (1971). Current patterns of parental authority. *Developmental Psychology Monographs*, **4**, 72.

Baumrind, D. (1973). The development of instrumental competence through socialization. In A.D. Pick (Ed.), *Minnesota Symposium on Child Psychology*, Vol. 7 (pp. 3–46). Minneapolis: University of Minnesota Press.

Baumrind, D. (1978). Parental disciplinary patterns and social competence in youth. *Youth and Society*, **9**, 239–76.

Baumrind, D. (1991). The influence of parenting style on adolescent competence and substance abuse. *Journal of Early Adolescence*, **11**, 56–95.

Baxter, J. (1992). Power attitudes and time: the domestic division of labor. *Journal of Comparative Family Studies*, **23**, 65–182.

Baxter, L.A. (1982). Strategies for ending relationships: two studies. *Western Journal of Speech Communication*, **46**, 223–41.

Baxter, L.A. (1984). An investigation of compliance-gaining as politeness. *Human Communication Research*, **10**, 427–56.

Baxter, L.A. (1985). Accomplishing relationship disengagement. In S.W. Duck & D. Perlman (Eds), *Understanding Personal Relationships* (pp. 243–65). London: Sage.

Baxter, L.A. (1987). Cognition and communication in the relationship process. In R. Burnett, P. McGhee & D.D. Clarke (Eds), *Accounting for Relationships* (pp. 192–212). London: Methuen.

Baxter, L.A. (1988). A dialectical perspective on communication strategies in relationship development. In S.W. Duck (Ed.) with D.F. Hay, S.E. Hobfoll, W. Ickes & B. Montgomery, *Handbook of Personal Relationships* (pp. 257–73). Chichester: Wiley.

Baxter, L.A. (1990). Dialectical contradictions in relationship development. *Journal of Social and Personal Relationships*, **7**, 69–88.

Baxter, L.A. (1992). Forms and functions of intimate play in personal relationships. *Human Communication Research*, **18**, 336–63.

Baxter, L.A. (1993). The social side of personal relationships: a dialectical perspective. In S.W. Duck (Ed.), *Social Contexts of Relationships [Understanding Relationship Processes 3]* (pp. 139–65). Newbury Park, CA: Sage.

Baxter, L.A. (1994). A dialogic approach to relationship maintenance. In D.J. Canary & L. Stafford (Eds), *Communication and Relational Maintenance* (pp. 233–54). New York: Academic Press.

Baxter, L.A. & Bullis, C. (1986). Turning points in developing romantic relationships. *Human Communication Research*, **12**, 469–93.

Baxter, L.A. & Clark, C. (1995). Perceived family rituals and personal authority in the family system: a dialectical analysis. Paper presented at the annual meeting of the Speech Communication Association, San Antonio.

Baxter, L.A. & Dindia, K. (1990). Marital partners' perceptions of marital maintenance strategies. *Journal of Social and Personal Relationship*, **7**, 187–208.

Baxter, L.A. & Montgomery, B.M. (1996). *Relational Dialectics: a Dialogic Approach to Communication in Personal Relationships*. New York: Guilford.

Baxter, L.A. & Simon, E.P. (1993). Relationship maintenance strategies and dialectical contradiction in personal relationships. *Journal of Social and Personal Relationships*, **10**, 225–42.

Baxter, L.A. & Widenmann, S. (1993). Revealing and not revealing the status of romantic relationships to social networks. *Journal of Social and Personal Relationships*, **10**, 321–38.

Baxter, L.A., Mazanec, M., Nicholson, L., Pittman, G., Smith, K. & West, L. (1996). Everyday loyalties and betrayals in personal relationships: a dialectical perspective. Paper presented to Western Speech Communication Association, Pasadena, CA, February.

Baxter, L.A., Wilmot, W.W., Simmons, C.A. & Swartz, A. (1993). Ways of doing conflict: a folk taxonomy of conflict events in personal relationships. In P.J. Kalbfleisch (Ed.), *Interpersonal Communication: Evolving Interpersonal Relationships* (pp. 89–107). Hillsdale, NJ: Erlbaum.

Baxter et al. (in press). Journal of Social and Personal Relationships (publication 1997).

Bazerman, C. (1987). Codifying the social scientific style: the *APA Publications Manual* as a behaviorist rhetoric. In J.S. Nelson, A Megill & D.N. McCloskey (Eds), *The Rhetoric of the Human Sciences: Language and Argument in Scholarship and Public Affairs* (pp. 125–44). Madison: UWisc Press.

Beach, F.A. (1976). Sexual attractivity, proceptivity and receptivity in female mammals. *Hormones and Behavior*, **7**, 105–38.

Beauvais, F. (1992). The consequences of drugs and alcohol use for Indian youth. *American Indian and Alaska Native Mental Health Research*, **5**, 32–7.

Becker, H.S. (1960). Notes on the concept of commitment. *American Journal of Sociology*, **66**, 32–40.

Bedford, V.H. (1989). Ambivalence in adult sibling relationships. *Journal of Family Issues*, **10**, 211–24.

Bedford, V.H. (1992). Memories of parental favoritism and the quality of parent–child ties in adulthood. *Journal of Gerontology*, **47**, 149–55.

Bedford, V.H. (1993, June). Attachment to a sibling in adulthood: Predisposing conditions. Paper presented at the Fourth Annual Conference of the International Network on Personal Relationships, Milwaukee.

Bedford, V.H. (1995). Sibling relationships in middle and old age. In R. Blieszner & V.H. Bedford (Eds), *Handbook of Aging and the Family* (pp. 201–22). Westport, CT: Greenwood.

Bednar, R.L. & Kaul, T. (1994). Experiential group research: can the cannon fire? In A.E. Bergin & S.L. Garfield (Eds), *Handbook of Psychotherapy and Behavior Change*, 4th Edn (pp. 631–63). New York: Wiley.

Beinstein-Miller, J. (1993). Learning from early relationship experiences. In S.W. Duck (Ed.), *Understanding Relationship Processes: Vol. 2. Learning about relationships* (pp. 1–29). Newbury Park, CA: Sage.

Beitel, A. & Parke, R.D. (1985). Relationships between preschoolers' sociometric factors and emotional decoding ability. Unpublished manuscript, University of Illinois, Urbana, IL.

Belk, R.W. (1988). Possessions and the extended self. *Journal of Consumer Research*, **15**, 139–68.

Bell, D.C. & Bell, L.G. (1983). Parental validation and support in the development of adolescent daughters. In H.D. Grotevant & C.R. Cooper (Eds), *Adolescent Development in the Family* (pp. 27–42). San Francisco: Jossey-Bass.

Bell, D.C. & Bell, L.G. (1989). Micro and macro measurement of family systems concepts. *Journal of Family Psychology*, **3**, 137–57.

Bell, R.A. & Healey, J.G. (1992). Idiomatic communication and interpersonal solidarity in friends' relational cultures. *Human Communication Research*, **18**, 307–35.

Bell, R.A., Buerkel-Rothfuss, N.L. & Gore, K.E. (1987). "Did you bring the yarmulke for the cabbage patch kid?" The idiomatic communication of young lovers. *Human Communication Research*, **14**, 47–67.

Bell, R.R. (1981). Friendships of women and of men. *Psychology of Women Quarterly*, **5**, 402–17.

Bellah, R.N., Madsen, R., Sullivan, W.M., Swindler, A. & Tipton, S.M. (1985). *Habits of the Heart: Individualism and Commitment in American Life*. San Francisco: Harper & Row.

Belle, D. (1987). Gender differences in the social moderators of stress. In R.C. Barnett, L. Biener & G. K. Baruch (Eds), *Gender and Stress* (pp. 257–77). New York: Free Press.

Belsky, J. (1984). The determinants of parenting: a process model. *Child Development*, **55**, 83–96.

Belsky, J. & Pensky, E. (1988). Marital change across the transition to parenthood. *Marriage and Family Review*, **12**, 133–56.

Belsky, J., Lang M.E. & Rovine, M. (1985). Stability and change in marriage across the transition to parenthood: a second study. *Journal of Marriage and the Family*, **47**, 855–65.

Belsky, J., Spanier, G.B. & Rovine, M. (1983). Stability and change in marriage across the transition to parenthood. *Journal of Marriage and the Family*, **45**, 553–6.

Belsky, J., Steinberg, L. & Draper, P. (1991). Childhood experience, interpersonal development, and reproductive strategy: an evolutionary theory of socialization. *Child Development*, **62**, 647–70.

Belsky, J., Ward, H. & Rovine, M. (1986). Prenatal expectations, postnatal experiences and the transition to parenthood. In R. Ashmore & D. Brodzinsky (Eds), *Perspectives on the Family*. Hillsdale, NJ: Earlbaum.

Belson, W.A. (1975). *Juvenile Theft: the Causal Factors*. London: Harper & Row.

Ben-Yoav, O. & Pruitt, D.G. (1984a). Accountability to constituents: a two-edged sword. *Organizational Behavior and Human Performance*, **34**, 283–95.

Ben-Yoav, O. & Pruitt, D.G. (1984b). Resistance to yielding and the expectation of cooperative future interaction in negotiation. *Journal of Experimental Social Psychology*, **34**, 323–35.

Bendtschneider, L. & Duck, S.W. (1993). "What's yours is mine and what's mine is yours": couple friends. In P. Kalbfleisch (Ed.), *Developments in Interpersonal Communication* (pp. 169–86). Hillsdale, NJ: Erlbaum.

Benedict, R. (1946). *The Chrysanthemum and the Sword: Patterns of Japanese Culture*. Boston: Houghton-Mifflin.

Benes, F.M., McSparren, J., Bird, E.D., SanGiovanni, J.P. & Vincent, S.L. (1991). Deficits in small interneurons in prefrontal and cingulate cortices of schizophrenic and schizoaffective patients. *Archives of General Psychiatry*, **48**, 996–1001.

Bengtson, V.L. & Kuypers, J.A. (1971). Generational differences and the developmental stake. *International Journal of Aging and Human Development*, **2**, 249–60.

Bengtson, V.L. & Mangen, D.J. (1988). Family intergenerational solidarity revisited: suggestions for future management. In D.J. Mangen, V.L. Bengtson & P.H. Landry, Jr (Eds), *Measurement of Intergenerational Relations* (pp. 222–38). Newbury Park, CA: Sage.

Bengtson, V.L. & Roberts, R.E.L. (1991). Parent–child relations. In D. Mangen & W.A. Peterson (Eds), *Research Instruments in Social Gerontology*, Vol. 2. Minneapolis: University of Minnesota Press.

Bengtson, V.L. & Schrader, S. (1982). Parent–child relations. In D. Mangen & W.A. Peterson (Eds), *Research Instruments in Social Gerontology*, Vol. 2. Minneapolis: University of Minnesota Press.

Bengtson, V.L., Olander, E.B. & Haddad, A.A. (1976). The "generation gap" and aging family members: toward a conceptual model. In J.E. Gubrium (Ed.), *Time, Roles and Self in Old Age* (pp. 237–63). New York: Human Sciences Press.

Bengtson, V., Rosenthal, C. & Burton, L. (1990). Families and aging: diversity and heterogeneity. In R.H. Binstock & L.K. George (Eds), *Handbook of Aging and the Social Sciences* (3rd Edn, pp. 263–87). New York: Academic Press.

Benjamin, L.S. (1993). *Interpersonal Diagnosis and Treatment of Personality Disorders.* New York: Guilford.

Benjamin, L.S. (1994). SASB: a bridge between personality theory and clinical psychology. *Psychological Inquiry*, **5**, 273–316.

Bennett, J. & Berry, J.W. (1992). Notions of competence in people of northern Ontario. Papers of the Twenty-Third Algonquian Conference, 36–50.

Benoit, D. & Parker, K.C.H. (1994). Stability and transmission of attachment across three generations. *Child Development*, **65**, 1444–57.

Benson, J.K. (1977). Organizations: A dialectical view. *Administrative Science Quarterly*, **22**, 1–21.

Berardo, D.H., Shehan, C.L. & Leslie, G.R. (1987). A residue of tradition: jobs, careers, and spouses' time in housework. *Journal of Marriage and the Family*, **49**, 381–90.

Berg, J.H. (1984). Development of friendship between roomates. *Journal of Personality and Social Psychology*, **46**, 346–56.

Berg, J.H. & Derlega, V.J. (1987). Themes in the study of self-disclosure. In V.J. Derlega & J.H. Berg (Eds), *Self-disclosure: Theory, Research and Therapy* (pp. 1–8). New York: Plenum.

Berger, C.R. (1988). Uncertainty and information exchange in developing relationships. In S.W. Duck, D.F. Hay, S.E. Hobfoll, W. Ickes & B. Montgomery (Eds), *Handbook of Personal Relationships* (pp. 239–56). Chichester: Wiley.

Berger, C.R. (1993). Goals plans and mutual understanding in personal relationships. In S.W. Duck (Ed.), *Understanding Relationship Processes 1: Individuals in Relationships* (pp. 30–59). Newbury Park: Sage.

Berger, C.R. & Bradac, J.J. (1982). Language and social knowledge: uncertainty in interpersonal relationships, London: Edward Arnold.

Berger, C.R. & Calabrese, R.J. (1975). Some explorations in initial interaction and beyond: toward a developmental theory of interpersonal communication. *Human Communication Research*, **1**, 99–112.

Berger, P.L. (1963). *Invitation to Sociology.* New York: Doubleday.

Berger, P.L. & Kellner, H. (1964). Marriage and the construction of reality: an exercise in the microsociology of knowledge, *Diogenes*, **46**, 1–23.

Berger, P.L. & Luckman, T. (1966). *The Social Construction of Reality.* Garden City, New York: Doubleday. .

Bergler, E. (1946). *Unhappy Marriage and Divorce: a Study of Neurotic Choice of Marriage Partners.* New York: International Universities Press.

Berk, R.A. & Berk, S.F. (1978). A simultaneous equation model for the division of household labor. *Sociological Methods & Research*, **6**, 431–68.

Berk, S.F. (1985). *The Gender factory: the Apportionment of Work in American Households.* New York: Plenum.

Berkman, L.F. (1985). The relationship of social networks and social support to morbidity and mortality. In S. Cohen & S.L. Syme (Eds), *Social Support and Health* (pp. 241–62). Orlando, FL: Academic Press.

Berkman, L.F. & Breslow, L. (1983). *Health and ways of living: findings from the Alameda Country Study.* New York: Oxford University Press.

Berkman, L.F. & Syme, S.L. (1979). Social networks, host resistance, and mortality: a nine-year follow-up study of Alameda Country residents. *American Journal of Epidemiology*, **109**, 186–204.

Berkowitz, L. & Daniels, L.R. (1963). Responsibility and dependency. *Journal of Abnormal Social Psychology*, **66**, 429–36.

Berlo, D.K. (1960). *The Process of Communication: an Introduction to Theory and Practice.* New York: Holt, Reinehart & Winston.

Berlyne, D.E. (1960). *Conflict, Arousal, and Curiosity.* New York: McGraw-Hill.

Berman, W.H. (1988). The role of attachment in the post-divorce experience. *Journal of Personality and Social Psychology*, **54**, 496–503.

Berman, W.H. & Sperling, M.B. (1994). The structure and function of adult attachment. In M.B. Sperling & W.H. Berman (Eds), *Attachment in Adults: Clinical and Developmental Perspectives* (pp. 1–30). New York: Guilford.

Bernard, J. (1972). *The Future of Marriage*. New York: World Publications.

Bernard, J. (1973). The *Sociology of Community*. Glenview, IL: Scott, Foresman.

Bernard, J.S. (1982). *The Future of Marriage* (2nd Edn). New Haven: Yale University Press.

Berndt, T.J. (1989). Obtaining support from friends during childhood and adolescence. In D. Belle (Ed.), *Children's Social Networks and Social Supports* (pp. 308–31). New York: Wiley.

Berndt, T.J. & Bulleit, T.N. (1985). Effects of sibling relationships on preschoolers' behavior at home and at school. *Developmental Psychology*, **21**, 761–7.

Berndt, T.J. & Perry, T.B. (1986). Children's perceptions of friendships as supportive relationships. *Developmental Psychology*, **22**, 640–48.

Berndt, T.J. & Savin-Williams, R.C. (1993). Peer relationships and friendships. In P.H. Tolan & B.J. Cohler (Eds), *Handbook of Clinical Research and Practice with Adolescents* (pp. 203–20). New York: Wiley.

Bernstein, B. (1964). Elaborated and restricted codes: their social origins and some consequences. *American Anthropologist*, **66**(2), 55–69.

Bernstein, I.S. (1964). The integration of rhesus monkeys introduced to a group. *Folia Primatologica*, **2**, 50–63.

Bernstein, I.S. (1969). Introductory techniques in the formation of pigtail monkey troops. *Folia Primatologica*, **10**, 1–19.

Bernstein, I.S. (1971). The influence of introductory techniques on the formation of captive mangabey groups. *Primates*, **12**, 33–44.

Berquier, A. & Ashton, R. (1991). A selective review of possible neurological etiologies of schizophrenia. *Clinical Psychology Review*, **11**, 645–61.

Berren, M., Santiago, J., Beigel, A. & Timmons S. (1989). A classification scheme for disasters. In R. Gist & B. Lubin (Eds), *Psychological Aspects of Disaster* (pp. 40–58). New York: Wiley.

Berry, J.W. (1994). An ecological perspective on cultural and ethnic psychology. In E.J. Trickett, R.J. Watts & D. Birman (Eds), *Human Diversity: Perspectives on People in Context* (pp. 115–41). San Francisco: Jossey-Bass.

Berry, J.W. & Annis, R.C. (1974). Acculturative stress. *Journal of Cross-Cultural Psychology*, **5**, 382–406.

Berry, J.W., Poortinga, Y.H., Segall, M.H. & Dasen, P.R. (1992). *Cross-cultural Psychology: Research and Applications*. New York: Cambridge University Press.

Berscheid, E. (1983). Emotion. In H.H. Kelley, E. Berscheid, A. Christensen, J.H. Harvey, T.L. Huston, G. Levinger, E. McClintock, L.A. Peplau & D.R. Peterson (Eds), *Close Relationships* (pp. 110–68). New York: Freeman.

Berscheid, E. (1985). Interpersonal attraction. In G. Lindzey & E. Aronson (Eds), *Handbook of Social Psychology* (3rd Edn, pp. 413–84). Reading, MA: Addison-Wesley.

Berscheid, E. (1986). Mea culpas and lamentations: Sir Francis, Sir Isaac and the "slow progress of soft psychology". In R. Gilmour & S.W. Duck (Eds), *The Emerging Field of Personal Relationships* (pp. 267–86). Hillsdale, NJ: Erlbaum.

Berscheid, E. (1994). Interpersonal relationships. In W. Porter & R. Rozenzweig (Eds), *Annual Review of Psychology*, **45**, 79–129. Palo Alto: Annual Reviews.

Berscheid, E. (1995). Help wanted: a grand theorist of interpersonal relationships, sociologist or anthropologist preferred. *Journal of Social and Personal Relationships*, **12**, 529–33.

Berscheid, E. & Graziano, W. (1979). The initiation of social relationships and social attraction. In R.L. Burgess & T.L. Huston (Eds), *Social exchange in developing relationships*. New York: Academic Press.

Berscheid, E. & Walster [Hatfield], E. (1969). *Interpersonal Attraction*. Reading, MA: Addison-Welsey.

Berscheid, E. & Walster, [Hatfield], E. (1978). *Interpersonal Attraction* (2nd Edn). Addison-Welsey: Reading, MA.

Berscheid, E., Snyder, M. & Omoto, A. (1989). Issues in studying close relationships: conceptualizing and measuring closeness. In C. Hendrick (Ed.), *Close Relationships* (pp. 63–91). Newbury Park: Sage.

Bertelsen, A., Harvald, B. & Hauge, M. (1977). A Danish twin study of manic-depressive disorders. *British Journal of Psychiatry*, **130**, 330–51.

Bertsch, T.D., Nagashima-Whalen, L., Dykeman, S., Kennell, J.H. & McGrath, S. (1990). Labor support by first time fathers: direct observations. *Journal of Psychosomatic Obstetric Gynecology*, **11**, 251–60.

Berzon, B. (1992). Developing a positive gay identity. In B. Berzon & R. Leighton (Eds), *Positively Gay* (pp. 3–15). Milrose, CA.

Betzig, L. (1989). Causes of conjugal dissolution: a cross-cultural study. *Current Anthropology*, **30**, 654–76.

Betzig, L. (1992). Roman polygyny. *Ethology and Sociobiology*, **13**, 309–49.

Beutler, I.V., Burr, W.R., Barr, K.S. & Herrin, D.A. (1989a). The family realm: theoretical contributions for understanding its uniqueness. *Journal of Marriage and the Family*, **51**, 805–15.

Beutler, I.V., Burr, W.R., Barr, K.S. & Herrin, D.A. (1989b). A seventh group has visited the elephant. *Journal of Marriage and the Family*, **51**, 826–30.

Bhavnagri, N. (1987). Parents as facilitators of preschool children's peer relationships. Unpublished doctoral dissertation, University of Illinois at Champaign-Urbana, IL.

Bhavnagri, N. & Parke, R.D. (1985). Parents as facilitators of preschool peer–peer interaction. Paper presented at the Biennial Meeting of the Society for Research in Child Development, Toronto.

Bhavnagri, N. & Parke, R.D. (1991). Parents as direct facilitators of children's peer relationships: effects of age of child and sex of parent. *Journal of Personal and Social Relationships*, **8**, 423–40.

Bielby, W. & Baron, J.(1984). A woman's place is with other women: sex segregation within organizations. In B. Reskin (Ed.) *Sex Segregation in the Workplace* (pp. 27–55). Washington DC: National Academy Press.

Bigelow, B.J. & La Gaipa, J.J. (1980). The development of friendship values and choice. In H.C. Foot, A.J. Chapman & J.R. Smith (Eds), *Friendship and Social Relations in Children*. Chichester: Wiley.

Billig, M. (1987). *Arguing and Thinking: a Rhetorical Approach to Social Psychology*. Cambridge, MA: Cambridge University Press.

Birman, D. (1994). Acculturation and human diversity in a multicultural society. In E.J. Trickett, R.J. Watts & D. Birman (Eds), *Human Diversity: Perspectives on People in Context* (pp. 261–84). San Francisco: Jossey-Bass.

Bischof-Kohler, D. (1988). Uber den Zusammenhang von Empathie und der Fahigkeit, sich im Spiegel zu erkennen [The relationship between empathy and mirror self-recognition]. *Schweizerische Zeitschrift fur Psychologie*, **47**, 147–59, cited in Asendorpf, J.B. & Baudonniere, P. (1993). Self-awareness and other awareness: mirror self-recognition and synchronic imitation among unfamiliar peers. *Developmental Psychology*, **29**, 88–93.

Bischof-Kohler, D. (1991). The development of empathy in infants. In M.E. Lamb & H. Keller (Eds), *Infant Development: Perspectives from German-speaking Countries* (pp. 1–33). Hillsdale, NJ: Erlbaum.

Black, D. (1993). *The Social Structure of Right and Wrong*. San Diego: Academic Press.

Blades, J. (1985). *Family Mediation*. Englewood Cliffs, NJ: Prentice-Hall.

Blair, S.L. (1993). Employment, family and perceptions of marital quality among husbands and wives. *Journal of Family Issues*, **14**, 189–212.

Blair, S.L. & Johnson, M.P. (1992). Wives' perceptions of the fairness of the division of household labor: the intersection of housework and idealogy. *Journal of Marriage and the Family*, **54**, 570–81.

Blake, R.R. & Mouton, J.S. (1964). *The Managerial Grid*. Houston: Gulf Publishing.

Bland, S.H., Krogh, V., Winkelstein, W. & Trevisan, M. (1991). Social network and blood pressure: a population study. *Psychosomatic Medicine*, **53**, 598–607.

Blankenship, V., Hnat, S., Hess, T. & Brown, D.R. (1984). Reciprocal interaction and similarity of personality attributes. *Journal of Social and Personal Relationships*, **1**, 415–32.

Blau, P.M. (1964). *Exchange and Power in Social Life*. New York: Wiley.

Blau, Z. (1973). *Old Age in a Contemporary Society*. New York: Viewpoints.

Blazer, D.G. (1982). Social support and mortality in an elderly community population. *American Journal of Epidemiology*, **115**, 684–94.

Bleicher, J. (1980). *Contemporary Hermeneutics: Hermeneutics as Method, Philosophy and Critique*. London: Routledge & Kegan Paul.

Blieszner, R. & Adams, R.G. (1992). *Adult Friendship*. Newbury Park, CA: Sage.

Blieszner, R. & Bedford, V.H. (Eds) (1995). *Handbook of Aging and the Family*. Westport, CT: Greenwood.

Bloch, S. & Crouch, E. (1985). *Therapeutic Factors in Group Psychotherapy*. New York: Oxford University Press.

Bloch, S., Reibstein, J., Crouch, E., Holroyd, P. & Themen, J. (1979). A method for the study of therapeutic factors in group psychotherapy. *British Journal of Psychiatry*, **134**, 257–63.

Block, J.D. (1980). *Friendship*. New York: Macmillan.

Block, J.H. & Block, J. (1980). The role of ego-control and ego-resiliency in the organization of behavior. In W.A. Collins (Ed.), *Development of Cognition, Affect, and Social Relations*. (Minnesota Symposia on Child Psychology (Vol. 13) (pp. 39–101). Hillsdale, NJ: Erlbaum.

Block, J., Block J.H. & Keyes, S. (1988). Longitudinally foretelling drug usage in adolescence: early childhood personality and environmental precursors. *Child Development*, **59**, 336–55.

Blood, R.O. (1969). Kinship interaction and marital solidarity. *Merrill-Palmer Quarterly*, **15**, 171–84.

Blood, R.O. & Wolfe, D.W. (1960). *Husbands and Wives*. Glencoe, IL: Free Press.

Bloom, B.L., Asher, S.J. & White, S.W. (1978). Marital disruption as a stressor: a review and analysis. *Psychological Bulletin*, **85**, 867–94.

Blos, P. (1967). The second individuation process of adolescence. *Psychoanalytic Study of the Child*, **22**, 162–86.

Blos, P. (1979). *The Adolescent Passage*. New York: International Universities Press.

Blumenthal, J.A., Burg, M., Barefoot, J., Williams, R.B., Haney, T. & Zimet, J.G. (1987). Social support, Type A behavior, and coronary artery disease. *Psychosomatic Medicine*, **49**, 331–40.

Blumstein, P. & Schwartz, P. (1983). *American Couples: Money, Work, Sex*. New York: William Morrow.

Blumstein, P. & Schwartz, P. (1991). Money and ideology. In R.L. Blumberg (Ed.), *Gender, Family, and Economy: the Triple Overlap* (pp. 261–88). Newbury Park, CA: Sage.

Bocharov, S. (1994). Conversations with Bakhtin. *PMLA*, **109**, 1009–24.

Bochner, A.P. (1982). On the efficacy of openness in closed relationships. In M. Burgoon (Ed.), *Communication Yearbook 5* (pp. 109–42). New Brunswick, NJ: Transaction Books.

Bochner, A.P. (1984). The functions of communication in interpersonal bonding. In C. Arnold & J. Bowers (Eds), *Handbook of Rhetorical and Communication Theory* (pp. 544–621). Boston: Allyn & Bacon.

Bochner, A.P. (1994). Perspectives on inquiry II: theories and stories. In M. Knapp & G. Miller (Eds), *Handbook of Interpersonal Communication* (2nd Edn) (pp. 21–41). Newbury Park, CA: Sage.

Bochner, A.P. & Eisenberg, E. (1987). Family process: system perspectives. In C.R. Berger & S. Chaffee (Eds), *Handbook of Communication Science* (pp. 540–63). Thousand Oaks, CA: Sage.

Bochner, A.P. & Ellis, C. (1992). Personal narrative as a social approach to interpersonal communication, *Communication Theory*, **2**, 165–72.

Bochner, A.P. & Ellis, C. (1995). Telling and living: narrative co-construction and the practices of interpersonal relationships. In W. Leeds-Hurwitz (Ed.), *Communication as Social Construction: Social Approaches to the Study of Interpersonal Interaction*. New York: Guilford.

Bochner, A.P. & Waugh, J. (1995). Talking with as a model for writing about: implications of Rortian pragmatism for communication theory. In L. Langsdorf & A. Smith (Eds), *Recovering Pragmatism's Voice: The Classical Tradition and the Philosophy of Communication* (pp. 211–33). Albany: SUNY Press.

Bock, R.D. (1989). *Multilevel Analysis of Educational Data*. San Diego: Academic Press.

Bolger, N. & Eckenrode, J. (1991). Social relationships, personality, and anxiety during a major stressful event. *Journal of Personality and Social Psychology*, **61**, 440–49.

Bolger, N. & Kelleher, S. (1993). Daily life in relationships. In S.W. Duck (Ed.) *Social Contexts of Relationships [Understanding Relationship Processes 3]* (pp. 100–108). Newbury Park, CA: Sage.

Bolger, N. & Zuckerman, A. (1994, August). Dynamics in adjustment in couples facing the bar examination. Paper presented at the 102th Annual Convention of American Psychological Association, Toronto, Canada.

Bolger, N., DeLongis, A., Kessler, R.C. & Wethington, E.(1989). The contagion of stress across multiple roles. *Journal of Marriage and the Family*, **51**, 175–83.

Bolger, N., Foster, M., Vinokur, A. & Ng, R. (1996). Close relationships and adjustment to a life crisis: the case of breast cancer. *Journal of Personality and Social Psychology*, **70**, 283–94.

Bolig, R., Stein, P.J. & McKenry, P.C. (1984). The self-advertisement approach to dating: male–female differences. *Family Relations*, **33**, 587–92.

Bolin, R. (1993). Natural and technological disasters: evidence of psychopathology. In A.M. Ghadirian & H.E. Lehmann (Eds), *Environment and Psychopathology* (pp.121–40). New York: Springer.

Bolin, R.C. (1982). *Long-term Family Recovery From Disaster*. Boulder, CO: Institute of Behavioral Science, University of Colorado.

Bolin, R.C. (1985a). Disaster and social support. In B.T. Sowder (Ed.), *Disaster and Mental Health: Selected Contemporary Perspectives* (pp. 150–57). National Institute of Mental Health, Rockville, MD.

Bolin, R.C. (1985b). Disaster characteristics and psychosocial impacts. In B.T. Sowder (Ed.), *Disasters and Mental Health: Selected Contemporary Perspectives* (pp. 3–28). National Institute of Mental Health, Rockville, MD.

Bolin, R. & Bolton, P. (1986). *Race, Religion, and Ethnicity in Disaster Recovery*. Boulder, CO: University of Colorado.

Bolin, R. & Stanford, L. (1990). Shelter and housing issues in Santa Cruz County. In R. Bolin (Ed.), *The Loma Prieta Earthquake: Studies of Short-term Impacts* (pp. 99–108). Boulder, CO: University of Colorado.

Bolin, R.C. & Trainer, P. (1978). Modes of family recovery following disaster: a cross-national study. In E.L. Quarantelli (Ed.), *Disasters: Theory and Research* (pp. 233–44). Beverly Hills, CA: Sage.

Bond, M.H. & Hwang, K.K. (1986). The social psychology of Chinese people. In M.H. Bond (Ed.), *The Psychology of the Chinese People* (pp. 213–66). Oxford: Oxford University Press.

Booth, A. & Hess, E. (1974). Cross-sex friendship. *Journal of Marriage and the Family*, 38–47.

Bopp, M.J. & Weeks, G.R. (1984). Dialectical metatheory in family therapy. *Family Process*, **23**, 49–61.

Bose, C.E. (1987). Devaluing women's work: the undercount of women's employment in 1900 and 1980. In C. Bose, R. Feldberg & N. Sokoloff (Eds), *Hidden Aspects of Women's Work* (pp. 95–115). New York: Praeger.

Bostrom, R. & Donohew, L. (1992). The case for empiricism: clarifying fundamental issues in communication theory. *Communication Monographs*, **59**, 109–29.

Bott, E. (1955). Urban families: conjugal roles and social networks. *Human Relations*, **8**, 345–84.

Bott, E. (1971). *Family and Social Network* (2nd Edn). New York: Free Press.

Bowen, S.P. & Michal-Johnson, P. (1995). HIV/AIDS: a crucible for understanding the dark side of sexual interaction. In S.W. Duck & J.T. Wood (Eds), *Confronting Relationship Challenges [Understanding Relationship Processes 5]* (pp. 150–80). Thousand Oaks, CA: Sage.

Bower, G.H. & Gilligan, S.G. (1979). Remembering information related to one's self. *Journal of Research in Personality*, **13**, 420–32.

Bowlby, J. (1944). Forty-four juvenile thieves: their characters and home life. *International Journal of Psychoanalysis*, **25**, 19–52.

Bowlby, J. (1969). *Attachment and Loss: Vol. 1. Attachment*. New York: Basic Books.

Bowlby, J. (1969/1982). *Attachment and Loss, Vol. I. Attachment* (2nd Edn). New York: Basic Books.

Bowlby, J. (1973). *Attachment and Loss, Vol. II. Separation: Anxiety and Anger*. New York: Basic Books.

Bowlby, J. (1979). *The Making and Breaking of Affectional Bonds*. London: Tavistock.

Bowlby, J. (1980a). *Attachment and Loss, Vol. III. Loss: Sadness and Depression*. New York: Basic Books.

Bowlby, J. (1980b). The making and breaking of affectional bonds. *British Journal of Psychiatry*, **130**, 201–10.

Bowlby, J. (1988a). *A Secure Base: Parent–Child Attachment and Healthy Human Development*. New York: Basic Books.

Bowlby, J. (1988b). Attachment, communication, and the therapeutic process. In J. Bowlby, *A secure base: Parent–child Attachment and Healthy Human Development* (pp. 137–57). New York: Basic Books.

Bowling, A. (1987). Mortality after bereavement: a review of the literature on survival periods and factors affecting survival. *Social Science and Medicine*, **24**, 24–117.

Bowman, M.L. (1990). Coping efforts and marital satisfaction: measuring marital coping and its correlates. *Journal of Marriage and the Family*, **52**, 463–74.

Boxer, A.M., Cook, J.A. & Cohler, B.J. (1986). Grandfathers, fathers, and sons: intergenerational relations among men. In K.A. Pillemer & R.S. Wolf (Eds), *Elder Abuse: Conflict in the Family* (pp. 9–121). Dover, MA: Auburn House.

Boyce, W.T., Kay, M. & Uitti, C. (1988). The taxonomy of social support: an ethnographic analysis among adolescent mothers. *Social Science Medicine*, **26**(11), 1079–85.

Boyce, W.T., Schaefer, C.H., Harrison, R.H., Haffner, W.H. J., Lewis, M. & Right, A.L. (1986). Social and cultural factors in pregnancy complications among Navajo women. *American Journal of Epidemiology*, **124**, 242–53.

Boyum, L. & Parke, R.D. (1995). Family emotional expressiveness and children's social competence. *Journal of Marriage and Family*, **57**, 593–608.

Bozormenyi-Nagy, I. & Spark, G.M. (1973). *Invisible Loyalties*. New York: Harper & Row.

Bradac, J. (1983). The language of lovers, flovers, and friends: communicating in social and personal relationships. *Journal of Language and Social Psychology*, **2**, 141–62.

Bradbury, T.N. & Fincham, F.D. (1989). Behavior and satisfaction in marriage: prospective mediating processes. *Review of Personality and Social Psychology*, **10**, 119–43.

Bradbury, T.N. & Fincham, F.D. (1990). Attributions in marriage: review and critique. *Psychological Bulletin*, **107**, 3–33.

Bradbury, T.N. & Karney, B.R. (1993). Longitudinal study of marital interaction and dysfunction: review and analysis. *Clinical Psychology Review*, **13**, 15–27.

Braha, V. & Rutter, D.R. (1980). Friendship choice in a mixed–race primary school. *Educational Studies*, **6**, 217–23.

Brain, R. (1976). *Friends and Lovers*. New York: Basic Books.

Braithwaite, D. & Baxter, L.A. (1995). "I do" again: the relational dialectics of renewing marriage vows. *Journal of Social and Personal Relationships*, **12**, 177–98.

Brake, S., Shair, H. & Hofer, M.A. (1988). Exploiting the nursing niche: the infant's sucking and feeding in the context of the mother–infant interaction. In E.M. Blass (Ed.), *Handbook of Behavioral Neurobiology*, Vol. 9 (pp. 347–88). New York: Plenum.

Brand, S. & Hirsch, B.J. (1990). The contribution of social networks, work–shift schedules, and the family life cycle to women's well-being. In S.W. Duck (Ed.), *Personal Relationships and Social Support* (pp. 159–72). London: Sage.

Brayfield, A.A. (1992). Employment resources and housework in Canada. *Journal of Marriage and the Family*, **54**, 19–30.

Brehm, S.S. (1985). *Intimate Relationships*. New York: Random House.

Brehm, S.S. (1988). Passionate love. In R.J. Sternberg & M.L. Barnes (Eds), *The Psychology of Love* (pp. 232–63). New Haven, CT: Yale University Press.

Brehm, S.S. (1992). *Intimate Relationships*, 2nd Edn. New York: McGraw-Hill.

Brennan, K.A., Shaver, P.R. & Tobey, A.E. (1991). Attachment styles, gender, and parental problem drinking. *Journal of Social and Personal Relationships*, **8**, 451–66.

Bretherton, I. (1985). Attachment theory: retrospect and prospect. In I. Bretherton & E. Waters (Eds), Growing points in attachment theory and research. *Monographs for the Society for Research in Child Development*, **50** (1–2), Serial No. 209, 3–35.

Bretherton, I. & Waters, E. (Eds) (1985). Growing points of attachment theory and research. *Monographs of the Society for Research in Child Development*, **50**(1–2), Serial No. 209.

Bretherton, I., Biringen, Z. & Rodgeway, D. (1991). The parental side of attachment. In K. Pillemer & K. McCartney (Eds), *Parent–Child Relations Throughout Life* (pp. 1–24). Hillsdale, NJ: Erlbaum.

Brewer, M. (1991). The social self: on being the same and different at the same time. *Personality and Social Psychology Bulletin*, **17**, 475–82.

Brewer, M.B. & Miller, N. (1987). Contact and cooperation: when do they work? In P.A. Katz & D.A. Taylor (Eds), *Eliminating Racism: Profiles in Controversy* (pp. 315–26). New York: Plenum.

Brickman, P., Dunkel-Schetter, C. & Abbey, A. (1987). The development of commitment. In P. Brickman (Ed.), *Commitment, Conflict, and Caring* (pp. 145–221). Englewood Cliffs, NJ: Prentice-Hall.

Bridge, K. & Baxter, L.A. (1992). Blended friendships: friends as work associates. *Western Journal of Communication*, **56**, 200–25.

Brock, D.M., Pierce, G.R., Sarason, I.G. & Sarason, B.R. (1995). Simultaneous assessment of perceived global and relationship-specific support. Manuscript submitted for publication.

Brockner, J. & Rubin, J.Z. (1985). *Entrapment in Escalating Conflicts: a Social Psychological Analysis*. New York: Springer-Verlag.

Broderick, C.B. (1993). *Understanding Family Process*. Newbury Park, CA: Sage.

Brody, E.M. & Farber, B.A. (1989). Effects of psychotherapy on significant others. *Professional Psychology: Research & Practice*, **20**, 116–22.

Brody, G.H., Stoneman, Z. & Mackinnon, C.E. (1982). Role asymmetries in interactions among school-aged children, their younger siblings and their friends. *Child Development*, **53**, 1364–70.

Brody, G.H., Stoneman, Z. & Burke, M. (1987). Child temperaments, maternal differential behavior, and sibling relationships. *Developmental Psychology*, **23**, 354–62.

Brody, G.H., Stoneman, Z. & McCoy, J.K. (1994). Forecasting sibling relationships in early adolescence from child temperaments and family process in middle childhood. *Child Development*, **65**, 771–84.

Brody, G.H., Stoneman, Z., McCoy, J.K. & Forehand, R. (1992). Contemporaneous and longitudinal associations of sibling conflict with family relationship assessments and family discussions about sibling problems. *Child Development*, **63**, 391–400.

Brody, G.H., Stoneman, A., MacKinnon, C.E. & MacKinnon, R. (1985). Role relationships and behavior among preschool-aged and school aged sibling pairs. *Developmental Psychology*, **7**, 225–36.

Brody, H. (1987). *Stories of Sickness*. New Haven, CT: Yale University Press.

Bromet, E.J. (1989). The nature and effects of technological failures. In R. Gist & B. Lubin (Eds), *Psychological Aspects of Disaster* (pp. 120–39). New York: Wiley.

Bronfenbrenner, U. (1970). *Two Worlds of Childhood: U.S. and U.S.S.R.* New York: Russell Sage.

Bronfenbrenner, U. (1979). *The Ecology of Human Development: Experiments by Nature and Design*. Cambridge, MA: Harvard University Press.

Bronfenbrenner, U. (1989). Ecological systems theory. In R. Vasta (Ed.), *Annals of Child Development*, Vol. 6 (pp. 187–250). Greenwich, CT: JAI Press.

Bronfenbrenner, U. & Weiss, H. (1983). Beyond policies without people: an ecological perspective on child and family policy. In E. Zigler, S.L. Kagan & E. Klugman (Eds), *Children, Families, and Government: Perspectives on American social policy*. Cambridge: Cambridge University Press.

Broude, G.J. (1992). The May–September algorithm meets the 20th century actuarial table. *Behavioral and Brain Sciences*, **15**, 94–5.

Brown, B., Altman, I. & Werner, C. (1992). Close relationships in the physical and social world: dialectical and transactional analyses. *Communication Yearbook*, **15**, 508–21.

Brown, C., Feldberg, R., Fox, E. & Kohen, J. (1976). Divorce: chance of a new lifetime. *Journal of Social Issues*, **32**, 119–34.

Brown, D.E. (1991). *Human Universals*. New York: McGraw-Hill.

Brown, G.W. (1985). The discovery of expressed emotion: induction or deduction? In J. Leff & C. Vaughn (Eds), *Expressed Emotion in Families*. New York: Guilford.

Brown, G.W. & Harris, T. (1978). Social origins of depression: a study of psychiatric disorder in women. London: Tavistock.

Brown, G.W. & Rutter, M. (1966). The measurement of family activities and relationships: a methodological study. *Human Relations*, **19**, 241–63.

Brown, G.W., Birley, J.L.T. & Wing, J.K. (1972). Influence of family life on the course of schizophrenic disorders: a replication. *British Journal of Psychiatry*, **121**, 241–58.

Brown, G.W., Carstairs, G.M. & Topping, G. (1958). Post-hospital adjustment of chronic mental patients. *Lancet*, **2**, 685–9.

Brown, G.W., Monck, E.M., Carstairs, G.M. & Wing, J.K. (1962). Influence of family life on the course of schizophrenic illness. *Journal of Preventive and Social Medicine*, **16**, 55–68.

Brown, J. & Dunn, J. (1991). "You can cry, mum": the social developmental implications of talk about internal states. *British Journal of Developmental Psychology*, **9**, 237–56.

Brown, J. & Dunn, J. (1992). Talk with your mother or your sibling? Developmental changes in early family conversations about feelings. *Child Development*, **63**, 336–49.

Brown, J.D. & McGill, K.L. (1989). The cost of good fortune: when positive life events produce negative health consequences. *Journal of Personality and Social Psychology*, **57**, 1103–10.

Brown, J.R. & Rogers, L.E. (1991). Openness, uncertainty, and intimacy: an epistemological reformulation. In N. Coupland, H. Giles & J.M. Wiemann (Eds), *"Miscommunication" and Problematic Talk* (pp. 146–65). Newbury Park: Sage.

Brown, P. & Levinson, S. (1987). *Politeness: Some Universals in Language Usage*. Cambridge: Cambridge University Press.

Brown, R. (1986). *Social Psychology*, 2nd Edn. New York: Free Press.

Brownell, C.A. & Carriger, M.S. (1990). Changes in cooperation and self-other differentiation during the second year. *Child Development*, **61**, 1164–74.

Bruess, C.J.S. & Pearson, J.C. (1993). "Sweet pea" and "pussy cat": an examination of idiom use and marital satisfaction over the life cycle. *Journal of Social and Personal Relationships*, **10**, 609–15.

Bruner, J. (1986). *Actual Minds, Possible Worlds*. Cambridge, MA: Harvard University Press.

Bruner, J. (1990). *Acts of Meaning*. Cambridge, MA: Harvard University Press.

Bryant, B. (1985). The neighborhood walk: sources of support in middle childhood. *Monographs of the Society for Research in Child Development*, **50**(3, Serial No. 210).

Bryant, B.K. (1989). The child's perspective of sibling caretaking and its relevance to understanding social-emotional functioning and development. In P.G. Zukow (Ed.), *Sibling Interaction Across Cultures: Theoretical and Methodological Issues*. New York: Springer-Verlag.

Bryant, B.K. & Crockenberg, S.B. (1980). Correlates and dimensions of prosocial behavior: a study of female siblings with their mothers. *Child Development*, **51**, 529–44.

Bryant, D. (1953). Rhetoric: its functions and its scope. *Quarterly Journal of Speech*, **39**, 401–24.

Bryk, A.S. & Raudenbush, S.W. (1992). *Hierarchical Linear Models: Applications and Data Analysis Methods*. Newbury Park: Sage.

Buber, M. (1937). *I and thou*. New York: Scribners.

Buchanan, R.M. (1994). Intergenerational and gender differences in acculturation: implications for adolescent–family adjustment. Unpublished master's thesis, University of Maryland, College Park, MD.

Buck, R. (1975). Non-verbal communication of affect in children. *Journal of Personality and Social Psychology*, **31**, 644–53.

Budman, S.H., Soldz, S., Demby, A., Feldstein, M., Springer, T. & Davis M.S. (1989). Cohesion, alliance and outcome in group psychotherapy. *Psychiatry*, **52**, 339–50.

Buehlman, K., Gottman, J.M. & Katz, L. (1992). How a couple views their past predicts their future: predicting divorce from an oral history interview. *Journal of Family Psychology*, **5**, 295–318.

Bugental, D. (1991). Affective and cognitive processes within threat-oriented family systems. In I.E. Sigel, A.V. McGillicuddy-DeLisi & J.J. Goodnow (Eds), *Parental Belief Systems: The Psychological Consequences for Children* (2nd Edn). Hillsdale, NJ: Erlbaum.

Buhrmester, D. (1990). Intimacy of friendship, interpersonal competence, and adjustment during preadolescence and adolescence. *Child Development*, **61**, 1101–11.

Buhrmester, D. & Furman, W. (1986). The changing functions of friends in childhood: a neo-Sullivanian perspective. In V. Derlega & B. Winstaed (Eds), *Friendship and Social Interaction* (pp. 41–62). New York: Springer.

Buhrmester, D. & Furman, W. (1987). The development of companionship and intimacy. *Child Development*, **58**, 1101–13.

Buhrmester, D. & Furman, W. (1990). Perceptions of sibling relationships during middle childhood and adolescence. *Child Development*, **61**, 1387–98.

Bukowski, W. & Hoza, B. (1989). Popularity and friendship: Issues in theory, measurement and outcome. In T. Berndt & G. Ladd (Eds), *Peer Relationships in Child Development* (pp. 15–45). New York: Wiley.

Bukowski, W.M., Nappi, B.J. & Hoza, B. (1987). A test of Aristotle's model of friendship for young adults' same-sex and opposite-sex relationships. *Journal of Social Psychology*, **127**, 595–603.

Bulcroft, K. & Bulcroft, R. (1991). The timing of divorce: effects on parent–child relationships in later life. *Research on Aging*, **13**, 226–43.

Burger, E. & Milardo, R.M. (1995). Marital interdependence and social networks. *Journal of Social and Personal Relationships*, **12**, 403–15.

Burgess, E.W. & Cottrell, L.S. (1939). *Predicting Success or Failure in Marriage*. Englewood Cliffs, NJ: Prentice-Hall.

Burks, V.M. & Parke, R.D. (in press). Parent and child representations of social relationships: Linkages between families and peers. *Merrill-Palmer Quarterly*.

Burks, V.M., Carson, J.L. & Parke, R.D. (1987). Parent–child interactional styles of popular and rejected children. Unpublished manuscript, University of Illinois, Urbana, IL.

Burleson, B.R. (1991). Review of *Studying Interpersonal Interaction*. *ISSPR Bulletin*, **8**, 29–31.

Burleson, B.R. (1994). Comforting messages: significance, approaches, and effects. In B.R. Burleson, T.L., Albrecht & I.G. Sarason (Eds), *Communication of Social Support: Messages, Interactions, Relationships, and Community*. Thousand Oaks: Sage.

Burman, B., Margolin, G. & John, R.S. (1993). America's angriest home videos: behavioral contingencies observed in home reenactments of marital conflict. *Journal of Consulting and Clinical Psychology*, **61**, 28–39.

Burnstein, E., Crandall, C. & Kitayama, S. (1994). Some neo-Darwinian rules for altruism: weighing cues for inclusive fitness as a function of the biological importance of the decision. *Journal of Personality and Social Psychology*, **67**, 773–89.

Burr, W.R., Herrin, D.A., Day, R.D., Beutler, I.F. & Leigh, G.K. (1987). An epistemological basis for primary explanations in family science. Paper presented at the Theory and Methods Workshop at the Annual Meetings of the National Council on Family Relations, Atlanta, GA.

Burt, R.S. (1983). Distinguishing relational contents. In R.S. Burt, M.J. Minor & Associates (Eds), *Applied Network Analysis: A Methodological Introduction* (pp. 35–74). Beverly Hills, CA: Sage.

Burton, L. (1992). Black grandparents rearing children of drug-addicted parents: stressors, outcomes and the social service needs. *The Gerontologist*, **32**, 744–51.

Burton, L.M. (1990). Teenage childbearing as an alternative life-course strategy in multigeneration black families. *Human Nature*, **1**(2), 123–43.

Burton, L.M. (1991). Caring for children. *The American Enterprise*, 34–7.

Burton, L.M. (in press). Intergenerational family structure and the provision of care in African-American families. In K.W. Schaie, V.L. Bengston & L.M. Burton (Eds), *Intergenerational Issues in Aging*. New York: Springer.

Burton, L.M. & Dilworth-Anderson, P. (1991). The intergenerational family roles of aged black Americans. *Marriage and Family Review*, **16**(3/4), 311–30.

Buss, A. (1980). *Self-consciousness and Social Anxiety*. San Francisco: W.H. Freeman.

Buss, A.R. (1979). *A Dialectical Psychology*. New York: Irvington.

Buss, D.M. (1988a). The evolution of human intrasexual competition: tactics of mate attraction. *Journal of Personality and Social Psychology*, **54**, 616–28.

Buss, D.M. (1988b). From vigilence to violence: tactics of mate retention in American undergraduates. *Ethology and Sociobiology*, **9**, 291–317.

Buss, D.M. (1989). Sex differences in human mate preferences: evolutionary hypotheses tested in 37 cultures. *Behavioral and Brain Sciences*, **12**, 1–49.

Buss, D.M. (1994). *The Evolution of Desire: Strategies of Human Mating*. New York: Basic Books.

Buss, D.M. (1995). Evolutionary psychology: a new paradigm for psychological science. *Psychological Inquiry*, **6**, 1–30.

Buss, D.M. & Barnes, M.F. (1986). Preferences in human mate selection. *Journal of Personality and Social Psychology*, **50**, 559–70.

Buss, D.M. & Kenrick, D.T. (in press). Evolutionary social psychology. In D. Gilbert, S. Fiske & G. Lindzey (Eds), *Handbook of Social Psychology* (4th Edn). New York: McGraw-Hill.

Buss, D.M. & Schmitt, D.P. (1993). Sexual strategies theory: an evolutionary perspective on human mating. *Psychological Review*, **100**, 204–32.

Buss, D.M., Larsen, R., Westen, D. & Semmelroth, J. (1992). Sex differences in jealousy: evolution, physiology, and psychology. *Psychological Science*, **3**, 251–5.

Butler, S. & Rosenblum, B. (1991). *Cancer in Two Voices*. San Francisco: Spinster.

Butzlaff, R.L. & Hooley, J.M. (1995). Expressed emotion and relapse: a meta-analysis. Unpublished manuscript.

Buunk, A.P. (1987). Conditions that promote breakups as a consequence of extradyadic involvements. *Journal of Social and Clinical Psychology*, **5**, 271–84.

Buunk, A.P. (1991). Jealousy in close relationships: an exchange-theoretical perspective. In P. Salovey (Ed.), *The Psychology of Jealousy and Envy* (pp. 148–77). New York: Guilford.

Buunk, A.P. & Hupka, R.B. (1987). Cross-cultural differences in the elicitation of sexual jealousy. *Journal of Sex Research*, **23**, 12–22.

Buunk, A.P. & VanYperen, N.W. (1991). Referential comparisons, relational comparisons, and exchange orientation: their relation to marital satisfaction. *Personality and Social Psychology Bulletin*, **17**, 709–17.

Buunk, A.P, Angleitner, A., Oubaid, V. & Buss, D.M. (in press). Sexual and cultural differences in jealousy: tests from The Netherlands, Germany, and the United States. *Psychological Science*.

Buunk, B. (1980). *Intieme relaties met derden. Ren sociaal Psychologische Studie* (Multiple Intimate Relationships: a Social Psychological Study). Alphen an den Rhein: Samsom.

Byers, J.A. & Byers, K.Z. (1983). Do pronghorn mothers reveal the locations of their hidden fawns? *Behavioral Ecology and Sociobiology*, **13**, 147–56.

Byrne, D. (1971). *The Attraction Paradigm*. New York: Academic Press.

Byrne, D. (1992). The transition from controlled laboratory experimentation to less controlled settings: surprise! Additional variables are operative. *Communication Monographs*, **59**, 190–98.

Callondann, A. (1995). Geschwister und Ärger—Eine Untersuchung zur Ärgerregulierung im Zusammenhang mit der Qualität der Geschwisterbeziehung. Unpublished MA thesis, Free University Berlin.

Cameron, C., Oskamp, S. & Sparks, W. (1977). Courtship American style—newspaper ads. *Family Coordinator*, **26**, 27–30.

Campbell, A., Converse, P.E. & Rodgers, W.L. (1976). *The Quality of American Life*. New York: Russell Sage.

Campbell, D.T. (1975). On the conflicts between biological and social evolution and between psychology and moral tradition. *American Psychologist*, **30**, 1103–26.

Campbell, K.E. & Lee, B.A. (1991). Name generators in surveys of personal networks, *Social Networks*, **13**, 203–21.

Campos, J.J., Barrett, K.C., Lamb, M.E., Goldsmith, H.H. & Stenberg, C. (1983). Socioemotional development. In P.H. Mussen (Series Ed.), M. Haith & J. Campos (Vol. Eds), *Handbook of Child Psychology*, Vol. 2 (pp. 273–314, 783–917). Hillsdale, NJ: Erlbaum.

Campos, J., Campos, R. & Barrett, K.C. (1989). Emergent themes in the study of emotional development and emotion regulation. *Developmental Psychology*, **25**, 394–402.

Camras, L. (1977). Facial expressions used by children in a conflict situation. *Child Development*, **48**, 1431–5.

Cappella, J.N. & Palmer, M.T. (1990). Attitude similarity, relational history, and attraction: the mediating effects of kinesic and vocal behaviors. *Communication Monographs*, **57**, 161–83.

Carnelley, K.B., Pietromonaco, P.R. & Jaffe, K. (1994). Depression, working models of others, and relationship functioning. *Journal of Personality and Social Psychology*, **66**, 127–40.

Carnevale, P.J. & Pruitt, D.G. (1992). Negotiation and mediation. *Annual Review of Psychology*, **43**, 531–82.

Carson, J. & Parke, R.D. (in press). Reciprocity of parent–child negative affect and children's social competence. *Child Development*.

Carson, R.C. (1969). *Interaction Concepts of Personality*. Chicago: Aldine.

Carstensen, L.L., Gottman, J.M. & Levenson, R.W. (1995). Emotional behavior in long-term marriage. *Psychology and Aging*, **10**, 140–49.

Carter, C.S. (1992). Oxytocin and sexual behavior. *Neuroscience and Biobehavioral Reviews*, **16**, 131–44.

Cartwright, D. & Harary, F. (1956). Structural balance: a generalization of Heider's theory. *Psychological Review*, **63**, 277–93.

Case, R. (1991). Stages in the development of the young child's first sense of self. *Developmental Review*, **11**, 210–30.

Caspi, A. & Silva, P.A. (1995). Temperamental qualities at age three predict personality traits in young adulthood: Longitudinal evidence from a birth cohort. *Child Development*, **66**, 486–98.

Caspi, A., Bem, D.J. & Elder, G.H. (1989). Continuities and consequences of interactional styles across the life course. *Journal of Personality*, **57**, 375–406.

Caspi, G.H., Elder, G.H. & Bem, D.J. (1987). Moving against the world: life courses of explosive children. *Developmental Psychology*, **23**, 308–13.

Cass, V.C. (1979). Homosexual identity formation: a theoretical model. *Journal of Homosexuality*, **4**, 219–35.

Cassel, J. (1976). The contribution of the social environment to host resistance. *American Journal of Epidemiology*, **104**, 107–23.

Cassidy, J. (1988). Mother–child attachment and the self at age six. *Child Development*, **57**, 331–7.

Cassidy, J., Parke, R.D., Butovsky, L. & Braungart, J. (1992). Family–peer connections: the roles of emotional expressiveness within the family and children's understanding of emotions. *Child Development*, **63**, 603–18.

Cates, R.M. & Lloyd, S.A. (1985). The developmental course of conflict in dissolution of premarital relationships. *Journal of Social and Personal Relationships*, **2**, 179–94.

Cates, R.M. & Lloyd, S.A. (1992). *Courtship*. Newbury Park, CA: Sage.

Cha, Y. (1994). Aspects of individualism and collectivism in Korea. In U. Kim, H.C. Triandis, C. Kagitcibasi, S. Choi & G. Yoon (Eds), *Individualism and Collectivism: Theory, Methods, and Applications* (pp. 157–74). Thousand Oaks, CA: Sage.

Chao, P. (1983). *Chinese Kinship*. London: Kegal Paul.

Chapman, A.J. (1976). Social aspects of humorous laughter. In A.J. Chapman & H.L. Foot (Eds), *Humor and Laughter: Theory, Research and Applications*. Chichester: Wiley.

Chapman, A.J., Smith, J.R. & Foot, H.L. (1980). Humor, laughter and social interaction. In P. McGhee & A.J. Chapman (Eds), *Children's Humor* (pp. 141–79). New York: Wiley.

Chapman, L.J. & Chapman, J.P. (1969). Genesis of popular but erroneous psychodiagnostic observations. *Journal of Abnormal Psychology*, **74**, 272–80.

Chatterjee, M. (1977). Conjugal roles and social networks in an Indian urban sweeper locality. *Journal of Marriage and the Family*, **39**, 193–202.

Chaudhary, B.K. & Sinha, R.B. (1992). The study of adjustment in relation to some personality factors. *Indian Journal of Psychometry and Education*, **23**, 33–6.

Chelune, G.J. (1979). Measuring openness in interpersonal communication. In G.J. Chelune & Associates (Eds), *Self-disclosure: Origins, Patterns, and Implica-*

tions of Openness in Interpersonal Relationships (pp. 1–27). San Francisco: Jossey-Bass.

Chen, C. & Uttal, D.H. (1988). Cultural values, parents' beliefs, and children's achievement in the United States and China. *Human Development*, **31**, 351–8.

Chen, X. & Rubin, K.H. (1992). Correlates of peer acceptance in a Chinese sample of six-year olds. *International Journal of Behavioral Development*, **15**(2), 259–73.

Chen, X., Rubin, K.H. & Li, Z.Y. (1994, July). Social functioning and adjustment in Chinese children: a longitudinal study. Paper presented at the meeting of the International Society for the Study of Behavioural Development, Amsterdam, The Netherlands.

Chen, X., Rubin, K.H. & Sun, Y. (1992). Social reputation and peer relationships in Chinese and Canadian children: a cross-cultural study. *Child Development*, **63**, 1336–43.

Cherlin, A. (1989). Remarriage as an incomplete institution. In J.M. Henslin (Ed.), *Marriage and Family in a Changing Society* (pp. 442–501). New York: Free Press.

Chesler, M.A. & Barbarin, O.A. (1984). Difficulties of providing help in a crisis: relationship between parents of children with cancer and their friends. *Journal of Social Issues*, **40**, 113–34.

Chiu, C.Y. (1990). Normative expectations of social behavior and concern for members of the collective in Chinese society. *The Journal of Psychology*, **124**(1), 103–11.

Chiu, C.Y., Tsang, S.C. & Yang, C.F. (1988). The role of face situation and attitudinal antecedents in Chinese consumer complaint behavior. *The Journal of Social Psychology*, **128**(2), 173–80.

Chown, S.M. (1981). Friendship in old age. In S. Duck & R. Gilmour (Eds), *Personal Relationships, Vol. 2: Developing Personal Relationships* (pp. 231–46). New York: Academic Press.

Christensen, A. (1988). Dysfunctional interaction patterns in couples. In P. Noller & M.A. Fitzpatrick (Eds), *Perspectives on Marital Interaction* (pp. 31–52). Clevedon, UK: Multilingual Matters.

Christensen, A. & Heavey, C.L. (1990). Gender and social structure in the demand/withdraw pattern of marital interaction. *Journal of Personality and Social Psychology*, **59**, 73–81.

Christopher, F.S. & Frandsen, M.M. (1990). Strategies of influence in sex and dating. *Journal of Social and Personal Relationships*, **7**, 89–105.

Chu, L. (1979). The sensitivity of Chinese and American children to social influences. *The Journal of Social Psychology*, **109**, 175–86.

Cialdini, R.B., Schaller, M., Houlihan, D., Arpts, K., Fultz, J. & Beaman, A.L. (1987). Empathy-based helping: is it selflessly or selfishly based? *Journal of Personality and Social Psychology*, **52**, 749–58.

Cicirelli, V.G. (1985). Sibling relationships throughout the life cycle. In L. L'Abate (Ed.), *Handbook of Family Psychology and Therapy*, Vol. 1 (pp. 177–214). Homewood, IL: Dorsey Press.

Cissna, K.N., Cox, D.E. & Bochner, A.P. (1990). The dialectic of marital and parental relationships within the stepfamily. *Communication Monographs*, **57**, 44–61.

Claiborn, C.D. (1993). Evaluating the interpersonal stage model: a reaction to Tracey (1993). *Journal of Counseling Psychology*, **40**, 413–15.

Clark, K. & Holquist, M. (1984). *Mikhail Bakhtin*. Cambridge, MA: The Belknap Press of Harvard University Press.

Clark, M.L. & Ayers, M. (1988). The role of reciprocity and proximity in junior high school friendships. *Journal of Youth and Adolescence*, **17**, 403–11.

Clark, M.L. & Ayers, M. (1992). Friendship similarity during early adolescence: gender and racial patterns. *Journal of Psychology*, **126**, 393–405.

Clark, M.S. & Mills, J. (1979). Interpersonal attraction in exchange and communal relationships. *Journal of Personality and Social Psychology*, **37**, 12–24.

Clark, M.S. & Reis, H.T. (1988). Interpersonal process in close relationships. *Annual Review of Psychology*, **39**, 609–72.

Clark, M.S., Mills, J. & Powell, M.C. (1986). Keeping track of needs in communal and exchange relationships. *Journal of Personality and Social Psychology*, **51**, 333–8.

Clark, R.D. & Hatfield, E. (1989). Gender differences in receptivity to sexual offers. *Journal of Psychology and Human Sexuality*, **2**, 39–55.

Clifford, E. (1959). Discipline in the home: a controlled observational study of parental practices. *Journal of Genetic Psychology*, **95**, 45–82.

Cline, R.J. (May, 1982). Revealing and relating: a review of self-disclosure theory and research. Paper presented at the International Communication Association Convention.

Cline, R.J. (1983a, November). Promising new directions for teaching and research: self disclosure. Paper presented at the annual convention of the Speech Communication Association, Washington, D.C.

Cline, R.J. (1983b). The acquaintance process as relational communication. In R.N. Bostrom (Ed.), *Communication Yearbook 7* (pp. 396–413). Beverly Hills, CA: Sage.

Cline, R.J., Johnson, S.J. & Freeman, K.E. (1992). Talk among sexual partners: interpersonal communication for risk reduction or risk enhancement. *Health Communication*, **4**, 39–56.

Cloke, K. (1987). Politics and values in mediation: the Chinese experience. *Mediation Quarterly*, **17**, 69–82.

Cobb, S. (1976). Social support as a moderator of life stress. *Psychosomatic Medicine*, **38**, 300–314.

Coble, H.M., Gantt, D.L. & Mallinckrodt, B. (1996). Attachment, social competency, and the capacity to use social support. In. G. Pierce, B.R. Sarason & I.G. Sarason (Eds), *Handbook of Social Support and the Family* (pp. 141–72). New York: Plenum.

Cochran, M. & Brassard, J.A. (1979). Child Development and personal social networks. *Child Development*, **50**, 601–16.

Cochran, M. & Davila, V. (1992). Societal influences on children's peer relationships. In R.D. Parke & G.W. Ladd (Eds), *Family–Peer Relationships: Modes of Linkage* (pp. 191–212). Hillsdale, NJ: Erlbaum.

Cochran, M., Larner, M., Riley, D., Gunnarsson, L. & Henderson, C. Jr (1990). *Extending Families: the Social Networks of Parents and Their Children*. Cambridge: Cambridge University Press.

Cody, M. (1982). A typology of disengagement strategies and an examination of the role intimacy: reactions to inequity and relational problems play in strategy selection. *Communication Monographs*, **49**, 148–70.

Cohen, J. (1988). *Statistical Power Analysis for the Behavioral Sciences* (2nd Edn). Hillsdale, NJ: Erlbaum.

Cohen, J.S. (1989). Maternal involvement in children's peer relationships during middle childhood. Unpublished doctoral dissertation, University of Waterloo, Waterloo, Ontario, Canada.

Cohen, S. (1988). Psychosocial models of the role of social support in the etiology of physical disease. *Health Psychology*, **7**, 269–97.

Cohen, S. & Edwards, J.R. (1989). Personality characteristics as moderators of the relationship between stress and disorder. In R.W.J. Neufeld (Ed.), *Advances in the Investigation of Psychological Stress* (pp. 235–83). New York: Wiley.

Cohen, S. & McKay, G. (1984). Social support, stress and the buffering hypothesis: a theoretical analysis. In A. Baum, S.E. Taylor & J.E. Singer (Eds), *Handbook of Psychology and Health* (pp. 253–67). Hillsdale, NJ: Erlbaum.

Cohen, S. & Syme, S.L. (1985). *Social Support and Health*. New York: Academic Press.

Cohen, S. & Wills, T.A. (1985). Stress, social support, and the buffering hypothesis. *Psychological Bulletin*, **98**, 310–57.

Cohen, S., Kaplan, J.R. & Manuck, S.B. (1994). Social support and coronary heart disease:

underlying psychologic and biologic mechanisms. In S.A. Shumaker & S.M. Czajkowski (Eds), *Social Support and Cardiovascular Disease* (pp. 195–221). New York: Plenum.

Cohen, S., Lichtenstein, E., Mermelstein, R., Kingsolver, K., Baer, J.S. & Kamarck, T.W. (1988). Social support interventions for smoking cessation. In B.H. Gottlieb (Ed.), *Marshaling Social Support: Formats, Processes, and Effects* (pp. 211–40). Newbury Park, CA: Sage.

Cohn, D.A. (1990). Child–mother attachment in six-year-olds and social competence at school. *Child Development*, **61**, 152–62.

Cohn, J.F. & Elmore, M. (1988). Effect of contingent changes in mothers' affective expression on the organization of behavior in 3-month-old infants. *Infant Behavior and Development*, **11**, 493–505.

Coie, J. (1985). Fitting social skills intervention to the target group. In B.H. Schneider, K. Rubin & J.E. Ledingham (Eds), *Children's Peer Relations: Issues in Assessment and Intervention*. New York: Springer-Verlag.

Colarusso, C.A. & Nemiroff, R.A. (1982). The father in midlife: crisis and the growth of paternal identity. In S.H. Cath, A.R. Gurwitt & J.M. Ross (Eds), *Father and Child: Developmental and Clinical Perspectives* (pp. 315–27). Boston: Little, Brown.

Cole, D.A. (1991). Change in self-perceived competence as a function of peer and teacher evaluation. *Developmental Psychology*, **27**, 682–8.

Coleman, E. (1982). Developmental stages of the coming out process. *Journal of Homosexuality*, **7**, 31–43.

Coleman, M. & Ganong, L.H. (1994). *Remarried Families*. Newbury Park, CA: Sage.

Coles, R. (1989). *The Call of Stories: Teaching and the Moral Imagination*. Boston: Houghton Mifflin.

Collett, P. (1971). On training Englishmen in the non-verbal behavior of Arabs: an experiment in intercultural communication. *International Journal of Psychology*, **6**, 209–15.

Colletta, N.D. & Lee, D. (1983). The impact of support for Black adolescent mothers. *Journal of Family Issues*, **4**(1), 127–43.

Collins, N.L. & Miller, L.C. (1994). The disclosure-liking link: from meta-analysis toward a dynamic reconceptualization. *Psychological Bulletin*, **116**, 457–75.

Collins, N.L. & Read, S.J. (1990). Adult attachment, working models, and relationship quality in dating couples. *Journal of Personality and Social Psychology*, **58**, 644–63.

Compas, B.E., Wagner, B.M., Slavin, L.A. & Vannatta, K. (1986). A prospective study of life events, social support, and psychological symptomatology during the transition from high school to college. *American Journal of Community Psychology*, **14**(3), 241–57.

Condon, R.G. (1990). The rise of adolescence: social change and life stage dilemmas in the central Canadian Arctic. *Human Organization*, **49**, 266–70.

Conger, R. (1994). Predicting marital instability. Paper presented at conference in intimate relationships at Iowa State, Ames, Iowa, September 29.

Conley, J.J. (1985). Longitudinal stability of personality traits: a multitrait–multimethod–multioccasion analysis. *Journal of Personality and Social Psychology*, **49**(5), 1266–82.

Conville, R. (1988). Relational transitions: an inquiry into their structure and functions. *Journal of Social and Personal Relationships*, **5**, 423–37.

Conville, R.L. (1983). Second-order development in interpersonal communication. *Human Communication Research*, **9**, 195–207.

Conville, R.L. (1991). *Relational Transitions: the Evolution of Personal Relationships*. New York: Praeger.

Cook, J. & Bickman, L. (1990). Social support and psychological symptomatology following a natural disaster. *Journal of Traumatic Stress*, **3**, 541–56.

Cook, W.L. (1993). Interdependence and the interpersonal sense of control: an analysis of family relationships. *Journal of Personality and Social Psychology*, **64**, 587–601.

Cooney, T.M. (1989). Coresidence with adult children: a comparison of divorced and widowed women. *The Gerontologist*, **29**, 779–84.

Cooney, T.M. (1994). Young adults' relations with parents: the influence of recent parental divorce. *Journal of Marriage and the Family*, **56**, 45–56.

Cooney, T.M. & Uhlenberg, P. (1992). Support from parents over the life course: the adult child's perspective. *Social Forces*, **71**, 63–84.

Cooney, T.M., Smyer, M.A., Hagestad, G.O. & Klock, R.C. (1986). Parental divorce in young adulthood: some preliminary findings. *American Journal of Orthopsychiatry*, **56**, 470–77.

Cooper, C.R., Grotevant, H.D. & Condon, S.M. (1983). Individuality and connectedness in the family as a context for adolescent identity formation and role-taking skill. In H.D. Grotevant & C.R. Cooper (Eds), *Adolescent Development in the Family* (pp. 43–59). San Francisco: Jossey-Bass.

Cooper, M., Corrado, R., Karlberg, A.M. & Pelletier Adams, L. (1992). Aboriginal suicide in British Columbia: an overview. *Canada's Mental Health*, **40**, 19–23.

Corey, G.R. (1994). *Theory and Practice of Group Psychotherapy* (4th Edn). Pacific Grove, CA: Brooks/Cole.

Cornforth, M. (1968). *Materialism and the Dialectical Method*. New York: International Publishers.

Cosmides, L. & Tooby, J. (1989). Evolutionary psychology and the generation of culture. II. Case study: a computational theory of social exchange. *Ethology and Sociobiology*, **10**, 51–97.

Costa, P.T. Jr & McCrae, R.R. (1987). Neuroticism, somatic complaints, and disease: is the bark worse than the bite? *Journal of Personality*, **55**, 299–316.

Costa, P.T. Jr & McCrae, R.R. (1988). From catalog to classification: Murray's needs and the five-factor model. *Journal of Personality and Social Psychology*, **55**, 258–65.

Cotton, S. (1995). Support networks and marital satisfaction. Unpublished manuscript, Macquarie University, Sidney, Australia.

Cotton, S., Antill, J. & Cunningham, J. (1993). Network structure, network support, and the marital satisfaction of husbands and wives. *Australian Journal of Psychology*, **45**, 176–81.

Courtwright, J.A., Millar, F.E. & Rogers-Millar, L.E. (1979). Domineeringness and dominance: replication and extension. *Communication Monographs*, **46**, 179–92.

Coverman, S. (1985). Explaining husbands' participation in domestic labor. *The Sociology Quarterly*, **26**, 81–97.

Coverman, S. & Sheley, J.F. (1986). Change in men's housework and child care time. *Journal of Marriage and the Family*, **48**, 413–22.

Cowan, C.P. & Cowan, P.A. (1988). Who does what when partners become parents: implications for men, women, and marriage. *Marriage and Family Review*, **12**, 105–31.

Cowan, C.P., Cowan, P.A., Heming G. & Miller N.B. (1991). Becoming a family: marriage, parenting, and child development. In P.A. Cowan & M. Hetherington (Eds), *Family Transitions*. Hillsdale, NJ: Erlbaum.

Cowan, C. & Kinder, M. (1985). *Smart Women; Foolish Choices*. New York: Clarkson N. Potter.

Cowan, M. & Murphy, S. (1985). Identification of postdisaster high risk bereavement predictors. *Nursing Research*, **34**, 71–5.

Cowan, P.A. & Cowan, C.P. (1994). Where's the romance? What happens to marriage when partners become parents. Paper presented at conference on intimate relationships at Iowa State, Ames, Iowa. September 29.

Cowan, P.A., Cowan, C.P., Shultz, M.S. & Hemming, G. (1994). Prebirth to preschool family factors in children's adaptation to kindergarten. In R.D. Parke & S.G. Kellam (Eds), *Exploring Family Relationships with Other Social Contexts*. Hillsdale, NJ: Erlbaum.

Coyne, J.C. & Bolger, N. (1990). Doing without social support as an explanatory concept. *Journal of Social and Clinical Psychology*, **9**, 148–58.

Coyne, J.C. & DeLongis, A. (1986). Going beyond social support: the role of social relationships in adaptation. *Journal of Consulting and Clinical Psychology*, **54**, 454–60.

Coyne, J.C. & Downey, G. (1991). Social factors and psychopathology: stress, social support, and coping processes. *Annual Review of Psychology*, **42**, 401–25.

Coyne, J.C. & Smith, D.A.F. (1991). Couples coping with a myocardial infarction: a contextual perspective on wives' distress. *Journal of Personality and Social Psychology*, **61**, 404–12.

Coyne, J.C., Burchill, S.A.L. & Stiles W.B. (1990). An interactional perspective on depression. In C.R. Snyder & D.R. Forsyth (Eds), *Handbook of Social and Clinical Psychology*. New York: Pergamon.

Coyne, J.C., Ellard, J.H. & Smith, D.A.F. (1990). Social support, interdependence, and the dilemmas of helping. In B.R. Sarason, I.G. Sarason & G.R. Pierce (Eds), *Social Support: an Interactional View* (pp. 129–49). New York: Wiley.

Coyne, J.C., Wortman, C.B. & Lehman, D.R. (1988). The other side of support: emotional overinvolvement and miscarried helping. In B.H. Gottlieb (Ed.), *Marshaling Social Support: Formats, Processes, and Effects* (pp. 305–30). Newbury Park, CA: Sage.

Crago, M.B., Annahatak, B. & Ningiuruvik, L. (1993). Changing patterns of language socialization in Inuit homes. *Anthropology and Education Quarterly*, **24**, 205–23.

Craig, R., Tracy, K. & Spisak, F. (1986). The discourse of requests: assessment of a politeness approach. *Human Communication Research*, **12**, 437–68.

Cramer, D. (1990). Psychological adjustment, close relationships and personality: a comment on McLennan & Omodei. *British Journal of Medical Psychology*, **63**, 341–3.

Cramer, D. (1993). Personality and marital dissolution. *Personality and Individual Differences*, **14**, 605–7.

Cramer, R.E., Weiss, R.F., Steigleder, M.K. & Balling, S.S. (1985). Attraction in context: acquisition and blocking of person-directed action. *Journal of Personality and Social Psychology*, **49**, 1221–30.

Crawford, C.B. & Anderson, J.L. (1989). Sociobiology: an environmentalist discipline. *American Psychologist*, **44**, 1449–59.

Crawford, D.W. & Huston, T.L. (1993). The impact of the transition to parenthood on marital leisure. *Personality and Social Psychology Bulletin*, **19**, 39–46.

Creamer, M. & Campbell, I.M. (1988). The role of interpersonal perception in dyadic adjustment. *Journal of Clinical Psychology*, **44**, 424–30.

Creighton, M. (1990). Revisting shame and guilt cultures: a forty-year pilgrimage. *Ethos*, **18**, 279–307.

Crites, S. (1971). The narrative quality of experience. *Journal of the American Academy of Religion*, **39**, 291–311.

Crites, S. (1986). Storytime: recollecting the past and projecting the future. In T. Sarbin (Ed.), *Narrative Psychology: the Storied Nature of Human Conduct* (pp. 152–73). New York: Praeger.

Crits-Christoph, P., Barber, J.P. & Kurcias, J.S. (1993). The accuracy of therapists' interpretations and the development of the therapeutic alliance. *Psychotherapy Research*, **3**, 25–35.

Crits-Christoph, P., Demorest, A. & Connolly, M.B. (1990). Quantitative assessment of interpersonal themes over the course of psychotherapy. *Psychotherapy*, **27**, 513–21.

Crits-Christoph, P., Luborsky, L., Dahl, L., Popp, C., Mellon, J. & Mark, D. (1987). Clinicians can agree in assessing relationship patterns in psychotherapy: the Core Conflictual Relationship Theme Method. *Archives of General Psychiatry*, **45**, 1001–5.

Crittenden, P.M. (1981). Abusing, neglecting, problematic, and adequate dyads: differentiating by patterns of interaction. *Merrill-Palmer Quarterly*, **27**, 201–18.

Crittenden, P.M. (1985). Social networks, quality of parenting, and child development. *Child Development*, **56**, 1299–1313.

Crittenden, P.M. (1988). Relationships at risk. In J. Belsky & T. Nezworski (Eds), *Clinical Implications of Attachment* (pp. 136–74). Hillsdale, NJ: Erlbaum.

Crittenden, P.M. (1990). Internal representational models of attachment relationships. *Infant Mental Health Journal*, **11**, 259–77.

Crittenden, P.M. (1992). Quality of attachment in the preschool years. *Development and Psychopathology*, **4**, 209–41.

Crittenden, P.M. (1995). Attachment and psychopathology. In S. Goldberg, R. Muir & J. Kerr (Eds), *Attachment Theory: Social, Developmental, and Clinical Perspectives* (pp. 367–405). Hillsdale, NJ: The Analytic Press.

Crittenden, P.M. (in press). The A/C pattern of attachment: risk of dysfunction versus opportunity for creative integration. In L. Atkinson & K.J. Zuckerman (Eds), *Attachment and Psychopathology*. New York: Guilford.

Crittenden, P.M. & Claussen, A.L. (June, 1994). Quality of attachment in the preschool years: alternative perspectives. Paper presented in the symposium "Quality of attachment in the preschool years", P.M. Crittenden, chair, International Conference on Infant Studies, Paris, France.

Crittenden, P.M. & DiLalla, D. (1988). Compulsive compliance: the development of an inhibitory coping strategy in infancy. *Journal Abnormal Child Psychology*, **16**, 585–99.

Crittenden, P.M., Partridge, M.F. & Claussen, A.H. (1991). Family patterns of relationship in normative and dysfunctional families. *Development and Psychopathology*, **3**, 491–512.

Crockenberg, S. & Litman, C. (1990). Autonomy as competence in two-year-olds: maternal correlates of child defiance, compliance, and self-assertion. *Developmental Psychology*, **26**, 961–71.

Crohan, S.E. (1988). The relationship between conflict behavior and marital happiness: conflict beliefs as moderators. Unpublished dissertation. Ann Arbor, Michigan: University of Michigan.

Crohan, S.E. (1992). Marital happiness and spousal consensus on beliefs about marital conflict: a longitudinal investigation. *Journal of Social and Personal Relationships*, **9**, 89–102.

Crosby, F. (1976). A model of egoistical relative deprivation. *Psychological Review*, **83**, 85–113.

Crouter, A.C. (1984a). Participative work as an influence on human development. *Journal of Applied Developmental Psychology*, **5**, 71–90.

Crouter, A.C. (1984b). Spillover from family to work: the neglected side of the work–family interface. *Human Relations*, **37**, 425–42.

Crouter, A.C. & Helms-Erikson (in press). Work and family from a dyadic perspective: variations in Inequality. In S.W. Duck (Ed.), *Handbook of Personal Relationships* (2nd Edn). Chichester: Wiley.

Crouter, A.C. & McHale, S.M. (1993). The long arm of the job: influences of parental work on child rearing. In T. Luster & L. Okagaki (Eds), *Parenting: an Ecological Perspective* (pp. 179–202). New York: Erlbaum.

Crouter, A.C. & McHale, S.M. (1994a). Gender role socialization in middle childhood. Proposal funded by the National Institute for Child Health and Human Development.

Crouter, A.C. & McHale, S.M. (1994b). Parental work, family dynamics, and adolescent development. Proposal funded by the National Institute for Child Health and Human Development.

Crouter, A.C., Manke, B. & McHale, S.M. (1995). The family context of gender intensification in early adolescence. *Child Development*, **66**, 317–29.

Cryderman, B.K. (1992). Chinese. In B.K. Cryderman & A. Fleras (Eds), *Police, Race, and Ethnicity: a Guide for Police Services* (pp. 191–208). Toronto: Butterworths.

Csikszentmihalyi, M. (1975). *Beyond Boredom and Anxiety*. San Francisco: Jossey Bass.

Cuellar, I., Harris, L.C. & Jasso, R. (1980). An acculturation scale for Mexican American normal and clinical populations. *Hispanic Journal of Behavioral Sciences*, **2**(3), 199–217.

Cummings, E.M. (1987). Coping with background anger in early childhood. *Child Development*, **58**, 976–84.

Cummings, E.M. & Cummings J.L. (1988). A process-oriented approach to children's coping with adults' angry behavior. *Developmental Review*, **8**, 296–321.

Cummings, E.M. & Davies, P.T. (1994). *Child and Marital Conflict: the Impact of Family Dispute and Resolution*. New York: Guilford.

Cummings, E.M., Ballard, M., El-Sheik, M. & Lake, M. (1991). Resolution and children's responses to interadult anger. *Developmental Psychology*, **27**, 462–70.

Cummings, E.M., Davies, P.T. & Simpson, K.S. (1994). Marital conflict, gender, and children's appraisals and coping efficacy as mediators of child adjustment. *Journal of Family Psychology*, **8**, 141–9.

Cummings, E.M., Iannotti, R.J. & Zahn-Waxler, C. (1985). The influence of conflict between adults on the emotions and aggression of young children. *Developmental Psychology*, **21**, 495–507.

Cummings, E.M., Simpson, K.S. & Wilson, A. (1993). Children's responses to interadult anger as a function of information about resolution. *Developmental Psychology*, **29**, 978–85.

Cummings, J.S., Pelligrini, D., Notarius, C. & Cummings, E.M. (1989). Children's responses to angry adult behavior as a function of marital distress and history of interparental hostility. *Child Development*, **60**, 1035–43.

Cunningham, M.R., Roberts, A.R., Barbee, A.P., Druen, P.B. & Wu, C. (1995). "Their ideas of beauty are, on the whole, the same as ours": consistency and variability in the cross-cultural perception of female physical attractiveness. *Journal of Personality and Social Psychology*, **68**, 261–79.

Cupach, W.R. & Metts, S. (1990). Remedial processes in embarrassing predicaments. In J.A. Anderson (Ed.), *Communication Yearbook 13* (pp. 323–52). Newbury Park, CA: Sage.

Cupach, W.R. & Metts, S. (1993, June). Correspondence between relationship partners on relationship beliefs and face predilections as predictors of relational quality. Paper presented at the conference of the International Network on Personal Relationships, Milwaukee, WI.

Cupach, W.R. & Metts, S. (1994). *Facework*. Thousand Oaks, CA: Sage.

Cupach, W.R. & Spitzberg, B.H. (1994). *The Dark Side of Interpersonal Communication*. Hillsdale, NJ: Erlbaum.

Curtis, R.C. & Miller, K. (1986). Believing another likes or dislikes you: behaviors making the beliefs come true. *Journal of Personality and Social Psychology*, **51**, 284–90.

Cuthbertson, B. & Nigg, J. (1987). Technological disaster and the nontherapeutic community: a question of true victimization. *Environment and Behavior*, **19**, 462–83.

Cutler, W.B., Garcia, C.R., Huggins, G.R. & Preti, G. (1986). Sexual behavior and steroid levels among gynecologically mature premenopausal women. *Fertility and Sterility*, **45**, 496–502.

Cutler, W.B., Preti, G., Huggins, G.R., Erickson, B. & Garcia, C.R. (1985). Sexual behavior frequency and biphasic ovulatory type menstrual cycles. *Physiology and Behavior*, **34**, 805–10.

Cutrona, C.E. (1986). Behavioral manifestations of social support: a microanalytic investigation. *Journal of Personality and Social Psychology*, **51**, 201–8.

Cutrona, C.E. (1990). Stress and social support: in search of optimal matching. *Journal of Social and Clinical Psychology*, **9**(1), 3–14.

Cutrona, C.E. (1994). Social support transactions in young married couples: preliminary results. Paper presented at conference on intimate relationships at Iowa State, Ames, Iowa, Sept 29.

Cutrona, C.E. & Russell, D.W. (1987). The provisions of social relationships and adaptation to stress. In W.H. Jones & D. Perlman (Eds), *Advances in Personal Relationships*, Vol. 1 (pp. 37–67). Greenwich, CT: JAI Press.

Cutrona, C.E. & Russell, D.W. (1990). Type of social support and specific stress: toward a theory of optimal matching. In B.R. Sarason, I.G. Sarason & G.R. Pierce (Eds), *Social Support: an Interactional View* (pp. 319–66). New York: Wiley.

Cutrona, C.E., Russell, D.W. & Rose, J. (1986). Social support and adaption to stress by the elderly. *Psychology and Aging*, **1**, 47–54.

Dakof, G.A. & Taylor, S.E. (1990). Victims' perceptions of social support: what is helpful from whom? *Journal of Personality and Social Psychology*, **58**, 80–89.

Daly, M. & Wilson, M. (1983). *Sex, Evolution, and Behavior* (2nd Edn). Belmont, CA: Wadsworth.

Daly, M. & Wilson, M. (1988a). *Homicide*. New York: Aldine de Gruyter.

Daly, M. & Wilson, M. (1988b). Evolutionary social psychology and family homicide. *Science*, **242** (October), 519–24.

Daly, M. & Wilson, M. (1989). Homicide and cultural evolution. *Ethology and Sociobiology*, **10**, 99–110.

Daly, M. & Wilson, M.I. (1994). Some differential attributes of lethal assaults on small children by stepfathers versus genetic fathers. *Ethology and Sociobiology*, **15**, 207–17.

Daly, M., Wilson, M. & Weghorst, S.J. (1982). Male sexual jealousy. *Ethology and Sociobiology*, **3**, 11–27.

Damico, S.B. & Sparks, C. (1986). Cross-group contact opportunities: impact on interpersonal relationship in desegregated middle schools. *Sociology of Education*, **59**, 113–23.

Daniels, P. & Weingarten, K. (1982). *Sooner or Later: the Timing of Parenthood in Adult Lives*. New York: Norton.

Darwin, C. (1859). *The Origin of Species.* London: Murray.

Darwin, C. (1872). *The Expression of the Emotions in Man and Animals.* London: Murray.

Darwin, C. (reprinted 1965). *The Expression of the Emotions in Man and Animals.* Chicago: University of Chicago Press (original work published 1872).

Davey, A.G. & Mullin, P.N. (1982). Inter-ethnic friendship in British primary schools. *Educational Research*, **24**, 83–92.

Davidson, J.R. (1992). Interracial marriages: a clinical perspective. *Journal of Multicultural Counseling and Development*, **20**, 150–57.

Davies, J.C. (1962). Toward a theory of revolution. *American Sociological Review*, **27**, 5–13.

Davies, P.T. & Cummings, E.M. (1994). Marital conflict and child adjustment: an emotional security hypothesis. *Psychological Bulletin*, **116**, 387–411.

Davis, J.A. (1970). Clustering and hierarchy in interpersonal relations: test two graph theoretical models on 742 sociomatrices. *American Sociological Review*, **35**, 843–51.

Davis, K.E. & Todd, M.J. (1985). Assessing friendship: prototypes, paradigm cases and relationship description. In S.W. Duck & D. Perlman (Eds), *Understanding Personal Relationships: an Interdisciplinary Approach* (pp. 17–38). London: Sage.

Davis, M.H. & Oathout, H.A. (1987). Maintenance of satisfaction in romantic relationships: empathy and relational competence. *Journal of Personality and Social Psychology*, **53**, 397–410.

Dawkins, R. (1976). *The Selfish Gene.* Oxford: Oxford University Press.

Dawson, M.E. & Nuechterlein, K.H. (1984). Psychophysiological dysfunctions in the developmental course of schizophrenic disorders. *Schizophrenia Bulletin*, **10**, 204–32.

Deag, J.M. (1977). Aggression and submission in monkey societies. *Animal Behaviour*, **25**, 465–74.

Deaux, K. & Major, B. (1987). Putting gender into context: an interactive model of gender-related behavior. *Psychological Review*, **94**, 369–89.

DeCasper, A.J. & Fifer, W. (1980). Of human bonding: newborns prefer their mothers' voices. *Science*, **208**, 1174–6.

Deci, E.L. (1975). *Intrinsic Motivation.* New York: Plenum Press.

Dehue, F.M.J., McClintock, C.G. & Liebrand, W.B.G. (1993). Social value related response latencies: unobtrusive evidence for individual differences in information processes. *European Journal of Social Psychology,* **23**, 273–94.

DeKeseredy, W.S. (1990a). Male peer support and woman abuse: the current state of knowledge. *Sociological Focus,* **23**, 129–39.

DeKeseredy, W.S. (1990b). Woman abuse in dating relationships: the contribution of male peer support. *Sociological Inquiry,* **60**, 236–43.

Delgado, P.L., Price, L.H., Heninger, G.R. & Charney, D.S. (1992). Neurochemistry. In E.S. Paykel (Ed.), *Handbook of Affective Disorders* (2nd Edn). New York: Guilford.

Delia, J.G. (1980). Some tentative thoughts concerning the study of interpersonal relationships and their development. *Western Journal of Speech Communication,* **44**, 97–103.

DeLongis, A., Folkman, S. & Lazarus, R.S. (1988). The impact of daily stress on health and mood: psychological and social resources as mediators. *Journal of Personality and Social Psychology,* **54**, 486–95.

Delphy, C. & Leonard, D. (1992). *Familiar Exploitation: a New Analysis of Marriage in Contemporary Western Societies.* Cambridge, MA: Polity.

DeMakis, G.J. & McAdams, D.P. (1994). Personality, social support, and well-being among first year college students. *College Student Journal,* **28**, 235–43.

Demo, D.H. & Acock, A.C. (1993). Family diversity and the division of domestic labor: how much have things changed? *Family Relations,* **42**, 323–31.

Denham, S.A. (1993). Maternal emotional responsiveness to toddlers social–emotional functioning. *Journal of Child Psychology and Psychiatry,* **34**, 715–28.

Denham, S.A., Cook, M. & Zoller, D. (1992). Baby looks very sad: implications of conversations about feelings between mother and preschooler. *British Journal of Developmental Psychology,* **10**, 301–15.

Denham, S., McKinley, M., Couchoud, E. & Holt, R. (1990). Emotional and behavioral predictors of preschool peer ratings. *Child Development,* **61**, 1145–52.

Denscombe, M. (1983). Ethnic group and friendship choice in the primary school. *Educational Research,* **25**, 184–90.

Denscombe, M., Szulc, H., Patrick, C. & Wood, A. (1986). Ethnicity and friendship: the contrast between sociometric research and fieldwork observation in primary school classrooms. *British Educational Research Journal,* **12**, 221–35.

Denzin, N.K. (1970). Rules of conduct and the study of deviant behavior: some notes on social relationships. In G.J. McCall, M. McCall, N. Denzin & S. Kurth (Eds), *Social Relationships* (pp. 62–94). Chicago: Aldine.

Denzin, N.K. (1989a). *Interpretive Biography.* Newbury Park, CA: Sage.

Denzin, N.K. (1989b). *Interpretive Interactionism.* Newbury Park, CA: Sage.

Denzin, N.K. (1991). *Images of Postmodern Society: Social Theory and Contemporary Cinema.* London: Sage.

Denzin, N.K. (1992). *Symbolic Interactionism and Cultural Studies: the Politics of Interpretation.* Oxford: Basil Blackwell.

Denzin, N.K. (1993). Narrative's phenomena. Paper presented at Midwest Sociological Society, Chicago.

Denzin, N.K. (1995). *The Cinematic Society: The Voyeur's Gaze.* London: Sage.

Denzin, N.K. & Lincoln, Y. (Eds) (1994). *Handbook of Qualitative Research.* Thousand Oaks, CA: Sage.

DePaulo, B.M. (1982). Social-psychological processes in informal help seeking. In T.A. Wills (Ed.), *Basic Processes in Helping Relationships* (pp. 255–79). New York: Academic Press.

DePaulo, B.M. (1992). Nonverbal behavior and self-presentation. *Psychological Bulletin,* **111**, 203–43.

Depner, C. (1978). Adult roles and subjective evaluation of life quality. Doctoral dissertation. Ann Arbor: University of Michigan.

Depner, C.E. & Ingersoll-Dayton, B. (1988). Supportive relationships in later life. *Psychology and Aging*, **3**, 348–57.

Derlega, V.J. & Chaikin, A. (1977). Privacy and self-disclosure in social relationships. *Journal of Social Issues*, **33**, 102–15.

Derlega, V.J., Hendrick, S.S., Winstead, B.A. & Berg, J.H. (1991). *Psychotherapy as a Personal Relationship*. New York: Guilford.

Derlega, V.J., Metts, S., Petronio, S. & Margulis, S.T. (1993). *Self-disclosure*. Newbury Park, CA: Sage.

Deutsch, F.M., Zalenski, C.M. & Clark, M.E. (1986). Is there a double standard of aging? *Journal of Applied Social Psychology*, **16**, 771–5.

Deutsch, M. (1975). Equity, equality, and need: what determines which value will be used as the basis of distributive justice? *Journal of Social Issues*, **31**, 137–49.

Dew, M.A., Bromet, E.J. & Schulberg, H.C. (1987). A comparative analysis of two community stressors' long-term mental health effects. *American Journal of Community Psychology*, **15**, 167–84.

deWaal, F. (1989). *Chimpanzee Politics*. Baltimore: Johns Hopkins University Press.

Diaz, R.M. & Berndt, T.J. (1982). Children's knowledge of a best friend: fact or fancy? *Developmental Psychology*, **18**, 787–94.

Dickens, D. & Fontana, A. (Eds) (1991). *Postmodernism and Sociology*. Chicago: University of Chicago Press.

Dickson, F.C. (1995). The best is yet to be: research on long-lasting marriages. In J. Wood & S. Duck (Eds), *Under-studied Relationships: Off the Beaten Track* (pp. 22–50). Thousand Oaks, CA: Sage.

Dillard, J.P. & Fitzpatrick, M.A. (1985). Compliance-gaining in marital interaction. *Personality and Social Psychology Bulletin*, **11**, 419–33.

Dilworth-Anderson, P. (1992). Extended kin networks in Black families. *Generations*, **XVI**, 29–32.

DiMatteo, M.R. & Hays, R. (1981). Social support and serious illness. In B.H. Gottlieb (Ed.), *Social Networks and Social Support* (pp. 117–48). Beverly Hills, CA: Sage.

Dindia, K. (1982). Reciprocity of self-disclosure: a sequential analysis. In M. Burgoon (Ed.), *Communication Yearbook 6* (pp. 506–30). Beverly Hills, CA: Sage.

Dindia, K. (1984, May). Antecedents and consequents of self-disclosure. Paper presented at the meeting of the International Communication Association, San Francisco.

Dindia, K. (1994). The intrapersonal–interpersonal dialectical process of self-disclosure. In S.W. Duck (Ed.), *Dynamics of Relationships (Understanding Relationship Processes 4)* (pp. 27–56). Thousand Oaks, CA: Sage.

Dindia, K. & Allen, M. (1992). Sex-differences in self-disclosure: a meta-analysis. *Psychological Bulletin*, **112**, 106–24.

Dindia, K. & Baxter, L.A. (1987). Strategies for maintaining and repairing marital relationships. *Journal of Social and Personal Relationships*, **4**, 143–58.

Dindia, K. & Canary, D.J. (1993). Definitions and theoretical perspectives on maintaining relationships. *Journal of Social and Personal Relationships*, **10**, 163–73.

Dindia, K., Fitzpatrick, M.A. & Kenny, D.A. (1989, May). Self-disclosure in spouse and stranger dyads: A Social Relations Analysis. Paper presented at the meeting of the International Communication Association, San Francisco.

Dion, K.L. & Dion, K.K. (1988). Romantic love: individual and cultural perspectives. In M.L. Sternberg & M.L. Barnes (Eds), *The Psychology of Love*. New Haven, CT: Yale University Press.

Dishion, T.J. (1990). The family ecology of boys peer relations in middle childhood. *Child Development*, **61**, 874–92.

Dishion, T.J. (1992). The peer context of troublesome child and adolescent behavior. In P.E. Leone (Ed.), *Understanding Troubled and Troubling Youth: a Multidisciplinary Perspective*. Newbury Park, CA: Sage.

Dixson, M. & Duck, S.W. (1993). Understanding relationship processes: uncovering the human search for meaning. In S.W. Duck (Ed.), *Understanding Relationship Processes 1: Individuals in Relationships* (pp. 175–206). Newbury Park, CA: Sage.

Doane, J.A., Falloon, I.R.H., Goldstein, M.J. & Mintz, J. (1985). Parental affective style and the treatment of schizophrenia: predicting course of illness and social functioning. *Archives of General Psychiatry*, **42**, 34–42.

Doane, J.A., Goldstein, M.J., Miklowitz, D.J. & Falloon, I.R.H. (1986). The impact of individual and family treatment on the affective climate of families of schizophrenics. *British Journal of Psychiatry*, **148**, 279–87.

Doane, J.A., West, K.L., Goldstein, M.J., Rodnick, E.H. & Jones, J.E. (1981). Parental communication deviance and affective style: predictors of subsequent schizophrenia spectrum disorders in vulnerable adolescents. *Archives of General Psychiatry*, **38**, 679–85.

Dobash, R.E. & Dobash, R.P. (1992). *Women, Violence, and Social Change*. New York: Routledge.

Docherty, N.M. (1993). Communication deviance, attention, and schizotypy in parents of schizophrenic patients. *Journal of Nervous and Mental Diseases*, **181**, 750–56.

Docherty, N.M. (1995). Expressed emotion and language disturbances in parents of stable schizophrenia outpatients. *Schizophrenia Bulletin*, **21**, 411–18.

Dodge, K.A. (1986). A social information processing model of social competence in children. In M. Perlmutter (Ed.), *Minnesota Symposium on Child Development*, Vol. 18 (pp. 77–125). Minneapolis: University of Minnesota Press.

Dodge, K.A. & Frame, C.L. (1982). Social cognitive biases and deficits in aggressive boys. *Child Development*, **53**, 620–35.

Dodge, K.A., Pettit, G.S., McClaskey, C.L. & Brown, M. (1986). Social competence in children. Monographs of the Society for Research, in *Child Development*, **51**(2, Serial No. 213).

Doherty, R.W., Hatfield, E., Thompson, K. & Chao, P. (1994). Cultural and ethnic influences on love and attachment. *Personal Relationships*, **1**, 391–8.

Dolan, R.T., Arnkoff, D.B. & Glass, C.R. (1993). Client attachment style and the psychotherapist's interpersonal stance. *Psychotherapy*, **30**, 408–12.

Dollard, J. & Miller, N.E. (1950). *Personality and Psychotherapy*. New York: McGraw-Hill.

Domino, G. & Hannah, M.T. (1987). A comparative analysis of social values of Chinese and American Children. *Journal of Cross-Cultural Psychology*, **18**(1), 58–77.

Dong, Q., Yang, B. & Ollendick, T.II. (1994). Fears in Chinese children and adolescents and their relations to anxiety and depression. *Journal of Child Psychology and Psychiatry*, **35**(2), 351–63.

Donner, A. & Koval, J.J. (1980). The estimation of intraclass correlation in the analysis of family data. *Biometrics*, **36**, 19–25.

Donohue, W.A., Lyles, J. & Rogan, R. (1989). Issue development in divorce mediation. *Mediation Quarterly*, **24**, 19–28.

Drabek, T.E. (1986). *Human System Responses to Disaster*. New York: Springer-Verlag.

Drabek, T.E. & Key, W.M. (1984). *Conquering Disaster: Family Recovery and Long-term Consequences*. New York: Irvington Publishers.

Dracup, K. (1994). Cardiac rehabilitation: the role of social support in recovery and compliance. In S.A. Shumaker & S.M. Czajkowski (Eds), *Social Support and Cardiovascular Disease* (pp. 333–53). New York: Plenum.

Drigotas, S.M. & Rusbult, C.E. (1992). Should I stay or should I go? A dependence model of breakups. *Journal of Personality and Social Psychology*, **62**, 62–87.

Drigotas, S.M., Rusbult, C.E., Wieselquist, J. & Whitten, S. (1995). Promotive interdependence in ongoing relationships. Unpublished manuscript, Southern Methodist University.

Driscoll, R., Davis, K.E. & Lipetz, M.E. (1972). Parental interference and romantic love:

the Romeo and Juliet effect. *Journal of Personality and Social Psychology*, **24**, 1–10.

Du Bois, W.E.B. (1903/1969). *The Souls of Black folk*. New York: Signet.

Du Bois, W.E.B. (1947/1965). *The World and Africa*. New York: International Publishers.

Du Bois, W.E.B. (1986). *Writings*. New York: Library of America.

DuBois, D.L. & Hirsch, B.J. (1990). School and neighborhood friendship patterns of blacks and whites in early adolescence. *Child Development*, **61**, 524–36.

Duck, S.W. (1977). Tell me where is fancy bred: some thoughts on the study of interpersonal attraction. In S.W. Duck (Ed.), *Theory and Practice in Interpersonal Attraction*. New York: Academic Press.

Duck, S.W. (1982). A topography of relationship disengagement and dissolution. In S.W. Duck (Ed.), *Personal Relationships 4: Dissolving Personal Relationship*s (pp. 1–30). London: Academic Press.

Duck, S.W. (Ed.) (1988a). *Handbook of Personal Relationships: Theory, Research and Interventions* (1st Edn). Chichester: Wiley.

Duck, S.W. (1988b). *Relating to Others*. Chicago: Dorsey Press.

Duck, S.W. (1990). Relationships as unfinished business: out of the frying pan and into the 1990s. *Journal of Social and Personal Relationships*, **7**, 5–29.

Duck, S.W. (1991). *Understanding Relationships*. New York: Guilford.

Duck, S.W. (1993a). Preface on social context. In S.W. Duck (Ed.), *Social Contexts of Relationships (Understanding Relationship Processes 3)* (pp. ix–xiv). Newbury Park: Sage.

Duck, S.W. (1993b). *Social Context and Relationships (Understanding Relationship Proceeses 3)*. Newbury Park, CA: Sage.

Duck, S.W. (1994a). *Meaningful Relationships: Talking, Sense, and Relating*. Thousand Oaks, CA: Sage.

Duck, S.W. (1994b). Stratagems, spoils and a serpent's tooth: on the delights and dilemmas of personal relationships. In W. Cupach & B.H. Spitzberg (Eds), *The Dark Side of Interpersonal Communication* (pp. 3–24). Hillsdale NJ: Erlbaum.

Duck, S.W. & Craig, G. (1978). Personality similarity and the development of friendship. *British Journal of Sociology and Clinical Psychology*, **17**, 237–42.

Duck, S.W. & Miell, D.E. (1986). Charting the development of personal relationships. In R. Gilmour & S.W. Duck (Eds), *The Emerging Field of Personal Relationships* (pp. 133–44). Hillsdale, NJ: Erlbaum.

Duck, S.W. & Montgomery, B.M. (1991). The interdependence among interaction substance, theory and methods. In B.M. Montgomery & S. Duck (Eds), *Studying Interpersonal Interaction* (pp. 3–15). New York: Guilford.

Duck, S.W. & Pittman, G. (1994). Social and personal relationships. In M. Knapp & G. Miller (Eds), *Handbook of Interpersonal Communication* (2nd Edn) (pp. 676–95). Thousand Oaks, CA: Sage.

Duck, S.W. & Sants, H.K.A. (1983). On the origin of the specious: are personal relationships really interpersonal states? *Journal of Social and Clinical Psychology*, **1**, 27–41.

Duck, S.W. & Wood, J.T. (1995). *Confronting Relationship Challenges (Understanding relationship processes 5)*. Newbury Park, CA: Sage.

Duck, S.W., Pond, K. & Leatham, G.B. (1994). Loneliness and the evaluation of relational events. *Journal of Social and Personal Relationships*, **11**, 253–76.

Duck, S.W., Rutt, D.J., Hurst, M.H. & Strejc, H. (1991). Some evident truths about conversations in everyday relationships: all communications are not created equal. *Human Communication Research*, **18**, 228–67.

Duckitt, J. (1994). *The Social Psychology of Prejudice*. Westport, CT: Praeger.

Duncan, S. & Fiske, D.W. (1977). Face-to-face interaction: research, methods, and theory. Hillsdale, NJ: Erlbaum.

Dunkel-Schetter, C. (1984). Social support and cancer: findings based on patient interviews and their implications. *Journal of Social Issues*, **40**, 77–98.

Dunkel-Schetter, C. & Barrett, T.L. (1990). Differentiating the cognitive and behavioral aspects of social support. In B.R. Sarason, I.G. Sarason & G.R. Pierce (Eds), *Social Support: an Interactional View* (pp. 267–96). Wiley: New York.

Dunkel-Schetter, C. & Bennett, T. (1990). Differentiating the cognitive and behavioral aspects of social support. In B.R. Sarason, I.G. Sarason & G.R. Pierce (Eds), *Social Support: an Interactional View* (pp. 267–96). New York: Wiley.

Dunkel-Schetter, C. & Skokan, L. (1990). Determinants of social support provisions in personal relationships. *Journal of Social and Personal Relationships*, **7**, 437–50.

Dunkel-Schetter, C. & Wortman, C. (1982).The interpersonal dynamics of cancer: problems in social relationships and their impact on the patient. In H. Friedman & M.R. Dimatteo (Eds), *Interpersonal Issues in Health Care* (pp. 69–100). New York: Academic Press.

Dunkel-Schetter, C., Blasband, D., Feinstein, L. & Bennett-Herbert, T. (1992). Elements of supportive interactions: when are attempts to help effective? In S. Spacapan & S. Oskamp (Eds), *Helping and Being Helped: Naturalistic Studies*. Newbury Park, CA: Sage.

Dunkel-Schetter, C., Folkman, S. & Lazarus, R.S. (1987). Correlates of social support receipt. *Journal of Personality and Social Psychology*, **53**, 71–80.

Dunn, J. (1983). Sibling relationships in early childhood. *Child Development*, **54**, 787–811.

Dunn, J. (1984). *Sisters and Brothers*. London: Fontana Paperbacks.

Dunn, J. (1988a). Relations among relationships. In S.W. Duck (Ed.), *Handbook of Personal Relationships: Theory, Research, and Interventions*. New York: Wiley.

Dunn, J. (1988b). *The Beginnings of Social Understanding*. Cambridge, MA: Harvard University Press.

Dunn, J. (1993). *Young Children's Close Relationships*. Newbury Park, CA: Sage.

Dunn, J. & Brown, J. (1991). Relationships, talk about feelings, and the development of affect regulation in early childhood. In J. Garber & K.A. Dodge (Eds), *The Development of Emotion Regulation and Dysregulation* (pp. 89–108). Cambridge: Cambridge University Press.

Dunn, J. & Brown, J. (1994). Affect expression in the family, children's understanding of emotions and their interactions with others. *Merrill-Palmer Quarterly*, **40**, 120–37.

Dunn, J. & Kendrick, C. (1981). Interaction between young siblings: association with the interaction between mother and firstborn. *Developmental Psychology*, **17**, 336–43.

Dunn, J. & Kendrick, C. (1982). *Siblings: Love, Envy and Understanding*. New York: Academic Press.

Dunn, J. & Munn, P. (1985). Becoming a family member: family conflict and the development of social understanding in the second year. *Child Development*, **56**, 764–74.

Dunn, J. & Munn, P. (1986). Siblings and the development of prosocial behavior. *International Journal of Behavioral Development*, **9**, 265–84.

Dunn, J. & Munn, P. (1987). Development of justifications in disputes with mother and sibling. *Developmental Psychology*, **23**, 791–8.

Dunn, J. & Plomin, R. (1990). *Separate Lives: Why Siblings Are So Different*. New York: Basic Books.

Dunn, J. & Shatz, M. (1989). Becoming a conversationalist despite (or because of) having an elder sibling. *Child Development*, **60**, 399–410.

Dunn, J., Brown, J. & Beardsall, L. (1991). Family talk about emotions and children's late understanding of others' emotions. *Developmental Psychology*, **27**, 448–55.

Dunn, J., Brown, J., Slomkowski, C., Tesla, C. & Youngblade, L. (1991). Young children's understanding of other people's feelings and beliefs: individual differences and their antecedents. *Child Development*, **62**, 1352–66.

Dunn, J., Slomkowski, C. & Beardsall, L. (1994). Sibling relationships from the preschool period through middle childhood and early adolescence. *Developmental Psychology*, **30**, 315–24.

Dunn, J., Slomkowski, C., Beardsall, L. & Rende, R. (1994). Adjustment in middle childhood and early adolescence: links with earlier and contemporary sibling relationships. *Journal of Child Psychology and Psychiatry*, **35**, 491–504.

Durkheim, E. (1893). *The Division of Labor in a Society* (G. Simpson, trans.). New York: Free Press.

Durkheim, E. (1897/1951). *Suicide: a Study in Sociology* (J. Spaulding & G. Simpson, trans.). New York: Free Press.

Durodoye, B. (1994). Intermarriage and marital satisfaction. *TCA Journal*, **22**, 3–9.

Durojaiye, M.O.A. (1969). Race relations among junior school children. *Educational Research*, **11**, 226–8.

Dutton, D.G. & Aron, A. (1974). Some evidence for heightened sexual attraction under conditions of high anxiety. *Journal of Personality and Social Psychology*, **30**, 510–17.

Dutton, D.G. & Aron, A. (1989). Romantic attraction and generalized liking for others who are sources of conflict-based arousal. *Canadian Journal of Behavioural Science*, **21**, 246–57.

Dwyer, J.W. (1995). The effects of illness on the family. In R. Blieszner & V.H. Bedford (Eds), *Handbook of Aging and the Family* (pp. 401–21). Westport, CT: Greenwood Press.

Dykstra, P.A. (1990). *Next of (Non)Kin*. Amsterdam: Swets & Zeitlinger.

Dykstra, P.A. (1993). The differential availability of relationships and the provision and effectiveness of support to older adults. *Journal of Social and Personal Relationships*, **10**, 355–570.

Early, G. (1993). Introduction. In G. Early (Ed.), *Lure and Loathing: Essays on Race, Identity, and the Ambivalence of Assimilation* (pp. xi–xxiv). New York: Penguin.

East, P.L. & Rook, K.S. (1992). Compensatory patterns of support among children's peer relationships: a test using school friends, nonschool friends, and siblings. *Developmental Psychology*, **28**, 163–72.

Eastburg, M.C., Williamson, M., Gorsuch, R. & Ridley, C. (1994). Social support, personality, and burnout in nurses. *Journal of Applied Social Psychology*, **24**, 1233–50.

Easterbrooks, M.A. (1987). Early family development: longitudinal impact of marital quality. Paper presented at the biennial meetings of the Society for Research in Child Development.

Easterbrooks, M.A. & Emde, R.N. (1988). Marital and parent–child relationships: the role of affect in the family system. In R. Hinde & J. Stevenson-Hinde (Eds), *Relationships Within Families* (pp. 83–103). Oxford, Clarendon.

Easterbrooks, M.A., Cummings, E.M. & Emde, R.N. (1994). Young children's responses to constructive marital disputes. *Journal of Family Psychology*, **8**, 160–69.

Eccles, J.S. & Midgley, C. (1989). Stage/environment fit: developmentally appropriate classrooms for young adolescents. In R.E. Ames & C. Ames (Eds), *Research on Motivation in Education*, Vol. 3 (pp. 139–86). New York: Academic Press.

Eccles, J.S. & Midgley, C. (1990). Changes in academic motivation and self-perception during early adolescence. In G.R. Adams & T.P. Gulotte (Eds), *Childhood to Adolescence: a Transitional Period?* Newbury Park, CA: Sage.

Eckenrode, J. & Wethington, E. (1990). The process and outcome of mobilizing social support. In S.W. Duck (Ed. with R.C. Silver), *Personal Relationships and Social Support* (pp. 83–103). London: Sage.

Edelmann, R.J. (1987). *The Psychology of Embarrassment*. Chichester: Wiley.

Edgar, T. (1994). Self-disclosure behaviors of the stigmatized: strategies and outcomes for the revelation of sexual orientation. In R.J. Ringer (Ed.), *Queer Words, Queer Images* (pp. 221–37). New York: New York University Press.

Edwards, C.P. & Whiting, B.B. (1993). "Mother, Older Sibling and Me"; the overlapping roles of caregivers and companions in the social world of two- and three-year-olds in Ngeca, Kenya. In K. MacDonald (Ed.), *Parent–Child Play: Descriptions and Implications*. Albany, NY: SUNY Press.

Egeland, B. & Farber, E.A. (1984). Infant–mother attachment: factors related to its development and changes over time. *Child Development*, **55**, 753–71.

Eggebeen, D.J. (1992). Family structure and intergenerational exchanges. *Research on Aging*, **14**, 427–47.

Eggebeen, D.J. & Hogan, D.P. (1990). Giving between generations in American families. *Human Nature*, **1**, 211–32.

Eggert, L.L. & Parks, M.R. (1987). Communication network involvement in adolescents' friendships and romantic relationships. In M.L. McLaughlin (Ed.), *Communication Yearbook 10* (pp. 283–322). Newbury Park, CA: Sage.

Eibl-Eibesfeldt, I. (1975). *Ethology: the Biology of Behavior* (2nd Edn). New York: Holt, Rinehart & Winston.

Eibl-Eibesfeldt, I. (1979). Human ethology: concepts and implications for the sciences of man. *Behavior and Brain Sciences*, **2**, 1–57.

Eibl-Eibesfeldt, I. (1989). *Human Ethology*. New York: Gruyter.

Eidelson, R.J. (1980). Interpersonal satisfaction and level of involvement: a curvilinear relationship. *Journal of Personality and Social Psychology*, **39**, 460–70.

Eidelson, R.J. & Epstein, N. (1982). Cognition and relationship maladjustment: development of a measure of relationship beliefs. *Journal of Consulting and Clinical Psychology*, **50**, 715–20.

Eisenberg, N. & Fabes, R.A. (1992). Young children's coping with interpersonal anger. *Child Development*, **63**, 116–28.

Eisenberg, N. & Fabes, R.A. (1994). Emotion, regulation and the development of social competence. In M. Clark (Ed.), *Review of Personality and Social Psychology*. Newbury Park, CA: Sage.

Eisenberg, N., Fabes, R.A., Schaller, M. & Miller, P. (1991). Personality and socialization correlates of vicarious emotional responding. *Journal of Personality and Social Psychology*, **61**, 459–70.

Eisenberg, N., Fabes, R.A., Nyman, M., Bernzweig, J. & Pinuelas, A. (1994). The relations of emotionality and regulation to children's anger-related reactions. *Child Development*, **65**, 109–28.

Ekblad, S. (1984). Children's thoughts and attitudes in China and Sweden: impacts of a restrictive versus a permissive environment. *Acta Psychiatrica Scandinavica*, **70**, 578–90.

Ekman, P. (1985). *Telling Lies. Clues to Deceit in the Marketplace, Politics, and Marriage.* New York: Norton.

Ekman, P. (1992). An argument for basic emotions. *Cognition and Emotion*, **6**, 169–200.

Ekman, P. & Friesen, W.V. (1971). Constants across cultures in the face and emotion. *Journal of Personality and Social Psychology*, **17**, 124–9.

Ekman, P., Davidson, R. & Friesen, W. (1990). The Duchenne smile: emotional expression and brain physiology II. *Journal of Personality and Social Psychology*, **58**, 343–53.

Ekman, P., Friesen, W.V., O'Sullivan, M., Chan, A., Diacoyanni-Tarlatzis, I., Heider, K., Krause, R., LeCompte, W.A., Pitcairn, T., Ricci-Bitti, P.E., Scherer, K., Tomita, M. & Tzavaras, A. (1987). Universals and cultural differences in the judgments of facial expressions of emotion. *Journal of Personality and Social Psychology*, **53**, 712–17.

El-Sheikh, M., Cummings, E.M. & Goetsch, V. (1989). Coping with adults' angry behavior: behavioral, physiological, a self-reported responding in preschoolers. *Developmental Psychology*, **25**, 490–98.

Elder, G., Modell, J. & Parke, R.D. (Eds) (1993). Children in time and place: developmental and historical insights. New York: Cambridge University Press.

Elias, M.J., Gara, M. & Ubriaco, M. (1985). Sources of stress and support in children's transition to middle school. *Journal of Clinical Child Psychology*, **14**, 112–18.

Eliasziw, M. & Donner, A. (1991). A generalized non-iterative approach to the analysis of family data. *Annals of Human Genetics*, **55**, 77–90.

Elicker, J., Egeland, M. & Sroufe, A. (1992). Predicting peer competence in childhood from early parent child relationships. In R. Parke & G.W. Ladd (Eds), *Family and Peer Relationships: Modes of Linkage*. Hillsdale, NJ: Erlbaum.

Ellis, B. J. & Symons, D. (1990). Sex differences in sexual fantasy: an evolutionary psychological approach. *Journal of Sex Research*, **27**, 527–56.

Ellis, C. (1991). Sociological introspection and emotional experience. *Symbolic Interaction*, **14**, 23–50.

Ellis, C. (1993). There are survivors: telling a story of sudden death. *The Sociological Quarterly*, **34**, 711–30.

Ellis, C. (1995a). *Final Negotiations: a Story of Love, Loss, and Chronic Illness*. Philadelphia: Temple University Press.

Ellis, C. (1995b). Speaking of dying: an ethnographic short story. *Symbolic Interaction*, **18**, 73–81.

Ellis, C. (1996). On the demands of truthfulness in writing personal loss narratives. *Journal of Personal and Interpersonal Loss*.

Ellis, C. & Bochner, A.P. (1992). Telling and performing personal stories: the constraints of choice in abortion. In C. Ellis & M. Flaherty (Eds), *Investigating Subjectivity* (pp. 79–101). Thousand Oaks, CA: Sage.

Ellis, L. & Ames, M.A. (1987). Neurohormonal functioning and sexual orientation: a theory of homosexuality–heterosexuality. *Psychological Bulletin*, **101**, 233–58.

Ellis, S. & Rogoff, B. (1982). The strategies and efficacy of child versus adult teachers. *Child Development*, **53**, 730–35.

Emery, R.E. (1988). *Marriage, Divorce, and Children's Adjustment*. Newbury Park, CA: Sage.

Emery, R.E. (1993). *Renegotiating Family Relationships*. New York: Guilford.

Emery, R.E. & O'Leary, K.D. (1984). Marital discord and child behavior problems in a nonclinic sample. *Journal of Abnormal Child Psychology*, **12**, 411–20.

Emery, R.E., Fincham, F.D. & Cummings, E.M. (1992). Parenting in context: systemic thinking about parental conflict and its influences on children. *Journal of Consulting and Clinical Psychology*, **60**, 909–12.

Emirbayer, M. & Goodwin, J. (1994). Network analysis and the problem of agency. *American Journal of Sociology*, **99**, 1411–54.

Endler, N.S. & Magnusson, D. (Eds) (1976). *Interactional Psychology and Personality*. Washington, DC: Hemisphere.

Endler, N., Hunt, J. McV. & Rosenstein, A.J. (1962). An S-R inventory of anxiousness. *Psychological Monographs*, **76** (17, Whole No. 536).

England, P. & McCreary, L. (1987). Gender inequality in paid employment. In B. Hess & M. Ferree (Eds), *Analyzing Gender: a Handbook of Social Science Research* (pp. 286–320). Newbury Park, CA: Sage.

Ensel, W. & Lin, N. (1991). The life stress paradigm and psychological distress. *Journal of Health and Social Behavior*, **32**, 321–41.

Epley, S.W. (1974). Reduction of the behavioral effects of aversive stimulation by the presence of companions. *Psychological Bulletin*, **81**, 271–83.

Epstein, A.L. (1969). The network and urban social organization. In J.C. Mitchell (Ed.), *Social Networks in Urban Situations*. Manchester: Manchester University Press.

Epstein, N., Baucom, D.H. & Rankin, L.A. (1993). Treatment of marital conflict: a cognitive-behavioral approach. *Clinical Psychology Review*, **13**, 45–57.

Eranen, L. & Liebkind, K. (1993). Coping with disaster: the helping behavior of communities and individuals. In J.P. Wilson & B. Raphael (Eds), *International Handbook of Traumatic Stress Syndromes* (pp. 957–64). New York: Plenum.

Erel, O. & Burman, B. (1995). Interrelatedness of marital relations and parent-child relations: a meta-analytic review. *Psychological Bulletin*, **118**, 108–32.

Ericksen, J.A., Yancey, W.L. & Ericksen, E.P. (1979). The division of family roles. *Journal of Marriage and the Family*, **41**, 301–13.

Erickson, M.F., Sroufe, L.A. & Egeland, B. (1985). The relationship between quality of attachment and behavior problems in preschool in a high risk sample. In I. Bretherton & E. Waters (Eds), *Growing Points in Attachment Theory and Research* (pp. 147–86). *Monographs of the Society for Research in Child Development*, **50**(1–2, Serial No. 209).

Eriksen, W. (1994). The role of social support in the pathogenesis of coronary heart disease: a literature review. *Family Practice*, **11**, 201–9.

Erikson, E.H. (1950). *Childhood and Society*. New York: Norton.

Erikson, E.H. (1963). *Childhood and Society* (2nd Edn). New York: Norton.

Erikson, E.H. (1968). *Identity, Youth and Crisis*. New York: Norton.

Erikson, K. (1976a). *Everything In Its Path*. New York: Simon and Schuster.

Erikson, K. (1976b). Loss of communality at Buffalo Creek. *American Journal of Psychiatry*, **133**, 302–5.

Erikson, K. (1991). A new species of trouble. In S.R. Couch & J.S. Kroll-Smith (Eds), *Communities at Risk: Collective Responses to Technological Hazards* (pp. 11–30). New York: Peter Lang.

Ervin-Tripp, J. (1989). Sisters and brothers. In P.G. Zukow (Ed.), *Sibling Interaction Across Cultures: Theoretical and Methodological Issues*. New York: Springer-Verlag.

Eshel, Y. & Kurman, J. (1990). Ethnic equity and asymmetry in peer acceptance. *Journal of Social Psychology*, **130**, 713–23.

Essed, P. (1991). *Understanding Everyday Racism: an Interdisciplinary Theory*. Newbury Park, CA: Sage.

Eysenck, H.J. (1967). *The Biological Basis of Personality*. Springfield, IL: Thomas.

Fabes, R.A. & Eisenberg, N. (1992). Young children's coping with interpersonal anger. *Child Development*, **63**, 116–28.

Fabes, R.A., Eisenberg, N., McCormick, S.E. & Wilson, M.S. (1988). Preschoolers' attributions of the situational determinants of others naturally ocurring emotions. *Developmental Psychology*, **24**, 376–85.

Fabes, R., Smith, M., Murphy, B. & Eisenberg, N. (1993). Peer relationships and the regulation of young children's anger. Paper presented at the Meeting of the Society for Research in Child Development, New Orleans, March 1993.

Fagot, B. & Paris, K. (1996, June). From infancy to seven years: continuities and change. *Development and Psychopathology*.

Fairchild, H.H. (1991). Scientific racism: the cloak of objectivity. *Journal of Social Issues*, **47**, 101–15.

Falbo, T. & Peplau, L.A. (1980). Power strategies in intimate relationships. *Journal of Personality and Social Psychology*, **38**, 618–28.

Falloon, I.R.H., Boyd, J.L., McGill, C.W., Ranzani, J., Moss, H.B. & Gilderman, A.M. (1982). Family management in the prevention of exacerbation of schizophrenia: a controlled study. *New England Journal of Medicine*, **306**, 1437–40.

Falloon, I.R.H., Boyd, J.L., McGill, C.W., Williamson, M., Ranzani, J., Moss, H.B., Gilderman, A.M. & Simpson, G.M. (1985). Family management in the prevention of morbidity of schizophrenia: clinical outcome of a two-year longitudinal study. *Archives of General Psychiatry*, **42**, 887–96.

Farrell, M.P. & Rosenberg, S.D. (1981). Parent–child relations at middle age. In C. Getty & W. Humphreys (Eds), *Understanding the Family: Stress and Change in American Family Life* (pp. 57–76). New York: Appleton-Century–Crofts.

Farrington, D.P. (1983). Offending from 10–25 years of age. In K.T. Van Dusen & S.A. Mednick (Eds), *From Children to Citizens: Vol. III, Families, Schools, and Delinquency Prevention* (pp. 27–51). New York: Springer-Verlag.

Fauber, R.L. & Long, N. (1991). Children in context: the role of the family in child psychotherapy. *Journal of Consulting and Clinical Psychology*, **59**, 813–20.

Feeney, J. & Noller, P. (1990). Attachment style as a predictor of adult romantic relationships. *Journal of Personality and Social Psychology*, **58**, 281–91.

Fehr, B. (1993). How do I love thee? . . . let me consult my prototype. In S.W. Duck (Ed.), *Understanding Relationship Processes 1: Individuals in Relationships* (pp. 87–120). Newbury Park: Sage.

Fehr, B. & Perlman, D. (1985). The family as a social network and support system. In L. L'Abate (Ed.), *Handbook of Family Psychology and Therapy*, Vol. 1 (pp. 323–56). Homewood, IL: Dorsey Press.

Feldlaufer, H., Midgley, C. & Eccles, J.S. (1988). Student, teacher, and observer perceptions of the classroom environment before and after the transition to junior high school. *Journal of Early Adolescence*, **8**(2), 133–56.

Felmlee, D.H. (1995). Fatal attractions: affection and disaffection in intimate relationships. *Journal of Social and Personal Relationships*, **12**, 295–311.

Felmlee, D., Sprecher, S. & Bassin, E. (1990). The dissolution of intimate relationships: a hazard model. *Social Psychology Quarterly*, **53**, 13–30.

Felner, R.D. & Adan, A.M. (1988). The School Transactional Environment Project: an ecological intervention and evaluation. In R.H. Price, E.L. Cowen, R.P. Lorion & J. Ramos-McKay (Eds), *Fourteen Ounces of Prevention: a Casebook for Practitioners* (pp. 111–22). Washington, DC: American Psychological Association.

Felner, R.D., Farber, S.S. & Primavera, J. (1983). Transitions and stressful life events: a model for primary prevention. In R.D. Felner, L.A. Jason, J.N. Moritsugu & S.S. Farber (Eds), *Preventive Psychology: Theory, Research, and Prevention* (pp. 191–215). New York: Pergamon.

Felner, R.D., Ginter, M. & Primavera, J. (1982). Primary prevention during school transitions: social support and environmental structure. *American Journal of Community Psychology*, **10**, 277–90.

Felner, R.D., Primavera, J. & Cauce, A.M. (1981). The impact of school transitions: a focus for preventive efforts. *American Journal of Community Psychology*, **9**, 449–59.

Felson, R.B. (1989). Parents and the reflected appraisal process: a longitudinal analysis. *Journal of Personality and Social Psychology*, **56**, 965–71.

Felton, B.J. & Berry, C.A. (1992). Do the sources of the urban elderly's social support determine its psychological consequences? *Psychology of Aging*, **7**, 89–97.

Fenzel, L.M. & Blyth, D.A. (1986). Individual adjustment to school transitions: an exploration of the role of supportive peer relations. *Journal of Early Adolescence*, **6**(4), 315–29.

Ferber, M.A., O'Farrell, B. & Allen, L. (Eds) (1991). *Work and Family: Policies for a Changing Work Force*. Washington, DC: National Academy Press.

Ferguson, T.J. & Stegge, H. (1995). Emotional states and traits in children: the case of guilt and shame. In J. Tangney & K. Fischer (Eds), *Self-conscious Emotions* (pp. 174–97). New York: Guilford.

Ferguson, T.J., Stegge, H. & Damhuis, I. (1991). Children's understanding of guilt and shame. *Child Development*, **62**, 827–39.

Fernandez, J.P. (1986). *Child Care and Corporate Productivity: Resolving Family/work Conflicts*. Lexington MA: Lexington Books.

Ferraro, K.F. (1989). Widowhood and health. In K.S. Markides & C.L. Cooper (Eds), *Aging, Stress, and Health* (pp. 69–90). Chichester: Wiley.

Ferree, M.M. (1987). The struggles of superwoman. In C. Bose, R. Feldberg & N. Sokoloff (Eds), *Hidden Aspects of Women's Work* (pp. 161–80). New York: Praeger.

Ferree, M.M. (1988, November). Negotiating household roles and responsibilities: resistance, conflict, and change. Paper presented at the annual meeting of the National Council on Family Relations, Philadelphia, PA.

Ferree, M.M. (1990). Beyond separate spheres: feminism and family research. *Journal of Marriage and the Family*, **52**, 866–84.

Ferree, M.M. (1991). The gender division of labor in two-earner marriages: dimensions of variability and change. *Journal of Family Issues,* **12**(2), 158–80.

Festinger, L. (1954). A theory of social comparison processes. *Human Relations*, 7, 117–40.

Festinger, L., Schachter, S. & Back, K.W. (1950). *Social Pressure in Informal Groups: a Study of Human Factors in Housing*. New York: Harper.

Field, D. & Minkler, M. (1993). The importance of family in advanced old age: the family is "forever". In P.A. Cowan, D. Field, D.A. Hansen, A. Skolnick & G.E. Swanson (Eds), *Family, Self, and Society: Toward a New Agenda for Family Research* (pp. 331–51). Hillsdale, NJ: Erlbaum.

Field, T.M. & Walden, T.A. (1982). Production and discrimination of facial expressions by preschool children. *Child Development*, 53, 1299–1311.

Field, T., Greenwald, P., Morrow, C., Healy, B., Foster, T., Gutherz, M. & Frost, P. (1992). Behavior state matching during interactions of preadolescent friends versus acquaintances. *Developmental Psychology*, 28, 242–50.

Field, T., Vega-Lahr, N., Scafidi, F. & Goldstein, S. (1986). Effects of maternal unavailablity on mother–infant interactions. *Infant Behavior and Development*, 9, 473–8.

Filsinger, E.E. (1991). Empirical typology, cluster analysis and family-level measurement. In T.W. Draper & A.C. Marcos (Eds), *Family Variables* (pp. 90–104). Newbury Park, CA: Sage.

Fincham, F.D. (1992). The account episode in close relationships. In M.L. McLaughlin, M.J. Cody & S.J. Read (Eds), *Explaining One's Self to Others: Reason-giving in a Social Context* (pp. 167–82). Hillsdale, NJ: Erlbaum.

Fincham, F.D. (1994). Understanding the association between marital conflict and child adjustment: Overview [Special section: contexts of interparental conflict and child behavior]. *Journal of Family Psychology*, 8, 123–7.

Fincham, F.D. & Bradbury, T.N. (1987). The impact of attributions in marriage: a longitudinal analysis. *Journal of Personality and Social Psychology*, 53, 510–17.

Fincham, F.D. & Bradbury, T.N. (1993). Marital satisfaction, depression, and attributions: a longitudinal study. *Journal of Personality and Social Psychology*, 64, 442–52.

Fincham, F.D. & Osborne, L.N. (1993). Marital conflict and children: retrospect and prospect. *Clinical Psychology Review*, 13, 75–88.

Fincham, F.D., Bradbury, T.N. & Scott, C.K. (1990). Cognition in marriage. In F.D. Fincham & T.N. Bradbury (Eds), *The Psychology of Marriage* (pp. 118–49). New York: Guilford.

Fine, M., Schwebel, A.I. & James-Myers, L. (1987). Family statishity in Black families: values underlying three different persepections. *Journal of Contemporary Family Studies*, 18, 1–23.

Finnie, V. & Russell, A. (1988). Preschool children's social status and their mothers' behavior and knowledge in the supervisory role. *Developmental Psychology*, 24, 789–801.

Fiore, J., Becker, J. & Coppell, D.A.B. (1983). Social network interactions: a buffer or a stress? *American Journal of Community Psychology*, 11, 423–40.

Fischer, C.S. (1982). *To Dwell Among Friends: Personal Networks in Town and City*. Chicago: University of Chicago Press.

Fischer, C.S., Jackson, R.M., Stueve, C.A., Gerson, K. & Jones, L.M., with Baldassare, M. (1977). *Networks and Places*. New York: Free Press.

Fischer, L.R. (1981). Transitions in the mother–daughter relationship. *Journal of Marriage and the Family*, 43, 613–22.

Fischer, L.R. (1986). *Linked Lives: Adult Daughters and Their Mothers*. New York: Harper & Row.

Fischmann-Havstad, L. & Marston, A.R. (1984). Weight loss maintenance as an aspect of family emotion and process. *British Journal of Clinical Psychology*, 23, 265–71.

Fisher, H.E. (1992). *Anatomy of Love*. New York: Norton.

Fisher, J.D., Goff, B.A., Nadler, A. & Chinsky, J.M. (1988). Social psychological influences on help-seeking and support from peers. In B.H. Gottlieb (Ed.), *Marshaling*

Social Support: Formats, Processes, and Effects (pp. 267–304). Newbury Park, CA: Sage.

Fisher, J.D., Nadler, A. & Whitcher-Alagna, S. (1982). Recipient reactions to aid. *Psychological Bulletin*, **91**, 27–54.

Fisher, R.A. (1925). *Statistical Methods for Research Workers*. Edinburgh: Oliver & Boyd.

Fisher, W. (1987). *Human Communication as Narration: Toward a Philosophy of Reason, Value, and Action*. Columbia: University of South Carolina.

Fiske, S.T. (1992). Thinking is for doing: portraits of social cognition from daguerreotype to laserphoto. *Journal of Personality and Social Psychology*, **63**, 877–89.

Fiske, S.T. (1993). Controlling other people: the impact of power on stereotyping. *American Psychologist*, **48**, 621–8.

Fiske, S.T. & Taylor, S.E. (1984). *Social Cognition*. Reading, MA: Addison-Wesley.

Fitch, K. (1994). Culture, ideology, and interpersonal communication research. *Communication Yearbook*, **17**, 104–35.

Fitch, K. (in preperation). *An Interpersonal Ideology of Connectedness: the Practice of Relationships in Urban Colombia*. New York: Guilford.

Fitness, J. & Strongman, K. (1991). Affect in close relationships. In G.J.O. Fletcher & F.D. Fincham (Eds), *Cognition in Close Relationships* (pp. 175–202). Hillsdale, NJ: Erlbaum.

Fitzpatrick, M.A. (1987). Marriage and verbal intimacy. In V.J. Derlega & J.H. Berg (Eds), *Self-disclosure: Theory, Research and Therapy* (pp. 131–54). New York: Plenum.

Fitzpatrick, M.A. (1993). Review of *Friendship Matters*. *Communication Theory*, **3**, 83–5.

Fitzpatrick, M.A. & Best, P. (1979). Dyadic adjustment in traditional, independent, and separate relationships: a validation study. *Communication Monographs*, **46**, 167–78.

Flaherty, J.A. & Richman, J.A. (1986). Effects of childhood relationships on the adult's capacity to form social supports. *American Journal of Psychiatry*, **143**, 851–5.

Flaherty, J. & Richman, J. (1989). Gender differences in the perception and utilization of social support: theoretical perspectives and an empirical test. *Social Science and Medicine*, **28**, 1221–8.

Flanagan, D.A.J. & Wagner, H.L. (1991). Expressed emotion and panic–fear in the prediction of diet treatment compliance. *British Journal of Clinical Psychology*, **30**, 231–40.

Fleming, R., Baum, A., Gisriel, M. & Gatchel, R. (1982). Mediating influences of social support on stress at Three Mile Island. *Journal of Human Stress*, **8**, 14–22.

Fletcher, G.J.O. & Fincham, F.D. (1991). Attribution processes in close relationships. In G.J.O. Fletcher & F.D. Fincham (Eds), *Cognition in Close Relationships* (pp. 7–35). Hillsdale, NJ: Erlbaum.

Fletcher, G.J.O. & Fitness, J. (1993). Knowledge structures and explanations in intimate relationships. In S.W. Duck (Ed.), *Understanding Relationship Processes 1: Individuals in Relationships* (pp. 121–43). Newbury Park: Sage.

Fletcher, G.J.O. & Kininmonth, L. (1991). Interaction in close relationships and social cognition. In G.J.O. Fletcher & F.D. Fincham (Eds), *Cognition in Close Relationships* (pp. 235–55). Hillsdale, NJ: Erlbaum.

Fogel, A. (1995). Relational narratives of the pre-linguistic self. In P. Rochat (Ed.), *The Self in Infancy: Theory and Research*. Amsterdam: Elsevier North Holland.

Fogel, A., Diamond, G.R., Langhorst, B.H. & Demos, V. (1982). Affective and cognitive aspects of the two-month-old's participation in face-to-face interaction with its mother. In E. Tronick (Ed.), *Social Interchanges in Infancy: Affect, Cognition, and Communication*. Baltimore: University Park Press.

Fonagy, P., Steele, M., Steele, H., Leigh, T., Kennedy, R., & Target, M. (in press). The predictive specificity of Mary Main's Adult Attachment Interview: implications for psychodynamic theories of normal and pathological emotional development. In S. Goldberg, R. Muir & J. Kerr (Eds), *Attachment Theory: Social, Developmental, and Clinical Perspectives*. Hillsdale, NJ: The Analytic Press.

Fonzi, A., Tomada, G. & Ciucci, E. (1994). Uso di indici informativi nell' interazione tra bambini del *nido* (Use of informative indexes in the interaction among creche children). *Eta-Evolutiva*, **47**, 5–13.

Foot, H.C., Chapman, A.J. & Smith, J.R. (1977). Friendship and social responsiveness in boys and girls. *Journal of Personality and Social Psychology*, **35**, 401–11.

Form, W.H. & Nosow, S. (1958). *Community in Disaster*. New York: Harper.

Foucault, M. (1970). *The Order of Things: An Archaeology of the Human Sciences*. New York: Random House.

Fowers, B.J. (1991). His and her marriage: a multivariate study of gender and marital satisfaction. *Sex Roles*, **24**, 209–21.

Frable, D.E.S., Blackstone, T. & Scherbaum, C. (1990). Marginal and mindful: deviants in social interactions. *Journal of Personality and Social Psychology*, **59**, 140–49.

Franck, D. (1993). *Separation*. New York: Alfred A. Knopf.

Frank, A. (1991). *At the Will of the Body: Reflections on Illness*. Boston: Houghton Mifflin.

Frank, A. (1993). The rhetoric of self-change: illness experience as narrative. *The Sociological Quarterly*, **34**, 39–52.

Frank, J.D. (1979). The present status of outcome studies. *Journal of Consulting and Clinical Psychology*, **47**, 310–16.

Frank, S.J., Avery, C.B. & Laman, M.S. (1988). Young adults' perceptions of their relationships with their parents: individual differences in connectedness, competence, and emotional autonomy. *Developmental Psychology*, **24**, 729–37.

Frederick, C. (1980). Effects of natural vs. human-induced violence upon victims. *Evaluation and Change*, Special Issue, 71–5.

Freedman, S. & Hurley, J. (1980). Perceptions of helpfulness and behavior in groups. *Group*, **4**, 51–8.

Freedy, J., Kilpatrick, D. & Resnick, H. (1993). Natural disasters and mental health. *Journal of Social Behavior and Personality*, **8**(5), 49–104.

Freeman, D. (1983). *Margaret Mead and Samoa*. Cambridge, MA: Harvard University Press.

French, M. (1985). *Beyond Power: On Women, Men, and Morals*. New York: Ballantine.

Freud, A. (1969). Adolescence as a developmental disturbance. In G. Kaplan & S. Lebovici (Eds), *Adolescence: Psychological Perspectives* (pp. 5–10). New York: Basic Books.

Freud, S. (1961). The ego and the id. In J. Strachey (Ed. and Trans.), *The Standard Edition of the Complete Psychological Works of Sigmund Freud*, Vol. 19 (pp. 3–66). London: Hogarth Press (original work published 1923).

Friedlander, M.L. (1993). When complementarity is uncomplementary and other reactions to Tracey (1993). *Journal of Counseling Psychology*, **40**, 410–12.

Friedlander, M.L., Siegel, S. & Brenock, K. (1989). Parallel processes in counseling and supervision: a case study. *Journal of Counseling Psychology*, **36**, 149–57.

Friedman, H.S. (1991). The self-healing personality: why some people achieve health and others succumb to illness. New York: Holt.

Friedman, H.S. (Ed.) (1992). Hostility, coping, and health. Washington, DC: American Psychological Association.

Friedman, H.S. & Rosenman, R. (1974). *Type A Behavior and Your Heart*. New York: Knopf.

Friedman, H.S., Tucker, J.S., Tomlinson-Keasey, C., Schwartz, J.E., Wingard, D.L. & Criqui, M.H. (1993). Does childhood personality predict longevity? *Journal of Personality and Social Psychology*, **65**, 176–85.

Friedrich, L.K. & Stein, A.H. (1973). Aggressive and prosocial television programs and the natural behavior of preschool children. *Monographs of the Society for Research in Child Development*, **38**(4, Serial No. 151).

Frieze, I.H. & McHugh, M.C. (1992). Power and influence strategies in violent and nonviolent marriages. *Psychology of Women Quarterly*, **16**, 449–65.

Frijda, N.H. (1988). The laws of emotion. *American Psychologist*, **43**, 349–58.

Fritz, C.E. (1961). Disasters. In R.K. Merton & R.A. Nisbet (Eds), *Contemporary Social Problems* (pp. 651–94). New York: Harcourt.

Fromm, E. (1956). *The Art of Loving*. New York: Harper & Row.

Fry, W.R., Firestone, I.J. & Williams, D.L. (1983). Negotiation process and outcome of stranger dyads and dating couples: do lovers lose? *Basic and Applied Social Psychology*, **4**, 1–16.

Fullinwider-Bush, N. & Jacobvitz, D.B. (1993). The transition to young adulthood: generational boundary dissolution and female identity development. *Family Process*, **32**, 87–103.

Funderberg, L. (1994). *Black, White, Other: Biracial Americans Talk about Race and Identity*. New York: Morrow.

Furman, L.G. (1986). Cross-gender friendships in the workplace: factors and components. Unpublished doctoral dissertation, Fielding Institute.

Furman, W. (1985). Compatibility and incompatibility in children's peer and sibling relationships. In W. Ickes (Ed.), *Compatible and Incompatible Relationships* (pp. 61–87). New York: Springer-Verlag.

Furman, W. & Buhrmester, D. (1985). Children's perception of the qualities of the sibling relationships. *Child Development*, **56**, 448–61.

Furman, W. & Robbins, P. (1985). What's the point? Issues in the selection of treatment objectives. In B. Schneider, K.H. Rubin & J.E. Ledingham (Eds), *Children's Peer Relations: Issues in Assessment and Intervention*. New York: Springer-Verlag.

Gadamer, H. (1989). *Truth and Method* (2nd Edn). New York: Crossroad.

Gaelick, L., Bodenhausen, G.V. & Wyer, R.S. (1985). Emotional communication in close relationships. *Journal of Personality and Social Psychology*, **49**, 1246–65.

Gaines, S.O. Jr (1994). Exchange of respect-denying behaviors among male–female friendships. *Journal of Social and Personal Relationships*, **11**, 5–24.

Gaines, S.O. Jr (1995). Relationships between measures of cultural minorities. In J.T. Wood & S.W. Duck (Eds), *Under-studied Relationships: Off The Beaten Track (Understanding Relationship Processes 6)* (pp. 51–88). Thousand Oaks, CA: Sage.

Gaines, S.O. Jr & Reed, E.S. (1994). Two social psychologies of prejudice: Gordon W. Allport, W.E.B. Du Bois, and the legacy of Booker T. Washington. *Journal of Black Psychology*, **20**, 8–28.

Gaines, S.O. Jr & Reed, E.S. (1995). Prejudice: from Allport to Du Bois. *American Psychologist*, **50**, 96–103.

Gaines, S.O. Jr, Marelich, W., Bledsoe, K., Barájas, L., Hicks, D., Lyde, M., Takahashi, Y. & Yum, N. (1995). The Individualism/Collectivism/Familism (ICF) Questionnaire: A multidimensional measure of cultural value orientations. Manuscript submitted for publication.

Gaines, S.O. Jr, Ríos, D.I., Granrose, C., Bledsoe, K., Farris, K., Page, M.S. & Garcia (1996). Reciprocity of affection and respect among interethnic married/cohabiting couples. Manuscript under review.

Gallimore, R., Boggs, J.W. & Jordan, C. (1974). *Culture, Behavior and Education: A Study of Hawaiian Americans*. Beverly Hills, CA: Sage.

Galvin, K.M. & Brommel, B.J. (1986). *Family Communication*. Glenview, IL: Scott, Foreman.

Gamson, W.A. (1979). Forword. In J.L. Davidson, *Political Partnerships: Neighborhood Residents and Their Council Members*. Beverly Hills: Sage.

Gangestad, S.W. & Simpson, J.A. (1990). Toward an evolutionary history of female sociosexual variation. *Journal of Personality*, **58**, 69–96.

Gard, L. (1990). Patient disclosure of human immunodeficiency virus (HIV) status to parents: clinical considerations, *Professional Psychology: Research and Practice*, **21**, 252–6.

Garmezy, N. & Rutter, M. (1983). *Stress, Coping and Development in Children*. New York: McGraw Hill.

Gaston, L. (1990). The concept of the alliance and its role in psychotherapy: theoretical and empirical considerations. *Psychotherapy*, **27**, 143–53.

Gecas, V. (1989). Social psychology of self-efficacy. *American Sociological Review*, **15**, 291–316.

Geen, R.G. & Gange, J.J. (1977). Drive theory of social facilitation: twelve years of theory and research. *Psychological Bulletin*, **84**, 1267–88.

Geertz, C. (1973). *The Interpretation of Cultures*. New York: Basic Books.

Gelles, R.J. (1979). *Family Violence*. Beverly Hills, CA: Sage.

Gelles, R.J. & Straus, M.A. (1985). Violence in the American family. In A.J. Lincoln & M.A. Straus (Eds), *Crime and the Family* (pp. 88–110). Springfield, IL: Thomas.

Gelso, C.J. & Carter, J.A. (1985). The relationship in counseling and psychotherapy. *The Counseling Psychologist*, **13**, 155–244.

Gelso, C.J. & Carter, J.A. (1994). Components of the psychotherapy relationship: their interaction and unfolding during treatment. *Journal of Counseling Psychology*, **41**, 296–306.

Genta, M.L., Menesini, E., Fonzi, A., Costabile, A. & Smith, P.K. (1996). Bullies and victims in schools in Central and Southern Italy. *European Journal of Psychology of Education*, **XI**, 91–110.

Georgoudi, M. (1983). Modern dialectics in social psychology: a reappraisal. *European Journal of Social Psychology*, **13**, 77–93.

Gergen, K.J. (1973). Social psychology as history. *Journal of Personality and Social Psychology*, **26**, 309–20.

Gergen, K.J. (1980). Toward generative theory. *Journal of Personality and Social Psychology*, **36**, 1344–60.

Gergen, K.J. (1982). *Towards Transformation in Social Knowledge*. New York: Springer-Verlag.

Gergen, K.J. (1994). *Realities and Relationships: Soundings in Social Construction*. Cambridge, MA: Harvard University Press.

Gergen, K.J. & Davis, K. (Eds) (1985). *The Social Construction of the Person*. New York: Springer-Verlag.

Gergen, K.J. & Gergen, M. (1986). Narrative form and the construction of psychological science. In T. Sarbin (Ed.), *Narrative Psychology: The Storied Nature of Human Conduct* (pp. 22–44). New York: Praeger.

Gergen, K.J. & Gergen, M. (1987). Narratives of relationship. In R. Burnett, P. McGhee & D. Clarke (Eds), *Accounting for Relationships: Explanation, Representation and Knowledge* (pp. 269–88). London: Methuen.

Gergen, M. (1992). Life stories: pieces of a dream. In G.C. Rosenwald & R.L. Ochberg (Eds), *Storied Lives: the Cultural Politics of Self-understanding* (pp. 127–44). New Haven, CT: Yale University Press.

Gershman, H. (1983). The stress of coming out. *The American Journal of Psychoanalysis*, **43**, 129–38.

Giddens, A. (1979). *Central Problems in Social Theory: Action, Structure and Contradiction in Social Analysis*. Berkeley: University of California Press.

Giddens, A. (1991). *Modernity and Self-Identity*. Cambridge: Polity.

Giel, R. (1990). Psychosocial process in disasters. *International Journal of Mental Health*, **19**, 7–20.

Gift, T.C., Cole, R.E. & Wynne, L.C. (1985). A hostility measure for use in family contexts. *Psychiatry Research*, **15**, 205–10.

Gilbert, D.T., Pelham, B.W. & Krull, D.S. (1988). On cognitive busyness: when person perceivers meet persons perceived. *Journal of Personality and Social Psychology*, **54**, 733–40.

Gilbert, S.J. & Horenstein, D. (1975). The communication of self-disclosure: level versus valence. *Human Communication Research*, **1**, 316–22.

Gilligan, C. (1977). In a different voice: women's conceptions of self and morality.

Harvard Educational Review, **47**, 481–517.

Gilligan, C. (1982). *In a Different Voice: Psychological Theory and Women's Development.* Cambridge, MA: Harvard University Press.

Ginsburg, G.P. (1988). Rules, scripts and prototypes in personal relationships. In S.W. Duck (Ed.), *Handbook of Personal Relationships* (1st Edn, pp. 23–40). Chichester: Wiley.

Givens, D.B. (1978). The nonverbal basis of attraction: flirtation, courtship, and seduction. *Psychiatry*, **41**, 346–59.

Glaser, R., Rice, L.J., Sheridan, J.H., Fertel, R., Stout, J., Speicher, C.E., Pinsky, D., Kotur, M., Post, A., Beck, M. & Kiecolt-Glaser, J.K. (1987). Stress related immune suppression: health implications. *Brain, Behavior, and Immunity*, **1**, 7–20.

Glass, J., Bengtson, V.L. & Dunham, C.C. (1986). Attitude similarity in three-generation families: socialization, status inheritance, or reciprocal influence. *American Sociological Review*, **51**, 685–98.

Glenn, N.D. (1990). Quantitative research on marital quality in the 1980s: a critical review. *Journal of Marriage and the Family*, **52**, 818–31.

Gleser, G.C., Green, B.L. & Winget, C.N. (1981). *Prolonged Psychological Effects of Disaster: a Study of Buffalo Creek.* New York: Academic Press.

Goffman, E. (1959). *The Presentation of Self in Everyday Life.* New York: Anchor Books.

Goffman, E. (1963). *Stigma: Notes on the Management of Spoiled Identity.* Englewood Cliffs, NJ: Prentice-Hall.

Goffman, E. (1967). *Interaction Ritual: Essays on Face-to-Face Behavior.* Garden City, NY: Anchor Books.

Goffman, E. (1974). *Stigma: Notes on the Management of Spoiled Identity.* New York: Jason Aronson.

Gold, D.T. (1989). Sibling relationships in old age: a typology. *International Journal of Aging and Human Development*, **28**, 37–51.

Gold, M. (1963). *Status Forces in Delinquent Boys.* Ann Arbor: University of Michigan Press.

Goldberg, L.R. (1981a). Language and individual differences: the search for universals in personality lexicons. In L. Wheeler (Ed.), *Review of Personality and Social Psychology*, Vol. 2 (pp. 141–65). Beverly Hills, CA: Sage.

Goldberg, L.R. (1981b). Unconfounding situational attributions from uncertain, neutral, and ambiguous ones: a psychometric analysis of descriptions of oneself and various types of others. *Journal of Personality and Social Psychology*, **41**, 517–52.

Goldenburg, S. (1984–5). An empirical test of Bott's hypotheses, based on analysis of ethnographic atlas data. *Behavioral Science Research*, **19**, 127–58.

Goldsmith, D. (1990). A dialectical perspective on the expression of autonomy and connection in romantic relationships. *Western Journal of Speech Communication*, **54**, 537–56.

Goldsmith, D. (1992). Managing conflicting goals in supportive interaction: an integrative theoretical framework. *Communication Research*, **19**, 264–86.

Goldsmith, D. (1994). The role of facework in supportive communication. In B.R. Burleson, T.L. Albrecht & I.G. Sarason (Eds), *Communication of Social Support: Messages, Interactions, Relationships, and Community* (pp. 29–49). Thousand Oaks, CA: Sage.

Goldsmith, D. & Parks, M.R. (1990). Communication strategies for managing the dilemmas of social support. In S.W. Duck & R.C. Silver (Eds), *Personal Relationships and Social Support* (pp. 104–21). Newbury Park, CA: Sage.

Goldstein, H. (1987). *Multilevel Models in Educational and Social Research.* New York: Oxford.

Goldstein, H. & McDonald, R.P. (1988). A general model for the analysis of multilevel data. *Psychometrika*, 53, 455–67.

Goldstein, M.J. (1987). Family interaction patterns that antedate the onset of schizophrenia and related disorders. In K. Hahlweg & M.J. Goldstein (Eds), *Understanding Major Mental Disorder: the Role of Family Interaction Research*. New York: Family Process Press.

Goldstein, M.J., Rodnick, E.H., Evans, J.R., May, P.R.A. & Steinberg, M.R. (1978). Drug and family therapy in the aftercare of acute schizophrenics. *Archives of General Psychiatry*, **35**, 1169–77.

Gollob, H.F. (1991). Methods for estimating individual- and group-level correlations. *Journal of Personality and Social Psychology*, **60**, 376–81.

Gonzalez, R. (1995). The statistics ritual in psychological research. *Psychological Science*, **5**, 321–6.

Gonzalez, R. & Griffin, D. (1995a). *An Approximate Significance Test for the Group-level Correlation*. University of Washington and University of Sussex.

Gonzalez, R. & Griffin, D. (1995b). *The Multiple Personalities of the Intraclass Correlation*. University of Washington and University of Sussex.

Goode, W.J. (1956). *Women in Divorce*. New York: Macmillan.

Goodenough, F. (1931). *Anger in Young Children*. Minneapolis: University of Minnesota Press.

Goodnow, J. & Collins, A. (1991). *Ideas According to Parents*. Hillsdale, NJ: Erlbaum.

Goodnow, J.J. & Warton, P.M. (1992). Understanding responsibility: adolescents' views of delegation and follow-through within the family. *Social Development*, **1**, 89–106.

Goodstein, L. & Reinecker, V. (1974). Factors affecting self-disclosure: a review of the literature. *Progress in Experimental Personality Research*, **7**, 49–77.

Goodwin, J.S., Hurt, W.C., Key, C.R. & Sarret, J.M. (1987). The effect of marital status on stage, treatment, and survival of cancer patients. *Journal of the American Medical Association*, **258**, 3125–30.

Goodwin, R. (1995). The privatization of the personal? I: Intimate disclosure in modern-day Russia. *Journal of Social and Personal Relationships*, **12**, 121–31.

Goodwin, R. & Emelyanova, T. (1995). The privatization of the personal? II: Attitudes to the family and child-rearing values in modern-day Russia. *Journal of Social and Personal Relationships*, **12**, 132–8.

Gordon, C. & Gaitz, C.M. (1976). Leisure and lives: personal expressivity across the life span. In R.H. Binstock & E. Shanas (Eds), *Handbook of Aging and the Social Sciences* (pp. 310–41). New York: Van Nostrand Reinhold.

Gordon, M. & Downing, H. (1978). A multivariate test of the Bott hypothesis in an urban Irish setting. *Journal of Marriage and the Family*, **40**, 585–93.

Gordon, S. (1976). *Lonely in America*. New York: Simon & Schuster.

Gottlieb, B.H. (1981). Preventive interventions involving social networks and social support. In B.H. Gottlieb (Ed.), *Social Networks and Social Support* (pp. 201–32). Beverly Hills, CA: Sage.

Gottlieb, B.H. (1983). *Social Support Strategies: Guidelines for Mental Health Practice*. Beverly Hills, CA: Sage.

Gottlieb, B.H. (1985). Social support and the study of personal relationships. *Journal of Social and Personal Relationships*, **2**, 351–75.

Gottlieb, B.H. (1988). Support interventions: a typology and agenda for research. In S.W. Duck (Ed.), *Handbook of Personal Relationships: Theory, Research, and Interventions* (1st Edn, pp. 519–41). Chichester: Wiley.

Gottlieb, B.H. (1992). Quandries in translating support concepts to intervention. In H.O.F. Veiel & U. Baumann (Eds), *The Meaning and Measurement of Social Support* (pp. 293–309). New York: Hemisphere.

Gottlieb, B.H. & Todd, D.M. (1979). Characterizing and promoting social support in natural settings. In R.F. Munoz, L.R. Snowden & J.G. Kelly (Eds), *Social and Psychological Research in Community Settings* (pp. 183–242). San Francisco: Jossey-Bass.

Gottman, J.M. (1979). *Marital Interaction: Experimental Investigations*. New York: Academic Press.

Gottman, J.M. (1982). Temporal form: toward a new language for describing relationships. *Journal of Marriage and the Family*, **44**, 943–62.

Gottman, J.M. (1983). How children become friends. *Monographs of the Society for Research in Child Development*, **48**(Serial No. 201).

Gottman, J.M. (1986). The world of coordinated play: same- and cross-sex friendship in young children. In J.M. Gottman & J.G. Parker (Eds), *Conversations of Friends: Speculations on Affective Development* (pp. 139–91). Cambridge, MA: Cambridge University Press.

Gottman, J.M. (1993). The roles of conflict engagement, escalation, and avoidance in marital interaction: a longitudinal view of five types of couples. *Journal of Consulting and Clinical Psychology*, **61**, 6–15.

Gottman, J.M. (1994). *What Predicts Divorce?* Hillsdale, NJ: Erlbaum.

Gottman, J.M. & Katz, L.F. (1989). Effects of marital discord on young children's peer interaction and health. *Developmental Psychology*, **25**, 373–81.

Gottman, J.M. & Krokoff, L.J. (1989). Marital interaction and satisfaction: a longitudinal view. *Journal of Consulting and Clinical Psychology*, **57**, 47–52.

Gottman, J.M. & Levenson, R.W. (1986). Assessing the role of emotion in marriage. *Behavioral Assessment*, **8**, 31–48.

Gottman, J.M. & Mettetal, G. (1986). Speculations about social and affective development: friendship and acquaintanceship through adolescence. In J.M. Gottman & J. Parker (Eds), *Conversations of Friends. Speculations on Affective Development* (pp. 192–237). Cambridge: Cambridge University Press.

Gottman, J.M., Katz, L.F. & Hooven, C. (April, 1995). Parental meta-emotion structure and the emotional life of families: theoretical model and preliminary data. Paper presented at the biennial meeting of the Society for Research in Child Development. Indianapolis, Indiana.

Gottman, J.M., Markman, H. & Notarius, C. (1977). The topography of marital conflict: a study of verbal and nonverbal behavior. *Journal of Marriage and the Family*, **39**, 461–77.

Gottschalk, L.A. & Gleser, G.C. (1969). *The Measurement of Psychological States through the Content Analysis of Verbal Behavior*. Berkeley, CA: University of California Press.

Gough, H.G. (1987). *California Psychological Inventory Administrator's Guide*. Palo Alto, CA: Consulting Psychologists Press.

Graham, S., Hudley, C. & Williams, E. (1992). Attributional and emotional determinants of aggression among African, American and Latino young adolescents. *Developmental Psychology*, **28**, 731–40.

Granovetter, M. (1973). The strength of weak ties. *American Journal of Sociology*, **78**, 1360–80.

Granovetter, M. (1979). The theory-gap in social network analysis. In P.W. Holland & S. Leinhardt (Eds), *Perspectives on Social Network Research*. New York: Academic Press.

Gratton, B. & Haber, C. (1993). In search of "intimacy at a distance": family history from the perspective of elderly women. *Journal of Aging Studies*, **7**, 183–94.

Gray-Little, B. & Burks, N. (1983). Power and satisfaction in marriage: a review and critique. *Psychological Bulletin*, **93**, 513–38.

Green, B. (1982). Assessing levels of psychological impairment following disaster: consideration of actual and methodological dimensions, *Journal of Nervous and Mental Disease*, **170**, 544–52.

Green, B. (1993). Identifying survivors at risk: trauma and stressors across events. In J.P. Wilson & B. Raphael (Eds), *International Handbook of Traumatic Stress Syndromes* (pp. 135–44). New York: Plenum.

Green, B. (1995). Long-term consequences of disasters. In S.E. Hobfoll & M.W. de Vries (Eds), *Extreme Stress and Communities: Impact and Intervention* (pp. 307–24). Dordrecht: Kluwer.

Green, B. & Solomon, S. (1995). The mental health impact of natural and technological disasters. In J.R. Freedy & S.E. Hobfoll (Eds), *Traumatic Stress: from Theory to Practice* (pp. 163–80). New York: Plenum.

Green, B., Lindy, J., & Grace, M. (1994). Psychological effects of toxic contamination. In R. Ursano, B. McCaughey & C. Fullerton (Eds), *Individual and Community Responses to Trauma and Disaster: the Structure of Human Chaos* (pp. 154–176). Cambridge: Cambridge University Press.

Greenbaum, P.E. (1985). Nonverbal differences in communication style between American Indian and Anglo elementary classrooms. *American Educational Research Journal*, **22**, 101–15.

Greenberg, J.R. & Mitchell, S.A. (1983). *Object Relations in Psychoanalytic Theory*. Cambridge, MA: Harvard University Press.

Greenberg, L. (1979). Genetic component of bee odor in kin recognition. *Science*, **206**, 1095–7.

Greenberg, L.S. (1994). What is "real" in the relationship? Comment on Gelso and Carter (1994). *Journal of Counseling Psychology*, **41**, 307–10.

Greenberg, M.T., Speltz, M.L. & DeKlyen, M. (1993). The role of attachment in the early development of disruptive behavior problems. *Development and Psychopathology*, **5**, 191–213.

Greene, A.L. & Boxer, A.M. (1986). Daughters and sons as young adults: restructuring the ties that bind. In N. Datan, A.L. Greene & H.W. Reese (Eds), *Life-span Developmental Psychology: Intergenerational Relations* (pp. 125–49). Hillsdale, NJ: Erlbaum.

Greenwald, A.G. (1980). The totalitarian ego: fabrication and revision of personal history. *American Psychologist*, **35**, 603–18.

Griesinger, D.W. & Livingston, J.W. (1973). Toward a model of interpersonal orientation in experimental games. *Behavioral Science*, **18**, 173–88.

Griffin, D. & Gonzalez, R. (1995a). The correlational analysis of dyad-level data in the exchangeable case. *Psychological Bulletin*, **118**, 430–39.

Griffin, D. & Gonzalez, R. (1995b). *Regression Models in Dyadic Research*. University of Sussex and University of Washington.

Gross, E. & Stone, G.P. (1964). Embarrassment and the analysis of role requirements. *American Journal of Sociology*, **70**, 1–15.

Gross, M. (1984). Sunfish, salmon, and the evolution of alternative reproductive strategies and tactics in fishes. In G. Potts & R. Wootton (Eds), *Fish Reproduction: Strategies and Tactics* (pp. 55–75). New York: Academic Press.

Grossmann, K., Fremmer-Bombik, E., Rudolph, J. & Grossmann, K.A. (1988). Maternal attachment representations as related to patterns of infant-mother attachment and maternal care during the first year. In R.A. Hinde & J. Stevenson-Hinde (Eds), *Relationships between Relationships within Families* (pp. 241–60). Oxford: Clarendon.

Grotevant, H.D. & Cooper, C.R. (1982). Identity formation and role-taking skill in adolescence: an Investigation of family structure and family process antecedents. Final report prepared for the National Institute of Child Health and Human Development, University of Texas at Austin.

Grotevant, H.D. & Cooper, C. (1986). Individuation in family relationships. *Human Development*, **29**, 82–100.

Grusec, J.E., Hastings, P. & Mammone, N. (1994). Parenting cognitions and relationship schemes. In J.G. Smetana (Ed.), *Beliefs about Parenting: Origins and Developmental Implications*. San Francisco: Jossey-Bass.

Grych, J.H. & Fincham, F.D. (1990). Marital conflict and children's adjustment: a cognitive-contextual framework. *Psychological Bulletin*, **101**, 267–90.

Grych, J.H. & Fincham, F.D. (1993). Children's appraisals of marital conflict: initial investigations of the cognitive-contextual framework. *Child Development*, **64**, 215–30.

Grych, J.H., Seid, M. & Fincham F.D. (1991, April). Children's cognitive and affective responses to different forms of interparental conflict. Paper presented at the biennial meetings of the Society for Research in Child Development, Seattle, WA.

Guarnacria, P.J., delaCancela, L. & Carrillo, E. (1989). The multiple meanings of ataques de nervios in the Latino community. *Medical Anthropology*, **11**, 47–62.

Guba, E.G. (1990). Carrying on the dialog. In E.G. Guba (Ed.), *The Paradigm Dialog* (pp. 368–78). Newbury Park: Sage.

Gudykunst, W.K. (1992). *Bridging Differences: Effective Intergroup Communication* (2nd Edn). Thousand Oaks, CA: Sage.

Gudykunst, W.K. & Ting-Toomey, S. (1988). *Culture and Interpersonal Communication*. Newbury Park, CA: Sage.

Gustavson, C., Garcia, J., Hankins, W. & Rusiniak, K. (1974). Coyote predation control by aversive stimulus. *Science*, **184**, 581–3.

Gutmann, D.L. (1987). *Reclaimed Powers: Toward a New Psychology of Men and Women in Later Life*. New York: Basic Books.

Guttentag, M. & Secord, P.F. (1983). *Too Many Women? The Sex Ratio Question*. Beverly Hills: Sage.

Haas, J., Kates, R. & Bowden, M. (Eds) (1977). *Reconstruction Following Disaster*. Cambridge, MA: MIT Press.

Haas, L. (1986). Wives' orientation toward breadwinning: Sweden and the United States. *Journal of Family Issues*, **7**, 358–81.

Haas, L. (1992). *Equal Parenthood and Social Policy*. Albany, NY: SUNY Press.

Hacker, H.M. (1981). Blabbermouths and clams: sex differences in self-disclosure in same-sex and cross-sex friendship dyads. *Psychology of Women Quarterly*, **5**, 385–401.

Hagestad, G.O. (1979). Patterns of communication and influence between grandparents and grandchildren in a changing society. Paper presented at the World Congress of Sociology, Uppsala, Sweden.

Hagestad, G.O. (1981). Problems and promises in the social psychology of inter-generational relations. In R.W. Fogel, E. Hatfield, S.B. Kiesler & E. Shanas (Eds), *Aging: Stability and Change in the Family* (pp. 11–46). New York: Academic Press.

Hagestad, G.O. (1982). Parent and child: generations in the family. In T.M. Field, A. Huston, H.C. Quay, L. Troll & G.E. Finley (Eds), *Review of Human Development* (pp. 485–99). New York: Wiley.

Hagestad, G.O. (1984). The continuous bond: a dynamic, multigenerational perspective on parent–child relations between adults. In M. Perlmutter (Ed.), *Parent–Child Inter-actions and Parent–child Relations in Child Development. The Minnesota Symposium on Child Psychology*, Vol. 17 (pp. 129–58). Hillsdale, NJ: Erlbaum.

Haggard, E.A. (1958). *Intraclass Correlation and the Analysis of Variance*. New York: Dryden Press.

Hahlweg, K., Goldstein, M.J., Nuechterlein, K.H., Magaña, A.B., Mintz, J., Doane, J.A., Miklowitz, D.J. & Snyder, K.S. (1989). Expressed emotion and patient–relative inter-action in families of recent-onset schizophrenics. *Journal of Consulting and Clinical Psychology*, **57**, 11–18.

Hahlweg, K., Reisner, L., Kohli, G., Vollmer, M., Schindler, L. & Revenstorf, D. (1984). Development and validity of a new system to analyse interpersonal communication (KPI). In K. Hahlweg & N.S. Jacobson (Eds.), *Marital Interaction: Analysis and Modi-fication* (pp. 182–98). New York: Guilford.

Haith, M.M., Bergman, T. & Moore, M.J. (1977). Eye contact and face scanning in early infancy. *Science*, **198**, 853–5.

Halberstadt, A.G. (1986). Family socialization of emotional expression and nonverbal communication styles and skills. *Journal of Personality and Social Psychology*, **51**, 827–36.

Haley, J. (1963). *Strategies of Psychotherapy*. New York: Grune & Stratton.

Hall, P. & Landreth, P. (1975). Assessing some long-term consequences of a natural disaster. *Mass Emergencies*, **1**, 55–61.

Hallinan, M.T. (1982). Classroom racial composition and children's friendships. *Social Forces*, **61**, 56–72.

Hallinan, M.T. & Smith, S.S. (1985). The effects of classroom racial composition on students' interracial friendliness. *Social Psychology Quarterly*, **48**, 3–16.

Hallinan, M.T. & Sorensen, A.B. (1985). Ability grouping and student friendships. *American Educational Research Journal*, **22**, 485–99.

Hallinan, M.T. & Teixeira, R.A. (1987a). Students' interracial friendships: individual characteristics, structural effects, and racial differences. *American Journal of Education*, **95**, 563–83.

Hallinan, M.T. & Teixeira, R.A. (1987b). Opportunities and constraints: black–white differences in the formation of interracial friendships. *Child Development*, **58**, 1358–71.

Hallinan, M.T. & Williams, R.A. (1987). The stability of students' interracial friendships. *American Sociological Review*, **52**, 653–64.

Hallinan, M.T. & Williams, R.A. (1989). Interracial friendship choices in secondary schools. *American Sociological Review*, **54**, 67–78.

Halpern, J. (1994). The sandwich generation: conflicts between adult children and their aging parents. In D.D. Cahn (Ed.), *Conflict in Personal Relationships* (pp. 143–60). Hillsdale, NJ: Erlbaum.

Halpern, R. & Covey, L. (1983). Community support for adolescent parents and their children: the parent-to-parent program in Vermont. *Journal of Primary Prevention*, **3**, 160–73.

Hamilton, D.L. & Rose, T.L. (1980). Illusory correlation and the maintenance of stereotypic beliefs. *Journal of Personality and Social Psychology*, **39**, 832–45.

Hamilton, W.D. (1964). The genetical evolution of social behavior. *Journal of Theoretical Biology*, **7**, 1–32.

Hammer, M. (1980). Predictability of social connections over time. Social Networks, **2**, 165–80.

Hammock, G.S. & Richardson, D.R. (1992). Aggression as one response to conflict. *Journal of Applied Social Psychology*, **22**, 298–311.

Handel, G. (1986). Beyond sibling rivalry: an empirically grounded theory of sibling relationships. In P.A. Adler & P. Adler (Eds), *Sociological Studies of Child Development*. (pp. 105–22). Greenwich, CT: JAI Press.

Hannan, D.F. & Katsiaouni, L.A. (1977). *Traditional Families? From Culturally Prescribed to Negotiated Roles in Farm Families*, Dublin: Economic and Social Research Institute.

Hansell, S. (1984). Cooperative groups, weak ties, and the integration of peer friendships. *Social Psychology Quarterly*, **47**, 316–28.

Hansell, S. & Slavin, R.E. (1981). Cooperative learning and the structure of interracial friendships. *Sociology of Education*, **54**, 98–106.

Hansson, R.O. & Carpenter, B.N. (1994). *Relationships in Old Age: Coping with the Challenge of Transition*. Guilford: New York.

Harber, K.D. & Pennebaker, J.W. (1992). Overcoming traumatic memories. In S.-A. Christianson (Ed.), *The Handbook of Emotion and Memory* (pp. 359–87). Hillsdale, NJ: Erlbaum.

Harlow, H. & Harlow, M.K. (1962). The effects of rearing conditions on behavior. *Bulletin of the Menniger Clinic*, **26**, 213–24.

Harlow, H. & Harlow, M.K. (1965). The affectional systems. In A.M. Schrier, H.F. Harlow & F. Stollnitz (Eds), *Behavior of Nonhuman Primates*, Vol. 2. New York: Academic Press.

Harpending, H. (1992). Age differences between mates in southern African pastoralists. *Behavioral and Brain Sciences*, **15**, 102–3.

Harre, R. (1995). Acting from a position: personal relations as aspects of complex discursive networks. Paper presented to annual convention of the International Network on Personal Relationships, Williamsburg, VA, June.

Harris, L.M. & Sadeghi, A. (1987). Realizing: how facts are created in human interaction. *Journal of Social and Personal Relationships*, **4**, 480–95.

Harris, L.M., Gergen, K.J. & Lannamann, J.W. (1986). Aggression rituals. *Communication Monographs*, **53**, 252–65.

Harris, M.B. & Siebel, C.E. (1975). Affect, aggression, and altruism. *Developmental Psychology*, **11**, 623–7.

Harris, P.L. (1989). *Children and Emotion.* Oxford: Basil Blackwell.

Harrison, A.A. & Saeed, L.(1977). Let's make a deal: analysis of revelations and stipulations in lonely hearts advertisements. *Journal of Personality and Social Psychology*, **35**, 257–64.

Harrist, A.W., Pettit, G.S., Dodge, K.A. & Bates, J.E. (1994). Dyadic synchrony in mother–child interaction–relation with children's subsequent kindergarten adjustment. *Family Relations*, **43**, 417–24.

Hart, C.H., Ladd, G.W., & Burleson, B.R. (1990). Children's expectations of the outcomes of social strategies: relations with sociometric status and maternal disciplinary styles. *Child Development*, **61**, 127–37.

Harter S. (1990). Developmental differences in the nature of self-representations: implications for the understanding, assessment, and treatment of maladaptive behavior. *Cognitive Therapy and Research*, **14**, 113–42.

Hartmann, H. (1981). The family as the locus of gender, class, and political struggle: the example of housework. *Signs,* **6**, 336–94.

Hartup, W.W. (1979). The social worlds of childhood. *American Psychologist*, **34**, 944–50.

Hartup, W.W. (1983). Peer relations. In P.H. Mussen (Ed.), *Handbook of Child Psychology*, Vol. 4 (pp. 103–96). New York: Wiley.

Hartup, W.W., French, D., Laursen, B., Johnston, M.K. & Ogawa, J. (1993). Conflict and friendship relations in middle childhood: behavior in a closed-field situation. *Child Development*, **64**, 445–54.

Hartup, W.W., Laursen, B., Stewart, M. & Eastenson, A. (1988). Conflict and the friendship relations of young children. *Child Development*, **59**, 1590–1600.

Harvey, J.H. (Ed.) (1996). *Journal of Personal and Interpersonal Loss.* Basingstoke: Taylor & Francis.

Harvey, J.H. & Uematsu, M. (1995). Why we must develop and tell our accounts of loss. Paper presented at Applied Research in Cognition and Memory Meeting, UBC.

Harvey, J.H., Agostinelli, G. & Weber, A.L. (1989). Account–making and the formation of expectations about close relationships. *Review of Personality and Social Psychology*, **10**, 39–62.

Harvey, J.H., Flanery, R. & Morgan, M. (1986). Vivid memories of vivid loves gone by. *Journal of Social and Personal Relationships*, **3**, 359–73.

Harvey, J.H., Hendrick, S. & Tucker, K. (1988). Self-report methods in studying personal relationships. In S. Duck (Ed.), *Handbook of Personal Relationships: Theory, Research and Interventions* (1st Edn, pp. 99–113). Chichester: Wiley.

Harvey, J.H., Ickes, W.J. & Kidd, R.F. (1976). A conversation with Fritz Heider. In J.H. Harvey, W.J. Ickes & R.F. Kidd (Eds), *New Directions in Attribution Research*, Vol. 1 (pp. 3–18). Hillsdale, NJ: Erlbaum.

Harvey, J.H., Orbuch, T. & Weber, A.L. (1990). A social psychological model of account-making in response to severe stress. *Journal of Language and Social Psychology*, **9**, 191–207.

Harvey, J.H., Orbuch, T. & Weber, A.L. (Eds) (1992). *Attributions, Accounts, and Close Relationships.* New York: Springer-Verlag.

Harvey, J.H., Orbuch, T., Weber, A.L., Merbach, N. & Alt, R. (1992). House of pain and hope: accounts of loss. *Death Studies*, **16**, 99–124.

Harvey, J.H., Stein, S., Olsen, N., Roberts, R., Lutgendorf, S. & Ho, J. (1995). Narratives of loss and recovery from a natural disaster. *Journal of Social Behavior and Personality*, **10**, 313–30.

Harvey, J.H., Weber, A.L. & Orbuch, T.L. (1990). *Interpersonal Accounts: a Social Psychological Perspective.* Oxford: Blackwell.

Harvey, J.H., Wells, G. & Alvarez, M. (1978). Attribution in the context of conflict and separation in close relationships. In J.H. Harvey, W. Ickes & R. Kidd (Eds), *New Directions in Attribution Research*, Vol. 2 (pp. 235–59). Hillsdale, NJ: Erlbaum.

Haskell, M. (1990). *Love and Other Infectious Diseases: A Memoir*, William Morrow and Company, Inc., New York.

Hatfield, E., Traupmann, J. & Sprecher, S. (1984). Older women's perceptions of their intimate relationships. *Journal of Social and Clinical Psychology*, **2**, 108–24.

Hatfield, E., Walster, G.W. & Berscheid, E. (1978). *Equity: Theory and Research*. Boston: Allyn & Bacon.

Hauser, R.M. (1974). Contextual analysis revisited. *Sociological Methods and Research*, **2**, 365–75.

Hay, T.H. (1977). The development of some aspects of the Ojibwa self and its behavioral environment. *Ethos*, **5**, 71–89.

Haynes, K. & Feinleib, M. (1980). Women, work, and coronary artery disease: prospective findings from the Framingham Heart Study. *American Journal of Public Health*, **70**, 133–41.

Hays, R.B. (1984). The development and maintenance of friendship. *Journal of Social and Personal Relationships*, **1**, 75–98.

Hays, R.B. (1988). Friendship. In S. Duck (Ed.), *Handbook of Personal Relationships: Theory, Research, and Interventions* (1st Edn, pp. 391–408). Chichester: Wiley.

Hazan, C. & Shaver, P. (1987). Romantic love conceptualized as an attachment process. *Journal of Personality and Social Psychology*, **52**, 511–24.

Hazan, C. & Shaver, P.R. (1990). Love and work: an attachment theoretical perspective. *Journal of Personality and Social Psychology*, **59**, 270–80.

Hazan, C. & Shaver, P.R. (1994a). Attachment as an organizational framework for research on close relationships. *Psychological Inquiry*, **5**, 1–22.

Hazan, C. & Shaver, P.R. (1994b). Deeper into attachment theory. *Psychological Inquiry*, **5**(1), 68–79.

Hazan, C. & Zeifman, D. (1994). Sex and the psychological tether. *Advances in Personal Relationships*, **5**, 151–77.

Hazan, C., Zeifman, D. & Middleton, K. (July, 1994). Attachment and sexuality. Paper presented at the International Conference on Personal Relationships, Gottingen, The Netherlands.

Healey, J.G. & Bell, R.A. (1990). Effects of social networks on individuals' responses to conflicts in friendship. In D.D. Cahn (Ed.), *Intimates in Conflict: a Communication Perspectiv* (pp. 121–50). Hillsdale, NJ: Erlbaum.

Heavey, C.L., Layne, C. & Christensen, A. (1993). Gender and conflict structure in marital interaction: a replication and extension. *Journal of Consulting and Clinical Psychology*, **61**, 16–27.

Heider, F. (1958). *The Psychology of Interpersonal Relations*. Hillsdale, NJ: Erlbaum.

Heinssen, R.K., Hooley, J.M., Minarik, M.E., Israel, S.B. & Fenton, W. (1994). Expressed emotion in psychiatric hospital staff: it's not all relative. Unpublished manuscript.

Heitzmann, C.A. & Kaplan, R.M. (1988). Assessment of methods for measuring social support. *Health Psychology*, **7**, 75–109.

Heller, K. (l979). The effects of social support: prevention and treatment implications. In A.P. Goldstein & F.H. Kanfer (Eds), *Maximizing Treatment Gains: Transfer Enhancement in Psychotherapy* (pp. 353–82). New York: Academic Press.

Heller, K. (1989). The return to community. *American Journal of Community Psychology*, **17**, 1–15.

Heller, K. (1990). Social and community intervention. *Annual Review of Psychology*, **41**, 141–68.

Heller, K. (1992). Ingredients for effective community change: some field observations. *American Journal of Community Psychology*, **20**, 143–63.

Heller, K. & Swindle, R.W. (1983). Social networks, perceived social support, and coping with stress. In R.D. Felner, L.A. Jason, J. Moritsuga & S.S. Farber (Eds), *Preventive Psychology: Theory, Research, and Practice in Community Intervention* (pp. 87–103). Elmsford, New York: Pergamon.

Heller, K., Price, R.H. & Hogg, J.R. (1990). The role of social support in community and clinical intervention. In I.G. Sarason, B.R. Sarason & G.R. Pierce (Eds), *Social Support: An Interactional View* (pp. 482–507). New York: Wiley.

Heller, K., Thompson, M.G., Trueba, P.E., Hogg, J.R. & Vlachos-Weber, I. (1991). Peer support telephone dyads for elderly women: was this the wrong intervention? *American Journal of Community Psychology*, **19**, 53–74.

Helsing, K.J., Szklo, M. & Comstock, G.W. (1981). Factors associated with mortality after widowhood. *American Journal of Public Health*, **71**, 802–9.

Helson, R. & Moane, G. (1987). Personality change in women from college to midlife. *Journal of Personality and Social Psychology*, **53**, 176–86.

Helson, R. & Wink, P. (1992). Personality change in women from the early 40s to the early 50s. *Psychology and Aging*, **7**, 46–55.

Henderson, A.S. (1977). The social network, support and neurosis: the function of attachment in adult life. *British Journal of Psychiatry*, **136**, 574–83.

Henderson, A.S. (1992). Social support and depression. In H.O.F. Veiel & U. Bauman (Eds), *The Meaning and Measurement of Social Support* (pp. 85–92). New York: Hemisphere.

Henderson, A.S., Byrne, D.G. & Duncan-Jones, P. (1981). *Neurosis and the Social Environment*. Sydney: Academic Press.

Henderson, A.S., Duncan-Jones, P., Byrne, D.G. & Scott, R. (1980). Measuring social relationships. The Interview Schedule for Social Interactions. *Psychological Medicine*, **10**, 723–34.

Hendrick, S.S. & Hendrick, C. (1992). *Romantic Love*. Newbury Park, CA: Sage.

Hendrick, S.S. & Hendrick, C. (1993). Lovers as friends. *Journal of Social and Personal Relationships*, **10**, 459–66.

Henggeler, S.W., Edwards, J.J., Cohen. R. & Summervile, M.B. (1991). Predicting changes in children's popularity: the role of family relations. *Journal of Applied Developmental Psychology*, **12**, 205–18.

Henry, W.P., Schacht, T.E. & Strupp, H.H. (1986). Structural analysis of social behavior: application to a study of interpersonal process in differential psychotherapeutic outcome. *Journal of Counseling and Clinical Psychology*, **54**, 27–31.

Henry, W.P., Schacht, T.E. & Strupp, H.H. (1990). Patient and therapist introject, interpersonal process, and differential psychotherapy outcome. *Journal of Consulting and Clinical Psychology*, **58**, 768–74.

Herdt, G. & Boxer, A. (1992). Introduction: culture, history, and life course of gay men. In G. Herdt (Ed), *Gay Culture in America* (pp. 1–28). Boston: Beacon Press.

Hermans, H.J.M., Kempen, H.J.G. & van Loon, R.J.P. (1992). The dialogical self. *American Psychologist*, **47**, 23–33.

Hernton, C.C. (1965/1988). *Sex and Racism in America*. New York: Anchor Books.

Herzberger, H. & Hall, J.A. (1993). Consequences of retaliatory aggression against siblings and peers:.urban minority children's expectations. *Child Development*, **64**, 1773–85.

Hetherington, E.M. (1988). Parents, children, siblings: six years after divorce. In R. Hinde & J. Stevenson-Hinde (Eds), *Relationships within Families: Mutual Influences*. New York: Oxford University Press..

Hetherington, E.M. (1989). Coping with family transitions: winners, losers, and survivors. *Child Development*, **60**, 1–14.

Hetherington, E.M., Cox, M. & Cox, R. (1979). Play and social interaction in children following divorce. *Journal of Social Issues*, **35**, 26–49.

Hetherington, E.M., Hagan, M.S. & Anderson, E.R. (1989). Marital transitions: a child's perspective. *American Psychologist*, **44**, 303–12.

Hewitt, J. & Stokes, R. (1975). Disclaimers. *American Sociological Review*, **40**, 1–11.

Higgins, E.T. (1989). Continuties and discontinuities in self-regulatory and self-evaluative processes: a developmental theory relating self and affect. *Journal of Personality*, **57**, 407–44.

Higgins, E.T. (1989). Self-discrepancy theory: what patterns of self-beliefs cause people to suffer? In L. Berkowitz (Ed.), *Advances in Experimental Social Psychology*, Vol. 22 (pp. 93–136). San Diego: Academic Press.

Hill, C.E. (1992). An overview of four measures developed to test the Hill process model: therapist intentions, therapist response modes, client reactions, and client behaviors. *Journal of Counseling and Development*, **70**, 728–39.

Hill, C.T., Rubin, Z. & Peplau, L.A. (1976). Breakups before marriage: the end of 103 affairs. *Journal of Social Issues*, **32**, 147–68.

Hill, K. & Hurtado, M. (1989). Hunter-gatherers of the new world. *American Scientist*, **77**, 437–43.

Hill, M.D. (1988). Class, kinship density, and conjugal role segregation. *Journal of Marriage and the Family*, **50**, 731–41.

Hill, M.S. (1988). Marital stability and spouses' shared time: a multidisciplinary hypothesis. *Journal of Family Issues*, **9**, 427–51.

Hillard, R.B., Henry, W.P. & Strupp, H.H. (June, 1995). Disaffiliative interpersonal process in psychotherapy. Paper presented at the annual conference of the Society for Psychotherapy Research, Vancouver Canada.

Hinde, R.A. (1979). *Towards Understanding Relationships*. Academic Press, London.

Hinde, R.A. (1981). The bases of a science of interpersonal relationships. In S.W. Duck & R. Gilmour (Eds), *Personal Relationships 1: Studying Personal Relationships* (pp. 1–22). New York: Academic Press.

Hinde, R.A. (1987). *Individuals, Rrelationships and Culture*. New York: Cambridge University Press.

Hinde, R.A. & Stevenson-Hinde, J. (Eds) (1988). *Relationships within Families*. Oxford: Oxford University Press.

Hinde, R.A. & Tamplin, A. (1983). Relations between mother–child interaction and behavior in preschool. *British Journal of Developmental Psychology*, **1**, 231–57.

Hirsch, B.J. (1980). Natural support systems and coping with major life changes. *American Journal of Community Psychology*, **8**, 159–72.

Hirsch, B.J. & Dubois, D.L. (1989). The school–nonschool ecology of early adolescent friendship. In D. Belle (Ed.), *Children's Social Networks and Social Supports* (pp. 260–74). New York: Wiley.

Hirsch, B.J. & Dubois, D.L. (1992). The relation of peer social support and psychological symptomatology during the transition to junior high school: a two-year longitudinal analysis. *American Journal of Community Psychology*, **20**(3), 333–47.

Hirsch, B.J. & Rapkin, B.D. (1986). Multiple roles, social networks, and women's well-being. *Journal of Personality and Social Psychology*, **51**, 1237–47.

Hirsch, B.J. & Rapkin, B.D. (1987). The transition to junior high school: a longitudinal study of self-esteem, psychological symptomatology, school life, and social support. *Child Development*, **58**, 1235–43.

Hirsch, S. & Leff, J. (1971). Parental abnormalities of verbal communication in the transmission of schizophrenia. *Psychological Medicine*, **1**, 118–27.

Hirschi, T. (1969). *Causes of Delinquency*. Berkeley, CA: University of California.

Hirschman, A.O. (1970). *Exit, Voice, and Loyalty: Responses to Decline in Firms, Organizations, and States*. Cambridge, MA: Harvard University Press.

Ho, D.Y.F. & Chiu, C.Y. (1994). Components ideas of individualism, collectivism, and social organization: an application in the study of Chinese culture. In U. Kim, H.C. Triandis, C. Kagitcibasi, S.C. Choi & G. Yoon (Eds), *Individualism and Collectivism* (pp. 137–56). Thousand Oaks, CA: Sage.

Ho, D.Y.F. & Kang, T.K. (1984). Intergenerational comparisons of child-rearing attitudes and practices in Hong Kong. *Developmental Psychology*, **20**(6), 1004–16.

Ho, M.K. (1984). *Building a Successful Intermarriage Between Religions, Social Classes, Ethnic Groups, or Races*. St. Meinrad, IN: St. Meinrad Archabbey.

Ho, M.K. (1990). *Intermarried Couples in Therapy*. Springfield, IL: Thomas.

Hobfoll, S.E. (1988). *The Ecology of Stress*. New York: Hemisphere.

Hobfoll, S.E. (1989). Conservation of resources: a new attempt at conceptualizing stress. *American Psychologist*, **44**, 513–24.

Hobfoll, S.E. & de Vries, M.W. (Eds) (1995). *Extreme Stress and Communities: Impact and Intervention*. Dordrecht: Kluwer.

Hobfoll, S.E. & Lerman, M. (1989). Predicting receipt of social support: a longitudinal study of parents' reactions to their child's illness. *Health Psychology*, **8**, 61–77.

Hobfoll, S.E. & Lilly, R. (1993). Resource conservation as a strategy for community psychology. *Journal of Community Psychology*, **21**, 128–48.

Hobfoll, S.E. & London, P. (1986). The relationship of self-concept and social support to emotional distress among women during war. *Journal of Social and Clinical Psychology*, **12**, 87–100.

Hobfoll, S.E. & Stokes, J.P. (1988). The process and mechanics of social support. In S.W. Duck, D.F. Hay, S.E. Hobfoll, B. Ickes & B. Montgomery (Eds), *The Handbook of Research in Personal Relationships*. Chichester: Wiley.

Hobfoll, S.E., Briggs, S. & Wells J. (1995). Community stress and resources: actions and reactions. In S.E. Hobfoll & M.W. de Vries (Eds), *Extreme Stress and Communities: Impact and Intervention* (pp. 137–58). Dordrecht: Kluwer.

Hochschild, A. (1989). *The Second Shift: Working Parents and the Revolution at Home*. New York: Viking.

Hofer, M.A. (1984). Relationships as regulators: a psychobiologic perspective on bereavement. *Psychosomatic Medicine*, **46**, 183–97.

Hofer, M.A. (1987). Early social relationships: a psychobiologist's view. *Child Development*, **58**, 663–47.

Hoffman, J.A. (1984). Psychological separation of late adolescents from their parents. *Journal of Counseling Psychology*, **31**, 170–78.

Hoffman, J.A. & Weiss, B. (1987). Family dynamics and presenting problems in college students. *Journal of Counseling Psychology*, **34**, 157–63.

Hoffman, L. (1981). *Foundations of Family Therapy*. New York: Basic Books.

Hoffman, M. (1976). Empathy, role-taking guilt and the development of altruistic motives. In T. Likona (Ed.), *Moral Development: Current Theory and Research* (pp. 124–43). New York: Holt, Rinehart, & Winston.

Hoffman, M. (1984). Parent discipline, moral internalization, and development of prosocial motivation. In E. Staub, D. Bar-Tal, J. Karylowski & J. Reykowski (Eds), *Development and Maintenance of Prosocial Behavior* (pp. 117–37). New York: Plenum.

Hoffman, M.L. (1970). Conscience, personality, and socialization techniques. *Human Development*, **13**, 90–126.

Hoffman, M.L. (1976). Empathy, role taking, guilt, and development of altruistic motives. In T. Lickona (Ed.), *Moral Development and Behavior*. New York: Holt.

Hogan, D.P. & Astone, N.M. (1986). The transition to adulthood. *Annual Review of Sociology*, **12**, 109–30.

Hogan, R. (1982). A socioanalytic theory of personality. In M. Page (Ed.), *Nebraska Symposium on Motivation* (pp. 55–89). Lincoln, NE: University of Nebraska Press.

Hogan, R. & Cheek, J. (1983). Self-concepts, self-presentations, and moral judgments. In J. Suls & A.G. Greenwald (Eds), *Psychological Perspectives on Self*, Vol. 2 (pp. 249–73). Hillsdale, NJ: Erlbaum.

Hogarty, G.E., Anderson, C.M. & Reiss, D.J. (1987). Family psychoeducation, social skill training and medication in schizophrenia: the long and short of it. *Psychopharmacology Bulletin*, **23**, 12–13.

Hogarty, G.E., Anderson, C.M., Reiss, D.J., Kornblith, S.J., Greenwald, D.P., Javna, C.D. & Madonia, M.J. (1986). Family psychoeducation, social skills training, and maintenance chemotherapy in the aftercare treatment of schizophrenia. *Archives of General Psychiatry*, **43**, 633–42.

Hollos, M. (1980). Collective education in Hungary: the development of competitive, cooperative, and role-taking behaviors. *Ethos*, **8**, 3–23.

Holloway, E.L. (1992). Supervision: a way of teaching and learning. In S.D. Brown & R.W. Lent (Eds), *Handbook of Counseling Psychology* (pp. 177–216). New York: Wiley.

Holman, T.B. & Jacquart, M. (1988). Leisure-activity patterns and marital satisfaction: a further test. *Journal of Marriage and the Family*, **50**, 69–77.

Holmes, J.G. (1981). The exchange process in close relationships: microbehavior and macromotives. In M. Lerner & S. Lerner (Eds), *The Justice Motive in Social Behavior: Adapting to Times of Scarcity and Change* (pp. 261–84). New York: Plenum.

Holmes, J.G. & Rempel, J.K. (1989). Trust in close relationships. In C. Hendrick (Ed.), *Review of Personality and Social Psychology*, Vol. 10 (pp. 187–220). London: Sage.

Holmes, T.H. & Rahe, R.H. (1967). The social readjustment scale. *Journal of Psychosomatic Research*, **11**, 213–18.

Holmes, W.G. & Sherman, P.W. (1983). Kin recognition in animals. *American Scientist*, **71**, 46–55.

Holohan, C.J. & Moos, R.H. (1981). Social support and psychological distress: a longitudinal analysis. *Journal of Abnormal Psychology*, **904**, 365–70.

Holquist, M. (1990). *Dialogism: Bakhtin and His World*. New York: Routledge.

Homans, G. (1950). *The Human Group*. New York: Harcourt Brace.

Homans, G.C. (1961). *Social Behavior: Its Elementary Forms*. New York: Harcourt Brace Jovanovich.

Homans, G.C. (1974). *Social Behavior: Its Elementary Forms* (revised Edn). New York: Harcourt Brace Jovanovich.

Honeycutt, J.M. (1993). Memory structures for the rise and fall of personal relationships. In S.W. Duck (Ed.), *Understanding Relationship Processes 1: Individuals in Relationships* (pp. 60–86). Newbury Park: Sage.

Honeycutt, J.M., Woods, B.L. & Fontenot, K. (1993). The endorsement of communication conflict rules as a function of engagement, marriage and marital ideology. *Journal of Social and Personal Relationships*, **10**, 285–304.

Hood, J.C. (1986). The provider role: its meaning and measurement. *Journal of Marriage and the Family*, **48**, 349–59.

Hooff, J.A.R.A.M. van (1972). A comparative approach to the phylogeny of laughter and smiling. In R.A. Hinde (Ed.), *Nonverbal Communication* (pp. 209–38). Cambridge: Cambridge University Press.

Hooley, J.M. (1986). Expressed emotion and depression: interactions between patients and high- versus low-expressed-emotion spouses. *Journal of Abnormal Psychology*, **95**, 237–46.

Hooley, J.M. (1987). The nature and origins of expressed emotion. In K. Hahlweg & M.J. Goldstein (Eds), Understanding Major Mental Disorder: the Contribution of Family Interaction Research. New York: Family Pruess Press.

Hooley, J.M. (1990). Expressed emotion and depression. In G.I. Keitner (Ed.), *Depression and Families: Impact and Treatment*. Washington, DC: American Psychiatric Press.

Hooley, J.M. & Hiller, J.B. (1994). Do high and low EE relatives differ in personality? Poster presented at the Annual Meeting of the Society for Research in Psychopathology, Coral Gables, FL, October 1994.

Hooley, J.M. & Richters, J.E. (1995). Expressed emotion: a developmental perspective. In

D. Cicchetti & S.L. Toth (Eds), *Rochester Symposium on Developmental Psychopathology*, Vol. 6. Rochester, NY: University of Rochester Press.

Hooley, J.M. & Teasdale, J.D. (1989). Predictors of relapse in unipolar depressives: expressed emotion, marital distress, and perceived criticism. *Journal of Abnormal Psychology*, **98**, 229–35.

Hooley, J.M., Orley, J. & Teasdale, J.D. (1986). Levels of expressed emotion and relapse in depressed patients. *British Journal of Psychiatry*, **148**, 642–7.

Hooley, J.M., Richters, J.E., Weintraub, S. & Neale, J.M. (1987). Psychopathology and marital distress: the positive side of positive symptoms. *Journal of Abnormal Psychology*, **96**, 27–33.

Hooley, J.M., Rosen, L.R. & Richters, J.E. (1995). Expressed emotion: toward clarification of a critical construct. In G.A. Miller (Ed.), *The Behavioral High-risk Paradigm in Psychopathology*. New York: Springer-Verlag.

Hoovern, C. & Katz, L.F. (1994). Parents' emotion, philosophies and their children peer and academic success. Unpublished paper, University of Washington.

Hopper, J. (1993). The rhetoric of motives in divorce. *Journal of Marriage and the Family*, **55**, 801–13.

Hopper, R., Knapp, M.L. & Scott, L. (1981). Couples' personal idioms: exploring intimate talk. *Journal of Communication*, **31**, 23–33.

Hormel, R., Burns, A. & Goodnow, J. (1987). Parental social networks and child development. *Journal of Social and Personal Relationships*, **4**, 159–77.

Horney, K. (1950). *Neurosis and Human Growth*. New York: Norton.

Hornstein, G.A. (1985). Intimacy in conversational style as a function of the degree of closeness between members of a dyad. *Journal of Personality and Social Psychology*, **49**, 671–81.

Horowitz, L.M. (1979). On the cognitive structure of interpersonal problems treated in , psychotherapy. *Journal of Consulting and Clinical Psychology*, **47**, 5–15.

Horowitz, L.M. (1994). Pschemas, psychopathology, and psychotherapy research. Annual International Meeting of the Society for Psychotherapy Research Presidential Address. *Psychotherapy Research*, **4**, 1–19.

Horowitz, L.M. & Vitkus, J. (1986). The interpersonal basis of psychiatric symptoms. *Clinical Psychology Review*, **6**, 443–69.

Horowitz, L.M., Rosenberg, S.E. & Bartholomew, K. (1993). Interpersonal problems, attachment styles, and outcome in brief dynamic psychotherapy. *Journal of Consulting and Clinical Psychology*, **61**, 549–60.

Horowitz, L.M., Rosenberg, S.E. & Kalehzan, B.M. (1992). The capacity to describe other people clearly: a predictor of interpersonal problems in brief dynamic psychotherapy. *Psychotherapy Research*, **2**, 37–51.

Horowitz, L.M., Rosenberg, S.E., Baer, B.A., Ureno, G. & Villasenor, V.S. (1988). Inventory of interpersonal problems: psychometric properties and clinical applications. *Journal of Consulting and Clinical Psychology*, **56**, 885–92.

Horvath, A.O. (1994). Research on the Alliance. In A.O. Horvath & L.S. Greenberg (Eds), *The Working Alliance: Theory, Research, and Practice* (pp. 259–86). New York: Wiley.

Horvath, A.O. & Symonds, B.D. (1991). Relation between working alliance and outcome in psychotherapy: a meta-analysis. *Journal of Counseling Psychology*, **38**, 139–49.

House, J.S. (1981). *Work Stress and Social Support*. Reading, MA: Addison-Wesley.

House, J.S., Landis, K.B. & Umberson, D. (1988). Social relationships and health. *Science*, **241**, 540–45.

House, J.S., Robbins, C. & Metzner, H.L. (1982). The association of social relationships and activities with mortality: prospective evidence from the Tecumseh Community Health Study. *American Journal of Epidemiology*, **116**, 123–40.

House, J.S., Umberson, D. & Landis, K. (1988). Structures and processes of social support. *Annual Review of Sociology*, **14**, 298–318.

Howard, J.A., Blumstein, P. & Schwartz, P. (1986). Sex, power, and influence tactics in intimate relationships. *Journal of Personality and Social Psychology*, **51**, 102–9.

Howe, N. (1991). Sibling directed internal state language, perspective taking and affective behavior. *Child Development*, **62**, 1503–12.

Howe, N. & Ross, H.S. (1990). Socialization perspective taking and the sibling relationship. *Developmental Psychology*, **26**, 160–65.

Howes, C. & Wu, F. (1990). Peer interactions and friendships in an ethnically diverse school setting. *Child Development*, **61**, 537–41.

Howes, C., Unger, O. & Matheson, C. (1992). *The Collaborative Construction of Pretend.* Albany: State University of New York Press.

Howitt, D. & Owusu-Bempah, J. (1994). *The Racism of Psychology: Time for Change.* New York: Harvester/Wheatsheaf.

Hsu, F.L.K. (1981). A social exchange view on the dissolution of pair relationships. In R.L. Burgess & T.L. Huston (Eds), *Social Exchange in Developing Relationships.* New York: Academic Press.

Hubbard, J.A. & Coie, J.D. (1994). Emotional correlates of social competence in children's peer relationships. *Merrill-Palmer Quarterly*, **40**, 1–20.

Huesmann, L.R. (1980). Toward a predictive model of romantic behavior. In K.S. Pope et al. (Eds), *On Love and Loving* (pp. 152–71). San Francisco, CA: Jossey-Bass.

Hughes, M. & Gove, W.R. (1981). Living alone, social integration, and mental health. *American Journal of Sociology*, **87**, 48–74.

Hull, J.G., Van Treuren, R.R. & Virnelli, S. (1987). Hardiness and health: a critique and alternative approach. *Journal of Personality and Social Psychology*, **53**, 1–13.

Hupka, R.B., Jung, J. & Silverthorn, K. (1987). Perceived acceptability of apologies, excuses and justifications in jealousy predicaments. *Journal of Social Behavior and Personality*, **2**, 303–14.

Huston, M. & Schwartz, P. (1995). Lesbian and gay male relationships. In J.T. Wood & S. Duck (Eds), *Understudied Relationships: Off the Beaten Track (Understanding relationship processes 6)* (pp. 89–121). Thousand Oaks, CA: Sage.

Huston, T.L. (1983). Power. In H.H. Kelley, E. Berscheid, A. Christensen, J.H. Harvey, T.L. Huston, G. Levinger, E. McClintock, L.A. Peplau & D.R. Peterson (Eds), *Close Relationships* (pp. 315–59). New York: W. H. Freeman.

Huston, T.L. & Ashmore, R.D. (1986). Women and men in personal relationships. In R.D. Ashmore & F.K. Del Boca (Eds), *The Social Psychology of Female–Male Relations: A Critical Analysis of Central Concepts* (pp. 167–210). Orlando, FL: Academic Press.

Huston, T.L. & Chorost, A.F. (in press). Behavioral buffers on the effect of negativity on marital satisfaction: a longitudinal study. *Personal Relationships.*

Huston, T.L. & Vangelisti, A.L. (1991). Socioemotional behavior and satisfaction in marital relationships: a longitudinal study. *Journal of Personality and Social Psychology*, **61**, 721–33.

Huston, T.L., McHale, S. & Crouter, A. (1986). When the honeymoon's over: changes in the marriage relationship over the first year. In R. Gilmour & S. Duck (Eds), *The Emerging Field of Personal Relationships* (pp. 109–32). Hillsdale, NJ: Erlbaum.

Huston, T.L., Surra, C.A., Fitzgerald, N.M. & Cate, R.M. (1981). From courtship to marriage: mate selection as an interpersonal process. In S.W. Duck & R. Gilmour (Eds), *Personal Relationships 2: Developing Personal Relationships* (pp. 53–88). London & New York: Academic Press.

Hutchins, G. & Norris, F.H. (1989). Life change in the disaster recovery period. *Environment and Behavior*, **21**, 33–56.

Huyck, M.H. (1995). Marriage and close relationships of the marital kind. In R. Blieszner & V.H. Bedford (Eds), *Handbook of Aging and the Family* (pp. 181–200). Westport, CT: Greenwood Press.

Ickes, W. (1984). Compositions in Black and White: determinants of interaction in interracial dyads. *Journal of Personality and Social Psychology*, **47**, 330–41.

Ickes, W. (Ed.) (1985). *Compatible and Incompatible Relationships.* New York: Springer-Verlag.

Ickes, W., Bissonnette, V., Garcia, S. & Stinson, L. (1990). Implementing and using the dyadic interaction paradigm. In C. Hendrick & M. Clark (Eds), *Review of Personality and Social Psychology*, Vol. 11 (pp. 16–44). Thousand Oaks, CA: Sage.

Ickes, W., Robertson, E., Tooke, W. & Teng, G. (1986). Naturalistic social cognition: methodology, assessment, and validation. *Journal of Personality and Social Psychology*, **51**, 66–82.

Ickes, W., Stinson, L., Bissonnette, V. & Garcia, S. (1990). Naturalistic social cognition: empathic accuracy in mixed-sex dyads. *Journal of Personality and Social Psychology*, **59**, 730–42.

Ickes, W., Tooke, W., Stinson, L., Baker, V. & Bissonnette, V. (1988). Naturalistic social cognition: intersubjectivity in same-sex dyads. *Journal of Nonverbal Behavior*, **12**, 58–84.

Ireys, H., Facchini, R., Stein, R. & Bauman, L. (1990). Implementing a lay prevention program for mothers of chronically ill children: how field experiences led to revisions in program theory. Working paper 90-07. Preventive Intervention Research Center, Albert Einstein College of Medicine, Bronx, NY.

Ironson, G., Greenwood, D., Wynings, C., Baum, A., Rodriquez, M., Carver, C., Benight, C., Evans, J., Antoni, M., LaPerriere, A., Kumar, M., Fletcher, M. & Schneiderman, N. (1993, August). Social support, neuroendocrine, and immune functioning during Hurricane Andrew. Paper presented at the 101th Annual Convention of American Psychological Association, Toronto, Canada.

Israel, J. (1979). *The Language of Dialectics and the Dialectics of Language.* Copenhagen: Munksgaard.

Jackson, M. (1989). *Paths Toward a Clearing: Radical Empiricism and Ethnographic Inquiry.* Bloomington: Indiana University Press.

Jackson, P. (1988). Personal networks, support mobilization and unemployment. *Psychological Medicine*, **18**, 397–404.

Jacobson, D.E. (1986). Types and timing of social support. *Journal of Health and Social Behavior*, **27**(3), 250–64.

Jacobson, N.S. (1990). Commentary: contributions from psychology to an understanding of marriage. In F.D. Fincham & T.N. Bradbury (Eds), *The Psychology of Marriage* (pp. 258–75). New York: Guilford.

Jacobson, N.S. & Margolin, G. (1979). *Marital Therapy: Strategies Based on Social Learning and Behavior Exchange Principles.* New York: Brunner/Mazel.

Jacobson, N.S. & Addis, M.E. (1993). Research on couples and couple therapy: What do we know? Where are we going? *Journal of Consulting and Clinical Psychology*, **61**, 85–93.

Jacobson, N.S. & Holtzworth-Munroe, A. (1986). Marital therapy: a social learning-cognitive perspective. In N.S. Jacobson & A.S. Gurman (Eds), *Clinical Handbook of Marital Therapy* (pp. 29–70). New York: Guilford.

Jacobvitz, D. & Sroufe, L.A. (1987). The early caregiver–child relationship and attention deficit disorder with hyperactivity in kindergarten: a prospective study. *Child Development*, **58**, 1488–95.

James, W. (1890). *The Principles of Psychology.* New York: Holt.

James, W. (1948). *Psychology.* Cleveland: Fine Editions Press (original work published 1890).

Jamison, R.N. & Virts, K.L. (1990). The influence of family support on chronic pain. *Behavioral Research and Therapy*, **28**, 283–7.

Janes, C.R. & Pawson, I.G. (1986). Migration and biocultural adaptation: Samoans in California. *Social Science and Medicine*, **22**, 821–34.

Jankowiak, W.R. & Fischer, E.F. (1992). A cross-cultural perspective on romantic love. *Ethnology*, **31**, 149–55.

Janoff-Bulman, R. (1992). *Shattered Assumptions: Towards a New Psychology of Trauma.* New York: Free Press.

Janson, B.S., Ferketich, S. & Benner, P. (1993). Predicting the outcomes of living with asthma. *Research in Nursing and Health,* **16**, 241–50.

Jason, L.A., Weine, A.M., Johnson, J.H., Warren-Sohlberg, L., Filippelli, L.A., Turner, E.Y. & Lardon, C. (1992). *Helping Transfer Students: Strategies for Educational and Social Readjustment.* San Francisco: Jossey-Bass.

Jelinek, M.M. & Brittan, E.M. (1975). Multiracial education: 1. Inter-ethnic friendship patterns. *Educational Research,* **18**, 44–53.

Jemmott, J.B. & Magloire, K. (1988). Academic stress, social support and secretory immunoglobulin A. *Journal of Personality and Social Psychology,* **55**, 803–10.

Jenkins, J. (1992). Sibling relationships in disharmonious homes: potential difficulties and protective effects. In F. Boer & J. Dunn (Eds), *Children's Sibling Relationships* (pp. 125–38). Hillsdale, NJ: Erlbaum.

Jenkins, J.M. & Smith, M.A. (1991). Marital disharmony and children's behavior problems: aspects of poor marriage that affect children adversely. *Journal of Child Psychology and Psychiatry,* **32**, 793–810.

Jerusalem, M., Kaniasty, K., Lehman, D., Ritter, C. & Turnbull, G. (1995). Individual and community stress: integration of approaches at different levels. In S.E. Hobfoll & M.W. de Vries (Eds), *Extreme Stress and Communities: Impact and Intervention* (pp. 105–29). Dordrecht: Kluwer.

Jessor, R., Donovan, J.E. & Costa, F.M. (1991). *Beyond Adolescence: Problem Behavior and Young Adult Development* (pp. 17–38). Cambridge: Cambridge University Press.

Joffe, C.E. (1977). *Friendly Intruders.* Berkeley: University of California Press.

John, O.P. (1990). The "Big Five" factor taxonomy: dimensions of personality in the natural language and in questionnaires. In L.A. Pervin (Ed.), *Handbook of Personality Theory and Research* (pp. 66–100). New York: Guilford.

Johnson, C.L. (1988). *Ex Familia.* New Brunswick: Rutgers University Press.

Johnson, C.L. (1993). The prolongation of life and the extension of family relationships: the families of the oldest old. In P.A. Cowan, D. Field, D.A. Hansen, A. Skolnick & G.E. Swanson (Eds), *Family, Self, and Society: Toward a New Agenda for Family Research* (pp. 317–30). Hillsdale, NJ: Erlbaum.

Johnson, C.L. & Barer, B.M. (1996). Childlessness and kinship organization: comparisons of very old Whites and Blacks. *Journal of Cross-cultural Gerontology,* **10**, 289–306.

Johnson, C.L. & Troll, L. (1996). Family structure and the timing of transitions from 70 to 103 years of age. *Journal of Marriage and the Family,* **58**(1), 178–87.

Johnson, D.B. (1982). Altruistic behavior and the development of the self in infants. *Merrill-Palmer Quarterly,* **28**, 379–88.

Johnson, D.J. (1992). Developmental pathways: toward an ecological theoretical formulation of race identity in Black–White biracial children. In M.P.P. Root (Ed.), *Racially Mixed People in America* (pp. 37–49). Newbury Park, CA: Sage.

Johnson, D.J. & Rusbult, C.E. (1989). Resisting temptation: devaluation of alternative partners as a means of maintaining commitment in close relationships. *Journal of Personality and Social Psychology,* **57**, 967–80.

Johnson, J.V. & Hall, E.M. (1994). Social support in the work environment and cardiovascular disease. In S.A. Shumaker & S.M. Czajowski (Eds), *Social Support and Cardiovascular Disease* (pp. 145–66). New York: Plenum.

Johnson, M.P. (1982). Social and cognitive features of the dissolution of commitment to relationships. In S.W. Duck (Ed.), *Personal Relationships 4: Dissolving Personal Relationships* (pp. 51–73). New York: Academic Press.

Johnson, M.P. (1991a). Commitment to personal relationships. In W.H. Jones & D.W. Perlman (Eds.), *Advances in Personal Relationships,* Vol. 3 (pp. 117–43). London: Jessica Kingsley.

Johnson, M.P. (1991b). Reply to Levinger and Rusbult. In W.H. Jones & D.W. Perlman

(Eds.), *Advances in Personal Relationships*, Vol. 3 (pp. 171–6). London: Jessica Kingsley.

Johnson, M.P. (1995). Patriarchal terrorism and common couple violence: two forms of violence against women. *Journal of Marriage and the Family*, **57**.

Johnson, M.P. & Ewens, W. (1971). Power relations and affective styles as determinants of confidence in impression formation in a game situation. *Journal of Experimental Social Psychology*, **7**, 98–110.

Johnson, M.P. & Kapinus, C.A. (1995). Gendered commitments: gender and family life-course as factors in the strength of relationship ties. Unpublished manuscript.

Johnson, M.P. & Milardo, R.M. (1984). Network interference in pair relationships: a social psychological recasting of Slater's theory of social regression. *Journal of Marriage and the Family*, **46**, 893–9.

Johnson, M.P., Huston, T.L., Gaines, S.O. Jr & Levinger, G. (1992). Patterns of married life among young couples. *Journal of Social and Personal Relationships*, **9**, 343–64.

Johnson, P.L. & O'Leary, K.D. (1987). Parental behavior patterns and conduct disorders in girls. *Journal of Abnormal Child Psychology*, **15**, 573–81.

Jones, E.E. & Davis, K.E. (1965). From acts to dispositions: the attribution process in person perception. In L. Berkowitz (Ed.), *Advances in Experimental Social Psychology*, Vol. 2 (pp. 283–329). New York: Academic Press.

Jones, E.E. & Gerard, H.B. (1967). *Foundations of Social Psychology*. Wiley: New York.

Jones, E.E. & Nisbett, R. (1971). The actor and the observer: divergent perceptions of the causes of behavior. In E.E. Jones, D. Kanouse, H. Kelley, R. Nisbett, S. Valins & B. Weiner (Eds), *Attribution: Perceiving the Causes of Behavior* (pp. 79–94). Morristown, NJ: General Learning Press.

Jones, E.E., Bell, L. & Aronson, E. (1972). The reciprocation of attraction from similar and dissimilar others: a study in person perception and evaluation. In C.G. McClintock (Ed.), *Experimental Social Psychology* (pp. 142–79). New York: Holt, Rinehart.

Jones, E. & Gallois, C. (1989). Spouses' impressions of rules for communication in public and private marital conflicts. *Journal of Marriage and the Family*, **51**, 957–67.

Jones, J.E. (1977). Patterns of transactional style deviance in the TATs of parents of schizophrenics. *Family Process*, **16**, 327–37.

Jones, J.M. (1987). Racism in Black and White: a bicultural model of reaction and evaluation. In P.A. Katz & D.A. Taylor (Eds), *Eliminating Racism: Profiles in Controversy* (pp. 117–35). New York: Plenum.

Jones, M.C. (1971). Personality correlates and antecedents of drinking patterns of adult males. *Journal of Consulting and Clinical Psychology*, **32**, 2–12.

Jones, S.S. & Hong, H. (1995, March). On the development of affective sharing from 8 to 12 months of age. Paper presented at the meeting of the Society for Research in Child Development, Indianapolis.

Jones, W.H., Kugler, K. & Adams, P. (1995). You always hurt the one you love: guilt and transgressions against relationship partners. In J. Tangney & K. Fischer (Eds), *Self-conscious Emotions* (pp. 301–21). New York: Guilford.

Jorm, A.F., Christensen, H., Henderson, A.S. & Korten-Ailsa, E. et al. (1993). Neuroticism and self-reported health in an elderly community sample. *Personality and Individual Differences*, **15**, 515–21.

Joseph, S., Yule, W., Williams, R. & Andrews, B. (1993). Crisis support in the aftermath of disaster: a longitudinal perspective. *British Journal of Clinical Psychology*, **32**, 177–85.

Josselson, R. (1988). The embedded self: I and Thou revisited. In D.K. Lapsley & F.C. Power (Eds), *Self, Ego, and Identity: Integrative Approaches* (pp. 91–106). New York: Springer-Verlag.

Josselson, R. (1992). *The Space Between Us: Exploring the Dimensions of Human Relationships*. San Francisco: Jossey-Bass.

Josselson, R. & Lieblich, A. (Eds) (1993). *The Narrative Study of Lives*. Newbury Park, CA: Sage.

Jourard, S.M. (1971a) *The Transparent Self* (revised Edn). New York: Van Nostrand Reinhold.

Jourard, S.M. (1971b). *Self-disclosure: an Experimental Analysis of the Transparent Self*. New York: Wiley.

Jouriles, E.N., Bourg, W.J. & Farris, A.M. (1991). Marital adjustment and child conduct problems: a comparison of the correlation across subsamples. *Journal of Consulting and Clinical Psychology*, **59**, 354–7.

Julien, D. & Markman, H. (1991). Social support and social networks as determinants of individual and marital outcomes. *Journal of Social and Personal Relationships*, **8**, 549–68.

Julien, D., Begin, J. & Chartrand, P.S. (1995). Networks' support and interference in marriage: a comparison of husbands' and wives' disclosures of marital problems to confidants. Paper presented at the annual convention of the International Communication Association, Albuquerque, NM, May.

Jung, C.G. (1959). Marriage as a psychological relationship. In V.S. DeLaszlo (Ed.), *The Basic Writings of C.G. Jung* (R.F.C. Hull, trans: pp. 531–44). New York: Modern Library (original work published 1925).

Kagan, J. (1991). The theoretical utility of constructs for self. *Developmental Review*, **11**, 244–50.

Kahn, R.L. (1979). Aging and social support. In M.W. Riley (Ed.), *Aging from Birth to Death: Interdisciplinary Perspectives* (pp. 77–91). Boulder, CO: Westview Press.

Kahneman, D. & Tversky, A. (1979). Prospect theory: an analysis of decision under risk. *Econometrica*, **47**, 263–91.

Kahneman, D., Slovik, P. & Tversky, A. (1982). *Judgment under Uncertainty: Heuristics and Biases*. New York: Cambridge University Press.

Kambon, K.K.K. & Hopkins, R. (1993). An African-centered analysis of Penn et al.'s critique of the own-racial preference assumption underlying Africentric models of personality. *Journal of Black Psychology*, **19**, 342–9.

Kamen-Siegel, L., Rodin, J., Seligman, M.E.P. & Dwyer, J. (1991). Explanatory style and cell-mediated immunity in elderly men and women. *Health Psychology*, **10**, 229–35.

Kamo, Y. (1988). Determinants of household division of labor: resources, power, and ideology. *Journal of Family Issues*, **9**, 177–200.

Kaniasty, K.Z. & Norris, F.H. (1992). Social support and victims of crime: matching event, support, and outcome. *American Journal of Community Psychology*, **20**, 211–41.

Kaniasty, K.Z. & Norris, F.H. (1993). A test of the support deterioration model in the context of natural disaster. *Journal of Personality and Social Psychology*, **64**, 395–408.

Kaniasty, K.Z. & Norris, F.H. (1994, July). Social support from family and friends following catastrophic events: the role of cultural factors. Paper presented at the 7th International Conference on Personal Relationships, Groningen, The Netherlands.

Kaniasty, K.Z. & Norris, F.H. (1995a). In search of altruistic community: patterns of social support mobilization following Hurricane Hugo. *American Journal of Community Psychology*, **23**, 447–77.

Kaniasty, K.Z. & Norris, F.H. (1995b). Mobilization and deterioration of social support following natural disasters. *Current Directions in Psychological Science*, **4**, 94–8.

Kaniasty, K.Z., Norris, F.H. & Murrell, S.A. (1990). Received and perceived social support following natural disaster. *Journal of Applied Social Psychology*, **20**, 85–114.

Kanter, R.M. (1968). Commitment and social organization: a study of commitment mechanisms in utopian communities. *American Sociological Review*, **33**, 499–517.

Kapferer, B. (1973). Social network and conjugal role in urban Zambia: towards a reformulation of the Bott hypothesis. In J. Bossevain & J. Mitchell (Eds), *Network Analysis: Studies in Human Interaction* (pp. 83–110). The Hague: Mouton.

Kaplan, G.A. & Comacho, T. (1983). Perceived health and mortality: a 9-year follow-up of the Human Population Laboratory Cohort. *American Journal of Epidemiology*, **117**, 292–304.

Karmack, T. & Jennings, J.R. (1994). Biobehavioral factors in sudden cardiac death. *Psychological Bulletin*, **109**, 42–75.

Karpel, M. (1976). Individuation: from fusion to dialogue. *Family Process*, **15**, 65–82.

Kashiwagi, K. & Azuma, H. (1977). Comparison of opinions on pre-school education and developmental expectations between Japanese and American mothers. *Japanese Journal of Educational Psychology*, **25**, 242–53.

Katz, L.F. & Gottman, J.M. (1991). Marital discord and child outcomes: a social psychophysiological approach. In J. Garber & K.A. Dodge (Eds), *The Development of Emotion Regulation and Dysregulation* (pp. 129–58). Cambridge: Cambridge University Press.

Katz, L.F. & Gottman, J.M. (1993). Patterns of marital conflict predict children's internalizing and externalizing behaviors. *Developmental Psychology*, **29**, 940–50.

Katz, L.F. & Kahen, V. (1993). Marital interaction patterns and children's externalizing and internalizing behaviors: the search for mechanisms. Paper presented at the Biennial meetings of Society for Research in Child Development, New Orleans, L.A.

Katz, L.F., Kramer, L. & Gottman, J.M. (1992). Conflict and emotions in marital, sibling, and peer relationships. In C.U. Shantz & W.W. Hartup (Ed.), *Conflict in Child and Adolescent Development*. Cambridge: Cambridge University Press.

Katz, P.A. & Taylor, D.A. (1987). Introduction. In P.A. Katz & D.A. Taylor (Eds), *Eliminating Racism: Profiles in controversy* (pp. 1–16). New York: Plenum.

Kayser, K. (1993). *When Love Dies*. New York: Guilford.

Keefe, E.K. (1977). *Area Handbook for Italy*. Washington, DC: American University.

Keenan, J.M. & Baillet, S.D. (1980). Memory for personally and socially significant events. In R.S. Nickerson (Ed.), *Attention and Performance*, Vol. 8 (pp. 652–69). Hillsdale, NJ: Erlbaum.

Keller, M. (1987). Resolving conflicts in friendship: the development of moral understanding in everyday life. In J. Gerwitz & W. Kurtines (Eds), *Morality and Moral Development*. New York: Wiley.

Kelley, H.H. (1972). Attribution in social interaction. In E.E. Jones, D.E. Kanouse, H.H. Kelley, R.E. Nisbett, S. Valins & B. Weiner (Eds), *Attribution: Perceiving the Causes of Behavior* (pp. 1–26). Morristown, NJ: General Learning Press.

Kelley, H.H. (1979). *Personal Relationships: their Structures and Processes*. Hillsdale, NJ: Erlbaum.

Kelley, H.H. (1983a). Love and commitment. In H.H. Kelley, E. Berscheid, A. Christensen, J.H. Harvey, T.L. Huston, G. Levinger, E. McClintock, L.A. Peplau & D.R. Peterson (Eds), *Close Relationships* (pp. 265–314). New York: W. H. Freeman.

Kelley, H.H. (1983b). The situational origins of human tendencies: a further reason for the formal analysis of structures. *Personality and Social Psychology Bulletin*, **9**, 8–30.

Kelley, H.H. (1984a). Affect in interpersonal relations. In P. Shaver (Ed.), *Review of Personality and Social Psychology*, Vol. 5 (pp. 89–115). Newbury Park, CA: Sage.

Kelley, H.H. (1984b). Interdependence theory and its future. *Representative Research in Social Psychology*, **14**, 2–15.

Kelley, H.H. (1984c). The theoretical description of interdependence by means of transition lists. *Journal of Personality and Social Psychology*, **47**, 956–82.

Kelley, H.H. (1991). Lewin, situations, and interdependence. *Journal of Social Issues*, **47**(2), 211–33.

Kelley, H.H. (1994). Personal commentary. *ISSPR Bulletin*, **11**(1), 1–3.

Kelley, H.H. & Grzelak, J.L. (1972). Conflict between individual and common interests in an *n*-person relationship. *Journal of Personality and Social Psychology*, **21**, 190–97.

Kelley, H.H. & Stahelski, A.J. (1970). Social interaction basis of cooperators' and competitors' beliefs about others. *Journal of Personality and Social Psychology*, **16**, 66–91.

Kelley, H.H. & Thibaut, J.W. (1969). Group problem solving. In G. Lindzey & E. Aronson (Eds), *Handbook of Social Psychology*, Vol. 4 (2nd Edn, pp. 1–101). Reading, MA: Addison-Wesley.

Kelley, H.H. & Thibaut, J.W. (1978). *Interpersonal Relations: a Theory of Interdependence*. New York: Wiley.

Kelley, H.H. & Thibaut, J.W. (1985). Self-interest, science, and cynicism. *Journal of Social and Clinical Psychology*, **3**, 26–32.

Kelley, H.H., Berscheid, E., Christensen, A., Harvey, J.H., Huston, T.L., Levinger, G., McClintock, E., Peplau, L.A. & Peterson, D.R. (1983). *Clothes Relationships*. New York: W. H. Freeman.

Kelley, M.L. & Tseng, H.M. (1992). Cultural differences in child rearing: a comparison of immigrant Chinese and Caucasian American mothers. *Journal of Cross-Cultural Psychology*, **23**(4), 444–55.

Kelly, D. & Main, F.O. (1979). Sibling conflict in a single parent family: an empirical case study. *American Journal of Family Therapy*, **7**, 39–47.

Kelly, G.A. (1955). *The Psychology of Personal Constructs*, Vol. 1. New York: Norton.

Kelly, J.G. (1968). Towards an ecological conception of preventive interventions. In J.W. Carter (Ed.), *Research Contributions from Psychology to Community Mental Health* (pp. 75–99). New York: Behavioral Publications.

Kelly, J.G. (1970). Antidotes for arrogance: training for a community psychology. *American Psychologist*, **25**, 524–31.

Kelly, J.G. (1979). *Adolescent Boys in High School: a Psychological Study of Coping and Adaptation*. Hillsdale, NJ: Erlbaum.

Kelly, J.G. & Hess, R. (1986). *The Ecology of Prevention: Illustrating Mental Health Consultation*. New York: Haworth Press.

Kempler, W. (1981). *Principles of Gestalt Family Therapy*. Salt Lake City, UT: Deseret Press.

Kendler, K.S. & Diehl, S.R. (1993). The genetics of schizophrenia: a current, genetic-epidemiologic perspective. *Schizophrenia Bulletin*, **19**, 261–85.

Kendrick, C. & Dunn, J. (1982). Protest or pleasure: the response of firstborn children to interactions between mothers and infant siblings. *Journal of Child Psychology and Psychiatry*, **23**, 117–29.

Kennell, J., Klaus, M., McGrath, S., Robertson, S. & Hinkley, C. (1991). Continuous emotional support during labor in a U.S. hospital: a randomized controlled trial. *Journal of the American Medical Association*, **265**, 2197–201.

Kenny, D.A. (1979). *Correlation and Causality*. New York: Wiley.

Kenny, D.A. (1988). The analysis of data from two-person relationships. In S.W. Duck (Ed.), *Handbook of Personal Relationships* (1st Edn, pp. 57–77). Chichester: Wiley.

Kenny, D.A. (1990). Design issues in dyadic research. In C. Hendricks & M.S. Clarke (Eds), *Review of Personality and Social Psychology*, Vol. 11 (pp. 164–84). Thousand Oaks, CA: Sage.

Kenny, D.A. (1995). *Models of Nonindependence in Dyadic Research*. University of Connecticut.

Kenny, D.A. & Albright, L.A. (1987). Accuracy in interpersonal perception: a social relations analysis. *Psychological Bulletin*, **102**, 390–402.

Kenny, D.A. & DePaulo, B.M. (1993). Do people know how others view them? An empirical and theoretical account. *Psychological Bulletin*, **114**, 145–61.

Kenny, D.A. & Judd, C.M. (1986). Consequences of violating the independence assumption in the analysis of variance. *Psychological Bulletin*, **99**, 422–31.

Kenny, D.A. & La Voie, L. (1984). The social relations model. In L. Berkowitz (Ed.), *Advances in Experimental Social Psychology*, Vol. 18 (pp. 141–82). Orlando: Academic Press.

Kenny, D.A. & La Voie, L. (1985). Separating individual and group effects. *Journal of Personality and Social Psychology*, **48**, 339–48.

Kenny, M.E. & Donaldson, G.A. (1992). The relationship of parental attachment and psychological separation to the adjustment of first-year college women. *Journal of College Student Development*, **33**, 431–8.

Kenrick, D.T. (1987). Gender, genes, and the social environment: a biosocial interactionist perspective. In P. Shaver & C. Hendrick (Eds), *Review of Personality and Social Psychology*, Vol. 7 (pp. 14–43). Newbury Park, CA: Sage.

Kenrick, D.T. (1994). Evolutionary social psychology: from sexual selection to social cognition. In M.P. Zanna (Ed.), *Advances in Experimental Social Psychology*, Vol. 26 (pp. 75–122). San Diego, CA: Academic Press.

Kenrick, D.T. & Brown, S. (1995). Al Capone, discrete morphs, and complex dynamic systems. *Behavioral and Brain Sciences*, **18**, 560–61.

Kenrick, D.T. & Cialdini, R.B. (1977). Romantic attraction: misattribution versus reinforcement explanations. *Journal of Personalty and Social Psychology*, **35**, 381–91.

Kenrick, D.T. & Gutierres, S.E. (1980). Contrast effects and judments of physical attractiveness: when beauty becomes a social problem. *Journal of Personality and Social Psychology*, **38**, 131–40.

Kenrick, D.T. & Keefe, R.C. (1992). Age preferences in mates reflect sex differences in reproductive strategies. *Behavioral and Brain Sciences*, **15**, 75–133.

Kenrick, D.T. & Sheets, V. (1994). Homicidal fantasies. *Ethology and Sociobiology*, **14**, 231–46.

Kenrick, D.T. & Trost, M.R. (1987). A biosocial model of relationship formation. In K. Kelley (Ed.), *Females, Males and Sexuality: Theories and Research* (pp. 58–100). Albany: SUNY Press.

Kenrick, D.T. & Trost, M.R. (1989). A reproductive exchange model of heterosexual relationships: putting proximate economics in ultimate perspective. In C. Hendrick (Ed.), *Review of Personality and Social Psychology*, Vol. 10. *Close Relationships* (pp. 92–118). Newbury Park: Sage.

Kenrick, D.T. & Trost, M.R. (1993). The evolutionary perspective. In A.E. Beall & R.J. Sternberg (Eds), *Perspectives on the Psychology of Gender* (pp. 148–72). New York: Guilford.

Kenrick, D.T., Dantchik, A. & MacFarlane, S. (1983). Personality, environment, and criminal behavior: an evolutionary perspective. In W.S. Laufer & J.M. Day (Eds), *Personality Theory, Moral Development and Criminal Behavior* (pp. 201–34). Lexington, MA: D.C. Heath & Co.

Kenrick, D.T., Engstrom, C., Keefe, R.C. & Cornelius, J.S. (in press). Adolescents' age preferences for dating partners: support for an evolutionary model of life-history strategies. *Child Development.*

Kenrick, D.T., Groth, G.E., Trost, M.R. & Sadalla, E.K. (1993). Integrating evolutionary and social exchange perspectives on relationships: effects of gender, self-appraisal, and involvement level on mate selection. *Journal of Personality and Social Psychology*, **64**, 951–69.

Kenrick, D.T., Gutierres, S.E. & Goldberg, L. (1989). Influence of popular erotica on judgments of strangers and mates. *Journal of Experimental Social Psychology*, **25**, 159–67.

Kenrick, D.T., Keefe, R.C., Bryan, A., Barr, A. & Brown, S. (1995). Age preferences and mate choice among homosexuals and heterosexuals: a case for modular psychological mechanisms. *Journal of Personality and Social Psychology*, **69**, 1166–72.

Kenrick, D.T., Neuberg, S.L., Zierk, K.L. & Krones, J.M. (1994). Evolution and social cognition: contrast effects as a function of sex, dominance, and physical attractiveness. *Personality and Social Psychology Bulletin*, **20**, 210–17.

Kenrick, D.T., Sadalla, E.K., Groth, G. & Trost, M.R. (1990). Evolution, traits, and the stages of human courtship: qualifying the parental investment model. *Journal of Personality*, **58**, 97–116.

Kenrick, D.T., Sadalla, E.K. & Keefe, R.C. (in press). Evolutionary cognitive psychology.

In C. Crawford & D. Krebs (Eds), *Evolution and Human Behavior*. Hillsdale, NJ: Erlbaum.

Kenrick, D.T., Stringfield, D.O., Wagenhals, W.L., Dahl, R.H. & Ransdell, H.J. (1980). Sex differences, androgyny, and approach responses to erotica: a new variation on the old volunteer problem. *Journal of Personality and Social Psychology*, **38**, 517–24.

Kephart, W.M. & Jedlicka, D. (1988). *The Family, Society, and the Individual*, 6th Edn. New York: Harper & Row.

Kerby, A. (1991). *Narrative and the Self*. Bloomington: Indiana University Press.

Kerckhoff, A.C. (1974). The social context of interpersonal attraction. In T.L. Huston (Ed.), *Foundations of Interpersonal Attraction* (pp. 61–77). New York: Academic Press.

Kerckhoff, A.C. & Davis, K.E. (1962). Value consensus and need complementarity in mate selection. *American Sociological Review*, **27**, 295–303.

Kernberg, O.F. (1974). Mature love: prerequisites and characteristics. *Journal of the American Psychoanalytic Association*, **22**, 743–68.

Kessler, R.C. & McLeod, J.D. (1984). Sex differences in vulnerability to undesirable life events. *American Sociological Review*, **49**, 620–31.

Kessler, R.C. & McLeod, J.D. (1985a). Social support and mental health in community samples. In S. Cohen & L. Syme (Eds), *Social Support and Health* (pp. 109–25). Orlando, FL: Academic Press.

Kessler, R.C. & McLeod, J.D. (1985b). Social support and psychological distress in community surveys. In S. Cohen & S.L. Syme (Eds), *Social Support and Health* (pp. 19–40). New York: Academic Press.

Kessler, R.C. & McRae, James A. Jr (1982). The effects of wives' employment on the mental health of married men and women. *American Sociological Review*, **47**, 216–17.

Kessler, R.C., McLeod, J.D. & Wethington, E. (1985). The costs of caring: a perspective on the relationship between sex and psychological distress. In I.G. Sarason & B.R. Sarason (Eds), Social Support: Theory, Research and Applications (pp. 491–506). Boston: Martinus Nijhoff.

Kessler, R.C., Turner, J.B. & House, J.S. (1988). Effects of unemployment on health in a community survey: main, modifying, and mediating effects. *Journal of Social Issues*, **44**, 69–85.

Kidd, V. (1975). Happily ever after and other relationship styles: advice on interpersonal relations in popular magazines, 1951–1973. *Quarterly Journal of Speech*, **61**, 31–9.

Kidwell, J., Fischer, J.L., Dunham, R.M. & Baranowski, M. (1983). Parents and adolescents: push and pull of change. In H.I. McCubbin & C.R. Figley (Eds), *Stress in the Family. Volume I: Coping with Normative Transitions (*pp. 74–89).

Kiecolt-Glaser, J.K., Dyer, C.S. & Shuttleworth, E.C. (1988). Upsetting social interactions and distress among Alzheimer's disease family care-givers: a replication and extension. *American Journal of Community Psychology*, **16**, 825–37.

Kiecolt-Glaser, J.K., Garner, W., Speicher, C., Penn, G.M., Holliday, J. & Glaser, R. (1984). Psychological modifiers of immunocompetence in medical students. *Psychosomatic Medicine*, **46**, 7–14.

Kiecolt-Glaser, J.K., Ricker, D., George, J., Messick, G., Speicher, G.E., Garner, W. & Glaser, R. (1984). Urinary cortisol levels, cellular immunocompetence, and loneliness in psychiatric inpatients. *Psychosomatic Medicine*, **46**, 15–23.

Kiesinger, C. (1995). The Anorexic and Bulimic Self. Unpublished PhD Dissertation, University of South Florida.

Kiesler, C.A. (1985). Policy implications of research on social support and health. In S. Cohen & L. Syme (Eds), *Social Support and Health* (pp. 347–64). Orlando, FL: Academic Press.

Kiesler, D. (1983). The 1982 interpersonal circle: a taxonomy for complementarity in human transactions. *Psychological Review*, **90**, 185–214.

Kiesler, D.J. & Watkins, L.M. (1989). Interpersonal complementarity and the therapeutic alliance: a study of relationship in psychotherapy. *Psychotherapy*, **26**, 183–94.

Kilbourne, B.S., Howell, F. & England, P. (1990). A measurement model for subjective marital solidarity: invariance across time, gender, and life cycle stage. *Social Science Research*, **19**, 62–81.

Kilijanek, T. & Drabek, T.E. (1979). Assessing long-term impacts of a natural disaster: a focus on the elderly. *The Gerontologist*, **19**, 555–66.

Killworth, P.D., Bernard, H.R. & McCarty, C. (1984). Measuring patterns of acquaintanceship. *Current Anthropology*, **25**, 381–97.

Kim, H.J. & Stiff, J.B. (1991). Social networks and the development of close relationships. *Human Communication Research*, **18**, 70–91.

Kim, U. (1994). Individualism and collectivism: conceptual clarification and elaboration. In U. Kim, H.C. Triandis, C. Kagitcibasi, S. Choi & G. Yoon (Eds), *Individualism and Collectivism: Theory, Methods, and Applications* (pp. 19–40). Thousand Oaks, CA: Sage.

King, A.Y.C. & Bond, M.H. (1985). The Confucian paradigm of Man: a sociological view. In W.S. Tseng & D.Y.H. Wu (Eds), *Chinese Culture and Mental Health* (pp. 29–45). Orlando: Academic Press.

Kingston, P.W. & Nock, S.L. (1987). Time together among dual-earner couples. *American Sociological Review*, **52**, 391–400.

Kinsella, K. (1995). Aging and the family: present and future demographic issues. In R. Blieszner & V.H. Bedford (Eds), *Handbook of Aging and the Family* (pp. 32–46). Westport, CT: Greenwood Press.

Kipnis, D., Castell, P.J., Gergen, M. & Mauch, D. (1976). Metamorphic effects of power. *Journal of Applied Psychology*, **61**, 127–35.

Kirkpatrick, L.A. & Davis, K.E. (1993). Attachment style, gender, and relationship stability: a longitudinal analysis. *Journal of Personality and Social Psychology*, **66**, 502–12.

Kirkpatrick, L.A. & Hazan, C. (1994). Attachment styles and close relationships: a four year prospective study. *Journal of Social and Personal Relationships*, **1**, 123–42.

Kirkwood, C. (1993). *Leaving Abusive Partners*. Newbury Park: Sage.

Kissel, S. (1965). Stress-reducing properties of social stimuli. *Journal of Personality and Social Psychology*, **2**, 378–84.

Kissman, K. & Shapiro, J. (1990). The composites of social support and well-being among adolescent mothers. *International Journal of Adolescence and Youth*, **2**(3), 165–73.

Kivett, V.R. (1989). Mother-in-law and daughter-in-law relations. In J.A. Mancini (Ed.), *Aging Parents and Adult Children* (pp. 17–32). Lexington, MA: Lexington Books.

Kivlighan, D.M. Jr & Angelone, E.O. (1992). Interpersonal problems: variables influencing participants' perception of group climate. *Journal of Counseling Psychology*, **39**, 468–72.

Kivlighan, D.M. Jr & Goldfine, D.C. (1991). Endorsement of therapeutic factors as a function of stage of group development and participant interpersonal attitudes. *Journal of Counseling Psychology*, **38**, 150–58.

Kivlighan, D.M. Jr & Mullison, D. (1988). Participants' perception of therapeutic factors in group counseling: the role of interpersonal style and stage of group development. *Small-Group-Behavior*, **19**, 452–68.

Kivlighan, D.M. Jr & Schmitz, P.J. (1992). Counselor technical activity in cases with improving working alliances and continuing-poor working alliances. *Journal of Counseling Psychology*, **39**, 32–8.

Kivlighan, D.M. Jr & Shaughnessy, P. (1995). Analysis of the development of the working alliance using hierarchical linear modeling. *Journal of Counseling Psychology*, **42**, 338–49.

Kivlighan, D.M. Jr, Marsh-Angelone, M. & Angelone, E.O. (1994). Projection in group counseling: the relationship between members' interpersonal problems and their perception of the group leader. *Journal of Counseling Psychology*, **41**, 99–104.

Klein, R. (1995). Conflict resolution in close relationships. Report to the German Science Foundation.

Klein, R. & Milardo, R.M. (1993). Third-party influences on the development and maintenance of personal relationships. In S.W. Duck (Ed.), *Understanding Relationship Processes: Vol. 3: Social Contexts of Relationships* (pp. 55–77). Newbury Park, CA: Sage.

Klein, R. & Milardo, R.M. (1995). The social context of pair conflict: paper presented at the International Network of Personal Relationships, 1995 Conference, Williamsburg, Virginia.

Kleinfeld, J.S. (1973). Classroom climate and the verbal participation of Indian and Eskimo students in integrated classrooms. *Journal of Educational Research*, **67**, 51–2.

Klerman, G.L., Weissman, M.M., Rounsaville, B.J. & Chevron, E.S. (1984). *Interpersonal Psychotherapy of Depression*. New York: Basic Books.

Knapp, M.L. & Taylor, E.H. (1994). Commitment and its communication in romantic relationships. In A.L. Weber & J.H. Harvey (Eds), *Perspectives on Close Relationships* (pp. 153–75). Boston: Allyn & Bacon.

Knapp, M.L. & Vangelisti, A.L. (1992). *Interpersonal Communication and Human Relationships*. Boston: Allyn & Bacon.

Kobak, R.R. & Sceery, A. (1988). Attachment in late adolescence: working models, affect regulation, and representations of self and others. *Child Development*, **59**, 135–46.

Kobak, R. & Hazan, C. (1991). Attachment in marriage: the effects of security and accuracy of working models. *Journal of Personality and Social Psychology*, **60**, 861–9.

Kobasa, S.C. (1979). Stressful life events, personality, and health: an inquiry into hardiness. *Journal of Personality and Social Psychology*, **37**, 1–11.

Kochanska, G. (1993). Toward a synthesis of parental socialization and child temperament in early development of conscience. *Child Development*, **64**, 325–47.

Kochanska, G. & Aksan, N. (1995). Mother–child mutually positive affect, the quality of child compliance to requests and prohibitions, and maternal control as correlates of early internalization. *Child Development*, **66**, 236–54.

Koenigsberg, H.W., Klausner, E., Pellino, D., Rosnick, P. & Campbell, R. (1993). Expressed emotion and glucose control in insulin-dependent diabetes mellitus. *American Journal of Psychiatry*, **150**, 114–15.

Köhler, W. (1947). *Gestalt Psychology: an Introduction to New Concepts in Modern Psychology*. New York: Liveright.

Kohn, M.L. (1969). *Class and Conformity: a Study in Values*. Homewood, IL: Dorsey Press.

Kohn, M.L. (1977). *Reassessment: a Preface to the Second Edition of Class and Conformity*. Chicago: University of Chicago Press.

Kohn, M.L. & Schooler, C. (1983). *Work and Personality: an Inquiry into the Impact of Social Stratification*. Norwood, NJ: Ablex.

Kokotovic, A.M. & Tracey, T.J. (1990). Working alliance in the early phase of counseling. *Journal of Counseling Psychology*, **37**, 16–21.

Kompter, A. (1989). Hidden power in marriage. *Gender & Society*, **3**, 187–216.

Kon, I. & Losenkov, V.A. (1978). Friendship in adolescence: values and behavior. *Journal of Marriage and the Family*, **40**, 143–55.

Kong, S.L. (1985). Counselling Chinese immigrants: issues and answers. In R.J. Samuda & A. Wolfgang (Eds), *Intercultural Counselling and Assessment: Global Perspectives* (pp. 181–9). Lewiston: C.J. Hogrefe.

Kopp, C.B. (1982). Antecedents of self-regulation: a developmental perspective. *Developmental Psychology*, **18**, 199–214.

Kopp, C.B. & Wyer, N. (1991). In D. Cicchetti & S.L. Toth (Eds), *Disorders and Dysfunctions of the Self* (pp. 31–56). Rochester, NY: University of Rochester Press.

Korolewicz, M. & Korolewicz, A. (1985). Effects of sex and race on interracial dating patterns. *Psychological Reports*, **57**, 1291–6.

Kotler, T. (1985). Security and autonomy within marriage. *Human Relations*, **38**, 299–321.

Köttgen, C., Sonischen, I., Mollenhauer, K. & Jurth, R. (1984). Group therapy with the families of schizophrenic patients: results of the Hamburg Camberwell Family Interview Study III. *International Journal of Family Psychiatry*, **5**, 83–94.

Kottler, J.A., Sexton, T.L. & Winston, S.C. (1994). *The Heart of Healing: Relationships in Therapy*. San Francisco: Jossey-Bass.

Kouri, K.M. & Lasswell, M. (1993). Black–White marriages: social change and intergenerational mobility. *Marriage and Family Review*, **19**, 241–55.

Kovecses, Z. (1986). *Metaphors of Anger, Pride, and Love: a Lexical Approach to the Structure of Concepts*. Amsterdam: John Benjamins.

Kovecses, Z. (1991). A linguist's quest for love. *Journal of Personal and Social Relationships*, **8**, 77–98.

Kraemer, H.C. & Jacklin, C.N. (1979). Statistical analysis of dyadic social behavior. *Psychological Bulletin*, **86**, 217–24.

Krain, M. (1977). A definition of dyadic boundaries and an empirical study of boundary establishment in courtship. *International Journal of Sociology of the Family*, **7**, 107–23.

Kramer, L. & Gottman, J.M. (1992). Becoming a sibling: "With a little help from my friends". *Developmental Psychology*, **28**, 685–99.

Krantz, D.S. & Manuck, S.B. (1984). Acute psychophysiological creativity and risk of cardiovasular disease: a review and methodological critique. *Psychological Bulletin*, **96**, 435–64.

Krappmann, L. (1986). Family relationships and peer relationships in middle childhood: an explanatory study of the association between children's integration into the social network of peers and family development. Paper presented at the Family Systems and Life-span Development Conference at the Max Planck Institute, Berlin, FRG.

Krappmann, L. (1989). Family relationships and peer relationships in middle childhood: an exploratory study of the associations between children's integration into the social network of peers and family development. In K. Kreppner & R. Lerner (Eds), *Family Systems and Life-span Development* (pp. 93–104). Hillsdale, NJ: Erlbaum.

Krappmann, L. (1995, April). Qualities of children's friendships in East and West Berlin. Paper presented to the Society for Research in Child Development, Indianapolis, IN.

Krappmann, L. (1996). The development of diverse relationships in the social world of childhood. In A.E. Auhagen & M. von Salisch (Eds), *The Diversity of Human Relationships*. New York: Cambridge University Press.

Krebs, D.L. & Miller, D.T. (1985). Altruism and aggression. In G. Lindzey & E. Aronson (Eds), *The Handbook of Social Psychology*, Vol. 2 (3rd Edn, pp. 1–71). New York: Random House.

Kreft, I., de Leeuw, J. & van der Leeden, R. (1994). Review of five multilevel analysis programs: bmdp-5v, genmod, hlm, ml3, varcl. *American Statistician*, **48**, 324–35.

Krokoff, L.J., Gottman, J.M. & Roy, A.K. (1988). Blue-collar and white-collar marital interaction and communication orientation. *Journal of Social and Personal Relationships*, **5**, 201–21.

Krol, B., Sanderman, R. & Suurmeijer, T.P. (1993). Social support, rheumatoid arthritis and quality of life: concepts, measurement and research. *Patient Education and Counseling*, **20**, 101–20.

Kroll-Smith, J.S. & Couch, S. (1990). *The Real Disaster is Above Ground: A Mine Fire and Social Conflict*. Lexington, KY: University Press of Kentucky.

Kroll-Smith, J.S. & Couch, S. (1993). Technological hazards: social responses as traumatic stressors. In J.P. Wilson & B. Raphael (Eds), *International Handbook of Traumatic Stress Syndromes* (pp. 79–91). New York: Plenum.

Kübler-Ross, E. (1969). *On Death and Dying*. New York: Macmillan.

Kuczynski, L., Kochanska, G., Radke-Yarrow, M. & Girnius-Brown, O. (1987). Developmental interpretation of young children's noncompliance. *Developmental Psychology*, **23**, 799–806.

Kuhn, T. (1970). Reflections on my critics. In E. Lakatos & A. Musgrave (Eds), *Criticism and the Growth of Knowledge* (pp. 231–78). Cambridge: Cambridge University Press.

Kuipers, L., Sturgeon, D., Berkowitz, R. & Leff, J. (1983). Characteristics of expressed emotion: its relationship to speech and looking in schizophrenic patients and their relatives. *British Journal of Clinical Psychology*, **22**, 257–64.

Kulik, J.A. & Mahler, H.I.M. (1989). Social support and recovery from surgery. *Health Psychology*, **8**, 221–38.

Kulik, J.A., Moore, P.J. & Mahler, H.I. (1993). Stress and affiliation: hospital roommate effects on preoperative anxiety and social interaction. *Health Psychology*, **12**, 118–24.

Kurdek, L.A. (1989). Relationship quality for newly married husbands and wives: marital history, stepchildren, and individual-difference predictors. *Journal of Marriage and the Family*, **51**, 1053–64.

Kurdek, L.A. (1993). Predicting marital dissolution: a 5-year prospective study of newly-wed couples. *Journal of Personality and Social Psychology*, **64**, 221–42.

Kurdek, L.A. (1994). Conflict resolution styles in gay, lesbian, heterosexual nonparent, and heterosexual parent couples. *Journal of Marriage and the Family*, **56**, 705–22.

Kurdek, L.A. (in press). Developmental changes in marital satisfaction: a 6-year prospective longitudinal study of newlywed couples. In T.N. Bradbury (Ed.), *The Developmental Course of Marital Dysfunction.* New York: Cambridge University Press.

L'Abate, K. & L'Abate, B. (1979). The paradoxes of intimacy. *Family Therapy*, **6**, 175–84.

La Gaipa, J.J. (1981). A systems approach to personal relationships. In S.W. Duck & R. Gilmour (Ed.), *Personal Relationships 1: Studying Personal Relationships* (pp. 67–90). London: Academic Press.

La Gaipa, J.J. (1990). The negative effects of informal support systems. In S. Duck (Ed.), *Personal Relationships and Social Support* (pp. 122–39). Newbury Park, CA: Sage.

Ladd, G.W. (1981). Effectiveness of a social learning method for enhancing children's social interaction and peer acceptance. *Child Development*, **52**, 171–8.

Ladd, G.W. (1990). Having friends, keeping friends, making friends, and being liked by peers in the classroom: predictors of children's early school adjustment? *Child Development*, **61**, 1081–1100.

Ladd, G.W. (1992). Themes and theories: perspective on processes in family–peer relationships. In R. Parke & G. Ladd (Eds), *Family–Peer Relationships: Modes of Linkage* (pp. 3–34). Hillsdale, NJ: Erlbaum.

Ladd, G.W. & Emerson, E.S. (1984). Shared knowledge in children's friendship. *Developmental Psychology*, **20**, 932–40.

Ladd, G.W. & Golter, B.S. (1988). Parents' management of preschoolers' peer relations: is it related to children's social competence? *Developmental Psychology*, **24**, 109–17.

Ladd, G.W. & Hart, C.H. (1991). Parents' management of children's peer relations: patterns associated with social competence. Paper presented at the 11th Meeting of the International Society for Behavioral Development, Minneapolis, MN.

Ladd, G.W. & Price, J.M. (1986). Promoting children's cognitive and social competence: the relations between parents' perceptions of task difficulty and children's perceived and actual competence. *Child Development*, **57**, 446–60.

Ladd, G.W., Hart, C.H., Wadsworth, E.M. & Golter, B.S. (1988). Preschoolers' peer network in nonschool settings: relationship to family characteristics and school adjustment. In S. Salzinger, J. Antrobus & M. Hammer (Eds), *Social Networks of Children, Adolescents, and College Students* (pp. 61–92). Hillsdale, NJ: Erlbaum.

Ladd, G.W., LeSieur, K. & Profilet, S.M. (1993). Direct parental influences on young children's peer relations. In S. Duck (Ed.), *Learning about Relationships*, Vol. 2. London: Sage.

Laing, R.D. (1969). *Self and Others.* Harmondsworth: Penguin.

Laird, R.D., Pettit, G.S., Mize, J., Brown, E.G. & Lindsey, E. (1994). Mother–child conversations about peers—contributions to competence. *Family Relations*, **43**, 425–32.

Lakey, B. & Cassady, P. (1990). Cognitive processes in perceived social support. *Journal of Personality and Social Psychology*, **59**, 337–43.

Lakoff, G. (1987). *Women, Fire and Dangerous Things: What Categories Reveal About the Mind.* Chicago: University of Chicago Press.

Lakoff, G. & Turner, M. (1989). *More than Cool Reason: a Field Guide to Poetic Metaphor.* Chicago: University of Chicago Press.

Lam, D.H. (1991). Psychosocial family intervention in schizophrenia: a review of empirical studies. *Psychological Medicine*, **21**, 423–41.

Lanaro, S. (1992). *Storia dell'Italia repubblicana dalla fine della guerra agli anni '90.* [History of Republican Italy from the end of the war through the '90s]. Venice: Marsilio.

Landry, P.H. Jr & Martin, M.E. (1988). Measuring Intergenerational Consensus. In D.J. Mangen, V.L. Bengtson & P.H. Landry Jr (Eds), *Measurement of Intergenerational Relations* (pp. 126–55). Newbury Park, CA: Sage.

Lane, C. & Hobfoll, S. (1992). How loss affects anger and alienates potential supporters. *Journal of Consulting and Clinical Psychology*, **60**, 935–42.

Langellier, K. & Peterson, E. (1993). Family storytelling as a strategy of social control. In D. Mumby's *Narrative and Social Control: Critical Perspectives* (pp. 49–76). Newbury Park, CA: Sage.

Langer, S.K. (1948). *Philosophy in a New Key: a Study of the Symbolism of Reason, Rite, and Art.* New York: Mentor.

Lannamann, J. (1991). Interpersonal communication research as ideological practice. *Communication Theory*, **1**, 179–203.

Lannamann, J.W. (1992). Deconstructing the person and changing the subject of interpersonal studies. *Communication Theory*, **2**, 139–48.

Lapsley, D.K., Rice, K.G. & Shadid, G.E. (1989). Psychological separation and adjustment to college. *Journal of Counseling Psychology*, **36**, 286–94.

Larson, L. (1974). System and subsystem perception of family roles. *Journal of Marriage and the Family*, **36**, 123–38.

Larson, R.W. & Bradney, N. (1988). Precious moments with family members and friends. In R.M. Milardo (Ed.), *Families and Social Networks* (pp. 107–26). Newbury Park, CA: Sage.

Larson, R. & Richards, M. (1991). Daily companionship in late childhood and early adolescence: changing developmental contexts. *Child Development*, **62**, 284–300.

Larson, R. & Richards, M.H. (1994). *Divergent Realities: the Emotional Lives of Mothers, Fathers, and Adolescents.* New York: Basic Books.

Larson, R., Mannell, R. & Zuzanek, J. (1986). Daily well-being of older adults with friends and family. *Psychology and Aging*, **1**, 117–26.

Lashley, K.S. (1958/60). Cerebral organization and behavior. In F.A. Beach, D.O. Hebb, C.T. Morgan & H.W. Nissen (Eds), *The Neuropsychology of Lashley*, pp. 529–43. New York: McGraw-Hill.

Latty-Mann, H. & Davis, K.E. (1996). Attachment theory and partner choice: preference and actuality. *Journal of Social and Personal Relationships*, **13**, 5.

Laverty, R. (1962). Reactivation of sibling rivalry in older people. *Social Work*, **7**, 23–30.

Laws, J.L. & Schwartz, P. (1981). *Sexual Scripts: the Social Construction of Female Sexuality.* Washington, DC: University Press of America.

Lawton, M.P. (1994, August). The aging family in multigenerational perspective. Paper presented at the Annual Convention of the American Psychological Association, Los Angeles.

Lazarus, A.A. (1993). Tailoring the therapeutic relationship, on being an authentic chameleon. *Psychotherapy*, **30**, 404–7.

Lazarus, R.S. (1991). *Emotion and Adaptation.* New York: Oxford University Press.

Lazarus, R.S. & Folkman, S. (1984). *Stress, Appraisal, and Coping.* New York: Springer.

Leary, M.R. & Kowalski, R.M. (1990). Impression management: a literature review and two-component model. *Psychological Bulletin*, **107**, 34–47.

Leary, T. (1957). *Interpersonal Diagnosis of Personality: a Functional Theory and Methodology for Personality Evaluation.* New York: Ronald.

Leatham, G. & Duck, S.W. (1990). Conversations with friends and the dynamic of social support. In S.W. Duck (Ed. with R. Silver), *Personal Relationships and Social Support* (pp. 1–29). London: Sage.

LeDoux, J.E. (1986). The neurobiology of emotion. In J.E. LeDoux & W. Hirst (Eds), *Mind and Brain: Dialogues in Cognitive Neuroscience* (pp. 301–54). Cambridge: Cambridge University Press.

Lee, G. (1979). Effects of social networks on the family. In W. Burr, R. Hill, F.I. Nye & I. Reiss (Eds), *Contemporary Theories about the Family,* Vol. 1 (pp. 27–56). New York: Free Press.

Lee, J.Y. & Welsh, M. (March, 1995). Parent's and childrens' social networks and childrens' social acceptance and social behavior. Paper presented at the Society for Research in Child Development, Indianapolis, Indiana.

Leeb, B., Hahlweg, K., Goldstein, M.J. & Feinstein, E. (1991). Cross-national reliability, concurrent validity, and stability of a brief method for assessing expressed emotion. *Psychiatry Research,* **39,** 25–31.

Lefcourt, H.M. (1981). *Research with the Locus of Control Concept,* Vol. 1. New York: Academic Press.

Lefcourt, H.M. & Martin, R.A. (1986). *Humor and Life Stress. Antidote to Adversity.* New York: Springer.

Leff, J.P., Kuipers, L., Berkowitz, R., Eberlein-Fries, R. & Sturgeon, D. (1982). A controlled trial of intervention in the families of schizophrenic patients. *British Journal of Psychiatry,* **141,** 121–34.

Leff, J. & Vaughn, C. (1980). The interaction of life events and relatives' expressed emotion in schizophrenia and depressive neurosis. *British Journal of Psychiatry,* **136,** 146–53.

Leff, J. & Vaughn, C. (1985). *Expressed Emotion in Families.* New York: Guilford.

Leff, J., Berkowitz, R., Shavit, A., Strachan, A., Glass, I. & Vaughn, C. (1989). A trial of family therapy versus a relatives' group for schizophrenia. *British Journal of Psychiatry,* **154,** 58–66.

Leff, J., Berkowitz, R., Shavit, N., Strachan, A., Glass, I. & Vaughn, C. (1990). A trial of family therapy versus a relatives' group for schizophrenia: two-year follow-up. *British Journal of Psychiatry,* **157,** 571–7.

Leff, J., Kuipers, L., Berkowitz, R. & Sturgeon, D. (1985). A controlled trial of social intervention in the families of schizophrenic patients: two-year follow-up. *British Journal of Psychiatry,* **146,** 594–600.

Leff, J., Wig, N.N., Ghosh, A., Bedi, H., Menon, D.K., Kuipers, L., Korten, A., Ernberg, G., Day, R., Sartorius, N. & Jablensky, A. (1987). Influence of relatives' expressed emotion in the course of schizophrenia in Chandigarh. *British Journal of Psychiatry,* **161,** 445–50.

Lehman, D.R., Davis, C.G., DeLongis, A., Wortman, C.B., Bluck, S., Mandel, D.R. & Ellard, J.H. (1993). Positive and negative life changes following bereavement and their relations to adjustment. *Journal of Social and Clinical Psychology,* **12,** 90–112.

Lehman, D.R., Ellard, J.H. & Wortman, C.B. (1986). Social support for the bereaved: recipients' and providers' perspectives on what is helpful. *Journal of Consulting and Clinical Psychology,* **54,** 438–46.

Leichty, G. & Applegate, J.L. (1991). Social-cognitive and situational influences on the use of face-saving persuasive strategies. *Human Communication Research,* **17,** 451–84.

Leigh, G.K. (1982). Kinship interaction over the family life span. *Journal of Marriage and the Family,* **44,** 197–208.

Leik, R.K. & Leik, S.K. (1976). Transition to interpersonal commitment. In R.L. Hamblin & J.H. Kenkel (Eds), *Behavioral Theory in Sociology* (pp. 299–322). New Brunswick, NJ: Transaction.

Lenington, S. (1981). Child abuse: the limits of sociobiology. *Ethology and Sociobiology*, **2**, 17–29.

Lennon, M.C. & Rosenfield, S. (1994). Relative fairness and the division of housework: the importance of options. *American Journal of Sociology*, **100**, 506–31.

Leonard, J.L. (1989). *Homo sapiens*: a good fit to theory, but posing some enigmas. *Behavioral and Brain Sciences*, **12**, 26–7.

Lepore, S.J., Evans, G.W. & Schneider, M.L. (1991). Dynamic role of social support in the link between chronic stress and psychological distress. *Journal of Personality and Social Psychology*, **61**, 899–909.

Leppin, A. & Schwarzer, R. (1991). Social support and physical health: an updated meta-analysis. In L.R. Schmidt, P. Schwenkmezger, J. Weinman & S. Maes (Eds), *Health Psychology: Theoretical and Applied Aspects* (pp. 185–202). London: Harwood.

Lerner, R.M. (1991). Changing organism–context relations as a basic process of development: a developmental contextual perspective, *Developmental Psychology*, **27**, 27–32.

Leslie, L.A. (1983). Parental influences and premarital relationship development (doctoral dissertation, Pennsylvania State University, 1982). *Dissertation Abstracts International*, **43**, 277A.

Leslie, L.A., Huston, T.L. & Johnson, M.P. (1986). Parental reactions to dating relationships: do they make a difference? *Journal of Marriage and the Family*, **48**, 57–66.

Leung, K. (1987). Some determinants of reactions to procedural models for conflict resolution: a cross-national study. *Journal of Personality and Social Psychology*, **53**(5), 898–908.

LeVay, S. (1993). *The Sexual Brain*. Cambridge, MA: MIT Press.

Levenson, R.W., Carstensen, L.L. & Gottman, J.M. (1994). The influence of age and gender on affect, physiology, and their interrelations: a study of long-term relationships. *Journal of Personality and Social Psychology*, **67**, 56–68.

Leventhal, H., Prohaska, T.R. & Hirschman, R.S. (1985). Preventive health behavior across the life span. In J.C. Rosen & L.J. Solomon (Eds), *Prevention in Health Psychology* (pp. 191–235). Hanover, NH: University Press of New England.

Levi, C. (1947). *Christ Stopped at Eboli*. New York: Times Books.

Levinger, G. (1965). Marital cohesiveness and dissolution: an integrative review. *Journal of Marriage and the Family*, **27**, 19–28.

Levinger, G. (1979). A social exchange view of the dissolution of pair relationships. In R.L. Burgess & T.L. Huston (Eds), *Social Exchange in Developing Relationships* (pp. 169–93). New York: Academic Press.

Levinger, G. (1980). Towards the analysis of close relationships. *Journal of Experimental Social Psychology*, **16**, 510–44.

Levinger, G. (1991). Commitment vs. cohesiveness: two complementary perspectives. In W.H. Jones & D.W. Perlman (Eds), *Advances in Personal Relationships*, Vol. 3 (pp. 145–50). London: Jessica Kingsley.

Levinger, G. & Pietromonaco, P. (1989). A measure of perceived conflict resolution styles in relationships. Unpublished manuscript. University of Massachusetts.

Levinger, G. & Rands, M. (1985). Compatibility in marriage and other close relationships. In W. Ickes (Ed.), *Compatible and Incompatible Relationships* (pp. 309–31). New York: Springer.

Levinger, G. & Snoek, D.J. (1972). *Attraction in Relationship: a New Look at Interpersonal Attraction*. Morristown, NJ: General Learning Press.

Levitt, M.J., Coffman, S. Guacci-Franco, N. & Loveless, S.C. (1994). Attachment relationships and life transitions: an expectancy model. In M.B. Sperling & W.H. Berman (Eds), *Attachment in Adults: Clinical and Developmental Perspectives* (pp. 232–55). New York: Guilford.

Lewin, K. (1936). *Principles of Topological Psychology*. New York: McGraw-Hill.

Lewis, H.B. (1971). *Shame and Guilt in Neurosis*. New York: International Universities Press.

Lewis, M. (1991a). Self-conscious emotions and the development of self. In T. Shapiro & R.N. Emde (Eds), New perspectives on affect and emotion in psychoanalysis. *Journal of the American Psychoanalytic Association (Suppl.)*, **39**, 45–73.

Lewis, M. (1991b). Ways of knowing: objective self-awareness or consciousness. *Developmental Review*, **11**, 231–43.

Lewis, M. (1995). Embarrassment: the emotion of self-exposure and evaluation. In J. Tangney & K. Fischer (Eds), *Self-conscious Emotions* (pp. 198–218). New York: Guilford.

Lewis, M., Alessandri, S. & Sullivan, M. (1992). Differences in shame and pride as a function of children's gender and task difficulty. *Child Development*, **63**, 630–38.

Lewis, M., Sullivan, M., Stanger, C. & Weiss, M. (1989). Self-development and self-conscious emotions. *Child Development*, **60**, 146–56.

Lewis, R.A. (1973). Social reaction and the formation of dyads: an interactionist approach to mate selection. *Sociometry*, **36**, 409–18.

Li, X. (1985). The effects of family on the mental health of the Chinese people. In W.S. Tseng & D.Y.H. Wu (Eds), *Chinese Culture and Mental Health* (pp. 85–93). Orlando: Academic Press.

Libby, R.W. (1977). Extramarital and comarital sex: a critique of the literature. In R.W. Libby & R.N. Whitehurst (Eds), *Marriage and Alternatives: Exploring Intimate Relationships*. Glenview: Scott, Foresman.

Lichtenberg, J.W. & Knox, P.L. (1991). Order out of chaos: a structural analysis of group therapy. *Journal of Counseling Psychology*, **38**, 279–88.

Lidz, T., Cornelison, A., Terry, D. & Fleck, S. (1958). Intrafamilial environment of the schizophrenic patient. VI. The transmission of irrationality. *Archives of Neurology and Psychiatry*, **79**, 305–16.

Lieberman, M.A. (1986). Social supports—the consequences of psychologizing: a commentary. *Journal of Consulting and Clinical Psychology*, **54**, 461–5.

Lieberman, M.A. & Kramer, J.H. (1991). Factors affecting decisions to institutionalize demented elderly. *The Gerontologist*, **31**, 371–4.

Liebowitz, M. (1983). *The Chemistry of Love*. New York: Berkeley Books.

Liebrand, W.B.G. & Van Run, G.J. (1985). The effects of social motives on behavior in social dilemmas in two cultures. *Journal of Experimental Social Psychology*, **21**, 86–102.

Lifton, R. & Olson, E. (1976). The human meaning of total disaster: the Buffalo Creek experience. *Psychiatry*, **39**, 1–18.

Lightfoot, S.L. (1978). *Worlds Apart: Relationships Between Families and Schools*. New York: Basic Books.

Lim, T.S. (1990). Politeness behavior in social influence situations. In J.P. Dillard (Ed.), *Seeking Compliance: the Production of Interpersonal Influence Messages* (pp. 75–86). Scottsdale, AZ: Gorsuch Scarisbrick.

Lim, T.S. (1994). Facework and interpersonal relationships. In S. Ting-Toomey (Ed.), *The Challenge of Facework: Cross-cultural and Interpersonal Issues* (pp. 209–30). Albany: State University of New York Press.

Lim, T.S. & Bowers, J.W. (1991). Facework: solidarity, approbation, and tact. *Human Communication Research*, **17**, 415–50.

Limandri, B. (1989). Disclosure of stigmatizing conditions: the discloser's perspective. *Archives of Psychiatric Nursing*, **III**, 69–78.

Lin, C.Y.C. & Fu, V.R. (1990). A comparison of child-rearing practices among Chinese, immigrant Chinese, and Caucasian-American parents. *Child Development*, **61**, 429–33.

Lin, R.C. (1986). A project for facilitating maternal adaptation with Chinese adolescent mothers in Taiwan. *Health Care for Women International*, **7**, 311–27.

Lin, Y.-H.W. & Rusbult, C.E. (1995). Commitment to dating relationships and cross-sex friendships in America and China. *Journal of Social and Personal Relationships*, **12**, 7–26.

Lind, E.A. & Tyler, T.R. (1988). *The Social Psychology of Procedural Justice.* New York: Plenum.

Lindemann, E. (1942). Symptomology and management of acute grief. *American Journal of Psychiatry,* **101,** 141–8.

Linden, R. (1993). *Making Stories, Making Selves: Feminist Reflections on the Holocaust.* Columbus, OH: Ohio State University Press.

Lindsay-Hartz, J., De Rivera, J. & Mascolo, M.F. (1995). Differentiating guilt and shame and their effects on motivation. In J. Tangney & K. Fischer (Eds), *Self-conscious Emotions* (pp. 274–300). New York: Guilford.

Lindy, J. & Grace, M. (1986). The recovery environment: continuing stressor versus a healing psychosocial space. In B. Sowder & M. Lystad (Eds), *Disasters and Mental Health* (pp. 147–60). Washington, DC: American Psychiatric Press.

Littlefield, C.H. & Rushton, J.P. (1986). When a child dies: the sociobiology of bereavement. *Journal of Personality and Social Psychology,* **51,** 797–802.

Littrell, D.W. & Hobbs, D. (1989). The self-help approach. In J.A. Christenson & J.W. Robinson Jr (Eds), *Community Development in Perspective* (pp. 48–68). Ames: Iowa State University Press.

Litwak, E. (1960). Geographic mobility and extended family cohesion. *American Sociological Review,* **25,** 9–21.

Livingston, K.R. (1980). Love as a process of reducing uncertainty—cognitive theory. In K.S. Pope (Ed.), *On Love and Loving* (pp. 133–51). San Francisco: Jossey-Bass.

Livingstone, M. & Hubel, D. (1988). Segregation of form, color, movement, and depth: Anatomy, physiology, and perception. *Science,* **240,** 740–49.

Lloyd, S.A. (1987). Conflict in premarital relationships: differential perceptions of males and females. *Family Relations,* **36,** 290–94.

Lloyd, S.A. & Cate, R.M. (1985). The developmental course of conflict in dissolution of premarital relationships. *Journal of Social and Personal Relationships,* **2,** 179–94.

Lloyd, S.A. & Emery, B.C. (1994). Physically aggressive conflict in romantic relationships. In D.D. Cahn (Ed.), *Conflict in Personal Relationships* (pp. 27–46). Hillsdale, NJ: Erlbaum.

Lockard, J.S. & Paulhus, D.L. (1988). *Self-deception: an Adaptive Mechanism?* Englewood Cliffs, NJ: Prentice-Hall.

Locke, H.J. (1951). *Predicting Adjustment in Marriage.* New York: Holt.

Locke, H.J. & Wallace, K.M. (1959). Short marital adjustment and prediction tests: their reliability and validity. *Marriage and Family Living,* **21,** 251–5.

Lofland, L.H. (1982). Loss and human connection: an exploration into the nature of the social bond. In W. Ickes & E.S. Knowles (Eds), *Personality, Roles, and Social Behavior* (pp. 219–42). New York: Springer-Verlag.

Lollis, S.P., Ross, H.S. & Tate, E. (1992). Parents regulation of children's peer interactions: direct influences. In R. Parke & G. Ladd (Eds), *Family–Peer Relationships: Modes of Linkage* (pp. 255–81). Hillsdale, NJ: Erlbaum.

Londerville, S. & Main, M. (1981). Security of attachment, compliance, and maternal training methods in the second year of life. *Developmental Psychology,* **17,** 289–99.

Long, N., Forehand, R., Fauber, R. & Brody, G.H. (1987). Self-perceived and independently observed competence of young adolescents as a function of parental marital conflict an recent divorce. *Journal of Abnormal Child Psychology,* **15,** 15–27.

Lopez, F.G., Campbell, V.L. & Watkins, C.E. Jr (1986). Depression, psychological separation, and college adjustment: an investigation of sex differences. *Journal of Counseling Psychology,* **33,** 52–6.

Lopez, F.G., Campbell, V.L. & Watkins, C.E. Jr (1989). Effects of marital conflict and family coalition patterns on college student adjustment. *Journal of College Student Development,* **30,** 46–52.

Lord, C.G. (1980). Schemas and images as memory aids: two modes of processing social information. *Journal of Personality and Social Psychology,* **38,** 257–69.

Lord, C.G. (1987). Imagining self and others: reply to Brown, Keenan, and Potts. *Journal of Personality and Social Psychology*, **53**, 445–50.

Lord, S.E., Eccles, J.S. & McCarthy, K.A. (1994). Surviving the junior high school transition: family processes and self-perceptions as protective and risk factors. *Journal of Early Adolescence*, **14**(2), 162–99.

Lorenz, K. (1970). *Studies in Animal and Human Behavior*. Cambridge, MA: Harvard University Press.

Lu, L. (1994). University transition: major and minor life stressors, personality characteristics and mental health. *Psychological Medicine*, **24**, 81–7.

Luborsky, L. (1984). *Principles of Psychoanalytic Psychotherapy: a Manual for Supportive-expressive Treatment*. New York: Basic Books.

Luborsky, L. & Crits-Christoph, P. (Eds) (1990). *Understanding Transference: the Core Conflictual Relationship Theme Method*. New York: Basic Books.

Luborsky, L., Barber, J.P. & Diguer, L. (1992). The meanings of narratives told during psychotherapy: the fruits of a new observational unit. *Psychotherapy Research*, **2**, 277–90.

Lumsden, C.J. & Wilson, E.O. (1981). *Genes, Mind, and Culture: the Coevolutionary Process*. Cambridge, MA: Harvard University Press.

Lundberg, G.A. & Dickson, L. (1952). Selective association among ethnic groups in a high school population. *American Sociological Review*, **17**, 23–35.

Lykes, M.B. (1985). Gender and individualistic vs. collectivist bases for notions about the self. *Journal of Personality*, **53**, 356–83.

Lynch, J.J. (1977). *The Broken Heart: the Medical Consequences of Loneliness*. New York: Basic Books.

Lyons, R.F. & Meade, D. (1995). Painting a new face on relationships: relationship remodelling in response to chronic illness. In S.W. Duck & J.T. Wood (Eds), *Confronting Relationship Challenges [Understanding Relationship Processes 5]* (pp. 181–210). Thousand Oaks, CA: Sage.

Lyons-Ruth, K. (1992). Maternal depressive symptoms, disorganized infant–mother relationships, and hostile-aggressive behavior in the preschool classroom: a prospective longitudinal view from infancy to age five. In D. Cicchetti & S. Toth (Eds), *Developmental Perspectives on Depression*. Rochester, NY: University of Rochester Press.

Lyotard, J. (1984). *The Postmodern Condition: A Report on Knowledge*. Minneapolis: University of Minnesota Press.

Maccoby, E. (1988). Gender as a social category. *Developmental Psychology*, **24**, 755–65.

Maccoby, E. (1990). Gender and relationships. *American Psychologist*, **45**, 513–20.

Maccoby, E. & Martin, J. (1983). Socialization in the context of the family: parent–child interaction. In P. Mussen (Ed.), *Handbook of Child Psychology: Vol. 4, Socialization, personality, and social development* (pp. 1–102).

MacDonald, K. (1987). Parent–child physical play with rejected, neglected and popular boys. *Developmental Psychology*, **23**, 705–11.

MacDonald, K. & Parke, R.D. (1984). Bridging the gap: parent–child play interaction and peer interactive competence. *Child Development*, **55**, 1265–77.

MacFarlane, A. (1975). Olfaction in the development of social preferences in the human neonate. In *Parent–Infant Interaction* (CIBA foundation Symposium No. 33). Amsterdam: Elsevier.

MacFarlane, I. & Krebs, S. (1986). Techniques for interviewing and evidence gathering. In K. MacFarlane & J. Waterman (Eds), *Sexual Abuse of Young Children* (pp. 67–100). New York: Guilford.

MacKenzie, K.R. & Livesley, W.I. (1983). A developmental model for brief group therapy. In R.R. Dies & K.R. MacKenzie (Eds), *Advances in Group Psychotherapy: Integrating Research and Practice* (pp. 101–16). Madison, CT: International Universities Press.

MacKinnon, C.E. (1989). An observational investigation of sibling interaction in married and divorced families. *Developmental Psychology*, **25**, 36–44.

MacKinnon-Lewis, J., Volving, B.L., Lamb, M.E., Dechman, K., Rabiner, D. & Curtner, M.E. (1994). A cross-contextual analysis of boys' social competence: from family to school. *Developmental Psychology*, **30**, 325–33.

MacLean, P.D. (1990). *The Triune Brain in Evolution: Role in Paleocerebral Functions*. New York: Plenum.

Magaña, A.B., Goldstein, M.J., Karno, M., Miklowitz, D.J., Jenkins, J. & Falloon, I.R.H. (1986). A brief method for assessing expressed emotion in relatives of psychiatric patients. *Psychiatry Research*, **17**, 203–12.

Mahler, M.S. (1958). Autism and symbiosis: two extreme disturbances of identity. *International Journal of Psychoanalysis*, **39**, 77–83.

Mahler, M.S. (1968). *On Human Symbiosis and the Vicissitudes of Individuation*. New York: International Universities Press.

Mahoney, J. & Heretick, D.M.L. (1979). Factor-specific dimensions in person perception for same- and opposite-sex friendship dyads. *The Journal of Social Psychology*, **107**, 219–25.

Main, M. & Goldwyn, R. (in preparation). Adult attachment classification system. In M. Main (Ed.), *A Typology of Human Attachment Organization: Assessed in Discourse, Drawing, and Interviews*. Cambridge: Cambridge University Press.

Main, M., Kaplan, N. & Cassidy, J. (1985). Security in infancy, childhood and adulthood: a move to the level of representation. In I. Bretherton & E. Waters (Eds), *Growing Points of Attachment Theory and Research*. Monographs of the Society for Research in Child Development. Serial No. 209, Vol. 50, Nos. 1–2, pp. 66–104.

Maines, D. (1993). Narrative's moment and sociology's phenomena: toward a narrative sociology. *The Sociological Quarterly*, **34**, 17–38.

Mairs, N. (1989). *Remembering the Bone House: An Erotics of Place and Space*. New York: Harper and Row.

Malamed, B.G. & Brenner, G.F. (1990). Social support and chronic medical stress: an interaction-based approach. *Journal of Social and Clinical Psychology*, **9**, 104–17.

Malatesta, C.Z. & Haviland, J. (1982). Learning display rules: the socialization of emotion expression in infancy. *Child Development*, **53**, 991–1003.

Malley, J. (1989). The balance of agency and communion: adjustmemt and adaptation. *Dissertation Abstracts International*, **50**, 2-B.

Mallinckrodt, B. (1989). Social support and the effectiveness of group therapy. *Journal of Counseling Psychology*, **36**, 170–5.

Mallinckrodt, B. (1991). Clients' representations of childhood emotional bonds with parents and formation of the working alliance. *Journal of Counseling Psychology*, **38**, 401–8.

Mallinckrodt, B. (1992). Childhood emotional bonds with parents, development of adult social competencies, and the availability of social support. *Journal of Counseling Psychology*, **39**, 453–61.

Mallinckrodt, B. (in press). Change in social support, working alliance, and psychological symptoms in brief therapy. *Journal of Counseling Psychology*.

Mallinckrodt, B. & Nelson, M.L. (1991). Counselor training level and the formation of the psychotherapeutic working alliance. *Journal of Counseling Psychology*, **38**, 133–8.

Mallinckrodt, B., Coble, H.M. & Gantt, D.L. (1995a). Working alliance, attachment memories, and social competencies of women in brief therapy. *Journal of Counseling Psychology*, **42**, 79–84.

Mallinckrodt, B., Coble, H.M. & Gantt, D.L. (1995b). Toward differentiating client attachment from working alliance and transference. *Journal of Counseling Psychology*, **42**, 320–22.

Mallinckrodt, B., Gantt, D.L. & Coble, H.M. (1995). Attachment patterns in the psychotherapy relationship: development of the Client Attachment to Therapist Scale. *Journal of Counseling Psychology*, **42**, 307–17.

Mallinckrodt, B., McCreary, B.A. & Robertson, A.K. (1995). Co-occurrence of eating disorders and incest: the role of attachment, family environment, and social competencies. *Journal of Counseling Psychology*, **42**, 178–86.

Malone, J.W. (1980). *Straight Women/Gay Men*. New York: Dial Press.

Mancini, J.A. & Blieszner, R. (1989). Aging parents and aging children: research themes in intergenerational relations. *Journal of Marriage and the Family*, **51**, 275–90.

Mandler, G. (1975). *Mind and Emotion*. New York: Wiley.

Manne, S. & Zautra, A.J. (1989). Spouse criticism and support: their association with coping and psychological adjustment among women with rheumatoid arthritis. *Journal of Personality and Social Psychology*, **56**, 608–17.

Mao, T. (1965). *On Contradiction*. Beijing: Foreign Languages Press.

Maret, E. & Finlay, B. (1984). The distribution of household labor among women in dual-earner families. *Journal of Marriage and the Family*, **46**, 357–64.

Margolin, G. (1988). Marital conflict is not marital conflict is not marital conflict. In R. De V. Peters et al. (Eds), *Social Learning and Systems Approaches to Marriage and the Family* (pp. 193–216). New York: Brunner/Mazel.

Margolin, G. & Wampold, B.E. (1981). Sequential analysis of conflict and accord in distressed and nondistressed marital partners. *Journal of Consulting and Clinical Psychology*, **49**, 554–67.

Margolin, G., Burman, B. & John, R.S. (1989). Home observations of married couples reenacting naturalistic conflicts. *Behavioral Assessment*, **11**, 101–18.

Margolin, G., John, R.S. & Gleberman, L. (1988). Affective responses to conflictual discussions in violent and nonviolent couples. *Journal of Consulting and Clinical Psychology*, **56**, 24–33.

Margulis, L. & Sagan, D. (1991). *Mystery Dance: On the Evolution of Sexuality*. New York: Summit Books.

Marin, G., Sabogal, F., Marin, B.V., Otero-Sabogal, R. & Perez-Stable, E.J. (1987). Development of a short acculturation scale for Hispanics. *Hispanic Journal of Behavioral Sciences*, **9**(2), 183–205.

Markman, H. (1994). Erosion theory: predicting and preventing decay in couples' satisfaction and divorce. Paper presented at conference on intimate relationships at Iowa State, Ames, Iowa, September 29, 1994.

Markman, H.J. (1991). Constructive conflict is NOT an oxymoron. *Behavioral assessment*, **13**, 83–96.

Markman, H.J. & Halweg, K. (1993). The prediction and prevention of marital distress: an international perspective. *Clinical Psychology Review*, **13**, 29–43.

Markman, H.J. & Kraft, S.A. (1989). Men and women in marriage: dealing with gender differences in marital therapy. *The Behavior Therapist*, **12**, 51–6.

Markman, H.J., Floyd, F.J., Stanley, S.M. & Jamieson, K. (1984). A cognitive-behavioral program for the prevention of marital and family distress: issues in program development and delivery. In K. Halweg & N.S. Jacobson (Eds), *Marital Interaction* (pp. 396–428). New York: Guilford Press.

Markman, H.J., Renick, M.J., Floyd, F.J. & Stanley, S.M. (1993). Preventing marital distress through communication and conflict management training: a 4- and 5-year follow up. *Journal of Clinical and Consulting*, **61**, 70–77.

Marks, G., Bundek, N., Richardson, J., Ruiz, M., Maldonado, N. & Mason, J. (1992). Self-disclosure of HIV infection: preliminary results from a sample of Hispanic men. *Health Psychology*, **11**, 300–6.

Marks, S.R. (1987). Critique of Burr et al: an epistemological basis for primary explanations in family science. Paper presented at the Theory and Methods Workshop at the annual meetings of the National Council on Family Relations, Atlanta, GA.

Marks, S.R. (1994). Studying workplace intimacy: havens at work. In D.L. Sollie & L.A.

Leslie (Eds), *Gender, Families, and Close Relationships: Feminist Research Journeys* (pp. 145–67). Thousand Oaks, CA: Sage.

Markus, H.R. (1977). Self-schemata and processing information about the self. *Journal of Personality and Social Psychology*, **35**, 63–78.

Markus, H.R. & Kitayama, S. (1994). The cultural construction of self and emotion: implications for social behavior. In S. Kitayama & H.R. Markus (Eds), *Emotion and Culture* (pp. 89–127).

Marsden, P. (1990). Network data and measurement. *Annual Review of Sociology*, **16**, 435–63.

Marshall, G. (1990). *In Praise of Sociology*. London: Unwin-Hyman.

Marshall, V.W., Matthews, S.H. & Rosenthal, C.J. (1993). Elusiveness of family life: a challenge for the sociology of aging. In G.L. Maddox & M.P. Lawton (Eds), *Annual Review of Gerontology and Geriatrics*, **13** (pp. 39–72). New York: Springer.

Martin, P., Poon, L.W., Clayton, G.M., Lee, H.S., Fulks, J.S. & Johnson, M.A. (1992). Personality, life events and coping in the oldest-old. *International Journal of Aging and Human Development*, **34**, 19–30.

Martin, R., Davis, G.M., Baron, R.S., Suls, J. & Blanchard, E. (1994). Specificity in social support: perceptions of helpful and unhelpful provider behaviors among irritable bowel syndrome, headache, and cancer patients. *Health Psychology*, **13**, 432–9.

Marvin, R.S. (1977). An ethological-cognitive model for attenuation of mother–child attachment behavior. In T.M. Alloway, L. Kramer & P. Pliner (Eds), *Advances in the Study of Communication and Affect, Vol. 3: The Development of Social Attachments* (pp. 25–60). New York: Plenum.

Maryanski, A. & Ishii-Kuntz, M. (1991). A cross-species application of Bott's hypothesis on role segregation and social networks. *Sociological Perspectives*, **34**, 403–25.

Mascolo, M.F. & Fischer, K.W. (1995). Developmental transformations in appraisals for pride, shame, and guilt. In J.P. Tangney & K.W. Fischer (Eds), *Self-conscious Emotions* (pp. 64–113). New York: Guilford.

Masheter, C. (1991). Postdivorce relationships between ex-spouses: the roles of attachment and interpersonal conflict. *Journal of Marriage and the Family*, **53**, 103–10.

Masheter, C. (1994). Dialogues between ex-spouses: evidence of dialectic relationship development. In R. Conville (Ed.), *Structure in Communication Study* (pp. 83–102). New York: Praeger.

Masheter, C. & Harris, L. (1986). From divorce to friendship: a study of dialectic relationship development. *Journal of Social and Personal Relationships*, **3**, 177–90.

Maslow, A.H. (1967). A theory of metamotivation: the biological rooting of the value-life. *Journal of Humanistic Psychology*, **7**, 93–127.

Maslow, A.H. (1968). *Toward a Psychology of Being* (2nd Edn). New York: Van Nostrand.

Massie, H.N. & Beels, C.C. (1972). The outcome and family treatment of schizophrenia. *Schizophrenia Bulletin*, **1** (Experimental Issue No. 6), 24–36.

Matas, L., Arend, R. & Sroufe, L.A. (1978). Continuity and adaptation in the second year: the relationship between quality of attachment and later competence. *Child Development*, **49**, 547–56.

Mather, L. & Yngvesson, B. (1981). Language, audience, and the transformation of disputes. *Law & Society Review*, **15**, 775–821.

Matsumoto, D., Haan, N., Yarbrove, G., Theodorou, P. & Carney, C.C. (1986). Preschoolers' moral actions and emotions in Prisoners' Dilemma. *Developmental Psychology*, **22**, 663–70.

Matthews, S.H. (1986). *Friendships Through the Life Course*. Beverly Hills: Sage.

Matthews, S.H. & Sprey, J. (1989). Older family systems: intra- and intergenerational relations. In J.A. Mancini (Ed.), *Aging Parents and Adult Children* (pp. 63–78). Lexington, MA: Lexington Books.

Maturana, H. (1991). Science and daily life: the ontology of scientific explanations. In F. Steier (Ed.), *Research and Reflexivity* (pp. 30–52). London: Sage.

May, R. (1973). *Love and Will*. New York: Delta.

Mayes, L.C. & Carter, A.S. (1990). Emerging social regulatory capacities as seen in the still-face situation. *Child Development*, **61**, 754–63.

Mayfield-Brown, L. (1989). Family status of low-income adolescent mothers. *Journal of Adolescent Research*, **4**(2), 202–13.

Maynard, D.W. & Zimmerman, D.H. (1984). Topical talk, ritual and the social organization of relationships. *Social Psychology Quarterly*, **47**, 301–16.

Mazanec, M.J. (1995, November). Border work by gays, lesbians, and bisexuals: Coming out on the borders of experience. Paper presented at the Speech Communication Association Convention, San Antonio.

McCabe, A. (Ed.) (1993). *Journal of Narrative and Life History*. Hillsdale, NJ: Erlbaum.

McCall, G.J. (1974). A symbolic interactionist approach to attraction. In T.L. Huston (Ed.), *Foundations of Interpersonal Attraction* (pp. 217–31). New York: Academic Press.

McCall, G.J. (1982). Becoming unrelated: the management of bond dissolution. In S.W. Duck (Ed.), *Personal Relationships 4: Dissolving Personal Relationships* (pp. 211–31). London: Academic.

McCall, G.J. (1988). The organizational life cycle of relationships. In S.W. Duck, D.F. Hay, S.E. Hobfoll, W.J. Ickes & B.M. Montgomery (Eds), *Handbook of Personal Relationships* (1st Edn, pp. 467–86). Chichester: Wiley.

McCall, G.J. & Simmons, J.L. (1991). Levels of analysis: the individual, the dyad, and the larger social group. In B.M. Montgomery & S. Duck (Eds), *Studying Interpersonal Interaction* (pp. 56–81). New York: Guilford.

McClelland, K.E. & Auster, C.J. (1990). Public platitudes and hidden tensions: racial climates at predominantly White liberal arts colleges. *Journal of Higher Education*, **61**, 607–42.

McClintock, C.G. & Liebrand, W.B.G. (1988). The role of interdependence structure, individual value orientation and other's strategy in social decision making: a transformational analysis. *Journal of Personality and Social Psychology*, **55**, 396–409.

McCoy, J.K., Brody, G.H. & Stoneman, Z. (1994). A longitudinal analysis of sibling relationships as mediators of the link between family processes and youths' best friendships. *Family Relations*, **43**, 400–8.

McCrae, R.R. & Costa, P.T. Jr (1987). Validation of the five-factor model of personality across instruments and observers. *Journal of Personality and Social Psychology*, **52**, 81–90.

McDonald, G.W. (1981). Structural exchange and marital interaction. *Journal of Marriage and the Family*, **43**, 825–39.

McDougall, W. (1908). *Social Psychology: an Introduction*. London: Methuen.

McFarlane, A. (1987). Family functioning and overprotection following a natural disaster: the longitudinal effects of post-traumatic morbidity. *Australian and New Zealand Journal of Psychiatry*, **21**, 210–18.

McFarlane, W.R., Link, B., Dushay, R., Marchal, J. & Crilly, J. (1995a). Psychoeducational multiple family groups: four-year relapse outcome in schizophrenia. *Family Process*, **34**, 127–44.

McFarlane, W.R., Lukens, E., Link, B., Dushay, R., Deakins, S.A., Newmark, M., Dunne, E.J., Horen, B. & Toran, J. (1995b). Multiple family groups and psychoeducation in the treatment of schizophrenia. *Archives of General Psychiatry*, **52**, 679–87.

McGhee, P. (1979). *Humor: Its Origin and Development*. San Francisco: WH Freeman.

McGoldrick, M. (1980). The joining of families through marriage: the new couple. In E.A. Carter & M. McGoldrick (Eds), *The Family Life Cycle* (pp. 93–120). New York: Gardner.

McGonagle, K.A., Kessler, R.C. & Gotlib, I.H. (1993). The effects of marital disagreement style, frequency, and outcome on marital disruption. *Journal of Social and Personal Relationships*, **10**, 385–404.

McHale, S.M. & Crouter, A.C. (1992). You can't always get what you want: incongruence between sex-role attitudes and family work roles and its implications for marriage. *Journal of Marriage and the Family*, **54**, 537–47.

McHale, S.M. & Crouter, A.C. (in press). The family contexts of children's sibling relationships. Chapter to appear in G. Brody (Ed.), *Sibling Relationships: their Causes and Consequences*. Norwood, NJ: Ablex.

McHale, S.M. & Huston, T.L. (1985). The effect of the transition to parenthood on the marriage relationship. *Journal of Family Issues*, **6**, 409–33.

McIntyre, A. (1981). *After Virtue: a Study in Moral Theory*. London: Duckworth.

McKenna, C. (1989). Marital satisfaction and sensation seeking in the first ten years of marriage: self-expansion versus boredom. Doctoral dissertation, California Graduate School of Family Psychology, San Francisco, CA.

McLanahan, S. & Bumpass, L. (1988). Intergenerational consequences of family disruption. *American Journal of Sociology*, **94**, 130–52.

McLaughlin, M.L., Cody, M.J. & O'Hair, H.D. (1983). The management of failure events: some contextual determinants of accounting behavior. *Human Communication Research*, **9**, 208–24.

McNamee, S. (1988). Accepting research as social intervention: implications of a systematic epistemology. *Communication Quarterly*, **36**, 50–68.

McNeal, J. & Aron, A. (1995, June). Exciting activities and relationship satisfaction: a comparison of married and dating couples. Paper presented at the International Network Conference on Personal Relationships, Williamsburg, VA.

McNulty, S.E. & Swann, W.B. Jr (1994). Identity negotiation in roommate relationships: the self as architect and consequence of social reality. *Journal of Personality and Social Psychology*, **67**, 1012–23.

Mead, G.H. (1934). *Mind, Self, and Society*. Chicago: Cambridge University Press.

Mealey, L. (1995). The sociobiology of psychopathy. *Behavioral and Brain Sciences*, **18**, 523–41.

Mechanic, D. (1974). Social structure and personal adaptation: some neglected dimensions. In G.V. Coelho, D.A. Hamburg & J.E. Adams (Eds), *Coping and Adaptation* (pp. 32–44). New York: Basic Books.

Mechanic, D. & Hansell, S. (1989). Divorce, family conflict, and adolescents' well-being. *Journal of Health and Social Behavior*, **30**, 105–16.

Meehl, P.E. (1962). Schizotaxia, schizotypy, schizophrenia. *American Psychologist*, **17**, 827–38.

Meissner, M., Humphreys, E.W., Meis, S.M. & Scheu, W.J. (1975). No exit for wives: sexual division of labour and the cumulation of household demands. *Canadian Review of Sociology and Anthropology*, **12**, 424–39.

Mellen, S.L.W. (1981). *The Evolution of Love*. Oxford: W.H. Freeman.

Mendelson, M.J. & Aboud, F.E. (1991, April). Kindergartners' personality, popularity, and relationships. Poster presented at the biennial meeting of the Society for Research in Child Development, Seattle, Washington.

Mendoza, J.L. & Graziano, W.G. (1982). The statistical analysis of dyadic social behavior: a multivariate approach. *Psychological Bulletin*, **92**, 532–40.

Mendoza, R.H. (1984). Acculturation and sociocultural variability. In J.R. Martinez Jr & R.H. Mendoza (Eds), *Chicano Psychology* (pp. 61–75). Orlando, FL: Academic Press.

Mendoza, R.H. & Martinez, J.L. (1981). The measurement of acculturation. In A. Baron Jr (Ed.), *Explorations in Chicano psychology*. New York: Holt.

Merleau-Ponty, M. (1945). *Phenomenologie de la Perception*. Paris: Gallimard.

Messick, D.M. & McClintock, C.G. (1968). Motivational bases of choice in experimental games. *Journal of Experimental Social Psychology*, **4**, 1–25.

Messner, M.A. (1992). Like family: power, intimacy, and sexuality in male athletes' friendships. In P. Nardi (Ed.), *Men's Friendships* (pp. 215–37). Newbury Park, CA: Sage.

Metts, S. (1992). The language of disengagement: a face-management perspective. In T.L. Orbuch (Ed.), *Close Relationship Loss* (pp. 111–27). New York: Springer-Verlag.

Metts, S. (1994). Relational transgressions. In B.R. Cupach & B.H. Spitzberg (Eds), *The Dark Side of Interpersonal Communication* (pp. 217–40). Hillsdale, NJ: Erlbaum.

Metts, S. & Cupach, W.R. (1989). Situational influence on the use of remedial strategies in embarrassing predicaments. *Communication Monographs*, **56**, 151–62.

Metts, S. & Mongeau, P. (1994, July). The management of critical events in continuing and noncontinuing relationships. Paper presented at the annual meeting of the Speech Communication Association, Atlanta, GA.

Metts, S., Backaus, S. & Kazoleas, D. (1995, February). Social support as problematic communication. Paper presented at the annual meeting of the Western States Speech Communication Association Convention, Portland, OR.

Metts, S., Cupach, W.R. & Bejlovec, R.A. (1989). "I love you too much to ever start liking you": redefining romantic relationships. *Journal of Social and Personal Relationships*, **6**, 259–74.

Miell, D.E. (1984). Cognitive and communicative strategies in developing relationships. Unpublished doctoral dissertation, University of Lancaster.

Miell, D.E. (1987). Remembering relationship development: constructing a context for interactions. In R. Burnett, P. McGhee & D. Clarke (Eds), *Accounting for Relationships* (pp. 60–73). London: Methuen.

Miell, D.E. & Duck, S.W. (1986). Strategies in developing friendships. In V.J. Derlega & B.A. Winstead (Eds), *Friends and Social Interaction* (pp. 129–43). New York: Springer.

Miklowitz, D.J. & Goldstein, M.J. (1990). Behavioral family treatment for patients with bipolar affective disorder. *Behavior Modification*, **14**, 457–89.

Miklowitz, D.J. & Stackman, D. (1992). Communication deviance in families of schizophrenic and other psychiatric patients: current state of the construct. In E.F. Walker, R.H. Dworkin & B.A. Cornblatt (Eds), *Progress in Experimental Personality and Psychopathology Research*, Vol. 15. New York: Springer.

Miklowitz, D.J., Goldstein, M.J. & Falloon, I.R.H. (1983). Premorbid and symptomatic characteristics of schizophrenics from families with high and low levels of expressed emotion. *Journal of Abnormal Psychology*, **92**, 359–67.

Miklowitz, D.J., Goldstein, M.J., Falloon, I.R.H. & Doane, J.A. (1984). Interactional correlates of expressed emotion in the families of schizophrenics. *British Journal of Psychiatry*, **144**, 482–7.

Miklowitz, D.J., Goldstein, M.J., Nuechterlein, K.H., Snyder, K.S. & Doane, J.A. (1987). The family and the course of recent onset mania. In K. Hahlweg & M.J. Goldstein (Eds), *Understanding Major Mental Disorder: the Role of Family Interaction Research*. New York: Family Process Press.

Miklowitz, D.J., Goldstein, M.J., Nuechterlein, K.H., Snyder, K.S. & Mintz, J. (1988). Family factors and the course of bipolar affective disorder. *Archives of General Psychiatry*, **45**, 225–31.

Miklowitz, D.J., Strachan, A.M., Goldstein, M.J., Doane, J.A. & Snyder, K.S. (1986). Expressed emotion and communication deviance in the families of schizophrenics. *Journal of Abnormal Psychology*, **95**, 60–66.

Miklowitz, D.J., Velligan, D.I., Goldstein, M.J., Nuechterlein, K.H. & Gitlin, M.J. (1991). Communication deviance in families of schizophrenic and manic patients. *Journal of Abnormal Psychology*, **100**, 163–73.

Mikula, G. (1983). Justice and fairness in interpersonal relations: thoughts and suggestions. In H. Tajfel (Ed.), *The Social Dimension* (pp. 204–27). Cambridge: Cambridge University Press.

Mikulincer, M. & Nachsohn, O. (1991). Attachment styles and patterns of self-disclosure. *Journal of Personality and Social Psychology*, **61**, 321–31.

Milardo, R.M. (1982). Friendship networks in developing relations: converging and diverging environments. *Social Psychology Quarterly*, **45**, 162–72.

Milardo, R.M. (1984). Theoretical and methodological issues in the identification of the social networks of spouses. *Journal of Marriage and the Family*, **51**, 165–74.

Milardo, R.M. (1986). Personal choice and social constraint in close relationships: applications of network analysis. In V.J. Derlega & B. Winstead (Eds), *Friendship and Social Interaction* (pp. 145–65). New York: Springer.

Milardo, R.M. (1987). Changes in social networks of women and men following divorce. *Journal of Family Issues*, **8**, 78–96.

Milardo, R.M. (1988). Families and social networks: an overview of theory and methodology. In R.M. Milardo (Ed.), *Families and Social Networks* (pp. 13–47). Newbury Park, CA: Sage.

Milardo, R.M. (1989). Theoretical and methodological issues in identifying the social networks of spouses. *Journal of Marriage and the Family*, **51**, 165–74.

Milardo, R.M. (1992). Comparative methods for delineating social networks. *Journal of Social and Personal Relationships*, **9**, 447–61.

Milardo, R.M. & Klein, R. (1992). Dominance norms and domestic violence: the justification of aggression in close relationships. Paper presented at the NCFR Preconference Workshop on Theory Construction and Research Methodology, Orlando, Flordia.

Milardo, R.M. & Lewis, R.A. (1985). Social networks, families, and mate selection: a transactional analysis. In L. L'Abate (Ed.), *Handbook of Family Psychology and Therapy*, Vol. 1 (pp. 258–83). Homewood, IL: Dorsey.

Milardo, R.M. & Wellman, B. (1992). The personal is social. *Journal of Social and Personal Relationships*, **9**, 339–42.

Milardo, R.M., Johnson, M.P. & Huston, T.L. (1983). Developing close relationships: changing patterns of interaction between pair members and social networks. *Journal of Personality and Social Psychology*, **44**, 964–76.

Milgram, N., Sarason, B., Schonpflug, U., Jackson, A. & Schwarzer, C. (1995). Catalyzing community support. In S.E. Hobfoll & M.W. de Vries (Eds), *Extreme Stress and Communities: Impact and Intervention* (pp. 473–88). Dordrecht: Kluwer.

Milgram, S. (1967). The small world problem. *Psychology Today*, **1**, 60–67.

Millar, F.E. & Rogers, L.E. (1988). Power dynamics in marital relationships. In P. Noller & M.A. Fitzpatrick (Eds), *Perspectives on Marital Interaction* (pp. 78–97). Clevedon: Multilingual Matters.

Miller, A.G. & Thomas, R. (1972). Cooperation and competition among Blackfoot Indian and Urban Canadian Children. *Child Development*, **43**, 1104–10.

Miller, G.A., Gallanter, E. & Pribram, K.H. (1960). *Plans and the Structure of Behavior*. New York: Holt, Rinehart, & Winston.

Miller, G.R. (1989). Paradigm dialogues: brief thoughts on an unexplored theme. In B. Dervin, L. Grossberg, B. O'Keefe & E. Wartella (Eds), *Rethinking Communication, Vol. 1: Paradigm Issues* (pp. 187–91). Newbury Park, CA: Sage.

Miller, G.R., Boster, F.J., Roloff, M.E. & Seibold, D.R. (1987). MBRS Rekindled: some thoughts on compliance gaining in interpersonal settings. In M.E. Rolof & G.R. Miller (Eds), *Interpersonal Processes: New Directions in Communication Research* (pp. 89–116). Newbury Park, CA: Sage.

Miller, J.B. (1976). *Toward a New Psychology of Women*. Boston: Beacon Press.

Miller, J.G. (1995, March). Rethinking problems of interdependence associated with individualism as compared with collectivism. In C. Raeff (Chair). Individualism and Collectivism as cultural contexts for developing different modes of independence and interdependence. Symposium presented at the meeting of the Society for Research in Child Development, Indianapolis.

Miller, K.A. & Kohn, M.L. (1983). The reciprocal effects of job conditions and the intellectuality of leisure-time activities. In M.L. Kohn & C. Schooler (Eds), *Work and Personality: an Inquiry into the Impact of Social Stratification*. Norwood, NJ: Ablex.

Miller, L.C. & Kenny, D.A. (1986). Reciprocity of self-disclosure at the individual and dyadic levels: a social relations analysis. *Journal of Personality and Social Psychology*, **50**, 713–19.

Miller, L.C. & Read, S.J. (1991). On the coherence of mental models of persons and relationships: a knowledge structure approach. In G.J.O. Fletcher & F.D. Fincham (Eds), *Cognition in Close Relationships* (pp. 69–99). Hillsdale, NJ: Erlbaum.

Miller, L.C., Berg, J.H. & Archer, R.L. (1983). Openers: individuals who elicit intimate self- disclosure. *Journal of Personality and Social Psychology*, **44**, 1234–44.

Miller, P.C., Lefcourt, H.M., Holmes, J.G., Ware, E.E. & Saleh, W.E. (1986). Marital locus of control and marital problem solving. *Journal of Personality and Social Psychology*, **51**, 161–9.

Miller, P.M., Danaher, D. & Forbes, D. (1986). Sex-related strategies for coping with interpersonal conflict in children aged five and seven. *Developmental Psychology*, **22**, 543–8.

Miller, R.S. (1994). Delineating the causes of embarrassment: awkward interaction versus social evaluation. Manuscript submitted for publication.

Miller, R.S. (1995). Embarrassment and social behavior. In J.P. Tangney & K.W. Fischer (Eds), *Self-conscious Emotions* (pp. 322–39). New York: Guilford.

Mills, C. (1963). In I. Horowitz (Ed.), *Power, Politics and People: the Collected Essays of C. Wright Mills*. New York: Ballantine.

Mills, R.S.L. & Rubin, K.H. (1993). Parental ideas as influences on children's social competence. In S.W. Duck (Ed.), *Learning about Relationships*. Newbury Park, CA: Sage.

Mink, L. (1969–1970). History and fiction as modes of comprehension. *New Literary History*, 1.

Minnett, A., Vandell, D. & Santrock, J.W. (1983). The effect of sibling status on sibling interaction: influence of birth order, age, spacing, sex of child and sex of sibling. *Child Development*, **54**, 1064–72.

Minuchin, P. (1985). Families and individual development: provocations from the field of family therapy. *Child Development*, **56**, 289–302.

Minuchin, S. (1974). *Familes and Family Therapy*. Cambridge, MA: Harvard University Press.

Mirkovic, D. (1980). *Dialectic and Sociological Thought*. St. Catherines, Ontario, Canada: Diliton Publications.

Mischel, W. (1974). Processes in delay of gratification. In L. Berkowitz (Ed.), *Advances in Experimental Social Psychology*, Vol. 7. New York: Academic Press.

Mishel, W. (1984). Convergence and challenges in the search for consistency. *American Psychologist*, **39**, 351–64.

Mishler, E. (1986). The analysis of interview-narratives. In T. Sarbin (Ed.), *Narrative Psychology: the Storied Nature of Human Conduct* (pp. 233–55). New York: Praeger.

Mishler, E. (1995). Models of narrative analysis: a typology. *Journal of Narrative and Life History*, **5**, 87–123.

Mitchell, J.C. (1969). The concept and use of social networks. In J.C. Mitchell (Ed.), *Social Networks in Urban Situations: Analyses of Personal Relationships in Central African Towns* (pp. 1–50). Manchester: Manchester University Press.

Mitchell, J.C. (1974). Social networks. *Annual Review of Anthropology*, **3**, 279–99.

Mitchell, R.E. & Trickett, E.J. (1979). Social networks as mediators of social support: an analysis of the effects and determinants of social networks. *Community Mental Health Journal*, **18**(1), 27–44.

Mitchell, R.E., Billings, A.G. & Moos, R.F. (1982). Social support and well-being: implications for prevention programs. *Journal of Primary Prevention*, **3**, 77–97.

Moghaddam, F.M., Taylor, D.M. & Wright, S.C. (1993). *Social Psychology in Cross-cultural Perspective*. New York: W. H. Freeman.

Molm, L.D. (1985). Relative effects of individual dependencies: further tests of the relation between power imbalance and power use. *Social Forces*, **63**, 810–37.

Monroe, S.M. & Depue, R.A. (1991). Life stress and depression. In J. Becker & A. Kleinman (Eds), *Psychological Aspects of Depression* (pp. 101–30). New York: Erlbaum.

Monroe, S.M. & Johnson, S.L. (1992). Social support and depression. In H.O.F. Veiel & U. Bauman (Eds), *The Meaning and Measurement of Social Support* (pp. 93–105). New York: Hemisphere.

Monsour, M. (1992). Meanings of intimacy in cross- and same-sex friendships. *Journal of Social and Personal Relationships*, **9**, 277–95.

Monsour, M. (1994). Challenges confronting cross-sex friendships: "Much ado about nothing?" *Sex Roles*, **31**, 55–77.

Monsour, M., Betty, S. & Kurzweil, N. (1993). Levels of perspectives and the perception of intimacy in cross-sex friendships: a balance theory explanation of shared perceptual reality. *Journal of Social and Personal Relationships*, **10**, 529–50.

Montemayor, R. (1983). Parents and adolescents in conflict: all families some of the time and some families most of the time. *Journal of Early Adolescence*, **3**, 83–103.

Montgomery, B. (1988). Quality communication in personal relationships. In S.W. Duck (Ed.), *Handbook of Personal Relationships: Theory, Research, and Interventions* (pp. 343–59). Chichester: Wiley.

Montgomery, B.M. (1984). Communication in intimate relationships: a research challenge. *Communication Quarterly*, **32**, 233–40.

Montgomery, B.M. (1986). Interpersonal attraction as a function of open communication and gender. *Communication Research Reports*, **3**, 27–36.

Montgomery, B.M. (1992). Communication as the interface between couples and culture. *Communication Yearbook*, **15**, 475–507.

Montgomery, B.M. (1993). Relationship maintenance versus relationship change: a dialectical dilemma. *Journal of Social and Personal Relationships*, **10**, 205–24.

Moore, E., Ball, R.A. & Kuipers, L. (1992). Expressed emotion in staff working with the long-term adult mentally ill. *British Journal of Psychiatry*, **161**, 802–8.

Moore, M.M. (1985). Nonverbal courtship patterns in women. *Ethology and Sociobiology*, **6**, 237–47.

Moos, R.H. (1979). *Evaluating Educational Environments*. San Francisco: Jossey-Bass.

Moran, D.K., Stockton, R. & Bond, L. (1991). Delivery of positive and corrective feedback in counseling groups. *Journal of Counseling Psychology*, **38**, 410–14.

Moras, K. & Strupp, H.H. (1982). Pretherapy interpersonal relations, patient's alliance, and outcome of brief therapy. *Archives of General Psychiatry*, **39**, 405–9.

Morgan, L.A. (1984). Changes in family interaction following widowhood. *Journal of Marriage and the Family*, **46**, 323–33.

Morley, I.E. (1992). Intra-organizational bargaining. In J.F. Hartley & G.M. Stephenson (Eds), *Employment*. Cambridge, MA: Blackwell.

Morris, D. (1972). *Intimate Behavior*. New York: Bantam.

Morris, L. (1985). Local social networks and domestic organizations: a study of redundant steel workers and their wives. *The Sociological Review*, **33**, 327–42.

Morson, G. & Emerson, C. (1990). *Mikhail Bakhtin: Creation of a Prosaics*. Palo Alto: Stanford University Press.

Mortimer, J.T., Lorence, J. & Kumka, D.S. (1986). *Work, Family, and Personality*. Norwood, NJ: Ablex.

Moss, L.W. (1981). The South Italian family revisited. *Central Issues in Anthropology*, **3**, 1–16.

Moss, M.S. & Moss, S.Z. (1995). Death and bereavement. In R. Blieszner & V.H. Bedford

(Eds), *Handbook of Aging and the Family* (pp. 422–39). Westport, CT: Greenwood Press.

Mueller, W.J. (1982). Issues in the application of "Supervision: a conceptual model" to dynamically oriented supervision: a reaction paper. *The Counseling Psychologist*, **10**, 43–6.

Mueller, W.J. & Kell, B.L. (1972). *Coping with Conflict: Supervising Counselors and Psychotherapists*. New York: Appleton-Century-Crofts.

Mueser, K.T. & Glynn, S.M. (Eds) (1995). *Behavioral Family Therapy for Psychiatric Disorders*. Boston: Allyn & Bacon.

Mueser, K.T., Glynn, S.M. & Liberman, R. (1994). Behavioral family management for serious psychiatric illness. In A.B. Hatfield (Ed.), *Family Interventions in Mental Illness: New Directions for Mental Health Services* (pp. 37–50). San Francisco: Jossey-Bass.

Mui, A.C. & Morrow-Howell, N. (1993). Sources of emotional strain among the oldest caregivers: differential experiences of siblings and spouses. *Research on Aging*, **15**, 50–69.

Mukaia, T. (1989). A call for our language: anorexia from within. *Women's Studies International Forum*, **12**, 613–38.

Mullen, B. & Copper, C. (1994). The relation between group cohesiveness and performance: an integration. *Psychological Bulletin*, **115**, 210–27.

Munn, P. & Dunn, J. (1989). Temperament and the developing relationship between siblings. *International Journal of Behavioral Development*, **12**, 433–51.

Muran, J.C., Segal, Z.V., Samstag, L.W. & Crawford, C.E. (1994). Patient pretreatment interpersonal problems and therapeutic alliance in short-term cognitive therapy. *Journal of Consulting and Clinical Psychology*, **62**, 185–90.

Murningham, K.J. & King, T.R. (1992). The effects of leverage and payoffs on cooperative behavior in asymmetric dilemmas. In W.B.G. Liebrand, D.M. Messick & H.A.M. Wilke (Eds), *Social Dilemmas: Theoretical Issues and Research Findings* (pp. 163–82). New York: Pergamon.

Murphey, E.B., Silber, E., Coelho, G.V., Hamburg, D.A. & Greenberg, I. (1963). Development of autonomy and parent–child interaction in late adolescence. *American Journal of Orthopsychiatry*, **33**, 643–52.

Murphy, B.C. (1989). Lesbian couples and their parents: the effects of perceived parental attitudes on the couple. *Journal of Counseling & Development*, **68**, 46–51.

Murphy, L.B. (1937). *Social Behavior and Child Personality*. New York: Columbia University Press.

Murphy, R. (1971). *The Dialectics of Social Life*. New York: Basic Books.

Murphy, S. (1986). Perceptions of stress, coping, and recovery one and three years after a natural disaster. *Issues in Mental Health Nursing*, **8**, 63–77.

Murphy, S. (1988). Mediating effects of intrapersonal and social support on mental health 1 and 3 years after a natural disaster. *Journal of Traumatic Stress*, **1**, 155–72.

Murray, L. & Trevarthen, C. (1985). Emotional regulation of interactions between two-month-olds and their mothers. In T. Field & N. Fox (Eds), *Social Perception in Infants* (pp. 177–97). Norwood, NJ: Ablex.

Murray, S. (1995). Is love blind? Positive illusions, idealization and the construction of satisfaction in close relationships. Doctoral Dissertation, University of Waterloo.

Murray, S.L. & Holmes, J.G. (1993). Seeing virtues in faults: negativity and the transformation of interpersonal narratives in close relationships. *Journal of Personality and Social Psychology*, **65**, 707–22.

Murray, S.L. & Holmes, J.G. (in press). The construction of relationship realities. In G. Fletcher & J. Fitness (Eds), *Knowledge Structures and Interactions in Close Relationships: a Social Psychological Approach*. Hillsdale, NJ: Erlbaum.

Murray, S.L., Holmes, J.G. & Griffin, D.W. (1996). The benefits of positive illusion:

idealization and the construction of satisfaction in close relationships. *Journal of Personality and Social Psychology*, **70**, 79–98.

Murstein, B.I. (1971). Critique of models of dyadic attraction. In B.I. Murstein (Ed.), *Theories of Attraction and Love* (pp. 1–30). New York: Springer .

Murstein, B.I. (1986). *Paths to Marriage*. Beverly Hills, CA: Sage.

Murstein, B.I. (1987). A clarification and extension of the SVR theory of dyadic pairing. *Journal of Marriage and the Family*, **49**, 929–33.

Muste, M.J. & Sharpe, D.F. (1947). Some influential factors in the determination of aggressive behavior in preschool children. *Child Development*, **18**, 11–28.

Myerhoff, B. (1978). *Number Our Days*. New York: Simon & Schuster.

Myrdal, G. (1944). *An American Dilemma*. New York: Harper & Row.

Nadler, A. (1986). Self-esteem and the seeking and receiving of help: theoretical and empirical perspectives. In B. Maher & W. Maher (Eds), *Progress in Experimental Personality Research*, Vol. 14 (pp. 115–63). New York: Academic Press.

Nardi, P.M. (1992). Sex, friendship, and gender roles among gay men. In P. Nardi (Ed.), *Men's Friendships* (pp. 173–85).

Nardi, P.M. & Sherrod, D. (1994). Friendship in the lives of gay men and lesbians. *Journal of Social and Personal Relationships*, **11**, 185–200.

National Center for Health Statistics (1991). Advance report of final marriage statistics, 1988. *Monthly Vital Statistics Report*, Vol. 39, No. 12, Suppl. 2. Hyattsville, MD: Public Health Service.

National Research Council (1989). *A Common Destiny: Blacks and American Society*. Washington, DC: National Academy Press.

Neisser, U. (1991). Two perceptually given aspects of the self and their development. *Developmental Review*, **11**, 197–209.

Nelson, J. (1966). Clique contacts and family orientations. *American Sociological Review*, **31**, 663–72.

Nelson, J.S., Megill, A. & McCloskey, D.N. (Eds) (1987). *The Rhetoric of the Human Sciences: Language and Argument in Scholarship and Public Affairs*. University of Wisconsin Press: Madison.

Nelson, K. (1986). Event knowledge and cognitive development. In K. Nelson (Ed.), *Event Knowledge: Structure and Function in Development*. Hillsdale, NJ: Erlbaum.

Nestle, J. & Preston, J. (1994). *Sister and Brother: Lesbians and Gay Men Write About their Lives Together*. San Francisco: Harper Collins.

Neuberg, S.L. & Fiske, S.T. (1987). Motivational influences on impression formation: outcome dependency, accuracy-driven attention, and individuating processes. *Journal of Personality and Social Psychology*, **53**, 431–44.

New, R.S. (1988). Parental goals and Italian infant care. In R.A. Levine, P.M. Miller & M.M. West (Eds), *Parental Behaviour in Diverse Societies*. San Francisco: Jossey-Bass.

Newcomb, M.D. (1990). Social support and personal characteristics: a developmental and interactional perspective. *Journal of Social and Clinical Psychology*, **9**, 54–68.

Newcomb, T.M. (1956). The prediction of interpersonal attraction. *American Psychologist*, **11**, 575–86.

Newcomb, T.M. (1961). *The Acquaintance Process*. New York: Holt Rinehart & Winston.

Newman, B.M. & Newman, P.R. (1975). *Development Through Life: a Psychosocial Approach*. Homewood, IL: Dorsey.

Niemi, P.M. (1988). Family interaction patterns and the development of social conceptions in the adolescent. *Journal of Youth and Adolescence*, **17**, 429–44.

Nisbet, R.A. (1973). Moral values and community. In R.L. Warren (Ed.), *Perspectives on the American Community* (pp. 85–93). Chicago: Rand McNally.

Nisbett, R.E. & Ross, L. (1980). *Human Inference: Strategies and Shortcomings of Social Judgment*. Englewood Cliffs, NJ: Erlbaum.

Nisbett, R.E., Caputo, C., Legant, P. & Marecek, J. (1973). Behavior as seen by the actor and as seen by the observer. *Journal of Personality and Social Psychology*, **27**, 154–64.

Noller, P. (1993). Gender and emotional communication in marriage: different cultures or differential social power. *Journal of Language and Social Psychology*, **12**, 132–52.

Noller, P. & Ruzzene, M. (1991). Communication in marriage: the influence of affect and cognition. In G.J.O. Fletcher & F.D. Fincham (Eds), *Cognition in Close Relationships* (pp. 203–33). Hillsdale, NJ: Erlbaum.

Noller, P., Feeney, J.A., Bonnell, D. & Callan, V.J. (1994). A longitudinal study of conflict in early marriage. *Journal of Social and Personal Relationships*, **11**, 233–52.

Norbeck, J.S. & Tilden, V.P. (1983). Life stress, social support and emotional disequilibrium in complications of pregnancy: a prospective, multi-variant study. *Journal of Health and Social Behavior*, **24**, 30–45.

Norbeck, J.S., Chaftez, L., Skodol-Wilson, H. & Weiss, S.J. (1991). Social support needs and family caregivers of psychiatric patients from three age groups. *Nursing Research*, **40**, 208–13.

Norman, C. & Aron, A. (1995, June). The effect of exciting activities on relationships satisfaction: A laboratory experiment. Paper presented at the International Network Conference on Personal Relationships, Williamsburg, VA.

Norris, F. & Kaniasty, K. (1992). Reliability of delayed self-report in disaster research. *Journal of Traumatic Stress*, **5**, 53–66.

Norris, F. & Kaniasty, K. (1996). Received and perceived social support in times of stress: a test of the social support deterioration deterrence model. *Journal of Personality and Social Psychology*, **71** (in press).

Norris, F. & Kearse, W. (1995, June). Ethnic differences in help seeking and receiving following disaster. Paper presented at 5th Biennial Conference of the Society for Community Research and Action, Chicago, IL.

Norris, F. & Thompson, M. (1995). Applying community psychology to the prevention of trauma and traumatic life events. In J.R. Freedy & S.E. Hobfoll (Eds), *Traumatic Stress: from Theory to Practice* (pp. 49–71). New York: Plenum.

Norris, F. & Uhl, G. (1993). Chronic stress as a mediator of acute stress: the case of Hurricane Hugo. *Journal of Applied Social Psychology*, **23**, 1263–84.

Norris, F., Phifer, J. & Kaniasty, K. (1994). Individual and community reactions to the Kentucky floods: Findings from a longitudinal study of older adults. In R. Ursano, B. McCaughey & C. Fullerton (Eds), *Individual and Community Responses to Trauma and Disaster: the Structure of Human Chaos* (pp. 378–400). Cambridge: Cambridge University Press.

Notarius, C.I. & Pellegrini, D.S. (1987). Differences between husbands and wives: implications for understanding marital discord. In K. Halweg & M. Goldstein (Eds), *Understanding Major Mental Disorder: the Contribution of Family Interaction Research*. New York: Family Process.

Notarius, C.I., Benson, P.R., Sloane, D., Vanzetti, N.A. & Hornyak, L.M. (1989). Exploring the interface between perception and behavior: an analysis of marital interactions in distressed and nondistressed couples. *Behavioral Assessment*, **11**, 39–64.

Nuechterlein, K.H. & Dawson, M.E. (1984). A heuristic vulnerability/stress model of schizophrenic episodes. *Schizophrenia Bulletin*, **10**, 300–12.

Nuechterlein, K.H., Snyder, K.S. & Mintz, J. (1992). Paths to relapse: possible transactional processes connecting patient illness onset, expressed emotion, and psychotic relapse. *British Journal of Psychiatry*, **161** (Suppl. 18), 88–96.

Nussbaum, J.F. (1989). Life-span communication: an introduction. In J.F. Nussbaum (Ed.), *Life-span Communication: Normative Processes* (pp. 1–4). Hillsdale, NJ: Erlbaum.

Nydegger, C.N. (1991). The development of paternal and filial maturity. In K. Pillemer & K. McCartney (Eds), *Parent–Child Relations Throughout Life* (pp. 93–112). Hillsdale, NJ: Erlbaum.

Nydegger, C.N. & Mitteness, L.S. (1991). Fathers and their adult sons and daughters. In S.K. Pfeifer & M.B. Sussman (Eds), *Families: Intergenerational and Generational Con-*

nections (pp. 249–66). New York: The Haworth Press.

O'Brien, R. (1991). Adolescents' perspectives on siblings and friends as resources. Paper presented at the Meeting of the Society for Research in Child Development, Seattle, WA.

O'Bryant, S.L. & Hansson, R.O. (1995). Widowhood. In R. Blieszner & V.H. Bedford (Eds), *Handbook of Aging and the Family* (pp. 440–58). Westport, CT: Greenwood Press.

O'Connor, P. (1992). *Friendships Between Women: a Critical Review*. Guilford, London.

O'Donnell, L. & Stueve, A. (1983). Mothers as social agents: structuring the community activities of school aged children. In H. Lopata & J.H. Pleck (Eds), *Research in the Interweave of Social Roles: Jobs and Families: Vol. 3. Families and Jobs*. Greenwich, CT: JAI.

O'Leary, K.D. & Vivian, D. (1990). Physical aggression in marriage. In F.D. Fincham & T.N. Bradbury (Eds), *The Psychology of Marriage* (pp. 323–48). New York: Guilford.

O'Meara, J.D. (1989). Cross-sex friendship: four basic challenges of an ignored relationship. *Sex Roles*, **21**, 525–43.

O'Meara, J.D. (1994). Cross-sex friendship's opportunity challenge: uncharted terrain for exploration. *Personal Relationship Issues*, **2**, 4–7.

O'Neill, M.K., Lance, W.J. & Freeman, S.J.J. (1986). Psychosocial factors and depressive symptoms. *Journal of Nervous and Mental Disease*, **174**, 15–23.

Oatley, K. (1992). *Best Laid Schemes. The Psychology of Emotions*. Cambridge: Cambridge University Press.

Ohbuchi, K., Kameda, M. & Agarie, N. (1989). Apology as aggression control: its role in mediating appraisal of and response to harm. *Journal of Personality and Social Psychology*, **56**, 219–27.

Okun, M.A., Melichar, J.F. & Hill, M.D. (1990). Negative daily events, positive and negative social ties, and psychological distress among older adults. *The Gerontologist*, **30**, 193–9.

Oliker, S.J. (1989). *Best Friends and Marriage: Exchange Among Women*. Berkeley, CA: University of California Press.

Oliveri, M.E. & Reiss, D. (1987). Social networks of family members: distinctive roles of mothers and fathers. *Sex Roles*, **17**, 719–36.

Olson, D.H. (1977). Insiders' and outsiders' views of relationships: research studies. In G. Levinger & H. Raush (Eds), *Close Relationships: Perspectives on the Meaning of Intimacy* (pp. 115–35). Amherst: UMass Press.

Olson, D.H. (1989). *The Circumplex Model: Systematic Assessment and Treatment of Families*. New York: Hawthorn Press.

Olson, D.H., Russell, C.S. & Sprenkle, D.H. (1979). Circumplex model of marital and family systems: cohesion and adaptability dimensions, family types, and clinical applications. *Family Process*, **8**, 3–28.

Olson, D.H., Russell, C.S. & Sprenkle, D.H. (1983). Circumplex model of marital and family systems: VI, theoretical update. *Family Process*, **22**, 69–83.

Olthof, T., Ferguson, T. & Luiten, A. (1989). Personal responsibility antecedents of anger and blame reactions in children. *Child Development*, **60**, 1328–36.

Omoto, A.M. & Gunn, D.O. (1994, May). The effect of relationship closeness on encoding and recall for relationship-irrelevant information. Paper presented at the May Meeting of the International Network on Personal Relationships, Iowa City, IA.

Orbell, J.M., Van de Kragt, A.J.C. & Dawes, R.M. (1988). Explaining discussion-induced cooperation. *Journal of Personality and Social Psychology*, **54**, 811–19.

Orbuch, T. & Custer, L. (1995). The social context of married women's work and its impact on black husbands and white husbands. *Journal of Marriage and the Family*, **57**, 333–45.

Orden, S.R. & Bradburn, N.M. (1968). Dimensions of marriage happiness. *American Journal of Sociology*, **73**, 715–31.

Orford, J. (1986). The rules of interpersonal complementarity: does hostility beget hostility and dominance, submission? *Psychological Review*, **93**, 365–77.

Orlick, T., Zhou, Q.Y. & Partington, J. (1990). Co-operation and conflict within Chinese and Canadian kindergarten settings. *Canadian Journal of Behavioral Science*, **22**(1), 20–25.

Ornstein, R. & Thompson, R.F. (1984). *The Amazing Brain*. New York: Houghton Mifflin.

Orth-Gomer, K. (1994). International epidemiological evidence for a relationship between social support and cardiovascular disease. In S.A. Shumaker & S.M. Czajowski (Eds), Social Support and Cardiovascular Disease (pp. 97–117). New York: Plenum.

Orth-Gomer, K. & Johnston, J.V. (1987). The measurement of social support in population studies. *Social Science and Medicine*, **24**, 83–94.

Orthner, D.K. (1975). Leisure activity patterns and marital satisfaction over the marital career. *Journal of Marriage and the Family*, **37**, 91–101.

Osborne, L.N. & Fincham, F.D. (1994). Conflict between parents and their children. In D.D. Cahn (Ed.), *Conflict in Personal Relationships* (pp. 117–41). Hillsdale, NJ: Erlbaum.

Osmond, M.W. & Thorne, B. (1993). Feminist theories: the social construction of gender in families and society. In P.G. Boss, W.J. Doherty, R. Larossa, W.R. Schumm & S.K. Steinmetz (Eds), *Sourcebook of Family Theories and Methods: a Contextual Approach* (pp. 591–623). New York: Plenum.

Oswald, K., Krappmann, L., Uhlendorff, H. & Weiss, K. (1994). Social relationships and support among children of the same age in middle childhood. In K. Hurrelmann & F. Nestmann (Eds), *Social Support and Social Networks in Childhood and Adolescence*. Berlin: De Gruyter.

Owen, W.F. (1987). Mutual interaction of discourse structures and relational pragmatics in conversational influence attempts. *Southern Journal of Speech Communication*, **52**, 103–27.

Paci, M. (1982). *La Struttura Sociale Italiana*. Bologna: Mulino.

Pagel, M.D., Erdly, W.W. & Becker, J. (1987). Social networks: we get by with (and in spite of) a little help from our friends. *Journal of Personality and Social Psychology*, **53**, 793–804.

Paget, M. (Ed. M.L. DeVault) (1993). *A Complex Sorrow: Reflections on Cancer and an Abbreviated Life*. Philadelphia: Temple University Press.

Paine, R. (1974). An exploratory analysis in "middle-class" culture. In E. Leylon (Ed.), *The Compact: Selected Dimensions of Friendship* (pp. 117–37). St. John's: Institute of Social and Economic Research.

Panksepp, J., Siviy, S.M. & Normansell, L.A. (1985). Brain opioids and social emotions. In M. Reite & T. Field (Eds), *The Psychobiology of Attachment and Separation* (pp. 3–50). London: Academic Press.

Papini, D.R. & Roggman, L.A. (1992). Adolescent perceived attachment to parents in relation to competence, depression, and anxiety: a longitudinal study. *Journal of Early Adolescence*, **12**(4), 420–40.

Paradis, B.A. (1991). Seeking intimacy and integration: gay men in the era of AIDS. *Smith College Studies in Social Work*, **61**, 260–74.

Parcel, T.L. & Menaghan, E.G. (1994). *Parents' Jobs and Children's Lives*. New York: Aldine de Gruyter.

Parham, T.A. (1993). Own-group preferences as a function of self-affirmation: a reaction to Penn et al. *Journal of Black Psychology*, **19**, 336–41.

Parke, R.D. (1978). Children's home environments: social and cognitive effects. In I. Altman & J.F. Wohlwill (Eds), *Children and the Environment* (pp. 33–81). New York: Plenum.

Parke, R.D. (1988). Families in life-span perspective: a multi-level developmental approach. In E.M. Hetherington, R.M. Lerner & M. Perlmutter (Eds), *Child Develop-*

ment in Life Span Perspective (pp. 159–90). Hillsdale NJ: Erlbaum.

Parke, R.D. (1994). Progress, paradigms and unresolved problems: a commentary on recent advances in our understanding of children's emotions. *Merrill Palmer Quarterly*, **40**, 157–69.

Parke, R.D. (1995). Fathers and families. In M. Bornstein (Ed.), *Handbook of Parenting*. New York: Wiley.

Parke, R.D. (1996). *Fathers* (Revised Edn). Cambridge: Harvard University Press.

Parke, R.D. & Bhavnagri, N. (1989). Parents as managers of children's peer relationships. In D. Belle (Ed.), *Children's Social Networks and Social Supports*. New York: Wiley.

Parke, R.D. & Neville, B. (1995). Late-timed fatherhood: determinants and consequences for children and families. In J. Shapiro, M. Diamond & M. Greenberg (Eds), *Becoming a Father: Social, Emotional and Psychological Perspectives*. New York: Springer.

Parke, R.D., Burks, V.M., Carson, J.L. & Cassidy, J. (1992). Family contributions to peer relationships among young children. In R.D. Parke & G. Ladd (Eds), *Family–Peer Relationships: Modes of Linkage*. Hillsdale, NJ: Erlbaum.

Parke, R.D., Burks, V., Carson, J., Neville, B. & Boyum, L. (1994). Family peer relationships: a tripartite model. In R.D. Parke & S. Kellam (Eds), *Advances in family research, Vol. 4. Family Relationships with Other Social Systems* (pp. 115–45). Hillsdale, NJ: Erlbaum.

Parke, R.D., MacDonald, K.B., Burks, V.M., Carson, J., Bhavnagri, N., Barth, J. & Beitel, A. (1989). Family and peer systems: in search of the linkages. In K. Kreppner & R.M. Lerner (Eds), *Family Systems and Life Span Development*. Hillsdale, NJ: Erlbaum.

Parke, R.D., MacDonald, K., Beitel, A. & Bhavnagri, N. (1988). The role of the family in the development of peer relationships. R. de V. Peters & R.J. McMahon (Eds), *Social Learning and Systems Approaches to Marriage and the Family* (pp. 17–44). New York: Brunner Mazel.

Parker, J.G. & Asher, S.R. (1993). Friendship and friendship quality in middle childhood: links with peer group acceptance and feelings of loneliness and social dissatisfaction. *Developmental Psychology*, **29**, 611–21.

Parkes, C.M., Benjamin, B. & Fitzgerald, R.G. (1969). Broken heart: a statistical study of increased mortality among widowers. *British Medical Journal*, **1**, 740–3.

Parkes, C.M., Stevenson-Hinde, J. & Marris, P. (1991). *Attachment Across the Life Cycle*. London: Tavistock/Routledge.

Parks, M.R. (1982). Ideology in interpersonal communication: off the couch and into the world. In M. Burgoon (Ed.), *Communication Yearbook 5* (pp. 79–108). New Brunswick, NJ: Transaction Books.

Parks, M.R. (1995). Webs of influence in interpersonal relationships. In C.R. Burger & M.E. Burgoon (Eds), *Communication and Social Influence Processes* (pp. 155–78). East Lansing: Michigan State University Press.

Parks, M.R. & Adelman, M.B. (1983). Communication networks and the development of romantic relationships: an expansion of uncertainty reduction theory. *Human Communication Research*, **10**, 55–79.

Parks, M.R. & Barnes, K.J. (1988). With a little help from my friends: The role of third parties in the initiation of interpersonal relationships. Paper presented at the annual convention of the Speech Communication Association, New Orleans.

Parks, M.R. & Eggert, L. (1991). The role of social context in the dynamics of personal relationships. In W. Jones & D. Perlman (Eds), *Advances in Personal Relationships*, Vol. 2 (pp. 1–34). London: Jessica Kingsley.

Parks, M.R. & Floyd, K. (1996). Friends in cyberspace. *Journal of Communication*, **46**(1), 80–97.

Parks, M.R. & Riveland, L. (1987). On dealing with disliked friends of friends: A study of the occurrence and management of imbalanced relationships. Paper presented at the annual convention of the International Communication Association. Montreal, Quebec, May.

Parks, M.R., Stan, C. & Eggert, L.L. (1983). Romantic involvement and social network involvement. *Social Psychology Quarterly*, **46**, 116–30.

Parpal, M. & Maccoby, E.E. (1985). Maternal responsiveness and subsequent child compliance. *Child Development*, **56**, 1326–34.

Parry, A. (1991). A universe of stories. *Family Process*, **30**, 37–54.

Parry, A. & Doan, R. (1994). *Story Re-Visions: Narrative Therapy in the Postmodern World*. New York: Guilford.

Patterson, C.J. & Stouthamer-Loeber, M. (1984). The correlation of family management practices and delinquency. *Child Development*, **55**, 1299–306.

Patterson, C.J., Griesler, P.C., Vaden, N.A. & Kupersmidt, J.B. (1992). Family economic circumstances, life transitions, and children's peer relations. In R.D. Parke & G. Ladd (Eds), *Family–Peer Relationships: Modes of Linkage* (pp. 385–424). Hillsdale, NJ: Erlbaum.

Patterson, C.J., Vaden, N.A. & Kupersmidt, J.B. (1991). Family background, recent life events, and peer rejection during childhood. *Journal of social and personal relationships*, **8**, 347–61.

Patterson, D.G. & Schwartz, P. (1994). The social construction of conflict in intimate same-sex couples. In D.D. Cahn (Ed.), *Conflict in Personal Relationships* (pp. 3–26). Hillsdale, NJ: Erlbaum.

Patterson, G.R. (1982). *A Social Learning Approach: Coercive Family Process*. Eugene, OR: Castalia.

Patterson, G.R. & Cobb, J.A. (1971). A dyadic analysis of aggressive behaviors. In J.P. Hill (Ed.), *Minnesota Symposium on Child Psychology*, Vol. 5. Minneapolis: University of Minnesota Press.

Patterson, G.R., DeBaryshe, B.D. & Ramsey, E. (1989). A developmental perspective on antisocial behavior. *American Psychologist*, **44**, 329–35.

Paulhus, D.L. (1991). Measurement and control of response bias. In J.P. Robinson, P.R. Shaver & L.S. Wrightsman (Eds), *Measures of Personality and Social Psychological Attitudes* (pp. 17–59). San Diego: Academic Press.

Pearce, W.B. (1989). *Communication and the Human Condition*. Carbondale, IL: Southern Illinois University Press.

Pearce, W.B. & Sharp, S.M. (1973). Self-disclosing communi cation. *Journal of Communication*, **23**, 409–25.

Pearlin, L. (1989). The sociological study of stress. *Journal of Health and Social Behavior*, **30**, 241–56.

Peck, R.F. & Havighurst, R. (1960). *The Psychology of Character Development*. New York: Wiley.

Peek, C.W., Fischer, J.J. & Kidwell, J.S. (1985). Teenage violence toward parents: a neglected dimension of family violence. *Journal of Marriage and the Family*, **47**, 1051–60.

Peeke, H.V.S. & Herz, M.J. (1973). *Habituation*. New York: Academic Press.

Peirce, R.S., Pruitt, D.G. & Czaja, S.J. (1991). Complainant–respondent differences in procedural choice. Unpublished manuscript.

Pence, E. & Paymar, M. (1993). *Education Groups for Men who Batter: the Duluth Model*. New York: Springer.

Penman, R. (1994). Facework in communication: conceptual and moral challenges. In S. Ting-Toomey (Ed.), *The Challenge of Facework* (pp. 15–46). New York: State University of New York Press.

Penn, M.L., Gaines, S.O. Jr & Phillips, L. (1993). On the desirability of own-group preference. *Journal of Black Psychology*, **19**, 303–21.

Pennebaker, J. & Harber, K. (1993). A social stage model of collective coping: the Loma Prieta Earthquake and the Persian Gulf War. *Journal of Social Issues*, **49**(4), 125–45.

Peplau, L.A. (1983). Roles and gender. In H.H. Kelley, E. Berscheid, A. Christensen, J.H.

Harvey, T.L. Huston, G. Levinger, E. McClintock, L.A. Peplau & D.R. Petersen (Eds), *Close Relationships* (pp. 220–64). New York: Freeman.

Perlman, D. (1986). Chance and coincidence in personal relationships. Paper presented to the Third International Conference on Personal Relationships, Herzlia, Israel, July.

Perper, T. & Weis, D.L. (1987). Proceptive and rejective strategies of U.S. and Canadian women. *Journal of Sex Research*, **23**, 455–80.

Perry, J.B., Hawkins, S.R. & Neal, D.M. (1983). Giving and receiving aid. *International Journal of Mass Emergencies and Disasters*, **1**, 171–88.

Perry-Jenkins, M. & Crouter, A.C. (1990). Men's provider-role attitudes: implications for household work and marital satisfaction. *Journal of Family Issues*, **11**, 136–56.

Perry-Jenkins, M. & Folk, K. (1994). Class, couples, and conflict: effects of the division of labor on assessments of marriage in dual-earner families. *Journal of Marriage and the Family,* **56**, 165–80.

Perry-Jenkins, M. & Gilman-Hanz, S. (1992, November). Processes linking work and the well-being of parents and children in single-parent and two-parent families. Paper presented at the annual meeting of National Council on Family Relations, Orlando, Florida.

Peters-Golden, H. (1982). Breast cancer: varied perceptions of social support in the illness experience. *Social Science and Medicine*, **16**, 483–91.

Peterson, C., Seligman, M.E.P. & Vaillant, G.E. (1988). Pessimistic explanatory style is a risk factor for physical illness: a thirty-five-year longitudinal study. *Journal of Personality and Social Psychology*, **55**, 23–7.

Peterson, D.R. (1983). Conflict. In H.H. Kelley, E. Berscheid, A. Christensen, J.H. Harvey, T.L. Huston, G. Levinger, E. McClintock, L.A. Peplau & D.R. Peterson (Eds), *Close Relationships* (pp. 360–96). New York: W.H. Freeman.

Peterson, J.L. & Zill, N. (1986). Marital disruption, parent–child relationships, and behavior problems in children. *Journal of Marriage and the Family*, **48**, 295–37.

Petillon, H. (1993). *Das Sozialleben des Schulanfängers. Die Schule aus der Sicht des Kindes*. Weinheim: Psychologie Verlags Union.

Petronio, S. (1988, November). The dissemination of private information: the use of a boundary control system as an alternative perspective to the study of disclosures. Paper presented at the Speech Communication Association Convention, New Orleans.

Petronio, S. (1991). Communication boundary management: a theoretical model of managing disclosure of private information between marital couples. *Communication Theory*, **1**, 311–35.

Petronio, S. (1994). Privacy binds in family interactions: the case of parental privacy invasion. In W.R. Cupach & B.H. Spitzberg (Eds), *The Dark Side of Interpersonal Communication* (pp. 241–57). Hillsdale, NJ: Erlbaum.

Petronio, S., Olson, C. & Dollar, N. (1988). Relational embarrassment: impact on relational quality and communication satisfaction. In D. O'Hair & B.R. Patterson (Eds), *Advances in Interpersonal Communication Research* (pp. 195–206). Las Cruces, NM: CRC Publications.

Pettigrew, T.F. (1987). Integration and pluralism. In P.A. Katz & D.A. Taylor (Eds), *Eliminating Racism: Profiles in Controversy* (pp. 19–30). New York: Plenum.

Pettit, G.S. & Mize, J. (1993). Substance and style: understanding the ways in which parents teach children about social relationships. In S.W. Duck (Ed.), *Learning about relationships (Understanding Relationship Processes 2)* (pp. 118–51). Thousand Oaks: Sage.

Pettit, G.S., Dodge, K.A. & Brown, M.M. (1988). Early family experience, social problem solving patterns, and children' social competence. *Child Development*, **59**, 107–20.

Phifer, J. & Norris, F.H. (1989). Psychological symptoms in older adults following natural disaster: nature, timing, duration, and course. *Journal of Gerontology*, **44**, 207–17.

Philips, S.V. (1972). Participant structures and communicative competence: Warm Springs children in community and classroom. In C.B. Cazden, V.P. John & D. Hymes (Eds), *Functions of Language in the Classroom* (pp. 370–94). New York: Teachers College Press.

Philipsen, G. (1987). The prospect for cultural communication. In D. Kincaid (Ed.), *Communication Theory: Eastern and Western Perspectives* (pp. 245–54). New York: Academic Press.

Phillips, L., Penn, M.L. & Gaines, S.O. Jr (1993). A hermeneutic rejoinder to ourselves and our critics. *Journal of Black Psychology*, **19**, 350–57.

Phinney, J.S. (1995). Ethnic identity and self-esteem: a review and integration. In A.M. Padilla (Ed.), *Hispanic Psychology: Critical Issues in Theory and Research* (pp. 57–70). Thousand Oaks, CA: Sage.

Piaget, J. (1952). *The Origins of Intelligence*. New York: International Universities Press.

Piaget, J. (1963). *The Origins of Intelligence in Children* (M. Cook, Trans.). New York: Norton (original work published 1952).

Piaget, J. (1986). *Das moralische Urteil beim Kinde* (2nd Edn: first published in Germany 1932). Munich: Klett-Cotta.

Pierce, G.R., Sarason, B.R. & Sarason, I.G. (1990). In S.W. Duck (Ed. with R.C. Silver), *Personal Relationships and Social Support* (pp. 173–89). Newbury Park, CA: Sage.

Pierce, G.R., Sarason, B.R. & Sarason, I.G. (1992). General and specific support expectations and stress as predictors of perceived supportiveness: an experimental study. *Journal of Personality and Social Psychology*, **63**, 297–307.

Pierce, G.R., Sarason, I.G. & Sarason, B.R. (1991). General and relationship-based expectations of social support: are two constructs better than one? *Journal of Personality and Social Psychology*, **63**, 297–307.

Pilisuk, M. & Minkler, M. (1980). Supportive networks: life ties for the elderly. *Journal of Social Issues*, **36**, 95–116.

Pina, D.L. & Bengtson, V.L. (1993). The division of household labor and wives' happiness: ideology, employment and perceptions of support. *Journal of Marriage and the Family*, **55**, 901–12.

Pincus, A.L. & Wiggins, J.S. (1990). Interpersonal problems and conceptions of personality disorders. *Journal of Personality Disorders*, **4**, 342–52.

Pinker, S. (1994). *The Language Instinct*. New York: William Morrow.

Pinkney, A. (1993). *Black Americans* (4th Edn). Englewood Cliffs, NJ: Prentice-Hall.

Piper, W.E., Azim, H.F.A., Joyce, A.S. & McCallum, M. (1991a). Transference interpretation, therapeutic alliance and outcome in short-term individual psychotherapy. *Archives of General Psychiatry*, **48**, 946–53.

Piper, W.E., Azim, H.F.A., Joyce, A.S., McCallum, M., Nixon, G.W.H. & Segal P.S. (1991b). Quality of object relations vs. interpersonal functioning as predictor of therapeutic alliance and psychotherapy outcome. *Journal of Nervous and mental Disease*, **179**, 432–8.

Pipp, S., Easterbrooks, M.A. & Harmon, R.J. (1992). The relation between attachment and knowledge of self and mother in one- to three-year-old infants. *Child Development*, **63**, 738–50.

Pipp, S., Robinson, J.L., Bridges, D., Bartholomew, S. (in press). Sources of individual differences in infant social cognition: Cognitive and affective aspects of self and other. In R.J. Sternberg & E.L. Grigorenko (Eds), *Intelligence: Heredity and Environment*. New York: Cambridge University Press.

Pipp, S., Shaver, P., Jennings, S., Lamborn, S. & Fischer, K.W. (1985). Adolescents' theories about the development of their relationships with parents. *Journal of Personality and Social Psychology*, **48**, 991–1001.

Pistole, M.C. & Watkins, C.E. (1995). Attachment theory, counseling process, and supervision. *The Counseling Psychologist*, **23**, 457–78.

Planalp, S. & Garvin-Doxas, K. (1994). Using mutual knowledge in conversation: friends as experts in each other. In S.W. Duck (Ed.), *The Dynamics of Relationship (Understanding Relationship Processes 4)* (pp. 1–26). Thousand Oaks, CA: Sage.

Platt, J. (1973). Social traps. *American Psychologist*, **28**, 641–51.

Pleck, J. (1985). *Working Wives/Working Husbands*. Beverly Hills, CA: Sage.

Plummer, K. (1975). *Sexual Stigma: an Interactionist Account*. London: Routledge and Kegan Paul.

Plutchik, R. (1967). Marriage as dynamic equilibrium: implications for research. In H.L. Silverman (Ed.), *Marital Counseling: Psychology, Ideology, Science* (pp. 347–67). Springfield, IL: Charles C. Thomas.

Polkinghorne, D. (1988). *Narrative Knowing and the Human Sciences*. Albany: SUNY Press.

Porter, B. & O'Leary, K.D. (1980). Marital discord and childhood behavior problems. *Journal of Abnormal Child Psychology*, **8**, 287–95.

Porterfield, E. (1978). *Black and White Mixed Marriages*. Chicago: Nelson-Hall.

Portes, A. & Rumbaut, R.G. (1990). *Immigrant America: A Portrait*. Berkeley, CA: University of California Press.

Post, R.M. & Kopanda, R.T. (1976). Cocaine, kindling, and psychosis. *American Journal of Psychiatry*, **133**, 627–34.

Post, R.M., Rubinow, D.R. & Ballenger, J.C. (1984). Conditioning, sensitization, and kindling: implications for the course of affective illness. In R.M. Post & J.C. Ballenger (Eds), *The Neurobiology of Mood Disorders*. Baltimore: Williams & Wilkins.

Power, T. & Chapieski, M.L. (1986). Childrearing and impulse control in toddlers: a naturalistic investigation. *Developmental Psychology*, **22**, 271–5.

Powless, D.L. & Elliot, S.N. (1993). Assessment of social skills of Native American preschoolers: teachers' and parents' ratings. *Journal of School Psychology*, **31**, 293–307.

Prager, K.J. (1991). Intimacy status and conflict conflict resolution. *Journal of Social and Personal Relationships*, **8**, 505–26.

Prager, K.J. (1995). *The Psychology of Intimacy*. New York: Guilford.

Pratt, M.W., Kerig, P.K., Cowan, P.A. & Cowan, P.A. (1992). Family worlds: couple satisfaction, parenting style, and mothers' and fathers' speech to young children. *Merrill-Palmer Quarterly*, **38**, 245–62.

Prentice, D.A. (1990). Familiarity and differences in self- and other-representations. *Journal of Personality and Social Psychology*, **59**, 369–83.

Presser, H.B. (1975). Age differences between spouses: trends, patterns, and social implications. *American Behavioral Scientist*, **19**, 190–205.

Prochanska, J.M. & Prochanska, J.O. (1985). Children's views of the causes and cures of sibling rivalry. *Child Welfare*, **64**, 427–33.

Procidano, M.E. & Heller, K. (1983). Measures of perceived social support from friends and from family: three validation studies. *American Journal of Community Psychology*, **11**, 1–24.

Pruitt, D.G. (1991). Complainant–respondent differences and procedural choice in asymmetrical social conflict. Paper presented at the Fifth Annual Conference of the International Association for Conflict Management, Minneapolis.

Pruitt, D.G. & Carnevale, P.J. (1993). *Negotiation in Social Conflict*. Pacific Grove, CA: Brooks/Cole.

Pruitt, D.G. & Kimmel, M.J. (1977). Twenty years of experimental gaming: critique, synthesis, and suggestions for the future. *Annual Review of Psychology*, **28**, 363–92.

Prusank, D.T., Duran, R.L. & DeLillo, D.A. (1993). Interpersonal relationships in women's magazines: dating and relating in the 1970s and 1980s. *Journal of Social and Personal Relationships*, **10**, 307–20.

Pulkkinen, L. (1981). Search for alternatives to aggression in Finland. In A.P. Medstein & M. Segall (Eds), *Aggression in Global Perspective* (pp. 104–44). New York: Pergamon.

Pulkkinen, L. (1996). Behavioral precursors to accidents and resulting physical impairment. *Child Development*, **70**(6).

Putallaz, M. (1987). Maternal behavior and sociometric status. *Child Development*, **58**, 324–40.

Putallaz, M. & Sheppard, B.H. (1992). Conflict management and social competence. In C.U. Shantz & W.W. Hartup (Ed.), *Conflict in Child and Adolescent Development*. Cambridge: Cambridge University Press.

Putnam, L.L. (1994). New developments in conflict styles and strategies. Paper presented at the annual conference of the International Association for Conflict Management, Eugene, Oregon.

Qualls, S.H. (1995). Clinical interventions with later-life families. In R. Blieszner & V.H. Bedford (Eds), *Handbook of Aging and the Family* (pp. 475–87). Westport, CT: Greenwood Press.

Quarantelli, E.L. (1960). A note on the protective function of the family in disasters. *Marriage and Family Living*, **22**, 263–4.

Quarantelli, E.L. (1985). An assessment of conflicting views on mental health: the consequences of traumatic events. In C. Figley (Ed.), *Trauma and Its Wake* (pp. 173–218). New York: Brunner-Mazel.

Quittner, A., Glueckauf, R. & Jackson, D. (1990). Chronic parenting stress: moderating versus mediating effects of social support. *Journal of Personality and Social Psychology*, **59**, 1266–78.

Rabinow, P. & Sullivan, W. (1987). *Interpretive Social Science: a Second Look*. Berkeley: University of California Press.

Radke-Yarrow, M., Cummings, E.M., Kuczynski, L. & Chapman, M. (1985). Patterns of attachment in two- and three-year-olds in normal families and families with parental depression. *Child Development*, **56**, 884–93.

Raffaelli, M. (1991). Sibling conflict in early adolescence. Unpublished doctoral dissertation, University of Chicago.

Rahim, M.A. (1983). A measure of styles of handling interpersonal conflict. *Academy of Management Journal*, **26**, 368–76.

Rajecki, D.W. (1985). Predictability and control in relationships: a perspective from animal behavior. In W. Ickes (Ed.), *Compatible and Incompatible Relationships* (pp. 11–31). New York: Springer-Verlag.

Rajecki, D.W., Bledsoe, S.B. & Rasmussen, J.L. (1991). Successful personal ads: gender differences and similarities in offers, stipulations, and outcomes. *Basic and Applied Social Psychology*, **12**, 457–69.

Ramey, J. (1976). *Intimate Friendships*. Englewood Cliffs, NJ: Prentice-Hall.

Rands, M. (1988). Changes in social networks following marital separation and divorce. In R.M. Milardo (Ed.), *Families and Social Networks* (pp. 127–46). Newbury Park, CA: Sage.

Raphael, B. & Wilson, J.P. (1993). Theoretical and intervention considerations in working with victims of disasters. In J.P. Wilson & B. Raphael (Eds), *International Handbook of Traumatic Stress Syndromes* (pp. 105–17). New York: Plenum.

Rapoport, A. (1966). *Two-person Game Theory*. Ann Arbor, MI: University of Michigan.

Raush, H., Barry, W., Hertel, R. & Swain, M.A. (1974). *Communication, Conflict, and Marriage*. San Francisco: Jossey-Bass.

Rawlins, W.K. (1981). Friendship as a communicative achievement: a theory and an interpretive analysis of verbal reports. Unpublished doctoral dissertation, Temple University.

Rawlins, W.K. (1982). Cross-sex friendship and the communicative management of sex-role expectations. *Communication Quarterly*, **30**, 343–52.

Rawlins, W.K. (1983a). Negotiating close friendship: the dialectic of conjunctive freedoms. *Human Communication Research*, **9**, 255–66.

Rawlins, W.K. (1983b). Openness as problematic in ongoing friendships: two conversational dilemmas. *Communication Monographs*, **50**, 1–13.

Rawlins, W.K. (1989). A dialectical analysis of the tensions, functions, and strategic challenges of communication in young adult friendships. *Communication Yearbook*, **12**, 157–89.

Rawlins, W.K. (1992). *Friendship Matters: Communication, Dialectics, and the Life Course*. New York: Aldine de Gruyter.

Rawlins, W.K. (1993). Communication in cross-sex friendships. In L.P. Arliss & D.J. Borisoff (Eds), *Women and Men Communicating* (pp. 51–70). Orlando, FL: Holt, Rinehart and Winston.

Rawlins, W.K. (1994a). Being there and growing apart: sustaining friendships during adulthood. In D.J. Canary & L. Stafford (Eds), *Communication and Relational Maintenance* (pp. 275–296). New York: Academic Press.

Rawlins, W.K. (1994b). Reflecting on cross-sex friendship: de-scripting the drama. *Personal Relationship Issues*, **2**, 1–3.

Rawlins, W.K. & Holl, M.R. (1987). The communicative achievement of friendship during adolescence: predicaments of trust and violation. *Western Journal of Speech Communication*, **51**, 345–63.

Rawlins, W.K. & Holl, M.R. (1988). Adolescents' interaction with parents and friends: dialectics of temporal perspective and evaluation. *Journal of Social and Personal Relationships*, **5**, 27–46.

Reandeau, S.G. & Wampold, B.E. (1991). Relationship of power and involvement in working alliance: a multiple-case sequential analysis of brief therapy. *Journal of Counseling Psychology*, **38**, 107–14.

Reed, D., McGee, D., Yano, K. & Feinleib, M. (1983). Social networks and coronary heart disease among Japanese men in Hawaii. *American Journal of Epidemiology*, **117**, 384–96.

Reedy, M.N., Birren, J.E. & Schaie, K.W. (1981). Age and sex differences in satisfying love relationships across the adult life span. *Human Development*, **24**, 52–66.

Reid, M., Landesmann, S., Treder, R. & Jaccard, J. (1989). "My family and friends": six-to-twelve-year old childrens' perceptions of social support. *Child Development*, **60**, 896–910.

Reik, T. (1944). *A Psychologist Looks at Love*. New York: Farrar & Reinhart.

Reis, H.T. & Shaver, P. (1988). Intimacy as an interpersonal process. In S. Duck (Ed.), *Handbook of Personal Relationships: Theory, Research, and Interventions* (1st Edn, pp. 367–89). Chichester: Wiley.

Reis, H.T., Senchak, M. & Solomon, B. (1985). Sex differences in the intimacy of social interaction: further exploration of potential explanations. *Journal of Personality and Social Psychology*, **48**, 1204–17.

Reis, H.T., Wheeler, L., Nazlek, J., Kernis, M.H. & Spiegel, N. (1985). On specificity in the impact of social participation on physical and psycholgical health. *Journal of Personality and Social Psychology*, **48**, 456–71.

Reisman, D. (1950). *The Lonely Crowd: a Study of the Changing American Character*. New Haven: Yale University Press.

Reiss, D., Plomin, R. & Hetherington, E.M. (1991). Genetics and psychiatry: an unheralded window on the environment. *American Journal of Psychiatry*, **148**, 283–91.

Reissman, C., Aron, A. & Bergen, M.R. (1993). Shared activities and marital satisfaction: causal direction and self-expansion versus boredom. *Journal of Social and Personal Relationships*, **10**, 243–54.

Rempel, J.K., Holmes, J.G. & Zanna, M.P. (1985). Trust in close relationships. *Journal of Personality and Social Psychology*, **49**, 95–112.

Repetti, R.L. (1993). The effects of daily social and academic experiences on children's subsequent interactions with parents. Poster presented at the Biennial Meeting of the Society for Research in Child Development, New Orleans, LA.

Repetti, R.L. (1994). Short-term and long-term processes linking job stressors to father–child interaction. *Social Development*, **3**, 1–15.

Repetti, R.L. & Wood, J. (1994). The effects of daily stress at work on mothers' interactions with preschoolers. Unpublished manuscript, University of California at Los Angeles.

Retzinger, S.M. (1995). Shame and anger in personal relationships. In S.W. Duck & J.T. Wood (Eds), *Relationship Challenges (Understanding Relationship Processes 5)* (pp. 22–42). Thousand Oaks, CA: Sage.

Revenson, T.A., Schiaffino, K.M., Majerovitz, D.S. & Gibofsky, A. (1991). Social support as a double-edged sword: the relation of positive and problematic support to depression among rheumatoid arthritis patients. *Social Science and Medicine*, **33**, 807–13.

Revenstorf, D., Hahlweg, K., Schindler, L. & Vogel, B. (1984). Interaction analysis of marital conflict. In K. Hahlweg & N.S. Jacobson (Eds), *Marital Interaction: Analysis and Modification* (pp. 159–81). New York: Guilford.

Reynolds, C.H. & Norman, R.V. (1988). *Community in America: The Challenge of Habits of the Heart*. Berkeley: University of California Press.

Rhodes, J.E., Ebert, L. & Fischer, K. (1992). Natural mentors: An overlooked resource in the social networks of young African American mothers. *American Journal of Community Psychology*, **20**(4), 445–61.

Riad, J. & Norris, F. (1996). The influence of relocation on the environmental, social, and psychological stress experienced by disaster victims. *Environment and Behavior*, **28**, 163–82.

Richards, E.F. (1980). Network ties, kin ties, and marital role organization: Bott's hypothesis reconsidered. *Journal of Comparative Family Studies*, **11**, 139–51.

Richardson, L. (1990). Narrative and sociology. *Journal of Contemporary Ethnography*, **19**, 116–35.

Richardson, L. (1994). Writing as a method of inquiry. In N. Denzin & Y. Lincoln (Eds), *Handbook of Qualitative Research*. Thousand Oaks, CA: Sage.

Richters, J.E. (1987). Chronic versus episodic stress and the adjustment of high-risk offspring. In K. Hahlweg & M. J. Goldstein (Eds), *Understanding Major Mental Disorder: the Role of Family Interaction Research*. New York: Family Process Press.

Ricoeur, P. (1983). *Hermeneutics and the Human Sciences: Essays on Language, Action and Interpretation* (Trans. J. Thompson). New York: Cambridge University Press.

Rieder, C. & Cicchetti, D. (1989). An organizational perspective on cognitive control functioning and cognitive-affective balance in maltreated children. *Developmental Psychology*, **25**, 482–93.

Riegel, K. (1976). The dialectics of human development. *American Psychologist*, **31**, 689–700.

Riessman, C. (1990). *Divorce Talk: Men and Women Make Sense of Personal Relationships*. New Brunswick, NJ: Rutgers University Press.

Riessman, C. (1992). Making sense of marital violence: one woman's narrative. In G.C. Rosenwald & R.L. Ochberg (Eds), *Storied Lives: the Cultural Politics of Self-understanding* (pp. 231–49). New Haven CT: Yale University Press.

Riley, D. (1990). Network influences on father involvement in child rearing. In M. Cochran, M. Larner, D. Riley, L. Gunnarsson & C.R. Henderson Jr (Eds), *Extending Families: the Social Networks of Parents and their Children* (pp. 131–53). New York: Cambridge University Press.

Riley, D. & Eckenrode, T. (1986). Social ties: subgroup differences in costs and benefits. *Journal of Personality and Social Psychology*, **51**, 770–78.

Riley, M.W. (1983). The family in an aging society: a matrix of latent relationships. *Journal of Family Issues*, **4**, 439–54.

Rimé, B., Philippot, P., Boca, S. & Mesquita, A. (1992). Long-lasting cognitive and social consequences of emotion: social sharing and rumination. In W. Stroebe & M. Hewstone (Eds), *European Review of Social Psychology*, Vol. 3, (pp. 225–58). Chichester: Wiley.

Rinehart, L. (1992). Coping with conflict: implications for relationship satisfaction. Paper presented at the Sixth International Conference on Personal Relationships, Orono, Maine.

Riordan, C.A. & Tedeschi, J.T. (1983). Attraction in aversive environments: some evidence for classical conditioning and negative reinforcement. *Journal of Personality and Social Psychology*, **44**, 684–92.

Risman, B.J. & Schwartz, P. (1989). Being gendered: a microstructural view of intimate relationships. In B.J. Risman & P. Schwartz (Eds), *Gender in Intimate Relationships: a Microstructural Approach* (pp. 1–9).

Rizzo, T. (1989). *Friendship Development Among Children in School.* Norwood, NJ: Ablex.

Robbins, S.B. & Jolkovski, M.P. (1987). Managing countertransference feelings: an interactional model using awareness of feeling and theoretical framework. *Journal of Counseling Psychology*, **34**, 276–82.

Roberts, C.S., Cox, C.E., Shannon, V.J. & Wells, N.L. (1994). A closer look at social support as a moderator of stress in breast cancer. *Health and Social Work*, **19**, 157–64.

Roberts, G.W. (1991). Schizophrenia: a neuropathological perspective. *British Journal of Psychiatry*, **158**, 8–17.

Roberts, M.K. (1982). Men and women: partners, lovers, friends. In K.E. Davis & T. Mitchell (Eds), *Advances in Descriptive Psychology*, **2**, 57–78.

Roberts, R.E.L. & Bengtson, V.L. (1990). Is intergenerational solidarity a unidimensional construct? A second test of a formal model. *Journal of Gerontology: Social Sciences*, **45**, S12–20.

Roberts, W. & Strayer, J. (1987). Parent's responses to the emotional distress of their children: relations with children's competence. *Developmental Psychology*, **25**, 415–22.

Robertson, J. (1953). Some responses of young children to the loss of maternal care. *Nursing Times*, **49**, 382–6.

Robertson, J.F. (1995). Grandparenting in an era of rapid change. In R. Blieszner & V. H. Bedford (Eds), *Handbook of Aging and the Family* (pp. 243–60). Westport, CT: Greenwood Press.

Robins, L.N. & Ratcliff, K.S. (1979). Risk factors in the continuum of childhood anti-social behavior to adulthood. *International Journal of Mental Health*, **7**, 96–116.

Robinson, J. (1977). *How Americans Use Time: a Social–Psychological Analysis.* New York: Praeger.

Robinson, W.S. (1950). Ecological correlations and the behavior of individuals. *American Sociological Review*, **15**, 351–7.

Robinson, W.S. (1957). The statistical measurement of agreement. *American Sociological Review*, **22**, 17–25.

Rochford, B. & Blocker, T. (1991). Coping with "natural" hazards as stressors. *Environment and Behavior*, **23**, 171–94.

Rocissano, L., Slade, A. & Lynch, V. (1987). Dyadic synchrony and toddler compliance. *Developmental Psychology*, **23**, 698–704.

Rogers, T.B., Kuiper, N.A. & Kirker, W.S. (1977). Self-reference and the encoding of personal information. *Journal of Personality and Social Psychology*, **35**, 677–88.

Rogler, L. & Procidano, M. (1986). The effects of social networks on marital roles. *Journal of Marriage and the Family*, **48**, 693–702.

Rohrbaugh, M. & Bartels, B. (1975). Participants' perceptions of "curative factors" in therapy and growth groups. *Small Group Behavior*, **6**, 430–56.

Rollins, B. & Feldman, H. (1970). Marriage satisfaction over the family life cycle. *Journal of Marriage and the Family*, **32**, 20–28.

Roloff, M.E. (1987). Communication and reciprocity within intimate relationships. In M.R. Roloff & G.R. Miller (Eds), *Interpersonal Processes: New Directions in Communication Research* (pp. 11–38). Newbury Park, CA: Sage.

Roloff, M.E. & Cloven, D.H. (1994). When partners transgress: maintaining violated relationships. In Canary, D.J. & Stafford, L. (Eds), *Communication and Relational Maintenance* (pp. 23–43). Academic Press: New York.

Roloff, M.E. & Janiszewski, C.A. (1989). Overcoming obstacles to interpersonal compliance: a principle of message construction. *Human Communication Research*, **16**, 33–61.

Roloff, M.E., Janiszewski, C.A., McGrath, M.A., Burns, C.S. & Manrai, L.A. (1988). Acquiring resources from intimates: when obligation substitutes for persuasion. *Human Communication Research*, **14**, 364–96.

Ronai, C.R. (1992). The reflexive self through narrative: a night in the life of an erotic dancer/researcher. In C. Ellis & M. Flaherty (Eds), *Investigating Subjectivity: Research on Lived Experience* (pp. 102–24). Newbury Park, CA: Sage.

Ronai, C.R. (1994). Multiple reflections on child sex abuse: an argument for a layered account, *Journal of Contemporary Ethnography*, **23**, 395–426.

Rook, K.S. (1984). The negative side of social interaction: impact on psychological well-being. *Journal of Personality and Social Psychology*, **46**, 109–18.

Rook, K.S. (1985). Functions of social bonds: perspectives from research on social support, loneliness and social isolation. In I.G. Sarason & B.R. Sarason (Eds), *Social Support: Theory, Research and Application*. The Hague: Martinus Nijhof.

Rook, K.S. (1987). Social support versus companionship: effects on life stress, loneliness, and evaluations by others. *Journal of Personality and Social Psychology*, **52**, 1132–47.

Rook, K.S. (1990). Social relationships as a source of companionship: implications for older adults' psychological well-being. In I.G. Sarason, B.R. Sarason & G.R. Pierce (Eds), *Social Support: an Interactional View* (pp. 219–50). New York: Wiley.

Rook, K.S. (1991). Facilitating friendship formation in late life: puzzles and challenges. *American Journal of Community Psychology*, **19**, 103–10.

Rook, K.S. (1992). Detrimental aspects of social relationships: taking stock of an emerging literature. In H. Veiel & U. Baumann (Eds), *The Meaning and Measurement of Social Support* (pp. 157–69). New York: Hemisphere.

Rook, K.S. & Dooley, D. (1985). Applying social support research: theoretical problems and future directions. *Journal of Social Issues*, **41**, 5–28.

Rook, K.S., Dooley, D. & Catalano, R. (1991). Stress transmission: the effects of husbands' job stressors on the emotional health of their wives. *Journal of Marriage and the Family*, **53**, 165–77.

Rorty, R. (1967). *The Linguistic Turn: Recent Essays in Philosophical Method*. Chicago: University of Chicago Press.

Rorty, R. (1979). *Philosophy and the Mirror of Nature*. Princeton, NJ: Princeton University Press.

Rorty, R. (1982). *Consequences of Pragmatism (Essays 1972–1980)*. Minneapolis: University of Minnesota Press.

Rorty, R. (1989). *Contingency, Irony, Solidarity*. Cambridge: Cambridge University Press.

Rosaldo, R. (1984). Grief and a headhunter's rage: on the cultural force of the emotions. In E. Bruner (Ed.), *Text, Play, and Story: the Construction and Reconstruction of Self and Society, Proceedings of the American Ethnological Society, Washington*, pp. 178–95.

Rosario, M., Shinn, M., Morch, H. & Huckabee, C. (1988). Gender differences in coping and social supports: testing socialization and role constraint theories. *Journal of Community Psychology*, **16**, 55–69.

Rose, S.M. (1985). Same- and cross-sex friendships and the psychology of homosociality. *Sex Roles*, **12**, 63–74.

Rosenau, P. (1992). *Postmodernism and the Social Sciences: Insights, Inroads, and Intrusions*. Princeton, NJ: Princeton University Press.

Rosenbaum, C.P. (1961). Patient–family similarities in schizophrenia. *Archives of General Psychiatry*, **5**, 120–26.

Rosenberg, S., Rosenberg, H. & Farrell, M. (1992). In the name of the father. In G.C.

Rosenwald & R.L. Ochberg (Eds), *Storied Lives: the Cultural Politics of Self-Understanding* (pp. 41–59). New Haven, CT: Yale University Press.

Rosenberger, N.R. (1989). Dialectic balance in the polar model of self: the Japan case. *Ethos*, **17**, 88–113.

Rosenblatt, P.C., Karis, T.A. & Powell, R.D. (1995). *Multiracial Couples: Black and White Voices*. Thousand Oaks, CA: Sage.

Rosenthal, D. (1970). *Genetic Theory and Abnormal Behavior*. New York: McGraw-Hill.

Rosenthal, D.A. & Feldman, S.S. (1990). The acculturation of Chinese immigrants: perceived effects on family functioning of length of residence in two cultural contexts. *The Journal of Genetic Psychology*, **15**(4), 495–514.

Rosenwald, G.C. (1992). Conclusion: reflections on narrative understanding. In G.C. Rosenwald and R.L. Ochberg (Eds), *Storied Lives: the Cultural Politics of Self-understanding* (pp. 265–89). New Haven, CT: Yale University Press.

Rosenwald, G.C. & Ochberg, R.L. (Eds) (1992). *Storied Lives: the Cultural Politics of Self-understanding*. New Haven, CT: Yale University Press.

Rosner, B. (1982). On the estimation and testing of interclass correlations: the general case of multiple replicates for each variable. *American Journal of Epidemiology*, **116**, 722–30.

Ross, C.E. (1987). The division of labor at home. *Social Forces*, **65**, 816–33.

Ross, C.E. (1995). Conceptualizing marital status as a continuum of social attachment. *Journal of Marriage and the Family*, **57**, 129–40.

Ross, H.S. & Goldman, B.D. (1976). Establishing new social relations in infancy. In T. Alloway, P. Pliner & L. Krames (Eds), *Advances in the Study of Communication and Affect: Attachment Behavior*, Vol. 3 (pp. 61–79). New York: Plenum.

Ross, L. (1977). The intuitive psychologist and his shortcomings: distortions in the attribution process. In L. Berkowitz (Ed.), *Advances in Experimental Social Psychology*, Vol. 10 (pp. 173–220). New York: Academic Press.

Rossi, A.S. & Rossi, P.H. (1990). *Of Human Bonding: Parent–Child Relations Across the Life Course*. New York: Aldine de Gruyter.

Rotenberg, K.J. (1985). Causes, intensity, motives, and consequences of children's anger from self reports. *The Journal of Genetic Psychology*, **146**, 101–6.

Roth, P. (1991). *Patrimony: a True Story*. New York: Simon and Schuster.

Rothbard, J.C. & Shaver, P.R. (1994). Continuity of attachment across the life span. In *Attachment in Adults: Clinical and Developmental Perspectives* (pp. 31–71). New York: Guilford.

Rotter, J.B. (1954). *Social Learning and Clinical Psychology*. Englewood Cliffs, NJ: Prentice-Hall.

Rowley, K.G. (1968). Social relations between British and immigrant children. *Educational Research*, **10**, 145–8.

Roy, A. (1978). Risk factors and depression in Canadian women. *Journal of Affective Disorders*, **3**, 69–70.

Ruan, F. & Matsumura, M. (1991). *Sex in China: studies in sexology in Chinese culture*. New York: Plenum.

Ruberman, W., Weinblatt, E., Goldberg, J.D. & Chaudhary, B. S. (1984). Psychosocial influences on mortality after myocardial infarction. *New England Journal of Medicine*, **311**, 552–9.

Rubin, C.M. & Rubin, J.Z. (1993). Dynamics of conflict escalation in families. In D. Perlman & W.H. Jones (Eds), *Advances in Personal Relationships*, Vol. 4 (pp. 165–91). London: Kingsley.

Rubin, J.Z. & Brown, B.R. (1975). *The Social Psychology of Bargaining and Negotiation*. New York: Academic Press.

Rubin, J.Z., Pruitt, D. & Kim, H.K. (1994). *Social Conflict* (2nd Edn). New York: McGraw-Hill.

Rubin, K.H. & Mills, R.S.L. (1990). Maternal beliefs about adaptive and maladaptive social behaviors in normal, aggressive and withdrawn preschoolers. *Journal of Abnormal Child Psychology*, **18**, 419–35.

Rubin, K.H., Mills, R.S.L. & Rose-Krasnor, L. (1989). Maternal beliefs and children's competence. In B. Schneider, G. Attili, J. Nadel & R. Weissberg (Eds), *Social Competence in Developmental Perspective* (pp. 313–31). Amsterdam: Kluwer Academic.

Rubin, L.B. (1983). *Intimate Strangers: Men and Women Together*. New York: Harper & Row.

Rubin, L.B. (1985). *Just Friends: the Role of Friendship in Our Everyday Lives*. New York: Harper & Row.

Rubin, Z. (1973). *Liking and Loving*. New York: Holt, Rinehart & Winston.

Rubonis, A.V. & Bickman, L. (1991). Psychological impairment in the wake of disaster: the disaster–psychopathology relationship. *Psychological Bulletin*, **109**, 384–99.

Ruch, W. (1993). Exhilaration and humor. In M. Lewis & J. Haviland (Eds), *Handbook of Emotions* (pp. 605–16). New York: Guilford.

Ruehlman, L.A. & Wolchik, S.A. (1988). Personal goals, interpersonal support and hindrance as factors in psychological distress and well-being. *Journal of Personality and Social Psychology*, **55**, 293–301.

Runciman, W.G. (1966). *Relative Deprivation and Social Justice*. Berkeley, CA: University of California Press.

Rusbult, C.E. (1980). Commitment and satisfaction in romantic associations: a test of the investment model. *Journal of Experimental Social Psychology*, **16**, 172–86.

Rusbult, C.E. (1983). A longitudinal test of the investment model: the development (and deterioration) of satisfaction and commitment in heterosexual involvements. *Journal of Personality and Social Psychology*, **45**, 101–17.

Rusbult, C.E. (1987). Responses to dissatisfaction in close relationships: the exit-voice-loyalty-neglect model. In D. Perlman & S.W. Duck (Eds), *Intimate Relationships* (pp. 209–37). Newbury Park, CA: Sage.

Rusbult, C.E. (1991). Comment on Johnson's "Commitment to personal relationships": what's interesting, and what's new? In W. H. Jones & D. Perlman (Eds), *Advances in Personal Relationships*, Vol. 3 (pp. 151–69). London: Kingsley.

Rusbult, C.E. & Buunk, A.P. (1993). Commitment processes in close relationships: an interdependence analysis. *Journal of Social and Personal Relationships*, **10**, 175–203.

Rusbult, C.E. & Martz, J.M. (1995). Remaining in an abusive relationship: an investment model analysis of nonvoluntary commitment. *Personality and Social Psychology Bulletin*, **21**, 558–71.

Rusbult, C.E., Van Lange, P.A.M., Verette, J. & Yovetich, N.A. (1995). A functional analysis of perceived superiority in close relationships. Unpublished manuscript, University of North Carolina at Chapel Hill.

Rusbult, C.E., Verette, J. & Drigotas, S.M. (1995). Absolute commitment level, mutuality of commitment, and couple adjustment in marital relationships. Unpublished manuscript, University of North Carolina at Chapel Hill.

Rusbult, C.E., Verette, J., Whitney, G.A., Slovik, L.F. & Lipkus, I. (1991). Accommodation processes in close relationships: theory and preliminary empirical evidence. *Journal of Personality and Social Psychology*, **60**, 53–78.

Rushton, J.P. (1989a). Genetic similarity, human altruism, and group selection. *Behavioral and Brain Sciences*, **12**, 503–59.

Rushton, J.P. (1989b). Genetic similarity in male friendships. *Ethology and Sociobiology*, **10**.

Russell, A. & Finnie, V. (1990). Preschool children's social status and maternal instructions to assist group entry. *Developmental Psychology*, **26**(4), 603–11.

Rutherford, E. & Mussen, P. (1968). Generosity in nursery school boys. *Child Development*, **39**, 755–65.

Rutter, M. (1971). Parent–child separation: psychological effects on children. *Journal of Child Psychology and Psychiatry*, **12**, 233–60.

Rutter, M. & Brown, G.W. (1966). The reliability and validity of measures of family life and relationships in families containing a psychiatric patient. *Social Psychiatry*, **1**, 38–53.

Ruvolo, A.P. (1990). Interpersonal ideals and personal changes in newlyweds. Unpublished doctoral dissertation. Ann Arbor, MI: University of Michigan.

Ruvolo, A.P. & Veroff, J. (1994). For better or worse: real–ideal discrepancies and the marital well-being of newlyweds (under review).

Ryan, A.S. (1985). Cultural factors in casework with Chinese-Americans. *Social Casework: the Journal of Contemporary Social Work*, **66**(6), 333–40.

Rychlak, J.F. (Ed.) (1976). *Dialectic: Humanistic Rationale for Behavior and Development*. New York: S. Karger.

Rychlak, J.F. (1988). *The Psychology of Rigorous Humanism* (2nd Edn). New York: New York University Press.

Ryder, R.G. & Bartle, S. (1991). Boundaries as distance regulators in personal relationships. *Family Process*, **30**, 393–406.

Saarni, C. (1995). Coping with aversive feelings. Paper presented at the Meeting of the Society for Research in Child Development, Indianapolis, IN.

Sabatelli, R.M. (1984). The marital comparison level index: a measure for assessing outcomes relative to expectations. *Journal of Marriage and the Family*, **46**, 651–61.

Sabatelli, R.M. & Shehan, C.L. (1993). Exchange and resource theories. In P.G. Boss, W.J. Doherty, R. LaRossa, W.R. Schumm & S.K. Steinmetz (Eds), *Sourcebook of Family Theories and Methods: a Contextual Approach* (pp. 385–411). New York: Plenum.

Sacks, H. (1972). An initial investigation of the usability of conversational data for doing sociology. In D. Sudnow (Ed), *Studies in Social Interaction* (pp. 31–75). New York: Free Press.

Sadalla, E.K., Kenrick, D.T. & Vershure, B. (1987). Dominance and heterosexual attraction. *Journal of Personality and Social Psychology*, **52**, 730–38.

Safran, J.D. (1990). Towards a refinement of cognitive therapy in light of interpersonal theory: I. Theory. *Clinical Psychology Review*, **10**, 87–105.

Safran, J.D. (1993). Breaches in the therapeutic alliance: an arena for negotiating authentic relatedness. *Psychotherapy*, **30**, 11–24.

Safran, J.D. & Segal, Z.V. (1990). *Interpersonal Process in Cognitive Therapy*. New York: Basic Books.

Safran, J.D., Muran, J.C. & Wallner-Samstag, L. (1994). Resolving therapeutic alliance ruptures: a task analytic investigation. In A.O. Horvath & L.S. Greenberg (Eds), *The Working Alliance: Theory Research and Practice* (pp. 225–58). New York: Wiley.

Sagi, A. & Hoffman, M. (1976). Empathic distress in the newborn. *Developmental Psychology*, **12**, 175–6.

Salisch, M. von (1989). Equality versus dominance within pairs of friends. Paper presented at the Meeting of the Society for Research in Child Development, Kansas City, MO.

Salisch, M. von (1991). *Kinderfreundschaften. Emotionale Kommunikation im Konflikt.* Göttingen: Hogrefe.

Salisch, M. von (1993). Self-worth and the experience and expression of anger. Paper presented at the Meeting of the Society for Research in Child Development, New Orleans, März 1993.

Salisch, M. von (1995). Ärger bei Kindern. Manuscript, Freie Universität Berlin.

Salisch, M. von (1996). Child–child relationships: symmetry and asymmetry among peers, friends and siblings. In A.E. Auhagen & M. von Salisch (Eds), *The Diversity of Human Relationships*. New York: Cambridge University Press.

Salzinger, L. (1982). The ties that bind: the effects of clustering on dyadic relationships. *Social Networks*, **4**, 117–45.

Sampson, E.E. (1988). The debate on individualism: indigenous psychologies of the individual and their role in personal and societal functioning. *American Psychologist*, **43**, 15–22.

Sancilio, M., Plumert, J. & Hartup, W.W. (1989). Friendship and aggressiveness as determinants of conflict outcomes in middle childhood. *Developmental Psychology*, **25**, 812–19.

Sande, G.N., Goethals, G.R. & Radloff, C.E. (1988). Perceiving one's own traits and others': the multifaceted self. *Journal of Personality and Social Psychology*, **54**, 13–20.

Sanford, S. & Eder, D. (1984). Adolescent humor during peer interaction. *Social Psychology Quarterly*, **47**, 235–43.

Sanjek, R. (1994). Intermarriage and the future of races in the United States. In S. Gregory & R. Sanjek (Eds), *Race* (pp. 103–30). New Brunswick, NJ: Rutgers University Press.

Sapadin, L.A. (1988). Friendship and gender: perspectives of professional men and women. *Journal of Social and Personal Relationships*, **5**, 387–403.

Saraceno, C. (1981). *Ritratto di famiglia degli anni '80*. Bari: Laterza.

Sarason, B.R., Pierce, G.R. & Sarason, I.G. (1990). Social support: the sense of acceptance and the role of relationships. In B.R. Sarason, I.G. Sarason & G.R. Pierce (Eds), *Social Support: an Interactional View* (pp. 97–128). New York: Wiley.

Sarason, B.R., Pierce, G.R. & Sarason, I.G. (1995). Personality, relationship, and task-related factors in parent–child interaction: two observational studies. Unpublished manuscript, University of Washington.

Sarason, B.R., Pierce, G.R., Bannerman, A. & Sarason, I.G. (1993). Investigating the antecedents of perceived social support: parents' view of and behavior toward their children. *Journal of Personality and Social Psychology*, **65**, 1071–85.

Sarason, B.R., Sarason, I.G. & Pierce, G.R. (1990). *Social Support: an Interactional View*. New York: Wiley.

Sarason, B.R., Sarason, I.G., Hacker, T.A. & Basham, R.B. (1985). Concomitants of social support: social skills, physical attractiveness and gender. *Journal of Personality and Social Psychology*, **49**, 469–80.

Sarason, B.R., Shearin, E.N., Pierce, G.R. & Sarason, I.G. (1987a). Interrelations of social support measures: Theoretical and practical implications. *Journal of Personality and Social Psychology*, **52**, 813–32.

Sarason, I.G., Levine, H.M., Basham, R.B. & Sarason, B.R. (1983). Assessing social support: the Social Support Questionnaire. *Journal of Personality and Social Psychology*, **44**, 127–39.

Sarason, I.G., Sarason, B.R. & Pierce, G.R. (1992). Three contexts of social support. In H. Veiel & U. Baumann (Eds), *The Meaning and Measurement of Social Support* (pp. 143–54). New York: Hemisphere.

Sarason, I.G., Sarason, B.R. & Pierce, G.R. (1994). Social support: global and relationship-based levels of analysis. *Journal of Social and Personal Relationships*, **11**, 295–312.

Sarason, I.G., Sarason, B.R. & Shearin, E.N. (1986). Social support as an individual difference variable: its stability, origins, and relational aspects. *Journal of Personality and Social Psychology*, **50**, 845–55.

Sarason, I.G., Sarason, B.R., Shearin, E.N. & Pierce, G.R. (1987b). A brief measure of social support: practical and theoretical implications. *Journal of Social and Personal Relationships*, **4**, 497–510.

Sarason, S.B. (1974). *The Psychological Sense of Community: Prospects for a Community Psychology*. San Francisco, CA: Jossey-Bass.

Saravia-Shore, M. & Arvitzu, S.F. (Eds) (1992). *Cross-cultural Literacy: Ethnographies of Communication in Multiethnic Classrooms*. New York: Garland.

Sarbin, T. (Ed.) (1986). *Narrative Psychology: the Storied Nature of Human Conduct*. New York: Praeger.

Satir, V. (1972). *Peoplemaking*. Palo Alto, CA: Science and Behavior Books.

Sattell, J. (1976). The inexpressive male: tragedy or sexual politics? *Social Problems*, **23**, 469–77.

Scanzoni, J., Polonko, K., Teachman, J. & Thompson, L. (1989). "Framing the problem" and "A fresh construct". In Scanzoni (Ed.), *The Sexual Bond* (pp. 12–50). Newbury Park, CA: Sage.

Scanzoni, L.D. & Scanzoni, J. (1981). *Men, Women and Change* (2nd Edn). New York: McGraw-Hill.

Schaap, C., Buunk, B. & Kerkstra, A. (1988). Marital conflict resolution. In P. Noller & M.A. Fitzpatrick (Eds), *Perspectives on Marital Interaction* (pp. 202–44). Clevedon, UK: Multilingual Matters.

Schachter, D. & Tulving, E. (1994). *Memory Systems 1994.* Cambridge, MA.

Schachter, S. (1959). *The Psychology of Affiliation: Experimental Studies of the Sources of Gregariousness.* Stanford, CA: Stanford University Press.

Schaffer, L., Wynne, L., Day, J., Ryckoff, I. & Halperin, A. (1962). On the nature and sources of the psychiatrists' experience with the family of the schizophrenic. *Psychiatry*, **25**, 32–45.

Schank, R.C. & Abelson, R.P. (1977). *Scripts, Plans, Goals and Understanding.* Hillsdale, NJ: Erlbaum.

Scheier, M.F. & Carver, C.S. (1992). Effects of optimism on psychological and physical well-being: theoretical overview and empirical update. *Cognitive Therapy and Research*, **16**, 201–28.

Scheier, M.F., Matthews, K.A., Owens, J.F., Magovern, G.J., Lefebvre, R.C., Abbott, R.A. & Carver, C.S. (1989). Dispositional optimism and recovery from coronary bypass surgery: the beneficial effects on physical and psychological wellbeing. *Journal of Personality and Social Psychology*, **57**, 1024–40.

Schellenberg, J.A. (1978). *Masters of Social Psychology: Freud, Mead, Lewin, and Skinner.* Oxford: Oxford University Press.

Scherer, K.R. (Ed.) (1988). *Facets of Emotion.* Hillsdale, NJ: Erlbaum.

Scherer, K.R., Wallbott, H. & Summerfield, A. (Eds) (1986). *Experiencing Emotion. A Cross-cultural Study.* Cambridge: Cambridge University Press.

Schneider, B.H. (1993). *Children's Social Competence in Context: the Contributions of Family, School and Culture.* Oxford: Pergamon.

Schneider, B. H. & Fonzi, A.F. (1995, September). La stabilita' dell'amicizia: uno studio cross culturale Italia–Canada [Friendship stability: A cross-cultural study (Italy–Canada)]. Presented to the Italian Psychological Society, Cesena (Bologna), Italy.

Schneider, B.H., Wiener, J. & Murphy, K. (1994). Children's friendships: the giant step beyond peer acceptance. *Journal of Social and Personal Relationships*, **11**, 323–40.

Schneider, W. & Larzelere, R. (1988, August). Effects of discipline strategies on delays of reoccurrences of misbehavior in toddlers. Paper presented at the meeting of the American Psychological Association, Atlanta, GA.

Schneider-Rosen, K. & Cicchetti, D. (1991). Early self-knowledge and emotional development: visual self-recognition and affective reactions to mirror self-images in maltreated and non-maltreated toddlers. *Developmental Psychology*, **27**, 471–8.

Schoenbach, V.J., Kaplan, B.H., Fredman, L. & Kleinbaum, D.G. (1986). Social ties and mortality in Evans County, Georgia. *American Journal of Epidemiology*, **123**, 577–91.

Schofield, J.W. & Sagar, H.A. (1977). Peer interaction patterns in an integrated middle school. *Sociometry*, **40**, 130–38.

Schonbach, P. (1980). A category system for account phases. *European Journal of Social Psychology*, **10**, 195–200.

Schonbach, P. & Kleibaumhuter, P. (1990). Severity of reproach and defensiveness of accounts. In M.J. Cody & M.L. McLaughlin (Eds), *The Psychology of Tactical Communication* (pp. 229–43). Clevedon, UK: Multilingual Matters.

Schreiber, R.D. (1984). Reactions to depressed individuals: an analogue study. Unpublished doctoral dissertation, Pacific Graduate School of Psychology, Palo Alto, CA.

Schutz, A. (1970). *On Phenomenology and Social Relations.* Chicago: Chicago University Press.

Schutz, A. (M. Natanson, Ed.) (1971). *Collected Papers: Volume I: The Problems of Social Reality*. The Hague: Matinus Nijoff.

Schutz, A. & Luckman, T. (1973). *The Structures of the Life-world* (R.M. Zaner & H.T. Englehardt, Trans.). Evanston: Northwestern University Press.

Schutz, W.C. (1958). *FIRO: a Three-dimensional Theory of Interpersonal Behavior*. New York: Holt, Rinehart & Winston.

Schwartz, P. (1994). *Peer Marriage: How Love Between Equals Really Works*. New York: Free Press.

Schwarz, N. (1990). Feelings as information: informational and motivational functions of affective states. In R. Sorrentino & E.T. Higgins (Eds), *Handbook of Motivation and Cognition: Foundations of Social Behavior*, Vol. 2 (pp. 527–61). New York: Guilford.

Schwarzer, R. & Leppin, A. (1989). Social support and health: a meta-analysis. *Psychology and Health: An International Journal*, **3**, 1–5.

Schwarzer, R. & Leppin, A. (1991). Social support and health: a theoretical and empirical overview. *Journal of Social and Personal Relationships*, **8**, 99–127.

Schwarzer, R. & Leppin, A. (1992). Possible impact of social ties and support on morbidity and mortality. In H.O.F. Veiel & U. Bauman (Eds). *The Meaning and Measurement of Social Support* (pp. 65–83). New York: Hemisphere.

Scopetta, M.A., King, O.E. & Szapocznik, J. (1977). *Relationship of Acculturation, Incidence of Drug Abuse, and Effective Treatment for Cuban Americans*. National Institute on Drug Abuse. Final Report of Research Contract No. 271-75-4136.

Scott, C.K., Fuhrman, R.W. & Wyer, R.S., Jr. (1991). Information processing in close relationships. In G.J.O. Fletcher & F.D. Fincham (Eds), *Cognition and Close Relationships* (pp. 37–68). Hillsdale, NJ: Erlbaum.

Scott, J. (1991). *Social Network Analysis: a Handbook*. London: Sage.

Scott, M.B. & Lyman, S.M. (1968). Accounts. *American Sociological Review*, **33**, 46–62.

Seattle Tiees (1994). They met at a wedding and later had their own (March 29, p. G2).

Secord, P.F. (1983). Imbalanced sex ratios: the social consequences. *Personality and Social Psychology Bulletin*, **9**, 525–43.

Sedikides, C., Olsen, N. & Reis, H.T. (1993). Relationships as natural categories. *Journal of Personality and Social Psychology*, **64**, 71–82.

Seeman, T.E. & Syme, S.L. (1987). Social networks and coronary artery disease: a comparison of the structure and function of social relations as predictors of disease. *Psychosomatic Medicine*, **49**, 340–53.

Segal, N. (1988). Cooperation, competition, and altruism in human twinships: a sociobiological approach. In K.B. MacDonald (Ed.), *Sociobiological Perspectives on Human Development* (pp. 168–206). New York: Springer-Verlag.

Segall, M.H. (1979). *Cross-cultural Psychology: Human Behavior in Global Perspective*. Monterey, CA: Brooks-Cole.

Segrin, C. (1993). Interpersonal reactions to dysphoria: the role of relationship with partner and perceptions of rejection. *Journal of Social and Personal Relationships*, **10**, 83–98.

Seidman, E., Allen, L., Aber, J.L., Mitchell, C. & Feinman, J. (1994). The impact of school transitions in early adolescence on the self-system and perceived social context of poor urban youth. *Child Development*, **65**(2), 507–22.

Seligman, M. (1971). Preparedness and phobias. *Behavior Therapy*, **2**, 307–20.

Selman, R.L. (1980). *The Growth of Interpersonal Understanding*. New York: Academic Press.

Selman, R.L. & Demorest, A.P. (1987). Putting thoughts and feelings into perspective: a developmental view of how children deal with disequilibrium. In D. Bearison & H. Zimiles (Eds), *Thought and Emotion* (pp. 93–128). Hillsdale, NJ: Erlbaum.

Seltzer, J.A. & Kalmuss, D. (1988). Socialization and stress explanations for spouse abuse. *Social Forces*, **67**, 473–92.

Selvini-Palazzoli, M., Boscola, L., Cecchin, G. & Prata, G. (1978). *Paradox and Counterparadox*. New York: Jason Aronson.

Selye, H. (1956). *The Stress of Life*. New York: McGraw Hill.

Selye, H. (1976). *The Stress of Life* (2nd Edn). New York: McGraw-Hill.

Semin, G.R. & Manstead, A.S.R. (1983). *The Accountability of Conduct: a Social Psychological Analysis*. London: Academic Press.

Sexton, C.S. & Perlman, D.S. (1989). Couples' career orientation, gender role orientation, and perceived equity as determinants of marital power. *Journal of Marriage and the Family*, **51**, 933–41.

Shantz, C.U. (1987). Conflicts between children. *Child Development*, **58**, 283–305.

Shantz, C.U. (1993). Children's conflicts: representations and lessons learned. In R.R. Coching & K.A. Renninger (Eds), *The Development and Meaning of Psychological Distance*. Hillsdale, NJ: Erlbaum.

Shantz, C.U. & Hartup, W.W. (Eds) (1992). *Conflict in Child and Adolescent Development*. Cambridge: Cambridge University Press.

Shantz, C.U. & Hobart, J. (1989). Social conflict and development. In T.J. Berndt & G.W. Ladd (Eds), *Peer Relationships in Child Development* (pp. 71–94). New York: Wiley.

Shantz, C.U. & Shantz, D. (1985). Conflicts between children: social-cognitive and sociometric correlates. In M. Berkowitz (Ed.), *Peer Conflict and Psychological Growth: New Directions for Child Development*, Vol. 29 (pp. 3–21). San Francisco: Jossey-Bass.

Shaver, P.R. & Hazan, C. (1988). A biased overview of the study of love. *Journal of Social and Personal Relationships*, **5**, 473–501.

Shaver, P.R. & Hazan, C. (1993). Adult romantic attachment: theory and evidence. In D. Perlman & W. Jones (Eds), *Advances in Personal Relationships: a Research Annual*, Vol. 4 (pp. 29–70). London: Jessica Kingsley.

Shaver, P.R., Hazan, C. & Bradshaw, D. (1988). Love as attachment: the integration of three behavioral systems. In R.J. Sternberg & M.L. Barnes (Eds), *The Psychology of Love* (pp. 68–99). New Haven, CT: Yale University Press.

Shaver, P., Schwartz. J., Kirson, D. & O'Connor, C. (1987). Emotion knowledge: further xploration of a prototype approach. *Journal of Personality and Social Psycholoy*, **52**, 1061–86.

Shea, L., Thompson, L. & Blieszner, R. (1988). Resources in older adults' old and new friendships. *Journal of Social and Personal Relationships*, **5**, 93–6.

Shedler, J. & Block, J. (1990). Adolescent drug use and psychological health: a longitudinal inquiry. *American Psychologist*, **45**, 612–30.

Shehan, C.L. & Dwyer, J.W. (1989). Parent–child exchanges in the middle years: attachment and autonomy in the transition to adulthood. In J.A. Mancini (Ed.), *Aging Parents and Adult Children*. Lexington, MA: Lexington Books.

Sheldon, A. (1992). Conflict talk: sociolinguistic challenges to self-assertion and how young girls meet them. *Merrill–Palmer Quarterly*, **38**, 95–117.

Shenkar, O. & Ronen, S. (1987). The cultural context negotiations: the implications of Chinese interpersonal norms. *The Journal of Applied Behavioral Science*, **23**(2), 263–75.

Shepher, J. (1971). Mate selection among second generation kibbutz adolescents and adults: incest avoidance and negative imprinting. *Archives of Sexual Behavior*, **1**, 293–307.

Sherbourne, C.D. & Hays, R.D. (1990). Marital status, social support, and health transitions in chronic disease patients. *Journal of Health and Social Behavior*, **31**, 328–43.

Sherbourne, C.D., Meredith, L.S., Rogers, W. & Ware, J.E. (1992). Social support and stressful life events: age differences in their effects on health-related quality of life among the chronically ill. *Quality of Life Research*, **1**, 235–46.

Sherer, M. & Adams, C.H. (1983). Construct validation of the Self-efficacy Scale. *Psychological Reports*, **53**, 899–902.

Sherwood, S., Smith, P. & Alexander, J. (1993). The British are coming . . . again! The hidden agenda of "cultural studies". *Cultural Studies*, **22**, 370–5.

Shihadeh, E.S. (1991). The prevalence of husband-centered migration: employment consequences for married women. *Journal of Marriage and the Family*, **53**, 432–44.

Shinn, M., Lehmann, S. & Wong, N.W. (1984). Social interaction and social support. *Journal of Social Issues*, **40**, 55–76.

Short, R.V. (1979). Sexual selection and its component parts: somatic and genital selection as illustrated in man and the great apes. *Advances in the Study of Behavior*, **9**, 131–55.

Shoshan, T. (1989). Mourning and longing from generation to generation. *American Journal of Psychotherapy*, **43**, 193–207.

Shotter, J. (1987). The social construction of an "us": problems of accountability and narratology. In R. Burnett, P. McGee, & D. Clarke (Eds), *Accounting for Relationships: Explanation, Representation, and Knowledge* (pp. 225–47). London: Methuen.

Shotter, J. (1992) What is a "personal relationship? A rhetorical-responsive account of "unfinished business". In J.H. Harvey, T.L. Orbuch & A.L. Weber (Eds), *Attributions, Accounts and Close Relationships* (pp. 19–39). New York: Springer-Verlag.

Shotter, J. (1993). *Conversational Realities: Constructing Life Through Language*. Thousand Oaks, CA: Sage.

Shotter, J. & Gergen, K.J. (Eds) (1989). *Texts of Identity*. London: Sage.

Shrout, P.E. & Fleiss, J.L. (1979). Intraclass correlations: uses in assessing rater reliability. *Psychological Bulletin*, **86**, 420–28.

Shulman, S., Elicker, J. & Sroufe, L.A. (1994). Stages of friendship growth in preadolescence as related to attachment history. *Journal of Social and Personal Relationships*, **11**, 341–62.

Shumaker, S.A. & Hill, D.R. (1991). Gender differences in social support and physical health. *Health Psychology*, **10**, 102–11.

Shweder, R., Mahapatra, M. & Miller, J. (1987). Culture and moral development. In J. Kagan & S. Lamb (Eds), *The Emergence of Morality in Young Children* (pp. 1–82). Chicago: University of Chicago Press.

Siebert, R., (1984). *Le ali di un elefante*. Milan: Angeli.

Siegel, K. & Krauss, B.J. (1991). Living with HIV infection: adaptive tasks of seropositive gay men. *Journal of Health and Social Behavior*, **32**, 17–32.

Sigelman, L. & Welch, S. (1994). *Black Americans' Views of Racial Inequality: the Dream Deferred*. Cambridge: Cambridge University Press.

Silka, L. & Tip, J. (1994). Empowering the silent ranks: the Southeast Asian experience. *American Journal of Community Psychology*, **22**, 497–529.

Sillars, A., Folwell, A.L., Hill, K.C., Maki, B.K., Hurst, A.P. & Casano, R.A. (1994). Marital communication and the persistence of misunderstanding. *Journal of Social and Personal Relationships*, **11**, 611–17.

Silver, R. (1978). The parental behavior of ring doves. *American Scientist*, **66**, 209–15.

Silver, R.C., Wortman, C.B. & Crofton, C. (1990). The role of coping in support provision: the self-presentational dilemma of victims of life crises. In B.R. Sarason, I.G. Sarason & G.R. Pierce (Eds), *Social Support: an Interactional View* (pp. 397–426). New York: Wiley.

Silverberg, S.B. & Steinberg, L. (1987). Adolescent autonomy, parent–adolescent conflict, and parental well-being. *Journal of Youth and Adolescence*, **16**, 293–312.

Silverman, I.W. & Ragusa, D.M. (1990). Child and maternal correlates of impulse control in 24-month-old children. *Genetic, Social, and General Psychology Monographs*, **116**, 435–73.

Silverman, P.R. (1988). In search of new selves: accommodating to widowhood. In L.A. Bond & B.M. Compas (Eds), *Families in Transition: Primary Prevention Programs that Work* (pp. 200–20). New York: Academic Press.

Simmel, G. (1950). *The Sociology of Georg Simmel* (K. Wolff, Trans.). Free Press: New York.

Simmons, R.G. & Blyth, D.A. (1987). *Moving into Adolescence: the Impact of Pubertal Change and School Context*. New York: Aldine De Gruyter.

Simmons, R.G., Carlton-Ford, S.L. & Blyth, D.A. (1987). Predicting how a child will cope with the transition to junior high school. In R.M. Lerner & T.T. Foch (Eds), *Biological–Psychosocial Interactions in Early Adolescence: a Life Span Perspective*. Hillsdale, NJ: Erlbaum.

Simon, H.A. (1990). A mechanism for social selection and successful altruism. *Science*, **250**, 1665–8.

Simpson, G.E. & Yinger, J.M. (1985). *Racial and Cultural Minorities: an Analysis of Prejudice and Discrimination* (5th Edn). New York: Plenum.

Simpson, J.A. (1987). The dissolution of romantic relationships: factors involved in relationship stability and emotional distress. *Journal of Personality and Social Psychology*, **53**, 683–92.

Simpson, J.A. (1990). The influence of attachment styles on romantic relationships. *Journal of Personality and Social Psychology*, **59**, 971–80.

Simpson, J.A. & Gangestad, S.W. (1992). Sociosexuality and romantic partner choice. *Journal of Personality*, **60**, 31–51.

Simpson, J.A., Gangestad, S.W. & Lerma, M. (1990). Perception of physical attractiveness: mechanisms involved in the maintenance of romantic relationships. *Journal of Personality and Social Psychology*, **59**, 1192–1201.

Simpson, J.A., Rholes, W.S. & Nelligan, J.S. (1992). Support seeking and support giving within couples in an anxiety-provoking situation: the role of attachment styles. *Journal of Personality and Social Psychology*, **62**, 434–46.

Singer, M.T. & Wynne, L.C. (1965a). Thought disorder and family relations of schizophrenics. III. Methodology using projective techniques. *Archives of General Psychiatry*, **12**, 187–200.

Singer, M.T. & Wynne, L.C. (1965b). Thought disorder and family relations of schizophrenics. IV. Results and implications. *Archives of General Psychiatry*, **12**, 201–12.

Singh, D. (1993). Adaptive significance of female physical attractiveness: role of waist-to-hip ratio. *Journal of Personality and Social Psychology*, **65**, 293–307.

Singleton, L.C. & Asher, S.R. (1979). Racial integration and children's peer preferences: an investigation of developmental and cohort differences. *Child Development*, **50**, 936–41.

Sinha, J.B.P. & Tripathi, R.C. (1994). Individualism in a collectivistic culture: a case of coexistence of opposites. In U. Kim, H.C. Triandis, C. Kagitcibasi, S. Choi & G. Yoon (Eds), *Individualism and Collectivism: Theory, methods, and applications* (pp. 123–36). Thousand Oaks, CA: Sage.

Sivadas, E. & Machleit, K.A. (1994). A scale to determine the extent of object incorporation in the extended self. *American Marketing Association*, **5**, 143–9.

Slater, P.E. (1963). On social regression. *American Sociological Review*, **28**, 339–64.

Slavin, R.E. (1979). Effects of biracial learning teams on cross-racial friendships. *Journal of Educational Psychology*, **71**, 381–7.

Slomkowski, C.L. & Dunn, J. (1992). Arguments and relationships within the family: differences in young children's disputes with mother and sibling. *Developmental Psychology*, **28**, 919–24.

Slomkowski, C.M. & Killen, M. (1992). Young children's conceptions of transgressions with friends and nonfriends. *International Journal of Behavioral Development*, **15**, 247–58.

Smith, A.L. & Weissman, M.M. (1992). Epidemiology. In E.S. Paykel (Ed.), *Handbook of Affective Disorders* (2nd Edn). New York: Guilford.

Smith, E. & Henry, S. (1994). An in-group becomes part of the self: response time evaluation. Manuscript under review.

Smith, M.D. (1990). Patriarchal ideology and wife beating: a test of a feminist hypothesis. *Violence and Victims*, **5**, 257–73.

Smith, P.K. (1995). Grandparenthood. In M.H. Bornstein (Ed.), *Handbook of Parenting*. Hillsdale, NJ: Erlbaum.

Smith, P.K., Bowers, L., Binney, V. & Cowie, H. (1994). Relationships of children involved in bully/victim relationships. In S. W. Duck (Ed.), *Learning About Relationships (Understanding Relationship Processes 2)* (pp. 186–212). Newbury Park, CA: Sage.

Smith, S.M. (1983). Disaster: family disruption in the wake of disaster. In C.R. Figley & H.I. McCubbin (Eds), *Stress and the Family: Vol. 2. Coping with Catastrophe* (pp. 120–47). New York: Brunner/Mazel.

Snyder, M. (1984). When belief creates reality. In L. Berkowitz (Ed.), *Advances in Experimental Social Psychology*, Vol. 18 (pp. 247–305). New York: Academic Press.

Snyder, M., Berscheid, E. & Glick, P. (1985). Focusing on the exterior and the interior: two investigations of the initiation of personal relationships. *Journal of Personality and Social Psychology*, **48**, 1427–39.

Snyder, M., Tanke, E. & Berscheid, E. (1977). Social perception and interpersonal behavior: on the self-fulfilling nature of social stereotypes. *Journal of Personality and Social Psychology*, **35**, 656–66.

Solomon, R.L. (1980). The opponent-process theory of acquired motivation: the costs of pleasure and the benefits of pain. *American Psychologist*, **35**, 691–712.

Solomon, S.D. (1986). Mobilizing social support networks in times of disaster. In C.R. Figley (Ed.), *Trauma and Its Wake: Vol. 2. Traumatic Stress Theory, Research, and Intervention* (pp. 232–63). New York: Brunner/Mazel.

Solomon, S.D., Bravo, M., Rubio-Stipec, M. & Canino, G. (1993). Effect of family role on response to disaster. *Journal of Traumatic Stress*, **6**, 255–69.

Solomon, S.D., Smith, E., Robins, L. & Fischbach, R. (1987). Social involvement as a mediator of disaster-induced stress. *Applied Journal of Social Psychology*, **17**, 1092–112.

Sorce, J., Emde, R., Campos, J. & Klinnert, M. (1985). Maternal emotional signaling: its effect on the visual cliff behavior of 1-year-olds. *Developmental Psychology*, **21**, 195–200.

Sorce, J.F., Emde, R.N., Campos, J. & Klinnert, M.D. (1985). Maternal emotional signalling: its effects on the visual cliff behavior of 1-year-olds. *Developmental Psychology*, **21**, 195–200.

Sorensen, T. & Snow, B. (1991). How children tell: the process of disclosure of child sexual abuse. *Journal of the Child Welfare League of America Inc.* **LXX**, 3–15.

Spanier, G.B. (1976). Measuring dyadic adjustment: new scales for assessing the quality of marriage and similar dyads. *Journal of Marriage and the Family*, **38**, 15–28.

Spanier, G.B. & Casto, R.F. (1979). Adjustment to separation and divorce: a qualitative analysis. In G. Levinger & O. Moles (Eds), *Divorce and Separation* (pp. 211–27). New York: Basic Books.

Spence, D. (1982). *Narrative Truth and Historical Truth*. New York: W.W. Norton.

Spence, J.T. & Helmreich, R.L. (1978). *Masculinity and Femininity: their Psychological Dimensions, Correlates, and Antecedents*. Austin, TX: University of Texas Press.

Spencer, T. (1993a, February). A new approach to assessing self-disclosure. Paper presented at the annual meeting of the Western States Communication Association, Albuquerque, NM.

Spencer, T. (1993b, June). The use of a turning point conversation task to stimulate nearly natural conversation. Paper presented at the Fourth International Network Conference on Personal Relationships, Milwaukee, WI.

Spencer, T. (1993c, November). Testing the self-disclosure reciprocity hypothesis within the context of conversational sequences in family interaction. Paper presented at the annual meeting of the Speech Communication Association, Miami, FL.

Spencer, T. (1994). Transforming relationships through ordinary talk. In S. Duck (Ed.), *Understanding Relationship Processes IV: Dynamics of Relationships* (pp. 58–85). Thousand Oaks, CA: Sage.

Spencer, T. & Derlega, V.J. (February, 1995). Important self-disclosure decisions: coming out to family and HIV-positive disclosures. Paper presented at the Western States Communication Association convention, Portland, OR.

Spickard, P.R. (1989). *Mixed Blood: Intermarriage and Ethnic Identity in Twentieth-century America*. Madison, WI: University of Wisconsin Press.

Spiegel, D., Bloom, J., Kraemer, H. & Gottheil, E. (1989). Effect of psychosocial treatment on survival of patients with metastic breast cancer. *Lancet*, **8668**, 888–91.

Spigner, C.C. (1994). Black/White interracial marriages: a brief overview of U.S. Census data, 1980–1987. In R. Staples (Ed.), *The Black Family: Essays and Studies*, 5th Edn (pp. 149–52). Belmont, CA: Wadsworth.

Spiro, A., Aldwin, C.M., Levenson, M.R. & Boss'e, R. (1990). Longitudinal findings from the Normative Aging Study. II. Do emotionality and extraversion predict symptom change? *Journal of Gerontology*, **45**, 136–44.

Spitz, R.A. (1946). Anaclitic depression. *Psychoanalytic Study of the Child*, **2**, 313–42.

Spitzberg, B.H., Canary, D.J. & Cupach, W.R. (1994). A competence based approach to the study of interpersonal conflict. In D.D. Cahn (Ed.), *Conflict in Personal Relationships* (pp. 183–202). Hillsdale, NJ: Erlbaum.

Spitze, G. & Logan, J.R. (1992). Helping as a component of parent–adult child relations. *Research on Aging*, **14**, 291–312.

Spitzer, S. & Parke, R.D. (1994). Family cognitive representations of social behavior and children's social competence. Paper presented at the American Psychological Society, Washington, DC.

Spitzer, S., Estock, S., Cupp, R., Isley-Paradise, S. & Parke, R.D. (1992). Parental influence and efficacy beliefs and children's social acceptance. Unpublished manuscript, University of California, Riverside.

Sprecher, S. (1985). Sex differences in bases of power in dating relationships. *Sex Roles*, **12**, 449–62.

Sprecher, S., Aron, A., Hatfield, E., Cortese, A., Potapova, E. & Levitskaya, A. (1994). Love: American style, Russian style, and Japanese style. Unpublished manuscript, Illinois State University.

Sprey, J. (1991). Studying adult children and their parents. *Marriage and Family Review*, **16**, 221–35.

Sroufe, L.A. (1979a). Socioemotional development. In J. Osofsky (Ed.), *Handbook of Infant Development*. New York: Wiley.

Sroufe, L.A. (1979b). The coherence of individual development. *American Psychologist*, **34**, 834–41.

Sroufe, L.A. (1982). Attachment and the roots of competence. In H.E. Fitzgerald & T.H. Carr (Eds), *Human Development: Annual Editions*. Guilford, CA: Dushkin.

Sroufe, L.A. & Fleeson, J. (1986). Attachment and the construction of relationships. In W.W. Hartup & Z. Rubin (Eds), *Relationships and Development* (pp. 51–72). Hillsdale, NJ: Erlbaum.

Sroufe, L.A. & Waters, E. (1977). Attachment as an organizational construct. *Child Development*, **48**, 1184–99.

Sroufe, L.A., Carlson, E. & Shulman, S. (1993). Individuals in relationships: development from infancy through adolescence. In D.C. Funder, R.D. Parke, C. Tomlinson-Keasey & K. Widaman (Eds), *Studying Lives Through Time* (pp. 315–42). Washington, DC: American Psychological Association.

Sroufe, L.A., Egeland, B. & Kreutzer, T. (1990). The fate of early experience following developmental change: longitudinal approaches to individual adaptation in childhood. *Child Development*, **61**, 1363–73.

Sroufe, L.A., Fox, J. & Pancake (1983). Attachment and dependency in developmental perspective. *Child Development*, **54**, 1615–27.

St. John, N.H. (1964). De facto segregation and interracial association in high school. *Sociology of Education*, **37**, 326–44.

Stacey, J. (1990). *Brave New Families*. New York: Basic Books.

Stack, C.B. (1972). *All Our Kin*. New York: Harper & Row.

Stack, C.B. & Burton, L.M. (1993). Kinscripts. *Journal of Comparative Family Studies*, **24**(2), 157–70.

Stack, D.M. & Muir, D.W. (1990). Tactile stimulation as a component of social interchange: new interpretations for the still-face effect. *British Journal of Developmental Psychology*, **8**, 131–45.

Stafford, L. (1994). Tracing the threads of spider webs. In D.J. Canary & L. Stafford (Eds), *Communication and Relational Maintenance* (pp. 297–305). New York: Academic Press.

Stafford, L. & Canary, D.J. (1991). Maintenance strategies and romantic relationship type, gender and relational characteristics. *Journal of Social and Personal Relationships*, **8**, 217–42.

Stallings, R. (1988). Conflict in natural disasters: a codification of consensus and conflict theories. *Social Science Quarterly*, 569–86.

Stamp, G.H. & Banski, M.A. (1992). The communicative management of constrained autonomy during the transition to parenthood. *Western Journal of Communication*, **56**, 281–300.

Staples, R. (1994). Interracial relationships: a convergence of desire and opportunity. In R. Staples (Ed.), *The Black Family: Essays and Studies* (5th Edn, pp. 142–9). Belmont, CA: Wadsworth.

Staples, R. & Mirandé, A. (1980). Racial and cultural variations among American families: a decentennial review of the literature on minority families. *Journal of Marriage and the Family*, **42**, 887–903.

Starr, R.H. (1979). Child abuse. *American Psychologist*, **34**, 872–8.

Stavig, G.R., Igra, A. & Leonard, A.R. (1984). Hypertension among Asians and Pacific Islanders in California. *American Journal of Epidemiology*, **119**, 677–91.

Staw, B.M. (1976). Knee-deep in the big muddy: a study of escalating commitment to a chosen course of action. *Organizational Behavior and Human Performance*, **16**, 27–44.

Steedman, P. (1991). On the relations between seeing, interpreting, and knowing. In F. Steier (Ed.), *Research and Reflexivity* (pp. 53–62). London: Sage.

Steier, F. (Ed.) (1991). *Research on Reflexivity*. London: Sage.

Stein, C.H. (1993). Felt obligation in adult family relationships. In S.W. Duck (Ed.), *Understanding Relationship Processes 3: Social Contexts of Relationships* (pp. 78–99). Thousand Oaks, CA: Sage.

Stein, C.H., Bush, E.G., Ross, R.R. & Ward, M. (1992). Mine, yours and ours: a configural analysis of the networks of married couples in relation to marital satifaction and individual well-being. *Journal of Social and Personal Relationships*, **9**, 365–83.

Steinberg, L. (1986). Latchkey children and susceptibility to peer pressure: an ecological analysis. *Developmental Psychology*, **22**, 433–9.

Steiner, I.D. (1974). Whatever happened to the group in social psychology. *Journal of Experimental Social Psychology*, **10**, 94–108.

Steiner, I.D. (1986). Paradigms and groups. In L. Berkowitz (Ed.), *Advances in Experimental Social Psychology*, Vol. 19 (pp. 251–89). New York: Academic Press.

Stephan, W.G. (1985). Intergroup relations. In G. Lindzey & E. Aronson (Eds), *The Handbook of Social Psychology*, Vol. 2 (3rd Edn, pp. 599–638). New York: Random House.

Stern, D.N. (1977). *The First Relationship: Mother and Infant*. Cambridge, MA: Harvard University Press.

Stern, D.N. (1986). *The Interpersonal World of the Infant*. New York: Basic Books.

Sternberg, R.J. & Barnes, M.L. (1985). Real and ideal others in romantic relationships: is four a crowd? *Journal of Personality and Social Psychology*, **49**, 1586–608.

Stets, J.E. & Pirog-Good, M.A. (1990). Interpersonal control and courtship aggression. *Journal of Social and Personal Relationships*, **7**, 371–94.

Stevenson, H.W., Chen, C., Lee, S.Y. & Fuligni, A.J. (1991). Schooling, culture and cognitive development. In L. Okagaki & R.J. Sternberg (Eds), *Directors of Development: Influences on the Development of Children's Thinking.* Hillsdale, NJ: Erlbaum.

Stevenson-Hinde, J. & Shouldice, A. (1995). Maternal interactions and self-reports related to attachment classification at 4.5 years. *Child Development,* **66,** 583–96.

Stewart, J. (1995). *Bridges Not Walls: a Book About Interpersonal Communication* (6th Edn). New York: McGraw-Hill.

Stewart, R.B. (1983). Sibling interaction: the role of the older child as teacher for the younger. *Merrill–Palmer Quarterly,* **29,** 47–68.

Stewart, R.B. & Marvin, R.S. (1984). Sibling relations: the role of conceptual perspective-taking in the ontogeny of sibling caregiving. *Child Development,* **55,** 1322–32.

Stiffman, A.R. (1991). Adolescent mothers: racial differences in childrearing support. *Child and Adolescent Social Work Journal,* **8**(5), 369–86.

Stiles, W.B., Shapiro, D. & Elliott, R. (1986). Are all psychotherapies equivalent? *American Psychologist,* **41,** 165–80.

Stinson, L. & Ickes, W. (1992). Empathic accuracy in the interactions of male friends versus male strangers. *Journal of Personality and Social Psychology,* **62,** 787–97.

Stipek, D.J. (1983). A developmental analysis of pride and shame. *Human Development,* **26,** 42–54.

Stipek, D.J. (1995). The development of pride and shame in toddlers. In J.P. Tangney & K.W. Fischer (Eds), *Self-conscious Emotions* (pp. 237–52). New York: Guilford.

Stipek, D.J., Recchia, S. & McClintic, S. (1992). Self-evaluation in young children. *Monographs of the Society for Research in Child Development,* **57**(1, Serial No. 226).

Stocker, C. & McHale, S. (1992). The nature and family correlates of preadolescents' perceptions of their sibling relationships. *Journal of Social and Personal Relationships,* **9,** 179–95.

Stocker, C. & Dunn, J. (1990). Sibling relationships in childhood: links with friendships and peer relationships. *British Journal of Developmental Psychology,* **8,** 227–44.

Stocker, C., Dunn, J. & Plomin, R. (1989). Sibling relationships: links with child temperament, maternal behavior, and family structure. *Child Development,* **60,** 715–27.

Stocker, C.M. (1994). Children's perceptions of relationships with siblings, friends, and mothers: compensatory processes and links with adjustment. *Journal of Child Psychology and Psychiatry,* **35,** 1447–59.

Stokes, J. & Wilson, D.G. (1984). The inventory of socially supportive behaviors: dimensionality, prediction, and gender differences. *American Journal of Community Psychology,* **12,** 53–70.

Stokols, D. & Altman, I. (Eds) (1987). *Handbook of Environmental Psychology.* New York: Wiley.

Stone, E. (1988). *Black Sheep and Kissing Cousins: How Our Family Stories Shape Us.* New York: Penguin.

Stone, L. (1988). Passionate attachments in the West in historical perspective. In W. Gaylin & E. Person (Eds), *Passionate Attachments* (pp. 15–26). New York: Free Press.

Stoneman, Z. & Brody, G. (1993). Sibling temperaments, conflict, warmth, and role asymmetry. *Child Development,* **64,** 1786–800.

Stoneman, Z., Brody, G.H. & MacKinnon, C. (1985). Naturalistic observations of children's activities and roles while playing with their siblings and friends. *Child Development,* **55,** 617–27.

Stonequist, E.V. (1937). *The Marginal Man: a Study in Personality and Culture Conflict.* New York: Russell & Russell.

Strachan, A.M., Leff, J.P., Goldstein, M.J., Doane, J.A. & Burtt, C. (1986). Emotional attitudes and direct communication in the families of schizophrenics: A cross-national replication. *British Journal of Psychiatry,* **149,** 279–87.

Strachan, C.E. & Dutton, D.G. (1992). The role of power and gender in anger responses to sexual jealousy. *Journal of Applied Social Psychology*, **22**, 1721–40.

Straus, M.A. & Gelles, R.J. (1990). *Physical Violence in American Families*. New Brunswick, NJ: Transaction.

Stroebe, W. & Stroebe, M. (in press). The social psychology of social support. In E.T. Higgins & A. Kruglanski (Eds), *Social Psychology: Handbook of Basic Principles*. New York: Guilford.

Strube, M.J. (1988). The decision to leave an abusive relationship: empirical evidence and theoretical issues. *Psychological Bulletin*, **104**, 236–50.

Strube, M.J. & Barbour, L.S. (1983). The decision to leave an abusive relationship: economic dependence and psychological commitment. *Journal of Marriage and the Family*, **45**, 785–93.

Strupp, H.H. & Binder, J.L. (1984). *Psychotherapy in a New Key: a Guide to Time-limited Dynamic Psychotherapy*. New York: Basic Books.

Studd, M.V. & Gattiker, U.E. (1991). The evolutionary psychology of sexual harassment in organizations. *Ethology and Sociobiology*, **12**, 247–90.

Sturgeon, D., Kuipers, L., Berkowitz, R., Turpin, G. & Leff, J. (1981). Psychophysiological responses of schizophrenic patients to high and low expressed emotion relatives. *British Journal of Psychiatry*, **138**, 40–45.

Sturgeon, D., Turpin, G., Kuipers, L., Berkowitz, R. & Leff, J. (1984). Psychophysiological responses of schizophrenic patients to high and low expressed emotion relatives: a follow-up study. *British Journal of Psychiatry*, **145**, 62–9.

Suggs, P.K. (1989). Predictors of association among older siblings: a black/white comparison. *American Behavioral Scientist*, **33**, 70–80.

Sullivan, H.S. (1953). In H.S. Perry & M.L. Gawel (Eds), *The Interpersonal Theory of Psychiatry*. New York: Norton.

Summit, R.C. (1983). The child sexual abuse accommodation syndrome. *Child Abuse and Neglect*, **7**, 177–93.

Sunnafrank, M. (1984). A communication-based perspective on attitude similarity and interpersonal attraction in early acquaintance. *Communication Monographs*, **51**, 372–80.

Suomi, S.J. (1982). Sibling relationships in nonhuman primates. In M.E. Lamb & B. Sutton-Smith (Eds), *Sibling Relationships*. Hillsdale, NJ: Erlbaum.

Surra, C.A. (1988). The influence of the interactive network on developing relationships. In R.M. Milardo (Ed.), *Families and Social Networks* (pp. 48–82). Newbury Park, CA: Sage.

Surra, C.A. & Longstreth, M. (1990). Similarity of outcomes, interdependence, and conflict in dating relationships. *Journal of Personality and Social Psychology*, **59**, 501–16.

Surra, C.A. & Milardo, R. (1991). The social psychological context of developing relationships: psychological and interactive networks. In D. Perlman & W. Jones (Eds), *Advances in Personal Relationships*, Vol. 3 (pp. 1–36). London: Jessica Kingsley.

Surra, C.A. & Ridley, C. (1991). Multiple perspectives on interaction: participants, peers and observers. In B.M. Montgomery & S. W. Duck (Eds), *Studying Interpersonal Interaction* (pp. 35–55). New York: Guilford.

Surra, C.A., Arizzi, P. & Asmussen, L. (1988). The association between reasons for commitment and the development and outcome of marital relationships. *Journal of Social and Personal Relationships*, **5**, 47–63.

Sutherland, L.E. (1990). The effect of premarital pregnancy and birth on the marital well-being of black and white newlywed couples. Unpublished doctoral dissertation (Microfilm # 28189). Ann Arbor, MI: University of Michigan.

Swados, E. (1991). *The Four of Us*. New York: Farrar, Straus and Giroux.

Swaim, R.C., Oetting, E.R., Thurman, P.J., Beauvais, F. & Edwards, R.W. (1993). American Indian adolescent drug use and socialization characteristics: a cross-cultural comparison. *Journal of Cross-Cultural Psychology*, **24**, 53–70.

Swain, S.O. (1992). Men's friendships with women: intimacy, sexual boundaries, and the informant role. In P. Nardi (Ed.), *Men's Friendships* (pp. 153–71). Newbury Park, CA: Sage.

Swann, W.B. Jr (1983). Self-aggrandisement: bringing social reality into harmony with the self. In J. Suls & A.G. Greenwald (Eds), *Social Psychology Perspectives*, Vol. 2 (pp. 33–66). Hillsdale, NJ: Erlbaum.

Swann, W.B. Jr. & Predmore, S.C. (1985). Intimates as agents of social support: sources of consolation or despair? *Journal of Personality and Social Psychology*, **49**, 1609–17.

Swindle, M. (1989). Predicting temperament-mental health relationships: a covariance structure latent variable analysis. *Journal of Research in Personality*, **23**, 118–44.

Symons, D. (1979). *The Evolution of Human Sexuality*. New York: Oxford University Press.

Syna, H. (1984). Couples in conflict: conflict resolution strategies, perceptions about sources of conflict and relationship adjustment. Doctoral dissertation, State University of New York at Buffalo.

Szapocznik, J. & Kurtines, W. (1980). Acculturation, biculturalism and adjustment among Cuban Americans. In A.M. Padilla (Ed.), *Acculturation: Theory, Models, and Some New Findings* (pp. 139–59). Boulder, CO: Westview Press.

Szapocznik, J. & Truss, C. (1978). Intergenerational sources of role conflict in Cuban mothers. In M. Montiel (Ed.), *Hispanic Families: Critical Issues for Policy and Programs in Human Services*. Washington, DC: National Coalition of Hispanic Mental Health and Human Services Organizations.

Szapocznik, J., Scopetta, M.A., Kurtines, W. & Aranalde, M.A. (1978). Theory and measurement of acculturation. *Interamerican Journal of Psychology*, **12**, 113–30.

Szmuckler, G.I., Eisler, I., Russell, G.F.M. & Dare, C. (1985). Anorexia nervosa, parental "expressed emotion" and dropping out of treatment. *British Journal of Psychiatry*, **147**, 265–71.

Tajfel, H. (1979). Individuals and groups in social psychology. *British Journal of Social Psychology*, **18**, 183–90.

Tajfel, H. & Turner, J.C. (1979). An integrative theory of intergroup conflict. In W. G. Austin & S. Worchel (Eds), *The Social Psychology of Intergroup Relations* (pp. 33–47). Monterey, CA: Brooks/Cole.

Tallman, I. (1994). The influence of family of origin on role negotiation in early marriage. Paper presented at conference on intimate relationships at Iowa State, Ames, Iowa September, 29.

Tallman, I. & Riley, A. (1995). Gender role expectations and couple interactions in newly married couples. Unpublished article, Washington State University.

Tallman, I., Burke, P.J. & Gecas, V. (in press). Socialization into marital roles: testing a contextual developmental model of marital functioning. In T.M. Bradbury (Ed.), *The Developmental Course of Marital Dysfunction*. New York: Cambridge University Press.

Tangney, J.P. (1995). Shame and guilt in interpersonal relationships. In J.P. Tangney & K.W. Fischer (Eds), *Self-conscious Emotions* (pp. 114–39). New York: Guilford.

Tangney, J.P. & Fischer, K.W. (Eds) (1995). *Self-conscious Emotions*. New York: Guilford.

Tarrier, N. (1989). Electrodermal activity, expressed emotion, and outcome in schizophrenia. *British Journal of Psychiatry*, **155** (Suppl. 5), 51–6.

Tarrier, N., Barrowclough, C., Porceddu, K. & Watts, S. (1988a). The assessment of psychophysiological reactivity to the expressed emotion of the relatives of schizophrenic patients. *British Journal of Psychiatry*, **152**, 618–24.

Tarrier, N., Barrowclough, C., Vaughn, C., Bamrah, J. S., Porceddu, K., Watts, S. & Freeman, H. (1988b). The community management of schizophrenia: a controlled trial of a behavioural intervention with families to reduce relapse. *British Journal of Psychiatry*, **153**, 532–42.

Tarrier, N., Barrowclough, C., Vaughn, C., Bamrah, J.S., Porceddu, K., Watts, S. & Freeman, H. (1989). Community management of schizophrenia: a two-year follow-up of a behavioural intervention with families. *British Journal of Psychiatry*, **154**, 625–8.

Tarrier, N., Vaughn, C., Lader, M.H. & Leff, J.P. (1979). Bodily reactions to people and events in schizophrenics. *Archives of General Psychiatry*, **36**, 311–15.

Tasca, G.A. & McMullen, L.M. (1992). Interpersonal complementarity and antitheses within a stage model of psychotherapy. *Psychotherapy*, **29**, 515–23.

Tashakkori, A. & Thompson, V. (1988). Cultural change and attitude change: an assessment of postrevolutionary marriage and attitudes in Iran. *Population Research and Policy Review*, **7**, 3–27.

Tavris, C. (1982). *Anger: the Misunderstood Emotion*. New York: Simon & Schuster.

Taylor, C. (1977). Interpretation and the sciences of man. In F. Dallmayr & T. McCarthy (Eds), *Understanding and Social Inquiry* (pp. 101–31). Notre Dame: University of Notre Dame Press.

Taylor, C.B., Bandura, A., Ewart, C.K., Miller, N.H. & DeBusk, R.F. (1985). Exercise testing to enhance wive's confidence in their husbands' cardiac capability after clinically uncomplicated acute myocardial infarction. *American Journal of Cardiology*, **55**, 635–8.

Taylor, D.A. (1968). Some aspects of the development of interpersonal relationships: social penetration processes. *Journal of Social Psychology*, **75**, 79–90.

Taylor, D.A. & Altman, I. (1987). Communication in interpersonal relationships: social penetration processes. In M.E. Roloff & G.R. Miller (Eds), *Interpersonal Processes: New Directions in Communication Research* (pp. 257–77). Newbury Park, CA: Sage.

Taylor, D.A. & Katz, P.A. (1987). Conclusion. In P.A. Katz and D.A. Taylor (Eds), *Eliminating Racism: Profiles in Controversy* (pp. 359–69). New York: Plenum.

Taylor, D.A., Altman, I. & Wheeler, L. (1972). Self-disclosure in isolated groups. *Journal of Personality and Social Psychology*, **26**, 39–47.

Taylor, D.M. & Moghaddam, F.M. (1994). *Theories of Intergroup Relations: International Social Psychological Perspectives* (2nd Edn). Westport, CT: Praeger.

Taylor, S.E. (1991). Asymmetrical effects of positive and negative events: the mobilization—minimization hypothesis. *Psychological Bulletin*, **110**, 67–85.

Taylor, S.E. & Brown, J.D. (1988). Illusion and well-being: a social psychological perspective on mental health. *Psychological Bulletin*, **103**, 193–210.

Taylor, V.A. (1977). Good news about disaster. *Psychology Today*, **11**, 93–4, 124–6.

Teger, A.I. (1980). *Too Much Invested to Quit*. New York: Pergamon.

Tennov, D. (1979). *Love and Limerence: the Experience of Being in Love*. New York: Stein and Day.

Terenzini, P.T., Rendon, L.I., Upcraft, M.L., Millar, S.B., Allison, K.W., Gregg, P.L. & Jalomo, R.(1994).The transition to college: diverse students, diverse stories. *Research in Higher Education*, **35**(1), 57–73.

Terkel, S. (1991). *Race: How Blacks and Whites Think and Feel About the American Obsession*. New York: Anchor Books.

Terman, L.M. & Oden, M.H. (1947). Genetic studies of genius. IV. The gifted child grows up: twenty-five years follow-up of a superior group. Stanford, CA: Stanford University Press.

Tesser, A. (1988). Toward a self-evaluation maintenance model of social behavior. In L. Berkowitz (Ed.), *Advances in Experimental Social Psychology*, Vol. 11 (pp. 288–338). San Diego, CA: Academic Press.

Teti, D.M. & Ablard, K.E. (1989). Security of attachment and infant–sibling relationships: a laboratory study. *Child Development*, **60**, 1519–28.

Teti, D.M., Gelfand, D.M., Messinger, D.S. & Isabella, R. (1995). Correlates of preschool attachment security in a sample of depressed and non-depressed mothers. *Developmental Psychology*, **31**, 364–78.

Teyber, E. (1992). *Interpersonal Process in Psychotherapy: a Guide to Clinical Training* (2nd Edn). Pacific Grove, CA: Brooks/Cole.

Thibaut, J.W. & Kelley, H.H. (1959). *The Social Psychology of Groups.* New York: Wiley.

Thibaut, J. & Faucheux, C. (1965). The development of contractual norms in a bargaining situation under two types of stress. *Journal of Experimental Social Psychology*, **1**, 89–102.

Thibaut, J. & Gruder, C.L. (1969). Formation of contractual agreements between parties of unequal power. *Journal of Personality and Social Psychology*, **11**, 59–65.

Thibaut, J. & Walker, L. (1975). *Procedural Justice: a Psychological Analysis.* New York: Wiley.

Thiessen, D., Young, R.K. & Burroughs, R. (1993). Lonely hearts advertisments reflect sexually dimorphic mating strategies. *Ethology and Sociobiology*, **14**, 209–29.

Thoits, P.A. (1982). Conceptual, methodological, and theoretical problems in studying social support as a buffer against life stress. *Journal of Health and Social Behavior*, **23**, 145–59.

Thoits, P.A. (1985). Social support and psychological well being: theoretical possibilities. In I. Sarason & B. Sarason (Eds), *Social Support: Theory, Research, and Application* (pp. 51–72). Dordrecht: Martinus Nijhoff.

Thoits, P.A. (1986). Social support as coping assistance. *Journal of Consulting and Clinical Psychology*, **54**, 416–23.

Thomas, J.B., Shankster, L.J. & Mathieu, J.E. (1994). Antecedents to organizational issue interpretation: the roles of single-level, cross-level, and content cues. *Academy of Management Journal*, **37**, 1252–84.

Thompson, B. & Vaux, A. (1986). The importance, transmission, and moderation of stress in the family system. *American Journal of Community Psychology*, **14**, 39–57.

Thompson, L. (1990). Family work: women's sense of fairness. *Journal of Family Issues*, **12**(2), 181–96.

Thompson, L. (1992). Feminist methodology for family studies. *Journal of Marriage and the Family*, **54**, 3–18.

Thompson, L. & Walker, A.J. (1982). The dyad as the unit of analysis: conceptual and methodological issues. *Journal of Marriage and the Family*, **44**, 889–900.

Thompson, L. & Walker, A.J. (1984). Mothers and daughters: aid patterns and attachment. *Journal of Marriage and the Family*, **46**, 313–22.

Thompson, L. & Walker, A.(1989). Gender in families: women and men in marriage, work and parenthood. *Journal of Marriage and the Family*, **51**, 845–71.

Thompson, M.G. & Heller, K. (1990). Facets of support related to well-being: quantitative social isolation and perceived family support in a sample of elderly women. *Psychology and Aging*, **5**, 535–44.

Thompson, M.S. & Peebles, W.W. (1992). The impact of formal, informal, and societal support networks on the psychological well-being of black adolescent mothers. *Social Work*, **37**(4), 322–8.

Thompson, M., Norris, F. & Hanacek, B. (1993). Age differences in the psychological consequences of Hurricane Hugo. *Psychology and Aging*, **8**, 606–16.

Thornes, B. & Collard, J. (1979). *Who Divorces?* London: Routledge & Kegan Paul.

Thornhill, R. & Thornhill, N.W. (1989). The evolution of psychological pain. In R.W. Bell & N.J. Bell (Eds), *Sociobiology and the Social Sciences* (pp. 73–103). Lubbock: Texas Tech University Press.

Thornhill, R. & Gangestad, S.W. (1994). Human fluctuating asymmetry and sexual behavior. *Psychological Science*, **5**, 297–302.

Thornton, A. (1989). Changing attitudes toward family issues in the United States. *Journal of Marriage and the Family*, **51**, 873–93.

Tienari, P., Lahti, I., Sorri, A., Naarala, M., Moring, J. & Wahlberg, K. (1989). The Finnish adoptive study of schizophrenia: possible joint effects of genetic vulnerability and family environment. *British Journal of Psychiatry*, **155** (Suppl. 5), 29–32.

Tienari, P., Sorri, A., Lahti, I., Naarala, M., Wahlberg, K., Moring, J., Pohjola, J. & Wynne, L.C. (1987). Genetic and psychosocial factors in schizophrenia: the Finnish adoptive family study. *Schizophrenia Bulletin*, **13**, 477–84.

Tienari, P., Wynne, L.C., Moring, J., Lahti, I., Naarala, M., Sorri, A., Wahlberg, K., Saarento, O., Seitamaa, M., Kaleva, M. & Läksy, K. (1994). The Finnish adoptive family study of schizophrenia: implications for family research. *British Journal of Psychiatry*, **164** (Suppl. 23), 20–26.

Tietjen, A. (1985). Relationships between the social networks of Swedish mothers and their children. *International Journal of Behavioral Development*, **8**, 195–216.

Timmer, S.G., Veroff, J. & Hatchett, S. (in press). Family ties and marital happiness: the different marital experiences of black and white newlywed couples. *Journal of Social and Personal Relationships*, **13**, 337–62.

Ting-Toomey, S., Gao, G., Trubisky, P., Yang, Z., Kim, H.S., Lin, S.-L. & Nishida, T. (1991). Culture, face maintenance, and styles of handling interpersonal conflict: a study in five cultures. *The International Journal of Conflict Management*, **2**, 275–96.

Tinsley, B.R. & Parke, R.D. (1984). The person–environment relationship: lessons from families with preterm infants. In D. Magnusson & V. Allen (Eds), *Human Development: an Interactional Perspective* (pp. 93–110). New York: Academic Press.

Titus, S.L. (1980). A function of friendship: social comparisons as a frame of reference for marriage. *Human Relations*, **33**, 409–31.

Tjosvold, D. (1981). Unequal power relationships within a cooperative or competitive context. *Journal of Applied Social Psychology*, **11**, 137–50.

Todd, J., McKinney, J.L., Harris, R., Chadderton, R. & Small, L. (1992). Attitudes toward interracial dating: effects of age, sex, and race. *Journal of Multicultural Counseling and Development*, **20**, 202–8.

Todorov, T. (1984). *Mikhail Bakhtin: the Dialogic Principle* (W. Godzich, Trans.). Minneapolis: University of Minnesota Press (original work published 1981).

Tolhuizen, J.H. (1989).Communication strategies for intensifying dating relationships: identification, use and structure. *Journal of Social and Personal Relationships*, **6**, 413–34.

Tomlinson-Keasey, C. & Little, T.D. (1990). Predicting educational attainment, occupational achievement, intellectual skill, and personal adjustment among gifted men and women. *Journal of Educational Psychology*, **82**, 442–55.

Tooby, J. & Cosmides, L. (1990). On the universality of human nature and the uniqueness of the individual: the role of genetics and adaptation. *Journal of Personality*, **58**, 17–67.

Tooby, J. & Cosmides, L. (1992). The psychological foundations of culture. In J.H. Barkow, L. Cosmides & J. Tooby (Eds), *The Adapted Mind: Evolutionary Psychology and the Generation of Culture* (pp. 19–136). New York: Oxford University Press.

Tooke, J. & Camire, L. (1991). Patterns of deception in intersexual and intrasexual mating strategies. *Ethology and sociobiology*, **12**, 345–64.

Toupin, E.S.W.A. (1980). Counseling Asians: psychotherapy in the context of racism and Asian-American history. *American Journal of Orthopsychiatry*, **50**(1), 76–86.

Tracey, T.J. (1993). An interpersonal stage model of the therapeutic process. *Journal of Counseling Psychology*, **40**, 396–409.

Tracey, T.J. (1994). An examination of the complementarity of interpersonal behavior. *Journal of Personality and Social Psychology*, **67**, 864–78.

Tracy, K. (1990). The many faces of facework. In H. Giles and W.P. Robinson (Eds), *Handbook of Language and Social Psychology* (pp. 209–26). New York: Wiley.

Trainer, P. & Bolin, R.C. (1976). Persistent effects of disasters on daily activities: a cross-cultural comparison. *Mass Emergencies*, **1**, 279–90.

Traupmann, J. & Hatfield, E. (1981). Love and its effect on mental and physical health. In J. March, S. Kiesler, R. Fogel, E. Hatfield & E. Shana (Eds), *Aging: Stability and Change in the Family* (pp. 253–74). New York: Academic Press.

Travisano, R. (1970). Alternation and conversion as qualitatively different transformations. In G. Stone & H. Farberman (Eds), *Social Psychology Through Symbolic Interaction*. Waltham, MA: Xerox College Publishing.

Trent, K. & Harlan, S.L. (1994). Teenage mothers in nuclear and extended households: differences by marital status and race/ethnicity. *Journal of Family Issues*, **15**, 309–37.

Triandis, H.C. (1986). Collectivism and individualism: a reconceptualization of a basic concept in cross-cultural psychology. In C. Bagley & G. Verma (Eds), *Personality, Cognition, and Values: Cross-cultural Perspectives of Childhood and Adolescence*. London: Macmillan.

Triandis, H.C. (1987). The future of pluralism revisited. In P.A. Katz and D.A. Taylor (Eds), *Eliminating Racism: Profiles in Controversy* (pp. 31–50). New York: Plenum.

Triandis, H.C. (1990). Cross-cultural studies of individualism and collectivism. *Nebraska Symposium on Motivation*, **39**, 41–133.

Triandis, H.C., Bontempo, R., Villareal, M.J., Asai, M. & Lucca, N. (1988). Individualism and collectivism: cross-cultural perspectives on self-ingroup relationships. *Journal of Personality and Social Psychology*, **52**, 323–38.

Trickett, E.J. (1978). Towards a social-ecological conception of adolescent socialization: normative data on contrasting types of public schools. *Child Development*, **49**, 408–14.

Trickett, E.J. (1984). Towards a distinctive community psychology: an ecological metaphor for training and the conduct of research. *American Journal of Community Psychology*, **12**, 261–79.

Trickett, E.J. (1986). Consultation as a preventive intervention: comments on ecologically based case studies. *Prevention in Human Services*, **4**(3–4), 187–204.

Trickett, E.J. & Birman, D. (1989). Taking ecology seriously: a community development approach to individually-based interventions. In L. Bond & B. Compas (Eds), *Primary Prevention in the Schools*. Hanover, NH: University of New England Press.

Trickett, E.J. & Schmid, K.D. (1993). The school as a social context. In P.H. Tolan & B.J. Cohler (Eds), *Handbook of Clinical Research and Practice with Adolescents* (pp. 173–202). New York: Wiley.

Trevarthen, C. (1979). Communication and cooperation in early infancy: a description of primary intersubjectivity. In M. Bullowa (Ed.), *Before Speech: The Beginnings of Human Communication*. Cambridge: Cambridge University Press.

Trickett, E.J., Kelly, J.G. & Todd, D.M. (1972). The social environment of the high school: guidelines for individual change and organizational development. In S. Golann & C. Eisdorfer (Eds) (pp. 331–406). *Handbook of Community Mental Health*. New York: Appleton Century Crofts.

Trivers, R. (1985). *Social Evolution*. Menlo Park, CA: Benjamin/Cummings Publishing.

Trivers, R.L. (1972). Parental investment and sexual selection. In B. Campbell (Ed.), *Sexual Selection and the Descent of Man 1871–1971* (pp. 136–79). Chicago: Aldine.

Troll, L.E. (1985). *Early and Middle Adulthood* (2nd Edn). Monterey, CA: Brooks Cole.

Troll, L.E. (1994). Family connectedness of old women: attachments in later life. In B.F. Turner & L.E. Troll (Eds), *Women Growing Older: Psychological Perspectives* (pp. 169–201). Thousand Oaks, CA: Sage.

Troll, L.E. (1996). Modified-extended families over time: discontinuity in parts, continuity in wholes. In V.L. Bengtson (Ed.), *Adulthood and Aging: Research on continuities and discontinuities* (pp. 246–68). New York: Springer.

Tronick, E.Z. (1989). Emotions and emotional communication in infants. *American Psychologist*, **44**, 112–19.

Tsui, P. & Schultz, G.L. (1988). Ethnic factors in group process: cultural dynamics in multi-ethnic therapy groups. *American Journal of Orthopsychiatry*, **58**(1), 136–42.

Tucker, M.B. & Mitchell-Kernan, C. (1995). Social structural and psychological correlates of interethnic dating. *Journal of Social and Personal Relationships*, **12**, 341–61.

Tucker, P. & Aron, A. (1993). Passionate love and marital satisfaction at key transition points in the family life cycle. *Journal of Social and Clinical Psychology*, **12**, 135–47.

Tuma, N.B. & Hallinan, M.T. (1979). The effects of sex, race and achievement on school children's friendships. *Social Forces*, **57**, 1265–85.

Turner, C. (1967).Conjugal roles and social networks: a re-examination of an hypothesis. *Human Relations*, **20**, 121–30.

Turner, R.J. (1983). Direct, indirect, and moderating effects of social support on psychological distress and associated conditions. In H.B. Kaplan (Ed.), *Psychosocial Stress: Trends in Theory and Research*. New York: Academic Press.

Turner, R.J. (1992). Measuring social support: issues of concept and method. In H.O.F. Veiel & U. Bauman (Eds). *The Meaning and Measurement of Social Support* (pp. 217–33). New York: Hemisphere.

Tversky, A. & Kahneman, D. (1982). Judgment under uncertainty: heuristics and biases. In D. Kahneman & A. Tversky (Eds), *Judgment Under Uncertainty: Heuristics and Biases* (pp. 3–20). Cambridge, UK: Cambridge University Press.

Tyler, F.B., Susswell, D. & Williams-McCoy, J. (1985). Ethnic validity in psychotherapy. *Psychotherapy*, **22**(2), 311–20.

US Bureau of the Census (1992). *Money Income of Households, Families, and Persons in the United States: 1992*. Current Population Reports, Series P60–184.

US Bureau of the Census (1994). *Statistical Abstract of the United States: 1994*. Washington, DC: US Department of Commerce.

Udry, J.R. & Hall, M. (1965). Marital role segregation and social networks in middle-class, middle-aged comples. *Journal of Marriage and the Family*, **27**, 392–5.

Udvari, S., Schneider, B.H., Labovitz, G. & Tassi, F. (1995, August). A multidimensional view of competition in relation to children's peer relations. Paper presented to the American Psychological Association, New York, NY.

Uehara, E. (1994). The influence of the social network's "second order zone" on social support mobilization: a case example. *Journal of Social and Personal Relationships*, **11**, 277–94.

Uehara, E. (1995). Reciprocity reconsidered: an application of Gouldner's concept of the moral norm of reciprocity to social support. *Journal of Social and Personal Relationships*, **12**, 483–90.

Uematsu, M. (1996). Giving voice to the account: the healing power of writing about loss. *Journal of Personal and Interpersonal Loss*, **1**, 17–28.

Ulin, M. & Milardo, R.M. (1992). Network interdependence and lesbian relationships. Paper presented at the National Council on Family Relations, Orlando, FL.

Umberson, D. (1987). Family status and health behaviors: social control as a dimension of social integration. *Journal of Health and Social Behavior*, **28**, 306–19.

Unger, D.G. & Wandersman, L.P. (1985). Social support and adolescent mothers: action research contributions to theory and application. *Journal of Social Issues*, **41**(1), 29–45.

Vaillant, G.E. (1977). *Adaptation to Life*. Boston, MA: Little, Brown.

Vaillant, G.E. (1992). *Ego Mechanisms of Defense*. Washington, DC: American Psychiatric Association.

Valone, K., Norton, J.P., Goldstein, M.J. & Doane, J.A. (1983). Parental expressed emotion and affective style in an adolescent sample at risk for schizophrenia spectrum disorders. *Journal of Abnormal Psychology*, **92**, 399–407.

van de Vliert, E. (1990). Positive effects of conflict: a field assessment. *The International Journal of Conflict Management*, **1**, 69–80.

Van Denburg, T.F. & Kiesler, D.J. (1993). Transactional escalation in rigidity and intensity of interpersonal behaviour under stress. *British Journal of Medical Psychology*, **66**, 15–31.

van der Poel, M.G.M. (1993).*Personal Networks: a Rational-choice Explanation of their Size and Composition*. Lisse: Swets & Zeitlinger B.V.

van Dijk, T.A. (1993). *Elite Discourse and Racism*. Newbury Park, CA. Sage.

van IJzendoorn, M. (1995). Adult attachment representations, parental responsiveness, and infant attachment: a meta-analysis on the predictive validity of the Adult Attachment Interview. *Psychological Bulletin*, **117**, 387–403.

Van Lange, P.A.M. & Rusbult, C.E. (1995). My relationship is better than—and not as bad as—yours is: the perception of superiority in close relationships. *Personality and Social Psychology Bulletin*, **21**, 32–44.

Van Lange, P.A., M., Rusbult, C.E., Drigotas, S.M. & Arriaga, B.A. (1995). Willingness to Sacrifice in Close Relationships. Unpublished manuscript, Free University, Amsterdam.

Van Lear, C.A. (1987). The formation of social relationships: a longitudinal study of social penetration. *Journal of Social and Personal Relationships*, **13**, 299–322.

Van Lear, C.A. (1991). Testing a cyclical model of communicative openness in relationship development: two longitudinal studies. *Communication Monographs*, **58**, 337–61.

van Tilburg, T. (1990). Support in close relationships: is it better to assess the content or the type of relationship? In C.P.M. Knipscheer & T.C. Antonucci (Eds), *Social Network Research* (pp. 151–9). Amsterdam: Swets & Zeitliner.

Vandell, D.L. & Bailey, M.D. (1992). Conflicts between siblings. In C.U. Shantz & W.W. Hartup (Eds), *Conflict in Childhood Adolescent Development* (pp. 242–69). Cambridge: Cambridge University Press.

Vangelisti, A.L. (1994). Family secrets: forms, functions and correlates. *Journal of Social and Personal Relationships*, **11**, 113–35.

Vangelisti, A.L. & Banski, M.A. (1993). Couples' debriefing conversations: the impact of gender, occupation, and demographic characteristics. *Family Relations*, **42**, 149–57.

Vangelisti, A.L. & Huston, T.L.(1994).Maintaining marital satisfaction and love, In D.J. Canary & L. Stafford (Eds), *Communication and Relational Maintenance* (pp.165–86). San Diego, CA: Academic Press.

Vaughan, K., Doyle, M., McConaghy, N., Blaszczynski. A., Fox, A. & Tarrier, N. (1992a). The relationship between relatives' expressed emotion and schizophrenia relapse: an Australian replication. *Social Psychiatry and Psychiatric Epidemiology*, **27**, 10–15.

Vaughan, K., Doyle, M., McConaghy, N., Blaszczynski, A., Fox, A. & Tarrier, N. (1992b). The Sydney intervention trial: a controlled trial of relatives' counseling to reduce schizophrenic relapse. *Social Psychiatry and Psychiatric Epidemiology*, **27**, 16–21.

Vaughn, B., Egeland, B. & Sroufe, L.A. (1979). Individual differences in infant–mother attachment at twelve and eighteen months: stability and change in families under stress. *Child Development*, **50**, 971–5.

Vaughn, C. (1986). Comments on Chapter 5. In M. Goldstein, I. Hand & K. Hahlweg (Eds), *Treatment of Schizophrenia: Family Assessment and Intervention*. New York: Springer.

Vaughn, C. & Leff, J. (1976a). The influence of family and social factors on the course of psychiatric illness: a comparison of schizophrenic and depressed neurotic patients. *British Journal of Psychiatry*, **129**, 125–37.

Vaughn, C. & Leff, J. (1976b). The measurement of expressed emotion in the families of psychiatric patients. *British Journal of Social and Clinical Psychology*, **15**, 157–65.

Vaughn, C., Snyder, K.S., Jones, S., Freeman, W.B. & Falloon, I.R.H. (1984). Family factors in schizophrenic relapse: replication in California of British research on expressed emotion. *Archives of General Psychiatry*, **41**, 1169–77.

Vaux, A. (1988). *Social Support: Theory, Research, and Intervention*. New York: Praeger.

Vaux, A., Phillips, J., Holly, L., Thomson, B. & Stewart, D. (1986). The Social Support Appraisals (SS-A) scale: studies of reliability and validity. *American Journal of Community Psychology*, **14**, 195–218.

Veiel, H.O.F. (1987). Dimensions of social support: a conceptual framework for research. *Social Psychiatry*, **20**, 156–62.

Veiel, H.O.F. & Bauman, U. (1992). The many meanings of social support. In H.O.F. Veiel & U. Bauman (Eds). *The Meaning and Measurement of Social Support* (pp. 1–9). New York: Hemisphere.

Veith, J.L., Buck, M., Getzlaf, S., Van Dalfsen, P. & Slade, S. (1983). Exposure to men influences the occurrence of ovulation in women. *Physiology and Behavior*, **31**, 313–15.

Ventura, J., Nuechterlein, K.H., Lukoff, D. & Hardesty, J.P. (1989). A prospective study of stressful life events and schizophrenic relapse. *Journal of Abnormal Psychology*, **98**, 407–11.

Veroff, J. (1994). Balance in the early years of marriage. Paper presented at conference in intimate relationships at Iowa State, Ames, Iowa. December 29.

Veroff, J. & Veroff, J.B. (1980). *Social Incentives*. New York: Academic Press.

Veroff, J., Douvan E. & Hatchett, S. (1995). *Marital Instability: a Social and Behavioral Study of the Early Years*. Westport, CT: Praeger.

Veroff, J., Douvan E. & Kulka, R. (1981). *The Inner American*. New York: Basic.

Veroff, J., Douvan, E., Orbuch, T. & Acitelli, L. (in press). Happiness in stable marriages: the early years. In T.M. Bradbury (Ed.), *The Developmental Course of Marital Dysfunction*. New York: Cambridge University Press.

Veroff, J., Sutherland, L., Chadiha, L. & Ortega, R. (1993). Newlyweds tell their stories. *Journal of Personal and Social Relationships*, **10**, 437–57.

Vinokur, A.D. & Van Ryn, M. (1993). Social support and undermining in close relationships: their independent effects on the mental health of unemployed person. *Journal of Personality and Social Psychology*, **65**, 350–59.

Volling, B. & Belsky, J. (1992). The contribution of the mother–child and the father–child relationship to the quality of sibling interaction: a longitudinal study. *Child Development*, **63**, 1209–22.

Voloshinov, V.N./Bakhtin, M.M. (1973). *Marxism and the Philosophy of Language* (L. Matejks & I.R. Titunik, Trans.). Cambridge, MA: Harvard University Press.

Vondracek, F.W., Lerner, R.L. & Schulenberg, J.E.(1986). *Career Development, a Life-Span Developmental Approach*. Hillsdale, NJ: Erlbaum.

Vormbrock, J.K. (1993). Attachment theory as applied to war-time and job-related marital separation. *Psychological Bulletin*, **114**, 122–44.

Vuorenkowski, V., Wasz-Hockert, O., Koivisto, E. & Lind, J. (1969). The effect of cry stimulus on the lactating breast of primipara: a thermographic study. *Experientia*, **25**, 1286–7.

Vygotskii, L.S. (1987). In R.W. Rieber & A.S. Carlton (Eds) (N. Minick, Trans.), *The Collected Works of L.S. Vygotskii*. New York: Plenum.

Vygotsky, L. (1986). *Thought and Language* (A. Kozulin, Trans.). Cambridge, MA: MIT Press.

Wagener, D.K., Hogarty, G.E., Goldstein, M.J., Asarnow, R.F. & Browne, A. (1986). Information processing and communication deviance in schizophrenic patients and their mothers. *Psychiatry Research*, **18**, 365–77.

Walker, A. (1982). Intermodal perception of expressive behaviors by human infants. *Journal of Experimental Child Psychology*, **33**, 514–35.

Walker, K. & Woods, M.(1976). *Time Use: a Measure of Household Production of Family Goods and Services*. Washington: Home Economics Association.

Walker, R.J. & Walker, M.G. (1972). *The English Legal System* (3rd Edn). Butterworth: London.

Walkover, B. (1992).The family as an overwrought object of desire. In G.C. Rosenwald & R.L. Oshberg (Eds), *Storied Lives: the Cultural Politics of Self-Understanding* (pp. 178–91). New Haven, CT: Yale University Press.

Wallach, M.A. & Wallach, L. (1983). *Psychology's Sanction for Selfishness: the Error of Egoism in Theory and Therapy*. San Francisco: W. H. Freeman.

Waller, W. (1938). *The Family: a Dynamic Interpretation*. New York: Dryden.

Walsh-Bowers, R.T. (1992). A creative drama prevention program for easing early adolescents' adjustment to school transitions. *The Journal of Primary Prevention*, **13**(2), 131–47.

Walster, E. & Walster, G.W. (1963). Effect of expecting to be liked on choice of associates. *Journal of Personality and Social Psychology*, **67**, 402–4.

Walster, E., Berscheid, E. & Walster, G.W. (1976). New directions in equity research. In L. Berkowitz & E. Walster (Eds), *Advances in Experimental Social Psychology*, Vol. 9 (pp. 1–42). New York: Academic Press.

Walters, R.W. (1993). *Pan Africanism in the African Diaspora: an Analysis of Modern Afrocentric Political Movements*. Detroit: Wayne State University Press.

Wapner, S. & Craig-Brey, L. (1992). Person-in-environment transitions: theoretical and methodological approaches. *Environment and Behavior*, **24**(2), 161–88.

Warner, R.R. (1984). Mating behavior and hermaphroditism in coral reef fishes. *American Scientist*, **72**, 128–34.

Wasserman, G.A., Brunelei, S.A. & Rauh, V.A. (1990). Social supports and living arrangements of adolescent and adult mothers. *Journal of Adolescent Research*, **5**, 54–66.

Watkins, S.C., Menken, J.A. & Bongaarts, J. (1987). Demographic foundations of family change. *American Sociological Review*, **52**, 346–58.

Watson, D.M. & Clark, L.A. (1984). Negative affectivity: the disposition to experience aversive emotional states. Psychological Bulletin, **96**, 465–90.

Watson, D. & Pennebaker , J.W. (1989). Health complaints, stress, and distress: exploring the central role of negative affectivity. *Psychological Review*, **96**, 234–54.

Watson, L. (1989). The affirmation of indigenous values in a Colonial education system. *Journal of Indigenous Studies*, **1**, 9–20.

Watzlawick, P., Beavin, J.H. & Jackson, D.D. (1967). *Pragmatics of Human Communication: a Study of Interactional Patterns, Pathologies, and Paradoxes*. New York: W.W. Norton.

Watzlawick, P., Weakland, J.H. & Fisch, R. (1974). *Change: Principles of Problem Formation and Resolution*. New York: Norton.

Weber, A.L. & Harvey, J.H. (1994). Accounts in coping with relationship loss. In A.L. Weber & J.H. Harvey (Eds), *Perspectives on Close Relationships*. Needham Heights, MA: Allyn and Bacon.

Weber, A.L., Harvey, J.H. & Stanley, M. (1987). The nature and motivations of accounts for failed relationships. In R. Burnett, P. McGhee & D. Clarke (Eds), *Accounting for Relationships* (pp. 114–35). London: Methuen.

Webster, P.S. & Herzog, A.R. (1995). Effects of parental divorce and memories of family problems on relationships between adult children and their parents. *Journal of Gerontology: Social Sciences*, **50B**, S24–34.

Wegner, D.M. (1980). The self in prosocial action. In D.M. Wegner & R.R. Vallacher (Eds), *The Self in Social Psychology* (pp. 131–57). New York: Oxford University Press.

Wegner, D.M., Erber, R. & Raymond, P. (1991). Transactive memory in close relationships. *Journal of Personality and Social Psychology*, **61**, 923–9.

Weigel, R.H., Wiser, P.L. & Cook, S.W. (1975). The impact of cooperative learning experiences on cross-ethnic relations and attitudes. *Journal of Social Issues*, **31**(1), 219–44.

Weinberger, D.R. (1987). Implications of normal brain development for the pathogenesis of schizophrenia. *Archives of General Psychiatry*, **44**, 660–69.

Weiner, B. (1986). *An Attributional Theory of Motivation and Emotion*. New York: Springer-Verlag.

Weiner, H. (1991). Stressful experience and cardiorespiratory disorders. *Circulation*, **83** (Suppl. II), 2–8.

Weinstein, A. (1988).*The Fiction of Relationship*. Princeton, NJ: Princeton University Press.

Weisfeld, G.E., Weisfeld, C. & Callaghan, J.W. (1984). Peer and Self Perceptions in Hopi and Afro-American Third- and Sixth-graders. *Ethos*, **12**(1), 64–85.

Weishaus, S. & Field, D. (1988). A half century of marriage: continuity or change? *Journal of Marriage and the Family*, **50**, 763–74.

Weisner, T.S. (1987). Socialization for parenthood in sibling caregiving societies. In J.B. Lancaster, J. Altmann, A.S. Rossi & L.R. Sherrod (Eds), *Parenting Across the Lifespan: Biosocial Dimensions*. New York: Aldine de Gruyter.

Weiss, R.L. (1980). Strategic behavioral marital therapy: toward a model for assessment and intervention. In J.P. Vincent (Ed.), *Advances in Family Intervention, Assessment and Theory*, Vol. 1 (pp. 229–71). Greenwich, CT: JAI Press.

Weiss, R.L. & Heyman, R.E.(1990). Observation of marital interaction. In F.D. Fincham & T.N. Bradbury (Eds), *The Psychology of Marriage* (pp. 87–117). New York: Guilford.

Weiss, R.S. (1973). *Loneliness: the Experience of Emotional and Social Isolation*. Cambridge, MA: MIT Press.

Weiss, R.S. (1974). Loneliness: the provisions of social relationships. In Z. Rubin (Ed.), *Doing Unto Others* (pp. 17–36). Englewood Cliffs, NJ: Prentice Hall.

Weiss, R.S. (1975). *Marital Separation*. New York: Basic Books.

Weiss, R.S. (1982). Attachment in adults. In C.M. Parkes & J. Stevenson-Hinde (Eds), *The Place of Attachment in Human Behavior* (pp. 171–84). New York: Basic Books.

Weiss, R.S. (1988). Loss and recovery. *Journal of Social Issues*, **44**, 37–52.

Weissman, M.M. (1987). Advances in psychiatric epidemiology: rates and risks for depression. *American Journal of Public Health*, **77**, 445–51.

Wellman, B. (1979). The community question: the intimate networks of East Yorkers. *American Journal of Sociology*, **84**, 1201–31.

Wellman, B. (1985). Domestic work, paid work and net work. In S.W. Duck & D. Perlman (Eds), *Understanding Personal Relationships: an Interdisciplinary Approach*. London: Sage.

Wellman, B. (1988). Structural analysis: from method and metaphor to theory and substance. In B. Wellman & S. Berkowitz (Eds), *Social Structures: a Network Approach*. (pp. 15–61). Cambridge: Cambridge University Press.

Wellman, B. & Wellman, B. (1992). Domestic affairs and network relations. *Journal of Social and Personal Relationships*, **9**, 385–409.

Wellman, B. & Wortley, S. (1989). Brothers' keepers: situating kinship relations in broader networks of social support. *Sociological Perspectives*, **32**, 273–306.

Wellman, B. & Wortley, S. (1990). Different strokes from different folks: which community ties provide what social support. *American Journal of Sociology*, **96**, 558–88.

Wellman, B., Carrington, P. & Hall, A. (1988). Networks as personal communities. In B. Wellman & S.D. Berkowitz (Eds), *Social Structures: a Network Approach* (pp. 130–84). Cambridge: Cambridge University Press.

Wells, A.J. (1988). Variations in mothers' self-esteem in daily life. *Journal of Personality and Social Psychology*, **55**(4), 661–8.

Wells, J.W. & Kline, W.B. (1987). Self-disclosure and homosexual orientation. *Journal of Social Psychology*, **127**, 191–7.

Werking, K.J. (1992). The communicative management of cross-sex friendship. Unpublished doctoral dissertation, Purdue University.

Werking, K.J. (1994a). Barriers to the formation of cross- sex friendship. Paper presented at the INPR annual conference [Professional Development], Iowa City, IA, May.

Werking, K.J. (1994b). Topics of talk and the activities of close cross-sex friends. Unpublished manuscript.

Werking, K.J. (1994c). Dissolving cross-sex friendships. Paper presented at the Speech Communication Association conference, New Orleans, LA, November.

Werking, K.J. (1995). "We're just good friends": Women and men in friendship. Unpublished manuscript.

Werner, C.M. & Baxter, L.A. (1994). Temporal qualities of relationships: organismic, transactional and dialectical views. In M.L. Knapp & G.R. Miller (Eds), *Handbook of*

Interpersonal Communication (2nd Edn, pp. 323–79). Newbury Park: Sage.

Werner, C.M., Altman, I. & Oxley, D. (1985). Temporal aspects of homes: a transactional perspective. In I. Altman & C.M. Werner (Eds), *Human Behavior and Environment: Advances in Theory and Research* (pp. 1–32). Beverly Hills: Sage.

Werner, C.M., Altman, I., Brown, B. & Ginat, J. (1993). Celebrations in personal relationships: a transactional/dialectical perspective. In S. Duck (Ed.), *Social Context and Relationships* (pp. 109–138). Newbury Park: Sage.

Werner, C.M., Altman, I., Oxley, D. & Haggard, L.M. (1987). People, place and time: a transactional analysis of neighborhoods. In W. Jones & D. Perlman (Eds), *Advances in Personal Relationships*, Vol. 1 (pp. 243–75). Greenwich, CT: JAI.

Werner, C.M., Brown, B., Altman, I. & Staples, J. (1992). Close relationships in their physical and social contexts: a transactional perspective. *Journal of Social and Personal Relationships*, **9**, 411–31.

Werner, C.M., Haggard, L.M., Altman, I. & Oxley, D. (1988). Temporal qualities of rituals and celebrations: a comparison of Christmas Street and Zuni Shalako. In J.E. McGrath (Ed.), *The Social Psychology of Time: New Perspectives* (pp. 203–31). Newbury Park: Sage.

Werner, E. & Smith, R. (1977). *Kawai's Children Come of Age*. Honolulu: The University of Hawaii Press.

West, C. (1993). *Race Matters*. Boston: Beacon Press.

West, C. & Fenstermaker, S. (1993). Power, inequality, and the accomplishment of gender: an ethnomethodological view. In P. England (Ed.), *Theory on Gender/fFminism on Theory* (pp. 151–74). New York: deGruyter.

West, C. & Fenstermaker, S. (1995). Doing difference. *Gender & Society*, **9**, 8–37.

West, C. & Zimmerman, D.H. (1987). Doing gender. *Gender & Society*, **1**, 125–51.

West, L. (1995). The construction of self and identities: examination of the shame construct. Paper presented at the Western Speech Association Conference, Portland, OR.

West, L., Anderson, J. & Duck, S.W. (1995). Crossing the barriers to friendship between men and women. In J.T. Wood (Ed.), *Gendered Relationships* (pp. 111–27). Mountain View, CA: Mayfield.

West, M.L. & Sheldon-Keller, A.E. (1994). *Patterns of Relating*. New York: Guilford.

Westerman, M.A. & Schonholtz, J. (1993). Marital adjustment, joint parental support in a triadic problem-solving task, and child behavior problems. *Journal of Clinical Child Psychology*, **22**, 97–106.

Weston, K. (1991). *Families We Choose*. New York: Columbia University Press.

Wethington E. & Kessler, R.C. (1986). Perceived support, received support, and adjustment to stressful life events, *Journal of Health and Social Behavior*, **27**, 78–89.

Wetzel, C.G. & Insko, C.A. (1982). The similarity-attraction relationship: is there an ideal one? *Journal of Experimental Social Psychology*, **18**, 253–76.

Wheaton, B. (1985). Models for stress-buffering functions of coping resources. *Journal of Health and Social Behavior*, **26**, 352–64.

Whitam, F.L., Diamond, M. & Martin, J. (1993). Homosexual orientation in twins: a report on 61 pairs and three triplet sets. *Archives of Sexual Behavior*, **22**, 187–206.

Whitbeck, L.B. & Hoyt, D.R. (1994). Social prestige and assortive mating: a comparison of students form 1956 and 1988. *Journal of Social and Personal Relationships*, **11**, 137–45.

Whitbeck, L.B., Simons, R.L. & Conger, R.D. (1991). The effects of early family relationships on contemporary relationships and assistance patterns between adult children and their parents. *Journal of Gerontology: Social Sciences*, **46**, 330–37.

White, G.L. & Kight, T.D. (1984). Misattribution of arousal and attraction: effects of salience of explanations of arousal. *Journal of Experimental Social Psychology*, **20**, 55–64.

White, G.L. & Mullen, P.E. (1989). *Jealousy: Theory, Research, and Clinical Strategies*. New York: Guilford.

White, G.L., Fishbein, S. & Rutstein, J. (1981). Passionate love and misattribution of arousal. *Journal of Personality and Social Psychology*, **41**, 56–62.

White, H. (1980). The value of narrativity in the representation of reality. *Critical Inquiry*, **7**, 5–27.

White, J.L. & Parham, T.A. (1990). *The Psychology of Blacks: an African-American Perspective* (2nd Edn). Englewood Cliffs, NJ: Prentice-Hall.

White, K.M., Speisman, J.C. & Costos, D. (1983). Young adults and their parents: individuation to mutuality. In H.D. Grotevant & C.R. Cooper (Eds), *Adolescent Development in the Family* (pp. 61–76). San Francisco: Jossey-Bass.

White, L.K. (1983). Determinants of spousal interaction: marital structure or marital happiness. *Journal of Marriage and the Family*, **45**, 511–19.

White, L.K. & Booth, A.V. (1985a). The quality and stability of remarriages: the role of stepchildren. *American Sociological Review*, **50**, 689–98.

White, L.K. & Booth, A.V. (1985b). The transition to parenthood and marital quality. *Journal of Family Issues*, **6**, 435–49.

White, R.W. (1959). Motivation reconsidered: the concept of confidence. *Psychological Review*, **66**, 297–333.

Whitesell, N.R. & Harter, S. (1994). *The Interpersonal Context of Emotion: Anger with Close Friends and Classmates*. MS, University of Denver.

Whiting, B. & Whiting J. (1975). *Children of Six Cultures*. Cambridge, MA: Harvard University Press.

Whiting, B.B. & Edwards, C.P. (1988). *Children of Different Worlds: the Formation of Social Behavior*. Cambridge, MA: Harvard.

Whitney, C. (1990). *Uncommon Lives: Gay Men and Straight Women*. New York: New American Library.

Wiederman, M.W. (1993). Evolved gender differences in mate preferences: evidence from personal advertisements. *Ethology and Sociobiology*, **14**, 331–52.

Wiederman, M.W. & Allgeier, E.R. (1993). Gender differences in sexual jealousy: adaptionist or social learning explanation? *Ethology and Sociobiology*, **14**, 115–40.

Wieselquist, J., Rusbult, C.E., Agnew, C. & Foster, C. (1995). Trust and commitment in close relationships. Unpublished manuscript, University of North Carolina at Chapel Hill.

Wiggins, J.S. (1982). Circumplex models of interpersonal behavior in clinical psychology. In P.C. Kendall & J.N. Butcher (Eds), *Handbook of Research Methods in Clinical Psychology* (pp. 183–221). New York: Wiley.

Wilkie, J.R., Ratcliff, K.S. & Ferree, M.M.(1992, November). Family division of labor and marital satisfaction among two -earner married couples. Paper presented at the annual conference of the National Council on Family Relations, Orlando, FL.

Wilkinson, G.S. (1988). Reciprical altruism in bats and other mammals. *Ethology and Sociobiology*, **9**, 85–100.

Wilkinson, G.S. (1990). Food sharing in vampite bats. *Scientific American*, **February**, 76–82.

Williams, N. (1990). *The Mexican-American Family: Tradition and Change*. Dix Hills, NJ: General Hall.

Wills, T.A. (1981). Downward comparison principles in social psychology. *Psychology Bulletin*, **90**, 245–71.

Wills, T.A. (1985). Supportive functions of interpersonal relationships. In S. Cohen & S.L. Syme (Eds), *Social Support and Health* (pp. 61–82). New York: Academic Press.

Wills, T.A. (1990). Multiple networks and substance use. *Journal of Social and Clinical Psychology*, **9**, 78–90.

Wills, T.A. & DePaulo, B. (1991). Interpersonal analysis of the help-seeking process. In C.R. Snyder & D. Forsyth (Eds), *Handbook of Social and Clinical Psychology: the Health Perspective* (pp. 350–75). New York: Pergamon Press.

Wilmot, W.W., Carbaugh, D.A. & Baxter, L.A. (1985). Communicative strategies used to terminate romantic relationships. *Western Journal of Speech Communication*, **49**, 204–16.

Wilson, E.O. (1975). *Sociobiology: the New Synthesis*. Cambridge, MA: Harvard University Press.

Wilson, M. & Daly, M. (1985). Competitiveness, risk taking, and violence: the young male syndrome. *Ethology and Sociobiology*, **6**, 59–73.

Wilson, M.N., Tolson, T.F., Hinton, I.D. & Kiernan, M. (1990). Flexibility and sharing of childcare duties in Black families. *Sex Roles*, **22**, 409–25.

Wilson, S.R. (1992). Face and facework in negotiation. In L.L. Putnam & M.E. Roloff (Eds), *Communication and Negotiation* (pp. 176–205). Newbury Park, CA: Sage.

Wimberley, H. (1973). Conjugal-role organization and social networks in Japan and England. *Journal of Marriage and the Family*, **35**, 125–30.

Winefield, H.R., Winefield, A.H. & Tiggemann, M. (1992). Social support and psychological well-being in young adults: the Multi-Dimensional Support Scale. *Journal of Personality Assessment*, **58**, 198–210.

Wirth, L. (1964). Urbanism as a way of life. In A.J. Reiss (Ed.), *On Cities and City Life* (pp. 60–83). Chicago: University of Chicago Press.

Wiseman, J.P. (1986). Friendship: bonds and binds in a voluntary relationship. *Journal of Social and Personal Relationships*, **3**, 191–211.

Wish, M., Deutsch, M. & Kaplan, S.J. (1976). Perceived dimensions of interpersonal relations. *Journal of Personality and Social Psychology*, **33**, 409–20.

Withycombe, J.S. (1973). Relationships of self-concept, social status and self-perceived social status and racial differences of Paiute Indian and white elementary school children. *Journal of Social Psychology*, **91**, 337–8.

Wolf, M. (1970). Child training and the Chinese family. In M. Freedman (Ed.), *Family and Kinship in Chinese Society* (pp. 37–62). Stanford: Stanford University Press.

Wolfgang, M.E. (1958). *Patterns in Criminal Homicide*. Philadelphia: University of Pennsylvania Press.

Wood, J.T. (1993a). *Gendered Lives: Communication, Gender and Culture*. Pacific Grove: Wadsworth.

Wood, J.T. (1993b). Engendered relations: interaction, caring, power and responsibility in intimacy. In S.W. Duck (Ed.), *Social Context and Relationships* (pp. 26–54). Newbury Park, CA: Sage.

Wood, J.T. (1994). *Who Cares? Women, Care, and Culture*. Carbondale, IL: Southern Illinois University Press.

Wood, J.T. (1995a). *Relational Communication: Continuity and Change in Personal Relationships*. New York: Wadsworth.

Wood, J.T. (1995b). Gender, relationships, and communication. In J.T. Wood (Ed.), *Gendered Relationships* (pp. 3–19). Mountain View, CA: Mayfield.

Wood, J.T. & Cox, J.R. (1993). Rethinking critical voice: materiality and situated knowledge. *Western Journal of Communication*, **57**, 278–87.

Wood, J.T. & Duck, S.W. (1995). Off the beaten track: new shores for relationship research. In J.T. Wood & S.W. Duck (Eds), *Understudied Relationships: Off the Beaten Track (Understanding relationship processes 6)* (pp. 1–21). Thousand Oaks: Sage.

Wood, J.T., Dendy, L.L., Dordek, E., Germany, M. & Varallo, S.M. (1994). Dialectic of difference: a thematic analysis of intimates' meanings for difference. In K. Carter & M. Presnell (Eds), *Interpretive Approaches to Interpersonal Communication*. New York: SUNY Press.

Wood, L.A. & Kroger, R.O. (1994). The analysis of facework in discourse: review and proposal. *Journal of Language and Social Psychology*, **13**, 248–77.

Wortman, C.B. & Dunkel-Schetter, C. (1979). Interpersonal relationships and cancer: a theoretical analysis. *Journal of Social Issues*, **35**, 120–55.

Wortman, C. & Lehman, D. (1985). Reactions to victims of life crises: support attempts that fail. In I.G. Sarason & B.R. Sarason (Eds), *Social Theory, Research, and Applications* (pp. 463–89). The Hague: Martinus Nijhoff.

Wortman, C. & Silver, R.C. (1989). The myths of coping with loss. *Journal of Consulting and Clinical Psychology*, **57**, 349–57.

Wright, P.H. (1989). Gender differences in adults' same- and cross-gender friendships. In R.G. Adams & R. Blieszner (Eds), *Older Adult Friendship* (pp. 197–221). Newbury Park, CA: Sage.

Wuerker, A.M. (1994). Relational control patterns and expressed emotion in families of persons with schizophrenia and bipolar disorder. *Family Process*, **33**, 389–407.

Wurmser, L. (1987). Shame: the veiled companion of narcissism. In D. Nathanson (Ed.), *The Many Faces of Shame* (pp. 64–92). New York: Guilford.

Wynne, L. (1984). The epigenesis of relational systems: a model for understanding family development. *Family Process*, **23**, 297–318.

Wynne, L.C. & Singer, M.T. (1963a). Thought disorder and family relations of schizophrenics. I. A research strategy. *Archives of General Psychiatry*, **9**, 191–8.

Wynne, L.C. & Singer, M.T. (1963b). Thought disorder and family relations of schizophrenics. II. A classification of forms of thinking. *Archives of General Psychiatry*, **9**, 199–206.

Wynne, L.C., Ryckoff, I.M., Day, J. & Hirsch, S.I. (1958). Pseudo-mutuality in the family relations of schizophrenics. *Psychiatry*, **21**, 205–20.

Wynne, L., Singer, M., Bartko, J. & Toohey, M. (1977). Schizophrenics and their families: recent research on parental communication. In J.M. Tanner (Ed.), *Developments in Psychiatric Research*. London: Hodder & Stoughton.

Yalom, I.D. (1989). *Love's Executioner & Other Tales of Psychotherapy*. New York: Harper Perennial.

Yalom, I.D. (1985). *The Theory and Practice of Group Psychotherapy* (3rd Edn). New York: Basic Books.

Yalom, I.D. (1995). *The Theory and Practice of Group Psychotherapy* (4th Edn). New York: Basic Books.

Yalom, I. & Elkin, G. (1974). *Every Day Gets a Little Closer: a Twice-told Therapy*. New York: Basic Books.

Yang, K.S. (1981). Social orientation and individual modernity among Chinese students in Taiwan. *The Journal of Social Psychology*, **113**, 159–70.

Yarrow, M.R. & Waxler, C.Z. (1976). Dimensions and correlates of prosocial behavior in young children. *Child Development*, **47**, 118–25.

Yee, A.H., Fairchild, H.H., Weizmann, F. & Wyatt, G.E. (1993). Addressing psychology's problems with race. *American Psychologist*, **48**, 1132–40.

Yerby, J., Buerkel-Rothfuss, N. & Bochner, A.P. (1990). *Understanding Family Communication*. Scottsdale, AZ: Gorsuch Scarisbrick.

Yerby, J., Buerkel-Rothfuss, N. & Bochner, A.P. (1995). *Understanding Family Communication*. Scottsdale, AZ: Gorsuch Scarisbrick.

Yi, E.K. (1986). Implications of conjugal role segregation for extrafamilial relationships: a network model. *Social Networks*, **8**, 119–47.

Yinger, J.M. (1994). *Ethnicity: Source of Strength? Source of Conflict?* Albany, NY: SUNY Press.

Young, H.B. & Ferguson, L.R. (1981). *Puberty to Manhood in Italy and America*. New York: Academic Press.

Youniss, J. (1980). *Parents and Peers in Social Development*. Chicago: University of Chicago Press.

Youniss, J. (1983). Social construction of adolescence by adolescents and parents. In H.D. Grotevant & C.R. Cooper (Eds), *Adolescent Development in the Family* (pp. 93–109). San Francisco: Jossey-Bass.

Youniss, J. & Smollar, J. (1985). *Adolescent Relations with Mothers, Fathers and Friends*. Chicago: University of Chicago Press.

Youniss, J. & Ketterlinus, R.D. (1987). Communication and connectedness in mother– and father–adolescent relationships. *Journal of Youth and Adolescence*, **16**, 265–80.

Yovetich, N.A. & Rusbult, C.E. (1994). Accommodative behavior in close relationships: exploring transformation of motivation. *Journal of Experimental Social Psychology*, **30**, 138–64.

Zack, N. (1993). *Race and Mixed Race*. Philadelphia: Temple University Press.

Zahn-Waxler, C., Radke-Yarrow, M. & King, R. (1979). Child rearing and children's prosocial initiations toward victims of distress. *Child Development*, **50**, 319–30.

Zahn-Waxler, C., Radke-Yarrow, M., Wagner, E. & Chapman, M. (1992). Development of concern for others. *Developmental Psychology*, **28**, 126–36.

Zajonc, R.B. (1965). Social facilitation. *Science*, **149**, 269–74.

Zajonc, R.B. (1968). Attitudinal effects of mere exposure. *Journal of Personality and Social Psychology Monograph Supplement*, **9** (2, Pt. 2), 1–27.

Zarbatany, L., Hartmann, D. & Rankin, B. (1990). The psychological functions of preadoloscent peer activities. *Child Development*, **61**, 1067–80.

Zarit, S.H. & Eggebeen, D.J. (1995). Parent–child relationships in adulthood and old age. In M.L. Bornstein (Ed.), *Handbook of Parenting, Vol. 1: Children and parenting*. Mahwah, NJ: Erlbaum.

Zavislak, N.M. & Sarason, B.R. (1992). Predicting parent–child relationships: influence of marital conflict and family behavior. Paper presented at the annual meeing of the American Psychological Association, Washington, DC.

Zelditch, M. (1964). Family, marriage and kinship. In R.E.L. Faris (Ed.), *Handbook of Modern Sociology* (pp. 680–733). Chicago: Rand McNally.

Zelkowitz, P. (1989). Parents and children as informants concerning children's social networks. In D. Belle (Ed.), *Children's Social Networks and Social Supports* (pp. 221–37). New York: Wiley.

Zicklin, G. (1969). A conversation concerning face to face interaction. *Psychiatry*, **August**, 236–49.

Ziegler, S. (1980). Report from Canada: adolescents' inter-ethnic friendships. *Children Today*, **9**(2), 22–4.

Ziegler, S. (1981). The effectiveness of cooperative learning teams for increasing cross-ethnic friendship: additional evidence. *Human Organization*, **40**, 264–8.

Zisman, P. & Wilson, V. (1992). Table hopping in the cafeteria: an exploration of "racial" integration in early adolescent social groups. *Anthropology & Education Quarterly*, **23**, 199–220.

Zola, I.K. (1982a). *Missing Pieces: a Chronicle of Living with a Disability*. Philadelphia: Temple University Press.

Zola, I.K. (Ed.) (1982b). *Ordinary Lives: Voices of Disability and Disease*. Cambridge: Applewood Books.

Zubin, J. & Spring, B.J. (1977). Vulnerability: a new view of schizophrenia. *Journal of Abnormal Psychology*, **86**, 103–26.

Zweigenhaft, R.L. & Domhoff, G.W. (1991). *Blacks in the White Establishment? A Study of Race and Class in America*. New Haven, CT: Yale University Press.

Author Index

Subject Index

Related titles of interest from Wiley...

Clinical Handbook of Marriage and Couples Interventions

Edited by **Kim Halford** and **Howard Markman**

Provides a comprehensive, analytic overview of research on marriage and couples interventions which is relevant to all clinicians working with psychological disorders, as well as those who specialise in couples problems.

0-471-95519-1　　1996　　696pp　　Hardback

Brief Therapeutic Consultations

An Approach to Systemic Counselling

Eddy Street and **Jim Downey**

Based on a life cycle perspective and within a systemic framework, this volume outlines the theory and practice of brief therapeutic consultations.

Wiley Series in Brief Therapy & Counselling
0-471-96343-7　　174pp　　1996　　Paperback

Brief Therapy with Couples

Maria Gilbert and **Diana Shmukler**

A concise, practical guide to brief therapy for couples and relationship problems, that relates therapy to the cultural, racial, and religious contexts of relationships, as well as key issues like parenting and same-sex relationships.

Wiley Series in Brief Therapy & Counselling
0-471-96206-6　　224pp　　1996　　Paperback

European Journal of Social Psychology

Chief Editor: **Eddy Van Avermaet**, University of Leuven, Belgium

An international forum for theoretical and empirical research, dedicated to fostering communication among social psychologists in Europe and to providing a bridge between European and other research traditions.

ISSN: 0046-2772